DAVID ALAN BARD
PRESIDING BISHOP

2020

MICHIGAN ANNUAL CONFERENCE

OF

THE UNITED METHODIST CHURCH

SECOND SESSION

Virtual

July 26 – 28, 2020

Bishop David Alan Bard, Presiding Bishop
Joy A. Barrett, Annual Conference Secretary

OFFICIAL MINUTES & RECORDS

VOLUME 2

— MAC Photos

MICHIGAN AREA EPISCOPAL OFFICE
1011 Northcrest Rd
Lansing, MI 48906-1262
517.347.4003

MICHIGAN CONFERENCE CENTER
1011 Northcrest Rd
Lansing, MI 48906-1262
517.347.4030

MICHIGAN CONFERENCE CENTER – NORTH
1161 E Clark Rd, Ste 212
DeWitt, MI 48820-8312
517.347.4030

MICHIGAN CONFERENCE CENTER – WEST
207 Fulton St E, Ste 6
Grand Rapids, MI 49503-3278
517.347.4030

MICHIGAN AREA EPISCOPAL OFFICE   517.347.4003

Resident Bishop
David A. Bard — bishop@michiganumc.org

Clergy Assistant to the Bishop — Ext. 4012
Rev. John W. Boley — jboley@michiganumc.org

Executive Assistant to the Bishop — Ext. 4011
Deana Nelson — dnelson@michiganumc.org

Executive Assistant to the Clergy Assistant to the Bishop — Ext. 4013
Aritha Davis — adavis@michiganumc.org

CONFERENCE OFFICERS OF THE ANNUAL CONFERENCE

Conference Chancellor
Andrew Vorbrich — Lennon, Miller, O'Connor, Bartosiewicz, PLC

Interim Director of Administrative Services and Treasurer
Rev. Donald J. Emmert — demmert@michiganumc.org

Conference Facilitator
Jennifer "Jen" Peters — jenpeters126@gmail.com

Conference Lay Leader
Annette Erbes — layleader@michiganumc.org

Conference Secretary
Rev. Joy Barrett — secretary@michiganumc.org

Conference Statistician
Pamela Stewart — statistician@michiganumc.org

DISTRICT OFFICES

CENTRAL BAY DISTRICT 3764 Fashion Square Blvd – Saginaw, MI 48603-2471
989.793.8838

Rev. John G. Kasper, District Superintendent jkasper@michiganumc.org
Teri Rice, Executive Assistant trice@michiganumc.org

EAST WINDS DISTRICT 624 W Nepessing St, Ste 201 – Lapeer, MI 48446-2088
810.396.1362

Rev. John H. Hice, District Superintendent jhice@michiganumc.org
Cheryl Rentschler, Executive Assistant crentschler@michiganumc.org

GREATER DETROIT DISTRICT 8000 Woodward Ave – Detroit, MI 48202-2528
313.481.1045

Rev. Dr. Charles S.G. Boayue, Jr., District Superintendent cboayue@michiganumc.org
Dwanda Ashford, Executive Assistant dashford@michiganumc.org

GREATER SOUTHWEST DISTRICT 2350 Ring Rd N, Ste B – Kalamazoo, MI 49006-5428
269.372.7525

Rev. Dwayne E. Bagley, District Superintendent dbagley@michiganumc.org
Mandana Nordbrock, Executive Assistant mnordbrock@michiganumc.org

HERITAGE DISTRICT PO Box 128, St. Clair Shores, MI 48080
734.663.3939

Rev. LuAnn L. Rourke, District Superintendent lrourke@michiganumc.org
Dar McGee, Executive Assistant dmcgee@michiganumc.org

MID-MICHIGAN DISTRICT 1161 E Clark Rd, Ste 216 – DeWitt, MI 48820-8312
517.347.4173

Rev. Dr. Jerome R. DeVine, District Superintendent jdevine@michiganumc.org
Sarah Gillette, Executive Assistant sgillette@michiganumc.org

MIDWEST DISTRICT 207 Fulton St E, Ste 6 – Grand Rapids, MI 49503-3278
616.459.4503

Rev. Dr. Margie R. Crawford, District Superintendent mcrawford@michiganumc.org
Liz Bode, Executive Assistant lbode@michiganumc.org

NORTHERN SKIES DISTRICT 927 W Fair Ave – Marquette, MI 49855-2611
906.228.4644

Rev. Scott A. Harmon, District Superintendent sharmon@michiganumc.org
Diana Byar, Executive Assistant dbyar@michiganumc.org

NORTHERN WATERS DISTRICT 1249 Three Mile Rd S – Traverse City, MI 49696-8307
231.947.5281

Rev. Jodie R. Flessner, District Superintendent jflessner@michiganumc.org
Jill Haney, Executive Assistant jhaney@michiganumc.org

CONFERENCE DIRECTORS — 517.347.4030

DIRECTOR OF CONNECTIONAL MINISTRY — Ext. 4070
Rev. Paul D. Perez — pperez@michiganumc.org

DIRECTOR OF CLERGY EXCELLENCE — Ext. 4050
Rev. Dr. Jennifer Browne — jbrowne@michiganumc.org

DIRECTOR FOR CONGREGATIONAL VIBRANCY — Ext. 4090
Rev. Dirk Elliott — delliott@michiganumc.org

INTERIM DIRECTOR OF ADMINISTRATIVE SERVICES AND TREASURER — Ext. 4110
Rev. Donald J. Emmert — demmert@michiganumc.org

DIRECTOR OF BENEFITS AND HUMAN RESOURCES — Ext. 4110
Rev. Donald J. Emmert — demmert@michiganumc.org

DIRECTOR OF COMMUNICATIONS — Ext. 4030
Mark Doyal — mdoyal@michiganumc.org

CONFERENCE OFFICE OF CONNECTIONAL MINISTRIES — 517.347.4030

Director of Connectional Ministries — Ext. 4070
Rev. Paul D. Perez — pperez@michiganumc.org

Executive Assistant to the Director of Connectional Ministries — Ext. 4071
Sus'ann Busley — sbusley@michiganumc.org

Associate Director for Mission and Ministry
TBD

Associate Director for Multi-Cultural Vibrancy — Ext. 4073
Rev. Brittney D. Stephan — bstephan@michiganumc.org

Children's Initiatives Coordinator — Ext. 4077
Rev. Kathryn L. Pittenger — kpittenger@michiganumc.org

Young Adult Initiatives Coordinator — Ext. 4078
Pastor Lisa M. Batten — lbatten@michiganumc.org

Missionary for Hispanic / Latino Ministries — Ext. 4074
Sonya Luna — sluna@michiganumc.org

Disaster Response Ministries Coordinator — Ext. 4082
Nancy Money — nmoney@michiganumc.org

Conference Events Planner — Ext. 4075
Nancy Arnold — narnold@michiganumc.org

CONFERENCE OFFICERS

Annual Conference Registrar   Ext. 4081
Sarah Vollmer   svollmer@michiganumc.org

Journal Clerical Assistant   Ext. 4072
Katherine Hippensteel   khippensteel@michiganumc.org

CONFERENCE OFFICE OF CLERGY EXCELLENCE   517.347.4030

Director of Clergy Excellence   Ext. 4050
Rev. Dr. Jennifer Browne   jbrowne@michiganumc.org

Executive Assistant to the Director of Clergy Excellence   Ext. 4051
Debbie Stevenson   dstevenson@michiganumc.org

CONFERENCE OFFICE OF CONGREGATIONAL VIBRANCY   517.347.4030

Director for Congregational Vibrancy   Ext. 4090
Rev. Dirk Elliott   delliott@michiganumc.org

Executive Assistant to the Director of Congregational Vibrancy   Ext. 4091
Jodi Fuller   jfuller@michiganumc.org

Associate Director for Congregational Vibrancy   Ext. 4092
Naomi García   ngarcia@michiganumc.org

Associate Director for Congregational Vibrancy   Ext. 4093
Rev. Gary G. Step   gstep@michiganumc.org

Associate Director for Lay Leadership Development   Ext. 4094
Laura Witkowski   lwitkowski@michiganumc.org

Youth Initiatives Coordinator   Ext. 4095
Christina "Christy" Miller White   cmillerwhite@michiganumc.org

CONFERENCE OFFICE OF FINANCE AND ADMINISTRATIVE SERVICES   517.347.4030

Interim Director of Administrative Services and Treasurer   Ext. 4110
Rev. Donald J. Emmert   demmert@michiganumc.org

Executive Assistant to Treasury   Ext. 4138
Kriss Salters   ksalters@michiganumc.org

Accountant   Ext. 4133
Jill Smith   jsmith@michiganumc.org

Accounts Payable Clerk   Ext. 4132
Kim Kemmis   kkemmis@michiganumc.org

Accounts Receivable Clerk　　Ext. 4134
Rich Pittenger　　rpittenger@michiganumc.org

IT Specialist　　Ext. 4136
Rev. Michael J. Mayo-Moyle　　mmayomoyle@michiganumc.org

Statistician / Ezra Database Specialist　　Ext. 4137
Pamela Stewart　　pstewart@michiganumc.org

CONFERENCE OFFICE OF BENEFITS AND HUMAN RESOURCES　　517.347.4030

Director of Benefits and Human Resources　　Ext. 4110
Rev. Donald J. Emmert　　demmert@michiganumc.org

Benefits Administrator and Payroll　　Ext. 4111
John Kosten　　jkosten@michiganumc.org

Executive Assistant to the Benefits and Human Resources Office　　Ext. 4135
Jennifer Gertz　　jgertz@michiganumc.org

CONFERENCE OFFICE OF COMMUNICATIONS　　517.347.4030

Director of Communications　　Ext. 4030
Mark Doyal　　mdoyal@michiganumc.org

Executive Assistant to the Director of Communications　　Ext. 4031
Kristen Gillette　　kgillette@michiganumc.org

Senior Content Editor　　Ext. 4032
Rev. Mariel Kay DeMoss　　kdemoss@michiganumc.org

Communications Production Assistant　　Ext. 4033
Valerie Mossman-Celestin, Deaconess　　vmossman-celestin@michiganumc.org

CHARGE LAY MEMBERS TO ANNUAL CONFERENCE

CENTRAL BAY DISTRICT

Alger	Not Represented
Arbela	Not Represented
Arenac Cnty: Christ	Not Represented
Auburn	Not Represented
Bay City: Grace	Monica Lebsak
	Not Represented
	Not Represented
Bayport, Hayes	Not Represented
Beaverton: First	Not Represented
Bentley	Not Represented
Birch Run	Not Represented
Blanchard-Pine River	Not Represented
Burt	Not Represented
Caro	Lisa Wightman
	Not Represented
Caseville	Not Represented
Cass City	Constance Schwaderer
Central Michigan Wesley Foundation	
	Not Represented
Churchill	Not Represented
Clare	Anita Kasper
	Barb Tyler
Coleman: Faith	Tammy Geek
Coomer, Winn	Not Represented
Elkton	Not Represented
Essexville: St Luke's	Not Represented
	Not Represented
Fairgrove	Not Represented
Farwell, Mt Pleasant: Trinity, Countryside	
	Ruth Wissinger
Frankenmuth	Not Represented
	Not Represented
	Not Represented
Freeland	Tatyana Spaulding
Gladwin: First	Not Represented
Glennie	Not Represented
Gordonville, Midland: Homer	Not Represented
	Not Represented
Hale: First	Charles Hamilton
Harrison: The Gathering	Kim Hollis
Harrisville, Lincoln	Not Represented
Kilmanagh, Owendale	Rhonda Powers
Kingston	Gayle Farver
Leaton	Carolyn Bohlmann
Mayville	Kathy Freeland
Midland Cnty: Hope, Edenville, Dale	
	Charlie Russian

Midland: Aldersgate	Not Represented
	Not Represented
	Not Represented
Midland: First	Brian Callihan
	Carol Hoffman
	Diane Lake
	Norm Lake
	Anne Wallin
	Chuck Goodman
	Pat Sedon
	Bethany Eicher
	Peggy Born
	Bethany Goodman
	Not Represented
Millington	Maurice Chapin
Mio	Robert Hegel
Mt Pleasant: Chippewa Indian	
	Not Represented
Mt Pleasant: First	John Skinner
	Kate Marsh
Oscoda, Oscoda: Indian Church	Julie Burrell
Pigeon: First	Peggy Mccormick
Pigeon: Salem	Not Represented
Pinconning, Garfield	John Oates
Port Austin Upc, Pinnebog	Janet Cameron
Reese	John Elsesser
Rose City: Trinity	Sharon Haynes
Rosebush	Not Represented
Saginaw: Ames	Not Represented
	Not Represented
	Not Represented
Saginaw: First	Robert Miller
	Not Represented
Saginaw: New Heart	Not Represented
Saginaw: Swan Valley, Laporte, Hemlock,	
Nelson	Mary Aaron
	Doris Simons
Sanford	George Farner
Sebewaing: Trinity	Not Represented
Shepherd	Linda Miller
St Charles	Linda Kube
Standish: Beacon Of Light	Rose Bledsoe
Sutton-Sunshine	Shelly Allan
Tawas	Howard Falker
Vassar: First	Linda Reimus
Wagarville: Community	Cathy Kennedy
Watrousville	Not Represented
Weidman	Not Represented

West Branch: First	Amy Merrick
Whittemore	Not Represented
Wilber	Not Represented
Wisner	Maryann Thompson

EAST WINDS DISTRICT

Applegate, Buel, Croswell: First	David Bokah
Armada, West Berlin	Daniel Farver
Atherton, Grand Blanc: Phoenix	John Howell
Attica	Harry Wilcox
Bad Axe: First, Minden City	Kathie Abke
Brown City, Omard	Not Represented
Byron: First, Gaines	Tom Atherton
Capac	Monica Standel
Clarkston	Ric Huttenlocher
	Laura Dake
	Barbara Trueman
	Not Represented
	Not Represented
	Not Represented
	Not Represented
	Not Represented
Clio: Bethany	Leona Lemmon
	Elizabeth Whiting
Columbiaville	Not Represented
Davisburg	Not Represented
Davison	Mike Hall
Dryden	Not Represented
Durand: First	Ron Craft
Fenton	Jim York
	Sandy York
	Stacey Highfield
	Tabitha Metreger
	Reuben Metreger
Flint: Asbury	Not Represented
Flint: Bethel	Janice Womack
	Terry Brannon
Flint: Bristol, Burton: Christ	Marilyn Wykes
Flint: Calvary	Gregory Timmons
Flint: Charity	Johny Lee Watkins
Flint: Court Street	Kevin Meinka
	Randeigh Dickinson
	David Lindsey
Flint: Hope	Peter Thoms
Flushing	Christian Anderson
	John Henson
Forester, Port Sanilac	Not Represented
Genesee, Thetford Center	Nancy Pelkey
Goodrich	Not Represented
	Not Represented

Grand Blanc	Tom Cerny
	Cecil Freels
Halsey, South Mundy	Marie Weaver
Harbor Beach, Port Hope	Not Represented
Holly: Calvary	Nancy Mills
Holly: Mt Bethel	Not Represented
Imlay City	Not Represented
Jeddo, Avoca	Not Represented
Lake Fenton, Lennon, Duffield	
	Not Represented
Lake Orion	Kathy Castillo
	Susan Montgomery
	Not Represented
	Not Represented
Lapeer: Trinity	Debi Lobb
	Carolyn Elzerman
	James Elzerman
Leonard	Not Represented
Lexington	Wayne Bank
Linden	Joan Tyree
Marlette: First	Not Represented
Marysville, Central Lakeport	Not Represented
	Not Represented
McGregor, Carsonville	Not Represented
Memphis: First, Lamb	Not Represented
Montrose	Not Represented
Mt Morris: First	Deborah Sprague
North Branch: First, Silverwood	
	Not Represented
North Street	Mike Connell
Oregon, Elba	Deborah Cowper
Ortonville	Not Represented
Otisville, Fostoria, West Deerfield	
	Venita Chapin
Oxford, Thomas	John Warren
Port Huron: First	Barbara Hurd
	Joseph Fetterly
	Robert Sult
	Not Represented
Port Huron: Gratiot Park	Nanette Miller
Richfield	Kristen Lapalm
Richmond: First	Glenn Quick
Romeo	Linda Eastman
	Evelyn Coker
Saint Clair: First	Nancy Wade
	Paul Wade
Sandusky: First, Deckerville	Mary Nichol
Seymour Lake	Courtney Miller
Shabbona	Not Represented
Snover: Heritage	Jan Watson

Swartz Creek	Rose Parks
	Not Represented
	Not Represented
West Forest	Not Represented
West Vienna	Not Represented
Worth Twp: Bethel	Carol Derby
Yale, Melvin, Cole	Not Represented

GREATER DETROIT DISTRICT

Beverly Hills	Alice Tucker
Birmingham: Embury	Not Represented
Birmingham: First	David Ruby
	Dawn Dulworth
	David Dale
	Sue Ruby
	Holly Pisano
	Bob Sutherland
	Ellie Sutherland
	W White
	Linda White
	Merrybeth Valliquet
	Karen Plants
	Bridgett Schipper
	Ted Mcclew
	Margaret Buccini
	Tyler Bouque
	James Valliquet
	Not Represented
Bloomfield Hls: St Paul	Not Represented
Clawson	Benjamin Clawson
Dearborn: First	Jill Sestok
	Richard Anderson
Dearborn: Good Shepherd	Martha Tamaroglio
Detroit: Calvary	George Campbell
Detroit: Cass Cmnty	Zachary Betthauser
	Rachel Stoney
	Not Represented
Detroit: Central	Cameron Davis
	Alex Oatley
Detroit: Centro Familiar Cristiano	
	Not Represented
Detroit: Conant Ave	Dianne Brown
Detroit: Ford Memorial	Not Represented
Detroit: French	Not Represented
	Not Represented
Detroit: Metropolitan	Jeanette Harris
	Sue Lawlis
Detroit: Mt Hope	Not Represented
Detroit: Resurrection	Not Represented
Detroit: Scott Memorial	Pearl Lewis
	Not Represented

Detroit: Second Grace	Gloria Gregory
	Tracey Moore
Detroit: St Paul	Audrey Sandford
Detroit: Trinity-Faith	Not Represented
Downriver	Patty Molloy
Eastpointe: Immanuel	Not Represented
Farmington: First	Not Represented
Farmington: First	Not Represented
Farmington: Nardin Park	Mike Marks
	Rachel Kain
	Dorothy Moore
	Michael Kain
	Not Represented
Farmington: Orchard	Cathy Albery
	David Albery
	Leslie Bonsky
	Melissa Chapman
Ferndale: First	Bonnie Kern
Flat Rock: First	Randall Ruppel
Franklin: Community	Not Represented
Fraser: Christ	Cori Mitchel
Garden City: First	Not Represented
Grosse Pointe	Venus Rembert-Karchin
	Vivian Anderson
	Bob Rossbach
Harper Woods: Redeemer	Barbara Davis
Hazel Park: First	Frank Cox
Howarth, Paint Creek	Not Represented
Livonia: Clarenceville	Barbara Bennett
Livonia: Newburg	Janice Gasaway
	Susan Adam
	Not Represented
Livonia: St Matthew's	April Gradowski
	Mary Beltzman
	Al Eardley
Macomb: Faith	Brent Ruby
Madison Hts	Not Represented
Madison Hts: Korean First Central	
	Not Represented
Madison Hts: Vietnamese Ministry	
	Not Represented
Motor City Wesley Wesley Foundation	
	Not Represented
Mt Clemens: First	Lois Hill
	Linda Johnston
Mt Vernon	Not Represented
Omo: Zion	Not Reprocented
Pontiac: Grace And Peace Cmnty	
	Karen Theriot
Pontiac: St John	Latonial Smith

Redford: Aldersgate, Brightmoor Campus	
	Chris Johnson
	Ed Mccall
Redford: New Beginnings	Larry Chapman
Riverview	Not Represented
Rochester Hls: St Luke's	Not Represented
Rochester: St Paul's	Ron Fisch
	Betsy Fisch
	Amy Heitman
	Roxanne Cleveland
	Kathy Lutey
	Jodi Stuermer
	Susan Sonye
	Garry Watson
	Leslie Bennett
	Mary Watson
	Peter Marsh
	Not Represented
	Not Represented
Romulus: Community	Not Represented
Roseville: Trinity	Not Represented
Royal Oak: First	Carrie Beerer
	Not Represented
	Not Represented
	Not Represented
	Not Represented
Southfield: Hope, Detroit: St Timothy	
	Not Represented
	Not Represented
	Not Represented
	Not Represented
	Not Represented
	Not Represented
Sterling Hts: First	David Lamb
Trenton: Faith	Not Represented
	Kathryn Korns
	Cynthia Allison
Trenton: First	Margaret Creekmore
Troy: Big Beaver	Not Represented
	Not Represented
Troy: First	Cathy Miller
	Christian Aurand
Troy: Korean	Not Represented
	Not Represented
	Not Represented
	Not Represented
	Not Represented
	Not Represented
	Not Represented
Utica	Peggy Miller
	David Miller

Warren: First	Paul Sadowski
	Carole Wesner
Washington	Not Represented
Waterford: Central	Larry Spiece
	Christy Painter
	Barbara Spiece
Waterford: Four Towns	Not Represented
Waterford: Trinity	Michael Feekart
Water's Edge Coop: Algonac: Trinity,	
New Baltimore:Grace	Charles Sullivan
	Not Represented
Wayne-Westland: First	Not Represented
West Bloomfield	Melodie Langford
Westland: St James, Detroit: Peoples	
	Not Represented
Wyandotte: First	Kirk Hayhurst
	Susan Hayhurst

GREATER SOUTHWEST DISTRICT

Allegan	Mark Bolyen
	Cathy Foune
Arden	Not Represented
Augusta: Fellowship	Not Represented
Bangor: Simpson	Karla Vassar
Battle Creek: Baseline, Bellevue	
	Not Represented
Battle Creek: Chapel Hill	Michael Johnson
	Linda Grap
	Carrie Morton
Battle Creek: Christ, Washington Heights	
	Not Represented
Battle Creek: Convis Union	Lynn King
Battle Creek: First	Not Represented
Battle Creek: Maple	Not Represented
Battle Creek: Newton	Sue Ratliff
Berrien Cnty: Lakeside	Not Represented
Berrien Springs, Pokagon	Not Represented
Bloomingdale	Not Represented
Bridgeman: Faith	Not Represented
Bronson: First, Colon	Not Represented
Buchanan: Faith	Wayne Wilcox
Buchanan: First	Tim Gowen
Burnips, Monterey Center	Not Represented
Burr Oak	Not Represented
Casco	Karl Andrews
Cassopolis	John Kelley
Centreville	Bernie Eash
Climax, Scotts	Not Represented
Coldwater	Lana Hunter
Coloma	Diane Hogue
Constantine, White Pigeon	Evelyn Connelly

Delton: Faith	Jeff Newman	Portage: Chapel Hill	Daryl Perkins
Dowagiac: First	Gloria Staten		Not Represented
Dowling: Country Chapel	Not Represented		Not Represented
Edwardsburg: Hope	Martha Bartels	Portage: Pathfinder	Not Represented
	Judy Denemark		Not Represented
	Dianna Graham	Riverside	Not Represented
Fennville: Fennville, Pearl	Not Represented	Saugatuck	Rick Vorel
Galesburg	Not Represented	Schoolcraft, Pleasant Valley	Not Represented
Galien: Galien, Olive Branch	Mary Kutemeier	Silver Creek	Gail Ward
Ganges	Marcia Tucker	Sodus: Chapel Hill	Marge Krieger
Girard	Not Represented	South Haven: First	Not Represented
Glenn	Not Represented	St Joseph: First	Lorie Kraus
Gobles, Almena	Jackie Coons		Keith Foote
	Cheryl Rumery	Stevensville	Not Represented
Gull Lake	Karen Morse		Not Represented
	Lorence Wenke		Not Represented
Hartford	Not Represented	Sturgis	Marcia Harrington
	Not Represented		Not Represented
Hinchman, Scottdale	Not Represented	Three Oaks	Not Represented
Hopkins, South Monterey	Amelia Green	Three Rivers: Center Park	Arlene Thompson
Kalamazoo: First	Molly Williams	Three Rivers: First	Not Represented
	John Clark	Three Rivers: Ninth Street	Not Represented
	Deborah Search-Willoughby	Townline	Not Represented
	Not Represented	Union City, Athens	Sally Thornton
	Not Represented	Vicksburg	Rachel Ball
Kalamazoo: Milwood	Vincent Wheat		Robert Ball
Kalamazoo: Northwest	Not Represented	Western Mi University Wesley Foundation	
Kalamazoo: Sunnyside	Christy Newhouse		Not Represented
	Not Represented		
Kalamazoo: Westwood	Roxanne Frey	**HERITAGE DISTRICT**	
	Not Represented	Adrian: First	Sherry Stone
Kendall	Not Represented		Not Represented
Lacota	Not Represented		Not Represented
Lawrence, Lawton: St Paul's	Not Represented	Albion: First	Cheryl Krause
Marcellus: Marcellus, Wakelee		Allen	Not Represented
	Not Represented	Ann Arbor: Calvary	Not Represented
Martin, Shelbyville	Ruth Schrier	Ann Arbor: First	Carrie Throm
Mendon	Patricia Kline		Rick Miller
New Buffalo: Water's Edge	Not Represented		Jillian Mortimer
Niles: Grace & Wesley, Morris Chapel			Shonagh Taruza
	Debra Litchfield		Wendy Everett
Nottawa	Not Represented		Em Howard
Oshtemo: Lifespring	Not Represented	Ann Arbor: Korean	Not Represented
Oshtemo: Oshtemo	Janet Snyder		Not Represented
Otsego: Otsego	Kay Strong	Ann Arbor: West Side	Debbie Gipson
	Nyla Merrill		Not Represented
Parchment	David Carr	Azalia, London	Not Represented
Paw Paw	Not Represented	Belleville: First	Not Represented
Plainwell: First	Stacy Levine		Not Represented
Portage Prairie	Not Represented	Blissfield: Emmanuel	Not Represented

Blissfield: First	Not Represented
Brighton: First	Suzanne Everett
	John Phillips
	Ann Birchmeier
	Brian Everett
	Not Represented
Britton: Grace, Macon	Sharon Scott
Camden, Montgomery, Stokes Chapel	
	Not Represented
Canton: Cherry Hill, Ypsilanti: St Matthews	
	Bob Simmons
Canton: Friendship	Not Represented
	Not Represented
Carleton	Not Represented
	Not Represented
Chelsea: First	Jeff Melvin
	Edith Wiarda
	Jeanne Franks
	Nolan Peterson
Clayton, Rollin Center	Esther Noffsinger
Clinton	Dottie Grzebik
Commerce	Not Represented
	Not Represented
	Not Represented
	Not Represented
Concord	Not Represented
Deerfield, Wellsville	Not Represented
Denton: Faith	Not Represented
Dexter	Karl Fink
	Jane Fink
	William Gordon
	Patricia Wikins
	Teena Gordon
	Steve Bringardner
	Not Represented
Dixboro	Brent Howlett
	Mary Turfe
Dundee	Aimee Luck
	Not Represented
Erie	Donna Foster
Frontier	Not Represented
Grass Lake	Not Represented
Hardy	Not Represented
Hartland	Not Represented
Highland	Connie Brinkerhoff
	Glen Betts
	Not Represented
Hillsdale: First	Marla Bowen
Hillside, Somerset Center	Beverly Clark
Homer, Lyon Lake	Not Represented
Howell: First	Sue Rice
	Not Represented
	Not Represented
Hudson: First	Not Represented
Ida, Samaria: Grace	Patti Mccarty
Jackson: Brookside, Trinity	Douglas Lawson
Jackson: Calvary	Not Represented
Jackson: First	Terri Reynolds
	Dawn Doerr
	Not Represented
	Not Represented
Jackson: Zion	Marge Clute
Jonesville, Napoleon	Shelly Snow
Lambertville	Not Represented
	Not Represented
Lasalle: Zion, Petersburg	David Wahr
Lee Center	Bruce Lack
Lulu	Not Represented
Manchester: First	Margaret Goodrich
Manchester: Sharon	Diana Parr
Marshall	Art Hill
	Ed Ramos
	Rachel Labram
Milan: Marble Mem.	Brenda Kempher
	Rodney Hill
Milford	Deb Bonnewell
	Linda Fraser
Monroe: Calvary, South Rockwood	
	Not Represented
Monroe: First, Heritage	Not Represented
Monroe: St Paul's	Cathy Butson
	Paula Vergowven
	Not Represented
Morenci, Weston	Not Represented
New Hudson	Susanne Hardy
North Adams, Jerome	Not Represented
North Lake	Richard Gorham
North Parma, Springport	Not Represented
Northville: First	Not Represented
	Not Represented
	Not Represented
	Not Represented
	Not Represented
	Not Represented
	Not Represented
Novi	April Vallerand
Oak Grove	Brenda Foltz
Pinckney: Arise	Rich Guyon
Pleasant Lake	Not Represented
Plymouth: First	Bradley Coyle
	Joy Coyle
	Not Represented
	Jan Kavulich

Pope, Griffith	Dennis Hoag
Quincy	Not Represented
Reading	Not Represented
Salem Grove	Dennis Drobeck
Saline: First	Not Represented
	Not Represented
	Not Represented
	Not Represented
South Lyon: First	Dave Smith
	Robin Fanning
	Stu Baker
	Not Represented
Stony Creek	David Mongson
Tecumseh	Edward Follas
	Not Represented
Univ Of Mi Wesley Foundation	Not Represented
Walled Lake	Not Represented
Waterloo Village	Nancy Hughes
Willow	Not Represented
Ypsilanti: First	Donna Mcgee
	Gerry Conti
Ypsilanti: Lincoln Cmnty	Not Represented

MID-MICHIGAN DISTRICT

Alma	Not Represented
Ashley, Bannister, Pompeii	Not Represented
Barry County: Woodland	Not Represented
Bath, Gunnisonville	Kathryn Reed
Breckenridge	Angela Sherwood
Brookfield Eaton	Not Represented
Carland	Not Represented
Carson City	Not Represented
	Waltha Leavitt
Charlotte: Lawrence Ave	Not Represented
Chesaning: Trinity	Ronita Newman
	Jill Shorkey
Corunna: Corunna	Not Represented
Corunna: Northwest Venice	Dawn Stroup
Delta Mills	Not Represented
Dimondale	Tonie Lokker
East Lansing: The Peoples Church	
	Not Represented
	Not Represented
East Lansing: University	Julie Bills
	Sue Abent
	Donald Jost
Eaton Rapids: First	Joanna Ballard
	Not Represented
Elsie	Not Represented
Ferris State Wesley Foundation	
	Not Represented

Fowlerville: First	Ann Reid
Freeport, Nashville: Peace, Hastings:	
Welcome Corners	Not Represented
Grand Ledge: First	Mary Daniels
	Not Represented
Gresham, Sunfield	Not Represented
Hastings: First	Not Represented
Hastings: Hope	James Frederick
Henderson, Chapin, Owosso: Trinity	
	Mark Keesler
Holt	Maynard Hamilton
	Annette Erbes
Ithaca, Beebe	Kathy Wilson
Juddville	Not Represented
Kalamo	Leon Everett
Laingsburg Parish: Laingsburg, Pittsburg	
	Carrie Rathbun Hawks
Lake Odessa: Central	John Gentner
Lake Odessa: Lakewood	Tom Raines
Lansing: Asbury	Not Represented
Lansing: Central	Patricia Bell
	Dennis Stoneman
Lansing: First	Darcy Bozen
Lansing: Grace	Carole Simmons
Lansing: Mount Hope	Judy Lott
	Ron Lott
	Joseph Groff
Leslie, Felt Plains	Not Represented
Livingston Circuit: Plainfield, Trinity	
	Not Represented
Maple River Parish: Maple Rapids, Lowe	
	Mona Kindel
Mason: First	Glenn Darling
	Deborah Fennell
	Not Represented
Mi State Wesley Foundation	Not Represented
Millville, Williamston: Wheatfield	
	Not Represented
Morrice, Bancroft	Barbara Medlock
Mulliken	Not Represented
Munith, Stockbridge	Randy Heatley
Nashville: Nashville	Jan Keech
New Lothrop: First	Becky Warren
Okemos Cmnty Church	Not Represented
	Not Represented
	Not Represented
Ovid United, Middlebury	Janell Kebler
Owosso: Burton	Not Represented
Owosso: First	Tom Moorhead
	Margie Moorhead

LAY MEMBERS

Perry, Shaftsburg	Rosalie Young
Portland	Beth Feldpausch
Redeemer Church: Dewitt Campus	
	Paul Blankenship
	Not Represented
	Not Represented
	Not Represented
	Not Represented
Riverdale: Lincoln Road	Rita Mason
Robbins	Carol Huntington
Shepardsville	Helen Squires Christmas
St Johns: Pilgrim	Not Represented
St Louis: First	Amber Maclaren
Sycamore Creek: Lansing Campus, Potterville	
Campus	Not Represented
	Not Represented
Vernon	Not Represented
Wacousta Community	Deanna Mccracken
	Not Represented
Webberville, Williamston: Crossroads	
	Douglas Elzerman
Williamston: Williamston	Nancy Ham

MIDWEST DISTRICT

Allendale: Valley Church	Not Represented
	Not Represented
Amble	Delores "Dee" Barringer
Barryton: Faith	Not Represented
Big Rapids: First	Randy Hahn
	Amanda Hahn
Big Rapids: Third Avenue, Paris, Rodney	
	Jean Huhtala
Bowne Center	Not Represented
Byron Center	James Brown
Caledonia	Thom Kohl
Carlisle	Not Represented
Cedar Springs	Keith Caldwell
Claybanks	Edith Bogart
Coopersville	Jessie Cypret
Courtland-Oakfield, Wyoming Park	
	Jeanne Bowser
	Karla Verhage
Crystal Valley, Walkerville	Not Represented
Dorr: Crosswind Cmnty	Not Represented
East Nelson	Sarah Zachow
Edmore: Faith	Cindi Scheiern
Fenwick, Palo, Vickeryville	Not Represented
Flat River Coop Parish: Turk Lake, Belding,	
Ionia:Easton	Not Represented

Fremont	Laurene Homsher
	Not Represented
Georgetown	Bill Stover
	Heather Blaszczyk
	Cyndi Hartley
Grand Haven: Church Of The Dunes	
	Shirey Chappell
Grand Haven: Church Of The Dunes	
	Blair Miller
	Richard Cole
Grand Rapids: Aldersgate	Not Represented
Grand Rapids: Cornerstone	Betsy Weems
	Bruce Smolenski
	Not Represented
	Not Represented
	Not Represented
	Not Represented
	Not Represented
	Not Represented
	Not Represented
Grand Rapids: Faith	Debra Hoek
Grand Rapids: First	Timothy Tuthill
	Sherah Eavy
	David Bloss
	Ken Peirce
	Jill Peirce
	Susan Bloss
Grand Rapids: Genesis	Not Represented
	Not Represented
Grand Rapids: La Nueva Esperanza	
	Not Represented
Grand Rapids: Northlawn	Sue Cleveland
Grand Rapids: Restoration	Not Represented
Grand Rapids: Saint Paul's	Peg Edvenson
Grand Rapids: South	Not Represented
Grand Rapids: Trinity	Bonnie Czuhajewski
	Kip Smalligan
	Not Represented
Grand Rapids: Vietnamese	Not Represented
Grandville	Judy Overmeyer
Grant Center	Not Represented
Greenville: First	Charles "Chuck" Hill
	Not Represented
	Not Represented
Hart	Maureen Huizing
Hesperia, Ferry	Not Represented
Holland: First	Not Represented
	Not Represented
	Not Represented
	Not Represented

Holton	Not Represented
Ionia Parish: LeValley, Berlin Center	
	Judy Huynh
Ionia: First, Lyons-Muir	Becky Brown
Ionia: Zion	Not Represented
Kent City: Chapel Hill	Not Represented
Lakeview: New Life	Doris Shaw
Leighton	Keith Pratt
Lowell: First	Not Represented
	Not Represented
Lowell: Vergennes	Elizabeth Wright
Marne	Not Represented
Mears, Shelby	Denise Schuitema
Mecosta: New Hope	Norvil Brown
Middleville	Susan Rietman
Montague	Thomas Hinken
	Michelle Vallier
Muskegon Hts: Temple	Not Represented
Muskegon: Central	Not Represented
Muskegon: Crestwood	Not Represented
Muskegon: Lake Harbor	Jason Colella
	Diane Thompson
Muskegon: Unity	Not Represented
Newaygo	Not Represented
North Muskegon: Community	Doug Wood
	Not Represented
Parmelee	Not Represented
Pentwater: Centenary	Susan Macgregor
Pierson: Heritage	Holly Fahner
Ravenna	Sarah Gilbert
Rockford	Not Represented
Rockford	Steve Laninga
Salem Indian Mission, Bradley Indian Mission	
	Not Represented
Sand Lake, South Ensley	Mary Johnson
Sitka	Not Represented
Sparta	Alan Hartman
Stanwood: Northland	Not Represented
Twin Lake	Ray Diehlman
Wayland	Not Represented
White Cloud	Barry Seabrook
Wolf Lake	Not Represented
Wyoming: Wesley Park	Not Represented
	Not Represented

NORTHERN SKIES DISTRICT

Bark River, Hermansville: First	Marjorie Meyers
Cheboygan: St Paul's	Joseph Mikula
Crystal Falls: Christ, Amasa: Grace	
	Dawn Payne
Emmett County: New Hope	Not Represented
Escanaba: Central	Not Represented
Escanaba: First	Not Represented
Gladstone: Memorial	Laurie Kaufmann
	Sue Lagina
Grand Marais, Germfask, Mcmillan	
	Devin Lawrence
Gwinn	Gayle Fike
Hancock: First	Jayne Nestell
	Not Represented
Houghton: Grace, Painesdale: Albert Paine Mem.	Anita Quinn
	Not Represented
Iron Mountain: First, Quinnesec	Paul Paulson
Iron Mountain: Trinity	Bruce Clark
	Beth Clark
Ironwood: Wesley, Wakefield	Thomas Brown
Ishpeming: Wesley	Connee Valente
	Not Represented
	Not Represented
Keweenaw Parish: Calumet, Lake Linden	
	Not Represented
L'anse, Sidnaw, Zeba	Not Represented
Mackinaw City: Church Of The Straits	
	Roger Moore
Manistique: First	Janet Helmbold
Marquette: Hope	Kim Fryzel
	Kurt Galbreath
Menominee: First, Stephenson	Keith Akins
Mohawk Ahmeek	Not Represented
Munising, Trenary	Not Represented
Negaunee: Mitchell	Not Represented
Newberry, Engadine	Not Represented
Northern Wesley Foundation	Not Represented
Norway: Grace, Faithorn	Chris Spence
Ontonagon, Greenland, Rockland: St. Paul	
	Not Represented
Paradise, Hulbert: Tahquamenon	
	Not Represented
Pickford	Neil Harrison
Republic, Woodland	Not Represented
Sault St Marie: Central, Algonquin	Raymond Bell
St Ignace	Walter Wilhide
White Pine, Bergland, Ewen	Jane Dickow

NORTHERN WATERS DISTRICT

LAY MEMBERS

Alden, Central Lake	Not Represented
Alpena: First	Pat Major
Arcadia	Not Represented
Avondale	Not Represented
Baldwin: Covenant Community, Chase-Barton	
	Janet Ball
Barnard, East Jordan	William Shapton
Bear Lake	Myrna Walter
Bellaire: Community	Not Represented
Boyne City, Boyne Falls, Epsilon	
	Not Represented
Brooks Corners	Not Represented
Cadillac	Don Rennie
	Not Represented
Charlevoix	Not Represented
Charlevoix: Greensky Hill	Robin Lees
Empire	Roy Pentilla
Evart, Sears	Kathy Galley
Frankfort, Elberta	Trudi Hook
Free Soil - Fountain	Not Represented
Gaylord: First	Richard Ross
	Nancy Ross
	Michael Cooper
Grant	Not Represented
Grawn	Fred Schlegel
Grayling: Michelson Mem.	Not Represented
Harbor Springs, Alanson	Not Represented
Harrietta	Not Represented
Hersey	Not Represented
Hillman	Cheryl Scramlin
Horton Bay	Liz Nortley
Houghton Lake	Kristy Carrick-Myers
	Dennis Dufford
	Donna Spencer
Indian River	Mark Fielder
	Not Represented
Kalkaska	Dee Miller
Keswick	Nancy Elmore
Kewadin: Indian Mission	Not Represented
Kewadin:Kewadin	Not Represented
Kingsley	Diane Walton
Lake Ann	Ruth Leckrone
Lake City	Cyndee Dubey
Leland	Joan Hook
	Not Represented
Ludington: St Paul	Not Represented
Ludington: United	Jane Mengot
	Karen Disegna
Mancelona, Alba	Robert Marsh
Manistee	Not Represented
	Not Represented
Manton	Not Represented
Marion, Cadillac: South Community	
	Not Represented
Mesick, Brethren: Epworth	Not Represented
NE Missaukee Parish: Merritt-Butterfield,	
Moorestown-Stittsville	Not Represented
Northport Indian Mission	Not Represented
Norwood	Not Represented
Old Mission Peninsula	Marge Long
Onaway, Millersburg	Colleen Whitsitt
Ossineke	Jeanette Schultz
Petoskey	Barb Angove
	Jane Sielski
	Sue Hutchinson
Pine River Parish: Leroy, Ashton, Luther	
	Mike Ramsey
Reed City	Cinda Locker
	Not Represented
Roscommon: Good Shepherd	
	Lenore Hoffmeyer
Scottville	Linda Starr
Spratt	Russ Robel
Traverse Bay	Cappy Potter
Traverse City: Central	Susan Cobb
	Carol Evans
	Allen Horstman
	Bob Blackmer
	Nan Horstman
	Amber Hassler
Traverse City: Mosaic	Toinette Wicks
Unified Parish: Williamsburg, Fife Lake, East	
Boardman, South Boardman	Denny Meyer

CONFERENCE EQUALIZATION LAY MEMBERS BY POSITION

Annual Conference Coordinator   Nancy Arnold
Annual Conference Trustee   David Apol
Annual Conference Trustee   Jorge Costales
Annual Conference Trustee   Jim LeBaron
Associate Director for Congregational
   Vibrancy   Naomi Garcia
Associate Director for Lay Leadership
   Development   Laura Witkowski
Board of Global Ministries, Chair
                 Brenda DuPree
Board of Ordained Ministry, Members:
                 Ruby Anderson
                 Sharon Appling
                 Ted Brainard
                 Carol Hodges
                 Laure Mieskooski
                 Sue Pung
                 Kelly Ross
                 Duane Townley
                 John Wharton
                 Jay Zylstra
Commission on Archives and History, Chair
                 Mary Whitman
Commission on Communications, Chair
                 Mark Doyal
Commission on the Annual Conference
   Session, Members: Donald Archambeau
                 Mara Marsman
                 Jennifer Peters
              Nichea Ver Veer Guy
Committee on African American Ministry,
   Co-Chair   Simmie Proctor
Committee on Rules, Members:
                 David Lundquist
                 Tonya Murphy
                 Todd Price
                 Keith Radak
                 Jim Searls
Committee on the Journal, Members:
          Mandana Nordbrock
                 Beth Snyder
Conference Chancellor   Andrew Vorbich
Conference Co-Director of Lay Servant
   Ministries   Jody Pratt
Conference Co-Lay Leader   Anne Soles
Conference Facilitator   Sue Buxton

Conference Leadership Council, Members:
                 Nick Arnold
                 Judith Coffey
                 Sung Yu
                 Carmen Zeigler
Conference Secretary of Global Ministries
                 Jackie Euper
Council on Finance & Administration,
   Members: Renae Clevenger
                 Cameron DeLong
                 Clayton Osburn
                 Patrick Tiedt
                 Andy Wayne
Deaconesses & Home Missioners Under
   Appointment:
                 Anne Hillman
        Valerie Mossman-Celestin
                 Amanda Mountain
Delegates to General or Jurisdictional
   Conference: Diane Brown
                 Gordon Grigg III
                 Lisa Hahn
                 Hoon-Yung Hopgood
                 Ruth Sutton
Diaconal Minister   Diane Griffin
District Co-Lay Leaders:
East Winds   Bonnie Potter
East Winds   Cynthia Rossman
Central Bay   Dennis Wissenger
Greater Southwest   Wynne Hurlbut
Heritage   John Seppanen
Mid-Michigan   Nona Spackman
Midwest   eb Hodges
Northern Skies   John Preston
Northern Waters   Denny Olin
Missionary for Hispanic/Latino Ministry
                 Sonya Luna
Persons Serving on General or Jurisdictional
   Agencies: Taylorie Bailey
           Diana Spitnale Miller
                 Linda Schramm
Protection Policy Implimentation Team, Chair
                 Judy Heriff
UMW Conference President   Linda Darrow

Young Adult Representatives:		Youth Representatives:	
Central Bay	Ethan Chu	Central Bay	Margaret Williams
East Winds	Peters Celia	East Winds	Ferguson Tramel
Greater Detroit	Amanda Funk	Greater Detroit	Angela Arnold
Greater Southwest	Olivia Bagley	Greater Southwest	Caleb Thomas
Heritage	Mary Comiskey	Heritage	Ken Labram
MidMichigan	Hannah Kinney	MidMichigan	Gerrard Leitelt
Midwest	Not Represented	Midwest	Sarah Delany
Northern Skies	Amilia Reed	Northern Skies	Represented Not
Northern Waters	David Hitts	Northern Waters	Elise Hitts

— MAC Photos

EQUALIZATION AT-LARGE LAY MEMBERS
ASSIGNED BY BOARD OF LAITY

CENTRAL BAY DISTRICT
Tsipporah Chu, Mary Fox, Jan Francis, Susan Franklin, Marge Hall Hall, Susan Hegel, Merry Henderson, Charles Huffman, Janice Huffman, Debbi Kasper, Jennifer Lane, Carla Long, Nancy Neuroth, Onita Oles, Teri Rice, Logan Romatz, Janet Shaffer, Deborah Skinner, Jacob Stone, Jeff Temple, Janet Wichert

EAST WINDS DISTRICT
Henry Allen, Minnie Armstrong, Becki Brice, Lois Bunton, Sandra Darby, Kathy Dorman, James Dover, Barbara Ernsberger, Alexandria Flores, Audrey Freels, Lynn Geer, Bruce Hurd, Lawrence Iseler, Carol Kandell, Bruce McCumons, Cyndi McDoniel, Linda Schenburn, Linda Schramm, Linda Squires, Paul Tiedeman, Suzanne Tinka, Dawn Titus, Connie Tosch, Marie Weaver, Michele Weston, Bob Wyatt, Dennis Youmans

GREATER DETROIT DISTRICT
Lenah Alghali, Regina Allie, Dwanda Ashford, Audrey Audrey Mangum, Shirley Bittings, Ernestine Campbell, Margaret Cantrell, Olivia Cato, Leonard Chapital, Jocelyn Davis, Kenneth Davis, John (Jack) Day, Rodney Diggs, Joshua Dixon, Ken Dowell, Isaac Garrigues-Cortelyou, Laura Gotham, Christopher Heldt, Carolyn Hildred, Lois Holman, Jimmie Jones, Mary Krentler, Sherman Louis, Diane Miles, Linda Owulette, Marchelle Phelps, Robin Rivers, Kimberly Ruppel, Ben Schornack, Kathy Sestok, Brenda Street, James Waldrop, James Westlake, Timothy Yu, Gary Zundel

GREATER SOUTHWEST DISTRICT
Sandra Belmore, Christi Blunt, JoAnn Bosserd Schroeder, Amy Brevitz, Jenna Brevitz, Michelle Brokaw, Karin Davis, Diane Garfield, Beth Griggs, Karen Grimes, Wendy Hernandez, Jane Knapp, Brian Lightner, Connie Luegge, Debby Mathis, Alexander Miller, Gail Phillips, Alice Reissmann, Donna Smith, Jean Szczypka, Cindy Thiele, Sarah Vollmer, Sally Wood

HERITAGE DISTRICT
Sally Ammerman, Julie Brunzell, Brooke Burns, Patricia Burns, Norman Colbry, Rene Crombez, Colleen Croxall, Marc Daly, Elisabeth Danielsons, Deanna Gaffney, BettieCarol Gorham, Anne Hanna, Aletha Hayes, Dick Hill, Ashlin Jackson, Elisa Jackson, Michelle McCalla, Dar McGee, Marianne McMunn, Joyce Mitchell, Cathy Montgomery, Stephanie Nichoff, Connie Perrine, James Rutherford, Richard Schaffer, Sandra Schmunk, Ellyn Simmons, Sherrie Snyder, Michelle Thompson, Sherry Wagenknecht, Michelle Walkup, Chuck Woolley, Dawn Wright

MID-MICHIGAN DISTRICT
Carole Armstrong, Theresa Austin, David Dekker, Andrea Gentner, Jennifer Hahm, Judy Herald, Shelia Huis, Tom Huis, Mary Lou Keenon, Donna Kleiver, Mary Jo Lott, Missy Noll, Cristy Omans, Jo Raines, Jackie Salsibury, Eric Simmons, Sharon Smith, Warren Wells, Ruth Whaley

MIDWEST DISTRICT
Joseph Brown, Tamara Brubacker, Wendy Clark, Julia Collingsworth, Mary Jo Delany, Terrie Eisenmann, Gail Gibbard, Max Gibbard, Kate Hanna, David Huhtala, John Huizing, Emil Jensen, Cookie Kramer, Steven Meredith, Reba Peterson, Leandro Robles, Linda Sbraccia, Jennifer Schumaker, Jean Sherman, Ray Wolfe, Sara Wolfsen, Paula Wright

NORTHERN SKIES DISTRICT
Kay Marie Bashore, Katja Falker, Robin Henry, Karen Kelly, Lawrence Molloy, Terri Reed, Robert Ross, Bruce Steinberg, Patti Steinberg, Mary Lou Vinson

NORTHERN WATERS DISTRICT
Leon Alberts, Randie Clawson, Darcy Dewling, Erin Fletcher, Neil Haney, Jeanette Hayes, Brian Highway, Debbie Highway, Anika Kasper, Steve Lett, Tim Locker, Bethany Maciejewski, Beth Pelkey, Linda Robel, Allison Thorton, Sandy Wegner-Mallory

MICHIGAN CONFERENCE EQUALIZATION SUMMARY

Clergy Members to Annual Conference

Clergy Members to the Annual Conference are as defined in ¶¶ 32 and 602 of *The Book of Discipline of the UMC – 2016*. These numbers are from the 2019 Michigan Annual Conference Journal using the Business of the Annual Conference, Part II: Pertaining to Ordained and Licensed Clergy, Question 57.

Deacons in Full Connection	57
Elders in Full Connection	883
Provisional Deacons	5
Provisional Elders	39
Associate Members & Affiliate Members with Vote	36
Full-time Local Pastors	134
Part-time Local Pastors	79
Total Clergy	1,233

Lay Members to Annual Conference

An equal number of Lay Members are invited to Annual Conference in accordance with ¶¶ 32 and 602 of *The Book of Discipline of the UMC – 2016*. Each Annual Conference determines and approves a process for equalization. The Michigan Conference outlines the process for equalization in the Standing Rules, § 5 Rules of Order, 5.2 Membership. In summary, Lay Members are gathered from local churches/charges, by virtue of their leadership office, or invited by the Board of Laity.

District	Members	Delegates
Central Bay	(12,515)	94
East Winds	(14,704)	100
Greater Detroit	(21,004)	151
Greater Southwest	(12,968)	104
Heritage	(19,420)	140
Mid-Michigan	(11,055)	88
Midwest	(15,469)	112
Northern Skies	(6,021)	41
Northern Waters	(9,476)	76
Equalization by Office		105
Equalization Invited by the Board of Laity		222
Total Laity		1,233

NOMINATIONS REPORT
for the
Michigan Conference
The United Methodist Church

Nominations Effective September 1, 2020 – June 30, 2021
(Year elected in parenthesis following name)

**The Annual Conference Granted the Nominations Committee
to Fill Vacancies Between Annual Conferences.
July 27, 2020**

AGENCIES RELATING TO
CHRIST-CENTERED MISSION AND MINISTRY

Annual Conference Session, Commission on the (1.1)

Eight voting members shall be nominated by the Committee on Nominations,
in consultation with the Executive Team, who shall be either Clergy Members of the Annual Conference
or Lay People who are members of a local church within the Annual Conference.

Members shall serve four-year terms, renewable twice, in annually staggered classes.

Commission shall elect from among its membership the following:
Chairperson: Rev. David Eardley
Vice Chairperson: Rev. Marsha Woolley
Head Usher: Mara Marsman
Worship Coordinator: Rev. Marsha Woolley

The Conference Secretary, Rev. Joy Barrett, shall serve as the Secretary of the Commission.
Annual Conference Coordinator/Events Planner: Nancy Arnold

Class	Laity	Clergy
2021	Mara Marsman (2018)	Anna Moon (2018)
2022	Don Archambeau (2018)	David Eardley, Chairperson (2018)
2023	**Lisa Poy (2020)**	Marsha Woolley (2018)
2024	**Elizabeth "Liz" Carr (2020)**	Leslee Fritz (2018)

Executive Committee: Bishop (Bishop David A. Bard), Clergy Assistant to the Bishop (Rev. John Boley), Chairperson (**Rev. David Eardley**), Worship Coordinator (Rev. Marsha Woolley, Director of Connectional Ministries (Rev. Benton Heisler), Legislative Coordinator (Diane Brown), Director of Communications (Mark Doyal), Conference Secretary (Rev. Joy Barrett), Annual Conference Coordinator/Events Planner (Nancy Arnold).

Ex officio **with vote**: Resident Bishop (Bishop David A. Bard) or representative, Conference Lay Leader (**Annette Erbes**) or Representative, Conference Secretary (Rev. Joy Barrett), Chair of the Committee on Rules (Todd Price), District Superintendent designated by the Cabinet (Rev. Jodie Flessner), Legislative Coordinator (Diane Brown), Conference Facilitator (**Jennifer "Jen" Peters**), A Representative of the Board of Ordained Ministry (Rev. Lindsey Hall).

Ex officio **with voice, but no vote**: Director of Connectional Ministries (Rev. Benton Heisler), Director of Communications (Mark Doyal).

Given voice, **per Commission Action:** Annual Conference Registrar (Sarah Vollmer)

Communications, Commission on (1.2)

Four persons who shall be Clergy Members or Local Pastors of the Annual Conference (if clergy) or Professing Members of a local church within the Annual Conference (if laity).

Members shall serve four-year terms, renewable once, in annually staggered classes.

Members shall be nominated by the Committee on Nominations, in consultation with the Director of Communications.

The Conference Director of Communications (Mark Doyal) shall chair the commission.

Class	Laity	Clergy
2022	Clayton Hardiman (2018)	Victoria "Vicky" Prewitt (2018)
2023	Oneika Mobley (2018)	_____
2024	_____	Dillon Burns (2018)

Ex officio with vote: Bishop (Bishop David A. Bard), or Clergy Assistant to the Bishop (Rev. John Boley), at the Bishop's discretion, Conference Lay Leader (**Annette Erbes**), Board Members of UM Communications residing within the bounds of the Annual Conference.

Ex officio with voice, but no vote: Senior Editor of Conference Communications (Rev. Mariel "Kay" DeMoss), IT Specialist (Rev. Michael Mayo-Moyle) or representative, Conference Director of Communications (Mark Doyal), Director of Connectional Ministries (Rev. Benton Heisler).

Journal, Committee on the (1.3)

Four people who shall be members of the Annual Conference (if clergy) or Professing Members of a local church within the Annual Conference (if laity).

Members shall serve four-year terms, renewable once, in annually staggered classes.

Members shall be nominated by the Committee on Nominations.

The Conference Secretary shall serve as Chairperson and Secretary: Rev. Joy Barrett
The committee shall elect from among its members a Vice Chairperson: _____.

Class	Laity	Clergy
2021	Blair Hunt (2018)	_____
2022	Beth Snyder (2018)	**Carol Freeland (2018)**
2023	_____	**Wilson "Drew" Hart (2018)**
2024	Mandana Nordbrock (2018)	**Ron Iris (2018)**

Ex officio with vote: Conference Secretary (Rev. Joy Barrett).

Ex officio with voice, but no vote: Conference Director of Communications (Mark Doyal).

Provided for Information Only: Annual Conference Secretarial Support – Rev. Kathryn "Kathy" Cadarette, Pastor Cheryl Mancier, Pastor Crystal Thomas

Justice, Board of (1.4)

Chairperson: Rev. George Covintree (2018)
(Chairperson of the Board is an additional member, chosen by Committee on Nominations)

Vice Chairperson: _____
(Convener shall serve as Vice Chairperson of the Board, chosen by the conveners)

Each Division shall elect a Convener.

NOMINATIONS REPORT

Church and Society, Division of (1.4.3.1)

Four people who shall be members of the Annual Conference (if clergy) or
Professing Members of a local church within the Annual Conference (if laity).

Members shall serve four-year terms, renewable once, in annually staggered classes.

Members shall be nominated by the Committee on Nominations.

Convener shall be elected among the members: Pastor Albert Rush

Class	Laity	Clergy
2021	Clarice McKenzie (2018)	_____
2022	_____	Albert Rush (2018)
2023	Joan Bosserd-Schroeder (2018)	_____
2024	_____	Corey Simon (2018)

Ex officio **with vote**: Mission Coordinator for Social Action of the Conference United Methodist Women (Alice Tucker), any Member of the General Board of Church and Society residing in the bounds of the Annual Conference (Rev. Paul Perez), the Conference Peace with Justice Coordinator, who shall be named by the Division of Church and Society and shall serve at the division's pleasure for up to eight years.

Religion and Race, Division on (1.4.3.2)

Two Clergy Members of the Annual Conference. Two Laymen who shall be Professing Members
of a local church within the Annual Conference. Two Laywomen who shall be Professing Members
of a local church within the Annual Conference.

Members shall serve four-year terms, renewable once, in annually staggered classes.

Members shall be nominated by the Committee on Nominations.

Convener shall be elected among the members: Ernestine "Tina" Campbell and Rev. Scott Manning

Class	Laity	Clergy
2021	Ernestine "Tina" Campbell (2018)	_____
2022	Kenneth "Ken" Dowell (2018)	Scott Manning (2018)
2023	Hoon-Yung Hopgood (2018)	**Ronald "Todd" Williamson (2020)**
2024	**Linda Darrow (2020)**	_____

Ex officio **with vote**: Any member of the General Commission on Religion and Race residing within the bounds of the Annual Conference.

Status and Role of Women, Division on the (1.4.3.3)

Two Clergy Women who shall be members of the Annual Conference. A Clergyman who shall be
a member of the Annual Conference. Three Laymen who shall be Professing Members of a local
church within the Annual Conference. Three Laywomen who shall be Professing Members of a local
church within the Annual Conference.

Members shall serve four-year terms, renewable once, in annually staggered classes.

Members shall be nominated by the Committee on Nominations.

Convener shall be elected among the members and shall be a woman: Patricia Bostic

Class	Laywomen (3)	Laymen (3)	Clergy
2021	Patricia Bostic (2018)	_____	Eric Stone (2018)
			Carol Blair Bouse (2018)
2022	Mary Blashill (2018)	_____	Kristine "Kristy" Hintz (2018)
2023	_____	_____	
2024	_____	_____	

***Ex officio* with vote**: Any member of the General Commission on the Status and Role of Women residing within the bounds of the Annual Conference.

Disability Concerns, Division on (1.4.3.4)

Four people who shall be members of the Annual Conference (if clergy) or Professing Members of a local church within the Annual Conference (if laity).

Members shall serve four-year terms, renewable once, in annually staggered classes.

Members shall be nominated by the Committee on Nominations.

At least one member of the division shall have a physical disability.
At least one member of the division shall have a mental disability.

Convener shall be elected among the members: _____

Class	Laity	Clergy
2021		Amee Paparella (2018)
2022		Frederick Sampson (2018)
2023		Ellen Brubaker (2018)
2024	**Greg Hicok (2020)**	

Global Ministries, Board of (1.5)

Twelve people who shall be members of the Annual Conference (if clergy) or Professing Members of a local church within the Annual Conference (if laity).

Members shall serve four-year terms, renewable once, in annually staggered classes.

Members shall be nominated by the Committee on Nominations.

Board will elect from its members the following:
Chairperson: Brenda DuPree   Vice Chairperson: **Rev. Julie Liske**
Secretary: Rev. Julie Elmore   Financial Secretary: Charles "Chuck" Woolley

Class	Laity	Clergy
2022	Brenda DuPree (2018)	
	Mildred Mallard (2018)	_____
	Charles "Chuck" Woolley (2018)	
2023	**Laurie Kaufman delaGarza (2019)**	**Dillon Burns**
	Ava Williams Euper (2019)	
2024	**Taylorie Bailey (2020)**	Julie Liske (2018)
	Lisa Poy (2019)	_____

***Ex officio* with vote**: Mission Coordinator for Education and Interpretation of the Conference United Methodist Women (Michele Weston), the Conference Secretary of Global Ministries, who shall be appointed by the Board and shall serve at its pleasure for up to eight years (**Rev. Julie Elmore**), Conference Disaster Response Coordinator (Dan O'Malley) selected by the Board of Global Ministries, **Conference Town and Country (Rev. Carol Freeland)**, Conference VIM Coordinator (Jody Pratt), District Superintendent (**Rev. John Kasper**). Any Member of the General Board of Global Ministries (GBGM) residing within the bounds of the Annual Conference.

Given voice, per Board of Global Ministries: Liberia Ministry Partnership (Rev. Jon Reynolds), Haiti Ministry Partnership (Rev. Karl Zeigler), Mission Intern Chairperson (_____), Conference Staff Liaisons (Pastor Lisa Batten, Nancy Money, and Rev. Paul Perez). GBGM Mission Personnel: Church and Community Worker (Randy Hildebrant), Global Mission Fellows/US-2s (Emily Burns, Lauren Norton, Kathryn Sappington, Jinnia Sirronen, Asti White, Yeo Jin Erika Yung)

Archives and History, Commission on (1.6)

Four Clergy Members of the Annual Conference.
Four Lay Persons who shall be Professing Members of a church within the Annual Conference.

Members shall be nominated by the Committee on Nominations.

Members shall serve four-year terms, renewable once, in annually staggered classes.

Commission will elect from its members the following:
Chairperson: Mary Whitman   Vice Chairperson: _____
Secretary: _____   Treasurer: _____

Class	Laity	Clergy
2020	Brian Lightner (2019)	William "Tom" T. Robinson (2018)
2021	William "Bill" McNitt (2018)	Melanie Young (2018)
2022	Mary Whitman (2018)	John Ross Thompson (2018)
2023	Kenneth Gackler (2018)	_____
2024		

Ex officio with voice and vote: TThe Archivists of the Conference Archives: Adrian College (Rebecca Mc-Nitt), Albion College (**Elizabeth Palmer**), President of the Michigan Area UMC Historical Society (Diana Spitnale Miller), Members of the General Commission on Archives and History (Diana Spitnale Miller, Linda Schramm).

AGENCIES RELATING TO BOLD AND EFFECTIVE LEADERS

Conference Leadership Council (2.1)

Four Clergy Members of the Annual Conference, at least one of whom shall be
a member of the Board of Ordained Ministry.
Five Lay People who are Professing Members of a congregation within the Annual Conference.

Members shall be nominated by the Committee on Nominations.

Members shall serve three-year terms, renewable thrice, in annually staggered classes.

In consultation with the Bishop, the Council shall elect from its voting members:
President: Rev. Amy Mayo-Moyle   Vice President: _____
Secretary: _____

Class	Laity	Clergy
2021	Carmen Zeigler (2018)	Eric Mulanda (2018)
2022	Judith "Judy" Coffey (2019)	Darryl Totty (2018)
		Megan Walther, BOM Rep (2019)
2023	Sung Yu (2018) _____	Amy Mayo-Moyle (2018)
	Katja Falker (2020)	

Ex officio with voice and vote: Conference Lay Leader (**Annette Erbes**), President of the Council on Finance and Administration (Rev. Bradley "Brad" Bartelmay), Chair of the Conference Board of Trustees or their designee (**George Lewis**), Chair of the Conference Human Resources Committee or their designee (**TBD**),

Chair of the Conference Board of Pension and Benefits or their designee (**TBD**), a representative of the Division on Religion and Race of the Board of Justice (Ernestine "Tina" Campbell), Any member of the Connectional Table residing within the bounds of the Annual Conference (Rev. Kennetha Bigham-Tsai and Rev. Dr. Jerome "Jerry" DeVine)

Ex officio **with voice only:** Director of Administrative Services and Conference Treasurer (TBD), Director of Connectional Ministries (Rev. Benton Heisler), Director of Communications (Mark Doyal), Bishop (Bishop David A. Bard), or Clergy Assistant to the Bishop (Rev. John Boley), Dean of the Appointive Cabinet (**Rev. Dr. Jerome "Jerry" DeVine**), Director of Benefits and Human Resources (Rev. Donald "Don" Emmert), any other Directors whose position may be created by the Conference Leadership Council (Rev. Dr. Jennifer "Jennie" Browne, Rev. Dirk Elliott).

Other Elections (Elected by AC as Conference Rep): North Central Jurisdictional Mission Council Member (**Laura Witkowski**)

Except for *ex officio* members listed hereinabove, Chairperson of Conference Agencies and employees of Conference Agencies shall be ineligible for membership on the Council.

Ordained Ministry, Board of (2.2)

At least twenty-five Full Clergy Members of the Annual Conference. At least one of whom shall be engaged in Extension Ministry. At least one of whom shall be age thirty-five or younger. At least two-thirds of whom shall be graduates of theological schools listed by the University Senate. A least one of whom shall be retired. At least three Clergy Persons who are either Associate Members or Local Pastors who have completed Course of Study. At least twelve Lay People who are Professing Members of a local church within the Annual Conference.

Members shall be nominated by the Bishop.

Members shall serve four-years terms (starting at the close of the Annual Conference Session following General Conference), renewable twice, with quadrennially staggered classes.

The Board shall elect from among its members:

Chairperson: Rev. Barry Petrucci   Vice Chairperson: Rev. Mark Erbes
Secretary: Rev. Amy Lee Terhune   Treasurer: Kelly Ross
Registrar for Full and Associate Members: **Rev. Kathy Brown**
Registrar for Provisional Members: **Rev. Briony Desotell**
Registrar for Local Pastors: Pastor Melody Olin
Registrar for Specialized Ministry Certification: Rev. Patricia "Pat" Catellier

CLERGY
2012 Quadrennium

Patricia "Pat" Catellier (2018)   Lynn Hasley (2018)
Thomas "Thom" Davenport (2018)   William "Bill" Johnson (2018)
Briony Desotell (2018)   Rob McPherson (2018)
Mark Erbes (2018)   Amy Lee Terhune (2018)
Annelissa "Lisa" Gray-Lion (2018)   Mark Thompson (2018)
Daniel "Dan" Hart (2019)   Christina Wright (2018)

2016 Quadrennium

Cora Glass (2019)   Scott Lindenberg (2018)
Paul Hahm (2018)   **Sue Pethoud (2019)**
Lindsey Hall (2018)   Barry Petrucci (2019)
M. Christopher "Chris" Lane (2019)   Megan Walther (2019)

2020 Quadrennium

Kathy Brown (2020)   **Barbara Lewis-Lakin (2020)**
Susanne "Suzie" Hierholzer (2020)   **Jeremy Peters (2020)**
Deborah "Deb" Johnson (2020)   **Euk Sik "Cloud" Poy (2020)**
John David "JD" Landis (2020)

ASSOCIATE MEMBERS OR LOCAL PASTORS / COMPLETED COURSE OF STUDY

Terri Bentley (2018)   Melody Olin (2019)
Marvin Herman (2020)   Susan "Sue" Platt (2019)

LAY PERSONS
2012 Quadrennium
Ruby Anderson (2018)

2016 Quadrennium
Sharon Appling (2018)   Sue Pung (2019)
Ted Brainard (2019)   Kelly Ross (2018)
Carol Hodges (2018)   Jay Zylstra (2019)
Laure Mieskowski (2019)

2020 Quadrennium

Executive Committee: Chairpersons of the Order of Elders (**Rev. M. Christopher "Chris" Lane**), the Order of Deacons (Rev. Sue Pethoud), the Fellowship of Local Pastors and Associate Members (**Pastor Marvin Herman**), Rev. Susan "Sue" Platt), Director of Clergy Excellence (Rev. Dr. Jennifer "Jennie" Browne).

Conference Relations shall be chaired by the Vice Chairperson, Rev. Mark Erbes. The Board shall determine membership. A District Superintendent shall not be a member.

***Ex officio* with voice and vote:** Chairpersons of the Order of Elders (**Rev. M. Christopher "Chris" Lane**), the Order of Deacons (Rev. Sue Pethoud), the Fellowship of Local Pastors and Associate Members (Rev. Susan "Sue" Platt), a District Superintendent named by the Bishop (Rev. Scott Harmon), Director of Clergy Excellence (Rev. Dr. Jennifer "Jennie" Browne).

Nominations, Committee on (2.3)

Two persons nominated by the Annual Conference Session.
Ten persons nominated by the Conference Leadership Council.
Members shall serve four-year terms, renewable once, staggered annually.

The Committee shall elect the following from among its members:
Chairperson: **Melissa Claxton**   Vice Chairperson: _____
Secretary: _____

Class	Laity	Clergy
2021	Simmie Proctor (2018)	Melissa Claxton (2018)
2022	Ruby Anderson (2018)	Michael "Mike" Conklin (2018)
2023	Laurie Kaufman delaGarza (2018)	_____
2024	Taylorie Bailey (2018)	_____
	_____	_____

Nominated by Annual Conference Session for Class of 2023: Beth Pelkey – Lay Member (2019)
Nominated by Annual Conference Session for Class of 2023: Rev. Scott Manning (2019)

***Ex Officio* with vote:** District Superintendent (Rev. Dwayne Bagley), Conference Lay Leader (**Annette Erbes**), Chairperson or Representative of Rules (**James "Jim" Searls**), Secretary of the Annual Conference (Rev. Joy Barrett).

***Ex officio* with voice, but no vote**: Director of Connectional Ministries (Rev. Benton Heisler).

Episcopacy, Committee on the (2.4)

Six Clergy Members of the Conference.
Six Lay Persons who shall be Professing Members of a local church within the conference, one of whom shall be the Conference Lay Leader.
Three members appointed by the Resident Bishop who, if laity, shall be Professing Members of a local church within the Conference and, if clergy, shall be members of the Annual Conference.

Members shall serve four-year terms, renewable once, in annually staggered classes.

The Committee shall elect from among its members the following:

Chairperson: John Wharton   Vice Chairperson: _____
Secretary: Rev. Dr. Darryl Totty

Class	Laity	Clergy
2021	Karl Jennings (2018)	Darryl Totty (2018)
	John Wharton (2018)	
2022	Koom Cho (2018)	Robert "Bob" Hundley (2018)
	Craig Schroeder (2018)	Brian West (2018)
2023	Linda Darrow (2019)	Erin Fitzgerald (2019)
	Marchelle "Micki" Phelps (2019)	Megan Walther (2019)
2024	**Mark Trierweiler (2020)**	Carolin Spragg (2018)

Selected by the Bishop:

Pastor Gregory "Greg" Timmons (2018)   Rev. Elbert Dulworth (2018)
Bruce Smolenski (2018)

Conference Lay Leader: **Annette Erbes**

Ex officio **with vote**: Members of the Jurisdictional Committee on the Episcopacy who reside within the bounds of the Annual Conference: Currently, Rev. Dr. Charles Boayue, Jacqueline "Jackie" Euper, Rev. Benton Heisler, Nichea VerVeer Guy.

Protection Policy Implementation Team (2.5)

Eight adults (at least 18 years of age) who shall be members of the Annual Conference (if clergy) or Professing Members of a local church within the Annual Conference (if laity).

Members shall serve four-year terms, renewable once, in annually staggered classes.

Members shall be nominated by the Committee on Nominations.

The Team shall elect the following from among its members:

Chairperson: Judy Heriff   Vice Chairperson: Marguerite Zawislak

Class	Laity	Clergy
2021	Ruth Sutton (2019)	
2022	Judy Herriff (2018)	
2023	Michael "Mike" Darby (2018)	
	Marguerite Zawislak (2018)	
2024	**Beth Pelkey (2020)**	Daniel "Dan" Colthorp (2019)

AGENCIES RELATING TO VIBRANT CONGREGATIONS

United Methodist Women (3.1)

Membership shall be composed of all members of the local United Methodist Women units existing within the bounds of the Conference.

The United Methodist Women shall elect from among its members:

President: Linda Darrow

Vice President: **Waltha Gaye Leavitt**

Secretary: Beth Mitchell

Treasurer: **Mary Danforth**

Ex officio **with vote**: Resident Bishop (Bishop David A. Bard), Members of the Board of Directors of the national office of the United Methodist Women residing within the bounds of the Annual Conference. Members of the United Methodist Women Program Advisory Group residing within the bounds of the Conference; Members of the North Central Jurisdiction United Methodist Women Leadership Team residing within the bounds of the Conference; District Superintendent (Rev. Scott Harmon).

United Methodist Men (3.2)

Membership of the United Methodist Men shall be made up of all men who are Professing Members of local churches within the bounds of the Annual Conference.

The United Methodist Men shall elect the following offices from among its members:

President: Donald "Don" Archambeau

Vice President: **John Huizing**

Secretary: Peter Thoms

Treasurer: Raymond "Ray" McClintic

Ex officio **Members**: Any Members of the North Central Jurisdiction United Methodist Men residing within the bounds of the Conference, any Members of the General Commission on United Methodist Men residing within the bounds of the Conference, Conference Lay Leader (or designated representative), Resident Bishop (Bishop David A. Bard), District Superintendent (Rev. Dr. Margie Crawford).

Laity, Board of (3.3)

Conference Lay Leader: Annette Erbes (2020)

District Lay Leaders:

Central Bay: **Dennis "Denny" Wissinger (2019)**

East Winds: Bonnie Potter, Co-Leader (2018)

Greater Detroit: Ruby Anderson (2018)

Greater Southwest: Wynne Hurlbut (2018)

Heritage: **John Seppanen (2019)**

Mid-Michigan: Nona Spackman (2018)

Midwest: **Deborah "Deb" Hodges (2019)**

Northern Skies: John Preston (2018)

Northern Waters: Denny Olin (2018)

Associate District Lay Leaders:

Cynthia Rossman (2020)

Kenneth Dowell (2018)

Associate Director for Lay Leadership Development: Laura Witkowski

Conference Co-Directors of Lay Servant Ministries: John Hart and Jody Pratt

President of the United Methodist Men (or representative): Donald Archambeau

President of the United Methodist Women (or representative): Linda Darrow, President

Convener of the Division of Young Adult Ministry of the Board of Young People's Ministries:

Convener of the Division of Youth Ministry of the Board of Young People's Ministries:

Conference Scouting Coordinator: Robert Sanders

Director of Connectional Ministries: Rev. Benton Heisler

District Superintendent designated by the Cabinet: Rev. Dwayne Bagley

NOMINATIONS REPORT

Young People's Ministries, Board of (3.4)

Chairperson: **Rev. Elizabeth Hurd**

(Chairperson of the Board is an additional member, chosen by Committee on Nominations.)

Vice Chairperson: _____

(Convener shall serve as Vice Chairperson of the Board, chosen by the conveners.)

Each Division shall elect a Convener.

***Ex officio* with voice, but no vote**: A representative of the Michigan Area Board of Christian Camping (TBD).

Youth Ministry, Division of (3.4.3.1)

Two clergy persons appointed in the Annual Conference,
who shall serve four-year terms, renewable once, in biennially staggered classes.

Two adult Laypersons who shall be Professing Members of a local church within the Annual Conference,
who shall serve four-year terms, renewable once, in biennially staggered classes.

Ten Youth (age 13-17) who shall be Professing Members of a local church within the Annual Conference,
who shall serve one-year terms, renewable as long as they are under age 18 at the start of a new term.

Members shall be nominated by the Committee on Nominations.

Convener shall be elected among the members: _____

Class	Laity	Clergy
2021		_____
2022		_____
2023		
2024	Daphne Mitchell (2019)	
	Rene Crombez (2019)	

Class	Youth	Youth
	Lenah Alghali (2019)	Isabelle Nowak (2019)
	Ethan Chu (2019)	Erin Stevens (2019)
	Mary Violet Comiskey (2019)	Elizabeth Storkey (2019)
	Elise Hitts (2019)	Kayla Sweeney (2019)
	Tyler Moody (2019)	_____

Given Voice, per Division Action: Youth Initiatives Coordinator, **Rev. Christina "Christy" Miller White** (Conference Staff).

Young Adult Ministry, Division of (3.4.3.2)

Two Young Adult (age 18-30) Clergy Persons of the Annual Conference who shall be
nominated by the committee on nominations.

Four Young Adult Lay Persons (age 18-30) who shall be nominated by the committee on nominations and who
shall be Professing Members of a local church within the Annual Conference.

Members shall serve one-year terms, renewable as long as they are age 30 or under
at the start of the new term.

Convener shall be elected among the members: _____

Class	Laity	Clergy
2021	_____	Jessica Davenport (2019)
2022	_____	Scott Marsh (2019)
2023	_____	
2024	**Anika Kasper (2020)**	

Given Voice, **per Division Action:** Young Adult Initiatives Coordinator, Pastor Lisa Batten (Conference Staff).

Higher Education and Campus Ministry, Division of (3.4.3.3)

Six people who shall be members of the Annual Conference (if clergy) or
Professing Members of a local church within the Annual Conference (if laity).

Members shall serve four-year terms, renewable once, in annually staggered classes.

Members shall be nominated by the Committee on Nominations.

Convener shall be elected among the members: Rev. Jeffrey "Jeff" Williams

Class	Laity	Clergy
2021	Blair Hunt (2018)	
2022		
2023	**Rick Miller (2019)**	Jeffrey "Jeff" Williams (2018)
2024		Katherine Fahey (2018)

Ex officio with vote: Any Member of the General Board of Higher Education and Ministry residing within the bounds of the Annual Conference.

Given Voice, **per Division Action:** Young Adult Initiatives Coordinator, Pastor Lisa Batten (Conference Staff).

Congregational Life, Board of (3.5)

Chairperson: Rev. Sherry Parker-Lewis
(Chairperson of the Board is an additional member, chosen by Committee on Nominations.)

Vice Chairperson: _____
(Convener shall serve as Vice Chairperson of the Board, chosen by the conveners.)

Each Division shall elect a Convener.

Given Voice, **per Board Action:** Director of Congregational Vibrancy, Rev. Dirk Elliott (Conference Staff).

Congregational Vibrancy, Division of (3.5.3.1)

Four people who shall be members of the Annual Conference (if clergy) or
Professing Members of a local church within the Annual Conference (if laity).

Members shall serve four-year terms, renewable once, in annually staggered.

Members shall be nominated by the Committee on Nominations.

Convener shall be elected among the members: _____

Class	Laity	Clergy
2020		Michael Sawicki (2018)
2021		Matthew "Matt" Stoll (2018)
2022		**James Noggle (2020)**
2023		
2024	**Cindy Thiele (2020)**	

Ex officio **with vote**: Any Member of Discipleship Ministries residing within the bounds of the Annual Conference, District Superintendent (**Rev. LuAnn Rourke**).

Small Membership Church, Division on the (3.5.3.2)

Four people who shall be members of the Annual Conference (if clergy) or
Professing Members of a local church within the Annual Conference (if laity).

Members shall serve four-year terms, renewable once, in annually staggered classes.

Members shall be nominated by the Committee on Nominations.

Convener shall be elected among the members: _____

Class	Laity	Clergy
2020		Kimberly "Kim" Metzer (2018)
2021		Matthew "Matt" Osborne (2018)
2022		Peggy Katzmark (2018)
2023		
2024		**Glenn Litchfield (2020)**

Christian Unity and Interreligious Relationships, Division on (3.5.3.3)

Six persons who shall be members of the Annual Conference (if Clergy) or Professing Members of a local church within the Annual Conference (if laity), one of whom shall serve as the District Coordinator for Christian Unity and Interreligious Relationships.

Members shall serve four-year terms, renewable once, in annually staggered classes.

Members shall be nominated by the Committee on Nominations.

Convener: Rev. Rodney "Rod" Gassaway

Class	Laity	Clergy
2021		Dianne VanMarter (2018)
2022		Rodney "Rod" Gasaway (2018)
2023	**Larry Edris (2020)**	
2024	**Mary Blashill (2020)**	**Melissa Claxton (2020)**
	Laurie Smith Del Pino (2018)	

Ex officio **with vote**: Any United Methodists residing within the bounds of the Annual Conference who are members of the following: The Office of Christian Unity and Interreligious Relationships of the Council of Bishops, the governing Board of the National Council of Churches of Christ in the U.S.A., the World Methodist Council, The United Methodist delegation to the most recent World Council of Churches Assembly, the United Methodist delegation to the most recent plenary meeting of Churches Uniting in Christ.

Hispanic/Latino Ministry, Committee on (3.6)

The committee shall define its membership and organize in any way it sees fit,
subject to the approval of the Conference Leadership Council.

Term: Four-year term, max two terms

Chairperson: Rev. Rey Mondragon

Class	Laity	Clergy
2020	Patsy Coffman (2018)	Jennifer Jue (2018)
2021	Lea Tobar (2018)	Ellen Zienert (2018)
		Sari Brown (2018)
2022	Victoria "Tori" Booker (2018)	Patricia Gandarilla (2018)
	Jorge Costales (2018)	Laura Feliciano (2018)
2023	Lawrence Iseler (2018)	Rey Mondragon (2018)
2024		**Nicolas Berlanga (2020)**

Co-Opted Members *(maximum of four; may be asked to fill the following positions such as but not limited to)*:
Training Coordinator:
Grant Application Coordinator:
Immigration Advisor:

Ex officio **with voice, but no vote**: District Superintendent (Rev. Dr. Margie Crawford), Conference Treasurer (TBD), Director of Connectional Ministries (Rev. Benton Heisler), Staff employed by the Conference Leadership Council and assigned to the Committee on Hispanic/Latino Ministry (Sonya Luna).

Asian-American Ministry, Committee on (3.7)

The committee shall define its membership and organize in any way it sees fit,
subject to the approval of the Conference Leadership Council.

Chairperson: Rev. Jung Eun Yum

Class	Laity	Clergy
2020		Latha Ravi (2018)
		Anna Moon (2018)
2021		Won Dong Kim (2018)
		Gunsoo Jung (2018)
2022		Jung Eun Yum (2018)
		Sang Chun (2018)
2023		
2024		

Co-opted Members: Rev. Dr. Darryl Totty (2018), Rev. Seung "Andy" Baek (2018), Rev. Dr. Jennifer Jue (2018), Prospero Tumonong (2018)

Ex officio **with voice, but no vote**: District Superintendent designated by Cabinet (**Rev. Dr. Jerome "Jerry" DeVine**), Director of Connectional Ministries or another Conference Representative (Sonya Luna).

Native American Ministry, Committee on (3.8)

"Insofar as possible, the majority of the committee's members should be Native Americans.

Taking into account the mandate of the purpose of this committee, the committee shall define its membership and organize in any way it sees fit, subject to the approval of the Conference Leadership Council."

The preliminary proposal that follows will need to be confirmed/revised by the Conference Leadership Council and the Committee on Native American Ministries/Indian Workers Conference at their next meeting,

The membership of the Committee on Native American Ministry (CONAM) shall include two persons elected by each Native American United Methodist congregation or ministry; the pastor may be a delegate or alternate, as determined by the church and at least four members at large selected by CONAM:

Executive Committee: Chairperson (Pastor Ronald "Todd" Williamson), Vice-Chairperson (Pastor George Pamp), Secretary (Valerie Maidens), Treasurer (Valerie Maidens), Cabinet Member Representative (Rev. Jodie Flessner, District Superintendent).

Bradley Indian Mission UMC
Chippewa Indian UMC
(Native American Elders Program)
Greensky Hill Indian Mission UMC
Kewadin Indian Mission UMC
Northport Indian Mission UMC

Oscoda UMC
PaWaTing MaGedwin Kikaajik

Salem Indian Mission UMC
Zeba Indian Mission UMC

Members-At-Large – Laity: Amy Alberts, Rose Bledsoe, Fran Church Pratt, Rich Guyon, Clara Lawrence

Ex Officio *Voice, but no vote (because of category)*: Bishop (Bishop David A. Bard), Cabinet Member Representative (Rev. Jodie Flessner), Director of Connectional Ministries (Rev. Benton Heisler).

African-American Ministry, Committee on (3.9)

The committee shall define its membership in any way it sees fit,
subject to the approval of the Conference Leadership Council.

Co-Chairs: Rev. Janet "Jan" Brown and Simmie Proctor
Recording Secretary: Rev. Janet "Jan" Brown
Communications Coordinator: Dwanda Ashford
Spiritual Formation Coordinator: Sharon Appling
Spiritual Care Coordinator: Pastor Anthony Ballah
Treasurer (Interim): Gregory "Greg" Keeler
Historian/BMCR Rep: Rev. Hilda Harris

Members:

Laity	Clergy
Loretta Lee	Sandra Bibilomo
Cecelia Tolliver	Willie "Will" Council
	B. Kevin Smalls
	Darryl Totty

***Ex officio* with voice, but no vote:** District Superintendent (Rev. Dr. Charles Boayue).

ADMINISTRATIVE AGENCIES

Finance and Administration, Council on (4.1)

Six Clergy Members of the Annual Conference.
Seven Lay People who are Professing Members of a local church within the Annual Conference.
At least one of the thirteen members shall be appointed to (in the case of a Clergy Person) or
a member of (in the case of a Lay Person) a church with fewer than two hundred members.

Members shall be nominated by the Committee on Nominations.

Members shall serve four-year terms (starting at the close of the Annual Conference Session
following General Conference), renewable once, with quadrennially staggered classes.

The Council shall elect from among its members the following:
President: Bradley "Brad" Bartelmay   Vice President: Andrew "Andy" Wayne
Secretary: Susan MacGregor

Laity
2020 Quadrennia
Jim Bosserd (2018)
Patrick Tiedt (2018)
Andrew "Andy" Wayne (2018)

2024 Quadrennia
Renae Clevenger (2018)
Cameron "Cam" DeLong (2018)
Susan MacGregor (2018)
Clayton Osborn (2018)

Clergy

Bradley "Bard" Bartelmay, President (2018)
Kristen Coristine (2020)
Donald "Don" Gotham (2019)
Janet Gaston Petty (2018)

Geraldine "Geri" Hamlen (2018)

Louis "Lou" Gretttenberger (2020)

Ex officio **with voice and vote**: Any Member of the General Council on Finance and Administration who resides within the bounds of the Annual Conference.

Ex officio **with voice, but no vote**: Director of Administrative Services and Conference Treasurer (TBD), Resident Bishop (Bishop David A. Bard), or Clergy Assistant to the Bishop (Rev. John Boley), District Superintendent (Rev. John Hice), Director of Connectional Ministries (Rev. Benton Heisler), Director of Benefits and Human Resources (Rev. Donald "Don" Emmert), any other Conference Directors as the Conference Leadership Council shall designate, any Director level benefits officer as determined by the Board of Pension and Health Benefits, Executive Director of the United Methodist Foundation of Michigan (Rev. David Bell), Chair of the Board of Trustees or their designee (**James "Jim" LeBaron**).

Pension and Health Benefits, Board of (4.2)

Six Clergy Members of the Annual Conference.
Six Lay Persons who shall be Professing Members of a local church within the Annual Conference.

Members shall be nominated by the Committee on Nominations.

Members shall serve one non-renewable eight-year term, in annually staggered classes.

The Board shall elect from among its members the following:
       Chairperson: Rev. Steven Buck   Vice Chairperson: _____
       Secretary: _____
       Treasurer: Director of Administrative Services/Conference Treasurer,

Class	Laity	Clergy
2021		Steven "Steve" Buck (2018)
2022	Kathleen Dorman (2018)	
2023	Kevin Dick (2018)	Carol Johns (2018)
2024		Gary Glanville (2018)
2025	Al Minert (2018)	Cornelius "Neil" Davis (2018)
2026	**Nancy Wyllis (2020)**	Joel Fitzgerald (2018)
2027	Dennis Stanek (2019)	**Deborah "Debbie" Thomas (2020)**

Ex officio **with vote**: Any Board Member of Wespath Benefits and Investments residing within the bounds of the Annual Conference (Rev. Joel Fitzgerald), a District Superintendent (Rev. Dr. Jerome "Jerry" DeVine) designated by the Cabinet.

Ex officio **with voice, but no vote**: Director of Administrative Services and Conference Treasurer (TBD), Director of Benefits and Human Resources (Rev. Donald Emmert), any other Conference Directors as the Conference Leadership Council shall designate, any Director level benefits officer as determined by the Board.

Administrative Review Committee (4.3)

Three Full Clergy Members of the Annual Conference.
Two additional Full Clergy Members of the Annual Conference who shall
serve as alternate committee members.
None of the foregoing shall be a District Superintendent (or a relative thereof) or
a member of the Board of Ordained Ministry (or relative thereof).

Members shall be nominated by the Bishop.

Members shall serve four-year terms, renewable once.

Class	Full Clergy Members
2020	Gerald Hagans (2018)
	Gloria Haynes (2019)
	George Lewis (2019)

Alternate Full Clergy Members

2020	Ellen Brubaker (2018)
	Catherine "Cathee" Miles (2019)

Trustees, Board of (4.4)

Six Clergy Members of the Annual Conference.
Six Lay Persons who are Professing Members of a local church within the Annual Conference.

All Board Members must be at least eighteen years of age.

All Board Members must fulfill any other criteria for serving on the Board of Directors of a corporation that the laws of the State of Michigan may require.

Members shall be nominated by the Committee on Nominations.

Except as otherwise required by law, members shall be elected to four-year terms,
renewable once, with annually staggered classes.

The Board shall elect from among its members the following:
Chairperson: **James "Jim" LeBaron**   Vice Chairperson: George Lewis
Secretary: Carolin Spragg

Except as otherwise required by law, the Director of Administrative Services/Conference Treasurer (TBD) shall serve as the Board Treasurer.

Consultant: Michael Belt

Class	Laity	Clergy
2021		Carolin Spragg (2018)
2022	Robert "Rob" Long (2018)	Matthew "Matt" Hook (2018)
2023	Jorge Costales (2018)	Joy Moore (2019)
	James "Jim" LeBaron (2019)	**Thomas "Tom" Ball (2020)**
2024	David Apol (2018)	George Lewis (2018)
	Karl Bauman (2018)	Clifford Radke (2018)
	Deborah "Deb" Federau (2020)	

Ex officio **with vote**: District Superintendent (Rev. John Hice).

Ex officio **with voice, but no vote**: Director of Administrative Services and Conference Treasurer (TBD), Director of Connectional Ministries (Rev. Benton Heisler), President of the Council on Finance and Administration or their designee (**TBD**).

Investigation, Committee on (4.5)

Four Ordained Clergy Members of the Annual Conference.
Three Lay People who are Professing Members of a local church within the Annual Conference.

Three Ordained Clergy Members of the Annual Conference shall serve as alternate members.
Six Lay People – three of whom, if possible, shall be Diaconal Ministers – who are Professing Members of a local church within the Annual Conference shall serve as alternate members.

Members shall be nominated by the Resident Bishop.

Members shall serve a one-quadrennium term.

Members of the following entities and their immediate family members shall be ineligible for members of the committee: Cabinet and Board of Ordained Ministry.

The Committee shall elect from among its members the following:
Chairperson: _____

Class	Laity	Clergy
2020	Minnie Armstrong (2019)	Richard "Rick" Blunt (2018)
	Murray Davis (2019)	G. Patrick England (2019)
	Paula Hines (2018)	Catherine "Cathi" Huvaere (2018)
	Wynne Hurlbut (2018)	Philip Tousley (2019)
	Michael Schlusler (2019)	Brian West (2019)
	Craig Schroeder (2018)	

Alternate Members:

Class	Laity	Clergy
2020	Louelle Burke (2018)	Glenn Litchfield (2018)
	Laura De La Garza (2019)	Julie Liske (2018)
	Fred Gray (2019)	
	Linda Polter (2019)	

Rules, Committee on (4.6)

Eight Voting Members who shall be either Clergy Members of the Annual Conference or Lay People who are Members of a local church within the Annual Conference.

Members shall be nominated by the Committee on Nominations.

Members shall serve four-year terms, renewable twice, in annual staggered classes.

The Committee shall elect from among its members the following:
Chairperson: Todd Price   Vice Chairperson: Tonya Murphy
Secretary: James "Jim" Searls

Class	Laity	Clergy
2021	C. David Lundquist (2018)	
	Herbert "Herb" Vanderbilt (2018)	
2022	James "Jim" Searls (2018)	Paula Timm (2018)
2023	Keith Radek (2019)	Richard "Rick" Blunt (2019)
	Tonya Murphy (2019)	
2024	Todd Price (2018)	

Ex officio with vote: Legislative Coordinator selected by the Commission on the Annual Conference (Diane Brown), Annual Conference Facilitator (**Jennifer "Jen" Peters**) a District Superintendent (Rev. Dr. Charles Boayue) designated by the Cabinet, Annual Conference Secretary (Rev. Joy Barrett), Conference Parliamentarian (if one is appointed by the Bishop).

Ex officio, but no vote: Director of Connectional Ministries (Rev. Benton Heisler).

Episcopal Residence Committee (4.7)

Chairperson of the Committee on Episcopacy (or representative): John Wharton
President of Council on Finance and Administration (or representative): Bradley "Brad" Bartelmay
Chairperson of Board of Trustees (or representative): Carolin Spragg
Others may be co-opted, with voice, but without vote, as needed.

Equitable Compensation, Commission on (4.8)

Four Clergy Members of the Annual Conference, at least one of whom shall be
appointed to a church with fewer than 200 members.
Four Lay Persons who shall be Professing Members of a church within the Annual Conference,
at least one of whom shall be a member of a church with fewer than 200 members.

Members shall serve four-year terms, renewable once, in annually staggered classes.

Members shall be nominated by the Committee on Nominations.

The Commission shall elect from among its members the following:
Chairperson: _____   Vice Chairperson: _____
Secretary: _____

The Director of Administrative Services/Conference Treasurer (TBD) shall serve as the Treasurer of the Commission.

Class	Laity	Clergy
2021	Molly Shaffer (2018)	_____
2022	Barry Trantham (2018)	Karen Williams (2018)
2023	_____	_____
2024	Robert "Bob" Bernum (2018)	Gerald Hagans (2018)

Ex officio with vote: A District Superintendent (Rev. Dwayne Bagley) designated by the Cabinet, a Member of the Council on Finance and Administration (Rev. Donald "Don" Gotham).

Ex officio with voice, but no vote: Director of Administrative Services and Conference Treasurer (TBD).

Human Resources, Committee on (4.9)

Eight people who shall be members of the Annual Conference (if Clergy) or
Professing Members of a local Church within the Annual Conference (if Laity).

Members shall serve four-year terms, renewable once, in annually staggered classes.

Members shall be nominated by the Committee on Nominations.

Chairperson chosen by the Committee on Nominations from among the Members: Rev. Ellen Zienert

Vice-Chairperson chosen by the Committee on Human Resources from among its members: Deborah "Deb" Fennell

Secretary chosen by the Committee on Human Resources from among its membership: Rev. J. Thomas Boutell

Class	Laity	Clergy
2021	Georgia Marsh (2018)	Ellen Zienert (2018)
2022	Deborah "Deb" Fennell (2018)	~~James "Tommy" Boutell~~ (2018)
2023	**Anne Soles (2020)**	Grant Lobb (2019)
		~~Nancy Powers (2019)~~
2024	Alice Tucker (2018)	

Ex officio **with vote**: Bishop (Bishop David A. Bard), or Clergy Assistant to the Bishop (Rev. John Boley), a District Superintendent (Rev. Dr. Margie Crawford) designated by the Cabinet.

Ex officio **with voice, but no vote**: Director of Connectional Ministries (Rev. Benton Heisler), Director of Administrative Services/Conference Treasurer (TBD), Director of Benefits and Human Resources (Rev. Donald Emmert), Chair of the Personnel Committee of the Council on Finance and Administration (**Rev. Janet Gaston Petty**).

Officers of The Annual Conference

Secretary (6.1): Rev. Joy Barrett (2017)
Four-year term, two terms maximum. Elected at first Annual Conference Session following General Conference.

Statistician (6.2): **Pamela Stewart** (07/15/2019)
Four-year term, two terms maximum. Elected at Annual Conference Session immediately preceding General Conference.

Facilitator (6.3): **Jennifer "Jen" Peters (2020)**
Four-year term, two terms maximum. Layperson.

Parliamentarian (6.4): None – May be appointed by the Bishop at his/her discretion.
May be appointed by the Bishop at his/her discretion.

Chancellor (6.5): Andrew Vorbrich (2017)
Nominated by the Bishop, elected quadrennially.

Director of Administrative Services and Conference Treasurer (6.6): _____ (2020)
Elected at first Annual Conference Session following each General Conference.

Lay Leader (6.7): **Annette Erbes (2020)**
Four-year term, one term. Nominated by the Bishop in consultation with the Board of Laity.

Associate Lay Leader: TBD

Please Note: The Annual Conference re-affirms the election of the General and Jurisdictional Delegation and Alternates from the 2019 Annual Conference.

In Order of Election:

2020 Elected General Conference Delegation
Clergy: Kennetha Bigham-Tsai (Chairperson), Paul Perez, Joy Barrett, Megan Walther
Laity: Laura Witkowski (Chairperson), Diane Brown, Jennifer "Jen" Peters, Nichea VerVeer Guy

2020 Elected North Central Jurisdictional Conference Delegation
Clergy: Charles Boayue, Joel Fitzgerald, Christina Wright, Brad Bartelmay
Laity: Ruby Anderson, Hoon-Yung Hopgood, Lisa Hahn, Ruth Sutton

2020 Elected NCJ Alternates
Clergy: Sherri Swanson, Matt Weiler
Laity: Brenda DuPree, Gordon Grigg III

2016 General Church Boards and Agencies:
The Connectional Table: Clergy-Kennetha Bigham-Tsai, Jerry DeVine
General Board of Church and Society: Clergy-Paul Perez
General Board of Pensions and Health Benefits: Clergy-Donald Emmert

2016 North Central Jurisdictional Committees:
Court of Appeals: Clergy-Benton Heisler (Vice Chairperson). Clergy Alternate: Joy Barrett
Committee on Investigation: Clergy-Melanie Carey, Alternate Clergy-Bill Dobbs
Committee on Episcopacy: Clergy-Charles Boayue, Benton Heisler. Laity-Jacqueline Euper, Nichea VerVeer Guy.
NCJ Mission Council: Clergy-Brad Bartelmay, At-Large: Laity-Alex Plum, Laura Witkowski
Directors of Connectional Ministries (as selected by the NCJ Association of DCMs): Clergy-Benton Heisler

AFFILIATE ENTITIES OF THE ANNUAL CONFERENCE
Elected UMC Board Members as Reported to the Committee on Nominations

Affiliated via the Board of Global Ministries (10.1)

Bronson Health Group (10.1.1) – Trustees of
(UMC Members are no longer a requirement, per change in their 2014 By-Laws)

Clark Retirement Community (10.1.2) – Trustees of
(Report Only, election is by Clark, per change in Clark's By-Laws.)

OFFICERS: Chair: Robert "Bob" Gillette (2013)

TRUSTEES:
[Tenure: By-Law terms are limited to 9 years.]
Suzeanne Benet (2015)
Jayne Courts (2016)
Kathleen "Kathy" Holt (2016)
     Only UMC Members Listed

Ex officio: **Rev. Dr. Margie Crawford, Sue Yoder**

Methodist Children's Home Society (10.1.3) – Directors
[Tenure: By-Law terms are limited to 10 years.]

Laity	Clergy
Marianne Conner (2016)	William "Bill" Amundsen (2008)
Eric Pelton (2017)	Charles Boayue (2001)
Doug Ross (2007)	
Carrie Russell (2014)	
Juli Stephens (2018)	
Christine Weemhoff (2000)	
Only UMC Members Listed	

Cabinet Assignment: A District Superintendent (Rev. Dr. Charles Boayue).

United Methodist Community House (10.1.4)
Taylorie Bailey (2016)
Kurt Kimball (2020)
     Only UMC Members Listed

Ex officio: Linda Darrow (UMW), Linda Burton-Collier (UMW).

United Methodist Retirement Communities, Inc. (10.1.5) – Board of Trustees

Laity	Clergy
Marianne Conner (2019)	Matthew "Matt" Hook (2007)
Steve Fetyko (2019)	
Mike Fritz (2019)	
Russ Ives (2009)	
Dick Lundy (1983)	

Cabinet Assignment: A District Superintendent (**Rev. LuAnn Rourke**).

Affiliated Via the Board of Young People's Ministries (10.2)

Adrian College (10.2.1) – Trustees of
[Tenure: By-Law terms are limited to 9 years.]

Laity	Clergy
	Elbert P. Dulworth (2019)
	Janet Gaston Petty (2019)
	Russell "Russ" McReynolds (2006) *

Area Bishop: Bishop David A. Bard

* Term extended by request of the Trustees of Adrian College.

[ ] Indicate names submitted for election of two by College in coordination with Board of Higher Education and Campus Ministry.

Albion College (10.2.2) – Trustees of
[Tenure: By-Law terms are limited to 12 years.]

Laity	Clergy
	Faith Fowler (2013)

Area Bishop: Bishop David A. Bard

[ ] Indicate names submitted for election of two by College in coordination with Board of Higher Education and Campus Ministry.

Michigan Area United Methodist Camping (10.2.4)
Elected by the Annual Conference, per Board By-Laws (no less than 60%):

Chairperson: **Stuart Smith**   Interim Director: Joel Wortley

Elected by the Board, per Board By-Laws: Deborah "Deb" Fennell (2018)

	Laity	Clergy
2021	Susan Witte (2017)	David Wichert (2017)
2022	Stuart Smith (2018)	Terry Euper (2019)
	Bob Wyatt (2018)	Anita Hahn (2019)
2023	Steve Steggerda (2019)	Joel Walther (2019)
		Patricia "Patti" Harpole (2019)
2024	**Rachel Dunlap (2020)**	

Designated by the Full Cabinet *(voice, but no vote)***:** District Superintendent (Rev. Dwayne Bagley).

Ex officio **with voice, but no vote:** Executive Director of Camping: Joel Wortley (interim).

Lake Louise Christian Community (10.2.5) – Board of Trustees
[Tenure: By-Law terms are limited to 9 years. Elect their own chair.]

Laity	Clergy
Christie Brewster (2019)	**Corey Simon (2020)**
Elizabeth "Liz" Carr (2014)	Hillary Thurston-Cox (2018)
Doug Clarke (2016)	**Alicia Williams (2020)**
Daphne Mitchell (2013)	
Linda Zeeb (2018)	

Affiliated via the Commission on Archives and History (10.3)

Michigan Area UMC Historical Society, Inc. (10.3)
Elected by Commission on Archives and History.

Chairperson: Diana Spitnale Miller

Laity	**Clergy**
Ken Gackler (2008)	Melanie Young (2012)
Sharon Scott (2007)	
Mary Whitman (2014)	
Dan Yakes (2008)	

Members At-Large: William McNitt, Lois Omundson, Rev. Lowell Peterson, Della Wilder

Ex officio **with voice and vote**: The Chairperson of the Commission on Archives and History (Mary Whitman), The Archivists of the Conference Archives – Rebecca McNitt (Adrian) and Elizabeth Palmer (Albion), Members of the General Commission on Archives and History residing in the Annual Conference: Diana Spitnale Miller, Linda Schramm; Member of the Historical Society of the UMC Board: Linda Schramm.

Affiliated via the Council on Finance and Administration (10.4)

Michigan Area Loan Funds (10.4.1)
Elected by the UM Foundation of Michigan

Chairperson:

Laity	**Clergy**
Nancy Craig (2019)	Bradley "Brad" Bartelmay (2019)
Ransom Leppink (2019)	Edward "Ed" Ross (2019)
Joy Stair (2019)	
Sue Woodard (2019)	

Ex officio: Rev. David Bell, Resident Agent.

United Methodist Foundation of Michigan (10.4.2)
12 Directors elected by the UM Foundation of Michigan

Class	Laity	Clergy
2020	Nancy Craig (2014)	
	Steve Peters (2020)	
	Sue Woodard (2011)	
	To Be Name	
2021	Ransom Leppink (2012)	Joel Fitzgerald (2018)
	Joy Stair (2012)	Edward "Ed" Ross (2015)
2022	**Pros Tumonong (2020)**	Bradley "Brad" Bartelmay (2015)
		Gary Glanville (2014)
		Mary McInnes (2019)

Ex officio: Rev. David Bell, President and Executive Director; Bishop David A. Bard, Resident Bishop; TBD, Conference Treasurer.

Disaster Response Team

Team Chairperson: Rev. Robert Miller
Disaster Response Coordinator: Dan O'Malley
Disaster Recovery Coordinator: Nancy Money
Conference Emotional and Spiritual Care Coordinator: _____
Conference Communications Director: Mark Doyal
Conference Finance Officer: _____
Conference VIM Coordinator: Jody Pratt

District Disaster Response Coordinators

Central Bay: _____
East Winds: **Rev. Eric Miller**
Greater Detroit: Dwanda Ashford
Greater Southwest: Rev. David "Dave" Morton
Heritage: **Robert "Bob" Ankrapp**
Mid-Michigan: _____
Midwest: _____
Northern Skies – East: **Randy Hildebrant**
Northern Skies – West: _____
Northern Waters: Dave Stockford

Ex officio **with voice, but no vote**: District Superintendent (**Rev. John Kasper**) and Director of Connectional Ministries (Rev. Benton Heisler).

Justice for Our Neighbors (JFON) – Michigan Board

Elected by Annual Conference, no less than 60% of Board:

Rev. Paul Perez, Chair   Sonya Luna
Kristine Faasse   Joan VanDessel
Hoon-Yung Hopgood

**Please e-mail any corrections/updates by September 1, 2020 to:
nominations@michiganumc.org**

If there is a correction, please include page number, agency, person's name, and explanation of the correction or change – i.e., "delete" or "add." If a person is to be added, please specify whether they are clergy/laity, male/female, and the beginning year of service.

**If you are interested in serving where vacancies exist, please contact:
nominations@michiganumc.org**

Thank you!

NOMINATIONS REPORT

DISTRICT COMMITTEES
Provided for Information Only

District Boards of Church Location and Building

Central Bay District – Rev. John Kasper, District Superintendent

Laity	Clergy
Karl Bauman, Chair (2018)	Jon Gougeon (2018)
Randy Hock (2018)	James "Jim" Payne (2018)
Darlene Levia (2018)	

East Winds District – Rev. John Hice, District Superintendent

Laity	Clergy
Bob Bernum (2018)	Barbara Benjamin (2018)
Kathy Dorman (2018)	*Jerry Griggs (2018), Co-Chair*
Peter Plum (2018)	David Reed (2018)
Doris Sain (2018)	
Dayna Wright (2018	
Robert Wyatt (2018), Co-Chair	

Greater Detroit District – Rev. Dr. Charles Boayue, District Superintendent

Laity	Clergy
Don Archambeau (2018)	Jean Snyder (2018)
John Lawrence (2018)	*Jonathan Combs, Vice Chair (2018)*
Pearl Lewis (2018)	Jinny Song (2018)
Eugene Paik, Chair (2018)	
Lynn Van De Putte (2018)	

Greater Southwest District – Rev. Dwayne Bagley, District Superintendent

Laity	Clergy
Wynne Hurlbut (2018)	Ronald "Ron" VanLente (2018)
Mark Crawford (2018)	
Nate Hawthorne (2018)	
Donald Weaver (2018)	

Heritage District – Rev. LuAnn Rourke, District Superintendent

Laity	Clergy
Nicolas Dever (2018)	**Robert "Bob" Freysinger (2019)**
Jim Jacobs (2018)	Peter "Pete" Harris (2019)
Doug Parr (2019)	Robert Hughes (2018)
	John Schneider (2019)
	Robert "Bob" Stover (2018)

Mid-Michigan District – Rev. Dr. Jerome "Jerry" DeVine, District Superintendent

Laity	Clergy
James "Jim" LeBaron, Chair (2018)	Jeanne Randels (2018)
William Blanchett (2018)	
Darcy Bozen (2018)	
Deborah Federau (2018)	
Dick Rice (2018)	

    Ex officio: District Treasurer (Betsy Mauk).

Midwest District – Rev. Dr. Margie Crawford, District Superintendent

Laity	Clergy
David Apol, Chair (2018)	Gregory "Greg" Buchner (2018)
Dennis Bekken (2018)	Diane Gordon (2018)
John Faas (2018)	Michael "Mike" Ramsey (2018)
Louann Hoffman (2018)	
Susan MacGregor (2018)	
Steve Meredith (2018)	

Northern Skies District – Rev. Scott Harmon, District Superintendent

Laity	Clergy
Rich Dahlin (2019)	James "Jim" Mathews (2018)
Randy Hildebrant (2019)	Geri Hamlin (2019)
Phillis Johnson (2020)	
Roger Tembreull (2020)	

Northern Waters District – Rev. Jodie Flessner, District Superintendent

Laity	Clergy
Tom Bowman (2018)	*John Scott, Chair (2018)*
Lyle Matteson (2018)	Eugene Baughan (2018)
Ann Porter (2018)	Patricia Haas (2018)
	George Spencer (2018)

District Committees on Ordained Ministry

Central Bay District

Ordained Ministry Representative: Rev. David Wichert
District Superintendent: **Rev. John Kasper**

Laity	Clergy
Mary Fox (2019)	Joseph Beaven (2019)
Larry Wyman, Sr. (2019)	Timothy Dibble (2019)
	Ernesto Mariona (2018)
	Robert "Rob" Richards (2018)
	Amy Lee Terhune (2019)

East Winds District

Ordained Ministry Representative: Rev. Susan Platt
District Superintendent: Rev. John Hice

Laity	Clergy	Clergy
Tom Cerny (2018)	**Sang Chum (2020)**	Susan Platt (2018)
Bonnie Potter (2018)	Richard "Rick" Dake (2018)	Tara Sutton (2019)
Bernie Schneider (2018)	Ann Emerson (2018), Vice Chair	Philip Tousley (2018)
	Patricia Hoppenworth (2018)	Joel Walther (2018), Secretary
	Catherine "Cathi" Huvaere (2018)	Karen Williams (2018)
	Charles "Chuck" Jacobs (2018)	Christine Wyatt (2018)
	Jeffrey Jaggers (2018), Chair	

Greater Detroit District
Ordained Ministry Representative: _____
District Superintendent: Rev. Dr. Charles Boayue

Laity	Clergy	Clergy
Ruby Anderson (2018)	*Steven McCoy, Chair (2018)*	Gregory Mayberry (2018)
Don Archambeau (2018)	*B. Kevin Smalls, Vice Chair (2018)*	**Anna Moon (2020)**
Cathy Hazen (2020)	Weatherly Burkhead-Verhelst (2018)	Jeffery Nelson (2018)
Carole Wesner (2018)	Melanie Carey (2018)	Latha Ravi (2018)
	Donald "Don" Gotham (2018)	**Dianna Rees (2020)**
	Carter Grimmett (2018)	**Jean Snyder (2020)**
	Jack Mannschreck (2018)	Joy Won (2018)
	Judith May (2018)	

Greater Southwest District
Ordained Ministry Representative: _____
District Superintendent: Rev. Dwayne Bagley

Laity	Clergy
Laurie Dahlman (2018)	*David Hills, Chair (2018)*
Wynne Hurlbut (2018)	Martin "Marty" Culver (2018)
	Julie Elmore (2018)
	Ronald Hansen (2018)
	Mona Joslyn (2018)
	Gregory Lawton (2020)
	Karen Wheat (2018)

Heritage District
Ordained Ministry Representative: _____
District Superintendent: **Rev. LuAnn Rourke**

Laity	Clergy
Lynne Pauer (2018)	Nancy Lynn, Chair (2018)
Ken Kneisel (2019)	**James "Jim" Britt (2019)**
John Seppanen, Lay Leader (2019)	**Jeanne Garza (2019)**
John Wharton (2018)	Annelisa Gray-Lion (2018)
	Loretta Job (2018)
	Mary Loring, Registrar (2020)
	Rob McPherson (2018)
	Marsha Woolley (2018)
	Timothy "Tim" Ziegler (2018)

Mid-Michigan District
Ordained Ministry Representative: Pastor Terri Bentley, Rev. Mark Erbes
District Superintendent: Rev. Dr. Jerome "Jerry" DeVine

Laity	Clergy
Fred Olmsted (2018)	*Patricia "Pat" Brook, Chair (2019)*
	Terri Bentley, BOM Rep (2018)
	Mark Erbes, BOM Rep (2018)
	Kathy Pittenger (2019)
	Irene Vittoz, Candidacy Registrar (2018)
	Ellen Zienert (2018)

Midwest District
  Ordained Ministry Representative: Rev. William "Bill" Johnson
  District Superintendent: Rev. Dr. Margie Crawford

Laity	Clergy
AnnMarie Buchner (2018)	*Jane Ellen Johnson, Chair (2019)*
Daniel "Dan" Davis (2018)	**Tommy Boutell (2019)**
	Taina Dozeman (2019)
	William "Bill" Johnson, Candidacy Registrar (2018)
	Nancy Patera, Local Pastor Registrar (2018)
	J. "Lynn" Pier-Fitzgerald (2018)
	Ryan Wieland, Secretary (2018)

Northern Skies District
  Ordained Ministry Representative: Rev. Scott Lindenberg
  District Superintendent: Rev. Scott Harmon

Laity	Clergy
Anine Bessolo (2018)	*Christopher Hintz, Chair (2018)*
Kelly Ross (2019)	James "Jim" Balfour (2018)
Rob Veale (2020)	J. Albert Barchue (2018)
	Victoria Hadaway (2020)
	Geraldine "Geri" Hamlen (2018)
	Scott Lindenberg (2018)
	Peggy Paige, Registrar (2018)
	Cathy Rafferty (2020)

Northern Waters District
  Ordained Ministry Representative: _____
  District Superintendent: Rev. Jodie Flessner

Laity	Clergy
Allen Horstman (2018)	*Dale Ostema, Chair (2018)*
Denny Olin (2018)	Deborah "Deb" Johnson (2019)
	Yoo Jin Kim (2019)
	James Mitchum (2018)
	Melody Olin, Registrar (2018)

District Committees on District Superintendency

Central Bay District
  District Superintendent: **Rev. John Kasper**
  District Lay Leader: **Dennis "Denny" Wissinger**

Laity	Clergy
Linda Doane (2010)	*Ernesto Mariona, Chair (2018)*
Al Gonzalez (2018)	Robert "Rob" Richards (2018)
Cathy Kelley (2018)	
Madison Meyer (2018)	

East Winds District
District Superintendent: Rev. John Hice
District Lay Leader: **Cynthia Rossman**

Laity
Lois Bunton, DS Appointee (2018)
James Dover (2018)
Bruce Hurd (2018)
Debra Lobb, DS Appointee (2018)
Cynthia Rossman (2020)
Dayne Walling, At-large (2018)

Clergy
Sari Brown, At-large (2018)
Julius Del Pino (2018), Secretary
Janine Plum (2018), Chair

Greater Detroit District
District Superintendent: Rev. Dr. Charles Boayue
District Lay Leader: Ruby Anderson

Laity
Ruby Anderson (2018)
Don Archambeau (2018)
Christopher Brown (2018)
Barbara DeGrazia (2020)
Alice Tucker (2019)

Clergy
Judith May, Chair (2018)
Carter Grimmett, Vice Chair (2018)
Diana Goudie (2018)
Cherlyn McKannders (2018)

Greater Southwest District
District Superintendent: Rev. Dwayne Bagley
District Lay Leader: Wynne Hurlbut

Laity
Michelle Brokaw (2018)
Lisa Coe (2018)
Marlene Cutler (2018)
Larry Edris (2018)
John Graves (2018)
Wynne Hurlbut (2018)
Deb Search Willoughby (2018), Chair
Donna Smith (2018)

Clergy
Joseph Shaler (2020)

Heritage District
District Superintendent: **Rev. LuAnn Rourke**
District Lay Leader: **John Seppanen**

Laity
Jane Case (2018)
Vicky Engelbert (2018)
Wendy Everett (2018)
John Phillips (2018)
John Seppanen (2019)
John Wharton (2018)

Clergy
Robert Miller, Chair (2018)
Mary Loring (2018)
Bradley "Brad" Luck (2018)

Mid-Michigan District

District Superintendent: Rev. Dr. Jerome "Jerry" DeVine
District Lay Leader: Nona Spackman

Laity	Clergy
Dean McCracken (2019)	*Deborah "Debbie" Thomas, Chair (2018)*
Marilyn Rothert (2018)	Russell "Russ" McReynolds (2018)
Nona Spackman (2018)	Molly Turner (2018)

Midwest District

District Superintendent: Rev. Dr. Margie Crawford
District Lay Leader: **Deborah "Deb" Hodges**

Laity	Clergy
Deborah "Deb" Hodges (2018)	*Dean Prentiss, Chair (2018)*
John Huizing (2018)	
Linda Sbraccia (2018)	

Northern Skies

District Superintendent: Rev. Scott Harmon
District Lay Leader: John Preston

Laity	Clergy
Janet Helmbold (2018)	*David "Dave" Wallis, Chair (2018)*
Dawn Payne (2018)	Kristine "Kristi" Hintz (2018)
John Preston (2018)	

Northern Waters District

District Superintendent: Rev. Jodie Flessner
District Lay Leader: Denny Olin

Laity	Clergy
Brian Highway, Chair (2018)	**Hyun-Jun Cho (2020)**
Chuck Corwin (2019)	**Kristen Coristine (2020)**
Valerie Maidens (2018)	Daniel Hofmann (2018)
Denny Olin (2018)	**Todd Shafer (2020)**

Please e-mail any corrections/updates by September 1, 2020 to:
nominations@michiganumc.org

If there is a correction, please include page number, agency, person's name, and explanation of the correction or change – i.e., "delete" or "add." If a person is to be added, please specify whether they are clergy/laity, male/female, and the beginning year of service.

If you are interested in serving where vacancies exist, please contact:
nominations@michiganumc.org

Thank you!

SPECIAL SESSION
of the Michigan Annual Conference
Saturday, March 7, 2020

A Special Session of the Michigan Annual Conference was called to order at 1:45 p.m. at the Goodrich Chapel, Albion College, by Bishop Bard. Nichea Ver Veer Guy, chair of the Commission on the Annual Conference, welcomed the members of the annual conference. She invited the conference to honor and express appreciation to the first peoples of Southwest Michigan who cared for this region of land. They include The Pokagon Band of Potawatomi, Nottawaseppi Huron Band of Potawatomi, and Match-e-Be-Nash-e-Wish Band of Pottawatomi.

Dave Atchison, Mayor of Albion, greeted the conference.

Dr. Mauri A. Ditzler, President of Albion College, brought a word of welcome from the college.

Opening Worship was led by Bishop Bard, organist Royal Ward.

Rules of Order: Nichea Ver Veer Guy, chair of the Commission on the Annual Conference, spoke. Following the motions, Ver Veer Guy clarified the nametag colors: Green: voice and vote; white: voice and no vote; pink: no voice and no vote and observers.

Motion: To open the March 7, 2020 Specially Call Session of the Michigan Annual Conference following the agenda in the program. **Motion adopted.**

Motion: The voting bar of the Michigan Specially Called Session shall be all the seats on the upper and lower levels of Goodrich Chapel. I would also include permission for any administrative assistants to the Bishop, Julie Bard, and General and Jurisdictional Conference Delegates and guests of the Bishop, who might be assisting with this session, to be allowed to be seated in the front of the chapel. **Motion adopted.**

Bishop Bard clarified the Michigan Annual Conference standing rule regarding the 3-minute length of debate speeches. Also, that our conference rules state that the conference may not amend the petition.

Conference Business: Laura Witkowski, co-chair of the Michigan Delegation to General Conference, made the following motion:

Motion: "Per The Book of Discipline of The United Methodist Church, ¶507.6, the Michigan Conference of the United Methodist Church hereby sends the petition entitled "Reconciliation and Grace Through Separation and Restructuring (BOD New ¶2556)" to the 2020 General Conference." **Motion adopted** (see below).

Vote on the motion. A vote was taken by paper ballet. Laura Witkowski, co-chair of the Michigan Delegation to General Conference, spoke to the motion. Joy Barrett, Michigan Annual Conference Secretary, explained the voting procedure. Voting is either "Yes" or "No" to the motion. Bishop Bard offered a prayer prior to the distribution of ballots.

Bishop Bard made announcements and called a break at 4:06 p.m. for the purpose of counting the ballots.

Business Session reconvened at 4:31 p.m. by Bishop Bard. He shared some thoughts about ways to respond to the coronavirus, and he expressed his gratitude for the way the Michigan Annual Conference responded to the request to hold a special annual conference session for the purpose of sending this petition to General Conference.

Report of the Vote:

Yes: 927
No: 92
Invalid: 0
TOTAL: 1019

Closing Prayer and Song: Bishop Bard led us in a closing prayer and we sang "You Are the Seed," accompanied by pianist Jan Fourn.

Conference Session was adjourned at 4:50 p.m. by Bishop Bard.

— MAC Photos

DAILY PROCEEDINGS

FIRST DAY – EVENING SESSION

Sunday, July 26, 2020

The Michigan Annual Conference Opening Worship and Memorial Service began at 7:00 p.m. at the Lansing Public Media Center in Lansing, Michigan, and streamed to annual conference delegates via Zoom Webinar, the Michigan Conference Facebook page, and 2020.MichiganUMC.org. Bishop David Bard preached, and Margie Crawford was the liturgist. Music was led by the musicians from Grand Rapids: Cornerstone United Methodist Church. Clergy, clergy spouses, and laity who passed away since the last annual conference session were memorialized by a reading of the names. The naming of the saints was led by Bishop Bard. Those memorialized were:

- **Clergy**: Sharyn Kay Rush-Osmond, Joyce A. Hanlon, Bruce M. Denton, Robert H. Bough, Donald S. Weatherup, Ross N. Nicholson, Margaret A. Kivisto, Charles F. Garrod, George R. Grettenberger, Clarence W. VanConant, Owen White-Pigeon, Kenneth D. McCaw, Webley J. Simpkins Jr., Ralph T. Barteld, O. William Cooper Jr., Theron E. Bailey, Ron L. Keller, Alfred T. Bamsey, Richard C. Cheatham, F. Richard MacCanon, John L. Andrews, A. Ray Grienke, Phylemon D. Titus, Anthony J. Shipley, Kenneth J. Bremer, David Cheyne, Robert E. Walton, George Fleming, John W. McNaughton, Georg F.W. Gerritsen, Robert P. Ward, and Gary Sanderson.
- **Clergy Spouses**: Matti R. Koivula, Deborah Ferris, Benjamin C. Wilson, Eileen L. Pohly, Carol A. Wingeier, Charlene F. Garrett, Mary Ten Have, Joanne R. Perez, Jean M. Schaaf, Nancy L. Mecartney, Jerry W. Daniel, Eloise M. Moore, Richard K. Osmond, Nancy J. Ellison, LeAnne Trebilcock, Janet Huddleson, Thomas L. Klacking, Donna M. Cozadd, and Wilma King.
- **Laity**: Jacquelin E. Washington, Janet E. Pool, Lucille R. Evans, Lucile M. Ogden, and Merna I. Francis.

An offering was received which will benefit our covenant partners, The Methodist Church of Haiti (45% to HAPI's 'Start Right' program) and The Liberia Annual Conference (45% to Bishop Judith Craig Children's Village). A 10% tithe of the offering will go the Michigan Disaster Relief and Recovery Fund.

Announcements were made by Nichea Ver Veer Guy, Commission on the Annual Conference Session chairperson.

Worship concluded at 8:10 p.m.

SECOND DAY – MORNING SESSION

Monday, July 27, 2020

Brad Kalajainen opened the morning session with a devotion at 9:30 a.m. on the theme of *Sowing Seeds: Rooting, Tending, and Reaping*. He suggested six seeds that will bear fruit if planted, nurtured, and tended over time:

1. We must become more *conversational*
2. We must become more *invitational*
3. We must become more *relational*
4. We must become more *'glocal'* (local & global)
5. We must become more *digital*
6. We must become more *foundational*

Nichea Ver Veer Guy, Chair on the Commission of Annual Conference, welcomed members to Annual Conference. She reminded the annual conference of our commitment to live into the Acts of Repentance to Native and Indigenous Peoples. On behalf of the conference, she apologized for past atrocities inflicted upon them and of racism and doctrinal abuse and asked for forgiveness. She led us in a moment of silence and prayer.

Episcopal welcome: Bishop Bard welcomed conference members, and introduced John Boley, Assistant to the Bishop, and Joy Barrett, Conference secretary.

Introduction to Zoom and Voting: Mark Doyal, Director of Communications, welcomed the members of the virtual annual conference and explained the process of virtually participating in today's session, drawing attention to pp. 8-9 of the legislative booklet.

Organization of Conference: Nichea Ver Veer Guy, Chair of the Commission on Annual Conference, spoke.
  Motion: Ver Veer Guy moved that the agenda for the business of Michigan Annual Conference 2020 to be as printed in the mailed program booklet that voting members have received. **Motion adopted**.
  Motion: Ver Veer Guy moved that the voting bar for this virtual plenary session will be within the capacity of this virtual Zoom meeting which includes phone participation, to all duly registered voting members. All duly registered voting members to Michigan Annual Conference should have received their paper ballot for use in the voting process. Some participants on this platform will have-voice but not vote and do not have a ballot. **Motion adopted.**

A 5-minute video break was called at 10:20 a.m. by Bishop Bard.

The business session reconvened at 10:25 a.m.

Report on Legislation. Bishop Bard explained the reasons behind the decision to limit resolutions this year to those which were essential business of the annual conference. He thanked those persons and groups who voluntarily withdrew their resolutions for this year's annual conference.

Pension and Benefits Resolutions: Don Emmert, Director of Conference Benefits and Human Resources, reported. Bishop Bard prayed prior to calling for the votes.
  Motion: Emmert moved the adoption of R#2020-1, "Authorization for CBOPHB to Address Claims." **R#2020-1 adopted.**
  Motion: Emmert moved the adoption of R#2020-2, "Establish the Housing/ Rental Allowance for Retired or Clergy on Medical Leave." **R#2020-2 adopted**.

Motion: Emmert moved to refer R#2020-3, "2021 Comprehensive Benefit Funding Plan," to the Board of Pensions and Health Benefits. **R#2020-3 adopted.**

Motion: Emmert moved the adoption of R#2020-4, "Establish Past Service Rate." **R#2020-4 adopted.**

Motion: Emmert moved the adoption of R#2020-23, "Guidelines for Equitable Compensation Support."

      Amendment: Gary Step moved to strike the words on page 17, line 10, "the Vital Church Initiative (VCI) or a Paragraph 213 Review" and replace them with "Roads to Vibrancy or Local Church Assessment". **Amendment adopted** (93% yes)

      R#2020-23 as amended adopted.

A 5-minute video break was called at 10:55 a.m. by Bishop Bard.

The business session reconvened at 11:00 a.m.

Legislative Work – Plan of Organization Amendments

R#2020-9 – *Amend Conference Plan of Organization – Conference Leadership Council Membership*

Amy Mayo-Moyle, chair of the Michigan Conference Leadership Council, spoke to the nature and purpose of the resolution. **R#2020-9 was adopted.**

R#2020-10 – *Amend Conference Plan of Organization – Council on Finance and Administration*

Brad Bartelmay, chair of the Michigan Conference Council on Finance and Administration, spoke to the nature and purpose of the resolution. **R#2020-10 was adopted.**

R#2020-11 – *Amend Conference Plan of Organization – Board of Trustees Membership*

Jim LeBaron, chair of the Michigan Conference Board of Trustees, spoke to the nature and purpose of the resolution. **R#2020-11 was adopted.**

CFA Report: Brad Bartelmay, President of the Council on Finance and Administration, reported, during which he thanked David Dobbs for his years of service as our Conference Treasurer. Two retirements were announced: Becky Emmert (Operations Manager) and Nancy Wyllys (Accounts Payable Officer). Three new employees were also announced: Kim Kemmis (Accounts Payable), Kriss Salters (administrative assistant), and Pamala Stewart (Statistician and Database Manager). See conference reports section of the journal for the full details of the CFA report.

A video was shown highlighting the search for a new Conference Treasurer. Bartelmay announced that that CFA is in currently doing a search with the support of the General Council on Finance and Administration. The title of the new position will be 'Chief Financial Officer of the Conference.' The job description has been updated. A first round of interviews has begun.

Nominations Report: Janet Larner, chair of the Nominations Committee, reported. The report was brought via video. Larner announced that the incoming chairperson will be Melissa Claxton. Bishop Bard prayed before calling for the vote.

Motion: Larner moved the acceptance of the report of the Committee on Nominations, with the understanding that the Committee is authorized to fill any vacancies between Conference sessions. **Motion adopted.**

The session was adjourned at 11:45 a.m. for lunch. John Boley offered grace for today's lunch.

SECOND DAY – AFTERNOON SESSION

Monday, July 27, 2020

Bishop Bard called the business session to order at 1:30 p.m.

Lay Leader Report: John Warton and Anne Soles, Co-Conference Lay Leaders, reported. Their report focused on congregational vitality. Warton emphasized the importance of a strong partnership between clergy and laity for vitality. Both clergy and laity play an important role in the making of disciples. He encouraged everyone to complete a spiritual gifts inventory, and specifically mentioned "Your Spiritual Gifts Inventory" by Charles V. Bryant. Soles spoke about the importance of practicing Wesley's 'General Rules,' specifically private acts of mercy and public acts of justice.

The business session was adjourned at 1:50 p.m. by Bishop Bard.

Michigan Annual Conference Corporate Session was called to order at 1:50 p.m. by Jim LeBaron, chair of Board of Trustees. Bishop Bard will facilitate the voting during the corporate session. The following is a brief summary of action taken by the Board of Trustees since the 2019 annual conference:

- George Lewis, vice-chair, oversaw the development of a comprehensive list of policies and procedures related to the ongoing care of conference-related properties (parsonages, offices, etc.).
- Worked with the Grand Rapids District and the Midwest District on a tax issue that relates to parsonages.
- Sold four properties.
- Oversaw the transfer of the title of the Saganing Indian Church to the Saginaw Chippewa Indian Tribe. Bishop Bard executed the deed on their behalf.
- Currently overseeing the sale of seven church buildings.
- Trying to expand the capacity for storage of church archives.
- Continue to be in conversations with Church Mutual regarding insurance regarding claims, risk analysis, and finding ways to enhance coverage.
- They have worked closely with the Camp Board and Stuart Smith, Camp Board chair, in the decisions around the disposition of camp properties.

Camp Ministry Report: Stuart Smith, Camp Board chair, reported. He briefly reviewed the strategic plan the Board recently adopted and then shared how we will be moving forward in the year ahead.

"Dowry" Reports: Jim LeBaron reported. Each district had the opportunity to be given a minimum of $250,000 in order to utilize their Board of Missions and apply those monies in missional support and extended grants. Each district is expected to submit to the Board of Trustees a report and a summary of what activities transpired. Mark Doyal has asked each district to provide him highlights which can be published in MIconnect throughout the year. The formal reports from each district will be included in future Annual Conference Journals.

"Legacy" Report: Elizabeth Hill reported. Hill named the four churches being closed this year and highlighted the legacies of each congregation.

Motion: On behalf of the appointive cabinet, Elizabeth Hill moved that in accordance with paragraph 2549 of the 2016 Book of Discipline, these four churches be closed as of the following dates. Bishop Bard offered prayer prior to calling for the vote. **Motion adopted**.
1. Owosso: Burton UMC - June 30, 2019
2. Ubly UMC - September 30, 2019
3. Muskegon: Unity UMC - December 31, 2019
4. Mulliken UMC - March 1, 2020.

LeBaron announced that in lieu of the fact that the process of disaffiliation outlined by paragraph 2553 of The Book of Discipline has not been ratified by the denomination, the Conference and the bishop have worked with the Conference Chancellor to define a formal Withdrawal Agreement for Michigan Annual Conference congregations which want to disaffiliate with The United Methodist Church.

Motion: LeBaron moved that in accordance with the Withdrawal Agreement worked out by the Board of Trustees and the Conference Chancellor, the following three churches be granted permission to withdraw from The United Methodist Church. Bishop Bard offered prayer. **Motion Adopted**.
1. Shabbona UMC
2. East Boardman UMC
3. North Adams UMC

Michigan Annual Conference Corporate Session was adjourned at 2:30 p.m.

Business session reconvened at 2:30 p.m.

Budget Motion: Brad Bartlemay, chair of CFA, moved to approve the 2021 Michigan Area Conference Budget, including the following highlights. **Motion adopted.**
1. The total budget is $12,617,521, a decrease of 14.17% from the prior year.
2. All cost of living increases have been eliminated from the budget.
3. There is no decrease in the Benefits Ministry Shares budget in 2021.
4. The Benefits Ministry Shares budget was reduced in 2020 by 50% ($1.86 million) through the BMS payment holiday from April-September.
5. The holiday effectively created a 25% total decrease for Benefits Ministry Shares receipts over 2020-2021.

Cabinet/Dean's Report: Elizabeth Hill, Dean of the Appointive Cabinet, reported.

<u>Word of appreciation</u>: Bishop Bard expressed his appreciation to Elizabeth Hill for her faithful service as the Dean of Cabinet, and to Jeff Maxwell for his service as a superintendent. Both are retiring. He announced that the next Dean of the Appointive Cabinet Dean is Jerry DeVine. He concluded his remarks with a special thank-you to Nichea Ver Veer Guy for her tireless and faithful work as the chair of the Commission on the Annual Conference.

<u>John Buxton Award for Creative Leadership</u>: Don Emmert presented the award to Susanne Buxton, sharing highlights of her leadership through the years, including:
- Sue served as the conference head usher from 1985-1997.
- Sue was the Conference President for the United Methodist Women from 1997-2000.
- Sue was a conference delegate for the North Central Jurisdiction and alternate to the 2000 General Conference.
- Since the early 2000's, Sue has occupied the chair and managed the table of Conference Facilitator with a creative proficiency, precision, and grace.
- Sue has served as a member of the Conference Program Committee/ Commission on Annual Conference for the last 35 years.

<u>A 5-minute break</u> was called at 2:51 p.m. by Bishop Bard.

<u>The business session</u> resumed at 2:58 p.m.

<u>"5K Run" Update</u>: Joy Barrett, Conference Secretary, reported that nearly 200 participants have raised $7495 to-date.

<u>Setting of Appointments</u> for the Michigan Annual Conference was led by Bishop Bard. All appointments are as shared online. He thanked John Boley for his service as the Assistant to the Bishop and announced that he will continue in this role on a part-time basis upon his retirement.

<u>Motion</u>: Nichea Ver Veer Guy moved the closing of this Michigan Annual Conference Annual Conference 2020 session. **Motion adopted.**

<u>A moment of silence</u> was observed in honor of John Lewis, the late senator of the state of Georgia.

THIRD DAY – CLERGY SESSION

Tuesday, July 28, 2020

<u>Digital clergy session [via Zoom] was called to order</u> at 9:30 a.m. at the Lansing Public Media Center in Lansing, Michigan, by Bishop Bard.

<u>Announcements</u> were given by Barry Petrucci, chair of the Board of Ordained Ministry.

<u>Enabling Motions</u>:
<u>Motion</u>: Petrucci moved to allow all Conference staff and technical support persons, both professional and volunteer who are necessary for the

functioning of this Clergy Session be granted voice but no vote. *Motion adopted.*

Motion: Petrucci moved that all lay members, local pastors, and associate pastors who serve on the Board of Ordained Ministry, in accordance with the Book of Discipline, be granted voice and vote in this clergy session. *Motion adopted.*

Motion: Petrucci moved that all Provisional Members, Associate Members, and all other clergy appointed to serve among us be granted voice, but no vote in this clergy session. *Motion adopted.*

Voting Procedure: Bishop Bard explained the procedure for voting during this clergy session.

Opening Message: Barry Petrucci, chair of the Board of Ordained Ministry, shared a message with the clergy.

A break was called at 9:50 a.m. by Bishop Bard.

The clergy session resumed at 9:55 a.m.

Preparation for the business ahead. Margie Crawford prayed. Bishop Bard clarified who has voice and vote, and who has voice and no vote.

Ordained and Licensed Clergy Status Action Items

Statement: Bishop Bard read the statement from the Appointive Cabinet in response to question **#17**.

Motion: Petrucci moved the adoption of question **#18a**. *Motion adopted.*

Motion: Petrucci moved the adoption of question **#20 #21a, and #21b**. *Motion adopted* by the required three-quarter vote.

Motion: Petrucci moved the adoption of question **#25**. *Motion adopted.*

Motion: Petrucci moved the adoption of question **#26b**. *Motion adopted* by the required two-thirds vote.

Motion: Petrucci moved the adoption of question **#28a** and **28b**. A video was shown of those to be elected as provisional members of The United Methodist Church. Introductions were made and a vote was taken for the whole class. *Motion adopted* by the required three-quarter vote.

Motion: Petrucci moved the adoption of question **#29**. *Motion adopted.*

Motion: Petrucci moved the adoption of question **#31a**. *Motion adopted.*

Motion: Petrucci moved the adoption of question **#32a** and **32b**. Candidates to be elected as members in full connection were introduced and a vote was taken for the whole class. *Motions adopted* by the required three-quarter vote. [note: on account of the COVID-19 pandemic, ordination listed for those in #32a and #32b has been delayed to annual conference 2021.]

Motion: Petrucci moved the adoption of question **#38**. *Motion adopted.*

Motion: Bishop Bard requested a "vote of affirmation" for question **#39**, which does not require a vote. *Motion adopted.*

Motion: Petrucci moved the adoption of question **#42a**. *Motion adopted.*

Motion: Petrucci moved the adoption of question **#44a**. *Motion adopted.*

Motion: Petrucci moved the adoption of question **#46a**. *Motion adopted.*

A 5-minute break was called by Bishop Bard.

Motion: Petrucci moved the adoption of question **#50a(1)**. *Motion adopted.*

Motion: Petrucci moved the adoption of question **#50a(2)**. *Motion adopted* with the required two-thirds vote.

Motion: Petrucci moved the adoption of question **#52**. *Motion adopted.* John Boley prayed for those on medical leave.

Motion: Petrucci moved the adoption of question **#53a**. *Motion adopted.* (¶357.3 two-thirds vote not required)

Motion: Petrucci moved the adoption of question **#53c**. *Motion adopted.* (¶357.3 two-thirds vote not required)

Motion: Petrucci moved the adoption of question **#54a**. *Motion adopted.*

Motion: Petrucci moved the adoption of question **#72a**. *Motion adopted.*

Motion: Petrucci moved the adoption of **#76c**. *Motion adopted* with the required two-thirds vote.

Naming of the Saints: Bishop Bard presented the names of the clergy who have died since the between the 2019 annual conference and the originally scheduled dates of the 2020 annual conference. The names are listed in question **#48c, 48d, & 48e**. Bishop Bard prayed.

Conference Cane (presented to oldest living member of the United Methodist clergy community): Bishop Bard shared that Art Spafford, who had been the keeper of the Conference cane, passed away on July 2, 2020, at the age of 94. Petrucci announced that the new keeper of the cane is Joseph H. Ablett.

Recognition of Retirees: Bishop Bard presented the names of those retiring this year, the names of which are listed in questions **#44a, 53a, 53c, 54a, & 56a**. Bishop Bard prayed for this year's retirees.

Information Items: Petrucci presented questions **18b, 18c, 19a, 19b, 19c, 21d, 22, 24a, 24b, 29a, 39, 40b, 41, 43a(2), 43b, 43c(2), 44b, 46c, 47, 48a, 49, 50a(5), 55, 57, 58, 59, 62, 63, 72b, 79, 80,** and **81** for information, with additions and corrections to the written report.

Petrucci announced that next year's Michigan Annual Conference is scheduled for June 3-6, 2021, at the Grand Traverse Resort in Acme, Michigan.

Motion to adopt the full report: Petrucci moved the adoption of the full clergy report. *Motion adopted.*

Bishop Bard expressed appreciation to Laura Speiran for her faithful work as the chair of the Board of Ordained Ministry, welcomed Barry Petrucci as the new chair, and announced the name of Chris Lane as the chair of the Order of Elders.

Motion: The Board of Ordained Ministry moved the affirmation of Chris Lane as the chair of the Board of Ordained Ministry. *Motion adopted.*

The conference adjourned *sine die* at 11:30 a.m. with prayer from Bishop Bard.

David A. Bard,
Presiding Bishop

Joy A. Barrett,
Conference Secretary

CORPORATE SESSION

Board of Trustees Report
to the 2020 Michigan Annual Conference

The conference Board of Trustees ("BoT") is blessed with a consolidated group comprised of former Detroit Annual Conference and West Michigan Annual Conference trustees. We have benefited from a seamless combination and very effective contributing members.

The board experienced an elevated work load during the past year necessitating two intervening full meetings (beyond the normal quarterly schedule) to ensure timely addressment of key issues. The primary focus was the determination of "Terms and Conditions" for the Disaffiliation process. This work entailed much interaction and input from the cabinet and affected directors.

When the Judicial Council did not opine on the new paragraph (**2553**), Bishop Bard stated he would honor the work done by the BoT and that the conference would proceed with a 'Withdrawal' process. This activity proved to be very time consuming.

Additionally, the held-properties (from closed churches) and their attendant oversight responsibilities presented a substantial challenge to the board.

Shown below is a high-level summary of activities and focus:

Work review:

- Vice chair George Lewis developed policies and procedures ("P&P") for all conference owned offices and parsonages.

- Worked extensively on property tax issue for parsonage(s)…To be determined as to resolving the issue through the appeals process with State of Michigan.

- Four properties were sold (one donated) in past year, one on LC w/ conference holding title (done w/ MI.Union)
  - Dearborn Stephens (Land Contract)
  - State Street parsonage
  - Kalamazoo Stockbridge
  - Saganing Indian Church donated & transferred to Saginaw/ Chippewa Indian Tribe

- Seven properties currently listed for sale – a challenging environment for commercial real estate and church properties in particular has arisen from the 'Covid world'. We know more properties will be added to this inventory due to the economic pressures on the local churches. Efforts are being made to find solutions other than closure which will help with the dispensation process.

- Developed in collaboration with cabinet representative DS John Hice a definitive itemization of roles for conference and district involvement re: closed properties.

- Working with DCM Benton Heisler on conference archive storage options pertaining to physical locations. The concern has grown due to both increased materials from closed churches and limitations of the current facilities.

- Conducted the annual 'Risk Management' review with Church Mutual Insurance in a full board meeting. There were no material claim-issues raised and the relationship is solid.

- **MAUMC (the camp board):** BoT's work last year involved substantial interaction with MAUMC management and included advisement on real estate related matters.

- MAUMC board chair Stuart Smith video was shown providing camping overview was a component of the Corporate Session.

- The Dowry legislation last year established a minimum $250,000 in missional funds per district. Each district is required to, and has, submitted a report detailing the application of funds. These reports will be included in the AC Journal and various highlight articles will be reflected in upcoming MIConnect issues.

Summary of closed churches requiring AC affirmative action to formally close with motions in accordance with paragraph 2549 of the *2016 Book of Discipline* submitted by Rev. Elizabeth Hill. The affirming petitions were distributed to the voting members and returned after adjournment.
- Owosso-Burton UMC – June 30, 2019
- Ubly UMC – September 30, 2019
- Muskegon Unity UMC – December 31, 2019
- Mulliken UMC – March 1, 2020

The three churches with completed Withdrawal Agreement terms and have submitted appropriate funds in accordance with paragraph 2549 of the *2016 Book of Discipline*; individual motions to close and withdraw presented by Rev. Elizabeth Hill. The affirming petitions were distributed to the voting members and returned after adjournment.
- Shabbona UMC – June 30, 2020
- East Boardman UMC – June 30, 2020
- North Adams UMC – June 30, 2020

A live question and answer session was held for the participating AC members.

Is there any other business to be brought before the corporate session?

I will entertain a motion to adjourn. We are adjourned.

James LeBaron, Chairperson
Michigan Conference Board of Trustees

THE UNITED METHODIST CHURCH
THE BUSINESS OF THE ANNUAL CONFERENCE

The Minutes of the **Michigan Annual Conference**
Held Virtually, July 26-28, 2020
Bishop David Alan Bard, Presiding
Date When Organized January 1, 2019 – First Session

PART I ORGANIZATION AND GENERAL BUSINESS

1. Who are elected for the quadrennium (¶¶603.7, 619)?

   Secretary?   **Joy Barrett**
      Mailing Address: 128 Park St., Chelsea, MI 48118
      Telephone: 734-475-8119 ext. 18
      Email: secretary@michiganumc.org
   Statistician?   **Pamela Stewart**
      Mailing Address: 1161 E Clark Rd Suite 212, DeWitt 48820
      Telephone: 517-347-4030
      Email: pstewart@michiganumc.org
   Treasurer?   **Donald Emmert (interim treasurer)**
      Mailing Address: 1161 East Clark Rd Suite 212; DeWitt, MI 48820
      Telephone: 517-347-4030
      Email: demmert@michiganumc.org

2. Is the Annual Conference incorporated (¶603.1)? Yes

3. Bonding and auditing:
   What officers handling funds of the conference have been bonded, and in what amounts (¶¶618, 2511)?

Name	Position	Amount Bonded
Donald Emmert	Conference Treasurer (interim)	$3,000,000.00
	Officers, Directors & Trustees	$2,000,000.00

   Have the books of said officers or persons been audited (¶¶617, 2511)? (See report, page 181 of Journal.)

4. What agencies have been appointed or elected?
   a) Who have been elected chairpersons for the mandated structures listed?

Structure	Chairperson	Mailing Address	Phone No.	Email
Council on Finance & Admin-istration (¶611)	Brad Bartelmay	57 W Tenth St Holland, MI 49423	616-396-5205	bradbartelmay @gmail.com
Board of Ordained Ministry (¶635)	Barry Petrucci	7028 Oakland Dr, Portage 49024	269-327-6643	barrypetrucci@pchum.org
Board of Pensions (¶639)	Steven Buck	6446 Prairie Dunes Dr Grand Blanc 48439	810-444-7089	sjbuck@comcast.net
Board of Trustees of the Annual Conference (¶2512)	Jim LeBaron	13401 Peacock Rd Laingsburg 48848	517-641-8042	jlebaronllc@aol.com
Committee on Episcopacy (¶637)	John Wharton	7409 Steeplechase Ct Saline MI 48176	734-429-5258	jwharton@comcast.net
Administrative Review Committee (¶636)	John Boley	1011 Northcrest Rd Okemos MI 48906	517-347-4003	jboley@michiganumc.org

b) Indicate the name of the agency (or agencies) and the chairperson(s) in your annual conference which is (are) responsible for the functions related to each of the following general church agencies (¶610.1):

General Agency	Conference Agency	Chairperson	Mailing Address	Phone No.	Email
General Board of Church and Society	Division on Church and Society	George Covintree	29835 Rock Creek Rd Southfield MI 48076	248-905-3448	georgecovintree@me.com
General Board of Discipleship	Conference Leadership Council	Amy Mayo-Moyle	30450 Farmington Rd Farmington Hills MI 48334	248-626-3620	amayomoyle@yahoo.com
General Board of Global Ministries	Board of Global Ministries	Brenda Dupree	8165 Holcomb Clarkston MI 48348	248-202-4746	bkdupree@comcast.net
General Board of Ordained Ministry	Board of Ordained Ministry	Barry Petrucci	7028 Oakland Dr, Portage 49024	269-327-6643	barrypetrucci@pchum.org
Higher Education and Campus Ministry	Division of Higher Education and Campus Ministry	Jeff Williams	204 W Cass St, Greenville 48838	269-944-9231	jeffwrev@gmail.com
General Commission on Archives and History	Commission on Archives and History	Mary Whitman	9155 Greenway Ct N222 Saginaw MI 48609	989-781-9223	librawhitman@yahoo.com
General Commission on Christian Unity and Interreligious Concerns	Division on Christian Unity & Interreligious Relationships	Rodney Gasaway	36522 Ann Arbor Trail Livonia MI 48150	743-578-6256	rodney@newburgumc.org
General Commission on Religion and Race	Division on Religion and Race	George Covintree	29835 Rock Creek Rd Southfield MI 48076	248-905-3448	georgecovintree@me.com
General Commission on the Status and Role of Women	Division on the Status and Role of Women	George Covintree	29835 Rock Creek Rd Southfield MI 48076	248-905-3448	georgecovintree@me.com
United Methodist Communications	Director of Communications	Mark Doyal	1011 Northcrest Rd Lansing MI 48906	517-347-4030	mdoyal@michiganumc.org

c) Indicate the conference agencies and chairpersons which have responsibilities for the following functions:

General Agency	Name of Agency	Chairperson	Mailing Address	Phone No.	Email
Criminal Justice and Mercy Ministries ¶657?	Board of Justice	George Covintree	29835 Rock Creek Rd Southfield MI 48076	248-905-3448	georgecovintree@me.com
Disability Concerns (¶653)?	Division on Disability Concerns	George Covintree	29835 Rock Creek Rd Southfield MI 48076	248-905-3448	georgecovintree@me.com

Equitable Compensation (¶625)?	Commission on Equitable Compensation	TBD			
Laity (¶631)?	Board of Laity	Annette Erbes	1951 Heatherton Dr, Holt 48842	517- 694-8277	layleader@ michiganumc. org
Native American Ministry (¶654)?	Committee on Native American Ministry	Ronald Todd Williamson	1146 Nicolson St, Wayland 49348	616-262-0358	revrtwilliamson @gmail.com
Small Membership Church (¶645)?	Division on Small Member-ship Church	Dirk Elliott	1161 East Clark Rd Suite 212 DeWitt MI 48820	517-347-4030	delliott@ michiganumc. org

d) Indicate the president or equivalent for the following organizations.

Organization	Name of Agency	Chairperson	Mailing Address	Phone No.	Email
Conference United Methodist Women (¶647)	Conference United Methodist Women	Linda Darrow	232 N Cooley St Mt. Pleasant MI 48858	989-763-8750	darrowlinda@ gmail.com
Conference United Methodist Men (¶648)	Conference United Methodist Men	Don Archambeau	28270 Elmira St Livonia 48150	734-422-2227	Donarcham beau@gmail. com
Conference Council on Youth Ministry (¶649)	Youth Ministry Development Coordinator	Christina Miller-White	7191 Birchwood Dr, Mount Morris 48458	989-488-3347	cmillerwhite@ michiganumc. org
	Board of Young People's Ministry, chair	Elizabeth Hurd	250 Vine St, Caledonia 49316	810-488-6300	pastor.elizabeth @caledoniaumc .org
Conference Council on Young Adult Ministry (¶650)?	Young Adult Initiatives Coordinator	Lisa Batten	1011 Northcrest Rd Lansing MI 48906	517-347-4030	lbatten@mich igan.org
	Board of Young People's Ministry, chair	Elizabeth Hurd	250 Vine St, Caledonia 49316	810-488-6300	pastor.elizabeth @caledoniaumc .org

e) Have persons been elected for the following district boards and committees? Answer yes or no.
   (1) District Boards of Church Location & Building (¶2518.2)? Yes
   (2) Committees on District Superintendency (¶669)? Yes
   (3) District Committees on Ordained Ministry (¶666)? Yes

f) What other councils, boards, commissions, or committees have been appointed or elected in the annual conference?

Structure	Chairperson	Mailing Address	Phone	Email
Conference Leadership Council	Amy Mayo-Moyle	30450 Farmington Rd Farmington Hills MI 48334	248-626-3620	amayomoyle@ yahoo.com
Protection Policy Team	Judy Herriff	5651 Bunker Rd Eaton Rapids MI 48827		jherriff@gmail. com

Michigan Area UM Camping Board	Stuart Smith	7486 Hunters Ridge Dr Jackson 49201	517-536-0363	smith4osu@ comcast.net
Conference Disaster Response Team	Dan O'Malley, Coordinator Robert Miller, Chair	9356 Enchantment Dr, Alto MI 49302 1401 Palmer Street Plymouth MI 48170	616-868-6193 810-623-0985	dano.omalley@ gmail.com pastorbobmiller@ comcast.net
Children's Initiative Coordinator	Kathy Pittenger	1011 Northcrest Rd Lansing MI 48906	517-347-4030	kpittenger@mich iganumc.org
Committee on Hispanic/Latino Ministries	Sonya Luna	1011 Northcrest Rd Lansing MI 48906	517-347-4030	sluna@michigan umc.org
Committee on Asian-American Ministry	Jung Eun Yum	315 W Larkin St PO Box 466 Midland MI 48640	989-835-6797	jeyum@hotmail. com
Committee on African-American Ministry	Jan Brown Simmie Proctor	1100 E Samaria Rd Erie MI 48133 73486 8th Ave South Haven MI 49090	313-303-1533 269-637-6053	januk99@gmail. com simmiepr@ hotmailcom
Comte on Native American Ministry	Ronald Todd Williamson	1146 Nicolson St, Wayland 49348	616-262-0358	revrtwilliamson@ gmail.com
Board of Congregational Life	Sherry Parker-Lewis, chair	48710 Apple Ln, Mattawan 49071	810-360-9995	sherry@umf michigan.org
Congregational Vibrancy, Division	Dirk Elliott	1161 E Clark Rd Ste 212 DeWitt MI 48820	517-347-4030	delliott@michi ganumc.org
Committee on Human Resources	Ellen Zienert	13015 Cedar St, Charlevoix 49720	517-515-9500	ekzienert@ gmail.com
Annual Conference Session Commission	David Eardley	620 Romeo St., Box 80307 Rochester 48308	248-651-9361	reveardley@ hotmail.com
Rules of Order Committee	Todd Price	9921 Seltzer Livonia MI 48150	734-834-4030	pencollector@ me.com
Conf Nominating Committee (CNC)	Melissa Claxton	5005 Chicago Rd, Warren 48092	586-264-4701	claxton517@ yahoo.com
Committee on Journal	Joy Barrett	128 Park St Chelsea MI 48118	734-475-8119	jbarrett@chelsea umc.org
United Methodist Foundation of MI	Ransom Leppink	PO Box 365 Lakeview MI 48850	989-352-6430	leppinks@ hotmail.com

5. Have the secretaries, treasurers, and statisticians kept and reported their respective data in accordance to the prescribed formats? (¶606.8)? Yes

6. What is the report of the statistician? (See report, page 579 of Journal.)

7. What is the report of the treasurer? (See report, page 579 of Journal.)

8. What are the reports of the district superintendents as to the status of the work within their districts? (See report, page 210 of Journal.)

9. What is the schedule of minimum base compensation for clergy for the ensuing year (¶¶342, 625.3)? (See legislation, page 208 of Journal.)

10. What amount has been apportioned to the pastoral charges within the conference to be raised for the support of the district superintendents for the ensuing year (¶614.1a)? $2,140,803

11. a) What amount has been apportioned to the pastoral charges within the conference to be raised for the support of the pension and benefit programs of the conference for the ensuing year (¶¶614.1d, 1507)? $3,720,000

    b) What are the apportionments to this conference for the ensuing year?
      (1) For the World Service Fund? $1,561,138
      (2) For the Ministerial Education Fund? $ 488,952
      (3) For the Black College Fund? $ 225,959
      (4) For the Africa University Fund? $ 50,800
      (5) For the Episcopal Fund? $ 626,855
      (6) For the General Administration Fund? $ 192,253
      (7) For the Interdenominational Cooperation Fund? $ 6,759

12. What are the findings of the annual audit of the conference treasuries? (See report, page 181 of Journal.)

13. Conference and district lay leaders (¶¶603.9, 660):
    a) Conference lay leader:
        Annette Erbes, 1951 Heatherton Dr, Holt 48842 layleader@michiganumc.org

    b) Associate conference lay leaders: NA

    c) District and associate district lay leaders:

CENTRAL BAY:	Dennis Wissinger	dowraw@charter.net
EAST WINDS	Cynthia Rossman	cynrosjam@hotmail.com
Associate:	Bonnie Potter	mpotter60@charter.net
GREATER DETROIT:	Ruby Anderson	rbydandrs@aol.com
Associate:	Kenneth Dowell	ken@dowell.ws
GREATER SOUTHWEST:	Wynne Hurlbut	wynne_hurlbut@frontier.com
HERITAGE:	John Seppanen	jseppanen313@gmail.com
MID-MICHIGAN:	Nona Spackman	nspackman12@gmail.com
MIDWEST:	Deborah Hodges	dhodges727@comcast.net
NORTHERN SKIES:	John Preston	johncarterpreston@gmail.com
NORTHERN WATERS:	Denny Olin	dennyolin@gmail.com

14. List local churches which have been:
    a) Organized or continued as New Church Starts (¶259,1-4, continue to list congregations here until listed in questions 14.c, d, or e)

GCFA #	Church Name	District	Mailing Address	Phone Number	Date
004793	Madison Heights: Vietnamese Ministry	Greater Detroit	500 W Gardenia Ave Madison Hts, MI 48071	?	07/01/2016
005992	Detroit: French	Greater Detroit	1803 E 14 Mile Rd Birmingham, MI 48009	?	07/01/2018
582123	Traverse City: Mosaic	Northern Waters	1249 Three Mile Rd S Traverse City, MI 49696-8307	231-946-3048	07/01/2017
581061	Detroit: Centro Familiar Cristiano	Greater Detroit	1270 Waterman St. Detroit, MI 48209	734-482-8374	02/01/2016
582635	Grand Rapids: Restoration	Midwest	2730 56th St SW S Wyoming, MI 49418	616.589.4793	01/01/2018

    b) Organized or continued as Mission Congregations (¶259,1-4, continue to list congregations here until listed in questions 14.c, d, or e)

GCFA #	Church Name	District	Mailing Address	Phone Number	Date
582761	Harrison: The Gathering	Central Bay	PO Box 86, Harrison, MI 48625-0086	989-539-1445	07/01/2004
597886	Mt Pleasant: Chippewa Indian	Central Bay	3490 S Leaton Rd, Mt Pleasant, MI 48858	517-773-0414	1974?

c) Organized or continued Satellite congregations (¶247.22, continue to list here until listed in questions 14.a, c, d, or e)

GCFA #	Church Name	Parent Church	District	Mailing Address	Date Launched
582282	Bay City: Grace - East Campus	Bay City: Grace 580897	Central Bay	4267 2 Mile Rd, Bay City, MI 48706-2332	07/01/2016
589330	Saginaw: Kochville	Midland: Aldersgate 589330	Central Bay	6030 Bay Rd, Saginaw, MI 48604-8703	09/01/2018
582293	Birmingham: First - Berkley 1St Campus	Birmingham: First 581881	Greater Detroit	1589 W Maple, Birmingham, MI 48009-4607	07/01/2015
582316	Detroit: Cass Cmnty - World Bldg Campus	Detroit: Cass Cmnty 582145	Greater Detroit	3901 Cass Ave, Detroit, MI 48201-1721	07/01/2017
582065	Redford: Aldersgate - Brightmoor Campus	Redford: Aldersgate 580501	Greater Detroit	10000 Beech Daly Rd, Redford, MI 48239	07/02/2012
582362	Troy: Korean – Troy Hope Campus	Troy: Korean 582830	Greater Detroit	42693 Dequindre, Troy, MI 48085-3960	07/01/2008
581527	Brighton: First - Whitmore Lake: Wesley Campus	Brighton: First 580306	Heritage	400 E Grand River, Brighton, MI 48116	01/01/2019
582453	Friendship - Shelby Twp Campus	Canton: Friendship 580476	Heritage	1240 Beck Rd, Canton, MI 48187-4811	01/01/2017
582338	Ann Arbor: First - Green Wood Campus	Ann Arbor: First 580226	Heritage	120 S State St, Ann Arbor, MI 48104-1606	06/07/1990
599806	Dewitt: Redeemer - St Johns: First Campus	Dewitt: Redeemer 598868	Mid-Michigan	13980 Schavey Rd, Dewitt, MI 48820-9013	07/01/2018
582373	Lansing: Sycamore Creek - Potterville Campus	Lansing: Sycamore Creek 583971	Mid-Michigan	1919 S Pennsylvania Ave, Lansing, MI 48910-3251	07/01/2017
005888	Grand Rapids: Cornerstone - Heritage Hill Campus	Grand Rapids: Cornerstone 599134	Midwest	1675 84th St SE, Caledonia, MI 49316-7939	10/06/2013
582418	Grand Rapids: Cornerstone - S Wyoming Campus	Grand Rapids: Cornerstone 599134	Midwest	1675 84th St SE, Caledonia, MI 49316-7939	10/04/2015
582087	Marquette: Hope - Connection Center Campus	Marquette: Hope 005753	Northern Skies	111 E Ridge, Marquette, MI 49855-4208	07/01/2016
582258	Marquette: Hope - Skandia Campus	Marquette: Hope 005753	Northern Skies	111 E Ridge, Marquette, MI 49855-4200	07/01/2016
582384	Free Soil-Fountain - Fountain Campus	Free Soil – Fountain 600600	Northern Waters	PO BOX 173, Free Soil, MI 49411-0173	06/01/2013

d)　Organized as Chartered (¶259.5-10, continue to list here until listed in questions 14.d or e)

GCFA #	Church Name	District	Mailing Address	Phone Number	Date Chartered
0					

e)　Merged (¶¶2546, 2547)

(1)　United Methodist with United Methodist

District	GCFA #	Name of First Church	GCFA #	Name of Second Church	GCFA #	Name of Merged Church	Date Merged
Greater Southwest	587843	Niles: Grace	583617	Niles: Wesley	587808	Niles: New Journey	01/01/2020
Northern Waters	600713	Alanson	600666	Harbor Springs	600666	Harbor Springs	01/01/2020
Greater Southwest	601466	Bloomingdale	601477	Townline	601477	Townline	01/01/2020
Central Bay	597226	Coomer	598403	Winn	598403	Winn	03/08/2020
Midwest	597421	Ferry	597567	Hesperia	597567	Hesperia	04/26/2020
Greater Detroit	582486	Mt. Hope	990192	Conant Ave.	990192	Detroit: Conant Ave.	07/01/2020
East Winds	990237	Flint: Charity	584020	Flint: Calvary	584020	Flint: Calvary	07/01/2020
Heritage	581620	Monroe: Heritage	581595	Monroe: First	581595	Monroe: Faith	07/01/2020
Heritage	580250	Ann Arbor: Calvary	580523	Dexter	580523	Dexter	07/01/2020

(2)　Other mergers (indicate denomination)

District	GCFA #	Name of First Church	GCFA #	Name of Second Church	GCFA #	Name of Merged Church	Date Merged

f)　Discontinued or abandoned (¶¶229, 341.2, 2549) (State which for each church listed.)

(1)　New Church Start (¶259.2,3)

GCFA #	Church Name	District	Location	Date Closed
0				

(2)　Mission Congregation (¶259.1a)

GCFA #	Church Name	District	Location	Date Closed
0				

(3)　Satellite Congregation

GCFA #	Church Name	District	Location	Date Closed
0				

(4)　Chartered Local Church (¶259.5)

GCFA #	Church Name	District	Location	Date Closed
584884	Owosso: Burton	Mid-Michigan	Owosso	6/30/2019
588027	Ubly	East Winds	Ubly	9/30/2019
599613	Muskegon: Unity	Midwest	Muskegon	12/31/2019
596346	Mulliken	Mid-Michigan	Mulliken	03/01/2020

g) Relocated and to what address

GCFA #	Church Name	District	Mailing Address	Physical Location	Date Relocated

h) Changed name of church? (Example: "First" to "Trinity")

GCFA #	Former Name	New Name	Address	District
602483	Niles: Wesley; Niles: Grace	Niles: New Journey	302 Cedar St, Niles, MI 49120	Greater Southwest
581595	Monroe: First; Monroe: Heritage	Monroe: Faith	312 Harrison St. Monroe, MI 48161	Heritage

i) Transferred this year into this conference from other United Methodist conference(s) and with what membership (¶¶41, 260)?

GCFA #	Name	Membership	Sending Conference

j) What cooperative parishes in structured forms have been established? (¶206)

GCFA #	Parish Name	Charge Name	Church Name	District
587945	Romeo	Romeo Regional	Leonard	East Winds

k) What other changes have taken place in the list of churches?

GCFA#	Name	Type of Change	District
586917	Shabbona	Disaffiliation (withdrawal from UMC)	East Winds
600633	East Boardman	Disaffiliation (withdrawal from UMC)	Northern Waters
596381	North Adams	Disaffiliation (withdrawal from UMC)	Heritage

15. Are there Ecumenical Shared Ministries in the conference? (¶207, 208)

a) Federated church (Membership is denomination specific.)

GCFA #	Name	District	Other Denomination(s)
601012	Church of the Straits	Northern Skies	Presbyterian
596404	Okemos Community Church	Mid-Michigan	Congregational Methodist
599726	Ovid United Church	Mid-Michigan	U.C.C.
599442	Lyons-Muir	Midwest	Presbyterian (PCUSA)

b) Union Church (Membership Unified.)

GCFA #	Name	District	Other Denomination(s)
599214	E. Lansing: Peoples Church	Mid-Michigan	Am. Bapt., U.C.C., Presb.
587724	Port Austin UPC	Central Bay	UPC

c) Merged Church (Membership separate, church related only to one denomination.)

GCFA #	Name	District	Other Denomination(s)
0			

d) Yoked Parish (Different denomination churches share pastor)

GCFA #	Name	District	Other Denomination(s)
600781	Lake City	Northern Waters	Lutheran

16. What changes have been made in district and charge lines (please list the GCFA # beside church name?)

Moved from Circuit to single Station:

584565 - Laingsburg
584920 - Pittsburg
581128 - Britton: Grace
595411 - Battle Creek: Baseline
494555 – Bronson: First
601683 - Colon
584587 - Lennon
583823 – Duffield
584634 – Lake Fenton
583880 - Fenton
588107 - Yale

584601 - Linden
595342 – Battle Creek: Christ
595364 – Battle Creek: Washington Heights
587626 - Oxford
587637 - Thomas
601980 - Gobles
601375 - Almena
586941 - Croswell
585662 - Hermansville
581505 - Williamston: Wheatfield

Moved to new multiple point Charge: (GCNO for Lead Church)

580317 – Blissfield: Emmanuel, Macon
595227 – Allen, Quincy
598141 – St. Louis, Breckenridge
580408 – Clinton, Stony Creek
595400 – Bellevue, Battle Creek: Convis Union
589523 – Pinconning, Alger
588723 – Bentley, Garfield
586837 – Applegate, Avoca
587205 – Jeddo, Buel

585525 – Escanaba: First, Bark River
586848 – Caseville, Hayes
582010 – Sebewaing: Trinity, Bay Port
584736 – West Vienna, West Forest
580693 – Millville, Leslie, Felt Plains
598788 – Cedar Springs, Kent City: Chapel Hill
596528 – Robbins, Brookfield Eaton
586906 – Cole, Melvin

Moved to new multiple station Circuit:

— MAC Photos

PART II – PERTAINING TO ORDAINED AND LICENSED CLERGY

(Note: A (**v**) notation following a question in this section signifies that the action or election requires a majority vote of the clergy session of the annual conference. If an action requires more than a simple majority, the notation (**v 2/3**) or (**v 3/4**) signifies that a two-thirds or three-fourths majority vote is required. Indicate credential of persons in Part II: FD, FE, PD, PE, and AM when requested.)

17. Are all the clergy members of the conference blameless in their life and official administration (¶604.4 and ¶605.7, The Book of Discipline of The United Methodist Church, 2016)

We take very seriously the call to moral excellence in the lives of clergy, knowing that only by the grace of God can any of us be blameless in our life and official administration. All persons stand in need of the grace of God and of the love and forgiveness of the Christian community.

In signing below and submitting this statement to the Board of Ordained Ministry, we the district superintendents, attest that all the clergy members of the conference are blameless in their life and official administration, or are involved in supervisory or complaint processes, and in signing below the Bishop David A. Bard attests the same for the district superintendents.

Herein signed, Rev. Dwayne Bagley, Rev. Dr. Charles S. G. Boayue, Jr., Rev. Dr. Margie Crawford, Rev. Dr. Jerome DeVine, Rev. Jodie Flessner, Rev. Scott A. Harmon, Rev. John H. Hice, Rev. Elizabeth Hill, Rev. Jeffrey R. Maxwell, Bishop David A. Bard

18. Who constitute:
  a) The Administrative Review Committee (¶636)? (**v**)

Clergy Name, Year Appointed, District	Clergy Alternate Name, Year Appointed, District
Gerald F. Hagans (Ret) ('18) [MW]	Ellen A. Brubaker (Ret) ('18) [MW]
Gloria Haynes (Ret) ('19) [CB]	Catherine J. Miles (Ret) ('19) [EW]
George H. Lewis (Ret) ('19) [HD]	

  b) The Conference Relations Committee of the Board of Ordained Ministry (¶635.1d)?
  2020-2021

Name	Position
Ms. Ruby Anderson (Lay)	
Mr. Ted Brainard (Lay)	
Rev. Mark Erbes (FE)	CRC Chair, BOM Vice-Chair
Rev. Suzie Hierholzer (FE)	
Rev. Bill Johnson (RE)	
Rev. JD Landis (RE)	
Rev. Amy Terhune (FE)	
Rev. Megan Walther (FE)	Conference Leadership Council Representative

  c) The Committee on Investigation (¶2703)? **2019-2020**

Clergy Name, Year Appointed, District	Professing Member Name, Year Appointed, District
1. Richard W. Blunt ('18) (MM)	1. Paula Hines ('18) (MW)
2. Cathi M. Huvaere ('18) (EW)	2. Wynne Hurlbut ('18) (GS)

3. Patrick England ('19) (GS)
4. Philip Tousley ('19) (EW)
5. Brian West ('19) (EW)

3. Craig Schroeder ('18) (GS)
4. Minnie Armstrong ('19) (EW)
5. Murray Davis ('19) (GD)
6. Michael Schlusler ('19) (EW)

**Clergy Alternate Name,
Year Appointed, District**
1. Glenn C. Litchfield ('18) (GS)
2. Julie A. Liske ('18) (MW)
3. Laura De La Garza ('19) (NS)
4. Linda Polter ('19) (HD)
5. Fred Gray ('19) (CB)

**Professing Member Alternate Name,
Year Appointed, District**
1. Louelle Burke ('18) (NW)
2. Max Waagner ('18) (HD)

19. Who are the certified candidates (¶ ¶ 310, 313, 314) (NOTE: Everyone who wants to become an LP, PE, or PD must first become a certified candidate.)
    a) Who are currently certified as candidates for ordained or licensed ministry?

Name	District	Date Certified
James Butler	Central Bay	03.31.2020
John Engler	Central Bay	04.14.2020
Ray Francis	Central Bay	01.15.2019
Sean M. Griffin	Central Bay	04.14.2016
Sharon Haynes	Central Bay	04.14.2020
Carla Long	Central Bay	03.14.2016
Janet E. Shaffer	Central Bay	12.10.2019
Theodore Alkins	East Winds	02.20.2020
Julia A. Cramer	East Winds	05.17.2019
Michelle Ettinger	East Winds	03.21.2019
Karen Harriman	East Winds	02.20.2020
Stacey Highfield	East Winds	03.21.2019
Vincent Slocum	East Winds	02.20.2020
Donald Beasley	Greater Detroit	05.17.2018
Rachael Dunlap	Greater Detroit	06.19.2015
Nadine Johnson	Greater Detroit	05.18.2017
Sean LaGuire	Greater Detroit	02.21.2019
Audrey Mangum	Greater Detroit	05.17.2018
George Marck	Greater Detroit	05.09.2019
Lydie Ngoie	Greater Detroit	04.30.2020
Michael Perez	Greater Detroit	12.12.2019
Robert Prud'homme	Greater Detroit	05.18.2017
Lenora Whitecotton	Greater Detroit	10.17.2019
Kelsey (Burns) French	Greater Southwest	04.25.2017
Sarah DeHaan	Greater Southwest	03.03.2020
Katelyn Hiscock	Greater Southwest	10.09.2018
Ashlei K. Horn	Greater Southwest	04.17.2018
Brian Lightner	Greater Southwest	04.09.2019
Dawn Oldenburg	Greater Southwest	04.09.2019
Ben Palmer	Greater Southwest	05.26.2020
Jennifer Ward	Greater Southwest	08.20.2019

Ann Birchmeier	Heritage	12.07.2017
Timothy Broyles	Heritage	06.11.2020
Elisabeth Danielsons	Heritage	05.09.2016
Crystal Fox	Heritage	11.15.2018
Denise Kasischke	Heritage	01.31.2019
Arthur David Korlapati	Heritage	11.15.2018
Reeve Segrest	Heritage	01.31.2019
Shonagh Taruza	Heritage	06.07.2018
Paula Vergowven	Heritage	05.02.2019
Mark Vorenkamp	Heritage	02.17.2020
Sarah Wheatley	Heritage	03.22.2018
Diana Carpenter	Mid-Michigan	02.18.2016
Ava (Williams) Euper	Mid-Michigan	06.03.2020
Steffani Glygoroff	Mid-Michigan	12.13.2018
Haley Hansen	Mid-Michigan	06.17.2019
Terry Melton	Mid-Michigan	09.16.2019
David Huhtala	Midwest	06.17.2020
Michelle Vallier	Midwest	02.19.2020
Melissa Sue Wagner	Midwest	03.31.2020
BJ Ash	Northern Skies	05.14.2018
Devin Lawrence	Northern Skies	06.03.2020
Larry Molloy	Northern Skies	06.17.2020
Keith Mullikin	Northern Skies	01.22.2020
Erica N. Thomas	Northern Skies	05.14.2018
Leon D. Alberts	Northern Waters	04.30.2020
Cynthia (Montague) Corey	Northern Waters	04.25.2019
M. Wava Hofmann	Northern Waters	01.23.2020
Angela M. Lovegrove	Northern Waters/ Central Bay	07.01.2020
Russell Poirier	Northern Waters	04.30.2020
Troy Trombley	Northern Waters	09.20.2018

b) Who have had their candidacy for ordained or licensed ministry accepted by a District Committee on Ordained Ministry in another annual conference? (Include name of accepting conference.)

Name	Receiving Conference	Date Originally Certified	Date Accepted by District in Other Conf.
Preston Watkins	East Ohio	10.17.2019	02.03.2020

c) Who have been discontinued as certified candidates for licensed or ordained ministry?

Name	District	Date Certified	Date Disc'd
Jonathon Brenner	Heritage	12.01.2016	05.13.2020
LaTonya (Candie) Johnson	Greater Detroit	04.02.2017	02.20.2020

(Note: Once a candidate is appointed as FL or PL, they are no longer listed as a certified candidate (except the first year they are appointed when they would need to be listed in 19 and in 20 or 21). Students appointed as Local Pastors (¶318.3) are the only people who are allowed to be listed as a candidate in one conference while being listed as an LP in a different conference. ¶318.3 stipulates that students appointed as local pastors can serve in either a full or part-time capacity).

20. Who have completed the studies for the license as a local pastor, are approved, but are not now appointed? (¶315 —Indicate for each person the year the license was approved.): **(3/4 v)**

Name	District	Year License Approved
Jack E. Balgenorth	Greater Southwest	2014
Frederick J. Bowden	East Winds	2019 *(0 COS)*
Kyle J. Bucholz	Heritage	2015
Gerald A. Erskine	Midwest	2014 *(5 COS)*
Theresa A. Fairbanks	Mid-Michigan	2016 *(2 COS)*
Everett L. Harpole	Greater Southwest	2015 *(6 COS)*
Rochelle J. Hunter	Greater Detroit	2013 *(*2016)*
David Kang	Greater Detroit	2018 *(17 COS)*
Donna J. Keyte	Greater Southwest	*2003
Trevor J. McDermont	Greater Southwest	2016 *(13 COS)*
Marianne McMunn	East Winds	2010 *(10 COS)*
Julius Nagy	Heritage	2014 *(4 COS)*
James Reinker	Greater Detroit	*2018
Noreen S. Shafer	Northern Waters	2010 *(7 COS)*
Charmaine Shay	East Winds	2015 *(4 COS)*
Ronald D. Slager	Greater Southwest	*2017
Daniel J. Wallington	Central Bay	2015 *(0 COS)*
Terry M. Wildman	Northern Waters	2017
Donna Zuhlke	Greater Detroit	2014 *(6 COS)*

21. Who are approved and appointed as: (Indicate for each person the first year the license was awarded. Indicate what progress each has made in the course of study or the name of the seminary in which they are enrolled. Indicate with an asterisk those who have completed the five-year course of study or the M.Div. (¶319.4)? PLEASE NOTE: Persons on this list must receive an episcopal appointment. **(3/4 v)**

a) Full-time local pastors? (¶318.1)

Name	First Year License Awarded	Number of Courses of Study Completed or Year Completed
Central Bay		
Joseph L. Beavan	2010	*2017
Carmen Cook	2014	17 COS
Robert P. Demyanovich	2019	2 COS
Laura E. Feliciano	2009	*M.Div. VUDS
Nickolas K. Genoff	2004	*2014
Cindy L. Gibbs	2008	*2014
Jon W. Gougeon	2002	*2010
Mark A. Harriman	2014	10 COS
Nathan Jeffords	2012	M.Div. ATS
Lisa Kelley	2013	*2019
Michael P. Kelley	2004	*2012
Heather M. Nowak	2017	M.Div. MTSO
Patrick R. Poag	2004	*M.Div. ATS
Clifford L. Radtke	2006	*2012

Jacqueline L. Raineri	2012	*2018
Robert G. Richards	1993	*2010
Melene E. Wilsey	2017	9 COS
Donald L. Wojewski	2004	*2012

East Winds

Lisa Jo Clark	2000	*2012
Curtis B. Clarke	2011	*2018
James I. Cogman	2020	M.Div. YDS
Christopher Grimes	2014	*M.Div. G-ETS
Brian K. Johnson	2011	*2018
Betty Kay Leitelt	2006	*2017
Tommy McDoniel	2010	*M.Div. G-ETS
Penelope R. Nunn	2014	12 COS
Patrick D. Robbins	1998	*2008
Christopher G.L. Titus	2010	*M.Div. UTS
Thomas Waller	2015	10 COS
Karen B. Williams	2002	*2012

Greater Detroit

Se Jin Bae	2015	*M.Div. RT
Anthony Ballah	2016	M.Div. G-ETS
Jonathan Combs	2009	*2016
Rachael M. Dunlap	2020	*M.Div. ATS
Robert F. Fuchs	2016	12 COS
Patricia Gandarilla	2012	*2012 Basic and Advanced COS
Markey C. Gray	2016	*M.Div. PTS
Marvin Herman	2007	*2015
Maurice R. Horne, Sr.	1999	*2010
Carolyn A. Jones	2016	8 COS
Myra Moreland	2018	4 COS
Marshall Murphy	2011	*M.Div. G-ETS
Michael R. Perez, Jr.	2020	0 COS
Albert Rush	2012	*2019

Greater Southwest

Lisa M. Batten	2009	MA G-ETS (¶344.1.d)
Ellen D. Bierlein	2018	4 COS
Ian Boley	2016	*M.Div. BU
Brian R. Bunch	1993	*M.Div. ESR
Daniel R. Colthorp	2018	15 COS
Cleoria Monique Renee French	2014	*M.Div. UTS
Kelsey B. (Burns) French	2020	M.Div. G-ETS
Samuel C. Gordy	2012	11 COS
Sean LaGuire	2020	0 COS
Wayne E. McKenney	1995	*M.Div. AMBS
Stephanie Norton	2019	M.Div. ATS
Dawn Oldenburg	2020	0 COS
James Palaszeski	2014	7 COS
Margaret Mallory Sandlin	2017	*M.Div. G-ETS
Scott B. Smith	2013	M.Div. UTS

Robert L. Snodgrass II	2014	9 COS
Nathaniel R. Starkey	2014	17 COS
Douglas A. Tipken	2019	1 COS
Craig H. VanBeek	2019	1 COS
Beverley J. Williams	2012	*2018
Janet S. Wilson	2018	1 COS

Heritage

Ann Birchmeier	2020	0 COS
Deborah S. Cole	2015	17 COS
Michael C. Desotell	2014	M.Div. G-ETS
Robert W. Dister	2012	*2018
Carol Abbott Freeland	2014	7 COS
Donna Galloway	2014	0 COS
April Gutierrez (Ext Ministry)	2020	M.Div Equivalent (¶344.1a)
Andrea L. Johnson	2018	6 COS
Todd Jones	2016	17 COS
Keith A. Lenard, Jr.	2014	*M.Div. ATS
Mark E. Mitchell	1995	*M.Div. AMBS
John J. Pajak	2009	*2019
Crystal C. Thomas	2013	M.Div. UTS
Matthew J. West	2018	4 COS
Kelly-Marie (Vergowven) Zawodni	2017	1 COS

Mid-Michigan

Mark D. Aupperlee	2018	8 COS
Billie Lou Gillespie	2000	*2007
Scott A. Herald	2016	11 COS
Naylo T. Hopkins	2020	*M.Div. WTS (see ¶324.3)
Karen L. Jensen-Kinney	2015	16 COS
Martin A. Johnston	2016	8 COS
Peggy A. Katzmark	2007	*2013
Matthew D. Kreh	2015	16 COS
Ian S. McDonald	2012	*2018
Kimberly S. Metzer	2017	9 COS
Heather L. Nolen	2017	M.Div. G-ETS
Rhonda Osterman	2012	12 COS
Steven C. Place	2011	16 COS
Jon L. Pohl	2006	*Completed COS

Midwest

Daniel L. Barkholz	2016	15 COS
Jeffrey J. Bowman	1995	*Completed COS
Terri L. Cummins	2010	*2016
Alejandro D. Fernandez	2015	15 COS
Thomas C. Fifer	2018	*M.Div. DDS
Lawrence J. French	2018	0 COS
Kevin K. Guetschow	2010	*2016
Zachary D. McNees	2019	1 COS
Daniel D. Nguyen	2012	M.Div. G-ETS

Nancy J. Patera	2007	*Completed COS
Michael J. Ramsey	2010	*2019
Anthony C. Shumaker	2002	*Completed COS
Edwin D. Snook	2002	M.Div. UTS
Donna J. Sperry	2014	M.Div. MTSO
Ronald "Todd" Williamson	2017	4 COS

Northern Skies

Timothy Bashore	2013	7 COS
Nelson Hall	1999	*2005
John P. Murray	2015	*M.Div. ATS
Matthew Osborne	2012	*2018
Victoria Prewitt	2019	4 COS
Nathan T. Reed	2011	*2018
Walter P. Reichle	2012	*2018
Irene R. White	1996	*2004

Northern Waters

Sean T. Barton	2017	M.Div. ATS
Bradley E. Bunn	2017	17 COS
Richard Hodgeson	2013	10 COS
Bryan K. Kilpatrick	2014	*M.Div. G-ETS
Duane A. Lindsey	2019	0 COS
Scott R. Loomis	2012	*2019
Angela M. Lovegrove (also serving CB)	2020	*M.Div. WTS
Joshua M. Manning	2014	11 COS
John D. Messner	2008	*Completed COS
Zelphia J. Mobley	2015	*M.Div. CST
Melody Lane Olin	2006	*Completed COS
Craig A. Pahl	2000	*Completed COS
Penny L. Parkin	2014	16 COS
Daniel J.W. Phillips	2015	*M.Div. G-ETS
Todd W. Shafer	2010	*2018
Katherine C. Waggoner	2011	*M.Div.
Jeremy J. Wicks	2011	15 COS
Colleen A. Wierman	2011	*2018

b) Part-time local pastors? (¶318.2) (fraction of full-time in one-quarter increments)

Name	First Year License Awarded	Fraction of Full Time to be Served	Number of Courses of Study Completed or Year Completed
Central Bay			
Helen Alford	2019	1/2	0 COS
James Butler	2020	1/2	0 COS
William C. Cleland	2014	3/4	9 COS
Raymond W. Francis	2020	1/4	0 COS
Douglas E. Hasse	2019	1/4	0 COS
Cheryl L. Mancier	2007	1/2	*2019
Keith Reinhardt	2014	1/4	6 COS

East Winds

Anika Bailey	2018	1/2	*M.Div. MTSO
Leah Caron	2018	1/4	M.Div. UTS
Julia A. Cramer	2020	1/2	0 COS
Donald R. Derby	*2001*	*1/4*	*Retired ¶320.5,*
			*Completed COS
Robert J. Easlick	*1989*	*1/2*	*HL ¶358.2, *M.Div.*
Linda L. Fuller	*2018*	*1/4*	*Retired ¶320.5,*
			*Completed COS
Jerry D. Griggs	1998	3/4	*2010
Patricia A. Hoppenworth	2002	1/2	*2007
Shelly A. Long	2016	1/2	M.Div. UTS
Eric J. Miller	2014	1/2	5 COS
Ronald Rouse	2013	1/2	*2019
Gregory E. Timmons	2019	1/2	0 COS
Brian Willingham	2014	3/4	6 COS

Greater Detroit

Donald Beasley	2020	1/2	0 COS
Mary Ellen Chapman	*2002*	*1/2*	*Retired ¶320.5,*
			*Completed COS
Willie Council	2014	1/2	15 COS
Rodney Diggs	2020	1/2	
Rosaline D. Green	*2017*	*1/2*	*Retired ¶320.5, 4 COS*
Kenneth Johnson	2017	1/4	0 COS
Laurie M. Koivula	2014	1/2	14 COS
George Marck	2018	1/4	0 COS
Cherlyn McKanders	2017	3/4	*M.Div.
Carol Ann Middel	2019	1/2	0 COS
Dale R. Milford	2015	1/4	5 COS
Nhan Duc (Nathan) Nguyen	2019	3/4	0 COS
Esrom Shaw	2013	1/4	5 COS
Dianne H. VanMarter	*2002*	*1/2*	*Retired ¶320.5, *M.Div.*

Greater Southwest

Scott M. Bouldrey	2003	1/4	*M.Div. MTSO
Sara L. Carlson	2015	1/4	M.Div. AMBS
Jodi M. Cartwright	2017	3/4	M.Div. G-ETS
Richard J. Foster	2012	1/2	14 COS
David L. Haase	2008	1/4	*Completed COS
Jason E. Harpole	2014	1/4	8 COS
Ashlei K. Horn	2020	1/2	0 COS
Brenda L. Ludwig (IN Conf)	*1999*	*3/4*	*Retired ¶320.5,*
			*Completed COS
James C. Robertson	2014	1/4	3 COS
Carolyn A. Robinson-Fisher	*1988*	*1/4*	*Retired ¶320.5,*
			*Completed COS
David E. Small	*1982*	*1/2*	*Retired, HL (¶358.2)*

Heritage

Beatrice S. Alghali	2019	1/2	M.Div. UTS
Mary Barrett	2016	3/4	3 COS

Lawrence J. Embury	2015	1/2	7 COS
Arthur David Korlapati	2018	1/4	0 COS
William Lass	2019	1/2	1 COS
Donald E. Lee	*2002*	*1/4*	*Retired ¶357.1*
Bradley R Vasey	2017	1/2	0 COS
Mark A. Vorenkamp	2020	3/4	M.Div. UTS
Kenny Walkup Jr.	2015	3/4	12 COS

Mid-Michigan

Jerry J. Bukoski	2014	1/4	8 COS
Zella M. Daniel	2019	1/2	1 COS
Steffani Glygoroff	2020	3/4	0 COS
Mark Huff	2017	1/2	3 COS
Kathryn L. Leydorf-Keck	2007	3/4	*2018
Kathleen Smith	*2002*	*1/2*	*Retired ¶320.5, *Completed COS*
Charlene Wagner	2019	1/4	1 COS
Coleen Wilsdon	2017	1/2	8 COS

Midwest

Mona J. Dye	*2007*	*1/2*	*Retired ¶320.5, *Completed COS*
William F. Dye	*2003*	*1/4*	*Retired ¶320.5, *Completed COS*
Jan Marie Johnson (Ext. Ministry)	2010	1/4	Western Theology Grad (¶316.1,344.1.d)
Michael E. Long	1983	1/2	RHL ¶358.2, *M.Div.
Eric L. Magner	2017	3/4	0 COS
Darryl L. Miller	2007	1/4	10 COS
Banza Mukalay	2018	1/2	0 COS
Larry W. Nalett	*1993*	*1/2*	*Retired ¶320.5, *Completed COS*
Gary L. Peterson	*2008*	*1/4*	*Retired ¶320.5, *Completed COS*
David O. Pratt	*1997*	*1/4*	*Retired ¶320.5, *Completed COS*
Marcus V. Schmidt	2016	1/2	5 COS
Inge E. Whittemore	2016	1/2	6 COS
Ronald L. Worley	2004	3/4	*2018

Northern Skies

BJ Ash	2020	1/2	0 COS
Rosemary R. DeHut	2002	1/4	*2011
Sandra J. Kolder	*2004*	*3/4*	*Retired ¶320.5, *Completed COS*
Peter LeMoine	2018	1/2	2 COS
Michelle K. Merchant	2016	1/2	2 COS
Keith P. Mullikin	2020	1/2	0 COS

Northern Waters

Lyle J. Ball	2010	3/4	*2018
Cynthia Corey	2019	1/4	0 COS

Lemuel O. Granada	2002	1/4	15 COS
Howard H. Harvey	2017	1/4	M.Div. MTSO
Randell J. Hitts	2017	1/2	10 COS
M. Wava Hofmann	2020	1/2	0 COS
Jonathan D. Mays	2015	1/2	0 COS
Richard D. Roberts	2015	1/4	0 COS
Jeffrey A. Swainston	2017	3/4	7 COS

c)   Students from other annual conferences or denominations serving as local pastors and enrolled in a school of theology listed by the University Senate (¶318.3,4)? **None**

d)   Students who have been certified as candidates in your annual conference and are serving as local pastors in another annual conference while enrolled in a school of theology listed by the University Senate (¶318.3)

Name	Serving Conference	Enrolled Seminary
Jennifer C. Ward	Susquehanna	Wesley Theological Seminary

e)   Persons serving as local pastors while seeking readmission to conference membership (¶¶365.4, 367, 368.3)? (If not in this conference indicate name of conference where serving.) **None**

22.   Who have been discontinued as local pastors (¶320.1)?

Name	Date Discontinued	District
Scott A. Clark	07.01.2020 (withdrawn by request)	East Winds
Patricia Elliott	07.01.2020 (withdrawn by request)	East Winds
Julie E. Fairchild	07.01.2020 (withdrawn by request)	Midwest
Cari Godbehere	01.01.2020 (withdrawn by request)	Mid-Michigan
Andrew B. Hollander	01.01.2020	Midwest
Eric L. Johnson	07.01.2020	Central Bay
Julie A. Krauss	07.01.2020 (withdrawn by request)	East Winds
Michael R. Neihardt	07.01.2020	Northern Waters
Jennifer J. Wheeler	07.01.2020	Midwest

23.   Who have been reinstated as local pastors (¶320.4) (v)? **None**

24.   What ordained ministers or provisional members from other Annual Conferences or Methodist denominations are approved for appointment in the Annual Conference while retaining their conference or denominational membership (¶¶331.8, 346.1)? (List alphabetically; indicate Annual Conference or denomination where membership is held. Indicate credential.)

a)   Annual Conferences

Name	Clergy Status	Home Conference
J. Albert Barchue	OE	Liberia
Daniel M. Bilkert	OR	East Ohio
Frederick G. Cain	OR	Indiana Conference
Linda J. Farmer-Lewis	OR	Wisconsin
Alice K. Ford	OE	Baltimore Washington
Victoria Hadaway	OE	Northern Illinois
Philip S. Harrington	OE	Pacific Northwest
Thomas L. Hoffmeyer	OE	Indiana
Daeki Kim	OE	Indiana
Steven W. Manskar	OE	Minnesota

Gertrude Mukalay	OE	North Katanga, Democratic Republic of Congo
John Kabala Ilunga Ngoie	OE	North Katanga, Democratic Republic of Congo
Mark J. Roberts	OE	Alabama-West Florida
Benjamin Kevin Smalls	OE	Baltimore Washington
Brittney Stephan	OP	Indiana
Lanette S. Van	OE	Iowa
Lawrence J. Wiliford	OR	Upper New York

b)   Other Methodist Denominations

Name	Clergy Status	Denomination
J. Albert Barchue	OE	Liberia
Luis Colozzo	OE	Puerto Rico
Diane Covington	OF (Ret)	Christian Methodist Episcopal
Leonard E. Davis	OR	Wesleyan Church
Travis Heystek	OE	Wesleyan Church
David Nellist	OE	British Methodist
Douglas M. Obwoge	OE	Kenyan Methodist Church

25.   What clergy in good standing in other Christian denominations have been approved to serve appointments or ecumenical ministries within the bounds of the Annual Conference while retaining their denominational affiliation (¶¶331.8, 346.2)? (v) (Designate with an asterisk those who have been accorded voting rights within the annual conference. Indicate credential.)

Name	Clergy Status	Denomination
Thomas C. Hartley	OF	Presbyterian Church USA
Derl G. Keefer	OF	Church of the Nazarene
Julie A. Kline	OF	United Church of Christ
Stephen Spina	OF	Presbyterian Church USA
Reggie A. White	OF	Progressive National Baptist Convention
Jeanne Harmon Wisenbaugh	OF	Christian Church (Disciples of Christ)

26.   Who are affiliate members: (List alphabetically; indicate annual conference or denomination where membership is held.)
      a)   With vote (¶586.4b [v])? **None**
      b)   Without vote (¶¶334.5, 344.4)? **(2/3 v)**

Name	Conference/ Denomination	First Year of Affiliation
David S. Bell	East Ohio	2011
Carol B. Cooley	West Ohio	2000
David A. Newhouse	Northern Illinois	2016
Joseph A. Perez	New York	1996
P. Kay Welsch	Wisconsin	2013

NOTE: If your conference has admitted or ordained persons as a courtesy to another conference, list these persons in Question 40 only. If persons have been admitted or ordained by another annual conference as a courtesy to your conference, list these persons in Questions 27-39, whichever are appropriate, giving the date and name of the accommodating conference.

27.   Who are elected as associate members? ¶322 **(3/4 v)** (List alphabetically-see note preceding Question 27): **None**

28. Who are **elected** as provisional members and what seminary are they attending, if in school? (under ¶¶322.4, 324, 325)

a)   Provisional Deacons under the provisions of ¶¶324.4a, c or ¶324.5 (**3/4 v**)

Name	Seminary
Michelle King	Garrett-Evangelical Theological Seminary

b)   Provisional Elders under the provisions of ¶¶324.4a, b or ¶324.6 (3/4v); ¶ 322.4 (**3/4 v**) (*indicates graduate of this school)

Name	Seminary
Nicolas R. Berlanga	Methodist Theological Seminary of Ohio
Martin T. Cobb	*Methodist Theological Seminary of Ohio
Jessica M. Davenport	*Wesley Theological Seminary
Eric M. Falker	*United Theological Seminary
Susan E. Hitts	*United Theological Seminary
Suzanne L. Hutchison	*Methodist Theological Seminary of Ohio
Ryan C. Low Edwardson	*Duke Divinity School
Scott W. Marsh	*Garrett-Evangelical Theological Seminary
Kellas D. Penny, III	*Asbury Theological Seminary
Paul C. Reissman	Garrett-Evangelical Theological Seminary
Joyce L. Vanderlip	Perkins Theological Seminary
Jenaba R. Waggy	*Vanderbilt University Divinity School

29. Who are **continued as** provisional members, in what year were they admitted to provisional membership, and what seminary are they attending, if in school (¶326 **v**)?

a)   In preparation for ordination as a deacon or elder? (¶326)

Name	Clergy Status	Date
Barbara Benjamin	PE	2018
Robert Blanchard	PE	2018
Nicholas E. Bonsky	PE	2019 MTSO
Kimberly M. Bos	PE	2019
Sari Brown	PE	2016
Christopher A. Butson	PE	2018
Jeffrey O. Cummings	PE	2016
Tania J. Dozeman	PE	2018
Katherine L. Fahey	PE	2016
Michelle N. Forsyth	PE	2018
Leslee J. Fritz	PE	2019
Amanda M. Hall *(Leave of Absence)*	PD	2015
LuAnne M. Stanley Hook	PD	2019 G-ETS
Julia R. Humenik	PE	2019
Elizabeth A. Hurd	PE	2019 BUST
Sean K. Kidd	PE	2018
Won Dong Kim	PE	2015
YooJin Kim	PE	2018
Heather A. McDougall	PE	2014
Tiffany M. Newsom	PE	2017
Alexander J. Plum	PD	2019 G-ETS
Marva Pope	PE	2015
Kayla M. Roosa	PE	2019
Taegyu Shin	PE	2019
Corey Simon	PE	2018
Jinny Song	PD	2016 G-ETS

Brian E. Steele	PE	2017
Linda J. Stephan	PE	2018
Mary A. Sweet	PE	2015
Hillary Thurston-Cox	PE	2019
Amy N. Triebwasser	PE	2019 MTSO
Ruth A. Irish VanderSande	PE	2019
Joan E. VanDessel	PE	2019
Michael W. Vollmer	PE	2016

    b)   Provisional deacons who became provisional elders? (v) **None**

    c)   Provisional elders who became provisional deacons? (v) (Indicate year) **None**

    d)   Provisional members who transferred from other conferences or denominations? (¶347.1, 347.2) (v) **None**

30.   What ordained clergy, coming from other Christian denominations, have had their orders recognized (¶347.6): (v) **A person's orders may be recognized when they are transferring their membership into your annual conference from another Christian denomination. A person who is listed in Q.30 must also be listed in either Q. 31 a or b, depending on the transfer status.**

31.   What ordained clergy have been received from other Christian denominations (¶347.3): (List alphabetically—see note preceding Question 27):

    a)   As provisional members (¶347.3c)? (v)

Name	Clergy Status	Previous Denomination
David Reed	PE – Received 2017	Missionary Church

    b)   As local pastors (¶347.3)? (v) **None**

32.   Who are elected as members in full connection? (List alphabetically-see note preceding Question 27. **Anyone appearing on this question must also be listed somewhere in questions 33-34 or 36, unless the clergy's orders from another denomination were recognized on question 30 in a previous year.) (3/4 v):**

    a)   Deacons

Name

Rodney G. Gasaway

    b)   Elders

Name

Dillon S. Burns

Matthew D. Chapman

Cydney Idsinga

Mary K. Loring

Elise R. Low Edwardson

33.   Who are ordained as deacons and what seminary awarded their degree? Or, if their master's degree is not from a seminary, at what seminary did they complete the basic graduate theological studies? (List alphabetically-see note preceding Question 27)

    a)   After provisional membership (¶330)? (3/4 v) *Ordination for those listed in 32.a has been delayed to Annual Conference 2021.*

    b)   Transfer from elder? (¶309) (v 3/4) **None**

34. Who are ordained as elders and what seminary awarded their degree?
    a) After provisional membership? (¶335) (**3/4 v**) *Ordination for those listed in 32.b has been delayed to Annual Conference 2021.*
    b) Transfer from deacon? (¶309) (**3/4 v**) **None**

35. What provisional members, previously discontinued, are readmitted (¶364)? (**v**) **None**

36. Who are readmitted (¶¶365-367 [**v**], ¶368 [**2/3 v**]): **None**

37. Who are returned to the effective relationship after voluntary retirement (¶357.7): (**v**) **None**

38. Who have been received by transfer from other annual conferences of The United Methodist Church (¶¶347.1, 416.5, 635.2n)? (List alphabetically. Indicate credential. See note preceding Question 27.): (**v**)

Name	Seminary
Jonathan E. Bratt Carle	Vanderbilt University Divinity School
Timothy L. Kobler	Candler School of Theology

39. Who are transferred in from other Methodist denominations (¶347.2)? (List alphabetically. Indicate credential.)

Name	Seminary
Eung Yong Kim	Methodist Theological University, Seoul, Korea
Vaughn W. Thurston-Cox	Asbury Theological Seminary

40. Who have been ordained as a courtesy to other conferences, after election by the other conference? (See note preceding Question 27. Such courtesy elections or ordinations do <u>not</u> require transfer of conference membership.)
    a) Deacons? **None**
    b) Elders?

Name	Conference	Date of Ordination
Lucinda Eastman	Liberia Conference	06.02.2019

41. Who have been transferred out to other annual conferences of The United Methodist Church (¶416.5)? (List alphabetically. Indicate credential. See note preceding Question 27.)

Name	Clergy Status	New Conference	Date of Transfer
Rebecca Farrester	FE	Oregon-Idaho Conference	07.01.2019

42. Who are discontinued as provisional members (¶327)? (**v**).
    a) By expiration of eight-year time limit (¶327)

Name	Clergy Status
Beth A. Reum	PE

    b) By voluntary discontinuance (¶327.6) (**v**) **None**
    c) By involuntary discontinuance (¶327.6) (**v**) **None**
    d) By reaching Mandatory Retirement Age (¶327.7) **None**

43. Who are on location?
    a) Who has been granted honorable location (¶358.1)?
       (1) This year? (**v**) **None**

(2) Previously?

Name	Year Originally Granted	Charge Conf. Membership	Year of Most Recent Report
Mary E. Isaacs Frost	1989	First UMC Oviedo, FL	2017
Melvin F. Hall	1986	South Bend, IN: First	2017
Clinton McKinven-Copus	2007	Ludington UMC	2020
Brian Rafferty	2016	Lansing: Mt. Hope UMC	2018
Rodney E. Rawson	1979	Davison UMC	2020
Timothy T. Tuthill	2017	Grand Rapids: First UMC	2020
Michelle Wisdom-Long	2011	Kalamazoo: First UMC	2020

b) Who on honorable location are appointed ad interim as local pastors? (¶358.2) (Indicate date and appointment.)

Name	Appointment	Year Originally Granted Location
Robert J. Easlick	Linden UMC – 07.01.2020	2004
Michael E. Long	Twin Lake UMC – 01.05.2020	1998
David E. Small	Paw Paw – 07.01.2016	1999

c) Who has been placed on administrative location (¶359)?
    (1) This year? (v) **None**
    (2) Previously?

Name	Year Originally Placed	Charge Conf. Membership	Year of Most Recent Report
Valerie M. Hill	1999	Greenville	

44. Who have been granted the status of honorable location–retired (¶358.3):
    a) This year? (v)

Clergy Name	Year H.L. Originally Status	Charge Conference Granted	Membership
Donald C. Schark	FE	1995	Menominee: First UMC

    b) Previously?

Clergy Name	Year H.L. Originally Status	Charge Conference Granted	Membership
Gordon B. Boyd	FE	2015	
William H. Brady	FE	1976	
Hayden K. Carruth, Jr	FE	1992	Ypsilanti: St. Matthews UMC
Jon M. Clapp	FE	1981	Clarkston: First
Thomas A. Crossman	FD	1991	St. Paul/St. Andrew, New York NY
Bruce W. Dempsey	FE	1993	Muskegon Heights: Temple
David L. Draggoo	FE	1086	Laingsburg UMC
James "Kyle" Elliott	FE	1964	Birmingham, AL: Riverchase
Ronald F. Ellis	FE	1971	Livonia: St. Matthew's
Harold G. Ford	FE	1974	Birmingham: First
C. David Hainer	FE	1996	Bowne Center UMC, Alto
Leon W. Herndon	FE	2010	Metropolitan UMC

Mary E. Howard	FE	1978	Richardson, TX: First
Terry L. MacArthur	FE	1985	Portage: Chapel Hill
Laurie J. McKinven-Copus	FE	2005	Ludington UMC
Charles D. McNary	FE	1977	Bangor Simpson UMC
Thurlan E. Meredith	FE	1993	Northlawn UMC, Grand Rapids
Allen C. Myers	RHL	1980	Trinity UMC, Grand Rapids
Louis E. Otter II	FE	1971	
Edward F. Otto	FE	1978	First UMC, Chicago IL
Robert L. Porter	FE	1980	Ferndale: First UMC
David P. Rahn	FE	1988	Grand Blanc UMC
Paul K. Scheibner	FE	1983	Good Shepherd of the North, Roscommon
Carl G. Silvernail	FE	1969	Kingston
Donald R. Silvis	FE	1972	Lowell UMC
David E. Small	FE	1999	Paw Paw UMC
Philip P. Steele	FE	1971	Milwood UMC, Kalamazoo
Charles E. Strawn	FE	1979	None available in Amsterdam
Ronald W. Tallman	FE	1981	Hope UMC, Greenwood Village CO
Bertran W. Vermeulen	FE	1984	Fremont UMC
George W. Versteeg	FE	1976	
Robert "Mel" Vostry	FE	1991	Palmer, Alaska
Harvard J. Warren	FE	1972	Bradenton, FL
Harold V. Whited	FE	1964	
Lawrence C. Whiting	FE	1981	None
Galen E. Wightman	FE	1969	Washington, D.C.: Foundry UMC
Kenneth B. Woodside	FE	1991	Southfield: Hope

45. Who have had their status as honorably located and their orders terminated (¶358.2)? (v)
None

46. Who have had their conference membership terminated?
   a) By withdrawal to unite with another denomination (¶360.1, .4)? (v)

Name	Date Effective	Prior Clergy Status
Michael J. Tupper	05.01.2020	RE

   b) By withdrawal from the ordained ministerial office (¶360.2, .4)? (v) **None**
   c) By withdrawal under complaints or charges (¶¶360.3, .4; 2719.2)?

Name	Date Effective	Clergy Status
David I. Kim	07.01.2020	FE

   d) By termination of orders under recommendation of the Board of Ordained Ministry (¶358.2, 359.3)? (v) **None**
   e) By trial (¶2713)? **None**

47. Who have been suspended under the provisions of ¶362.1d, ¶2704.2c or ¶2711.3? (Give effective dates. Indicate credential.)

Name	Date Effective	Clergy Status
David I. Kim	12.01.2019 – 03.31.2020	FE

48. Deceased (List alphabetically)

  a)   What associate members have died during the year?
       Active: **None**
       Retired:

Name	Date of Birth	Date of Death
Elaine M. Buker	06.04.1933	06.04.2020

  b)   What provisional members have died during the year? (Indicate credential.)
       Active: **None**
       Retired: **None**

  c)   What elders have died during the year?
       Active:

Name	Date of Birth	Date of Death
Ronald D. VanLente	09.29.1953	07.01.2020

       Retired:

Name	Date of Birth	Date of Death
Emerson W. Arntz	09.04.1942	06.04.2018
J. Leon Andrews	02.03.1929	01.20.2020
Theron E. Bailey	11.02.1928	11.17.2019
Alfred T. Bamsey	05.18.1936	11.26.2019
Ralph T. Barteld	10.24.1930	10.19.2019
Kenneth J. Bremer	09.10.1953	04.03.2020
Richard C. Cheatham	05.24.1930	11.30.2019
David A. Cheyne	12.07.1942	04.11.2020
Oscar W. Cooper, Jr.	05.24.1939	11.11.2019
George W. Fleming	09.14.1939	04.16.2020
Charles F. Garrod	10.07.1929	07.25.2019
Georg F.W. Gerritsen	09.11.1934	05.15.2020
George R. Grettenberger	04.16.1930	07.28.2019
A. Ray Grienke	08.10.1937	03.10.2020
Ron L. Keller	03.14.1936	11.25.2019
D. Keith Laidler	05.19.1932	07.01.2020
F. Richard MacCanon	10.06.1925	12.18.2019
Kenneth D. McCaw	06.02.1934	09.05.2019
John W. McNaughton	01.25.1939	05.11.2020
Ross N. Nicholson	01.05.1933	06.29.2019
Gary L. Sanderson	10.05.1936	05.28.2020
Anthony J. Shipley	05.19.1939	04.01.2020
Webley J. Simpkins, Jr.	09.27.1930	09.17.2019
David A. Stout	04.22.1939	05.29.2020
Phylemon D. Titus	12.04.1937	03.23.2020
Daniel J. Wallace	06.02.1927	06.09.2020
Robert E. Walton	09.03.1936	04.13.2020
Robert P. Ward	08.13.1927	05.27.2020

  d)   What deacons have died during the year?
       Active: **None**
       Retired:

Name	Date of Birth	Date of Death
Joyce Hanlon	05.28.1937	04.26.2019

e)   What local pastors have died during the year?
       Active: **None**
       Retired:

Name	Date of Birth	Date of Death
Margaret A. Kivisto	02.06.1941	07.07.2019
Clarence W. VanConant	06.13.1944	07.29.2019

49.   What provisional or ordained members (elders and deacons) have received appointments in other Annual Conferences of The United Methodist Church while retaining their membership in this Annual Conference (¶¶331.8, 346.1)?

Name	Clergy Status	Conference Where Appointed	Appointment	Year
Susan D. Amick	FD	North Georgia	Chaplain, Wesley Woods Senior Living	2018
Thomas Beagan	FE	Western Pennsylvania	Charter Oak UMC	
Jeremy P. Benton	FE			
Eric Burton-Krieger	FE	Indiana	Central-Indianapolis St. Luke's	2015
Catherine Christman	FE	Wisconsin	South West-Stoughton	2016
Donald R. Ferris-McCann	FE	Virginia	Bruen Chapel UMC	2019
Charles D. Farnum	FE	South Carolina Conference	Wesley Foundation, Winthrop College	2020
Chul-Goo Lee	FE	Florida	South Florida Korean UMC	
April McGlothin-Eller	FD	North Georgia	Newnan Office of the UM Children's Home	2017
Vince McGlothin-Eller	FD	North Georgia	Newnan First UMC	2019

50.   Who are the provisional, ordained members or associate members on leave of absence and for what number of years consecutively has each held this relation (¶353)? (Indicate credential. Record Charge Conference where membership is held.)
       a)   Voluntary?
             (1)   Personal, 5 years or less (¶353.2a 3) (**v**)

Name	Clergy Status	Date Effective	Years	Charge Conference
Kenneth Dunstone	FE	07.01.2017	2	
Tyson G. Ferguson	FE	07.01.2016	4	
Margaret R. Garrigues	FE	09.01.2016	4	Ann Arbor: First
Devon R. Herrell	FE	07.01.2020	0	Big Rapids: First
Amanda Hall	PD	07.01.2017	3	Rochester: St. Paul's
Emily K. Hansson	FE	07.01.2020	0	Vicksburg UMC
Janice T. Lancaster	FD	03.31.2017	3	Northlawn
Gregory W. Lawton	FD	01.01.2020	0	Georgetown UMC
Jane R. Lippert	FE	09.01.2015	4	Traverse City Central
T. Bradley Terhune	FE	07.01.2020	0	Saginaw: First
Colleen R. Treman	FD	07.01.2016	4	Kalamazoo First
Timothy W. Trommater	FE	04.03.2020	0	DeWitt: Redeemer

             (2)   Personal, more than 5 years (¶353.2a 3) (**2/3 v**)

Name	Clergy Status	Date Effective	Years	Charge Conference
Jennifer L. Bixby	FE	09.15.2006	14	
Michael Coffey	FE	04.30.2012	8	
Christopher D. Cowdin	FE	05.01.2003	17	Troy: First

(3)   Family, 5 years or less (¶353.2b 3) (v) **None**
(4)   Family, more than 5 years (¶353.2b 3) (2/3 v) **None**
(5)   Transitional (¶353.2c)

Name	Clergy Status	Date Effective	Years	Charge Conference
Michelle M. King	PD	07.01.2020	0	Chelsea First UMC
Nathaniel W. Johnson	FE	07.01.2020	0	Lowell: Vergennes
Todd Query	FD	01.01.2020	0	Wellspring UMC
Caleb B. Williams	FD	01.05.2020	0	Royal Oak: First

b)   Involuntary? (¶354)? (2/3 v) **None**

51.   Who are granted sabbatical leave (¶351)? (**v**) **None**

52.   Who have been granted medical leave due to medical or disabling conditions (¶356)? (**v**)

Name	Clergy Status	Date Effective	Charge Conference
Marshall Dunlap	FE	02.01.2016	Farmington: Nardin Park
David J. Goudie	FE	09.01.2017	
Faith Green-Timmons	FE	04.01.2018	Flint: Calvary
Tracy N. Huffman	FE	07.01.2019	Monroe: St. Paul
Lynda B. Liles	FD	07.01.2011	Rochester: St. Paul's
Theresa "Little Eagle" Oyler-Sayles	FE	04.15.2009	
Beth A. Reum	LP	01.15.2016	Berrien Springs
Frederick G. Sampson, III	OF	01.01.2020	Bloomfield Hills: St. Paul / Hazel Park
Laura C. Speiran	FD	05.01.2020	Clarkston UMC
Colin P. Stover	FE	01.01.2011	Lapeer: Trinity
Thomas L. Taylor	FE	02.01.2013	
Tamara S.M. Williams	FE	07.01.2017	N Muskegon Community

53.   What members in full connection have been retired (¶357): (**List** alphabetically. If retiring in the interim between conference sessions (¶357.2d), indicate the effective date of retirement.) (**Under ¶357.1, no vote required; under ¶357.2, v; under ¶357.3, 2/3 v**)
Deacons
a)   This year?

Name	Date Effective
Janet S. Carter	07.01.2020
Patricia L. Catellier	07.01.2020
Julie A. Liske	07.01.2020

b)   Previously?

Name	Date Effective
Grace Ann Beebe	2017
Jane A. Berquist	2006
Dorothy M. Blakey	1999
Pamela L. Buchholz	2013
Charlotte A. Cowdin	2003
Murphy S. Ehlers	2018

Catherine M. Freeman	2014
Annelissa M. Gray-Lion	2018
Loretta M. Job	2019
Janet A. Lee	2002
Pamela J. Mathieu	2012
Judith Y. Mayo	2014
Dorothy D. Mercer	2003
Catherine J. Miles	2017
Betsy Myers	2002
Johncie K. Palmer	2008
Jaye A. Reisinger	2018
Carolyn Wik	2014
Christine Wyatt	2015

Elders
c)   This year?

Name	Date Effective
Seung (Andy) Ho Baek	07.01.2020
Pamela A. Beedle-Gee	07.01.2020
Daniel W. Biteman	07.01.2020
John W. Boley	07.01.2020
John Britt	07.01.2020
Mary S. Brown	07.01.2020
Margaret E. Bryce	01.01.2020
Stephen M.G. Charnley	07.01.2020
Lisa L. Cook	07.01.2020
Julius E. Del Pino	10.01.2019
Carter M. Grimmett	07.01.2020
Kevin J. Harbin	03.27.2020
Trevor A. Herm	07.01.2020
Elizabeth A. Hill	07.01.2020
Janet M. Larner	07.01.2020
George H. Lewis	07.01.2020
Jane D. Logston	07.01.2020
Ernesto Mariona	07.01.2020
June M. Marshall-Smith	07.01.2020
Jon R. Powers	07.31.2019
Nancy G. Powers	06.01.2020
Dianna L. Rees	07.01.2020
Robert D. Schoenhals	07.01.2020
Cynthia A. Skutar	07.01.2020
Kathryn S. Snedeker	07.01.2020
Donald E. Spachman	07.01.2020
David K. Stewart	07.01.2020
Paula M. Timm	07.01.2020
Dominic A. Tommy	07.01.2020
Philip L. Tousley	07.01.2020
Gary S. Wales	07.01.2020
James J. Walker	07.01.2020
Steven L. Woodford	07.01.2020

d) Elders Previously?

1.	Joseph H. Ablett	1985	50.	J. Melvin Bricker	1995
2.	Gordon E. Ackerman	2001	51.	Patricia L. Bromberek	2011
3.	Craig L. Adams	2010	52.	Patricia L. Brook	2018
4.	Pegg Ainslie	1997	53.	Wayne W. Brookshear	1983
5.	Terry W. Allen	2006	54.	Colon R. Brown	2019
6.	Andrew A. Allie	2009	55.	Dale E. Brown	2014
7.	Jana Lynn Almeida	2016	56.	Janet J. Brown	2018
8.	David D. Amstutz	2018	57.	Lawrence P. Brown	2014
9.	William J. Amundsen	2003	58.	Tom Brown II	1997
10.	Richard C. Andrus	1999	59.	Ellen A. Brubaker	2001
11.	Joy E. Arthur	1991	60.	Wesley L. Brun	2006
12.	Wayne H. Babcock	2003	61.	Vivian C. Bryant	2003
13.	Eugene K. Bacon	2016	62.	Steven J. Buck	2013
14.	Thomas G. Badley	2002	63.	Donald L. Buege	2017
15.	Paul F. Bailey	2001	64.	Tommy Burdette	2016
16.	Wilson C. Bailey	2007	65.	Ray W. Burgess	2000
17.	Maureen V. Baker	2019	66.	Linda J. Burson	2019
18.	Melanie J. Baker	2016	67.	Bonnie D. Byadiah	1997
19.	Peggy J. Baker	2018	68.	Kathryn S. Cadarette	2019
20.	James R. Balfour II	2010	69.	William A. Cargo	2011
21.	Glenn C. Ball	1996	70.	Donna J. Cartwright	2003
22.	Martha C. Ball	2002	71.	H. Reginald Cattell	1994
23.	James W. Barney	2005	72.	Lynn F. Chappell	2009
24.	Marilyn B. Barney	2008	73.	Kathy R. Charlefour	2014
25.	Wayne C. Barrett	2011	74.	Victor D. Charnley	2013
26.	B. Gordon "Gordie" Barry	2015	75.	David E. Church	1995
27.	Jack M. Bartholomew	1995	76.	Saundra J. Clark	2013
28.	William P. Bartlett	2011	77.	William V. Clegg, Jr.	2011
29.	Joseph R. Baunoch	2004	78.	William M. Clemmer	2014
30.	William M. Beachy	2014	79.	Leonard A. Clevenger	2015
31.	Eric S. Beck	2019	80.	James D. Cochran	1998
32.	Norman R. Beckwith, Sr.	2008	81.	Bufford "Buff" W. Coe	2017
33.	Gary L. Bekofske	2014	82.	Roger L. Colby	2008
34.	John K. Benissan	2011	83.	David C. Collins	2011
35.	Kenneth W. Bensen	2003	84.	Michael T. Conklin	2012
36.	Evans C. Bentley	2018	85.	Frederick P. Cooley	2000
37.	Elwood J. Berkompas	1995	86.	Kathryn M. Coombs	2002
38.	Bruce L. Billing	2011	87.	George E. Covintree, Jr.	2015
39.	Joseph J. Bistayi	2005	88.	Ramona E. Cowling	2002
40.	Eugene A. Blair	2012	89.	Lawson D. Crane	2009
41.	Paul F. Blomquist	1996	90.	Wallace "Pete" Crawford	2015
42.	James W. Boehm	1998	91.	Doris Crocker	1998
43.	Gilbert R. Boersma	2011	92.	Anthony N. Cutting	2011
44.	Benjamin Bohnsack	2006	93.	Billie R. Dalton	2013
45.	Sylvia A. Bouvier	2006	94.	Reva H. Daniel	2005
46.	Keith A. Bovee	1994	95.	Robert Davis	1997
47.	Dianne M. Bowden	2013	96.	Gary C. Dawes	2014
48.	Benjamin H. Breitkreuz	2008	97.	Donald J. Daws	1997
49.	Robert D. Brenner	2013	98.	Alan W. DeGraw	2000

99. Lynn A. DeMoss	1997	150. Michelle A. Gentile	2019
100. Jerry P. Densmore	2014	151. Max L. Gibbs	2009
101. Isabell M. Deppe (Involuntary)	2000	152. Jack e. Giguere	1999
102. David A. Diamond	2006	153. David G. Gladstone	2012
103. James A. Dibbet	2011	154. Daniel L. Gonder	2018
104. William D. Dobbs	2015	155. Diane L. Gordon	2018
105. Robert D. Dobson	1991	156. Diana Kay Goudie	2009
106. William R. Donahue, Jr.	2014	157. Robert F. Goudie	2003
107. Linda J. Donelson	2015	158. Michael Grajcar, Jr.	1991
108. Paul G. Donelson	2015	159. James C. Grant	1999
109. William H. Doubblestein	2006	160. Ronald B. Grant	2012
110. David L. Dryer	2006	161. Joseph M. Graybill	2011
111. Paula Jane Duffey	2005	162. Patricia A. Green	2013
112. Robert Duggan	2005	163. James E. Greer II	2013
113. Daniel M. Duncan	2014	164. Robert C. Grigereit	1999
114. Susan Defoe Dunlap	2013	165. Kathleen A. Groff	2008
115. Mary M. Eckhardt	2010	166. James M. Gysel	2011
116. Eldon K. Eldred	2003	167. Gerald F. Hagans	2006
117. Joe D. Elenbaas	2010	168. Susan J. Hagans	2006
118. John W. Ellinger	2007	169. William E. Haggard	2018
119. Hydrian Elliott	2011	170. Gary T. Haller	2017
120. John W. Elliott	2014	171. A. Theodore Halsted, Jr.	1992
121. Gene Patrick England	2018	172. John N. Hamilton	2016
122. Janet M. Engler	2015	173. Frederick G. Hamlin	1994
123. Richard R. Erickson	2006	174. Eric S. Hammar	1991
124. Terry A. Euper	2010	175. Claudette I. Haney	2005
125. Thomas J. Evans	2013	176. Randall R. Hansen	2014
126. Haldon D. Ferris	2002	177. Ronald W. Hansen	2011
127. John C. Ferris	2012	178. Alan J. Hanson	2013
128. Raymond D. Field	2003	179. John "Jack" E. Harnish	2013
129. Harold F. Filbrandt	1994	180. Duane M. Harris	2018
130. Garrison "Fred" Finzer	2012	181. Hilda L. Harris	2004
131. Frederick H. Fischer	1996	182. Caroline F. Hart	2018
132. John W. Fisher	2013	183. Pauline S. Hart	2008
133. David L. Flagel	2013	184. Thomas E. Hart	2002
134. David L. Fleming	2014	185. Robert D. Harvey	1999
135. Barbara J. Flory	2011	186. Lynn Hasley	2016
136. Carolyn Floyd	2008	187. Robert C. Hastings	2004
137. Valerie A. Fons	2017	188. Timothy S. Hastings	2012
138. Tat-Khean Foo	2003	189. Carl L. Hausermann	2001
139. James E. Fox	1995	190. Ronda L. Hawkins	2014
140. Thomas P. Fox	2012	191. Wayne A. Hawley	2007
141. Nancy K. Frank	2015	192. Geoffrey L. Hayes	2009
142. Barbra L. Franks	2007	193. Stanley L. Hayes	1999
143. Bea B. Fraser-Soots	2015	194. Gloria Haynes	2015
144. Lynda F. Frazier	2015	195. Leonard B. Haynes	1998
145. Lillian T. French	2010	196. Lyle D. Heaton	2016
146. Donald R. Fry	2008	197. Constance L. Heffelfinger	2016
147. Charles W. Fullmer	1997	198. Keith W. Heifner	2006
148. Elizabeth Gamboa	2008	199. Robert J. Henning	2011
149. Roger F. Gedcke	2010	200. John R. Henry	2011

201. Theodore W. Hepner	2002	
202. William A. Hertel	2001	
203. Timothy R. Hickey	2000	
204. Duane J. Hicks	1997	
205. Howard Higgins	2015	
206. John W. Hinkle	1999	
207. Robert L. Hinklin	2001	
208. Lawrence E. Hodge	2000	
209. Harris J. Hoekwater	2018	
210. Jacqueline Holdsworth	2011	
211. Laurence E. Hubley	2002	
212. John C. Huhtala, Sr.	2009	
213. James R. Hulett	1998	
214. Gerald S. Hunter	2015	
215. Joel W. Hurley	1998	
216. David M. Hurst	1998	
217. Joseph D. Huston	2009	
218. James L. Hynes	2000	
219. Roger W. Ireson	2001	
220. Ronald L.F. Iris	2006	
221. Andrew Jackson	2006	
222. Charles R. Jacobs	2010	
223. James D. Jacobs	2011	
224. James P. James	2007	
225. Jerry L. Jaquish	2012	
226. Curtis E. Jensen	2010	
227. Carol J. Johns	2015	
228. Deborah M. Johnson	2014	
229. Jane Ellen Johnson	2016	
230. Mark G. Johnson	2015	
231. William C. Johnson	2012	
232. David L. Johnston	2009	
233. Jack E. Johnston	2012	
234. Mark G. Johnston	2012	
235. Donald W. Joiner	2010	
236. Charles Jones	1997	
237. Margaret Zee Jones	2006	
238. Robert E. Jones	2009	
239. Emmett Kadwell, Jr.	2011	
240. Pamela S. Kail	2012	
241. Mark A. Karls	2014	
242. Thomas F. Keef	2014	
243. James G. Kellermann	2013	
244. Dwayne L. Kelsey	2000	
245. O. Jay Kondall	2012	
246. Robert L. Kersten	1995	
247. Charles W. Keyworth	2017	
248. David E. Kidd	1997	
249. Susan M. Kingsley	2016	
250. Bruce R. Kintigh	2018	
251. Dean A. Klump	2007	

252. David G. Knapp	2009
253. Kenneth A. Kohlmann	2001
254. Norman C. Kohns	2005
255. Robert I. Kreger	2013
256. James P. Kummer	2016
257. Kathleen S. Kursch	2017
258. Sally J. LaFrance	2004
259. Frederick LaMere	2002
260. John D. Landis	2019
261. Wayne T. Large	2003
262. Jean M. Larson	2010
263. Mary G. Laub	2010
264. Melvin L. Leach	2015
265. Hoon K. Lee	2013
266. John Hyung Lee	2011
267. Jung Kee Lee	2013
268. S. Douglas Leffler	1994
269. Ben B. Lester	2011
270. Alger T. Lewis	1999
271. Bradford K. Lewis	2010
272. Eugene A. Lewis	2003
273. Kendall A. Lewis	1990
274. Barbara Lewis-Lakin	2015
275. Donald L. Lichtenfelt	1994
276. Olaf R. Lidums	2007
277. Johnny S. Liles	2004
278. Paul B. Lim	2000
279. Donna J. Lindberg	2004
280. David M. Liscomb	1998
281. Carl Q. Litchfield	2017
282. David L. Litchfield	2006
283. Glenn C. Litchfield	2016
284. Calvin D. Long	2018
285. Leicester R. Longden	2013
286. John D. Lover	2000
287. Paul E. Lowley	2000
288. Carole S. Lyman	2010
289. Frank W. Lyman Jr.	2010
290. Gary V. Lyons	1996
291. Elizabeth A. Macaulay	2018
292. Thomas P. Macaulay	2010
293. Mary Lynch Mallory	2009
294. Paul J. Mallory	2014
295. Charles R. Marble	2000
296. Beverly L. Marr	2017
297. Douglas E. Mater	2019
298. Edrye A. Eastman Maurer	2016
299. Jeffrey R. Maxwell	2016
300. Judith A. May	2016
301. William R. Maynard	2009
302. Robert J. Mayo	2013

303. Paul D. Mazur	1990	
304. William P. McBride	2016	
305. Marvin H. McCallum	2002	
306. J. Patrick McCoy	2014	
307. Allen D. McCreedy	2000	
308. Brent L. McCumons	2011	
309. Ginethea D. McDowell	2002	
310. Martin A. McEntarfer	1992	
311. A. Faye McKinstry	2014	
312. David R. McKinstry	2010	
313. Sandra B. Hoffman McNary	2007	
314. Russell F. McReynolds	2007	
315. John M. Mehl	2019	
316. David W. Meister	2016	
317. Paul J. Melrose	2011	
318. Douglas K. Mercer	2000	
319. Patricia A. Meyers	2014	
320. Kevin L. Miles	2017	
321. Dale M. Miller	2016	
322. Duane E. Miller	2011	
323. Sylvester Miller III	2003	
324. David H. Minger	2006	
325. Daniel J. Minor	2011	
326. Frederick B. Moore, Sr.	2008	
327. John L. Moore	1995	
328. Richard D. Moore	2015	
329. Robert S. Moore-Jumonville	2019	
330. Rebecca K. Morrison	2019	
331. Richard A. Morrison	2007	
332. Harold S. Morse	2011	
333. John D. Morse	2012	
334. David L. Morton	2001	
335. Meredith T. Moshauer	1997	
336. David G. Mulder	2018	
337. Elias N. Mumbiro	2015	
338. Marjorie H. Munger	2013	
339. Nanette Myers-Cabeen	2014	
340. John E. Naile	2014	
341. David B. Nelson	1998	
342. Lance E. Ness	2017	
343. Frederick D. Neumann	2017	
344. Sharon G. Scott Niefert	2001	
345. R. Ivan Niswender	1994	
346. Karen Y. Noel	2018	
347. James C. Noggle	2019	
348. Arthur V. Norris	2001	
349. Bruce L. Nowacek	2016	
350. Gordon W. Nusz	2003	
351. Dorothy Okray	2007	
352. William W. Omansiek	2010	
353. Karen K. Orr	2014	
354. Donna J. Osterhout	2016	
355. James E. Paige, Jr.	2008	
356. Margaret "Peggy" Paige	2012	
357. Wade S. Panse	2012	
358. John G. Park	2011	
359. Gerald R. Parker	1994	
360. James F. Parker	1994	
361. Roger A. Parker	2008	
362. Cynthia M. Parsons	2018	
363. Edward L. Passenger	1999	
364. Margaret A. Passenger	2005	
365. J. Douglas Paterson	2018	
366. Paul E. Patterson	1990	
367. Mark R. Payne	2016	
368. William V. Payne	1996	
369. Richard A. Peacock	2008	
370. Douglas L. Pedersen	2005	
371. A. Edward Perkins	2006	
372. Susan M. Petro	2014	
373. Warren D. Pettis	1998	
374. Janet Gaston Petty	2012	
375. Ralph H. Pieper II	2012	
376. J. "Lynn" Pier-Fitzgerald	2017	
377. Thomas M. Pier-Fitzgerald	2016	
378. Robert B. Pierce	2007	
379. Keith I. Pohl	1993	
380. Gerald A. Pohly	1996	
381. Karen B. Poole	2006	
382. Linda Jo Powers	2015	
383. Carl E. Price	1998	
384. W. Cadman Prout	1981	
385. Blaine B. Rader	2004	
386. Douglas E. Ralston	2019	
387. Jeanne M. Randels	2014	
388. David E. Ray	2012	
389. Kenneth B. Ray	2010	
390. Wayne G. Reece	2000	
391. Kenneth C. Reeves	2006	
392. Jeffrey D. Regan	2013	
393. James L. Rhinesmith	1969	
394. Stephen E. Rhoades	2019	
395. Clifford Rice	2002	
396. Philip A. Rice	2002	
397. Richard M. Riley	2014	
398. William A. Ritter	2005	
399. Archie T. Roberts	1997	
400. Stanley "Joe" Robertson	2002	
401. Beatrice K. Robinson	2007	
402. William Tom Robinson	2004	
403. Edward C. Ross	2012	
404. Robert H. Roth, Jr.	2018	

405.	Edwin A. Rowe	2013	456. Robert W. Stark	2008
406.	Gregory E. Rowe	2016	457. Ethel Z. Stears	1999
407.	Larry W. Rubingh	2012	458. Jerry L. Stewardson	2003
408.	James L. Rule	2012	459. Carlyle F. Stewart III	2014
409.	Meredith Rupe	2006	460. Linda D. Stoddard	2016
410.	James Russell Rupert	2009	461. Arthur R. Stone	2006
411.	Donald A. Russell	1996	462. Robert P. Stover	2012
412.	William P. Sanders	2003	463. Dana R. Strall	2017
413.	Donald A. Scavella, Sr.	2005	464. Michael P. Streevy	2010
414.	John G. Schleicher	2006	465. David R. Strobe	2013
415.	Margery A. Schleicher	2007	466. Donald B. Strobe	1990
416.	Leonard R. Schoenherr	2013	467. David T. Strong	1998
417.	W. Thomas Schomaker	2004	468. Verne Carl Summers	1992
418.	William D. Schoonover	1992	469. Royal J. Synwolt	1991
419.	James P. Schwandt	2008	470. Thomas E. Tarpley, Sr.	2015
420.	Robert B. Secrist	1991	471. Edmond G. Taveirne	2018
421.	David A. Selleck	2015	472. Roy G. Testolin	2013
422.	Gerald L. Selleck	2018	473. Wayne N. Thomas	2010
423.	Richard A. Selleck	1996	474. J. Todd Thompson	2010
424.	Priscilla J. Seward	2003	475. James M. Thompson	2006
425.	Merton W. Seymour	1999	476. John Ross Thompson	2010
426.	Philip M. Seymour	2011	477. R. John Thompson	2010
427.	Jane B. Shapley	1996	478. Ronald J. Thompson	1995
428.	Maurice D. Sharai, Jr.	2005	479. Dorothy J. Thon	2017
429.	Isaac Yong-Cheol Shin	2010	480. Duane G. Thon	2007
430.	Gary R. Shiplett	2000	481. Phylemon D. Titus	2002
431.	Larry R. Shrout	1998	482. Karen Hien Thi Vo To	2018
432.	Robert J. Sielaff	2018	483. William J. Torrey	1993
433.	Jay K. Six	2016	484. Gerald L. Toshalis	2006
434.	Edward H. Slate	2012	485. Kenneth L. Tousley	1995
435.	Harold J. Slater	2010	486. Raymond J. Townsend	2009
436.	Dennis E. Slattery	2012	487. Ted P. Townsend	1998
437.	Linda J. Slaughter-Titus	2010	488. Douglas R. Trebilcock	2006
438.	Stephen C. Small	2004	489. Keith R. Treman	2015
439.	Betty A. Smith	2004	490. Saul C. Trinidad	2013
440.	Charles W. Smith	2011	491. Arthur R. Turner	2006
441.	James A. Smith	1993	492. Molly C. Turner	2012
442.	Jerome K. Smith	2011	493. Richard A. Turner	1995
443.	Russell L. Smith	1994	494. James E. Tuttle	2016
444.	William M. Smith	2005	495. Diane E. Vale	1990
445.	Dorraine S. Snogren	1990	496. Oscar Ventura	2009
446.	David P. Snyder	2014	497. William A. Verhelst	2006
447.	Jean R. Snyder	2002	498. Douglas W. Vernon	2010
448.	G. Charles Sonquist, Jr.	2002	499. Rony S. Veska	2013
449.	Harlan E. Sorensen	2006	500. Alonzo E. Vincent	2013
450.	Joseph L. Spackman	2013	501. Paul T. Wachterhauser	2009
451.	Arthur L. Spafford	1991	502. Glenn M. Wagner	2017
452.	Sandra Lee Spahr	2006	503. Lynn W. Wagner	2002
453.	Gordon E. Spalenka	1993	504. Joyce E. Wallace	2013
454.	Carolin S. Spragg	2013	505. Suzanne B. Walls	2016
455.	Lynette Stallworth	2002	506. Lowell F. Walsworth	2002

507.	Maurice E. Walworth, Jr.	2006	527. Theodore D. Whitely, Sr.	2015
508.	George F. Ward	2006	528. Bobby Dale Whitlock	2009
509.	Kenneth E. Ward	2005	529. Myron K. Williams	1994
510.	Grant A. Washburn	1995	530. Richard K. Williams	2001
511.	Brent L. Webster	2012	531. Sondra B. Willobee	2017
512.	Roy "LaVere" Webster	1995	532. Margaret Halls Wilson	2009
513.	Harold E. Weemhoff, Jr.	2015	533. Richard D. Wilson	2008
514.	Glenn R. Wegner	2004	534. Douglas E. Wingeier	2000
515.	Stephan Weinberger	2016	535. David A. Winslow	2008
516.	Edward C. Weiss, Jr.	1994	536. Chong Y. Won	2015
517.	James D. Weiss	1993	537. Gregory B. Wood	2015
518.	Barbara E. Welbaum	2019	538. Robert D. Wright	2015
519.	Karen A. (Mars) Welch	2008	539. William R. Wright	2017
520.	Gerald L. Welsh	1994	540. William A. Wylie-Kellermann	2017
521.	Robert L. Wessman	1999	541. Deborah A. Line Yencer	2018
522.	Charles H. West	2009	542. Richard A. Youells	1995
523.	Margaret Rodgers West	2009	543. Lee F. Zachman	2010
524.	Karen S. Wheat	2015	544. Karl L. Zeigler	2010
525.	Randy J. Whitcomb	2019	545. Ellen K. Zienert	2018
526.	Robert A. White	2016		

54. What associate members have been retired (¶357): (List alphabetically. If retiring in the interim between conference sessions (¶357.2d), indicate the effective date of retirement.) **(Under ¶357.1, no vote required; under ¶357.2, v; under ¶357.3, 2/3 v)**
   a)   This year?

Name	Effective Date
Barbara J. Fay	01.01.2020

   b)   Previously?

Name	Year	Name	Year
John R. Allan	1998	Walter H. Miller	2004
Eugene L. Baughan	2002	Gerald E. Mumford	1993
John T. Charter	1999	Harold V. Phillips	2017
Jane A. Crabtree	2003	Darlene Kay Pratt	2016
Jean Arthur Crabtree	1994	Merlin H. Pratt	2019
Walter David	1992	James A. Rencontre	1997
Roy G. Forsyth	1991	Randall E. Roose	1993
Marcos A. Gutierrez	2010	Terrill M. Schneider	2018
Patricia A. Harpole	2017	Nicholas W. Scroggins	2010
Catherine W.J. Hiner	2009	Howard Seaver	2012
Dale F. Jaquette	1992	Brian K. Sheen	2004
Geraldine M. Litchfield	2014	Theodore A. Trudgeon	2019
Michael W. Luce	2012	Charles R. VanLente	2010
James M. Mathews	2003	Nola R. Williams	2000
Clyde E. Miller	1987		

55. What provisional members have been previously retired (¶358, 2008 *Book of Discipline*)?

Name	Effective Date
Carol L. Bourns	2007

56. Who have been recognized as retired local pastors (¶320.5):

a) This year? * **indicates completed COS or M.Div**

Name	COS or M.Div.	Date Effective
Terri L. Bentley	*2006	07.01.2020
Christine J. Bergquist	*2003	07.01.2020
Carleton R. Black	*2019	07.01.2020
John M. Brooks	8 COS	01.01.2020
Paul A. Damkoehler	*M.Div.	07.01.2020
Howard H. Harvey	M.Div.	07.01.2020
Judith A. Hazle	10 COS	07.01.2020
James E. Huff, Jr.	*2007	07.01.2020
Ronald G. Hutchinson	*2011	07.01.2020
Esther A. Irish	*2017	07.01.2020
Brenda K. Klacking	*2005	07.01.2020
Bruce W. Malicoat	*2018	07.01.2020
Patricia A. Pebley	*M.Div.	07.01.2020
Timothy R. Puckett	*M.Div.	06.01.2020
Ellen O. Schippert	*2012	07.01.2020

b) Previously? (*Those with an asterisk have completed the Course of Study)

Name	Year	Name	Year
L. Cecile Adams	2013	*Richard J. Duffey	2005
L. Cecile Adams	2013	*Mona J. Dye	2017
*Sheila F. Baker	2014	*William F. Dye	2017
James E. Barnett	2013	James A. Fegan	2005
*Donald E. Bedwell	2011	*Edna M. Fleming	2011
Virginia B. Bell	2005	*David C. Freeland	2017
*Leo "Bud" Elwood Bennett	1993	Richard A. Fritz	2014
*Nancy J. Bitterling	2018	*Linda L. Fuller	2018
Betty M. Blair	2009	*Joyce F. Gackler	2012
*Nancy L. Boelens	2009	*Sandra J. Gastian	2011
*Peggy Ann Boltz	2014	*Sue J. Gay	2007
*Connie R. Bongard	2015	*Donald J. Graham	2019
Carole A. Brown	2019	Rosaline D. Green	2019
*Debra K. Brown	2015	*Carl E. Greene	2011
*Richard B. Brown	2010	*Sueann K. Hagan	2017
Ronald A. Brown	1994	*Paul E. Hane	2018
*Ellen F. Burns	2010	*Carolyn G. Harris	2013
*Linda J. Burton-Collier	2014	Daniel W. Harris	2003
*Roberta W. Cabot	2014	Patricia A. Harton	2010
David Gunnar Carlson	2010	*Jacque Hodges	2017
*Linda J. Carlson	2009	*Dale A. Hotelling	2019
*Mary Ellen Chapman	2016	*Clare Walter Huyck	2015
*Robert D. Chapman	2012	*Raymond A. Jacques	2008
*Paulette G. Cheyne	2008	*Thomas H. John, Sr.	2012
*Esther Cox	1988	Charles B. Jones	1997
*Martin H. Culver	2011	*J. Robert Keim	2011
Bonita Davis	2008	*Sandra J. Kolder	2017
*Merlin Delo	1997	*Robert I. Kreger	2013
*Donald R. Derby	2018	*Suzanne P. Kornowski	2011
*Judy K. Downing-Siglin	2001	Jeanne N. Laimon	2015

*Bonny J. Lancaster	2006	*Michael J. Simon	2017
*George W. Lawton	2007	*Kathleen Smith	2012
Margaret A. Martinez	2019	*Mary E. Spencer	2009
Ruth A. McCully	2009	*Cherrie A. Sporleder	2013
James B. Montney	2012	*Robert A. Srock	2012
*Dianne Doten Morrison	2016	Bruce Steinberg	2018
*Larry W. Nalett	2004	John R. Sternaman	2002
*Lawrence A. Nichols	2016	*James W. Stilwell	2017
Judith A. Nielsen	2007	*Diane E. Stone	2010
*Gary L. Peterson	2016	*Stanley Patrick Stybert	2010
Kathy Phillips	2016	*Kenneth E. Tabor	2010
*Ralph A. Posnik, Jr.	2019	Earleen A. VanConant	2000
*David O. Pratt	2016	*Sandra K. VandenBrink	2013
*Jean B. Rencontre	2008	*Herbert J. VanderBilt	2017
*O'Ryan Rickard (¶327.7)	2013	*Dianne H. Van Marter	2015
*John F. Ritter	2001	*Irene L. Vittoz	2018
*Carolyn A. Robinson-Fisher	2011	*Donald R. Wendell	2009
*Deanna M. Sailor-Petit	2006	Calvin "Herb" Wheelock	2019
Cecelia L. Sayer	2019	*Betty J. Whitely	2007
*Jeffrey J. Schrock	2016	*Henry Williams	2012
*William Schuman	2001	Roberta L. Willson	2014
Allen F. Schweitzer	2000	*Donald Woolum	2003
Edward C. Seward	2004	*David L. Youngs	2006
*Connie E. Shatz	2012	*Gayle Sue (Berntsen) Zaagman	2014
*Alice J. Sheffield	2012	*Mark E. Zender	2019

57. What is the number of clergy members of the Annual Conference: 1,219
    a)   By appointment category and conference relationship?
            (NOTES:
            (1)   Where applicable, the question numbers on this report form corresponding to each category have been placed in parenthesis following the category title. Where these question numbers appear, the number reported in that category should agree with the number of names listed in the corresponding questions.

            (2)   For the three categories of Appointments to Extension Ministries, report as follows:

                ¶344.1a, c): the number of clergy members appointed within United Methodist connectional structures, including district superintendents, or to an ecumenical agency.

                ¶344.1b): the number of clergy members appointed to extension ministries, under endorsement by the Division of Chaplains and Related Ministries of the General Board of Higher Education and Ministry.

                ¶344.1d): the number of clergy members appointed to other valid ministries, confirmed by a two-thirds vote of the Annual Conference.

            Note: Report those in extension ministry in one category only.

            See the Discipline paragraphs indicated for more detailed description of these appointment categories.)

            Note: Those approved to serve as a local pastor, but not currently under appointment, are not counted as clergy members of the conference.

Categories	Deacons in Full Connection	Elders in Full Connection	Provisional Deacons	Provisional Elders	Associate Members & Affiliate Members with Vote	Full-time Local Pastors	Part-time Local Pastors
Pastors and deacons whose primary appointment is to a Local Church (¶¶331.4a, 331.1c, 339, 345) (74)	11	224	3	44	5	135	70
Deacons (in full connection and provisional) serving Beyond the Local Church (¶331.1a, b) (77a,b)	14	XXXXX XXXXX XXXXX	0	XXXXX XXXXX XXXXX	XXXXX XXXXX XXXXX	XXXXX XXXXX XXXXX	XXXXX XXXXX XXXXX
Appointments to Extension Ministries (¶316.1; 344.1a, c) (76a)	XXXXX XXXXX XXXXX	19	XXXXX XXXXX XXXXX	0	0	2	0
Appointments to Extension Ministries (¶316.1; 344.1b) (76b)	XXXXX XXXXX XXXXX	8	XXXXX XXXXX XXXXX	0	0	0	0
Appointments to Extension Ministries (¶316.1; 344.1d) (76c)	XXXXX XXXXX XXXXX	9	XXXXX XXXXX XXXXX	0	0	1	0
Appointments to Attend School (¶331.3) (79)	0	0	0	0	0	XXXXX XXXXX	XXXXX XXXXX
Appointed to Other Annual Conferences (49)	3	5	0	0	0	XXXXX XXXXX	XXXXX XXXXX
On Leave of Absence (50a1, a2)	2	9	1	0	0	XXXXX XXXXX	XXXXX XXXXX
On Family Leave (50a3, a4)	0	0	0	0	0	XXXXX XXXXX	XXXXX XXXXX
On Sabbatical Leave (51)	0	0	0	0	0	XXXXX XXXXX	XXXXX XXXXX
On Medical Leave (52)	2	9	0	0	0	0	0
On Transitional Leave (50a5)	3	1	1	0	0	XXXXX XXXXX	XXXXX XXXXX
Retired (53, 54, 55)	22	588	0	1	32	XXXXX XXXXX	XXXXX XXXXX
Total Number, Clergy Members	57	867	5	45	37	138	70
Grand Total, All Conference Clergy Members	1219						

b) By gender and racial/ethnic identification? (NOTE: See the instruction for item 57 for guidelines to assist in the racial/ethnic identification count.)

	Clergy Demographics														
Categories	Deacons in Full Connection		Elders in Full Connection		Provisional Deacons		Provisional Elders		Associate Members & Affiliate Members with Vote		Full-time Local Pastors		Part-time Local Pastors	
	Male	Female	Male	Female	Male	Female	Male	Female	Male	Female	Male	Female	Male	Female
Asian	0	0	23	5	0	1	3	0	0	0	3	0	1	1
Black	0	1	31	13	0	0	0	1	0	0	7	3	6	2
Hispanic	1	0	3	0	0	0	1	0	1	0	1	2	0	0
Native American	0	0	0	1	0	0	0	0	0	0	0	0	0	0
Pacific Islander	0	0	0	0	0	0	0	0	0	0	0	0	1	0
White	10	45	605	204	2	2	16	24	25	10	74	46	36	22
Multi-Racial	0	0	1	0	0	0	0	0	0	0	2	0	1	0
Grand Total-All Conference Clergy Members*	11	46	645	223	2	3	20	25	26	10	87	51	45	25

PART III – CERTIFICATION IN SPECIALIZED MINISTRY

Note: Indicate credential of persons in Part III: FD, FE, PD, PE, AM, FL, PL, and LM.

58. Who are the candidates in process for certification in specialized ministry?

Name	Clergy/Lay Status	Specialized Ministry
Andrew Schleicher	FD	Christian Education
Diana Carpenter	Lay	Spiritual Formation
Julie Lawhead	Lay	Spiritual Formation

59. Who is certified in specialized ministry? (List the areas of specialized ministry. Indicate by an asterisk those certified this year.)

Name	Clergy/Lay Status	Specialized Ministry
M. Kay DeMoss	FD	Christian Education
I. Naomi Garcia	Laity	Christian Education
Diane MA Griffin	Diaconal	Christian Education
Colleen T. Treman	FD	Christian Education
Michele Ettinger	Lay	Youth Ministry
Brian K. Johnson	FL	Youth Ministry
Sue A. Pethoud	FD	Youth Ministry
Mark R. Babb	FD	Music Ministry
John Potter	Lay	Music Ministry
Susan D. Amick	FD	Spiritual Formation
Annelissa M. Gray-Lion	RD	Spiritual Formation
Sueann K. Hagan	RL	Spiritual Formation
Jennifer J. Jue	FE	Spiritual Formation
Nancy LeValley	Laity	Spiritual Formation
Jack L. Mannschreck	FE	Spiritual Formation
Andrew J. Schleicher	FD	Christian Communications

60. Who are transferred in as a certified person in specialized ministry? **None**

61. Who are transferred out as a certified person in specialized ministry? **None**

62. Who have been removed as a certified person in specialized ministry?

Name	Clergy/Lay Status	Specialized Ministry
Lisa M. Batten	FL	Spiritual Formation
Pamela L. Buchholz	RD	Christian Education
Daniel R. Colthorp	FL	Youth Ministry
Philip L. Tousley	FE	Spiritual Formation
Christine E. Wyatt	RD	Spiritual Formation

PART IV CERTIFIED LAY MINISTRY

(¶¶268, and 666.10 *The Book of Discipline*)

63. Who are certified as lay ministers (¶¶268, and 666.10)? (List alphabetically, by district)

Name	District	Certified / Re-Certified
Merry Henderson *(DSA 07.01.2020)*	Central Bay	2019
Sharon Appling	Greater Detroit	2018 / 2020
Barbara Bennett	Greater Detroit	2020
Sherman Louis	Greater Detroit	2020
Diane Miles	Greater Detroit	2020
Alan Muniz Ugalde	Greater Detroit	2020
Eugene Paik	Greater Detroit	2020
Robin Rivers	Greater Detroit	2020
Evelyn Summerville	Greater Detroit	2020
Ellena Totty	Greater Detroit	2020
Steven P. Beukema	Greater Southwest	2017 / 2019
Patricia Bird	Greater Southwest	2015 / 2018
Linda S. Depta	Greater Southwest	2016 / 2019
Wynne L. Hurlbut	Greater Southwest	2017 / 2019
Alexander Miller *(DSA 2014)*	Greater Southwest	2014 / 2020
Simmie N. Proctor	Greater Southwest	2017 / 2020
Marcia Tucker *(DSA 07.01.2014)*	Greater Southwest	2016 / 2020
Richard Vorel *(DSA 01.01.2020)*	Greater Southwest	2015 / 2020
Beverly Clark *(DSA 01.01.2020)*	Heritage	2015 / 2020
Lois Fenmore	Heritage	2011 / 2020
Joseph Keith Caldwell	Midwest	2015 / 2018
Larry Molloy *(DSA 07.01.2019)*	Northern Skies	2019
Randie Clawson	Northern Waters	2019
Nancy LeValley	Northern Waters	2011 / 2018
Donna Stone	Northern Waters	2009 / 2019

PART V DIACONAL MINISTERS

(Paragraph numbers in questions 64-71 refer to *The 1992 Book of Discipline*)

64. Who are transferred in as diaconal ministers (¶312)? **None**

65. Who are transferred out as diaconal ministers (¶312)? **None**

66. Who have had their conference relationship as diaconal ministers terminated by Annual Conference action (¶313.3)? **(Under ¶313.3a, no vote; under ¶313.3b, 2/3 v) None**

67. What diaconal ministers have died during the year?
    a) Effective: **None**
    b) Retired: **None**

68. What diaconal ministers have been granted leaves of absence under ¶313.1a, c, d) (disability, study/sabbatical, or personal leave): **(v) None**

69. What diaconal ministers have been granted an extended leave (¶313.1e): **None**

70. Who have returned to active status from extended leave (¶313.1e)? **(v)**? **None**

71. Who have taken the retired relationship to the Annual Conference as diaconal ministers (¶313.2): **(Under ¶313.2b, 2/3 v)**
   a)   This year? **None**
   b)   Previously?

Name	Date Effective
Barbara A. Brooks	2007
Janice E. Caldwell	1999
Jane Case	2011
Thelma M. Childress	1994
Daphna Lee Flegal	2018
Margaret L. Foster	1999
George W. Gish	2003
Mary Levack Quick	2002
Beverly W. Rice	1997

PART VI APPOINTMENTS AND CONCLUDING BUSINESS

72. Who are approved for less than full-time service?
   a)   What associate members and elders (full and provisional) are approved for appointment to less than full-time service, what is the total number of years for which such approval has been granted to each, and for what fraction of full-time service (in one-quarter, one-half, or three-quarter increments) is approval granted (¶¶338.2, 342.2, 1506)? **(2/3 v; after 8 years 3/4 v)**:

Name	Current Appointment	Years	Fraction of Full-Time Service
John W. Ball	Lake Orion	1	3/4
Shawn P. Lewis-Lakin	Birmingham: First UMC	1	3/4
Ryan C. Low Edwardson	Escanaba: First/Bark River	0	3/4
Marva Pope	Wayne: First UMC	2	1/2
Latha Ravi	Cass Community	1	1/4
Heidi Reinker	Trenton: First	4	3/4
Linda "Lyne" K. Stull-Lipps	Riverdale: Lincoln Road	4	3/4
Beth Titus	Nardin Park	6	1/2
Susan J. Trowbridge	Battle Creek: First UMC	6	1/2

   b)   What deacons in full connection and provisional deacons are approved for appointment to less than full-time service (¶331.7)?

Name	Current Appointment	Years	Fraction of Full-Time Service
Mark R. Babb	Sturgis: First UMC	1	1/2
M. Kay DeMoss	MI Area Communications	5	3/4
Nancy V. Fancher	Exec Dir Maple Valley Comm Center of Hope	0	1/2
Mary Hagley	Dixboro UMC	7	1/2
Georgia N. Hale	Grand Rapids: Genesis	5	1/4

Christina L. Miller-White	Court St, Conference Staff	0	1/2
Cara Beth Ann Weiler	Kalamazoo: Sunnyside	11	1/2 and 1/4
Alicea Williams	Mount Clemens: First	3	1/2

73. Who have been appointed as interim pastors under the provisions of ¶338.3 since the last session of the annual conference, and for what period of time? **None**

74. What elders, deacons (full connection and provisional), associate members, local and supply pastors are appointed to ministry to the local church and where are they appointed for the ensuing year? (Attach a list.)

75. What changes have been made in appointments since the last annual conference session? (Attach list. Include and identify Appointments Beyond the Local Church (Deacons) and Appointments to Extension Ministries (Elders). Give effective dates of all changes.)

76. What elders (full connection and provisional), associate members, and local pastors are appointed to extension ministries for the ensuing year? (Attach a list)
    a) Within the connectional structures of United Methodism (¶344.1a, c)?
    b) To ministries endorsed by the Board of Higher Education and Ministry (¶344.1b)?
    c) To other valid ministries under the provisions of ¶344.1d? **(2/3 v)**

Name	Clergy Status	Date Eff.	Extension Ministry Assignment	Charge Conference
John W. Ball	FE	2019	Celebrate Hope Consultant	Lake Orion
Kenneth C. Dunstone	FE	2020	Psychiatrist, VA Eastern Kansas Health Care System	
David G. Elmore	FE	2016	Chaplain for Ascension at Home/Reverence Hospice, Portage	Coldwater
Emmanuel J. Giddings, Sr.	FE	2006	Director of Alfalit International/ Liberia Literacy Program	
Melody Johnson	FE	2002	Corporate Chaplain, Porter Hills Retirement Community	Birmingham: First
Kristen J. Leslie	FE	2010	Professor, Eden Seminary	
Russell K. Logston	FE	2019	Pastor: St. John's Lutheran Church	Lake City UMC
Stacy R. Minger	FE	2004	Associate Prof, Asbury Theological Seminary	Girard UMC
Joy J. Moore	FE	2019	Luther Seminary, Associate Professor of Biblical Preaching	Flint: Bethel
Kenneth J. Nash (¶345)	FE	2016	Wesleyan Church of Hamburg, Hamburg, NY	Grand Rapids: Cornerstone
Matthew R. Schlimm	FE	2019	Professor of Old Testament, University of Dubuque Theological Seminary	Kalamazoo: Westwood
Barbara L. Smith-Jang	FE	2003	Pastoral Counselor, Taejon Christian International School, Taejon South Korea	Grand Ledge: First
Alice Fleming Townley (¶345)	FE	2010	Parish Associate, Okemos Presbyterian Church, Okemos	East Lansing: University

77. Who are appointed as deacons (full connection and provisional) for the ensuing year? (Attach a list.)
    a) Through non-United Methodist agencies and settings beyond the local church (¶331.1a)?
    b) Through United Methodist Church-related agencies or schools within the connectional structures of The United Methodist Church (¶331.1b)?

78. Who are appointed to attend school (¶416.6)? (List alphabetically all those whose prime appointment is to attend school.)

79. Where are the diaconal ministers appointed for the ensuing year (¶310) [**1992 Discipline**]?

Name	**Appointment**
Diane Griffin	Howell: First UMC – Director of Educational Ministries
Matthew Packer	Fenton UMC Chancel Choir Director and Music Coordinator

80. What other personal notations should be made? (Include such matters as changes in pension credit (¶1506.5), corrections or additions to matters reported in the "Business of the Annual Conference" form in previous years, and legal name changes of clergy members and diaconal ministers.)
    Patricia Elliott – went from NL in 2019 to Discontinued in 2020.
    Donald E. Lee – should have been listed as RL in 2019

81. Where and when shall the next Conference Session be held (¶603.2, 3)?
    Grand Traverse Resort in Acme, Michigan, June 3-6, 2021

— MAC Photos

APPOINTMENTS
Appointments by District

DM – Diaconal Minister
PD – Provisional Deacon
PM – Provisional Member
FD – Deacon in Full Connection
DP – Deacon from other denomination serving UM probation
OD – Deacon Member of Other Annual Conference
PE – Provisional Elder
FE – Elder in full connection
EP – Elder/full minister from other denomination serving UM probation
OE – Elder member of other annual conference

OF – Full member of other denomination
AF – Affiliated Member
AM – Associate Member
FL – Full Time Local Pastor
PL – Part Time Local Pastor
SP – Student Local Pastor
RA – Retired Associate Member
RE – Retired Full Member
RD – Retired Deacon
RP – Retired Provisional Member

RL – Retired Local Pastor
RLA – Retired Local Pastor Under Appointment
OR – Retired Member of Other Conference
HL – Honorable Location
HLOC – Honorable Location Other Conference
DSA – District Superintendent Assignment (name)
CLM – Certified Lay Minister
++ – Ad Interim Appointment
*Home Address

CENTRAL BAY DISTRICT

District Superintendent	John G. Kasper FE1
Executive Assistant	Teri Rice

DS Email: jkasper@michiganumc.org
Office Email: trice@michiganumc.org

Office: (989) 793-8838
3764 Fashion Square Blvd, Saginaw 48603

CHARGE	PASTOR		ADDRESS	TELEPHONE	
				CHURCH	HOME
Arbela	Gloria Haynes	RE3	Box 252, 8496 Barnes, Millington 48746	(989) 793-5880	
			*2152 Village West Dr., S, Lapeer 48466		(734) 626-0070
Arenac County: Christ	James A. Payne (part-time ½)	AM2	3322 E. Huron Rd., Box 145, AuGres 48703	(989) 876-7449	
			*124 N. Chestnut, PO Box 167, Sterling 48659		(989) 654-9001
Auburn	Robert D. Nystrom	FE3	207 S. Auburn, Auburn 48611	(989) 662-6314	
			*201 S. Auburn, Auburn 48611		(269) 535-2481

CENTRAL BAY DISTRICT

CHARGE	PASTOR		ADDRESS	CHURCH	HOME
BAY CITY					
Grace	Eric D. Kieb	FE6	4267 S. Two Mile Rd, Bay City 48706	(989) 684-1101	
			*2161 Niethammer Dr. Bay City 48706		(989) 671-8951
Beaverton: First	Lynn F. Chappell	RE6	150 West Brown, Beaverton 48612	(989) 435-4322	(989) 435-9403
			*148 W Brown, Beaverton 48612		
Birch Run	Laura E. Feliciano	FL1	Box 277, 12265 Church St, Birch Run 48415	(989) 624-9340	
Burt			Box 96, 2799 Nichols Rd, Burt 48417	(989) 770-9948	
			*8196 Poellet, Birch Run 48415		(734) 645-8991
Blanchard-Pine River	William W. Chu	FE1	7655 West Blanchard Road, Blanchard 49310	(989) 561-2864	
			*1109 Glenwood Dr, Mt Pleasant 48858		(517) 992-5038
Caro	Anthony Tomasino	FE5	670 Gilford, Caro 48723	(989) 673-2246	
			*208 W. Burnside, Caro 48723		(989) 673-4355
Caseville	Donald L. Wojewski	FL1	PO Box 1027, 6490 Main St., Caseville 48725	(989) 856-4009	
Hayes			7001 Filion Rd., Pigeon 48755	(989) 553-2161	
			*PO Box 1027, 6474 Main, Caseville 48725		(989) 856-2626
Cass City	Robert P. Demyanovich	FL3	5100 N. Cemetery, Box 125, Cass City 48726	(989) 872-3422	
			*6339 Brenda Dr., Cass City 48726		(248) 636-5679
Churchill	Michelle N. Forsyth	PE1	501 E. State Rd., West Branch 48661	(989) 345-0827	
	(part-time ½)		*1005 W. Eighth St., Mio 48647		(989) 826-5521
Clare	Jaqueline L. Raineri	FL1	105 E Seventh Street, Clare 48617-1301	(989) 386-2591	
			*714 S Rainbow Dr, Clare 48617-9605		(989) 386-7683
Coleman: Faith	Scott W. Marsh	PE2	310 Fifth St., Box 476, Coleman 48618	(989) 465-6181	
			*209 E. Jefferson St, Coleman 48618		(231)-760-0601
Elkton	Won D. Kim	PE4	150 South Main St., Box 9, Elkton 48731	(989) 375-4113	
			*134 S. Main St., Elkton 48731		(989) 375-4185
Essexville: St. Luke's	Jenaba Waggy	PE1	206 Scheurmann St., Essexville 48732	(989) 893-8031	
			*212 Hart St., Essexville 48732		(317) 534-7248

CHARGE	PASTOR		ADDRESS	CHURCH	HOME
Fairgrove	James Butler	PL1	5116 W. Center, Box 10, Fairgrove 48733	(989) 693-6564	
			*2024 Liberty, Fairgrove 48733		(248) 881-6294
Farwell	Martin T. Cobb	PE4	PO Box 709, 281 E Ohio Street, Farwell 48622	(989) 588-2931	
			*511 N Superior St, Farwell 48622		
Frankenmuth	Ryan L. Wenburg	FE5	346 East Vates, Frankenmuth 48734	(989) 652-6858	(989) 598-5438
			*326 East Vates, Frankenmuth 48734		
Freeland	Kayla J. Roosa	PE6	205 E. Washington, Box 207, Freeland 48623	(989) 695-2101	(989) 573-8357
			*7801 N. River Road, Freeland 48623		
Bentley	Merry Henderson	DSA1	7209 N Main St, Bentley 48613	(989) 233-5529	
Garfield			701 N Garfield Road, Linwood 48634	(989) 879-6992	(989) 447-1874
			*10601 Carr Rd, Saint Charles 48655		
GLADWIN					
First	Carmen L. Cook	FL3	309 S. M-18, Gladwin 48624	(989) 426-9619	(989) 426-2698
			*1271 Chatterton, Gladwin 48624		
Wagarville Community	Douglas E. Hasse	PL3	2478 W. Wagarville Rd., Gladwin 48624		(989) 598-0716
			*5943 Weiss St # 58, Saginaw 48603		
Glennie	Keith Reinhardt	PL5	5094 Bamfield Rd., Box 189, Glennie 48737	(989) 735-3951	(989) 710-1976
			*7620 Spruce, Hale 48739		
Gordonville	Michael P. Kelley	FL1	76 E. Gordonville Rd., Midland 48640	(989) 631-4388	
Midland: Homer			507 S. Homer Rd., Midland 48640	(989) 835-5050	
			*7770 W Scott Rd, Hubbard Lake 49747		(989) 297-7242
Hale: First	Melvin L. Leach	RE3	201 West Main St., Box 46, Hale 48739	(989) 728-9522	(586) 212-2802
			*7540 O'Connor, Box 334, Hale 48739		
Harrison: The Gathering	Ray McClintic	DSA1	PO Box 86, 426 N First St. Suite 106, Harrison 48625	(989) 539-1445	(989) 249-6158
	(Sept. 1)		*3781 Peninsular Drive, Gladwin 48624		
Harrisville	Angela M. Lovegrove	FL1	107 W Church St., Harrisville 48740	(989) 724-5450	(616) 295-7546
Lincoln			101 East Main St., PO Box 204, Lincoln 48742	(989) 736-6910	
			*216 5th St, Harrisville 48740		

CENTRAL BAY DISTRICT

CENTRAL BAY DISTRICT

CHARGE	PASTOR		ADDRESS	CHURCH	HOME
Hope	Patrick R. Poag	FL16	5278 North Hope Rd., Hope 48628	(989) 689-3811	
Edenville			455 W. Curtis Rd., Box 125, Edenville 48620	(989) 689-6250	
Dale			4688 S. Freeman Rd., Box 436, Beaverton 48612	(989) 435-4829	(989) 689-4788
			*5302 N. Hope Rd., Hope 48628		
Kilmanagh	William C. Cleland	PL7	2009 S. Bay Port Rd., Bay Port 48720	(989) 453-3520	
Owendale			7370 Main St., Box 98, Owendale 48754	(989) 678-4172	(989) 975-1500
			*129 S. Silver St., Bad Axe 48413		
Kingston	Mark A. Harriman	FL	PO Box 196, 3453 Washington St., Kingston 48741	(989) 683-2832	(989) 683-2929
			*3442 Washington St., Box 243, Kingston 48741		
Mayville	Nathan J. Jeffords	FL2	601 East Ohmer, PO Box 189, Mayville 48744	(989) 843-6151	(989) 781-0860
			*860 E. Brown Rd, Mayville 48744		
MIDLAND					
Aldersgate	Michael T. Sawicki	FE8	2206 Airfield Lane, Midland 48642	(989) 631-1151	(989) 492-4464
Saginaw: Kochville Campus *(became satellite campus 9/1/18)*			6030 Bay Rd., Saginaw 48604	(989) 792-2321	
			*415 Coolidge Dr., Midland 48642		
First	Anita K. Hahn	FE2	315 W. Larkin St., Box 466, Midland 48640	(989) 835-6797	(989) 708-8894
			*3217 Noeske, Midland 48640		
Associate	Jung Eun Yum	FE7	315 W. Larkin St., Box 466, Midland 48640	(989) 835-6797	(989) 486-9307
			*1010 Pepperidge Ct. Midland 48642		
Associate	Ruth A. VanderSande	PE1	315 W. Larkin St., Box 466, Midland 48640	(989) 835-6797	(810) 335-3962
			*		
Millington	Nickolas K. Genoff	FL1	Box 321, 9020 State, Millington 48746	(989) 871-3489	(810) 537-5028
			*4851 W. Main St., Millington 48746		
Mio	Michelle N. Forsyth	PE1	1101 W. Eighth St., Mio 48647	(989) 826-5598	(989) 826-5521
	(part-time ½)		*1005 W. Eighth St., Mio 48647		
MT. PLEASANT					
Chippewa Indian	TO BE SUPPLIED		3490 S Leaton Rd, Mt Pleasant 48858-7995		(989) 621-8867
			*3490 S Leaton Rd, Mt Pleasant 48858-7995		

CHARGE	PASTOR		ADDRESS	CHURCH	HOME
First	Julie A. Greyerbiehl	FE3	400 S Main Street, Mount Pleasant 48858-2598	(989) 773-6934	
			*1109 Glenwood Dr, Mt Pleasant 48858-4325		(517) 655-2321
Leaton	Deborah A. Line Yencer	RE3	6890 E Beal City Road, Mt Pleasant 48858	(989) 773-3838	
			*17429 Summit Ct, Barryton 49305		(248) 425-4684
Trinity	Martin T. Cobb	PE2	202 S Elizabeth St, Mt Pleasant 48858-2820	(989) 772-5690	
Countryside			202 S. Elizabeth St (4264 S Leaton Rd), Mt Pleasant 48858	(989) 773-0359	
			*511 N Superior St, Farwell 48622		(231) 215-3596
Oscoda	William R. Seitz	FE10	120 W. Dwight, Oscoda 48750	(989) 739-8591	
Oscoda Indian Church			7994 Alvin Rd., Mikado 48750		
			*108 W. Dwight St, Oscoda 48750		(989) 739-5213
PIGEON					
First	Cindy L. Gibbs	FL6	7102 Michigan Ave., Box 377, Pigeon 48755	(989) 453-2475	
			*7090 Scheurer St., Box 377, Pigeon 48755		(989) 453-3232
Salem	David K. Stewart, Sr (until 9/1)	RE7	23 Mabel, Box 438, Pigeon 48755	(989) 453-2552	
	J. Albert Barchue (begin 9/1)	OE1	*7065 Clabuesch St., Box 438, Pigeon 48755		(570) 267-6513
Pinconning	Janet Shaffer	DSA1	314 Whyte St., Pinconning 48650	(989) 879-3271	
Alger			7786 Newberry St, Alger 48610	(989) 836-2291	
			*7786 Newberry St, Alger 48610		989-362-6536
Port Austin	Clifford L. Radtke	PL3	8625 Arch, Box 129, Port Austin 48467	(989) 738-5322	
Pinnebog			4619 Pinnebog Rd., Kinde 48445		
			*114 Washington St., Port Austin 48467		(269) 545-2275
Reese	Jon W. Gougeon	FL12	9859 Saginaw St., PO Box 7, Reese 48757	(989) 868-9957	
			*1968 Rhodes, Reese 48757		(989) 868-9957
Rose City: Trinity	Helen Alford	PL2	125 West Main St., PO Box 130, Rose City 48654	(989) 685-2350	
			*163 Hayes St., Rose City 48654		
Rosebush	Joseph L. Beavan	FL7	PO Box 187, 3805 School Street, Rosebush 48878	(989) 433-2957	
			*3272 E Weidman Rd, Rosebush 48878-9715		(989) 433-5509

CENTRAL BAY DISTRICT

CENTRAL BAY DISTRICT

CHARGE	PASTOR		ADDRESS	CHURCH	HOME
SAGINAW					
Ames	David A. Wichert	FE2	801 State St., Saginaw 48602	(989) 754-6373	
First	Amylee B. Terhune	FE5	*1477 Vancouver, Saginaw 48638	(989) 799-0131	(989) 401-6622
			4790 Gratiot Road, Saginaw 48638		(989) 793-5880
New Heart	Melene E. Wilsey	FL5	*4674 Village Drive, Saginaw 48638		
			1802 W. Michigan Ave., Saginaw 48602	(989) 792-4689	(989) 839-4798
Swan Valley	Robert G. Richards	FL2	*1304 W. Stewart, Midland 48640		
LaPorte			9265 Geddes Rd., Saginaw 48609	(989) 781-0860	
Hemlock			3990 Smith's Crossing, Freeland 48623	(989) 695-9692	
Nelson			406 W. Saginaw, Box 138, Hemlock 48626	(989) 642-5932	
			5950 S Hemlock Rd, Hemlock 48626	(989) 642-8285	
			*16344 Nothern Pintail Trail, Hemlock 48626		(989) 642-4560
St. Charles	Karen J. Sorden	FE4	301 W. Belle, Box 87, St. Charles 48655	(989) 865-9091	(989) 865-8144
			*510 Christy Drive, St. Charles 48655		
Sanford	Lisa L. Kelley	FL1	2560 W. River Rd., Sanford 48657	(989) 687-5353	(989) 280-0627
			*7770 W Scott Rd, Hubbard Lake 49747		
Sebewaing: Trinity	Heather M. Nowak	FL1	513 Washington, Sebewaing 48759	(989) 883-3350	(586) 275-7522
Bay Port			838 Second St., Bay Port 48720	(989) 656-2151	
			*525 Washington, Sebewaing 48759		
Shepherd	William W. Chu	FE1	PO Box 309, 107 W Wright Ave, Shepherd 48883	(989) 828-5866	(517) 992-5038
			*1109 Glenwood Dr, Mt Pleasant 48858		
Standish: Beacon of Light	James A. Payne (part-time ½)	AM2	201 S. Forest, Standish 48658	(989) 846-6277	(989) 654-9001
Sutton-Sunshine	James Butler	PL1	*124 N. Chestnut, PO Box 167, Sterling 46659	(989) 673-6695	
			2996 N. Colwood Rd., Caro 48723		(248) 881-6294
Tawas	Kris S. Kappler	FE3	*2024 Liberty, Fairgrove 48733	(989) 362-4288	(859) 858-8233
			20 East M-55, Tawas City 48763		
Vassar: First	Scott Sherrill	FE5	*801 W. Franklin St., East Tawas 48730	(989) 823-8811	(906) 370-5937
			139 N. Main, Box 71, Vassar 48768		
			*706 Cork Pine Lane, Vassar 48768		

CHARGE	PASTOR		ADDRESS	CHURCH	HOME
Watrousville	William P. Sanders	RE7	4446 W. Caro Rd., Caro 48723 *6116 Slocum Ave, Unionville 48767	(989) 673-3434	(989) 693-6564
Weidman	Cynthia S.L. Greene	FE2	PO Box 98, 3200 N Woodruff Rd., Weidman 48893 *9532 W Saint Charles Rd, Sumner 48889-8729	(989) 644-3148	
West Branch: First	Timothy C. Dibble	FE7	2490 W. State Rd., West Branch 48661 *2458 W. State Rd., West Branch 48661	(989) 345-0210	(248) 622-9514
Whittemore	Gary Gillings	DSA2	Box 155, 110 North St., Whittemore 48770 *205 W State St, Whittemore 48770	(989) 756-2831	(989) 756-3981
Wilber	Keith Reinhardt	PL7	3278 N. Sherman Rd., East Tawas 48730 *7620 Spruce, Hale 48739	(989) 362-7860	(989) 710-1976
Winn	Raymond W. Francis	PL5	8187 S Winn Rd, Mt Pleasant 48858 *812 W Center St, Alma 48801-2140	(989) 866-2417	(989) 330-9135
Wisner	In Beom Oh	FE4	5375 N. Vassar Rd., Akron 48701 *5363 N. Vassar Rd., Akron 48701	(989) 691-5277	

NAME	POSITION		ADDRESS	OFFICE	HOME

APPOINTMENTS TC EXTENSION MINISTRIES LOCATED IN THE CENTRAL BAY DISTRICT:
(further information at end of appointment section)

Timothy Hastings	Chaplain, St. Mary's of Michigan Medical Center, Saginaw	RE17	*1908 Stark St., Saginaw 48602		(989) 752-7898
John G. Kasper	District Superintendent, Central Bay District Office	FE1	3764 Fashion Square Blvd, Saginaw 48603	(989) 793-8838	
Lisa M. McIlvenna	Executive Director	FE13	315 W. Larkin, Midland 48640	(989) 835-7511	
	Fresh Aire Counseling Services		*614 Fisher St., Saginaw 48604		(248) 224-4296

CENTRAL BAY DISTRICT

EAST WINDS DISTRICT

District Superintendent	John H. Hice FE3	DS Email: jhice@michiganumc.org
Executive Assistant	Cheryl Rentschler	Office Email: crentschler@michiganumc.org
		Office: (810) 396-1362
		624 West Nepessing Ste 201, Lapeer 48446

CHARGE	PASTOR		ADDRESS	TELEPHONE CHURCH	HOME
Applegate	Joseph Fetterly	DSA1	4792 Church, Box 1, Applegate 48401	(810) 633-9700	
Avoca			8905 Avoca Rd, Box 233 Avoca 48006	(810) 327-6144	
			*2844 17th Ave, Port Huron 48060		(810) 982-0798
Armada	Christopher G.L. Titus	FL2	23200 E. Main, Box 533, Armada 48005	(586) 784-5201	
West Berlin			905 Holmes Rd., Box 91, Allenton 48002	(810) 395-2409	
			*23234 E. Main St., Box 533, Armada 48005		(586) 784-9484
Atherton	Sang Y. (Abraham) Chun	FE5	4010 Lippincott Blvd., Burton 48519	(810) 742-5644	
Grand Blanc: Phoenix			4423 S. Genesse Rd., Grand Blanc 48439	(810) 743-3370	
			*6105 Wilderness Point, Grand Blanc 48439		(734) 856-3151
Attica	Ronald W. Rouse	PL8	27 Elk Lake Rd., Attica 48412	(810) 724-0690	
			*26789 Dayton Rd., Richmond 48062		(248) 379-2509
BAD AXE COOPERATIVE PARISH					
Bad Axe: First	Timothy G. Callow	FE1	216 East Woodworth, Bad Axe 48413	(989) 269-7671	
Minden City			PO Box 126, 3346 Main St, Minden City 48456	(810) 648-4155	
			*1165 Thompson Dr., Bad Axe 48413		(906) 290-2251
BROWN CITY COOPERATIVE PARISH					
Brown City	Patrick D. Robbins	FL2	7043 Lincoln, PO Box 39, Brown City 48416	(810) 346-2010	
Omard			2055 Peck Rd., Brown City 48416	(810) 346-3448	
			*6931 George St., Brown City 48416		(810) 346-2555
Byron: First	Barbara S. Benjamin	PE3	Box 127, 101 S Ann, Byron 48418	(810) 266-4976	
Gaines			117 Clinton St., Box 125, Gaines 48436	(989) 271-9131	
			*10214 Bath Rd., Byron 48418		(810) 370-1157

CHARGE	PASTOR		ADDRESS	CHURCH	HOME
Capac	Lisa J. Clark	FL21	14952 Imlay City Rd., Capac 48014	(810) 395-2112	
			*211 W. Mill, Capac 48014		(810) 247-0946
Clarkston	Richard L. Dake	FE16	6600 Waldon Rd., Clarkston 48346	(248) 625-1611	(248) 625-1727
			*6599 Church St., Clarkston 48346		
Associate	Megan Jo Crumm Walther	FE4	6600 Waldon Rd., Clarkston 48346	(248) 625-1611	
			*7228 Chapel View Dr., Clarkston 48346		(734) 751-6836
Clio: Bethany	Catherine M. Huvaere	FE4	353 E. Vienna St., Box 327, Clio 48420	(810) 686-5151	(616) 550-2570
			*10480 Varna, Clio 48420		
Cole	Julia A. Cramer	PL2	7015 Carson Rd., Yale 48097	(810) 387-4400	(810) 304-2310
Melvin			1171 E. Main St., Melvin 48454		
			*7656 Melvin Rd, Melvin 48454		
Columbiaville	Philip L Tousley	RE1	4696 Pine, PO Box 98, Columbiaville 48421	(810) 793-6363	(989) 553-3790
			216 East Woodworth, Bad Axe 48413		
Croswell: First	Linda L. Fuller	RLA1	13 North Howard St., Croswell 48422	(810) 679-3595	(810) 679-3576
			*254 N Howard Ave, Croswell 48422		
Davisburg	Thomas C. Hartley, Sr.	OF3	803 Broadway, Davisburg 48350	(248) 634-3373	(248) 698-4502
	(LTFT ½)		*711 Oxhill Drive, White Lake 48386		
Davison	Bo Rin Cho	FE4	207 E. Third St., Davison 48423	(810) 653-5272	(517) 775-5436
			*819 Alana Court, Davison 48423		
Duffield	Jason Dover	DSA1	7001 Duffield Rd, PO Box 19, Durand 48449	(810) 621-3676	(810) 635-9067
			*5222 Don Shenk Dr, Swartz Creek 48473		
Dryden	Patricia A. Hoppenworth	PL13	5400 W. Main St., Box 98, Dryden 48428	(810) 796-3341	(810) 734-1171
			*1421 Poplar, LL, Port Huron 48060		
Durand: First	Aaron B. Kesson	FE5	10016 E. Newburg Rd, Durand 48429	(989) 288-3880	(989) 288-4364
			*302 Hampton, Durand 48429		
Fenton	Jeffrey L. Jaggers	FE7	119 S. Leroy St., Fenton 48430	(810) 629-2132	(810) 354-8430
			*11310 Greenview, Fenton 48430		
Diaconal	Matthew J. Packer	DM4	*6020 Creekside Dr., Swartz Creek 48473		(810) 610-3692

EAST WINDS DISTRICT

EAST WINDS DISTRICT

CHARGE	PASTOR		ADDRESS	CHURCH	HOME
FLINT					
Asbury	Tommy L. McDoniel	FL10	1653 Davison Rd., Flint 48506	(810) 235-0016	
			*2050 Covert Rd. Burton 48529		(248) 705-4401
Bethel	James I. Cogman	FL1	1309 N. Ballenger, Flint 48504	(810) 238-3843	
			*5424 Sycamore Ln, Flint 48532		(248) 682-9879
Bristol	Brian K. Willingham	PL2	G-5285 Van Slyke Rd., Flint	(810) 238-9244	
Burton: Christ			4428 Columbine Ave., Burton 48529	(810) 743-1770	
			*1884 Springfield St., Flint 48503		(810) 513-1407
Calvary	Gregory Timmons	PL3	2111 Flushing Rd., Flint 48504	(810) 238-7685	
			*2327 Limestone Lane, Flushing 48433		(810) 250-4304
Court Street	Jeremy T. Peters	FE6	225 W. Court St., Flint 48502	(810) 235-4651	
			*1827 Overhill, Flint 48503		(810) 407-8333
Hope	Carol M. Blair Bouse	FE8	G-4467 Beecher Rd., Flint 48532	(810) 732-4820	
			*601 Leland, Flushing 48433		(810) 867-4033
Flushing	Jeremiah J. Mannschreck	FE3	413 E. Main St., Flushing 48433	(810) 659-5172	
			*1159 Clearview Dr., Flushing 48433		(810) 659-6231
Forester	Anika Bailey	PL3	2481 N. Lakeshore Rd., Carsonville 48419		
Port Sanilac			7225 Main St., Box 557, Port Sanilac 48469		
			*7209 Main, Port Sanilac 48469		(313) 543-9434
Genesee	Karen B. Williams	FL11	7190 N. Genesee Rd., Box 190, Genesee 48437	(810) 640-2280	
Thetford Center			G-11394 N. Center Rd., Genesee 48437	(810) 687-0190	
			*7472 Roger Thomas Dr., Mt Morris 48458		(810) 547-1706
Goodrich	Joel L. Walther	FE4	8071 S. State Road, Goodrich 48438	(810) 636-2444	
			*7228 Chapel View Dr., Clarkston 48346		(734) 625-4077
Grand Blanc	Brian G. West	FE1	515 Bush Ave., Grand Blanc 48480	(810) 694-9040	
			*12110 Francesca Dr, Grand Blanc 48439		(586) 419-1178
Halsey	Tara R. Sutton	FE5	10006 Halsey Rd., Grand Blanc 48439	(810) 694-9243	
South Mundy			10018 S. Linden Rd., Grand Blanc 48439		
			*10030 Halsey Rd., Grand Blanc 48439		(810) 694-9243

CHARGE	PASTOR		ADDRESS	CHURCH	HOME
Harbor Beach	Sari L. Brown	PE4	PO Box 25, 253 S. First St., Harbor Beach 48441	(248) 634-9711	(989) 479-6053
Port Hope			PO Box 25, 4521 Main St., Port Hope 48468		
			*PO Box 25, 247 First St., Harbor Beach 48441		
HOLLY					
Calvary	Clifford J. Schroeder III	FE9	15010 N. Holly Rd., Holly 48442	(248) 634-9711	(248) 245-8155
			*3464 Quick Rd., Holly 48442		
Mt. Bethel	Leah Caron	PL3	3205 Jossman Rd., Holly 48442	(248) 627-6700	(248) 520-0884
			*735 Vivian Ln, Oxford 48371		
Imlay City	Marcel A. Lamb	FE8	210 North Almont Ave., Imlay City 48444	(810) 724-0687	(810) 721-7149
			*280 Bancroft St., Imlay City 48444		
Jeddo	Karen A. Harriman	DSA1	8533 Wildcat Rd., Box 7, Jeddo 48032	(810) 327-6644	(810) 633-9374
Buel			2165 E. Peck Rd., Croswell 48422		
			*2990 Applegate Rd, Applegate 48401		
Lake Fenton	Vincent Slocum	DSA1	2581 N. Long Lake Rd., Fenton MI 48430	(810) 629-5161	810-210-8589
			*11494 Torrey Rd, Fenton 48430		
Lake Orion	Lawrence A. Wik	FE7	140 East Flint, Lake Orion 48362	(248) 693-6201	(248) 391-0930
			*3691 Hi Crest, Lake Orion 48360		
Associate	John W. Ball	FE8	140 East Flint, Lake Orion 48362	(248) 693-6201	(248) 393-1520
	(LTFT ¾)		*2647 Orbit Dr, Lake Orion 48360		
Lapeer: Trinity	Grant R. Lobb	FE9	1310 North Main St., Lapeer 48446	(810) 664-9941	(810) 664-2213
			*804 Fourth St., Lapeer 48446		
Lennon	Joyce E. Wallace	RE1	1014 Oak St., PO Box 19, Lennon 48449	(810) 621-3676	(810) 208-0648
			* 9921 Belcrest Blvd, Fenton 48430		
Lexington	Susan M. Youmans	FE3	5597 Main St., Lexington 48450	(810) 359-8215	(248) 912-4660
			*7051 Greenbush Ln, Lexington 48450		
Linden	Robert J. Easlick	PL/HL	201 S Bridge St, PO Box 488, Linden 48430	(810) 735-5858	(810) 397-1376
	(LTFT ½)		*701 Tickner, Linden 48451		

EAST WINDS DISTRICT

EAST WINDS DISTRICT

CHARGE	PASTOR		ADDRESS	CHURCH	HOME
Marlette: First	George H. Ayoub	FE3	3155 Main St., Marlette 48453	(989) 635-2075	
			*3169 Main St., Marlette 48453		(989) 635-2436
MARYSVILLE COOPERATIVE PARISH					
Marysville	Curtis B. Clarke	FL2	721 West Huron Blvd., Marysville 48040	(810) 364-7391	
Central Lakeport			3597 Milwaukee, Lakeport 48059	(810) 385-9446	(313) 570-4442
			*683 18th St., Marysville 48040		(989) 280-5553
McGregor	Jerry D. Griggs	PL23	2230 Forester Rd., Deckerville 48427	(810) 657-9168	
Carsonville			3953 Sheldon, Carsonville 48419		(810) 378-5686
			*5800 Paldi, Peck 48466		
Memphis: First	Luis M. Collazo	OE1	81265 Church St, PO Box 29, Memphis 48041	(810) 392-2294	
Lamb			1209 Cove Rd, Wales 48027		(248) 895-8699
			*3216 Woodview Circle, Lake Orion 48362		
Montrose	Harold V. Phillips	RA5	158 E. State St., Box 3237, Montrose 48457	(810) 639-6925	(810) 639-6924
			*12012 Vienna Rd., Montrose 48457		
Mt. Morris: First	Ralph H. Pieper II	RE3	808 E. Mt. Morris St., Mt. Morris 48458	(810) 686-3870	(586) 260-7538
			*3373 Brookgate Dr., Flint 48507		
North Branch: First	Theodore A. Adkins	DSA1	4195 Huron St., PO Box 156, North Branch 48461	(810) 688-2610	(810) 837-1646
Silverwood			2750 Clifford Rd, Silverwood 48760	(989) 761-7599	
			*1506 S Townline Rd., Sandusky 48471		
North Street	David A. Reed	PE6	4580 North Rd., Clyde 48049	(810) 385-4027	(810) 385-8366
			*4584 North Rd., Clyde 48049		
Oregon	Jeanne H. Wisenbaugh	OF3	2985 German Rd., Columbiaville 48421	(810) 793-6828	
Elba			154 S. Elba Rd., Lapeer 48446	(810) 664-5780	
			*1457 Westerrace Dr, Flint 48532		(810) 732-8123
Ortonville	Brian K. Johnson	FL6	93 Church St., Box 286, Ortonville 48462	(248) 627-3125	(248) 627-3347
			*319 Sherman Ct., Ortonville 48462		

CHARGE	PASTOR		ADDRESS	CHURCH	HOME
Otisville	Betty "Kay" Leitelt	FL11	Box 125, 200 W. Main St., Otisville 48463	(810) 631-2911	
Fostoria			Box 67,7435 Willits Rd., Fostoria 48435	(989) 795-2389	
West Deerfield			PO Box 185, 383 Otter Lake Rd. Fostoria 48435	(810) 793-2116	(810) 631-8395
Oxford	Julius E. Del Pino (Sept 1)	RE1	*9622 Hammil Rd., Otisville 48463 21 E. Burdick St., Oxford 48371 *7346 Chipmunk Hollow, Clarkston 48346	(248) 628-1289	(248) 807-2397
PORT HURON					
First	Wilson (Drew) A. Hart	FE1	828 Lapeer Ave., Port Huron 48060 *3014 E. Woodland Dr., Port Huron 48060	(810) 985-8107	(734) 904-9775
Gratiot Park	Eric J. Miller	PL3	811 Church St., Port Huron 48060 *48212 Cardinal, Shelby Twp. 48317	(810) 985-6206	(586) 206-4527
Richfield	Shelly Ann Long	PL5	10090 E. Coldwater, PO Box 307, Davison 48423 *11564 Kings Coach Rd., Grand Blanc 48439	(810) 653-3644	(248) 417-1196
Richmond: First	Tom Waller	FL3	69495 Main St., Box 293, Richmond 48062 *35675 Pound Rd., Richmond 48062	(586) 727-2622	(586) 727-6555
ROMEO COOPERATIVE PARISH					
Romeo	Devin R. Smith	FE1	280 North Main St., Romeo 48065	(586) 752-9132	
Leonard			245 E. Elmwood, Box 762, Leonard 48367 *289 North Bailey St., Romeo 48065	(248) 628-7983	(734) 707-1792
St. Clair: First	John N. Grenfell III	FE3	415 North Third St., Saint Clair 48079 *3202 S Shoreview, Fort Gratiot 48059	(810) 329-7186	(734) 787-7539
SANDUSKY COOPERATIVE PARISH					
Sandusky: First	Susan E. Platt	AM3	68 Lexington St., Sandusky 48471 *155 Bella Ave., Sandusky 48471	(810) 648-2606	(989) 802-2684
Deckerville	TO BE SUPPLIED		3354 Main St., Deckerville 48427 *	(810) 376-2029	
Seymour Lake	Janine Plum	FE6	3050 Sashabaw, Oxford 48371 *3191 Clipper Court, Oxford, 48371-5405	(248) 628-4763	(810) 624-1404

EAST WINDS DISTRICT

EAST WINDS DISTRICT

CHARGE	PASTOR		ADDRESS	CHURCH	HOME
Snover: Heritage	Penelope R. Nunn	FL3	3329 W. Snover Rd., PO Box 38, Snover 48472	(810) 672-9101	
			*1571 N. Main St., Box 65, Snover 48472		(810) 672-9233
Swartz Creek	Daniel J. Bowman	FE1	7400 Miller Rd., Swartz Creek 48473	(810) 635-4555	(810) 441-1600
			*4187 Mountain Ash Court, Swartz Creek 48473		(810) 287-9861
Thomas	Gary Glanville (until 9/1)	RE6	*4945 Deerfield Meadows, Almont 48003		
	Kristen LePalm	DSA1	504 First St., PO Box 399, Oxford 48371	(248) 628-7636	(810) 429-3269
			*10266 E Stanley Rd, PO Box 307, Davison 48423		
West Vienna	Christopher M.Grimes	FL1	5485 W. Wilson Rd., Clio 48420	(810) 686-7480	(313) 399-4530
West Forest			7297 E. Farrand Rd., Millington 48746	(989) 871-3456	
			*5445 W. Wilson Rd., Clio 48420		
Worth Township: Bethel	Donald R. Derby	RLA3	8020 Babcock Rd., Box 143, Croswell 48422	(810) 327-1440	(810) 990-5544
			*1014 St Joseph Ln, Marysville 48040		
Yale	Joseph R. Baunoch	RE1	2 South Main St., Yale 48097	(810) 387-3962	(810) 841-4745
			*4333 24th Ave Lot 9, Fort Gratiot 48059-3844		

NAME	POSITION	ADDRESS	OFFICE	HOME
APPOINTMENTS TO EXTENSION MINISTRIES LOCATED IN THE EAST WINDS DISTRICT:				
(further information at end of appointment section)				
Ann Emerson	Director, Lake Huron Retreat Center FD21	8794 Lakeshore Dr., Lakeport 48059	(810) 327-6272	(810) 327-6468
John H. Hice	District Superintendent, East Winds District Office FE3	624 West Nepessing Ste 201, Lapeer 48446	(810) 396-1362	

GREATER DETROIT DISTRICT

District Superintendent	Charles S.G. Boayue FE3
Executive Assistant	Dwanda Ashford

DS Email: cboayue@michiganumc.org
Office Email: cboayue@michiganumc.org

Office: (313) 481-1045
8000 Woodward Avenue, Detroit 48202

CHARGE	PASTOR		ADDRESS	TELEPHONE	
				CHURCH	HOME
Beverly Hills	Anthony J. Ballah	FL6	20000 W. 13 Mile Rd., Beverly Hills 48025	(248) 646-9777	(248) 327-6276
			*30700 Old Stream, Southfield 48076		
BIRMINGHAM					
Embury	Esrom Shaw	PL1	1803 E. 14 Mile Rd., Birmingham 48009	(248) 644-5708	(313) 868-1352
			*29600 Franklin #40, Southfield 48034		
First	Elbert P. Dulworth	FE5	1589 W. Maple, Birmingham 48009	(248) 646-1200	(248) 258-0903
			*1043 Chesterfield, Birmingham 48009		
Senior Associate	Shawn Lewis-Lakin (LTFT ¾)	FE4	1589 W. Maple, Birmingham 48009	(248) 646-1200	
			*154 S. Cranbrook Cross Road, Bloomfield Hills 48301		
Associate	Susanne E. Hierholzer	FE2	1589 W. Maple, Birmingham 48009	(248) 646-1200	(989) 326-0766
			*361 Pleasant St, Birmingham 48009		
Associate	Rachael M. Dunlap	FL1	1589 W. Maple, Birmingham 48009	(248) 646-1200	(248) 399-3698
			*3485 Kipling, Berkley 48072		
Associate	Zachary L. Dunlap	PE6	1589 W. Maple, Birmingham 48009	(248) 646-1200	(734) 272-5667
			*3485 Kipling, Berkley 48072		
Deacon	Sarah Alexander	FD2	1589 W. Maple, Birmingham 48009	(248) 646-1200	(734) 649-7043
			*8925 Sudbury St. Livonia 48150		
Bloomfield Hills: St. Paul Hazel Park: First	Maurice R. Horne	FL1	165 E. Square Lake Rd., Bloomfield Hills 48302	(248) 338-8233	(313) 550-5810
			315 E. Nine Mile Rd., Hazel Park 48030	(248) 546-5955	
			*208 Barrington Rd., Bloomfield Hills 48302		
Clawson	Michael R Perez, Jr. (½ time)	FL2	205 N. Main, Clawson 48017	(248) 435-9090	(586) 252-7257
			*442 Marias Ave, Clawson 48017		

GREATER DETROIT DISTRICT

CHARGE	PASTOR		ADDRESS	CHURCH	HOME
DEARBORN					
First	David Nellist	OE3	22124 Garrison, Dearborn 48124	(313) 563-5200	
Deacon	Carl T.S. Gladstone (LTFT ½)	FD2	*301 S. Silvery Lane, Dearborn 48124 22124 Garrison, Dearborn 48124	(313) 563-5200	(313) 562-8220
Good Shepherd	Stephen K. Perrine	FE1	*542 W Grand Blvd, Detroit 48216-1439 1570 Mason, Dearborn 48124	(313) 278-4350	(586) 295-3055
DETROIT			*23435 Oak Glen Dr, Southfield 48034		(248) 827-7110
Calvary	Will G. Council	PL7	15050 Hubbell, Detroit 48227	(313) 835-1317	
Cass Community	Faith E. Fowler	FE27	*7796 Surrey Dr., Romulus 48174 3901 Cass Ave., Detroit 48201	(313) 833-7730	(734) 641-8711
Associate	Latha Ravi (LTFT ¼)	FE2	*2245 Wabash, Detroit 48216 3901 Cass Ave., Detroit 48201	(313) 833-7730	(313) 408-1980
Deacon	Sue Pethoud	FD4	*533 Hill St, Rochester 48307 3901 Cass Ave., Detroit 48201	(313) 833-7730	(248) 464-4600
Central	Jill Hardt Zundel	FE7	*4529 Pleasant Valley Rd,, Brighton 48114 23 E. Adams, Detroit 48226	(313) 965-5422	(810) 278-1235
Deaconess	Anne M. Hillman	DC2	2013 Hyde Park, #33, Detroit 48207 23 E. Adams, Detroit 48226	(313) 965-5422	(313) 393-8899
Centro Familiar Cristiano	Patricia Gandarilla-Becerra (part-time ½)	FL9	*111 Cadillac Square11D, Detroit 48226 1270 Waterman, Detroit 48209	(313) 843-4170	(616) 617-6722
Conant Avenue	Willie Smith	FE6	*8961 Niver, Allen Park 48101 18600 Conant, Detroit 48234	(313) 891-7237	(402) 699-1325
Ford Memorial	Donald Beasley	PL5	*16876 Braile, Detroit 48219 16400 W. Warren, Detroit 48228	(313) 584-0035	(313) 566-7226
French	Gertrude M. Mukalay (LTFT ¾)	OE3	*13969 Fielding, Detroit 1803 E 14 Mile Rd, Birmingham 48009		(313) 475-3416
(New Church Start)	John K. Ilunga Ngoie (LTFT ¼)	OE3	*1858 Estates Dr, Detroit 48206 1803 E 14 Mile Rd, Birmingham 48009 *1858 Estates Dr, Detroit 48206		(517) 703-3035

CHARGE	PASTOR		ADDRESS	CHURCH	HOME
Metropolitan	Janet Gaston Petty	FE5	8000 Woodward Ave., Detroit 48202	(313) 875-7407	
Resurrection	Carolyn A. Jones (part-time ½)	FL2	26110 Hendrie Blvd, Huntington Woods 48070		(248) 546-9749
			8150 Schaefer, Detroit 48228	(313) 582-7011	
			*2466 Edison, Detroit 48206		(313) 573-0043
St. Paul	Kenneth M. Johnson	PL3	8701 W. Eight Mile Rd., Detroit 48221	(313) 342-4656	
			*30700 Old Stream, Southfield 48076		(248) 327-6276
Scott Memorial	Cornelius Davis, Jr.	FE5	15361 Plymouth, Detroit 48227	(313) 836-6301	
			*531 New Town-Victoria Park, Detroit 48215		(313) 331-8075
Second Grace	Darryl E. Totty	FE6	18700 Joy Rd., Detroit 48228	(313) 838-6475	
			*29193 Northwestern Hwy, #388, Southfield 48034		(313) 215-3841
Trinity-Faith	Markey C. Gray	FL3	19750 W. McNichols, Detroit 48219	(313) 533-0101	
			*23470 Meadow Park, Redford 48239		(313) 533-8423
DownRiver	Robert F. Fuchs	FL1	14400 Beech Daly, Taylor 48180	(734) 442-6100	
			*20433 Foxboro, Riverview 48192		(810) 571-0185
Eastpointe: Immanue	Albert Rush	FL9	23715 Gratiot, Eastpointe 48021	(586) 776-7750	
			*22839 Linwood Eastpointe 48021		(586) 871-2025
FARMINGTON First	Anthony R. Hood	FE5	33112 Grand River, PO Box 38, Farmington 48326	(248) 474-6573	
			25766 Livingston Circle, Farmington Hills 48335		(248) 474-7568
Nardin Park	Melanie L. Carey	FE5	29887 W. 11 Mile Rd., Farmington Hills 48336	(248) 476-8860	
			*25109 Lyncastle Ln., Farmington Hills 48336		(248) 476-8860
Associate	Beth D. Titus (LTFT ½)	FE7	29887 W. 11 Mile Rd., Farmington Hills 48336	(248) 476-8860	
			*6771 Kestral Ridge, Brighton 48116		(586) 665-4333
Orchard	Amy E. Mayo Moyle	FE6	30450 Farmington, Farmington Hills 48334	(248) 626-3620	
			*32979 Thorndyke Court, Farmington Hills 48334		(517) 918-2215
Associate	Nicholas E. Bonsky	PE2	30450 Farmington, Farmington Hills 48334	(248) 626-3620	
			*29221 Aranel St, Farmington Hills 48334		(586) 944-3292

GREATER DETROIT DISTRICT

GREATER DETROIT DISTRICT

CHARGE	PASTOR		ADDRESS	CHURCH	HOME
Ferndale: First	Robert D. Schoenhals	RE8	22331 Woodward, Ferndale 48220	(248) 545-4467	
			*657 W. Oakridge, Ferndale 48220		(248) 542-5598
Flat Rock: First	Amy Triebwasser	PE4	28400 Evergreen, Flat Rock 48134	(734) 782-2565	
			*29451 Evergreen, Flat Rock 48134		
Franklin: Community	David Huseltine	FE5	26425 Wellington, Franklin 48025	(248) 626-6606	(248) 761-4327
Fraser: Christ	Dennis E. Irish	FE1	*2423 Ogden W., Farmington Hills 48323		
			34385 Garfield, Fraser 48026	(586) 293-5340	(810) 300-3963
			*34355 Garfield, Fraser 48026		
Garden City: First	Jonathan Combs	FL6	6443 Merriman Rd., Garden City 48135	(734) 421-8628	(734) 422-5375
	(part-time ¾)		*31515 Windsor, Garden City 48135		
Grosse Pointe	Ray McGee	FE5	211 Moross Rd., Grosse Pte Farms 48236	(313) 886-2363	(313) 881-1129
			*64 Moross Rd., Grosse Pte Farms 48236		
Harper Woods: Redeemer	Marshall C. Murphy	FL4	20571 Vernier Rd., Harper Woods 48225	(313) 884-2035	
			*20572 Anita, Harper Woods 48225		
Howarth	Marvin L. Herman	FL3	550 E. Silverbell Rd., Lake Orion 48360	(248) 373-2360	
Paint Creek			4420 Collins Rd., Rochester 48306	(248) 652-1583	
			*137 Stratford Ln, Lake Orion 48362		(810) 908-0373
LIVONIA					
Clarenceville	Donald R. Sperling	FE11	20300 Middlebelt Rd., Livonia 48152	(248) 474-3444	
			*34184 Haldane, Livonia 48152		(248) 615-1435
Newburg	Steven E. McCoy	FE8	36500 Ann Arbor Trail, Livonia 48150	(734) 422-0149	(734) 424-4593
			*33652 Trillium Court, Livonia 48150		
Deacon	Rodney Gasaway	FD4	36500 Ann Arbor Trail, Livonia 48150	(734) 422-0149	
	(LTFT ½)		*36522 Ann Arbor Trail, Livonia 48150		(734) 578-6256
St. Matthew's	Jeremy P. Africa	FE6	30900 W. Six Mile Rd., Livonia 48152	(734) 422-6038	(734) 855-4882
			*31000 W Six Mile, Livonia 48152		
Macomb: Faith	Dianne H. VanMarter	RLA6	56370 Fairchild Rd., Macomb 48042	(586) 749-3147	(810) 488-0608
			*20100 Cushing, Detroit 48205		

CHARGE	PASTOR		ADDRESS	CHURCH	HOME
MADISON HEIGHTS					
Korean First Central	Daeki Kim	OE3	500 W. Gardenia Ave., Madison Heights 48071	(248) 545-5554	
			*30150 Shoreham St., Southfield 48076		
Madison Heights	Rodney K. Diggs	PL1	246 E. Eleven Mile Rd., Madison Heights 48071	(248) 544-3544	
	(Aug 1)		*31711 Kenwood Ave, Madison Heights 48071		(615) 300-1195
Vietnamese Ministry	Nhan Duc Nguyen	OF5	246 E. Eleven Mile Rd., Madison Heights 48071		(714) 501-0323
			*38108 Charwood Dr., Sterling Heights 48312		
Mount Clemens: First	Daniel J.C. Hart	FE2	57 S.B. Gratiot Ave., Mt. Clemens 48043	(586) 468-6464	(586) 863-3646
			*110 Belleview St., Mt. Clemens 48043		
Deacon	Alicea Lynn Williams	FD5	57 S.B. Gratiot Ave., Mt. Clemens 48043	(586) 468-6464	(810) 694-8318
	(LTFT ½)		*21515 Bay Hills Dr., Macomb 48044		
Mount Vernon	Cherlyn McKanders	PL4	3000 28 Mile Rd., Washington 48094	(248) 650-2213	(248) 881-8541
			*59989 Whitman N Apt D, Washington 48094-2261		
Omo: Zion	Mary Ellen Chapman	RLA2	63020 Omo Rd., Box 344, Richmond 48062	(810) 233-2824	(586) 291-6552
			*19059 Carmelo Dr N, Clinton Township 48038		
PONTIAC					
Grace & Peace Community	Laura M. Koivula	PL2	451 W Kennett, Pontiac 48340	(248) 334-3280	(248) 559-3053
			*1851 Birchcrest Rd., Waterford 48328		
St. John	Lester Mangum	FE8	620 University Dr., Pontiac 48342	(248) 338-8933	(248) 217-9071
			*622 University Dr., Pontiac 48342		
REDFORD					
Aldersgate	Benjamin J. Bower	FE5	10000 Beech Daly Rd., Redford 48239	(313) 937-3170	(313) 531-7487
			*11328 Arnold, Redford 48239		
Assoc. Brightmoore Campus	Jonathan Combs	FL6	12065 W. Outer Dr, Detroit 48223.	(313) 937-3170	(734) 422-5375
	(part-time ¼)		*31515 Windsor, Garden City 48135		
New Beginnings	Diane Covington	OF6	16175 Delaware, Redford 48240	(313) 255-6330	(248) 943-0534
			*18261 University Pk. Dr., Livonia 48152		

GREATER DETROIT DISTRICT

GREATER DETROIT DISTRICT

CHARGE	PASTOR		ADDRESS	CHURCH	HOME
Riverview	Carol A. Middel	PL2	13199 Colvin, Riverview 48193	(734) 284-2721	
			*42018 Woodbrook Dr, Canton 48188-2612		(734) 397-2332
Rochester: St. Paul's	David A. Eardley	FE8	620 Romeo St., Box 80307, Rochester 48308	(248) 651-9361	(248) 651-9770
			*632 Romeo St., Rochester 48307		
Associate	Erin L. Fitzgerald	FE3	620 Romeo, Box 80307, Rochester 48308	(248) 651-9361	(616) 510-7941
			*632 Romeo Rd, Rochester 48307		
Rochester Hills: St. Luke's	Scott E. Manning	FE5	3980 Walton Blvd., Rochester Hills 48309	(248) 373-6960	(248) 366-1937
			*6161 Mission Dr., West Bloomfield 48324		
Romulus: Community	Carolyn A. Jones (part-time ½)	FL3	11160 Olive St., Romulus 48174	(734) 941-0736	(313) 573-0043
			*2466 Edison, Detroit 48206		
Roseville: Trinity	Stephen T. Euper	FE9	18303 Common, Roseville 48066	(586) 886-2363	(586) 776-1459
			*30455 Progress, Roseville 48066		
Royal Oak: First	Jeffrey S. Nelson	FE5	320 W. Seventh, Royal Oak 48067	(248) 541-4100	(248) 629-7185
			*3113 Marion Dr, Royal Oak 48073		
Co-Pastor	Myra Moreland	FL3	320 W. Seventh, Royal Oak 48067	(248) 541-4100	
			*		
Associate	George Marck	PL1	320 W. Seventh, Royal Oak 48067	(248) 541-4100	
			*4309 N Verona Cir, Royal Oak 48073		(248) 682-0211
Southfield: Hope	Benjamin Kevin Smalls	OE3	26275 Northwestern Hwy., Southfield 48076	(248) 356-1020	
			*5704 N. Pinnacle, West Bloomfield 48322		(301) 512-4075
Associate	Reggie A. White (LTFT ¼)	OF2	26275 Northwestern Hwy., Southfield 48076	(248) 356-1020	
			*		
Associate	Rosaline D. Green	RLA4	26275 Northwestern Hwy., Southfield 48076	(248) 356-1020	(248) 470-4042
			*29476 Briar Bank Ct, Southfield 48034		
Associate	Christopher M. Grimes	FL4	26275 Northwestern Hwy., Southfield 48076	(248) 356-1020	(313) 399-4530
			*14314 Artesian St, Detroit 48223		
Associate	Dale R. Milford	PL2	26275 Northwestern Hwy., Southfield 48076	(248) 356-1020	(248) 626-4368
			*29229 Utley Rd, Farmington Hills 48334		

CHARGE	PASTOR		ADDRESS	CHURCH	HOME
St. Timothy	Benjamin Kevin Smalls	OE3	15888 Archdale, Detroit 48227	(313) 837-4070	(301) 512-4075
Associate	Reggie A. White (LTFT ¼)	OF2	*5704 N. Pinnacle, West Bloomfield 48322	(313) 837-4070	
Sterling Heights	Joel T. Fitzgerald	FE3	15888 Archdale, Detroit 48227 *11333 16½ Mile, Sterling Heights 48312 *632 Romeo Rd, Rochester 48307	(586) 268-3130	(616) 848-9759
TRENTON Faith	Wayne A. Price	FE2	2530 Charlton, Trenton 48183 *1641 Edsel Drive, Trenton 48183	(734) 671-5211	(269) 330-6768
First	Heidi C. Reinker (LTFT ¾)	FE5	2610 W. Jefferson, Trenton 48183 *2604 Lenox Rd., Trenton 48183	(734) 676-2066	(734) 676-0041
TROY Big Beaver	Gregory M. Mayberry	FE5	3753 John R, Troy 48083 *2050 Fairfield, Troy 48085	(248) 689-1932	(248) 689-2839
First	Weatherly Burkhead Verhelst	FE6	6363 Livernois, Troy 48098 *6339 Vernmoor, Troy 48098	(248) 879-6363	(989) 598-6506
Korean TroyHope Campus	Eung Yong Kim	FE2	42693 Dequindre, Troy 48085 42693 Dequindre, Troy 48085 *974 Hillsborough Dr, Rochester Hills 48307	(248) 879-2240 (248) 879-2240	
Associate	Se Jin Bae	PE6	42693 Dequindre, Troy 48085 *1940 Flagstone Circle, Rochester 48307	(248) 879-2240	(248) 841-1595
Associate TroyHope Campus	Anna Moon	FE8	42693 Dequindre, Troy 48085 *17377 Averhill Blvd., Macomb 48042	(248) 879-2240	
Deacon	Jinny Song	PD5	42693 Dequindre, Troy 48085 *3200 Olde Franklin Dr., Farmington 48334	(248) 879-2240	
Utica	Donald D. Gotham	FE10	8650 Canal Rd., Sterling Hts. 48314 *8506 Clinton River Rd., Sterling Hts. 48314	(586) 731-7667	(586) 739-2726

GREATER DETROIT DISTRICT

GREATER DETROIT DISTRICT

CHARGE	PASTOR		ADDRESS	CHURCH	HOME
Warren: First	Melissa J. Claxton	FE3	5005 Chicago Rd., Warren 48092	(586) 264-4701	
Washington	Cherlyn E. McKanders	PL2	*32006 Wellston, Warren 48093		(586) 264-2212
			58430 Van Dyke, Box 158, Washington 48094	(586) 781-9662	
			*59989 Whitman N Apt D, Washington 48094		(248) 881-8541
WATERFORD					
Central	Jack L. Mannschreck	FE8	3882 Highland Rd., Waterford 48328	(248) 681-0040	
			*3720 Shaddick, Waterford 48328		(248) 683-2986
Deacon	Cora E. Glass	FD3	3882 Highland Rd., Waterford 48328	(248) 681-0040	
			*4011 Shaddick, Waterford 48328		(248) 410-2645
Four Towns	George Marck	PL1	6451 Cooley Lake Rd., Waterford 48327	(248) 682-0211	
			*4309 N Verona Cir, Royal Oak 48073		(248) 682-0211
Trinity	Michael R. Perez, Jr. (½ time)	FL2	6440 Maceday Dr., Waterford 48329	(248) 623-6860	
			**442 Marias Ave, Clawson 48017		(586) 252-7257
WATER'S EDGE COOPERATIVE PARISH					
New Baltimore: Grace	Brian E. Steele	PE3	49655 Jefferson, New Baltimore 48047	(586) 725-1054	
			*33840 Hooker Rd., New Baltimore 48047		(586) 648-6242
	Christopher J. Heldt	DSA1	49655 Jefferson, New Baltimore 48047	(586) 725-1054	
			*43748 Donley Dr, Sterling Heights 48314		(586) 206-2684
Algonac: Trinity	Christopher J. Heldt	DSA1	424 Smith St., Algonac 48001	(810) 794-4379	
			*43748 Donley Dr, Sterling Heights 48314		(586) 206-2684
Wayne: First	Marva C. Pope (LTFT ½)	FE3	3 Town Square, Wayne 48184	(734) 721-4801	
			*3017 Flora Lane, Wayne 48184		(248) 629-0746
West Bloomfield	Monica L. William	FE2	4100 Walnut Lake Rd., West Bloomfield 48323	(248) 851-2330	
			*5553 Fox Hunt Lane, West Bloomfield 48322		(248) 851-0149
Westland: St. James	Rahim O. Shabazz	FE3	30055 Annapolis, Westland 48186	(734) 729-1737	
Detroit: People's			19370 Greenfield Rd., Detroit 48235	(313) 342-7868	
			*3722 Heritage Parkway, Dearborn 48124		(313) 570-6292

CHARGE	PASTOR		ADDRESS	CHURCH	HOME
Wyandotte: First	Mark D. Miller	FE1	72 Oak, Wyandotte 48192	(734) 282-9222	
			*2210 20th St., Wyandotte 48192		(734) 282-9222

NAME	POSITION		ADDRESS	OFFICE	HOME

APPOINTMENTS TC EXTENSION MINISTRIES LOCATED IN THE GREATER DETROIT DISTRICT:
(further information at end of appointment section)

Charles S.G. Boayue	District Superintendent, Greater Detroit District Office				
		FE3	8000 Woodward Avenue, Detroit 48202	(313) 481-1045	
Carl T.S. Gladstone	Director of Motor City Wesley, Young Leaders Initiative Board (LTFT ½)				
		FD2	8000 Woodward, Detroit 48202	(313) 718-2275	
			*542 W Grand Blvd. 48216		(586) 295-3055
Lisa M. McIlvenna	Samaritan Counseling Center		29887 W. 11 Mile Rd, Farmington Hills 48336	(248) 474-4701	
		FE12	*5601 Houghton, Troy 48098		(248) 879-3220
Alexander J. Plum	Director Clinical and Social Health Integration, Henry Ford Health Care				
		PD1	3901 Cass Ave, Detroit 48201	(313) 833-7730	

APPOINTMENT TO LOCAL CHURCH FOR DEACON TO MISSIONAL WORK (331.5)

Susan Pethoud	Detroit: Cass Community Social Services				
		FD6	3901 Cass Ave. Detroit 48201	(313) 833-7730	(810) 278-1235

GREATER DETROIT DISTRICT

GREATER SOUTHWEST DISTRICT

GREATER SOUTHWEST DISTRICT

District Superintendent	Dwayne E Bagley FE3	DS Email: dbagley@michiganumc.org	Office: (269) 372-7525	
Executive Assistant	Mandana Nordbrock	Office Email: mnordbrock@michiganumc.org	2350 Ring Road North, Ste B, Kalamazoo 49006	

				TELEPHONE	
CHARGE	PASTOR		ADDRESS	CHURCH	HOME
Allegan	Robert K. Lynch	FE9	409 Trowbridge St., Allegan 49010	(269) 673-4236	
			*1310 South M 40, Allegan 49010		(269) 673-2512
Almena	Leonard R. Schoenherr	RE1	27503 County Rd 375, Paw Paw 49079	(269) 668-2811	
			*4500 Mountain Ash Lane, Kalamazoo 49004		(269) 903-2182
Arden	(TO BE SUPPLIED)		6891 M 139, Berrien Springs 49103	(269) 429-4931	
			*		
Augusta: Fellowship	Scott M. Bouldrey	PL4	PO Box 337, 103 N. Webster, Augusta 49012	(269) 731-4222	
			*109 N Webster St, Augusta 49012		(269) 275-2633
Bangor: Simpson	Mona K. Joslyn	FE5	507 Joy St., Bangor 49013	(269) 427-7725	
			*9177 South Gullway, Richland 49083		(269) 484-4060
BATTLE CREEK					
Baseline	(TO BE SUPPLIED)		9617 E Baseline Rd, Battle Creek 49017	(269) 963-7710	
Chapel Hill	Chad M. Parmalee	FE8	157 Chapel Hill Drive, Battle Creek 49015	(269) 963-0231	
			*192 Brentwood Dr, Battle Creek 49015		(517) 281-0362
Associate	Janet S. Wilson	FL3	157 Chapel Hill Drive, Battle Creek 49015	(269) 963-0231	
			*20515 Bedford Rd N, Battle Creek 49017		(269) 317-5591
Christ	Carolyn Robinson-Fisher (until 7/22)	RLA1	65 Bedford Road N, Battle Creek 49037	(269) 965-3251	
	Janet S. Wilson (begin 9/8)	FL1	*20515 Bedford Rd N, Battle Creek 49017		(269) 317-5591
First	Susan J. Trowbridge	FE2	111 E Michigan Ave, Battle Creek 49014	(269) 963-5567	
	(LTFT ½)		*PO Box 151, 329 S Main St, Vermontville 49096		(517) 667-8414

CHARGE	PASTOR		ADDRESS	CHURCH	HOME
Maple	Linda D. Stoddard	RE13	342 Capital Ave NE, Battle Creek 49017	(269) 964-1252	(269) 965-1671
Newton	Cori R. Clevenger (7/15)	DSA1	*126 Heather Ridge, Battle Creek 49017		
			8804 F Drive South, Ceresco 49033	(269) 979-2779	(936) 391-2204
Washington Heights	Cleora M. French	FL1	*403 Maple St, Colon 49040		
			153 N. Wood St, Battle Creek 49037	(269) 968-8773	(810) 814-6487
Bellevue	Margaret M. Sandlin	FL1	*26 W. Roosevelt Ave, Battle Creek 49037		
			122 W Capital Ave, Bellevue 49021	(269) 763-9421	(989) 387-1494
BC: Convis Union			18990 12 Mile Rd, Battle Creek 49014	(269) 965-3787	
			*523 Sherwood Rd, Bellevue 49021		
Berrien County: Lakeside	Brenda L. Ludwig	RLA1	14970 Lakeside Rd, Lakeside 49116	(269) 469-8468	(269) 369-0696
			*8000 Warren Woods Rd #81, Three Oaks 49128		
Berrien Springs	William Walters	DSA3	310 West Mars, Berrien Springs 49103	(269) 471-7220	(269) 479-5561
Pokagon			31393 Kansas St, Dowagiac 49047	(269) 683-8515	
			*609 Rynearson St, Buchanan, MI 49107		
Bridgman: Faith	Bradley K. Heiple	DSA1	PO Box 414, 9156 Red Arrow Hwy, Bridgman 49106	(269) 465-3696	(517) 270-1664
			*2909 Yankee, Niles 49120		
Bronson: First	Samuel C. Gordy	PL3	312 E. Chicago St, Bronson 49028	(517) 369-6555	(269) 330-6054
			*330 E Cory St, Bronson 49028		
BUCHANAN					
Faith	Edward H. Slate	RE9	728 North Detroit Street, Buchanan 49107	(269) 695-3261	(269) 262-0011
			*1358 Honeysuckle Ln, Niles 49120		
First	Ellen D. Bierlein	FL3	132 S Oak Street, Buchanan 49107	(269) 695-3282	(269) 695-3896
			*304 Pontiac Court, Buchanan 49107		
Burnips	Craig H. VanBeek	FL4	PO Box 30 4237 30th St, Burnips 49314	(616) 896-8410	(616) 299-6668
Monterey Center			PO Box 30, (3022 130th Ave, Hopkins) Burnips 49314	(616) 896-8410	
			*4290 Summer Creek Dr, Dorr 49323		
Burr Oak	Carl Q. Litchfield	RE3	PO Box 91, 105 S. Fourth St., Burr Oak 49030	(269) 489-2985	(269) 275-5296
			*27435 Michigan Ave, Mendon 49072		

GREATER SOUTHWEST DISTRICT

GREATER SOUTHWEST DISTRICT

Church	Pastor	Code	Address	Phone	Phone
Casco	Jodi M. Cartwright	PL2	880 66th Street, South Haven 49090	(269) 227-3328	
			*870 66th St, South Haven 49090		(517) 282-9642
Cassopolis	Wade S. Panse	RE6	PO Box 175, 209 South Rowland St, Cassopolis 49031	(269) 445-3107	(269) 449-5335
			*1218 Riverwood Terrace, St. Joseph 49085		
Centreville	Joyce L. Vanderlip	PE1	305 E Main Street, Centreville 49032	(269) 467-8645	(810) 813-9200
			*304 E Market St, Centreville 49032		
Climax	Beverley J. Williams	FL5	PO Box 125, 133 East Maple, Climax 49034	(269) 746-4023	
Scotts			PO Box 112, 8458 Wallene, Scotts 49088	(269) 626-9757	(269) 746-8728
			*331 Prairie Drive, Climax 49034		
Coldwater	Julie Yoder Elmore	FE4	26 Marshall St, Coldwater 49036	(517) 279-8402	(517) 607-6977
			*20 Parsons Ct, Coldwater 49036		
Coloma	Christine M. Beaudoin	FE3	PO Box 670, 144 South Church St, Coloma 49038	(269) 468-6062	(480) 659-1472
			*331 Tannery Dr, Coloma 49038		
Colon	Cori R. Clevenger (7/15)	DSA1	PO Box 646, 224 N. Blackstone, Colon 49040	(269) 432-2783	(936) 391-2204
			*403 Maple St, Colon 49040		
Constantine	Lanette S. Van	OE1	285 White Pigeon St., Constantine 49042	(269) 435-8151	
White Pigeon			PO Box 518, 204 N Kalamazoo St, White Pigeon 49099	(269) 483-9054	
			*265 White Pigeon St, Constantine 49042		
Delton: Faith	Brian R. Bunch	FL9	PO Box 467, 503 S Grove, Delton 49046	(269) 623-5400	(269) 623-5335
			*146 Bush St, Delton 49046		
Dowagiac First	Christopher M. Momany	FE2	PO Box 393, 326 N Lowe, Dowagiac 49047	(269) 782-6157	(248) 462-5317
			*207 Michigan Ave, Dowagiac 49047		
Dowling: Country Chapel	Richard J. Foster	PL5	PO Box 26, Dowling 49050	(269) 721-8077	(269) 721-3400
			*3400 Lacey Rd, Dowling 49050		
Edwardsburg: Hope	Nathaniel R. Starkey	FL1	PO Box 624, 69941 Elkhart Rd., Edwardsburg 49112	(269) 663-5321	(586) 229-5767
			*69862 Roy Dr, Edwardsburg 49112		
Fennville	Douglas A. Tipken	FL3	PO Box 407, 5849 124th Ave, Fennville 49408	(269) 561-5048	(269) 873-0014
Pearl			PO Box 407, Fennville 49408	(269) 561-5048	
			*687 W Fennville St, Fennville 49408		

CHARGE	PASTOR		ADDRESS	CHURCH	HOME
Galesburg	Leonard E. Davis	OR5	PO Box 518, 111 W Battle Creek St, Galesburg 49053	(269) 665-7952	
			*10998 Pleasant Lake Rd, Delton 49046		(269) 623-4412
Galien	Cynthia L. Veilleux	DSA3	PO Box 266, 208 N Cleveland Ave, Galien 49113	(269) 545-2275	
Olive Branch			PO Box 266, 2289 Olive Branch Rd, Galien 49113		
			*72 Sycamore Bnd, Union City 49094		(517) 741-9041
Ganges	Marcia A. Tucker	DSA7	PO Box 511, 2218 68th Street, Fennville 49408	(269) 543-3581	
			*6948 Colver, Fennville 49408		(269) 857-4797
Girard	Sean LaGuire	FL1	990 Marshall Rd., Coldwater 49036	(517) 279-9418	
			*992 Marshall Rd, Coldwater 49036		(313) 926-2498
Glenn	Philip S. Harrington	OE2	PO Box 46, 1391 Blue Star Hwy, Glenn 49416	(269) 227-3930	
	(LTFT ¼)		*1395 Blue Star Hwy, Glenn 49416		(425) 495-6419
Gobles	Ashlei K. Horn	PL1	PO Box 57, 210 E Exchange St, Gobles 49055	(269) 628-2263	
			*31880 Jefferson Ave, Gobles 49055		(269) 364-8545
Gull Lake	Ian J. Boley	FL1	8640 Gull Rd, Richland 49083-9647	(269) 629-5137	
			*8405 Hemel Lane, Richland 49083		(989) 400-1268
Hartford	Stephanie E. Norton	FL2	425 East Main Street, Hartford 49057	(269) 621-4103	
			*143 Paras Hill Dr, Hartford 49057		(269) 532-4741
Hinchman	Dawn Marie Oldenburg	FL3	8154 Church St, Berrien Springs 49103	(269) 471-5492	
Scottdale			4276 Scottdale Rd, St. Joseph 49085	(269) 429-7270	
			*9862 Vineyard St, Bridgman, MI 49106		(269) 208-9673
Hopkins	Kelsey Burns French	FL1	PO Box 356, 322 N Maple St, Hopkins 49328	(269) 793-7323	
South Monterey			PO Box 356, Hopkins 49328 (Corner of 26th St & 127th Ave)	(269) 793-7323	
			*216 Elm St, Hopkins 49328		(248) 613-0366
KALAMAZOO					
First	Julie A. Kline	OF2	212 South Park Street, Kalamazoo 49007	(269) 381-6340	
			*1724 Nichols Rd, Kalamazoo 49006		(269) 330-8502
Associate	John Matthew Weiler	FE1	212 South Park Street, Kalamazoo 49007	(269) 381-6340	
			*3090 Vliet Ln, Kalamazoo 49004		(269) 599-2274

GREATER SOUTHWEST DISTRICT

GREATER SOUTHWEST DISTRICT

CHARGE	PASTOR		ADDRESS	CHURCH	HOME
Milwood	Billie R. Dalton	RE4	3919 Portage Road, Kalamazoo 49001	(269) 381-6720	
			*6585 San Gabriel Dr, Kalamazoo 49009		(269) 615-6945
Northwest	Mark J. Roberts	OE3	3140 N 3rd Street, Kalamazoo 49009	(269) 290-1312	
	(LTFT ¼)		*22980 64th Ave, Mattawan 49071		(406) 217-2237
Sunnyside	Amee A. Paparella	FE1	2800 Gull Road, Kalamazoo 49048	(269) 349-3047	
			*9755 N Division Ave, Sparta 49345		(517) 862-2599
Westwood	Sean K. Kidd	PE2	538 Nichols Road, Kalamazoo 49006	(269) 344-7165	
			*1003 Greenway Terrace, Kalamazoo 49006		(616) 401-8576
Deacon	Sandra V. Bibilomo	FD10	538 Nichols Road, Kalamazoo 49006	(269) 344-7165	
	(LTFT ¼)		*2021 March St, Kalamazoo 49001		(269) 369-8803
Kendall	Glenn C. Litchfield	RE2	PO Box 57, 26718 County Road 388, Gobles 49055	(269) 628-2263	
			*61470 County Road 657, Lawton 49065		(269) 436-0023
Lacota	Michael A. Pinto	DSA14	PO Box 7, 01160 CR 681, Lacota 49063	(269) 253-4382	
			*2321 Tamarack, Kalamazoo 49006		(269) 342-2747
Lawrence	Wayne E. McKenney	FL7	PO Box 276, 122 S Exchange St, Lawrence 49064	(269) 674-8381	
Lawton: St Paul's			PO Box 456, 63855 N. M-40, Lawton 49065	(269) 624-1050	
			*45520 24th St, Mattawan 49071		(269) 669-7062
Marcellus	TO BE SUPPLIED		PO Box 396, 197 W Main St, Marcellus 49067	(269) 646-5801	
Wakelee			15921 Dutch Settlement, Marcellus 49067	(269) 646-2049	
			*224 Davis St, Marcellus 49067		(269) 646-7791
Martin	Corey M. Simon	PE2	PO Box 154, 969 E Allegan, Martin 49070	(269) 672-7097	
Shelbyville			PO Box 154, 938 124th Ave, Shelbyville 49344	(269) 672-7097	
			*948 Lee St, Martin 49070		(231) 622-2070
Mendon	Carl Q. Litchfield	RE3	PO Box 308, 320 W Main St, Mendon 49072	(269) 496-4295	
			*27435 Michigan Ave, Mendon 49072		(269) 275-5296
New Buffalo: Water's Edge	Kellas D Penny III	PE4	18732 Harbor Country Dr, New Buffalo 49117	(269) 469-1250	
			*19603 Oak Dr, New Buffalo 49117		(616) 209-2828

CHARGE	PASTOR		ADDRESS	CHURCH	HOME
NILES					
Portage Prairie	Scott B. Smith	FL2	2450 Orange Road, Niles 49120	(269) 695-6708	(269) 357-3693
			*3310 Chicago Rd, Niles 49120		
New Journey	Robert L. Snodgrass II	FL7	302 Cedar Street, Niles 49120	(269) 683-7250	
Morris Chapel			1730 Holiday, Niles 49120	(269) 684-5194	
			*16270 Lewis Rd, Vandalia 49095		(574) 261-5139
Nottawa	Alexander (Sandy) Miller	DSA18	PO Box 27, 25838 M-86, Nottawa 49075	(269) 467-7134	(269) 467-7134
			*61616 Filmore Rd, Sturgis 49091		
OSHTEMO					
LifeSpring	Jason E. Harpole	PL5	1560 S 8th Street, Oshtemo 49009	(269) 353-1303	(269) 388-8312
			*205 Amos Ave, Portage 49002		
Oshtemo	John W. Fisher	RE8	PO Box 12, 6574 Stadium Dr, Oshtemo 49077	(269) 375-5656	(269) 327-3277
			*3506 East Shore Dr, Portage 49002		
Otsego	Joseph D. Shaler	FE20	PO Box 443, 223 E Allegan St, Otsego 49078	(269) 694-2939	(269) 806-9087
			*411 Walden Dr, Otsego 49078		
Parchment	Thomas A. Davenport	FE5	225 Glendale Blvd, Parchment 49004	(269) 344-0125	(269) 762-3159
			*1227 Grand Ave, Kalamazoo 49006		
Paw Paw	David E. Small	PL/RHL5	420 W Michigan Ave, Paw Paw 49079	(269) 657-7727	(269) 303-8062
	(LTFT ½)		*52333 Ackley Terrace, Paw Paw 49079		
	· Kathy E. Brown				
Plainwell: First		FE11	PO Box 85, 200 Park St., Plainwell 49080	(269) 685-5113	(269) 312-1378
			*714 E Gun River Dr, Plainwell 49080		
PORTAGE					
Chapel Hill	Barry T. Petrucci	FE20	7028 Oakland Dr, Portage 49024	(269) 327-6643	(269) 276-0482
			*5300 Bronson Blvd, Portage 49024		
Associate	Jessica M. Davenport	PE1	7028 Oakland Dr, Portage 49024	(269) 327-6643	(309) 262-3469
	(LTFT ½)		*1836 Waite Ave, Kalamazoo 49008		
Pathfinder	Donald W. Wolfgang	FE5	8740 S Westnedge Ave, Portage 49002	(269) 327-6761	(912) 674-8155
			*8731 Newhouse, Portage 49024		

GREATER SOUTHWEST DISTRICT

GREATER SOUTHWEST DISTRICT

CHARGE	PASTOR		ADDRESS	CHURCH	HOME
Riverside	David L. Haase	PL7	PO Box 152 (4401 Fikes Rd Benton Harbor) Riverside 49084 *211 W Saint Joseph St, Watervliet 49098	(269) 849-1131	(269) 463-3536
Saugatuck	Richard Vorel	DSA1	PO Box 647, 250 Mason St, Saugatuck 49453 *2315 Forest Trail Circle, Fennville 49408	(269) 857-2295	(616) 990-4717
Schoolcraft Pleasant Valley	Julia R. Humenik	PE6	PO Box 336, 342 N Grand Ave, Schoolcraft 49087 PO Box 517, 9300 West XY Ave, Schoolcraft 49087 *318 Willow Ct, Schoolcraft 49087	(269) 679-4845 (269) 679-5352	(269) 679-4501
Silver Creek	Sara Louise Carlson	PL5	31994 Middle Crossing Rd, Dowagiac 49047 *4229 Mahoney St, Portage 49002	(269) 782-7061	(269) 329-1072
Sodus: Chapel Hill	Brenda E. Gordon	FE3	4071 Naomi Road, Sodus 49126 *4033 Naomi Rd, Sodus 49126	(269) 927-3454	(269) 925-4528
South Haven	TO BE SUPPLIED		429 Michigan, South Haven 49090 *12320 76th St, South Haven 49090	(269) 637-2502	(269) 468-9378
St. Joseph: First	Daniel R. Colthorp	FL3	2950 Lakeview Ave, St. Joseph 49085 *5835 Demorrow Rd, Stevensville 49127	(269) 983-3929	(269) 369-8475
Deacon	James W. Kraus Jr	FD20	2950 Lakeview Ave, St. Joseph 49085 *2820 Willa Dr, St Joseph 49085	(269) 983-3929	(269) 983-5798
Stevensville	David F. Hills	FE6	5506 Ridge Rd, Stevensville 49127 *1418 Lake Blvd #1, St. Joseph 49085	(269) 429-5911	(989) 330-3730
Sturgis	Susan J. Babb	FE2	200 Pleasant Ave., Sturgis 49091 *1332 Rolling Ridge Ln, Sturgis 49091	(269) 651-5990	(989) 287-1770
Deacon	Mark R. Babb (LTFT ½)	FD2	200 Pleasant Ave., Sturgis 49091 *1332 Rolling Ridge Ln, Sturgis 49091	(269) 651-5990	(989) 287-1956
Three Oaks	Stephen J. Shimek	DSA1	2 Sycamore Street E, Three Oaks 49128 *112 E Sycamore, Three Oaks 49128	(269) 756-2053	(269) 756-3724

CHARGE	PASTOR		ADDRESS	CHURCH	HOME
THREE RIVERS					
Center Park	Derl G. Keefer	OF2	18662 Moorepark Rd., Three Rivers 49093	(269) 279-9109	
	(LTFT)		*318 E St, Three Rivers 49093		(816) 519-1473
First	Heather A. McDougall	PE2	215 N Main St, Three Rivers 49093	(269) 278-4722	(269) 352-4857
	(LTFT ¼)		*61644 Windridge Ct, Centreville 49032		
Ninth Street	Edward C. Ross	RE4	704 9th St, Three Rivers 49093	(269) 278-2065	(269) 382-0870
			*4231 Persian Dr, Kalamazoo 49006		
Townline	James C. Robertson	PL7	41470 24th Ave, Bloomingdale 49026	(269) 521-4559	(269) 838-3500
			*55130 County Rd 384, Grand Junction 49056		
Union City	James Palaszeski	FL3	PO Box 95, 200 Ellen St, Union City 49094	(517) 741-7028	
Athens			PO Box 267, 123 Clark St, Athens 49011	(269) 729-9370	(989) 912-5738
			*72 Sycamore Bend, Union City 49094		
Vicksburg	Gregory P. Culver	FE4	217 S Main Street, Vicksburg 49097	(269) 649-2343	(231) 651-9309
			*7794 TS Ave E, Scotts 49088		

GREATER SOUTHWEST DISTRICT

GREATER SOUTHWEST DISTRICT

NAME	POSITION	ADDRESS	OFFICE	HOME
APPOINTMENTS TO EXTENSION MINISTRIES LOCATED IN THE GREATER SOUTHWEST DISTRICT:				
(further information at end of appointment section)				
Dwayne E. Bagley	District Superintendent, Greater Southwest District Office			
	FE3	2350 Ring Road North, Suite B, Kalamazoo 49006	(269) 372-7525	(269) 370-2800
Lisa M. Batten	Young Adult Initiatives Coordinator, Michigan Conference			
	FL3	1810 N Drake Rd, Kalamazoo 49006	(517) 347-4030	(269) 491-1799
Sandra V. Bibilomo	Representative Payee, Guardian Finance and Advocacy Services			
	FD9	1000 S Burdick, Kalamazoo 49001	(269) 364-6759	(269) 369-8803
Jessica M. Davenport	Co-Executive Director & Co-Pastor, Wesley Foundation of Kalamazoo (LTFT ½)			
	PE1	2350 Ring Road North, Kalamazoo 49006	(269) 344-4076	(309) 262-3469
David G. Elmore	Chaplain, Ascension at Home Hospice			
	FE2	5220 Lovers Ln, Ste 140, Portage 49002	(800) 343-1396	(517) 817-8855
Heather A. McDougall	Chaplain, Beacon Health System			
	PE5	*61644 Windridge Ct, Centreville 49032		(269) 352-4857
Sherry L. Parker-Lewis	Senior Director of Church Relations, United Methodist Foundation of Michigan			
	FE1	*48710 Apple Ln, Mattawan 49071		(810) 360-9995
Cara Beth Ann Weiler	Associate Director of Site Services, Communities In Schools of Kalamazoo			
	FD4	125 W Exchange Pl, Kalamazoo 49007	(269) 337-1601	
APPOINTMENT FROM OTHER CONFERENCES:				
Mark J. Roberts	Chaplain, Borgess Medical Center, Kalamazoo (3/4 time)			
(Alabama-West Florida Conf.)	OE3	1521 Gull Rd, Kalamazoo 49048	(406) 217-2237	

HERITAGE DISTRICT

| District Superintendent | LuAnn L. Rourke FE1 | DS Email: lrourke@michiganumc.org | Office: (734) 663-3939 |
| Executive Assistant | Dar McGee | Office Email: dmcgee@michiganumc.org | PO Box 128, St. Clair Shores 48080 |

| | | | | TELEPHONE | |
CHARGE	PASTOR		ADDRESS	CHURCH	HOME
Adrian: First	Eric A. Stone	FE1	1245 W. Maple Ave., Adrian 49221	(517) 265-5689	
			*4580 S. Clubview Dr., Adrian 49221		(734) 355-7486
Albion: First	Leslee J. Fritz	PE4	600 E. Michigan, Albion 49224	(517) 629-9425	
			*11184 29 Mile Rd, Albion 49224-9735		(517) 629-6531
Allen	Larry W. Rubingh	RE1	PO Box 103, 167 W Chicago Rd, Allen 49227	(517) 200-8416	
Quincy			32 W. Chicago St., Quincy 49082	(517) 639-5035	
			*2480 N Portage Rd, Jackson 49201		(517) 812-6636
ANN ARBOR					
First	Nancy S. Lynn	FE3	120 S. State St., Ann Arbor 48104	(734) 662-4536	
			*3475 Glazier Way, Ann Arbor 48105		(734) 730-2421
Associate	Nicolas R. Berlanga	PE3	120 S. State St., Ann Arbor 48104	(734) 662-4536	
			*1507 Warwick, Ann Arbor 48103		(734) 983-8677
Korean	Joonshik Yoo	PE2	1526 Franklin St., Ann Arbor 48103	(734) 662-0660	
			*1811 Avondale, Ann Arbor 48103		
Associate	Steve H. Khang	FE14	1526 Franklin St., Ann Arbor 48103	(734) 662-0660	
			*4131 Inglewood Dr, Ypsilanti 48197		(734) 482-0460
West Side	Timothy R. Ziegler	FE8	900 S. Seventh St., Ann Arbor 48103	(734) 663-4164	
			*3023 Appleridge Dr, Ann Arbor 48103		(734) 645-3623
Azalia	Beatrice S. Alghali	PL2	9855 Azalia Rd., Box 216, Milan 48160	(734) 529-3731	
London			11318 Plank Rd., Milan 48160	(734) 439-2680	
			*22492 Pontchartrain Dr, Southfield 48034		(248) 281-3157
Belleville: First	Mary K. Loring	FE1	417 Charles St., Belleville 48111	(734) 697-9288	
			*455 High St., Belleville 48111		(734) 697-7398

HERITAGE DISTRICT

HERITAGE DISTRICT

CHARGE	PASTOR		ADDRESS	CHURCH	HOME
BLISSFIELD					
Emmanuel	Kelley-Marie Zawodni	FL1	215 E. Jefferson St., Blissfield 49228	(517) 486-3020	
Macon			11964 Macon Hwy., Clinton 49236	(517) 423-8270	(734) 497-3560
First	Gunsoo Jung	FE2	*302 E. Jefferson St., Blissfield 49228		
			201 W. Adrian St., Blissfield 49228	(517) 486-4040	
			*403 Brenot Ct., Blissfield 49228		(517) 486-3805
Brighton: First			400 E. Grand River, Brighton 48116	(810) 229-8561	
Whitmore Lake Campus			9318 Main St., Box 431, Whitmore Lake 48189	(734) 449-2121	
Co-Pastor	Lindsey M. Hall	FE1	*7608 Brookview Ct., Brighton 48116		(248) 648-0542
Co-Pastor	Jonathan E. Reynolds	FE1	*7608 Brookview Ct., Brighton 48116		(248) 891-2788
Britton: Grace	William R. Lass	PL1	9250 E. Monroe, Britton 49229	(517) 451-8280	
			*5423 N Stoney Creek Rd, Monroe 48162		(734) 735-1669
Camden	Frederick G. Cain	RE8	PO Box 272, 201 S Main St, Camden 49232	(517) 368-5406	
Montgomery			PO Box 272, 201 S Main St, Camden 49232	(517) 269-4232	
Stokes Chapel			PO Box 272, 201 S Main St, Camden 49232	(517) 368-5406	
			*PO Box 155, 201 S Main St, Camden 49232		(517) 797-5530
CANTON					
Cherry Hill	Michael Desotell	FL7	321 S. Ridge Rd., Canton 48188	(734) 495-0035	
St. Matthew's			1344 Borgstrom, Ypsilanti 48198	(734) 483-5876	
			*1110 Ruth, Ypsilanti 48198		(734) 730-6746
Friendship	Michael K. Norton	FE24	1240 Beck Rd., Canton 48187	(734) 710-9370	
			*1237 Lotz Rd. South, Canton 48188		(734) 722-0183
Carleton	Taek H. Kim	FE9	11435 Grafton Rd., Box 327, Carleton 48117	(734) 654-2833	
			*1424 Monroe St., Box 327, Carleton 48117		(734) 654-2001
Chelsea: First	Joy A. Barrett	FE17	128 Park St., Chelsea 48118	(734) 475-8119	
			*10 Sycamore Dr., Chelsea 48118		(734) 475-8449
Deacon	Rodney Gasaway (LTFT ½)	PD2	128 Park St., Chelsea 48118	(734) 475-8119	
			*36522 Ann Arbor Trail, Livonia 48150		(734) 578-6256

CHARGE	PASTOR		ADDRESS	CHURCH	HOME
Clayton	Robert W. Dister	FL9	3387 State St., PO Box 98, Clayton 49235	(517) 445-2641	
Rollin Center			3988 Townley Rd., Box 98, Manitou Beach 49253		(517) 445-4009
Clinton	Michael W. Vollmer	PE1	*3282 State St., PO Box 98, Clayton 49235		
			10990 Tecumseh-Clinton Rd., Clinton 49236	(517) 456-4972	
Stony Creek			8635 Stony Creek Rd., Ypsilanti 48197	(734) 482-0240	(989) 600-6148
			*5493 Willis Rd, Ypsilanti 48197		
Commerce	Andrew H. Lee	FE2	1155 N Commerce Rd., Commerce Township 48382	(248) 363-3935	(248) 977-0400
			*840 Morella, Commerce Twp. 48382		
Concord	Robert M. Hughes	FE5	PO Box 366, 119 S. Main St., Concord 49237	(517) 524-6156	(517) 677-6381
			*361 Calhoun St, Union City 49194		
Deerfield	Bradley R. Vasey	PL2	110 Williams St., Box 395, Deerfield 49238	(517) 447-3420	(419) 704-1884
Wellsville			2509 S. Wellsville, Blissfield 49228	(517) 486-4777	
			*4322 Corey Hwy, Blissfield 49228		
Denton: Faith	Arthur D. Korlapati	PL3	6020 Denton Rd., Belleville 48111	(734) 483-2276	(248) 444-6529
			*7338 Talbot Drive Apt 102, Lansing 48917		
Dexter	Matthew J. Hook	FE18	7643 Huron River Dr., Dexter 48130	(734) 426-8480	(734) 426-8420
			*7605 Grand Ave., Dexter 48130		
Deacon	Thomas Snyder	FD7	7643 Huron River Dr., Dexter 48130	(734) 426-8480	(734) 476-8954
			*8650 Huron River Dr., Dexter 48130		
Dixboro	E. Jeanne Garza	FE2	5221 Church Rd., Ann Arbor 48105	(734) 665-5632	(269) 503-2099
			*3350 Oak Dr, Ann Arbor 48105		
Deacon	Mary Hagley	FD8	5221 Church Rd., Ann Arbor 48105	(734) 665-5632	(734) 652-5389
	(LTFT ½)		*2929 Brandywine Dr., Ann Arbor 48103		
Dundee	Bradley S. Luck	FE3	645 Franklin, Dundee 48131	(734) 529-3535	(734) 625-6693
			*241 Sidney St., Dundee 48131		
Erie	Janet J. Brown	RE3	1100 E. Samaria Rd., Erie 48133	(734) 856-1453	(313) 533-8423
			*23470 Meadow Park, Redford 48239		

HERITAGE DISTRICT

HERITAGE DISTRICT

CHARGE	PASTOR		ADDRESS	CHURCH	HOME
Frontier	Donald Lee	RLA4	PO Box 120, 9925 Short St, Frontier 49239 *PO Box 127, 106 E Maple St, Camden 49232	(269) 233-0631	(517) 398-3082
Grass Lake	Lawrence J. Wiliford	OR2	449 E Michigan Ave, Grass Lake 49240 *4273 Indian Trl, Jackson 49201	(517) 522-8040	(585) 409-3546
Hardy	John H. Schneider Jr.	FE8	6510 E. Highland Rd., Howell 48843 6520 E. Highland Dr., Howell 48843	(517) 546-1122	(517) 579-2526
Hartland	Charles A. Williams	FE1	10300 Maple St, Hartland 48353 *1403 Odette, Hartland 48353	(810) 632-7476	(810) 991-1032
Highland	Thomas C. Anderson	FE5	680 W. Livingston Rd., Highland 48357 *650 W. Livingston Rd., Highland 48357	(248) 887-1311	(248) 887-1311
Hillsdale: First	Rob A. McPherson	FE3	45 N Manning, Hillsdale 49242 *1079 Markris Dr, Hillsdale 49242	(517) 437-3681	(269) 845-5221
Hillside Somerset Center	Crystal C. Thomas	FL1	6100 Folks Rd, Horton 49246 PO Box 277, 12095 E Chicago Rd, Somerset Center 49282 *6094 Folks Rd, Horton 49246	(517) 563-2835 (517) 688-4330	(517) 563-8920
Homer Lyon Lake	Robert P. Stover	RE9	101 E Adams St, Homer 49245 8493 17 Mile Rd, Marshall 49068 *105 E Adams St, Homer 49245	(517) 568-4001 (269) 789-0017	(517) 568-1126
Howell: First	Scott K. Otis	FE1	1230 Bower St., Howell 48843 *2774 Bogues View Drive, Howell 48843	(517) 546-2730	(616) 307-9765
Diaconal	Diane M. Griffin	DM	1230 Bower St., Howell 48843 *247 S. Mill St., Pinckney 48169	(517) 546-2730	(734) 878-9414
Hudson: First	Carol J. (Abbott) Freeland	FL3	420 W. Main St., Hudson 49247 *428 W. Main St., Hudson 49247	(517) 448-5891	(517) 306-6236
Ida Samaria: Grace	Robert J. Freysinger	FE2	Box 28, 8124 Ida East, Ida 48140 Box 37, 1463 Samaria Rd., Samaria 48177 *3276 Lewis Ave, PO Box 28, Ida 48140	(734) 269-6127 (734) 856-6430	(517) 812-0762

CHARGE	PASTOR		ADDRESS	CHURCH	HOME
JACKSON					
Brookside	Jennifer J. Jue	FE1	4000 Francis, Jackson 49203	(517) 782-5167	
Trinity	Jennifer J. Jue	FE1	1508 Greenwood Ave, Jackson 49203	(517) 782-7937	
Calvary			925 Backus St, Jackson 49202	(517) 782-0543	(734) 272-1780
			*217 Mohawk, Jackson 49203		
First	Tonya M. Arnesen	FE2	275 W Michigan Ave, Jackson 49201	(517) 787-6460	(586) 292-1036
			*1734 Malvern Dr, Jackson 49203-5341		
Deacon	Greg W. Lawton (8/15) (LTFT ½)	FD1	275 W Michigan Ave, Jackson 49201	(517) 787-6460	(269) 317-7183
			*525 S Alpine Lake Dr Apt A, Jackson 49201		
Zion	TO BE SUPPLIED		7498 Cooper St, Jackson 49201	(517) 769-2570	
			*		
Jonesville	Mary A. Sweet	PE2	203 Concord Rd, Jonesville 49250-9824	(517) 849-9565	
Napoleon			PO Box 337, 210 Nottawasepee, Napoleon 49261	(517) 536-8609	
			*969 Adams St, Litchfield 49252-9779		
Lambertville	James E. Britt	FE3	8165 Douglas Rd., Box 232, Lambertville 48144	(734) 847-3944	(231) 881-7367
			*8116 Michelle Ln., Lambertville 48144		
LaSalle: Zion	Keith A. Lenard, Jr.	FL1	1603 Yargerville Rd., LaSalle 48145	(734) 243-5940	(810) 282-8081
Petersburg			152 Saline St., PO Box 85, Petersburg 49270	(734) 279-1118	
			*1607 Yargerville Rd, LaSalle 48145		(734) 778-0835
Lee Center	James M. Gysel	RE7	22392 24 Mile Road, Olivet 49076-9533	(517) 857-3447	(269) 209-4795
			*3239 Nighthawk Lane, Battle Creek 49015		
Lulu	Robert J. Freysinger	FE1	12810 Lulu Rd, PO Box 299, Ida 48140	(734) 269-9076	(517) 812-0762
			*3276 Lewis Ave, PO Box 28, Ida 48140		
MANCHESTER					
Manchester	Dillon S. Burns	PE4	501 Ann Arbor Rd., Manchester 48158	(734) 428-8495	(734) 428-4780
			*330 Ann Arbor St., Manchester 48158		
Sharon	Peter S. Harris	FE14	Box 543, 19980 Pleasant Lk. Rd., Manchester 48158	(734) 428-0996	(517) 431-3908
			*16181 Wellwood Ct., Tipton 49287		

HERITAGE DISTRICT

HERITAGE DISTRICT

CHARGE	PASTOR		ADDRESS	CHURCH	HOME
Marshall	Melany A. Chalker	FE8	721 Old US 27N, Marshall 49068	(269) 781-5107	
Milan: Marble Memorial	Matthew J. West	FL1	*762 N Kalamazoo Ave, Marshall 49068 8 Park St., Milan 48160	(734) 439-2421	(517) 403-8528 (269) 967-4444
Milford	Douglas J. McMunn	FE10	*835 Faith Ct., Milan 48160 1200 Atlantic St., Milford 48381	(248) 684-2798	(248) 685-1737
Deacon	Sheryl A. Foster (LTFT ½)	FD11	*350 Cabinet St., Milford 48381 1200 Atlantic St., Milford 48381 *5821 Selske Dr., Brighton 48116	(248) 628-1002	(248) 318-5613
MONROE					
Calvary	Andrea L. Johnson	FL1	790 Patterson Dr., Monroe 48161	(734) 242-0145	
Faith			312 Harrison, Monroe 48161	(734) 241-6070	
St.Paul's	Melodye S. VanOudheusden	FE2	*PO Box 1925, 577 Augusta Dr, Monroe 48161 201 S. Monroe St., Monroe 48161	(734) 242-3000	(269) 317-1937 (517) 250-1879
Morenci	Donna Galloway	FL7	*212 Hollywood Dr., Monroe 48162 110 E. Main St., Morenci 49256	(517) 458-6923	
Weston	(part-time ½ + ½)		4193 Weston Rd., Box 96, Weston 49289	(517) 436-3492	(517) 458-6687
New Hudson	John J. Pajak	FL1	*111 E. Main St., Morenci 49256 56730 Grand River, Box 803, New Hudson 48165	(248) 437-6212	(248) 640-6987
Jerome	Beverly Clark	CLM/DSA1	*56730 Grand River Ave, New Hudson 48165 8768 Jerome Rd N, Jerome 49249		(517) 474-2679
North Lake	Todd Wesley Jones	FL5	*PO Box 355, 216 Spink St, Hanover 49241 14111 N. Territorial, Chelsea 48118	(734) 475-7569	(734) 475-9348
North Parma	Mark E. Mitchell	FL3	*14130 Wagon Wheel Ct., Chelsea 48118 11970 Devereaux, PO Box 25, Parma 49269	(517) 531-4619	
Springport			127 W Main St, PO Box 1004, Springport 49284 *258 Green St, Springport 49284	(517) 857-2777	(517) 414-0180

CHARGE	PASTOR		ADDRESS	CHURCH	HOME
Northville: First	Marsha M. Woolley	FE8	777 W. 8 Mile Rd., Northville 48167	(248) 349-1144	(248) 349-1143
Associate	Alice K. Ford (LTFT ½)	OE1	*20490 Lexington Blvd., Northville 48167 777 W 8 Mile Rd., Box 55, Northville 48167	(248) 349-1144	(301) 541-7630
Novi	Carter L. Cortelyou	FE1	*1483 Colonade Ct, Canton 48187 41671 W. Ten Mile Rd., Novi 48375	(248) 349-2652	(248) 629-0746
Oak Grove	Mark A. Vorenkamp	PL1	*40755 Oakwood Dr, Novi 48375 6686 Oak Grove Rd., Oak Grove 48855	(517) 546-3942	(810) 772-1987
Pinckney: Arise	Reed P. Swanson	FE3	*6893 Sanford Rd., Howell 48855 11211 Dexter-Pinckney Rd., Pinckney 48169	(734) 878-1928	(586) 202-1894
Pleasant Lake	Christine L. Pease	CLM/DSA7	*11267 Dexter-Pinckney Rd., Pinckney 48169 PO Box 83, 4815 E Territorial Rd, Pleasant Lake 49272		(517) 543-5618
Plymouth: First	Robert A. Miller, Jr.	FE3	*340 Pleasant St, Charlotte 48813 45201 N. Territorial Rd., Plymouth 48170	(734) 453-5280	(810) 623-0985
Associate	Suzanne L. Hutchison	PE3	*1401 Palmer St., Plymouth 48170 45201 N. Territorial Rd., Plymouth 48170	(734) 453-5280	(810) 923-1649
Pope Griffith	Lawrence J. Embury	PL3	*44698 Maidstone, Canton 48187 10025 N Parma Rd, Springport 49284 9537 S Clinton Trail, Eaton Rapids 48827	(517) 857-3655 (517) 663-6262	(517) 206-2952
Reading	Deborah Sue Cole	FL7	*PO Box 86, 1855 Sarossy Lake Rd, Grass Lake 49240 PO Box 457, 312 E Michigan St, Reading 49274	(517) 283-2443	(517) 283-2775
Salem Grove Waterloo: Village	Mary Barrett	PL5	*317 First Street, Reading 49274 3320 Notten Rd., Grass Lake 49240 8110 Washington St, Grass Lake 49240-9241	(734) 475-2370 (734) 475-1171	(517) 521-3939
Saline: First	Thomas H. Zimmerman	FE5	*305 N. Howard, PO Box 530, Webberville 48892 1200 N. Ann Arbor St., Saline 48176	(734) 429-4730	(419) 262-5575
South Lyon: First	Mary Ann McInnes	FE4	*3020 Aspen Lane, Ann Arbor 48108 640 S. Lafayette, South Lyon 48178	(248) 437-0760	(586) 515-0013
			*650 S. Lafayette, South Lyon 48178		

HERITAGE DISTRICT

HERITAGE DISTRICT

CHARGE	PASTOR		ADDRESS	CHURCH	HOME
Willow 　South Rockwood	Ann Birchmeier	FL1	36925 Willow Rd., Box 281, New Boston 48164 6311 S. Huron River Dr., South Rockwood 48033	(734) 654-9020 (734) 379-3131	313-318-8581
Springville	Evans C. Bentley	RE3	*13392 Wingate Lane, Brighton 48116 10341 Springville Hwy., Onsted 49265	(517) 467-4471	(734-552-5064
Tecumseh	Mark A. Miller	FE11	*1109 N River Ct, Tecumseh 49286 605 Bishop Reed Dr., Tecumseh 49286	(517) 426-2523	(517) 423-3767
Walled Lake	Kenny R. Walkup Jr.	PL1	*808 Derby Dr., Tecumseh 49286 313 Northport St., Walled Lake 48390	(248) 624-2405	(248) 361-6658
YPSILANTI 　First	Briony P. Desotell	FE7	*1115 Paddock, South Lyon 48178 209 Washtenaw Ave., Ypsilanti 48197	(734) 482-8374	(734) 730-6747
Lincoln Community	Christopher A. Butson	PE2	*1110 Ruth, Ypsilanti 48198 9074 Whittaker Rd., Ypsilanti 48197	(734) 482-4446	(734) 735-4892
			*9066 Whittaker Rd., Ypsilanti 48197		

NAME	POSITION	ADDRESS	OFFICE	HOME
APPOINTMENTS TO EXTENSION MINISTRIES LOCATED IN THE HERITAGE DISTRICT:				
(further information at end of appointment section)				
April Gutierrez	Chaplain, Adrian College FL1	Valade Hall 133, 110 S Madison St, Adrian 49221	(517) 265-5761	
LuAnn L. Rourke	District Superintendent, Heritage District Office FE1	PO Box 128, St. Clair Shores 48080	(734) 663-3939	
Roy Testolin	Pastoral Counselor, Heritage Interfaith Counseling Center RE22	*12884 E Dr S, Marshall 49068	(269) 979-5180	(269) 781-9257
Teresa J. Zimmerman	Associate Director Spiritual Life, Chelsea Retirement Community FD4	805 W. Middle St., Chelsea 48118	(734) 433-1000	(734) 428-0576
Christina L. Wright	Associate Director, Dept of Spiritual Care, Michigan Medicine U of M FD2	1500 E Medical Center Dr, Ann Arbor 48109	(734) 936-4041	
APPOINTMENT FROM OTHER CONFERENCES:				
David Bell	President and Executive Director, United Methodist Foundation of Michigan			
(East Ohio Conference)	AF10	840 W Grand River Ave, Brighton 48116	(810) 534-3001	(888) 451-1929
Timothy L. Kobler	Chaplain, Wesley Foundation, University of Michigan FE3	602 E Huron, Ann Arbor 48104	(734) 668-6881	

HERITAGE DISTRICT

MID-MICHIGAN DISTRICT

MID-MICHIGAN DISTRICT

		DS Email: jdevine@michiganumc.org	Office (517) 347-4173
District Superintendent	Jerome R. DeVine FE3	Office Email: sgillette@michiganumc.org	1161 E Clark Rd Ste 216, DeWitt 48820
Executive Assistant	Sarah Gillette		

CHARGE	PASTOR		ADDRESS	CHURCH	TELEPHONE	HOME
Alma	Lori J. Sykes	FE1	501 Gratiot Ave, Alma 48801	(989) 463-4305	
			*627 Woodworth Ave, Alma 48801		(517) 775-6556
Ashley	Zella M. Daniel	PL3	PO Box 7, 112 N New St, Ashley 48806	(989) 862-4392	
Bannister			103 Hanvey St, Bannister 48807	(989) 862-4392	
Pompeii			PO Box 125, 135 Burton St, Pompeii 48874	(989) 838-4159	
			*2415 E Tobias, Clio 48420		(810) 869-8815
Barry County: Woodland	Kathleen Smith	RLA6	203 N Main St, Woodland 48897	(269) 367-4061	
			*7500 Bayne Rd, Woodland 48897		(269) 367-4123
Bath	Matthew D. Kreh	FL6	PO Box 308, 13777 Main St, Bath 48808	(517) 641-6551	
Gunnisonville			2031 E Clark Rd, Bath 48808	(517) 482-7987	
			*2025 Cumberland Rd, Lansing 48906		(517) 440-8178
Carland	Charlene S. Wagner	PL3	4002 Carland Rd., Elsie 48831	(989) 494-7763	(989) 494-7763
			*587 N Baldwin Rd, Owosso 48867		
Carson City	Ian S. McDonald	FL2	PO Box 298, 119 E Elm Street, Carson City 48811	(989) 584-3797	(906) 322-5318
			*121 S Abbott St, Carson City 48811		
Charlotte: Lawrence Avenue	John J. Conklin	FE1	PO Box 36, Charlotte 48813	(517) 543-4670	(517) 231-6775
			*1072 N Stonehill Dr, Charlotte 48813		
Chesaning: Trinity	Timothy S. Woycik	FE9	1629 W. Brady, Chesaning 48616	(989) 845-3157	(989) 845-2227
			*1701 W. Brady Rd., Chesaning 48616		
CORUNNA					
Corunna	Stephen Spina	OF4	200 W. McArthur, Corunna 48817	(989) 743-5050	
			*225 W. Corunna Rd., Corunna 48817		(715) 374-0078

CHARGE	PASTOR		ADDRESS	CHURCH	HOME
Northwest Venice	David Owen (July 15)	PL1	6001 E. Wilkinson Rd, Corunna 48817 *13425 Dawn Dew Dr Apt 7, DeWitt 48820	(989) 661-2377	(989) 384-1200
Delta Mills	Joseph L. Spackman	RE8	6809 Delta River Dr, Lansing 48906 *3806 Cornice Falls Dr Apt 6, Holt 48842	(517) 321-8100	(517) 694-8346
DeWitt: Redeemer	Rodney J. Kalajainen	FE33	13980 Schavey Rd, DeWitt 48820 *2155 Longwoods Dr, DeWitt 48820	(517) 669-3430	(517) 669-9140
Co-Pastor	Deborah S. Thomas	FE1	13980 Schavey Rd, DeWitt 48820 *3505 W Clark Rd R103, DeWitt 48820	(517) 669-3430	(989) 285-4212
St. Johns Campus	Kalajainen / Thomas		200 E State Street, St Johns 48879	(989) 224-6859	
Dimondale	Linda Farmer-Lewis	OR2	PO Box 387, 6801 Creyts Rd, Dimondale 48821 *6747 Creyts Rd, Dimondale 48821	(517) 646-0641	(517) 581-5595
EAST LANSING Peoples Church	served by another denomination		200 W Grand River Ave, East Lansing 48823	(517) 332-5073	
University	William C. Bills	FE5	1120 S Harrison Rd, East Lansing 48823 *405 Green Meadows Dr, Lansing 48917	(517) 351-7030	
Eaton Rapids: First	Martin M. DeBow	FE7	600 S Main St, Eaton Rapids 48827 *702 State St, Eaton Rapids 48823	(517) 663-3524	(517) 663-8256
Elsie	Jung Du Paik (July 15)	DSA1	PO Box 189, 160 W Main St, Elsie 48831 *2653 N Elm St, Onaway 49765	(989) 862-5239	(989) 733-8434
Fowlerville: First	Scott A. Herald	FL5	201 S. Second, Box 344, Fowlerville 48836 *18521 Daymon Dr., Gregory 48137	(517) 223-8824	(734) 545-2276
Freeport Nashville: Peace Hastings: Welcome Corners	Mickey Ann Cousino	DSA6	PO Box 142, 193 Cherry St, Freeport 49325 6043 E M-79 Hwy, Nashville 49073 3185 N M-43 Hwy, Hastings 49058 *1713 W Sisson Rd, Hastings 49058	(616) 765-5316 (517) 852-1993 (269) 945-2654	(616) 765-5322
Grand Ledge: First	Ronald K. Brooks	FE1	411 Harrison St, Grand Ledge 48837 *912 E Scott St, Grand Ledge 48837	(517) 627-3256	(269) 779-6131

MID-MICHIGAN DISTRICT

MID-MICHIGAN DISTRICT

CHARGE	PASTOR		ADDRESS	CHURCH	HOME
Gresham	Heather L. Nolen	FL4	4800 Lamie Highway, Charlotte 48813	(517) 652-1580	
Sunfield			PO Box 25, 227 Logan St, Sunfield 48890	(517) 566-8448	(734) 846-3491
			*235 Dunham St, Sunfield 48890		
HASTINGS					
First	Bryce E. Feighner	FE4	209 W Green St, Hastings 49058	(269) 945-9574	
			*220 N Chester Rd, Charlotte 48813		(517) 588-1619
Hope	Kimberly S. Metzer	FL4	PO Box 410, 2920 S M-37 Hwy, Hastings 49058	(269) 945-4995	
			*121 W North St, Hastings 49058		
Henderson	Steffani Glygoroff	PL2	218 E. Main, Henderson 48841	(989) 723-5729	
Chapin			19848 S. Chapin Rd., Elsie 48831	(989) 661-2497	
Owosso: Trinity			720 S. Shiawassee St., Owosso 48867	(989) 723-2664	
			*302 E Main St, Henderson 48841		
Holt	Mark R Erbes	FE7	PO Box 168, 2321 Aurelius Rd, Holt 48842	(517) 694-8168	(248) 805-3597
			*1951 Heatherton Dr, Holt 48842		(517) 694-8277
Ithaca	Gary L. Simmons	FE6	327 E Center Street, Ithaca 48847	(989) 875-4313	
Beebe			327 E Center Street, (2975 N Baldwin) Ithaca 48847		
			*601 N Union St, Ithaca 48847-1311		
Juddville	Wallace "Peter" Crawford	RE5	3907 N. Durand Rd., Box 152, Corunna 48817	(810) 638-7498	(517) 388-2286
			*4934 Center St., Millington 48746		(989) 882-3084
Kalamo	Jerry J. Bukoski	PL7	1475 S Ionia Rd, Vermontville 49096	(810) 986-0240	(517) 588-8415
			*1069 S Ionia Rd, Vermontville 49096		
Laingsburg	Tiffany M. Newsom	PE1	210 Crum St., Laingsburg 48848	(517) 651-5531	(517) 917-5705
			*214 Crum St., Laingsburg 48848		
LAKE ODESSA					
Central	Vaughn W. Thurston-Cox	PE1	PO Box 485, 912 4th Ave, Lake Odessa 48849	(616) 374-8861	(231) 250-3924
			*9590 Looking Glass Brook Dr, Grand Ledge 48837		
Lakewood	Steven C. Place	FL4	10265 E Brown Rd, Lake Odessa 48849	(269) 367-4800	(269) 367-4161
			*10121 E Brown Rd, Lake Odessa 48849		

CHARGE	PASTOR		ADDRESS	CHURCH	HOME
Associate	Kathleen Smith	RLA6	10265 E Brown Rd, Lake Odessa 48849	(269) 367-4800	(269) 367-4123
LANSING			*7500 Bayne Rd, Woodland 48897		
Asbury	Jon L. Pohl	FL4	2200 Lake Lansing Rd, Lansing 48912	(517) 484-5794	(231) 748-4330
			*2412 Post Oak Ln, Lansing 48912		
Central	Naylo T. Hopkins	FL1	215 N Capitol Ave, Lansing 48933	(517) 485-9477	(734) 972-4334
			*2828 Woodview Dr, Lansing 48911		
First	Robert P. Blanchard	FE1	3827 Delta River Dr, Lansing 48906	(517) 321-5187	(517) 775-6556
			*3727 Delta River Dr, Lansing 48906		
Grace	Paul SungJoon Hahm	FE5	1900 Boston Blvd, Lansing 48910	(517) 482-5750	(517) 484-0227
			*2915 S Cambridge Rd, Lansing 48910		
Mt Hope	Eric Nduwa Mulanda	FE6	501 E Mt Hope Ave, Lansing 48910	(517) 482-1549	(847) 868-6687
			*545 N. Dexter Dr. Lansing 48910		
Sycamore Creek	Thomas F. Arthur	FE12	1919 S Pennsylania Ave, Lansing 48910	(517) 394-6100	(517) 889-5540
			*5058 Glendurgan Ct, Holt 48842		
Associate	Mark D. Aupperlee	FL3	1919 S Pennsylania Ave, Lansing 48910	(517) 394-6100	(517) 643-1161
			*420 Ardson Rd, E Lansing 48823		
Potterville Camp us	Arthur / Aupperlee		105 N Church St, Potterville 48876	(517) 645-7701	
Livingston Circuit:					
Plainfield	Mark Huff	PL4	17845 M-36, Gregory 48137	(517) 851-7651	(517) 223-3150
Fowlerville: Trinity			8201 Iosco Rd., Fowlerville 48836	(517) 223-9601	
			*8233 Iosco Rd., Fowlerville 48836		
MAPLE RIVER PARISH					
Maple Rapids	Kathryn L. Leydorf-Keck	PL14	330 S Maple Ave, Maple Rapids 48853	(989) 224-4460	(517) 282-4446
Lowe			5485 W Lowe Rd, St. Johns 48879		
			*10886 S Woodbridge Rd, Bannister 48807		
Mason: First	Suzanne K. Goodwin	FD2	201 E Ash St, Mason 48854	(517) 676-9449	(248) 318-4869
			*616 Hall Blvd, Mason 48854		

MID-MICHIGAN DISTRICT

MID-MICHIGAN DISTRICT

CHARGE	PASTOR		ADDRESS	CHURCH	HOME
Millville	Rhonda J. Osterman	FL1	1932 N M-52, Stockbridge 49285	(517) 851-8785	
Leslie			401 S Main St, Leslie 49251-9402	(517) 589-9211	
Felt Plains			401 S Main St (3523 Meridian Rd), Leslie 49251	(517) 589-9211	(586) 243-9240
			*1956 N M 52, Stockbridge 49285		
Morrice	Coleen Wilsdon	PL4	204 Main, Box 301, Morrice 48857	(517) 625-7715	
Bancroft			101 S. Beach St., Box 175, Bancroft 48414	(989) 634-5291	(989) 413-9850
			*8452 E. Cole Rd., Durand 48420		
Munith	Stephan Weinberger	RE2	PO Box 189, 224 N Main St, Munith 49259	(517) 596-2441	(517) 242-5020
			*3880 Lone Pine Dr Apt 3, Holt 48842		
Nashville	Karen Jensen-Kinney	FL6	PO Box 370, 210 Washington St, Nashville 49073	(517) 852-2043	(517) 852-0685
			*540 Chapel Dr, Nashville 49073		
New Lothrop: First	Stephen Spina	OF4	7495 Orchard, Box 247, New Lothrop 48460	(810) 638-5702	(715) 374-0078
			*225 West Corunna Ave., Corunna 48817		
Okemos: Community Church	Richard W. Blunt	FE7	PO Box 680, 4734 Okemos Rd, Okemos 48805	(517) 349-4220	(517) 721-1301
			*2441 S Wild Blossom Ct, East Lansing 48823		
Ovid: United Church	Melanie S. Young	FE3	PO Box 106, 131 West Front Street, Ovid 48866	(989) 834-5958	(231) 301-2055
			*141 W Front St, Ovid 48866-9601		
Middlebury			PO Box 7, 8100 W. Hibbard Rd., Ovid 48866	(989) 834-2573	(810) 208-0648
			*9921 Belcrest Blvd., Fenton 48430		
OWOSSO					
First	Deane B. Wyllys	FE3	1500 N. Water St., Owosso 48867	(989) 725-2201	
			*1415 N. Water St., Owosso 48867		
Perry	Rey C. Mondragon	FE1	PO Box 15, 131 Madison St, Perry 48872	(517) 675-1567	(248) 860-7385
Shaftsburg			PO Box 161, 12821 Warner Rd, Shaftsburg 48882		
			*121 S Madison St, Perry 48872		
Pittsburg	Terry Melton	DSA1	2960 Grand River, Owosso 48867	(810) 208-0648	(517) 625-3444
			*5069 Bell Oak Rd, Webberville 48892		(517) 468-0113

CHARGE	PASTOR		ADDRESS	CHURCH	HOME
Portland	Letisha M. Bowman	FE6	310 E Bridge St, Portland 48875 *309 Grape St, Portland 48875	(517) 647-4649	(517) 647-6460
Riverdale: Lincoln Road	Linda K. Stull-Lipps (LTFT ¾)	FE5	9479 W Lincoln Rd, Riverdale 48877 *9437 W Lincoln Rd, Riverdale 48877	(989) 463-5704	(269) 830-1136
Robbins Brookfield Eaton	Peggy A. Katzmark	FL1	6419 Bunker Rd, Eaton Rapids 48827 PO Box 430, 7681 Brookfield, Charlotte 48813 *827 S Waverly Rd, Eaton Rapids 48827	(517) 663-5226 517-420-3903	(517) 663-8417
St. Johns: Pilgrim	Andrew L. Croel	FE7	2965 W Parks Road, St Johns 48879 *2917 W Parks Rd, St. Johns 48879	(989) 224-6865	(989) 224-4423
St Louis: First Breckenridge	Billie Lou Gillespie	FL1	116 S Franklin Street, St. Louis 48880 PO Box 248, Breckenridge 48615 *116 N East St, St Louis 48880	(989) 681-3320 (989) 842-3632	(810) 241-3160
Shepardsville	Jung Du Paik (July 15)	DSA1	6990 East Winfield Road, Ovid 48866 *2653 N Elm St, Onaway 49765	(989) 834-5104	(989) 733-8434
Stockbridge	Stephan Weinberger	RE2	219 E Elizabeth St, Stockbridge 49285 *3880 Lone Pine Dr Apt 3, Holt 48842	(517) 851-7676	(517) 242-5020
Vernon	David Owen (July 15)	FL1	202 E. Main St., PO Box 155, Vernon 48476 *13425 Dawn Dew Dr Apt 7, DeWitt 48820	(989) 288-4187	(989) 384-1200
Wacousta Community	Hillary Thurston-Cox	PE5	9180 Herbison Rd, Eagle 48822 *235 Dunham St, Sunfield 48890	(517) 626-6623	(517) 566-2066
Webberville Williamston: Crossroads	Martin A. Johnston	FL4	4215 E Holt Rd, Webberville 48892 5491 N Zimmer Rd, Williamston 48895 *120 E Beech St, Webberville 48892	(517) 521-3631 (517) 655-1466	(517) 521-3434
Williamston	Linda J. Stephan	PE3	211 S Putnam St, Williamston 48895 *733 Orchard Dr, Williamston 48895	(517) 655-2430	(616) 617-9419
Williamston: Wheatfield	TO BE SUPPLIED		520 E Holt Rd, Williamston 48895	(517) 851-7853	

MID-MICHIGAN DISTRICT

MID-MICHIGAN DISTRICT

APPOINTMENTS TO EXTENSION MINISTRIES LOCATED IN THE MID-MICHIGAN DISTRICT:
(further information at end of appointment section)

NAME	POSITION	ADDRESS	OFFICE	HOME
Kennetha J. Bigham-Tsai	Chief Connectional Ministries Officer of the Connectional Table			
	FE3	*6137 Horizon Dr, East Lansing 48823		(517) 242-2442
John W. Boley	Clergy Assistant to the Bishop, Michigan Area Episcopal Office			
	RE5	1011 Northcrest Rd, Lansing 48906	(517) 347-4003	(989) 400-0355
Jennifer Browne	Director of Clergy Excellence, Michigan Conference			
	FE3	161 E Clark Rd Ste 212, DeWitt 48820	(517) 347-4030	(517) 898-4575
William W. Chu	Director, Wesley Foundation – Michigan State University			
	FE10	1118 S. Harrison, East Lansing 48823	(517) 332-0861	(517) 996-2207
M. Kay DeMoss	Senior Writer & Content Editor, MI Conference Communications Team			
	FD6	1011 Northcrest Rd, Lansing 48906	(517) 347-4030	(231) 670-5921
Jerome R. DeVine	District Superintendent, Mid-Michigan District Office			
	FE3	1161 E Clark Rd Ste 216, DeWitt 48820	(517) 347-4173	
Dirk Elliott	Director of Congregational Vibrancy, Michigan Conference			
	FE3	161 E Clark Rd Ste 212, DeWitt 48820	(517) 347-4030	(810) 965-2349
Donald J. Emmert	Director of Benefits & Human Resources, Michigan Conference; Interim Director of Administrative Services and Treasurer			
	FE3	161 E Clark Rd Ste 212, DeWitt 48820	(517) 347-4030	
Nancy Fancher	Director, Maple Valley Community Center of Hope (LTFT ½)			
	FD4	501 E Mt Hope Ave, Lansing 48915	(251) 748-2154	(517) 371-3311
Benton R. Heisler	Director of Connectional Ministries, Michigan Conference			
	FE3	1011 Northcrest Rd, Lansing 48906	(517) 347-4030	
Paul D. Perez	Associate Director for Mission & Ministry, Michigan Conference			
	FD3	1011 Northcrest Rd, Lansing 48906	(517) 347-4030	(810) 347-6363
Kathryn L. Pittenger	Children's Initiatives Coordinator, Michigan Conference			
	FD3	161 E Clark Rd Ste 212, DeWitt 48820	(517) 347-4030	(248) 505-5848

NAME	POSITION	ADDRESS	OFFICE	HOME
Alice Fleming Townley	Parish Associate, Okemos Presbyterian Church			
	FE11	2258 Bennett Rd, Okemos 48823	(517) 507-5117	(517) 324-5432
Michael J. Mayo-Moyle	IT Specialist, Michigan Conference			
	FE3	161 E Clark Rd Ste 212, DeWitt 48820	(517) 347-4030	(810) 444-9439
Christina M. White	Conference Youth Ministry Initiatives Coordinator (LTFT ½)			
	FD1	7191 Birchwood Dr, Mount Morris 48458	(517) 347-4030	(989) 488-3347
APPOINTMENT FROM OTHER CONFERENCES:				
Brittney D. Stephan	Associate Director for Multi-Cultural Vibrancy			
(Indiana Conf.)	OP3	1161 E Clark Rd, Ste 212, DeWitt 48820	(517) 357-4030	

MID-MICHIGAN DISTRICT

MIDWEST DISTRICT

MIDWEST DISTRICT

District Superintendent	Margie R. Crawford FE3	DS Email: mcrawford@michiganumc.org	Office (616) 459-4503
Executive Assistant	Elizabeth M. Bode	Office Email: lbode@michiganumc.org	207 Fulton St E Suite 6, Grand Rapids 49503

CHARGE	PASTOR		ADDRESS	TELEPHONE CHURCH	HOME
Allendale: Valley	Matthew J. Bistayi	FE12	5980 Lake Michigan Dr, Ste B, Allendale 49401-9576	(616) 892-1042	
			*10811 Lance Ave, Allendale 49401-7317		(616) 892-6240
Associate	Zach D. McNees (part-time ½)	FL2	5980 Lake Michigan Dr, Ste B, Allendale 49401-9576	(616) 892-1042	
			*1141 Northlawn St NE, Grand Rapids 49505		(269) 986-0108
Bowne Center	Robert D. Wright	RE5	12051 84th St. SE, Alto 49302	(616) 868-6778	
			*10187 Mulberry Dr, Middleville 49333		(269) 205-2609
Amble	Ronald L. Worley	PL1	PO Box 392, 15207 Howard City Edmore Rd, Howard City 49329 (231) 580-6304		
			*PO Box 254, 76 W Muskegon St NW, Kent City 49330		(616) 485-4441
Barryton: Faith	TO BE SUPPLIED		95 E Marion Ave, Barryton 49305-5115	(989) 382-5431	
BIG RAPIDS					
First	Tae Gyu Shin	PE1	304 Elm Street, Big Rapids 49307	(231) 796-7771	
			*14080 Wildwood Dr, Big Rapids 49307		(909) 472-7802
Third Avenue	Morgan William (Bill) Davis	DSA2	226 N Third Ave, Big Rapids 49307	(231) 796-4157	
Paris			109 Lincoln, Paris 49338	(231) 796-4157	
Rodney			PO Box 14, 12135 Charles St, Rodney 49342	(231) 796-4157	
			*1764 Kettle Lake Rd, Kalkaska 49646		(231)384-0040
Byron Center	Jeffrey O. Cummings	PE5	2490 Prescott SW, Byron Center 49315	(616) 878-1618	
			*8650 Meadow Haven Dr SW, Byron Center 49315		(616) 878-9739
Caledonia	Elizabeth A. Hurd	PE2	250 Vine St, Caledonia 49316	(616) 891-8669	
			*260 Vine St, Caledonia 49316		(616) 891-8167
Carlisle	Gary M. Zinger	CLM/DSA4	1084 76th St SW, Byron Center 49315	(616) 878-1836	
			*6559 Burlingame Ave SW, Byron Center 49315		(616) 890-2744

CHARGE	PASTOR		ADDRESS	CHURCH	HOME
Cedar Springs	Lawrence J. French	FL1	PO Box K, 140 S Main St, Cedar Springs 49319	(616) 696-1140	
Kent City: Chapel Hill			14591 Fruit Ridge Ave NW, Kent City 49330	(616) 675-7184	(616) 551-9280
			*140 S. Main St, Cedar Springs 49319		
Claybanks	Gary L. Peterson	RLA5	PO Box 104, 9197 S 56th Ave, Montague 49437	(231) 923-0573	(231) 893-5210
			*8054 S 56th Ave, Montague 49437		
Coopersville	Cori Lynn Conran	FE9	105 68th Ave N, Coopersville 49404	(616) 997-9225	(269) 986-0732
			*422 Harrison St., Coopersville 49404		
Courtland-Oakfield	Kimberly A. DeLong	FE4	10295 Myers Lake Ave NE, Rockford 49341	(616) 866-4298	
Wyoming Park			2244 Porter St SW, Wyoming 49519	(616) 532-7624	(616) 443-5210
			*4934 Brownstone Dr NE, Rockford 49341		
Crystal Valley	David O. Pratt	RLA3	PO Box 125, Walkerville 49459	(231) 873-5422	
Walkerville			PO Box 125, Walkerville 49459	(231) 873-4236	(810) 404-0085
			*409 3rd St, Ludington 49431		
Dorr: CrossWind Community	Kevin K. Guetschow	FL4	1683 142nd Ave, Dorr 49323	(616) 681-0302	(269) 365-2926
			*4380 Tracy Trail, Dorr 49323		
East Nelson	Inge E. Whittemore	PL5	9024 18 Mile Rd NE, Cedar Springs 49319	(616) 696-0661	(616) 897-6525
			*590 Wildview, Lowell 49331		
Edmore: Faith	Daniel L. Barkholz	FL4	833 S First Street, Edmore 48829	(989) 427-5575	(269) 903-9665
			*320 S Maple St, Edmore 48829		
Fenwick	Melissa S. Wagner	DSA1	PO Box 241, 235 W Fenwick Rd, Sheridan 48884	(989) 291-5547	
Palo			PO Box 241, 8445 Division St., Sheridan 48884	(989) 291-5547	
Vickeryville			PO Box 241, 6850 S Vickeryville Rd, Sheridan 48884	(989) 291-5547	(616) 302-3406
			*141 Lafayette St, Ionia 48846		
FLAT RIVER COOPERATIVE PARISH					
Turk Lake	Donna Jean Sperry	FL5	8900 W Colby Road, Greenville 48838	(616) 754-3718	
Belding			301 South Pleasant, Belding 48809	(616) 794-1244	
Ionia: Easton		FL7	4970 Potters Rd, Ionia 48846	(616) 527-6529	(586) 255-6228
			*319 Pearl St, Ionia 48846		

MIDWEST DISTRICT

MIDWEST DISTRICT

CHARGE	PASTOR		ADDRESS	CHURCH	HOME
Fremont	Donna J. Minarik	FE1	351 Butterfield St, Fremont 49412	(231) 924-0030	
			*352 Butterfield, Fremont 49412		
Georgetown	Sherri L. Swanson	FE3	2766 Baldwin St, Jenison 49428	(616) 669-0730	
			*6105 Balcom Ln, Allendale 49401		(269) 405-0002
Deacon	Mariel Kay DeMoss	FD3	2766 Baldwin St, Jenison 49428	(616) 669-0730	
			*1520 Sherman St SE, Grand Rapids 49506		(231) 670-5921
Deacon	Gregory W. Lawton	FD3	*10 N 160th Ave, Holland 49424		(616) 805-5407
Grand Haven: Church	Louis W. Grettenberger	FE4	717 Sheldon Road, Grand Haven 49417	(616) 842-7980	
of the Dunes			*633 Hillock Ct, Grand Haven 49417		(616) 883-9806
GRAND RAPIDS					
Aldersgate	James E. Hodge	FE8	4301 Ambrose Ave NE, Grand Rapids 49525	(616) 363-3446	
			*5160 Windcrest Ct SW, Wyo-ming 49418		(616) 308-9925
Cornerstone	Bradley P. Kalajainen	FE31	1675 84th St SE, Caledonia 49316	(616) 698-3170	
			*7810 Golf Meadows Dr SE, Caledonia 49316		(616) 891-8443
Assoc. Heritage Hill Campus	Alejandro D. Fernandez	FL6	1675 84th St SE, Caledonia 49316	(616) 698-3170	
			*10160 Alaska Ave SE, Cale-donia 49316		(616) 891-5611
Assoc. South Wyoming Campus	Marcus V. Schmidt	PL5	1675 84th St SE, Caledonia 49316	(616) 698-3170	
			*5482 Fieldstone Dr SW, Wyoming 49418		(616) 443-9257
Faith	Daniel M. Bilkert	OR3	2600 Seventh St NW, Grand Rapids 49504	(616) 453-0693	
	(LTFT ½)		*2239 Ducoma St NW, Grand Rapids 49504		(419) 606-0640
First	Robert L. Hundley	FE8	227 Fulton St E, Grand Rapids 49503	(616) 451-2879	
			*3035 Grenada Dr SE, Grand Rapids 49546		(616) 427-3749
Associate	Joan E. VanDessel	PE2	227 Fulton St E, Grand Rapids 49503	(616) 451-2879	
			*2005 Collingwood Ave SW, Wyoming 49519		(616) 818-9295
Genesis	James Thomas Boutell	FE3	3189 Snow Ave, Lowell 49331	(616) 974-0400	
			*1805 Forest Lake Dr, SE, Grand Rapids 49546		(616) 678-7664
Deacon	Georgia Noel Hale	FD6	1601 Galbraith Ave SE Ste 304, Grand Rapids 49546	(616) 974-0400	
	(LTFT ¼)		*272 S Ball Creek Rd, Kent City 49330		(616) 678-7664

CHARGE	PASTOR		ADDRESS	CHURCH	HOME
Iglesia Metodista Unida La Nueva Esperanza	Ricardo Angarita-Oviedo	DSA1	1005 Evergreen St. SE, Grand Rapids 49507	(616) 560-4207	
Northlawn	Zach D. McNees (part-time ½)	FL2	*324 Griswold SE, Grand Rapids 49507 1157 Northlawn NE, Grand Rapids 49505 *1141 Northlawn St NE, Grand Rapids 49505	(616) 361-8503	(734) 680-5185 (269) 986-0108
Restoration	Banza Mukalay	PL3	2730 56th St SW, South Wyoming 49418 *4217 Norman Dr SE, Grand Rapids 49508	(616) 589-4793	(616) 589-4793
St Paul's	Virginia L. Heller	FE3	3334 Breton Rd SE, Grand Rapids 49512 *3509 Bromley SE, Kentwood 49512	(616) 949-0880	(269) 274-9416
South	Michael J. Ramsey	FL1	4500 S Division Ave, Grand Rapids 49548 *4777 10th St, Wayland 49348	(616) 534-8931	(616) 293-9831
Trinity	Steven W. Manskar	OE3	1100 Lake Dr SE, Grand Rapids 49506 *2128 Monroe Ave NW, Grand Rapids 49505	(616) 456-7168	(615) 948-0650
Vietnamese	Daniel Dung Nguyen	FL9	212 Bellevue St SE, Wyoming 49548 *497 Harp St SE, Kentwood 49548	(616) 534-6262	(616) 288-3007
Grandville	Ryan B. Wieland	FE5	3140 S Wilson, Grandville 49418 *2000 Frontier Ct. SW, Wyoming 49519	(616) 538-3070	(616) 258-2001
Grant Center	TO BE SUPPLIED		15260 21 Mile Road, Big Rapids 49307 *	(231) 796-8006	
Greenville: First	Jeffrey C. Williams	FE1	204 W Cass Street, Greenville 48838 *405 W Grant St, Greenville 48838	(616) 754-8532	(616) 712-6024
Hart	Steven R. Young	FE6	308 S State St, Hart 49420 *3818 Melody Lane, Hart 49420	(231) 873-3516	(231) 873-4766
Hesperia	Donna J. Minarik	FE1	187 E South Ave, Hesperia 49421 *352 Butterfield, Fremont 49412	(231) 854-5345	
Holland: First	Bradley S. Bartelmay	FE4	57 West 10th St, Holland 49423 *6105 Balcom Ln, Allendale 49401	(616) 396-5205	(269) 266-2221
Associate	Tania J. Dozeman	PE3	57 West 10th St, Holland 49423 *66 Crosswind Dr, Holland 49424	(616) 396-5205	(616) 566-4165

MIDWEST DISTRICT

MIDWEST DISTRICT

CHARGE	PASTOR		ADDRESS	CHURCH	HOME
Deacon	Luanne M. Stanley-Hook	PD2	57 West 10th St, Holland 49423	(616) 396-5205	
			*6618 Butternut Dr, West Olive 49460		(616) 994-0085
Holton	Matthew T. Stoll	FE3	9530 Holton-Duck Lake Rd, Holton 49425	(231) 821-2323	
			*8670 Ward St, Holton 49425		(231) 821-0374
IONIA					
First	Jonathan Bratt Carle	PE4	105 E Main Street, Ionia 48846	(616) 527-1860	
Lyons-Muir Church			1074 Olmstead Road, Muir 48860	(989) 855-2247	
			*2536 Union Ave SE, Grand Rapids 49507		(901) 417-2844
IONIA PARISH					
LeValley	Nancy J. Patera	FL4	4018 Kelsey Highway, Ionia 48846	(616) 527-1480	
Berlin Center			4018 Kelsey Hwy, Ionia 48846 (3042 Peck Lake Rd, Saranac) (616) 527-1480		
			*6232 Sunset Beach, Lake Odessa 48849		(616) 902-6973
Zion	Larry Nalett	RLA3	423 W Washington Street, Ionia 48846	(616) 527-1910	
			*620 N Rich St, Ionia 48846		(616) 527-2025
Lakeview: New Life	Timothy B. Wright	FE2	6584 M 46, Six Lakes 48886	(989) 352-7788	(989) 352-6728
			*8544 Howard City-Edmore Rd, Lakeview 48850		
Leighton	David L. McBride	FE15	4180 Second St, Caledonia 49316	(616) 891-8028	
			*4180 Second St, Caledonia 49316		(616) 891-1646
LOWELL					
First	James Bradley Brillhart	FE7	621 E Main St, Lowell 49331	(616) 897-5936	
			*640 Shepard Dr, Lowell 49331		(616) 897-8267
Deacon	Cheryl A. Mulligan (LTFT ¼)	FD7	621 E Main St, Lowell 49331	(616) 897-5936	
Vergennes	Thomas C. Fifer	FL3	*3170 Buttrick Ave SE, Ada 49301	(616) 897-6141	(616) 340-7995
			10411 Bailey Dr NE, Lowell 49331		
Marne	Cydney M. Idsinga	FE3	*2445 Almont Ave SE, Grand Rapids 49507	(616) 677-3957	
			PO Box 85, 14861 Washington, Marne 49435		(616) 560-3914
			*14861 Washington St, Marne 49435		
Mears	Anne W. Riegler	AM4	PO Box 100, 1990 N Joy St, Mears 49436	(231) 873-0875	
Shelby			68 E Third St, Shelby 49455	(231) 861-2020	(616) 677-3991

CHARGE	PASTOR		ADDRESS	CHURCH	HOME
Mecosta: New Hope	Carman J. Minarik	FE2	*5181 Hancock St, Montague 49437		(231) 631-0573
			7296 9 Mile Road, Mecosta 49332	(231) 972-2838	(248) 921-2714
Middleville	Anthony C. Shumaker	FL9	*3955 9 Mile Rd, Remus 49340		(269) 650-5112
			PO Box 400, 111 Church St, Middleville 49333	(269) 795-9266	
Montague	Michael A. Riegler	FE4	*1497 120th Ave, Hopkins 49328		(231) 631-4712
			8555 Cook St, Montague 49437	(231) 894-5789	
MUSKEGON			*5181 Hancock St, Montague 49437		
Central	Robert B. Cook	FE1	1011 Second Street, Muskegon 49440	(231) 722-6545	(517) 449-4826
Crestwood	William F. Dye	RLA1	* Home: 2353 E Riverwood Dr, Twin Lake 49457		(231) 429-1891
			1220 Creston, Muskegon 49442	(231) 773-9696	
Lake Harbor	Mary Letta-Bement Ivanov	FE7	*550 Western Ave Apt 424, Muskegon 49440		(231) 780-3951
			4861 Henry St, Muskegon 49441	(231) 798-2181	
Muskegon Heights: Temple	Jeffrey J. Bowman	FL9	*1322 Clayton Ave, Muskegon 49441		(231) 798-9309
			2500 Jefferson St, Muskegon Heights 49444	(231) 733-1065	
Newaygo	Eric L. Magner	PL4	*1205 Yorkshire Dr, Muskegon 49441		(231) 750-3488
			PO Box 366, 101 W State Road, Newaygo 49337	(231) 652-6581	
North Muskegon: Community	Jeremy PH Williams	FE4	*PO Box 366, 104 State Rd, Newaygo 49337		(517) 554-1836
			1614 Ruddiman Dr, North Muskegon 49445	(231) 744-4491	
Parmelee	William V. Clegg Jr	RE9	*2317 Marquard Ave, North Muskegon 49445		(616) 366-2486
			PO Box 237, 9266 W Parmelee Rd, Middleville 49333	(269) 795-8816	
Pentwater: Centenary	William E. Haggard	RE3	*4593 N Camrose Court, Wy-oming 49519		(231) 301-2055
			PO Box 111, 82 S Hancock, Pentwater 49449	(231) 869-5900	
Pierson: Heritage	Terri L. Cummins	FL5	*124 S Rutledge St, Pentwater 49449		(231) 903-5139
			19931 W Kendalville Rd, Pierson 49339	(231) 937-4310	
Ravenna	David A. Selleck	RE1	*18985 W Coral Rd, Howard City 49329		(231) 299-5374
			PO Box 191, 12348 Stafford St, Ravenna 49451	(231) 853-6688	
			*13687 Pinewood Dr, Grand Haven 49417		

MIDWEST DISTRICT

MIDWEST DISTRICT

CHARGE	PASTOR		ADDRESS	CHURCH	HOME
Rockford	Gregory L. Buchner	FE2	159 Maple St, Rockford 49341	(616) 866-9515	
			*PO Box 894, 1105 West Pickard, Mt Pleasant 48804		(989) 621-7782
Salem Indian Mission	R. Todd Williamson	FL6	3644 28th St, Hopkins 49328	(269) 397-1780	
Bradley Indian Mission			695 128th Ave, Shelbyville 49344		
			*1146 Nicolson St, Wayland 49348		(616) 262-0358
Sand Lake	Darryl L. Miller	PL14	PO Box 97, 65 W Maple St, Sand Lake 49343	(616) 636-5673	
South Ensley			PO Box 97, Sand Lake 49343	(616) 636-5659	
			*1568 Solon, Cedar Springs 49319-9438		(616) 696-4057
Sitka	TO BE SUPPLIED		9606 S. Dickinson Rd., Holton 49425	(231) 744-1767	
			*		
Sparta	Phillip J. Friedrick	FE4	54 E Division St, Sparta 49345	(616) 887-8255	
			*1960 Skyview Dr, Sparta 49345		(231) 670-7796
Stanwood: Northland	Gary D. Bondarenko	FE7	PO Box 26, 6842 Northland Dr, Stanwood 49346	(231) 629-4590	
			*PO Box 26, 18835 Fillmore Rd, Stanwood 49346		(231) 823-2514
Twin Lake	Michael E. Long	PL/RHL1	PO Box 352, 5940 S Main St, Twin Lake 49457	(231) 828-4083	
			*1303 6th St, Muskegon 49441		(231) 645-9584
Wayland	Paul C. Reissman	PE1	200 Church St, Wayland 49348	(269) 792-2208	
			*220 Church St, Wayland 49348		(269) 621-5333
White Cloud	Edwin D. Snook	FL9	PO Box 188, 1125 Newell St, White Cloud 49349	(231) 689-5911	
			*718 E Pine Hill Ave, White Cloud 49349		(231) 689-6774
Wolf Lake	Mona J. Dye	RLA3	378 Vista Terrace, Muskegon 49442	(231) 788-3663	
			*550 Western Ave Apt 424, Muskegon 49440		(231) 429-1892
Wyoming: Wesley Park	Dean N. Prentiss	FE10	1150 32nd St SW, Wyoming 49509	(616) 988-6738	
			*2664 Borglum Ave NE, Grand Rapids 49505		(616) 514-7124

APPOINTMENTS TO EXTENSION MINISTRIES LOCATED IN THE MIDWEST DISTRICT:
(further information at end of appointment section)

NAME	POSITION / ADDRESS	OFFICE	HOME
Janet Carter	Chaplain, Pine Rest Christian Mental Health Services		
	FD 300 68th St SE, Grand Rapids 49508	(616) 281-6363	(616) 260-9604
Margie Crawford	District Superintendent, Midwest District Office		
	FE3 207 Fulton St E Suite 6, Grand Rapids 49503	(616) 459-4503	
Kimberly M. Bos	Director, Wesley Foundation – Ferris State University (LTFT 1/2)		
	PE2 628 S Warren Ave, Big Rapids 49307	(231) 796-8315	(231) 557-0574
Jan Johnson	Chaplain, Mercy Health Partners		
	FL PO Box 358, 1500 E Sherman Blvd, Muskegon 49443	(231) 672-3629	
Cheryl Mulligan	Respiratory Therapist, Helen DeVos Pediatric Pulmonary Clinic		
	FD 35 Michigan St NE, Ste 3003, Grand Rapids 49503	(616) 267-2200	
Gary G. Step	Associate Director of Congregational Vibrancy, Michigan Conference		
	FE3 6666 Crown Point Drive, Hudsonville 49426	(517) 347-4030	(231) 420-2676

MIDWEST DISTRICT

NORTHERN SKIES DISTRICT

NORTHERN SKIES DISTRICT

District Superintendent	Scott A. Harmon FE3	DS Email: sharmon@michiganumc.org
Executive Assistant	Diana Byar	Office Email: dbyar@michiganumc.org
		Office: (906) 228-4644
		927 W. Fair Avenue, Marquette 49855

CHARGE	PASTOR		ADDRESS	TELEPHONE CHURCH	HOME
Hermansville: First	Jeff Gagne	DSA1	W 5494 Second St., Hermansville 49847		
			N14020 Co Rd. 577, Vulcan 49852		(906) 438-2252
Cheboygan: St. Paul's	John D. Bailey	FE4	531 E. Lincoln Ave., Cheboygan 49721	(231) 627-9710	
			*568 O'Brien Dr., Cheboygan 49721		(231) 627-9710
Crystal Falls: Christ	Victoria I. Prewitt	FL3	500 Marquette Ave., Box 27, Crystal Falls 49920	(906) 875-3123	
Amasa: Grace			PO Box 144, 209 Pine St., Amasa 49903		(906) 875-6134
			*110 Elm Grove, Crystal Falls 49920		
ESCANABA					
Central	Elise Rodgers Low Edwardson	FE5	322 S. Lincoln, Escanaba 49829	(906) 786-0643	
			*1814 22nd Ave., Escanaba 49829		(906) 789-1874
First	Ryan C. Edwardson	PE1	302 S. Sixth St., Escanaba 49829	(906) 786-3713	
Bark River			3716 "D" Rd., Bark River 49807		(906) 789-1874
			*1814 22nd Ave South, Escanaba 49829		
Gladstone: Memorial	Cathy L. Rafferty	FE2	1920 Lakeshore Dr., Gladstone 49837	(906) 428-9311	
			*1006 Lakeshore Dr., Gladstone 49837		(906) 420-8096
GOD'S COUNTRY COOPERATIVE PARISH					
Grand Marais	Devin T. Lawrence	DSA2	N 14226 M-77, PO Box 268, Grand Marais 49839	(906) 494-2751	
Germfask			1212 Morrison St., PO Box 135, Germfask 49836	(906) 586-3162	
McMillan			7406 Co. Rd. 415, PO Box 54, McMillan 49853	(906) 293-8933	
			*719 Garden Ave, Manistique 49854-1615		(906) 202-3231
Newberry	Jacquelyn A. Roe	FE1	110 W. Harrie St., Newberry 49868	(906) 293-5711	
Engadine			13970 Park Ave., PO Box 157, Engadine 49827	(906) 477-9989	
			*PO Box 157, N6828 Elm St., Engadine 49827		(906) 293-5497

Paradise	Mary D. Brooks	DSA8	7087 N. M-123, PO Box 193, Paradise 49768	(906) 492-3585	
Hulbert:Tahquamenon			10505 W 6th St., PO Box 91, Hulbert 49748		(906) 293-1966
			*207 W Ave. B, Newberry 49868		
Gwinn	Ronald A. Fike	FE7	251 W. Jasper, Box 354, Gwinn 49841	(906) 346-6314	(906) 346-3441
			*252 W. Carbon, PO Box 352, Gwinn 49841		
Hancock: First	Scott P. Lindenberg	FE5	401 Quincy, Box 458, Hancock 49930	(906) 482-4190	(906) 482-1404
			*1631 Portage Dr., Hancock 49930		
Houghton: Grace	Eric M. Falker	PE1	201 Isle Royale, Houghton 49931	(906) 482-2780	
Painesdale: Albert Paine Memorial			156 Iroquois St., Painesdale 49955		(906) 482-1751
			*807 Oak Grove Pkwy., Houghton 49931		
IRON MOUNTAIN					
First	Walter P. Reichle	FL9	106 Fourth St., Iron Mountain 49801	(906) 774-3586	
Quinnesec			677 Division, PO Box 28, Quinnesec 49876	(906) 774-7971	(906) 828-1228
			*901 Fairbanks St.,Iron Mountain 49801		
Trinity	Geraldine G. Hamlen	FE7	808 Carpenter Ave., Iron Mountain 49801	(906) 774-2545	(906) 774-0064
			*421 Woodward, Kingsford 49802		
Ironwood: Wesley	Keith P. Mullikin	PL2	500 E. McLeod Ave., PO Box 9, Ironwood 49938	(906) 932-3900	
Wakefield			706 Putnam St., Wakefield 49968	906-988-2533	(906) 285-9847
			*600 Garvey, Ironwood 49938		
Ishpeming: Wesley	Matthew L. Osborne	FL3	PO Box 342, 801 Hemlock, Ishpeming 49849	(906) 486-4681	(906) 475-9337
			*220 Shoreline Dr., Negaunee 49866		
KEWEENAW PARISH					
Calumet	James M. Mathews	RA2	57235 Calumet Ave., Calumet 49913	(906) 337-2720	
Lake Linden			53237 N. Hecla St., Lake Linden 49945	(906) 296-0148	(906) 337-0539
			*26350 Wyandotte, Laurium 49913		
L'Anse	Nathan T. Reed	FL2	304 N. Main, L'Anse 49946	(906) 524-7939	
Sidnaw			S 121 W. Milltown Rd., Sidnaw 49961	(906) 524-6967	(906) 524-7936
Zeba			16024 Zeba Rd., L'Anse 49946		
			*227 N. Front, L'Anse 49946		

NORTHERN SKIES DISTRICT

NORTHERN SKIES DISTRICT

CHARGE	PASTOR		ADDRESS	CHURCH	HOME
Mackinaw City: Church of the Straits	David M. Wallis	FE15	PO Box 430, 307 N. Huron, Mackinaw City 49701	(231) 436-8882	
			*309 East Jamet, PO Box 718, Mackinaw City 49701		(231) 436-5484
Manistique: First	B.J. Ash	PL1	190 N. Cedar St., Manistique 49854	(906) 341-6662	
			*9344 W State Hwy M149, Manistique 49854		(906) 341-6287
Marquette: Hope	Kristine K. Hintz co-pastor	FE7	111 E. Ridge St., Marquette 49855 (Main campus)	(906) 225-1344	
			927 W. Fair, Marquette 49855 (Connection Center)		
			189 Kreiger Dr, Skandia, 49885 (Skandia Campus)	(906) 942-7310	
			*619 Mesnard, Marquette 49855		(906) 226-3683
	Christopher P. Hintz co-pastor	FE5	111 E. Ridge St., Marquette 49855 (Main Campus)	(906) 225-1344	
			927 W. Fair, Marquette 49855 (Connection Center)		
			189 Kreiger Dr, Skandia, 49885 (Skandia Campus)	(906) 942-7310	
			*619 Mesnard, Marquette 49855		(906) 226-3683
Menominee: First Stephenson	John P. Murray	FL2	601 Tenth, PO Box 323, Menominee 49858	(906) 864-2555	
			S 111 Railroad St., Box 205, Stephenson 49887	(906) 753-6363	
			*1801 17th Ave., Menominee 49858		(814) 366-0239
Mohawk-Ahmeek	Larry Molloy	DSA2	PO Box 76, 120 Stanton Ave., Mohawk 49950		
			*226 Fourth St, Eagle Harbor 49950		(906) 284-4221
Munising	Sandra J. Kolder	RLA10	312 S. Lynn, Munising 49862	(906) 387-3394	
Trenary			PO Box 201, N 1133 E.T. Rd., Trenary 49891	(906) 446-3599	
			*PO Box 130, W18394 H-42 Rd., Curtis 49820		
Negaunee: Mitchell (merged w/ Marquette: Hope 9/1)	J. Albert Barchue (until 8/31)	OE5	207 Teal Lk Ave., Box 190, Negaunee 49866	(906) 475-4861	
New Hope of Emmett County	Michelle K. Merchant	PL6	PO Box 72, 4516 N US 31, Levering 49755	(231) 537-2000	
			*3224 Hill Road NW, Rapid City 49676		(231) 564-0723
Norway: Grace	Irene R. White	FL10	130 O'Dill Dr., Norway 49870	(906) 563-8917	
Faithorn			W8601 Blum Rd., Vulcan 49892		
			*725 Norway St., Norway 49870		(906) 563-9877

NORTHERN SKIES DISTRICT

CHARGE	PASTOR		ADDRESS	CHURCH	HOME
Ontonagon	Nelson L. Hall	FL3	109 Greenland, PO Box 216, Ontonagon 49953	(906) 884-4556	
Greenland			1002 Ridge Rd., Greenland 49929	(906) 883-3141	
Rockland: St. Paul			50 National Ave., PO Box 339, Rockland 49960	(906) 886-2851	(906) 884-2789
			*1101 Pine St., Ontonagon 49953		
Pickford	Timothy T. Bashore	FL7	115 E. Church St., Box 128, Pickford 49774	(906) 647-6195	(906) 647-7231
			230 W. Townline Rd., Pickford 49774		
Republic	Peter A. LeMoine	PL3	216 S. Front St., PO Box 395, Republic 49879	(906) 376-2389	(906) 390-0521
Michigamme: Woodland			3533 US 41E, Michigamme 49861	(906) 323-6151	(906) 376-2085
			*356 Maple St., Republic 49879		
St. Ignace	Mark E. Thompson	FE1	615 W. U.S. 2, PO Box 155, St. Ignace 49781	(906) 643-8088	(269) 591-0731
			*90 Spruce St., St. Ignace 49781		
SAULT STE. MARIE					
Central	Victoria L. Hadaway	OE3	111 E. Spruce St., Sault Ste. Marie 49783	(906) 632-8672	
Algonquin			1604 W. 4th Ave., Sault Ste. Marie 49783	(906) 632-8672	(906) 632-3125
			*1513 Augusta, Sault Ste. Marie 49783		
White Pine	Rosemary R. DeHut	PL2	9 Tamarack, PO Box 158, White Pine 49971	(906) 885-5419	
Bergland			108 Birch St., PO Box 142, Bergland 49910		
Ewen			621 M28, PO Box 272, Ewen 49925		(906) 884-2871
			*22358 Norwich Trail, Ontonagon 49953		

NAME	POSITION		ADDRESS	OFFICE	HOME

APPOINTMENTS TO EXTENSION MINISTRIES LOCATED IN THE NORTHERN SKIES DISTRICT:
(further informatior at end of appointment section)

Scott A. Harmon	District Superintendent, Northern Skies District Office				
	FE3		927 W. Fair Avenue, Marquette 49855	(906) 228-4644	

NORTHERN WATERS DISTRICT

NORTHERN WATERS DISTRICT

District Superintendent	Jodie R. Flessner FE2	DS Email: jflessner@michiganumc.org
Executive Assistant	Jill Haney	Office Email: jhaney@michiganumc.org.
		1249 Three Mile Rd S, Traverse City 49696-8307
		Office: (231) 947-5281

				TELEPHONE	
CHARGE	PASTOR		ADDRESS	CHURCH	HOME
Alden	Katherine C. Waggoner	FL1	PO Box 130, 9015 Helena Street, Alden 49612	(231) 331-4132	
Central Lake			PO Box 213, 8147 W State Rd, Central Lake 49622		(517) 215-4846
			*9022 Franklin, Alden 49612		
Alpena: First	Seok Nam Lim	FE3	167 S. Ripley Blvd., Alpena 49707	(989) 354-2490	(989) 356-1846
			*1320 Hobbs Dr., Alpena 49707		
Arcadia	TO BE SUPPLIED		PO Box 72, 3378 Division, Arcadia 49613	(231) 864-3680	(231) 923-6476
			*5763 W 9th St, Mears 49436		
Avondale	TO BE SUPPLIED		PO Box 388, 6976 14 Mile Rd, Evart 49631		
Baldwin: Covenant Community	Lyle J. Ball	PL6	PO Box 250, 5330 S M-37, Baldwin 49304	(231) 745-3232	
Chase: Barton			PO Box 104, 6957 S Depot St, Chase 49623	(231) 832-5069	(231) 972-7335
			*6874 5 Mile Rd, Blanchard 49310		
Barnard	Craig A. Pahl	FL7	PO Box 878, East Jordan 49727	(231) 547-5269	
East Jordan			PO Box 878, 201 4th St, East Jordan 49727	(231) 536-2161	(231) 536-7596
			*PO Box 238, 305 Esterly, East Jordan 49727		
Bear Lake	Cynthia Montague-Corey	PL3	PO Box 157, 7861 Main St, Bear Lake 49614	(231) 864-3680	(231) 645-1244
			*8340 Zosel St, Onekama 49675		
Bellaire: Community	Daniel J.W. Phillips	FL2	PO Box 235, 401 N Bridge St, Bellaire 49615	(231) 533-8133	(810) 986-0240
			*4046 Grass Lake Rd, Bellaire 49615		
Boyne City	Eun Sik Poy	FE6	324 S Park St, Boyne City 49712	(231) 582-9776	
Boyne Falls			3057 Mill St, Boyne Falls 49713	(231) 582-9776	

Charge	Minister	Code	Address	Phone	Phone
Epsilon			8251 E Mitchell Rd, Petoskey 49770	(231) 347-6608	(231) 347-5382
Brooks Corners	Douglas Mochama Obwoge	OE2	*4979 Boyne City Rd, Boyne City 49712 5951 30th Ave, Sears 49679 *5951 30th Ave, Sears 49679	(231) 734-2733	(231) 734-2733
Cadillac	Thomas E. Ball	FE14	PO Box 37, 1020 E Division St, Cadillac 49601 *114 Barbara St, Cadillac 49601	(231) 775-5362	(231) 775-1851
Associate	Travis Heystek	OF3	PO Box 37, 1020 E Division St, Cadillac 49601 *210 Blodgett St, Cadillac 49601	(231) 775-5362	(540) 819-5712
CHARLEVOIX					
Charlevoix	Randell J. Hitts	PL4	104 State St, Charlevoix 49720 *1206 State St, Charlevoix 49720	(231) 547-2654	(231) 622-3565
Greensky Hill	Jonathan D. Mays	PL8	8484 Green Sky Hill Rd, Charlevoix 49720 *409 Prospect St, Charlevoix 49720	(231) 547-2028	(231) 459-8067
Empire	Melody Lane Olin	FL2	PO Box 261, 10050 W Michigan St, Empire 49630 *PO Box 261, 10205 Aylsworth Rd, Empire 49630	(231) 326-5510	(231) 970-2048
Evart	Jean M. Smith	AM2	PO Box 425, 619 N Cherry St, Evart 49631	(231) 734-2130	(231) 734-2003
Sears			5951 30th Ave, 4897 Pratt St, Sears 49679 *8543 Seven Mile Rd, Evart 49631	(231) 734-2733	
Frankfort	Penny L. Parkin	FL1	PO Box 1010, 537 Crystal Ave, Frankfort 49635	(231) 352-7427	(231) 352-4724
Elberta			PO Box 405, 555 Lincoln Ave, Elberta 49628 *320 Maple Street, Frankfort 49635	(231) 352-4311	
Free Soil-Fountain	Richard D. Roberts	PL8	PO Box 173, 2549 E Michigan St, Free Soil 49411 *2415 E Michigan St, Free Soil 49411	(231) 690-4591	(231) 233-8954
Gaylord: First	Paul J. Gruenberg	FE1	215 South Center, Box 617, Gaylord 49734 *915 Five Lakes Rd., Gaylord 49735	(989) 732-5380	(989) 635-2075
Grant	TO BE SUPPLIED		PO Box 454, Interlochen 49643 (10999 Karlin Rd, Buckley 49620) (231) 269-3981 *		
Grawn	Sean T. Barton	FL3	PO Box 62, Grawn 49637 (1260 S West Silver Lake Rd, TC 49685) (231) 943-8353 *1222 S West Silver Lake Rd, Traverse City 49685		(269) 908-7313

NORTHERN WATERS DISTRICT

NORTHERN WATERS DISTRICT

CHARGE	PASTOR		ADDRESS	CHURCH	HOME
Grayling: Michelson Memorial	Richard E. Burstall	FE7	400 Michigan Ave., Grayling 49738	(989) 348-2974	(989) 348-9697
Harbor Springs	Susan E. Hitts	PE5	*142 Barbara St., Grayling 49738 343 East Main St, Harbor Springs 49740	(231) 526-2414	(231) 548-5774
Harrietta	Travis Heystek	OF3	*1881 Ellinger Rd, Alanson 49706 PO Box 13, 116 N Davis St, Harrietta 49638	(231) 389-0267	(540) 819-5712
Hersey	Lemuel O. Granada	PL9	*210 Blodgett St, Cadillac 49601 PO Box 85, 200 W Second Street, Hersey 49639	(231) 832-5168	(231) 723-2763
Hillman	Duane A. Lindsey (part-time ½)	FL1	*351 2nd St, Manistee 49660-1747 PO Box 638, 111 Maple St, Hillman 49746	(989) 742-3014	(810) 730-6861
Horton Bay	Kathryn S. Cadarette	RE1	*23910 Lowell St, Hillman 49746 4961 Boyne City Rd, Boyne City 49712-9217	(231) 582-9262	(231) 675-2172
Houghton Lake	George R. Spencer	FE5	*5925 Horton Bay Rd N, Boyne City 49712 7059 W. Houghton Lake Dr., Houghton Lake 48629	(989) 422-5622	(989) 422-4365
Indian River	Todd W. Shafer	FL4	*316 Superior, Houghton Lake 48629 PO Box 457, 956 Eagles Nest Rd, Indian River 49749	(231) 238-7764	(231) 258-6916
Kalkaska	Yong Choel Woo	FE2	*5954 Berry Lane, Indian River 49749 2525 Beebe Rd, Kalkaska 49646	(231) 258-2820	(231) 258-5995
Keswick	Patricia Ann Haas	FE10	*2301 Shawn Rd NW, Kalkaska 49646 3376 S Center Hwy, Suttons Bay 49682	(231) 271-3755	(231) 271-4117
Kewadin	Howard Harvey	RLA6	*3400 S Center Hwy, Suttons Bay 49682 PO Box 277, 7234 Cairn Hwy, Kewadin 49648	(231) 264-9640	(231) 709-5481
Kewadin Indian Mission	George Pamp	DSA4	*701 Chippewa St, Apt 6, Elk Rapids 49629 PO Box 227, 7250 Cairn Hwy, Kewadin 49648	(231) 347-9861	(231) 838-9375
Kingsley	Colleen A. Wierman	FL7	*851 W Conway, Harbor Springs 49740-9585 PO Box 395, 113 W Blair Street, Kingsley 49649	(231) 263-5278	(231) 263-4145
Lake Ann	Joshua Manning	FL4	*8658 Hency Rd, Kingsley 49649-9736 6583 First St, Lake Ann 49650	(231) 275-7236	(334) 320-9603
			*6596 First St, Lake Ann 49650-9549		

CHARGE	PASTOR		ADDRESS	CHURCH	HOME
Lake City	Russell K. Logston	FE2	PO Box - Drawer P, 301 E John St, Lake City 49651	(231) 839-2123	(231) 839-7542
			*133 N Park St, Lake City 49651-9702		
Leland	Daniel B. Hofmann	FE7	PO Box 602, 106 N 4th St, Leland 49654	(231) 256-9161	(231) 994-2159
			*PO Box 1134, 4840 Golfview Dr, Leland 49654		
LUDINGTON					
St Paul	Bradley E. Bunn	FL4	3212 W Kinney Rd, Ludington 49431	(231) 843-3275	(404) 625-6802
			*3257 W Kinney Rd, Ludington 49431		
United	Dennis B. Bromley	FE8	5810 Bryant Road, Ludington 49431	(231) 843-8340	(231) 425-4386
			*914 Seminole Dr, Ludington 49431		
Mancelona	Bryan K. Kilpatrick	FL4	PO Box 301, 117 E Hinman St, Mancelona 49659	(231) 587-8461	
Alba			PO Box 301, Mancelona 49659 (5991 Barker St, Alba 49611)	(231) 587-8461	
			*406 Sunnyside St, Mancelona 49659		
Manistee	John A. Scott	FE6	387 First St, Manistee 49660-1749	(231) 723-6219	(231) 723-3304
			*819 Elm St, Manistee 49660-2035		
Manton	Jeff A. Swainston	PL4	PO Box B, 102 N Michigan Ave, Manton 49663	(231) 824-3593	(616) 813-8746
			*PO Box 77, 102 N. Michigan, Manton, MI 49663		
Marion	James J. Mort	FE14	PO Box C, 216 W Main St, Marion 49665	(231) 743-2834	(231) 743-0062
Cadillac South Community			PO Box C, Marion 49665 (11800 47 Mile Rd, Cadillac 49601)	(231) 775-3067	
			*205 Flemming St, Marion 49665		
Mesick	Russell W. Poirier	DSA1	PO Box 337, 121 S Alvin St, Mesick 49668	(231) 885-1699	
Brethren: Epworth			PO Box 177, 3939 High Bridge Rd, Brethren 49619	(231) 477-5486	
			*PO Box 325, Onekama 49675		
NE MISSAUKEE PARISH					
Merritt-Butterfield	Hyun-Jun Cho	FE2	428 S Merritt Rd, Merritt 49667	(231) 328-4598	(231) 301-2692
Moorestown-Stittsville			4509 E Moorestown Rd, Lake City 49651	(231) 328-4598	
			*7037 E Houghton Lake Rd, Merritt 49667		
Northport Indian Mission	Mary Wava Hofmann	PL2	PO Box 401, 8626 N Manitou Trail, Northport 49670	(231) 941-2360	(231) 994-2159
			*4840 Golfview Dr, Leland 49654		

NORTHERN WATERS DISTRICT

NORTHERN WATERS DISTRICT

CHARGE	PASTOR		ADDRESS	CHURCH	HOME
Norwood	TO BE SUPPLIED		667 4th St, Norwood Village, Charlevoix 49720	(517) 262-4595	
Old Mission Peninsula	Zelphia J. Mobley	FL2	16426 Center Rd, Traverse City 49686-9775	(231) 223-4393	
			*14432 Peninsula Dr, Traverse City 49686		(586) 441-2274
Onaway	Yoo Jin Kim	PE3	3647 North Lynn St., PO Box 762, Onaway 49765	(989) 733-8811	
Millersburg			5484 Main St., Box 258, Millersburg 49759		
			*3653 N. Elm, Box 762, Onaway 49765		(989) 733-8434
Ossineke	Angela M. Lovegrove	FL1	13095 US-23, Ossineke 49766	(989) 471-2334	
			*216 5th St, Harrisville 48740		(616) 295-7546
Petoskey	James P. Mitchum	FE24	1804 E Mitchell Road, Petoskey 49770	(231) 347-2733	
			*900 Jennings Ave, Petoskey 49770		(231) 374-4747
Pine River Parish	Scott R. Loomis	FL9			
LeRoy			PO Box 38, 310 West Gilbert St, LeRoy 49655	(231) 768-4972	
Ashton			PO Box 38, 20862 11 Mile Rd, LeRoy 49655	(231) 832-8347	
Luther			PO Box 175, 315 State St, Luther 49656	(231) 797-0073	
			*PO Box 234, 400 W Gilbert St, LeRoy 49655		(231) 768-4512
Reed City	Kristen I. Coristine	FE2	503 S Chestnut, Reed City 49677	(231) 832-9441	
			*219 S State St, Reed City 49677		(231) 675-4172
Roscommon: Good Shepherd of the North	Thomas L. Hoffmeyer	OE2	149 W. Robinson Lake Rd., Roscommon 48653	(989) 275-5577	(989) 821-6056
			*303 Rising Fawn Trail, Roscommon 48653		
Scottville	Richard J. Hodgeson	FL4	114 W State St, Scottville 49454	(231) 757-3567	
			*301 W Maple Ave, Scottville 49454		(231) 757-4781
Spratt	Duane A. Lindsey (part-time ½)	FL1	PO Box 323, 7440 M-65 South, Lachine 49743	(989) 742-4372	(810) 730-6861
			*23910 Lowell St, Hillman 49746		

CHARGE	PASTOR		ADDRESS	CHURCH	HOME
TRAVERSE CITY					
Central	Dale P. Ostema	FE14	222 Cass St, Traverse City 49684	(231) 946-5191	
			*1713 Indian Woods Dr, Traverse City 49686		(231) 933-4026
Associate	M Christopher Lane	FE12	222 Cass St, Traverse City 49684	(231) 946-5191	
			*10160 E Pickwick Ct, Traverse City 49684		(231) 947-5594
Mosaic (New Church Start)	Jeremy J. Wicks	FL4	1249 Three Mile Rd. S, Traverse City 49696	(231) 946-3048	
			*PO Box 395, 449 N. Brownson St, Kingsley 49649		(517) 851-1494
Traverse Bay	Matthew D. Chapman	FE1	1200 Ramsdell St, Traverse City 49684	(231) 946-5323	
			*10160 E Pickwick Ct, Traverse City 49684		(231) 947-5594
UNITED PARISH	John D. Messner	FL1	PO Box 40, 5750 Williamsburg Rd, Williamsburg 49690	(231) 267-5792	
Williamsburg			PO Box 69, 206 Boyd St, Fife Lake 49633	(231) 879-4270	
Fife Lake			PO Box 112, 5488 Dagle St, South Boardman 49680	(231) 879-6055	
South Boardman			*124 Boyd St, Fife Lake 49633		(231) 757-4780

NAME	POSITION		ADDRESS	OFFICE	HOME

APPOINTMENTS TO EXTENSION MINISTRIES LOCATED IN THE NORTHERN WATERS DISTRICT:
(further information at end of appointment section)

Jodie R. Flessner	District Superintendent, Northern Waters District Office				
	FE3		1249 Three Mile Rd S, Traverse City 49696	(231) 947-5281	
Kathryn M. Steen	Lead Hospital Chaplain, Munson Medical Center				
	FE13		1105 Sixth Street, Traverse City 49684	(231) 935-7163	(231) 421-5138

APPOINTMENTS TO OTHER VALID MINISTRIES

Russell K. Logston	St John's Lutheran Church (Para 345)				
	FE2				

NORTHERN WATERS DISTRICT

APPOINTMENTS TO OTHER CONFERENCES

MEMBERS OF THE MICHIGAN ANNUAL CONFERENCE APPOINTED TO OTHER CONFERENCES

(Paragraph 346.1, Book of Discipline)

CHARGE	PASTOR	ADDRESS	CHURCH	HOME
FLORIDA CONFERENCE				
Chul-Goo Lee FE8		Korean American UMC, 4905 W. Prospect Rd., Ft. Lauderdale FL 33309	(954) 739-8581	
INDIANA CONFERENCE				
Eric Burton-Krieger FE4		Indianapolis St. Luke's UMC (Assoc.), 100 W 86th St, Indianapolis IN 46260	(317) 846-3404	(615) 934-0068
OREGON-IDAHO CONFERENCE				
Rebecca L. Wieringa FE5		Milwaukie St. Paul's UMC, 11631 SE Linwood Ave, Milwaukie OR 97222	(503) 654-1705	(269) 615-4527
ROCKY MOUNTAIN CONFERENCE				
Sandra L. Spahr RE8		Avondale UMC, 233 Highway 50 East, PO Box 237, Avondale CO 81022		(719) 568-5858
SOUTH CAROLINA CONFERENCE				
Charles D. Farnum FE1		Wesley Foundation, Winthrop College, 406 Stewart Ave, Rock Hill SC 29730		(989) 545-1761
VIRGINIA CONFERENCE				
Donald Ferris-McCann FE2		Bruen Chapel, 3035 Cedar Ln, Fairfax VA 22031	(703) 560-1665	(989) 640-6969
WESTERN PENNSYLVANIA CONFERENCE				
Thomas M. Beagan FE9		Charter Oak UMC, 405 Frey Rd., Pittsburgh, PA 15235	(412) 372-1341	
WEST OHIO CONFERENCE				
Yong Choel Woo FE7		Madisonville Korean, 32 Wesley Blvd., Worthington, OH 43085	(614) 844-6200	
WISCONSIN CONFERENCE				
Catherine M. Christman FE5		Stoughton UMC, 525 Lincoln Ave, Stoughton WI 53589	(608) 873-3273	(608) 205-2214

APPOINTMENTS BEYOND THE LOCAL CHURCH
APPOINTMENTS TO EXTENSION MINISTRIES
2020–2021

Appointment to Extension Ministries
(¶316.1 *The Book of Discipline 2016)*

(Lisa M. Batten) Young Adult Initiatives Coordinator

(April R. Gutierrez) Chaplain, Adrian College

(Jan M. Johnson) Palliative Care Chaplain, Mercy Health / Trinity Health. Montague - Missional C.C.

Appointment Beyond the Local Church
(¶331.1 a., b. *The Book of Discipline 2016)*

Susan D. Amick (FD) Chaplain, Wesley Woods Senior Living, Atlanta, GA. Decatur First - Missional C.C.

Grace Ann Beebe (RD) Consultant, Disability Awareness and Accessibility

M. Kay DeMoss (FD) Senior Content Editor, Michigan Conference Communications (LTFT ¾). Georgetown - Missional C.C.

Ann E. Emerson (FD) Director, Lake Huron Retreat Center.
Lexington - Missional C.C.

Carl T.S. Gladstone (FD) Missional and Young Leaders Initiative, Motor City Wesley (LTFT ½). Dearborn: First - Missional C.C.

April K. McGlothin-Eller (FD) Church Engagement Manager, Newnan Office of the UM Children's Home of North Georgia Conference.
Royal Oak: First - Missional C.C.

Vincent W. McGlothin-Eller (FD) Associate Pastor, Newnan First UMC, La-Grange, North Georgia (½ time) / GETS Registration Services & Data Specialist (½ time). Royal Oak: First - Missional C.C.

Christina L. Miller-White (FD) (LTFT ½) Youth Ministry Initiatives Coordinator. Flint: Court Street – Missional C.C.

Paul D. Perez (FD) Associate Director for Mission and Ministry.
Northville - Missional C.C.

Sue A. Pethoud (FD) Church & Community Relations Liaison, Cass Community Social Services. Cass Community - Missional C.C.

Kathryn L. Pittenger (FD) Children's Initiatives Coordinator.
DeWitt: Redeemer - Missional C.C.

Andrew J. Schleicher (FD) Senior Project Specialist, United Methodist Communications, Nashville, TN. Denton: Faith - Missional C.C.

Cara B. Weiler (FD) Associate Director of Site Services, Communities In Schools of Kalamazoo. Sunnyside - Missional C.C.

Christina L. Wright (FD) Associate Director, Department of Spiritual Care, Michigan Medicine, University of Michigan. Royal Oak First - Missional C.C.

APPOINTMENTS

Teresa J. Zimmerman (FD) Associate Director of Spiritual Life, Chelsea Retirement Community. Manchester - Missional C.C.

Appointment Beyond the Local Church
(¶331.4a The Book of Discipline 2016)

Sandra V. Bibilomo (FD) (LTFT ¾) Representative Payee of Guardian Finance and Advocacy Services. Westwood - Missional C.C.

Nancy V. Fancher (FD) (LTFT ½) Maple Valley Community Center of Hope. Lansing Mt Hope - Missional C.C.

Cheryl A. Mulligan (FD) Field Clinical Specialist, RespirTech Medical. Lowell First – Missional C.C.

Alexander J. Plum (PD) Director, Clinical & Social Health Integration, Henry Ford Health System. Cass Community Health Care Ministries Liaison – Missional C.C.

Appointment to Attend School
(¶338.4 The Book of Discipline 2016)

Appointment within the Connectional Structure
(¶344.1.a The Book of Discipline 2016)

John H. Amick, Director, Global Migration, UMCOR/Global Ministries, Atlanta, GA

Dwayne E. Bagley, Greater Southwest District Superintendent

Kennetha J. Bigham-Tsai, Chief Connectional Ministries Officer, Connectional Table

Jeremy P. Benton, Director & Campus Minister, Wesley Foundation of Greenville, Greenville, NC. Ortonville C.C.

Charles S.G. Boayue, Greater Detroit District Superintendent

John W. Boley (RE), Clergy Assistant to Bishop (LTFT)

Kimberly M. Bos (PE), Director, Wesley Foundation at Ferris State University

Jennifer Browne, Director of Clergy Excellence

Margie R. Crawford, Midwest District Superintendent

Jessica M. Davenport (PE) (LTFT ½) Co-Executive Director and Co-Pastor, Wesley Foundation of Kalamazoo

Jerome R. DeVine, Mid-Michigan District Superintendent

Dirk Elliott, Director of Congregational Vibrancy. Fenton C.C.

Donald J. Emmert, Director of Benefits and Human Resources

Katherine L. Fahey (PE), Director of Admissions & Recruitment, Garrett-Evangelical Theological Seminary.

Jodie R. Flessner, Northern Waters District Superintendent

Scott A. Harmon, Northern Skies District Superintendent

Benton R. Heisler, Director of Connectional Ministries. Cornerstone C.C.

John H. Hice, East Winds District Superintendent

John G. Kasper, Central Bay District Superintendent

Timothy L. Kobler, Chaplain, Wesley Foundation at the University of Michigan

Michael J. Mayo-Moyle, IT Specialist. Farmington: Orchard C.C.

Sherry L. Parker-Lewis, Senior Director of Church Relations, United Methodist Foundation of Michigan

LuAnn L. Rourke, Heritage District Superintendent

Gary G. Step, Associate Director for Congregational Vibrancy. Valley C.C.

Appointment to Extension Ministries
(¶344.1.b, c *The Book of Discipline 2016*)

Adam W. Bissell, Chaplain/Spiritual Care Coordinator, The Good Samaritan Society Prescott Hospice, Prescott AZ. Eastpointe: Immanuel C.C.

Herbert Lee Griffin, Jr., Chaplain, US Navy. Battle Creek: Washington Heights C.C.

Timothy Hastings, (RE) Chaplain, St. Mary's of Michigan. Saginaw: Ames C.C.

Jayme L. Kendall, Staff Chaplain, United States Air Force. Indian River C.C.

Heather A. McDougall, (PE) (LTFT ¾) Chaplain, Beacon Health System.

Lisa M. McIlvenna, Clinical Director/Pastoral Counselor, Fresh Aire Samaritan Counseling Center. Midland: First C.C.

Kathryn M. Steen, Lead Staff Hospital Chaplain, Munson Medical Center, Traverse City. Traverse City: Central C.C.

Roy G. Testolin, (RE) Pastoral Counselor, Heritage Interfaith Counseling Center, Battle Creek. Battle Creek: First C.C.

Jonathan D. VanDop, Chaplain, VA-Middleton Veteran's Hospital, Madison, WI. Coopersville C.C.

Randy J. Whitcomb (RE), Chaplain, In House Hospice Solutions. Bloomfield Hills: St. Paul's C.C.

Steven L. Woodford, Readjustment Counselor, Veterans Administration. Bay City: Grace C.C.

Appointment to Extension Ministries
(¶344.1.d *The Book of Discipline 2016*)

John W. Ball, (LTFT ¼) Consultant, Celebrate Hope. Lake Orion C.C.

Kenneth Dunstone, Psychiatrist, Eastern Kansas Veteran's Administration, Topeka, KS

David G. Elmore, Chaplain, Ascension Home Hospice. Coldwater C.C.

Alice M. Fleming-Townley, Associate Pastor, Presbyterian Church of Okemos (¶345 *The Book of Discipline 2016*). East Lansing University C.C.

Valerie A. Fons, (RE) Chaplain, Bread and Water and L.A.U.N.C.H. Wisconsin Conference. St Joseph: First C.C.

Emmanuel J. Giddings, Director, Afalit International/Liberia Literacy Program.

Melody P. Johnson, Director of Pastoral Care, Porter Hills Retirement Communities & Services, Grand Rapids. Birmingham: First C.C.

Kristen J. Leslie, Professor of Pastoral Theology and Care, Eden Theology Seminary. Adrian: First C.C.

Russell K. Logston, Pastor, St. John's Lutheran Church (¶345 *The Book of Discipline 2016*). Lake City C.C.

Stacy R. Minger, Associate Professor of Preaching, Asbury Theological Seminary, Wilmore, KY. Girard C.C.

Joy J. Moore, Vice President of Academic Affairs and Academic Dean, Luther Seminary, Saint Paul MN. Flint: Bethel C.C.

Kenneth J. Nash, Lead Pastor, Watermark Wesleyan, New York, (¶345 *The Book of Discipline 2016*). Cornerstone C.C.

Matthew R. Schlimm, Professor of Old Testament, University of Dubuque Theological Seminary, Dubuque, IA. Westwood C.C.

Barbara L. Smith-Jang, Pastoral Counselor/Parent Liaison, Taejon Christian International School, Daejeon South Korea. East Lansing: University C.C.

Appointment from Other Conferences
(¶346.1 *The Book of Discipline 2016*)

East Ohio Conference:
David S. Bell, President and Director United Methodist Foundation of Michigan. Brighton: First C.C.

Indiana Conference:
Brittney D. Stephan, (PE), Associate Director for Multi-Cultural Vibrancy

Appointment of Deaconesses
(¶1913 *The Book of Discipline 2016*)

Valerie Mossman-Celestin, Executive Director, Haitian Artisans for Peace International

Michelle White, Co-Director 5Loaves2Fish Outreach Ministries

William White, Co-Director, 5Loaves2Fish Outreach Ministries

(   ) indicates Local Pastor

AUDITOR'S REPORT

The report from the auditor is not complete at the time of publication.

Financial Policies

**as Presented by the
Council on Finance and Administration**

The following index is provided as a quick method to access this important document.

Note: For other specific rules of a financial nature please check the following:
    Board of Equitable Compensation
    Board of Pension & Health Benefits

Stewardship Recommendation

The members of the Annual Conference strongly urge each local church to conduct an every-member commitment program as outlined by Discipleship Ministries or some other effective means of involving the congregation in the needs and program of the church. (Resources are also available through Discipleship Ministries of the United Methodist Church.)

Ministry Shares Calculation

Ministry Shares represent the connectional commitment of the United Methodist Church. All United Methodist churches share in support of the programs and ministries of the UMC as it offers Christ through district, conference, or worldwide activities. The Ministry Share components addressed through these policies include ministries managed by the Michigan Conference, the Ministerial Pension Fund, Church World Service, and the Episcopal Fund.

1. For the purpose of establishing a uniform system of financing the Conference, all Ministry Shares made by the Conference and Districts shall be based on the Grade Figure System employed by the Conference for the common budget.

2. The Council on Finance and Administration shall apportion the amount comprising the annual budget among the churches of the Michigan Annual Conference for the fiscal year (January through December.) These Ministry Shares shall be based on the Grade Figure System and in conformity with the requirements of *The Book of Discipline of The United Methodist Church* and rules adopted by the Annual Conference.

3. The Grade Figure System has been chosen because it allows Ministry Shares for the local church to be based upon the financial relationship of the local church to the total of the churches in the Conference. Each church is expected to assume its portion of the common budget. Giving in addition to Ministry Shares, such as designated special day offerings, authorized General and Conference Advance Specials, etc. is to be made in keeping with the *Discipline* affirmation that "payment in full [of the World Service apportionment] by local churches is the first benevolent responsibility of the church (¶812)."

4. The grade figure for the common budget shall be determined by the current operating expense budget (lines 40 - 47 of the Local Church Report) plus non-United Methodist benevolent giving (line 38 of the Local Church Report), except that in any year when the Ministry Shares are paid in full, the non-United Methodist benevolent giving amount will be excluded from the calculation. Annual variances in the resulting calculation will be moderated by using a four-year rolling average of these numbers. (Note: the line numbers can change based upon changes to the Statistical Report.)

5. Steps in determining the grade figure for the common budget:
   a. For each local church, for each of the four most recent years reported, find the sum of lines 40 through 47 of the Local Church Report (plus line 38 non UMC benevolences – unless ministry shares are paid in full). For each year that Ministry Shares were paid in full, exclude the amount from Line 38. Add the four annual sums and find the simple average.
   b. Divide the simple average by the Conference total (simple average) for the same lines.
   c. Example:

Local church total 2017 = $89,750	Conference total 2017 = $57,147,624
Local church total 2016 = $86,317	Conference total 2016 = $58,487,020
Local church total 2015 = $71,725	Conference total 2015 = $56,025,720
Local church total 2014 = $75,726	Conference total 2014 = $51,369,385
Sum divided by four = $80,879	Sum divided by four = $55,757,437

Local church average $80,879 divided by Conference average $55,757,437 equals grade figure of .001451; multiply by the total common budget to calculate the Ministry Shares.

6. Benefits Ministry Shares provide funding for the following areas: contributions for the denomination's retirement plan; premiums for the denomination's welfare plan; all expenses related to operations of the Conference Benefits Office and Conference Board of Pension & Health Benefits. Therefore, every local church will be administered a Benefits Ministry Share in connectional support of these conference ministries. The calculation for Benefits Ministry Shares shall be separate from the grade figure for the common budget and shall be based upon the annual compensation paid by each local church to it Appointed Clergyperson or District Superintendent Assignment. The Conference Benefits Office will bill the Benefits Ministry Share to each local church monthly.

7. Steps in calculating the Benefits Ministry Shares billing:
   a. For the purpose of Benefits Ministry Shares calculations, compensation includes base cash salary plus housing if provided. Twenty-five (25) percent of the base cash salary is added to the salary to determine compensation if a parsonage is provided. If a housing allowance is provided, the actual amount of the housing allowance is added to the salary to determine total compensation.
   b. A fixed percentage of total compensation is used to calculate Benefits Ministry Shares. The fixed percentage will be established annually by CFA in collaboration with the Conference Board of Pensions and Health Benefits.
   c. A reduced percentage will be used in situations of Retired Clergy Appointments, District Superintendent Assignments (DSA), or temporary situations of no appointment/assignment.
   d. Benefits Ministry Share amounts will be adjusted the first of the month following a change in compensation or appointment status.
   e. Example with Benefits Ministry Share percentage fixed at 12%:
      1. Compensation = $40,000 salary plus parsonage
         Local church Benefits Ministry Share compensation is $40,000 + 25% of $40,000 or $50,000 x 12% = $6,000 annually, billed $500 monthly
      2. Compensation = $27,000 salary plus $15,000 housing allowance
         Local church Benefits Ministry Share compensation is $27,000 + $15,000 or $42,000 x 12% = $5,040 annually, billed $420 monthly
      3. Compensation = $34,000 salary with no housing
         Local church Benefits Ministry Share is $34,000 x 12% = $4,080 annually, billed $340 monthly
      4. Compensation = $18,000 with no housing for a DSA
         Benefits Ministry Share percentage is reduced to 4% to reflect the DSA
         Local church Benefits Ministry Share is $18,000 x 4% = $720 annually, billed $60 monthly

8. Overpayment of a church's Benefits Ministry and Common Budget Ministry Shares will be carried over to that church's Benefits Ministry and Common Budget Ministry Shares for the following year.

9. Special policies are further set out below for churches without a 4-year history:
   a. Calculation of Ministry Shares for new churches: a new church will be assigned Ministry Shares by the Conference and the District 20% of its "full" amount during the first calendar year after the effective charter year. During the second calendar year, the Ministry Shares will be at 40%; during the third year 60%, fourth year 80%; fifth year and thereafter 100%. Prior to the end of the year of their chartering, new church starts are expected to send a tithe (10%) of their giving receipts to the Conference on a quarterly basis.

b. Calculation of Ministry Shares for <u>merged churches</u>: the statistics of the merging churches will be added together before calculating the Ministry Shares of the newly formed church for the ensuing year. Reasons for departure from this procedure will be reviewed by CF&A upon appeal, and adjustments may be made on a case-by-case basis.

c. Calculation of Ministry Shares for <u>vital merger churches</u>: a new classification of merged churches will be "Vital Mergers." Those mergers fulfilling the Vital Merger qualifications will be considered a new church start by the New Church Development Committee. As part of the Vital Merger process, the congregations involved will create a proposed budget for the merged church which will go into effect on the date the merged church begins worshipping and meeting as one congregation. This budget will be developed in consultation with, and given approval by, the District Superintendent and the District Committee on Church Building and Location. This budget will then be forwarded to the Conference Treasurers office to be used to formulate Ministry Share figures for the newly merged church. A new total base figure will be calculated for the merged church based on the formula outlined in paragraph 6. This new total base figure will be in effect until the actual financial records of the merged church are reported for the first full year of its existence and can be used to calculate a total base figure based on actual expenditures. The Vital Merger church will be assigned Ministry Shares by the Conference and District at 25% of its "full" amount during the first calendar year after the merger. During the second calendar year, the Ministry Shares will be 50%; 75% for the third calendar year; and 100% for the fourth calendar year and thereafter. The church must submit to the District Superintendent and Conference Treasurer's offices and the Board of Pensions a plan for managed debt repayment for any conference pension or health care arrearages.

d. Calculation of Ministry Shares for <u>adoption merger churches</u>: a new classification of merged churches will be "Adoption Mergers." In an Adoption Merger, a larger, healthy congregation (known as the parent congregation) agrees to partner with a smaller, usually struggling congregation (known as the partner congregation), assuming leadership and all assets and liabilities of the partner church, with the intention that the partner church is absorbed by the parent church but remains open and the church becomes a multi-site congregation. The adoption will be approved by the New Start Team, the District Superintendent, and the District Committee on Church Building and Location. The Ministry Shares for churches involved in the Adoption will be calculated as follows: 1) the year the Adoption becomes effective the Ministry Shares calculation will be calculated on the parent church only, using the standard calculation of a four-year rolling average, 2) the second year the Ministry Shares will be calculated on the parent church's expenses for the four preceding years, which will include one year of the combined expenses of both campuses, 3) the third year the Ministry Shares will be calculated on the parent church's expenses for the four preceding years, which will include two years of the combined expenses, 4) the fourth year the Ministry Shares will be calculated on the parent church's expenses for the four preceding years, which will include three years of the combined expenses. The church must submit to the District Superintendent, the Conference Treasurer's office and the Director of Benefits and Human Resources a plan for managed debt repayment for any conference pension or health care arrearages.

10. As Ministry Shares are received during the year, the <u>World Service</u> apportionment from the General church shall be paid at the level of receipts.

11. The portion of the Ministry Share for each local church designated for the Episcopal Fund shall be paid in the same proportion as the church pays its pastor. (¶818.3 of *The Book of Discipline of The United Methodist Church 2016)*

12.Funds received in excess of expenses for the Conference fiscal year shall be placed in the reserves of the respective Ministry Share funds and maintained by the Conference Treasurer.

13. During the Conference fiscal year, the Council on Finance and Administration, by a two-thirds (2/3) vote of its members, may use for the benefit of, or distribute to, Conference agencies and causes from the respective funds, such amounts as the Council by its action, upon concurrence with the Bishop, shall determine are required for use or distribution before the next session of the Annual Conference.

Section I - **Administration**

A.   **Local Church Contributions**

1. All ministry shares apportioned to individual churches for the conference fiscal year shall be divided in ten (10) monthly installments. A statement will be sent from the treasurer's office 12 times a year.

2. All contributions, whether apportioned or un-apportioned, for Michigan Conference agencies and institutions, and for all benevolent causes of The United Methodist Church, shall be sent to the Conference Treasurer for distribution.

B.   **Clergy Support Items**

1. Travel Reimbursement - Churches shall reimburse pastors of local congregations for travel expenses using a voucher system based on reimbursement equivalent to the IRS allowance for business mileage.

2. Expense Reimbursement - Churches may reimburse pastors of local congregations for professional expenses as defined by IRS code. A voucher system shall be used for such reimbursement.

3. Utilities - Churches shall pay all utilities in full for their parsonages, including heat, electricity, water, sewage, and basic telephone service.

4. Annual Conference – The Michigan Conference recommends that the local church pay living expenses for their clergy and lay members who attend Annual Conference. Such expenses should be paid at the rate specified for registration, meals and lodging as shown on the Annual Conference registration materials.

5. Health Insurance

   a. Enrollment in the conference active group health care plan in most situations will be mandatory for all eligible participants. Enrollment of eligible dependents is optional at the discretion of the participant.

   b. Each charge or conference-approved group shall share with the participant the full cost of conference group health insurance covering the pastor/conference lay employee and his/her dependents according to the approved premium sharing schedule.

   c. Even if a pastor is enrolled as a dependent in a spouse's health care plan, the church will be expected to share a portion of the cost of the conference active group health care.

   d. In the case of health benefits coverage for dependents when there is a legal separation or divorce, please refer to the conditions established by the healthcare policy of the Conference Board of Pension & Health Benefits.

   e. At the time of a pastoral move, the insurance should be paid to the end of the billing period by the church from which the pastor is moving.

   f. If a pastor chooses to be enrolled as a dependent on a spouse's health insurance plan, the pastor must have a signed waiver of coverage placed in the file in the

Benefit's office. Joining the active conference group health care plan during the open enrollment period is always an option. Enrollment since the last previous open enrollment period is a prerequisite to receiving certain retirement benefits.

6. Effective dates for salary and Clergy Retirement Security Plan/Comprehensive Protection Plan (CRSP/CPP) Payments for Ministerial Appointment Changes

   a. The salary shall be paid through June 30 when an appointment change is made at the session of Annual Conference. Salary payments for mid-year appointments will coincide with the effective date of the appointment.

   b. Payment on CRSP/CPP billing from the General Board of Pension and Health Benefits shall be made for the entire month of June for those appointment changes made during the session of Annual Conference. CRSP/CPP payments for mid-year appointments with an effective date of the first of the month shall be made for the previous month for the outgoing pastor and for the current month for the incoming pastor. Payments for appointment changes effective the 15th of a month shall be made for half of the current month for the outgoing pastor and half of the current month for the incoming pastor.

7. United Methodist Personal Investment Plan (UMPIP) - This is the pastor's recommended contribution (at least three percent) to his/her own personal retirement account. The local church is not required to contribute to this. Where churches do, however, it shall be considered as part of the total cash salary and so reported.

C. **Cabinet Level Salaries**

   The salaries of District Superintendents, Director of Connectional Mission and Ministries, Director of Conference Benefits and Human Resources Services, Director of Administrative Services and Conference Treasurer, Director of Communications, Director of Clergy Excellence, and the Director of Congregational Vibrancy shall be set by Council of Finance & Administration. Council of Finance & Administration shall consider the best information available, including, but not limited to, the denominational average compensation, Conference average compensation, the average salary of the top 10 highest paid pastors, and the US Consumer Price index or inflation rate.

Section I – **Travel Expense Policies**

A. Conference travel

   Expenses incurred due to travel on behalf of the Michigan Conference of the United Methodist Church may be reimbursed. All persons who are entitled to travel and other expense reimbursements must complete and submit an expense reimbursement form on a regular basis. Expenses within the appropriate budget limits will be reimbursed. Each form should include detailed explanations of trip expenses and mileage. Receipts for all expenses exceeding $10 must be attached to the report. According to IRS regulations, reimbursed expenses which are inadequately supported or un-documented may be considered additional compensation and thus be taxable to the recipient.

   1. Who May Request Travel Reimbursement – Any Conference employee or member of a Commission, Board, or agency who has traveled for a required Conference purpose may request travel reimbursement. Such amounts must be reasonable. Expenses relating to commuting will not be reimbursed.

   2. Information and Documentation Requirements
      a) Airlines – Receipt from airline must be provided. Electronic tickets may be documented with the emailed receipt from the airline company. Air travel insurance is not a reimbursable expense.

b) Auto Expenses – Includes parking fees, tolls, car rental (see below), taxicab, shuttles and other expense incurred in ground transportation; all of which are eligible to be reimbursed. No police or court fines or tickets for parking violations will be reimbursed.

c) Car Rental – Rental cars are reimbursable where common carriers are not available or feasible due to scheduling needs, or actual rental cost including gas and other charges are less than the standard mileage rate or common carrier cost.

d) Dates of Travel – The expense report should clearly indicate the dates of travel for each trip.

e) Incidentals – Tips for baggage handling, porters, bellhops, restaurant service, and business telephone charges are reimbursable. Incidentals should not exceed $10 per day.

f) Lodging – Lodging should be obtained at the most reasonable rate available for the location. A copy of the bill should be submitted with the expense report. Actual cost will be reimbursed when a copy of the bill is submitted. Entertainment expenses are not reimbursable.

g) Meals – Meals are reimbursable when travel begins prior to or ends after the normal meal time. Reimbursement will not be made for alcoholic beverages. Generally, meals should not exceed $40 per day. The maximum daily meal allowance begins when you leave your office. The trip ends when you arrive back at your office but excludes personal travel during the total trip.

h) Mileage – Miles traveled on Conference business will be reimbursed at the appropriate rate approved by the Internal Revenue Service. Total miles per trip should be itemized for each day reported. Mileage to be reimbursed is the round-trip miles from the primary office location unless the trip originates from home in a different city in which case the mileage to be reimbursed **is the lesser** of the round-trip miles from the primary office location or the home location. Odometer readings are not required but may be reported. Commuting miles and miles incurred for personal business enroute for Conference business are not reimbursable. A group mileage report may be completed for committee meetings where there are no other expenses which require receipts to be attached to the report. Any expense reimbursement requiring a receipt must be reported separately by individuals.

i) Purpose – The business purpose of each trip must be clearly documented on the travel expense report. Confidential information need not be disclosed but should be maintained in a personal log or diary for your own records. Group meal receipts must document all individuals included in the expense.

j) Receipts – Receipts must be submitted for all expenses exceeding $10. The receipt should report individual items purchased. The original detailed receipts and the credit card authorization receipt showing the partial card number and any tip amounts must accompany any requisition submitted for expenses paid by credit card. Please submit original receipts only. If costs are being shared by another organization and receipts are required for that entity, a copy of the shared items and corresponding expense report submitted to the second organization may be submitted.

k) Registration Fees – Evidence of fees paid must be submitted.

l) Spouse Expenses – Spousal travel expenses will only be reimbursed in situations where their presence is required by the Conference on Conference business. To avoid any perception that personal expenses are being reimbursed, Board minutes or other written documentation should document a spouse's required presence.

3. Who May Approve Expense Reports
   The Bishop may approve travel reimbursement of District Superintendents; the Director of Connectional Ministries may approve travel reimbursement request for Associate Directors and Treasurer. The Treasurer may approve reimbursement requests by any employee of the Conference and the Bishop. No individual may approve a reimbursement to themselves.
   Group Mileage Reports may be approved by an officer of the committee, Director of Connectional Ministries or Treasurer. The individual approving the group travel should not be listed as a payee for travel on the same report.

4. Timing of Check Requests and Processing
   Forms for each month should be received in the Treasurer's Office as soon as feasible after the month's travel is completed. Travel expense reimbursement requests will be processed in the normal processing schedule. Forms which are incomplete or improperly filled out may result in a delay in processing the check or may be returned for further information.

5. Travel and other expense advances are issued only in very rare instances, except for District Superintendents and conference staff. Upon signing a promissory note, an advance may be obtained, which will be due and payable when the person leaves the staff position.

6. Conference personnel who draw travel allowance by voucher shall receive reimbursement equivalent to the federal IRS allowance for business mileage. This is designed to cover the cost of automobile operation.

7. All others drawing travel expenses from conference funds shall receive reimbursement equivalent to the federal IRS allowance for moving and medical care mileage for car and travel and $.02 per mile per passenger up to five people. This is designed to cover out-of-pocket expenses (i.e. gas and oil).

B. Travel expense by conference agencies

   1. The travel expense of authorized representatives of conference agencies attending meetings convened by conference agencies drawing their full budget from the conference shall be paid by the agency which calls the meeting.

   2. Dependent reimbursement cost necessary for dependents (children, sick or elderly) may be distributed from the Administrative budget for a member of any board, commission or committee meeting. The amount reimbursed shall not exceed $40 per day, per member.

   3. Travel to non-United Methodist agencies - The travel expenses of authorized conference representatives attending meetings convened by non-United Methodist agencies within the state of Michigan, shall be paid by the conference, as provided in Part 1 of this section, to the extent the expenses are not borne by the convening agency.

Section III – **Moving Expense Policy**

A. Eligible Persons and Moves

   1. No moving expenses will be approved until the Appointment Status Sheet is received by the Conference Treasurer's office.

   2. All pastors under active appointment within the Michigan Conference structure are eligible to receive moving expense benefits. This will include local church pastors, district superintendents, staff members of conference or district councils, boards, and agencies, treasurers, bishop's assistants, superintendents or directors of parish development, conference-approved evangelists, and campus ministers.

3. Seminary students and pastors from outside the Michigan Conference who are accepting appointment in the conference are eligible for moving expense benefits as provided in this code up to a limit of 750 miles.

4. The conference will pay for one retirement move for pastors who have retired or plan to retire from Episcopal appointment in the conference. The move must be taken within five years of the retirement date. The designation of a retirement move must be declared in writing before the moving expenses are incurred. A move within the state of Michigan shall be paid in accordance with the provisions of this code. A move outside the state shall be paid up to the cost equivalent of 600 miles beyond the state border. Pastors called out of retirement and assigned to a charge will be granted an additional retirement move.

5. A disability move or the move of the surviving spouse of an eligible pastor shall be paid in accordance with the policy for retiring pastors. The conference shall pay for the move out of the parsonage or other approved housing, to another residence in the event of an eligible pastor's death, in accordance with the policy for retiring pastors.

6. When a separation or pending divorce action makes a move advisable, the spouse of a pastor is entitled to reimbursement for one move. Benefits are the same as those available to a surviving spouse of a deceased pastor.

7. Moves within a charge from one parsonage to another are the responsibility of the local charge unless ordered by the cabinet.

8. Pastors not eligible for moving expense benefits include those:
   a. under appointment outside the structure of the conference.
   b. on sabbatical, leave of absence, or location.
   c. who no longer have membership in the annual conference.

B. Policy for Moves

1. Interstate moves – Moves to or from states other than Michigan. Interstate moves are very competitive, and 2 or 3 estimates should be obtained before choosing a moving company to get the lowest rate available. Most movers will provide a "Not to Exceed" estimate.

2. Intrastate moves - Moves greater than 40 miles within the State of Michigan. These moves are regulated by State Law and the cost is based solely on weight and distance. Multiple estimates are not required.

3. Local zone moves (40 miles outside of corporate limits) - Local zone moves are not regulated as are other moves within the state. Therefore, 2 or 3 estimates should be obtained to get the lowest rate available. Charges will be based on an hourly rate times the number of employees involved. Most movers will provide "Not To Exceed" estimates if asked.

4. Family travel - Family travel for pastors covered by this policy will be paid upon request, for one car, at the IRS rate (except the first 100 miles), plus tolls. One overnight lodging will be paid for moves of more than 350 miles upon presentation of receipts.

5. Expenses covered by this code:
   a. Normal state tariff provision for loading, transporting and unloading of household goods up to a maximum weight of 20,000 pounds, including professional books and equipment. Reasonable additional weight will be allowed for clergy couples to enable movement of professional books and equipment for each clergy person. Handwritten weight certificates will not be accepted.
   b. Up to $150 will be paid by the conference to cover needed packing materials, including wardrobes and dish packs. Mattress boxes will be provided.
   c. One extra pickup and one extra delivery for each clergy person defined as the church office or local storage unit within 15 miles of the clergy member's housing.
   d. Reasonable charges for necessary handling of special items such as a piano or freezer.
   e. Standard liability insurance of 60 cents per pound which is furnished by the moving company, at no extra charge, under basic tariff provisions.

NOTE: It is now required that the householder sign a release statement on the Bill of Lading on the day of the move to release the shipment to a value of 60 cents per pound per article. Failure to do this will allow the moving company to charge a premium for insurance to cover the shipment at a value of up to $1.50 per pound.

    f.   Where there are medically recognized physical limitations, up to $1,000 additional shall be allowed for packing. A physician's authorization must be provided. Contact the Conference Treasurer for authorization.

    g. Storage charges are the responsibility of the local church if the parsonage is not ready for occupancy. The conference will pay only to the place of storage.

    h. When a moving company has been selected and an estimate given, contact the treasurer's office for authorization to be given to the mover. Because Michigan in-state moves are regulated by tariff, only one estimate is needed if items 1 and 2 above do not apply to the move.

6. Expenses NOT covered by this code:

    a. Moving of items other than normal household goods and books, such as boats, trailers, autos, building materials, firewood, fishing shanties, dog houses, etc.

    b. Packing and/or unpacking services, except as noted in 5.f.

    c. Full value insurance beyond standard liability insurance provided by the moving company.

    d. Charges for waiting time, extra labor, connecting and disconnecting appliances.

    e. Consequential damages resulting from any part or aspect of the move.

    f. Emotional or pain and suffering damages arising directly or indirectly, from any part or aspect of the move.

C. Miscellaneous Policies

1. No moving company shall employ a pastor or an immediate member of his/her family to solicit business at any time for the purpose of receiving a commission or other consideration.

2. No company shall be allowed to establish an office at the seat of the conference for the purpose of soliciting business.

3. Each pastor is advised to request a copy of his/her inventory sheet from the mover at the time of loading and that it be signed by both the pastor and the moving company.

4. Pastors may want to check with their moving company or home insurance company and request an all-risk policy that would cover all damages in the moving of their household goods from one residence to another.

D. Administration

1. The Conference Treasurer shall administer the Moving Expense Fund.

2. Pastors anticipating a move shall consult with the Conference Treasurer's office to review the guidelines of this code.

3. The pastor shall be responsible for contacting a moving company and for scheduling the loading and unloading of household goods.

4. A written estimate of the cost of moving services shall be made by the moving company and a copy shall be sent to the conference treasurer's office in advance of the move.

5. A letter of authorization shall be sent from the Conference Treasurer's office in advance of the move.

6. Billing for the cost of moving expenses covered by this code shall be made directly to the Conference Treasurer's office. Moving expenses not covered by this code shall be billed directly to the pastor.

7. Provision for payment of any unusual expenses which are not defined by this code shall be arranged through consultation with the Conference Treasurer prior to the move.

CFA FINANCIAL POLICY

8. Requests for exception to the provisions of this code shall be made to the Conference Treasurer in advance of the move. The Treasurer shall review and decide on each exception after consultation with the cabinet and/or CFA, as necessary.

9. **Pursuant to IRS rules, employer paid moves are considered taxable to the employee. The treasurer's office will provide 1099-MISC to the employee in accordance with the IRS rules.**

Approved Moving Companies
(Listed Alphabetically)

1.** Corrigan Moving Systems
United Van Lines

    4204 Holiday Dr.
    Flint 48507
    810-235-9700 / 800-695-0540

    7409 Expressway Court St
    Grand Rapids 49548
    616-455-4500
    www. Corriganmoving.com

2. Escanaba Moving Systems
United Van Lines
2601 Danforth
Escanaba 49829
906-786-8205

3. Frisbie Moving and Storage
United Van Lines
14225 Schaefer Hwy
Detroit 48227
313-837-0808

4. Guindon Moving & Storage Co.
1600 3rd Ave. N.
Escanaba 49829
800-562-1075 / 906-786-6560

5. Palmer Moving & Storage
North American Van Lines
24660 Dequindre
Warren 48091-3332
800-521-3954

6.** Rose Moving & Storage
Allied Van Lines
41775 Ecorse Road, #190
Belleville, MI 48111
800-521-2220
www.rosemoving.com

7. Stevens Worldwide Van Lines
Clergy Move Center
527 Morley Drive
Saginaw 48601
989-755-3000 / 800-678-3836
www.stevensworldwide.com

8. Taylor Moving & Storage
8320 Hilton Rd.
Brighton, MI 48114
810-229-7070 / 800-241-7122
www.taylormoving-storage.com

** These companies are "Preferred Movers" and may offer additional services. Please contact the movers directly to find out what additional services they may be able to offer.

Section IV – **Investment Policy**

A.   **Statement of Purpose**

The purpose of this Investment Policy (IP) is to provide governance and oversight to investments of conference funds under the control and responsibility of the Michigan Conference Council of Finance & Administration. The intent is to facilitate and not hinder conference agencies in the execution of their duties related to the management of their investment portfolios and in the use of their funds as provided in the *2016 Book of Discipline of The United Methodist Church.* In recognition of its fiduciary responsibilities and the mandate of the *2016 Book of Discipline of The United Methodist Church (613.5)*, the Council of Finance & Administration has developed this IP governing investment of their respective conference funds.

B.   **Delineation of Responsibilities**

1.   Under the *2016 Book of Discipline of The United Methodist Church (612.1)*, the purpose of the Council of Finance & Administration shall be to develop, maintain, and administer a comprehensive and coordinated plan of fiscal and administrative policies, procedures, and management services for the conference. Accordingly, the Council of Finance & Administration is responsible for establishing principles, policies, standards and guidelines for the investment of all monies, assets and properties of the conference.
2.   The Council of Finance & Administration is ultimately responsible for the financial integrity and oversight of conference financial resources. Under this IP all operational and implementation of policy decisions may be delegated to the Investment Committee.
3.   The Council of Finance & Administration shall at least once per year review the IP, the effectiveness of the Investment Committee and the overall results of the investments and will acknowledge in writing that they have done so.

C.   **Members of the Investment Committee**

The Conference Investment Committee shall be a sub-committee of Council of Finance & Administration and be composed of five Council of Finance & Administration members selected by Council of Finance & Administration. The members' individual terms shall not exceed eight years and shall be staggered to provide for continuity and experienced leadership. The chairperson and other offices shall be nominated by the Committee from among its members and approved by the Council of Finance & Administration.

Responsibilities of the Investment Committee:

1.   To define and develop investment goals, and other operational guidelines.
2.   To recommend to the Council of Finance & Administration the selection and discharge of the Investment Managers.
3.   To monitor and evaluate the performance results and risk posture of the Investment Manager(s).
4.   To provide semi-annually to the Council of Finance & Administration a written account of the investment results, accounting summary and any significant developments.
5.   To provide annually to the Council of Finance & Administration a written annual evaluation of the Investment Managers.
6.   To require all portfolios will be managed with the aim of maximizing funds available for mission in a manner consistent with the preservation of capital, the

Policies Relative to Socially Responsible Investments and the Social Principles of The United Methodist Church.

7. To establish effective communication procedures between the Committee, Council of Finance & Administration, the staff and the outside service providers.

8. To monitor and control investment expenses.

9. To delegate the execution and administration of certain Committee responsibilities as appropriate to the Conference Treasurer who serves as its staff.

10. To carry out any other duties required for the legal operations of the investments, including but not limited to hiring outside vendors to perform various services.

11. To report to the Council of Finance & Administration any significant deviations from this policy for prior approval before they are implemented.

D. **Investment Managers**

To achieve its investment objectives and to ensure alignment with United Methodist Policies Relative to Socially Responsible Investments and Social Principles, the Investment Managers of Conference Funds, shall be The United Methodist Foundation of Michigan and Wespath Benefits and Investments.

E. **Investment Performance Benchmarks**

The investment performance of total portfolios and asset class components will be measured against the published benchmark for the respective investment funds, as well as, against commonly accepted performance benchmarks. Consideration shall be given to the extent to which the investment results are consistent with the investment objectives and guidelines as set forth in this IP. The standard of care when making decisions is the Prudent Expert Standard, defined as:

"...the care, skill, prudence and diligence under the circumstances then prevailing that a prudent person acting in a like capacity and familiar with such matters would use in the conduct of an enterprise of a like character and with like aims."

F. **Responsibilities of Investment Managers**

The Investment Managers shall provide the Investment Committee quarterly or as necessary the following written reports:

1. the portfolio's complete holdings;

2. a review of the investment performance measured against the respective benchmarks;

3. a commentary on investment results in light of the current investment environment on the goals and guidelines;

4. a review of the key investment decisions and the rationale for these decisions;

5. a discussion of the manager's outlook and what specific decisions this outlook may indicate;

6. any recommendations as to changes in goals and guidelines in light of material and sustained changes in the capital market; and any significant change in the manager's investment outlook, ownership or key employees.

G. **Socially Responsible Investment Guidelines**

As an Annual Conference of The United Methodist Church we are committed to implementation of the socially responsible investment policies in *2016 Book of Discipline of The United Methodist Church (717)*. (We encourage all of our congregations to be socially responsible investors.)

"Sustainable and Socially Responsible Investments-In the investment of money, it shall be the policy of The United Methodist Church that all general boards and agencies, including Wespath Benefits and Investments, and all administrative agencies and institutions, including hospitals, homes, educational institutions, annual conferences, foundations, and local churches, make a conscious effort to invest in institutions, companies, corporations, or funds with policies and practices that are socially responsible, consistent with the goals outlined in the Social Principles. All United Methodist institutions shall endeavor to seek investments in institutions, companies, corporations, or funds that promote racial and gender justice, protect human rights, prevent the use of sweatshop or forced labor, avoid human suffering, and preserve the natural world, including mitigating the effects of climate change. In addition, United Methodist institutions shall endeavor to avoid investments in companies engaged in cored business activities that are not aligned with the Social Principles through their direct or indirect involvement with the production of anti-personnel weapons and armaments (both nuclear and conventional weapons), alcoholic beverages or tobacco; or that are involved in privately operated correctional facilities, gambling, pornography or other forms of exploitative adult entertainment. The boards and agencies are to give careful consideration to environmental, social, and governance factors when making investment decisions and actively exercise their responsibility as owners of the companies in which they invest. This includes engaging with companies to create positive change and hold them accountable for their actions, while also considering exclusion if companies fail to act responsibly."

H. **Target Asset Allocations and Rebalancing Guidelines**

The purpose of allocating among asset classes is to ensure the proper level of diversification and risk for each portfolio. The primary considerations in the asset allocation decision process are:

1. maintaining inflation-adjusted purchasing power;
2. growing the corpus of the funds to meet future obligations;
3. achieving a minimum return in excess of inflation but with minimal annual fluctuations in the corpus; and,
4. maintaining the longevity of the assets and their distributions while taking into consideration that there may be no additional contributions.

I. **General Investment Policies**

a. Not less than 30% nor more than 70% of the market value of the assets of the fund shall be in equity securities, unless otherwise determined by the Investment Committee.
b. Not more than 20% of the market value of the assets of the fund shall be in cash or cash equivalents, unless otherwise determined by the Investment Committee.
c. No more than 10% of the market value of the assets are in the securities of any one issuer, except for securities of the U.S. Government or its agencies.
d. No more than 20% of the market value of the equity assets are in the equity issues of companies in any one industry.
e. Periodically market conditions may cause the portfolio's investments in various equities (mutual funds) to temporarily vary from the established industry allocation policy.

J. **General Investment Policies**

a. Fixed-Income securities may be held only is such securities are issued by the U.S. Treasury or any agency of the U.S. Government, or are corporate bonds rated in one of the top two letter classifications by Moody's or Standard and Poor's. Convertible securities will be considered as equity securities.
b. Short-term securities may be held only if such securities are issued by the U.S. Treasury or an agency of the U.S. Government; are commercial paper rated P-1 by Moody's, A-1 by Standard and Poor's or F-1 by Fitch's; or are certificates of deposit of U.S. banks which have or whose holding companies have a Standard and Poor's rating of A+ or better.

    c. No direct investments shall be made in foreign currency denominated securities, including American Depository Receipts except as follows: Investments may be made in common stocks, bonds and American Depository Receipts of those foreign securities listed on the New York, American or NASDAQ exchanges. Investments in a foreign securities pooled fund operated by a U.S. based money manager is also permitted provided that all transactions are in dollars.

    d. Investments shall not be made in commodities, real estate (except Real Estate Investment Trusts [REITS]), commodity contracts, financial futures, oil, gas mineral leases, mineral rights or royalty contracts.

    e. Margin transactions, short sales, options, put, calls, straddles, and/or spreads shall not be used.

    f. Investments shall not be made in the securities of an issuer which, together with any predecessor, has been in operation for less than three years.

    g. Investments shall not be made in securities for which market quotations are not readily available.

    h. Investments shall not be made in securities for the purpose of exercising control or management.

    i. Private placements of debt or equity will not be purchased.

    j. Investments shall not knowingly be made in securities of companies which have significant interest in the following activities: alcoholic beverages, tobacco, or gambling.

    k. Investments shall not knowingly be made in voting securities of companies which derive more than 15% of revenue from military contracts including both domestic and foreign customers. In the case of nonvoting securities, the limit shall be 5% of revenue.

    l. Investments shall not knowingly be made in companies which derive more than 3% of revenue from nuclear weapons contracts.

    m. Investments shall not be made if such investments will result in income which would require the filing of federal, state or local tax returns.

K. **Amendments and Revisions**

Amendments or changes to this IP may be made by the Council of Finance & Administration and incorporated directly into the policy as a revision and restatement or acknowledged and noted in an addendum until such time as the IP is revised and restated.

L. **Investment of Other Conference Funds**

The Conference Board of Pensions and Health Benefits and the Board of Trustees are given separate authority and responsibility in *2016 Book of Discipline of The United Methodist Church* for the management and investment of funds under their control. In carrying out their investment responsibilities, they may, if they determine, engage the services of the Investment Managers under this Policy to manage their funds, provided such funds shall be maintained in separate accounts. They shall also acknowledge that the responsibilities of the Investment Committee and Investment Managers and other investment guidelines as outlined in the Policy shall apply to their separate funds.

Section V – Miscellaneous Policies

A. **Conference-Wide Appeal for Funds**

No proposal for apportionments or conference-wide appeals for funds shall be recognized from the conference floor until it has first been submitted to the Council on

Finance and Administration prior to completion by the Council of its annual budget recommendation to the conference [See ¶614.5 a-c of *The 2016 Book of Discipline*.]

B. **World Service Apportionment**
   1. Special attention should be given to the *2016 Book of Discipline* which reads in part: "The World Service Fund is basic in the financial program of The United Methodist Church. World Service on apportionment represents the minimum needs of the general agencies of the church. Payment in full of these apportionments by local churches and annual conferences is the first benevolent responsibility of the church." (¶812 of *The 2016 Book of Discipline*).
   2. Likewise, attention is called to ¶820.5 which reads: "Churches and individuals shall give priority to the support of the World Service and conference benevolences and other apportioned funds."

C. **General Church Apportionments** - Recognizing the importance of ministries supported by the General Church apportionments, the Michigan Conference shall make every effort to support all apportioned items at 100%. If the level of receipts in any year is insufficient to do so, the CFA shall use general reserve funds to achieve the 100% goal, at the discretion of the Council of Finance & Administration. The Episcopal Fund shall be paid at 100%.

The Michigan Conference will continue to make monthly remittance on General Church Apportionments and challenges its churches to do the same. Interpretive, educational and motivational assistance will be given to local church leaders in an effort to improve understanding of and support for all Ministry Shares.

D. **Presentation of Proposed Budgets** - The budgets of all conference boards, commissions, committees, institutions and agencies seeking support from the conference or from churches, groups or individual members of the churches of the conference, shall present their proposed budget for the ensuing year to the Council on Finance and Administration for recommendation to and approval by the annual conference. Conference program budgets will be processed by the Conference Leadership Council.

The following limitations shall apply only to those conference boards, commissions, committees, institutions, and agencies which receive their total budget support from the conference through Ministry Shares, fees, or gifts.
   1. No annual conference agency expense of the budget under Connectional Ministry and Administration shall exceed the annual amount budgeted except as authorized by the conference Council on Finance and Administration.
   2. Gifts and Bequests
      a) No board, agency or commission may accept gifts or bequests that will obligate that board, agency or commission beyond its present budget.
      b) If the receipt of such gifts or bequests could obligate the annual conference in the future, it cannot be received or accepted until it has been approved by the board, agency or commission, the Council on Finance and Administration, and the Annual Conference.
      c) If the acceptance of such a gift or bequest must be determined prior to a session of the annual conference, approval may be given by a two-thirds vote each of the Board of Trustees and the Council on Finance and Administration voting separately.
   3. Within the budget approved by the Annual Conference, the various conference boards, commissions, committees, institutions and agencies are individually given the task of distributing this in ways consistent with their assigned responsibilities.

4. No funds shall be shifted between budget areas of administration, program, and projects without the approval of the Council of Finance & Administration.
5. No program should be initiated or continued unless there is a reasonable assurance of adequate funds on a continuing basis to allow the program to be successful.

E. **Auditing Requirements** - All agencies receiving financial support from conference benevolences, or from any other authorized conference-wide appeal, shall make audited reports (as defined in the *2016 Book of Discipline*) to the Council on Finance and Administration concerning all such receipts and the disbursement thereof in such detail and at such times as the Council may direct. Furthermore, the books of the Conference Treasurer shall be audited annually as defined in the *2016 Book of Discipline of The United Methodist Church.*

F. **Bonding of Treasurers** - The conference contracts for fidelity bonds covering financial personnel of the conference agencies located in the conference headquarters and the conference treasurer as required by the *2016 Book of Discipline of The United Methodist Church.* In addition, a fidelity bond is provided for each conference trustee and for related staff up to $1,000,000 by the General Council on Finance and Administration through the General Church Insurance Program.

G. **Control System** -The Council on Finance and Administration shall have a system of control in the disbursement of funds apportioned for conference staff, boards and agencies to ensure that they remain within their allocated budget. During the first six months of the fiscal year, the conference treasurer's office will honor vouchers presented for expenditures up to 70% of the amount approved by the annual conference for that board or agency. For the remainder of the year, spending by a board or agency may not exceed that board or agency's prorated amount of Ministry Shares receipts to date not yet expended, with the exception of salaries and like expenses. Exceptions will be made only with the approval of the appropriate supervising council or its executive committee (Conference Leadership Council or the Council on Finance and Administration) as documented in its minutes.

There shall be no carrying forward of budgeted funds from Ministry Shares receipts from one year to the next by any agency or board of the conference without approval of the Council on Finance and Administration. The following exceptions have been approved:
a. A fund of up to $10,000 may be accumulated for transitional activities at the time of a change of bishop, administered by the Episcopacy Committee.
b. A fund of up to $25,000 may be accumulated for maintenance of conference-owned properties, administered by the Board of Trustees.
c. A fund of up to $25,000 may be accumulated for counseling needs, administered by the Conference Treasurer at the direction of the Episcopal Office, for victims of clergy sexual misconduct.
d. A fund of up to $14,000 may be accumulated for district office equipment, to be administered by the Cabinet, and $7,500 for equipment for the Conference Treasurer's office.

H. **Housing/Furnishing Allowance** - An amount of the salaries of the District Superintendents, Director of Connectional Mission and Ministries, Director of Conference Benefits and Human Resources Services, Director of Administrative Services and Conference Treasurer, Director of Communications, Director of Clergy Excellence, Director of Congregational Vibrancy, Associate Directors, assistant to the bishop and director of the United Methodist Foundation (if listed under the appointments) may be designated by that person and approved by CFA as a fair housing/furnishing allowance for Internal Revenue Service Section 107 purposes.

I.   **Conflict of Interest** - Michigan Conference officials, employees and/or members of the various boards and commissions of the conference shall not, during their time of service, receive any compensation or have any financial interest in any contract or in any firm or corporation which provides goods or services (excluding publicly held companies where the official employee or member owns less than 1 percent of the voting stock thereof) or in any contract for the supply of goods or services or the procurement of furnishings or equipment, interest in any construction project of the conference, site procurement by the conference, or any other business whatsoever unless approved in writing in advance by the official's or employee's immediate supervisor and/or the board or commission upon which the member participates after full disclosure of the conflict including the amount of compensation and/or benefit the official, employee, or member will receive.

The term "official" "employee" or "member of the board or commission" shall include the official's, employee's or member's immediate family. Immediate family shall be defined as any person residing with the official, employee or member and their mother, father, and/or sons or daughters.

J.   **Depositories** – Depositories for the funds of Central Treasury shall be determined by the Council of Finance & Administration upon recommendation by the Conference.

K.   **Interest Earnings** – All interest earned on General Funds carried in Central Treasury shall be accumulated in a General Funds Interest Account. (This does not include funds in Central Treasury which are being held for specific purposes and have been designated as Interest Earning Funds by the Council.) At the end of each fiscal year, this General Interest Account shall be transferred and accumulated in the Conference Contingency Fund to be administered by the Council of Finance & Administration.

L.   **Policy on Electronic Mail and Internet Usage.** Conference employees are provided with e-mail and Internet access for the purpose of furthering the business of the Michigan Conference. All computing equipment provided to employees for their use remains the property of the Michigan Conference, and use thereof is subject at any time to monitoring by management without notice.

Use of conference e-mail accounts is limited to business purposes. As such, they may not be used to solicit participation in any non-conference-sponsored activities. Employees who engage in personal use of conference e-mail do so at their own risk and expense. The Michigan Conference will neither assume nor share any responsibility for any harassment, defamation, copyright violation, or other violations of civil or criminal law that may occur as a result of personal and/or inappropriate e-mail use. Responsibility for such incidents shall rest solely with the person who engages in such activities. Employees are prohibited from accessing other employees' files without the express consent of appropriate management personnel. Employees are also prohibited from using conference computer equipment and e-mail accounts to forward chain letters, jokes, or "spam."

Employees are reminded that e-mail communications should be drafted with the same thought and concern that would be devoted to other types of written communications, such as letters or memoranda.

The conference reserves the right at any time and without notice to access and disclose all messages, sent from and received by conference e-mail accounts.

Employee access to the Internet on conference-owned computer equipment is strictly limited to business purposes. Employees are expressly prohibited from accessing any illegal websites. Accessing websites with racist, pornographic, defamatory, sexist, or otherwise offensive content is strictly prohibited. Employees who download copyrighted material in violation of the Copyright Act of 1976, 17 U.S.C. §101, *et seq.*, are reminded that they are subject to federal criminal prosecution. The Michigan Conference will not assume any responsibility for any civil or criminal prosecutions of employees in connection with improper Internet activity, nor will the Detroit Annual Conference bear any portion of any legal fee's employees may incur in connection with such improper activity.

The use of chat rooms with conference-owned computer equipment is strictly prohibited.

Conference employees are urged to exercise caution in opening e-mail attachments from unknown persons due to the risk of computer worms and viruses. Any conference employees who knowingly allow conference computer equipment to become infected by a virus or worm shall be subject to disciplinary action, up to and including immediate termination. Such employees may also be held legally and financially liable for these actions. The Detroit Annual Conference reserves the right to commence civil litigation or to press criminal charges in such circumstances.

Violation of any conference rule regarding e-mail and Internet usage may result in disciplinary action, up to and including immediate discharge from employment.

Special Offerings

The annual conference recommends:

A.   The support of general and conference Advance Specials as particularly approved by the annual conference (see *Jubilee/Spotlight Book*).

B.   The special days designated in the *Discipline* and by the Michigan Conference with offerings for:

1	Human Relations Sunday	January 17, 2021
2.	UMCOR Sunday	March 14, 2021
3.	Native American Sunday	April 18, 2021
4.	Golden Cross Sunday	May 16, 2021
5.	Peace With Justice Sunday	May 30, 2021
6.	Christian Education Sunday	August 22, 2021
7.	Rural Life Sunday	September 12, 2021
8.	World Communion Sunday	October 3, 2021
9.	Disability Awareness Sunday	October 17, 2021
10.	United Methodist Student Sunday	November 28, 2021

Calendar

The following dates are established:

A.   January 11, 2021   Last day for submitting payments to the conference treasurer for credit on the previous conference fiscal year.

B.   January 22, 2021   Deadline for all boards, commissions, committees, and agencies to submit their budget requests for the ensuing conference fiscal year to the Council on Finance and Administration.

C.   January 30, 2021   Last day for receiving pastor's annual report by the conference statistician and treasurer.

SUBJECT: Michigan Conference Budget Recommendation for 2021

MOTION: The Council on Finance & Administration recommends the following:

1. The amount of $12,617,521 shall be the Conference budget for 2021 which is a decrease of 14.17% from prior year.
2. The amount of $3,720,000 shall be the Benefits budget for 2021 which is the same as the prior year.
3. The salary of District Superintendents and Directors shall be $87,394, which is a 0% increase, and the housing allowance will remain at $20,000.
4. There will be no increase in Support Staff wages for 2021.

2021 Michigan Conference Budget

	2019 - Michigan Budget	2020 - Michigan Budget	2021 - Michigan Budget	Increase/ (Decrease)	% Change to 2020
A) Clergy Support Budget					
1) District Superintendents	$ 2,102,743	$ 2,126,446	$ 2,140,803	14,357	0.68%
2) **Episcopal Fund**	$ 562,632	$ 568,025	$ 626,855	58,830	10.36%
3) **Ministerial Education Fund**	$ 641,692	$ 647,843	$ 488,952	(158,891)	-24.53%
4) Episcopal Residence Committee	$ 7,500	$ 7,500	$ 7,500	-	0.00%
5) Equitable Compensation Committee	$ 125,000	$ 120,000	$ 150,000	30,000	25.00%
6) Clergy Advocacy	$ 2,000	$ 2,000	-	(2,000)	-100.00%
7) Abuse Prevention Team	$ 10,500	$ 10,500	-	(10,500)	-100.00%
8) Clergy Moving Expense Fund	$ 350,000	$ 300,000	$ 300,000	-	0.00%
Sub-total Clergy Support Budget	$ 3,802,067	$ 3,782,314	$ 3,714,110	(68,204)	-1.80%
Provision for Unpaid Ministry Shares	$ 601,976	$ 597,042	$ 614,316	17,274	2.89%
Total Clergy Support Budget	**$ 4,404,043**	**$ 4,379,356**	**$ 4,328,426**	**(50,930)**	**-1.16%**
B) Administration Budget					
1) Council on Finance & Administration	$ 2,000	$ 2,000	$ 2,000	-	0.00%
2) Treasurer's Office	$ 684,164	$ 734,900	$ 577,700	(157,200)	-21.39%
3) Jurisdictional Conference	$ 36,723	$ 36,723	$ 36,723	-	0.00%
4) General Conference Delegation	$ 20,000	$ 28,000	$ 8,000	(20,000)	-71.43%
5) **General Church Administration**	$ 225,596	$ 227,758	$ 192,253	(35,505)	-15.59%
6) Area Administration	$ 556,453	$ 556,453	$ 316,703	(239,750)	-43.09%
7) Operations	$ 332,783	$ 312,783	$ 302,783	(10,000)	-3.20%

8) Conference Secretary	$ 18,300	$ 18,300	$ 1,000	(17,300)	-94.54%
9) Conference Statistician	$ 3,600	$ -	$ -	-	0.00%
10) Conference Trustees	$ 1,000	$ 1,000	$ 1,000	-	0.00%
11) Committee on Archives & History	$ 40,586	$ 45,000	$ 40,000	(5,000)	-11.11%
12) Committee on Human Resources	$ 5,000	$ 5,000	$ 5,000	-	0.00%
13) Legal Fees	$ 55,000	$ 55,000	$ 55,000	-	0.00%
14) Contingency Funds	$ 50,000	$ 50,000	$ -	(50,000)	-100.00%
Sub-total Administration Budget	$ 2,031,205	$ 2,072,917	$ 1,538,162	(534,755)	-25.80%
Provision for Unpaid Ministry Shares	$ 343,926	$ 351,459	$ 256,364	(95,095)	-27.06%
Total Administration Budget	**$ 2,375,131**	**$ 2,424,376**	**$ 1,794,526**	**(629,850)**	**-25.98%**

C) Conference Benevolences Budget

1) *Agencies Relating to Christ-Centered Mission and Ministry*

a) Commission on Annual Conference Session	$ 325,000	$ 275,000	$ 100,000	(175,000)	-63.64%
b) Commission on Communications	$ 396,000	$ 427,000	$ 1,000	(426,000)	-99.77%
c) Committee on Journal	$ 11,220	$ 11,220	$ 5,000	(6,220)	-55.44%
d) Board of Justice	$ 15,000	$ 15,000	$ 10,500	(4,500)	-30.00%
e) Board of Global Ministries	$ 210,000	$ 210,000	$ 147,000	(63,000)	-30.00%
f) Engage Program Promotion	$ -	$ -	$ -	-	0.00%

2) *Agencies Relating to Bold and Effective Leaders*

a) Conference Leadership Council	$ 10,000	$ 10,000	$ 5,000	(5,000)	-50.00%
b) Board of Ordained Ministry	$ 95,279	$ 66,500	$ 59,900	(6,600)	-9.92%
c) Committee on Nominations	$ 7,500	$ 7,500	$ 5,000	(2,500)	-33.33%
d) Committee on the Episcopacy	$ 2,000	$ 2,000	$ 2,000	-	0.00%
e) Protection Policy	$ 5,000	$ 5,000	$ 2,000	(3,000)	-60.00%
f) Clergy Excellence Program Funds	$ -	$ 15,000	$ 10,000	(5,000)	-33.33%

3) *Agencies Relating to Vibrant Congregations*

a) United Methodist Men	$ -	$ -	$ -	-	0.00%
b) United Methodist Women	$ -	$ -	$ -	-	0.00%
c) Board of Laity	$ 10,000	$ 10,000	$ 5,000	(5,000)	-50.00%
d) Board of Young People's Ministry	$ 350,000	$ 363,000	$ 254,000	(109,000)	-30.03%
e) Board of Congregational Life	$ 581,000	$ 533,000	$ 373,000	(160,000)	-30.02%
f) Committee on Hispanic/Latino Ministry	$ 39,000	$ 39,000	$ 25,300	(13,700)	-35.13%
g) Committee on Asian-American Ministry	$ 47,000	$ 47,000	$ 30,900	(16,100)	-34.26%
h) Committee on Native American Ministry	$ 115,000	$ 115,000	$ 80,500	(34,500)	-30.00%

CONFERENCE BUDGET

i) Committee on African-American Ministry	$ 66,000	$ 66,000	$ 44,200	(21,800)	-33.03%
j) Racial & Ethnic Local Churches	-	-	-	-	0.00%
4) Administrative Expenses/Compensation	$ 2,147,841	$ 2,172,000	$ 2,645,627	473,627	21.81%
5) World Service Fund	1,899,882	1,918,093	1,561,138	(356,955)	-18.61%
6) Pathways Funding	$ -	$ -	$ -	-	0.00%
7) MI Area Camping	400,000	300,000	100,000	(200,000)	-66.67%
8) Contigency Funds	$ 25,000	$ 25,000	$ -	(25,000)	-100.00%
9) Assets Released from Restrictions	-	-	-	-	0.00%
Sub-total Conference Benevolences Budget	$ 6,757,722	$ 6,632,313	$ 5,467,065	(1,165,248)	-17.57%
Provision for Unpaid Ministry Shares	$ 925,303	$ 897,947	$ 743,986	(153,961)	-17.15%
Total Conference Benevolences Budget	**$ 7,683,025**	**$ 7,530,260**	**$ 6,211,051**	**(1,319,209)**	**-17.52%**
D) Other Apportioned Causes					
1) Black College Fund	$ 255,965	$ 258,419	$ 225,959	(32,460)	-12.56%
2) Africa University Fund	$ 57,284	$ 57,833	$ 50,800	(7,033)	-12.16%
3) Interdenominational Fund	$ 50,185	$ 50,666	$ 6,759	(43,907)	-86.66%
Sub-total Other Apportioned Caused	$ 363,434	$ 366,918	$ 283,518	(83,400)	-22.73%
Provision for Unpaid Ministry Shares	$ -	-	$ -	-	0.00%
Total Other Apportioned Causes	$ 363,434	$ 366,918	$ 283,518	(83,400)	-22.73%
Total Conference Common Budget	**$ 14,825,633**	**$ 14,700,910**	**$ 12,617,521**	**(2,083,389)**	**-14.17%**
E) Benefits Ministry Shares Budget					
1) Pension/Welfare Payments to Wespath	$ 3,128,220	$ 3,020,000	$ 3,020,000	-	0.00%
2) Benefits Office	$ 711,780	$ 700,000	$ 700,000	-	0.00%
Total Benefits Ministry Shares Budget	**$ 3,840,000**	**$ 3,720,000**	**$ 3,720,000**	**-**	**0.00%**

Michigan Conference (160)
2020 Comprehensive Benefit Funding Plan

Conference Benefit Officer (or equivalent)	Donald Emmert	12/19/2019
Conference Treasurer	David Dobbs	12/19/2019
Conference Board of Pension Chair	Steven Buck	12/26/2019
Council on Finance and Administration Chair		

Opinion on **Michigan Conference 2020** Comprehensive Benefit Funding Plan

The funding plan meets the standards for a Pre-82 funding plan as established by Wespath Benefits and Investments and the favorable opinion requirements for a funding plan. Note: The statement above and any written opinion provided by Wespath do not imply any representation as to the ability or probability of the applicable plan sponsor to fulfill the obligations included in the funding plan.

Wespath Benefits and Investments

Wespath Benefits and Investments
1901 W Chestnut Ave
Glenview, IL 60025

2020 MICHIGAN ANNUAL CONFERENCE
IMPLEMENTATION OF RESOLUTIONS

Resolution	Page	Follow up agency/person
R #1 – Authorize CBOPHB Health Insurance Benefits Claims	206	The Michigan Conference Board of Pension & Health Benefits
R #2 – Housing/Rental Allowance for Retired or Clergy on Disability	206	The Michigan Conference Board of Pension & Health Benefits
R #3 – 2021 Comprehensive Benefits Funding Plan	207	The Michigan Conference Board of Pension & Health Benefits
R #4 – Establish Past Service Rate	207	The Michigan Conference Board of Pension & Health Benefits
R #9 – Amend Conference Plan of Organization – Conference Leadership Council Membership	207	Conference Leadership Council Membership
R #10 – Amend Conference Plan of Organization	208	Council on Finance and Administration, Membership
R #11 – Amend Conference Plan of Organization	208	Board of Trustees, Membership
R #23 – Guidelines for Equitable Compensation Team	208	MI Conf. Comm. on Equitable Compensation

2020 RESOLUTIONS

R #1 – Authorization for CBOPHB to address claims

It was resolved by the Michigan Conference:

The Michigan Conference Board of Pension and Health Benefits moves to:

Authorize The Conference Board of Pension and Health Benefits (CBOPHB) to negotiate, compromise, or submit to arbitration any claims for benefits that may arise under the Michigan Conference Health Care Plan, the Michigan Conference Lay Employee Welfare Plan (death and disability), the United Methodist Retirement Plans (Pre-82, Ministerial Pension Plan, Clergy Retirement Security Program, United Methodist Personal Investment Plan), the United Methodist Clergy Welfare Plan (Comprehensive Protection Plan); and for that purpose to retain legal counsel as needed. The CBOPHB will be considered the final appeal and have final authority to decide any issue in the event of a dispute or disagreement by a participant.

R #2 – Establish the Housing/Rental allowance for retired clergy or clergy on medical leave

It was resolved by the Michigan Conference:

The Michigan Conference Board of Pension and Health Benefits moves to establish the Housing/Rental Allowance for retired or clergy on medical leave status (receiving disability benefits) in the Michigan Conference as follows:

1. An amount equal to 100% of the pension/disability payments received during the year 2021 is hereby designated as a rental/housing allowance for each retired and disabled ordained or licensed minister of The United Methodist Church who is or was a member of the Michigan Conference at the time of his or her retirement or disability;
2. This rental/housing allowance shall apply to each retired and disabled ordained or licensed minister who has been granted the retired relationship or placed on medical leave by the Michigan Conference and whose name and relationship to the conference is recorded in the Journal of the Michigan Conference or in other appropriate records maintained by the conference;
3. The pension/disability payment to which this rental/housing allowance applies shall be the pension/disability payment resulting from all service of such retired and disabled ordained or licensed ministers from all employment by any local church, annual conference or institution of The United Methodist Church, or from any other employer who employed the minister to perform services related to the ministry and who elected to make contributions to the pension and welfare funds of The United Methodist Church for such retired minister's pension or disability benefits;
4. The amount of the housing/rental allowance that may be excluded is limited to the lesser of: a) the amount designated as the housing/rental allowance, or b) the amount actually expended for housing/rent, or c) the fair rental value of housing, if required by law.

R #3 – 2020 Comprehensive Benefit Funding Plan

It was resolved by the Michigan Conference:

The Michigan Conference Board of Pension and Health Benefits moves to authorize the Conference Board of Pension and Health Benefits to review and approve the 2021 Comprehensive Benefit Funding Plan (CBFP) upon successful completion of the CBFP and receipt of a favorable "letter of opinion" from Wespath Benefits & Investments.

[NOTE: Due to Wespath's timeline, their review and "letter of opinion" cannot be completed by the conference deadline for submitting resolutions. The "letter of opinion" will be available online and in the final printed materials once it is received from Wespath.]

R #4 – Establish Past Service Rate

It was resolved by the Michigan Conference:

The Michigan Conference Board of Pension and Health Benefits moves to establish the 2021 Past Service Rate (PSR) for the Ministers' Reserve Pension Fund (Pre-82) at $860. The surviving spouse benefit shall remain at 85 percent.

R #0 – Amend Conference Plan of Organization

It was resolved by the Michigan Conference:

Amend the Plan of Organization of the Michigan Conference, Section 2.1.3.2, "Conference Leadership Council Membership, Ex officio with voice and vote" by adding:

2.1.3.2.5 Chair of the Conference Board of Trustees or their designee

2.1.3.2.6 Chair of the Conference Human Resources Committee or their designee

2.1.3.2.7 Chair of the Conference Board of Pension and Benefits or their designee

R #10 – Amend the Plan of Organization of the Michigan Conference

It was resolved by the Michigan Conference:

Amend the Plan of Organization of the Michigan Conference, Section 4.1.3.3, "Council on Finance and Administration, Membership, Ex officio with voice only", by adding:

4.1.3.3.8 Chair of the Board of Trustees or their designee

R #11 – Amend Conference Plan of Organization

It was resolved by the Michigan Conference:

Amend the Plan of Organization of the Michigan Conference, Section 4.4.3.3, "Board of Trustees, Membership, Ex officio with voice, but not vote," by adding:

4.4.3.3.3 President of the Council on Finance and Administration, or their designee

R #23 – Guidelines for Equitable Compensation Support

It was resolved by the Michigan Conference:

The Commission on Equitable Compensation moves the Conference Guidelines for Equitable Compensation Support for 2021.

1. Local congregations shall conduct an annual stewardship campaign. Congregations receiving Equitable Compensation support are expected to participate in ongoing stewardship education and planning through programs such as the Stewardship Academy offered through the United Methodist Foundation of Michigan, Roads to Vibrancy or Local Church Assessment, as provided in ¶213 of the United Methodist Book of Discipline.
2. Local congregations receiving Equitable Compensation grants shall annually counsel with the District Superintendent (DS) concerning levels of pastoral support. Completed applications are to be submitted to the DS for approval.
3. Local congregations requesting equitable compensation support shall voucher pastors' travel and business expenses according to the guidelines of the Council on Finance and Administration.
4. Local congregations may receive Equitable Compensation support for up to four consecutive years, reducing the original grant amount by 25% each year. Equitable Compensation funds shall not be used to fund more than the Conference minimum salary.
5. Congregations receiving Equitable Compensation are encouraged to show progress in full payment of ministry shares.
6. Churches receiving or applying for Equitable Compensation that have planned or are planning to enter into building or remodeling projects that require permission of the District Board of Church Location and Building, or which exceed 10% of the total annual budget of the local congregation, shall not proceed with proposed projects and/or related capital campaigns until such time as a

plan for ending Equitable Compensation support has been presented and approved by the Commission on Equitable Compensation and the district superintendent. Exceptions to this guideline shall be given greater consideration when proposed projects are related to building accessibility.
7. Exceptions to these guidelines may be considered upon recommendation of the Bishop and the Cabinet.

	Local Pastor		Associate Member		Provisional Member		Full Member			Increase
Years	2020	2021	2020	2021	2020	2021	2020	2021		1.60%
1	$37,394	$37,992	*	*	$41,730	$42,397	**	**		
2	$37,768	$38,372	*	*	$42,145	$42,819	**	**		
3	$38,143	$38,753	*	*	$42,562	$43,243	$44,526	$45,238		
4	$38,516	$39,132	*	*	$42,981	$43,668	$44,980	$45,700		
5	$38,891	$39,514	$40,646	$41,296	$43,397	$44,091	$45,431	$46,158		
6	$39,267	$39,895	$41,049	$41,706	$43,813	$44,514	$45,879	$46,613		
7	$39,640	$40,274	$41,453	$42,116	$44,230	$44,937	$46,286	$47,026		
8	$40,014	$40,654	$41,861	$42,531	$44,648	$45,362	$46,779	$47,528		
9	$40,389	$41,035	$42,274	$42,951	$45,065	$45,787	$47,232	$47,988		
10	$40,763	$41,415	$43,652	$44,350	$45,483	$46,211	$47,684	$48,447		
			Recommended	(Years	11-40)					
11	$41,578	$42,244	$44,525	$45,237	$46,393	$47,135	$48,638	$49,416		
12	$42,395	$43,073	$45,399	$46,125	$47,302	$48,059	$49,592	$50,385		
13	$43,210	$43,901	$46,272	$47,013	$48,213	$48,985	$50,546	$51,354		
14	$44,026	$44,731	$47,145	$47,899	$49,123	$49,909	$51,500	$52,324		
15	$44,841	$45,559	$48,019	$48,787	$50,033	$50,833	$52,455	$53,294		
16	$45,658	$46,388	$48,893	$49,675	$50,944	$51,759	$53,409	$54,263		
17	$46,473	$47,216	$49,765	$50,562	$51,853	$52,683	$54,363	$55,232		
18	$47,289	$48,046	$50,639	$51,450	$52,763	$53,607	$55,317	$56,202		
19	$48,105	$48,875	$51,513	$52,337	$53,674	$54,533	$56,271	$57,171		
20	$48,920	$49,703	$52,386	$53,224	$54,584	$55,457	$57,226	$58,141		
21	$49,737	$50,532	$53,260	$54,112	$55,493	$56,381	$58,180	$59,111		
22	$50,552	$51,361	$54,133	$55,000	$56,404	$57,307	$59,134	$60,080		
23	$51,368	$52,190	$55,006	$55,886	$57,314	$58,231	$60,088	$61,049		
24	$52,183	$53,018	$55,880	$56,774	$58,225	$59,156	$61,042	$62,018		
25	$53,000	$53,848	$56,754	$57,662	$59,135	$60,081	$61,997	$62,989		
26	$53,815	$54,676	$57,627	$58,549	$60,044	$61,005	$62,951	$63,958		
27	$54,631	$55,505	$58,500	$59,436	$60,955	$61,931	$63,905	$64,927		
28	$55,447	$56,334	$59,373	$60,323	$61,865	$62,855	$64,859	$65,896		
29	$56,262	$57,163	$60,247	$61,211	$62,775	$63,779	$65,813	$66,866		
30	$57,079	$57,992	$61,121	$62,099	$63,686	$64,705	$66,768	$67,836		
31	$57,894	$58,820	$61,994	$62,985	$64,595	$65,629	$67,722	$68,805		
32	$58,710	$59,649	$62,867	$63,873	$65,505	$66,553	$68,676	$69,774		
33	$59,525	$60,478	$63,741	$64,761	$66,416	$67,479	$69,630	$70,744		
34	$60,342	$61,307	$64,614	$65,648	$67,326	$68,403	$70,584	$71,713		
35	$61,158	$62,136	$65,488	$66,536	$68,237	$69,328	$71,539	$72,683		
36	$61,973	$62,965	$66,362	$67,423	$69,146	$70,253	$72,493	$73,652		
37	$62,789	$63,794	$67,234	$68,310	$70,056	$71,177	$73,446	$74,622		
38	$63,604	$64,622	$68,108	$69,198	$70,967	$72,102	$74,400	$75,591		
39	$64,421	$65,451	$68,982	$70,086	$71,877	$73,027	$75,354	$76,560		
40	$65,236	$66,280	$69,855	$70,972	$72,787	$73,951	$76,309	$77,530		

CABINET DEAN'S REPORT

Dear Bishop Bard, the Appointive Cabinet and Michigan Annual Conference, Grace and Peace in the name of Jesus Christ!

It has been my honor and pleasure to be the Dean of the Appointive Cabinet this past year. Thank you, Bishop, for this opportunity! Also, thank you Appointive Cabinet for your support.

I must say, however, "what a year it has turned out to be!" As we entered our second year as the Michigan Conference, we left the 2019 Michigan Annual Conference with mixed emotions regarding the actions of the conference and the uncertainty of the next General Conference around the issues of inclusivity of the LGBTQI community. Personally, I wondered how this would affect the work of the local church, and I prayed fervently that God's peace and love would permeate the conference, so that we could focus on the work of being the Christian Church for the people in our community and out into the world.

By fall, some of the churches of the conference were laying out plans to begin their participation in the Local Church Assessment and Church Unique, while there were others who were continuing to be vital churches as they implemented ways in which to reach their community, to welcome new people into the life of the church through their learned experience with Vital Church Initiative. Our congregational excellence director and associate directors were busy. The Local Church Assessments led some churches to begin conversations regarding how they might be able to work together on missions and ministry, while others began conversations on how a merger might allow them to be healthier and more vital in their work of making disciples of Jesus Christ for the transformation of the world.

As charge conference season ended, many churches from Northern Skies District to Greater Southwest District were providing food pantries and clothing stores; and churches from Mid-Michigan District to Central Bay District to East Winds District were opening free stores, and tutoring programs for children; while Northern Waters District to Heritage District provided free meals, and English as a Second Language tutoring was offered; and from Midwest District to Greater Detroit District church home repair and feeding their neighbors with community gardens. Many of these missions were shared among several congregations. Issues that divided churches theologically did not keep God's work from happening, nor did it stop the love that God showed the world through his son Jesus the Christ. The winter was full of promise and hope and many churches were implementing or continuing their practice of vital welcome, worship and mission. While others, remembering what it means to be a connectional denomination, began working together in their communities.

As things were moving forward, we received word of a virus that was beginning to cause concern in our nation. Soon, the virus began to hit some areas of our state very hard. It wasn't long before the church doors were closed, for the safety of all. BUT through hard work and the grace of God, the church did not close! Instead pastors, staff, and laity worked together to find ways of offering daily devotions, and meaningful worship on Sunday morning. It was the church being the church working together and taking the word of God through Christ to the nation. Yes, it was a struggle at first, but with webinars provided by conference directors, associate directors and coordinators allowing laity, clergy and staff to became more proficient with their ability to Facebook live stream, to record messages and upload to YouTube, and to provide phone conference calls while teaching their members how to use these technologies. Most individuals became aware of the word Zoom. Churches set up zoom coffee hours, prayer groups, Bible study, children's ministry, youth groups and meetings for church business. It was amazing to see how creative the churches became. Laity joined their pastor and staff and began checking on their shut-ins to see if there were needs they could meet. In addition to this the laity began reaching further out into the community, offering to pick up food and medication for all who could not go out. The church was the church into the world! It was exciting to hear how the churches were meeting the needs of those around them while working together to offer worship in a format that fit their community's need. For some, worries over attendance were relieved when responses to Sunday morning worship came in from the congregation and from people outside of the congregation! Members invited family, friends and neighbors to worship with them, while others connected on their own. God's message was being amplified by online worship! Monies were a worry and yet in many churches the members were faithful in their tithing, allowing the work of the church to strongly continue. God provided! God was faithful! Church is alive and well as each congregation determines the needs of their community to return to in-person worship. The lesson was learned well, that the church can no longer close its doors on Sunday morning at the start of worship, as if all who want to be there are present. Now we know that we must continue online worship for those who, for whatever reason, cannot be present in worship with us in the pews! We have learned and continue to learn more, but we know that God is faithful! Even when the days are dark, and the future is uncertain. God walks with us.

Then, as summer began, the news of a horrific death came across our newsfeed. We were able to watch video of George Floyd dying before our eyes. Through George Floyd's death we are reawakened to the racism that exists in our nation. Over the next weeks, we continued to learn of other black lives lost, while the action was being hidden by those involved. However, the news spread, and we watched and learned of many an innocent black life being senselessly ended! The nation responded. Black Lives Matter protests took place around the nation, around the state, in our communities. Congregations and pastors joined together to raise our voices to yet another challenge for the people of God. The Christian church works to be a people of justice for all of God's people. Jesus set the example of all are welcome at God's table, regardless of their race or skin color. A wound was opened, our eyes were opened, that even though we have made progress there is still much more work to be done. The work of dismantling racism, the work of being an anti-racist white person, needs to be active in the life of our churches. As the Michigan Conference of The United Methodist Church, we must continue to do our own work as well as work together and raise our voices sharing the voice of Jesus to the nation that racism is not a part of God's kingdom!

I leave you with these words shared in Acts 2:42-47: The believers devoted themselves to the apostles' teaching, to the community, to their shared meals, and to their prayers. A sense of awe came over everyone. God performed many wonders and signs through the apostles. All the believers were united and shared everything. They would sell pieces of property and possessions and distribute the proceeds to everyone who needed them. ...they met together in the temple and shared food with gladness and simplicity. They praised God and demonstrated God's goodness to everyone!

Church, this is our work! Thanks be to God!

Elizabeth A. Hill, Dean of the Cabinet
Michigan Conference

— MAC Photos

CONFERENCE LAY LEADERS' ADDRESS

Thanks, John. Thank you, Bishop.

I would like to thank each of the members of the Board of Laity. This has been quite a year. Their work has been above and beyond their original remit! We sit down together – District Lay Leaders, UMW President, Lay Servants and UMM – and try and make sense of things on the districts and from the conference. That sense has changed across the year. The catch phrase at each meeting has been, "Guess what." Thank you all for making things work. I think this is called "adapting." What ever it is, thanks for your flexibility.

The church – when you get down to it – is 98% laity! We have pastors, we have district superintendents, we have committees. Methodists have a system for everything. We've taken some ribbing for that over the years. But those systems can and sometimes do work. When you get right down to it, making disciples is making one-to-one connections. How is it with your soul? The spirit of love flows through the touch, one person to another. And don't we know that now!

To be a disciple, John Wesley's General Rule calls for private acts of mercy – flood buckets, how to use ZOOM, bringing a casserole, and making a phone call. Each disciple is called to private action. It might be sharing conversation. It might be sharing a chain saw. As disciples we have gifts and skills to share. As laity, we each have a toolbox. Sometimes with some pretty interesting tools inside. Praise the Lord of double entry bookkeeping – among other tools.

Discipleship does not stop with our private acts.

Wesley calls for public acts of justice. How is it with our community? And guess what? We have some challenges. Virus lock down, social distance in the hardware store, old fault lines of inequality and racism exposed. How is our community? And the answer comes back, "a little tattered" "I hope it holds together!" "We need some changes here." Do we have a toolbox, a tool shed, hardware store for all this?

The author William Least Heat Moon wrote a book called, "Blue Highways," in praise of those two-lane highways usually blue on the map. Traffic flows both ways, lots of stops and local attractions. You don't save much time on M-46 or 115, US 2 across the UP or US 12 downstate. Those blue highways and local roads spread out to every corner and every driveway. Traffic in both directions.

And at those driveways (or apartment lobbies or nursing home entrances) – the hardest, most expensive connection in communications is the last mile. Post your number on a billboard – will they call? Dig a cable, will it make it to the house. Give an iPad, can they use it? Last mile barriers, building a network takes time and tools. This moves at "walk speed" not warp speed.

Jesus walked. He was a blue highways man. He was always stopping to talk with the likes of Zacchaeus who may have been a "wee little man" but Jesus saw him in his tree. He saw the woman at the well in detail. He didn't send a mass mailing or a tweet.

Jesus calls us to be disciples and to make disciples in the same slow manner. No short cuts and lots of labor. Even fishers of men don't catch on every cast.

Disciples need worship – private prayer and public worship. We trust in this grace and we need this lifegiving renewal. But the last mile is still there and calling. As you listen to a sermon or connect with Facebook Live with a thumbs-up, there is still the "making" to do. Church is a verb and "making" has come to include mending and patching and reweaving community fabric as well.

Tip O'Neil, speaker of the house way before Nancy Pelosi, famously said, "All politics is local." Almost right. For disciples, all church is local. The transformation of the world begins with the making of disciples. With the one-on-one connections. With last mile of connection. With the messages of love and concern, hope and joy that travel on these two lanes of connection. That's the work of it.

Guess what? We have some changes coming. I do not know "what's next," only that we have the tools, we have the charge, quite literally have the charge, spark of energy, of insight and power to bring light and hope and even comfort. Although you don't want to be too comfortable, as we have also learned in the last year.

We give thanks for this year past and a message of hope for the year ahead. John and I were privileged to light the new conference candle last year. It is burning today, brighter perhaps as the world has grown darker. So, we say – go forth in confidence. And keep your tool kit with you.

Anne Soles and John Wharton,
Conference Lay Leaders

— MAC Photos

CFA REPORT TO ANNUAL CONFERENCE
July 27, 2020

Good Day, Conference! I'm Brad Bartelmay, the President of the Council on Finance and Administration. Over the next few minutes I would like to give you a brief overview of the state of the conference's financial well-being.

Before I do, I want to begin with a few words of thanks. As you may be aware, Conference Treasurer David Dobbs resigned late last February to pursue a new career in the nonprofit sector with an organization in Arizona. David faithfully stewarded the finances of the Detroit Conference prior to the establishment of the new Michigan Conference. He played a critical role in setting up the financial structures of our conference. We wish David and his family well in their new life in Arizona, though if you are watching, David, there are some in the annual conference who question your choice of moving to the city of "Buckeye" – not me though.

A bit later today, I will be updating you on the search for a new chief financial officer.

I want to thank the Treasury Staff for their hard work on behalf of the conference throughout the year, and particularly since David left. Your tireless efforts in the ministry of administration are essential in creating the foundation for all other conference ministries. We have had two retirements in the treasurer's office: Operations Manager, Becky Emmert and Accounts Payable Officer Nancy Wyllys. We are grateful for their service, as we are grateful for the new additions to the team: Kim Kemmis in accounts payable, Kriss Salters as an administrative assistant and Pamela Stewart as our Statistician and Database Manager.

I want to offer special thanks to Benton Heisler who each year plays a pivotal role in creating the conference budget and who was especially helpful this year.

I also want to thank Don Emmert who has helped manage the treasurer's office during this transition period. He has taken on this task in addition to his responsibilities as Director of Benefits and Human Resources. Don, your generous gift of time and service has been remarkable and on behalf of the Council on Finance and Administration, and the whole conference, I offer our deepest appreciation and thanks.

Finally, I want to thank the members of the Council on Finance and Administration for their efforts on behalf of the conference in the ministry of generosity. These servants are working hard and making difficult decisions on your behalf during these challenging times.

In his book, "Canoeing the Mountains," Tod Bolsinger quotes Ronald Heifetz and Marty Linsky about one key element of adaptive leadership: "Leadership is disappointing your own people at a rate they can absorb." My report today shares disappointing news – there is no way to soft pedal the financial challenges we are facing. Yet, as we absorb this difficult news we can, and are, choosing to take steps to address these trials.

The central challenge we face concerns remittance of Ministry Shares. Each congregation is called to pay a proportional share of the conference and general church budget – its Ministry Share. Unfortunately, payment of Ministry Shares is weakening each year. In 2018 the churches of our conference remitted approximately $11.4 million for the ministries of the conference and the general church. In 2019 the amount shrank by over $800,000. In response, reductions of 15% were put in place for all conference ministries.

2020, with the outbreak of COVID-19, has seen Ministry Shares pay-in decline dramatically. At the end of May, payment of Ministry Shares is 23.1% behind where it was on the same date last year. While the Trustees have applied for, and the conference has received, a Paycheck Protection Loan, the amount, even if all of it is forgiven, will not be sufficient to address the deficiency in Ministry Share remittances. Consequently, the 15% reduction has grown to 30% in many areas of the budget. We will be presenting, later in this annual conference, a 2021 Budget which is significantly smaller than the 2020 Budget.

The Council on Finance and Administration is also examining the process by which the conference creates its budget. Our goal is to outline procedures where we begin by setting realistic expectations for income, and then budget within those expectations – much the same way you would when creating a household budget. As the Council on Finance and Administration enters into this task, we will work hand-in-hand with the Conference Leadership Council that interprets the overall direction of conference ministries based on the actions taken by you, the Annual Conference.

When Ministry Shares go unpaid, ministries both here in Michigan and globally go unfunded or underfunded. As a pastor serving a local church, I am fully aware of the challenges churches are facing. Our culture is shifting and growing more secular. Worship attendance is declining (In our conference it declined by 5% in 2018 alone.).

The COVID-19 outbreak has brought new trials upon our churches. Seemingly overnight, we have had to learn new skills, we have attempted to make plans adjusting to the new realities, only to see them change again and again as the outbreak expanded. But, we are now in a moment when Michigan is beginning to open up. Churches are relaunching. As you begin to gather again, I implore you to remember your commitment to the ministries of the Michigan Conference and The United Methodist Church.

I am also asking each district superintendent to highlight at church conferences this fall the amount in Ministry Shares each congregation has remitted to date and to specifically work with each congregation struggling with remittances to create plans wherein efforts are redoubled in addressing Ministry Shares. Absent a renewed commitment to Ministry Shares the conference will need to take dramatic steps which will fundamentally alter and contract the way we do ministry.

In addition to the overall decline in Ministry Shares payment, the number of churches who do not pay their shares in full remains very high. Only 58% of churches remitted their ministry shares in full in 2018 and 59% paid in full in 2019. In other words, over 40% of our churches do not remit their full share. Furthermore, churches who are remitting their Ministry Shares in full are actually paying a premium that helps partially fund the underpayment of others.

In response to these uneven Ministry Share remittances, the Council on Finance and Administration is establishing a task force which will be examining the formula for calculating ministry shares. This team, which will be made up of CFA members as well as outside lay and clergy representatives, will examine the challenges we are facing in getting our churches to remit their Ministry Shares. It will explore the practices of conferences which achieve high pay-in rates, and it will report back to you at the next annual conference with specific recommendations on realigning the Ministry Share formula so as to create greater buy-in from all our churches and to improve the overall pay-in rate.

We have no illusion that every church will pay its full share every year. There will always be unforeseeable events which will cause short-term deficiencies in remittances, but a situation where this chronically occurs is simply not just, and it must be addressed.

If you have questions about Ministry Shares or about this task force, please feel free to contact me through the treasurer's office.

Undoubtedly, this has been a disappointing report to receive. I hope and pray it has not been overwhelmingly so. We face difficult challenges, we live in challenging times, but our current challenges need not define our future. One of my favorite quotes comes from Abraham Lincoln, who, as he was drafting the Emancipation Proclamation, foreshadowed this liberating act in these words which he wrote in his annual message to Congress:

"The dogmas of the quiet past, are inadequate to the stormy present. The occasion is piled high with difficulty, and we must rise – with the occasion. As our case is new, so we must think anew, and act anew."

In this stormy present let us remember that we are Wesleyans who believe in free will. We can choose to think anew, we can choose to act anew and rise to the occasion. We can choose to act faithfully in our mission and ministry and in our generosity as we support the furtherance of God's reign through the Michigan Conference and The United Methodist Church.

Thank you.

Brad Bartelmay, President
Council on Finance and Administration

STATE OF THE CHURCH

— MAC Photos

MEMOIRS

Clergy

JOHN L. ANDREWS – Born February 3, 1929, Rev. Andrews served: 1951 Blanchard; 1955 Riverdale; 1960 Oshtemo; 1962 Coloma; 1968 Jackson: Calvary; 1972 Big Rapids: First; 8/16/80 Grand Traverse District Superintendent; 1986 Grandville; 1989 Marshall; 1992 Retired. Died January 20, 2020.

John Leon ("Lee") Andrews was born February 3, 1929, in Superior, Wisconsin, and died at home in Grand Rapids, Michigan, on January 20, 2020. His ministry spanned 42 years in the West Michigan Conference. He completed a Master of Divinity degree at Garrett-Evangelical School of Theology and was ordained a full Elder of the West Michigan Conference in 1960. He also served as District Superintendent for the Grand Traverse District (1980-1986). He served churches in Blanchard, Riverdale and Elwell, Oshtemo, Coloma, Jackson Calvary, Big Rapids, Grandville, and Marshall prior to his retirement in 1992. He and his wife Arlene retired to a home he built on Lake Louise and later moved to Clark Retirement Community. He is survived by his wife of 70 years, Arlene and four sons.

THERON E. BAILEY – Born November 2, 1928. Rev. Bailey served: 1955 Kewadin; 1957 Union City; 1964 Ogdensburg/Wesley Foundation; 1966 Hart/Mears; 12/15/1969 Wyoming: Wesley Park; 9/1/1977 Sabbatical Leave; 8/1/1978 Empire (interim); 9/15/1978 Lansing: First; 3/1/1982 Conf Staff Program Coordinator; 1989 Grand Rapids: St. Paul's; 1994 Retired. Died November 17, 2019.

Ted held several jobs before entering ministry including grease monkey at his father's gas station, a factory job at Eaton Manufacturing and driving a laundry truck. He met and married Evelyn Dolph, and they attended Urbandale UMC. Rev. Lester Bailey (no relation) asked Ted to help with worship and urged him to enter ministry.

Although never having preached a sermon, he accepted his first appointment to three churches, while a full-time student at Northwestern Community College in Traverse City.

Ted was a member of the first graduating class at MTSO (1963). During his ministry, he and Evelyn led many marriage enrichment classes.

A man of deep faith, Ted loved ministering to and touching the lives of those he served.

ALFRED T. BAMSEY – Born May 18, 1936. Rev. Dr. Bamsey served for 39 years: 1961 Grosse Pointe (assoc.); 1964 Detroit: Bethany; 1969 Troy: First; 1976 Detroit West District Superintendent; 1982 Conference Program Director; 1990 Ann Arbor: First 2000 Retired. Died in the early morning of November 26, 2019.

Al is survived by wife, Karen, sons Scott and Craig and deeply loved step-children, Will MacFarland and Amy Heikkila. His wit, wisdom, and deep thinking as a man of God and his influence upon this conference, its clergy, and its churches will not be soon forgotten. Well done, good and faithful servant.

RALPH T. BARTELD – Born October 24, 1930. Rev. Barteld served: 1958 Lakeville; 1966 Forrester; 1966 Essex, Mt. Olive (Ohio); 1970 Mayville, Silverwood, Fostoria; 2/1979 Cheboygan; 1985 Escanaba: Central; 1991 Marysville; 1979 Retired. Died October 19, 2019.

Reverend Ralph T. Barteld, 88, of Marysville, died Saturday, October 19, 2019. He was born October 24, 1930 in Bay City to the late Fred and Cora Barteld. He married the love of his life, Diane A. Lockwood on November 24, 1951 in Detroit. She preceded him in death on March 8, 2012.

Ralph wore many "hats" throughout his life which included husband, father, grandfather, son, brother, uncle, minister in the United Methodist Church, Michigan State Police Chaplain, director of Michigan Christian Ashram, dean of Church Camps and member of many boards and committees. In Ralph's own words, preaching, teaching and calling on people, were his favorite pastoral duties. Retiring in June 1997 from full-time ministry, Ralph continued to preach at two churches in a part-time capacity.

Psalm 127 says that children are a reward from God and "Blessed is the man whose quiver is full of them." Ralph and his wife Diane took this scripture to heart as they had eleven children of their own. They had one very busy household!

Throughout Ralph's life, he had a love for trains, classical music, travel and the beaches of our Great Lakes. His top priority was always that of serving our Heavenly Father.

ROBERT H. BOUGH – Born November 23, 1934. Rev. Bough served: 1965 Westfield (Ohio); 1967 Pontiac: Covert; 1968 Vassar; 1972 Madison Heights; 1976 Honorable Location; 2004 Honorable Location Retired. Died May 13, 2019.

Bob graduated from MSU in May 1958 and in June married his soulmate Carolyn. He worked for the Detroit Alcohol & Tobacco Commission and shortly after Bob and Carolyn began seminary. Upon graduation in 1967, he headed to Pontiac, pastoring his first church. Then to the next church in Vassar, and then to Madison Heights. In the early 70's Bob took a counseling position at Henry Ford Hospital in Detroit for Alcohol and Drug Abuse. In 1981 he helped open Henry Ford Maple Grove Center in West Bloomfield, a substance abuse facility. He later decided his clients needed more time than what was being given, and he left MapleGrove to begin his own private practice along with assisting with Samaritan Counseling Center at Nardin Park UMC in Farmington Hills. He was very proud of his wife Carolyn, and his daughters Cynthia and Kathryn. Family time was most enjoyed on the lakes of Michigan, sailing, water-skiing, and picnics.

KENNETH J. BREMER – Born September 10, 2953. Rev. Bremer served: 06/01/92 Holton; 2006 St Johns: Pilgrim; 2014 Rockford; 2017 Retired. Died April 3, 2020.

Pastor Kenneth "Ken" John Bremer, age 66, died on Friday, April 3, 2020, in Grand Rapids, Michigan, after fighting a six- year battle with prostate cancer.

Ken was born on September 10, 1953, in Hastings, MI, to Tom and Lois Bremer. He was raised in Middleville, Michigan, and graduated from Thornapple Kellogg

High School in 1971. Ken trained to be an electrician and worked in the skilled trades division of GM. When he was called to a second career as a pastor in The United Methodist Church, he moved his family to Wilmore, Kentucky to attend Asbury College and Theological Seminary. Returning to Michigan, he faithfully served congregations in Holton, St. Johns, and Rockford.

Ken will be remembered for his love of the Lord, his fondness for the outdoors, and his investment in the lives of his family and those he served.

Ken will be sadly missed by his wife of 46 years, Vicky Bremer, their three children, 10 grandchildren, and two great-grandchildren.

RICHARD C. CHEATHAM – Born May 24, 1934. Rev. Dr. Cheatham served: 1961 Napoleon; 1967 Ann Arbor: Glacier Way; 5/1974 Detroit: St. James; 1977 Brighton; 1988 Franklin: Community; 7/31/1998 Retired. Died November 30, 2019.

Reverend Dr. Richard C. ("Dick") Cheatham was a multitalented man loved by many. Born May 24, 1930 in Detroit, he lived an abundant life filled with his faith, family and friends. He gave freely to others, championed the CROP Walk, volunteered on mission trips and devoted his time to working with incarcerated juveniles. He lived his life based on The Beatitudes.

In 1967 he and his wife Diane moved to Ann Arbor where he began a church in his home and launched Glacier Way UMC. He received a double doctorate in Sacred Theology from Garrett Theological Seminary and Northwestern University and authored seven books. Dick retired in 1998 and moved to San Antonio, Texas, where he was an associate pastor for 12 years at University UMC. Dick's other passion was playing "Clara" his clarinet in jazz groups and the church orchestra.

Wife Diane (Schleicher) who has shared in his mission for 68 years survives him along with their three daughters, seven grandchildren, and several nieces and nephews.

DAVID A CHEYNE – He was born December 7, 1942 in Grand Rapids, Michigan. Rev. Cheyne served: 1972 Mulliken; 1975 Sand Lake/South Ensley; 1977 Hersey/Grant Center; 1982 Alden/Central Lake; 1991 Webberville; 1995 Hillside; 1998 Three Oaks; 01/16/99 Baldwin: Covenant Community/Luther; 1999 Pine River Parish: Leroy/Ashton; 2003 Sodus: Chapel Hill; 2005 Retired. He died April 11, 2020.

David, received his undergraduate degree from Owosso College and his Master of Divinity from Asbury Theological Seminary in Wilmore, Kentucky. As a pastor, he led many to Christ serving in Michigan churches starting at Newberry Wesleyan and then at United Methodist churches. He retired in 2005. David was also an emergency medical technician and a volunteer firefighter in Hersey, Alden and Webberville, Michigan.

After retirement, he frequented his grandson's band, choir and sporting events. He took up oil painting. He attended performances at the Lansing Symphony Orchestra, Michigan State University jazz students, and Jazz Tuesdays at Moriarty's Pub. He was a founding member of the Jazz Alliance of Mid-Michigan.

David was known as a kind and generous person who loved visiting with everyone he met. He is survived by his children, grandchildren and his former wife Paulette Cheyne.

O. WILLIAM COOPER, JR. – Born May 31, 1929. Rev. Dr. Cooper served: 1961 Ypsilanti: First; 1965 Manchester; 1969 Manchester: Sharon; 1970 Elkton; 1974 Port Huron: First; 1979 Warren: First; 1985 Saginaw: Ames. 1989 Retired. Died November 11, 2019.

The Reverend Dr. Oscar William (Bill) Cooper, Jr passed away on November 11, 2019 at his home in Fort Collins, Colorado. He was born on May 24, 1939. In June 1953 he married Ruth Zimmermann. She survives him along with his brother, Dr. Terrence Cooper (Dr. Martha) and his sister, Corliss Mick (Rodney), his two children, Dr. Ruth Mannschreck (The Reverend Dr. Jack) and Kiel Cooper (Tauna), six grandchildren, and two great grandchildren.

Bill was an insatiable student. He received a Bachelor of Theology from Nyack College, a Bachelor of Art from Wayne State University, a Master of Divinity from Biblical Seminary in New York City and his Doctor of Ministries from Asbury Theological Seminary.

He served the following churches: Ypsilanti: St. Matthew's, Manchester/Sharon, Elkton, Port Huron: First, Warren: First, and Saginaw: Ames. After his retirement, ministry took an international turn. He served seminaries in six different countries: Ukraine, Moscow, India, Indonesia, Kazakhstan, and Haiti. In Haiti he started and built the Emmaus Biblical Seminary.

The scripture that would best describe Bill is Jeremiah 15:16 "Your words came to me and I ate them, and your words became a joy and the delight of my heart." To this he would say, "Amen!"

BRUCE M. DENTON – October 12, 1950. Rev. Denton served: 1975 Iron River; 1978 Harrisville, Lincoln; 1983 West Branch; 4/15/88 Birmingham: First (assoc.); 1995 Flushing; 2004 Lake Orion; 2012 Retired. Died May 5, 2019.

Bruce grew up in Livonia St Matthews Church and was a graduate of Adrian College and Garrett-ETS. He married his high school sweetheart, Jeannine Churchill, daughter of Rev Ralph & Jean Churchill. He loved music, computers, travel, humor and had a heart for people which served him well in ministry.

He was a loving grandson, son, brother, husband, father and grandpa in addition to his ministry to his church families, District and Conference. He sought to live daily by his faith and to leave each place better than he found it. In his ten-year battle with rare neuroendocrine cancer he sought out experts in the field and advocated for himself and others. A clinical trial he participated in resulted in a new treatment being available in the U.S. to give others hope.

"A man leaves all kinds of footprints when he walks through life." –Margaret Lee Runbeck

MEMOIRS

GEORGE W. FLEMING – Born September 14, 1939. Rev. Fleming served: 1965 Turk Lake/Greenville; 08/01/1975 Sodus: Chapel Hill; 1987 Charlotte; 2002 Retired. Died April 16, 2020.

George Fleming was born September 14, 1939, in South Haven. George was active with his family in the Casco United Methodist Church. George attended Buys School and South Haven High School graduating in the class of 1958. George attended North Central College in Naperville and American University in Washington, D.C. where he majored in Political Science. He graduated from seminary in 1965 from Evangelical Theological Seminary. On November 28, 1970, George married Edna Abel of Cedar Springs. George's marriage to Edna was the highlight of his life. George and Edna became parents to Alice Mary on October 20, 1972 and Christina Joy on August 10, 1977.

George served as pastor of the Turk Lake (EUB) United Methodist Church and Assistant Pastor at the Greenville United Methodist Church in 1965, then at the Sodus Chapel Hill United Methodist Church, 1975-1987. George and Edna served as co-pastors of the Lawrence Avenue United Methodist Church in Charlotte, 1987-2002. In retirement, George once more returned to blueberry farming.

CHARLES (Chuck) F. GARROD – Born October 7, 1929. Rev. Dr. Garrod served: 1955 Lawton/Porter; 1962 Kalamazoo: Simpson; 1/1/1967 St Louis: First; 1972 Church of the Dunes; 1978 Grand Rapids: Trinity; 1984 District Superintendent, Central District; 1990 Lansing: Asbury; 10/1/1992 District Superintendent, Grand Rapids District; Retired 1995. Died July 25, 2019.

Chuck was a compassionate, caring, gentle and humble man. He loved his family deeply; wife Marcile and their four children. Over time he was blessed with a growing family to love as precious new members were added through marriages and births.

The things he most cared about had little to do with his own life and welfare. He worked tirelessly to advance God's work through the UMC, at his various appointments, in congregants' hearts and souls and lives. In the church at large, he was described by colleagues as a "gentle giant" for his deep insights and wise counsel regarding the business and future of the church. And his influence reached around the globe as he and his wife Marcile were instrumental in organizing the start-up of a UMC in Cameroon.

Chuck's love of his Lord was evident in his daily walk of ministry, to everyone he met.

GEORG F.W. GERRITSEN – Born September 11, 1934. Rev. Gerritsen served: 1972 Howarth, Thomas; 1978 Saginaw: West Michigan Avenue; 1980 Monroe: Calvary; 1985 Jeddo, Central-Lakeport; 1988 Caring Covenant Group Ministry: Oregon, Elba; 1996 Port Huron: Gratiot Park, Washington Avenue; 2000 Retired. Died May 15, 2020.

He was born in Batavia, Indonesia on September 11, 1934, son of the late Gerrit and Maya (Barbara) Gerritsen. Georg married Barbara Foulks on September 23, 1961, in Pemberton, New Jersey.

After graduation from high school in The Netherlands, Georg graduated from Calvin College in 1959. He studied at Westminster Theological Seminary and graduated with a Bachelor of Divinity degree in 1963 obtained his Master of Divinity in 1974. In 1980, Georg graduated with a Doctor of Ministry degree from San Francisco Theological Seminary. Georg liked listening to classical music, traveling, and most importantly spending quality time with his friends and family.

He is survived by his wife Barbara of 59 years; his son, Greg; sisters, Maya (Bourke) Lyklema of The Netherlands, and Ruth Schneider of Germany; as well as several nieces, nephews, cousins, and dear friends.

GEORGE R. GRETTENBERGER – Born April 16, 1930. Rev. Grettenberger served: 1955 Middleville; 1959 Transferred to Argentina Conf; 1965 Transferred from Argentina Conf; 1965 Potter Park; 11/01/1967 Cadillac; 1970 Cadillac United; 1980 Mason: First; 1989 Jackson Calvary; 1992 Retired. Died July 28, 2019.

George enjoyed his boyhood days in Grand Rapids. He graduated from high school and went to the University of Michigan. He earned a Master of Divinity in 1955 at Boston University and also met his future wife Diane.

Middleville, Michigan was George's first pastorate. His love of missions led him to Cordoba, Argentina with his wife and three children (John, Susan, and Charlotte) to serve as a missionary for five years. His son Louis was born there. George also led mission trips to Bolivia, Haiti, and Nicaragua. He served as chair of the Michigan Area Haiti Task Force and the Board of Global Ministries.

George served churches in Lansing, Cadillac, Mason, and Jackson. In his retirement, he became Associate Pastor of Okemos Community Church and in 2015 Pastor Emeritus.

He enjoyed working puzzles, gardening, reading, going to the cottage, traveling, and most of all, eating ice cream. He always said that his greatest joy was having a loving wife and children.

A. RAY GRIENKE – Born August 10, 1937. Rev. Grienke served: 1971 transferred from South Indiana Conf; 1971 Battle Creek: Sonoma/Newton; 01/15/1974 Boyne City/Boyne Falls; 1981 Kent City: Chapel Hill; 1985 Carson City; 08/16/1999 Retired. Died March 10, 2020.

Ray was born on August 10, 1937, in Alta, Iowa. He graduated from Alta High School in 1956. He received his BA in Social Services from Indiana University in 1964, and his Master of Theology from Southern Seminary in Louisville, Kentucky, in 1969.

He and Beverly married in 1967. They lived in New Castle, Indiana, for two years where he pastored New Castle UMC, then in Michigan for 29 years where he pastored in Battle Creek, Boyne City and Boyne Falls, Kent City, and Carson City.

Ray and Beverly had three children, Beth, Daniel, and Paul. Upon retirement in 1999, Ray and his wife moved to St. Joseph, Missouri, his wife's hometown. He served intermittently as interim minister of First Presbyterian Church.

He enjoyed fishing, especially several times each year in Canada. Ray earned his Master Gardener certification and took pride in his fruit trees and flowers. His unselfish love for others will be forever remembered and deeply missed by all.

JOYCE A. HANLON – Born May 28, 1937. Rev. Hanlon served: 1992 Deacons Appointed Beyond the Local Church(¶331.1a) Psychotherapist, Psychology Assoc. of GR 1992; 1995 Deacons Appointed w/in UM Connectional Structure (¶331.1b) GR Reflections Counseling & Consultant Services; 2001 Retired. Died April 26, 2019.

Rev. Joyce A. Hanlon, age 81, of Jenison, died on Friday, April 26, 2019. She is lovingly remembered by her husband of 58 years, Charles B. Hanlon, children, grandchildren, great-granddaughter, and brother. Joyce received her B.S. in Nursing (with Honors) from Michigan State University, and her M.S.N. in Psychiatric Mental Health Nursing from Wayne State University. Joyce was a life-long learner, and shared her talents in many positions including Psychiatric and Medical-Surgical Nursing instructor at Gloucester County College, New Jersey; Psychiatric and Medical-Surgical Nursing Instructor at Blodgett Memorial Medical Center in Grand Rapids; Director of Counseling Services at Hope College; Consecrated as a Diaconal Minister in the UMC; founded and developed her own business as Reflections Counseling and Consultations Services; Clinical Nursing instructor for Ferris State University in Big Rapids, in Bachelor of Science, nursing program, at Pine Rest Hospital in Grand Rapids; implemented E.M.D.R. therapy techniques while working with P.T.S.D. clients; and retired in 2001 from her own psychotherapy practice.

RON L. KELLER – Born March 14, 1936. Rev. Keller served: 1956 Battle Creek: Washington Heights; 1958 Appointed to Northeast Ohio Conference, Republic; 1962 Union City; 1966 Battle Creek: Birchwood; 1970 Rockford; 1973 Conference Staff Director; 1/1/1982 Kalamazoo: Milwood; 1988 Muskegon: Central; 1993 Battle Creek: First; 1998 Retired; 1/1/200-6/1/2000 Kalamazoo: First (interim). Died November 25, 2019.

Ron L Keller was born in Morenci, MI. He attended a one-room country schoolhouse and Morenci High School. He attended Albion College and Oberlin School of Theology. He loved to tell the story that he had a diploma from a school he never attended. Oberlin merged with Vanderbilt after he graduated, and Vanderbilt sent him a new diploma.

Ron's passion in ministry was two-fold. He felt strongly that Christian education should be life long and encouraged adult education in every church he served. He also was passionate about every church being welcoming. He recently wrote that he wanted to be a part of a congregation that welcomes everyone and whom loudly and clearly makes that known within and beyond the church. He was an ally of the LGBTQ+ community.

Ron was an amateur candlemaker for 50 years giving away hundreds of candles. He loved to travel and had visited 48 states. He leaves his wife, Pat, a daughter, three sons, three daughter-in-loves and seven precious grandchildren.

MARGARET A. KIVISTO – Born February 6, 1941. Rev. Kivisto served: 8/1/2004 Linden, Argentine; 1/1/2009 Linden (LTFT ¼); 2013 Retired. Died July 7, 2019.

Kivisto, Margaret 2/6/1941 - 7/7/2019 Brighton, MI. Margaret Amelia Kivisto, born February 6, 1941 in Detroit, Michigan, the daughter of Roy and Neva Dodd, passed suddenly while walking through her beloved

Mount Brighton subdivision. She met Jeffrey Kivisto in high school and after six years of dating, they wed and spent 55 wonderful years of marriage together. Margo and Jeff had two children: Eric and Megan. Margo set an example by always seeking knowledge, striving to learn and study, and to be productive by using the skills God gave her to help others. She thought life without these two blessings would be hollow and a frightening prospect. Anyone who knew Margo knew her love of silliness and irreverent humor. One of her greatest joys was spontaneous laughter, finding and embracing the foolishness in life. Margo is survived by her husband (Jeffrey), children Eric (Cheri) and Megan, grandson Carter, sister Carolyn (Robert), beloved nieces and nephews, and cats Augustine and Henry.

F. RICHARD MACCANON – Born October 6, 1925. Rev. MacCanon served: 1947 Laurel; 1949 Seminary; 1952 Center Point; 1957 Located; 1969 Readmitted, Mich. Conf., EUB, Dearborn: First (assoc.); 1974 Detroit: Thoburn; Mar. 1978 Detroit: Zion; Dec. 1978 River Rouge: Epworth, Detroit: Woodmere; Apr. 1983 Oscoda, Oscoda Indian Mission; 1988 Retired. Died December 18, 2019.

Rev. F. Richard MacCanon was born October 6, 1925 Ames, Iowa. During his pastoral ministry in Iowa and Michigan, Rev. MacCanon faithfully served both Evangelical United Brethren and then United Methodist Churches. In retirement, he enjoyed his time in Florida with family and friends. He died December 18, 2019 in Lakeland, FL. He is survived by his wife Shirley Glover-MacCanon and son David MacCanon, three grandchildren, and one great-grandson.

KENNETH D. MCCAW – Born June 2, 1934. Rev. McCaw served: 1962 Transferred from Indiana Conf; 1962 Caledonia 1962; 1966 Muskegon Parish; 1969 Grand Rapids: South; 1975 Portage; 1983 District Superintendent, Kalamazoo District; 1989 Conference Council Director; 1991 Kalamazoo: First; 1/1/2000 Medical Leave; 2000 Retired. Died September 5, 2019.

Born June 2, 1934. Married Jeanne Smith August 25, 1955. Died September 5, 2019.

Ken attended Wesley Theological Seminary in Washington, DC. He served as Kalamazoo District Superintendent, West Michigan Conference Council Director, and as pastor in the West Michigan Conference.

Ken had a great sense of humor and a unique combination of administrative and people skills. While traveling the world, it was not unusual for him to run into someone he knew! Ken offered experiential worship long before it was common. He found ways to bring popular music, props, humor, and other elements into worship. His preaching always called for an active response from the listener.

Ken enjoyed many hobbies including reading, classical music, woodworking, travel, and camping. He and Jeanne often used their singing voices in programs. A great husband, father, pastor, and friend, Ken handled his health struggles these past 20 years with grace and was an example of faith and perseverance for us all.

JOHN W. MCNAUGHTON – Born January 25, 1939, Rev. McNaughton served: 1973 Webberville; 1973 Bell Oak; 1979 Oakwood; 1982 Concord; 1984 Plainfield; 1986 Kendall; 1986 Gobles; 1987 Blackhearth Circuit, England; 1993 Elberta, Frankfort; 1996 Lane Boulevard; 1998 Kalamazoo: Stockbridge Ave; 2000 Kalamazoo: Northwest; 2003 Retired; 2008 Bloomingdale – Interim; Died May 11, 2020.

ROSS N. NICHOLSON – Born January 5, 1933. Rev. Dr. Nicholson served: 1958 Mt. Freedom, NJ (Newark Conf); Stroudsburg, PA (assoc.) (Phila. Conf); 1961 Melvindale; 1967 Madison Heights; 1972 Bad Axe; 12/1977 Conference Staff: Education; 1984 Detroit: North Detroit (LTFT-1/2); 1985 Leave of Absence; 1990 Retired. Died June 29, 2019.

Ross Neil Nicholson had wonderful friends, grandchildren, and great grandchildren. He had a good life. In the end, it is said of those like Ross, "Well done, good and faithful servant."

RUSH-OSMOND, SHARYN K. – Born February 19, 1951. Rev. Rush-Osmond served: 1996 Rochester Hills: First; 1/16/1999 Rochester Hills: St. Luke's (assoc); 2002 Dansville, Wheatfield (W. MI Conf.); Oct 10, 2008 disability leave. Died April 19, 2019.

Rev. Sharyn Kay Rush-Osmond, age 68, of Farwell went to be with her Lord and Savior on Friday, April 19, 2019. Sharon leaves behind her beloved husband Rick, and Daughters Fran and Alexandria, and a large family including her dearly loved grandchildren. Sharyn attended The Methodist Theological School in Ohio and Duke School of Divinity and was very proud to serve as a United Methodist Pastor. She served churches in Rochester Hills, Dansville, Wheatfield, Trinity, Leaton and Countryside.

After retirement, Sharyn was a member of Farwell United Methodist Church. Sharyn was a published author of poetry. She also loved to sing and was in a quartet called "The Five of Us" while living in Novi. Her greatest accomplishments in her eyes were being a mother, grandmother, and most recently, a great-grandmother.

GARY L. SANDERSON – Born October 5, 1936. Rev. Sanderson served: 1966 Goodrich; 1970 Durand, Duffield; 1979 Wyandotte: First; 1989 Flushing; 1995 Ann Arbor: West Side; 1999 Retired. Died May 28, 2020.

Gary was born in Owosso on October 5, 1936. He married Caroline Warner on August 8, 1964, in Owosso. He earned a bachelor's degree from Michigan State University and attended Chandler School of Theology, at Emory University in Atlanta, GA. Gary was ordained an Elder and served the Goodrich, Durand, Wyandotte First, Flushing and Ann Arbor West Side UMCs. In retirement, Gary served at Flint Court Street UMC as an Associate Pastor of Pastoral Care.

Gary served on the Flint District Board of Church Building and Location, the Flint District Committee on the Superintendency, the DAC Division of Evangelism, the United Methodist Foundation and the DAC Board of Pensions.

Gary is survived by his loving wife, Caroline; son, Marc and wife Marie and special grandsons, Riley, Grayson and Nicholas Sanderson of Sartell, MN; sister, Mildred and husband Ron Smith of Owosso; and nephews, Jeffrey and Matthew Smith.

ANTHONY J. SHIPLEY – Born May 19, 1939. Rev. Shipley served: 1964 NY: Metropolitan-Duane; 1966 Brooklyn, NY: Union; 1968 Assistant Program Director, NY Conf.; 1971 Trans. to Detroit Conf., Conference Staff, Program Director; 1982 Detroit West District Superintendent; 1987 Detroit: Scott Memorial; Mar. 1, 1992 Deputy General Secretary, National Division, Gen. Bd. of Global Ministries; 1994 Eastside Covenant Cooperative Parish: Detroit: Christ; 2007 Retired. Died April 1, 2020.

The Rev. Dr. Anthony J. Shipley went to be with his Lord on April 1, 2020 at the age of 80. Anthony was a Retired Elder of the Michigan Conference who served first in the New York Conference before transferring to the Michigan Conference where he served as a Program Director; Detroit West District Superintendent; Detroit: Scott Memorial; Deputy General Secretary, National Division, General Board of Global Ministries; Eastside Covenant Cooperative Parish: Detroit: Christ. Anthony retired in 2007.

WEBLEY J. SIMPKINS, JR. – Born September 27, 1930. Rev. Simpkins, Jr. served: 1952 Victoria, Colonial Manor; 1954 Aldine; 1956 Sharptown, Hainesneck; 1958 Eldbrooke; 1959 Woodside; 1961 Transfer to NW IN Conf, Grave; 1956 Transfer to Detroit Conf. Birminghan: First (assoc.); 1966 Midland: First (assoc.); 1970 Pigeon: First; 1975 Marquette: First; 1980 Marysville; 1985 Trenton: First; 1994 Retired. Died September 17, 2019.

Webley started pastoring about 52 years ago in the New Jersey, Philadelphia area after graduating from Wesley Seminary. He pastored in serval small churches in the area. He worked his way west with a stop in Indiana to Michigan starting in Midland as an Associate pastor. Then on to Pigeon, Marquette, Marysville and ending in Trenton. After retiring June of 1994, Web and his wife Betty traveled the country in their motorhome for five years then ended up settling in Malabar, FL by one of their daughters. Web worked part time for several years at the Methodist church in Palm Bay, FL as an Associate Pastor. Web's favorite services were the music services. He would lead the congregation in singing for the whole service out of the hymn book. He loved to sing and had a beautiful Baritone voice. Web's singing and love of music and birds will be greatly missed.

PHYLEMON D. TITUS – Born December 4, 1937. Rev. Titus served: 1969 Trans. to Detroit Conf., Detroit: Fourteenth Avenue; 1971 Detroit: Henderson Memorial; 1974 Conference Staff, Urban Missioner; 1984 Detroit: Conant Avenue; 1988 Detroit East District Superintendent; 1995 Detroit: St. Timothy 2002 Detroit: St. Timothy, West Outer Drive; Dec 31, 2002 Retired. 7/1/06-3/1/07 Inkster: Christ. Died March 23, 2020.

The Reverend Phylemon DePriest Titus, Retired (Dec. 31, 2002) Elder of the Michigan Conference, passed away on Monday, March 23, 2020 in Waycross, Goergia, with his wife (Rev. Linda Slaughter-Titus, Waycross) and daughter (Iyana Titus-Richards, New York, New York).

Although 'Tite' was ordained in the Texas Conference, he served in pastoral ministry in the Georgia Conference (1967-69) and the Detroit Annual Conference (06/1969-12/31/2002). His pastorates included: Augusta: St. Marks UMC, Detroit: Fourteenth Avenue, Detroit: Henderson Memorial, Detroit: Conant Avenue, Detroit: St. Timothy, West Outer Drive and Inkster Christ (after retirement). He also served the Methodist connection church as Detroit Conference Urban Missioner, Detroit East District Superintendent, NCJ Town and Country President, NCJ Judicial Council, Conference Delegate to Jurisdictional Conference (four times) Conference Delegate to General Conference (four times) Conference Delegate to World Methodist Conference (6 times) as well as serving as Trustee to Garret Evangelical Seminary (Life Trustee) and Adrian College.

CLARENCE W. VANCONANT – Born June 13, 1944. Rev. VanConant served: 1/1/1993 White Pine, Bergland, Ewen, Trout Creek Presb; 1997 Kilmanaugh, Unionville; 1999 Harbor Beach, Port Hope; 2004 Sanilac, Forrester; 2007 Monroe: First; 2010 Retired. Died July 29, 2019.

Clarence saw active duty as a Navy SeaBee during the Vietnam War.

He and his wife, Earleen, served four churches in the Upper Peninsula: White Pine, Bergland, Ewen, and Trout Creek Presbyterian. He also served Kilmanagh/Unionville, Harbor Beach/Port Hope, Port Sanilac/Forester, and Monroe: First. He is survived by his wife Earleen, six children, five step-children, 33 grandchildren, and 26 great grandchildren.

He lived his faith and shared the love of God with everyone he met. He did woodworking, making toys to give away and loved playing with his great grandchildren. He retired in 2010 and spent winters in Arizona where he rode his special tricycle around as he spread the good news of the gospel of Jesus Christ. No matter where he lived everyone in the neighborhood knew him. He brought joy to a lot of people.

ROBERT E. WALTON – Rev. Walton served: 1977 transfer to Detroit Conf., Detroit: Central (assoc.); 1981 Wesley Foundation, Wayne State University; 1986 Program Secretary, United Methodist Volunteer Services, National Division, Gen. Board of Global Ministries; 2002 Retired. Died April 13, 2020.

Rev. Robert Earl Walton, age 83 years, passed away on April 13, 2020 after battling illnesses for several years. He is survived by his wife Alice Walton and is a father of three, grandfather of eight, great-grandfather of one and a beloved friend of many.

Born in Loogootee, Indiana, Bob was an ordained Methodist minister and worked in international relief during his later years. He lived and worked in Cincinnati, Detroit as the Wayne State University Wesley Foundation Campus Pastor, and New York City as the Assistant General Secretary at the National Division of the General Board of Global Ministries.

ROBERT P. WARD – Born August 13, 1927. Rev. Ward served: 1952 Detroit: Westlawn; 1954 Troy: First; 1957 Marquette: First; 1961 Ypsilanti: First; 1965 Adrian: First; 1969 Flint: Court Street; 1972 Ann Arbor District Superintendent; 1978 Grosse Pointe; 1982 Birmingham: First; 1993 Retired. Died May 26, 2020.

Rev. Dr. Robert Paul Ward died May 26, 2020. He was 92 years old.

His first appointment was Westlawn where he met Joan, his wife of 62 years, who predeceased him in 2016. He served as senior pastor at the First UMCs of Troy, Marquette, Ypsilanti, Adrian and Flint Court Street, as District Superintendent of the Ann Arbor district, Grosse Pointe, and Birmingham First where he retired in 1993. While there, Dr. Ward was nominated for Bishop at the North Central Jurisdictional Conference.

He was instrumental in securing funding for underprivileged students to attend Adrian College on full scholarships. When the college opened its new admissions building, it bore the name "Ward Admissions House" in his honor.

He is survived by his daughters Wendy and Carolyn Ward who will remember him as a faithful servant of the church, devoted husband and loving father. In recent weeks, he told his daughters that he had lived a perfect life.

DONALD S WEATHERUP – Born September 14, 1961. Rev. Weatherup served: 2002 Flushing (assoc.); 2006 Pinckney: Arise; 2018 Commerce. Died May 13, 2019.

We extend our condolences to the family and friends of Rev. Donald S. Weatherup who died on May 13, 2019 at the age of 57. Don served at Flushing UMC, Pinckney: Arise UMC and Commerce UMC. He is survived by his wife Shelley and his extended family.

OWEN L. WHITE-PIGEON – Born January 21, 1957. Rev. White-Pigeon served in the Northern Waters District as a District Superintendent Assignment (DSA) at Kewadin: Indian Mission and as a Part-time Local Pastor and DSA in the Central Bay District at Mt. Pleasant: Chippewa Indian Mission. Died August 26, 2019.

Clergy Spouses

MARGARET C. BEAN – Passed away on April 22, 2019. Margaret was born in Ann Arbor. She attended Western Michigan University where she met the love of her life and husband of 69 years, Rex E. Bean. Margaret taught elementary music for 30 years and retired from Mona Shores Schools. Margaret was an accomplished musician, playing the piano, organ, violin and viola. She performed from a young age, to her university days and with the West Shore Symphony in Muskegon. She was an energetic grandmother that was always filled with excitement for her grandchildren's life events. Her love for animals, especially cats, was passed down to the whole family. Margaret never left the house without her trademark jewelry and festive sweaters. She will be greatly missed and remembered as a loving wife, mother, grandmother and wonderful friend to so many. She had a wonderful smile and her kindness and faith showed in everything she did. She is survived by her two daughters, three grandchildren.

DONNA M. COZADD – Donna Marie Cozadd passed away on May 4, 2020. She was born May 24, 1929. She was married to the late Rev. William B Cozadd. They served the following United Methodist churches in Michigan: Eagle, Ravenna, Hope and Edenville, West Vienna and Burton: Christ. She served the Lord in these churches by doing secretarial work, leading women's groups and making visits.

She was preceded in death by her husband Bill and daughter Patricia Lewis. She leaves behind two daughters Victoria Cozadd and Bilene (Greg) Crabill and one son-in-law Rev. George Lewis (Howell First UMC) along with eight grandchildren and fifteen great-grandchildren. She enjoyed singing in choirs and as a soloist. For the last 30 years she lived in Palmetto FL where she loved to swim and ride her bike.

"But seek ye first the kingdom of God, and his righteousness; and all these things shall be added unto you." Matthew 6:33

JERRY W. DANIEL – Jerry Wayne Daniel died February 4, 2020. He was born July 9, 1938 in Hughey, Tennessee. While still in high school, he joined the National Guard and later served in the reserves at Fort Bragg, North Carolina. He attended Draughons School of Business in Nashville, Tennessee and managed stations for Esso Oil. In 1959, he married Sandra Huffines with whom he raised three children. The family moved to Warren, Michigan where he was a tool maker and soccer coach. His boys' team won the AYSO state championship in 1977. In 1999, he married Rev. Reva Wykes Hawke. After retirement, he became a security guard at Sandy Pines Resort and Checker Motors.

Jerry Wayne is survived by his wife Reva, his two daughters, one son; and their mother Sandra Daniel. He leaves eight grandchildren, and a great-grandchild. He is also survived by his wife's three children; her eleven grandchildren, including Andrew J. Hawke whom he helped raise; and her 13 great-grandchildren.

NANCY J. ELLISON – Nancy graduated from Dearborn High, obtained her RN from Lansing's Sparrow Hospital, and worked as a nurse. She married Floyd in December 1951 at Dearborn First Methodist, where both grew up. They were married for 56 years. Floyd and Nancy served 11 churches across Michigan over Floyd's 30+ year career. Together they grew their family, raised them well, and as doting grandparents watched them raise families of their own. Being in the Detroit area in the 70s and 80s allowed Nancy to join the staff of Dearborn First as financial secretary, a position she held and which her mother had held before her. Nancy continued her commitment to Methodism following Floyd's retirement, joining Detroit's Metropolitan United Methodist where she served as Administrative Council chair. She later become a member of Birmingham UMC. Nancy died the committed Methodist she was raised, supporting the church both locally and globally. She will be missed by her children, grandchildren, great grandchildren, and friends.

DEBORAH KAY (KENNEDY) FERRIS – Deb was born in Western Pennsylvania and attended Adrian College, where she met John Ferris. They were married August 22, 1970. When John felt God's call Deb supported him through seminary (where daughter Sonya was born) and through thirty-nine years of ordained ministry (where son Jeremy was born during his first appointment).

MEMOIRS

Deb's series of careers demonstrated her interests and diverse skills: high school teacher; Office of Missions and Church Extension of the Detroit Annual Conference; Director of the Senior Citizen Center of the Cass Community UMC; Planning Commission Member for the City of Detroit; Director of Fund Raising for Alternatives for Girls. Beyond volunteer work where John pastored, she was a dedicated advocate for peace and justice.

Deb loved and was loved by God, her husband, their children and grandchildren, her sister, and many other relatives, and seemingly countless friends, including a great many four-legged friends.

CHARLENE F. GARRETT – Charlene was wonderful! Loved life, people, but mostly loved the Lord. She ministered along with her husband Robert for over 55 years, most of them in the Thumb. Charlene took great joy in capturing memories through writing poetry. One favorite she shared during Robert's retirement moment at Annual Conference, "Ministers Wives Don't Chew Gum." She taught her four children and grandchildren a legacy of kindness. In the last 10 years, she had cognitive impairment, living the last two in memory care. Even there she brought joy and smiles with her love. Her doll, "Baby Angel," was her comfort when we couldn't be there. She sang "Jesus Loves Me" to her and made her dance after dinner which brought smiles to her community. Oh and by the way..." Minister's wives do chew gum!"

JANET L. HUDDLESON – Janet Lee Huddleson, beloved wife of Reverend Robert "Bob" Kemp Townley, died April 30, 2020 in Wichita Falls, Texas, after a prolonged illness. We rejoice that she is once again reunited with Bob in Heaven and her pain has ended.

Born November 6, 1949 in Grosse Pointe, Michigan, Janet married Bob in 1973 and supported his ministries in East Lansing and Bay City, Michigan. Janet graduated from Michigan State University and together they built a 40' trimaran "Winds of Change" by hand, and sailed off through the St. Lawrence Seaway, eventually landing in Providenciales, Turks & Caicos Islands in 1980 where they lived for 40 years. There Bob served as Pastor and counselor, and Janet found special delight teaching young children English as a second language. Her gentle warmth and kindness drew people to her; she bloomed and thrived wherever life took her.

Following Bob's death on August 29, 2017, Janet lived first with her sister in Colorado and later with her brother in Texas. Janet's love and kindness lives on in brother Jim (Dorothy) Huddleson, sister Judy Ladd, stepson Michael Scott Townley, grandsons David Townley and Matthew Townley, and all who knew her.

MAGGIE J. KALLWEIT – Maggie Jean Kallweit, beloved mother, grandmother and great grandmother, passed away April 17, 2019 at the age of 85. Maggie will be sorely missed, but her family rejoices knowing she is now reunited in Heaven with her husband, Ralph. Maggie was also preceded in death by her son, Daniel.

Surviving to cherish her memory are children, Debbie, David Wayne (Leanne), Peggy (Mike); grandchildren, Trevor (fiancé Rona), Robert, Tony (Kara),

Lisa (Andy), Tim (fiancé, Holly), Megean, Alea, Bobby (Alissa), Thomie (Nick), Ryan (Melissa), Adam (Krystal); great grandchildren, AJ, Braylon, Keyli, Hazel, Madison, Jona, Jacob, Callen, Henry, Rhiyan; and her devoted dog, Annie.

Maggie loved to travel. She also enjoyed picking apples to create her famous pies and strawberries for her delicious jam. Maggie liked Precious Moments figurines and put together an extensive collection over the years.

WILMA J. KING – Wilma King, age 82, died Wednesday, May 27, 2020. Wilma Jean Ross was born May 28, 1937 in Deckerville, Michigan. She is the daughter of the late Leroy and the late Dorothy (Innes) Ross. Wilma grew up in Deckerville and Marlette, Michigan. She is a graduate of Marlette High School, Class of 1955. Wilma married Rev. Willard Arthur King on June 4, 1955 in Marlette, Michigan. He preceded her in death on April 29, 2012.

Wilma has lived in the Capac area for 22 years. She held several different positions throughout the years: teacher assistant for Imlay City High School, a store clerk at Dean's Pharmacy, bus driver for Peck Schools, and a teacher aide for Genesee Schools. Wilma was a member of Capac United Methodist Church where she played the organ and piano and was also a preschool assistant.

Wilma is survived by three daughters, Karen, Connie, and Brenda, her sister Wanda, and seven grandsons and eight great-grandsons.

THOMAS L. KLACKING – Thomas Lee Klacking passed away April 30, 2020. He was born in Garden City, MI on February 1, 1938 to Wallace and Bessie Klacking. Tom graduated from West Branch High School, Class of 1956.

Tom was a dairy farmer for over 40 years and a U.S. Air Force veteran. He was an avid golfer and bowler. Tom was well known as a high-pitch softball pitcher for Wangler's Trucking. He also enjoyed hunting, fishing and Thursday coffee with the Jacksons.

Tom is survived by his wife of 42 years, Pastor Brenda Klacking; children, Gary Klacking and Annet (DeWayne) Culbertson of West Branch, Tammy Bell (Sean Averna) of Post Falls, ID, and Terry Klacking of Howell, MI. He had six grandchildren; Ben Klacking, Jessica Sheppard, Christina Grell, Mitchell, Mason and Mallory Bell and nine great-grandchildren. He also had a sister, Mary Hughes of Arlington, TX and many nieces, nephews and extended family and friends.

MATTI R. KOIVULA – Matti Richard Koivula, 62, of Mesick, husband of Rev. Laurie Koivula, passed away on Wednesday, May 15th surrounded by family and friends. He was born March 4, 1957, in Ypsilanti. He spent his life troubleshooting and repairing computers in various industries. His favorite was his last place of employment which was Detroit Public Schools where he loved putting smiles on the faces of the children. Matt was an active member of Mesick United Methodist Church. He was baptized and became a member of The United Methodist Church Easter Sunday 2016 at West Goodland UMC in Imlay City.

Matt loved his family and enjoyed spending time with his grandchildren. He was an avid reader and enjoyed helping others.

MEMOIRS

The most important things in his life was his faith and his family. He will be remembered as a loving husband, father, brother, uncle, friend and most importantly Papa.

BETTY J. LUCE – Betty, age 89, passed away Friday, April 19, 2019. She was born December 30, 1929 in Munger Michigan to the late Jay and Louise (Morel) Briggs and was an area resident all of her life.

She married Michael Luce February 13, 1971 in Reese Michigan and he survives her. She is also survived by her children, Terry Shooltz, Barb (Gary) Behmlander, David (Susan) Shooltz, and Stacey (Randy) LaPreze; grandchildren, Zachary, Casey, Jennifer (Bryan), Kevin, Brooke, Richard, Andrew (Kristine), Jessica (Mark), and Andrew, and Landrie, Sydnie, Clint (Jennifer), and Ali LaPreze; 10 great-grandchildren; daughter-in-law, Michelle Shooltz; mother-in-law, Inez Luce; several nieces, nephews, cousins; and many friends. She was predeceased by her son Larry Shooltz; siblings, Dorothy VanTol, Arthur Briggs, & Mary Helmreich; and father-in-law, Robert Luce.

NANCY L. MECARTNEY – Nancy Lee Mecartney died February 1, 2020 in Irvine, California. Nancy was born in Ferndale, Washington on September 16, 1924.

Nancy graduated from Ferndale High School in 1942 and Seattle Pacific College in 1946, majoring in psychology. She met John Mecartney at a peace meeting in Chicago. They married on September 17, 1951. While John served churches in Wisconsin, they welcomed four daughters, Mary, Martha, Susan and Crystal. In Albion, Nancy went to work part time as a teacher in 1966. She then received her teaching credential and began her career as an elementary school teacher.

Nancy and John were members of Detroit Metropolitan UMC where Nancy helped run the Good Samaritan program and volunteered with the Detroit Institute of Arts.

They moved to the Chelsea Retirement Community in 2002. John passed away on their 53rd wedding anniversary September 17, 2004. Nancy continued to be an active member. She moved to Irvine, California in December 2017, to be closer to her family.

ELOISE (ELLIE) M. MOORE – Eloise (Ellie) Janette Millikan Moore was born in Rensselaer, Indiana on Feb 1, 1935. Ellie died Feb 15, 2020 in Lawrenceville, GA.

She married Paul Millikan in Upland, Indiana on June 3, 1957, and they were married for 20 years. Ellie and Paul had three children and five grandchildren. The family enjoyed their lives in Upland Indiana, Fredericksburg, Virginia and Portage, Michigan, following Paul's assignments and teaching career.

Ellie married Rev. John Moore in Portage, Michigan on Sep 27, 1982. Ellie and John lived in Portage, Berrien Springs, Kalamazoo, Galesburg, Union City and back to Portage following John's pastoral assignments. Ellie lovingly welcomed John's four children and five grandchildren into her life.

Ellie always put family first. Her children, grandchildren, great grandchildren (one in utero), stepchildren and all their families were all the light of Ellie's life. There were always stories and there was always laughter. She was an amazing Mom, Grandma and "G-G".

RICHARD K. OSMOND – Richard Kenneth Osmond died on Saturday, March 14, 2020. Rick was born on May 27, 1945 to parents Aubrey and Gwendolyn Osmond in Washington D.C. He graduated from Glen Burnie High School in Maryland. Rick worked for and retired from Detroit Edison. Rick was married several times and had two children; Keli Su Mills and Kristopher Kenneth Osmond with his second wife and two children; Frances Owens and Alexandria Blain with his third wife, Rev. Sharyn Kay Osmond.

After retiring Rick enjoyed singing in his church choir, helping with church functions, attending bible studies and prayer groups, as well as singing with a Barbershop Quartet. He had an extensive record collection, and he loved singing and music of all types.

Rick was preceded in death by his wife of 34 years, Rev. Sharyn Kay Osmond. He is survived by his children, step mother, siblings, step siblings, half-brother, grandchildren, great granddaughter, and many nieces and nephews.

JOANNE R. PÉREZ – Joanne Robinson Pérez, 88, died October 24th, 2019. Born and raised in Clarksburg, WV she graduated with a BA from West Virginia Wesleyan, MA from Ohio Wesleyan and Specialist Degree in Educational Administration from Eastern Michigan University. Joanne was an elementary music teacher and principal in the Adrian Public Schools. She was a member of the Adrian First UMC and was President of the UMW at Adrian FUMC, the president of the Ann Arbor District UMW, Vice-president of the Detroit Conference UMW, Vice-president of the North Central Jurisdiction UMW, trustee of the District Board of Missions and Church Extension, and member of the Detroit Conference COSROW. In 1967 Joanne co-founded the Adrian Community Preschool and was the first President of their board of directors.

She is survived by her husband of 65 years Joseph A Pérez; daughter Sarah A Pérez of San Francisco CA; son John W Pérez and grand-daughter Julia M Pérez of Little Rock, AR; and other family and friends.

KARLEEN J. PETTIS – Age 80, a resident of Lyndonville, VT, died, April 19, 2019. She was born May 27, 1938 in Midland, Michigan to Carl and Eileen Strayer (Bowsher). A graduate of Midland High School in 1956; and a graduate of Albion College of Michigan in 1960. She worked with the Summer Migrant Ministry program through the Michigan Council of Churches, teaching and leading the Summer Program for migrant children. She taught Elementary School in Royal Oak and Petersburg Public Schools prior to her marriage to seminarian, Warren Pettis in 1964. She was a faithful homemaker and pastor's wife in all the churches her husband was appointed to in the Detroit Conference of The United Methodist Church. She led the Children's Church ministry and was involved in the United Methodist Women. In retirement, she was a member of the Lyndonville UMC Tuesday Ladies Bible Study group.

She is survived by her husband, Warren Pettis; three children; five grandchildren; and many nieces, nephews, cousins and friends.

EILEEN L. POHLY – Eileen Lois (Hamilton) Pohly, age 88, died on July 2, 2019 at Clark on Keller Lake in Grand Rapids. Before her marriage to Gerald Pohly, she began her working career at Addressograph-Multigraph Corporation in Cleveland, Ohio. Later, following a pivotal faith event at Linwood Park, Ohio, she became a Secretary at the Master's UMC in Euclid, Ohio. Eventually, she became the Director of Christian Education where Gerald's brother, Dr. Kenneth Pohly, was Senior Pastor. Eileen was very active in Christian Education, United Methodist Women and in other activities where her husband was appointed. She enjoyed gardening and traveling. She was known for her loving spirit, compassionate mind and heart, and self-giving spirit to her immediate family, extended family and many others in her wide circle of friends.

JEAN M. SCHAAF – Jean (McDonald) Deal Stine Schaaf passed away on October 29, 2019. She was born June 16, 1932. Jean traveled many complex paths in her life with one common theme, service.

After graduating from her beloved Oberlin College, she married Ralph Deal and moved to Baltimore, where she served as a social worker. Jean gave birth to three daughters: Rebecca, Heather and Deborah. While in Kalamazoo, Jean was active in the Peace Center, ACLU and People's Unitarian Fellowship youth group. She was elected County Commissioner. She later married Reverend Wendell Stine. Wendell's children Cynthia, David, Wendell Jr and Rebecca were very much a part of their lives. After Wendell passed in 2004, Jean met and married George Schaaf. George and Jean enjoyed five years together.

Jean's life was filled with music and she lived in service to helping her fellow human beings. Her family is very proud of her accomplishments, her passions, her feistiness, her durability, and the amazing example she left for her family and all who met her.

NANCY L. STEELE – Nancy Lou-Ellen (Wheeler) Steele died April 13, 2019. Nancy was born October 23, 1939 in Kalamazoo to Coramay and Richard O Wheeler. Nancy graduated from Mattawan HS in 1957. In 1983 she received her Associate in Applied Science with a General Marketing Major from Kalamazoo Valley Community College. She married Rev. Philip P. Steele on June 20, 1957, supporting him as he served Schoolcraft, Wolf Lake Muskegon, Sitka, Cooper UCC, Portage, Coopersville, Battle Creek Birchwood, Portage Chapel Hill, Almena, Climax-Scotts, Oakwood, Lane Boulevard, and Milwood UMC.

She was an accomplished pianist, seamstress and artist. She worked as the assistant accompanist for the St Luke's Choristers in Kalamazoo and the Oakwood UMC Organist. She shared love, faith, hope and joy through the piano strings and into our souls. She loved animals and was dedicated to caring for many feral barn cats. Her greatest loves and joys were her children Mark, Melody and Genipher, grandchildren Rhiannon, Katelyn, Brandyn and Miranda, and great grandson Shadow.

MARY E. TEN HAVE – Mary was carried by the angels into heaven on August 31, 2019 at the age of 91. Mary was born in Howell, Michigan, November 7, 1927, the daughter of Alfred and Helen (Whittaker) Shaffier. She was an affiliate member of the many United Methodist churches where she served alongside her husband, Milton. Mary was also a member of the Eaton Rapids Holiness Camp Meeting and was active in church leadership. She was a 4-H leader and devoted her life not only to church and fellowship but also as a licensed practical nurse caring for countless others.

Mary is survived by her daughters, Dawn (Charles) Kissack of Texas, Katherine (Thomas) Davis on Indiana, Helen (David) Jones of Haslett; son, Milton (Tammy) Ten Have of Riverdale; numerous grandchildren and great grandchildren. She was preceded in death by her husband, Pastor Milton Ten Have and a son, Harold Ten Have.

LEANNE TREBILCOCK – Born January 17, 1942. Leanne was a member of the Escanaba: First UMC (8/26/92 – 7/13/01) and Corunna UMC (6/1/00 – 7/13/07), while her late husband, Rev. Michael Peterlin, served those churches as pastor. She died April 3, 2020.

BENJAMIN C. WILSON – Benjamin Charles Wilson, a man of devout faith and ardent patriotism, died on June 30th. A native of Traverse City, Ben graduated from High School in 1962 and enlisted in the U.S. Army where he served with the Corps of Engineers for three years. Ben married his first wife in 1971 and had two daughters who describe him as a gentle, guiding father who took great pride in his family. Ben remarried in 2000 to Pastor Margaret "Meg" Wilson and, together, they fostered several children and adopted others. For many children, Ben would be the only father figure they would know. He was a man with the "patience of Job", who gave of his time to help his neighbors and strangers alike. He never raised his voice, was a good listener and had Christian values that impressed even the pastor whom he called his wife. Ben will be missed by his wife, Meg Wilson, his children, grandchildren, brothers, and sisters.

CAROL A. WINGEIER – Carol Ann (Wise) Wingeier, spouse of Rev. Dr. Douglas E. Wingeier, passed away in Asheville, North Carolina, on July 4, 2019, at the age of 89. Born in Calhoun, GA, she is survived by her husband of 67 years, two daughters, two sons, nine grandchildren, and one great-grandchild. Graduating from Georgia College (BS), and Roosevelt University (MEd), Carol served ten years as a Methodist missionary in Singapore, founding a bilingual kindergarten, then publishing a mission study book, "Where the Jungle Meets the Street." Carol taught preschool and worked as education enabler in Chicago churches.

Upon retirement, they returned to her beloved Appalachia, where she took up the banjo and gardening, volunteered in church and social action activities, and did extensive hiking, canoeing, camping, travel, and roughing it at her Minnesota log cabin. Carol will be remembered for her love of nature, creative teaching skills, faith-based dedication to peace and justice, global perspective, devotion to family and her heartfelt, engaging smile.

Lay Persons (Professionally Related to the Conference)

LUCILLE R. EVANS – Lucille Ruth Evans was born on May 8, 1937, in Elkhart, Indiana, the daughter of the late Clarence and Lilia Fuss. Lucy graduated from Adrian High School in 1955. Lucy and George Evans were married on June 8, 1957, at the Baptist Church in Adrian.

Together, Lucy and George raised their family in Dearborn and Royal Oak. Lucy eventually went to work in the radiology department for Beaumont Royal Oak. During her career with Beaumont, she even spent a couple of years at the West Bloomfield location. Lucy retired after having put in 30 years of service with Beaumont Health Systems. In retirement, Lucy kept busy working as a receptionist here at Birmingham First for the last several years.

Lucy will be greatly missed by her family, her church family, her friends, and all those whose lives she touched as she lived out the life that God had first shared with her in Jesus Christ.

MERNA I. FRANCIS – Merna died January 17, 2020. Merna was born in Cairo, Iowa, on August 22, 1933 to Royce and Ruby Partington. Merna and Aden Francis were married on October 24, 1954. While their children were growing up, Merna volunteered her secretarial skills at church and community organizations. She was employed as a secretary at the Upjohn Company, retiring as executive secretary in 1995. Merna became an active member of the International Association of Administrative Professionals (IAAP). She was proud to attain the Certified Professional Secretary certification.

Merna was a member of the Gull Lake UMC, where she was active in the UMW, sang in the choir, and served on many committees. She enjoyed attending the West Michigan Annual Conference and served on the Commission on Archives and History for the North Central Jurisdiction of the UMC. Merna also served on the Conference Journal Committee and the Conference Historical Society.

LUCILE M. OGDEN – Lucile Marie Ogden was born June 3, 1921 in Port Hope and passed away November 26, 2019 in Port Huron, moving there in 1938. A family that Lucile lived with suggested she go to First Methodist Church. She found a home there, including meeting her future husband Floyd Ogden in a Sunday School class. When they married in Port Hope, Dwight Large, who taught that class, officiated.

United Methodist Women were always special to Mrs. Ogden. She served at the District level in the 60's, the Conference as Secretary and as Treasurer from 1972-1980, and the Jurisdiction from 1981-1984. She also was active in their Schools of Christian Mission. She served the Detroit Conference Commission on Archives and History and the Historical Society of the UMC.

She took to heart a verse from Luke 24:24 "...some of our womenfolk have disturbed us profoundly...". It became her life's mission at a time when a woman's contributions were not always appreciated or heard.

JANET E. POOL – Janet Eileen Pool, prior employee of the former West Michigan Conference of the United Methodist Church, passed away on September 4, 2019 at the age of 63 years at Masonic Pathways Nursing Home in Alma, Michigan, after nearly eight years of illnesses.

Janet was born at Gratiot Community Hospital, Alma on December 7, 1955 to James Robert Whitman and Shirley Jean (Root) Whitman of Ithaca, Michigan. She married Brien Belanger on October 18, 1980. Brien passed away on January 2, 2000. Janet married Willard Pool on July 9, 2005 and he preceded her in death on November 10, 2011.

Janet worked in the former West Michigan Conference Treasurer's Office as an Accounts Payable Coordinator from October 1999 until December 2005 and from February 2008 to October 2008 as a Receptionist.

JACQUELIN E. WASHINGTON – Jacquelin E. Washington, a pioneering leader for women's rights and equal justice, died on April 27, 2019. She was 87.

In 1970, she organized and chair the first Violence Against Women Committee for the National Organization for Women (NOW) Detroit Chapter. She co-founded the personnel agency New Options in 1975. In 2000, she was elected to the Wayne State University Board of Governors, serving as president. She was inducted into the Michigan Women's Hall of Fame in 1995. For 17 years she served on the ACLU Michigan Executive Board, serving 4 years as president, and representing Michigan on ACLU's national board.

For nearly 50 years, she was an active member of Central United Methodist Church in Detroit.

She is survived by her three children, a granddaughter, a brother-in-law, a cousin, six nieces and nephews, and other relatives and friends. She was preceded in death by her husband, Kenneth B. Washington, DDS in 2004.

— MAC Photos

MEMOIRS

ROLL OF DECEASED CLERGY MEMBERS

For Roll of Deceased prior to July 1, 2018, consult West Michigan Conference or Detroit Conference Minutes of 2018 and before.

Name	Date of Death	Place of Death	Age	Conference & Admission Date	
Dennis G. Buwalda	*12/21/2017**	*Holt, MI*	*74*	*West Michigan*	*1968*
* correction of death date in previous entry: 2017, not 2018					
James G. Simmons	4/24/2018	Chelsea, MI	90	Detroit	1952
Gilson M. Miller	4/25/2018	Heber City, UT	70	Detroit	1971
Michael L. Raymo	5/1/2018	Hoover, AL	70	Detroit	1978
Bert Hosking	5/17/2018	Louisville, KY	95	Detroit	1956
James F. Thomas	6/2/2018	Grand Rapids, MI	82	N. Indiana	1952
Amerson W. Arntz	6/4/2018	Macomb Township, MI	75	Detroit	2000
Gerald M. Sever, Jr.	6/19/2018	Grand Blanc, MI	71	Detroit	1997
Douglas K. Olsen	7/15/2018	Dundee, MI	71	Detroit	1970
Bernard R. Randolph	7/21/2018	Mecosta, MI	102	West Michigan	1956
Young Bong Yoon	7/24/2018	Moreno Valley, CA	93	Korea	1951
Harold M. Taber	8/18/2018	Grand Rapids, MI	89	West Michigan	1950
Susan Bennett Stiles	8/31/2018	Charlotte, NC	66	Detroit	1975
Sally A. LaFrance	9/15/2018	Spring Lake, MI	82	West Ohio	1995
Ward N. Scovel, Jr.	10/13/2018	Penn Valley, CA	82	West Michigan	1976
Francis F. Anderson	10/18/2018	Holt, MI	92	West Michigan	1960
Juanita J. Ferguson	11/18/2018	Detroit, MI	75	Detroit	1972
Paton M. Zimmerman	11/27/2018	Southfield, MI	93	Detroit	1978
Richard C. Kuhn	12/8/2018	Perrinton, MI	82	Minnesota	1959
Marvin R. Rosa	2/11/2019	Lake Ann, MI	81	West Michigan	1968
Gary V. Lyons	2/17/2019	Gallatin, TN	79	Detroit	1972
Mark E. Spaw	3/8/2019	Farmington Hills, MI	61	Detroit	1982
Gregory R. Wolfe	4/15/2019	Napoleon, MI	71	West Michigan	1973
Brian K. William	4/16/2019	West Bloomfield, MI	43	Detroit	2004
Joyce Hanlon	4/26/2019	Jenison, MI	81	West Michigan	1997
Bruce M. Denton	5/5/2019	Lake Orion, MI	68	Detroit	1973
Robert H. Bough	5/13/2019	West Bloomfield, MI	84	Detroit	1965
Donald S. Weatherup	5/13/2019	Canton, MI	57	Detroit	2002
Ross Neil Nicholson	6/29/2019	Marquette, MI	86	Detroit	1959
Margaret A. Kivisto	7/7/2019	Brighton, MI	78	Detroit	2004
Charles F. Garrod	7/25/2019	Grand Rapids, MI	89	West Michigan	1957
George R. Grettenberger	7/28/2019	Okemos, MI	89	West Michigan	1954
Clarence W. VanConant	7/29/2019	Macomb, MI	75	Detroit	1993
Kenneth D. McCaw	9/5/2019	Grand Rapids, MI	85	West Michigan	1962
Webley J. Simpkins, Jr	09/17/2019	Palm Bay, FL	88	New Jersey	1957
Ralph T. Barteld	10/19/2019	Marysville, MI	88	Detroit	1967

continued on next page

ROLL OF THE DECEASED

Name	Date	Location	Age	Conference	Year
Oscar W. Cooper, Jr.	11/11/2019	Fort Collins, CO	80	Detroit	1961
Theron E. Bailey	11/17/2019	Kentwood, MI	91	West Michigan	1961
Ron L. Keller	11/25/2019	Flint, MI	83	West Michigan	1956
Alfred T. Bamsey	11/26/2019	Ann Arbor, MI	83	Detroit	1958
Richard C. Cheatham	11/30/2019	San Antonio, TX	89	Detroit	1964
F. Richard MacCanon	12/18/2019	Lakeland, FL	94	Iowa EUB	1947
J. Leon Andrews	01/20/2020	Grand Rapids, MI	90	West Michigan	1959
A. Ray Grienke	03/10/2020	St. Joseph, MO	82	South Indiana	1969
Phylemon D. Titus	03/23/2020	Waycross, GA	82	Texas	1967
Anthony J. Shipley	04/01/2020	Southfield, MI	80	New York	1962
Kenneth J. Bremer	04/03/2020	Grand Rapids, MI	66	West Michigan	1990
David A. Cheyne	04/11/2020	Grand Rapids, MI	77	West Michigan	1973
Robert E. Walton	04/13/2020	Brooklyn, NY	83	West Ohio	1959
George W. Fleming	04/16/2020	South Haven, MI	80	West Michigan	1965
John W. McNaughton	05/11/2020	Kalamazoo, MI	81	Detroit	1971
Georg F.W. Gerritsen	05/15/2020	Port Huron, MI	85	Detroit	1972
Robert P. Ward	05/26/2020	Bloomfield Hills, MI	92	Detroit	1949
Gary L. Sanderson	05/28/2020	Flushing, MI	83	Detroit	1964
David A. Stout	05/29/2020	Gladwin, MI	81	Detroit	1969
Elaine M. Buker	06/04/2020	Pensacola, FL	87	West Michigan	1985
Daniel J. Wallace	06/09/2020	Davison, MI	93	Detroit	1956
D. Keith Laidler	07/01/2020	Holland, MI	88	West Michigan	1957
Ronald D. VanLente	07/01/2020	South Haven, MI	66	W North Carolina	1991

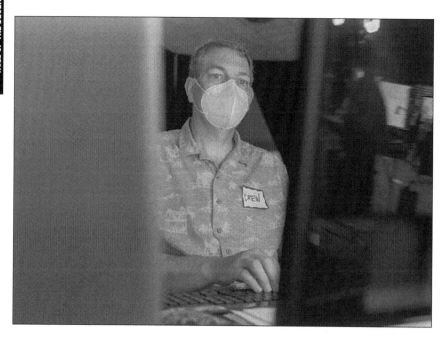

— MAC Photos

HISTORICAL SESSIONS OF THE ANNUAL CONFERENCE

For the listing of previous sessions of the former Detroit Annual Conference and West Michigan Annual Conference of The United Methodist Church, please refer to each conference's 2018 Journal, pages 322 and 298 respectively.

For information regarding previous sessions of the former Conferences of Evangelical United Brethren Church, refer to the Journal of the 107th Annual Session of the Michigan Conference (EUB) pages 25 and 26 dated May 20-23, 1968.

No.	Date Began	Place	Bishop	Secretary
1	May 30, 2019	Traverse City, MI	David A. Bard	Joy A. Barrett
2	July 26, 2020	Virtual	David A. Bard	Joy A. Barrett

— MAC Photos

CONFERENCE CANE

The Michigan Conference Cane replaces the two canes previously awarded by the Detroit and West Michigan Conferences. It will be used in ceremonies to honor the oldest living clergy person who has been under appointment to the Conference (and predecessor Michigan Area conferences) for a minimum of thirty (30) years). The thirty years need not be continuous, and the recipient need not be a resident of the state of Michigan at the time the award is made. The Commission on Archives and History sponsors the presentation. The current holder of the conference cane is Joseph H. Ablett.

The body of the cane is made of wood from the church in Adrian where the Detroit Conference was organized. There are inserts representing different historical periods, including: wood from the first Methodist Episcopal Church erected in Michigan in 1818 at River Rouge; wood from the desk of Reverend Seth Reed, who joined the Michigan Conference in its earliest years and died at the age of 100; wood from a tree near the resting place of Barbara Heck, a pioneering Methodist woman in America; wood from the church where Judson Collins, our first missionary to China, was converted; and wood from the pulpit used by Robert Strawbridge, pioneer of Methodism on the American continent.

The Detroit and West Michigan conferences both began the tradition of presenting canes to a senior member in 1904, during the celebration of the centennial of the first two visits to Michigan by Methodist preachers. Over the years, fifty-nine retired ministers received these cane awards (28 in West Michigan and 31 in Detroit). Recipients have included ministers not only from the United Methodist Church, but also some who began their careers in the Methodist Episcopal Church, Methodist Protestant Church, Evangelical Church, United Brethren in Christ, and the former Lexington Conference (a segregated African-American conference). The two older canes have been retired to the Conference archives.

Detroit Conference Cane holders and year presented: David A. Curtis, 1904; Francis A. Blades, 1904; Seth Reed, 1905; Phillip I. Wright, 1924; David Casler, 1928; David B. Millar, 1929; James E. Jacklin, 1941; Samuel Graves, 1944; George Tripp, 1948; Thomas Mott, 1950; Carl S. Risley, 1951; David N. Earl, 1953; Edwin D. Dimond, 1954; James T.M. Stephens, 1959; H. Addis Leeson, 1960; Richard C.G. Williams, 1964; Charles Bragg, 1966; William A. Gregory, 1967; Frank Purdy, 1971; Henry I. Voelker, 1973; Russell D. Hopkins, 1975; Benjamin F. Holmes, 1984; Myron R. Everett, 1990; George M. Jones, 1993; Walter C.B. Saxman, 1998; Ira L. Wood, 2002; Alvin Burton, 2003; Konstantin Wipp, 2005; William D. Rickard, 2013; Donald O. Crumm, 2014; Arthur L. Spafford, 2014 (died July 2, 2020)

West Michigan Conference Cane holders and year presented: John H. Pitezel, 1904; Riley C. Crawford, 1906; Lorin M. Bennett, 1911; Daniel S. Haviland, 1912; Thomas T. George, 1917; John K. Stark, 1919; John Graham, 1920; James H. Potts, 1921; Leander S. Matthews, 1942; William D. Rowland, 1949; Howard D. Skinner, 1950; August H. Coors, 1953; Harley H. Harris, 1955; Charles P. Ostrom, 1964; Albert T. Cartland, 1965; Grant L. Jordan, 1971; Floyd M. Barden, 1974; Lloyd A. Mead, 1975; Alvin G. Doten, 1980; Edward F. Rhoades, 1986; Richard D. Wearne, 1988; Harley L. Lane, 1989; Glenn M. Frye, 1991; Wayne M. Palmer, 1996; Chester J. Erickson, 1999; William A. Blanding, 2005; H. James Birdsall, 2007; Bernard R. Randolph, 2008 (died 2018)

Michigan Conference Cane holders and year presented:Joseph H. Ablett, 2020

SURVIVING SPOUSES

Abbott, Carol (Freeland) – 428 W Main Street, Hudson, MI 49247 ....(313) 231-0300
Amstutz, Jean – 4495 Calkins Rd., Apt 109, Flint, MI 48532-3574 ....(810) 230-0514
Anderson, Virginia A – 4090 Tall Oaks Dr, Grand Ledge, MI 48837 ....(517) 627-7895
Anderson, Winona – Great Lakes Christian Homes, 2050 S Washington Rd Apt 1012,
    Holt, MI 48842-8634 ....(517) 694-3084
Andrews, Arlene – 741 Clark Crossing SE, Grand Rapids, MI 49506 ....(616) 245-1589
Arntz, Ellen – 47280 Savannah Dr, Macomb, MI 48044-2792 ....(586) 468-6464
Atherton, Tom – 10400 Smith Rd., Gaines, MI 48436 ....(989) 271-8757
Atkins, Gertrude – 6206 S. Friends Ave., Whittier, CA 90601-3726
Baggs, Betty L – Timberline Lodge, 3770 Colwood Road, Caro, MI 48723 ....(989) 672-2525
Bailey, Cheryl – 3086 Slater Ave SE, Kentwood, MI 49512-1989 ....(616) 956-5678
Bamberger, Fern – 2439 Winona Street, East Tawas, MI 48730 ....(989) 362-5810
Bamsey, Karen – 1736 Weatherstone Dr., Ann Arbor, MI 48108 ....(734) 997-0421
Bank, Dorothy – 255 Mayer Rd., 266 Loehe Haus, Frankenmuth, MI 48734 ....(989) 652-4266
Bates, Barbara (Joyce) – 2525 N Elm St Apt 38, Miami, OK 74354-1421
Bates, Wanda – 6321 Noel Dr., Brentwood, TN 37027
Beach, Barbara – 200 Fairway West, Nicholasville, KY 40356-9414
Becker, Jeanne – 2985 Hillcrest Drive, New Era, MI 49446 ....(231) 861-5799
Beeker, Carol – 17425 Bunker Hill, Mt., Clemens, MI 48044 ....(586) 263-1712
Beers, Helen – 553 Gidley Ave Apt H, Grand Haven, MI 49417-2358 ....(616) 844-4272
Benner, Joan – 21660 Meadow Lane, Franklin, MI 48025-4850..................................(248) 723-0676
Benton, Katherine – 8530 Elkwood St., Byron Center, MI 49315...............................(616) 878-1405
Betts, Shirley – 501 King St. #114, Eaton Rapids, MI 48827 ....(517) 663-1626
Beynon, Hester W – 212 Chandler, Flint, MI 48503-2140
Blankenburg, Marilyn Jean – 9459 Orchard Street, PO Box 394, New Lothrop,
    MI 48460-0247 ....(810) 638-5722
Blue, Joan – 12198 SW Torch Lake Dr, Rapid City, MI 49676-9330 ....(231) 322-4420
Boal, Linda – 320 W. Main St, Marquette, MI 49855..(231) 871-0781
Bolitho, Mabel – 2315 40th St., R.F.D.#2, Hudsonville, MI 49426-9626
Bollinger, Evelyn – 201 Bedford Trail, Apt. 132, Sun City Center, FL 33573
Bough, Carolyn – 7341 Villamuer Rd, West Bloomfield, MI 48322-3307 ....(248) 788-1431
Bourns, Carol Lynn – 144 W 4th St Apt 403, Clare, MI 48617-1483 ....(989) 544-2719
Bowen, Barbara – 9387 Oakley Rd., St. Charles, MI 48655
Bracken, Claudia – 54 S. Avery, Waterford, MI 48328-3400 ....(248) 894-5902
Braid, Judith – 1850 Helena Ave., Hartland, MI 48353...(248) 887-4312
Branstner, Virginia – 210 E Sherwood Rd, Williamston, MI 48895-9323
Braun, Carol – 2730 Clyde Road, Ionia, MI 48846...(616) 527-0034
Bray, Jeannette – 16806 Lochmoor Circle W., Northville, MI 48167 ....(734) 667-4802
Breithaupt, Kathy – 18829 Lakewood Circle, Lake Ann, MI 49650 ....(231) 620-5508
Bremer, Vicky – 1527 G Hidden Creek Circle Dr NE, Grand Rapids, MI 49505 ....(989) 980-0903
Brooks, Alice –
Brooks, Kimberly – 216 Fifth St., Harrisville, MI 48740
Brooks, Nancy – 3845 Longfore Drive, Bay City, MI 48706
Brown, Esther – 162 Lakewood Dr, East Leroy, MI 49058 ....(269) 979-9303
Browne, Llwewellyn – 20100 Murray Hill, Detroit, MI 48235
Buker, Elaine M. – 10100 Hillview Dr. Apt.1213, Pensacola, FL 32514 ....(850) 607-7743
Bunce, Barbara – 717 Petoskey St., Gaylord, MI 49735
Burgess, Eula Jean – 422 Seaman Street, St Louis, MI 48880 ....(989) 681-4129

Burkey, Beth – 45182 W Park Dr Apt 46, Novi, MI 48377-1302
Burton-Collier, Linda J – 2574 127th Ave, Allegan, MI 49010-9250 ....(269) 793-7340
Butters, Pamela – 2204 2nd St, Connellsville, PA 15425-5313
Buwalda, Carol – 3983 Sierra Hts, Holt, MI 48842-7701 ....(517) 663-4418
Cameron, Doris J – 1103 SW 11th Street, Boca Raton, FL 33486............................(561) 395-5827
Carr, Carolyn – 5536 Ivy Path, Stevensville, MI 49127 ....(263) 686-0290
Cermak, Adele – 10540 N Shore Dr, PO Box 839, Northport, MI 49670....................(231) 386-5204
Chappell, Marilyn – 2401 Stobbe St, Saginaw, MI 48602-4081
Cheatham, Diane – 6331 Penwoods, San Antonio, TX 78240 ....(210) 697-1978
Christler, Betty – 801 W. Middle St. DH 461, Chelsea, MI 48118..............................(810) 338-9696
Christler, Bonnie – 2500 River Rd. #15, Marysville, MI 48040 ....(810) 841-5296
Cobb, Betty – 6711 Embassy Blvd, 106, Port Rickey, FL 34668-4739......................(813) 842-3447
Cole, Susan – 25 Arrowhead Estates Ln, Chesterfield, MI 63017-1824 ....(636) 536-2585
Coleman, Marge – 235 Gateway Dr. #507, Clare, MI 48817
Collins, Mary – PO Box 17, Northport, MI 49670 ....(231) 386-5169
Collins, Olo R – 15827 Maddelein, Detroit, MI 48205-2535
Collver, Joanne – 5619 Bayshore Rd. #135, Palmetto, FL 34221-9232
Conn, Judith – 1738 E Front St, Traverse City, MI 49686 ....(231) 995-5294
Cook, Anne – 1013 Castle Drive, Weidman, MI 48893..(989) 644-5903
Cooper, Ruth (Zimmermann) – 909 Centre Ave, Fort Collins, CO 80526
Cowing, Della – 3800 Shamrock Drive, Charlotte, NC 28215
Cozadd, Fay – 2450 S. Ridgewood #10, Edgewater, FL 32141
Crawford, Shirley – 3849 William Hume Dr, Zephyrhills, FL 33541-2351 ....(813) 788-0534
Crotser, Doris Lee – 109 N. 2nd Street, Lawrence, MI 49064-9697 ....(269) 674-4249
Crum, Grace – 2000 32nd St. SE, Grand Rapids, MI 49508 ....(616) 284-5445
Crumm, Barbara – 12640 Holly Rd., Apt B211, Grand Blanc, MI 48439 ....(810) 771-7319
Damberg, Marion – 495 McBride St, Dundee, MI 48131-1120....................................(734) 529-2157
Daniels, Gail – 4282 Occidental Hwy., Adrian, MI 49221 ....(517) 266-9377
Darling, Thomas – 44013 Winthrop Dr., Novi, MI 48375-8375....................................(248) 348-9039
Dennis, Barbara – 11444 Clark Rd, Davisburg, MI 48350..(810) 625-5981
Denton, Jeannine – 2401 Canoe Circle Dr, Lake Orion, MI 48360 ....(586) 482-9372
Dickins, Sally – 102 Hitchcock St., Aplena, MI 49707 ....(989) 356-4982
Diehl, Ruth – Core Bldg., Po Box 126, Cokesbury Village, Hockessin, DE 19707
Dimmick, Ann – 944 Grindle Drive, Lowell, MI 49331 ....(616) 897-5326
Doane, Helen Jeanne – 801 W. Middle St. #361, Chelsea, MI 48118........................(734) 475-6324
Douglas, Gertrude – 2700 Magnolia Ave., LaVerna, CA 91750
Dunstan, Bonnie – 5760 Pine Dr, Caseville, MI 48725 ....(989) 856-3263
Eckert, Mary – 1300 Benjamin Ave. SE, Grand Rapids, MI 49506 ....(616) 245-7108
Eddy, Ginger – 8020 Erie Ave, Chanhassen, MN 55317-9752 ....(952) 974-2092
Elford, Coral – 225 Capel St. #108, Sarnia, CANADA
Emelianov, Jenella – 3942 Tamarack Dr, Port Huron, MI 48060-1564
Engerbretson, Mrs. Otto – Flan unit-sompson Hs, Belmount Monument Rd., Philadelphia, PA 19131
Evan, Edna – 575 E. Lincoln, Apt. #8, Birmingham, MI 48009
Everett, Annabelle – 4465 35th Terrace, N., St. Petersburg, FL 33713
Fassett, Mary Lou – 1551 Franklin SE Apt 2028, Grand Rapids, MI 49506...............(616) 285-4795
Faust, Wilma – 8881 Bever Road, Delton, MI 49046 ....(269) 623-5520
Ferrigan, Debbie – 169 Helen St, Montrose, MI 48457-9426
Finkbeiner, Betty – 1551 Franklin St SE Apt 2017, Grand Rapids, MI 49506 ....(616) 887-2189
Fleming, Edna M. – 793 68th St, South Haven 49090 ....(269) 637-4406
Foldesi, Deb – 582 W Deerfield Road, Mt Pleasant, MI 48858....................................(989) 772-2548

Francis, Donna – 1551 Franklin SE Apt 4001, Grand Rapids, MI 49506 ....(616) 245-7402
Francis, Lois – 11 Pontiac St., Oxford, MI 48371
Franke, Charles – 2555 Amelia Lane, Lansing, MI 48917 ....(517) 322-0484
Fraser-Soots, Bea Barbara – 33762 Colony Park Dr, Farmington Hills, MI 48331-2732 ....(248) 320-5108
Frederick, Jody – 28450 Tiffin Dr, Chesterfield, MI 48047-6203 ....(586) 598-9887
Frey, Kenneth – 3907 Grodi Rd, Erie, MI 48133-9763 ....(734) 848-3411
Frick, Bonnie – 116 Wilmen Rd, Quincy, MI 49082 ....(517) 639-4496
Fry, Betty Jean – 4253 Embassy Dr SE, Grand Rapids, MI 49546 ....(616) 956-5653
Furness, Jerie – 618 W. Corunna Ave., Corunna, MI 48817-1200.............................(863) 655-1610
Gamber, Joanne – 1208 N Peniel Ave, Avon Park, FL 33825-2336...........................(863) 453-3172
Gerritsen, Barbara – 2915 16th Ave., Port Huron, MI 48060 ....(810) 987-2864
Gierman, Adrianne – c/o Kristen Reed, 5324 Stanford Rd, Jacksonville, FL 32207
Gilroy, Grace – 39 Park Ave, Battle Creek, MI 49017-5615 ....(269) 965-8830
Gjerstad, Flo – 5165 Spinning Wheel Dr., Grand Blanc, MI 48439-8439
Gladding, Irene – 15177 W Center Lake Dr, Tustin, MI 49688...................................(231) 829-3661
Glasgow, Joan M – 1351 Arch Road, Eaton Rapids, MI 48827 ....(517) 663-1612
Glasgow, Marion – 225 E Bort St, Long Beach, CA 90805-2234
Glover-MacCanon, Shirley – 9624 Park Ave, Allen Park 48101
Goodwin, Alice – 23708 Nilan Dr, Novi, MI 48375...(313) 475-0727
Graham, Jean – 748 Clark Crossing SE, Grand Rapids, MI 49506 ....(616) 248-0639
Grant, Gertrude – 25671 Sherwood Rd., Warren, MI 48091-4157
Grauer, Patricia – 11442 East River Dr, DeWitt, MI 48820.......................................(517) 669-3483
Grenfell, Jeannine – 2966 Sylvan Dr, Fort Gratiot, MI 48059-2853
Grettenberger, Diane – 1931 Osage Dr, Okemos, MI 48864 ....(517) 347-4604
Grienke, Beverly – 1920 Wank Ave, St Joseph MO 64507
Griffith, Nan – 29518 Westbrook Pkwy, Southfield, MI 48076-5073..........................(810) 559-0333
Griner, Beth – 6533 S. Betsie River Road, Interlochen, MI 49643-9508 ....(231) 276-9960
Guilliat, Eva – Box 144, Hillman, MI 49746-9746
Hanlon, Charles – 7797 Teakwood, Jenison, MI 49428 ....(616) 457-2901
Hanna, Anne Marie – 341 Lafayette, PO Box 787, Manchester, MI 48158................(734) 428-8212
Hansen, Beth – 1551 Franklin St SE Apt 4005, Grand Rapids, MI 49506 ....(616) 776-1281
Hart, Katherine – 6813 15th Avenue Dr W, Bradenton, FL 34209-4443
Hartley, Beatrice – 519 Round Tree, Sarasota, FL 33578
Haskell, Janet –
Hatch, Lois – 536 Poplar St, Ishpeming, MI 49849-1041 ....(906) 485-4355
Helm, Charlene – 7372 Main St., Box 98, Owendale, MI 48754
Higgins, Marie – 68 Reservoir, Holden, MA 01520-1520
Hilliard, Viola – 801 W. Middle St. DH-467, Chelsea, MI 48118
Hinkston, Kay – 226 Greenview, Cadillac, MI 49601-9601
Hippensteel, Johanna – 695 E Girard Road, Quincy, MI 49082 ....(517) 278-2118
Hocking, Hettie – 42 Smith St, Mount Clemens, MI 48043-2338
Hodgson, Ariel – 873 W. Avon Rd., #210, Rochester Hills, MI 48307-2705
Hoff, Mary – 850 W Huron River Dr, Belleville, MI 48111-4298
Hoffmaster, M. Jean – 9236 Tallapoosa Highway, Cedartown, GA 30125
Hollies, Charles – 1403 W. Broadway Ave. PMB 418, Apache Junction, AZ 85220 ....(517) 780-4503
Hoon, Fannie – 228 The Western Way, Princeton, NJ 08540
Host, Margery H – 6136 Co Rd 413, McMillan, MI 49853..(906) 293-1670
Houk, Anna Belle – 4585 S Lakeshore Dr, Ludington, MI 49431 ....(231) 845-7510
Imms, Carolyn – 65 Harbor Oaks Dr, Fruitland Park, FL 34731 ....(352) 728-1052
James, Phyllis – C/o Kathryn Mccurdy, Romeo, MI 48065
Janka, Mildred – 09780 Meadows Trail, Boyne Falls, MI 49713

Jensen, Yvonne – 349 Ardussi St, Frankenmuth, MI 48734
Johns, Marlene – 3127 Heather Glynn Drive, Mulberry, FL 33860 ....(863) 425-9691
Johnson, Elouise – 3317 Sir Thomas Drive #24, Silver Springs, MD 20904...............(301) 890-3478
Johnson, Judy – 9459-32 Mission Gorge Rd, Santee, CA 92071 ....(619) 749-7859
Jones, Ruth – 540 Georgetown Dr Apt 36, Traverse City, MI 49684-4479..................(231) 645-1761
Jones, Shirley – 910 Fairmead Rd Apt B, Plainfield, IN 46168-2415
Jongeward, Elaine – 574 Belltower Ave, Deltona, FL 32725....................................(386) 574-0373
Jorgensen, Lenna (Daniel) – 3420 Nathan Ct, Rocklin, CA 95677-2351
Karlzen, Martha Jane – PO Box 3, Charlotte, MI 48813 ....(517) 541-0653
Keller, Patricia – 10532 Pine Tree Ln, Goodrich, MI 48438 ....(810) 820-7021
Kivisto, Jeffrey – 7144 Brentwood Dr., Brighton 48116 ....(810) 227-6371
Kline, Tina – 28955 Pujol St Apt 10-B, Temecula, CA 92590-2837 ....(951) 506-0609
Kline-Hunt, Janet W – 7630 W St Andrews Circle, Portage, MI 49024 ....(269) 373-1588
Kolb, Dena – RR 5 Box 5032, Grayling, MI 49738-8713
Kramer-Schurman, Donna – 696 N. State Route 741, Lebanon, OH 45036
Kraushaar, Doris – 5621 Blue Grass Lane, Saline, MI 48176-8176
Krichbaum, Susan – 24082 Bingham Pointe Dr., Bingham Farms, MI 48025
Kuhn, Mary Beth – 10143 Lakeside Dr, Perrinton, MI 48871-9647 ....(989) 682-4814
Kye, Yang Ja – 14715 San Jacinto Dr, Moreno Valley, CA 92555-6366...................(951) 242-8484
LaFrance, David – 15132 Snowberry Ct, Spring Lake, MI 49456-2814 ....(616) 850-2157
Laidler, Judy – 3335 Starboard Dr, Holland 49424..(616) 786-2774
Lamb, Ollie – 801 W Middle St # DH 372, Chelsea, MI 48118-1341
Lantz, Melinda – Hubbard Manor, Apt.#912, 22077 Beech St., Dearborn, MI 48124
Laphew, Geneva V. – 19438 Beech Daly Rd, Detroit, MI 48240-1321
Leach, Marie – 2025 Charter Oaks Dr, Clearwater, FL 33763-4209
Leach, Peggy – 3398 Crestwood Dr, Salt Lake City, UT 84109-3202
Lemmons, Barbara – 410 3rd Ave S, #D9, Hurley, WI 54534-1527 ....(715) 561-3310
Lester, Maridelle – 3128 N. Harding Ave., Indianapolis, IN 46208-4800
Lewis, Ann – 6393 Little Lake Geneva Road, Keystone Heights, FL
Lindley, Shirley – 454 Hickory Court, Leipsic, OH 45856-5856
Logsdon (VanLente), Kathleen – 467 Mary Knoll Dr #83, Fennville 49408 269-308-1032
Lovejoy, Lorraine – 224 SR 13, Wesley Manor, Jacksonville, FL 32223
Lowes, Carol – 27145 County Road 364, Mattawan, MI 49071-9558.........................(269) 668-6526
Luciani, Carolyn – 801 W Middle St Apt 560, Chelsea, MI 48118-1374 ....(734) 475-5926
Lutz-Sempert, Joyce – 7651 W. Chelsea Ct, PO Box 5066, Homosassa Springs, FL 34447
Magnuson, Edla – 714 Parkvies, Saint Paul, MN 55117-4156
Mahan, Marcia – 1555 N. Main St., Frankfort, IN 46041
Malstrom, Esther – c/o Joseph Malstrom, 1392 Van Buren St., St. Paul, MN 55101-5101
Mannino, Barbara – 8732 Huckleberry Lane, Lansing, MI 48917 ....(517) 449-3413
Marbly, Mayme S. – 8328 S Indiana Ave, Chicago, IL 60619-4727
Marshall, Esther – 2611 Wildwood Dr Apt 519, Brunswick, GA 31520-4250
Martin, Martha – 1368 Grayton St, Grosse Pointe Park, MI 48230-1128 ....(313) 885-3974
Martin, Mary – Balmoral Skilled Nursing Home, 5500 Fort St., Trenton, MI 48183
Matson, Jacqueline – 5792 Leisure South Dr SE, Kentwood, MI 49548....................(616) 437-3022
Matthews, Edith – 18190 W. Outer Dr., Dearborn, MI 48128-1349
Maurer, Edrye A. Eastman – 10101 Jackson Square, Decatur, GA 30030 ....(269) 459-5223
McCaw, Jeanne – 4211 Embassy Dr SE, Grand Rapids, MI 49546-2438 ....(616) 975-1875
McKanders, Cherlyn – PO Box 158, Washington, MI 48094-0158 ....(313) 640-8498
McLellan, Virginia – 4640 Shaw Road, Harrisville, MI 48740......................................(989) 724-6248
McLennan, Mary – 241 Bravado Lane, Palm Beach Shores, FL 33404
McNally, Bessie – 1852 Union Ave, Benton Harbor, MI 49022-6264

McNaughton, Donna Lee – 2910 Bronson Blvd, Kalamazoo, MI 49008 ....(269) 383-3433
McVety, Elizabeth – 1932 Stimson Rd, Brown City, MI 48416-8181 ....(810) 346-3384
Meines, Noreen – 11279 Whispering Creek Dr, Allendale, MI 49401.........................(616) 895-5297
Meredith, Gertrude A. – 1701 Mallery, Flint, MI 48501
Michael, Helen – 170 Grove, Coopersville, MI 49404
Middleton, Betty – 344 Persimmon Way, Harrodsburg, KY 40330
Milano, Regina – 12 1/2 Applegrove Dr, Nicholasville, KY 40356
Miles, Louise K. – 5915 Cartago Dr, Lansing, MI 48911-6480 ....(989) 777-1248
Miles, Marilyn – 309 Fieldstone Dr., Hemlock, MI 48626-9104 ....(989) 642-3075
Miller, Beth – 175 Timber Lakes Est, Heber City, UT 84032-9694
Miller, Deborah Reid – 554 Faraday Dr SE, Grand Rapids, MI 49548-8500..............(616) 350-2991
Miller, Phyllis – 37644 Pinata Avenue, Zephyr Hills, FL 33541 ....(813) 788-1676
Millet, Edna – 776 Newberry Rd, Nashville, TN 37205-1129 ....(313) 582-8483
Mirmak, Letha – 804 Maurice, Alton, IL 62002-1957
Mitchell, Coral – C/o Mrs. H. Mccoy, 1702 Francis, Jackson, MI 49201
Mitchell, Hazel – 16631 Mendota, Detroit, MI 48221
Mohr, Phyllis – 4070 York Ln, Jackson, MI 49201
Morse, Lorna – 833 S Ausable Trl, Grayling, MI 49738-9166 ....(989) 348-7037
Mosher, Sharry – 510 Village W Apt B, Midland, MI 48642-9343.........................(810) 627-3055
Mulder, Lydia – 219 Highland, Dearborn, MI 48128 ....(313) 278-8634
Murphy, Patricia – 1892 Jasper Place, Ocala, FL 34472 ....(352) 694-1892
Myers, Beth – 262 Pennbrook, Battle Creek, MI 49017 ....(269) 274-9120
Myers, Linda – 7463 Navajo Valley Dr., Byron Center, MI 49315
Myette, Ruth – 211 1/2 S. Spruce St, Traverse City, MI 49684 ....(231) 946-5993
Nachtrieb, Evelyn – 1616 W Glendale Ave # 380, Phoenix, AZ 85021-8948
Nelson, Juanita – 1145 College Ave, Columbus, OH 43209-2858
Nicholson, Patricia – 392 Shot Point Dr, Marquette, MI 49855-9554 ....(906) 343-6506
Noordhof, Barbara – 14297 Leonard Rd, Spring Lake, MI 49456..............................(616) 935-9718
Olde, Grace – 4137 Morehouse Raod, West Lafayette, IN 47906
Olsen, Robert – 175 Cherry Street, Freeport, MI 49325 ....(616) 765-3838
Olsen, Sandy – 557 McBride St, Dundee, MI 48131-8131 ....(734) 529-5389
Osborne, Pearl E. – 6830 E 19th Ave, Denver, CO 80220-1725
Page, Mildred – 8111 E Broadway Blvd Apt 307, Tucson, AZ 85710-3929 ....(520) 495-5880
Palmer Turner, Johncie – 1039 Crestwood Ln, Jackson, MI 49203 ....(517) 769-2329
Patton, Louine – Sayre Christain Village, 580 Greenfield Dr., #107A, Lexington, KY 40517
Paulson, Gerrie – 1414 Woodcock Pass, Alger, MI 48610
Penzien, Jo – 7414 Wall Ct, Dexter, MI 48130-1338
Petersen, Elsie – Masonic Pathways, 1200 Wright Ave #233, Alma, MI 48801-1133.......(989) 875-4665
Pillow, Lorraine – 5133 Hoffman Street, PO Box 68, Elkton, MI 48731-0068
Porter, Nancy Hicok – 9514 Bluewater Hwy Rt #3, Lowell, MI 49331-9298
Preston, Sally – 4491 E Park Dr, Bay City, MI 48706-2549.....................................(989) 667-4438
Price, Martha – 5057 Woodlands Ct, Flint, MI 48532-4078
Pumfery, Carole – 21345 52nd St, Grand Junction, MI 49056-9755.........................(269) 427-5513
Quick, Mary Levack – 1941 Wellesley Dr, Detroit, MI 48203-1428 ....(313) 891-2861
Raymo, Muriel – 1215 Riverford Dr, Voctavia Hills, AL 35216-6101 ....(205) 985-4912
Reese, Carin – 558 Lawrence Ave, Wayland, MI 49348
Reese, Janice – 3302 SE Alder St, Hillsboro, OR 97123-7435.................................(503) 648-6134
Regier, Hinako – 30 Seven Star Lane, Concord, MA 1742
Reinhart, Ruth – 9136 Flamingo Circle, N. Ft. Myers, FL 33903.................................(239) 652-9188
Reyner, Beverly – 4500 Killarney Park Dr, Burton, MI 48529-1832 ....(810) 744-4265
Rhoads, Annie Ruth Callis – 3800 Shamrock Dr., Charlotte, NC 28215

Rice, Birdie – 2662 Columbus Street, Detroit, MI 48206 ....(313) 871-7918
Rice, Dorotohy – 478 4th St Apt 202, Beaver, PA 15009-2235
Rice, Shan – 10333 W. Olive Ave. #146, Peoria, AZ 85345
Rice, Susan – 533 Kern Rd, Fowlerville, MI 48836-9251
Richards, Helen – 3700 E Allen Rd, Howell, MI 48855-8224
Richards, Ruth – 733 Gilead Shores Dr, Bronson, MI 49028
Richie, Alice – 208 Freeman Forest Dr, Newnan, GA 30265-3399 ....(770) 683-9506
Ritchie, Dorothy – PO Box 274, Hesperia, MI 49421-0274
Ritchie, Florence K. – 129 Smachbar Bldg., Champaign, IL 61820
Robinson, Carole – 1710 14th St, Wyandotte, MI 48192-3612
Rosa, Annette – 19558 Maple, PO Box 123, Lake Ann, MI 49650-0123
Rothfuss, Jackie (Jacqueline) – 2049 Rowland Ave SE #8, Grand Rapids, MI 49546 ......(616) 202-7206
Ruotsalainen, Jenny – PO Box 1268, Twentynine Palms, CA 92277-0980
Salisbury, Marylin – 1551 Franklin SE #4004, Grand Rapids, MI 49506.....................(616) 246-6360
Sanderson, Caroline – 319 Sunburst, Flushing, MI 48433...(810) 659-4523
Schloop, Patricia – 1551 Franklin SE Apt 2022, Grand Rapids, MI 49506 ....(616) 246-1006
Schroeder, Carolyn – 2019 Ter Van Dr NE, Grand Rapids, MI 49505-6369
Scovel, Mary A – 14176 Lake Wildwood Dr, Penn Valley, CA 95946-9592
Scranton Bassett, Vivian – 1551 Franklin SE Apt. 3025, Grand Rapids, MI 49506.........(616) 247-0950
Seitz, Oneida – 10590 Wadsworth Rd., Reese, MI 48757
Selberg, Linda – 640 S Lafayette St, Dearborn, MI 48124-1594
Sever, Diane – 920 D Ave, Central City, NE 68826
Shamblen, Audrey – Centerline Park Towers #8-18, 8033 E 10 Mile Rd, Centerline, MI 48015
Sheppard, Sandy – 7420 Majestic Wood Dr, Linden, MI 48451-8836.........................(989) 823-8996
Sheridan, Nancy – 604 Ames Ct., Bay City, MI 48708
Shields, Ida – 6851 Goldenrod Ave NE, Rockford, MI 49341-9436............................(616) 874-2113
Shipley, Gwendolyn – 23711 Clarkson, Southfield, MI 48033 ....(313) 861-9180
Siders, Vesta – 904 Piper Dr, Saginaw, MI 48604-1833 ....(989) 753-8806
Silvernail, Florence – 3832 Perrine Rd, Rives Junction, MI 49277-9642 ....(517) 569-3715
Simmons, Charlotte – 801 West Middle #373, Chelsea, MI 48118 ....(734) 433-9879
Skinner, Bill – 460 S Edgar Rd, Mason, MI 48854-9744 ....(517) 676-1529
Slaughter-Titus, Linda – 1108 Suwannee Dr., Waycross GA 31501 ....(912) 283-5908
Smith, Beverly – 514 E Roselawn Dr, Logansport, IN 46947-2134............................(269) 679-4646
Smith, Diana – 10275 Strasburg Rd., Erie, MI 48133
Smith, Dorothy J. – 3341 Woodwind Dr NE, Grand Rapids, MI 49525-9752 ....(616) 719-2131
Smith, Jennella – 3942 Tamarack Dr, Port Huron, MI 48060-1564
Smith, Phyllis – Beacon Hill, 1845 Boston SE Apt 308, Grand Rapids, MI 49506-4400....(616) 805-3560
Snow, Dorothy – 501 Leorie Street, North Muskegon, MI 49445 ....(231) 744-2659
Soderholm, David – 216 5th St, Harrisville, MI 48740-9673 ....(231) 450-0901
Sommer (Spafford), Lois – 47197 Manhattan Circle, Novi 48374 ....(248) 773-8341
Stone, Helen – 1428 Roosevelt Dr, Venice, FL 34293-6853 ....(248) 835-1301
Stout, Ruthanne – 4721 7th Ave, Sacramento, CA 95820
Strait, Janet Sue – 1402 Suncrest Dr. NE, Grand Rapids, MI 49503 ....(616) 245-1099
Stricker, Edith – c/o Jacqueline Wisman, 1218 West E St., North Platte, NE 69101
Stubbs, Caroline – 104 E Mechanic, Yale, MI 48097-3454
Sundell, Jennifer – 3289 Hitching Post Rd Apt 40, Dewitt, MI 48820-9664 ....(616) 527-9656
Sursaw, Margaret – 37737 Hixford Pl Apt G-20, Westland, MI 48185-3365
Sutton, Helen – 1000 Manhattan Ave., Dayton, OH 45406
Syme, Judy – 250 Marcell Dr NE Apt 6, Rockford, MI 49341-1380
Taber, Miriam – 1551 Franklin St SE Apt 3305, Grand Rapids, MI 49506 ....(616) 475-0717
Taylor, Josephine – c/o Gilford Taylor, 17682 Cooley Ave., Detroit, MI 48219

Teague, Lillie Mae – 331 Franklin Blvd, Pontiac, MI 48340-8340
Tester, Lydia – 455 S. College Drive, Heston, KS 67062-8105
Thomas, Ann – 1890 Ashley Dr, Ypsilanti, MI 48198-9412
Thornton, June – 512 Englewood Drive, Roscommon, MI 48653
Timm, Ann – 5110 Autumn Ln, North Street, MI 48049-4459 ....(810) 987-5124
Timmons, Doris – 8822 Richfield Ave., Livonia, MI 48150 ....(734) 953-9208
Tingland, Edith R. – 4447 Wisner, Saginaw, MI 48601
Tomlinson, Karan – 36 Rockhampton Ridge, Battle Creek, MI 49014 ....(269) 968-4930
Trevarthen, Amanda – 2501 Broadway, Huntington Park, CA 90255-6343
Truran, Donna – 5884 Augusta Lane, Grand Blanc, MI 48439-9472 ....(231) 955-0257
Turner, Johncie Kay (Palmer) – 1039 Crestwood Ln, Jackson, MI 49203 ....(517) 769-2329
Van Wormer, Dennis – 3013 Oakwood Dr, Port Huron, MI 48060
VanConant, Earleen – 55209 Fallbrooke Dr., Macomb 48042 ....(586) 243-6176
Vandlen, Gerry – 1551 Franklin St SE Apt 3027, Grand Rapids, MI 49506 ....(616) 475-0125
Vaught, Helen – 1641 S Broadway St, Hastings, MI 49058-2561 ....(269) 945-9392
Vuurens, Florence – 2685 Forest Hills Drive, Muskegon, MI 49441-3441 ....(231) 828-4341
Wagner, Noreen – 3534 Conger St., Port Huron, MI 48060
Walker, Lorna – 2753 E. Waterview Dr., Avon Park, FL 33825-6015 ....(863) 314-6502
Walton, Alice – 33010 West Chicago, Livonia, MI 48150
Wangdahl, Agnes – 1252 Doubleday Drive, Arnold, MD 21012
Ward, Olive – 3202 Meridian Rd, Leslie, MI 49251-9520
Weatherup, Shelley – 40460 Cinnamon Cir, Canton, MI 48187-4588
Weeks, Martha – 429 Center St, PO Box 404, Manistique, MI 49854-1111 ....(906) 341-3423
Wehrli, Kitty – 32805 Garfield Rd, Fraser, MI 48026-3848
Westfall, Geraldine – 1001 Lynn, Kalamazoo, MI 49008-2952
White, Joanne – 158 LaSiesta, Edgewater, FL 32141-2141 ....(904) 428-0900
White, Sharon – 745 Clark Crossing SE, Grand Rapids, MI 49506 ....(616) 425-0045
Whyte, Blanche – 17387 Plainview, Detroit, MI 48219-8219......................................(313) 538-1194
William, Monica – 4100 Walnut Lake Rd, West Bloomfield, MI 48323 ....(248) 851-0149
Williams, Virginia – 36615 Cherry St, Newark, CA 94560
Wolfe, Sue – 245 Highland Dr, Jackson, MI 49201 ....(517) 926-6041
Wong, Patricia – 326 - 5th Street, Ann Arbor, MI 48103-6209....................................(734) 741-8160
Wood, Judith – 1842 Live Oak Court, Avon, IN 46123
Wood, Una – 4300 Martin Rd., Box 462, Capac, MI -
Woodward, Eva D. – 1609 - 21st Ave. West, Braderton, FL 33505
Yarlott, Irene – 2946 Creek Park Dr NE, Marietta, GA 30062 ....(770) 321-5310
Yearby, Joan – 250675 Meadowbrook Rd, Novi, MI 48375
Yoh, Mary – 5026 Village Gardens Drive, Sarasota, FL 34234 ....(616) 392-3942
Young, Harry – 700 N. LeRoy, Fenton, MI 48430

ADDRESSES

ELECTED LAYPERSONS ON CONFERENCE COMMITTEES

Alberts, Amy – 6929 Curtis Rd, PO Box 102, Hale 48739 (989) 728-5772 ......myfaithalberts@juno.com

Anderson, Ruby – 25180 Thorndyke, Southfield 48033 (248) 352-9246 ....rbydandrs@aol.com

Angarita-Oviedo, Ricardo – 247 S 1st Street, Harbor Beach 48441 (734) 680-5185
....vida7plena@gmail.com

Apol, David – 3246 Wayburn Ave SW Frnt Apt, Grandville 49418 (616) 292-6687
....apoldavid@aol.com

Appling, Sharon – 882 Rivard Blvd, Grosse Pointe 48230 (313) 671-8974 ...sea0704@comcast.net

Archambeau, Don – 28270 Elmira St, Livonia 48150 (734) 422-2227.......donarchambeau@gmail.com

Armstrong, Minnie – 18107 Baldwin Rd., Holly 48442 (810) 877-0511minibstrong1975@gmail.com

Arnold, Nancy – 350 Riviera Terrace, Waterford 48328 (248) 682-6140 .narnold@michiganumc.org

Ashford, Dwanda – 8000 Woodward Ave, Detroit 48202 (313) 481-1045 .....ashford@michiganumc.org

Bailey, Taylorie – 16855 Rosemont, Detroit 48219 (313) 531-0751 ....etbailey77@sbcglobal.net

Ball, Janet – 6874 5 Mile Rd, Blanchard 49310 (231) 250-1084 ....ljball6@hotmail.com

Baumann, Karl – 5010 N. Magrudder Rd., Coleman 48618 (989) 465-1557 ....karlbauman@hotmail.com

Bennett, David – 2471 Veltema Dr, Holt 48842 (517) 694-0517 ....bennettd41@ameritech.net

Bernum, Robert – 3209 Monticello Dr, Port Huron 48060 (810) 984-2771 ...BBernum@comcast.net

Blashill, Mary – 07909 M-43, South Haven 49090 (269) 767-6060 ....maryblashill@gmail.com

Bledsoe, Rose – 1106 Nine Mile Road, Sterling 48659 (989) 324-8514........bledsoerm@gmail.com

Booker, Victoria – Beverly Hills UMC, 20000 W. 13 Mile Rd., Beverly Hills 48025
....director@jfonsemi.org

Bosserd, Jim – 3631 13 Mile Rd NW, Sparta 49345 (616) 887-7805 ....Bosserdjim@gmail.com

Bosserd-Schroeder, Joan – 7515 W Hickory Rd, Hickory Corners 49060 (269) 623-5762
....joanlbs@gmail.com

Bostic, Patricia – 4106 W. 13 Mile, Apt.D, Royal Oak 48073 (248) 677-4940 ....pbostic02@att.net

Brainard, Ted – 7358 S Lake Bluff O.5 Dr, Gladstone 49837 (906) 428-2806
....sallybrainard732@gmail.com

Brewster, Christie – 3810 Syracuse, Dearborn 48124 (313) 585-5615christiebrewster@yahoo.com

Brown, Diane – 4512 Cottonwood Dr., Ann Arbor 48108 (734) 662-0469 ....dlb4512@yahoo.com

Burton-Collier, Linda – 2574 127th Ave, Allegan 49010 (269) 793-7340
....lindaburtoncollier@gmail.com

Busley, Sus'ann – 555 S Williamston Rd, Dansville 48819 (517) 623-6239 ...sbusley@michiganumc.org

Campbell, Ernestine – 20300 Westmoreland Rd., Detroit 48219 (313) 529-5686
....ecampbe16@yahoo.com

Carr, Liz – 2267 Sunset Bluff Dr, Holland 49424 (317) 847-3661 ....Lizcarr@charter.net

Cho, Koom – 819 Alana Ct, Davison 48423...mathchampion@gmail.com

Chu, Ethan – 733 Orchard Dr, Williamston 48895 ....ethanichu@gmail.com

Clarke, Doug – 2147 Bluffton Ave, Muskegon 49441 (231) 759-0682 ....dpclarke@comcast.net

Clawson, Randie – 384 Lind Dr., Traverse City 49696 (231) 929-7808.......randie.clawson@yahoo.com

Clevenger, Renae – 2302 Longfellow Ln., Midland 48640 (989) 430-8562.......renaeclev76@gmail.com

Coffey, Judith – 128 Forest Lawn Dr, Cadillac 49601 (231) 775-6095 ....jcoffeyumc@yahoo.com

Coffman, Patsy – 206 S Swegles St, St Johns 48879 (989) 224-7692 ....patsymcoffman@gmail.com

Comiskey, Mary – 1321 Beamer Rd, Blissfield 49228 (517) 918-8252

Costales, Jorge – 9841 Woodlawn Dr, Portage 49002 (269) 324-0697................chumyc@aol.com

Craig, Nancy – 1428 Safire Court, East Lansing 48823 (517) 351-1391 ....craign@msu.edu

Crombez, Rene – 2223 Allen St, Adrian 49221 (734) 904-4146

Dahlman, Laurie – 1228 Southern Ave, Kalamazoo 49001 (269)343-1490 ......ladmsu1@gmail.com

Darby, Michael – 5133 Scott Rd., Mr. Morris 48458 (810) 610-8500 ......1stnaturalsolutions@gmail.com

Darrow, Linda – 232 N. Cooley St., Mt. Pleasant 48858 (989) 763-8750 ....darrowlinda@gmail.com

Davis, Murray – 26225 Fordson Hwy, Redford 48239 (313) 937-3453 ....mbdavisinc@aol.com

DeLong, Cameron – 4934 Brownstone Drive NE, Rockford 49341 (616) 866-3191 ...cdelong@wnj.com
Dick, Kevin – 606 W Sunset Dr, Muskegon 49445 (231) 719-8006 ....kevin@j-fins.com
Donley, Lee – 1977 N 2700 East Rd, Moweaqua, IL 62550..............................leedonley2@aol.com
Dorman, Kathleen – 2596 Vatter Rd., Snover 48472 (810) 404-9630.............khdflame@icloud.com
Dowell, Kenneth – 19080 San Jose Blvd., Lathrup Village 48076 (248) 559-7047 ...ken@dowell.ws
Downer, Holly – 3733 Bantam Dr, Hudsonville 4942-8669 (616) 669-6794....Holly@grmetroministry.org
Doyal, Mark – 525 University Dr, East Lansing 48823 (517) 927-5920 ...mdoyal@michiganumc.org
Dunlap, Rachel – 1589 W Maple, Birmingham 48009 (734) 620-3566.........dunlap.r.m@gmail.com
DuPree, Brenda – 8165 Holcomb, Clarkston 48348 (248) 625-5141 ....bkdupree@comcast.net
Edris, Larry – 2534 Lakeshore Dr, Fennville 49408 (269) 543-4182...............cledris@comcast.net
Erbes, Annette – 1951 Heatherton Dr, Holt 48842 (517) 694-8277 ......layleader@michiganumc.org
Euper, Jacqueline – 11463 S State Rd., Morrice 48857 (517) 625-2920 ....tjeuper@tm.net
Falker, Katja – 807 Oak Grove Pkwy, Houghton 49931 (906) 281-4129...........ksfalker@gmail.com
Federau, Deborah – , (517) 202-3533...debfederau@aol.com
Fennell, Deborah – 3409 Rolfe Rd, Mason 48854 (517) 676-1887......debontheweb@wowway.com
Fielder, Sue – 2010 Maca Vista Dr, Indian River 49749 (231) 238-4751 ....sue.irumc@gmail.com
Gackler, Kenneth – 410 Johnson St., Caledonia 49316 (616) 891-5682 ....gackler@iserv.net
Garbrecht, Bonnie – 153 Garrison Ave, Battle Creek 49017 (269) 964-9828
....garbrechtab@comcast.net
Gillette, Robert – 4091 12 Mile Road, Rockford 49341 (616) 866-0934....gillette@wuattorneys.com
Gray, Fred – 2100 Norwood Dr., Midland 48640 (989) 631-0763 ....hhs69@aol.com
Guy, Nichea – (616) 456-7168...orangecelt00@aol.com
Guyon, Rich – 3289 Outback Tr., Pinckney 48169 (734) 751-7719 ....rich.guyon@charter.net
Hahn, Lisa – 3317 Noeske St, Midland 48640 ....funny.laugh.88@gmail.com
Hardiman, Clayton – ....chardiman@muskegonchronicle.com
Hart, John – 1894 Chatham Dr., Troy 48084 (248) 649-2396........................johnfhart@hotmail.com
Hazen, Catharine – 2150 Teggerdine Rd, White Lake 48386 (248)698-9326.......cathzen@comcast.net
Herriff, Judy – 5651 Bunker Rd, Eaton Rapids 48827 ....jherriff@gmail.com
Hewitt, Suzanne – 2250 Knapp St NE, Grand Rapids 49505 (616) 361-9565...suzmckhew@att.net
Hicok, Greg – #514, 25701 West 12 Mile Rd, Southfield 48034
Hildebrant, Randy – 110 W Harrie St, Newberry 49868 (906) 492-3680.....rhildebrant@umcmission.org
Hines, Paula – 925 35th St. SW, Wyoming 49509 (616) 235-7001...............paulahines@gmail.com
Hitts, Elise – 1881 Ellinger Rd., Alanson 49706 (231) 548-5774 ....21hitelie@rayder.org
Hodges, Carol – 222 N Kalamazoo Mall Apt 320, Kalamazoo 49007
....carolhodges.kalamazoo@gmail.com
Hodges, Deborah – 7057 Amber Springs Dr SW, Byron Center 49315 (616) 443-3728
....dhodges727@comcast.net
Holt, Kathy – 2376 Belle Glade Ct, Fenton 48430 (810) 750-1931 ....kathleenholt@charter.net
Hopgood, Hoon-Yung – PO Box 30036, Lansing 48909 (855) 347-8006
....senhhopgood@senate.michigan.gov
Huizing, John – 40 N. Plum Street, Hart 49420 (231) 873-0418 ....huizingathart@charter.net
Hunt, Blair – 2110 Palm Dale Dr SW, Wyoming 49519 (269) 341-0467 ....blair.r.hunt@gmail.com
Hurlbut, Wynne – 36146 Cherry St, Gobles 49055 (269) 628-2944 .....wynne_hurlbut@frontier.com
Iseler, Lawrence – 5606 Minden Rd N, Port Hope 48468 (989) 428-4229....mciseler70@gmail.com
Ives, Russ – ....russives@comcast.net
Jennings, Karl – 8711 Pebble Creek Dr., Pinckney 48169 (517) 404-0058.......karl@borekjennings.com
Kasper, Anika – 3851 N 15 Rd, Mesick 49668 (231) 885-1179 ....anikakasper@gmail.com
Kaufman de la Garza, Laurie – 1306 Michigan Ave., Gladstone 49837 (906) 428-4623
....laurie.kdlg@sbcglobal.net
Keeler, Gregory – 25170 Circle Dr, Southfield 48075 (248) 350-3659 ....tron_9990@yahoo.com
Kimball, Kurt – 4552 Koinonia Ct NE, Grand Rapids 49525 (616) 401-5100 ..kurt.kimball@comcast.net

Lawrence, Clara – 20222 Sunset Street, Livonia 48152 (248) 863-7705 ....claralaw4peace@gmail.com
Leavitt, Waltha Gaye – 8524 E. Colby Rd., Crystal 48818 (989) 640-0238........wally@cmsinter.net
LeBaron, Jim – 13401 Peacock Rd, Laingsburg 48848 (517) 641-8042...........jlebaronllc@aol.com
Lee, Loretta – 142 Greenwood Ave, Battle Creek 49037 (269) 317-7377
....weatherBY2000@sbcglobal.net
Leppink, Ransom – PO Box 365, Lakeview 48850 (989) 352-6430...............leppinks@hotmail.com
Long, Robert – 10 Sycamore Dr., Chelsea 48118 (734) 475-8449....................rlquizzy@gmail.com
Luna, Sonya – 1467 Collegewood St, Ypsilanti 48197 (734) 961-7314 ......sluna@michiganumc.org
Lundquist, C David – 1400 N Drake Rd Apt 347, Kalamazoo 49006 (616) 372-4772
....dlundquist@ameritech.net
MacGregor, Susan – 5432 Monroe Rd, PO Box 914, Pentwater 49449 (231) 869-4364
....jsmac1@frontier.com
Machesky, Lisa – Baldwin Avenue Center, PO Box 420700, Pontiac 48340 (248) 642-6343
....lmachesky@umcampingboard.org
Maidens, Valerie – 1639 Black Bark Ln, Traverse City 49686 (231) 941-2360 ...vjmaidens@yahoo.com
Mallard, Mildred – 18525 Division, Marshall 49068 (269) 781-4689 ....Abcboutique@aol.com
Mangum, Audrey – 3591 W Outer Dr, Detroit 48221 (912) 432-3001 ....amangumsav@gmail.com
Marsh, Georgia – 212 Chauncey Court, Marshall 49068 (269) 781-2501.....georgiamarsh212@gmail.com
Marsman, Mara – 1675 84th St SE, Caledonia 49316 (616) 890-1810..........maram@cornerstonemi.org
McClintic, Raymond – 3781 Peninsular Dr, Gladwin 48624 (989) 426-7019.....raymcclintic@hotmail.com
McCormick, Robert – 13185 Wilkes Rd, Yale 48097 ....mccor1958@gmail.com
McKenzie, Clarice – 396 Ford St., Bitely 49309 (727) 536-1888....................cjmckum@gmail.com
McNitt, Rebecca – 110 S. Madison St., Adrian 49221 (517) 265-5161 ....dcumcarchives@adrian.edu
McNitt, William – 3400 LaSalle Dr., Ann Arbor 48108 (734) 971-7045 ....mmmcnitt@umich.nedu
Mieskowski, Laure – (616) 308-6335 ....mieskowskilaure@gmail.com
Miller, Diana – 3352 W. River Dr., Gladwin 48624 (989) 426-2644.....................diana@ddmiller.net
Miller, Rick – 411 Sommerset Court, Ann Arbor 48103 (734) 972-4317 ....urmiller@umich.edu
Minert, Al – 104 E. 29th Street, Holland 49423 (616) 396-3751........................apminerthm@att.net
Mitchell, Beth – 3813 Rockwood Dr, Kalamazoo 49004 (269) 343-6806....bmitchell@lewisreedallen.com
Mitchell, Daphne – 29926 Robert Dr., Livonia 48150 (734) 425-5926..........daphnehmyd@aol.com
Mobley, Oneika – 21420 Indian Creek Dr, Farmington Hills 48335 (313) 728-9496
....Mobley318@yahoo.com
Money, Nancy – 2996 N Waldo Rd, Midland 48642 (517) 347-4030 ......nmoney@michiganumc.org
Nordbrock, Mandana – 3412 Willow Lake Dr, Apt 302, Kalamazoo 49008 (269) 720-6152
....mnordbrock@michiganumc.org
Norton, Kenneth – 748 Bowers Rd, Bronson 49028 (517) 369-1803 .....klnorton@kendalefarm.com
Olin, Denny – 10205 Aylsworth Rd, PO Box 223, Empire 49630 (231) 223-4141 ...dennyolin@gmail.com
O'Malley, Dan – 9356 Enchantment Dr, Alto 49302 (616) 915-6301.........dano.omalley@gmail.com
Osburn, Clayton – 5785 Marble Dr., Troy 48085 (248) 879-6371 ....clayosburn@aol.com
Paik, Eugene – 2253 Chalgrove Dr, Troy 48098 (248) 766-0379 ....eugenepaik@me.com
Palmer, Elizabeth – Stockwell-Mudd Library Albion College, 611 E Porter St, Albion 49224
        (517) 629-0487
Pelkey, Beth – 7011 Long Rapids Rd, Alpena 49707 (989) 379-3386..........eapelkey53@gmail.com
Pelton, Eric – 3260 Kernway Ct, Bloomfield Hills 48304 (248) 594-7293...........epelton@kohp.com
Peters, Jennifer – 1827 Overhill Dr, Flint 48503 (810) 288-7363...............jenpeters126@gmail.com
Phelps, Marchelle "Micki" – 19622 Syracuse St, Detroit 48234............marchellephelps@gmail.com
Polter, Linda – 413 Giles Ave., Blissfield 49228 (517) 486-2947 ....linda.polter@emich.edu
Potter, Bonnie – 5140 Scott Rd., Mt Morris 48458 (810) 687-2318 ....mpotter60@charter.net
Poy, Lisa – 8204 E Mitchell Rd, Petoskey 49770 (248) 891-3583..................lisa.h.poy@gmail.com
Pratt, Fran – 2644 Seymour Drive, Shelbyville 49344 (269) 792-4145..........fechurchp@gmail.com
Pratt, Jody – 2984 5th St, Shelbyville 49344 (616) 292-4908.........................prattgji09@gmail.com

Preston, John – 16931 Baraga Plains Rd, Baraga 49908 (906) 353-6439 ...johncarterpreston@gmail.com
Price, Todd – 9921 Seltzer, Livonia 48150 (734) 834-4030 ....pencollector@me.com
Proctor, Cheryl – 104 Tuttle Park Dr, Sherwood 49089 (517) 741-3125 ......seldominn_1@juno.com
Proctor, Simmie – 73486 8th Ave, South Haven 49090 (269) 637-6053.......simmiepr@hotmail.com
Pung, Susan – 4325 Water's Edge Dr, Mt Pleasant 48858 (989) 817-8884 ....susanepung@yahoo.com
Radak, Keith – 834 Courtland, Ypsilanti 48197 (734) 483-8124........................kradak@provide.net
Ross, Kelly – 5628 N Helen Lake Rd, Ishpeming 49849 (906) 376-8086 ....pinkgiraffe@hughes.net
Rossman, Cynthia – 4273 Grant St, Brown City 48416 586-757-5146 ....cynrosjam@hotmail.com
Russell, Carrie – 16622 Woodside St, Livonia 48154 (734) 632-0247 ....ca.russell@att.net
Sanders, Robert – 5597 Eugene Drive, Dimondale 78821 (810) 621-5214....bob.scout@lentel.com
Schlusler, Michael – 1576 Ru-Lane Drive, Lapeer 48446 (810) 664-9899....mschlusler@gmail.com
Schramm, Linda – 244 S. Elk St., Sandusky 48471 (810) 648-4696.................lars@greatlakes.net
Schroeder, Craig – 7517 W Hickory Rd, Hickory Corners 49060 (269) 760-4604......ccraigls5@aol.com
Searls, James – 53 East Central, Zeeland 49464 (616) 772-4306.....................jrs@macatawa.org
Seppanen, John – 141 Shadowood Lane, Battle Creek 49014 (269) 965-4931
....jseppanen313@gmail.com
Shaffer, Molly – 33053 Crystal Springs St, Dowagiac 49047 (269) 684-6347 ....orcf@aol.com
Smith, Stuart – 7486 Hunters Ridge Dr, Jackson 49201 (517) 536-0363 ...smith4osu@comcast.net
Smith-Del Pino, Laurie – 12110 Francesca Dr, Grand Blanc 48439 (248) 366-1937
....laurieowl@hotmail.com
Smolenski, Bruce – 76 Union Ave SE Apt 202, Grand Rapids 49503 (586) 850-6540....bmsmo@mail.com
Snyder, Beth – 8650 Huron River Dr., Dexter 48130 (734) 663-4164 ....secretary@dexterumc.org
Soles, Anne – 217 Old State Rd, PO Box 467, Pentwater 49449 (231) 869-7651...annesoles@charter.net
Spackman, Nona – 3806 Cornice Falls Dr Apt 6, Holt 48842 (517) 694-8346
....nspackman12@gmail.com
Stair, Joy – 2756 Aspen Court, Ann Arbor 48108 (734) 327-8370 ....joystair@aol.com
Stanek, Dennis – 7238 Lake Bluff O.75 Ln, Gladstone 49837 (906) 428-2407....dstanek@nmu.edu
Steggerda, Steve – 8507 S. Maple, Zeeland 49464 (616) 748-9989..............steggs76@gmail.com
Stephens, Juli – 19206 Berkley, Detroit 48221 (248) 563-6161 ....julis1111@aol.com
Stevenson, Debbie – 4585 Round Lake Rd, Laingsburg 48848 (517) 420-7032
....dstevenson@michiganumc.org
Stewart, Pamela – 1161 E Clark Rd, Dewitt 48820 (616) 299-6484....pstewart@michiganconference.org
Stockford, Dave – 8544 Gedman Rd, Mancelona 49659 (231) 587-8694 ...dsstockford@freeway.net
Sutton, Ruth – 2335 N. Meridian Rd., Sanford 48657 (989) 687-5646 ....suttonr1@charter.net
Thiele, Cindy – 319 River Street, Allegan 49010 (269) 673-4514 ....cindahthiele@gmail.com
Thoms, Peter – 1213 Carter Dr., Flint 48532 (810) 732-7719 ....psthoms59@gmail.com
Tiedt, Patrick – 5755 30th Ave, Sears 49679 (231) 734-2932 ....patiedt@hotmail.com
Tobar, Lea – 2430 Highridge Ln SE, Grand Rapids 49546 (616) 940-0406 ....flt62@hotmail.com
Trantham, Barry – 3158 N. McKinley Rd, Flushing 48433 (810) 659-5354
....barrytrantham@sbcglobal.net
Trierweiler, Mark – 6378 Iroquois St., Pentwater (231) 899-6330 ....mark.trierweiler@gmail.com
Tucker, Alice – 22289 Woodwill St., Southfield 48075 (313) 618-3173...........fayerich@comcast.net
Tumonong, Prospero – 1908 Firethorn Ct. SE, Grand Rapids 49546 (616) 883-6397
....ptumonong@att.net
Vanderbilt, Herbert 2204 Goc Dr, Lowell 40331 (616) 897-0642 ....hvanderbilt@comcast.net
Vollmer, Sarah – 304 E Market St, Centreville 49032 (815) 600-4785...svollmer@michiganumc.org
Vorbrich, Andrew – Comerica Building, 151 S Rose St Ste 900, Kalamazoo 49007 (269) 343-1906
....AVorbrich@LennonMiller.com
Wayne, Andrew – 32800 Cadillac St., Farmington Hills 48336 (248) 615-1205 ....acwayne@hotmail.com
Weemhoff, Christine – ....cweem@sbcglobal.net

Wesner, Carole – 6642 Guildford Dr., Shelby Twp. 48316 (586) 731-0870 ....carole.wesner@gmail.com
Weston, Michele – 5158 Sandalwood Circle, Grand Blanc 48439 (810) 694-6266 ....mweston38@att.net
Wharton, John – 7409 Steeplechase Ct., Saline 48176 (734) 429-5258 ....jwharton@comcast.net
Whitman, Mary – 9155 Greenway Ct., N222, Saginaw 48609 (989) 781-9223
....librawhitman@yahoo.com
Wilder, Della – 6130 Garfield Rd, Freeland 48623 (989) 695-5808 ....dellaw@yahoo.com
Wissinger, Dennis – 2797 Lone Pine Rd, Farwell 48622 (989) 386-8900 ....dowraw@charter.net
Witkowski, Laura – 1164 Treeway Dr NW, Sparta 49345 (616) 540-3795
....lwitkowski@michiganumc.org
Witte, Susan – 5961 Sunfish Lake Ave NE, Rockford 49341 (616) 446-1570
....switte@umcampingboard.org
Woodard, Sue – 3815 Delano Dr, Eaton Rapids 48827 (517) 628-2628...suecwoodard@gmail.com
Woolley, Charles – 20490 Lexington Blvd, Northville 48167 (734) 646-6245 .....cbwoolley@gmail.com
Wortley, Joel – 220 East Scott, Grand Ledge 48837 (517) 881-6466
....ExecutiveDirector@umcamping.org
Wyatt, Robert – 8181 Deerwood, Clarkston 48346 (248) 625-5326
Wyllys, Nancy – 1415 N Water St, Owosso 48867 (248) 860-7386.................nlwyllys@yahoo.com
Yakes, Dan – 409 Mill Pond Road, Whitehall 49461 (231) 894-9279....................yakesd@iserv.net
Yoder, Sue – 1126 Billings Ct SE Apt 1B, Grand Rapids 49508
Yu, Sung – 3571 Cedar Brook Dr, Rochester Hills 48309 (248) 688-1403 .....sungyu0063@gmail.com
Zawislak, Marguerite – 3932 Wayfarer Dr., Troy 48083 (248) 524-9323......mozawislak@gmail.com
Zeeb, Linda – 13084 Torrey Rd, Fenton 48430 (810) 252-6091 ....zeeblinda@yahoo.com
Zeigler, Carmen – 4273 Port Autin Rd, Caseville 48725 (810) 241-1296 .....carmenszeigler@gmail.com
Zylstra, Jay – 5842 Julie St, Hudsonville 49426 (616) 667-0911 ....jay.zylstra@gmail.com

— MAC Photos

PASTORAL RECORD

This Pastoral Record indicates appointments, including clergy of other annual conferences and denominations serving within the Michigan Conference, but is **not necessarily a pension record**. The date given before/after each appointment represents the initial year of that appointment, with changes occurring immediately following Annual Conference unless otherwise noted.

The Michigan Conference has been transitioning database systems. Please know we are still in the process of cleaning the data and verifying data syncs. If you find significant errors in a record, please email khippensteel@michiganumc.org and also pstewart@michiganumc.org. Thank you for your patience while we transition.

Membership status codes:

AF = Affiliated Member
AM = Associate Member
CC = Certified Candidate
DM = Diaconal Minister (consecrated under provisions of 1992 or earlier Discipline)
DR = Retired Diaconal Minister (consecrated under provisions of 1992 or earlier Discipline)
FD = Deacon in Full Connection
FL = Full Time Local Pastor
NL = Local Pastor (Approved but Not Appointed)
OA = Associate Member of Other Conference
OD = Deacon Member of Other Conference
OE = Elder Member of Other Conference
OF = Other Denomination
OR = Retired Member of Other Conference
PD = Provisional Deacon
PL = Part Time Local Pastor
RD = Retired Deacon in Full Connection
RHL = Retired Honorable Location
RP = Retired Provisional Member
DSA = District Superintendent Assignment

AL = Administrative Location
BH = Bishop

FE = Elder in Full Connection
HL = Honorable Location

PE = Provisional Elder
RA = Retired Associate Member
RE = Retired Elder
RL = Retired Local Pastor
SP = Student Local Pastor

Retired status is also indicated with an asterisk (*) before the name.

Pertaining to the former West Michigan Conference clergy, D stands for year of ordination as Deacon, FE for the year of ordination as Elder, PE for the year of Provisional Elder, PD for the year of Provisional Deacon, R for the year of Retirement.

The following pertains to how the former Detroit Conference clergy are shown:
Last name, first name (spouse)　　　　　　　　　　　　　　　　email address
[(Membership Status) "X" year; "Y" year]. Appointment service record; **present appointment**

Codes for "x" or "y" are in the Detroit Conference, unless otherwise noted:

F	Full Member	P	Probationary Member
FD	Deacon/Full Connection	PD	Provisional Deacon
FE	Elder/Full Connection	PE	Provisional Elder
FL	Full-time Local Pastor	PL	Part-time Local Pastor
LD	Local Deacon	SP	Student Local Pastor
LE	Local Elder	T	Received on Trial (probationary member, 1968 and prior)
LP	Local Pastor		

"P," "F," and "T" are exclusive to the former Detroit Conference.
"D" is exclusive to the former West Michigan Conference.

*Ablett, Joseph H. (Wilma) –
[(RE) T 1950; F 1956] 1950 Minooka IL; 1952 Deer Park MD; 1956 Saginaw: Kochville; 1963 Oscoda; 1969 Escanaba; 1971 Marysville; 1980 Auburn; **1985 Retired**.<> Home: 20311 Pemberville Rd Apt 735, Pemberville OH 43450 (419) 833-1320

*Ackerman, Gordon Earl –
[(RE) T 1962; F 1964] 1959 E.U.B. IL Conf; 1960 Symerton IL; 1962 North Detroit; 1964 Detroit: Rice; Sept 1966 Detroit: West Outer Drive; Oct 1969 Frankenmuth; 1983 Tecumseh; 1988 Clawson; **2001 Retired**.<> Home: 2696 Blue Heron Lane, Wixom 48393. ackermange@sbcglobal.net

*Adams, L. Cecile Adams (Donald Ott) –
[(RL) PL 2010] 2010 Laporte, Mapleton; **2013 Retired**.<> Home: S77W 12929 D212, Muskego WI 53150 (912) 658-0253. 1pastorcecile@gmail.com

*Adams, Craig L. (Robin) –
[(RE) D-1973; FE-1977; R-2010] Wolf Lake 1975; Saugatuck/Ganges 1979; Horton Bay 1984; Ionia: Zion 1994; Weidman 09/16/1999; Carlisle 2006; Mt Pleasant: Trinity/Countryside/Leaton 12/01/2009; Retired 2010; Grand Rapids: Northlawn 2018-2019.<> Home: 5073 Rum Creek Ct SE, Grand Rapids 49508 (616) 514-7474. craigadams1@me.com

Africa, Jeremy Paul (Kaura) –
[(FE) PE 2005; FE 2008] June 1, 2005 Plymouth: First (assoc); 2006 Midland: First (assoc); 2010 Goodrich; **2015 Livonia: St. Matthew's**.<> 30900 W. Six Mile Rd., Livonia 48152 (734) 422-6038. Home: 31000 W. Six Mile Rd., Livonia 48152 (734) 855-4882. jafrica@stmatthewslivonia.com

*Ainslie, Pegg –
[(RE) D-1975; FE-1978; R-1997] Okemos Community Church (Assoc) 11/01/1991; Lansing: Central (Assoc) 1993; Retired 1997.<> Home: 2000 Pleasant Grove Rd, Lansing 48910 (517) 574-4175

Alexander, Sarah Barrett-Nadeau (Matthew) –
[(FD) PD 2016; FD 2019] May 23, 2016 Young Leaders Initiative Motown Mission Director; **2019 Birmingham: First Director of Young Adult & High School Ministries (¶331.1c)**.<> 1589 W Maple Rd, Birmingham 48009 (248) 646-1200. Home: 8925 Sunbury, Livonia 48150. sarahbalexander@gmail.com

Alford, Helen –
[(PL) PL 2019] **2019 Rose City: Trinity (LTFT ½)**.<> 125 W Main St, Rose City 48654 (989) 685-2350. Home: 163 Hayes St., Rose City 48654. pastorhelenea@gmail.com

Alghali, Beatrice S. –
[(PL) PL 2019] **2019 Azalia/London (LTFT ½)**.<> (A) 9855 Azalia Rd, PO Box 216, Azalia 48110 (734) 529-3731, (L) 11318 Plank Rd, Milan 48160 (734) 439-2680. Home: 22492 Pontchartrain Dr, Southfield 48034 (248) 281-3157. sierraintl@peoplepc.com

*Allan, John Richard (Karen Jean) –
[(RA) LD 1964; LE 1966] 1960 Farwell; Jan 1966 Croswell; 1979 Marlette; **Retired**.<> 7227 W. Marlette, Marlette 48453 (989) 635-7227

PASTORAL RECORDS

*Allen, Terry Wayne (Sandra) –
[(RE) P 1971; F 1974] 1973 Birmingham: Embury (assoc); 1974 Flint: Flint Park; Jan 1976 Hemlock, Nelson; 1978 Regional Director, Pacific Northwest Area for Church World Service/CROP; 1980 Southfield: Hope; 1983 Ferndale: First; 1989 Executive Director, United Methodist Foundation of the Detroit Annual Conference; 1990 Troy: First; 1997 Ypsilanti: First; 2000 Detroit: Metropolitan (assoc); 2002 Livonia: Newburg; Sept 1, 2005 leave of absence; **2006 Retired**.<> 586 Riverbank Circle, Zeeland 49464 (616) 239-1503. revtwa@yahoo.com

*Allie, Andrew Amadu (Madeir Boothe) –
[(RE) P 1976; F 1977] Detroit: Westlawn 1976; Detroit: Peoples 1977; Pontiac: St. John's Feb 1981; Detroit: Scott Memorial May 1, 1992; Flint District Superintendent 2001; Pontiac: St. John 2009; **Retired Dec 31, 2009**; Crossroads District Superintendent 4/1-6/30/2012; Flint: Bethel Apr 1-June 20, 2018; Flint: Bethel (interim) 2019-2020.<> Home: 5424 Sycamore Lane, Flint 48532 (810) 732-6653. A.Allie@comcast.net

*Almeida, Jana Lynn (Gabriel) –
[(RE) D-1996; FE-1999; R-2016] Vicksburg (Assoc) 1995; Grand Ledge: First 1997; Mt Pleasant: Trinity/ Countryside 10/16/1999; UM Connectional Structures (¶344.1a,c) Conference Ministry Consultant (LTFT ½) 2004; Transitional Leave (¶354.2c.2) 01/01/2010; Riverdale: Lincoln Road (LTFT ¾) 2010; Retired 2016.<> Home: 1509 Tallywood Dr, Sarasota FL 34237 (616) 430-0414. janalynn@me.com

Amick, John Harvey (Susan) –
[(FE) PE 2006; FE 2010] 2006 Allen Park: Trinity; 2007 Redford: New Beginnings; 2008 Rochester: St. Paul's (assoc); 2012 Flint: Hope; 2013 Deputy General Secretary, International Disaster Relief, UMCOR; 2016 Senior Director, Disaster Relief UMCOR 2016; **Director, Global Migration, UMCOR/Global Ministries 2020**.<> GBGM 458 Ponce de Leon, Atlanta GA 30308 (615) 916-2225. Home: 221 Missionary Drive, Decatur GA 30030 (248) 613-9296. jamick@umcor.org

Amick, Susan D. (John) –
[(FD) PD 2014; FD 2018] 2014 Office of Christian United and Interreligious Relationships, UM Council of Bishops; Aug 1, 2014 Transitional Leave; 2016 Chaplaincy – Emory Spiritual Health/Missional; 2018 Chaplin, Wesley Woods Sr. Living (¶331.4b), Missional: Grace UMC; **2019 Chaplin, Wesley Woods Sr. Living (¶331.4b), Missional: Decatur: First**.<> 1825 Clifton Rd. NE, Atlanta GA 30329. Home: 221 Missionary Drive, Decatur GA 30030 (248) 613-9294. susan.amick@emory.edu

Amstutz, David DeWayne (Carrie) –
[(FE) P 1976; F 1979] 1977 Riley Center, Berville, West Berlin; 1981 North Street; Mar 1, 1987 New Baltimore: Grace; 1990 Lambertville; 1997 Marysville; Feb 15, 1999 leave of absence; 1999 Davisburg; 2001 Riverview; 2012 Gladwin: First; **2018 Retired**.<> Home: 312 McIntosh, Almont 48003 (989) 246-0137. therevdav777@gmail.com

*Amundsen, William J. (Catherine) –
[(RE) D-1967; FE-1970; R-2003] Edwardsburg: Hope 1969; Mesick/Harrietta 1972; Grand Rapids: Trinity (Assoc) 1979; Lowell: First 05/01/1982; Grand Ledge: First 1993; Retired 2003.<> Home: 735 Maycroft Rd, Lansing 48917 (517) 285-9640. wjamundsen@juno.com

Anderson, Thomas Craig (Karen) –

[(FE) P 1981; F 1986] 1984 Deerfield, Petersburg; Jan 1, 1990 Seven Churches United Group Ministry: Durand; 1995 Houghton: Grace; Aug 1, 2009 Houghton Lake; **2016 Highland.**<> 680 W. Livingston Rd., Highland 48357 (248) 887-1311. Home: 650 W. Livingston Rd., Highland 48357. anderson810@gmail.com

*Andrus, Richard C. (Jean) –

[(RE) P 1973; F 1976] Sept 1967 Morrice, Bennington; 1972 Jasper, Weston; 1975 Bayport, Hayes; 1979 New Baltimore: Grace; Feb 1, 1987 Warren: Wesley; Jan 16, 1990 Warren: First (assoc); 1992 Mt. Clemens: First; **1999 Retired.**<> Home: 3551 Wilson St., New Baltimore 48047 (586) 716-2123. rjandrus@avci.net

Arnesen, Tonya Morris (David) –

[(FE) P 1995; F 1997] 1995 Plymouth: First (assoc); June 1, 2000 New Baltimore: Grace; 2006 Detroit: Metropolitan; 2011 Dixboro; **2019 Jackson: First.**<> 275 W Michigan Ave, Jackson 49201 (517) 787-6460. Home: 19734 Malvern Dr, Jackson 49203. Revtonya95@comcast.net

*Arthur, Joy Eldon (Dorothy) –

[(RE) T N. IN, 1955; F N. IN, 1959] 1953 Alexandria Circuit; 1958 DeSoto; 1961 Muncie: College Avenue; 1964 trans. to Detroit Conf, Saginaw: Jefferson Avenue (assoc); 1969 Highland Park: First; 1973 Belleville; Sept 1982 Detroit East District Superintendent; 1988 Coleman: Faith, Geneva: Hope; 1990 Coleman: Faith; **Jan 1, 1991 Retired.**<> Home: 183 Spring St., Midland 48640 (989) 631-1039

Arthur, Thomas F. (Sarah) –

[(FE) PE-2009; FE-2012] Lansing: Sycamore Creek 2009; Lansing: Sycamore Creek/Potterville 09/01/2016; Lansing: Sycamore Creek 12/08/2016.<> 1919 S Pennsylvania Ave, Lansing 48910 (517) 394-6100. Home: 5058 Glendurgan Ct, Holt 48842 (517) 889-5540. tomarthur@sycamorecreekchurch.org

Ash, B.J. –

[(PL) PL 2020] **Manistique (PTLP ½) 2020.**<> 190 N. Cedar St., Manistique 49854 (906) 341-6662. Home: 9344 W State Hwy M149, Manistique 49854 (906) 341-6287. pastorbjash@gmail.com

Aupperlee, Mark D. –

[(FL) FL-2018] Lansing: Sycamore Creek (assoc) 01/01/2018.<> 1919 S Pennsylvania Ave, Lansing 48910 (517) 394-6100. Home: 420 Ardspm Rd, E Lansing 48823 (517) 643-1161. markaupperlee@sycamorecreekchurch.org

Ayoub, George H. (Elizabeth) –

[(FE) D-1984; FE-1987] Appointed To Extension Ministries (¶344.1b,c) Masonic Pathways Senior Living Services, St. Johns 09/24/1999; (Transferred to WMC 2014) UM Connectional Structures (¶344.1a,c) Executive Director of Camps 03/01/2014; UM Connectional Structures (¶344.1a,c) Interim Executive Director of Camp, Michigan Area 2015; UM Connectional Structures (¶344.1a,c) Executive Director of Camping, Michigan 2018; Transitional Leave 08/01/2018; Marlette: First Oct 1, 2018.<> 3155 Main St, Marlette 48453 (989) 635-2075. Home: 3169 Main St., Marlette 48453. a.georgepastor@gmail.com

Babb, Mark R. (Susan) –

[(FD) D-1991; FE-1993; FD-2002] Coldwater (Deacon) 2002; (Transferred from West Ohio Conf 2005) Coldwater (Deacon FT) and Albion College, Music Dept Manager (LTFT) 09/01/2005; Coldwater (Deacon LTFT) and Albion College, Music Dept Manager (LTFT) 01/01/2006; Albion College (LTFT ½) 2006; St. Paul UCC, Director Of Music Ministries, Waterloo IL 01/20/2008; Transitional Leave 06/01/2009; University of Phoenix, Associate Faculty (LTFT ½), Westminster Presbyterian Church, Choir Director (LTFT ¼) and Jackson: First Spiritual Formation Consultant (LTFT ¼) 06/01/2010; University Of Phoenix, Associate Faculty (LTFT ½) Director of Music Federated Church Of Grass Lake (LTFT ¼) and Jackson: First Spiritual Formation Consultant (LTFT ¼) 2013; Transitional Leave 2015; University Of Phoenix, Adjunct Faculty (LTFT ½) 2016; Lakeview: New Life (Deacon) Music And Worship Leader (LTFT ¼ - Missional Service) 11/15/2016; Sturgis: First as Administrativie Assistant (deacon) (¶331.1c).<> 200 Pleasant St, Sturgis 49091 (269) 651-5990. Home: 1332 Rolling Ridge Ln, Sturgis 49091 (989) 287-1770. lighthousemusician@gmail.com

Babb, Susan J. (Mark) –

[(FE) D-1993; FE-1995] Transferred from West Ohio Conf 2004; Jackson: First (Assoc) 01/16/2004; Lakeview: New Life 2015; Sturgis: First 2019.<> 200 Pleasant St, Sturgis 49091 (269) 651-5990. Home: 1332 Rolling Ridge Ln, Sturgis 49091 (989) 287-1770. pastorsueb@gmail.com

*Babcock, Wayne H. (Lois) –

[(RE) D-1972; FE-1976; R-2003] Townline/Bloomingdale 09/01/1969; Scottdale/Bridgman: Faith 1972; Marcellus/Wakelee 01/01/1975; Kingsley/Grant 1978; Webberville/Bell Oak 1983; Webberville 01/16/1987; Berrien Springs 1991; Lawrence 1998; Retired 01/01/2003.<> Home: 32052 County Road 687, Bangor 49013 (269) 427-2681. way.loisbabcock@gmail.com

*Bacon, Eugene Kalman (Karen) –

[(RE) P 1976; F 1980] 1978 Flushing (assoc); 1982 Flint: Bristol, Dimond; 1988 Madison Heights; July 1, 1995 Hancock: First; 2006 Alpena; **2016 Retired**.<> Home: 100 N. Brooke St., Alpena 49707 (989) 340-0358. ekbacon@chartermi.net

*Badley, Thomas G. (Darlene) –

[(RE) T 1968; F 1971] 1965 Rea, Cone, Azalia; 1968 Macon; 1970 Harbor Beach, Port Hope; Nov 1973 Rochester: St. Paul (assoc); 1975 Pontiac: Aldersgate, Elmwood; 1978 Roseville; 1984 Hancock; 1988 Clio: Bethany; 1997 Livonia: Newburg; **2002 Retired**.<> Home: 6617 Wire Rd. Zephyrhills FL 33542 (810) 300-1252. tdbadley65@att.net

Bae, Se Jin (Mi Hyang Jeong) –

[(FL) OE 2015, Florida; FL Jan 1, 2019] **Troy: Korean (assoc) Mar 1, 2015**.<> 42693 Dequindre, Troy 48084 (248) 879-2440. Home: 1940 Flagstone Circle, Rochester 48307 (248) 841-1595

*Baek, Seungho "Andy" (Hehyoung "Sarah") –
[(RE) D-1987; FE-1993; RE 2020] Transferred from Wisconsin Conf 1997; Grand Rapids Suhbu Korean New Church Ministry 07/16/1997; Appointed to Extension Ministries (¶344.1b,c) GBGM New Church Ministry-Suhbu Korean Congregation 2001; Suhbu Korean UMC (Re-named Church of All Nations 2006) 2005; Church of All Nations/ Oakdale 2006; Schoolcraft 2008; Appointed in Other Annual Conferences (¶346.1) West Ohio Conf, Columbus Korean 2010; Union City (¾ Time)/ Athens (¼ Time) 2012; Appointed in Other Annual Conferences (¶331.8, ¶346.1) Detroit Conference, Ann Arbor District, Dundee 2015; New Hudson 2018; **Retired 2020**.<> Home: 1575 Hillcrest Dr, Sugar Hill GA 30518 (614) 440-5404. baekandy@hotmail.com

Bagley, Dwayne E. (Michele) –
[(FE) D-1998; FE-2001] Webberville 1995; Albion: First 2002; Mason: First 2009; UM Connectional Structures (¶344.1a,c), Kalamazoo District Superintendent 2016; UM Connectional Structures (¶344.1a,c), Greater Southwest District Superintendent 01/01/2019.<> 2350 Ring Rd North Suite B, Kalamazoo 49006 (269) 372-7525. Home: 7228 Bolingbrook Dr, Portage 49024 (269) 370-2800. dbagley@michiganumc.org

Bailey, Anika –
[(PL) PL 2018] **2018 Forester/Port Sanilac**.<> (PS) 7225 Main St., PO Box 557, Port Sanilac 48469, (F) 2481 N. Lakeshore Rd., Carsonville 48419. Home: 7209 Main, Port Sanilac 48469 (313) 543-9434. puppetpower28@aol.com

Bailey, John D. (Karen) –
[(FE) FL 1999; PE 2000; FE 2003] 1996 Custer/South Liberty, W. OH Conf;1999 Ossineke, Hubbard Lake; Jan 1, 2005 Ossineke; 2005 Seven Churches United Group Ministry: Gaines, Duffield; 2010 Clio: Bethany; 2015 Romeo; **2017 Cheboygan: St. Paul's**.<> 531 E. Lincoln Ave., Cheboygan 49721 (231) 627-2424. Home: 578 O'Brien Dr., Cheboygan 49721 (231) 627-9710. Jbailey57@hotmail.com

*Bailey, Paul F. (Lynn) –
[(RE) D-1962; FE-1967; R-2001] Transferred to West MI Conf 1978; Associate Director, MiCAP 1978; Honorable Location 1979; Transferred to N NY Conf 1984; Transferred to Detroit Conf 1988; Transferred to West MI Conf 1995; Potterville/West Benton 1995; Retired 05/01/2001; Ionia: Easton 04/13/2003-09/01/2004.<> Home: 2500 Breton Woods Dr SE Apt 1065, Grand Rapids 49512 (517) 930-3743. pfbpadre@gmail.com

*Bailey, Wilson Charles (Noreen) –
[(RE) PE 1999; FE 2002] 1999 Deerfield, Wellsville; Sept 1, 1999 Wisner; 2005 leave of absence; **Sept 30, 2007 Retired**.<> Home: 4901 Squirrel Run, Farwell 48622 (989) 588-4695. wilson.bailey@att.net

*Baker, Maureen Vickie (Robert) –
[(RE) PL Dec 1, 2002; PE 2007; FE 2010; RE 2019] Dec 1, 2002 Applegate; 2007 Brown City; 2013 Lexington; 2017 Mount Clemens: First; **2019 Retired**.<> Home: 1804 Sunflower Circle, Sebring FL 33872 (810) 488-2390. revbakerm@yahoo.com

*Baker, Melanie J. –
[(RE) D-1984; FE-1987; R-2016] Empire 1985; Leave Of Absence 1988; North Adams/Jerome 10/01/1988; Battle Creek: Birchwood 1995; Sabbatical Leave 2003; Lansing: First 2004; Alma 07/15/2012; Personal Leave 2013; Retired 2016.<> Home: 3813 ½ W Willow St, Lansing 48917 (517) 204-5870. MBSmicah68@aol.com

*Baker, Peggy J. (Forrest) –
[(RE) D-1999; FE-2003; R-2018] Comstock 1999; Outland Harper Creek (New Church Start) 2006; Battle Creek: Baseline/Bellevue 2011; Retired 2018.<> Home: 8039 Allison Ln, Battle Creek 49014 (269) 387-1494. pegbkr@gmail.com

*Baker, Sheila F. (Keith P) –
[(RL) PL-2005; RL-2014] Riverside (DSA 07/01-12/01/04) (LTFT PT) 12/01/2004; Breedsville (LTFT PT) 2005; Townline (LTFT PT) 2005; Kalamazoo: Northwest (¼ Time 01/03/08) (LTFT PT) 2007; Otsego: Trowbridge (LTFT PT) 2012; Retired 02/02/2014.<> Home: 27399 22nd Ave, Gobles 49055 (269) 628-4882. sf-baker1031@gmail.com

*Balfour, James Robert, II (Mary) –
[(RE) P 1970; F 1974] 1973 Royal Oak: First (assoc); 1975 Rose City, Churchill; 1982 Marquette: Grace, Skandia; Sept 15, 1986 school; 1988 Leave of Absence; 1989 Pastoral Counselor/Administrator, Preventive & Rehabilitative Center, Burns Medical Center; 2002 St. Ignace; **2010 Retired**.<> Home: N 7014 K-1 Dr., Stephenson 49887 (906) 298-0352. mjbalf@gmail.com

*Ball, Glenn Charles –
[(RE) T Mich 1956; F Mich 1961] 1954 Bingham, Solon; 1956 Horton Bay, North Bay; 1958 Adamsville, Kessington; 1961 Grand Rapids: Northlawn; 1966 Caro; 1972 Onaway, Millersburg; 1983 Frankenmuth; **1996 Retired**.<> Home: 255 Mayer Rd., #375L, Frankenmuth 48734 (989) 652-4375

Ball, John W. (Cyndi) –
[(FE) PE 1999; FE 2002] 1999 Mayville; 2007 Leave of Absence; Apr 15, 2009 Elkton (assoc); 2009 Brighton: First (assoc); 2013 Lake Orion (assoc); **2019 Lake Orion (assoc) (LTFT ¾), Celebrate Hope Consultant (¶344.1d) (LTFT ¼)**.<> 140 East Flint, Lake Orion 48362 (248) 693-6201. Home: 2647 Orbit Dr., Lake Orion 48362 (248) 393-1520. john.ball@lakeorionumc.org

Ball, Lyle J. (Janet) –
[(PL) PL-2010] Chase Barton/Grant Center (DSA) 2010; Chase: Barton/Grant Center (PTLP ½) 11/01/10; Baldwin: Covenant Community (PTLP ½) and Chase Barton (PTLP ¼) 2015.<> (BCC) PO Box 250, 5330 S M-37, Baldwin 49304 (231) 745-3232. (CB) PO Box 104, 6957 S Depot St, Chase 49623 (231) 832-5069. Home: 6874 5 Mile Rd, Blanchard 49310 (231) 972-7335. ljball6@hotmail.com

*Ball, Martha C. –
[(RE) P 1983; F 1987] 1984 Wayne: First (assoc); Nov 1, 1985 Britton: Grace; Apr 1, 1991 Henderson Settlement, Kentucky District, Red Bird Missionary Conf; July 16, 1993 Hudson: First (LTFT ½); Jan 15, 1996 Oneida: First, Oneida TN; 1997 leave of absence; **2002 Retired**.<> Home: 4298 Hillside, Ann Arbor 48105 (734) 213-0443

Ball, Thomas E. (Kelly) –
[(FE) D-1982; FE-1986] Girard/Ellis Corners 1984; Climax/Scotts 12/01/1988; Farwell 1994; Howard City: Heritage 2000; Cadillac 2007.<> PO Box 37, 1020 E Division St, Cadillac 49601 (231) 775-5362. Home: 114 Barbara St, Cadillac 49601 (231) 775-1851. tebpastor@yahoo.com

Ballah, Anthony J. (Miatta Buxton-Ballah) –
[(FL) FL Nov 2016] Apr 16, 2016 Detroit: St. Paul, Beverly Hills; **2018 Beverly Hills**.<>
20000 W. 13 Mile Rd., Beverly Hills 48025 (248) 646-9777. Home:30700 Old Stream,
Southfield 48076 (248) 327-6276. ajballa@gmail.com

Barchue, J. Albert –
[(OE) OE, 2016 Liberia Conference] Negaunee: Mitchell 2016; **Pigeon: Salem Sept
1, 2020**.<> 23 Mabel, Box 438, Pigeon 48755 (989) 453-2552. Home: 7065 Clabuesch
St., Box 438, Pigeon 48755 (570) 267-6513. revbarchue@yahoo.com

Barkholz, Daniel L. (Mary Beth) –
[(FL) CC-2013; FL-2016] Fennville/Pearl 2016; Edmore: Faith 2017.<> 833 S 1st St,
Edmore 48829 (989) 427-5575. Home: 320 S Maple St, Edmore 48829 (269) 903-
9665. pastordanbarkholz@gmail.com

***Barnett, James E.** (Valerie) –
[(RL) PL 2002; FL 2005] Jan 1, 2002 Washington; June 1, 2002 Washington, Mt. Vernon; Jan 1, 2002 Washington; Jan 1, 2006 Washington/Mount Vernon (LTFT ¾); Nov
1, 2006 Washington/Mount Vernon (LTFT ½); Jan 1, 2007 Mount Vernon; 2007 Applegate; **2013 Retired**.<> 12275 Jeddo Rd., Yale 48097 (810) 387-2431.
jvbarnett@umich.edu

***Barney, James W.** (Marilyn) –
[(RE) D-1972; FE-1975; R-2005] Transferred from New Hampshire Conf 1979; Mu-
nith/Pleasant Lake 1979; Quincy 1983; Wayland 1987; Constantine 09/15/1991; Somerset Center 1998; Retired 08/31/2005.<> Home: 1713 Linden Trail, Kalamazoo 49009
(269) 251-1187. deriter2@charter.net

***Barney, Marilyn B.** (James) –
[(RE) D-1985; FE-1990; R-2008] Burnips/Monterey Center 1987; Three Rivers: Ninth
Street/Jones 10/01/1991; Hillside 1998; Retired 2008.<> Home: 1713 Linden Trail,
Kalamazoo 49009 (269) 251-1021. deriter2@charter.net

Barrett, Joy Anna (Robert Long) –
[(FE) P 1982; F 1985] 1983 Gordonville; 1988 Sterling Heights; 1993 Saginaw: State
Street; 1998 Ann Arbor District Superintendent; **2004 Chelsea**.<> 128 Park St. Chelsea
48118 (734) 475-8119. Home: 10 Sycamore Dr., Chelsea 48118 (734) 475-8449. jbar-
rett@chelseaumc.org

Barrett, Mary J. –
[(PL) DSA-2016; PL-2016] Waterloo Village (DSA) 2016; Waterloo Village (PTLP)
11/15/2016; Waterloo Village (PTLP) and Salem Grove (PTLP) 2017.<> (WV) 8110
Washington St, Grass Lake 49240 (734) 475-1171. (SG) 3320 Notten Rd, Grass Lake
49240 (734) 475-2370. Home: PO Box 530, 305 N Howard, Webberville 48892 (517)
521-3939. marybarrett29@yahoo.com

***Barrett, Wayne C.** (Linda) –
[(RE) D-1972; FE-1975; R-2011] Snow 1969; Bloomingdale/Townline 1972; Muskegon:
Central (Assoc) 11/01/1974; Plainfield 1978; Plainfield/UM Connectional Structures
(¶344.1a,c) Director of United Methodist Foundation 02/01/1982; Executive Director,
United Methodist Foundation (Re-named United Methodist Foundation of MI 2006)
1982; Retired 2011.<> 3347 Eagle Run Dr. NE, Ste B, Grand Rapids 49525 (888) 451-
1929. Home: 1517 Heathfield NE, Grand Rapids 49505 (616) 458-9975.
wayne@umfmichigan.org

*Barry, B. Gordon (Susan) –
[(RE) D-1982; FE-1985; R-2015] Remus/Halls Corner/Mecosta 1982; New Buffalo/Berrien County: Lakeside 1985; New Buffalo/Bridgman: Faith 1988; Lowell: First 1993; Stevensville 06/06/2003; Retired 2015.<> Home: 5798 Whites Bridge Road, Belding 48809 (616) 244-3233. gordiebarry@gmail.com

Bartelmay, Bradley S. (Sherri Swanson) –
[(FE) FL-1990; D-1996; FE-2002] Stevensville (Assoc) 1990; New Buffalo/Bridgman: Faith 1993; New Buffalo: Water's Edge (Church Name Changed To Water's Edge UMC 1/1/12) 05/01/2000; Holland First 2017.<> 57 W 10th St, Holland 49423 (616) 396-5205. Home: 2600 7th St NW, Grand Rapids 49504 (269) 266-2221. bradbartelmay@gmail.com

*Bartlett, William Peter (Lee Ann) –
[(RE) SP 1985; P 1991; F 1994] 1985 Lake Linden, Painesdale; 1987 Middletown, Ohio: Pleasant Ridge (W. OH Conf); 1992 Stephenson, Hermansville: First; 1996 God's Country Cooperative Parish: Newberry (Parish Director); 2001 Onaway, Millersburg; **2011 Retired**.<> Home: 358 West Northland, Ironwood 49938 (906) 285-9541. bartlettwmpeter@gmail.com

*Bartholomew, Jack M. (Mildred) –
[(RE) SP-1969; D-1975; FE-1979; R-1995] Quincy/Fisher Hill 1969-1974; Elk Rapids/Kewadin 1978; Hastings: Hope 02/16/1983; Lansing Calvary 02/15/1986; Stanwood: Northland 1992; Retired 1995.<> Home: 1133 Yeomans St #96, Ionia 48846 (616) 527-8852. jbart96@att.net

Barton, Sean T. –
[(FL) FL-2017] Grawn/Grant 2017; Grawn 2018.<> PO Box 62, Grawn 49637 (231) 943-8356. Home: 1222 S West Silber Lake Rd, Traverse City 49685 (269) 908-7313. sean_barton@ymail.com

Bashore, Timothy T. (Kay) –
[(FL) PL Nov 2013; FL 2014] Nov 9, 2013 Bethel (Worth Twp.); **2014 Pickford**.<> 115 E. Church St., Box 128, Pickford 49774 (906) 647-6195. Home: 230 W. Townline Rd., Pickford 49774 (906) 647-7231

Batten, Lisa M. (Jim) –
[(FL) FL-2009] UM Connectional Structures (¶344.1a,c) Director Wesley Foundation of Kalamazoo 11/15/2009; Young Adult Intiatives Coordinator 07/15/2018.<> 1810 N Drake Rd, Kalamazoo 49006 (517) 347-4030 ext. 4078. Home: 1810 N Drake Rd, Kalamazoo 49006 (269) 344-4076. lbatten@michiganumc.org

*Baughan, Eugene L. (Philis) –
[(RA) PL-1974; FL-1987; AM-1993; RA-2002] NE Missaukee Parish: Moorestown-Stittsville/Merritt-Butterfield 1974; Springport/ Lee Center 1987; Brooks Corner/Sears 1991; Barnard/East Jordan/Norwood 1997; Retired 2002; Kewadin 11/01/2009-2015.<> Home: 400 Heartland Dr, Traverse City 49684 (231) 943-0354. reverendgeneb@aol.com

*Baunoch, Joseph Robert (Betty) –
[(RE) P 1984 (N. IN); F 1987 (N. IN)] Saratoga, Mt. Zion 1981; Elkhart: First (assoc) 1983; Elkhart: Albright 1985; Whiting/Centenary 1990; Chaplain, St. Mary Medical Center, Hobart IN 1993; Samaritan Counseling Center, Munster IN: Wheeler 1996; Portage: First 1999; trans to Detroit Conf 2002, Oxford 2002; **Retired 2004; Yale Apr 1, 2020**.<> 2 South Main St., Yale 48097 (810) 387-3962. Home: 4333 24th Ave Lot 9, Fort Gratiot 48059-3844 (810) 841-4745. drjoe@yaleumc.org

*Beachy, William M. (Barbara) –
[(RE) D-1982; FE-1985; R-2014] Transferred from West Ohio Conf 2001; Lansing: Trinity 2001; Retired 2014.<> Home: 230 E Knight St, Eaton Rapids 48827 (517) 441-9456. wbeachy@comcast.net

Beagan, Thomas Michael –
[(FE) P 1982; F 1985; FL 1992; F 1993] 1983 Utica (assoc); 1986 Leave of Absence; 1988 Honorable Location; 1992 Northville (assoc); 1993 reinstated Northville (assoc); **2000 CEO/Executive Director, Logos Associates**.<> 1405 Frey Rd., Pittsburgh PA 15235 (412) 372-1341. Home: 6790 Stephanie Ct., Delmont PA 15626 (724) 327-4653. tombeagan@thelogosministry.org

Beasley, Donald –
[(PL) PL Jan 1, 2020] Detroit: Ford Memorial (DSA) (¼ time) 2016; **Detroit: Ford Memorial (½ time) Jan 1, 2020**.<> 16400 W Warren Ave, Detroit 48228 (313) 584-0035. Home: 13969 Fielding St, Detroit 48223 (313) 475-3416. revdonaldjbeasley@yahoo.com

Beaudoin, Christine M. (Michael) –
[(FE) PL-2013; PE-2014; FE-2017] Salem Grove 2013; Velda Rose Sept 1, 2015; **Coloma 2018**.<> PO Box 670, 144 S Church St, Coloma 49037 (269) 468-6062. Home: 331 Tannery Dr, Coloma 49038 (480) 659-1472. cmbeau81@aol.com

Beavan, Joseph L. (Darcy) –
[(FL) FL-2010] Brooks Corners/Sears/Barryton: Faith 01/15/2010; Rosebush 2014.<> PO Box 187, 3805 School Rd, Rosebush 48878 (989) 433-2957. Home: 3272 E Weidman Rd, Rosebush 48878 (989) 433-5509. icmkck@yahoo.com

*Beck, Eric S. (Heather) –
[(RE) D-1979; FE-1983; R-2019] Eaton Rapids: First (Assoc) 12/01/1980; Muskegon: Unity 1983; Union City 1986; Kalamazoo: Westwood 08/01/1995; Lake Odessa: Central 2007; Jackson: First 2012; Retired 2019.<> Home: 376 Vansickle, Charlottee 48813 (517)c962-2451 (517) 962-2451. revdrebeck@gmail.com

*Beckwith, Norman Richard, Sr. (Christina) –
[(RE) P 1967; F 1970] 1967 Homersville OH; 1970 Lapeer: Trinity (assoc); 1972 Denton: Faith; 1976 Erie; 1981 trans. W. OH, Peebles; 1984 South Salem; 1987 Union Plains; 1988 Stryker; 1994 trans. to Detroit Conf, Bay Port, Hayes; 1998 Owosso: Trinity; **Retired 2008**; Corunna: Northwest Venice, Nov. 1, 2014-2020; Vernon 2016-2020.<> Home:18571 W. Brady Rd., Oakley 48649 (989) 277-1289. NBeckwithSr@msn.com

*Bedwell, Donald Eugene (Polly) –
[(RL) PL Dec 1, 2002] Ishpeming: Salisbury Dec 1, 2002; Manistique: First 2004-2020; **Retired 2011**.<> Home:141 New Delta, Manistique 49654 (906) 341-5812. car54mhpd@hotmail.com

*Beebe, Grace Ann –
[(RD) PD 2004; FD 2007] 2004 Consultant, Disability Awareness and Accessibility Concerns; 2015 Trenton: Faith; **2017 Retired**.<> Home: 2225 Emeline, Trenton 48183 (734) 676-3863. beebega@aol.com

*Beedle-Gee, Pamela A. (John) –
[(RE) PE 2003; FE 2006; RE 2020] Grosse Pointe (assoc) 2003; Garden City: First 2009; Clinton 2014; Sebewaing: Trinity 2018; **Retired 2020**.<> Home: 2808 Downderry Ct, Bloomfield 48304. pastorpam@live.com

*Bekofske, Gary L. (Nancy) –
[(RE) D-1972; FE-1976; R-2014] Tranferred from Eastern Pennsylvania Conf 1989; Hillsdale: First 06/01/1989; Lansing: Grace 1996; Montague 2005; Muskegon: Central 08/16/2009; Delton: Faith 2010; Pentwater: Centenary 2012; Retired 2014.<> Home: 733 W Elmwood Ave, Clawson 48017 (248) 435-5027. garyleeb@hotmail.com

Bell, David S. (Ethel) –
[(AF) AF-2009] [East Ohio Conf] Vice President of Stewardship of the United Methodist Foundation of MI 09/01/2007; President and Executive Director, United Methodist Foundation of MI 2011.<> 840 W Grand River Ave, Brighton 48116 (888) 451-1929. Home: 5527 Timber Bend Drive, Brighton 48116 (248) 435-5027 (810) 534-3001. david@umfmichigan.org

*Bell, Virginia B. (Jack) –
[(RL) PL 2001] 2001 God's Country Cooperative Parish: Paradise, Hulbert: Tahquamenon; Jan 1, 2002 God's Country Cooperative Parish: Paradise, Hulbert: Tahquamenon; **Oct 30, 2005 Retired**.<> Home: PO Box 198, Paradise 49768 (906) 492-3202. vbellagain@yahoo.com

*Benissan, John Kodzo (Janis) –
[(RE) P N. IL, 1979; F N. IL, 1981] 1978 Harvey: Wesley Memorial; Aug 1984 trans. to Detroit Conf, Detroit: Henderson Memorial; 1987 Saginaw: New Church Development; 1998 Cooperative Ministries of Northwest Flint: Flint: Trinity; 2003 Beverly Hills; Aug 1, 2008 Flat Rock; **2011 Retired**.<> Home: 15919 Petros Drive, Brownstown 48173 (734) 379-1746. benissanjk@gmail.com

Benjamin, Barbara S. (Raymond) –
[(PE) PL 2012; FL 2016; PE 2018] Aug 1, 2012 Richfield; 2014 Richfield, Elba; 2016 Byron: First, Lennon; **2018 Bryon: First, Gaines**.<> (BF) Box 127, 101 S. Ann, Byron 48418 (810) 266-4976, (G) 117 Clinton St., PO Box 125, Gaines 48436 (989) 271-9131. Home: 10214 Bath Rd., Byron 48418 (810) 433-1096. mrsbenjix@aol.com

*Bensen, Kenneth W. (Sandra) –
[(RE) D-1990; FE-1992; R-2003] Lansing: Faith 05/01/1987; Retired 2003.<> Home: 502 W Calle Artistica, Green Valley AZ 85614 (517) 819-7511. kbensen@gmail.com

*Bentley, Evans Charles (Betsy) –
[(RE) P 1980; F 1982; RE 2018] 1980 Birmingham: First (assoc); 1983 Manchester: Sharon; Jan 15, 1988 Morenci; 1995 Flat Rock: First; 2004 Monroe: St. Paul's; **2018 Retired; 2018 Springville**.<> 10341 Springville Hwy., Onsted 49265 (517) 467-4471. Home: 1109 N River Ct, Tecumseh 49286 (734) 552-5064. evansbentley27@gmail.com

*Bentley, Terri L. (Tom) –
[(RL)– FL-2002; RL 2020] Stevensville (Assoc) 05/31/2002; St Louis: First 02/01/2008; **Retired 2020**.<> Home: 9735 W Taft Rd, St Johns 48879 (989) 388-6303. pastorterrib@gmail.com

Benton, Jeremy P. (Rachel) –
[(FE) PE 2008; FE 2011] 2008 Morrice, Pittsburg, Bancroft; 2011 Ortonville; **2013 Campus Minister, Wesley Foundation of Greenville SC**.<> 501 E. 5th Street, Greenville SC 27858 (252) 758-2030. Home: 606A Spring Forest Road, Greenville SC 27834 (252) 412-6214. revjeremybenton@gmail.com

*Bergquist, Christine J. (Gary) –
[(RL) PL 1990; RL 2020] Bark River 1990; Bark River, Hermansville: First 2009; **Retired 2020**.<> Home: 1290 10th Rd., Bark River 49807 (906) 241-7154. 1chris1cross1@att.net

*Berkompas, Elwood Jay (Donna Lindberg) –
[(RE) P Mich., 1954; F Mich., 1957] 1956 Adamsville; 1957 Adamsville, Kessington; 1958 Grand Rapids: Northlawn; 1962 Detroit: Trinity; 1965 Monroe: First; 1972 Detroit: Zion; 1976 Troy: First; 1982 Ann Arbor: West Side; **1995 Retired**.<> Home: 1530 W. Ridge St., Apt. #47, Marquette 49855 (906) 273-1026. woodyberk@charter.net

Berlanga, Nicolas Rey –
[(PE) PL 2012; FL 2015; PE 2020] Dec 9, 2012 Melvindale: New Hope; Feb 15, 2014 Plymouth: First (assoc); 2018 Ann Arbor: First (assoc); **2018 Ann Arbor: First (assoc)**.<> 120 S. State, Ann Arbor 48104 (734) 662-4536. Home: 1507 Warwick Ct., Ann Arbor 48103 (734) 983-8677. nick@phfum.org

*Berquist, Jane A. (George) –
[(RD) CE CRT Assoc. CE 1993; CON 1994; DFM 1997; RD 2006] 1994 Royal Oak: First; 1995 Farmington Hills: Nardin Park (deacon); **2006 Retired**.<> Home: 26375 Halstead, #198, Farmington Hills 48331 (248) 473-0184. jgberquist@aol.com

Bibilomo, Sandra V. (Jimoh) –
[(FD) PD-2008; FD-2011] Benton Harbor Peace Temple (Deacon LTFT ¼) and Deacons Appointed w/in UM Connectional Structure (¶331.1b) Executive Director Harbor Harvest Urban Ministries 2008; Deacons Appointed w/in UM Connectional Structure (¶331.1b) Executive Director Harbor Harvest Urban Ministries (LTFT ¾) and Battle Creek: Washington Heights (Interim LTFT ¼) 2009; Deacons Appointed w/in UM Connectional Structure (¶331.1b) Executive Director Harbor Harvest Urban Ministries (LTFT ¾) and Kalamazoo: Westwood (Deacon LTFT ¼) 2011; Kalamazoon Westwood (Deacon LTFT ¼) 01/01/2012; Deacons Appointed Beyond the Local Church (¶331.6) Guardian Finance and Advocacy Services Representative Payee (LTFT ¾) and Kalamazoo Westwood (Deacon LTFT ¼) 2012.<> 538 Nichols Rd, Kalamazoo 49006 (269) 344-7165. Home: 2021 March St, Kalamazoo 49001 (269) 369-8803. sandra.douglas73@yahoo.com

Bierlein, Ellen D. –
[(FL) FL-2018] Buchanan: First 2018.<> 132 S Oak St, Buchanan 49107 (269) 695-3282. Home: 304 Pontic Court, Buchanan 49107 (269) 695-3896. PastorEllenB@BuchananFirstUMC.org

Bigham-Tsai, Kennetha J. (Kee Tsai) –
[(FE) PE-2006; FE-2009] East Lansing: University (Assoc) 2006; Kalamazoo: Milwood 2011; UM Connectional Structures (¶344.1a,c) Lansing District Superintendent 2013; UM Connectional Structures (¶344.1a,c) Chief Connectional Officer of the Connectional Table 01/22/2018.<> Home: 6137 Horizon Dr, East Lansing 48823 (517) 347-4173. kbighamtsai@umc.org

*Bilkert, Daniel M. –
[(OR) OR 2018] East Ohio Conference, Grand Rapids: Faith 2018; Grand Rapids: Faith (LTFT ½) 2019.<> 2600 7th St NW, Grand Rapids 49504 (616) 453-0693. Home: 2239 Ducoma St NW, Grand Rapids 49504 (419) 606-0640. dgbilkert@gmail.com

*Billing, Bruce Lee (Linda) –
[(RE) P 1974; F 1978] 1977 Otisville, West Forest; 1982 Howarth, Paint Creek; 1993 Burton: Atherton; 2001 Atherton, Phoenix; **2011 Retired**; Feb 1, 2018-June 30, 2018 Mt. Morris: First.<> Home: 5231 Sandalwood Circle, Grand Blanc 48439 (810) 694-0992. clgbbrewski@aol.com

Bills, William C. (Julie) –
[(FE) D-1990; FE-1993] Burr Oak 07/16/1988; Marshall (Assoc) 1991; Martin/Shelbyville 1994; Georgetown 2007; East Lansing: University 2016.<> 1120 S Harrison Rd, East Lansing 48823 (517) 351-7030. Home: 405 Green Meadows Dr, Lansing 48917 (616) 706-6050. bbills@eluumc.org

Birchmeier, Ann –
[(FL) FL 2020] **Willow, South Rockwood 2020**.<> (W) 36925 Willow Rd., Box 281, New Boston 48164 (734) 654-9020. (SR) 6311 S. Huron River Dr., South Rockwood 48033 (734) 379-3131. Home: 13392 Wingate Lane, Brighton 48116 313-318-8581. rabirch1995@hotmail.com

Bissell, Adam Winthrop (Shannon) –
[(FE) FL 2000; PE 2002; FE 2005] 1997-1998 Flushing (assoc); 2000 Brighton: First (assoc); 2003 Eastpointe: Immanuel; 2007 leave of absence; Feb 1, 2008 Chaplain, Lifepath Hospice, Tampa FL; Nov 1, 2008 leave of absence; June 2009 Bereavement Coordinator, Hospice of the Pines (AZ Conf); **June 2013 Support Services Manager/Chaplain Good Samaritan Society Prescott Hospice**.<> 1065 Ruth St., Prescott AZ 86301 (928) 710-5532. Home: 7444 N. Pinnacle Pass Dr., Prescott Valley AZ 86315 (928) 592-5681. adamwbissell@yahoo.com

*Bistayi, Joseph J. (Cheryl) –
[(RE) D-1970; FE-1973; R-2005] Transferred from Detroit Conf 1978; Portage: Chapel Hill 10/01/1978; Battle Creek: Chapel Hill 1985; UM Connectional Structures (¶344.1a,c) Conference Staff Person for Spiritual Formation 1993; Georgetown 08/16/1999; **Retired 2005**; Bloomfield Hills: St. Paul, Hazel Park Mar 15-June 30, 2020.<> Home: 47049 Manhattan Circle, Novi 48374 (616) 550-4374. joecheryl@prodigy.net

Bistayi, Matthew J. (Shellie) –
[(FE) FL-2002; PE-2007; FE-2015] Brandywine Trinity 01/01/1999; Kalamazoo: First (Assoc) 05/31/2002; Bronson: First 2006; Allendale: Valley Church 2009.<> 5980 Lake Michigan Dr, Ste B, Allendale 49401 (616) 892-1042. Home: 10811 Lance Ave, Allendale 49401 (616) 892-6240. mbistayi@valleychurchallendale.org

*Biteman, Daniel W., Jr. (Kellie Lynn) –
[(RE) FL-1983; D-1988; FE-1996; RE 2020] Fife Lake/South Boardman 1983; Dewitt: Redeemer (assoc) 1987; Lane Boulevard 1988; Grawn 1996; Lawton: St Paul's 2006; Alden/Central Lake 2010; **Retired 2020.**<> Home: PO Box 157, Alden MI 49612 (231) 409-8015. dbiteman@outlook.com

*Bitterling, Nancy J. (Curtis) –
[(RL) SP 2000; FL 2002; PL 2013; RL 2018] Niles: Grace 2000; Riverdale Lincoln Road May 31, 2002; Nashville 2010; Port Austin, Pinnebog 2013; **Retired 2018;** Shabbona (LTFT ¼) 2019-2020.<> Home: 3610 Bluff Rd, PO Box 533, Port Austin 48467 (989) 738-6322. njbit1@yahoo.com

Bixby, Jennifer Lynn –
[(FE) PE 2000; FE 2003] Northville: First (assoc) 2000; leave of absence 2004; Chaplain, US Navy Aug 1, 2004; **Leave of Absence Sept 15, 2006.**<> Home: 3034 S. Navel Ave., Yuma AZ 85365 (928) 269-6422. jennifer777@wwnet.com

*Black, Carleton R. (Barbara) –
[(RL) FL-2012; RL 2020] Ravenna (DSA ½ Time) 2011; Ravenna PTLP ¾) 11/12/11; Ravenna (FTLP) 2012; **Retired 2020.**<> Home: 6236 Staple Rd, Twin Lake 49457 (231) 343-1581. carl.black77@gmail.com

*Blair, Betty Montel (Coulson) –
[(RL) FL 2002] Lexington 2002; **Retired June 30, 2009.**<> Home: 5674 Gov. Sleeper Ct, Lexington 48450 (810) 359-3419. bcbean@att.net

*Blair, Eugene A. (Dawn) –
[(RE) P W. OH 1982; F W. OH 1985] 1980 Columbus: Hilltop; Toledo: New Horizon; 1986 Dean of the Chapel, UPPER ROOM; 1992 Methodist Church of Kenya, West; 1993 Columbus: Livingston Avenue; 1995 Northern Illinois Conference Staff, Congregational Development; Jan 1, 2004 transf to Detroit Conference; Jan 1, 2004 Associate Council Director, in American Spiritual Formation; 2009 Flint District Superintendent; 2011 Crossroads District Superintendent; **Apr 1, 2012 Retired.**<> Home: 3631 Meadow Grove Trail, Ann Arbor 48108 (734) 748-0287. jabulaney3@gmail.com

*Blakey, Dorothy M. –
[(RD) DM-1994; FD-1997; RD-1999] Holland: First (Deacon) (LTFT ¼) 1997; Retired 1999.<> Home: 5054 Maple Creek SE, Kentwood 49508 (616) 455-8503. dorothy.m.blakey@gmail.com

Blanchard, Robert P. –
[(PE) PE 2018] Clinton 2018; **Lansing: First 2020.**<> 3827 Delta River Dr, Lansing 48906 (517) 321-5187. Home: 3727 Delta River Dr, Lansing 48906 (517) 775-6556. reverendblanchard@gmail.com

*Blomquist, Paul Frederick (Beatrice) –
[(RE) T MI, 1957; F MI, 1959] 1955 Niles: First (assoc); 1957 Coloma; 1962 trans to N. Eng. Conf, Pittsfield; 1964 trans. to Detroit Conf, Ferndale: First (assoc); 1966 Troy: Big Beaver; 1969 Warren: First; 1973 Flint District Superintendent; 1979 Port Huron: First; 1985 Farmington: Orchard; **1996 Retired.**<> Home: 5578 Hummingbird Lane, Clarkston 48346 (248) 620-1713. SagePaul@comcast.net

Blunt, Richard W. (Natalie) –
[(FE) D-1985; FE-1988] Ogdensburg (Old Mission Peninsula) 1986; Manton 1993; Reed City 02/01/1999; Lowell: First 2008; Okemos Community Church 2014.<> PO Box 680, 4734 Okemos Rd, Okemos 48864 (517) 349-4220. Home: 2441 S Wild Blossom Ct, East Lansing 48823 (517) 721-1301. rickblunt@hotmail.com

Boayue, Charles S.G., Jr. (Elizabeth) –
[(FE) FL 1990; P 1991; F 1993] 1990 Detroit: Metropolitan (assoc). 1991 Detroit: Metropolitan (assoc.-LTFT), Jefferson Avenue (LTFT); 1993 Associate Council Director: Urban Missioner; 1999 Detroit: Second Grace; 2015 Detroit Renaissance District Superintendent; **Jan 1, 2019 Greater Detroit District Superintendent**.<> 8000 Woodward Ave., Detroit 48202 (313) 481-1045. Home: 35361 Stratton Hill Court, Farmington Hills 48331. cboayue@michiganumc.org

*Boehm, James W. –
[(RE) D-1966; D-1973; FE-1976; R-1998] Gobles/Kendall 04/01/1967-09/01/1969; Withdrew 1970; Readmitted 1973; Transferred from Detroit Conf 1975; Newaygo 1975; Plainwell: First 1984; UM Connectional Structures (¶344.1a,c) Kalamazoo District Superintendent 1989; Okemos Community Church 1996; Retired 09/01/1998.<> Home: PO Box 663, 73 N Eldridge Rd, Beulah 49617 (231) 882-7074. hrboehm712@gmail.com

*Boelens, Nancy L. –
[(RL) FL-2000; PL-2007; RL-2009] Bath/Gunnisonville 1998; Wayland 06/06/2003-11/01/2006; Sitka 11/1/2006-7/1/2008; Muskegon: Unity 11/01/2006-1/1/2009; Personal Leave 1/1/2009-4/12/2009; Retired 4/12/2009; Salem Indian Mission / Bradley Indian Mission 2013-12/15/2015.<> Home: 1875 Parkcrest Dr. SW, Apt. 2, Wyoming 49519 (616) 914-9300. boelensnancy5@gmail.com

*Boersma, Gilbert R. (Sara Jayne) –
[(RE) D-1982; FE-1984; R-2011] Frontier/Osseo 1982; Middleville/Freeport (Assoc) 1985; Wolf Lake 01/01/1989; Other Valid Ministries (¶344.1d) Pastoral Care Coordinator, Hospice Of Oceana & Muskegon Counties 02/01/1995; Clergy Appointed to Attend School, CPE Residency Program, Bronson Medical Center 1997; Appointed to Extension Ministries (¶344.1b,c) Chaplain, Hackley Hospital 06/15/1998; Appointed to Extension Ministries (¶344.1b,c) Manager, Spiritual Care Services, Hackley Hospital 2004; Transitional Leave 04/17/2009; Muskegon: Unity (LTFT ¼) 2009; Retired 10/31/2011.<> Home: 3364 Davis Rd, Muskegon 49441 (231) 557-5640. boersma49@gmail.com

*Bohnsack, Benjamin (Marcia) –
[(RE) P 1969; F 1971] 1970 Livonia: Newburg (assoc); 1973 Hardy; 1980 Marquette: First; 1988 Brighton: First; 1997 Farmington: Nardin Park; **2006 Retired**.<> 3140 State Highway M-28 East, Marquette 49855 (906) 343-6638. bohnsack@sandriverfriends.com

Boley, Ian J. (Jessica Korpela) –
[(FL) FL 2016] Walled Lake 2016; **Gull Lake 2020**.<> 8640 Gull Rd, Richland 49083-9647 (269) 629-5137. Home: 8405 Hemel Lane, Richland 49083 (989) 400-1268. ianboley@gmail.com

*Boley, John W. (Diane) –

[(RE) D-1991; FE-1994; RE 2020] Mancelona/Alba 06/16/1992; Lansing: Central 1997; Mt Pleasant: First 2002; Kalamazoo: First 2010; UM Connectional Structures (¶344.1a,c) Kalamazoo District Superintendent 2014; **Clergy Assistant to the Bishop 2016; Retired 2020; Clergy Assistant to the Bishop (LTFT ½) 2020**.<> 1011 Northcrest Rd, Lansing 48906 (517) 347-4030. Home: 2717 Frederick Ave, Kalamazoo 49008 (989) 400-0355. jboley@michiganumc.org

*Boltz, Peggy A. –

[(RL) FL-1995; RL-2014] Marcellus 08/01/1995; Shelby 2002; Lawton: St Paul's 2010; Oshtemo 2011; Bellaire: Community 2013; Retired 07/16/2014.<> PO Box 26, 6842 Northland Dr, Stanwood 49346 (231) 629-4590. Home: PO Box 26, 18835 Fillmomre Rd, Stanwood 49346 (231) 823-2514. bondo5@sbcglobal.net

*Bongard, Connie R. (Frank) –

[(RL) FL-1992; RL-2015] Leaton 05/01/1992; Mt Pleasant: First (Assoc) 08/01/1994; Edmore: Faith 07/16/1997; Farwell 01/01/2007; Retired 2015.<> Home: 1007 Lincoln Dr., Weidman 48893 (989) 506-6659. rev_crab@hotmail.com

Bonsky, Nicholas E. –

[(PE) PE 2019] **Farmington: Orchard (assoc) 2019**.<> 30450 Farmington Rd, Farmington Hills 48334 (248) 626-3620. Home: 29221 Aranel, Farmington Hills 48334 (586) 944-3292

Bos, Kimberly Mae –

[(PE)] UM Connectional Structures (¶344.1a,c) Director of Wesley Foundation at Ferris State University 2019.<> FSU Wesley Foundation, 628 S Warren Ave, Big Rapids 49307 (231) 796-8315. Home: 14610 Tomahawk Ln, Big Rapids 49307 (231) 557-0574. PastorKimBos@gmail.com

*Bourns, Carol Lynn –

[(RP) D-1992; RP-2007] North Evart/Sylvan (¼ Time) 09/01/1991; Leave of Absence 01/01/1995; Medical Leave 1997; Retired 2007.<> Home: 144 W 4th St Apt 403, Clare 48617 (989) 544-2719. fpm-dave@hotmail.com

Bouse, Carol Marie Blair (Allen) –

[(FE) P 1995; F 1997] 1995 Owendale, Gagetown; Oct 1, 1996 Fenton (assoc); 2001 Lake Orion (assoc); 2002 Dearborn: Mt. Olivet; 2006 Bay City: Christ; **2013 Flint: Hope**.<> G-4467 Beecher Rd., Flint 48532 (810) 732-4820. cmbblogos@aol.com

Boutell, James (Tommy) T. (Shelly) –

[(FE) PL-2008; PE-2010; FE-2016] Olivet (PTLP) 2008; Marne 2010; Grand Rapids: Genesis 2018.<> 3189 Snow Ave, Lowell 49331 (616) 974-0400. Home: 1805 Forest Lake Dr SE, Grand Rapids 49546 (616) 678-7664. tomboutell@yahoo.com

*Bouvier, Sylvia Ann (Carl) –

[(RE) P 1985; F 1987] 1985 Lakeville, Leonard; 1987 Pontiac: Aldersgate; 1987 Oakland County Jail Chaplain; May 1, 1989 Pontiac United Ministries Association, parish director; 1992 Flint: Oak Park; 1998 Howarth, Paint Creek; **2006 Retired**.<> 1855 Brentwood Pointe, Franklin TN (615) 427-8562. sylvia13bouvier@gmail.com

*Bovee, Keith A. –
[(RE) D-1956; FE-1958; R-1994] Frontier 1952; Centreville 1954; Muskegon: Central (Assoc) 1957; North Muskegon 1959; Lowell: First 1963; St Johns: First 1965; Voluntary Location 1968; Left Appointment 1974; Marne 1982; Ionia: First 1985; Shelby 1991; Retired 1994.<> Home: 1551 Franklin St SE, 3010 Manor, Grand Rapids 49506 (616) 805-3682. keith6451@att.net

*Bowden, Dianne M. (Jeff) –
[(RE) PE-2002; FE-2005; R-2013] Nashville 01/16/2002; Muskegon: Crestwood 2007; Medical Leave 05/01/2008; Retired 2013.<> Home: 2310 Avenal Ct, Murfreesboro TN 37129 (615) 410-3399. Pastordi46@gmail.com

Bower, Benjamin J. R. (Mallory) Missing changes with statuses?
[(FE) FL 2013; PE 2014; FE 2017] 2013 Trenton: First; **2016 Redford: Aldersgate**.<> 10000 Beech Daly Rd., Redford 48239 (313) 937-3170. Home: 11328 Arnold, Redford 48239 (313) 531-7487

Bowman, Daniel James (Celina) –
[(FE) PL 1991; P 1993; F 1995] LaSalle: Zion May 16, 1991; Lapeer: Trinity (assoc) Jan 1, 1995; Marlette: First Sept 1, 1998; Gaylord: First 2014; **Swartz Creek 2020**.<> 7400 Miller Rd., Swartz Creek 48473 (810) 635-4555. Home: 4187 Mountain Ash Court, Swartz Creek 48473 (810) 441-1600. preacherdb@gmail.com

Bowman, Letisha M. (Brian) –
[(FE) PL-2007; PE-2011; FE-2014] Saugatuck (DSA) 2005; Saugatuck (PTLP) 2007; Grand Rapids: First (Assoc) 2011; Portland 2015.<> 310 E Bridge St, Portland 48875 (517) 647-4649. Home: 309 Grape St, Portland 48875 (517) 647-6460. pastortish@gmail.com

Bowman, Jeffrey J., Sr. (Cheryl) –
[(FL) FL-2000] Vermontville/Gresham 1995; White Cloud 2002; Muskegon Heights: Temple 2012.<> 2500 Jefferson St, Muskegon Heights 49444 (231) 733-1065. Home: 1205 Yorkshire Dr, Muskegon 49441 (231) 798-9309. pjbowman400@att.net

Bratt Carle, Jonathan E. –
[(FE) PE-2017; FE 2020] [Tennessee Conference] **Ionia First, Lyons-Muir 2017**; transferred from Tennessee Conference 2020.<> (IF) 105 E Main St, Ionia 48846 (616) 527-1860. (LM) 1074 Olmstead Rd, Muir 48860 (989) 855-2247. Home: 2536 Union Ave SE, Grand Rapids 495074 (901) 417-2844. jonathan.brattcarle@gmail.com

*Breitkreuz, Benjamin H. (Sharlene) –
[(RE) trans. from American Baptist Assn 1977; F 1982] 1978 Indiana University Hospital, Chaplain; Director of Dept. of Pastoral Care, Parkland Memorial Hospital; Jan 1, 1993 Department of Pastoral Care and Education, Medical University of South Carolina; 1997 Community Donation Coordinator, Transplant Center; 2000 leave of absence; Aug 1, 2001 Chaplain, Clinical Pastoral Educator, Bon Secours, St. Francis Xavier Hospital (335.1); Sept 1, 2002 leave of absence; 2004 Chaplain, Clinical Pastoral Educator; Jan 1, 2007 voluntary leave of absence; **2008 Retired**.<> Home: 22 D Foxwood Dr., Morris Plains NJ 07950

*Brenner, Robert Dale (Joyce) –
[(RE) PL 2000; PE 2002; FE 2005] 2000 Denton: Faith; Sept 1, 2002 Carleton; 2010 Farmington: First; **2013 Retired**.<> Home: 25766 Livingston Circle, Farmington Hills 48335 (248) 474-7568. revrdbrenner@gmail.com

*Bricker, J. Melvin –
[(RE) D-1966; FE-1968; R-1995] Kalamazoo: First (Assoc) 1966; Frankfort/Elberta 1971; Rockford 1980; Grandville 1989; Retired 1995.<> Home: 1216 Oakmont Dr #8, Walnut Creek CA 94595 (925) 482-0555

Brillhart, James (Brad) B. (Julia) –
[(FE) D-1999; FE-2004] Hesperia/Ferry 1999; Howard City: Heritage 2007; Lowell: First 2014.<> 621 E Main St, Lowell 49331 (616) 897-5936. Home: 640 Shepard Dr, Lowell 49331 (616) 897-8267. thewayofxp@gmail.com

Britt, James Edward (Denise) –
[(FE) P 1986; F 1989] 1986 Owosso: Central; 1990 Algonac: Trinity; 1992 West Vienna; 2001 Livonia: Clarenceville; Aug 16, 2006 Norway Grace, Faithhorn; 2011 Flint: Calvary; **2018 Lambertville**.<> 8165 Douglas Rd., Box 232, Lambertville 48144 (734) 847-3944. Home: 8116 Michelle Ln, Lambertville 48144 (810) 282-8081. jbritt@norwaymi.com

*Britt, John Joseph (Janine) –
[(RE) P 1982; F 1984; RE 2020] Warren: First (assoc) 1982; Sterling, Alger, Bentley Nov 1982; Mio, Curran Sunnyside 1990; Pigeon: First 2005; Millington 2015; **Retired 2020**.<> Home: 1054 Northwood Dr, Caro 48723. rev_jjb@yahoo.com

*Bromberek, Patricia L. (Glen Brown) –
[(RE) FL-2002; PE-2004; FE-2009; R-2011] Niles: Grace 2002; Center Park 2004; Newaygo 2006; Newaygo (LTFT ¾) 02/01/2011; Retired 2011.<> Home: 5793 Zebra Longwing Path, The Villages FL 32163. plbromberek@hotmail.com

Bromley, Dennis B. (JoAnn) –
[(FE) D-2000; AM-2000; PE-2014; FE-2016] Epsilon/Levering (DSA) 1993; Epsilon/Levering/11/16/1993; Epsilon/Levering/ Pellston 09/01/1997; Clare 2003; Ludington United 2013.<> 5810 Bryant Rd, Ludington 49431 (231) 843-8340. Home: 914 Seminole Dr, Ludington 49431 (231) 425-4386. pastord@ludingtonumc.org

*Brook, Patricia L. (Roger) –
[(RE) PE-2001; FE-2004; R-2018] Dewitt: Redeemer (Assoc) 1999; Marne 02/01/2002; Hillsdale: First 2010; Retired 2018; Carson City (LTFT ¼) 08/01/2018-06/30/2019.<> Home: 1653 Dr, E Lansing 48823 (517) 607-5770. plb331@gmail.com

*Brooks, John M. (Terri Ann) –
[(RL) PL-2015; FL-2016; RL-2020] Gobles/Kendall (PTLP ¾) 2015; Gobles/Kendall 2016; not appointed 2019; **Retired Jan 1, 2020**.<> 1106 Poplar Grove Pl, Summerville SC 29483 (269) 271-0856. johnbrookspastor@gmail.com

Brooks, Ronald K. (Penny) –
[(FE) D-1985; FE-1988] Center Eaton/Brookfield 1985; Nashville 1988; Lawrence 05/16/1991; Lansing: Mount Hope (Assoc) 1998; Lansing: Mount Hope 1999; Lawton: St Paul 2000; Carson City 2006; Voluntary Leave of Absence 2008; Lansing: Central 2009; Jackson: Brookside 2013; Jackson: Brookside/Trinity 2015; Jackson: Calvary (Director, Cooperative Parish para. 206.3 and 206.6) Nov 1, 2019; **Grand Ledge 2020**.<> 411 Harrison St, Grand Ledge 48837 (517) 627-3256. Home: 912 E Scott St, Grand Ledge 48837 (269) 779-6131. revbrooks.ron@gmail.com

*Brookshear, Wayne Walker (Margie) –
[(RE) T 1958; F 1960] 1956 Lennon; 1960 Pontiac: St. Luke's, Oakland University Wesley Foundation; 1968 Detroit: St. Mark's; 1972 Milford; **1983 Retired**.<> Home: 1920 Northeast 18th St, Crystal River, FL 34428 305-304-9352

*Brown, Carole A. –
[(RL) PL Apr 1, 2005; FL 2006; RL 2019] Apr 1, 2005 Oregon; 2006 Owosso: Burton, Carland; 2011 Mayville; **2019 Retired**.<> 3001 Oklahoma Ave, Flint 48506 (989) 277-2306. carolebrown@intouchmi.com

*Brown, Colon Robert (Lisa) –
[(RE) P, N. IN, 1987; F N. IN, 1991; RE 2019] 1985 Michigan City; 1987 Mishawaka; 1992 trans. to Detroit Conf, Burton: Burton; Dec 15, 1995 Grand Blanc: Phoenix; 1997 Associate Council Director, Director of Congregational Development; 2005 Associate Executive Director, United Methodist Union; Feb 1, 2006 incapacity leave; **Retired 2019**.<> Home: 2109 Breeze Dr., Holland 49424 (616) 820-4053. cbrown1@mac.com

*Brown, Dale E. (Margaret) –
[(RE) P 1971; F 1974] 1973 AuGres, Turner, Twining; Mar 1979 Mayville, Fostoria, Silverwood; Jan 8, 1984 Hardy; 1989 Birch Run; 1999 Bay City: Fremont Avenue; 2002 Macon; Mar 1, 2004 Macon (LTFT ¾); 2007 Capac: First, Zion Community; 2011 Menominee: First; **2014 Retired**.<> Home: 4622 Weswilmar Dr., Holt 48842 (517) 742-7067. dalemargebr@gmail.com

*Brown, Debra Kay (Dennis) –
[(RL)] PL Oct 1, 2000] Oct 1, 2000 Cole; 2002 Cole, Melvin; Aug 1, 2010 Kingston; 2014 medical leave; **Mar 15, 2015 Retired**.<> Home: 2357 Snover Rd., Deckerville 49427 (810) 366-0430. pastordebi2000@yahoo.com

*Brown, Janet Jacqueline –
[(RE) PE 2007; FE 2010; RE 2018] 2007 Detroit: Trinity Faith; **2018 Retired; 2018 Erie**.<> 1100 E. Samaria Rd., Erie 48133 (734) 856-1453. Home: 23470 Meadow Park, Redford 48239 (313) 533-8423. januk99@gmail.com

Brown, Kathy E. –
[(FE) D-1985; FE-1987] Traverse City: Central (Assoc) 1985; Litchfield 1990; Hastings: First 02/01/2001; Plainwell: First 2010.<> PO Box 85, 200 Park St, Plainwell 49080 (269) 685-5113. Home: 714 E Gun River Dr, Plainwell 49080 (269) 312-1378. kathyebrown935@gmail.com

*Brown, Lawrence P. (Beverly) –
[(RE) D-1988; FE-1992; R-2014] Somerset Center/Moscow Plains 1989; Somerset Center 01/01/1993; Lakeview Asbury/Belvidere 1996; Lakeview: New Life 01/01/1998; Ionia: First 2006; Retired 2014.<> Home: 564 Indiana Ave, South Haven 49090 (517) 526-7958. Larrybev@outlook.com

Brown, Mary S. (Carl) –
[(RE) FD-1994; FE-1997; RE 2020] Baldwin/Luther (¶426.1) 1995; Transferred from Detroit Conf 1996; Baldwin/ Luther 1996; Bellaire: Community 10/16/1998; Traverse City Christ and Kewadin 2009; Grawn 11/01/2009; Montague 2014; Medical Leave 12/01/2016; **Retired 2020**.<> Home: 16843 Shawano Dr, Sand Lake 49343 (231) 357-4506. pastormaryb@gmail.com

*Brown, Richard B. (Randi) –
[(RL) PL 2000; FL 2003] Mar 16, 2000 Calumet, Mohawk-Ahmeek, Lake Linden, Laurium (assoc); 2003 Vernon, Bancroft; 2005 Kingston, Clifford; Dec 1, 2009 Kingston; **2010 Retired**.<> Home: 4257 Mill Ridge Circle, Eau Claire WI 54703. richardblackstock.brown@gmail.com

*Brown, Ronald Alex (Joan) –
[(RL) PL 1987] 1987 Keego Harbor: Trinity; **1994 Retired**.<> Home: 294 Draper, Pontiac 48341 (248) 681-8470

Brown, Sari L. (Ricardo Angarita Oviedo) –
[(PE) PE 2016] 2016 Grosse Pointe (assoc); **2017 Harbor Beach, Port Hope**.<> (HB) PO Box 25, 253 S. First St., Harbor Beach 48441, (PH) PO Box 25, 4521 Main St., Port Hope 48468. Home: PO Box 25, 247 First St., Harbor Beach 48441 (989) 479-6053. revsaribrown@gmail.com

*Brown, Tom, II –
[(RE) T 1957; F 1959] 1959 Dearborn: First (assoc); 1960 St. Clair Shores: Good Shepherd; 1965 River Rouge: Epworth; 1968 Iron Mountain: Trinity; 1973 Roseville; 1978 Hemlock, Nelson; 1984 Warren: Wesley; Dec 1, 1986 Flint: Oak Park; 1992 Burton: Emmanuel; **1997 Retired**.<> Home: 801 W Middle St, Apt 177, Chelsea 48118 (517) 554-0645. tbrown@albion.edu

Browne, Jennifer (Eric Strand) –
[(FE) D-1998; FE-2008] Reed City (Assoc) 01/15/1997; Transferred from United Church of Christ 1998; Clergy Appointed To Attend School (¶416.6) 12/01/1998; UM Connectional Structures (¶344.1a,c) Albion College, Assistant to the President (¶335.1a LTFT ½) 2000; Leave of Absence 03/01/2003; Appointed in Other Annual Conferences (¶337.1) (Assoc) Detroit Conference, Brighton First 2003; Grand Rapids: First (Assoc) 2006; East Lansing: University 2011; Georgetown 2016; UM Connectional Structures (¶344.1a,c), Conference Director of Clergy Excellence 2018.<> 1161 E Clark Rd, DeWitt 48820 (517) 347-4030 ext. 4050. Home: 434 Creston Ave, Kalamazoo 49001 (517) 898-4575. jbrowne@michiganumc.org

*Brubaker, Ellen A. (John Ross Thompson) –
[(RE) D-1974; FE-1976; R-2001] Transferred from Detroit Conf 1975; Traverse City: Central (Assoc) 1975; Traverse City: Central (Assoc) / Ogdensburg (Re-named Old Mission Peninsula 1978; Belding 1981; UM Connectional Structures (¶344.1a,c) Grand Rapids District Superintendent 1983; Church of the Dunes 1989; Grand Rapids: Aldersgate 1992; Retired 12/31/2001; Grand Rapids: Trinity (Assoc) (LTFT 1/8) 2015-9/1/2016.<> Home: 4114 Sawkaw Dr NE, Grand Rapids 49525 (616) 822-5383. johnellen5@comcast.net

*Brun, Wesley LeRoy –
[(RE) P MO E., 1963; F MO E, 1965] 1965 school (Yale); 1966 Monroe City, Florida (Missouri); 1968 St. Louis: Grace (assoc); 1974 Pastoral Counseling Center, Lutheran General Hospital, Park Ridge IL; 1986 Executive Director, Samaritan Counseling Center of Southeastern Michigan (1999 trans to Det Conf); **2006 Retired**.<> Home: 41120 Fox Run Rd #308, Novi 48337 (248) 956-7889. wesbrun@gmail.com

*Bryant, Vivian C. (William) –
[(RE) P 1997 on recognition of orders AME; FE 2000] 1997 Southfield: Hope (assoc); **June 30, 2003 Retired**.<> Home: 313 Castlemere Ct., Murfreesboro TN 37130 (615) 605-7636. revvcb@yahoo.com

*Bryce, Margaret E. (Craig) –
[(RE) PL 2008; PE 2012 (Church of the Nazarene); FE 2014; RE 2020] Attica Aug 1, 2008; Downriver 2013; leave of absence July 1, 2018; Adjunct Professor of Practical Theology, Ashland Theological Seminary, Detroit Campus Aug 1, 2018; **Retired Jan 1, 2020.**<> Home: 824 Inverness Dr, Oxford 48371 (810) 338-2373. drmbryce@gmail.com

*Buchholz, Pamela Leigh (Fredric) –
[(RD) PD 2006; FD 2009] 2006 Midland: First, Minister of Christian Education (deacon); **Sept 1, 2013 Retired.**<> Home: 256 E. Youngs Ct., Midland 48640 (989) 835-3203. pam06@charter.net

Buchner, Gregory L. (AnnMarie) –
[(FE) FL-1999; PE-2005; FE-2008] Three Oaks (DSA) 11/15/1997; Wakelee (DSA) 1998; Wakelee 11/16/1999; Rosebush 2005; Ovid United Church 2008; Mecosta: New Hope 2013; Rockford 2019.<> 59 Maple St, Rockford 49341 (616) 866-9515. Home: 1105 West Pickard, PO Box 894, Mt Pleasant 48804 (989) 621-7782. pastorgreg.ncd@gmail.com

*Buck, Steven J. (Susan) –
[(RE) trans. from Wesleyan Methodist, 1977; F 1979] 1977 Yale, Greenwood; Jan 15, 1982 Royal Oak: First (assoc); 1988 Marquette: First; 1993 Flint: Court Street; 2008 Northville: First; **2013 Retired.**<> 6446 Prairie Dunes Dr., Grand Blanc 48439 (810) 444-7089. sjbuck@comcast.net

*Buege, Donald L. (Cynthia) –
[(RE) D-1977; FE-1981; R-2017] Vergennes/Lowell: First (Assoc) 1979; Mesick/Harrietta 09/01/1980; Keeler/ Silver Creek 01/01/1984; Evart/Avondale 1990; Avondale/North Evart/Sylvan (LTFT ¼) 2000; Leslie/Felt Plains (LTFT ¾) 01/15/2006; Fife Lake Parish: Fife Lake/East Boardman/South Boardman 2014; Retired 2017.<> Home: 124 Boyd St, Fife Lake 49633 (231) 879-6055. dbuege76@gmail.com

Bukoski, Jerry J. (Sandra) –
[(PL) PL-2014] Barry-Eaton Cooperative Ministry: Quimby (DSA) (LTFT ¼) 2013; Barry-Eaton Cooperative Ministry: Quimby (PTLP ¼) 2014; Kalamo/Quimby (PTLP 45%) 2015; Kalamo (LTFT ¼) 2018.<> 1475 S Ionia Rd, Kalamo 49096 (810) 986-0240. Home: 1069 S Ionia Rd, Vermontville 49096 (517) 588-8415. jerry.bukoski@gmail.com

Bunch, Brian R. (Kendra) –
[(FL) FL-1997] Brooks Corners and Sears 1997; Brooks Corners/Barryton-Chippewa Lake/Sears 03/01/2002; NE Missaukee Parish: Merritt-Butterfield/ Moorestown-Stittsville 08/01/2005; Delton: Faith 2012.<> PO Box 467, 503 S Grove St, Delton 49046 (269) 623-5400. Home: 146 Bush St, Delton 49046 (269) 623-5335. brbunch@mei.net

Bunn, Bradley E. –
[(FL) CC-2017; DSA-2017; FL-2017] Ludington: St. Paul (DSA) 2017; Ludington: St. Paul (FL) 2017.<> 3212 W Kinney Rd, Ludington 49431 (231) 843-3275. Home: 3257 W Kinney Rd, Ludington 49431 (404) 625-6802. bunnbrad5@gmail.com

Burdette, Tom Glenn (Gail) –
[(FE) P 1975; F 1979] 1977 Ypsilanti: First (assoc); 1983 Lincoln Community; Nov 1, 1985 Chaplain, M. J. Clark Home, Grand Rapids; Dec 1, 1986 Staff Chaplain, University of Michigan Health System' **Dec 2, 2016 Retired**.<> Home: 8424 Crestshire, Ypsilanti 48197 (734) 484-6004. tburd@med.umich.edu

*Burgess, Ray W. –
[(RE) D-1961; FE-1965; R-2000] Transferred from Detroit Conf 01/01/1970; UM Connectional Structures (¶344.1a,c) Wesley Foundation Director, Ferris State College 01/01/1970; Grand Rapids: South 1979; Sturgis 1988; Muskegon: Central 1993; Retired 2000.<> Home: 10915 Pioneer Trail, Boyne Falls 49713 (231) 549-3066. Winter: 8701 S Kolb 7-232, Tuscon AZ 85706 (520) 574-6692. mrburgess2@nmo.net

Burns, Dillon Selby –
[(FE) PE 2017; FE 2020] **Manchester: First 2017**.<> 501 Ann Arbor St., Manchester 48158 (734) 428-8495. Home: 330 Ann Arbor St., Manchester 48158 (734) 428-4780. pastordillionburns@gmail.com

*Burns, Ellen Florence (William) –
[(RL) PL 1996; FL 2000] 1996 Eastern Thumb Cooperative Parish: Minden City, Forester; 2000 Decker, Argyle, Shabbona, Ubly; Jan 1, 2006 Parish Director, DASU Parish (Decker, Argyle, Shabbona, Ubly); **2010 Retired**.<> Home: 60 Chippewa St., Port Sanilac 48469 (810) 404-2444. burns2444@att.net

*Burson, Linda J. (Douglas Rose) –
[(RE) D-1987; FE-1990; RE-2019] Transferred from New York Conf 1997; Homer/Lyon Lake 1997; Leave of Absence 1/1/2000; UM Connectional Structures (¶344.1a,c) Conference Staff Ministry Consultant 8/1/2000; Leave of Absence 2008; Kalamazoo: Sunnyside 3/1/2009; Personal Leave 2009; Appointed in Other Annual Conferences (¶331.8, ¶346.1) Mallory, Tennessee Conf 2017; Retired 02/04/2019.<> Home: 240 Cullom Way, Clarksville TN 37043 (931) 302-6760. LindaJBurson@gmail.com

Burstall, Richard Erich –
[(FE) PL May 15, 2005; FL 2005; PE 2008; FE 2013] May 15, 2005 Azalia, London; 2007 Morenci; 2010 Britton: Grace; **2014 Grayling: Michelson Memorial**.<> 400 Michigan Ave., Grayling 49738 (989) 348-2974. Home: 142 Barbara St., Grayling 49738 (989) 348-9697. gvnit2god@yahoo.com

*Burton-Collier, Linda J. (Earl Collier) –
[(RL) PE-2005; FL-2010; RL-2014] White Pigeon (DSA 07/01/01-07/01/02) 2002; Hopkins 2005; South Monterey 2005; Retired 2014.<> Home: 2574 127th Ave, Allegan 49010 (269) 793-7340. lindaburtoncollier@gmail.com

Burton-Krieger, Eric M. (Meagan) –
[(FE) PE-2012; FE-2015] Appointed in Other Annual Conferences (¶331.8, ¶346.1) Tennessee Conference, Brentwood (assoc) 2012; Appointed in Other Annual Conferences (¶331.8, ¶346.1) Indiana Conference, Indianapolis St. Luke's (assoc) 2015.<> 100 W 86th St, Indianapolis IN 46260 (317) 846-3404. Home: 520 N Rangeline Rd, Carmel IN 46032 (615) 934-0068. eric.burton.krieger@gmail.com

Butler, James –
[(PL) PL 2020] **Fairgrove, Sutton-Sunshine (PTLP ½) Jun 1, 2020**.<> (F) 5116 W. Center, Box 10, Fairgrove 48733 (989) 693-6564. (SS) 2996 N Colwood Rd, Caro 48723 (989) 673-6695. Home: 2024 Liberty, Fairgrove 48733 (248) 881-6294. jim3956@gmail.com

Butson, Christopher A. –
[(PE) PL Aug 1, 2014; PE 2-18] Jan 1, 2014 Azalia, London (LTFT ½); **2019 Ypsilanti: Lincoln Community**.<> 9074 Whittaker Rd., Ypsilanti 48197 (734) 482-2226. Home: 9066 Whittaker Rd., Ypsilanti 48197 (734) 657-2490. christopherbutson@live.com

*Byadiah, Bonnie D. (Cleg Bordeaux) –
[(RE) P 1980; F 1983] 1981 Caro (assoc); 1983 Burton; 1992 Pontiac Cooperative Parish: First; **1997 Retired**.<> Home: 664 Nichols, Auburn Hills 48326 (248) 852-2711

*Cabot, Roberta W. –
[(RL) FL-2001; PL-2010; FL-2011; RL-2014] Wolf Lake 11/15/2001 (PTLP 05/10/10); Bear Lake 2011; Arcadia 2011; Retired 2014.<> Home: Kingdom Life Healing Ministries, 28 Caberfae Hwy, Manistee 49660 (231) 557-0166

*Cadarette, Kathryn S. (David) –
[(RE) D-1994; FE-1996; RE-2019] Horton Bay 1994; Horton Bay/Greensky Hill Indian Mission 02/01/1998; Leave of Absence 2000; Harbor Springs/Alanson 2003; Reed City 2011; Retired 2019; **Horton Bay 2020**.<> 4961 Boyne City Rd, Boyne City 49712-9217 (231) 582-9262. Home: 5925 Horton Bay Rd N, Boyne City 49712 (231) 675-2172. kathycad60@gmail.com

*Cain, Frederick G. –
[(OR) D-1976; OE-1980; OR-2013] [Indiana Conference, Retired Elder] Camden/Montgomery/Stokes Chapel (LTFT ½) 2013.<> PO Box 155, 201 S Main St, Camden 49232 (517) 797-5530. revfgcain@yahoo.com

Callow, Timothy G. –
[(FE) FL 2013; PE 2014; FE 2017] God's Country Cooperative Parish: Newberry, Engadine 2013; **BAD AXE COOPERATIVE PARISH: Bad Axe: First, Minden City 2020**.<> (BA) 216 East Woodworth, Bad Axe 48413 (989) 269-7671. (MC) 3346 Main St, PO Box 126, Minden City 48456 (810) 648-4155. Home: 1165 Thompson Dr., Bad Axe 48413 (906) 290-2251. tgcallow@gmail.com

Carey, Melanie Lee (Jonathan) –
[(FE) P 1990; F 1993] 1991 Hudson: First; 1993 Livonia: Newburg (assoc); 2000 Ypsilanti: First; 2011 Detroit Renaissance District Superintendent; 2015 Clergy Assistant to the Bishop; **2016 Farmington Hills: Nardin Park**.<> 29887 W. 11 Mile Rd., Farmington Hills 48336 (248) 476-8860. Home: 25109 Lyncastle Ln., Farmington Hills 48336 (248) 477-8891. Revmelaniecarey@yahoo.com

*Cargo, William Abram (Alice Jo) –
[(RE) P 1971; F WIS., 1975] 1973 Waukaw, Elo, Eureka (Wisconsin); 1974 Admin. Sec. Office Pres, Union Seminary NY; 1975 school, Nunnelly, Bethel TN; 1976 Trans. to Detroit Conf, Detroit: Jefferson Avenue; 1981 Riverview; 1988 Oscoda, Oscoda Indian Church; 2006 Grayling: Michelson Memorial; **2011 Retired**.<> 816 S. Gondola Dr., Venice FL 34293 (615) 739-1595. waCargo@chartermi.net

*Carlson, David 'Gunnar' (Normajean) –
[(RL) PL-2007; RL-2010] Grass Lake (LTFT PT) 2007; Retired 2010; Montague 12/1/2016-2017; Grass Lake (LTFT ¼) 12/1/2018-6/30/2019.<> Home: 2185 Moon St, Muskegon 49441 (231) 755-8168. dgcarlson1947@comcast.net

*Carlson, Linda J. (Ted) –
[(RL) PL-1993; FL-1999; RL-2009] Jackson Calvary (assoc) (LTFT PT) 1993; Manton 02/16/1999; Retired 2009.<> Home: 1720 SE 72nd Ave, Portland OR 97215

Carlson, Sara Louise –
[(PL) PL-2015] Kalamazoo: Stockbridge Ave (LTFT ¼) 2015; Silver Creek (LTFT ¼) 2/01/2016.<> 31994 Middle Crossing Rd, Dowagiac 49047 (269) 782-7061. Home: 4229 Mahoney St, Portage 49002 (269) 329-1072. sara.carlson@wmich.edu

Caron, Leah –
[(PL) PL 2018] **Holly: Mt. Bethel 2018**.<> 3205 Jossman Rd. Holly 48442 (248) 627-7600. Home: 735 Vivian Ln, Oxford 48371 (248) 520-0884. caron.leagh@yahoo.com

*Carter, Janet S. (Lee Copenhaver) –
[(RD) PD-2005; FD-2009; RD-2020] Deacons Appointed Beyond the Local Church (¶331.1a) Chaplain, Heartland Home Health Care & Hospice and Pine Rest Christian Mental Health Services 2005; Deacons Appointed Beyond the Local Church (¶331.1a) Chaplain, Pine Rest Christian Mental Health Services (¶331.1a) 10/23/2006; Deacons Appointed Beyond the Local Church (¶331.1a) Chaplain, Pine Rest Christian Mental Health Services (¶331.1a) and Grand Rapids: First (Deacon) 2009; Deacons Appointed Beyond the Local Church (¶331.1a) Chaplain, Pine Rest Christian Mental Health Services (¶331.1a) 2011; **Retired 2020**.<> Home: 4367 Cottage Trl, Hudsonville 49426 (616) 260-9604. labarnabas@hotmail.com.

Cartwright, Jodi M. –
[(PL) CC-2016; PL-2017] Dowagiac: First (LTFT ¾) 2017; Casco (LTFT ¾) 2019.<> 880 66th St, South Haven 49090 (269) 227-3328. Home: 870 66th St, South Haven 49090 (517) 282-9642. jodicartwright5@gmail.com

*Catellier, Patricia L. –
[(RD) PD-2010; FD-2014; RD-2020] Deacons Appointed w/in UM Connectional Structure (¶331.1b) Chaplain, Borgess Medical Center (LTFT ½) 2010; Transitional Leave 09/01/2015; Portage: Chapel Hill (Deacon) (LTFT ¼) 01/01/2016; **Retired 2020**.<> Home: 7146 Oakland Dr, Portage 49024 (269) 382-0708. pcatellier7711@charter.net

*Cattell, H. Reginald (Dorothy) –
[(RE) Trans. from Missouri, Nov 1972] 1972 Imlay City, Attica; 1974 Imlay City, Goodland, E. Goodland; 1975 Hazel Park; Feb 1979 Detroit: Zion; Nov 1, 1983 Swartz Creek; **Sept 1, 1994 Retired**.<> Home: 29 St. Thorman Terrace, St. Thomas, Ontario (519) 637-3937

Chalker, Melany A. (Darryl) –
[(FE) FL-2004; PE-2005; FE-2008] Appointed in Other Annual Conferences (¶346.1) Detroit Conference, Springville 2005; Concord 2006; Marshall 2013.<> 721 Old US 27N, Marshall 49068 (269) 781-5107. Home: 762 N Kalamazoo Ave, Marshall 49068 (517) 403-8528. pastormelany@gmail.com

*Chapman, Mary Ellen (James) –
[(RL) FL Mar 2002] Hazel Park Mar 1, 2002; Lincoln Community 2010; **Retired 2016;** Omo: Zion, Washington (LTFT ½) Sept 3, 2018; **Omo: Zion (LTFT ¼) 2019**.<> 63030 Omo Rd., PO Box 344, Richmond 48062 (810) 233-2824. Home: 19059 Carmelo Dr., N, Clinton Township 48038 (586) 291-6552. pastor@wowway.com

Chapman, Matthew D. (Abigail) –
[(FE) FL 2016; PE 2017; FE 2020] Bay Port, Hayes 2016; **Traverse Bay 2020**.<> 1200 Ramsdell St, Traverse City 49684 (231) 946-5323. Home: 10160 E Pickwick Ct, Traverse City 49684 (231) 947-5594. pastor.matthew.chapman@gmail.com

*Chapman, Robert David (Sandy) –
[(RL) PL 1995; RL 2012] 1995 Avoca, Ruby; disability leave; 2001 Port Huron: Gratiot Park; 2009 Port Huron: Gratiot Park and Port Huron: Washington Ave; **2012 Retired**.<> Home: 4458 Atkins Rd., Port Huron 48060 (810) 982-2049. rsmbchap@yahoo.com

*Chappell, Lynn Francis (Caren) –
[(RE) P 1972; F 1975] 1974 Sterling, Alger, Bentley; 1981 Wisner; 1984 Whittemore, Prescott; 1989 Kingston, Deford; 1996 Pickford; May 1, 2003 Gladwin; **2009 Retired; 2009 Beaverton: First**.<> 150 West Brown, Beaverton 48612 (989) 435-4322. Home: 9723 E. Townline Lake Rd. Harrison 48625 (989) 329-0317. chappell_2@charter.net

*Charlefour, Kathy Ruth (John) –
[(RE) PL 2001; PE 2002; FE 2005] 2001 Monroe: East Raisinville Frenchtown; Sept 1, 2002 Monroe: East Raisinville Frenchtown (LTFT ¾) Carleton (assoc) (LTFT ¼); Nov 1, 2005 Dearborn: Good Shepherd; **2014 Retired**.<> Home: 43314 Hanford, Canton 48187 (734) 788-3022. revkrc@gmail.com

*Charnley, Stephen M.G. (Cynthia) –
[(RE) D-1978; FE-1982; RE-2020] Transferred from Wisconsin Conf 1988; Newaygo 1988; Gull Lake 1994; Greenville: First 2008; Greenville: First, Turk Lake/Belding Cooperative Parish 2013; Kalamazoo: First 2014; **Retired 2020**.<> Home: 471 W South St #403, Kalamazoo 49007 (269) 312-8633. thecharnleys@sbcglobal.net

*Charnley, Victor D. –
[(RE) D-1979; FE-1981; RE-2013] Church of the Dunes (Assoc) 1978; Received from American Baptist Church 1979; Church of the Dunes (Assoc) 1979; Battle Creek: Trinity 1984; Muskegon: Crestwood 1995; Mecosta: New Hope 2004; Retired 2013.<> Home: 1361 Overseas Highway Lot A13, Marathon FL 33050 (616) 512-5936. pastvic@yahoo.com

*Charter, John T. (Murelann) –
[(RA) AM-1972; RA-1999] Battle Creek: Calvary 1972; Homer/Lyon Lake/Marengo 1973; Homer/Lyon Lake 1975; Mendon 1978; Niles: Grace 1981; Battle Creek: Christ 11/16/1992; Retired 1999.<> Home: 4240 Keewahdin Rd, Fort Gratiot 48059. johncharterhi@comcast.net

*Cheyne, Paulette G. –
[(RL) PL-1992; FL-1995; RL-2008] Bell Oak / Williamston: Wheatfield (DSA 07/01/91; PTLP ½ 09/01/92; PTLP ¾ 01/01/95) (LTFT PT) 09/01/1992; Parmelee (assoc) 06/01/1995; Freeport / Middleville (Assoc) 06/01/1995; Winn / Coomer 2005; Blanchard-Pine River 2005; Comstock 2006; Aldersgate 11/15/2006-4/1/2008; Delta Mills 2007-4/1/2008; Delta Mills (LTFT ¼) 04/01/2008-2013; Retired 04/01/2008.<> Home: 3041 E Frost Rd, Williamston 48895 (517) 896-3787. paulettecheyne@gmail.com

Cho, Bo Rin (Koom) –
[(FE) D-1990; OE-2004; FE-1992] East Lansing: Korean 03/01/2004; Transferred from Minnesota Conf 2013; Lansing: Asbury 2014; Appointed in Other Annual Conferences, Detroit, Davison 2017.<> 207 E 3rd St, Davison 48423 (810) 653-5272. Home: 819 Alana Ct, Davison 48423 (517) 775-5436. borincho@comcast.net

Cho, Hyun Jun (Kyung Ran) –
[(FE) 2010 (Korean Methodist) FE 2016] Ann Arbor: Korean 2010; **NE Missaukee Parish: Merritt-Butterfield, Moorestown-Stittsville Aug 1, 2019**.<> (MB) 428 S Merritt Rd, Merritt 49667 (231) 328-4598. (MS) 4509 E Moorestown Rd, Lake City 49651 (231) 328-4598. Home: 7037 E Houghton Lake Rd, Merritt 49667 (231) 301-2692. pastor.hjcho@gmail.com

Christman, Catherine M. (Michael) –
[(FE) PL-2007; FL-2008; PE-2009; FE-2014] Nashville (PTLP) 2007; Nashville (FTLP) 4/1/08; Nashville 2009; Appointed in Other Annual Conferences (¶346.1) Detroit Conference, Midland: First (Assoc) 2010; Vassar: First 2013; Appointed in Other Annual Conferences (¶331.8, ¶346.1) Wisconsin Conference, Stoughton 2016.<> 525 Lincoln Ave, Stoughton WI 53589 (608) 873-3273. Home: 520 N Van Buren St, Stoughton WI 53589 (231) 342-3728. cchristman2006@hotmail.com

Chu, William W. (Julie Greyerbiehl) –
[(FE) PE-2005; FE-2008] Burr Oak (Student Local Pastor) 2001; LP w/o Appointment - Garrett-Evangelical Theological Seminary Coordinator of Educational Technologies 2003; Elk Rapids/ Kewadin/Williamsburg 2005; Elk Rapids/Kewadin/Williamsburg (Co-Pastor) 2008; Coloma/Watervliet 2009; East Lansing: University (Assoc) (½ Time) and UM Connectional Structures (¶344.1a,c) MSU Wesley Foundation, Director (½ Time) 2011; East Lansing: University (Assoc) (¼ Time) and UM Connectional Structures (¶344.1a,c) MSU Wesley Foundation, Director (¾ Time) 2013; UM Connectional Structures (¶344.1a,c) MSU Wesley Foundation, Director 01/01/2016; **Shepherd, Blanchard-Pine River 2020**.<> (S) PO Box 309, 107 W Wright Ave, Shepherd 48883 (989) 828-5866. (BPR) 7655 W Blanchard Rd, Blanchard 49310 (989) 561-2864. Home: 1109 Glenwood Dr, Mt Pleasant 48858 (517) 992-5038. wmwchu@gmail.com

Chun, Sang Yoon (Jinah) –
[(FE) P 1988; F 1990] 1988 Reese, Watrousville; 1992 Elkton; 1996 Korean United Methodist Church of Greater Washington (Virginia Conference), (para 426.1); 1999 Birch Run; 2005 Monroe: First; 2007 Ida, Samaria: Grace; **2016 Atherton, Phoenix**.<> (A) 4010 Lippincott Blvd., Burton 48519 (810) 742-5644. (P) 4423 S. Genesse Rd., Grand Blanc 48439 (810) 743-3370. Home: 6105 Wilderness Point, Grand Blanc 48439 (734) 856-3151. saychun@netzero.com

*Church, David E. (Winona) –
[(RE) T 1955; F 1960] 1958 Grass Lake; 1962 Houghton; 1968 Wesley Foundation, Oakland University, Rochester: St. Luke's; 1969 Rochester: St. Luke's; 1970 Walled Lake; 1978 Dearborn: Mt. Olivet; 1988 Livonia: Newburg; 1992 Highland; **1995 Retired**.<> Home: 717 W. Middle St., Chelsea 48118 (734) 475-8667. wecdec@sbcglobal.net

Clark, Lisa J. (Hollis) –
[(PL) PL 2000] Oct 1, 2000 Capac: First and Zion Community (assoc); 2008 Capac: Zion Community (assoc), Ruby; 2011 Capac: First, Capac: Zion Community; **2016 Capac**.<> 14952 Imlay City Rd., Capac 48018 (810) 395-2112. Home: 211 W. Mill St., Capac 48018 (810) 247-0946. plisaj@gmail.com

*Clark, Saundra Jean (Mike) –
[(RE) PE 2003; FE 2006] 2003 God's Country Cooperative Parish: Newberry, Engadine; **2013 Retired**.<> Home: PO Box 343, Powers 49874 (906) 203-1314. revsonie@gmail.com

Clarke, Curtis B. (Rita) –
[(FL) FL 2011] Nov 12, 2011 Armada/West Berlin; **2019 Marysville, Central Lakeport**.<> (M) 721 W Huron Blvd, Marysville 48040 (810) 364-7391. (CL) 3597 Milwaukee Rd., Lakeport 48059. Home: 683 18th St, Marysville 48040 (313) 570-4442. cbclarke95@gmail.com

Claxton, Melissa J. (Edward) –
[(FE) SP-2009; FL-2010; PE-2011; FE-2016] North Parma (Student Local Pastor) 2009; Springport/North Parma 2010; Appointed in Other Annual Conferences (¶331.8, ¶346.1) Detroit Conference, Warren: First 2018.<> 5005 Chicago Rd, Warren 48092 (586) 264-4701. Home: 32006 Wellston, Warren 48093. claxton517@yahoo.com

*Clegg, William V., Jr. (Joni) –
[(RE) D-1981; FE-1986; R-2011] Haslett Mission 01/16/1984; Haslett Aldersgate 1985; Wyoming: Wesley Park 1994; Retired 2011; Parmelee (¼ Time) 11/11/2012.<> PO Box 237, 9266 W Parmalee Rd, Middleville 49333 (269) 795-8816. Home: 4593 N Camrose Court, Wyoming 49519 (616) 366-2486. wvcleggjr@gmail.com

Cleland, William C. (Deb) –
[(PL) PL Dec 1, 2014] 2014 Gagetown, Owendale; **2017 Owendale, Kilmanagh**.<> (O) 7370 Main St., Box 98, Owendale 48754 (989) 678-4172. (K) 2009 S. Bay Port Rd., Bay Port 48720 (989) 453-3520. Home: 129 S. Silver St., Bad Axe 48413 (989) 975-1500. bcleland@comcast.net

*Clemmer, William Michael (Susan) –
[(RE) P 1981; F 1983] 1979 Samaria, Lulu; Jan 1, 1981 Deerfield, Petersburg; 1984 Asst. Admin., Chelsea Retirement Home; Feb 1, 1987 Detroit: Metropolitan (assoc ½ Time); 1988 leave of absence; 1989 honorable location; 1994 readmitted; Sept 1, 1994 Azalia, London; Feb 1, 2003 incapacity leave; Feb 16, 2003 disability leave; 2005 Deerfield, Wellsville; **Jan 1, 2014 Retired**.<> Home: 15300 Dixon, Dundee 48131 (734) 529-3213. wmclemmer@hotmail.com

*Clevenger, Leonard A. (Renae) –
[(RE) PL Nov 15, 2007; PE 2010; FE 2013] Nov 15, 2007 Mapleton; 2010 Bloomfield Hills: St. Paul; 2013 Bay City: Grace; **2015 Retired;** Oct 1, 2018-2019 Mapleton (LTFT ¼).<> Home: 2302 Longfellow Lane, Midland 48640 (989) 631-7277. revlenmod21@gmail.com

Cobb, Martin T. (Jessica) –
[(PE) SP-1999; FL-2001; PE-2007; FL-2015; PE 2020] Burr Oak 1999; Middleton/Maple Rapids/Christian Crossroads Cooperative Parish 2001; Old Mission Peninsula 2006; Litchfield/Quincy 2010; Fremont 2013; **Farwell 2017; Mt. Pleasant: Trinity, Mt. Pleasant: Countryside Oct 1, 2019**.<> (F) PO Box 709; 281 E Ohio St, Farwell 48622 (989) 588 2031. (MPT) 202 S Elizabeth St, Mt Pleasant 48858 (989) 772-5690. (MPC) 4264 S Leaton Rd, Mt Pleasant 48858 (989) 773-0359. Home: 511 N Superior St, Farwell 48622. pastorcobb@gmail.com

*Cochran, James D. (Theresa) –
[(RE) P 1963 W.MI; F 1965 W.MI] 1963 Lexington Conf: Scott Methodist, Maysville KY; 1963 Trans. to W. MI Conf, Grand Rapids: St. Paul (Co-Pastor); 1965 Grand Rapids: Church of the Redeemer; 1968 Trans. to Detroit Conf, Detroit: Central (assoc); 1970 Detroit West District Superintendent; 1976 school; 1980 Trans. to W. MI Conf, Conference Staff: Program Coordinator; 1986 Flint: Court St. (assoc); 1987 Trans. to Detroit Conf; 1988 Detroit: Conant Avenue; 1992 Dixboro; **1998 Retired.**<> Home: 8203 Berkshire Dr., Ypsilanti 48198 (734) 483-5939

*Coe, Bufford W. (Lisa) –
[(RE) D-1974; FE-1978; R-2017] Transferred from Detroit Conf 1994; Hastings: First 1994; Vicksburg 10/15/2000; Retired 2017.<> Home: 1751 Grovenberg Ct, Vicksburg 49097 (269) 626-4610. buffordc@aol.com

Coffey, Michael –
[(FE) AF 2007 (Missouri Conf), FE 2008 transfer to Detroit Conf from Missouri Conf] Executive Director, Bay Shore Camp 2007; **voluntary leave of absence Apr 30, 2012.**<>

Cogman, James I. –
[(FL) PL 5/1/2020; FL 2020] Royal Oak: First (interim assoc) May 1, 2020; **Bethel 2020.**<> 1309 N. Ballenger, Flint 48504 (810) 238-3843. Home: 5424 Sycamore Ln, Flint 48532 (248) 682-9879. james.cogman@yale.edu

*Colby, Roger L. (Dorothy) –
[(RE) P 1969; F 1976] 1975 Genesee, Thetford Center; 1980 Coleman: Faith, Geneva: Hope; 1986 Houghton Lake; 1992 Flint: Central; 1998 Grand Blanc; **2008 Retired.**<> Home: 6444 Kings Pointe Dr., Grand Blanc 48439 (810) 694-6873. rlcolby@comcast.net

Cole, Deborah S. –
[(FL) DSA-2014; FL-2015] Reading (DSA) 09/01/2014; Reading 2015.<> PO Box 457, 312 Michigan St, Reading 49274 (517) 283-2443. Home: 317 First Street, Reading 49274 (517) 283-2775. deb.cole@readingumc.com

Collazo, Luis –
[(OE) OE-2008] Detroit: El Buen New Creations Ministry 2008-2012; **Memphis: First, Lamb 2020.**<> (MF) 81265 Church St., PO Box 29, Memphis 48041 (810) 392-2294. (L) 1209 Cove Rd., Wales 48027. Home: 3216 Woodview Circle, Lake Orion 48362 (248) 895-8699. luiscollazomd@outlook.com

*Collins, David Clark (Roberta) –
[(RE) P 1983; F 1987] June 1, 1980 Bradfordsville Circuit (Louisville Conf); June 1, 1984 North Lake, Salem Grove; Nov 1, 1985 Lincoln Community; 1991 Saginaw: West Michigan Avenue, Sheridan Avenue; 1997 Montrose; 2006 Elkton; Apr 15, 2009 incapacity leave; **2011 Retired.**<> Home: 10195 W. Stanley Rd., Flushing 48433 (810) 487-1949. pastordave@comcast.net

Colthorp, Daniel R. (Kristina) –
[(FL) CC-2008; PD-2016; FL-2018] St Joseph: First (Deacon) Minister Of Youth & Children's Ministries 2016-2018; St Joseph: First 2018.<> 2950 Lakeview Ave, St Joseph 49085 (269) 983-3929. Home: 5835 Demorrow Rd, Stevensville 49127 (269) 369-8475. dancolthorp@sjfirstumc.org

Combs, Jonathan –
[(FL) PL 2009 FL 2016] Oak Park: Faith Nov 7, 2009; **Redford: Aldersgate - Brightmoore Campus (LTFT ¼ time), Garden City (LTFT ¾) 2015.**<> (B) 12065 W. Outer Dr, Detroit 48223 (313) 937-3170. (GC) 6443 Merriman, Garden City 48135 (734) 421-8628. Home: 18261 University Pk. Dr., Livonia 48152 (248) 943-0534. JSCombs_99@yahoo.com

*Comer, Michael P. (Anne) –
[(OR) D1972-; FE-1975; OE-1982; OR-2009] North Central New York Conference; Pastoral Counselor, Samaritan Center of Battle Creek 1982; Pastoral Counselor (Private Practice) 1989; Police Psychologist, Michigan State Police 3/17/2002; Retired 2009; Police Psychologist Michigan State Police and Psychologist with the Michigan Department of Natural Resources 2011-2013.<> Home: 5153 Oak Hills Dr, Eaton Rapids 48827 (517) 663-1571

Conklin, John "Jack" J. (Pattie) –
[(FE) FL-2002; AM-2008; PE-2014; FE-2016] Mesick/Harrietta (DSA) 2001; Mesick/Harrietta 12/01/2001; Scottville 2009; Williamsburg/Fife Lake Boardman Parish: Fife Lake, East Boardman, South Boardman 2017 (2018 Williamsburg, Fife Lake, East Boardman, South Boardman formed Unified Parish); **Charlotte: Lawrence Avenue 2020.**<> PO Box 36, 210 E Lawrence Ave, Charlotte 48813 (517) 543-4670. Home: 1072 N Stonehill Dr, Charlotte 48813 (231) 920-2908. jack49668@gmail.com

*Conklin, Michael T. (Deborah) –
[(RE) D-1979; FE-1983; R-2012] Pokagon 1981; Boyne City/Falls 1983; Centreville 1989; Coopersville 08/01/1997; Jackson Calvary 1999; Lowell: First 2003; Courtland-Oakfield 2008; Middleville/ Snow 2009; Retired 2012; Battle Creek: First (Assoc) (Ltft ¼) 2016; Battle Creek: First 2017-2018.<> Home: 125 Heather Ridge Rd, Battle Creek 49017 (616) 204-8125. conklinmichael4@gmail.com

Cook, Carmen (Todd) –
[(FL) FL 2014] Onaway, Millersburg2014; **Gladwin: First 2018.**<> 1300 Bartlett Drive, Gladwin 48624 (989) 426-9619. Home: 1271 Chatterton, Gladwin 48624. cook.carmen34@gmail.com

*Cook, Lisa L. (Ron) –
[(RE) PM 1997; FM 2000; RE 2020] Tawas (assoc) 1997; Saginaw: Kochville May 1, 2000; Northville: First (assoc) 2004; West Branch: First 2009; Sanford 2014; **Retired 2020.**<> Home: 2550 N West River Rd, Sanford 48657 (989) 701-7240. revlisacook@gmail.com

Cook, Robert B. (Lisa Richey) –
[(FE) FL-2001; PE-2003; FE-2006] Grand Rapids: Trinity (Assoc) 05/31/2001; Leave of Absence 2006; Muskegon Heights: Temple 09/01/2006; Lansing: Mount Hope 2012; **Muskegon: Central 2020.**<> 1011 Second St, Muskegon 49440 (231) 722-6545. Home: 2353 E Riverwood Dr, Twin Lake 49457 (517) 449-4826. rob@muskegoncentralumc.org

*Cooley, Frederick Paul (Margot) –
[(RE) P 1962; F 1965] 1965 Mayfield Village OH; 1969 Brook Park OH; 1975 Garfield Heights OH; Aug 1979 Trans. from E. OH Conf, Bay Port, Hayes; 1984 Mt. Clemens: First (assoc); 1988 Hancock: First; 1995 Wayne: First; **Aug 1, 2000 Retired.**<> 915 Egret Dr, Chelsea 48118 (734) 751-0296. fredpc@comcast.net

*Coombs, Kathryn M. (James) –

[(RE) D-1977; FE-1983; R-2002] Transferred from Iowa Conf 1977; Quincy 1977; Leave of Absence 1979; Watervliet 12/01/1981; Ionia: Zion/Easton 09/16/1984; Ionia: Easton (LTFT ¾) 11/01/1986; Leave of Absence 1990; Empire 1991; Elk Rapids/Kewadin 1998; Frankfort/Elberta 1999; Leave of Absence 03/01/2002; Retired 2002; Northport Indian Mission (DSA) 2003-2005; Traverse City: Christ (DSA) 2010-2011.<> Home: 11127 Oviatt Rd, Honor 49640 (231) 326-5852. kathryn.coombs4@gmail.com

Coristine, Kristen I. [Parks] (Chris) –

[(FE) FL 2010; PE 2015; FE 2018] 2010 Columbiaville (¾), Flint District Project Director; 2013 Blissfield: First; **2019 Reed City**.<> 114 W State St, Reed City 49677 (231) 832-9441. Home: 219 S State St, Reed City 49677 (231) 675-4172. kristencoristine@gmail.com

Cortelyou, Carter Louis (Andrea) –

[(FE) P 1990; F 1992] South Central Cooperative Ministry: Linden, Argentine 1990; Rose City: Trinity, Churchill Sept 1, 1994; Manchester: Sharon 1998; Otisville, West Forest 2007; Birmingham: Embury, Royal Oak: St. John's, Waterford: Trinity 2010; New Hope 2013; Wayne: First 2014; LaSalle, Petersburg 2018; **Novi 2020**.<> 41671 W 10 Mile Rd, Novi 48375 (248) 349-2652. Home: 40755 Oakwood Dr, Novi 48375 (248) 629-0746. clcortelyou@gmail.com

Council, Willie G. (Denice) –

[(PL) PL Dec 1, 2014] **Detroit: Calvary 2014**.<> 15050 Hubbell, Detroit 48227 (313) 835-1317. Home: 7796 Surrey Dr., Romulus 48174 (734) 641-8711. pastorwillcouncil@gmail.com

*Covington, Diane –

[OR] 2015 Redford: New Beginnings; **2018 Retired; 2018 Redford: New Beginnings (LTFT ½)**.<> 16175 Delaware, Redford 48240 (313) 255-6330. Home: 18261 University Pk. Dr., Livonia 48152 (248) 943-0534

*Covintree, George E., Jr. (Winifred) –

[(RE) SP, S. NE, 1985; P 1989; F 1991] 1985 Rockland MA: Heatherly; 1989 Waterford: Central (assoc); Sept 1, 1993 Detroit: Redford; 1997 Pontiac: Baldwin Avenue; 2005 Berkley: First; 2010 Livonia: St. Matthew's; **2015 Retired**.<> 29835 Rock Creek Rd., Southfield 48076 (248) 905-3448. georgecovintree@me.com

*Cowdin, Charlotte A. (Douglas) –

[(RD) CRT 1984; CON (CE) 1990; FD 2000] 1980 Clarkston; Feb 1, 1991 Leave of Absence; 1992 Study Leave; Aug 1, 1994 Coordinator of Diaconal Ministry Education, Ecumenical Theological Seminary; Jan 1, 1995 Retreat Leader Consultant in CE (LTFT); **May 1, 2003 Retired**.<> Home: 6132 Wildrose Lane, Lakeport 48059 (810) 385-3852. cowdinatthelake@comcast.net

Cowdin, Christopher Douglas –

[(FE) P 1988; F 1991] 1989 Utica (assoc); 1996 Family Leave; Jan 1, 1999 Warren: Wesley (LTFT ¾); 2002 Eastpointe: Immanuel (assoc), Parish Director, Eastside Covenant Cooperative Parish; 2002 Troy: Fellowship (LTFT ¾); **May 1, 2003 leave of absence**.<> Home: 3099 Cherry Creek Lane, Sterling Heights 48314 (586) 731-3599. christop_cowdin@sbcglobal.net

PASTORAL RECORDS

*Cowling, Ramona Elizabeth –
[(RE) P 1984; F 1988] 1985 McMillan, Engadine, Germfask; 1987 Inkster: Christ; 1989 Disability Leave; 1993 Macon; Sept 1, 1997 disability; **2002 Retired**.<> Home: 1131 N. Maple, #2, Ann Arbor 48103 (734) 585-5156. ramonacowling2224@comcast.net

*Cox, Esther –
[(RL) FL-1969; RL-1988] Hastings: Welcome Corners 1969; Quimby 1970; Not Appointed 1975; Retired 1988

*Crabtree, Jane A. (Jean) –
[(RA) D-1994; AM-2000; RA-2003] North Evart/Sylvan 01/16/1988; Turk Lake 1990; Lake City 1996; Fennville/ Pearl 2000; Family Leave 2002; Retired 07/16/2003; Olivet (DSA) 7/1/2010-12/12/2010.<> Home: 2538 N Mundy Ave, White Cloud 49349 (231) 689-3415. janecrabtree90@yahoo.com

*Crabtree, Jean Arthur (Jane) –
[(RA) FL-1955; D-1962; E-1964; AM-1969; RA-1994] Stanwood: Northland 09/01/1955; Fenwick Circuit: Fenwick/Orleans/ Vickeryville 1959; Howard City 1962; Newaygo 1967; Hartford 1972; Mesick/ Harrietta 1979; Parma/North Parma 09/01/1980; Barryton/Chippewa Lake 1984; Six Lakes/Millbrook 1990; Six Lakes (LTFT ¾) 1993; Retired 03/31/1994; North Evart/Sylvan 1996; Fennville/Pearl (Assoc) 2000; Avondale/North Evart/ Sylvan (DSA) 11/05/2006-07/01/2007; Olivet (DSA) 2010-2/12/2010.<> Home: 2538 N Mundy Ave, White Cloud 49349 (231) 689-3415. janecrabtree90@yahoo.com

Cramer, Julia Ann (Don) –
[(PL) PL 1/1/2020] Yale, Cole, Melvin (assoc) (DSA) (¼ time) 2019; Yale, Cole (PTLP) Jan 1, 2020; **Cole, Melvin (PTLP ½) Apr 1, 2020**.<> (C) 7015 Carson Rd, Yale 48097 (810) 387-4400. (M) 1171 Main St, Melvin 48454 (810) 376-4581. Home: 7656 Melvin Rd, Melvin 48454 (810) 304-2310. cramerjuliann@gmail.com

*Crane, Lawson D. (Beverly) –
[(RE) P 1971; F 1974] Clayton, Rollin Center 1968; Oak Grove Feb 1, 1976; Pickford 1986; Auburn 1993; **Retired 2009**.<> 1334 Beamer, Blissfield 49228 (517) 486-2082. lawsonandbev@frontier.net

Crawford, Margie R. –
[(FE) PE-2005; FE-2009] Flint: Court Street (assoc) 2005; St. Clair Shores: First 2008; St. Clair: First 2011; Grand Rapids District Superintendent 2018; **Midwest District Superintendent Jan 1, 2019**.<> 207 Fulton St E Ste 6, Grand Rapids 49503 (616) 459-4503. Home: 1630 Millbank St SE, Grand Rapids 49508. mcrawford@michiganumc.org

*Crawford, Wallace Peter (Alice Kay) –
[(RE) P 1985; F 1988] Decker, Argyle, Shabbona 1986; Saginaw: Swan Valley May 1, 1991; Elkton 1996; Millington 2006; **Retired 2015**.<> Home: 4934 Center St., Millington 48746 (989) 882-3084. walcrawford@charter.net

*Crocker, Doris (Wesley) –
[(RE) SP 1990; P 1991; F 1993] Wyandotte: First (assoc) 1990; Samaria: Grace, Lulu 1991; **Retired 1998**.<> Home: 6295 Monroe Ct., Belleville 48111 (734) 547-5722. dorisandwesley@gmail.com

Croel, Andrew L. (Anne) –

[(FE) PE-2005; FE-2008] Dimondale/Grovenburg 2005; Carson City 2008; St Johns: Pilgrim 2014.<> 2965 W Parks Rd, Saint Johns 48879 (989) 224-6865. Home: 2917 W Parks Rd, St. Johns 48879 (989) 224-4423. pastorandycroel@yahoo.com

Culver, Gregory P. –

[(FE) D-2000; FE-2006] Muskegon: Central (Assoc) 07/20/1999; Frankfort/Elberta 2002; Charlevoix 2010; Horton Bay 2016; Vicksburg 2017.<> 217 S Main St, Vicksburg 49097 (231) 649-2343. Home: 7794 TS Ave E, Scotts 49088 (231) 651-9309. gpculver@mac.com

*Culver, Martin H. (Barbara) –

[(RL) FL-1991; RL-2011] Keswick (DSA) 1991; Keswick 08/01/1991; Ionia: First 2000; Kalamazoo: Milwood 2006; Lane Boulevard (DSA) 03/18/2007-03/25/2008; Retired 2011; Center Park (LTFT ¼) 2011; Center Park/Three Rivers: First (Part Time) 2017; Center Park (LTFT ¼) 2018-2019.<> Home: 511 Landsdowne Ave, Portage 49002 (269) 615-1360. pastormartyc@charter.net

Cummings, Jeffrey O. (Bridget) –

[(PE) PL-2013; PE-2016] Galien/Olive Branch (DSA ¾ Time) 1/1/2012; Galien/Olive Branch (PTLP ¾) 2013; Byron Center 2016.<> Home: 8650 Meadowhaven Dr, Byron Center 49315 (269) 588-9081. cummings.jeffrey91@gmail.com

Cummins, Terri L. –

[(FL) FL-2010] Shelby 2010; Shelby/Claybanks 2014; Pierson: Heritage 2016.<> 19931 W Kendaville Rd, Pierson 49339 (231) 937-4310. Home: 18985 W Coral Rd, Howard City 49329 (231) 903-5139. tlcummins5@aol.com

*Cutting, Anthony Navaro (Joan) –

[(RE) P 1985; F 1986] Trans. to Detroit Conf from Free Methodist, Detroit: St. Timothy's 1985; Detroit: Second Grace 1986; Bay City: First 1993; **Retired 2011**.<> 1659 Honeychuck Ln, Kent OH 44240 (330) 986-6203. anthonlycutting@gmail.com

Conran, Cori Lynn [Cypret] –

[(FE) PE-2012; FE-2015] Coopersville 2012.<> 105 68th Ave N, Coopersville 49404 (616) 997-9225. Home: 422 Harrison St, Coopersville 49404 (269) 986-0732. pastorcori@coopersvilleumc.org

Dake, Richard Lee (Laura) –

[(FE) P 1979; F 1982] Springville 1980; Ypsilanti: St. Matthew's Feb 1, 1985; Chelsea: First Sept 1, 1992; **Clarkston 2004**.<> 6600 Waldon Rd., Clarkston 48346 (248) 625-1611. Home: 6599 Church St., Clarkston 48346 (248) 625-1727. rdake@clarkstonumc.org

*Dalton, Billie R. (Georgia) –

[(RE) SP-1965; FL-1971; D-1985; FE-1989; R-2013] Pompeii/Perrinton/Newark 09/01/1965; Mt Pleasant: First (Assoc) 1970; Lawton/ Almena 1987; South Haven: First 1995; Kalamazoo: Sunnyside (LTFT ¾) 2004; Kalamazoo: Sunnyside (Full Time) 2006; Kalamazoo: Sunnyside (LTFT ¾) 2007; Battle Creek: First 03/01/2009; Retired 2013 09/01/2013; Battle Creek: First (LTFT ½) 09/01/2013-3/4/2014; Kalamazoo Milwood (Part Time) 2017.<> 3919 Portage St, Kalamazoo 49001 (269) 381-6720. Home: 6585 San Gabriel Dr, Kalamazoo 49009 (269) 615-6945. billierdalton@milwoodunitedmethodistchurch.org

*Damkoehler, Paul A. (Paula) –
[(RL) FL-2008; PL-2015; RL 2020] Webberville 01/01/2008; United Church of Ovid 2013; Leslie (PTLP ¼) 2015; Felt Plains (LTFH ¼) 2018; **Retired 2020**.<> Home: 2417 Pattengill Ave, Lansing 48910-2627. pdamkoehler@gmail.com

*Daniel, Reva Hawke –
[(RE) PL-1984; D-1987; FE-1990; R-2005] Pokagon (PTLP) 1984; Transferred from Detroit Conf 1988; Three Rivers: Ninth Street/Jones 1988; Leslie/Felt Plains 10/01/1991; Baldwin/Luther 05/01/1993; Jonesville/Allen 1995; West Mendon 1997; Hopkins/South Monterey 2001; Retired 2005.<> Home: 1140 138th Ave, Wayland 49348 (616) 550-2645. revarev@live.com

Daniel, Zella Marie –
[(PL) DSA-2017; PL-2019] Ashley / Bannister / Pompeii (DSA) 10/03/2017; Ashley / Bannister / Pompeii (LTFT ½) 01/01/2019.<> (A) 112 N New St, Ashley 48806 (989) 862-4392. (B) 103 E Hanvey St, Bannister 48807 (989) 862-4392. (P) 135 Burton St, PO Box 125, Pompeii 48874 (989) 838-4159. Home: 2415 E Tobias, Clio 48420 (810) 869-8815. zella.daniel@ge.com

Davenport, Jessica M. –
[(PE) FL-2018; PE 2020] UM Connectional Structures (¶344.1a,c) Executive Director & Campus Pastor, Kalamazoo Wesley Foundation 2018; **Co-Executive Director & Co-Pastor, Wesley Foundation of Kalamazoo (LTFT ½), Portage: Chapel Hill (assoc) (LTFT ½) 2020**.<> 2350 Ring Rd N, Kalamazoo 49006 (269) 344-4076. (PCH) 7028 Oakland Dr, Portage 49024 (269) 327-6643. Home: 1836 Waite Ave, Kalamazoo 49008 (309) 262-3469. jessica.m.davenport@wmich.edu

Davenport, Thomas A. (Elyse Connors) –
[(FE) D-1987; FE-1991] UM Connectional Structures (¶344.1a,c) Director, WMU Wesley Foundation 2002; Bangor: Simpson 2007; Transferred from Detroit Conf 2011; Parchment 2016.<> 225 Glendale Blvd, Parchment 49004 (269) 344-0125. Home: 1227 Grand Ave, Kalamazoo 49006 (269) 762-3159. pastorthomm@hotmail.com

*David, Walter –
[(RA) AM 1967] Sterling Township 1967; Sterling Heights 1969; Escanaba: First, Bark River 1973; Mt. Morris Aug 1978; Saginaw: Jefferson Avenue 1986; **Retired 1992**.<> Home: 327 Nickless, Frankenmuth 48734 (989) 652-3979. wwdavid@fmuth.com

*Davis, Bonita C. –
[(RL) PL Sept 16, 2007] LaPorte Sept 7, 2007; **Retired 2008**.<> Home: 2200 Cleveland Ave., #2330, Midland 48640 (989) 488-2787

Davis, Cornelius (Neil), Jr. (Lela Brown-Davis) –
[(FE) FL-1999; PE-2002; FE-2005] [Northern Illinois Conference, Rust Memorial 1998] Plainfield 1999; Lansing: Faith Connections (New Church Start) 2002; Lansing: Faith Connections (¼ Time), Lansing: New Church Start ¾ Time) 2003; Faith UMC/South Lansing Ministries 2005; UM Connectional Structures (¶344.1a,c) Kalamazoo District Superintendent 2008; Detroit Conference, Southfield Hope 2014; Personal Leave 09/22/2015; Farmington First (interim) 02/01/2016; Detroit: Scott Memorial 2016.<> 15361 Plymouth Rd, Detroit 48227 (313) 836-6301. Home: 531 New Town-Victoria Park, Detroit 48125 (517) 712-4066. Frontedge7@yahoo.com

*Davis, Leonard E. –

[(OR) OR-2016] [retired elder of Wesleyan Church] Galesburg (LTFT ¼) 2016.<> PO Box 518, 111 W Battle Creek St, Galesburg 49053 (269) 665-7952. Home: 10998 Pleasant Lake Rd, Delton 49046 (269) 623-4412

*Davis, Robert F. (Sue) –

[(RE) T 1959; F 1962] 1962 Detroit: Aldersgate (assoc); 1964 Whitmore Lake; 1967 Veterans' Administration; 1968 Holly; 1973 Warren: First; 1979 Conference Staff: Parish Developer; Jan 1, 1987 trans to W. MI Conf: Conference Staff: Coordinator of New Church Development; 1993 trans to Detroit Conf, Lake Orion; **1997 Retired**.<> Home: 09844 Meadows Trail, Boyne Falls 49713 (231) 549-2530. bobsue58@icloud.com

*Dawes, Gary Carl (Barbara) –

[(RE) P 1982; F 1986] Dec 1, 1983 Saginaw: First (assoc); Oct 18, 1987 Saginaw: Kochville; Dec 1, 1992 Ypsilanti: St. Matthew's; 1996 Berkley; 2005 Adrian: First; **2014 Retired**.<> Home: 30011 Barwell Rd., Farmington Hills 48334 (248) 893-7512

*Daws, Donald J. –

[(RE) P 1972; F 1976] 1965 Glennie, Curran; 1973 Byhalia OH; 1975 LaSalle; 1980 Imlay City, E. Goodland, W. Goodland, Lum; 1989 Cass City: Salem; Jan 16, 1992 Coleman: Faith; **Aug 1, 1997 Retired**.<> 23661 Wilmarth Ave., Farmington 48335. dzdaws@pocketmail.com

Debow, Martin M. (Cynthia) –

[(FE) D-1985; FE-1988] Grovenburg 1986; Coopersville 1990; Robbins 1997; Lansing: Asbury 2008; Eaton Rapids: First 2014.<> 600 S Main St, Eaton Rapids 48827 (517) 663-3524. Home: 702 State St, Eaton Rapids 48823 (517) 663-8256. marty@fumer.org

*DeGraw, Alan Wilford –

[(RE) T 1964; F 1966] 1964 Chicago: St. Stephens (assoc); 1966 Oak Grove; 1967 Calumet; Jan 1972 Essexville: St. Luke's; Feb 1975 Pontiac: Central (assoc); 1978 Allen Park: Trinity, Detroit: Simpson; 1980 Allen Park: Trinity; 1983 Vassar; 1991 Flat Rock: First; 1995 Oak Grove; **2000 Retired**.<> Home: 2574 Kerria Dr., Howell 48855 (517) 540-0715. jadegraw@sbcglobal.net

DeHut, Rosemary Ruth –

[(PL) PL Aug 1, 2002; FL 2008; PL Sept 1, 2018] Aug 1, 2002 White Pine; 2008 White Pine, Ironwood: Wesley; Sept 1, 2018 White Pine Community; **2019 White Pine Community, Bergland, Ewen (LTFT ¼)**.<> (WPC) 9 Tamarack, PO Box 158, White Pine 49971 (906) 885-5419. (B) 108 Birch, PO Box 142, Bergland 49910 (906) 988-2533. (E) 621 M28, Ewen 49925 (906) 988-2533. Home: 22358 Norwich Trail, Ontonagon 49953 (906) 884-2871. rrdehut@up.net

*Delo, Merlin Keith (Juanita) –

[(RL) FL-1964; RL-1997] Sethton / Middleton 1964; Hesperia / Ferry 1966; East Jordan 1986; Retired 1997.<> Home: 2706 S Maple Island Rd, Fremont 49412 (231) 924-4182

Delong, Kimberly A. (Cameron) –
[(FE) PL-1998; CC-2003; PD-2009; FD-2012; FE-2016] Muskegon: Unity (Part Time) 1998; Grand Rapids: First (Deacon-Director of Education LTFT ½) 2009; Turk Lake/Belding 08/15/2012; Greenville: First, Turk Lake/Belding Cooperative Parish (Deacon LTFT ½) 2013; Big Rapids: Third Avenue/Paris/Rodney (Para. 315.4) 2015; Wyoming Park/Courtland-Oakfield 2017.<> (WP) 2244 Porter St SW, Wyoming 49519 (616) 532-7624. (CO) 10295 Myers Lake Ave NE, Rockford 49341 (616) 866-4298. Home: 4934 Brownstone Dr NE, Rockford 49341 (616) 443-5210. kim.delong.1113@gmail.com

*Del Pino, Julius E. (Laurie Smith) –
[(RE) P 1970; F 1976 (Cal. Pacific); RE 2019] trans. from California-Pacific Conf 1998; Detroit: Metropolitan 1998; incapacity leave Jan 1, 2004; Dearborn: First 2005; Rochester Hills: St. Luke's 2008; Grand Blanc 2016; **Retired 2019**; Grand Blanc Oct 1, 2019-Jun 30, 2020; **Oxford Sept 1, 2020**.<> 21 E Burdick St, Oxford 48371 (248) 628-1289. Home: 7346 Chipmunk Hollow, Clarkston 48346. (248) 807-2397. julius-delpino47@gmail.com

*DeMoss, Lynn A. (M. Kay) –
[(RE) D-1961; FE-1963; R-1997] Coleman/North Bradley 1963; Fremont 1966; Albion: First 1969; Muskegon: Central 1979; Grand Rapids: First 04/16/1988; Lansing: Central 1993; Retired 1997.<> Home: 1520 Sherman Court SE, Grand Rapids 49506 (231) 670-0993. puzisha4lynn@att.net

DeMoss, Mariel Kay (Lynn) –
[(FD) DM-1985; D-1997] Kalamazoo: First Coordinator Of Education and Lay Development 1985; Editor/Publisher, Michigan Christian Advocate 1987; Editor/Publisher, Blodgett Press 1995; Deacons Appointed Beyond the Local Church(¶331.1a) Mission to Area People, Coordinator Of Volunteers, Muskegon Heights 1997; Deacons Appointed Beyond The Local Church(¶331.1a) Editor/Publisher, Blodgett Press 1998; Deacons Appointed Beyond the Local Church(¶331.1a) Editor/Publisher, Blodgett Press (LTFT ½) and Minister of Education, Muskegon Central (LTFT ½) 01/01/2003; Minister of Adult Education, Muskegon Central (LTFT ¼) and Deacons Appointed w/in UM Connectional Structure (¶331.6) Conference Secretary Of Global Ministries (LTFT ¼) 2005; Muskegon: Central (Deacon) Minister Of Discipleship (LTFT ½) 2009; Muskegon: Central (Deacon) Minister Of Discipleship (LTFT ½) and Deacons Appointed w/in UM Connectional Structure (¶331.1b) Conference Web-Editor (LTFT ¼) 2012; Muskegon: Central (Deacon) Minister Of Discipleship (LTFT ¼) and Deacons Appointed w/in UM Connectional Structure (¶331.1b) Area Communications Team (LTFT ½) 2013; Deacons Appointed Within Um Connectional Structure (¶331.1b) Senior Writer & Content Editor, MI Area Communications Team Annual Conference (LTFT ½) 2015; Deacons Appointed Within UM Connectional Structure (¶331.1b) Senior Writer & Content Editor, MI Area Communications Team Annual Conference (LTFT ½) and Missional: Grand Rapids: Trinity (Deacon) (Part Time) 2016; Deacons Appointed Within UM Connectional Structure (¶331.1b) Senior Writer & Content Editor, MI Area Communications Team Annual Conference (LTFT ½) and Missional: Georgetown (Part-Time) 10/22/2018; Senior Content Editor, MI Conference Communications Team (LTFT ¾) and Missional: Georgetown 01/01/2019.<> 1011 Northcrest Rd, Lansing 48906 (517) 347-4030 x4032. Home: 1520 Sherman Court SE, Grand Rapids 49506 (231) 670-5921. kdemoss@michiganumc.org

Demyanovich, Robert P. –
[(FL) FL Jan 1, 2019] Cass City (DSA) 2018; **Cass City Jan 1, 2019**.<> 5100 Cemetery Rd, PO Box 125, Cass City 48726 (989) 872-3422. Home: 6339 Brenda Dr, Cass City 48726 (248) 636-5679. PastorRobertPaul@gmail.com

*Densmore, Jerry P. –
[(RE) FE IN] trans to Detroit Conf 2001; Croswell: First 2001; Hemlock, Nelson 2009; **Retired 2014**.<> Home: 3470 Williamson Rd, Saginaw 48601 (989) 777-7025. JDA-gape@aol.com

*Deppe, Isabell M. –
[(RE) D-1984; FE-1992; R-2000] Transferred from New York Conf 1990; Center Eaton/Brookfield 1990; Potter Park 1991; Sabbatical Leave (¶ 349) 01/01/1998; Vicksburg 1998; Involuntary Retirement 09/01/2000.<> Home: 11492 Fordyce Rd, Farwell 48622 (989) 588-3467

*Derby, Donald Raymond (Carol) –
[(RL) PL Nov 1, 2002; FL Oct 1, 2008; RL 2018] Whittemore Nov 1, 2002; St. Clair Shores: First 2005; Hillman, Spratt 2008; Heritage 2013; **Retired 2018; Worth Twp: Bethel (LTFT ¼) 2018**.<> 8020 Babcock Rd., Box 143, Croswell 48422 (810) 327-1440. Home: 1014 St Joseph Ln, Marysville 48040 (810) 990-5544. revdderb@gmail.com

Desotell, Briony Erin Peters (Michael) –
[(FE) PE 2006; FE 2009] Oscoda, Oscoda Indian Mission 2006; **Ypsilanti: First 2014**.<> 209 Washtenaw, Ypsilanti 48197 (734) 482-8374. Home: 1110 Ruth, Ypsilanti 48198 (734) 483-0460. pastorbri@hotmail.com

Desotell, Michael C. –
[(FL) PL 2014; FL 2017] Ypsilanti: St. Matthew's 2014; **Ypsilanti: St. Matthew's, Canton: Cherry Hill 2016**.<> (Y) 1344 Borgstrom, Ypsilanti 48198 (734) 483-5876, (CH) 321 S. Ridge Rd., Canton 48188 ((734) 495-0035. Home: 1110 Ruth, Ypsilanti 48198 (734) 730-6746. pastormikedesotell@gmail.com

DeVine, Jerome R. (Ruth) –
[(FE) PD 1984 (N. Dakota); FE 1987 (Peninsula-Delaware); transf to W.MI 1999] 1981 Cambridge MD, Grace; Wilmington DE; 1985 St. Paul's: (assoc); Newark DE, Kingswood; 1993 Coordinator for Mission Leaders, General Board of Global Ministries; 1995 Chestertown MD, First; 1999 transf to W. MI Conf, Ministry Consultant; 2004 Albion District Superintendent; 2009 Director of Connectional Ministries; 2014 transf to Detroit Conference; **Feb 1, 2018 Lansing District Superintendent; Jan 1, 2019 Mid-Michigan District Superintendent**.<> 1161 E Clark Rd Ste 216, DeWitt 48820 (517) 347-4173. Home: 16170 Pleasant St, Linden 48451. jdevine@michiganumc.org

*Diamond, David Arthur (Barbara) –
[(RE) P 1971; F 1974] 1973 Detroit: Strathmore (assoc); 1976 Pontiac: Baldwin Avenue; 1980 Mio; 1986 Oak Grove; 1988 Rochester: St. Paul (assoc); 1994 Utica; 2003 Alpena; **2006 Retired**.<> Home: 503 Adams St, Decatur GA 30030 (404) 747-2605. ddiamond@columbus.rr.com

*Dibbet, James A. (Gloria) –
[(RE) FL-1999; PE-2001; FE-2004; R-2011] St Johns: Salem/Greenbush/Lowe 1999; Sodus: Chapel Hill 2005; Retired 2011.<> Home: 220 Whitetail Dr, Prudenville 48651 (989) 400-2055

Dibble, Timothy C. (Fiona) –
[(FE) LP 1997; PE 1998; FE 2000] West Marquette County Parish: White Pine, Berg-land, Ewen, Trout Creek Presbyterian 1997; British Methodist Church 2000; Ortonville 2005; Ypsilanti: First 2011; **West Branch: First 2014**.<> 2490 W. State Rd., West Branch 48661 (989) 345-0210. Home: 2458 W. State Rd., West Branch 48661 (248) 622-9514. revtcd@yahoo.com

Diggs, Rodney K. Diggs –
[((PL) PL 2020] (formerly at Jackson Parish, TN; Tennessee Conference) Madison Heights: First (PTLP ½) 2020.<> 246 E. Eleven Mile Rd., Madison Heights 48071 (248) 544-3544. Home: 31711 Kenwood Ave, Madison Heights 48071 (615) 300-1195. dr-rkdiggs@gmail.com

Dister, Robert W. (Patricia) –
[(FL) FL 2012] **Clayton, Rollin Center 2012**.<> (C) 3387 State St., Clayton 49235 (517) 445-2641, (RC) 3988 Townley Rd., Manitou Beach 49253. Home: 3282 State St., PO Box 98, Clayton 49235 (517) 445-4009. dister.r@gmail.com

*Dobbs, William D. (Janice) –
[(RE) P 1973; F 1978 (W.MI)] 1972 West Mendon (DSA); 1973 West Menden; 1978 Lansing: Calvary; 1983 Ludington: United; 1991 East Lansing: University; 1996 Hol-land: First; 2005 Central District Superintendent (renamed Heartland District 2009); 2010 Clergy Assistant to the Bishop; **2015 Retired**.<> Home: 1271 Masonic Ct, Alma MI 48801 (517) 898-9791. bjdobbs2863@gmail.com

*Dobson, Robert Dale (Ethel) –
[(RE) T 1965; F 1967] Jan 1965 Kingsley (OH); 1966 Director, Wesley Foundation, Michigan Technological University; 1968 Marquette: First (assoc); Feb 1972 Taylor: West Mound; 1976 Menominee; 1986 Leave of Absence; **1991 Retired**.<> Home: 224 Shoreline Dr., Negaunee 49866 (906) 475-5752. rdejdobson@charter.net

*Donahue, William Richard, Jr. (Nancy) –
[(RE) P 1977; F 1981] 1978 Grace Church, Piqua OH (student assist.); 1979 Utica (assoc); 1982 Livingston Circuit: Plainfield, Trinity; Jan 1, 1988 Hale; June 1, 1993 Dexter; 2003 Utica; 2011 Fenton; Mar 11, 2014 medical leave; **May 1, 2014 Retired**.<> Home: 10139 Kress, Pinckney 48169 (586) 651-0550. donahuebill@comcast.net

*Donelson, Linda Jeanne (Paul) –
[(RE) P IA, 1973; F IA, 1976] 1975 Hope Parish; 1978 Leave of Absence; 1982 Strawberry Point (LTFT 1/3); 1984 West Bend, Mallard (LTFT ¾); 1986 Kumrur, Loebster City, Asbury; 1987 Leave of Absence; 1989 Trans. to Detroit Conf, South Central Cooperative Ministry: Linden, Argentine; 1990 Owosso: Central (LTFT ¾); 1992 Dundee; 1997 Birmingham: Embury; Oct 1, 2000 medical disability; **2015 Retired**.<> Home: 37273 Woodsman Trail, Detour Village 49275 (989) 872-2945. linda@umcs.org

*Donelson, Paul Gregory (Linda) –
[(RE) P 1973; F IA, 1976] 1974 Trans. to Iowa Conf, Hope Parish; 1978 Strawberry Point; 1984 West Bend; 1987 Trans. to W. MI Conf, Centerville; 1989 Trans. to Detroit Conf, Caring Covenant Group Ministry: Richfield, Otter Lake; 1990 Corunna; 1992 Saline: First (assoc); 1995 Monroe: Calvary; 1997 Pontiac Cooperative Parish: Pontiac: First, St. James; Apr 19, 2000 Pontiac: First, Aldersgate; 2000 Roseville; 2001 Ro-seville, Warren: Wesley; Oct 1, 2001 Ishpeming: Wesley; 2006 Cass City; 2010 Bliss-field: First; 2013 Birch Run (¾), Burt (¼); **2015 Retired**.<> Home: 37273 Woodsman Trail, Detour Village 49275 (989) 928-8825. donelson@umcs.org

*Doubblestein, William H. (Karen) –
[(RE) D-1978; FE-1982; R-2006] Grandville (Assoc) 1974; Galien/Olive Branch 1980; Springport/Lee Center 10/16/1983; Byron Center 1987; Dowagiac: First 2004; Retired 2006.<> Home: 3350 100th St, Byron Center 49315 (616) 481-3881. william_doubblestein@yahoo.com

*Downing, Judy K. –
[(RL) FL-1988; RL-2001] Kendall / Gobles (DSA) 1987; Kendall / Gobles 1988; Marshall (Assoc) 1998; Ionia: Easton 1999; Lyons-Muir 07/20/1999; Retired 05/31/2001.<> Home: 5959 Barnhart Rd, Ludington 49431 (231) 425-3314

Dozeman, Tania J. (Ted) –
[(PE) CC-2015; PE-2018] Holland: First (assoc) 2018.<> First 57 W 10th St, Holland 49423 (616) 396-5205. Home: 66 Crosswind Dr, Holland 49424 (616) 566-4165. taniadozeman@gmail.com

*Dryer, David L. (Tudie) –
[(RE) D-1963; FE-1966; R-2006] Osseo 1963; Mendon 1966; Pine River Parish: Leroy/Ashton/Luther 04/01/1968; Dansville/Vantown 1974; Hesperia/Ferry 1980; Lake City 1985; Battle Creek: Trinity 1996; Retired 2006; Battle Creek: Birchwood 01/01/2007-06/30/2007.<> Home: 2150 Gethings Road, Battle Creek 49015 (269) 441-0456. ddryerdeerrange@comcast.net

*Duffey, Paula Jane (Richard) –
[(RE) D-1992; FE-1994; R-2005] Maple Hill (PTLP) 11/01/1980-1988; Winn/Blanchard/Pine River/Coomer (FTLP) 1990; Blanchard/Pine River/Coomer (LTFT ¾) 1994; Blanchard/Pine River/Coomer 1996; Calvary Lansing 1998; Retired 2005; Grant Center (LTFT <¼) 08/01/2015-2016.<> Home: 13599 Deaner Rd, Howard City 49329 (989) 330-0251. dopper1921@aol.com

*Duffey, Richard J. (Jane) –
[(RL) PL-1980; NL-1988-1994; RL-2005] Maple Hill (LTFT PT) 11/01/1980; Not Appointed 1988; Six Lakes (LTFT PT) 1994; Lakeview: New Life (Co-Pastor) 01/01/1998; Grovenburg (LTFT PT) 1998; Retired 2005.<> Home: 13599 Deaner Rd, Howard City 49329 (989) 330-0251

*Duggan, Robert (June) –
[(RE) P 1989, on recognition of orders, Presbyterian Church, USA; F 1992, on recognition of orders, Presbyterian Church, USA] June 1964 (ordained Presbytery of New York City) Weston WV: First Presbyterian; Mar 1969 Detroit: St. James United Presbyterian; July 1977 Paris IL; Jan 1, 1983 Sandusky: Presbyterian; Mar 1987 Sagola: Grace (Interim), Florence WI; Sept 1988 Republic, Woodland; 1989 Trans. to Detroit Conf from Presbyterian Church; 1990 Redford: Rice Memorial; Dec 1, 1994 Wyandotte: Glenwood; **2005 Retired**.<> Home: 5801 Holly Oak Ct., Louisville KY 40291 (502) 290-1754. duggan3434@twc.com

Dulworth, Elbert P. (Dawn) –
[(FE) PE 2000; FE 2003] Crystal Falls: Christ, Amasa: Grace 2000; Marquette: First (Intentional Interim ¶329.3) 2004; Laingsburg 2006; Marquette District Superintendent 2012; **Birmingham: First June 11, 2017**.<> 1589 W. Maple, Birmingham 48009 (248) 646-1200. Home: 1043 Chesterfield Birmingham 48009 (248) 258-0903. dulworth@cablespeed.com

*Duncan, Daniel M. (Mary Whittaker) –
[(RE) D-1983; FE-1988; R-2014] Transferred from Detroit Conf 1986; Snow/Vergennes 1986; Muskegon: Central (Assoc) 1989; Fremont 1994; Church of the Dunes 2003; Retired 2014.<> Home: 909 Warren Place, Kalamazoo 49006 (616) 502-5092. danduncan56@gmail.com

*Duncan, Jean-Pierre (Noreen) –
[(OR)] New Baltimore: Grace; New Cooperative: New Baltimore Grace (parish director) 2014; **Retired 2018**.<> Home: 2282 18th St, Wyandotte 48192 (570) 407-1304. gracepastorjp@yahoo.com

Dunlap, Marshall Grant (Susan DeFoe Dunlap) –
[(FE) P 1981; F 1985] 1983 Detroit: Thoburn; 1986 Detroit: Mt. Hope (LTFT); 1989 Trenton: Faith (LTFT ½); Jan 1, 1999 Conference Pension Officer (LTFT), Trenton: Faith (co-pastor) (LTFT ½); 1999 Royal Oak: First (co-pastor) (LTFT ½), Conference Pension Officer (LTFT ½); 2003 Royal Oak: First (co-pastor) (LTFT ¾), Conference Pension Officer (LTFT ¼); Nov 1, 2005 Royal Oak: First; 2008 Harper Woods Redeemer (LTFT ¾), Dearborn: First (co-pastor) (LTFT ¼); 2011 Retired; 2013 returned from voluntary retirement (para 358.7), Farmington: First; **Feb 1, 2016 medical leave**.<> Home: 28851 Millbrook Rd, Farmington Hills 48334 (248) 515-7064. revmgdunlap@gmail.com

Dunlap, Rachael M. (Zachary) –
[(FL) FL 2020] **Birmingham: First (assoc), Berkley 1st Campus (assoc) 2020**.<> (BF) 1589 W. Maple, Birmingham 48009 (248) 646-1200. (BFC) 2820 12 Mile Rd, Berkley 48072 (248) 646-1200. Home: 3485 Kipling, Berkley 48072 (248) 399-3698. rdunlap@berkleyfirst.org

*Dunlap, Susan DeFoe (Marshall) –
[(RE) P 1974; F 1977] Denton: Faith 1976; Detroit: Mt. Hope 1983; Detroit: Mt. Hope (LTFT) 1986; Trenton: Faith (LTFT ½) 1989; Royal Oak: First (co-pastor) 1999; Dearborn: First (co-pastor) (LTFT ¾) 2008; Dearborn: First 2011; **Retired 2013**.<>. RevSDunlap@aol.com

Dunlap, Zachary L. (Rachael) –
[(FE) PL 2011; PE 2013; FE 2016] Allen Park: Trinity 2011; Blissfield: Emmanuel (½), Lambertville (assoc) (½) Jan 1, 2013; **Birmingham: First (assoc) (Path One Internship) 2015**.<> 1589 W. Maple, Birmingham 48009 (248) 646-1200. Home: 3485 Kipling, Berkley 48072 (734) 272-5667. zld@comcast.net

Dunstone, Kenneth Curtis (Tracy) –
[(FE) P 1996; FE 1999] Stephenson, Hermansville: First 1996; US Army Chaplain (para 335.1b) 10th Mountain Division, Fort Drum Dec 16, 1999; school (para 416.6) Jan 1, 2003; leave of absence 2017; **Psychiatrist, Eastern Kansas Veteran's Administration, Topeka, KS 2020**.<> 2200 S W Gage Blvd, Topeka KS 66622 (785) 350-4335. dusntone@gmail.com

*Dye, Mona J. (William) –
[(RL) PL-2007; FL-2011; RL-2017] Fountain (PTLP) 12/01/2007; Fountain/Free Soil (PTLP) 2009; Ashley/Bannister /Greenbush 2011; Ashley/Bannister 2015; Ashley/Bannister/Pompeii 2016-2018; **Retired Oct 1, 2017**; Wolf Lake (PTLP ½) 2018.<> 378 Vista Terrace, Muskegon 49442 (231) 788-3663. Home: 550 Western Ave Apt 424, Muskegon 49440 (231) 429-1892. billmona3@msn.com

*Dye, William F. (Mona) –
[(RL) FL-2003; PL-2012; FL-2015; RL-2017] Empire 2/1/2003; Bear Lake / Arcadia 2006; Vickeryville / Palo / Fenwick 2011; Pompeii / Middleton / North Star / Perrinton 7/15/2012; Breckenridge 9/1/2015; **Retired 2017**; Twin Lake (LTFT ½) 2018; **Muskegon: Crestwood (PTLP ¼) 2020**.<> 1220 Creston, Muskegon 49442 (231) 773-9696. Home: 550 Western Ave Apt 424, Muskegon 49440 (231) 429-1891. billmona3@gmail.com

Eardley, David Anthony (Sara) –
[(FE) P 1992; F 1995] Britton: Grace 1993; Ann Arbor: First (assoc) 1997; Bay City: Christ 2001; Frankenmuth 2006; **Rochester: St. Paul's 2013**.<> 620 Romeo St., Box 80307, Rochester 48308 (248) 651-9361. Home: 1450 Oakstone Dr, Rochester Hills 48309 (248) 651-9770. reveardley@hotmail.com

*Eckhardt, Mary Margaret (Robert) –
[(RE) P 1976; F 1979] Lake Orion (assoc) Apr 1978; Lake Orion (assoc) (LTFT ½) 1981; Leave of Absence 1983; Lake Orion (assoc) (LTFT ¼) 1985; Thomas (LTFT ½), Lake Orion (assoc) (LTFT ¼) 1988; Thomas, Lakeville Nov 1, 1992; leave of absence 2002; Livonia: St. Matthew's Sept 1, 2002; **Retired 2010**.<> Home: 110 Gorge Ct, Cary NC 27518. revmme@earthlink.net

Ehlers, Murphy Schieman (David) –
[(FD) CRT, 1997; CON (CE) 1998; FD 2001] 1998 Human Sexuality Consultant; Nov 1, 1998 Franklin: Community; 2001 Flint: Court Street; Feb 2, 2002 leave of absence; 2002 Retreat and Educational Ministries (LTFT ½), Rochester Hills: St. Luke's (LTFT ½); Dec 1, 2002 Retreat and Educational Ministries (LTFT ½), Warren: First (assoc); Feb 15, 2007 family leave; Oct 1, 2011 Detroit: Second Grace (deacon); Nov 30, 2015 transitional leave; Jan 1, 2016 Clawson; **Dec 31, 2017 Retired**.<> Home: 3425 Hawk Woods Circle, Auburn Hills 48336 (248) 371-9010. murphyehlers@aol.com

*Elders, Marcia L. (David) –
[(OR) OF-2003; OR-2017] [Reformed Church of America] Wyoming: South Wyoming (LTFT ¼) 2003; Wyoming: South Wyoming (LTFT ½) 10/01/2006; Wyoming: South Wyoming (LTFT ¾) 01/01/2009; Grand Rapids: Cornerstone South Wyoming Campus (LTFT ¾) 01/01/2015; Hastings: Hope (LTFT ¾) 2015; Retired 2017.<> Home: 3246 Wayburn Ave SW, Grandville 49418 (616) 292-6712. revmom436@aol.com

*Eldred, Eldon K. (Rhea) –
[(RE) D-1966; FE-1968; R-2003] Perrinton/Pompeii 1963; Farwell 12/01/1967; Edmore 1969; Sparta 1973; Fremont 03/01/1979; Appointed to Extension Ministries (¶344.1b,c) District Superintendent, Albion District 03/01/1987; Church of the Dunes 1992; Retired 2003.<> Home: 130 Woodslee Court, Norton Shores 49444 (616) 402-3169. eldon616@gmail.com

*Elenbaas, Joe D. (Mary) –
[(RE) D-1986; FE-1988; R-2010] Transferred from Minnesota Conf 2000; Ludington 2000; Medical Leave 11/30/2006; Retired 2010.<> (231) 499-8578. moonlitpines@yahoo.com

*Ellinger, John W. (Sally) –

[(RE) D-1968; FE-1971; R-2007] Transferred from New York Conf 1972; Jackson: First (Assoc) 01/15/1972; Kalamazoo: Sunnyside 1976; Lansing: Grace 1981; Albion: First 1985; Holland: First 1990; UM Connectional Structures (¶344.1a,c) District Superintendent, Lansing District 1996; Traverse City: Central 2002; Retired 2007; Traverse City: Christ 12/01/2009-6/1/2010.<> Home: 820 Red Dr. Suite 112, Traverse City 49686 (231) 631-9237. johnwe1@charter.net

Elliott, Dirk (Tricia) –

[(FE) transferred from West Ohio Conf 2018] Director of New Faith Communities and Congregational Development 2011; trans to Detroit Conf 2018; **Conference Director of Congregational Vibrancy 2018**.<> 1161 E Clark Rd, Ste 212, DeWitt 48820 (517-347-4030 ext. 4090). Home: 6831 Oak Leaf Trail, Linden 48451 (810) 965-2349. delliott@michiganumc.org

*Elliott, Hydrian (Emma) –

[(RE) P 1980; F 1985] 1982 Detroit: East Grand Boulevard; 1985 Detroit: Conant Avenue (assoc); Feb 27, 1986 Chaplain, Navy, USN Reserve, Station Chaplain, Naval Training Center, San Diego CA; Nov 15, 1993 Detroit: Resurrection; Jan 16, 1998 Detroit: Trinity-Faith; May 1, 2000 Westland: St. James; 2003 Flint: Charity, Dort-Oak Park Ministry; **2011 Retired**.<> Home: 18425 South Drive, Apt 1531, Southfield 48076 (313) 671-6272. dopnh@gfn.org

*Elliott, John Wilson (Carla) –

[(RE); P 1972; F 1975] 1974 Mt. Clemens: First (assoc); 1977 North Lake; 1982 Bay City: First (assoc); 1984 Poseyville; Mar 1, 1986 Goodrich; Sept 1, 1994 St. Ignace; Apr 16, 2002 incapacity leave; **2014 Retired**.<> Home: 3517 Lorna Rd., Apt. 3, Rocky Ridge Retirement Center, Vestavia Hills AL 35216 (205) 989-9230. johnwelliott@comcast.net

Elmore, David G. (Julie) –

[(FE) PE-2009; FE-2012; OE-2013; FE-2015] Concord 2013; Transferred from Alaska Missionary Conf 2015; Personal Leave 2016; Ascension at Home Hospice Chaplain (¶344.1d), Missional: Coldwater 2019.<> Ascension at Home Hospice, 5220 Lovers Ln, Ste 140, Portage 49002 (800) 343-1396. Home: 20 Parsons Ct, Coldwater 49036 (517) 817-8855. dgelmore@gmail.com

Elmore, Julie Yoder (David G.) –

[(FE) FE-2012; OE-2013; FE-2015] Litchfield/Quincy 2013; Transferred from Alaska Missionary Conf 2015; Coldwater 2017.<> 26 Marshall St, Coldwater 49036 (517) 279-8402. Home: 20 Parsons Ct, Coldwater 49036 (517) 607-6977. jyelmore@gmail.com

Embury, Lawrence J. –

[(PL) PL-2015] Griffith 2015; Pope/Griffith (LTFT ½) 2018.<> (G) 9537 S Clinton Tr, Eaton Rapids 48827 (517) 663-6262. (P) PO Box 419, Eaton Rapids 48827 (517) 857-3655. Home: 1855 Sarossy Lake Rd, PO Box 86, Grass Lake 49240 (517) 206-2952. frn89sdka@frontier.com

Emerson, Ann E. –

[(FD) PD W.OH 1998; FD Det., 1999] New Albany (West Ohio) 1998; trans to Detroit 1999; **Director Lake Huron Adult Retreat Center 1999**.<> 8794 Lakeshore Dr., Burtchville 48059 (810) 327-6272. Home: (810) 327-6468 [local church appointment: Lexington]. annbythelakeshore@comcast.net

Emmert, Donald Joseph (Becky) –

[(FE) P 1983; F 1986] 1984 Ontonagon, Greenland, Rockland; Feb 16, 1990 Pinconning; 1995 New Baltimore: Grace; June 1, 2000 North Central Macomb Regional Ministry: Mt. Vernon (assoc); 2001 Treasurer's Office Staff; 2003 Conference Benefits Administrator (LTFT ¾), Associate Treasurer (LTFT ¼); 2006 Conference Benefits Officer; Jan 1, 2017 Michigan Area Benefits Officer; **2018 Director of Benefits and Human Resources**.<> 1161 E Clark Rd, Ste 212, DeWitt 48820 (517-347-4030 ext. 4110). demmert@michiganumc.org

*England, Gene Patrick (Lisa) –

[(RE) P 1980; F 1984; RE 2018] 1982 Detroit: Redford (assoc); Sept 1, 1985 Caring Covenant Group Ministry: Otisville, West Forest; Mar 1988 Caring Covenant Group Ministry, Parish Director; 1993 Hale; 2008 Grand Blanc; 2016 Lambertville; **2018 Retired**.<> Home: 2963 Bayberry Ct, Holland 49424 (810) 265-8677. pastorpat1982@gmail.com

*Engler, Janet M. –

[(RE) FL 2001; PE 2002; FE 2005] 1998 Mt. Zion (VA Conf); 2000 Manassas: Grace (assoc), (VA Conf); 2001 Memphis: First, Lamb; 2004 Monroe: Calvary; 2006 Burton: Christ; Mar 1, 2009 disability leave; 2011 New Lothrop, Juddville; 2013 Mt. Morris: First; **Oct 1, 2015 Retired**.<> Home: 261 Fox Haven Dr Unit 5, Somerset KY 42501 (586) 255-9132. jengler@aol.com

Erbes, Mark R. (Annette) –

[(FE) D-1996; FE-2000] Appointed in Other Annual Conferences West Ohio Conference, Faith Community (Assoc), Xenia OH (¶426.1-*1992 Discipline*) 1996; Mt Pleasant: First (Assoc) 1997; Constantine 2001; Muskegon: Lake Harbor 2007; Holt 2014.<> PO Box 168, 2321 Aurelius Rd, Holt 48842 (517) 694-8168. Home: 1951 Heatherton Dr, Holt 48842 (517) 694-8277. pastormark@acd.net

*Erickson, Richard R. (Jayne) –

[(RE) D-1969; FE-1973; R-2006] Barry County: Woodland 1972; Woodland/Hastings: Welcome Corners 1975; Jackson: First (Assoc) 1976; Manistee 1982; UM Connectional Structures (¶344.1a,c) Director, Wesley Foundation, Michigan State University 1990; Retired 2006.<> Home: 3028 Hamlet Circle, East Lansing 48823 (517) 420-5841. rrerickson1301@gmail.com

Euper, Stephen T. –

[(FE) PE 2005; FE 2008] Ossineke 2005; New Hope 2010; incapacity disability leave Aug 9, 2010; **Eastside Covenant Cooperative Parish: Roseville: Trinity 2012**.<> 18303 Common, Roseville 48066 (586) 776-8828. Home: 30455 Progress, Roseville 48066 (586) 776-1459. steveeuper@gmail.com

*Euper, Terry A. (Jackie) –

[(RE) P 1969; F 1973] Morrice, Bennington, Pittsburg 1972; Troy: Big Beaver 1976; Saginaw Bay District Superintendent 1989; Lapeer: Trinity 1994; Clergy Assistant to the Bishop 2003; **Retired 2010**.<> Home: 11463 S. State Rd., Morrice 48857 (517) 625-2920. tjeuper@tm.net

*Evans, Thomas J. (Judy) –

[(RE) D-1974; FE-1977; R-2013] Comstock/Portage (Assoc) 1976; Comstock 10/01/1980; Leland/Keswick 1984; Leland 1988; Eaton Rapids: First 02/01/1994; Ludington 2007; Retired 2013; Hastings First (49%) 01/01/2017-06/30/2017.<> Home: 8630 Lake Drive, Springport 49284 (231) 233-6355. pastortom1948@yahoo.com

Fahey, Katherine L. –
[(PE) CC-2013; PE-2016] UM Connectional Structures (¶344.1a,c) Director of Residential Ministries, Garrett-Evangelical Theological Seminary 2016.<> Home: 4524 N Wolcott Ave Apt 3A, Chicago IL 60640 (269) 277-4894. katherinelfahey@gmail.com

Falker, Eric M. (Katja) –
[(PE) FL-2014; PE 2020] Bellaire: Community (DSA) 09/24/2014; Bellaire: Community (FTLP) 11/10/2014; Saint Ignace 2019; **Houghton: Grace / Painesdale: Albert Paine Memorial 2020**.<> (HG) 201 Isle Royale, Houghton 49931 (906) 482-2780. (PAPM) 54385 Iroquois, Painesdale 49955 (906) 482-1470. Home: 807 Oak Grove Pkwy, Houghton 49931. (906) 482-1751. emfalker@gmail.com

Fancher, Nancy V. –
[(FD) PD-2013; FD-2017] Peace (DSA) 03/16/2005; Peace (PTLP) 11/15/2005; LP w/o Appointment 03/31/2006; Transitional Leave 2013-06/20/2014; Nashville (¼) and Vermontville (¼) and Woodland (¼) (Deacon) (Missional Service: Maple Valley Community Center of Hope – Deacon) July 1-31/2014; Nashville (½) and Vermontville (¼) (Deacon) (Missional Srvice: Maple Valley Community Center of Hope – Deacon) 08/01/2014; Other Valid Ministries (¶344.1d) Missional Service: Maple Valley Community Center (LTFT ½) 2015; Deacons Appointed Beyond the Local Church(¶331.1a) Executive Director of Maple Valley Community Center of Hope (LTFT ½) 2017 and Misisonal Service: Lansing Grace (LTFT ½) 2017; Missional Service: Director of Children's Ministry Lansing: Mt Hope (LTFT ½) 2018; **Director Maple Valley Community Center of Hope (LTFT ½), Missional C.C. Lansing: Mt Hope, 2020**.<> 501 E Mt Hope Ave, Lansing 48915 (251) 748-2154. Home: 1317 W Saginaw St, Lansing 48915 (517) 371-3311. fancher11@yahoo.com

*Farmer-Lewis, Linda J. (Bill Lewis) –
[(OR) D-1981; FE-1985; OE-2011; OR-2017 (Wisconsin Conf)] Munith/Pleasant Lake 1983; Jaskcon: First (assoc) 1986; Homer/Lyon Lake 1987; Lansing: Trinity (Assoc) 1992; Deanof the Chapel, Albion College 1994; Leland (¶346.1) 2011; Lansing Central 2013; Retired 2017; Battle Creek: First (LTFT ¾) 2018; Dimondale (LTFT ½) 2019.<> 6801 Creyts Rd, PO Box 387, Dimondale 48821 (517) 646-0641. Home: 6747 Creyts Rd, Dimondale 48821 (517) 783-9003. farmlewis@aol.com

Farnum, Charles D. (Kendall) –
[(FE) D-1997; FE-2002] Middleton/Maple Rapids 1997; Battle Creek: Maple 2001; Leave of Absence 07/01-16/2006; UM Connectional Structures (¶344.1a,c Director, Wesley Foundation Central Michigan University (LTFT ½) and Mt Pleasant: First (Assoc) (LTFT ½) 07/16/2006; UM Connectional Structures (¶344.1a,c) Director, Wesley Foundation Central Michigan University (LTFT ¾) 2007; UM Connectional Structures (¶344.1a,c) Director, Wesley Foundation Central Michigan University (FT) 1/1/2008; UM Connectional Structures (¶344.1a,c) Director, Wesley Foundation Central Michigan University (LTFT ¼) 1/1/2014; **Appointed to South Carolina Conference, Director Wesley Foundation, Winthrop College 2020**.<> 406 Stewart Ave, Rock Hill, SC 29730. Home: 1765 Alyce Lane Apt 203, Rock Hill SC 29732 (989) 545-1761. charlie.farnum@gmail.com

*Fay, Barbara Jo (Fred) –
[(RA) FL-1997; PL-2007; AM-2009; RA-2020] Ganges (FTLP) 1997; LP w/o Appointment 12/31/2004; Plainwell: First (Assoc) (PTLP) 2007; Frankfort/Elberta 2010; **Retired Jan 1, 2020**.<> Home: 326 Park St, Wayland 49348 (616) 318-5684. barbf55@gmail.com

*Fegan, James A. –

[(RL) FL 12/1/2001] Stephenson, Hermansville Dec 1, 2001; Iron River: Wesley June 16, 2002; Republic, Woodland 2004; **Retired 2005**.<> Home: 8825 M5 Rd., Gladstone 49837. lorpman@aol.com

Feighner, Bryce E. (Eileen) –

[(FE) PL-2004; PE-2007; FE-2013] Kalamo (¼ Time) 2004; Kalamo (LTFT ½) 1/1/2007; Kalamo (LTFT ¼) and Quimby (LTFT ¼) 2011; Barry-Eaton Cooperative Ministry: Gresham (LTFT ½) 2013; Hastings: First 2017.<> 209 W Green St, Hastings 49058 (269) 945-9574. Home: 935 N Taffee Dr, Hasting 49058 (517) 588-1619. brycefeighner@yahoo.com

Feliciano, Laura E. –

[(FL) FL-2018] Grand Rapids: Iglesia Metodista Unida La Nueva Esperanza and Conference Staff, New Church and Hispanic-Latino Committee (¶361.1) 2018; **Birch Run, Burt 2020**.<> (BR) 12265 Church St., PO Box 277, Birch Run 48415 (989) 624-9340, (B) 2799 Nicholas Rd., PO Box 96, Burt 48417 (989) 770-9948. Home: 8196 Poellet, Birch Run 48415 (615) 218-8187. laurafeliciano@yahoo.com

Ferguson, Tyson Geoffrey (Erin) –

[(FE) FL 2002; PE 2003; FE 2008] Saline: First (assoc) 2002; Director, Penn State University Wesley Foundation 2004; Vassar: First 2010; Campus Minister, Wesley Foundation, Middle Tennessee State University 2013; **leave of absence 2016**.<>. tferguson@stpaulsc.org

Fernandez, Alejandro (Alex) D. (Bethann) –

[(FL) PL-2015; FL-2016] Grand Rapids: Cornerstone (Assoc) Campus Pastor (LTFT ½) 01/01/2015; Grand Rapids: Cornerstone (Assoc) Campus Pastor, Heritage Hill Campus 02/29/2016.<> 48 Lafayette Ave SE, Grand Rapids 49503 (616) 698-3170. Home: 10160 Alaska Ave SE, Caledonia 49316 (616) 891-5611. alexf@cornerstonemi.org

*Ferris, Haldon Dale (Kathryn Snedeker) –

[(RE) P MI, 1960; F MI, 1967] Cloverdale 1959; Pipestone 1962; Portage Prairie 1966; Trans. to Detroit Conf, Livonia: St. Matthew's (assoc) 1968; Romulus, New Boston 1971; Dixboro 1974; Sanford 1985; Dearborn: Mt. Olivet 1988; Saginaw: First (co-pastor) June 16, 1996; **Retired 2002**.<> Home: 7364 Williams Ct., Elk Rapids 49629 (231) 264-6278. revdoc3@aol.com

*Ferris, John Clair –

[(RE) P 1973; F 1977] Livonia: Newburg: (assoc) 1976; Detroit: Rice Memorial Apr 1979; Highland Park: First 1986; Pontiac Cooperative Parish: Waterford: Trinity (Parish Director) 1990; Dixboro 1998; Flint: Hope 2006; **Retired 2012**.<> Home: 3766 River Birch, #10, Flint 48532 (810) 733-3233. ferris.1637@comcast.net

Ferris-McCann, Donald R. (Lisa) –

[(FE) D-1983; FE-1986] Mason: First (Assoc) 1984; Frankfort/Elberta 04/01/1989; Cassopolis 1993; Lake Odessa: Central 2000; Battle Creek: First 2007; Medical Leave 02/01/2009; Elsie (LTFT ¾) 2013; Elsie/Salem 5/1/2014; Leave Of Absence 2016; **appointed to Virginia Conference, Bruen Chapel 2019**.<> 3035 Cedar Ln, Fairfax VA 22031 (703) 560-1665. Home: 7346 Robert Lane, Falls Church VA 22042 (989) 640-6969

*Field, Raymond D. –
[(RE) D-1980; FE-1986; R-2003] Eagle (LTFT ¼) 1988; Eagle (LTFT ½) 1989; Transferred from Detroit Conf 1990; Eagle (LTFT ¼) 1990; Bath/Gunnisonville 1993; Herperia/Ferry 1998; Hopkins/South Monterey 1999; Hersey 2001; Retired 05/01/2003.<> Home: 8659 W. Thomas St, Shelby 49455 920-210-8132. ray_field2003@yahoo.com

Fifer, Thomas C. –
[(FL) CC-2013; FL-2018] Vergennes 2018.<> 10411 Bailey Dr NE, Lowell 49331 (616) 897-6141. Home: 2445 Almont Ave SE, Grand Rapids 49507 (616) 560-3914. thomas.fifer@gmail.com

Fike, Ronald A. (Gayle) –
[(FE) PL 2010; PE 2013; FE 2016] Springville 2010; **Gwinn 2014.**<> 251 W. Jasper, Box 354, Gwinn 49841 (906) 346-6314. Home: 252 W. Carbon, PO Box 655, Gwinn 49841 (906) 346-3441. basketlifter@yahoo.com

*Filbrandt, Harold F. (Marian) –
[(RE) D-1959; FE-1962; R-1994] Twelve Corners Church 1950; Lacota/Casco 1955; Gobles/Kendall 1959; Frankfort 12/01/1964; Ludington First 1967; Marshall 1974; St Joseph First 02/16/1983; Holland: First 04/01/1987; Fremont 1990; Retired 1994; Glenn (LTFT ¼) 2014 – 12/31/2018.<> Home: 77020 County Road 380, South Haven 49090 (269) 637-3087. harold77020@comcast.net

*Finzer, Garrison Fred (Lois) –
[(RE) PL 1994; PE 1997; FE 1999] Rochester Hills: First July 15, 1994; Dexter (assoc) 1996; Seven Churches United Group Ministry: Byron: First 2000; Hartland 2006; **Retired 2012.**<> Home: 1665 Carlson Lane SW, Marietta GA 30064. pastorfred2351@yahoo.com

*Fischer, Frederick H. –
[(RE) D-1958; FE-1961; R-1996] Suttons Bay (EUB) 1958; Maple Hill (EUB) 1962; Berrien Springs/Arden (EUB) 05/10/1965; Rosebush/Leaton 01/01/1970; Leave of Absence 1978; Williamston Center/Wheatfield 1980; Elsie/Duplain 1985; Elsie 01/01/1990; Retired 1996; Leslie/Felt Plains (LTFT 49%) 09/14/2014-2015.<> Home: 3123 E Grand River Rd, Williamston 48895 (517) 655-4896. fischbones@frontier.com

*Fisher, John W. (Corinne) –
[(RE) D-1975; FE-1980; R-2013] Niles: Wesley (Assoc) 1977; Schoolcraft/Pleasant Valley 1978; Casco 1980; North Muskegon 1986; Kalamazoo: Sunnyside 1992; South Haven: First 2004; Retired 2013; Oshtemo (LTFT ½) 2013.<> PO Box 12, 6574 Stadium Dr, Kalamazoo 49009 (269) 375-5656. Home: 3506 East Shore Dr, Portage 49002 (269) 214-0276. revjwfisher@hotmail.com

Fitzgerald, Erin Lea Brodhagen (Joel) –
[(FE) PE-2012; FE-2016] Grand Rapids: Saint Paul's 2012; Rochester: St Paul's (assoc) 2018.<> 620 Romeo Rd, PO Box 80307, Rochester, 48308 (248) 651-9361. Home: 632 Romeo Rd, Rochester 48307. erin.lb.fitzgerald@gmail.com

Fitzgerald, Joel Thomas Pier (Erin) –
[(FE) FL-2012; PE-2016; FE-2019] Wyoming Park 2012; Hopkins/South Monterey 2017; Sterling Heights 2018.<> 1133 16 1/2 Mile Rd, Sterling Heights 48312 (586) 268-3130. Home: 632 Romeo Rd, Rochester 48307 (616) 848-9759. pierfitz@gmail.com

*Flagel, David L. (Rebecca) –
[(RE) D-1975; FE-1977; R-2013] North Adams/Jerome 09/01/1975; Coopersville 1980; Ionia Parish LeValley/ Berlin Center 03/01/1989; Lake Odessa: Lakewood 2003; Retired 2013.<> Home: 13566 Hill Country Dr SE, Lowell 49331 (616) 821-7743. drflagel@yahoo.com

*Fleming, David L. (Lani) –
[(RE) LP 1995; PE 1996; FE 1998] Seven Churches United Group Ministry: Gaines, Duffield 1995; Memphis: First, Lamb 1999; Heritage 2001; New Lothrop, Juddville 2003; Davisburg 2011; **Retired Feb 15, 2014.**<> Home: 2622 San Rosa Drive, St. Clair Shores 48081 (586) 776-2019. DavidLFleming@gmail.com

*Fleming, Edna M. –
[(RL) PL-1995; NL-2002; RL-2011] Charlotte: Lawrence Ave (Assoc) (LTFT PT) 1995; Not Appointed 2002; Retired 2011.<> Home: 793 68th St, South Haven 49090 (269) 637-4406. gandefleming@gmail.com

Flessner, Jodie R. –
[(FE) D-1993; FE-1997] Pompeii/ Perrinton/North Star 1994; Pompeii/ Perrinton/North Star/Christian Crossroads Cooperative Parish 2001; Pine River Parish:Leroy/Ashton 2003; Caledonia 2012; UM Connectional Structures (¶344.1a,c) District Superintendent, Northern Waters District 2019.<> 1249 3 Mile Rd S, Traverse City 49696 (231) 947-5281. Home: 4505 Stone Ridge Ct, Traverse City 49684. jflessner@michiganumc.org

*Flory, Barbara J. (Robert) –
[(RE) D-1989; FE-1992; R-2011] Concord 01/01/1990; Holt (Assoc)/Alaiedon Township New Church Start 1998; Lansing: Sycamore Creek 2000; UM Connectional Structures (¶344.1a,c) New Church Development (LTFT ½) 2009; Retired 2011.<> Home: 3819 Cornice Falls #5, Holt 48842 (517) 648-0277. barbflory@gmail.com

*Floyd, Carolyn C. –
[(RE) FD-1992; FE-1995; R-2008] West Mendon 1990; Mancelona/Alba 1997; St Johns: First 2000; Perry/ Shaftsburg 2003; Retired 2008; Appointed in Other Annual Conferences (¶331.8, ¶346.1) Detroit Conf, Eastpointe Immanuel (LTFT ½) 01/01/2012-06/30/2012; Appointed in Other Annual Conferences (¶331.8, ¶346.1) Detroit Conf, Algonac Trinity (LTFT ¼) and Marine City (LTFT ¼) 2013; (Marine City closed 02/01/2014) Appointed in Other Annual Conferences (¶331.8, ¶346.1) Detroit Conf, Algonac Trinity (LTFT ¼) 02/01/14-6/1/2014.<> Home: 3437 Gratiot Ave, Port Huron 48060 (810) 982-1629. k_kid@sbcglobal.net

*Fons, Valerie (Joseph Ervin) –
[(RE) FL-1995; D-1998; FE-2002; R-2017] Bell Oak/Webberville 1995; Galien/Olive Branch 1999; Pokagon (LTFT ½) 2001; Family Leave 2003; Other Valid Ministries (¶344.1d) Bread & Water LLC and L.A.U.N.C.H. (Lake Adventures Uniting Nature & Children With Hospitality) WI 10/01/2009; Retired 02/14/2017; Other Valid Ministries (¶344.1d) Bread & Water LLC and L.A.U.N.C.H. (Lake Adventures Uniting Nature & Children With Hospitality) WI 02/14/2017.<> 1275 Main Rd, Washington Island WI 54246 (920) 535-0077. Home: 987 Townline Rd, Washington Island WI 54246 (920) 847-2393. breaduponthewaters@gmail.com

*Foo, Tat-Khean (Kim) –
[(RE) P Malaysian Conf, 1967; F 1974] Sept 18, 1972 Henderson, Chapin; 1973 Trans. to Detroit Conf; 1976 Waterford: Trinity; 1990 Walled Lake; 1996 Dearborn: Mt. Olivet; Oct 1, 2002 leave of absence; **Apr 1, 2003 Retired**.<> Home: 32 Blair Lane, Dearborn 48120 (313) 336-1988. tkfkgf@sbcglobal.net

Ford, Alice K. –
[(OE) OE 2020, Baltimore Washington Conference para. 346.1] Northville: First (assoc) (LTFT ½).<> 777 W 8 Mile Rd, Box 55, Northville 48167 (248) 349-1144. Home: 1483 Colonade Ct, Canton 48187 (301) 541-7630. pastoralice@gmail.com

Forsyth, Michelle N. (Robert) –
[(PE) FL 2015; PE 2018] Fenton (assoc) 2015; Fenton (assoc) (LTFT ¾), Linden (LTFT ¼) 2018; **Churchill, Mio 2020**.<> (C) 501 E State Rd, PO Box 620, West Branch 48661 (989) 312-0105. (M) 1101 W. Eighth St., Mio 48647 (989) 826-5598. Home: 1005 W. Eighth St., Mio 48647 (989) 826-5521. fumc.mnforsyth@gmail.com

Foster, Richard J. (Renee) –
[(PL) PL-2012; FL-2013; PL-2020] Williamston Crossroads (DSA LTFT ¼) 08/01/2012; Williamston Crossroads (PTLP ¼) 11/10/2012; M-52 Cooperative Ministry: Webberville (LTFT ¾)/ Williamston Crossroads (LTFT ¼) 2013; [M-52 Cooperative Ministry renamed Connections Cooperative Ministry 2015] Dowling: Country Chapel 2016; **Dowling: Country Chapel (PTLP ½) May 1, 2020**.<> PO Box 26, 9275 S M 37 Hwy, Dowling 49050 (269) 721-8077. Home: 3400 Lacey Rd, Dowling 49050 (269) 721-3400. rjfoster0206@ymail.com

Foster, Sheryl A. –
[(FD) PD 2008; FD 2015] 2008 Milford, Pastoral Assistant (½), Milford High School; **2015 Milford (deacon)**.<> 1200 Atlantic, Milford 48381 (248) 684-2798. Home: 5821 Felske Drive, Brighton 48116 (248) 318-5613. sherylafoster@gmail.com

Fowler, Faith Ellen –
[(FE) P 1986; F 1988] 1986 Detroit: Ford Memorial; **July 1, 1994 Detroit: Cass Community**.<> 3901 Cass Avenue, Detroit 48201 (313) 833-7730 (shelter: 11850 Woodrow Wilson, Detroit 48206 (313) 883-2277. Home: 2245 Wabash, Detroit 48216 (313) 408-1980. ccumcac@aol.com

*Fox, James E. (Helen) –
[(RE) D-1965; FE-1968; R-1995] Leaton Community 1961; Rosebush/Center 1962; Grand Rapids Epworth/ Westgate 1964; Lansing: Trinity 1968; Shelby 11/15/1971; Wyoming: Wesley Park 09/01/1977; Three Rivers: First 05/01/1985; Fennville/Pearl 1990; Hastings: Hope 1992; Retired 1995; Barry County: Woodland 07/22/2008-2011.<> Home: 1112 N Hanover St, Hastings 49058 (269) 945-0190. jfox@broadstripe.net

*Fox, Thomas P. (Kathleen) –
[(RE) D-1986; FE-1992; R-2012] Mesick/Harrietta 1986; Reading 1992; Portage Prairie 1999; Portage Prairie (LTFT ¾) 01/01/2008; Homer/Lyon Lake 2008; Retired 2012.<> Home: 1626 Lake Dr Apt 189, Haslett 48840 (517) 331-2287. preacher1947@yahoo.com

Francis, Raymond –
[(PL) PL Jan 1, 2020] Coomer / Winn (CLM/DSA) (¼ time) 2016; Coomer / Winn (PTLP ½) Jan 1, 2020 [Coomer merged w/ Winn 3-8-2020]; **Winn (PTLP ¼) Mar 8, 2020**.<> 8187 S. Winn Rd, Mt Pleasant 48858 (989) 866-2440. Home: 812 W Center St, Alma 48801 (989) 330-9135. drrayfrancis@yahoo.com

*Frank, Nancy Kathleen (Daniel) –
[(RE) P 1991; F 1993] 1991 Norway: Grace, Faithorn; Nov 1, 1994 Fenton (assoc); 1996 Saginaw: Swan Valley; 2000 Dearborn: Good Shepherd; Oct 1, 2005 incapacity leave; **2015 Retired**.<> Home: 4605 Robindale Dr., Knoxville TN 37921. NKFrank@msn.com

*Franks, Barbara L. –
[(RE) P KY, 1976; F KY, 1979] 1976 school; 1978 Mt. Olivet KY; 1980 Tower, Dayton KY (LTFT ½), Director, United Methodist Advisory Council of Northern Kentucky (LTFT ½); 1984 Tower, Dayton KY; 1986 Maysville: Scott; 1987 Director, Ida Spence United Methodist Mission, Covington KY; 1989 Trans. to Detroit Conf, Rose City: Trinity, Churchill; Sept 1, 1994 LaPorte, Mapleton; Oct 1, 1996 God's Country Cooperative Parish: Paradise, Hulbert; 1998 Bay Port, Hayes; 2000 Hardy; 2005 leave of absence; **2007 Retired**.<> Home: 7533 Grand River Rd Apt 144, Brighton MI 48114 (517) 579-4383

*Fraser-Soots, Bea Barbara –
[(RE) P 1991; F 1993] 1991 Detroit: Cass Community (assoc); 1994 Detroit: Zion; 1997 Detroit: Mt. Hope; Sept 1, 1997 Washington, Davis; Jan 1, 1999 Ferndale: Campbell Memorial (LTFT ¼); 2000 Detroit: Redford; 2005 sabbatical leave;2006 Pontiac: Grace & Peace Community, Four Towns; 2014 Garden City: First; **Mar 2, 2015 Retired**.<> Home: 20225 True Vista Circle, Monument CO 80132 (248) 320-5108. beasoots@gmail.com

*Frazier, Lynda Frances (Kevin) –
[(RE) PE 2006; FE 2010] 2005 Gordonville (LTFT ¼); June 20, 2010 leave of absence; 2012 Freeland; Feb 15, 2014 leave of absence; **Dec 1, 2015 Retired**.<> Home: 1105 Tanwood Ct., Midland 48462 (989) 835-8290. lynfrazier1120@gmail.com

Freeland, Carol Joan [Abbott] (David) –
[(FL) PL 2014; FL 2015] Iron River: Wesley 2014; Kingston 2015; **Hudson: First 2018**.<> 420 W. Main St., Hudson 49247 (517) 448-5891. Home: 428 W. Main St., Hudson 49247 (517) 306-6236. pastorcjabbott@frontier.com

Freeland, David C. (Carol) –
[(FL) PL 1998; FL 2000] Peck, Buel, Melvin (co-pastor) Jan 1, 2000; Port Austin, Pinnebog/Grindstone 2002; Livingston Circuit: Plainfield, Trinity 2013; **Retired 2017**.<> Home: 5250 Swaffer Rd., Millington 48746 (810) 569-3669. davecf@gmail.com

*Freeman, Catherine M. (Tom) –
[(RD) PD 2008; FD 2011; RD 2014] 2008: Dixboro; Dixboro: Pastoral Assistant (½), Project Manager Avalon Housing Sept 29, 2008; Dixboro (½), Ann Arbor Women's Group (½) 2010; **Retired 2014**.<> Home: 3381 Alan Mark, Ann Arbor 48105 (734) 665-8471. cathyfreeman27@yahoo.com

French, Cleoria Monique Renee [Turner] (Cedric) –
[(PL) FL 2015; PL 2019; FL 2020] Saginaw: State Street 2015; Breckenridge 2019; **Battle Creek: Washington Heights 2020**.<> 153 Wood St N, Battle Creek 49037 (269) 968-8773. Home: 26 W. Roosevelt Ave, Battle Creek 49037 (810) 814-6487. monique.turner21@gmail.com

French, Kelsey Beatrice Burns –
[(FL) FL 2020] **Hopkins, South Monterey 2020**.<> (H) 322 N Maple St, PO Box 356, Hopkins 49328 (269) 793-7323. (SM) Corner of 26th St & 127th Ave, PO Box 356, Hopkins 49328 (269) 793-7323. Home: 216 Elm St, Hopkins 49328 (248) 613-0366. pastorkelseyfrench@gmail.com

French, Lawrence James (Sharon) –
[(FL) PL-2019; FL-2019] Kalamazoo: Milwood (assoc) (LTFT ½) 01/01/2019; Gobles, Almena 2019; **Cedar Springs, Kent City: Chapel Hill 2020**.<> (CS) PO Box K, 140 S Main St, Cedar Springs 49319 (616) 696-1140. (KC) 14591 Fruit Ridge Ave, Kent City 49330 (616) 675-7184. Home: 140 S. Main St, Cedar Springs 49319 (616) 551-9280. pastorlarryfrench@gmail.com

*****French, Lillian T.** (Michael) –
[(RE) PE-2002; FE-2005; R-2010] Dimondale 11/16/1999; St Louis: First 2002; Jackson Calvary 01/01/2008; Retired 09/01/2010.<> Home: 4151 Lancashire Dr, Jackson 49203 (517) 990-0395. LillianFrench@msn.com

Freysinger, Robert J. (Marion Robin) –
[(FE) D-1981; FE-1985] Center Eaton/Brookfield 10/16/1982; Lane Boulevard 1985; Napoleon 1988; Millville 2004; Millville (LTFT ¾) and Stockbridge (LTFT ¼) 2011; Kalkaska 2013; Appointed in Other Annual Conferences (¶331.8, ¶346.1) Detroit Conf, Fowlerville First 2015; Battle Creek: Newton (LTFT ¼) 2016; Ida/Samaria: Grace 2019; **Ida, Samaria: Grace, Lulu (Regional Director of Co-op Parish, para 206.3 and 206.6) 2020**.<> (I) 8124 Ida E, PO Box 28, Ida 48140 (734) 269-6127. (SG) 1463 Samaria, PO Box 37, Samaria 48177 (734) 269-6127. (L) 12810 Lulu Rd, PO Box 299, Ida 48140 (734) 269-9076. Home: 3276 Lewis Ave, PO Box 28, Ida 48140 (517) 812-0762. pastorrjf913@yahoo.com

Friedrick, Phillip J. (Gail) –
[(FE) D-1984; FE-1988] Appointed in Other Annual Conferences (¶331.8, ¶346.1) Highland Park (Assoc), Dallas TX 1984-1985; Galien/Olive Branch 1986; Battle Creek: Birchwood 1991; Alma 1995; N Muskegon: Community 07/15/2012; Sparta 2017.<> 54 E Division St, Sparta 49345 (616) 887-8255. Home: 1960 Skyview Dr, Sparta 49345 (231) 670-7796

Fritz, Leslee J. –
[(PE) CC-2016; PL-2017; PE-2019] Albion: First (PTLP ¾) 2017; Alboin: First 2019.<> 600 E Michigan Ave, Albion 49224 (517) 629-9425. Home: 11184 29 Mile Rd, Albion 49224 (517) 629-6531. fritzleslee@yahoo.com

*****Fritz, Richard A** (Marjean) –
[(RL) FL-2009; RL-2014] Monterey Center / Burnips 2008; Retired 2014.<> Home: 589 Peterson, Muskegon 49445

*Fry, Donald R. (Anna) –
[(RE) D-1967; FE-1970; R-2008] Waterloo Village/First 1969; Sonoma/Battle Creek: Newton 1970; Ionia Parish: LeValley/Berlin Center 1971; Marne 1973; White Pigeon 11/22/1977; Marion/ Cadillac: South Community 1981; Newaygo 1994; Three Rivers: First 2000; Ovid United 2006; Retired 2008; Dansville (LTFT ¼) 2008-2011.<> Home: 775 N Pine River St, Ithaca 48847 (517) 749-9304. anna_don@charter.net

Fuchs, Robert F. (Susan) –
[(FL) FL 2017] **Brighton (assoc) Campus Pastor - Whitmore Lake Campus Jan 1, 2017; DownRiver 2020.**<> 14400 Beech Daly, Taylor 48180 (734) 442-6100. Home: 20433 Foxboro, Riverview 48193 (810) 571-0185. bobiof59@gmail.com

*Fuller, Linda L. (Gale) –
[(RL) FL 2000; RL 2018] Worth Twp.: Bethel 2000; Caseville 2010; **Retired 2018; Croswell: First (PTLP ¼) 2020.**<> 13 N Howard Ave, Croswell 48422 (810) 679-3595. Home: 254 N Howard Ave, Croswell 48422 (810) 679-3576. urmy2@greatlakes.net

*Fullmer, Charles W. (Margaret) –
[(RE) D-1957; FE-1959; R-1997] Lyon Lake/Marengo Fall 1956; Lyon Lake 1957; Kalamazoo: First (Assoc) 1959; Grand Rapids: Valley 1962; Reed City 1966; Ionia: First 1970; Grandville 1977; Petoskey 1986; Appointed to Extension Ministries (¶344.1b,c) Chaplain, Clark Retirement Community 03/01/1994; Retired 1997; Amble 08/01/1999-10/31/2001.<> Home: 733 Clark Crossing SE, Grand Rapids 49506 (562) 607-2375. Summer: PO Box 239, Lakeview 48850 (989) 352-7002. cwfmjf3235@gmail.com

*Gackler, Joyce F. (Ken) –
[(RL) PL-2005; RL-2012] Plainfield 06/01/2005; Retired 2012.<> Home: 410 Johnson St, Caledonia 49316 (616) 891-5682. joycef2@msn.com

Galloway, Donna –
[(FL) FL Aug 1, 2014] Aug 1, 2014 Morenci; **2016 Morenci, Weston.**<> (M) 110 E. Main St., Morenci 49256 (517) 458-6923. (W) 4193 Weston Rd., Box 96, Weston 49289 (517) 436-3492. Home: 111 E. Main St., Morenci 49256 (517) 458-6687. donagalloway@msn.com

*Gamboa, Elizabeth M. (Stephan) –
[(RE) (FE, PA)] 2000 trans to Detroit Conf, Flint: Bristol, Dimond; 2003 Mt. Morris: First; **2008 Retired.**<> Home: 1601 W. 34th St., N., Wichita KS 67204. gamboapersephone@aol.com

Gandarilla-Becerra, Patricia –
[(FL) FL 2012] 2012 Detroit: El Buen, Alpha and Omega Faith Community; 2015 Ypsilanti: First (assoc), Detroit: El Buen Pastor, Revive, 50 Communities of Faith; 2016 Ypsilanti: First, New Church Development (¶344.1a,c) Detroit: Centro Familiar Cristo; **Feb 1, 2016 Detroit: Centro Familiar Cristiano.**<> 1270 Waterman, Detroit 48209 (313) 843-4170. Home: 8961 Niver, Allen Park 48101 (313) 551-4003. carpagabe@gmail.com

Garrigues, Margaret "Peggy" Ruth –
[(FE) P 1990; F 1992; HL 2000; FE 2009] 1990 Howell: First (assoc); 1992 Fenton (assoc) (LTFT ½); Sept 1, 1994 Wagarville: Community/Wooden Shoe; 1995 family leave; 1998 Chelsea: First (assoc); 2000 Honorable Location; 2009 Fostoria, West Deerfield (LTFT ½); (2009 readmitted) 2010 Clawson; 2013 Berkley (½), Clawson (½); Jan 1, 2015 Clawson; Oct 1, 2015 Clawson (LTFT ½); Mar 16, 2016 Clawson (LTFT ¼); **Sept 1, 2016 voluntary leave of absence**.<>. revpeggyg@gmail.com

Garza, E. Jeanne [Koughn] –
[(FE) D-1996; FE-1998] UM Connectional Structures (¶344.1a,c) Director, Wesley Foundation, Ferris State University 2003; [Transferred from Iowa Conf 2004] Traverse Bay (Assoc) 2008; Hillside/Somerset Center 2009; Sturgis 2014; Dixboro 2019.<> 5221 Church Rd, Ann Arbor 48105 (734) 665-5632. Home: 3350 Oak Dr, Ann Arbor 48105 (517) 745-2490. pstrjg@gmail.com

Gasaway, Rodney Glenn (Janice) –
[(FD) PD 2017; FD 2020] Joy Southfield, Director Community & Economic Dev 2017-Jan 31, 2018; **Livonia: Newburg, Adult Education Program and Outreach (½) Feb 1, 2018; Chelsea: First, Director of Adult Ministries (½)Jan 13, 2019**.<> 36500 Ann Arbor Trail, Livonia 48150 (734) 422-0149

*Gastian, Sandra J. –
[(RL) PL-1991; RL-2011] Athens (LTFT ½) 08/01/1991; Retired 01/01/2011.<> Home: 416 22nd St, Springfield 49037 (269) 964-9050

*Gay, Sue J. (David) –
[(RL) FL-1994; PL-2005; RL-2007] Augusta: Fellowship (DSA 6/1/93-7/1/94) 1994; Augusta: Fellowship (LTFT PT) 01/01/2005; Retired 2007.<> Home: 4222 NE 129 Pl, Portland OR 97230

*Gedcke, Roger Franklin (Donna) –
[(RE)] Detroit: Bethel 1968; Ferndale: St. Paul's 1969; Ontonagon County Larger Parish 1972; North Branch, Clifford 1979; Clio: Bethany 1997; **Retired 2010**.<> Home: 13078 Golfside Ct., Clio 48420 (810) 547-1538. drgedcke@gmail.com

Genoff, Nickolas Kelly (Tina) –
[(FL) FL Jan 1, 2004; PL 2013; FL 2020] Port Huron: Washington Ave Jan 1, 2004; Port Huron: Washington Avenue, Avoca 2007; Croswell: First, Avoca 2009; Applegate, Buel, Croswell: First 2013; Medical Leave Jan 1, 2019; **Millington 2020**.<> Box 321, 9020 State, Millington 48746 (989) 871-3489. Home: 4851 W. Main St., Millington 48746 (810) 537-5028. nkg111015@gmail.com

Gentile, Michelle Annette (Randy Whitcomb) –
[(FE) P 1984; F 1987] Dearborn: First (assoc) 1985; Denton: Faith 1988; disability leave 1990; **Retired 2019**.<> Home: 2772 Roundtree Dr., Troy 48083 (248) 229-8383. arejayrev@aol.com

Gibbs, Cindy L. (Jim) –
[(FL) PL Jan 1, 2008; FL 2010] Churchill Jan 1, 2008; Romulus 2010; **Pigeon: First 2015**.<> 7102 Michigan Ave., PO Box 377, Pigeon 48755 (989) 453-2475. Home: 7090 Scheurer St., PO Box 377, Pigeon 48755 (989) 453-3232. cindygibbs1957@gmail.com

*Gibbs, Max L. (Jean) –
[(RE) P 1977; F 1980] 1978 Pontiac: Central (assoc); 1980 Flint: Oak Park (assoc); 1982 Akron, Unionville; 1983 Director, Camp Reynoldswood IL; 1987 Minister of the Word, Uniting Church in Australia; Feb 1, 1990 Deerfield, Petersburg; 1991 Deckerville, Minden City; 1996 Akron; Oct 1, 1996 disability leave; **2009 Retired**.<> Home: 5671 Galbraith Line Rd, Croswell 48422 (810) 404-9726

Giddings Sr., Emmanuel J. –
[(FE) P 1993 (on recognition of orders, Liberia Annual Conference); F 1994] 1992 Detroit: Central (assoc); 1995 Detroit: Conant Avenue; 1997 St. Clair Shores: Good Shepherd; Oct 1, 1999 Associate Council Director: Urban Missioner; Jan 1, 2003 leave of absence; **Sept 1, 2006 Director of Alfalit International/Liberia Literacy Program, Liberian Conference para 344.1**.<>. enw@earthlink.net

*Giguere, Jack Eugene (Joyce) –
[(RE) T 1959; F 1962] 1959 Baltimore: Brooklyn (assoc) (Baltimore Conf); 1962 Clarkston (assoc); 1965 Bad Axe; 1971 Flushing; 1980 Livonia: Newburg; 1984 Ann Arbor District Superintendent; 1989 Grosse Pointe; **1999 Retired**.<> Home: (summer) PO Box 1313, Bay View 49770 (231) 347-8277; (winter) 410-A Goldsborough St., Easton MD 21601. je.giguere@hotmail.com

Gillespie, Billie Lou (Roger Brown) –
[(FL) FL 2000] Henderson, Chapin 2000; West Vienna Oct 15, 2006; **St Louis: First, Breckenridge 2020**.<> (SL) 116 S Franklin Street, St. Louis 48880(989) 681-3320. (B) PO Box 248, Breckenridge 48615 (989) 842-3632. Home: 116 N East St, St Louis 48880 (810) 241-3160. spiritdancer1216@gmail.com

Gladstone, Carl Thomas Stroud (Anna) –
[(FD) PD 2004; FD 2007] Birmingham: First (deacon) (LTFT ¾) 2004; Birmingham: First (deacon); Director, Young Leaders Initiative 2007; Youth Leaders Initiative (½), Jurisdictional Coordinator Youth and Young Adult Ministries (½) Jan 1, 2010; Discipleship Ministries: Regional Staff Jan 1, 2016; **Dearborn: First Director of Youth & Adult Ministries & Missional and Young Leaders Initiative (deacon) (LTFT ½) 2019; Director of Motor City Wesley (LTFT ½) (para 331.1a) 2019**.<> (DF) 22124 Garrison St, Dearborn 48124 (313) 563-5200. (MCW) 8000 Woodward, Detroit 48202 (313) 757-0471. Home: 542 W. Grand Blvd, Detroit 48216 (586) 295-3055. carl@motorcity-wesley.org

*Gladstone, David G. –
[(RE) SP 1989; P 1990; F 1993] Detroit: Metropolitan (assoc) 1989; Eastpointe: Immanuel 1991; Warren: First 1997; Port Huron: First 2003; **Retired 2012**.<> 2017-2018 Lexington. Home: 10850 Pioneer Trl, Boyne Falls 49713 (231) 549-2728. dgladstone517@gmail.com

*Glanville, Gary R. (Lisa) –
[(RE) P 1980; F 1983] Saginaw: Ames (assoc) 1981; Saginaw: Swan Valley 1983; Utica (assoc) Mar 1, 1987; Ann Arbor: Calvary 1989; Romeo 1996; Swartz Creek 2015; **Retired Sept 1, 2020**.<> 4945 Deerfield Meadows, Almont 48003 (810) 287-9861. dr.gg@sbcglobal.net

Glass, Cora Elizabeth –
[(FD) PD 2016; FD 2019] Wesley Foundation, Resident Director of Intentional Living and Director of Discipleship Ministries/ Area Board of Higher Education and Campus Ministry Fund Developer 2016; Garrett-Evangelical Theological Seminary, Assistant Director of Annual Giving and Alum Relations (¶331.1b) July 31, 2017; **Waterford: Central, Director of Life-Long Faith Formation 2018**.<> 3882 Highland Rd., Waterford 48328 (248) 681-0040. Home: 4011 Shaddick, Waterford 48328 (248) 410-2645. glass.cora@gmail.com

Glygoroff, Steffani –
[(PL) PL-Jan 1, 2020] Henderson/Chapin/Owosso: Trinity (DSA) (¾ time) 2019; **Henderson, Chapin, Owosso: Trinity (PTLP ¾ time) Jan 1, 2020** .<> (H) 218 E Main, Henderson 48841 (989) 723-5729. (C) 19848 S Chapin Rd, Elsie 48831 (989) 661-2497. (OT) 720 S Shiawassee St, Owosso 48867 (989) 723-2664. Home: 302 E Main St, Henderson 48841 (248) 805-3597. trinityumc@michonline.net

*Gonder, Daniel L. (Pamela) –
[(RE) PL 2006; PE 2010; FE 2013; RE 2018] Fairgrove 2006; Fairgrove, Watrousville Mar 1, 2010; Tawas 2013; **Retired 2018;** Grant (LTFT ¼) 2018-2019.<> 10999 Karlin Rd, Buckley 49620 (231) 269-3981. Home: PO Box 24, Interlochen 49643 (989) 415-0537 (989) 415-0537. revdonnow@att.net

Goodwin, Suzannne Kuenzli (James) –
[(FD) PD 2007; FD 2011] Farmington: Orchard (deacon) (¾ Time) 2007; deacon full-time 2011; **Mason: First 2019**.<> 201 E Ash St, Mason 48854 (517) 676-9449. Home: 616 Hall Blvd, Mason 48854 (248) 318-4869. revsuzanne@masonfirst.org

Gordon, Brenda E. –
[(FE) D-2000; FE-2007] Hinchman/Oronoko 2000; Empire 2006; Berrien Springs/Pokagon 2014; Berrien Springs/Pokagon and Hinchman/Oronoko 2017; Sodus: Chapel Hill 2018.<> 4071 Naomi Rd, Sodus 49126 (269) 927-3454. Home: 4033 Naomi Rd, Sodus 49126 (269) 925-4528. begordon68@hotmail.com

*Gordon, Diane L. (Tom) –
[(RE) FL-2003; PE-2004; FE-2007; R-2018] Ashley/Bannister 2003; Battle Creek: Trinity 2006; Muskegon: Central 2010; Mt Pleasant: First 2013; Retired 2018.<> Home: 114 Lillybell Ct, Spring Lake 49456 (231) 457-3744. PastorDiane7@me.com

*Gordon, Linda R. (Bruce) –
[(OR) OR-2014] [Illionis Great Rivers Conf, Retired AM 2011] Hinchman/Oronoko (LTFT ½) 2014-2017.<> Home: 116 S Detroit St, Buchanan 49107 (269) 815-6094. yes2six@gmail.com

Gordy, Samuel C. (Elizabeth) –
[(FL) PL-2015; FL-2018; PL-2020] Morris Chapel (PTLP ¼) 03/11/2012; Kalamazoo: Northwest (PTLP ¼) 2013; Bronson: First (PTLP ½) 2015; Bronson: First/Colon 2018; **Bronson: First (PTLP ½) 2020**.<> 312 E Chicago St, Bronson 49028 (517) 369-6555. Home: 330 E Cory St, Bronson 49028 (260) 330 6054. sgordy1062@gmail.com

Gotham, Donald D. (Laura) –
[(FE) P 1994; F 1997] Sutton-Sunshine, Bethel 1995; Sutton-Sunshine, Bethel, Akron Oct 1, 1996; Sandusky: First 1997; Saint Clair: First Sept 1, 2004; **Utica 2011**.<> 8650 Canal Rd., Sterling Heights 48314 ((586) 731-7667. Home: 8506 Clinton River Rd., Sterling Heights 48314 (586) 739-2726. dongotham@sbcglobal.net

Goudie, David J. (Andee) –

[(FE) PE 1999; FE 2002] 1999 Monroe: Calvary; 2004 Utica (assoc); Aug 1, 2009 Houghton: Grace; 2013 Hale: First; **Medical Leave Sept 1, 2017**.<> Home: 16296 Picton Ct., Clinton Twp., 48038. pastordavidgoudie@gmail.com

*Goudie, Diana Kay (Robert) –

[(RE) PL 1983; SP 1988; P 1991; F 1993] 1983 Milan: Marble Memorial (assoc) (LTFT); Sept 1, 1991 Azalia, London; Sept 1, 1994 Redford: Aldersgate (co-pastor); 2003 Redford: Redford Aldersgate; **2009 Retired**.<> Home: 19710 W. 13 Mile Rd., #108, Beverly Hills 48025 (248) 220-4046. dianagoudie09@comcast.net

*Goudie, Robert F. (Diana) –

[(RE) T 1964; F 1966] 1966 Detroit: St. James (assoc); 1970 Waterford: Trinity; Apr 1976 Monroe: First; 1983 Milan: Marble Memorial; Sept 1, 1994 Redford: Aldersgate (co-pastor); **2003 Retired**.<> Home: 19710 W. 13 Mile Rd., #108, Beverly Hills 48025 (248) 220-4046. bobgoudie09@comcast.net

Gougeon, Jon W. (Kitty) –

[(FL) (FL) 2003] 2003 Sterling, Alger, Garfield; **Mar 1, 2010 Reese**.<> 9859 Saginaw St., PO Box 7, Reese 48757 (989) 868-9957. Home: 1968 Rhodes, Reese 48757 (989) 868-9957. pastorgougeon@gmail.com

*Grajcar, Michael, Jr. (Sharon) –

[(RE) T Pitts., 1961; F 1964] 1959 Renaker, Sadieville KY; 1960 Sinking Spring OH; 1963 Trans. to Detroit Conf, Linden; 1969 Troy: Big Beaver; 1976 Holly: Calvary; 1982 Pontiac: St. James; 1988 Riverview; 1989 Onaway, Millersburg; **1991 Retired**.<> Home: 17867 St. Pierre, Arcadia 49713 (231) 889-4234. mikegraj34@gmail.com

*Graham, Donald J. (Judy) –

[(RL) FL-2001; RL 2019] Ionia: Zion 2001; Colon/Burr Oak 2007; Martin/Shelbyville 2012; Muskegon Lakeside 2014; Casco 2016; Retired 2019.<> Home: 4457 Marshall Rd, Muskegon 49441 (269) 503-0354. pastordongraham@gmail.com

Granada, Lemuel O. (Colleen) –

[(PL) PL-2002; NL-2007; PL-2012] Fountain (DSA) 2002; Fountain 11/15/2002; Brethren Epworth 2003; Fountain 2005; LP w/o Appointment 11/30/2007; Hersey (PTLP ¼) 07/29/2012.<> PO Box 85, 200 W 2nd St, Hersey 49639 (231) 832-5168. Home: 351 2nd St, Manistee 49660 (231) 723-2763. LGranada@charter.net

*Grant, James Clyde –

[(RE) D-1958; FE-1959; R-1999] Almena/Glendale 1957; Dowagiac: First 1960; Grand Rapids: Second 1966; Kalamazoo Oakwood 1972; Byron Center 03/01/1975; Otsego 1985; Leave of Absence 03/06/1992; Otsego 08/01/1992; Marion/Cadillac: South Community 1994; Retired 06/23/1999.<> Home: 1029 Wedgewood Drive, Plainwell 49080 (269) 685-0079

*Grant, Ronald B. (Carol) –

[(RE) D-1973; FE-1976; R-2012] Concord 1975; UM Connectional Structures (¶344.1a,c) Director, Wesley Foundation WMU 1982; Leave of Absence 08/15/1992; Other Valid Ministries (¶344.1d) Limited License Psychologist, New Directions Counseling Kalamazoo 02/01/1995; Retired 11/01/2012.<> Home: 1815 Quail Cove Dr, Kalamazoo 49009 (269) 375-0321. msu2kzoo@hotmail.com

Gray, Markey C. –
[(FL) FL 2018] **Detroit: Trinity Faith 2018**.<> 19750 W McNichols Rd, Detroit 48219 (313) 533-0101. Home: 23470 Meadow Park, Redford 48239

*Gray-Lion, Annelissa Marie –
[(RD) PD 2006; FD 2013; RD 2018] Jan 1, 2007 Chelsea: First (deacon); 2009 leave of absence; 2012 Chelsea: First (deacon); **2018 Retired**.<> Home: 258 Harrison St, Chelsea 48118 (734) 945-2097. lgraylion@gmail.com

*Graybill, Joseph M. (Sue) –
[(RE) D-1982; FE-1984; R-2011] Transferred from Free Methodist Church 1982; Dansville/Vantown 1980; Edmore: Faith 04/01/1987; Leland 1997; Retired 2011.<> Home: 386 York View Lane NW, Comstock Park 49321 (231) 342-2222. sueandjoegraybill@gmail.com

*Green, Patricia A. –
[(RE) PL 1986; SP 1990; P 1992; F 1995] 1986 Detroit: North Detroit; 1990 Second UMC, First UMC (associate youth pastor), North Vernon IN, under para 426.1; 1992 Ebenezer, Madison IN, under para. 426.1; 1993 Brighton: First (assoc); 1995 Erie; 1999 Madison Heights; 2008 Milan: Marble Memorial; **2013 Retired**.<> 24353 Tamarack Tr., Southfield 48075 (248) 809-6644. pgreen5188@att.net

*Green, Rosaline D. –
[(RL) FL 2017; RL 2019] Dec 1, 2017 Southfield: Hope (assoc); **2019 Retired; 2019 Southfield: Hope (assoc) (LTFT ½)**.<> 27275 Northwestern Hwy., Southfield (248) 356-1020. Home: 29476 Briar Bank Ct, Southfield 48034 (248) 470-4042. rgreen@hopeumc.org

*Greene, Carl E. (Deanna) –
[(RL) PL-2005; RL-2011] Brethren: Epworth (DSA 7/1-11/11/05) (LTFT PT) 11/11/2005; Grant (LTFT PT) 03/15/2006; Retired 2011.<> Home: 3021 Glen Malier Drive, Beulah 49617 (231) 375-1006

Greene, Cynthia S.L. –
[(FE) D-1993; FE-1995] Transferred from Origon-Idaho Conf 1998; Lansing: Trinity (Assoc) 05/01/1998; Byron Center 2003; Ithaca/Beebe 2010; Lake Odessa: Lakewood 2015; Rockford 2017; Weidman 2019.<> 3200 N Woodruff Rd, PO Box 98, Weidman 48893 (989) 644-3148. Home: 9532 W Saint Charles Rd, Sumner 48889. cingreene01@gmail.com

*Greer, James Edward, II (Madeline) –
[(RE) P 1982; F 1985] 1983 Rochester: St. Paul's (assoc); 1987 Farmington: Orchard (assoc); 1990 New Baltimore: Grace; 1995 Bloomfield Hills: St. Paul; Nov 16, 2000 Franklin: Community; **2013 Retired**.<> Home: 106 Chota Hills Trace, Loudon TN 37774 (248) 227-7599. JEGreer@aol.com

Grenfell, John Nicholas, III (Shelley) –
[(FE) P 1987; F 1989] Jan 1, 1987 God's Country Cooperative Parish: Grand Marais, Germfask; Feb 1, 1992 Menominee: First; 1994 school; 1995 Menominee: First; 1998 Belleville: First; 2007 Plymouth: First; **2018 St. Clair: First**.<> 415 N 3rd St, St Clair 48079 (810) 329-7186. Home: 3202 S Shoreview, Fort Gratiot 48059. john@pfumc.org

Grettenberger, Louis W. (Karen) –
[(FE) D-1987; FE-1989] Manton 1987; Traverse City: Christ 1993; Sparta 2009; Grand Haven Church of the Dunes 2017.<> 717 Sheldon Rd, Grand Haven 49417 (616) 842-7980. Home: 633 Hillock Ct, Grand Haven 49417 (231) 883-9806. louis.grettenberger@gmail.com

Greyerbiehl, Julie A. (William W. Chu) –
[(FE) FL-2005; PE-2009; FE-2013] Elk Rapids/ Kewadin/Williamsburg (Assoc) 2005; Elk Rapids/Kewadin/ Williamsburg (Co-Pastor) 2008; Silver Creek/Keeler 2009; Williamston 2011; Mt Pleasant: First 2018.<> 400 S Main St, Mt Pleasant 48858 (989) 773-6934. Home: 1109 Glenwood Dr, Mt Pleasant 48858 (517) 655-2321. pastor-julieg@gmail.com

Griffin, Herbert L., Jr. (Ellainia) –
[(FE) D-1991; FE-1993] Battle Creek: Washington Hts (Assoc) 1990; Appointed to Extension Ministries (¶344.1b,c) Chaplain/Wing Chaplain, US Navy, US Marine Corps 1993.<> Home: 11334 Village Ridge Rd, San Diego CA 92131 (858) 397-2532. herbertgriffin911@yahoo.com

*Grigereit, Robert Charles (Carolyn) –
[(RE) P 1960 W.MI; F 1962 W.MI] 1960 Deerfield: Bethlehem; 1962 Ludington: Zion; 1965 Ludington: Grace, Zion; 1967 Ludington: St. Paul; 1967 Grand Rapids: Griggs Street; 1968 Trans. to Detroit Conf, Ann Arbor: Calvary; 1976 Garden City; 1987 Midland: First (assoc); **1999 Retired**.<> Home: 7355 S. Shugart Rd., Traverse City 49684 (231) 946-8551. cgrigereit@aol.com

Griggs, Jerry Dwight (Cherie) –
[(PL) PL 1998] 1998 Eastern Thumb Cooperative Parish: McGregor, Carsonville; **2004 McGregor, Carsonville**.<> (M) 2230 Forest R., Deckerville 48427; (C) 3953 Sheldon, Carsonville 48419 (810) 657-9168. Home: 5791 Paldi, Peck 48466 (810) 378-5686. mcrgegorumc@airadvantage.net

Grimes, Christopher M. –
[(FL) FL 2015] Detroit: St. Timothy 2013; Westland: St. James 2015; Southfield: Hope (assoc) 2017; **West Vienna, West Forest 2020**.<> (WV) 5485 W Wilson Rd, Clio 48420 (810) 686-7480. (WF) 7297 E. Farrand Rd., Millington 48746; 129 E Vates, Frankenmuth 48734 (989) 871-3456. Home: 5445 W Wilson Rd, Clio 48420 (313) 399-4530. pastorchris208@gmail.com

*Grimmett, Carter Mansfield (Toni) –
[(RE) PL 2003; PE 2007; FE 2010; RE 2020] Dec 2002 Detroit: Conant Avenue; Sept 1, 2003 Westland: St. James (LTFT ½); Jan 1, 2006 Westland: St. James (LTFT ¾); Mar 1, 2007 Westland: St. James, Inkster: Christ; 2008 Detroit: People's; Nov 1, 2013 Detroit Peoples, Calvary; 2014 St. Clair Shores: Good Shepherd; 2017 Rochester: St. Paul; **Retired 2020**.<> Home: 598 Jacob Way, #103, Rochester 48307 (313) 303-0617. cartergrimmett@att.net

*Groff, Kathleen A. (Joseph) –
[(RE) P 1997; FE 1999] 1997 Farmington: Nardin Park (assoc); Sept 1, 2002 Dundee; **2008 Retired**; 2011 Newaygo (LTFT ¾); 01/01/2014 Newaygo (LTFT 45%); 05/08/2014-2017 Newaygo (LTFT ¾).<> Home: 2524 Windbreak Ln, Lansing 48910 (989) 339-7887. kthgrff@gmail.com

Gruenberg, Paul J. (Lyent) –
[(FE) PE 2003; FE 2006] Pickford 2003; Hartland 2012; **Gaylord: First 2020.**<> 215 South Center, Box 617, Gaylord 49734 (989) 732-5380. Home: 915 Five Lakes Rd., Gaylord 49735 (989) 635-2075. fumcoffice@winntel.net

Guetschow, Kevin K. (Karen) –
[(FL) FL-2010] Kent City: Chapel Hill 2010; Dorr Crosswind Community 2017.<> 1683 142nd Ave, Dorr 49323 (616) 681-0302. Home: 4380 Tracy Trail, Dorr 49323 (616) 227-5567. keving@crosswindcc.org

Gutierrez, April –
[(FL) FL 2020] **Chaplain, Adrian College Jan 1, 2020.**<> Adrian College, Valade Hall 133, 110 S Madison St, Adrian 49221 (517) 265-5761. Home: 664 Stonecrest Dr, Adrian 49221. april.gutierrez@garrett.edu

Gutierrez, Dora (Marcos) –
[(PL) PL Sept 1, 1998] Sept 1, 1998 New Creations Ministries 2003 El Buen Pastor/New Creations Ministries; **Jan 1, 2005 without appointment.**<> Home: 11550 Willow, Southgate 48195 (734) 284-8052. marcosdorag@yahoo.com

*Gutierrez, Marcos A. (Dora) –
[(RA) P 1980 (Puerto Rico Conf); AM 1999] 1966 Villa Fontana Carolina; 1967 San Juan Apostor, Villa Palmeras; 1968 Los Angeles Carolina; 1969 Villa Palmeras; 1975 Patillas; 1983 Caguas; 1985 trans to Wisconsin Conference, Madison; Sept 1, 1998 Detroit: El Buen New Creations Ministry; Aug 16, 1998 trans to Detroit Conference; Apr 15, 2005 incapacity leave; **2010 Retired.**<> Home: 11550 Willow, Southgate 48195 (734) 284-8052. marcosdorag@yahoo.com

*Gysel, James M. (Shari) –
[(RE) D-1977; FE-1981; R-2011] Quincy 1979; Lansing: Central (Assoc) 1983; Battle Creek: Chapel Hill 1993; Retired 2011; Lee Center (LTFT ¼) 2014.<> 22386 24 Mile Rd, Olivet 49076 (517) 857-3447. Home: 3239 Nighthawk Lane, Battle Creek 49015 (269) 209-4795. jamesgysel@mac.com

Haas, Patricia A. –
[(FE) PL-2003; PE-2011; FE-2014] Pokagon 2003; Keswick 2011.<> 3376 S Center Hwy, Suttons Bay 49682 (231) 271-3755. Home: 3400 S Center Hwy, Suttons Bay 49682 (231) 271-4117. pastorphaas@gmail.com

Haase, David L. (Linda) –
[(PL) PL-2008] Townline (DSA) (¼ Time) and Breedsville (DSA) (¼ Time) 01/03/2008; Townline (PTLP ¼) and Breedsville (PTLP ¼) 2008; Riverside (PTLP ¼) and Coloma (Assoc) (PTLP ¼) 2014; Riverside (PTLP ¼) 01/01/2016.<> PO Box 152 (4401 Fikes Rd, Benton Harbor), Riverside 49084 (269) 849-1131. Home: 211 W Saint Joseph St, Watervliet 49098 (269) 463-3536. davehaase55@gmail.com

Hadaway, Victoria L. –
[(OE) Northern Illinois] **Sault Ste. Marie: Central, Algonquin 2018.**<> (SSM) 111 E. Spruce St., Sault Ste. Marie 49783 (906) 632-8672. (A) 1604 W. 4th Ave., Sault Ste. Marie 49783 (906) 632-8672. Home: 1513 Augusta, Sault Ste. Marie 49783 (906) 632-3125. vickie.31.hadaway@gmail.com

*Hagan, Sueann K. (Lloyd) –
[(RL) FL-2003; RL-2017] Chase: Barton / Grant Center 10/16/2003; Battle Creek: Convis Union 2006; Retired 2017.<> 5987 Heron Pond Dr, Port Orange FL 32128. sueannhagan@yahoo.com

*Hagans, Gerald F. (Susan) –
[(RE) D-1983; FE-1986; R-2006] Appointed in Other Annual Conferences (¶331.8, ¶346.1) Gordon/Pitsburg, West Ohio Conf 1981-1984; Muskegon: Central (Assoc) 1984; Constantine 1989; Muskegon Heights: Temple 08/01/1991; Retired 09/01/2006; Sitka (LTFT ¼) 11/15/2009-6/30/2019.<> Home: 1249 Lakeshore Dr #305, Muskegon 49441 (231) 755-1767. francis1491@aol.com

*Hagans, Susan J. (Gerald) –
[(RE) D-1986; FE-1989; R-2006] Muskegon: Unity (LTFT) 1986; Muskegon: Unity 1987; Holland: First (Assoc) 11/15/1988; Muskegon: Lake Harbor 1995; UM Connectional Structures (¶344.1a,c) District Superintendent, Grand Rapids District 2000; Retired 2006; Wolf Lake (LTFT 45%) 09/07/2014-08/31/2017.<> Home: 1249 Lakeshore Dr #305, Muskegon 49441 (231) 750-0135. susanj1491@aol.com

*Haggard, William E. (Robin) –
[(RE) D-1980; FE-1984; R-2018] Lake Ann 1982; Cedar Springs/East Nelson 1989; Traverse City Asbury 1995; Lansing: Mount Hope 2002; UM Connectional Structures (¶344.1a,c) District Superintendent, Grand Rapids District 2012; Retired 2018; Pentwater: Centenary 2018.<> 82 S Hancock, PO Box 111, Pentwater 49449 (231) 869-5900. Home: 124 S Rutledge St, Pentwater 49449 (616) 430-9964. billh5955@comcast.net

Hagley, Mary K. (Jeffrey) –
[(FD) PD 2011; FD 2016] Plymouth: First (assoc). Transitional leave 2011; **Dixboro (Deacon LTFT ½) 2013**.<> 5221 Church St., Ann Arbor 48105. Home: 2929 Brandywine Dr., Ann Arbor 48104 (734) 652-5389. revmaryhagley@gmail.com

Hahm, Paul Sungjoon (Jennifer) –
[(FE) FL 2011; PE 2014; FE 2017] Wayne: First 2011; Brighton: First (assoc) 2013; Resident—Discipleship Ministries Urban Village Church, Chicago, Northern Illinois Conference 2015; **Lansing: Grace 2016**.<> 1900 Boston Blvd, Lansing 48910 (517) 482-5750. Home: 2915 S Cambridge Rd, Lansing 48911 (517) 484-0227. Paul.hahm@gmail.com

Hahn, Anita K. (Kevin) –
[(FE) D-1998; FE-2001] Whitehall/Claybanks 1998; Lakeview: New Life 2006; UM Connectional Structures (¶344.1a,c) District Superintendent, Grand Traverse District 2011; UM Connectional Structures (¶344.1a,c) District Superintendent, Northern Waters District 01/01/2019; Midland: First 2019.<> 315 W Larkin St, Midland 48640 (989) 835-6797. Home: 3217 Noeske St, Midland 48640 (989) 708-8894. glue4evr@yahoo.com

Hale, Georgia N. (Dwayne Glisson) –
[(FD) PD-2012; FD-2017] Transferred from Great Plains Conf 2015; Missional Appointment: Grand Rapids Genesis (Deacon) Serving Coordinator/Bridges Program (Unpaid Position) 2015.<> 3189 Snow Ave, Lowell 49331 (616) 974-0400. Home: 272 S Ball Creek Rd, Kent City 49330 (616) 678-7664. gnhale@sprintmail.com

Hall, Amanda (Chris) –
[(PD) PD 2015] leave of absence (family leave) 2015; **personal leave 2017**.<> 2030 Chester Blvd, #241, Richmond 47374. mandymmcneil@gmail.com

Hall, Lindsey M. (Jon Reynolds) –
[(FE) FL 2013; PE 2014; FE 2017] Birmingham: First (assoc) Apr 1, 2013; 2016 Birmingham: First (assoc) (LTFT ½) 2016; Birmingham: First (assoc) 2019; **Brighton: First (co-pastor, Whitmore Lake Campus) 2020**.<> 400 E. Grand River, Brighton 48116 (810) 229-8561. Home: 7608 Brookview Ct., Brighton 48116 (248) 648-0542. lhall@brightonfumc.org

Hall, Nelson L. –
[(FL) PL-1999; FL-2018] Baldwin/Luther (DSA) 1999; Baldwin/Luther 11/16/1999; Marcellus: Wakelee 2005; Augusta: Fellowship (PTLP ½) 2007; Gobles/Kendall 2013; Kalamazoo: Northwest (PTLP ¼) 2015; **Ontonagon, Greenland, Rockland: St. Paul 2018**.<> (O) PO Box 216, 109 Greenland Rd., Ontonagon 49953 (906) 884-4556. (G) 1002 Ridge Rd., Greenland 49953 (906) 883-3141. (RSP) 50 National Ave., PO Box 339, Rockland 49960 (906) 886-2851. Home: 1101 Pine, Ontonagon 49953 (906) 884-2789. nelsonlhall@gmail.com

*Haller, Gary T. (Laurie) –
[(RE) D-1979; FE-1983; R-2017] Traverse City: Central (Assoc)/Ogdensburg 1981; Traverse City: Central 01/01/2982; Pentwater: Centenary 1985; Grand Rapids: First (Co-Pastor) 1993; Appointed in Other Annual Conferences (¶331.8, ¶346.1) Detroit Conference, Birmingham First (Senior Pastor) 2013, Retired 2017.<> Home: 4521 NW 167th St, Clive IA 50325 (616) 308-7762. ghaller273@aol.com

*Halsted, Alfred Theodore, Jr. –
[(RE) T S.India, 1950; F 1956] 1948 Gosport IN; 1949 Missionary in S. India Conf; 1952 school; 1954 Stamford Circuit CT; 1956 Dixboro; 1960 Dexter; 1965 Hemlock, Nelson; 1970 Marlette; Nov 1, 1975 Lincoln Park: First; 1980 Redford; 1986 Marquette District Superintendent; **1992 Retired**.<> Home: 2030 Chester Blvd., #241, Richmond IN 47374 (765) 244-0524. athalsted@aol.com

*Hamilton, John Norman (Linda) –
[(RE) P 1978; F 1982] 1980 Adrian: First (assoc); Apr 1981 Stephenson, Hermansville; 1986 Caseville; 1990 Blissfield: Emmanuel; 1995 Onaway, Millersburg June 16, 2001 Saulte Ste. Marie: Central; Algonquin; 2004 incapacity leave; 2014 medical leave; **2016 Retired**.<> 1580 Track Iron Dr., Gladwin 48624 (989) 329-0382. johnhamiltonusaf@hotmail.com

Hamlen, Geraldine Gayle –
[(FE) PE 2006; FE 2009] Gwinn 2006; **Iron Mountain: Trinity 2014**.<> 808 Carpenter Ave., Iron Mountain 49801 (906) 774-2545. Home: 421 Woodward, Kingsford 49802 (906) 774-0064. pastorimtrinity@gmail.com

*Hamlin, Frederick G. –
[(RE) D-1982; FE-1987; R-1994] Benton Harbor: Grace 1978-1982; Watervliet 11/20/1984; Byron Center 1985; Camden/Montgomery/Stokes Chapel 1987; Retired 1994; Saugatuck 1996-1998.<> Home: PO Box 458, Douglas 49406 (269) 543-4790. fredandjoan@frontier.com

*Hammar, Eric S. –
[(RE) T 1952; F 1955] 1953 Stephenson; 1957 White Pine; 1958 Ishpeming: Wesley; 1967 Farmington: Orchard; 1977 Saginaw Bay District Superintendent; 1983 Northville; **1991 Retired**.<> Home: 6356 Richalle, Brighton 48116 (810) 229-3367

*Hane, Paul E. (Julie Spurlin-Hane) –
[(RL) FL-2003; RL-2018] North Adams/Jerome (DSA) 2002; North Adams/Jerome 06/01/2003; Hesperia/ Ferry 2011; **Retired 2018**; Hesperia/Ferry (LTFT ½) 2018-Apr 26, 2020.<> Home: 14218 Wilson Dr, Plymouth 48170 (734) 233-7719. haulpane@yahoo.com

*Haney, Claudette I. Kerns –
[(RE) D-1991; FE-1993; R-2005] Harbor Springs/Alanson 1990; Homer/Lyon Lake 04/16/1993; Lawton/Almena 1995; Lawton 1996; Cassopolis 2000; Retired 2005.<> Home: 51 Las Yucas, Green Valley AZ 85614 (520) 829-6002. haney1@cox.net

*Hansen, Randall R. (Susan) –
[(RE) FE-1982; R-2014] Albion: First (Assoc) 1983-1985; Fennville/Pearl 07/16/1992; Transferred from Uruguay Evangelical Methodist Conf 1993; Fennville: Pearl 07/16/1992; Fennville/Pearl 1993; Muskegon: Central 2000; Montague 08/16/2009; Medical Leave 2014; Retired 10/20/2014.<> Home: 1319 Chicago Ave Unit #301, Evanston IL 60201 (847) 868-8029. rshansen50@hotmail.com

*Hansen, Ronald W. (Jan) –
[(RE) D-1977; FE-1980; R-2011] Fennville/Pearl 1978; Ovid United 02/01/1984; Leave of Absence 1993; Hartford 1999; Retired 2011; Kalamazoo: Northwest (LTFT ¼) 2012-2013; Portage First (Pathfinder) (LTFT ¾) 2015-2016.<> Home: 7615 Andrea Lane, Portage 49024 (269) 208-5410. revronhansen@gmail.com

*Hanson, Alan J. (Judy) –
[(RE) P 1970; F 1973] 1972 Marquette: First (assoc); 1973 Morenci; 1981 school; 1984 Associate Staff Counselor, Fayetteville Family Life Center, North Carolina Baptist Hospital; 1985 school; Aug 1986 Executive Director, Samaritan Counseling Center, Toledo OH; Sept 1, 2001 Macon; 2002 Bloomfield Hills: St. Paul; 2007 Wyandotte: First; **2013 Retired**.<> 802 Bailey Dr., Papillion NE 68046 (419) 377-6406. drajhanson@sbc-global.net [6/10/08]

Hansson, Emily K. [Slavicek] (Scott) –
[(FE) FL-2010; PE-2012; FE-2016] Girard 09/01/2010; Centreville 2014; Medical Leave 01/01/2019; **Personal Leave 2020**.<> Home: 705 E Osterhout Ave, Portage 49032 (269) 743-7487. pastor.emilysb@gmail.com

*Harbin, Kevin J. (Ellen) –
[(RE) P 1996; FE 1999; RE 2020] school (Asbury) 1996; Fairgrove, Gilford Jan 1, 1997; St. Charles, Brant 1999; Imlay City 2002; Swartz Creek 2011;**Fraser: Christ 2015; Retired Mar 27, 2020**.<> 16751 Braile St, Detroit 48219 810-790-9812. kevin-harbin8@gmail.com

Harmon, Scott A. (Bron) –
[(FE) P 1996; FE 1998] 1996 Iron Mountain: Trinity (assoc) (LTFT ¼); Quinnesec: First; 1998 Negaunee: Mitchell; 2002 Birmingham: First (assoc); 2003 Escanaba: Central; 2013 Frankenmuth; 2017 Marquette District Superintendent; **Jan 1, 2019 Northern Skies District Superintendent**.<> 927 W. Fair Avenue, Marquette 49855 (906) 228-4644. Home: 2916 Parkview, Marquette 49855 (906) 228-2976. sharmon@michiganumc.org

*Harnish, John "Jack" E. (Judy) –
[(RE) P W. PA, 1970; F 1973] 1974 Trans. to Detroit Conf, Washington, Davis; Dec 1979 Dexter; 1990 Flint: Court Street; July 1, 1993 General Board of Higher Education; 2000 Ann Arbor: First; 2005 Birmingham: First; **2013 Retired**.<> 7341 Deadstream Rd., Honor 49640 (231) 325-2948. jackharnish1@gmail.com

Harpole, Jason E. (Sharla) –
[(PL) PL-2014] Breedsville (PTLP ¼) 2014; Oshtemo: Lifespring (LTFT ¼) 2016.<> 1560 S 8th St, Kalamazoo 49009 (269) 353-1303. Home: 205 Amos Ave, Portage 49002 (269) 388-8312. PastorJHarpole@gmail.com

*Harpole, Patricia A. (Everett) –
[(RA) FL-1993; NL-1994; AM-2002; RA-2017] Brandywine Trinity 1993; LP w/o Appointment 04/17/1994; Transferred to Ohio Conf 01/01/1999; Transferred from Ohio Conf 05/01/2002; Townline/Breedsville 11/01/2002; Dowling: Country Chapel 2004; Oshtemo: Lifespring 2009; Indian River 2014; Retired 2017.<> Home: 2461 Bay Pointe, St Joseph 49085 (269) 806-2814. patti.harpole@gmail.com

Harriman, Mark A. (Karen) –
[(FL) PL Dec 1. 2014; FL 2018] Dec 1, 2014 Bethel (Worth Twp.); 2016 Bethel (Worth Twp.), Port Sanilac, Forester; **2018 Kingston**.<> PO Box 196, Kinston 48741 (989) 683-2832. Home: 3442 Washington St, Kingston 48741 (989) 683-2929. time691@hotmail.com

Harrington, Philip S. –
[(OE) OE 2019 Pacific Northwest Conference] **Glenn (LTFT ¼) 2019**.<> PO Box 46, 1391 Blue Star Hwy, Glenn 49416(269) 227-3930. Home: 1395 Blue Star Hwy, Glenn 49416(425) 495-6419. psharringtonnow@gmail.com

*Harrington, Sally K. –
[(OR) OR-2012] [South German Methodist Conf, RE] Galesburg (LTFT ½) 11/1/2010-2012; Sonoma/Newton (LTFT ½) 2012-2014; Newton 2014-03/31/2016.<> Home: 32 Spaulding Ave W, Battle Creek 49037 (269) 548-7803. RevSallyH@gmail.com

*Harris, Carolyn G. (Daniel) –
[(RL) PL 1995; RL 2013] June 1, 1995 Monroe: East Raisinville Frenchtown (co-pastor). 1998 Salem Grove (co-pastor); 2003 Salem Grove; **2013 Retired**.<> Home: 5229 W. Michigan Ave. #198, Ypsilanti 48197 (734) 528-9657. grannyharris@yahoo.com

*Harris, Daniel Wayne (Carolyn) –
[(RL) PL 1987] 1987 Monroe: East Raisinville; June 1, 1995 Monroe: East Raisinville Frenchtown (co-pastor). 1998 Salem Grove (co-pastor); **2003 Retired**.<> Home: 5229 W. Michigan Ave., #198, Ypsilanti 48197 (734) 528-9657. papaw@peoplepc.com

*Harris, Duane Marshall (Lynn) –
[(RE) P 1984; F 1988; R 2018] 1986 Sutton, Sunshine; Nov 1, 1988 Midland: First (assoc); 1997 Essexville; 2005 Owosso: First; 2009 Auburn; **2018 Retired**.<> Home: 213 Meadow Ln, Midland 48640 (989) 600-9150. dmh8181@gmail.com

*Harris, Hilda L. –
[(RE) SP 1992; P 1994; F 1996] 1992 River Rouge: John Wesley; 1993 Detroit: St. Timothy's; 1995 Southfield: Hope (assoc); 1997 Detroit: Calvary; **Sept 1, 2004 Retired**.<> Home: 12654 Santa Rosa, Detroit 48238 (313) 933-3342. divabish831@gmail.com

Harris, Peter Scouton (Jan) –
[(FE) P 1982; F 1987] 1984 Owosso: First (assoc); 1986 Flint: Eastwood; 1989 Lincoln Park: Dix; 1996 Stony Creek; **2007 Manchester: Sharon**.<> Box 543, 19980 Pleasant Lake Rd., Manchester 48158 (734) 428-0996. Home: 16181 Wellwood Ct., Tipton 49287 (517) 431-3908. revpharris@aol.com

*Hart, Caroline F. (James) –
[(RE) PE 1999; FE 2002; RE 2018] 1999 Warren: First (assoc); 2008 Coleman: Faith; **2015** Gladstone: Memorial; **2018 Retired**.<> Home: 3542 Madison Ave, Orion Twp 48359 (586) 899-6421. revchart@me.com

Hart, Daniel "JC" Joseph Charnley (Autumn) –
[(FE) PE 2012; FE 2015] 2012 Grosse Pointe (assoc); Apr 1, 2016 Birmingham: First (assoc); **2019 Mt. Clemens: First**.<> 57 SB Gratiot Ave, Mt Clemens 48043 (586) 468-6464. Home: 110 Belleview St., Mt. Clemens 48043 (586) 863-3646. daniel.hart@garrett.edu

*Hart, Pauline Sue (Thomas) –
[(RE) P 1983; F 1986] 1984 Detroit: Waterman-Preston; 1989 Bloomfield Hills: St. Paul; 1995 South Lyon: First (co-pastor); 2002 disability leave; **2008 Retired**.<> Home: 302 Wellington Dr. South Lyon 48178 (248) 437-1608. Harts1mi@sbcglobal.net

*Hart, Thomas Everett (Pauline) –
[(RE) T Balt Conf, 1967; F 1970] Nov 1970 Trans. to Detroit Conf, Livingston Circuit: Plainfield, Trinity; 1975 Vernon, Bancroft; Sept 1980 Manchester; 1984 West Bloomfield; 1991 Detroit: St. Timothy's; 1995 South Lyon: First (Co-pastor); **Sept 1, 2002 Retired**.<> Home: 302 Wellington Dr. South Lyon 48178 (248) 437-1608. harts1mi@sbcglobal.net

Hart, Wilson Andrew (F. Caroline) –
[(FE) PE 1992; FE 1995; HL 2009; FE 2014] Lake Orion (assoc) 1993; Mackinaw City: Church of the Straits May 1, 1996; Millington 2001; leave of absence 2006; Honorable Location 2009; Adrian: First 2014; **Port Huron: First 2020**.<> 828 Lapeer Ave, Port Huron 48060 (810) 985-8107. Home: 3014 E. Woodland Dr., Port Huron 48060 (734) 904-9775. revdrewhart@gmail.com

Hartley, Thomas C., Sr. –
[(OF) DSA 2018, Presbyterian Church USA OF 2019] Davisburg (DSA) (LTFT ¼) 2018; **Davisburg 2019**.<> 803 Broadway, Davisburg 48350 (248) 634-3373. Home: 711 Oxhill Dr, White Lake 48386 (248) 698-4502

*Harton, Patricia A. (Bruce) –
[(RL) PL Feb 1, 2006] Mt. Bethel Feb 1, 2006; **Retired 2010**.<> Home: 10415 Lee Ann Ct., Brighton 48114 (810) 588-6303. pbharton@comcast.net

*Harvey, Howard –
[(RL) PL-1983; NL-2000; DSA-2015; PL-2017; RL 2020] South Wyoming 1982-1988; Fenwick/Palo/Vickeryville 1991; Sand Lake/South Ensley 1996; Marion/Cadillac South Community 1999; LP w/o Appointment Aug 21, 2000; Kewadin (DSA) (¼ time) 2015; **Kewadin (PTLP ¼) Jan 1, 2017; Retired 2020, still serving Kewadin.**<> PO Box 277, Kewadin 49648 (231) 264-9640. Home: 701 Chippewa St Apt 6, Elk Rapids 49629 (231) 709-5481. kewadinumc@elkrapidsnet.com

*Harvey, Robert Dale (Ruth Ann) –
[(RE) SP 1990; P 1993; F 1996] Caring Covenant Group Ministry: Richfield, Otter Lake 1990; Bay City: Fremont Avenue July 1, 1994; **Retired 1999.**<> Home: 12 Sovey Court, Essexville 48732 (989) 891-9335

*Hasley, Lynn Marie (Gary) –
[(RE) PE 2004; FE 2008] 2004 Birmingham: First (assoc); Oct 1, 2008 Eastpointe: Immanuel; Jan 9, 2012 Sabbatical leave; Jan 1, 2013 Farmington: Orchard (assoc); 2013 Franklin: Community; **2016 Retired.**<> Home: 6690 West Ridge Drive., Brighton 48116 (248) 227-6119. lynnhasley@gmail.com

Hasse, Doug E. –
[(PL) PI Jan 1, 2019] Sept 1, 2017 Wagarville: Community (DSA); **Jan 1, 2019 Gladwin: Wagarville Community (LTFT ¼).**<> 2478 Wagarville Rd, Gladwin 48624 (989) 426-2971. Home: 5943 Weiss St, # 58, Saginaw 48603 (989) 598-0716. dshasse@aol.com

*Hastings, Robert Curtis (Phyllis) –
[(RE) T 1965; F 1967] 1965 Grosse Pointe (assoc); 1967 Flint: Graham, Dimond; 1968 Highland Park: St. Paul's; 1970 Centerline; Apr 1975 Essexville: St. Luke's; 1980 Saginaw: Kochville; 1983 Hazel Park; Aug 1, 1987 Sabbatical Leave; Aug 1, 1988 Dearborn Heights: Stephens; 1994 Saginaw: Jefferson Avenue; **2004 Retired.**<> Home: 1441 Cedar St, Saginaw 48601 (989) 777-2365. Hastybob@concentric.net

*Hastings, Timothy Stewart (Deborah) –
[(RE) P 1980; F 1982] 1980 Saginaw: First (assoc); 1983 Manistique; 1986 Pigeon: Salem; 1990 Saginaw: Ames (assoc); Sept 1, 1993 leave of absence; Sept 1, 1994 school; 1996 Chaplain: St. Luke's Hospital (Saginaw); Dec 1, 1997 LaPorte, Mapleton; Sept 1, 2000 LaPorte, Mapleton (LTFT ¾); Dec 1, 2003 Mapleton; 2004 Chaplain, St. Mary's of Michigan, Saginaw; **2012 Retired.**<> Home: 1908 Stark St., Saginaw 48602 (989) 752-7898. Thastings@stmarysofmichigan.org

*Hausermann, Carl L. (Marcia) –
[(RE) D-1964; FE-1967; R-2001] Galien 1964; Grand Rapids: First (Assoc) 1967; Coloma/Riverside 1971; Ionia: First 1977; Jackson Calvary 1983; Portage: Chapel Hill 1989; Retired 2001.<> Home: 1551 Franklin Street SE, Apt 2814, Grand Rapids 49506. clhauser@charter.net

*Hawkins, Ronda L. –
[(RE) P 1995; F 1997] 1995 Hardy; June 1, 2000 incapacity leave; **2014 Retired.**<> 1223 Mountain Ash Dr., Brighton (810) 220-5854. revronda@beeeky.com

*Hawley, Wayne Alton (Pamela) –
[(RE) P 1977; F 1979 (E. PA. Conf)]; Tans. to Detroit Conf from E. PA, Harbor Beach, Port Hope 1983; 1991 North Lake; 2001 Ida, Samaria: Grace; **2007 Retired.**<> 401 N. Hill St, Burnet TX 78611 (830) 637-9132. whawley@austin.rr.com

*Hayes, Geoffrey L. (Pamela) –
[(RE) D-1970; FE-1974; R-2009] Grand Rapids: First (Assoc) 1973; Lansing: Asbury 1978; Stevensville 1987; Surrender of Credentials 03/23/1994; Re-admitted 1998; Grand Rapids: Faith 1998; Retired 2009.<> Home: 112 Woodruff Ct, Cary NC 27518 (919) 233-6950. geoffhayes@att.net

*Hayes, Stanley L. (Joyce) –
[(RE) D-1963; FE-1965; R-1999] Leaton 1959; Grand Traverse Larger Parish 1964; Kingsley Circuit 1965; East Jordan 10/15/1966; Cedar Springs 1970; Cedar Springs/East Nelson 1972; Evart/ Avondale 10/15/1975; Fennville/Pearl 04/01/1984; Breckenridge 1990; Grass Lake 1994; Retired 1999; Kalkaska 10/01/1999; Old Mission Peninsula (Ogdensburg) 2002.<> Home: PO Box 67, 316 N Main St, Fife Lake 49633 (231) 879-3884. sjhayes239@charter.net

*Haynes, Gloria –
[(RE) P 1990; F 1993] 1991 Port Sanilac, Forester, McGregor; 1996 Brown City: First, Immanuel; Jan 1, 1997 Brown City; Oct 1, 1998 South Central Cooperative Ministry: Lake Fenton (parish director); 2002 Thomas, Lakeville; 2005 Lapeer: Trinity (assoc); 2009 Pigeon: Salem; 2012 Riverview; Feb 15, 2014 Riverview (LTFT ¾), Melvindale: New Hope (LTFT ¼); **2015 Retired; 2018 Arbela (LTFT ¼).**<> 8496 Barnes Rd, PO Box 252, Millington 48746 (989) 793-5880. Home: 2152 Village West Dr., S, Lapeer 48466. glorev0070@gmail.com

*Haynes, Leonard B. (Birute) –
[(RE) D-1970; FE-1973; R-1998] Riverside 1970; Kingscreek 1972; Appointed to Extension Ministries (¶344.1b,c) Pine Rest Christian Hospital 1975; Appointed to Extension Ministries (¶344.1b,c) Bethesda Hospital 1976; Transferred from West Ohio Conf 1979; Appointed to Extension Ministries (¶344.1b,c) Chaplain, Director of Pastoral Care, Bronson Methodist Hospital 1979; Leave of Absence 03/24/1983-06/15/1983; Hinchman/ Oronoko 1983; Shepherd/Pleasant Valley 1986; Calvary Lansing 1992; Leave of Absence 03/01/1998; Retired 1998.<> Home: 13630 W Meath Dr, Homer Glen IL 60491 (708) 828-7653. Truckermanlen@comcast.net

*Hazle, Judith A. (Stuart) –
[(RL) LM-2009; PL-2012; RL-2020] Shepardsville (CLM ¼ Time) 08/01/2009; Shepardsville (PTLP ¼) 11/10/2012; **Retired 2020.**<> Home: 1795 W Centerline Rd, St Johns 48879 (989) 640-1436. pastorjudy777@gmail.com

*Heaton, Lyle D. (Sylvia) –
[(RE) D-1978; FE-1982; R-2016] Barryton 1979; Barryton/Chippewa Lake 1980; Middleton/Maple Rapids 1984; Delta Mills 1990; Wacousta Community 01/01/1999; Lansing: Christ 2013; Mulliken/Sunfield 01/01/2016; Retired 2016.<> Home: 4747 W Stoll Rd, Lansing 48906 (517) 580-5058. lyledheaton@gmail.com

*Heffelfinger, Constance L. (Randy Wedeven) –
[(RE) D-1976; FE-1980; R-2016] Transferred from East Ohio Conf 1977; Fremont (Assoc) 1978; Barry County: Woodland/Hastings: Welcome Corners 1981; Saugatuck/Ganges 1984; Saugatuck (LTFT ½) 01/01/1990; Medical Leave 09/01/1995; Retired 2016.<> Home: 199 W 20th St, Holland 49423 (616) 393-0919. constance.heffelfinger@gmail.com

*Heifner, Keith W. (Becky) –

[(RE) D-1971; FE-1973; R-2006] Maplewood 1977; Transferred from Missouri East Conf 1980; Appointed to Extension Ministries (¶344.1b,c) Counselor, Samaritan Counseling Center Ad Interim 1980; Appointed to Extension Ministries (¶344.1b,c) Pastoral Counselor, Samaritan Counseling Center, Battle Creek 1981; Appointed to Extension Ministries (¶344.1b,c) Director, Samaritan Center of South Central MI, Battle Creek 1986; Appointed to Extension Ministries (¶344.1b,c) Pastoral Counselor, Battle Creek Pastoral Counseling 01/01/1990; Big Rapids: First 1993; Marshall 1996; Parma/North Parma 1999; Galesburg 2003; Retired 2006.<> Summer: 3164 Brimstead Dr, Franklin TN 37064. Home: 4985 Sandra Bay Dr Apt 101, Naples FL 34109 (239) 287-0828. Heifskb@yahoo.com

Heisler, Benton R. (Linda) –

[(FE) D-1985; FE-1988] St Joseph First (Assoc) 1986; Charlevoix/Greensky Hill 08/16/1988; Lansing: Asbury 11/16/1992; Mt Pleasant: First 1997; District Superintendent, Lansing District 2002; Director of Connectional Ministries, West MI Conf 01/01/2009 and Detroit Conf 02/01/2018; Director of Connectional Ministries, Michigan Conference 01/01/2019.<> 1011 Northcrest Rd, Lansing 48906 (517) 347-4030. Home: 106 S Whittemore, St. Johns 48879. etnagreen@sbcglobal.net

Heller, Virginia L. –

[(FE) D-1996; FE-1999] Muskegon: Central (Assoc) 1996; Keeler/Silver Creek 1998; Battle Creek Baseline/Bellevue 2004; Portage: Chapel Hill (Assoc) 2011; Leland 2013; South Haven: First 2014; Grand Rapids: St. Paul's 2018.<> 3334 Breton Rd SE, Grand Rapids 49512 (616) 949-0880. Home: 3509 Bromley SE, Kentwood 49512 (269) 274-9416. pastorgini54@yahoo.com

Henderson, Joshua (Emily) –

[(OF) OF-2016] NE Missaukee Parish: Merritt-Butterfield (LTFT ½) and Moorestown-Stittsville (LTFT ½) 09/01/2016; NE Missaukee Parish: Merritt-Butterfield and Moorestown-Stittsville 01/01/2017-07/31/2019

*Henning, Robert James (Barbara) –

[(RE) P 1985; F 1988] 1985 Trans. to Detroit Conf from Free Methodist Church, New Lothrop, Juddville; July 2, 1990 Assistant Coordinator of Prison Education Program and Assistant Professor of Interdisciplinary Studies, Spring Arbor College; 1996 Stockbridge (W MI Conference); 2007 Ludington: St. Paul (W MI conference) (para 337.1); **2011 Retired**.<> 140 Morgan St., Oberlin OH

*Henry, John R. (Robin) –

[(RE) P W. OH, 1973; F 1976] 1975 Trans. to Detroit Conf, Stephenson, Hermansville; Mar 1981 L'Anse, Sidnaw, Zeba; 1986 Canton: Cherry Hill; 1988 Alaska Missionary Conference, Fairbanks AK: St. Paul's; 1989 Pastor-Missionary, East Anchorage UMC; 1997 North Star UMC; 2004 L'Anse, Sidnaw, Zeba; **2011 Retired**.<>14876 State Hwy. M-38 Pelkie 49958 (906) 338-2430. outreach@up.net

*Hepner, Theodore Warren –
[(RE) P 1962; F 1965] 1965 Detroit: Trinity; 1968 Chaplain, Army, US Army Garrison, Fort Riley, Kansas; 1969 Chaplain, Vicenze, Italy; 1973 H.Q. John F. Kennedy Center for Military Assistance, Fort Bragg NC; 1974 HW 7th Special Forces Group (ABN), Fort Bragg NC; 1975 US Army Chaplain (Colonel) 82D Airborne Division, Fort Bragg NC; Aug 1987 Stuttgart, Germany, Greater Stuttgart Military Command; 1990 Office of the Command Chaplain; 1992 Director of Endorsement & Administration; 1996 Section of Chaplains & Related Ministries; **2002 Retired**.<> Home: 1015 Wyndham Hill Lane, Franklin TN 37064 (615) 791-5887. BaronTed@aol.com

Herald, Scott A. –
[(FL) FL 2017] **Fowlerville: First 2016**.<> 201 S. Second, Box 344, Fowlerville 48836 (517) 223-8824. Home: 18521 Daymon Dr., Gregory 48137 (734) 545-2276

*Herm, Trevor Allen (Carol) –
[(RE) P 1984; F 1988; RE 2020] Port Huron: First (assoc) Jan 1, 1986; Yale, Greenwood 1989; Burton: Christ 1994; Richmond: First 2004; Cheboygan: St Paul's 2010; Romeo 2017; **Retired 2020**.<> Home: 242 Chippendale Dr, Houghton Lake 48629 (810) 275-3277. hermtrevor@gmail.com

Herman, Marvin L. –
[(FL) PL 2007; FL 2018] Flint: Bristol (LTFT ½) Oct 1, 2007; **Howarth, Paint Creek 2018**.<> (H) 550 E. Silverbell Rd., Lake Orion 48360 (248) 373-2360. (PC) 4420 Collins Rd., Rochester 48306 (248) 652-1583. Home: 137 Stratford Ln, Lake Orion 48362. Hmarvherman@aol.com

Herrell, Devon R. –
[(FE) PE-2005; FE-2008] Traverse Bay (Assoc) 2005; Lake Ann 06/15/2008; South Haven: First 2013; UM Connectional Structures (¶344.1a,c) Director, Wesley Foundation, Ferris State University 2014; UM Connectional Structures (¶344.1a,c) Director, Wesley Foundation, Ferris State University (LTFT ½) 2014 and Big Rapids: Third Ave/Paris/Rodney (LTFT ½) 2017; Big Rapids: First 2019; **Personal Leave 2020**.<> Home: (231) 649-2302. devonherrell@gmail.com

*Hertel, William A. (Janet) –
[(RE) D-1963; FE-1966; R-2001] Allen 1961; Niles (Assoc) 1964; White Cloud/East Denver 1966; White Cloud 1968; Grand Rapids: Saint Paul's 1969; Lake Odessa: Central 1974; Traverse City: Asbury 09/16/1980; Lansing: Asbury 1987; Delton: Faith 1990; Retired 2001.<> Home: 858 Pine Grove Ave, Traverse City 49686 (931) 260-7697. wjhertel@gmail.com

Heystek, Travis (Hannah) –
[(OF) OF-2018] Harrietta 2018; Cadillac (assoc) 2018.<> (H) 116 N Davis St, PO Box 13, Harrietta 49638 (231) 389-0267. (C) 1020 E Division St, PO Box 37, Cadillac 49601 (231) 775-5362. Home: 210 Blodgett St, Cadillac 49601 (540) 819-5712. travis.heystek@gmail.com

Hice, John H. (Laura) –
[(FE) P 1976; F 1980 W.MI] 1977 Kalamazoo: Millwood (assoc); 1978 trans. to W. MI. conf; 1979 Hartford; 1987 Traverse City: Asbury; 1995 Grand Rapids District Superintendent; 2000 transf to Detroit Conf, Northville: First; 2008 Royal Oak: First; **2016 Crossroads District Superintendent; Jan 1, 2019 East Winds District Superintendent**.<> 624 W Nepessing, Ste 201, Lapeer 48446 (810) 396-1362. Home: 5420 Misty Creek Court, Flint 48532 (810) 820-9545. jhice@michiganumc.org

*Hickey, Timothy Roy (Betty Lou) –
[(RE) T 1960; F 1962] 1960 Sandhill Circuit, Jackson Springs NC; 1962 Saginaw: Jefferson Avenue; 1964 school; 1965 Ypsilanti: First (assoc); 1967 Waterford: Trinity; 1969 Birmingham: Embury; 1973 Rochester: St. Paul's; **Oct 1, 2000 Retired**.<> Home: Hammock Dunes, 15 Avenue de la Mer #2505, Palm Coast FL 32137 (386) 447-1319. timandbettylou@gmail.com

*Hicks, Duane James (Susan) –
[(RE) P 1975; F 1980] 1978 Rochester: St. Paul's (assoc); 1981 Detroit: St. Andrew's; Jan 1, 1982 Centerline: Bethel; 1986 Detroit: Rice Memorial; 1990 school, Walden University, Minneapolis MN; 1991 Insight Recovery Center; 1995 Mental Health/Substance Abuse Therapist, Genesee Regional Medical Center; **1997 Retired**.<> Home: 8201 Sawgrass Trail, Grand Blanc 48439 (810) 695-2729

Hierholzer, Susanne E. (Craig) –
[(FE) PE 2013; FE 2016] 2013 St. Ignace; **2019 Birmingham: First (assoc)**.<> 1589 W Maple Rd, Birmingham 48009 (248) 646-1200. Home: 361 Pleasant St, Birmingham 48009. susiethepastor@yahoo.com

*Higgins, Howard (Elouise) –
[(RE)] Retired.<> Home: 107 Cedar Park Dr, Linn MO 65051

*Hill, Elizabeth A. (Richard) –
[(RE) PE 2006; FE 2009; RE 2020] Birmingham: Embury 2006; Royal Oak: St. John's 2006; Gladstone: Memorial 2010; Blue Water District Superintendent 2015; Ann Arbor District Superintendent 2018; Heritage District Superintendent Jan 1, 2019; **Retired 2020**.<> Home: 4176 Oxford Dr, Leland 49654 . revelizabethhill@gmail.com

Hills, David F. (Claire) –
[(FE) D-1992; FE-1994] Big Rapids: Third Avenue/Paris/ Rodney 1992; Climax/Scotts 1994; Coloma/ Watervliet 08/01/1999; Delton: Faith 2007; UM Connectional Structures (¶344.1a,c) District Superintendent, Heartland District 2010; Stevensville 08/01/2015.<> 5506 Ridge Rd, Stevensville 49127 (269) 429-5911. Home: 1418 Lake Blvd #1, St. Joseph 49085 (989) 330-3730. dfhills@gmail.com

*Hiner, Catherine Wanita Jean –
[(RA) PL 1991; FL 1994; Deacon, AM 1998] 1991 Ubly; 1993 Memphis: First, Lamb; 1999 Eastern Thumb Cooperative Parish, Port Sanilac, Deckerville, (Parish Director); 2004 Jeddo, Buel; **2009 Retired**.<> Home: 870 Marseilles, Upper Sandusky OH 43351 (419) 429-9909. umcrev@yahoo.com

*Hinkle, John W. (Ginger) –
[(RE) T W. OH, 1959; F W. OH, 1962] 1958 Donnelsville, Pitchin Charge; 1960 Springfield: Northridge; 1962 West Unity; 1967 Norwood: First; 1972 Toledo: St. Paul's; 1977 Leave of Absence; 1978 Trans. to Detroit Conf, Detroit: St. Timothy's (assoc); 1981 Flat Rock: First; 1989 Saginaw: Ames; 1994 Saline: First; **1999 Retired**.<> Home: 1302 Catalani Lane, The Villages, Lady Lake FL 32162 (352) 750-0001. jwhinkle@aol.com

*Hinklin, Robert L. (Christine) –
[(RE) D-1963; FE-1966; R-2001] Jasper (EUB) 1966; Jasper/Weston 1968; Napoleon 1969; Grand Rapids Plainfield/Epworth 1972; Georgetown 02/01/1976; Lansing: Mount Hope 1984; Portage: First 03/01/1987; Grandville 1998; Retired 2001; Fennville/Pearl 2002.<> Home: 20131 Balleylee Ct, Estero FL 33928 (239) 719-0029. rhinklin@aol.com

Hintz, Christopher P. (Kristine) –
[(FE) PE 1997; FE 2000 (W. OH.). Trans to Detroit Conference 2016] 2014 Marquette: Grace, Skandia; **2016 Marquette: Hope**.<> 111 E. Ridge, Marquette 49855 (906) 225-1344. Home: 619 Mesnard, Marquette 49855 (906) 226-3683. chintz@mqthope.com

Hintz, Kristine Kim (Christopher) –
[(FE) P 1994; FE 1997; HL 2011; FE 2014] 1995 Brighton: First (assoc); 2000 family leave; 2003 Milan: Marble Memorial; Oct 1, 2007 leave of absence; 2011 Honorable Location; 2014 Marquette: First; **2016 Marquette: Hope**.<> 111 E. Ridge, Marquette 49855 (906) 225-1344. Home: 619 Mesnard, Marquette 49855 (906) 226-3683. khintz@mqthope.com

Hitts, Randall J. (Susan) –
[(PL) DSA-2016; CC-2017; PL-2017] Harbor Springs/Alanson (DSA Co-Pastor) 2016; Charlevoix (PTLP ½ Time) 2017.<> 104 State St, Charlevoix 49720 (231) 547-2654. Home: 1206 State St, Charlevoix 49720 (231) 622-3565. rjhitts@aol.com

Hitts, Susan E. (Randall) –
[(PE) DSA-2016; CC-2017; FL-2017; PE 2020] Harbor Springs/Alanson (DSA Co-Pastor) 2016; Harbor Springs/Alanson 2017 (Alanson merged w/ Harbor Springs 1/1/2020).<> 343 E Main St, Harbor Springs 49740 (231) 526-2414. Home: 1881 Ellinger Rd, Alanson 49706 (231) 548-5774. missburtlake@aol.com

Hodge, James E. (Kathleen) –
[(FE) D-1984; FE-1986] Somerset Center/Moscow Plains 1984; Bangor: Simpson 1989; Bangor: Simpson/ Breedsville 1990; Shelby 1994; Grandville (Assoc) 2001; Caledonia 2005; Voluntary Leave Of Absence 2012; Grand Rapids: Aldersgate 2013.<> 4301 Ambrose Ave NE, Grand Rapids 49525 (616) 363-3446. Home: 5160 Windcrest Ct SW, Wyoming 49418 (616) 308-9925. contemporaryjim@gmail.com

*Hodge, Lawrence E. (Ruth) –
[(RE) D-1965; FE-1966; R-2000] Bloomingdale/Townline 1960; Keeler 1963; Elk Lake Parish 1966; Muskegon: Central (Assoc) 11/01/1968; Battle Creek: Birchwood 1971; Muskegon: Crestwood 1980; Hillside 1983; Ionia: First 1991; Retired 2000.<> Home: 9947 Huntington Rd, Battle Creek 49017 (269) 969-9483

*Hodges, Jacque (Clifford) –
[(RL) PL Dec 2012] Dec 1, 2011 Port Huron: New Beginnings; 2014 Mt. Vernon; Lakeville; **2017 Retired**.<> Home: 3494 Serenade Cmns NW, Kennesaw GA 30152 (586) 786-4909. nomadgm@aol.com

Hodgeson, Richard J. –
[(FL) FL Nov 21, 2013] Saginaw: Kochville, Mapleton Nov 21, 2013; **Scottville 2017**.<> 114 W State St, Scottville 49454 (231) 757-3567. Home: 301 W Maple Ave, Scottville 49454 (231) 757-4781. richard.hodgeson@aol.com

*Hoekwater, Harris J. (Jane) –
[(RE) FD-1980; FE-1985; R-2018] Perry/Shaftsburg 1983; Sunfield 01/15/1992; Concord 1998; Pentwater: Centenary 2006; St Joseph: First 2012; Retired 2018.<> Home: 2515 Tower Rd, Vanderbilt 49795 (269) 932-5390. hoekster73@yahoo.com

Hoffmeyer, Thomas Leo –
[(OE) OE Indian Conf Apr 1, 2019] Roscommon: Good Shepherd of the North Apr 1, 2019.<> 149 W Robinson Lake Rd, Roscommon 48653 (989) 275-5577 Home: 303 Rising Fawn, Roscommon 48653 (989) 821-6056

Hofmann, Daniel B. (Mary) –
[(FE) D-1993; FE-1996] Appointed in Other Annual Conferences (¶426.1) Ithaca, Arcanum OH, West Ohio Conf (LTFT ¾) 1993; Ravenna 1994; Delton: Faith 2001; Eaton Rapids: First 2007; Leland 2014.<> PO Box 602, 106 N 4th St, Leland 49654 (231) 256-9161. Home: PO Box 1134, 4840 Golfview Dr, Leland 49654 (231) 994-2159. rotsap@lelandcumc.com

Hofmann, Mary Wava (Daniel) –
[(PL) PL-Feb 1, 2020] Northport Indian Mission (DSA) (½ time) 4/1/2019; **Northport Indian Mission (PTLP ½) Feb 1, 2020.**<> 8626 N Manitou Trl, PO Box 401, Northport 49670 (231) 715-1280. Home: PO Box 1134, 4840 Golfview Dr, Leland 49654 (231) 994-2159. mwavahofmann@gmail.com

*Holdsworth, Jacqueline Elaine –
[(RE) P 1981; F 1983] 1981 Port Huron: First (assoc); 1983 Allen Park: Trinity; 1991 Ann Arbor: West Side (assoc)/Dexter (assoc); Sept 1, 1992 Ann Arbor: West Side (assoc); 1995 Monroe: St. Paul's (co-pastor) 2003 Monroe: St. Paul's; 2004 Novi; Mar 1, 2007 incapacity leave; **May 1, 2011 Retired.**<> Home: 901 Gadwall Way, Chelsea 48118 (517) 917-4089. jackieholdsworth@gmail.com

Hood, Anthony R. –
[(FE) FL 1999; PE 2001; FE 2004] Southfield: Hope (assoc) Oct 1, 1999; Highland Park: Berea-St. Paul 2002; Detroit: Scott Memorial 2005; **Farmington: First 2016.**<> 33112 Grand River, Farmington 48326 (248) 474-6573. Home: 25766 Livingston Circle, Farmington Hills 48335 (248) 474-7568. drarhood@yahoo.com

Hook, Matthew James (Leigh) –
[(FE) P 1994; F 1996] Christ UMC, Memphis TN 1994; Birmingham: First (assoc) Aug 16, 1995; school (Beeson Program, Asbury Theological Seminary) 2002; **Dexter 2003** [Ann Arbor: Calvary merged w/ Dexter 7/1/2020].<> 7643 Huron River Dr., Dexter 48130 (734) 426-8480. Home: 7605 Grand Ave., Dexter 48130 (734) 426-8420. matt@dexterumc.org

Hoppenworth, Patricia Ann (Chris) –
[(FL) FL Dec 1, 2002] Dec 1, 2002 Marine City; Jan 1, 2005 Marine City (LTFT ¾); Jan 1, 2008 Marine City (LTFT ½); **2008 Dryden, Leonard.**<> (D) 5400 W. Main St., Box 98, Dryden 48428 (810) 796-3341. (L) 245 E. Elmwood, Box 9, Leonard 48367 (248) 628-7983. Home: 1421 Poplar LL, Port Huron 48060 (810) 734 1171. revhopp@gmail.com

Hopkins, Naylo T. –
[(FL) NL 2016; FL May 1, 2020] **Lansing: Central 2020.**<> 215 N Capitol Ave, Lansing 48933 (517) 485-9477. Home: 2828 Woodview Dr, Lansing 48911 (734) 972-4334. pastornaylo@gmail.com

Horn, Ashlei Kristin –
[(PL) PL Jan 1, 2020] Bridgman: Faith (DSA) (¼ time) 10/28/2018; Bridgman: Faith (PTLP ¼) Jan 1, 2020; **Gobles (PTLP ½) 2020**.<> PO Box 57, 210 E Exchange St, Gobles 49055 (269) 628-2263. Home: 31880 Jefferson Ave, Gobles 49055 (269) 364-8545. AshleiUMC@yahoo.com

Horne, Maurice R., Sr. (Mae) –
[(FL) PL 1999; FL 2006] Eastside Covenant Cooperative Parish: Detroit: Mt. Hope 1999; Saginaw: Jefferson Avenue, Calvary 2004; Saginaw: Jefferson Avenue Jan 1, 2006; Flint: Lincoln Park 2009; Flint Mission Zone Minister of Outreach Jan 1, 2018; **Bloomfield Hills: St. Paul, Hazel Park 2020**.<> (BH) 165 E. Square Lake Rd., Bloomfield Hills 48302 (248) 338-8233. (HP) 315 E. Nine Mile Rd., Hazel Park 48030 (248) 546-5955. Home: 208 Barrington Rd., Bloomfield Hills 48302 (313) 550-5810. pastorhorne55@yahoo.com

*Hotelling, Dale A. (Beth) –
[(RL) FL-1996; PL-2005; FL-2008; PL-2011; NL-8/31/2012; RL-2019] Old Mission Peninsula (DSA) 1995; Old Mission Peninsula Ogdensburg 06/18/1996; Kalamazoo: First (Assoc) 07/16/2000; Not Appointed 2004; Um Connectional Structures (¶344.1A,C) Conference Ministry Consultant 01/01/2005; Muskegon: Crestwood 2008; Not Appointed 2010; White Pines New Church (LTFT ½) 2011; Not Appointed 08/31/2012; Retired 01/01/2019.<> Home: 3256 Dorais Dr NE, Grand Rapids 49525. dale.hotelling@gmail.com

*Hubley, Laurence E. –
[(RE) FE-1991; R-2002] Colon 11/01/1985, Transferred from Free Methodist 1991; Hillside 1991; Hastings: Hope 1995; Wolf Lake 2000; Medical Leave 2001; Retired 06/01/2002.<> Home: 17283 Rosy Mound Ln, Apt 315, Grand Haven 49417 (269) 501-6887. l_hubley@yahoo.com

*Huff, James E., Jr. (Darlene) –
[(RL) PL Jan 1, 2005; RL 2020] Memphis: First, Lamb Jan 1, 2005; **Retired 2020**.<> Home: 952 Liberty St, Algonac 48001 (248) 459-9625. huff11@aol.com

Huff, Mark W. (Aurora) –
[(PL) PL Nov 12, 2017] **Livingston Circuit: Plainfield, Trinity (LTFT ½) Nov 12, 2017**.<> (P) 17845 M-36, Gregory 48137 (517) 851-7651. (T) 8201 Iosco Rd., Fowlerville 48836 (517) 223-3803. Home: 8233 Iosco Rd., Fowlerville 48836 (248) 825-2887. mawihu11@aol.com

Huffman, Tracy Nichols (Robert) –
[(FE) P 1994; F 1997] 1995 Clarkston (assoc); 1999 Ann Arbor: West Side; 2013 Dearborn: First; 2018 Monroe: St. Paul's; **2019 Clergy Medical Leave ¶356**.<> Home: 400 Illinois Dr., Tecumseh 49286 (734) 276-3656. revtracyhuffman@gmail.com

Hughes, Robert M. (Becky) –
[(FE) PE-2006; FE-2009] Union City 2004; Reading 2012; Leave of Absence 07/13/2014; Allen 2015; Leave of Absence/Concord (DSA) (LTFT ½) 2016; Concord 2019.<> 119 S Main St, PO Box 366, Concord 49237 (517) 524-6156. Home: 361 Calhoun St, Union City 49094 (517) 677-6381. rhughes36@yahoo.com

*Huhtala, John Collins, Sr. (Karen) –
[(RE) T 1965; F 1968] 1968 Samaria; 1969 Manchester: Sharon (assoc); 1970 Hemlock, Nelson; Jan 1976 Marquette: First (assoc), Conf Staff, Marquette District Specialist; 1980 Sault Ste. Marie: Central, Algonquin; 1992 Port Huron: First; 1996 Flint District Superintendent; 2001 Director of Connectional Ministries; **2009 Retired**.<> Home: 819 St. Paul St., Marysville 48040 (810) 364-8485. jhuhtala2625@comcast.net

*Hulett, James R. (Linda) –
[(RE) D-1964; FE-1967; R-1998] Transferred from North Dakota Conf 1978; Lake Odessa: Lakewood 1978; Sparta 1985; Vicksburg 1998; Retired 1998.<> Home: 674 Gardenview Ct SW, Byron Center 49315. jcottage@localnet.com

Humenik, Julia R. –
[(PE) FL-2015; PE-2019] Schoolcraft/Pleasant Valley 2015.<> (S) PO Box 336, 342 N Grand Ave, Schoolcraft 49087 (269) 679-4845. (PV) PO Box 517, 9300 West XY Ave, Schoolcraft 49087 (269) 679-5352. Home: 318 Willow Ct, Schoolcraft 49087 (269) 679-4501. jrhumenik@gmail.com

Hundley, Robert L., Jr. (Ruth Pigeon) –
[(FE) PL-1980; D-1982; FE-1989] Center Eaton/Brookfield 1980; East Lansing: University (Assoc) 08/01/1982; Other Valid Ministries (¶344.1d) Director of Pastoral Care, Michigan Capital Medical Center 09/01/1990; Lansing: First 1996; Mason: First 2000; UM Connectional Structures (¶344.1a,c) District Superintendent, Lansing District 2009; Grand Rapids: First 2013.<> 227 Fulton St E, Grand Rapids 49503 (616) 451-2879. Home: 3035 Grenada Dr SE, Grand Rapids 49546 (616) 427-3749. bobh@grandrapidsfumc.org

*Hunter, Gerald Stanley (Tracey) –
[(RE) P 1989; F 1992] 1990 Denton: Faith; May 15, 1995 Leave of Absence; 1995 Pinconning; 1999 Hartland; Oct 2, 2000 General Board of Global Ministries: Field and Finance Representative (337.1); 2002 New Hudson; **Oct 15, 2015 Retired**.<> 10/01-10/30/2018 Grass Lake (LTFT ¼).<> Home: 11357 Weatherwax Dr., Jerome 49249 (517) 688-5323. boomerchinde@sbcglobal.net

Hurd, Elizabeth Ann –
[(PE) PE-2019] Caledonia 2019.<> 250 Vine St, Caledonia 49316 (616) 891-8669. Home: 260 Vine St, Caledonia 49316 (810) 488-6300. pastor.elizabeth@caledoniaumc.org

*Hurley, Joel W. (Donna) –
[(RE) F 1974] 1974 Trans. to Detroit Conf from Free Methodist; Aug 1974 Kingston, Deford; 1978 Elkton; 1983 Associate Director: Marquette District, Munising; 1986 Gladwin; 1992 Saginaw: Jefferson Avenue; 1994 Honorable Location; 1995 Roscommon: Good Shepherd of the North; **June 4, 1998 Retired**.<> Home: 6945 E. Main St., #1101, Mesa AZ 85207 (408) 982-0546. joelhccjl@gmail.com

*Hurst, David M. (Susan) –
[(RE) P, E. PA 1961; F, E. PA 1964] 1960 Landonburg PA; 1963 West Grover PA; 1967-70 Chaplain, Haverford State Hospital PA; 1980 Executive Director, Pastoral Care Services of Southeastern Michigan; Nov 1, 1983 Leave of Absence; 1986 Executive Director, Dearborn Pastoral Counseling Center; July 1, 1990 Hospital Chaplain, Supervisor of Programs in Clinical Pastoral Education, William Beaumont Hospital, Royal Oak; **1998 Retired**.<> Home: 2305 Pittsfield, Ann Arbor 48104 (734) 677-3612. dhurst@beaumonthospitals.com

Huseltine, David Earl (Elizabeth Deacon) –
[(FE) P 1986; F 1989] 1987 Melvindale: First; Nov 15, 1989 Melvindale: First, Detroit: Woodmere; 1990 Farmington: Orchard (assoc); 1994 Royal Oak: St. John's; 2001 Tawas; 2004 Flat Rock: First; Aug 1, 2008 Beverly Hills; 2010 Beverly Hills, Berkley: First; 2013 Troy: Big Beaver; **2016 Franklin Community**.<> 26425 Wellington, Franklin 48025 (248) 626-6606. Home: 2423 Ogden W., Farmington Hills 48323 (248) 761-4327. davidhuseltine@gmail.com

*Huston, Joseph D. –
[(RE) D-1970; FE-1973; R-2009] Camden Charge 09/01/1970; Concord 1972; Transferred to Detroit Conf 1975; Transferred from Detroit Conf 1977; Robbins/Grovenburg 10/15/1977; Grand Rapids: Saint Paul's 02/16/1982; Holt 1989; UM Connectional Structures (¶344.1a,c) District Superintendent, Central District 1999; Georgetown 2005; Lansing: Central 2007; Retired 2009; Dimondale (¼ Time)/Grovenburg (¼ Time) 2009; Dimondale (½ Time) 2017-Feb 1, 2019.<> Home: 3032 Kay Dr SE, Grand Rapids 49508 (517) 646-6530. jdhuston56@gmail.com

*Hutchinson, Ronald Glenn (Tammy) –
[(RL) PL 1998; RL 2020] Silverwood 1998; Silverwood, North Branch (LTFT) Apr 16, 2008; **Retired 2020**.<> Home: 3049 Burnside Rd., North Branch 48461 (810) 614-7928. ronhutchinson50@aol.com

Hutchison, Suzanne L. (David) –
[(PE) FL 2014; PE 2020] Richmond: First 2014; **Plymouth: First (assoc) 2018**.<> 45201 N. Territorial, Plymouth 48170 (734) 453-5280. Home: 44698 Maidstone, Canton 48187 (810) 923-1649. suzy.hutchison@yahoo.com

Huvaere, Catherine (Cathi) M. –
[(FE) D-1996; FE-2002] Marne 1993; Grand Rapids: Aldersgate 02/01/2002; Grand Rapids: Saint Paul's 2005; Niles: Wesley 2012; Clio: Bethany 2017.<> PO Box 327, 353 E Vienna St, Clio 48420 (810) 686-5151. Home: 10480 Varna St, Clio 48420 (810) 550-2570. camahu93@gmail.com

*Huyck, Clare –
[(RL) FL-2007; RL-2015; RLA-2015; RL-2017] Perrinton / Pompeii / Middleton / North Star (DSA) 7/1/2007-11/10/2007; Perrinton / Pompeii / Middleton / North Star (DSA) 11/10/2007-2012; Sunfield / Sebewa Center 2012-2013; Sunfield / Mulliken 2013-2015; Retired 2015; Allen 2016-2017.<> Home: 6812 Cooper Rd, Jackson 49201 (517) 795-5465. pastorclare@gmail.com

*Hynes, James L. (Bernadine) –
[(RE) D-1966; FE-1968; R-2000] Transferred from Detroit Conf 1986; Wacousta Community 1986; Leave of Absence 1992; Nashville 1994; Retired 2000.<> Home: 1551 Franklin St SE Apt 3025, Grand Rapids 49506 (616) 943-0979. hyneshome@sbcglobal.net

Idsinga, Cydney M. –
[(FE) PE-2015; FE 2020] Girard 2014; Marne 2018.<> 14861 Washington, PO Box 85, Marne 49435 (616) 677-3957. Home: 14861 Washington, Marne 49435 (616) 677-3991. cydinga@gmail.com

Ilunga Ngoie, John Kabala (Gertrude M. Mukalay) –
[(OE) OE 2017, North Katanga Conf, Democratic Republic of Congo] **2018 Detroit: French (New Church Start) (LTFT ¼).**<> 1803 E 14 Mile Rd, Birmingham 48009. Home: 1858 Estates Dr, Detroit 48206 (517) 703-3035. johnkabala2008@yahoo.fr

*Ireson, Roger W. (Judy) –
[(RE) T 1963; F 1966] 1962 Putnamville IN; 1963 Zion IL, Assistant Pastor: Memorial Church; 1966 school (England); 1970 Franklin (assoc); 1975 Bloomfield Hills: St. Paul's; 1979 Detroit: St. Timothy's; Jan 1, 1988 General Secretary, Board of Higher Education and Ministry; **2001 Retired.**<> Home: 4200 Jackson Ave, Apt 4008, Austin TX 78731 (615) 207-3042. rwireson@aol.com

*Iris, Ronald Lewis Figgins (Carla) –
[(RE) P 1970; F 1974; RE-2006; AF-2013] 1970 Rushsylvania OH (W. OH); 1972 Hartland; 1975 Melvindale; 1980 Manchester: Sharon; 1983 Elkton; 1985 Millington, Arbela; Sept 1, 1991 Gwinn; 1995 Allen Park: Trinity; **2006 Retired;** 12/01/2013-2015 Crystal Valley/Walkerville (LTFT ¼).<> Home: 2774 W Victory Dr, Ludington 49431 (231) 843-8352. DRRoniris@aol.com

Irish, Dennis Eric (Sherri) –
[(FE) FL 1/1/04; PE 2008; FE 2011] Algonac: Trinity Jan 1, 2004; Algonac: Trinity, Marine City 2008; New Hope 2011; Brown City 2013; Yale, Cole, Melvin 2019; **Fraser: Christ Apr 1, 2020.**<> 34385 Garfield Rd, Fraser 48026 (586) 293-5340. Home: 34355 Garfield, Fraser 48026 (810) 300-3963. deirishman@yahoo.com

*Irish, Esther A. –
[(RL) PL 2008; FL 2017; RL 2020] Flint: Dimond 2008; Caring Covenant Group Ministry: Columbiaville 2013; **Retired 2020.**<> Home: 1108 Collins, Mt Morris 48458 (810) 241-6934. irishe67@yahoo.com

Ivanov, Mary LB (Ivan) –
[(FE) PE-2001; FE-2004] Ravenna 2001; Cedar Springs 2008; Muskegon: Lake Harbor 2014.<> 4861 Henry St, Muskegon 49441 (231) 798-2181. Home: 1322 Clayton Ave, Muskegon 49441 (231) 780-3951. mary_ivanov@hotmail.com

*Jackson, Andrew (Phyllis) –
[(RE) D-1997; FE-1999; R-2006] Grand Rapids: Saint Paul's (Assoc) (Part Time) 02/01/1987; Carlisle (Part Time) 1994; Carlisle 1997; Retired 2006; Carlisle (LTFT ½) 12/01/2009-2010; Alto/ Bowne Center (LTFT ¾) 2014-2016.<> Home: 978 Amber View Dr SW, Byron Center 49315 (616) 878-1284. chaplainjackson@comcast.net

*Jacobs, Charles Richard (Ann) –
[(RE) P 1967; F 1970] 1969 Ypsilanti: First (assoc); 1972 Davisburg; 1976 Harper Woods; 1980 Hancock; 1984 Novi; 1997 Howell: First; **2010 Retired.**<> Home: 115 Victoria Ct., St. Clair 48079 (810) 637-8166. ca.jacobs@comcast.net

*Jacobs, James Douglas (Joanna) –
[(RE) P W. PA, 19; F 1977] 1975 Trans. to Detroit Conf, Port Huron: First (assoc); Feb 1977 Brown City: First, Immanuel; 1980 Birch Run; 1989 Monroe: First; Sept 1, 1999 school; June 1, 2000 Director of Pastoral Care, Mercy Memorial Hospital System, Monroe; **2011 Retired.**<> Home: 1109 N. Roessler, Monroe 48162 (734) 384-0719. jdjacobs98@yahoo.com

*Jacques, Raymond Allen (Doris) –
[(RL) FL 1992] Mar 1, 1992 Port Austin, Pinnebog, Grindstone City; 1997 Sutton-Sunshine, Bethel, Akron; 2001 Midland: Homer; **2008 Retired**.<> Home: 384 W. Island Dr., Beaverton 48612 (989) 689-3489. paparay384@yahoo.com

Jaggers, Jeffrey Lee (Keri Lynn) –
[(FE) P 1988; F 1992] Jan 1, 1990 Port Huron: First (assoc); 1994 Snover: Heritage; 1998 Grayling: Michelson Memorial; 2004 Flushing; **2014 Fenton**.<> 119 S. Leroy St., Fenton 48430 (810) 629-2132. Home: 11310 Greenview, Fenton 48430 (810) 354-8463. revjagg@gmail.com

*James, James Price (Norma Jane) –
[(RE) P 1983; F 1986] 1984 Henderson, Chapin; May 1, 1989 Elkton; 1992 Reese, Watrousville; 1996 Lincoln Park: Dix; 2000 Lincoln Park: Dix, Taylor: West Mound; 2005 Caring Covenant Ministry: Otisville, West Forest; **2007 Retired**.<>. captjimjames@comcast.net

*Jaquette, Dale F. (Betty) –
[(RA) D-1986; AM-1986; RA-1992] Pompeii/Perrinton/North Star 08/16/1981; Reading 04/16/1990; Retired 1992.<> Home: 504 Palm Ave, Wildwood FL 34785 (352) 330-1670. betjaq@atlantic.net

*Jaquish, Jerry L. (Joy) –
[(RE) D-1981; FE-1984; R-2012] Epsilon/Levering 1981; Leave of Absence 1987; White Cloud 1988; Manistee 2002; Retired 2012.<> Home: PO Box 144, 956 N Thornapple Ave, White Cloud 49349 (231) 689-0079. jerryjaquish@yahoo.com

Jeffords, Nathan J. –
[(FL) FL 2012] 2012 Byron; 2016 Rose City: Trinity, Whittemore; **2019 Mayville**.<> 610 East Ohmer, PO Box 189, Mayville 48744 (989) 843-6151. Home: 860 E. Brown Rd., Mayville 48744 (989) 781-0860

*Jensen, Curtis Eugene (Anne) –
[(RE) D-1970; FE-1975; R-2010] Mt Pleasant: First (Assoc) 1972; Mancelona/Alba 1975; Berrien Springs 1983; Buchanan: First 1987; Pentwater: Centenary 01/16/1996; Lake Odessa: Lakewood 2001; Hillsdale: First 2003; Retired 2010.<> Home: 915 Meadowbrook Dr, Mt Pleasant 48858 (517) 425-1606. annecurtjensen@gmail.com

Jensen-Kinney, Karen L. (David Kinney) –
[(FL) FL-2015] Nashville / Vermontville (DSA) 2015; Nashville/Vermontville 12/01/2015; Nashville 2018.<> PO Box 370, 210 Washington St., Nashville 49073 (517) 852-2043. Home: 540 Chapel Dr, Nashville 49073 (517) 852-0685. karenkinney66@gmail.com

*Job, Loretta M. (Larry) –
[(RD) PD 2007; FD 2010; RD 2019] 2007 Brighton: First (deacon); 2018 Personal Leave of Absence; **2019 Retired**.<> Home: 208 Sisu Knoll, Brighton 48116 (810) 229-4604. loretta@brightonfumc.org

*John, Thomas H., Sr. (Phyllis) –
[(RL) FL-1998; RLA-2012-2015; RL-2012] Kewadin: Indian Mission 1998; Northport Indian Mission 2005; Retired 2012.<> Home: 313 Davis St. Apt. 1, Traverse City 49686 (231) 632-4920

*Johns, Carol J. –
[(RE) P 1970; F 1973] 1972 Saginaw: First (assoc); Oct 1978 Bay City: Christ; 1985 Owosso: First; 1996 Farmington: Orchard; **2015 Retired**.<>. Caroljohns@orchardumc.org

Johnson, Andrea L. –
[(FL) PL-2018; FL 2020] Battle Creek: Convis Union (LTFT ½) 01/01/2018; **Monroe: Calvary, Monroe: Faith 2020**.<> (MC) 790 Patterson Dr., Monroe 48161 (734) 242-0145. (MF) 312 Harrison, Monroe 48161 (734) 241-6070. Home: PO Box 1925, 577 Augusta Dr, Monroe 48161 (269) 317-1937. pastorandreajohnson@gmail.com

Johnson, Brian Keith (Jenny) –
[(FL) FL Jan 1, 2013] Jan 1, 2013 Bay Port Hays; **2016 Ortonville**.<> 93 Church St. Box 286, Ortonville 48462 (248) 627-3125. Home: 319 Sherman Ct., Ortonville 48462 (248) 627-3347. pastorbrian@ortonvilleumc.org

*Johnson, Deborah M. –
[(RE) D-1979; FE-1983; R-2014] Manton 1981; Marne 1985; Hudsonville, Organizing Pastor 09/01/1990; Lansing: Asbury 1997; Sturgis 2008; Retired 07/08/2014.<> Home: 22849 110th Ave, Tustin 49688 (231) 825-2580. debjohn386@aol.com

Johnson, Jan M. (James) –
[(FL) FL-2010] Appointed to Extension Ministries (¶344.1b,c) Chaplain, Mercy Health Partners 11/13/2010.<> PO Box 358, 1500 E Sherman Blvd, Muskegon 49443 (231) 672-3629. Home: 1541 Fifth St, Muskegon 49444 (231) 343-8268. johnjm@mercy-health.com

*Johnson, Jane Ellen (Charles) –
[(RE) FL-2000; PE-2001; FE-2005; R-2016] Farwell 2000; Lansing: Grace 01/01/2007; Retired 2016.<> Home: 4014 Grandview Terrace SW, Grandville 49418 (616) 259-9896. JaneEllen@hotmail.com

Johnson, Kenneth M. –
[(PL) PL 2018] **Detroit: St. Paul (LTFT ¼) 2018**.<> 8701 W 8 Mile Rd, Detroit 48228 (313) 342-4656. kennjohn07@yahoo.com

*Johnson, Mark G. (Johnie) –
[(RE) D-1983; FE-1985; R-2015] Fenwick/Palo/Vickeryville 03/16/1982; Lawrence 1986; Kent City: Chapel Hill 05/01/1991; Hillsdale: First 1996; Ionia Parish: LeValley/Berlin Center 2003; Bath/Gunnisonville 2007; Retired 2015; LeValley/Berlin Center 12/01/2016-2017; Breckenridge 2017-2019.<> PO Box 248, 125 3rd St, Breckenridge 48615 (989) 842-3632. Home: 2396 Houghton Hollow Dr, Lansing 48911 (517) 898-6960. mark123johnson@gmail.com

Johnson, Melody Pierce Hurley –
[(FE) P N. IL, 1974; F W. NC, 1976] 1974 school (Duke); 1975 school, C.P.E., NC Baptist Hospital; 1976 Haw River Parish (assoc); 1978 Greensboro: Morehead; 1984 Director of Religious Life, Epworth Heights; Sept 1, 1994 transf to Detroit Conf; Sept 1, 1994 Birmingham: First (assoc); 1998 Epworth Heights Assembly: Director of Religious Life (para. 335.1A), Epworth Heights Assembly, Ludington; **2002 Corporate Chaplain, Porter Hills Presbyterian Retirement Community**.<> 3600 Fulton St E, Grand Rapids 49546 (616) 954-1799. Home: 2018 N Cross Creek Ct SE, Grand Rapids 49508 (616) 682-0253. mjohnson@porterhills.org

Johnson, Nathaniel W. (Lisa) –

[(FE) D-1990; FE-1993] Transferred from North Indiana Conf 1991; Belding 1991; Vergennes 09/01/1996; Appointed to Extension Ministries (¶326.1,3) Pastoral Counselor, CPE, Bronson Methodist Hospital, Kalamazoo 2010; Leave of Absence 09/06/2011; Appointed to Extension Ministries (¶344.1d) Chaplain, Heartland Home Care And Hospice, Spiritual Care 10/04/2011; Other Valid Ministries (¶344.1d) Chaplain, Heartland Home Health Care & Hospice (LTFT ¾) and Other Valid Ministries (¶344.1d) Chaplain, Spectrum United Memorial Hospital, Greenville (LTFT ¼) 07/09/2012; Other Valid Ministries (¶344.1d) Chaplain, Pediatrics/NICU, Helen DeVos Children's Hospital, Grand Rapids 10/10/2012; Appointed to Extension Ministries (¶344.1b,c) Chaplain, Helen DeVos Children's Hospital & Spectrum Health United Hospital, Grand Rapids 2014; Appointed to Extension Ministries (¶344.1b,c) Manager of Pastoral Care & Bereavement for Spectrum Health System 10/16/2016; **Transitional Leave May 1, 2020.**<> Home: 2821 Boynton Ave NE, Ada 49301 (616) 710-9703. pastorthan@aol.com

*****Johnson, William C.** (Judy) –

[(RE) D-1972; FE-1975; R-2012] Jonesville/Allen 1974; Holland: First (Assoc) 1977; Grand Rapids: Aldersgate 1981; Marshall 1992; Wyoming Park 1996; **Retired 2012;** Courtland-Oakfield (LTFT 45%) 11/01/2016-2017; Cedar Springs (LTFT 45%) 01/01/2018-2020.<> Home: 4390 Summerlane Ave NE, Grand Rapids 49525 (616) 366-2421. bjinside@gmail.com

*****Johnston, David L.** (Ann Marie) –

[(RE) D-1975; FE-1976; RE-2009] Bellevue/Kalamo 1977, DeWitt Redeemer 05/01/1983; Lansing Grace 1985; Jackson Brookside 1992; Personal Leave 06/24/2005; Retired 2009.<> Home: 122 Bingham Dr, Brooklyn 48230 (517) 784-1346. johnston254@comcast.com

*****Johnston, Jack Edson** –

[(RE) P Neb., 1977; F Neb., 1979] 1977 Ogallola (assoc); 1978 Bradshaw, Lushton; 1981 Indianola, Garden Prairie; 1983 Springview, Long Pine; 1987 Eddyville, Oconto, Miller; 1989 Trans. to Detroit Conf, Lake Linden, Larium; 1992 Hillman, Spratt; Nov 1, 2005 leave of absence; 2006 Seven Churches United Group Ministry: Byron; 2010 Ossineke; **2012 Retired.**<> 11630 Alfred St, Atlanta 49709 (989) 727-8202

*****Johnston, Mark Gordon** (Jane Ann) –

[(RE) P 1978 W.MI; F 1982 W.MI] 1980 Ashley, Bannister; 1982 Camp Director, Judson Collins; 1983 Trans. to Detroit Conf, Director, Manager, Judson Collins Camp; Feb 1, 1996 Hudson: First; 2008 Chesaning: Trinity; **2012 Retired.**<> Home: 15950 Wellwood Rd., Tipton 49287 (989) 280-9188. mjohnston159@yahoo.com

Johnston, Martin A. –

[(FL) PL-2016; FL 2017] Frontier (DSA) 09/01/2017; Frontier (PTLP) 11/15/2016; Connections Cooperative Ministry: Webberville/Williamston: Crossroads 2017.<> (W) 4215 E Holt Rd, Webberville 48892 (517) 521-3631. (WC) 5491 Zimmer Rd, Williamston 48895 (517) 655-1466. Home: 120 E Beech St, Webberville 48892 (517) 521-3434. pastormartyj@yahoo.com

*Joiner, Donald Wesley (Catherine) –
[(RE) T 1968; F 1971] 1970 Melvindale; 1975 Flint: Atherton; Jan 1978 Staff Consultant, Evangelism and Stewardship; Nov 1, 1985 Gen. Bd. of Discipleship, Director of
Stewardship; Nov 1, 1999 Operations Officer and Director of Fund Development, Discipleship Ministries; **Apr 1, 2010 Retired**.<> Home: 1225 Chloe Dr., Gallatin TN 37066
(615) 206-8659

Jones, Carolyn –
[(FL) FL 2016; PL 2018; FL 2019] Nov 15, 2016 Howarth, Paint Creek; 2018 Dearborn
Heights: Stephens (LTFT ¾); Dec 1, 2018 Romulus: Community (LTFT ½), Dearborn
Heights: Stephens (LTFT ½); Jan 1, 2019 Romulus: Community (LTFT ½); **2019 Ro-
mulus: Community, Detroit: Resurrection**.<> (DR) 11160 Olive St, Romulus 48174
(734) 941-0736; (DR) 8150 Schaefer Hwy, Detroit 48228 (313-582-7011. Home: 2466
Edison, Detroit 48206 (313) 573-0043. jonescat1@juno.com

*Jones, Charles B. (Jewel) –
[(RL) FL 1986] 1986 Detroit: Resurrection; Oct 1, 1993 disability leave; **1997 Retired**.<> Home: 8367 Carlin, Detroit 48228 (313) 581-7147

*Jones, Margaret Zee (John "Jack") –
[(RE) PE-2002; FE-2005; R-2006] Other Valid Ministries (¶335.1.D) Chaplain and Bereavement Coordinator, McLaren-Ingham Visiting Nurse and Hospice Services
09/01/2002; Other Valid Ministries (¶335.1.D) Chaplain and Bereavement Coordinator,
McLaren-Ingham Visiting Nurse and Hospice Services and Retired (¶344.1.a)
06/24/2006.<> Home: 599 Pebblebrook Ln, East Lansing 48823 (517) 351-0728. mar-
garetzeejones@comcast.net

*Jones, Robert E. (Carol) –
[(RE) D-1970; FE-1973; R-2009] Frontier/Osseo 1971; Mendon 11/15/1973; Grand
Rapids: First (Assoc) 1978; Montague 1983; Lansing: Christ 1992; Big Rapids: First
1996; Scottville 2004; Retired 2009.<> Home: 5648 Nancy Dr SW, Wyoming 49418
(616) 719-3935. jonesr5648@gmail.com

Jones, Todd Wesley –
[(FL) FL 2017] **2016 North Lake**.<> 14111 North Territorial Rd., Chelsea 48118 (734)
475-7569. Home: 14130 Wagon Wheel Ct., Chelsea 48118 (734) 475-9348

Joslyn, Mona K. –
[(FE) D-1998; FE-2001] Nottawa (DSA) / Leonidas (DSA) 10/01/1994; Waterloo
First/Waterloo Village 08/01/1997; Bronson: First 1998; Galesburg 2006; Gull Lake
2010; Voluntary Personal Leave of Absence 2015; Bangor: Simpson 2016.<> 507 Joy
St, Bangor 49013 (269) 427-7725. Home: 28760 Hillside Dr, Bangor 49013 (269) 484-
4060. mojoslyn2@gmail.com

Jue, Jennifer J. (Erik Wong) –
[(FE) PE-2007; FE-2010] Napoleon 2007; Wayne First 2013; Oxford 2014; Oxford,
Thomas 2019; **Jackson: Brookside, Trinity, Calvary 2020**.<> (B) 4000 Francis, Jack-
son 49203 (517) 782-5167 (T) 1508 Greenwood Ave, Jackson 49203 (517) 782-7937.
(C) 925 Backus St, Jackson 49202 (517) 782-0543. Home: 217 Mohawk, Jackson
49203 (734) 272-1780. jenjue@prodigy.net

Jung, Gun Soo –
[(FE) Iowa Conf; transfer to Detroit Conf, 2016] Oct 1, 2013 Madison Heights: Korean First Central; 2018 Keweenaw Parish: Calumet, Mohawk-Ameek, Lake Linden; **2019 Blissfield: First**.<> 201 W. Adrian, Blissfield 49228 (517) 486-4040. Home: 403 Brenot Ct., Blissfield 49228 (515) 250-6456. gsj0925@yahoo.com

*Kadwell, Emmett H., Jr. (Mary) –
[(RE) D-1973; FE-1978; R-2011] Ashley/Bannister 1975; Empire 10/01/1978; Stanwood: Northland 1982; Lake Odessa: Central 1992; Niles: Wesley 01/01/2000; Reed City 2008; Retired 2011; Saugatuck (LTFT ¼) 09/01/2011-1/1/2020.<> PO Box 647, 250 Mason St, Saugatuck 49453 (269) 857-2295. Home: 2794 6th St, Shelbyville 49344 (231) 912-0806. pastor_emmett@yahoo.com

*Kail, Pamela Sue –
[(RE) P 1990; F 1993] 1991 Ravenna (W. MI Conf, under para. 426.1); July 1, 1994 school; 1995 Ironwood: Wesley, Wakefield; 1998 Dearborn: First (assoc); 2001 Ypsilanti: St. Matthew's; 2009 South Central Cooperative Ministry: Lake Fenton, Mt. Bethel; **2012 Retired**.<> Home: 601 Manor Dr, Albion 49224 (517) 680-0387. reverend2kail@yahoo.com

Kalajainen, Bradley P. (Colleen) –
[(FE) D-1982; FE-1984] Freeport/Middleville/Parmalee (Assoc) 01/01/1981; Freeport 1982; Grand Rapids: First (Assoc) 1985; Grand Rapids: Cornerstone 1990.<> 1675 84th St SE, Caledonia 49316 (616) 698-3170. Home: 7810 Golf Meadows Dr SE, Caledonia 49316 (616) 891-8443. BradK@cornerstonemi.org

Kalajainen, Rodney J. (Janet) –
[(FE) D-1979; FE-1981] St Johns Parish 1978; Shepardsville/Price 1978; Mt Pleasant: First (Assoc) 1981; Battle Creek: Birchwood 1984; DeWitt: Redeemer 1988.<> 13980 Schavey Rd, Dewitt 48820 (517) 669-3430. Home: 2155 Longwoods Dr, Dewitt 48820 (517) 669-9140. rod@dewittredeemer.org

*Kaliszewski, Charles R. –
[(OR) OR-2016] [East Ohio Conference] Pierson: Heritage 03/01/2016; Carson City 2016.<> PO Box 298, 119 E Elm St, Carson City 48811 (989) 584-3797. Home: 2816 Meadowwood St, Mt Pleasant 48858 (989) 317-8421. revchuckkal@hotmail.com

Kappler, Kris Stewart (Sarah) –
[(FE) FL 1991; P 1993; F 1995] 1991 Harbor Beach, Port Hope; 1997 Missionary, OMS International, Inc; **2018 Tawas**.<> 20 East M-55, Tawas City 48763 (989) 362-4288. Home: 801 W. Franklin St., Tawas City 48763 (859) 858-8233

*Karls, Mark A. (Sandy) –
[(RE) P 1979; F 1983] 1978 Norway, Faithorn; 1983 Pigeon: Salem; 1986 Wisner; 1997 Saginaw: Ames; **2014 Retired**.<> 74 W. Corral, Saginaw 48638 (989) 598-5438. pastorkarls@msn.com

Kasper, John G. (Deb) –
[(FE) FL-2000; PE-2005; FE-2008] Hersey (DSA) 08/01/1994; Hersey 1995; Galien/Olive Branch 2001; Dowagiac: First 2006; Clare 2013; **Central Bay District Superintendent 2020**.<> 3764 Fashion Square Blvd, Saginaw 48603 (989) 793-8838. Home: 6120 Londonberrie Midland 48640 (269) 228-0921. jkasper@michiganumc.org

Katzmark, Peggy A. –
[(FL) PL-2007; FL-2014] Omard 2007; Omard, Peck 2011; Robbins 2014; **Robbins, Brookfield Eaton 2020**.<> (R) 6419 Bunker Rd, Eaton Rapids 48827 (517) 663-5226. (BE) PO Box 430, 7681 Brookfield, Charlotte 48813 517-420-3903. Home: 827 S Waverly Rd, Eaton Rapids 48827 (517) 663-8417. pastorpeggy@robbinsumc.org

*Keef, Thomas Frank –
[(RE) P 1976; F 1978] 1977 Detroit: Aldersgate (assoc); 1980 Utica: Hope, New Haven: Faith; 1982 Utica: Hope, Mount Vernon; 1988 Burton: Christ; 1994 Millington, Arbela; Jan 1, 1996 Millington; 2001 Clawson; 2010 Richmond: First; **2014 Retired**.<> 12409 Pine Mesa, Canadian Lake 49346 (231) 972-5132. Keefguys@comcast.net

*Keefer, Derl G. –
[(OF) OF-2018] [Retired Chruch of Nazarene] Three Rivers: First (LTFT ¼) 2018; Three Rivers: Center Park (¶346.1) (LTFT ¼) 2019.<> 18662 Moorepark Rd, Three Rivers 49093 (269) 279-9109. Home: 318 E St, Three Rivers 49093 (816) 519-1473. derlkeefer@gmail.com

*Keim, J. Robert (Judi) –
[(RL) FL-2000; PL-2009; RL-2011] Sturgis (assoc) (PTLP 7/1/09-12/31/11) 12/16/1999; Retired 12/31/2011.<> Home: 344 Hazelwood Ct., Muskegon 49442 (269) 467-7541

*Kellermann, James Garfield (Polly Strosahl) –
[(RE) P 1975; F 1978] 1977 Redford (assoc); 1980 Melvindale; 1985 Burton: Emmanuel; 1992 Bay City: Christ; Nov 1, 2000 Waterford: Central; **2013 Retired**.<> Home: 2149 Lakeside Place, Green Bay WI 54302 (248) 390-2416. kelstrowater@comcast.net

Kelley, Lisa L. (Michael) –
[(FL) FL 2013] Hillman, Spratt 2013; **Sanford 2020**.<> 2560 W. River Rd., Sanford 48657 (989) 687-5353. Home: 7770 W Scott Rd, Hubbard Lake 49747 (989) 280-0627. (248) 760-9590. pastorlisakelley@outlook.com

Kelley, Michael P. (Lisa) –
[(FL) PL Dec 1, 2004; FL 2009] Mapleton Dec 1, 2004; Mapleton, Burt 2006; Burt, Saginaw: West Michigan Avenue 2007; Jeddo, Buel 2009; Ossineke 2012; **Gordonville, Midland: Homer 2020**.<> (G) 76 E Gordonville Rd, Midland 48640 (989-486-10640. (MH) 507 S Homer Rd, Midland 48640 (989) 835-5050. Home: 7770 W Scott Rd, Hubbard Lake 49747(989) 297-7242. pastormikekelley@yahoo.com

*Kelsey, Dwayne Lee (Ruth) –
[(RE) P 1975; F 1977] 1976 Plymouth (assoc); 1978 Howarth, Thomas; Oct 15, 1981 Flint: Lincoln Park; 1987 Caring Covenant Group Ministry: Davison; 1991 Romeo; 1996 Dearborn: Good Shepherd; **Jan 1, 2000 Retired**.<> Home: 89 Randolph Rd., Rochester Hills 48309. dlkelc@wowway.com

Kendall, Jayme L. –
[(FE) PE-2004; FE-2008] Elsie 2004; Appointed to Extension Ministries (¶344.1.c) Chaplain, MI Army National Guard 07/11/2005; Appointed in Other Annual Conferences (¶331.8, ¶346.1) Pastoral Counselor, CPE, Covenant Counseling and Family Resource Center, Snellville GA 06/01/2007; Appointed in Other Annual Conferences (¶331.8, ¶346.1) Chaplain, Abbey Hospice, Social Circle GA 09/01/2008; Appointed to Extension Ministries (¶344.1d) Chaplain, United States Air Force, Kirtland Air Force Base 06/01/2010.<> 230 Missile Ave, Minot AFB ND 58705 (701) 723-2456. Home: 3311 8th St NE Apt 208, Minot ND 58703 (505) 319-7873. jayme.abq@icloud.com

*Kendall, O. Jay (Janis) –
[(RE) D-1984; FE-1986; R-2012] Transferred from Central Illinois Conf 1993; NE Missaukee Parish: Moorestown-Stittsville/Merritt-Butterfield 09/01/1993; Leave of Absence 2005; Indian River (Assoc) (LTFT ¼) 2007; Retired 09/01/2012.<> Home: PO Box 2038, 3300 M 68 Hwy, Indian River 49749 (231) 238-0816

*Kersten, Robert L. –
[(RE) D-1963; FE-1968; R-1995] Stanwood/Higbee 10/01/1960; Burr Oak 1962; Napoleon 1967; Transferred to Detroit Conf 1969; Transferred from Detroit Conf 1987; Barry County: Woodland/Hastings: Welcome Corners 1987; Vermontville/Gresham 1991; Retired 1995.<> Home: 1601 W Queen Creek Rd, Chandler AZ 85248 (623) 910-0134

Kesson, Aaron Bertel (Maria) –
[(FE) FL 2008; PE 2011; FE 2014] Blissfield: Emmanuel (LTFT ¾), Lambertville (assoc) (LTFT ¼) 2008; Manchester 2012; Chaplain Army Reserve (¶344.1b) Mar 14, 2012; Durand, Swartz Creek (assoc) 2017; **Durand 2020**.<> 100016 E. Newburg Rd., Durand 48429 (989) 288-3880. Home: 302 Hampton, Durand 48429 (989) 288-4364. pastoraaronumc@gmail.com

*Keyte, Donna J. (Steven) –
[(RL) PL-2003; RL-2019] Lacota 09/01/2003; Almena (LTFT ½) 01/01/2006; Almena (PTLP ¼) 01/01/2007; Almena (PTLP ½) 01/01/2008; LP w/o appointment 2019; Retired Aug 18, 2020.<> Home: 7632 Sandyridge St, Portage 49024 (269) 329-1560. djkeyte@yahoo.com

*Keyworth, Charles Wesley (Della Jane) –
[(RE) P 1983; F 1986] Piqua OH: Grace (student associate); 1984 Republic, Woodland; 1988 Gordonville; Sept 1, 1994 St. Charles, Brant; 1999 Midland: First (assoc); **2017 Retired**.<> Home: 630 Wood Run Dr., Marysville OH 43040 (989) 859-5654. churckkeywort@gmail.com

Khang, Steve Hongsup –
[(FE) PE 2007; FE 2010] Ann Arbor: Korean (assoc) 2007; Ann Arbor: Korean (assoc) (LTFT), Ypsilanti: St. Matthews (LTFT) 2009; Ann Arbor: Korean (assoc) (LTFT) 2014; **Ann Arbor: Korean (assoc) (full-time) Jan 1, 2020**.<> 1526 Franklin St, Ann Arbor 48103 (734) 483-5876. Home: 4131 Inglewood Dr, Ypsilanti 48197 (734) 482-0460. steverkhang@gmail.com

*Kidd, David Earl (Ada) –
[(RM) T 1961; F 1964] 1960 Broadway, E. Baltimore Parish (Baltimore Conf); 1962 Kensington MD (Baltimore Conf): St. Paul's, Minister of Education; 1964 Wesley Foundation, Flint; 1966 Wesley Foundation, Wayne State University; 1974 Flint: Trinity; Oct 1980 Detroit: Central; 1990 Ypsilanti: First; **1997 Retired**.<> Home: 2767 Del Mar Drive, Okemos 48864 (517) 351-7510. adkidds@gmail.com

Kidd, Sean K. (Nicole) –
[(PE) FL-2014; PE-2018] Pokagon (DSA) (LTFT ½) 2011; Martin/Shelbyville 2014; Kalamazoo: Westwood 2019.<> 538 Nichols Rd, Kalamazoo 49006 (269) 344-7165. Home: 1003 Greenway Ter, Kalamazoo 49006 (616) 401-8576. seankidd1970@gmail.com

Kieb, Eric Douglas (Lisa) –
[(FE) FL 2001; PE 2003; FE 2006] 2001 Owosso: First (assoc); 2003 Negaunee: Mitchell; 2010 Roscommon: Good Shepherd of the North; **2015 Bay City: Grace**.<> 4267 S. Two Mile Rd., Bay City 48708 (989) 684-1101. Home: 2161 Neithammer Dr., Bay City 48706 (989) 671-8951. edkieb@sbcglobal.net

Kilpatrick, Bryan K. (Ashley) –
[(FL) FL-2014] Brooks Corners/Barryton: Faith/Sears 2014; Mancelona/Alba 2017.<> (M) PO Box 301, 117 E Hinman St, Mancelona 49659 (231) 587-8461. (A) 5991 Barker St, Alba 49611. Home: 406 Sunnyside St, Mancelona 49659. bkilpatrickministry@gmail.com

Kim, Daeki –
[(OE) OE 2018, Indiana Conf] **Madison Heights: Korean First Central 2018**.<> 500 W Gardenia Ave, Madison Heights 48071. Home: 30150 ShorehamSt, Southfield 48076. skydk033@gmail.com

Kim, Eung Yong –
[(FE) OE 2019; FE 2020] Troy: Korean Jan 1, 2019; transferred from Korean Methodist 2020; **Troy: Korean, Troy: Korean - TroyHope Campus 2020**.<> 42693 Dequindre Rd, Troy 48085 (248) 879-2240. Home: 974 Hillsborough Dr., Rochester Hills 48307 (248) 525-5979. eykim11@gmail.com

Kim, Taek Han (Jamie) –
[(FE) PE 2002; FE 2005] Birmingham: First (assoc) 2002; Walled Lake 2004; **Carleton 2012**.<> 11435 Grafton Rd., Box 327, Carleton 48117 (734) 654-2833. Home: 1424 Monroe St., Box 327, Carleton 48117 (734) 654-2001. revtaekkim@gmail.com

Kim, Won Dong (Jessie) –
[(PE) FL 2014; PE 2015] Troy: Korean (assoc) 2014; Goodrich 2015; **Elkton Jan 1, 2017**.<> 150 South Main St., Box 9, Elkton 48731 (989) 375-4113. Home: 134 S. Main St., Elkton 48731 (989) 375-4185. coolgod80@hotmail.com

Kim, Yoo Jin –
[(PE) PL 2016; FL Sept 1, 2016; PE 2018] Madison Heights: Korean Central (assoc) 2016; Madison Heights: Korean Central (assoc) (LTFT ½), Clawson (LTFT ½) Sept 1, 2016; **Onaway, Millersburg 2018**.<> (O) 3647 N. Lynn St., PO Box 762, Onaway 49765 (989) 733-8811, (M) 5484 Main St., Box 258, Millersburg 49759 (989) 733-6946. Home: 3653 N. Elm, PO Box 762, Onaway 49765. yjphaha@bu.edu

King, Michelle M. –
[(PD) PD 2020] Not appointed Mar 30, 2020; **Transitional Leave 2020**.<> Home: 140 Church St Apt 103, Belleville 48111 (734) 536-6695. mmking108@gmail.com

*Kingsley, Susan M. –
[(RE) FL Sept 1, 1999; PE 2000; FE 2003] Midland: First (assoc) Sept 1, 1999; Owosso: Trinity 2008; **Retired 2016**.<> Home: 4110 Belaire St., Midland 48642 (989) 859-6223. Kings2ley@yahoo.com

*Kintigh, Bruce R. (Paula) –
[(RE) D-1979; FE-1983; R-2018] Shepardsville/Price 1981; Kingsley/Grant 1988; Hart 1993; Battle Creek: Christ 01/01/1999; Girard/Ellis Corners 2007; [Ellis corners Closed 12/31/2007] Girard 01/01/2008; Battle Creek: Trinity 2010; Battle Creek: Birchwood/Trinity 2012; **Retired 2018**.<> Home: 17102 11 Mile Rd, Battle Creek 49014 (269) 209-3633. b_kintigh@comcast.net

*Klacking, Brenda K. –
[(RL) PL 2000; FL 2013; RL 2020] Glennie, Curran: Sunnyside 2000; Whittemore. Wilber 2008; Whittemore, Wilber, Churchill 2013; Churchill, Mio 2014; **Retired 2020**.<> Home: 489 N Cambell Rd, West Branch 48661. Brendakk@hotmail.com

Kline, Julie A. –
[(OF) UCC Elder] Kalamazoo: First (assoc) (¶346.2) 2019; **Kalamazoo: First 2020**.<> 212 S Park St, Kalamazoo 49007 (269) 381-6340. Home: 1724 Nichols Rd, Kalamazoo 49006 (269) 330-8502. jkline@umc-kzo.org

*Klump, Dean Alan (Linda) –
[(RE) P 1970; F 1972] Plymouth (assoc) 1971; Lambertville 1974; Romeo 1981; Monroe: St. Paul's 1991; Plymouth: First 1995; **Retired 2007**.<> Home: 2740 Cypress Trace Circle #2711, Naples, FL 34119 (734) 927-4762. klumpdean@gmail.com

*Knapp, David G. (Jane) –
[(RE) D-1976; FE-1980; R-2009] Hopkins/South Monterey 1978; Adamsville 10/16/1982; Jackson: First (assoc) 1986; Appointed in Other Annual Conferences (¶331.8, ¶346.1) Waterman/ Preston, Detroit Conf 1989; Transferred to Detroit Conf 1990; Transferred From Detroit Conf 1992; Grand Rapids: Pawating Magedwin And Salem/Bradley Indian Mission 1992; Benton Harbor: Peace Temple 1995; Climax/Scotts 2003; Retired 2009; Mendon/West Mendon (Interim) (LTFT ¼) 1/1/-6/30/2013.<> Home: 7792 Kilowatt Dr, Kalamazoo 49048 (269) 775-1387. dgkcreations@outlook.com

Kobler, Timothy L. –
[(FE) OE 2018, Holston Conference; FE 2020] UM Connectional Structures (¶344.1a,c) Director, University of Michigan Wesley Foundation 2018; transferred from Holston Conference 2020; **Chaplain, Wesley Foundation, University of Michigan 2020**.<> 602 E Huron, Ann Arbor 48104 (734) 668-6881. H: 2884 Sorrento Ave, Ann Arbor 48104 (276) 614-8141. timkobler@umichwesley.org

*Kohlmann, Kenneth Arlan (Barbara) –
[(RE) P 1972; F 1975] 1974 Flint: Court Street (assoc); 1977 Mt. Clemens (assoc); 1981 Detroit: Messiah; Sept 1, 1985 Detroit: Redford (assoc); 1988 Utica: Hope, Mt. Vernon; 1992 Marine City; 1996 Midland: Homer; **2001 Retired**.<> Home: 50525 Abbey Dr., New Baltimore 48047 (586) 716-0262. kennethkohlmann4@gmail.com

*Kohns, Norman C. (Carole) –
[(RE) D-1967; FE-1969; R-2005] Transferred from Detroit Conf 1974; Grand Rapids: Aldersgate 01/01/1974; Grand Rapids: Aldersgate/Westgate 1977; Grand Rapids: Aldersgate 1978; Kalamazoo: Sunnyside 1981; Appointed to Extension Ministries (¶344.1b,c) Resident Therapist, Care and Counseling, Eden Theological Seminary, St. Louis MO 1986; Appointed to Extension Ministries (¶344.1b,c) Samaritan Counseling Center of South Bend IN 1988; Riverside/Scottdale 11/16/1992; Appointed to Extension Ministries (¶344.1b,c) Director Of Pastoral Counseling, Hospice of Greater Kalamazoo 1993; Caledonia 1996; Retired 2005.<> Home: 5845 Lyn Haven Dr SE, Kentwood 49512 (616) 554-1244. normankohns@yahoo.com

Koivula, Laurie M. –
[(PL) PL Dec 1, 2014; FL-2016; PL-2018] Dec 1, 2014 West Goodland; 2016 Harrietta, Mesick, Brethren: Epworth, (W. MI Conf); 2018 Mesick, Brethren: Epworth (LTFT ½); **2019 Pontiac: Grace and Peace Cmnty (LTFT ½).**<> 451 W Kennett, Pontiac 48340 (248) 334-3280. Home: 1851 Birchcrest Dr, Waterford 48328 (231) 557-8131. lkoivula@ymail.com

Kolder, Sandra J. –
[(PL) PL Dec 2005] Dec 4, 2005 God's Country Cooperative Parish: Paradise/Hulbert: Tahquamenon; 2011 Munising, Trenary; **2017 Retired**.<> Home: PO Box 130, W18394 H-42 Rd., Curtis 49820 (906) 586-9696. skolder@att.net

Korlapati, Arthur "David" David –
[(PL) PL Jan 1, 2020] Denton: Faith (DSA) (¼ time) 2018; **Denton: Faith (PTLP ¼) Jan 1, 2020.**<> 6020 Denton Rd, Belleville 48111 (734) 483-2276. Home: 7338 Talbot Dr Apt 102, Lansing 48917 (248) 444-6529. davidk@friendshipchurchinfo.com

*Kornowski, Suzanne P. (James Ferguson) –
[(RL) PL-2002; FL-2004; RL-2011] Oakwood (DSA) (LTFT PT) 06/01/2000-12/1/2002; Oshtemo (DSA) (LTFT PT) 2000; Oshtemo (PTLP 12/1/02-3/21/04) 12/01/2002; Retired 2011.<> Home: 252 Bobwhite Dr, Pensacola FL 32514

Kraus, James W., Jr. (Lorie) –
[(FD) DM-1998; FD-2001] Director of Music and Director of Leadership Development, Diaconal Minister, St Joseph First 1998; St Joseph First (Deacon) 05/31/2001.<> 2950 Lakeview Ave, Saint Joseph 49085 (269) 983-3929. Home: 2820 Willa Dr, Saint Joseph 49085 (269) 983-5798. jameskrausjr@hotmail.com

*Kreger, Robert Ivan (Karen) –
[(RL) PL Dec 1, 2002] Dec 1, 2002 Avoca, Ruby; 2003 Ruby; 2008 Sterling Heights; **2013 Retired**.<> Home: 4747 Lakeshore Rd., Fort Gratiot 48059 (810) 334-6520. rkdataman2@live.com

Kreh, Matthew D. (Lori Lou) –
[(FL) FL-2015] Bath/Gunnisonville (DSA) 2015; Bath/Gunnisonville 12/01/2015.<> (B) PO Box 308, 13777 Main St, Bath 48808 (517) 641-6551. (G) PO Box 308, 2031 Clark Rd, Bath 48808 (517) 482-7987. Home: 2025 Cumberland Rd, Lansing 48006 (517) 449-8178. mattkreh@gmail.com

*Kummer, James Philip (Pamela) –
[(RE) P 1980; F 1983] Dec 1980 Port Sanilac, Forester, McGregor; 1985 Elkton; Apr 15, 1989 Flint: Calvary (assoc); Feb 1, 1992 Livonia: Clarenceville; 1995 Highland; **2016 Retired**.<> Home: 2864 Bullard Rd., Hartland 48353 (810) 632-9026. jkummer@humc.us

*Kursch, Kathleen S. –
[(RE) D-1999; FE-2003; R-2017] Waterloo First/Waterloo Village 1998; Grand Ledge: First (Assoc) 02/01/2000; Grand Ledge: First (Assoc) (LTFT ½) / Delta Mills (LTFT ½) 2003; Grand Rapids: South 09/01/2004; Shepherd 2007; Retired 2017.<> Home: 11134 Barnsley, Lowell 49331 (989) 506-4601. kskursch@juno.com

*Lafrance, Sally J. (David) –
[(RE) D-1995; FE-1997; R-2005] Transferred from West Ohio Conf 1999; Climax/Scotts 10/01/1999; Old Mission Peninsula (Ogdensburg) 2001; Twin Lake 2002; Retired 10/01/2004.<> Home: 15132 Snowberry Ct, Spring Lake 49456 (616) 850-2157. davidsally@chartermi.net

LaGuire, Sean –
[(PL) PL-Jan 1, 2020; FL 2020] Waterford: Four Towns (DSA) (¼ time) 2019; Waterford: Four Towns (PTLP ¼) Jan 1, 2020; **Girard 2020.**<> 990 Marshall Rd., Coldwater 49036 (517) 279-9418. Home: 992 Marshall Rd, Coldwater 49036 (313) 926-2498. pastorseanlaguire@gmail.com

*Laimon, Jeanne (John W.) –
[(RL) PL-2008; FL-2013; RL-2015] Williamston: Wheatfield (DSA) (LTFT PT) 2007; Williamston: Wheatfield (LTFT ¼) 12/01/2007; Munith (¼ Time) 2012; Waterloo First (¼ Time) 2013-2/16/2014; Pleasant Lake (¼ Time) 2013; Stockbridge (¼ Time) 2013; Not Appointed 2014; Retired 2015.<> Home: 6701 Hawkins Rd., Jackson 49201 (517) 769-6570. jeannelaimon@yahoo.com

Lamb, Marcel A. (Michelle) –
[(FE) OF Wesleyan; PE 2010; FE 2011] Sept 16, 2005 Mio; 2012 AuGres, Twining: Trinity; **2013 Imlay City.**<> 210 North Almont Ave., Imlay City 48444 (810) 724-0687. Home: 280 Bancroft St., Imlay City 48444 (810) 721-7149. revmarcel@msn.com

*LaMere, Frederick –
[(RE) P 1991, VA] 1991 Potts Valley Charge; 1993 trans to Detroit Conf, Republic, Woodland; 1996 disability leave; Aug 1, 2000 Beaverton: First, Dale; **2002 Retired.**<> Home: 3578 W. Riley Rd., Gladwin 48624. falamere@charter.net

*Lancaster, Bonny Joy –
[(RL) FL 1992] Sept 1, 1992 Mayville, Fostoria, Silverwood; Feb 1, 1997 Mayville; 1999 Macon; 2001 West Vienna; **Oct 1, 2006 Retired.**<> Home: 4134 N State Rd, PO Box 476, Davison 48423 (810) 240-1257

Lancaster, Janice T. –
[(FD) PD-2010; FD-2013] Holland Hospital, Psychiatric Nurse/Holland: First (Deacon – Assoc Congregational Care LTFT ¼ unpaid) 2010; Deacons Appointed Beyond the Local Church(¶331.1a) Emmanuel Hospice of Grand Rapids, Clinical Nurse/ Northlawn (Assoc Congregational Care LTFT ¼ unpaid) 02/01/2014; Deacons Appointed Beyond the Local Church(¶331.1a) Emmanuel Hospice of Grand Rapids, Clinical Nurse/Northlawn (Assoc Congregational Care LTFT ¼ paid) 01/01/2015; Leave of Absence 03/31/2017.<> Home: 0-660 Krystal Kove, Grand Rapids 49534 (616) 784-5662. lantock@yahoo.com

*Landis, John David (Carolyn) –
[(RE) P 1982; F 1988; RE 2019] 1980 Buel, Peck, Melvin; 1986 school (United Theological Seminary), Ashland OH: Trinity; 1987 Romulus: Community; 1994 Detroit: Metropolitan (assoc); 2000 Swartz Creek; 2011 Midland: First; **2019 Retired**.<> Home: 9535 Hill Rd., Swartz Creek 48473 (989) 948-9838. jlandis902@gmail.com

Lane, M. Christopher (Jane Lippert) –
[(FE) D-1982; FE-1988] Transferred from Holston Conf 1986; Winn/Blanchard-Pine River/Coomer 1986; Muskegon: Crestwood 1990; Grand Rapids: Genesis (Co-Pastor) 1995; Martin/ Shelbyville 2007; Traverse City: Central (Assoc) 2009.<> 222 Cass St, Traverse City 49684 (231) 946-5191. 965 Fenton Road, Kingsley 49649 (231) 313-4480. chris@tccentralumc.org

*Large, Wayne Thomas (Joy) –
[(RE) T 1964; F 1969] 1967 Newberry; Sept 1970 Midland: First (assoc); 1974 Gladstone; 1981 Director, Wesley Foundation, University of Michigan; 1995 Farmington: First; June 1, 2001 incapacity leave (para 355); 2002 Royal Oak: First (assoc); **2003 Retired**.<> Home: 8504 Old Wilsey Bay 12 Lane, Rapid River 49878. wlarge@up.net

*Larner, Janet M. (Peter J. Sivia) –
[(RE) P 1979; F 1984; RE 2020] Sterling, Alger, Bentley 1981; Sutton- Sunshine, Bethel Oct 1982; Beaverton: First, Dale 1986; Bay City: First (assoc) (LTFT ½) 1991; Wagarville Aug 1994; Gordonville Sept 1, 1994; sabbatical leave 2002; Sanford 2003; voluntary leave of absence 2011; Churchill 2011; Corunna 2013; Shepherd, Blanchard-Pine River 2017**; Retired 2020**.<> Home: 3728 E Douglas Dr, Midland 48642 (989) 245-8846. jmlarner@gmail.com

*Larson, Jean M. (Warren) –
[(RE) PL 1988; P 1995; F 1998] 1988 Painesdale: Albert Paine; 1990 Wesley Foundation, Northern Michigan University; school; June 16, 1996 Owosso: Burton, Carland; Jan 1, 2000 Stephenson, Hermansville: First; Nov 16, 2001 leave of absence; 2002 Plover Charge (WI conf); 2003 Reese; Jan 1, 2008 leave of absence; **2010 Retired**.<> Home: 1633 River St., Niagara WI 54151 (989) 863-0148. bjtools@charter.net

Lass, William –
[(PL) DSA 2018; PL 2019] Lulu (DSA) (¼ time) Jan 15, 2018; Lulu (PTLP ¼) Jan 1, 2019; **Britton: Grace (PTLP ½) 2020**.<> 9250 E Monroe Rd, Britton 49229 (517) 451-8280. Home: 5423 N Stoney Creek Rd, Monroe 48162 (734) 735-1669

*Laub, Mary Grace –
[(RE) PL 1990; FL 1992; Deacon, AM 1998; FE 2000] 1990 Painesdale: Albert Paine Memorial; Feb 15, 1992 God's Country Cooperative Parish: Grand Marais, Germfask; 1998 Heritage; 2001 Escanaba: First; **2010 Retired**.<> Home: 204 W. Douglass Ave., Houghton 49931 (906) 483-2363. revlaub@dsnet.us

PASTORAL RECORDS

*Lawton, George W. –
[(RL) PL-2001; RL-2007] Berrien County: Lakeside (DSA) Sept 1, 1999; Berrien County: Lakeside 2001; **Retired 2007;** Berrien County: Lakeside (RLA ¼) 2007-Sept 2, 2019; Berrien County: Lakeside (RLA) Dec. 1, 2019-2020.<> Home: 8000 Warren Woods Rd #79, Three Oaks 49128 (269) 336-9430. geolawton@csinet.net

Lawton, Gregory W. –
[(FD) PD-2007; FD-2010] Deacons Appointed Within UM Connectional Structure (¶331.1b) Resolution Services Center of CMU (½ Time) / Grand Ledge: First (Deacon) (½ Time) 2007; Grand Ledge First (Deacon) (LTFT ½) and Deacons Appointed Within UM Connectional Structure (¶331.1b) Interim Director of Campus Ministry, Wesley Foundation at MSU (LTFT ½) 12/05/2010; UM Connectional Structures (¶344.1a,c) Director, Campus Ministry Wesley Fellowship Grand Valley State University (LTFT ¾) 2011; Deacons Appointed Beyond the Local Church (¶331.1a) Director, Wesley Fellowship at Grand Valley State University (Full-Time) 2012; Deacons Appointed Beyond the Local Church (¶331.1a) Director, Wesley Fellowship at Grand Valley State University (¼ Time) 04/01/2017; Deacons Appointed Beyond the Local Church (¶331.1a) Assoc Dean of Students, Lithuania Christian College International University 08/10/2017 and Georgetown (Missional) 12/1/2018; Transitional Leave 01/01/2019; Personal Leave Jan 1, 2020; **Jackson: First, Minister of Spiritual Formation (Deacon) (LTFT ½) Aug 15, 2020.**<> 275 W Michigan Ave, Jackson 49201 (517) 787-6460. Home: 525 S Alpine Lake Dr Apt A, Jackson 49201(269) 317-7183. gregorywlawton@gmail.com

*Leach, Melvin L. (Judy) –
[(RE) P 1973; F 1975] 1973 West Vienna; 1981 Davisburg; Jan 1, 1995 Eastside Covenant Cooperative Parish: Fraser: Christ; 2002 Parish Director; **2015 Retired; Sept 1, 2017 Hale: First.**<> 201 W Main, PO Box 46 Hale 48739 (989) 728-9522 Home: 7540 O'Connor, Box 334, Hale 48739. pastormel48@gmail.com

Lee, Andrew H. (Grace) –
[(FE) FL 2013; PE 2014; FE 2017] 2013 Ann Arbor: Calvary; **2019 Commerce.**<> 1155 N. Commerce Rd., Commerce Twp. 48382 (248) 363-3935. Home: 840 Morella St., Commerce Twp. 48382 (248) 977-0400. leeandr5@gmail.com

Lee, Chul-Goo –
[(FE) Korean Methodist Church, PE 2008; FE 2009] Madison Heights: Korean First Central Mar 1, 2004 (trans to Detroit Conf from Korean Methodist Church May 17, 2007); **Korean American UMC of South Florida 2013.**<> 4905 W. Prospect Rd., Ft. Lauderdale FL 33309 (954) 739-8581. eglee1320@yesu.org

*Lee, Donald–
[(RLA) DSA-2002; PL-2003; R-2010; RLA-2017] Frontier/Osseo (DSA) 2002; Frontier/Osseo (PTLP) 2003; Discontinued 2010; Readmitted 2017; Frontier PTLP (¼) (¶357.1) 2017.<> PO Box 120, 9925 Short St, Frontier 49239 (269) 223-0631. Home: PO Box 127, 106 E Maple St, Camden 49232 (517) 398-3082. donlee@dmcibb.net

*Lee, Hoon Kyong (Kyong Ja) –
[(RE) P MN, 1980; F MN, 1983] 1980 S. NJ Conf, Mays Landing: Korean; Sept 1, 1985 S. NJ Conf, Cherry Hill: First Korean; Jan 1, 1995 Troy: Korean (transfer to Detroit Conference); **2013 Retired.**<> Chicago IL (NCJ Korean Missions). 631 Hapsfield Ln, Buffalo Grove IL 60089. hklee722@yahoo.com

*Lee, Janet A. –
[(RD) D-1997; PL-2000; RD-2002] Transferred from Detroit Conf 1986; Hillsdale: First, Minister of Music and Arts and Hillsdale Daily News, Religion and Lifestyles Editor 1988; Retired 2002; Hillsdale First, Minister of Music and Arts 2002-12/31/2012.<> Home: 4300 W Bacon Rd, Hillsdale 49242 (517) 437-4949. Janet_lee@comcast.net

*Lee, John Hyung (Jae Hyang) –
[(RE) P E. Annual Conf of Korea, 1977; F E. Annual Conf of Korea, 1979] 1974-79 Jung-gu, Korea: Zion UMC (assoc); 1975-77 Assistant Professor, Christian Social Ethics, Methodist Theological Seminary, Seoul, Korea; 1978-79 Professor of Christian Social Ethics, Methodist Theological Seminary, Seoul, Korea; 1980 Trans. to Western NC Conf, Greensboro: Korean; Sept 1, 1988 Trans. to Detroit Conf, Ann Arbor: Korean; 1992 Madison Heights: Korean First Central; Feb 1, 2004 Detroit West District Superintendent; **2011 Retired**.<> Home: 2064 Christopher Ct., West Bloomfield 48324 (248) 366-1948. mgmxbop@aol.com

*Lee, Jung Kee (Eun Su) –
[(RE) D-1989; FE-1991; R-2013] Transferred from East Ohio Conf 1998; Lansing: Korean 1998; Other Valid Ministries (¶344.1d) Seoul Theological University 01/01/2004; Retired 02/28/2013.<> Home: 808 N Springs St, Apt 702, Los Angeles CA 90012

*Leffler, Stephen Douglas (Marilyn) –
[(RE) T IN, 1955; F IN, 1958] 1958 Vincennes; 1961 Merom; 1963 Carrollton; 1966 Indianapolis: Union Chapel (assoc); 1968 Chaplain, VA Medical Center, Butler PA; 1981 Trans. to W. PA Conf; 1981 Chaplain, VA Medical Center, Saginaw; 1988 Trans. to Detroit Conf; 1988 Chaplain, VA Medical Center, Saginaw; Jan 11, 1992 sabbatical leave; 1992 Bay Port, Hayes; **1994 Retired**.<> Home: 4392 Ann Street, Saginaw 48603

Leitelt, Betty Kay –
[(FL) PL 2006; FL 2010] 2006 Corunna: Northwest Venice; **2010 Caring Covenant Group Ministry: Otisville, Fostoria, West Deerfield**.<> (O) Box 125, 200 W. Main St., Otisville 48463 (810) 631-2911, (F) Box 67, Fostoria 48435. Home: 9622 Hammil Rd., PO Box 125, Otisville 48463 (810) 631-8395. pastor.kay@live.com

LeMoine, Peter A. –
[(PL) PL 2018] **2018 Republic, Michigamme: Woodland (LTFT ½)**.<> (R) 216 Front, PO Box 395 Republic 49879, (906) 376-2389. (MW) 3533 US 41E, Michigamme 49861 (906) 323-6151. Home: 356 Maple S, Republic 49879 (906) 376-2085. hdrider2@chartermi.net

Lenard, Keith A., Jr. –
[(FL) PL Mar 2014; FL 2016] Wyandotte: Glenwood Mar 1, 2014; Melvindale: New Hope, Downriver (assoc) Jan 1, 2016; Riverview, Downriver (assoc) 2016; Grosse Pointe (assoc) 2017; **LaSalle, Petersburg 2020**.<> (L) 1603 Yargerville Rd., LaSalle 48145 (734) 243-5940. (P) 152 Saline St., PO Box 85, Petersburg 49270 (734) 279-1118. Home: 1607 Yargerville., LaSalle 48145 (734) 778-0835. k19redice@aol.com

Leslie, Kristen Jane (Michael Boddy) –
[(FE) P, E. OH, 1986; F, E. OH, 1988] 1988 Westlake (assoc), (E. OH Conf); 1989 Chaplain: Adrian College; 1990 Trans. to Detroit Conf, Chaplain: Adrian College; July 1, 1993 school (School of Theology of Claremont); Jan 1, 1998 Professor of Pastoral Theology, Yale Divinity School; **2010 Professor of Pastoral Theology and Care, Eden Theological Seminary**.<> 475 Lockwood Ave., St. Louis MO 63119 (314) 918-2513. Home: 540 Lee Ave. St. Louis MO 63119 (203) 376-4537. kleslie@eden.edu

*Lester, Ben B. (Linda) –
[(RE) D-1990; FE-1993; R-2011] Howard City First/Amble/Coral 1988; Cedar Springs/East Nelson 1995; Hart 2003; Retired 2011.<> Home: 1575 Hess Lake Dr, Grant 49327 (231) 834-8868. hesslakeben@yahoo.com

*Lewis, Alger T. (Ruth) –
[(RE) FL 1986; AM 1991; FM 1998] 1986 Bay Port, Hayes; 1992 North Street; **1999 Retired**.<> Home: 9906 Lakeside Dr., Bay Port 48720 (989) 656-3151. revatl@airadv.net

*Lewis, Bradford K. (Deborah) –
[(RE) LP 1992; P 1993; F 1996] Sept 1, 1992 Wellsville; 1994 Romulus: Community; 1998 Roscommon: Good Shepherd of the North; **2010 Retired**.<> Home: 1980 Teton Ave., Monroe 48162 (989) 906-5213. bklewis2105@charter.net

*Lewis, Eugene A. (Marilyn) –
[(RE) D-1965; FE-1967; R-2003] Glenn-Pearl 1963; Glenn/Pearl/Casco 1965; Hanover/Horton/Hillside 12/01/1966; Belding/Orleans 07/15/1972; Grand Rapids: Faith 1977; Wacousta Community 1984; Clare 1986; Stevensville 1994; Retired 2003.<> Home: 25080 27 1/2 St, Gobles 49055 (269) 628-1482. ealewis25080@gmail.com

*Lewis, George Henry (Sherry Parker-Lewis) –
[(RE) P 1989; F 1992; RE 2020] Kilmanagh, Unionville 1990; Carleton 1993; Cheboygan: St. Paul's 1998; Howell: First 2010; **Retired 2020**.<> Home: 48710 Apple Ln, Mattawan 49071 (231) 268-9991. revgeorgelewis@gmail.com

*Lewis, Kendall A. (Doris) –
[(RE) D-1970; FE-1974; R-1990] Transferred from Detroit Conf 1973; Banfield/Briggs/Dowling-South Maple Grove 1973; Country Chapel/Banfield 1975; Marion/ Cadillac: South Community 1977; White Pigeon 1981; Mendon 01/01/1985; Big Rapids: Third Avenue/Paris/ Rodney 1986; Retired 1990.<> Home: 179 Summer Street, Battle Creek 49015 (269) 441-1921. lewiskendall2803@yahoo.com

*Lewis-Lakin, Barbara (Shawn) –
[(RE) P 1980; F 1983] 1981 Detroit: Aldersgate (assoc); 1985 Melvindale; 1986 Detroit: Central (assoc); 1990 school; 1997 Pastoral Counselor, Samaritan Counseling Center; 2004 Pastoral Psychotherapist, Samaritan Counseling Center of Southeastern Michigan (LTFT ½), Chelsea: First (assoc) (LTFT ½). 2010 Samaritan Counseling Center of S. E. Michigan; **Sept 1, 2015 Retired**.<> Home: 154 S. Cranbrook Cross Road, Bloomfield Hills 48301 (248) 629-6232. blewislakin@gmail.com

Lewis-Lakin, Shawn Patrick (Barbara) –
[(FE) P 1987; F 1990] 1988 Pontiac: St. James; 1990 Dearborn: First (assoc); 1994 Trenton: First; 1997 leave of absence; **2017 Birmingham: First (senior assoc) (2019 LTFT ¾)**.<> 1589 W. Maple, Birmingham 48009 (248) 646-1200. Home: 2221 Maplewood, Royal Oak 48073 (734) 717-8947. slewis-lakin@fumcbirmingham.org

Leydorf-Keck, Kathryn L. (Roger Keck) –
[(PL) FL-2012; PL-2014] Salem/Lowe/Maple Rapids (DSA) 2007; Salem/Lowe/Maple Rapids 11/10/2007; Lowe/Maple Rapids (¾ Time) 5/1/2014.<> (L) 5485 W Lowe Rd, Saint Johns 48879 (989) 224-4460. (MR) 330 S Maple Ave, Maple Rapids 48853 (989) 224-4460. Home: 10886 S Woodbridge Rd, Bannister 48807 (517) 282-4446. kathyleydorf@gmail.com

*Lichtenfelt, Donald Lloyd –
[(RE) T N. Iowa, 1955; F N. Iowa, 1959] 1954 Calamus, Ground Mound; Dec 1961 Trans. to Detroit Conf, Fraser; 1967 Mayville, Clifford, Silverwood; 1969 Mayville; 1970 Sabbatical; 1971 Honorable Location; 1974 reinstated; 1974 Utica: Hope, Meade, New Haven; 1980 Harper Woods; 1988 Royal Oak: St. John's; **1994 Retired**.<> Home: 1417 Copper Glen Dr., Lexington KY 40519 (859) 224-3236. donlichtenfelt@yahoo.com

*Lidums, Olaf R. (Susan) –
[(RE) PL Apr 1998; FL 1998; recognition from ELCA, 1999; FE 2001] Apr 1, 1998 Detroit: Ford Memorial, Waterman-Preston; Apr 16, 1999 Ford Memorial, Director, New Creations Ministries; 2000 New Lothrop, Juddville; 2003 Flint: Bristol, Dimond; **Apr 1, 2007 Retired**.<> Home: 4103 Lapeer Rd., Burton 48509 (810) 742-3480. slidums@aol.com

*Liles, Johnny S. (Lynda) –
[(RE) P 1989, on recognition of orders, General Baptist Convention; F 1991] 1988 Warren: First (assoc); Mar 16, 1990 Rochester Hills: St. Luke's; **2004 Retired**.<> Home: 434 Taylor Ave., Rochester 48307 (248) 601-3369. JLiles1208@aol.com

Liles, Lynda B. (Johnny) –
[(FD) CON (SM) 1999; FD 2002] 1986 Howarth; 1975 Paint Creek; 1999 Rochester: St. Luke's; June 15, 2006 transitional leave of absence (para. 357); Sept 1, 2006 Troy Fellowship (deacon); **2011 leave of absence**.<> Home: 434 Taylor Ave., Rochester 48307 (248) 601-3369. liles731@wowway.com

*Lim, Paul Byungioo (Susie) –
[(RE) P C. IL, 19__; F C. IL, 19__] 1983 Korean Church; 1985 Korean, North Detroit; 1986 Gwinn; 1987 Hazel Park; 1992 Freeland; Apr 1, 1996 Kum Ran Methodist Church, Seoul, Korea; 1998 Henderson, Chapin; **2000 Retired**.<> 23480 Lahser Rd., Southfield 48034 (248) 356-4677

Lim, Seok Nam (Soon-Shil) –
[(FE) PE 2015; FE 2018] (2015 serving in West Michigan Conference). 2016 Dearborn: Good Shepherd; **2018 Alpena: First**.<> 167 S. Ripley, Alpena 49707 (989) 354-2490. Home: 1320 Hobbs Dr., Alpena 49707

*Lindberg, Donna Jeanne (Elwood Berkompas) –
[(RE) T 1967; F 1971] 1970 Beverly Hills (assoc); 1972 Port Huron: First (assoc); 1973 Livonia: Newburg (assoc); Mar 1974 Detroit: Rice Memorial; Apr 1979 Hazel Park; 1983 Gaylord; 1989 Ann Arbor District Superintendent; 1993 Ishpeming: Wesley; 1997 Manistique: First (LTFT 2/3); Marquette district, project director; **2004 Retired**.<> Home: 1530 W. Ridge St., Apt. #47, Marquette 49855 (906) 273-1026. djlind@charter.net

Lindenberg, Scott Paul (Jill) –
[(FE) PE 2006; FE 2009] 2006 Ishpeming: Wesley; 2014 Saginaw: Ames; **2016 Hancock: First**.<> 401 Quincy, Box 158, Hancock 49930 (906) 482-4190. Home: 1631 Portage Dr., Hancock 49930 (906) 482-1404. pastor.lindenberg@gmail.com

Lindsey, Duane A. –
[(FL) PL Jan 1, 2019; FL 2020] Lennon, Duffield (DSA) 2018; Lennon, Duffield (PTLP ½) Jan 1, 2019; Lake Fenton, Lennon, Duffield 2019; **Hillman (½ time) and Spratt (½ time) 2020**.<> (H) 111 Maple St, PO Box 638, Hillman 49746 (989) 742-3014. (S) PO Box 323, 7440 M-65 South, Lachine 49743 (989) 742-4372. Home: 23910 Lowell St, Hillman 49746 (810) 730-6861. dualind@yahoo.com

*Line Yencer, Deborah A. (Ron Yencer) –
[(RE) PE 1999; FE 2002; RE 2018] 1999 Seymour Lake; 2009 Caring Covenant Group Ministry: Davison; 2013 Davison; 2014 Flushing; 2018 Retired; **2018 Mt. Pleasant: Leaton (LTFT ½)**.<> 6890 E Beal City Rd, Mt Pleasant 48858 (989) 773-3838. Home: 17429 Summit Ct, Barryton 49305 (248) 425-4684. revdebiline@gmail.com

Lippert, Jane R. (Christopher Lane) –
[(FE) D-1984; FE-1988] Riverdale: Lincoln Road 1986; Muskegon: Unity (LTFT ½) 1990; Grand Rapids: Genesis (Co-Pastor) (LTFT ½) 1995; Leave of Absence 2007; Traverse Bay 2009; Personal Leave 09/01/2015.<> Home: 965 Fenton Road, Kingsley 49649 janerobertalippert@gmail.com

*Liscomb, David M. (Arlene) –
[(RE) T 1965; F 1968] 1955 Disco; 1956 (without appointment at his request); 1957 Paint Creek; 1958 Paint Creek, Howarth; 1964 Gambier, Hopewell (NE OH Conf); 1967 Clinton; 1969 Escanaba: First, Bark River; 1973 Iron Mountain: Trinity; 1982 Troy: First; 1986 Mt. Clemens: First; 1992 Sault Ste. Marie: Central, Algonquin; 1993 disability leave; **1998 Retired**.<> Home: 600 Marquette, Crystal Falls 49920 (906) 875-6140. dliscomb@cox.net

*Liske, Julie A. –
[(FD) D-1994; FE-1996; FD-2008; RD 2020] Transferred from Detroit Conf 1994; Portage: Chapel Hill (Assoc) 1994; Appointed to Extension Ministries (¶344.1b,c) Chaplain, Clark Retirement Home 12/01/1997; Wayland 08/01/2001; Leave of Absence 2003; Other Valid Ministries (¶335.1d) Chaplain, Spectrum Health (LTFT) 2004; Leave of Absence 03/08/2005; Kalamazoo: First (Assoc) 2006; Deacons Appointed w/in UM Connectional Structure (¶331.1b) Executive Director, United Methodist Metropolitan Ministry of Greater Grand Rapids (LTFT ¾) and Grand Rapids: Trinity (Deacon, Assoc) (¼ Time) 11/08/2010; Deacons Appointed w/in UM Connectional Structure (¶331.1b) Executive Director, United Methodist Metropolitan Ministry of Greater Grand Rapids (¾ Time) and Chapter Director Of Circles Grand Rapids (LTFT ¼) 2015; Deacons Appointed Beyond the Local Church (¶331.1a) Director, Circles Grand Rapids 03/01/2016; **Retired 2020**.<> Home: 1323 Suncrest Dr NE, Grand Rapids 49525 (616) 299-0115. liskejulie@gmail.com

*Litchfield, Carl Q. (Geri) –
[(RE) D-1985; FE-1988; R-2017] Brooks Corners/Sears 1986; Barry County: Woodland/Hastings: Welcome Corners 1991; Boyne City/Boyne Falls 2000; Litchfield 2005; Bellaire: Community 2009; Kingsley 2013; Retired 2017; Colon/Burr Oak 02/15/2018; Mendon 2018; Mendon, Burr Oak 10/01/2018.<> 320 W Main St, PO Box 308, Mendon 49072 (269) 496-4295. Home: 27435 Michigan Ave, Mendon 49072 (269) 275-5296. litch2revdup@hotmail.com

*Litchfield, David L. (Vera) –
[(RE) D-1966; FE-1969; R-2006] Scottdale (EUB) 1966; West Mendon 12/15/1968; Mendon/West Mendon 1969; Elsie/Duplain 11/15/1970; Niles: Grace 1976; Bellaire: Community 01/15/1981; Kalamazoo Oakwood/Oshtemo 1987; Keeler/Silver Creek 1992; Springport/Lee Center 1998; Battle Creek: Convis Union 2001; Retired 2006.<> Home: 103 Hubbard Dr, New Carlisle IN 46552 (574) 654-2297. daveralit@tds.net

*Litchfield, Geraldine M. (Carl) –
[(RA) FL-2000; AM-2001; RA-2014] Barry County: Woodland/Hastings: Welcome Corners (Assoc) 01/01/1993-1994; Brookfield (½ Time) 1995; Horton Bay/Charlevoix: Greensky Hill 2000; Leave of Absence 07/01-08/31/2005; Somerset Center 09/01/2005; Quincy 2007; Williamsburg/Elk Rapids 2009; Retired 2014.<> Home: 27435 Michigan Ave, Mendon 49072 (269) 275-5239. revgmlitchfield@yahoo.com

*Litchfield, Glenn C. (Dorie) –
[(RE) D-1981; FE-1985; R-2016] Vermontville/Gresham 1983; Ashley/Bannister 1990; Kent City: Chapel Hill 1996; Cassopolis 2005; Climax/Scotts 2009; Retired 2016; Kendall 2019.<> 26718 Cnty Rd 388, Gobles 49055; PO Box 6, Kendall 49062 (269) 628-2303. Home: 61470 CR 657, Lawton 49065 (269) 436-0023. glennlitchfield52@gmail.com

Lobb, Grant Richard (Debra) –
[(FE) P 1983; F 1986] 1984 LaSalle: Zion; 1988 Croswell: First; 1996 Owosso: First; 2005 Marquette District Superintendent; **2012 Lapeer: Trinity**.<> 1310 North Main St., Lapeer 48446 (810) 664-9941. Home: 804 Fourth St., Lapeer 48446 (810) 660-7386. revgrant9@gmail.com

*Logston, Jane D. (Russell) –
[(RE) D-1988; FE-1991; RE 2020] Transferred from West Virginia Conf 1994; Quincy 1994; Mason: First (Assoc) 1996; Family Leave 1998; Appointed in Other Annual Conferences (¶337.1) Newberry, Detroit Conf 2001; Lawrence 2003; Hinchman/Oronoko 2006; Berrien Springs/Hinchman/Oronoko 2012; Bear Lake/Arcadia 2014; Medical Leave 09/01/2018; **Retired 2020**.<> Home: 133 N Park St, Lake City 49651 (269) 419-7917. jdlogston@yahoo.com

Logston, Russell K. (Jane) –
[(FE) D-1986; FE-1991] Transferred from West Virginia Conf 1994; Camden/Montgomery/Stokes Chapel 1994; Dansville/Vantown 1996; Constantine 1998; Family Leave 2001; Riverside (LTFT ¼) 01/01/2005; Riverside (LTFT ½) 01/01/2006; Galien/Olive Branch 2006; Sodus: Chapel Hill 2011; Empire 2014; Lake City and St. John's Lutheran Church (¶345) 2019.<> 301 E John St, PO Box Drawer P, Lake City 49651 (231) 839-2123. Home: 133 N Park St, Lake City 49651 (231) 839-7542. lcumc301@gmail.com

*Long, Calvin D. (Beth) –
[(RE) P 1983; F 1985; R 2018] 1980-81 Albany Circuit (Louisville Conf); 1983 Saginaw: Ames (assoc); Mar 1, 1987 Saginaw: Swan Valley; Apr 1, 1991 Monroe: Frenchtown; June 1, 1995 Pigeon: Salem; 2000 Houghton Lake; 2009 Owosso: First; **2018 Retired**.<> Home: 5531 Timothy Ln, Bath Wwp 48808 (989) 954-5485. calvin-long@hotmail.com

Long, Shelly Ann (Steven) –
[(PL) PL 2017] **Nov 15, 2016 Richfield**.<> 10090 E. Coldwater, PO Box 307, Davison 48423 (810) 653-3644. Home: 11564 Kings Coach Road, Grand Blanc 48439. pastor-shellyrumc@comcast.net

*Longden, Leicester R. (Linda) –
[(RE) D-1973; FE-1976; R-2013] Transferred from Oregon-Idaho Conf 1992; Lansing: Trinity 1992; Other Valid Ministries (¶335.1a) Assoc Professor of Evangelism & Discipleship, University of Dubuque Theological Seminary 2001; Retired 2013.<> Home: 3549 Polonaise Dr, Muskegon 49442 (563) 5647274. LLongden@dbq.edu

Loomis, Scott R. (Kimberly) –
[(FL) FL-2012] Pine River Parish: Ashton/Leroy (DSA) 2012; Pine River Parish: Ashton/Leroy 11/10/2012; Pine River Parish: Ashton/Leroy/Luther 06/01/2015.<> (A) PO Box 38, 20862 11 Mile Rd, Leroy 49655 (231) 832-8347. (Le) PO Box 38, 310 West Gilbert St, Leroy 49655 (231) 768-4512. (Lu) PO Box 175, 315 State St, Luther 49656 (231) 797-0073. Home: PO Box 234, 400 W Gilbert St, Leroy 49655 (231) 768-4512. srloomis1@gmail.com

Loring, Mary K. (Mark) –
[(FE) PL-2010; PE-2015; FE 2020] Twin Lake (PTLP ½) 2010; Appointed to Extension Ministries (¶344.1b,c) Chaplain, Clark Retirement Community 2013; Appointed to Extension Ministries (¶344.1b,c) Coordinator Of Pastoral Care, Clark Retirement Community (FTLP) 06/01/2014; Jackson: Calvary and Jackson: First (Assoc) 2017; Ann Arbor: Calvary 2019; **Belleville 2020**.<> 417 Charles St., Belleville 48111 (734) 697-9288. Home: 455 High St., Belleville 48111 (616) 307-0369. mkloring23@gmail.com

Lovegrove, Angela M. –
[(FL) FL 2020] **Ossineke (½ time) and Harrisville, Lincoln (½ time) 2020**.<> (O) 13095 US Hwy 23 S, Ossineke 49766; 7770 Scott Rd, Hubbard Lake 49747 (989) 471-2334. (H) 217 N State St, Harrisville 48740 (989) 724-5450. (L) 101 E Main St, PO Box 204, Lincoln 48742 (989) 736-6910. Home: 216 5th St, Harrisville 48740 (616) 295-7546. lovegra1ferris@gmail.com

*Lover, John D. (Grace) –
[(RE) D-1960; FE-1963; R-2000] Transferred from Nebraska Conf 1994; Indian River/Pellston 1994; Indian River Indian River 09/01/1997; Retired 2000.<> Home: 725 Highland Terrace, Sheboygan WI 53083 (920) 395-2055. gracie08@charter.net

Low Edwardson, Elise Rodgers (Ryan) –
[(FE) FL 2016; PE 2017; FE 2020] **Escanaba: Central 2016**.<> 322 S. Lincoln, Escanaba 49829 (906) 786-0643. Home: 1814 22nd Ave, Escanaba 49829 (906) 789-1874. reveliselowedwardson@gmail.com

Low Edwardson, Ryan Casey (Elise) –
[(PE) FL 2016; PL 2019; PE 2020] Escanaba: First, Menominee: First 2016; Escanaba: First (LTFT ½) 2019; **Escanaba: First, Bark River 2020**.<> (EF) 302 S. Sixth St., Escanaba 49829 (906) 786-3713. (BR) 3716 "D" Rd, Bark River 49807. Home: 1814 22nd Ave, Escanaba 49829 (906) 789-1874. ryan.c.edwardson@gmail.com

*Lowley, Paul E. (Marjan) –
[(RE) D-1960; FE-1963; R-2000] Transferred from Northern Illinois Conf 1991; Ludington United 1991; Retired 2000.<> Home: 211 Bear Creek Lane, Georgetown TX 48633 (231) 347-9373

*Luce, Michael W. (Janet) –
[(RA) PL 1995; AM 2006] Garfield 1995; Poseyville 2001; **Retired 2012**.<> Home: 4510 Flajole Rd, Midland, MI 48642 (989) 225-8692. fathermikeusa@gmail.com

Luck, Bradley S. (Aimee) –
[(FE) PL 2011; PE 2014; FE 2017] 2011 Troy: Fellowship; **2013 Hudson: First; 2018 Dundee**.<> 645 Franklin St, Dundee 48131 (734) 529-3535. Home: 241 Sidney St., Dundee 48131. blucky33@comcast.net

*Ludwig, Brenda L. –
[(RL) RL-2018] [Indiana Conference, Retired Local Pastor] Three Oaks (PTLP ¾) 2018; **Berrien County: Lakeside (PTLP) 2020**.<> PO Box 402, Union Pier 49129 (269) 469-8468. Home: 8000 Warren Woods Rd #81, Three Oaks 49128 (269) 369-0696. brenda.ludwig@inumc.org

*Lyman, Carole Strobe (Frank) –
[(RE) D-1985; FE-1989; R-2010] Muskegon: Lake Harbor (Assoc LTFT ½) 11/01/1984; Muskegon: Lake Harbor (Assoc LTFT ¾) 01/01/1991; Plainwell: First (Co-Pastor) 1991; East Lansing: University (Co-Pastor) 1996; Grand Rapids: Trinity 2006; Retired 2010.<> Home: 29543 Seahorse Cove, Laguna Niguel CA 92677 (616) 558-1924. carolelyma@aol.com

*Lyman, Frank W. (Carole) –
[(RE) D-1976; FE-1980; R-2010] Transferred from Detroit Conf 1981; Muskegon: Lake Harbor 1981; Plainwell: First (Co-Pastor) 1991; East Lansing: University (Co-Pastor) 1996; Grand Rapids: Trinity 2006; Retired 2010.<> Home: 29543 Seahorse Cove, Laguna Niguel CA 92677 (616) 558-1924. franklyma@aol.com

Lynch, Robert K. (Leslie) –
[(FE) D-1993; FE-1995] Mason: First (Assoc) 1992; Paw Paw 1995; Kalamazoo: Milwood 1999; N Muskegon: Community 2006; Allegan 2012.<> 409 Trowbridge St, Allegan 49010 (269) 673-4236. Home: 1310 South M 40, Allegan 49010 (269) 673-2512. blynch4551@gmail.com

Lynn, Nancy S. –
[(FE) PE 2010; FE 2013] 2010 Ann Arbor: First (assoc); **2018 Ann Arbor: First**.<> 120 S. State, Ann Arbor 48104 (734) 662-4536. Home: 3475 Glazier Way, Ann Arbor 48105 (734) 730-2421. nancy@fumc-2a.org

*Lyons, Gary V. –
[(RE) D-1972; FE-1975; R-1996] Transferred from Detroit Conf 1972; Vermontville/Gresham 1972; Other Valid Ministries (¶344.1d) Chaplain, US Navy 04/05/1976; Retired 1996.<> Home: 522 Albion Circle, Gallatin TN 37066 (615) 230-9754

*Macaulay, Elizabeth Ann –
[(RE) PE 1999; FE 2002; RE 2018] June 16, 1999 Sterling Heights; 2008 Trenton: First; Apr 15, 2013 medical leave; **2018 Retired**.<> Home: 250 McDougall St, Apt 425, Detroit 48207. Pastorbeth0528@gmail.com

*Macaulay, Thomas Paul (Mary) –
[(RE) P 1972; F 1975] 1973 Detroit: Boulevard Temple; 1974 Birmingham: Embury (assoc); Jan 1977 Detroit: Waterman, Preston; 1979 Carleton; July 15, 1984 Lincoln Park: First; July 1, 1990 Warren: First; 1997 Lake Orion; 2004 Ann Arbor District Superintendent; **2010 Retired**.<> Home: 624 Maple Oaks Court, Saline 48176 (734) 730-1742. tommac223@aol.com

Magner, Eric Lee (Amy) –
[(PL) CC-2017; DSA-2017; PL-2017] Newaygo (DSA) (LTFT ¾) 2017; Newaygo (LP) (LTFT ¾) 12/01/2017.<> 101 State Rd., Newaygo 49337 (231) 652-6581. Home: 104 State Rd., Newaygo 49337 (231) 750-3488. e1972magner@gmail.com

*Malicoat, Bruce W. –
[(RL) PL Nov 2006; FL 2010; RL 2020] Nov 1, 2006 Arbela (¼); Jan 1, 2008 Arbela (½); 2010 Arbela, West Forest; 2016 West Forest; **Retired 2020.**<> Home: 129 E. Vates, Frankenmuth 48734 (989) 860-7378. Bruce.malicoat@gmail.com

*Mallory, Mary Lynch –
[(RE) P N. Ill, 1979; F Cent. IL, 1986] 1982 Carthage-Burnside; 1984 Minonk-Dana; 1988 Piper City; July 1, 1993 trans to Detroit Conf, Iron River: Wesley; Feb 1, 2001 Birmingham: Embury; 2006 West Branch: First; **2009 Retired.**<> Home: #10 Penny Lane, St. Helen 48656 (989) 387-0372. revmlm05@yahoo.com

*Mallory, Paul J. (Kathy) –
[(RE) P Cent. IL, 1980; F Cent. IL, 1984; FL 2006; FE 2008] 1981 Coluse-Dallas City-Nauvoo; 1984 Streator: First (Assoc); 1988 Chastsworth; July 1, 1993 trans to Detroit Conf, Crystal Falls-Amasa: Grace; [Nov 1, 1993 surrender of credentials]; 2006 reinstated; 2006 God's Country Cooperative Parish (Parish Director): Grand Marais, Germfask, McMillan; 2011 Iron Mountain: Trinity; **2014 Retired.**<> Home: 305 S. Steele, Ontonagon 49953. thevicar@yahoo.com

Mangum, Lester (Tina) –
[(FE) P NY, 1983; F 1986] 1983 New York City: Willis Avenue; 1985 Trans. to Detroit Conf, Detroit: Central (assoc); 1986 Director, Young Adult Housing Project of Metropolitan Community Church, NYC (NY Conf, under par. 425.1); 1988 Detroit Human Services; 1989 River Rouge: John Wesley; 1992 Detroit: People's; Jan 1, 2003 Detroit: St. Timothy, West Outer Drive; 2005 Detroit: St. Timothy; Oct 18, 2012 medical leave; **Oct 1, 2013 Pontiac: St. John.**<> 620 University Dr., Pontiac 48342 (248) 338-8933. Home: 622 University Dr., Pontiac 48342 (248) 335-7093. stjohnpontiac@sbcglobal.net

Manning, Joshua –
[(FL) FL-2017] Lake Ann 2017.<> 6583 First St, Lake Ann 49650 (231) 275-7236. Home: 6596 First St, Lake Ann 49650 (334) 320-9603. alpacacries@yahoo.com

Manning, Scott E. –
[(FE) FL-2005; PE-2007; FE-2011] Middleville/Freeport 2004; Middleville 2006; Constantine/White Pigeon 2009; Rochester Hills: St. Luke 2016.<> 3980 Walton Blvd, Rochester Hills 48309 (248) 373-6960. Home: 59180 Hamilton Circle, Washington Township 48094 (586) 371-4950. revscottemanning@gmail.com

Mannschreck, Jack Lester (Ruth) –
[(FE) P 1983; F 1986] 1984 Grosse Pointe (assoc); 1992 Oxford; 2002 Troy: Big Beaver; **2013 Waterford: Central.**<> 3882 Highland Rd., Waterford 48328 (248) 681-0040. Home: 3720 Shaddick, Waterford 48328 (248) 683-2986. jmannschreck@waterfordcumc.org

Mannschreck, Jeremiah J. (Sara) –
[(FE) FL 2014; PE 2015; FE 2019] 2014 Ishpeming: Wesley; **2018 Flushing.**<> 413 E. Main St., Flushing 48433 (810) 659-5172. Home: 1159 Clearview Dr., Flushing 48472 (810) 659-6231. pastor@flushingumc.org

Manskar, Steven W. –
[(OE) OE-2018] [Minnestoa Conference, Elder] Grand Rapids: Trinity 2018.<> 1100 Lake Dr SE, Grand Rapids 49506 (616) 456-7168. Home: 2128 Monroe Ave NW, Grand Rapids 49505 (615) 948-0650. steven.manskar@gmail.com

*Marble, Charles Robert (Janice) –
[(RE) T 1961; F 1963] 1961 school; Feb 1963 Detroit: Westlawn (assoc); 1965 Flint: Central (assoc); 1967 Inkster: Christ; 1971 Bay City: Fremont Avenue; Jan 1978 Burton: Atherton; 1985 Dixboro; 1992 Houghton Lake; **2000 Retired**.<> 2129 Knights Circle, Gladwin 48624 (989) 426-4580

Marck, George –
[(PL) PL Jan 1, 2020] **Royal Oak: First (assoc) (PTLP ¼) Jan 1, 2020; Waterford: Four Towns (PTLP ¼) 2020**.<> (ROF) 320 W 7th St, Royal Oak 48067 (248) 541-4100. (WFT) 6451 Cooley Lake Rd, Waterford 48327 (248) 682-0211. Home: 4309 N Verona Cir, Royal Oak 48073 (248) 682-0211. gmarck@rofum.org

*Mariona, Ernesto –
[(RE) FL May 16, 2008, American Baptist Convention; FE 2011; RE 2020] 2008-Sept 30, 2017 St. Charles; 2008-2015 Brant; Oct 1, 2017 Midland: Homer, Gordonville; **Retired 2020**.<> Home: 8225 Beaver Rd, Saint Charles 48655 (248) 760-9590. netomariona@gmail.com

*Marr, Beverly Louise (Fred) –
[(RE) PE 2003; FE 2006] 2003 Lincoln Community; 2010 Seven Churches United Group Ministry: Durand: First (Parish Director); **2017 Retired**.<> Home: 3910 Norton Road, Howell 48843 (810) 923-6860. revbevmarr@hotmail.com

Marsh, Scott W. (Meagan) –
[(PE) FL 2019; PE 2020] **Coleman: Faith 2019**.<> 310 N 5th St, Coleman 48618 (989) 465-6181. Home: 209 Jefferson St, Coleman 48618 (231) 760-0601. smarsh3386@gmail.com

Marshall, Murphy C. –
[(LP) LP 2015] **2017 Harper Woods: Redeemer**.<> 20571 Vernier Rd., Harper Woods 48225 (313) 884-2035. Home: 20572 Anita, Harper Woods 48225

*Marshall-Smith, June M. –
[(RE) PL 2006; PE 2007; FE 2011; RE 2020] Dearborn: Mt. Olivet 2006; Novi 2007; **Retired 2020**.<> Home: 40755 Oakwood Dr., Novi 48375 (248) 349-6117. junesmith48124@yahoo.com

*Martinez-Ventour, Margaret A. –
[(RL) PL 9/1/03; PE 2004; LP 2012; RL 2019] Sept 1, 2003 Detroit: Jefferson Avenue; 2005 Detroit: Mt. Hope; 2010 Detroit: Resurrection; **2019 Retired**.<> Home: 7623 Danbury Cir, W Bloomfield 48322 (313) 342-3027. pastormmv@comcast.net

*Mater, Douglas E. (Margaret) –
[(RE) FL 2003; PE 2004; FE 2007; RE 2019] 2003 Bay Port, Hayes; 2010 Negaunee. Mitchell; 2016 Saginaw: Ames; **Retired 2019**.<> Home: 6061 Foxwood Ct, Saginaw 48638 (989) 906-1463. spamd5@aol.com

*Mathews, James M. (Coryn) –

[(RA) FL 1981; LD, AM 1986; RA 2003] 1981 Republic, Woodland; June 1, 1984 Iron Mountain: First, Quinnesec; Dec 1, 1989 Leave of Absence; 1990 L'Anse, Sidnow, Zeba; 1993 Pickford; 1996 Leave of Absence; Aug 1, 1997 Seven Churches United Group Ministry: Vernon, Bancroft; Oct 1, 2001 Roseville: Trinity, Warren: Wesley; 2002 incapacity leave; **2003 Retired;** 2003 Stephenson: First (LTFT ½); **2019 Keweenaw Parish: Calumet, Lake Linden (LTFT ½).**<> (C) 57235 Calumet Ave., Calumet 49913 (906) 337-2720. (LL) 53237 N. Hecla, Lake Linden 49945 (906) 296-0148. Home: 26350 Wyandotte St., Laurium 49913 (906) 337-0539. revmathews@yahoo.com

*Mathieu, Pamela J. –

[(RD) D-1997; RD-2012] Transferred from Detroit Conf 1995; Lansing: Mount Hope, Director of Visitation and Adult Ministries 1995; Transitional Leave 12/31/2005; Medical Leave 03/01/2006; Retired 2012.<> Home: 5824 Merritt Rd, Ypsilanti 48197 (517) 214-4441. pmath2@peoplepc.com

*Maurer, Edrye A. Eastman –

[(RE) FL-2000; PE-2003; FE-2006; R-2017] Lake City 2000; Jackson Calvary 09/01/2010; Jackson Calvary/Zion 2013; Coldwater 2015; Retired 2017.<> Home: 10101 Jackson Square, Decatur GA 30030 (269) 459-5223. edryemaurer@gmail.com

*Maxwell, Jeffrey R. (Janet) –

[(RE) LP 1982; P 1986; F 1989] Garfield 1982; Kilmanagh, Unionville 1987; Holly: Calvary Jan 15, 1990; Farmington: First 2001; Saginaw Bay District Superintendent 2010; **Retired 2016;** Interim Central Bay District Superintendent Jan 1-July 1, 2020.<> Home: 304 Meadow Lane, Midland 48640 (989) 750-7035. jffmxwll@yahoo.com

*May, Judith Ann –

[(RE) P 1990; F 1993] 1989 Four Towns (LTFT); Jan 1, 1991 Four Towns; 1992 Pontiac Cooperative Parish, Parish Director: Four Towns; Feb 1, 1996 Dearborn: First (assoc); 1998 Walled Lake; 2003 Warren: First; 2008 Grosse Pointe; **2016 Retired.**<> Home: 52843 Sable Drive, Macomb 48042 (586-242-1555. judymay1947@yahoo.com

Mayberry, Gregory Mark –

[(FE) P 1984; F 1986] 1984 Iron River; 1990 Caseville; May 1, 1998 Milford; 2011 Caro; **2016 Troy: Big Beaver.**<> 3753 John R, Troy 48083 (248) 689-1932. Home: 2050 Fairfield, Troy 48085 (248) 689-2839. gmayberry@bbumc.org

*Maynard, William Robert (Janis) –

[(RE) P 1972; F 1980] Sept 1978 Kilmanagh; 1980 Flint: Eastwood; 1986 Mayville, Fostoria, Silverwood; Sept 1, 1992 Mt. Morris; 1996 Corunna; 2001 Davisburg; Jan 1, 2004 incapacity leave; **2009 Retired.**<> Home: PO Box 163, East Tawas 48730. RevBill02@aol.com

*Mayo, Judith Y. (James) –

[(RD) CE CRT 1990; CON 1992; DFM 1997; RD 2014] 1984 Livonia: Newburg; 1998 Detroit: Christ; 1999 East Side Covenant Cooperative Parish, parish deacon; Jan 1, 2001 leave of absence; 2001 Ypsilanti: First (deacon); Jan 1, 2007 Ypsilanti: First (deacon); Dec 5, 2007 incapacity leave; **2014 Retired.**<> Home: 6065 Vista Dr., Ypsilanti 48197 (734) 482-0776. jymayo1@comcast.net

*Mayo, Robert J. (Sharon) –

[(RE) D-1980; FE-1983; R-2013] Transferred from Northern Indiana Conf 1981; Marcellus/Wakelee 1981; Hastings: Hope 04/01/1986; Traverse City Emmanuel 1992; Grand Rapids: Saint Paul 1999; UM Connectional Structures (¶344.1a,c) District Superintendent, Grand Traverse District 2005; Battle Creek: Chapel Hill 2011; Retired 2013.<> Home: 4651 Springmont Dr SE, Kentwood 49512 (616) 228-3075. rmayo777@yahoo.com

Mayo-Moyle, Amy E. (Michael) –

[(FE) PE 2000; FE 2003] 2000 Detroit: Metropolitan (assoc); 2002 Britton: Grace; Sept 16, 2007 Britton: Grace (LTFT ½); Jan 1, 2009 Britton: Grace (LTFT ¾);2010 Clarkston (assoc); **2015 Farmington: Orchard**.<> 30450 Farmington, Farmington Hills 48334 (248) 626-3620. Home: 32979 Thorndyke Court, Farmington Hills 48334 (517) 918-2215. AMayomoyle@yahoo.com

Mayo-Moyle, Michael James (Amy) –

[(FE) FL 2001; PE 2002; FE 2005] 2001 Ann Arbor: First (assoc); Feb 1, 2003 Blissfield: First; 2010 Seven Churches United Group Ministry: Byron: First; 2012 Voluntary leave of absence; **2017 Michigan UMC IT Specialist**.<> 1161 E Clark Rd, Ste 212, DeWitt 48820 (517-347-4030 ext. 4136). Home: 32979 Thorndyke Court, Farmington Hills 48334 (517) 918-2215. mmayomoyle@michiganumc.org

Mays, Jonathan D. –

[(PL) PL-2015] Charlevoix: Greensky Hill (DSA) (½ Time) 2012; Charlevoix: Greensky Hill (PTLP ½) 2015.<> 8484 Green Sky Hill Rd, Charlevoix 49720 (231) 547-2028. Home: 409 Prospect St, Charlevoix 49720 (231) 459-8067. jonmays7@gmail.com

*Mazur, Paul D. (Margaret) –

[(RE) D-1968; FE-1971; R-1990] Frontier 1963; Girard 1966; Battle Creek: Baseline 1969; Hillside 09/15/1972; Climax/Scotts 09/01/1974; Carson City/Hubbardston 1978; Buchanan: First 1985; Frankfort/Elberta 1987; Coopersville 04/01/1989; Retired 1990.<> Home: 536 Harwood Ct, Eaton Rapids 48827 (517) 663-2687. paulmazur12@att.net

McBride, David L. (Bonnie) –

[(FE) D-1985; FE-1987] Holton/Sitka 1983; Holton 01/01/1985; Marshall (Assoc) 1988; Ithaca/Beebe 1991; Leighton 2006.<> 4180 2nd St, Caledonia 49316 (616) 891-8028. Home: (616) 891-1646. office@leightonchurch.org

*McBride, William Parker –

[(RE) P 1975; F 1981] 1978 Owendale, Gagetown; 1980 Flint: Faith; 1985 Monroe: Calvary; 1995 Seven Churches United Group Ministry (Parish Director): Durand: First; 2002 North Street; Nov 1, 2014 disability leave; **2016 Retired**.<> 3900 Aspen Dr., #316, Port Huron 48060 (810) 434-3494. mbill@shianet.org

*McCallum, Marvin H. (Joyce) –

[(RE) T 1959; F 1961] 1961 Pigeon; 1966 Oxford; 1972 Manistique; Nov 1975 Chelsea; 1983 Monroe: St. Paul's; 1991 Royal Oak: First; 1995 Port Huron District Superintendent; **2002 Retired**.<> Home: 5385 Burtch Rd., Jeddo 48032 (810) 327-2691. joyce.mccallum@gmail.com

*McCoy, J. Patrick (Susan) –
[(RE) D-1977; FE-1982; R-2014] Three Rivers: First/Ninth Street (Assoc) 10/01/1980; Other Valid Ministries (¶344.1d) Resident Supervisory CPE, North Carolina Memorial Hospital 1983; Other Valid Ministries (¶344.1d) Director of Clinical Chaplaincy Iowa Methodist Medical Center 10/15/1985; Other Valid Ministries (¶344.1d) Director of Chaplaincy, Dartmouth-Hitchcock Medical Center, Lebanon NH 11/01/1993; Retired 09/01/2014.<> Home: 32 Sargent St, Norwich VT 05055 (802) 649-3736

McCoy, Steven E. (Deborah) –
[(FE) PE 1999; FE 2002] 1999 Midland: First (assoc); 2006 Marquette: First; **2013 Livonia: Newburg.**<> 36500 Ann Arbor Trail, Livonia 48150 (734) 422-0149. Home: 33652 Trillium Court, Livonia 48150 (734) 424-4593

*McCreedy, Allen D. (Mina Ann) –
[(RE) D-1965; FE-1970; R-2000] Kalamazoo: Sunnyside 1967; Kalamazoo: Westwood 1973; Reed City 1977; Cadillac 1990; Retired 2000.<> Home: 2015 Kaylynn Dr, Cadillac 49601 (231) 775-8254. 2015kaylyn@gmail.com

*McCully, Ruth Alida –
[(RL) FL 1998] 1998 Samaria: Grace, Lulu; 2001 Lulu; 2003 Retired; Nov 1, 2007 Azalia, London; **Oct 30, 2009 Retired.**<> Home: 510 E. Monroe, Dundee 48131 (734) 529-5130. ruthmccully@live.com

*McCumons, Brent Lee (Marlene) –
[(RE) P 1976; F 1980] Jan 1, 1975 Second Creek, Edenton OH (W OH Conf); 1978 Royal Oak: First (assoc); 1981 Caseville; 1986 Chesaning: Trinity; 1993 Ann Arbor District Superintendent; 1998 Midland: First **2011 Retired.**<> Home: 909 Ruddy Duck Lane, Chelsea 48118. bmccumons@aol.com

McDonald, Ian S. –
[(FL) FL 2012] 2012 God's Country Cooperative Parish: Grand Marais, Germfask, McMillian; **Carson City 2019.**<> 119 E Elm St, PO Box 298, Carson City 48811. Home: 121 S Abbott St, Carson City 48811 (906) 322-5318

McDoniel, Tommy L. –
[(FL) FL 2010] **2010 Flint: Asbury.**<> 1653 Davison Rd., Flint 48506 (810) 235-0016. Home: 2050 Covert Rd., Burton 48509 (810) 705-4401. revmcdoniel@gmail.com

McDougall, Heather A. –
[(PE) FL-2011; PE-2014] Silver Creek/Keeler 2011; Kalamazoo: Milwood 2013; Appointed to Extension Ministries (¶344.1b,c) PRN Chaplain, Bronson Healthcare Group 09/01/2015; Appointed to Extension Ministries (¶344.1b,c) Chaplain, Bronson Methodist Hospital 02/08/2016; Appointed to Extension Ministries (¶344.1b,c) Chaplain Beacon Health System (LTFT ¾) and Three Rivers: First (LTFT ¼).<> 215 N Main St, Three Rivers 49093 (269) 278-4722. Home: 61644 Windridge Ct, Centreville 49032 (269) 352-4857. chaplainheathermcdougall@gmail.com

*McDowell, Ginethea D. –
[(RE) PL 1989; P 1994; F 1996] 1989-91 Caring Covenant Group Ministry: West Deerfield; 1992 no appointment; 1994 Yale, Greenwood; Dec 1, 1998 family leave **2002 Retired.**<> Home: 124 Happy Haven Dr., Lot 46, Osprey FL 34229

*McEntarfer, Martin A. –
[(RE) FL, Erie, 1950; T. MI, 1953; F 1960] 1950 Franklin Center; 1951 Lyon Lake; 1953 Delton; 1956 Burton Heights (assoc); Dec 1956 Trans. to Detroit Conf, Menominee; 1960 Centerline: Bethel; 1966 Chaplain, Plattsburg AFB, NY; 1969 Site Chaplain, Alaskan Air Command; 1970 Chaplain, Kitty Hawk Center, Wright Patterson AFB, Ohio; 1972 Chaplain, Pilot Training Program, Reese AFB, TX; 1973 Chaplain, Utapoa AB, Thailand; 1974 Chaplain, Regional Medical Center, March AFB, CA; 1978 Senior Chaplain, Irakion AB, Crete, Greece; 1980 Senior Chaplain, David Grant Medical Center, Travis AFB, CA; 1984 Senior Chaplain, March AFB, CA; 1986 USAF Retired; 1986 Service Director, American Cancer Society; 1989 Cancer Control Director, American Cancer Society; **1992 Retired.**<> Home: 20505 Claremont Ave., Riverside CA 92507 (951) 686-5846

McGee, Ray Thomas (Darlene) –
[(FE) LP 1995; FL 1998; AM 2000; FE 2003] Jan 1, 1995 LaSalle: Zion; Aug 15, 2000 Sebewaing: Trinity; 2004 Flint: Calvary; 2011 Detroit: Metropolitan; **2016 Grosse Pointe.**<> 211 Moross Rd., Grosse Pointe Farms 48236 (313) 886-2363. Home: 64 Moross Rd., Grosse Pointe Farms 48236 (313) 881-1129. mcgreeray4@gmail.com

McGlothin-Eller, April K. (Vincent) –
[(FD) PD 2006; FD 2009] Young Leaders Initiative June 1, 2006; leave of absence Jan 31, 2008; Student Coordinator for Interfaith Worker Justice, Highland Park Presbyterian Mar 16, 2008; Stewardship Associate, Garrett-Evangelical Seminary June 14, 2010; **Church Engagement Manager, Newnan Office of the UM Children's Home (Par 331.1b) North Georgia Conf 2018.**<> (313) 610-1980. Home: 6572 Oakwood Dr., Douglasville GA 30135 (313) 384-3158. april.mcgel@gmail.com

McGlothin-Eller, Vincent W. (April) –
[(FD) PD 2009; FD 2012] Registrar, Garrett Evangelical Theological Seminary 2009; Director of Academic Studies and Registrar GETS June 1, 2010; Director: Academic Studies and Registrar GETS 2018; **Newnan: First (N Georgia Conf) (½ time) Jan 1, 2019; GETS Registration Services & Data Specialist (½ time) Jul 13, 2020.**<> 33 Greenville St., Newnan GA 30263 (770) 253-7400. Home: 6572 Oakwood Dr., Douglasville GA 30135 (313) 384-3158. vincemcgel@gmail.com

McIlvenna, Lisa M. (Patrick) –
[(FE) P 1990; F 1993] 1991 Owendale, Gagetown; 1995 Saginaw: Kochville; Sept 1, 1999 Birmingham: First (assoc); 2004 Rochester Hills: St. Luke's; 2008 Samaritan Couseling Center, Southeast Michigan; **Jan 2010 Midland: First (assoc) (½), Clinical Director/Pastoral Therapist, Samaritan Counseling Center (½).**<> 315 W. Larkin, Midland 48640 (989) 835-7511. Home: 531 Morningside Dr, Midland 48640 (248) 224-4296. lisamcilvenna@yahoo.com

McInnes, Mary G. (Damon) –
[(FE) P 1996; F 1998] 1996 Grosse Pointe (assoc); Nov 1, 2002 Farmington: Nardin Park (assoc); 2008 Tawas; 2013 Mount Clemens: First; **2017 South Lyon: First.**<> 640 S. Lafayette, South Lyon 48178 (248) 437-0760. Home: 650 S. Lafayette, South Lyon 48178 (586) 515-0013. revmarymcinnes@att.net

McKanders, Cherlyn E. –
[(PL) PL 2017] 2017 Mount Vernon (LTFT ½); **2019 Mt Vernon (LTFT ½), Washington (LTFT ¼).**<> (MV) 3000 28 Mile Rd., Washington 48094 (248) 650-2213. (W) 58430 Van Dyke, PO Box 158, Washington 48094 (586) 781-9662. Home: 59989 Whitman N. #D, Washington 48094 (248) 881-8541. cmckanders@comcast.net

McKenney, Wayne E. (Sally) –
[(FL) FL-1995] Chase Barton/Grant Center (DSA) 1995; Chase: Barton/Grant Center 11/16/1995; Webberville 08/01/2002; Boyne City/Boyne Falls 2005; Oshtemo: Life-spring/Lawton: St Paul's 2014; Lawrence/Lawton: St Paul's 2016.<> (L) PO Box 276, 122 S Exchange St, Lawrence 49064 (269) 674-8381. (LSP) PO Box 456, 63855 N M-40, Lawton 49065 (269) 624-1050. Home: 45520 24th St, Mattawan 49071 (269) 669-7062. skinnypreacher@me.com

***McKinstry, A. Faye** (David) –
[(RE) P 1988; F 1992] 1988 St. Clair Shores: First (assoc) (LTFT½); 1990 East Detroit: Peace; July 1, 1995 Madison Heights; 1999 Manchester; 2005 Clinton; **2014 Re-tired**.<> Home: 35 Ridgemont Dr., Adrian 49221 (517) 815-1172. fayemckinstry@com-cast.com

***McKinstry, David Robert** (A. Faye) –
[(RE) P 1979; F 1982] 1980 Oregon, Elba; 1988 St. Clair Shores: First; 1999 Tecumseh; **2010 Retired**.<> Home: 35 Ridgemont Dr., Adrian 49221 (517) 815-1172. drmck-instry@gmail.com

McMunn, Douglas Jay (Marianne) –
[(FE) P 1985; F 1988] 1986 Plymouth: First (assoc); Feb 16, 1990 Iron Mountain: First, Quinnesec: First; Jan 1, 1996 Pinckney: New Church Development (Arise); Sept 28, 2001 Pinckney: Arise; 2006 Oxford; **2011 Milford**.<> 1200 Atlantic St. Milford 48381 (248) 684-2798. Home: 350 Cabinet St., Milford 48381 (248) 685-1737. doug.mc-munn@gmail.com

***McNary, Sandra B. Hoffman** (Charles) –
[(RE) D-1984; FE-1988; R-2007] Transferred from Tennessee Conf 1994; Bangor: Simpson 1994; Retired 2007. 6117 Santa Fe Trail NE, Rio Rancho NM 87144 (269) 427-0766. <> sandramcnary@live.com

McNees, Zachary D. (Sarah) –
[(FL) FL 2019] Grand Rapids: Northlawn (LTFT ½) and Allendale: Valley Church (Assoc) (LTFT ½) 2019.<> (N) 1157 Northlawn St NE, Grand Rapids 49505 (616) 361-8503. (V) 5980 Lake Michigan Dr, Ste B, Allendale 49401 (616) 892-1042. Home: 1141 Northlawn St NE, Grand Rapids 49505 (269) 986-0108. zmcnees@valleychurchallen-dale.org

McPherson, Rob A. (Kristi) –
[(FE) D-1997; FE-2001] Grandville (Assoc) 1994; Ovid United Church 1999; Buchanan: First 2006; Hillsdale: First 2018.<> 45 N Manning St, Hillsdale 49242 (517) 437-3681. Home: 1079 Markris Dr, Hillsdale 49242 (269) 845-5221. revrobmac@sbcglobal.net

***McReynolds, Russell F.** –
[(RE) D-1971; FE-1974; R-2007] Transferred from Detroit Conf 1991; Battle Creek: Washington Heights 06/16/1991; UM Connectional Structures (¶344.1a,c) District Su-perintendent, Kalamazoo District 1996; Lansing: Central 2002; Retired 2007; Lansing: Faith & S Lansing Ministries 2008-2015.<> Home: 1721 Dover Place, Lansing 48910 (517) 483-2727. russellfmcreynolds@comcast.net

***Mehl, John Matthew, Jr.** (Terrie) –
[(RE) P 1980; F 1984; RE 2019] 1982 Argentine, Linden; 1989 Ida; 1996 Ida, Peters-burg; 2001 Petersburg (LTFT ½); Jan 1, 2010 incapacity leave; **June 1, 2019 Re-tired**.<> Home: 16645 Dixon Rd., Petersburg 49270 (734) 279-2662. mudbug@cass.net

*Meister, David W. (Denise) –
[(RE) D-1977; FE-1980; R-2016] Transferred from East Ohio Conf 1978; Rosebush/Leaton 1978; Lakeview/ Belvidere 1980; Litchfield 1985; Leave of Absence 03/16/1990; Haslett: Aldersgate 1994; Union City 08/01/1995; Centreville 08/16/1997; Buchanan: First 2003; Casco 2006; Retired 2016.<> Home: 6775 107th Ave, South Haven 49090 (269) 876-7204. revdmeister@gmail.com

*Melrose, Paul J. (Sue Ellis Melrose) –
[(RE) P 1971 NY; F 1974 NY] 1971 school; 1973 Bristol: Prospect (assoc); 1975 Bronx: City Island; Jan 1981 school; 1982 Associate Director, Lakeland Counseling Center, FRMH, Dover NJ; 1986 Co-Director, Lakeland Counseling Center, FRMH, Dover NJ; 1993 Director, FRMH Counseling Center, NW New Jersey; 1996 Director, FRMH, New Jersey; 1998 Coordinator, Pastoral Psychotherapy, NW Covenant Medical Center, NJ; 1999 Coordinator, Pastoral Psychotherapy, St. Clares Hospital, Boonton NJ; Feb 2, 2000 Staff Counselor, Samaritan Counseling Center, Southeast Michigan (transferred to Detroit Conf, 2001); 2006 Executive Director, Samaritan Counseling Center, Southeast Michigan; **2011 Retired**.<> Home: 1624 N. Golf Glen, Unit A, Madison WI 53704 (248) 231-7229. paul.melrose@gmail

*Mercer, Dorothy M.D. (David) –
[(RD) D-1997; RD-2003] Grand Rapids: Faith, Director of Music 1987; Stanwood (LTFT ¼) 1997; Retired 03/01/2003.<> Home: 8651 Mohawk Ct, Stanwood 49346 (231) 972-7175

*Mercer, Douglas Keith (Barbara F.) –
[(RE) T 1966; F 1968] 1962 Wellsville; Oct 1963 Rea, Cone, Azalia; 1966 Concord Charge (Peninsula Conf); 1968 Port Huron: Washington Avenue; 1970 Algonac; 1974 Flint: Court Street (assoc); 1977 South Lyon; Jan 15, 1988 Gladstone: Memorial; 1990 Flint District Superintendent; 1996 Frankenmuth; **2000 Retired**.<> 10117 Hawthorne Lane, Byron 48418 (810) 919-6147. dougbarbmercer@gmail.com

Merchant, Michelle K. –
[(PL) PL-2016] New Hope of Emmett County (DSA) 12/01/2015; New Hope of Emmett County (PTLP ½) 11/15/2016.<> PO Box 72, 4516 N US 31, Levering 49755 (231) 537-2000. Home: 3224 Hill Road NW, Rapid City 49676 (231) 564-0723. michellekm64@outlook.com

Messner, John D. (Sally) –
[(FL) FL-2008] Marcellus/Wakelee (DSA) 2007; Marcellus/Wakelee 01/01/2008; **Williamsburg, Fife Lake Boardman Parish: Fife Lake, South Boardman 2020**.<> (W) PO Box 40, 5750 Williamsburg Rd, Williamsburg 49690 (231) 267-5792. (FL) PO Box 69, 206 Boyd St, Fife Lake 49633 (231) 879-4270. (SB) PO Box 112, 5488 Dagle St, S Boardman 49680 (231) 879-6055. Home: 124 Boyd St, Fife Lake 49633 (231) 757-4780. jdmessner@gmail.com

Metzer, Kimberly S. (Steve) –
[(FL) FL-2017] Hastings Hope 2017.<> PO Box 410, 2920 S M37, Hstings 49058 (269) 945-4995. Home: 121 W North St, Hastings 49058. pastorkimmetzer@gmail.com

*Meyers, Patricia A. (Lee Hearn) –
[(RE) P 1977; F 1979] 1977 Flint: Central (assoc); 1978 Dearborn: First (assoc); 1980 Pontiac: Baldwin Avenue; 1997 Ferndale: First; 1999 Mt. Clemens: First; Aug 1, 2006 incapacity leave; **2014 Retired**.<> Home: 15821 19 Mile Rd, Apt 309, Clinton Twp 48038 (586) 884-6538. patbeaches@comcast.net

Middel, Carol Ann –
[(PL) PL Jan 1, 2019] 2017 Thomas (DSA) (LTFT ½); Jan 1, 2019 Thomas (LTFT ½); **2019 Riverview (LTFT ½).**<> 13199 Colvin, Riverview 48193 (734) 284-2721. Home: 42018 Woodbrook Dr, Canton 48188 (734) 765-8143. bmiddel@aol.com

*Miles, Catherine J. (Kevin) –
[(RD) PD 2009; FD 2012] May 17, 2009 Detroit: Metropolitan (deacon); Aug 1, 2013 Fraser: Christ (deacon); **2017 Retired.**<> Home: 906 Hollis St., Port Huron 48060 (586) 453-7209. revcjmm7@gmail.com

*Miles, Kevin Lee (Catherine) –
[(RE) P 1990; F 1993] 1991 Plymouth: First (assoc); 1995 Blissfield: Emmanuel; 2002 Eastside Covenant Cooperative Parish: Roseville: Trinity; 2012 Oxford; 2014 Davison; **2017 Retired.**<> Home: 906 Hollis St., Port Huron 48060 (586) 453-3275. revkevm@gmail.com

Milford, Dale R. –
[(LP) LP 2015] 2015 Waterford: Four Towns; **2019 Southfield: Hope (assoc) (LTFT ¼).**<> 26275 Northwestern Hwy, Southfield 48076 (248) 356-1020. Home: 29229 Utley Rd, Farmington Hills 48334 (248) 417-5905

*Miller, Clyde E. (Judith) –
[(RA) D-1964; E-1966; AM-1973; RA-1987] Transferred from South Indiana Conf 1973; Pentwater/Smith Corners 1973; Pentwater 1976; Pentwater/Smith Corners 1977; Dowagiac: First 12/01/1979; Lansing Christ 04/16/1983; Leave of Absence 01/31/1987; Retired 1987.<> Home: 1117 Park St, Pentwater 49449 (231) 869-2151. clydemiller@chartermi.net

*Miller, Dale M. (Susan) –
[(RE) P N. IN, 1972; F 1975] 1974 Trans. to Detroit Conf, Plymouth: First (assoc); 1976 Stony Creek; 1981 Gladstone: Memorial; Jan 1, 1988 Flint: Central; 1992 Pontiac Cooperative Parish, Waterford: Central; Oct 1, 2000 Detroit East: District Superintendent; 2006 Farmington: Nardin Park; **2016 Retired.**<> Home: 129 Chauncey Ct., Marshall 49068 (248) 943-0699. dalemmiller@gmail.com

Miller, Darryl L. (Shari Ann) –
[(PL) PL-2007] Sand Lake/South Ensley (DSA PTLP ½) 01/01/2007; Sand Lake/South Ensley (PTLP ½) 12/01/2007; Sand Lake/South Ensley (PTLP ¼) 2011.<> (SL) PO Box 97, 65 W Maple Street, Sand Lake 49343 (676) 636-5673. (SE) PO Box 97, 13600 Cypress Ave, Sand Lake 49343 (616) 365-5659. Home: 1568 Solon, Cedar Springs 49319 (616) 696-4057. parsonmiller@charter.net

*Miller, Duane E. (Diana) –
[(RE) P 1968; F 1973] Mar 1972 Memphis, Lamb; Nov 1977 Gwinn, Ishpeming: Salisbury; Jan 1, 1986 Associate Council Director: Evangelism/Stewardship; Jan 1, 1996 Macomb Community Church; Jan 1, 1999 Seymour Lake; 1999 Caro; 2006 Detroit East District Superintendent; **2011 Retired.**<> Home: 3352 W. River Dr., Gladwin 48624 (989) 426-2644. duane@ddmiller.net

Miller, Eric John –
[(PL) PL Dec 1, 2014] Dec 1, 2014 Davisburg; **2018 Port Huron: Gratiot Park, Port Huron: Washington Avenue (LTFT ½).**<> (GP) 811 Church St., Port Huron 48060 (810) 985-6206, (WA) 1217 Washington Ave., Port Huron 48060 (810) 982-7812. Home: 48212 Cardinal, Shelby Twp. 48317 (586) 206-4527. pastorericjmiller@gmail.com

Miller, Mark Alan (Sharon) –
[(FE) PE 2006; FE 2009] 2006 Romulus: Community; **2010 Tecumseh.**<> 605 Bishop Reed Dr, Tecumseh 49286 (517) 423-2523. Home: 808 Derby Dr., Tecumseh 49286 (517) 423-3767. tecumcpastor@gmail.com

Miller, Mark Douglas (Kelly) –
[(FE) P 1983; F 1986] Blissfield: Emmanuel (assoc), Wellsville 1984; Owosso: Trinity May 1, 1989; West Branch: First 1998; Midland: Aldersgate 2006; Muskegon: Central 2013; **Wyandotte: First 2020.**<> 72 Oak, Wyandotte 48192 (734) 282-9222. Home: 2210 20th St., Wyandotte 48192 (734) 282-9222. revmarkmiller@yahoo.com

Miller, Robert A., Jr. –
[(FE) PL 2010; PE 2012; FE 2015] Jan 1, 2010 Livingston Circuit: Plainfield, Trinity; 2013 Milan: Marble Memorial; **2018 Plymouth: First.**<> 45201 N. Territorial Rd., Plymouth 48170 (734) 453-5280. Home: 1401 Palmer St., Plymouth 48170 (810) 623-0985. pastorbobmiller@comcast.net

*Miller, Sylvester, III –
[(RE) P N. Miss., 1968; F N. Miss., 1977] 1969—73 Boyd Chapel, Sturgis; 1979 Pleasant Grove, Louisville MS; 1983 Director, Holmes County Parish; Aug 1, 1985 Trans. to Detroit Conf, Detroit: Second Grace (assoc); Mar 1, 1986 Flint: E.L. Gordon Sr. Memorial; 1988 Leave of Absence; 1990 Flint: Faith; Aug 1, 2002 leave of absence; **2003 Retired.**<> Home: PO Box 28185, Birmingham AL 35228 (205) 426-8457. PastorSylMil3@aol.com

*Miller, Walter Harry (Sandra) –
[(RA) FL 1982; Deacon, AM 1987] Nov 1, 1981 Clayton, Rollin Center; 1994 Blissfield: First Dec 1, 2002 leave of absence; **Dec 1, 2004 Retired.**<> Home: 3805 Townley Highway, Manitou Beach 49253 (517) 547-4544

Miller-Black, Christina Lee (see White, Christina Miller) –

Minarik, Carman John (Donna) –
[(FE) P 1997, W. OH; FE 2000] 1995 Essex (W. OH); 1997 school; 1998 Carleton; Sept 1, 2002 South Lyon (co-pastor); 2007 Mount Clemens: First (co-pastor); 2013 Escanaba: First; 2016 Owosso: Trinity; **2019 Mecosta: New Hope.**<> 7296 9 Mile Rd., Mecosta 49332 (231) 972-2838. Home: 3955 9 Mile Rd., Remus 49340 (989) 967-8801. pastorcarman.newhope@gmail.com

Minarik, Donna Jo (Carman) –
[(FE) SP 1998, W. OH; PE 2001; FE 2005] Richwood Central (W. OH) 1996; Carleton (assoc) 1998; South Lyon (co-pastor) Sept 1, 2002; leave of absence Sept 16, 2006; Mount Clemens: First (co-pastor) 2007; Escanaba: Central 2013; Mason: First (W. MI Conf) 2016; Voluntary Leave of Absence 2019; **Fremont, Hesperia 2020.**<> (F) 351 Butterfield St, Fremont 49412 (231) 924-0030. (H) 187 E South Ave, Hesperia 49421 (231) 854-5345. Home: 352 Butterfield St, Fremont 49412. pastordonnaminarik@gmail.com

*Minger, David H. –
[(RE) D-1991; FE-1993; R-2006] Nottawa (Part Time) 10/01/1983; Athens 09/01/1987; Springport/Lee Center 01/01/1991; Traverse City Emmanuel 1999; Old Mission Peninsula (Ogdensburg) 02/01/2003; Retired 2006; Pleasant Lake/Jackson: Zion 2008; Griffith (LTFT ¼) 2013-10/16/2014.<> Home: 806 Emmaus Rd, Eaton Rapids 48827 (517) 256-5857. dhminger@yahoo.com

Minger, Stacy R. –
[(FE) D-1988; FE-1991] Girard/Ellis Corners 1989; Wayland 1995; Clergy Appointed to Attend School Student, University of Kentucky 08/01/2001; Appointed to Extension Ministries (¶344.1b,c) Associate Professor, Preaching, Asbury Theological Seminary 2004.<> Asbury Theo Sem, 204 N Lexington Ave, Wilmore KY 40390 (859) 858-2000. Home: 406 Wabarto Way, Nicholasville KY 40356 (859) 229-0059. Stacy.Minger@asburyseminary.edu

*Minor, Daniel J. (Jolene) –
[(RE) D-1968; FE-1970; R-2011] Transferred from East Ohio Conf 1974; East Jordan/Barnard/Norwood 4/15/1974; Shelby 1981; Parchment 1989; Retired 2011; Gobles/Kendall 09/16/2012-2013.<> Home: 719 Bayberry Ln, Otsego 49078 (269) 962-2119. revdminor@att.net

Mitchell, Mark E. (Joyce) –
[(FL) FL-1995] Howard City First/Amble/Coral 1995; Howard City: Maple Hill/First/Coral (Assoc) 08/01/1999; Homer/Lyon Lake 2000; Evart 2008; Fife Lake Parish: East Boardman/South Boardman 2012; Sodus: Chapel Hill 2014; North Parma/Springport 2018.<> (NP) 11970 Devereaux, PO Box 25, Parma 49269 (517) 531-4619. (S) 127 W Main St, PO Box 1004, Springport 49284 (517) 857-2777. Home: 258 Green St, Springport 49284 (517) 414-0180. mjmjumc@gmail.com

Mitchum, James P. (Michelle) –
[(FE) D-1984; FE-1986] Charlotte (Assoc) 04/16/1983; Robbins 06/01/1987; Petoskey 1997.<> 1804 E Mitchell Rd, Petoskey 49770 (231) 347-2733. Home: 900 Jennings Ave, Petoskey 49770 (231) 374-4747. james.mitchum@petoskeyumc.org

Mobley, Zelphia J. –
[(FL) PL 2014; FL 2015] Pontiac: Grace & Peace Community, Waterford: Trinity **Old Mission Penisula 2019**.<> 16436 Center Rd. Traverse City 49686 (231) 223-4393. Home: 14432 Peninsula Dr., Traverse City 49686 (248) 223-4141. zemobley@gmail.com

Momany, Christopher P. (Elizabeth) –
[(FE) D-1986; FE-1989] Mecosta: New Hope 1987; Pentwater: Centenary 1993; UM Connectional Structures (¶344.1a,c) Chaplain & Director of Church Relations, Adrian College 01/01/1996; Dowagiac: First 2019.<> 326 N Lowe St, PO Box 393, Dowagiac 49047 (269) 782-5167. Home: 207 Michigan Ave, Dowagiac 49047 (248) 462-5317. christopherpmomany@gmail.com

Mondragon, Rey Carlos Borja (Rosa Escudero) –
[(FE) PE 2007; FE 2011] school; Ypsilanti: First (assoc) 2007; Hartford (West Michigan Conference) 2014; Birch Run, Burt 2015; **Perry, Shaftsburg 2020**.<> (P) PO Box 15, 131 Madison St, Perry 48872 (517) 625-3444. (S) PO Box 161, 12821 Warner Rd, Shaftsburg 48882 (517) 675-1567. Home: 121 S Madison St, Perry 48872 (517) 625-3444. mondragonrey2000@yahoo.com

Montague-Corey, Cynthia –
[(PL) PL Jan 1, 2020] Bear Lake (DSA) (¼ time) 11/18/2018; **Bear Lake (PTLP ¼) Jan 1, 2020**.<> 7861 Main St, PO Box 157, Bear Lake 49614 (231) 864-3680. Home: 8340 Zosel St, PO Box 645, Onekama 49675 (231) 645-1244. pastorcynthia2019@gmail.com

*Montney, James B. –
[(RL) PL Feb 1, 2006] Elba Feb 1, 2006; **Retired 2012**.<> Home: 5033 N. Washburn, Davison 48423 (810) 653-1866. jbja4047@hotmail.com

Moon, Anna Mi-Hyun –
[(FE) PE 2012; FE 2015] North Lake 2012; **Troy: Korean (assoc) Hope Ministry 2016**.<> 42693 Dequindre, Troy 48085 (248) 879-2240. inpottershand12@gmail.com

*Moore, Frederick Boyce, Sr., (Delores) –
[(RE) P 1974; F 1980] 1976 River Rouge: John Wesley; Mar 1981 Detroit: People's; 1992 Pontiac: St. John (LTFT ¾); **2008 Retired**.<> 2897 Onagon Circle, Waterford 48328 (248) 681-4748. Fmoore54@comcast.net

*Moore, John Lewis –
[(RE) FE-1981; R-1995] Transferred from Free Methodist 1981; Arden 11/01/1980; Kalamazoo: Stockbridge Ave 03/16/1988; Galesburg 1992; Retired 1995; Center Park 1995-1997; Union City 08/16/1997-2004; Portage First (Assoc) 10/01/2006; Portage First (Assoc ¾ Time) and Kalamazoo Stockbridge Ave (¼ Time) 2007; Portage First (Assoc ¾ Time) 2010; Portage First (Assoc ½ Time) and Galesburg (½ Time) 2012-2013; Otsego: Trowbridge (LTFT ¼) 2014-2018.<> Home: 10100 Commons St Apt 1007, Lone Tree CO 80124 (269) 501-8181. johnmoore2924@gmail.com

Moore, Joy Jittaun –
[(FE) D-1989; FE-1991] Jackson: First (Assoc) 1988; Battle Creek: Baseline 1990; UM Connectional Structures (¶344.1a,c) Chaplain and Director of Church Relations, Adrian College 08/16/1993; Battle Creek: Trinity 1995; Lansing: Trinity (Assoc) 05/01/1996; Other Valid Ministries (¶344.1d) Director of Women's Ministries and Ethnic Concerns, Asbury Theo Sem 1997; Other Valid Ministries (¶344.1d) Director of Student Life 1998; Other Valid Ministries (¶335.1a) Instructor of Preaching, Asbury 08/16/2000; Other Valid Ministries (¶344.1d) Professor of Preaching, Asbury Asbury Theo Sem 07/01/2003; Greenville: First 2007; UM Connectional Structures (¶344.1a,c) Assoc Dean for Lifelong Learning, Duke Divinity 2008; UM Connectional Structures (¶344.1a,c) Assoc Dean for Black Church Studies and Church Relations 2009; UM Connectional Structures (¶344.1a) Associate Dean for African-American Church Studies and Assistant Professor of Preaching, Fuller Theological Seminary 09/01/2012; UM Connectional Structures (¶344.1b) Associate Professor of Homiletics and Christian Ministry 2017-04/30/2018; Transitional Leave 05/01/2018-06/30/2018; Appointed in Other Annual Conferences (¶331.8, ¶346.1) Detroit Conference, Flint: Bethel 2018; Associate Professor of Biblical Preaching Luther Seminary (¶344.1d) 2019; **Vice President of Academic Affairs and Academic Dean, Luther Seminary Sept 1, 2020**.<> Luther Seminary, 2481 Como Ave, St Paul MN 55108 (651) 641-3476. drjoyjmoore@gmail.com

*Moore, Richard D. (Margo) –
[(RE) D-1988; FE-1992; R-2015] Howard City Maple Hill 1989; Howard City Maple Hill/First/Coral 08/01/1999; Hastings: Hope 2000; Retired 2015.<> Home: 930 W Broadway St, Hastings 49058 (269) 908-0210. moore82@att.net

*Moore-Jumonville, Robert S. (Kimberly) –
[(RE) D-1989; FE-1992; RE-2019] Transferred from Illinois Great Rivers Conf 2008; Other Valid Ministries (¶344.1d) Assoc Professor of Religion, Spring Arbor Univ 2007; Appointed to Extension Ministries (¶344.1b,c) Associate Professor of Religion, Spring Arbor University and Pope (LTFT ¼) 2010; Appointed to Extension Ministries (¶344.1b,c) Associate Professor of Religion, Spring Arbor University 2018; Retired Apr 1, 2019.<> Home: 21 Dickens Street, Spring Arbor 49283 (517) 524-6818. rmooreju@arbor.edu

Moreland, Myra
[(FL) PL 2018; FL Feb 2020] Royal Oak: First (assoc) (PTLP ¼) Jan 1, 2018; Royal Oak: First (assoc) (PTLP ½) Jan 1, 2020; **Royal Oak: First (assoc) (FT) Feb 2, 2020.**<> 320 W. Seventh, Royal Oak 48067 (248) 541-4100. Home: 1763 Dorchester Rd, Birmingham 48009 (248) 835-5873. mmoreland@rofum.org

*Morrison, Dianne Doten (Richard) –
[(RL) PL-1996; NL-12/31/1997-1998; FL-1998; PL-2007; RL-2016] Sturgis (Assoc) (LTFT PT) 01/01/1996; Not Appointed 12/31/1997; Gull Lake (Assoc) 1998; Dowling: Country Chapel 02/01/2001; Muskegon: Crestwood 2004; Ferry (LTFT PT) 2007; Hesperia (LTFT PT) 2007; Traverse City: Christ 2011-1/1/2015; Retired 01/01/2016.<> Home: 7750 S West Bayshore Dr, Traverse City 49684 (231) 709-2382. Ddotenmorr@aol.com

*Morrison, Rebecca K. –
[(RE) FL-2002; PE-2003; FE-2008; RE-2019] Potterville 01/16/2002; Big Rapids: First 2011; Retired 2019.<> Home: 1625 Meijer Dr, Apt 206, Greenville 48838 (517) 712-4508. bkmorrison2019@gmail.com

*Morrison, Richard A. (Dianne Doten) –
[(RE) D-1967; FE-1969; R-2007] Jackson: First (Assoc) 1969; Bainbridge Newhope 1971; Appointed in Other Annual Conferences (¶331.8, ¶346.1) Missioner, Alaska Missionary Conference 1972; Transferred to West Ohio Conf 1975; Transferred from West Ohio Conf 1992; Alden/Central Lake 06/01/1992; Sturgis 1995; UM Connectional Structures (¶344.1a,c) District Superintendent, Albion District 01/01/1998; Muskegon: Lake Harbor 2004; Retired 2007; Hesperia/Ferry 2007-2011.<> Home: 7750 S West Bayshore Dr, Traverse City 49684 (231) 944-5503. adosuper@aol.com

*Morse, Harold S. (Linda) –
[(RE) P 1970; F 1973] 1972 Rochester: St. Luke's; 1979 Chaplain Supervisor, St. Louis Children's Hospital; **2011 Retired**.<> Home: 703 Muir Kirk Lane, Manchester MO 63011 (314) 394-1663

*Morse, John D. (Darleen) –
[(RE) D-1971; FE-1975; R-2012] Center Eaton/Brookfield 1973; Sunfield/Sebewa Center 02/01/1976; Frankfort/ Elberta 1982; Traverse City: Christ 1987; Jackson: First (Assoc) 1993; Coopersville 1999; Retired 2012; Twin Lake (LTFT ½) 2013; Twin Lake (LTFT 45%) 01/01/2014-2018.<> Home: 215 Dee Rd, Muskegon 49444 (231) 798-6943. jdm14879@gmail.com

Mort, James J. (Janet) –
[(FE) PE-2007; FE-2010] Marion/Cadillac: South Community 2007.<> (M) PO Box C, 216 W Main St, Marion 49665 (231) 743-2834. (CSC) 11800 47 Mile Rd, Cadillac 49601 (231) 775-3067. Home: 205 Flemming St, Marion 49665 (231) 743-0062. jim.mort@sbcglobal.net

***Morton, David L.** (Carrie) –
[(RE) D-1959; FE-1966; R-2001] Gilead (EUB) 1961; Scottdale (EUB) 1963; Vicksburg (EUB) 1965; Hillsdale: First (Assoc) 1969; Kent City: Chapel Hill 1970; Delta Mills/Eagle 01/15/1974; Jackson: First (Assoc) 1982; Battle Creek: Maple 1986; Other Valid Ministries (¶344.1d) Chaplain, Battle Creek Health System 05/01/1996; Retired 2001; Battle Creek: First (LTFT ¼) 03/05/2014-6/30/2014; Coldwater 01/01/2017-6/30/2017.<> Home: 4285 E Kirby Rd, Battle Creek 49017 (269) 964-7098. RevMorton62@yahoo.com

***Moshauer, Meredith T.** –
[(RE) T W. NY, 1969; F] 1969 Farmington: Nardin Park (assoc); 1977 Leave of Absence; Jan 1981 Livingston Circuit: Plainfield, Trinity; 1982 Leave of Absence; 1984 Durand Cluster: Lennon, Duffield (part- time); 1988 Detroit: West Outer Drive (LTFT ½); 1990 Highland Park: First (LTFT ½); 1995 Detroit: Waterman-Preston (LTFT ¾); **Aug 31, 1997 Retired.**<> Home: 1740 Nemoke Trail, #1, Haslett 48840

Mukalay, Gertrude Mwadi (John Kabala Ilunga Ngoie) –
[(OE) OE 2017, North Katanga Conf, Democratic Republic of Congo] **Detroit: French (New Church Start) (LTFT ¾) 2018.**<> 1803 E 14 Mile Rd, Birmingham 48009. Home: 1858 Estates Dr, Detroit 48206. mukalaymk@yahoo.fr

Mulanda, Eric Nduwa (Mafo Sonyi Corinne) –
[(FE) OE-2015; FE-2017] [SW Katanga Annual Conf, Elder] Greenville First, Turk Lake/Belding Cooperative Parish (Assoc) (LTFT ¼) 02/01/2015-06/30/2015; Greenville: First, Turk Lake/Belding Cooperative Parish (Assoc) (LTFT ¼) 2015; Lansing: Mount Hope (Assoc) 08/01/2015; Transferred from South Congo and Zambia 2017; **Lansing: Mount Hope 2020.**<> 501 E Mount Hope Ave, Lansing 48910 (517) 482-1549. Home: 545 N Dexter Dr, Lansing 48910. reveric79@gmail.com

***Mulder, David George** (Patricia) –
[(RE) P 1987; F 1990; R 2018] 1988 Flint: Court Street (assoc); 1992 Fairgrove, Gilford; 1996 Ypsilanti: St. Matthew's; 2001 Fenton (assoc); 2008 Midland: Homer; 2014 Marlette: First; **2018 Retired.**<> Home: 308 18th Ave NE, Waseca MN 56093. dmulder3@yahoo.com

Mulligan Armstrong, Cheryl A. –
[(FD) PD-2012; FD-2015] Deacons Appointed Beyond the Local Church (¶331.1a) Respitory Therapist at Helen DeVos Ped Pulmonary Clinic and Grand Rapids: Genesis (Deacon) Pastoral Care Minister 2012; Deacons Appointed Beyond the Local Church (¶331.1a) Respitory Therapist at Helen DeVos Ped Pulmonary Clinic and Missional at Lowell: First (Deacon Unpaid) 01/01/2014; Deacons Appointed Beyond the Local Church (¶331.1a) Respiratory Therapist, Helen DeVos Pediatric Pulmonary Clinic and Lowell: First (Deacon) Pastor of Discipleship (Paid) 10/09/2015; Deacons Appointed Beyond the Local Church (¶331.4a) Field Clinical Specialist for RespirTech Medical and Lowell: First (LTFT ¼ - Missional Service) 2018.<> (L) 621 E Main St, Lowell 49331 (616) 897-5936. 35 Michigan St NE, Suite 3003, Grand Rapids 49503 (616) 267-2200. Home: 3170 Buttrick Ave SE, Ada 49301 (616) 340-7995. mulliganfore@att.net

Mullikin, Keith Paul –
[(PL) PL Jan 22, 2020] Ironwood: Wesley (DSA) (¼ time) 10/01/2018; Ironwood: Wesley, Wakefield (DSA) (½ time) 2019; **Ironwood: Wesley, Wakefield (PTLP ½) Jan 22, 2020**.<> (IW) 500 E McLeod Ave, PO Box 9, Ironwood 49938 (906) 932-3900. (W) 706 Putnam St, Wakefield 49968 (906) 988-2533. Home: 600 Garvey, Ironwood 49938 (906) 285-9847. mullik81@gmail.com

*****Mumbiro, Elias N.** (Tapuwa) –
[(RE) P Zimbabwe 1977; F N. IN 1977] Jan 1, 1975-Dec 31, 1975 Associate Pastor, School Chaplain, Mutambara United Methodist Mission Center, Mutambara, Cashel, Zimbabwe; Jan 1, 1976-Dec 31, 1977 Missionary to South Indiana Conference; Jan 1, 1978-Aug 31, 1981 Evansville IN: St. John's and St. Andrews; 1983 to Dec 15, 1983 Itinerant Missioner to Iowa Conference and Southern District, Minnesota Conference; Jan 1, 1983-Dec 31, 1986 Mission Administrator/Chaplain Old Mutare Mission, Mutare, Zimbabwe; Jan 1, 1987-Aug 31, 1992 Mutasa-Makoni District Superintendent; Sept 1, 1992 River Rouge: John Wesley; 1995 transfer to Detroit Conference, Westland: St. James; Nov 1, 1999 Eastside Covenant Cooperative Parish: St. Clair Shores: Good Shepherd; 2009 Saginaw: State Street; **2015 Retired**.<>. mumbiro7@gmail.com

*****Mumford, Gerald Edward** (Dorothy) –
[(RA) LD 1966; LE 1968; AM 1989] 1964 West Forest, Otter Lake; 1976 West Deerfield; 1989 Mt. Bethel (part-time); **1993 Retired**.<> Home: 283 Inner Dr., E., Venice FL 34292 (941) 488-4312

*****Munger, Marjorie H.** (Dennis) –
[(RE) P 1991; F 1993] 1991 Flint: Bristol, Dimond; 1993 Canton: Cherry Hill; 1998 Troy: Fellowship; 2002 Lake Orion (assoc); **2013 Retired**.<> 1317 Gemstone Square, E., Westerville OH 43081 (614) 726-5061. margemunger@yahoo.com

Murphy, Marshall C. (Marian) –
[(FL) PL-2011; FL-2017] Battle Creek: Washington Heights (PTLP ¼) 2011; Battle Creek: First (PTLP ½) and Washington Heights (PTLP ¼) 2014; Appointed in Other Annual Conference (¶331.8, ¶346.1) Harper Woods Redeemer, Detroit Conf 2017.<> 20571 Vernier Rd, Harper Woods 48225 (313) 884-2035. Home: 20592 Anita, Harper Woods 48225 (269) 753-8056. mmurphy19@comcast.net

Murray, John Paul (Linn) –
[(FL) FL-2014] Kalkaska 2015; Menominee: First, Stephenson 2019.<> (MF) 601 10th Ave, PO Box 323, Menominee 49858 (906) 864-2555. (S) S 111 Railroad St, PO Box 205, Stephenson 49887 (906) 753-6363. Home: 1801 17th Ave, Menominee 49858 (814) 366-0239. jmurray16365@gmail.com

*****Myers-Cabeen, Nanette D.** (James Sterling Cabeen) –
[(RE) P 1986; F 1989] 1987 Royal Oak: First (assoc); 1991 Flushing (assoc). 1992 Flushing (assoc., LTFT ¾); Jan 1, 1997 Flushing (assoc); 1997 school; **2014 Retired** (Bay Regional Medical Center).<> Home: 353 Old Orchard Dr., Essexville 48732 (989) 895-8955

*****Naile, John Edmund** (Myrna) –
[(RE) P 1972; F 1974] 1973 Carsonville, Applegate, Watertown; 1977 St. Ignace; 1985 St. Clair: First; 1998 Gaylord; **2014 Retired**.<> Home: 2431 Rainswood Dr., Gaylord 48734 (989) 732-5325. therev74@hotmail.com

*Nalett, Larry W. (Elaine) –
[(RL) PL-1993; FL-1998; RL-2004] Eagle 1993; Vickeryville / Fenwick / Palo 1998; Retired 8/8/2004; Middleton 9/15/2015-11/29/2015; Carson City 2/22/16-6/30/2016; Ionia: Zion 2018.<> 423 W Washington St, Ionia 48846 (616) 527-1910. Home: 620 Rich St, Ionia 48846 (616) 527-2025. larrynal62@gmail.com

Nash, Kenneth J. (Christine Frances) –
[(FE) PE-2000; FE-2004] Transferred from Kentucky Conf 2000; Carson City 2000; Grand Rapids: Cornerstone (Assoc) 2006; Grand Rapids: Cornerstone (Assoc) (LTFT ¼) 2011; Grand Rapids: Cornerstone (Assoc) 2012; Appointed to Extension Ministries (¶345) Wesleyan Church Of Hamburg NY (Appt to Ecumenical Shared Ministries) 2016.<> 4999 McKinley Parkway, Hamburg NY 14075 (716) 649-6335. pknash@wchamburg.org

Nellist, David (Glenys) –
[(OE) OE-2000, British Methodist Conf] Schoolcraft 2000; Gull Lake 2008; Grand Rapids: Trinity 2010; **Dearborn: First 2018**.<> 22124 Garrison, Dearborn 48124 (313) 563-5200. Home: 301 S. Silvery Lane, Dearborn 48124 (269) 903-8560. pastor@dearbornfirstumc.org

*Nelson, David B. (Jean Freeland) –
[(RE) D-1961; FE-1964; R-1998] UM Connectional Structures (¶344.1a,c) Director, Mt Pleasant: CMU Wesley Foundation 1959; Camden/Montgomery 1960; Saugatuck/New Richmond 1962; Coopersville/Nunica 01/01/1965; Portage: Chapel Hill 03/01/1968; Ithaca 1972; Ithaca/Beebe 1976; Lansing: Faith 09/16/1980; Hastings: First 1985; Plainwell: First 1989; UM Connectional Structures (¶344.1a,c) West MI Conference Council Director 1991; Retired 1998.<> Home: 1220 Pine Ave # B, Alma 48801 (989) 297-0257. Mail: c/o Sarah Kettelhohn, 5469 George St, Saginaw 48603. dbnelson@iserv.net

Nelson, Forest "Bert" Bertran (Susan Garbarind) –
[(OF) OF-2005] [Presbyterian Church USA] Lyons-Muir Church (LTFT ¾) (¶346.2), 1/1/2005-01/01/2016.<> Home: 1074 Olmstead Road, Muir 48860 (616) 891-8918. fbertnelson@charter.net

Nelson, Jeffrey Scott (Bridget) –
[(FE) PE 2004; FE 2006] Feb 1, 2004 Birmingham: First (assoc); 2009 Redford: Aldersgate; **2016 Royal Oak: First**.<> 320 W. Seventh, Royal Oak 48067 (248) 541-4100. Home: 3113 Marion Dr., Royal Oak 48073 (248) 629-7185. detroitnelsons@aol.com

*Ness, Lance E. –
[(RE) SPL Peninsula-Delaware 1990; LP 1994; PM 1998; FE 2003; RE 2017] 1990 East New Market MD (Peninsula-Delaware Conf); July 1, 1994 Ontonagon, Greenland, Rockland; Jan 1, 2000 Owosso: Burton, Carland; Aug 1, 2004 Brown City; 2007 Macon; **2017 Retired**.<> Home: 1203 Middle Neck Drive, Salisbury MD 21804 (517) 902-4609. revness1966@gmail.com

*Neumann, Fredrick D. (Kay) –
[(RE) LP 1994; P 1995; F 1998; R 2017] Aug 1, 1994 Ossineke, Hubbard Lake, Wilson; Aug 1, 1994 Ossineke, Hubbard Lake; 1999 North Street; 2002 Bay City: Fremont Avenue; 2006 Wisner; 2010 Hudson: First; 2013 medical leave of absence; **2017 Retired**.<> 3046 Camino Real, Las Cruces NM 88001 (989) 884-1776. fdneumann@yahoo.com

Newsom, Tiffany M. –
[(PE) CC-2014; PE-2017] Constantine/White Pigeon 2017; **Laingsburg 2020**.<> (L) 210 Crum St., Laingsburg 48848 (517) 651-5531. Home: 214 Crum St, Laingsburg 48848 (517) 917-5705. newsom.tiffany@gmail.com

Nguyen, Daniel Dung (Minh Ha Le) –
[(FL) FL-2014] Grand Rapids: Vietnamese 2012.<> 212 Bellevue St SE, Wyoming 49548 (616) 534-6262. Home: 497 Harp St. SE, Kentwood 49548 (616) 288-3007

Nguyen, Nhan Duc –
[(PL) DSA Apr 1, 2014; PL Jan 1, 2019] Apr 1, 2014 Madison Heights: Vietnamese Ministry (DSA); **Jan 1, 2019 Madison Heights: Vietnamese Ministry (LTFT ¾)**.<> 500 W Gardenia Ave, Madison Heights 48071 (248) 545-5554. Home: 38108 Charwood Dr, Sterling Heights 48312 (714) 501-0323. ducnhan234@yahoo.com

*Nichols, Lawrence A. –
[(RL) FL-1979; NL-1988; PL-1994; FL-2003; RL-2016] Waterloo Village / Waterloo First (DSA) 1978; Waterloo Village / Waterloo First 1979; Not Appointed 1988; Jackson: Zion (LTFT PT) 02/01/1994; Hersey 2003; Byron Center 2010; Retired 2016.<> Home: 921 Roselle Street, Jackson 49201 (517) 745-4224. nichols.larry64@comcast.net

*Nielsen, Judith A. –
[(RL) FL-1998; NL-2000; RL-2007] Munith 1998; Pleasant Lake 1998; Not Appointed 2000; Retired 2007.<> Home: 3024 Norwich Rd, Lansing 48911 (517) 882-0608

*Niswender, R. Ivan (Phyllis) –
[(RE) FE-1958; HL-1971; FE-1989; R-1994] Hersey (EUB) 1958; Hersey/Grant Center (EUB) 1960; Battle Creek: Calvary (EUB) 1962; Grand Rapids: Northlawn (EUB) 1966; Perry/Shaftsburg 1969; Honorable Location 1971; Otsego: Trowbridge 1981; Readmitted 1989; Otsego: Trowbridge (LTFT ¾) 1989; Otsego: Trowbridge 1993; Retired 1994.<> Home: 191 Grace Village Dr, Winona Lake IN 46590 (574) 372-6191. ivephyl@gmail.com

*Noel, Karen Y. (Phares) –
[(RE) PE 2001; FE 2004; RE 2018] 2001 Detroit: St. Paul's (LTFT ½); 2010 Pontiac: St. John's; Sept 29, 2013 voluntary leave of absence; Mar 2, 2015 Garden City: First (interim); 2015 Birmingham: Embury (LTFT ¼); 2016 Birmingham Embury, Sterling Heights; **2018 Retired**.<> Home: 4673 Walnut Glen Ct, W Bloomfield 48323 (313) 595-4051. revdustynoel@msn.com

*Noggle, James C. (Karen) –
[(RE) D-1995; AM-1995; PE-2014; FE-2016; RE-2019] Nashville Parish: Peace and Quimby 1989; Millville 03/01/1993; Mecosta: New Hope 1997; Harrison: The Gathering (New Church Start) 2004; The Gathering, Wagarville/Wooden Shoe 2009; Grand Rapids: Northlawn 2010; Lake Odessa: Lakewood 2013; Roscommon: Good Shepherd of the North 2015; Retired Apr 1, 2019.<> Home: 10290 N Polk Ave, Harrison 48625 (231) 250-8707. jnoggle@macharcc.com

Nolen, Heather L. –
[(FL) CC-2017; DSA-2017; FL-2017] Gresham / Sunfield (DSA) 2017; Gresham / Sunfield (FL) 12/01/2017.<> (G) 5055 Mulliken Rd, Charlotte 48813. (S) 227 Logan St, Sunfield 48890 (517) 566-8448. Home: PO Box 25, Sunfield 48890 (734) 846-3941. hauble23@gmail.com

*Norris, Arthur Vernon (Evelyn) –
[(RE) P Mich., 1959; F Mich., 1964] 1963 Howe: Lima; 1966 Novi: Willowbrook; 1969 Owosso: First (assoc); 1971 Millington, Arbela; 1976 Pontiac: First; 1980 Blissfield: First; 1983 Wyandotte: Glenwood; 1991 Iron Mountain: Trinity; July 1, 1994 Hemlock, Nelson; **2001 Retired.**<> Home: 5900 S. Hemlock, Hemlock 48626

Norton, Michael Kent (Susan) –
[(FE) P 1987; F 1992] 1987 Snover: Moore, Trinity, Elmer; 1992 Heritage; 1994 Sebewaing: Trinity; **1997 Canton: Friendship.**<> 1240 Beck Rd., Canton 48187 (734) 710-9370. Home: 1237 Lotz Rd., Canton 48188 (734) 722-0183. mikenorton@cantonfriendship.org

Norton, Stephanie Elaine (Ash) –
[(FL) FL 2019] (Great Plains Conference) Hartford 2019.<> 425 E Main St, Hartford 49057 (269) 621-4103. Home: 143 Paras Hill Dr, Hartford 49057 (269) 532-4741. stephanie.e.norton@gmail.com

*Nowacek, Bruce L. (Candy) –
[(RE) FL 2003; PE 2007; FE 2011] 2003 Genesee-Thedford Center; 2010 Bay Port, Hayes; 2012 Yale; Feb 1, 2014 Transitional leave; 2014 Menominee: First; **2016 Retired.**<> Home: 1728 Cowan, National City 48748 (906) 792-9051. b_nowacek@yahoo.com

Nowak, Heather M. –
[(FL) DSA Oct 1, 2016; FL 2017] Pinconning, Garfield (DSA) Oct 1, 2016-Nov 20, 2017; Pinconning, Garfield Dec 1, 2017; **Sebewaing: Trinity, Bay Port 2020**.<> (ST) 513 Washington, Sebewaing 48759 (989) 883-3350. (BP) 838 Second St., Bay Port 48720 (989) 656-2151. Home: 525 Washington, Sebewaing 48759 (586) 275-7522. heathermarienowak@gmail.com

Nunn, Penelope R. –
[(FL) PL Dec 1, 2014; FL 2018] Port Huron: Gratiot Park, Port Huron: Washington Avenue Dec 1, 2014; **Snover: Heritage 2018**.<> 3329 W. Snover Rd., PO Box 38, Snover 48472 (810) 672-9101. Home: 1571 N. Main St., PO Box 65, Snover 48472 (810) 672-9233. peasweet1961@yahoo.com

*Nusz, Gordon Wayne (Shirley) –
[(RE) L Mich., 1966; P 1968; F 1971] 1970 Detroit: St. James (assoc); 1974 Swan Valley; 1980 Pigeon: First; 1988 West Branch: First; 1993 Marquette: First; 2000 Northville: First (assoc); May 1, 2002 involuntary leave of absence; **May 1, 2003 involuntary retirement.**<> Home: 2813 Laurel Hill Dr., Flower Mound TX 75028 (972) 691-1335

Nystrom, Robert D. (Ronda) –
[(FE) D-1989; FE-1992] Hopkins/South Monterey 1989; Traverse City: Central 1992; Bronson: First 1994; St Louis: First 1998; Dimondale and East Lansing Chapel Hill 2002; East Lansing Chapel Hill (LTFT ½) 01/16/2004; Webberville 2005; Battle Creek: Birchwood 2007; Battle Creek Birchwood (LTFT ¾) and Athens (LTFT ¼) 2011; Three Rivers: First/Mendon 2013; Ovid United Church 2015; Ovid United Church/Elsie 2016; Appointed in Other Annual Conferences (¶331.8, ¶346.1) Detroit Conference, Aburn 2018.<> 207 S. Auburn, PO Box 66, Auburn 48611 (989) 662-6314. Home: 201 S. Auburn, Auburn 48611 (269) 535-2481. rnr@comcast.net

Obwoge, Douglas Mochama –
[(OE) OE Jan 1, 2020 Methodist Church in Kenya] Brooks Corners (DSA) (¼ time) Jul 7, 2019; Brooks Corners (DSA) (½ time) Oct 1, 2019; **Brooks Corners (LTFT ½) Jan 1, 2020.**<> 5951 30th Ave, Sears 49679 (231) 734-2733. Home: 5951 30th Ave, Sears 49679 (231) 734-2733. dmochamaobwoge@gmail.com

Oh, In Beom (Jooyeun Lim) –
[(FE) FL 2013; FE 2016, transferred from Korean Methodist Church] Troy: Korean (assoc) Apr 1, 2013; **Wisner 2016.**<> 5375 N. Vassar Rd., Akron 48701 (989) 691-5277. Home: 5363 N Vassar Rd, Akron 48701 (248) 840-3683. mt1016@hotmail.com

***Okray, Dorothy –**
[(RE) PE Troy 1997; FE Troy, 2000] 1997 Newcomb NY: Newcomb, Calvary, Long Lake NY; 2001 Johnstown (NY): First, Gloversville (NY); 2003 Morenci; **2007 Retired.**<> 7318 Kensington Ct., University Park FL 34201. djokray@comcast.net

Oldenburg, Dawn (Thomas) –
[(FL) FL Jan 1, 2020] Hinchman (DSA) (½ time) 2018; Hinchman, Scottdale (DSA) 10/1/2018; **Hinchman, Scottdale Jan 1, 2020.**<> (H) 8154 Church St, Berrien Springs 49103 (269) 471-5492. (S) 4271 Scottdale Rd, St Joseph 49085 (269) 429-7270. Home: 9862 Vineyard St, Bridgman 49106 (269) 208-9673. zambonidrvr1218@aol.com

Olin, Melody L. (Denny) –
[(FL) FL-2006] Blanchard-Pine River/Coomer/Winn (DSA) 2006; Blanchard-Pine River/Coomer/ Winn (FTLP) 11/16/2006; Old Mission Peninsula 2010; Empire 2019.<> 10050 W Michigan St, PO Box 261, Empire 49630 (231) 326-5510. Home: 10205 Aylsworth Rd, PO Box 261, Empire 49630 (231) 970-2048. MelodyOlin@yahoo.com

***Omansiek, William Walter –**
[(RE) T 1967; F 1971; HL 1986; FL 2005; FE Jan 1, 2006] Jan 1970 Flint: Flint Park; 1971 Chaplain, Methodist Children's Home; 1974 Detroit: St. James (assoc); 1975 Inkster: Christ; 1979 St. Charles, Brant; 1986 Honorable Location; Jan 1, 2005 Harrisville, Lincoln; 2005 Wisner;2006 Bay City: Fremont Avenue; **2010 Retired.**<> 801 Pendleton Street, Bay City 48708 (989) 778-1405. omansiek@chartermi.net

***Orr, Karin K. –**
[(RE) PE-2003; FE-2006; R-2014] Centreville 2003; Retired 2014.<> Home: 4207 Embassy Drive SE, Grand Rapids 49546 (616) 901-4382. pastorrkarin@gmail.com

Osborne, Matthew L. (Melissa) –
[(FL) FL 2012] 2012 Algonac: Trinity, Marine City; 2013 Sandusky: First; **2018 Ishpeming: Wesley.**<> 801 Hemlock, PO Box 342, Ishpeming 49849 (906) 486-4681. Home: 220 shoreline Dr., Negaunee 49866 (906) 475-9337. matthewlosborne@gmail.com

Ostema, Dale P. (Deborah) –
[(FE) D-1987; FE-1990] Baldwin: Covenant Cmnty 1988; Charlevoix/Greensky Hill 02/01/1993; Charlevoix 02/01/1998; Cadillac 2000; Traverse City: Central 2007.<> 222 Cass St, Traverse City 49684 (231) 946-5191. Home: 1713 Indian Woods Dr, Traverse City 49686 (231) 933-4026. dale@tccentralumc.org

*Osterhout, Donna Joan –
[(RE) P 1978; F 1981] 1979 Inkster; Jan 1983 Taylor: West Mound; Sept 1, 1987 Lexington, Bethel; 1991 Lincoln Community; 1996 Marine City; Feb 1, 2002 incapacity leave; **2003 Retired**.<> 801 W Middle St, Apt 470, Chelsea 48118. donnao3928@gmail.com

Osterman, Rhonda J. –
[(FL) PL Nov 2012; FL 2020] Madison Heights Nov 10, 2012; **Millville, Leslie, Felt Plains 2020**.<> (M) 1932 N M-52, Stockbridge 49285(517) 851-8785. (L) 401 S Main St, Leslie 49251 (517) 589-9211. (FP) 3523 Meridian Rd, Leslie 49251. Home: 1956 N M 52, Stockbridge 49285 (586) 243-9240. rhonda8776@gmail.com

Otis, Scott K. (Carolyn) –
[(FE) D-1988; FE-1991] Lyons/Muir (Student Appt) 07/16/1988; Lyons/Muir (Full Time) 11/16/1988; Lyons/Muir/Ionia: Easton 1990; Mecosta: New Hope 1993; Portland 1997; Grand Rapids: Cornerstone (Assoc) 2003; Dorr: Crosswind Community (New Church Start)10/01/2004; Edwardsburg: Hope 2017; **Howell: First 2020**.<> 1230 Bower St, Howell 48843 (517) 546-2730. Home: 2774 Bogues View Drive, Howell 48843 (616) 307-9765. pastorscott@howellfumc.com

Owen, David –
[(PL) PL 2020] **Corunna: Northwest Venice, Vernon (PTLP ½) Jul 15, 2020**.<>(NV) 6001 E. Wilkinson Rd, Corunna 48817 (989) 661-2377. (V) 202 E. Main St., PO Box 155, Vernon 48476 (989) 288-4187. Home: 13425 Dawn Dew Dr Apt 7, DeWitt 48820 (989) 384-1200. adown@bellsouth.net

Oyler-Sayles, Theresa Little Eagle (Ed) –
[(FE) PE-2000; FE-2006] Oakdale/Pa Wa Ting Ma Ged Win 2003; Battle Creek: Maple 2006; Niles: Portage Prairie 2008-2009; Medical Leave 4/15/2009.<> Home: 256 Nottingham Rd, Elkton MD 21921 (269) 967-7145. littleeagle77@hotmail.com

Pahl, Craig A. –
[(FL) PL-2000; FL-2004] Jonesville/Allen 2000; Jonesville/Allen/Moscow Plains 2001; Jonesville/Allen/ Moscow Plains (FT) 2004; Jonesville/Allen 2007; Barnard/East Jordan/Norwood 2014; East Jordan/Barnard 2017.<> (EJ) PO Box 878, 201 4th St, East Jordan 49727 (231) 536-2161. (B) PO Box 878, East Jordan 49727 (231) 547-5269. Home: PO Box 238, 305 Esterly, East Jordan 49727 (231) 536-7596. cappahl@netzero.net

*Paige, James E., Jr. (Margaret "Peggy") –
[(RE) P 1971; F 1978] 1974 Stephenson, Hermansville; 1976 Morrice, Bennington, Pittsburg; 1980 Jeddo, Central-Lakeport (Co-Pastor, LTFT ½); 1985 Leave of Absence; 1986 Glennie, Curran, Wilber (LTFT ½); Jan 1, 1992 Salem Grove; 1998 Caring Covenant Group Ministry: Oregon, Elba (LTFT) 2002 parish director; Oct 1, 2003 incapacity leave; Jan 1, 2007 Capac: First, Zion Community; 2007 Richfield (LTFT ½); **2008 Retired**.<> Home: N7344 County Road 577, Ingalls 49848 (231) 421-4208. Revspaige@yahoo.com

*Paige, Margaret Ann "Peggy" (James) –
[(RE) P 1975; F 1978] Jan 1977 Morrice, Bennington, Pittsburg (Co-Pastor); 1980 Jeddo, Central-Lakeport (Co-Pastor, LTFT ½); 1985 Glennnie, Curran, Wilber (LTFT ½); Nov 15, 1991 Manchester: Sharon; 1998 Caring Covenant Group Ministry: Columbiaville (parish director); 2002 Port Huron District Superintendent; 2009 Iron Mountain: First, Quinnesec; **2012 Retired**.<> Home: N7344 County Road 577, Ingalls 49848 (231) 421-4208 or (906) 221-7677. mapaige49@yahoo.com

Pajak, John J. (Connie) –
[(PL) PL 2009] Redford: New Beginnings Apr 1, 2009; New Cooperative: Algonac: Trinity 2016**; New Hudson 2020**.<> 56730 Grand River, PO Box 803, New Hudson 48165 (248) 437-6212. Home: 56730 Grand River Ave, New Hudson 48165 (248) 640-6987 jpajak@palacenet.com

Palaszeski, James (Nikki) –
[(FL) PL Dec 1, 2014; FL 2016] Ubly/Shabbona/Argyle Dec 1, 2014; Keweenaw Parish: Calumet, Mohawk-Ameek, Lake Linden, Laurium 2016; **Union City, Athens 2018**.<> (UC) 200 Ellen St, PO Box 878, Union City 49094 (517) 741-7028. (A) 123 Clark St, PO Box 267 Athens 49011 (269) 729-9370. Home: 72 Sycamore Bend, Union City 49094 (989) 912-5738. pastor.ucaumc@gmail.com

*Panse, Wade S. (Patti) –
[(RE) D-1978; FE-1980; R-2012] Burr Oak 1978; Robbins 03/01/1982; Lansing: Mount Hope 05/01/1987; Appointed in Other Annual Conferences (¶331.8, ¶346.1) Director of Alumni, Asbury Theological School 10/16/1992; Mt Pleasant: First 1995; St Joseph First 1997; Retired 01/01/2012; Cassopolis (LTFT ½) 08/23/2015.<> PO Box 175, 209 South Rowland St, Cassopolis 49031 (269) 445-3107. Home: 1218 Riverwood Terrace, Saint Joseph 49085 (269) 449-5335. wadepanse@hotmail.com

Paparella, Amee A. (James) –
[(FE) PE-2009; FE-2016] Williamston 2009; Clergy Appointed to Attend School (¶416.6) MSU 2011; UM Connectional Structures (¶344.1a,c) Director/Organizer for Women's Advocacy, General Board of Church and Society 08/27/2012; Wacousta Community 2013; Leave of Absence To Attend School 2016; Grand Rapids First (Assoc) 2017; Leave of Absence 02/28/2018; **Kalamazoo: Sunnyside 2020**.<> 2800 Gull Road, Kalamazoo 49048 (269) 349-3047. Home: 9755 N Division Ave, Sparta 49345 (517) 862-2599. pastoramee@sunnysideumc.com

*Park, John G. (Madeline) –
[(RE) P E.OH., 1970; F 1973] 1972 Trans. to Detroit Conf, LaSalle: Zion; 1975 Royal Oak: First (assoc); 1978 Fairgrove, Gilford; May 1981 Commerce; 1992 Berkley; 1996 Flint: Hope; 2006 Dixboro; **2011 Retired**.<> 2268 Willow Tree Drive, Brighton 48116 (734) 660-4238. Jgpark@aol.com

*Parker, Gerald R. (Holly Craig) –
[(RE) P 1969; F 1973] 1972 Britton: Grace, Wellsville; 1973 University of Michigan Law School; 1975 Salem Grove; 1978 Ann Arbor: First (assoc); 1986 Chelsea; July 16, 1992 Saline; **1994 Retired**.<> Home: 1500 Hillridge Ct., Ann Arbor 48103 (734) 913-4937. ParkerGrld@netscape.net

*Parker, James Floyd (Ines) –
[(RE) P 1969; F 1972] 1971 General Board of Pensions; Apr 1987 General Secretary, General Board of Pension; **1994 Retired**.<> Home: 1248 Wickie Pl. SE, Tumwater WA 98501 (360) 754-3384. jparker150@comcast.net

*Parker, Roger Allen (Judith) –
[(RE) T 1967; F 1970] 1969 Livingston Circuit: Plainfield, Trinity; Oct 1970 Stony Creek; 1976 Bay City: Madison Avenue; 1983 Flint: Trinity; Feb 1, 1993 Director: Cooperative Ministry of Northwest Flint, Flint: Trinity; 1998 sabbatical leave; Oct 1, 1998 LaVergne UMC; 1998 Franklin: First (assoc) (TN Conf, para 337.1); **2008 Retired**.<> Home: 8522 Parkridge Drive, Dexter 48130 (734) 580-2134. roger.parker07@comcast.net

Parker-Lewis, Sherry Lynn (George Lewis) –
[(FE) PL 1991; P 1996; FE 1999] Wagarville: Community, Wooden Shoe (part-time—½) Sept 1, 1991; Hardy, Hartland (assoc) 1994; Ann Arbor: First (assoc) 1995; Dundee 1997; Chesaning: Trinity Aug 1, 2002; Brighton: First 2008; **Senior Director of Church Relations, United Methodist Foundation of Michigan (LTFT ½) 2020**.<> Home: 48710 Apple Ln, Mattawan 49071 (810) 360-9995. sherry@umfmichigan.org

Parkin, Penny L. –
[(FL) PL Sept 1, 2014; FL 2017] Fairgrove Sept 1, 2014; Fairgrove, Sutton-Sunshine 2017; **Frankfort, Elberta Jun 1, 2020**.<> (F) PO Box 1010, 537 Crystal Ave, Frankfort 49635 (231) 352-7427. (E) PO Box 405, 555 Lincoln Ave, Elberta 49628 (231) 352-4311. Home: 320 Maple St, Frankfort 49635 (231) 352-4724. pastorpennyparkin@gmail.com

Parmalee, Chad M. (Roschenne) –
[(FE) FL-2006; PE-2014; FE-2017] Jackson: Brookside 09/01/2005; Battle Creek: Chapel Hill 2013.<> 157 Chapel Hill Dr, Battle Creek 49015 (269) 963-0231. Home: 192 Brentwood Dr, Battle Creek 49015 (517) 281-0362. pastorchad@thehillbc.com

*Parsons, Cynthia M. (Jeff) –
[(RE) D-1988; FE-1992; R-2018] North East Missaukee Parish 1989; Williamsburg 1993; Kalamazoo: First (Assoc) 1997; Casco 2001; Berrien Springs (LTFT ½) 2006; Appointed in Other Annual Conferences (¶346.1) Owendale (½) / Gagetown (¼) (LTFT ¾) 2012; Sebewaing: Trinity 2014; Retired 2018.<> Home: 450 N Miller, PO Box 563, Sebewaing 48759 (989) 883-2350. RevCindy47@gmail.com

*Passenger, Edward L. (Sally) –
[(RE) D-1959; FE-1962; HL-1971; FE-1987; R-1999] Northport/Leland/Northport Indian Mission 1962; Alden 09/15/1965; Caledonia/ Parmelee 12/01/1966; Hart/Mears 12/01/1969; Honorable Location 06/01/1971; Appointed to Extension Ministries (¶344.1b,c) Chaplain, Ionia Temporary Correctional Facility 1987; Appointed to Extension Ministries (¶344.1b,c) Chaplain, Carson City Temporary Correctional Facility 12/28/1987; Retired 1999.<> Home: 526 Ferry St, Spring Lake 49456 (616) 566-8833. revedpass@gmail.com

*Passenger, Margaret Ann (Henry) –
[(RE) P 1997; FE 1999] 1997 Kingston, Deford; 2001 Pigeon: First; **2005 Retired**.<> Home: 44 E. Elm Ave., Monroe 48162 (734) 242-6944. revmarg@gmail.com

Patera, Nancy J. (Greg) –
[(FL) PL-2007; FL-2014] Ionia: Easton (PTL P ½) 01/01/2007; Burnips/Monterey Center 2014; Ionia Parish: LeValley/ Berlin Center 2017.<> (L) 4018 Kelsey Hwy, Ionia 48846 (616) 527-1480. (BC) 3042 Peck Lake Rd, Saranac 48881 (616) 527-1480. Home: 6232 Sunset Beach, Lake Odessa 48849 (616) 642-0966. nancypatera@mac.com

*Paterson, John Douglas (Karla) –
[(RE) P 1981; F 1985; R 2018] Mar 1983 Seymour Lake; Sept 15, 1986 Marquette: Grace, Skandia; 1993 Grayling: Michelson Memorial; 1998 Marquette District Superintendent; 2005 Ann Arbor: First; **2018 Retired**.<> Home: 729 Lakewood Ln, Marquette 49855 (734) 474-4100. jdpaterson@me.com

*Patterson, Paul E. –
[(RE) D-1951; FE-1953; R-1990] Edwardsburg: Hope 10/01/1950; Grand Rapids: First (Assoc) 1955; Wacousta Community 1957; Cedar Springs 1958; Grand Rapids: South 09/07/1960; Ludington 1964; Kalamazoo: Westwood 1967; Sparta 1968; Allegan 1973; Paw Paw 1979; Grand Rapids: Faith 1984; St Johns: First 1987; Barryton/Chippewa Lake 07/01-10/01/1990; Retired 10/01/1990.<> Home: 1551 Franklin SE, Apt 4065, Grand Rapids 49506 (616) 243-2967. rgulbranson@sbcglobal.net

Payne, James A. –
[(AM) PL 2005; FL 2010; AM 2018] 2005 Watrousville; Mar 2, 2010 Sterling, Alger, Garfield; Jan 1, 2013 Sterling, Alger, Standish: Community; Apr 1, 2019 Standish: Beacon of Light, Alger; **2019 Standish: Beacon of Light, Arenac Cnty: Christ**.<> (BOL) 201 S. Forest, Standish 48658 (989) 846-6277, (ACC) 3322 E. Huron Rd., PO Box 145, AuGres 48703 (989) 876-7449. Home: 124 N. Chestnut, PO Box 167, Sterling 48659 (989) 654-9001. Pastorjimpayne@gmail.com

*Payne, Mark R. (Nola) –
[(RE) D-1994; FE-1997; R-2016] Rosebush 1992; Rosebush (LTFT ½) 1994; Rosebush (LTFT ¾) 01/01/1995; Rosebush (LTFT ¾) and Clare (Assoc) (LTFT ¼) 1995; Rosebush 1996; Oshtemo: Lifespring (New Church Start) 2001; Robbins 2009; Hastings: First 2014; Retired 12/31/2016.<> markp@broadstripe.net

*Payne, William V. (Jayne) –
[(RE) FL-1951; FD-1960; FE-1962; R-1996] East Osceola Circuit 1951; Middle Branch 1954; Leave of Absence 1955; Dowagiac: First 1957; Decatur 1960; Edmore: Faith 1961; Paw Paw 1965; Hillsdale: First 1979; Sodus: Chapel Hill 1987; Retired 1996.<> Home: 8000 Warren Woods Rd, Lot 64, Three Oaks 49128 (269) 469-7643. wvpayne@triton.net

*Peacock, Richard A. (Janis) –
[(RE) P 1970; F 1974] 1973 Utica (assoc); 1978 Ortonville; July 1982 Lake Orion; 1993 Farmington: Nardin Park; 1997 Troy: First; **2008 Retired**.<> Home: 40198 Riverbend Dr., Sterling Heights 48310 (248) 321-7480. rjpeacock@wowway.com

*Pebley, Patricia A. (Allen D) –
[(RL) FL-2014; RL 2020] Jackson: Trinity/Parma (LTFT ½) 2012; Hillside/Somerset Center 2014; **Retired 2020**.<> Home: 4485 Springbrook Rd, Jackson 49201 (517) 740-6694. patpebley@gmail.com

*Pedersen, Douglas L. (Darlene) –
[(RE) D-1970; FE-1972; R-2005] Center Park 1970; Transferred from Minnesota Conf 1971; St Joseph First (Assoc) 1971; Saugatuck 10/15/1973; Saugatuck/Ganges 10/15/1973; Turk Lake 08/15/1975; Wyoming: Wesley Park (Assoc) 1979; Wayland 1982; Grand Rapids: Faith 1987; Leland 02/16/1994; Williamsburg 1997; Emmanuel Traverse City 02/01/2003; Traverse Bay/Williamsburg 01/01/2005 (TC Emmanuel Merged w/ Tc Asbury Becoming Traverse Bay); Retired 2005.<> Home: PO Box 314, 102 W Terrace LN Commons, Leland 49654 (231) 256-9088. PedersenL5@aol.com

Penny, Kellas D., III (Leanne) –
[(PE) PL-2013; FL-2014; PE 2020] Harrison: The Gathering (PTLP ½) 2013; Grand Rapids: Rivercrest (New Church Start) 01/01/2014; Dowagiac: First and UM Connectional Structures (¶344.1a,c) WMC New Church Position 02/01/2015; Dowagiac: First 2015; Water's Edge (New Buffalo) 2017.<> 18732 Harbor Country Dr, New Buffalo 49117 (269) 469-1250. Home: 19603 Oak Dr, New Buffalo 49117 (616) 209-2828. kel@h2oedge.org

Perez, Joseph Anthony –
[(AF) New York] Home: 1330 Trenton, Adrian 49221 (517) 263-1807. joeandjo@tc3net.com

Perez, Michael R., Jr. –
[(FL) FL 2019] Clawson (DSA) (¼ time) 1/01/2019; **Clawson (½ time), Waterford: Trinity (½ time) 2019**.<> (C) 500 E McLeod Ave, PO Box 9, Ironwood 49938 (906) 932-3900. (WT) 6440 Maceday Dr, Waterford 48329 (248) 623-6860. Home: 442 N Marias Ave, Clawson 48017 (586) 252-7257. perezm1551@yahoo.com

Perez, Paul David (Anne) –
[(FD) PD 2006; FD 2010] Wesley Theological Seminary; 2006 Director of Youth Ministry, Dulin United Methodist Church; 2008 Livonia: Newburg (deacon); 2013 Conference Director of Mission and Justice Engagement and Leadership Recruitment; **2018 Associate Director for Mission & Ministry**.<> 1011 Northcrest Rd, Lansing 48906 (517) 347-4030 ext. 4070. pperez@michiganumc.org

*Perkins, A. Edward (Shirley) –
[(RE) D-1967; FE-1970; R-2006] Transferred from Detroit Conf 1981; Bronson: First 1980; Fremont 04/01/1987; UM Connectional Structures (¶344.1a,c) District Superintendent, Lansing District 1990; Grand Rapids: Trinity 1996; Retired 2006; UM Connectional Structures (¶344.1a,c) Interim Conference Director 10/01/2008-12/31/2008.<> Home: 3052 Bonita Dr SE, Grand Rapids 49508 (616) 606-5060. perksperch@gmail.com

Perrine, Stephen Kendall (Connie) –
[(FE) P 1974; F 1976] 1975 Flushing (assoc); Oct 1977 Honorable Location; 1995 reinstated; 1995 Warren: Wesley (LTFT ¾); 1998 Beverly Hills; 2003 leave of absence; Aug 16, 2006 South Rockwood; South Rockwood (LTFT ½), Monroe: Calvary (LTFT ½) 2016; **Dearborn: Good Shepherd 2020**.<> 1570 Mason, Dearborn 48124 (313) 278-4350. Home: 23435 Oak Glen Dr, Southfield 48034 (248) 827-7110. sperrine@sbcglobal.net

Peters, Jeremy Troy (Jennifer) –
[(FE) PE 2003; FE 2006] 2003 Minister of Religion, British Methodist Church Wakefield Circuit (para 336); Sept 1, 2004 Morrice, Bennington, Pittsburg; 2005 Morrice, Pittsburg, Bancroft; 2008 Fenton (assoc); 2012 Fenton (assoc); South Central Cooperative Ministry: Lake Fenton; **2015 Flint: Court Street**.<> 225 W. Court St., Flint 48502 (810) 235-4651. Home: 1827 Overhill, Flint 48503 (810) 407-8333. revjtp@hotmail.com

*Peterson, Gary L. (Reba) –
[(RL) FL-2008; RL-2016] Olivet (DSA) 2006; Fennville/Pearl 2008; Retired 2016; Claybanks (LTFT ¼) 2016.<> PO Box 104, 9197 S 56th Ave, Montague 49437 (231) 923-0573. Home: 6337 Cheyenne Rd, Pentwater 49449 (231) 869-3373. glpeterson32@frontier.com

Pethoud, Sue Ann (Rick) –
[(FD) PD 2014; FD 2017] Detroit: Cass Community (deacon) 2014; **Detroit: Cass Community and Social Services Community Relations liaison (deacon) 2016**.<> (CC) 3901 Cass Ave., Detroit 48201 (313) 833-7730. (SSCR) 11745 Rosa Parks Blvd., Detroit 48206 Home: 4529 Pleasant Valley Rd., Brighton 48114 (810) 278-1235. spethoud@casscommunity.org

*Petro, Susan M. –
[(RE) D-1994; FE-1996; R-2014] Gull Lake (Assoc) 01/01/1994; Portage: Chapel Hill (Assoc) 01/01/1998; Grand Rapids: Genesis 2007; Retired 2014.<> Home: 7799 Glenwood Pond Dr SE, Alto 49302 (616) 550-6850. suempetro@gmail.com

Petrucci, Barry T. (Lesa) –
[(FE) D-1984; FE-1988] Grandville (Assoc) 1986; Olivet 1989; UM Connectional Structures (¶344.1a,c) Executive Director of UM Metro Mininistries, Greater Grand Rapids 01/01/1995; Portage: Chapel Hill 2001.<> 7028 Oakland Dr, Portage 49024 (269) 327-6643. Home: 5300 Bronson Blvd, Portage 49024 (269) 276-0482. barrypetrucci@pchum.org

*Pettis, Warren Donald –
[(RE) T 1963; F 1965] 1961 Weston; 1962 Samaria, Lulu; 1968 Saginaw: Ames (assoc); 1971 Brown City: First, Emmanual; Jan 1977 Caseville; 1980 Essexville; 1987 Monroe: First; 1989 Gaylord; **1998 Retired**.<> Home: 1202 Cotton Road, Lyndonville VT 05851 (802) 626-3845. warrenpettis@myfairpoint.net

*Petty, Janet Gaston –
[(RE)] 2002 Detroit: Metropolitan (assoc) (para. 337.1); Feb 1, 2004 Commerce (interim); 2004 trans from CA-Pacific conf; 2004 Southfield: Hope (assoc); **2012 Retired**.<> Home: 26110 Hendrie, Huntington Woods 48070 (248) 546-9749. petty65@msn.com

Phillips, Daniel J.W. –
[(FL) PL 2013; FL 2019] 2013 Kalamo; 2015 Felt Plains, Williamston: Wheatfield; 2017 Riverview; **2019 Bellaire: Community**.<> 401 N. Bridge St., PO Box 235, Bellaire 49615 (231) 533-8133. Home: 4046 Grass Lake Rd., Bellaire 49615 (231) 533-4228. dan.jw.phillips@gmail.com

Phillips, Harold V. (Kathy) –
[(AM) FL 1994 from Missionary Church; AM 2001] 1993 Omard/Cole; Aug 1, 1996 Capac: First & Zion; 2006 South Central Cooperative Ministry: Halsey, South Mundy; 2016 Montrose; **Dec 31, 2016 Retired**.<> Home: 9788 Boucher Rd., Otter Lake 48464 (810) 410-7234. hal.phillips334@gmail.com

*Phillips, Kathy M. (Harold) –
[(RL) PL 2009] 2009 Seven Churches United Group Ministry: Lennon; **2016 Retired**.<> Home: 9788 Boucher Rd., Otter Lake 48464 (989) 795-1024. kphillips9788@gmail.com

*Pieper, Ralph Howard, II (Mary) –
[(RE) P 1972; F 1974] 1972 Genesee, Thetford Center; 1975 Pigeon: Salem; 1983 Blissfield: First; 1989 Flint: Hope; 1996 Port Huron: First; 2003 Lapeer: Trinity; **2012 Retired; 2018 Mt. Morris: First (LTFT ¼)**.<> 808 E. Mt. Morris Rd, Mt Morris 48458 (810) 686-3870. Home: 3373 Brookgate Dr., Flint 48507 (586) 260-7538. RMPieper@aol.com

PASTORAL RECORDS

*Pierce, Robert Bruce (Sandie) –
[(RE) P 19__ W.MI; F 19__ W.MI] 1974 Trans. to Detroit Conf, Gwinn, Ishpeming, Salisbury; Sept 1977 Chaplain, Navy, David Adams Memorial Chapel, Naval Station, Norfolk VA, Group Chaplain, Stop 19, MAG32; 1990 Chaplain, NavSuppAct, Naples, Italy; 1993 Chaplain, Submarine Group 10; 1997 Regional Chaplain; Command Chaplain, Pearl Harbor; 2000 Command Chaplain, US Navy, Keflavik, Iceland; Sept 1, 2004 Eastern US Regional Field Director, Military Youth Ministry; **Feb 1, 2007 Retired**.<> Home: 45 Longyear Drive, Negaunee 49866 (906) 236-2547. rbrucepierce@gmail.com

*Pier-Fitzgerald, J. Lynn (Tom) –
[(RE) D-1977; FE-1980; R-2017] East Lansing Chapel Hill/Gunnisonville 1978; White Cloud (LTFT ½) 05/16/1984; Wyoming Park (Assoc) (LTFT ½) 1988; Leave of Absence 1989; Plainfield 08/16/1991; UM Connectional Structures (¶344.1a,c) District Superintendent,Grand Traverse District 1999; Holland: First 2005; Retired 2017.<> Home: 83 West 18th St, Holland 49423 (616) 393-6242. lynn.pier.fitzgerald@gmail.com

*Pier-Fitzgerald, Thomas M. (Lynn) –
[(RE) D-1977; FE-1980; R-2016] East Lansing: University (Assoc) 1978; East Lansing Chapel Hill/Gunnisonville 1982; White Cloud (LTFT ½) 05/16/1984; Grand Rapids: South 1988; Sabbatical Leave 1998; Elk Rapids/Kewadin (LTFT ¾) 1999; Grandville 2005; Retired 2016.<> Home: 83 West 18th St, Holland 49423 (616) 393-6242. tpfitz5169@sbcglobal.net

Pittenger, Kathryn L. (Richard) –
[(FD) PD 2008; FD 2011] Waterford: Central (deacon) 2008; **Children's Initiatives Coordinator, DeWitt: Redeemer (missional) 2018**.<> 1161 E Clark Rd, Ste 212, DeWitt 48820 (517-347-4030 ext. 4030). Home: 4551 Seneca Dr., Okemos 48864 (248) 505-5848. kpittenger@michiganumc.org

Place, Steven C. (Ilse) –
[(FL) NL-2010; FL-2011] LP w/o Appointment 2010; Grand Rapids: Mosaic 01/01/2011; Lake Odessa Lakewood 2017.<> 10265 Brown Rd, Lake Odessa 48849 (269) 367-4800. Home: 10121 Brown Rd, Lake Odessa 48849 (616) 901-7633. splaceman@gmail.com

Platt, Susan E. –
[(AM) FL 2011; AM 2013] Bay City: Fremont Avenue 2011; Alpena: First 2016; **Sandusky: First 2018**.<> 68 Lexington St., Sandusky 48471 (810) 648-2606. Home: 155 Bella Ave., Sandusky 48471. sueeplatt@gmail.com

Plum, Alexander J. –
[(PD) PD 2019] Director Global Health Initiatives Henry Ford Health Systems, Detroit: Cass Community Missional Charge Conference (para 331.4a) 2019; **Director Clinical and Social Health Integration, Henry Ford Health Care / Missional – Cass Community Health Care Ministries Liaison, Jan 5, 2020**.<> 3901 Cass Ave, Detroit 48201 (313) 833-7730. Home: 285 Ashland St, Detroit 48215 (810) 210-0090. plumalex@gmail.com

Plum, Janine L. (Peter) –
[(FE) PL 2008; PE 2015; FE 2018] 2008 Caring Covenant Group Ministry: Richfield; Aug 1, 2012 school (Asbury); **2015 Seymour Lake**.<> 3050 Sashabaw, Oxford 48371 (248) 628-4763. Home: 3191 Clipper Ct., Oxford 48371 (810) 624-1404. revjanine1@gmail.com

Poag, Patrick R. –
[(FL) FL July 2, 2002] Hemlock, Nelson; July 1, 2002 Hope, Edenville; 2004 Hope, Edenville; **2005 Midland Cnty: Hope, Edenville, Dale**.<> (H) 5278 N Hope Rd., Hope 48628 (989) 689-3811, (E) W. State Rd., Box 125, Edenville 48620 (989) 689-6250, (D) 4688 S. Freeman Rd, Beaverton 48612 (989) 435-4829. Home: 5302 N. Hope Rd., Hope 48628 (989) 689-4788. churchladylisa@aol.com

Pohl, Jon L. (Diane) –
[(FL) FL-2006] Avondale/North Evart/Sylvan (DSA) 01/15/2006; Ashley/Bannister/Greenbush 2006; Ludington: St Paul 2011; Lansing Asbury 2017.<> 2200 Lake Lansing Rd, Lansing 48912 (517) 484-5794. Home: 2412 Post Oak Ln, Lansing 48912 (616) 894-4461. jpohl333@gmail.com

*Pohl, Keith I. (Roberta) –
[(RE) D-1958; FE-1960; R-1993] Nashville 1958; Grand Rapids: First (Assoc) 1961; Rockford 1964; UM Connectional Structures (¶344.1a,c) Director, Wesley Foundation, Michigan State University 10/01/1966; UM Connectional Structures (¶344.1a,c) Associate Editor, Michigan Christian Advocate 1972; UM Connectional Structures (¶344.1a,c) Editor, Michigan Christian Advocate 10/01/1973; UM Connectional Structures (¶344.1a,c) Editor-Publisher, Michigan Christian Advocate 1977; East Lansing: University 08/01/1980; Appointed to Extension Ministries (¶344.1b,c) Editor, Circuit Rider 09/01/1986; Retired 12/31/1993.<> Home: 665 N Aurelius Rd, Mason 48854 (517) 244-0389. pohlkirj@cs.com

*Pohly, Gerald A. –
[(RE) D-1952; FE-1957; R-1996] Battle Creek: Calvary (EUB) 1956; Magnolia (EUB) 1961; Wyoming Park 04/01/1969; UM Connectional Structures (¶344.1a,c) District Superintendent, Central District 03/01/1973; Church of the Dunes 1978; Grand Rapids: Trinity 1989; Retired 1996.<> Home: 2529 Grove Bluff Dr SE, Grand Rapids 49546 (616) 308-0071. gedu32@att.net

*Poole, Karen B. (Gary) –
[(RE) P 1983; F 1988] 1985 school, St. John's Seminary, Plymouth; 1986 Monroe: St. Paul's (assoc); 1988 Brighton: First (assoc); 1993 Farmington: Nardin Park (assoc); 1997 Trenton: First 2003 sabbatical leave; 2004 Waterford: Four Towns, Trinity (Intentional Interim ¶329.3); **2006 Retired**.<> Home: 30029 Barwell, Farmington Hills 48334 (248) 471-9586. kbpoole@twmi.rr.com

Pope, Marva C. –
[(PE) PL 2014; PE 2015] 2014 Detroit: People's; **2018 Wayne: First**.<> 3 Towne Square St, Wayne 48184 (734) 721-4801. Home: 29875 Rambling Rd., Southfield 48076. marpo0828@yahoo.com

*Posnik, Ralph A., Jr. (Karen) –
[(RL) FL-2010; RL-2019] Barnard/East Jordan/Norwood (DSA) 05/15/2009; Barnard/East Jordan/Norwood 11/15/2009; Niles: Portage Prairie 2014; Retired 2019.<> Home: 137 Lakeshire Dr, Fairfield Glade TN 38558 (231) 883-1985. servant1@reagan.com

*Powers, Jon R. (Susan Speer-Powers) –
[(RE) D 1972; FE 1975; RE 2019] East Lansing: University (Assoc) 1974; Portage: Chapel Hill 1978; Hillside 09/16/1978; UM Connectional Structures (¶344.1a,c) Chaplain and Director of Church Relations, Adrian College 08/16/1981; UM Connectional Structures (¶344.1a,c) Chaplain, Ohio Wesleyan University 08/16/1988; **Retired Jul 31, 2019.**<> Home: 104 W Winter St, Delaware OH 43015 (614) 369-1709. jrpowers@owu.edu

*Powers, Linda Jo –
[(RE) P 1995; F 1998] June 16, 1996 Whittemore, Prescott; 2000 Lexington; 2002 Beaverton: First, Dale; 2005 Beaverton: First, Wagarville: Community, Wooden Shoe; 2009 Clayton, Rollin Center; 2012 Glennie, Harrisville, Lincoln; Nov 1, 2014 medical leave; **Oct 1, 2015 Retired.**<> Home: 139 Northbrook Ct., Decatur IN 46733 (260) 301-9222. lp05@mediacombb.net

*Powers, Nancy G. (Paul) –
[(RE) PE-2006; FE-2010; RE 2020] Reading 2006; Battle Creek: Sonoma/Newton 2008; Perry/Shaftsburg 2012; **Retired Jun 1, 2020.**<> Home: 2444 Kimberly Dr, Muskegon 49444 (517) 375-7479. pastornancy@live.com

Poy, Eun Sik –
[(FE) PL-2015; PE-2016; FE-2019] Boyne City/Boyne Falls/Horton Bay (LTFT ¾) 09/01/2015; Boyne City/Boyne Falls/Epsilon 2016.<> (BC) 324 S Park St, Boyne City 49712 (231) 582-9776. (BF) 3057 Mill St, Boyne Falls 49713 (231) 582-9776. (E) 8251 E Mitchell Rd, Petoskey 49770 (231) 347-6608. Home: 8204 E Mitchell Rd, Petoskey 49770 (231) 347-5382. cloud.sik@asburyseminary.edu

*Pratt, David Orville –
[(RL) PL Nov 16, 1997; FL 2003] Nov 16, 1997 Clifford; 2003 Heritage; 2013 Ortonville; **Mar 1, 2016 Retired; 2018 Crystal Valley, Walkerville (LTFT ¼).**<>(CV) 1547 E Hammett Rd, Hart 49420 (231) 873-5422. (W) 189 E Main St, PO Box 125, Walkerville 49459 (231) 873-4236. Home: 8331 E Johnson Rd, Branch 49402 (810) 404-0085. gooey@tir.com

*Pratt, D. Kay (Merlin) –
[(RA) PL-1992; FL-1996; AM-2002; RA-2016] Transferred from South Indiana Conf 1992; Dowling: Country Chapel/Banfield (Co-Pastor) (LTFT ¼) 1992; Shepardsville/Price 1996; St Johns: Pilgrim (Assoc) 2004; Leave of Absence 2006; Appointed in Other Annual Conferences (¶331.8, ¶346.1) Detroit Conference, Denton: Faith 08/15/2008; Leave of Absence 2010; Other Valid Ministries (¶344.1d) Vice-President, Pastors and Priests Available for Service (PAPAS), Jamaica 2011; Retired 2016.<> Home: 1857 S Co Rd 50W, Brownstown IN 47220 (812) 498-7147. mpratteumc@juno.com

*Pratt, Merlin H. (Kay) –
[(RA) FL-1991; AM-1997; RA-2019] Waterloo Village/First (DSA) (Part Time) 1988-02/01/1991; Dowling: Country Chapel/Banfield 1991; Elsie 1996; St Johns: Pilgrim 2003; Leave of Absence 2006; Appointed in Other Annual Conferences (¶331.8, ¶346.1) Detroit Conference, Canton Cherry Hill 08/15/2008; Leave of Absence 2011; Other Valid Ministries (¶344.1d) Port Antonio Circuit, Jamaica District of the Methodist Church in the Caribbean and the Americas 09/01/2011; Appointed in Other Annual Conferences (¶331.8, ¶346.1) Detroit Conference, Ypsilanti: Lincoln Community 2016; Retired 2019.<> Home: 1857 S Co Rd 50W, Brownstown IN 47220 (734) 482-4446. cowtownpreacher@hotmail.com

Prentiss, Dean N. –
[(FE) D-1998; FE-2000] Transferred from Detroit Conf 2003; Mt Pleasant: Trinity/Countryside 1995; Williamston 09/15/1999; Big Rapids: First 2008; Wyoming: Wesley Park 2011.<> 1150 32nd St SW, Wyoming 49509 (616) 988-6738. Home: 2664 Borglum Avenue NE, Grand Rapids 49505 (616) 514-7124. deanprentiss1@gmail.com

Prewitt, Victoria Irene –
[(FL) DSA 2018; FL Jan 1, 2019] 2018 Crystal Fall: Crist, Amasa: Grace (DSA); **Jan 1, 2019 Crystal Fall: Crist, Amasa: Grace.**<> (CFC) 500 Marquette Ave, PO Box 27, Crystal Falls 49920, (AG) 209 Pine St, Amasa 49903. Home: 110 Elm Grove, Crystal Falls 49920 (906) 362-0460. gooey@tir.com

*Price, Carl Edwin (Patricia) –
[(RE) T W. VA, 1957; F W. VA, 1959] 1953 Palestine; 1956 school; 1959 Trenton NJ: Broad Street; 1960 Allentown; Oct 1962 Trans. to Detroit Conf, Birmingham: First (assoc); 1965 Detroit: St. Mark's; 1968 Pontiac: Central; Nov 1973 Midland: First; **1998 Retired.**<> Home: 1107 Timber Dr, Midland 48642 (989) 948-2277. 09cep31@gmail.com

Price, Wayne A. (Joy) –
[(FE) D-1988; FE-1993] Transferred from North Carolina Conf 2000; Keswick 2000; Shepherd 2004; Kalamazoo: Westwood 2007; Trenton: Faith 2019.<> 2530 Charlton, Trenton 48183 (734) 671-5211. Home: 1641 Edsel Dr, Trenton 48183 (269) 330-6768. pastorwaynewumc@gmail.com. waynepricefumc@gmail.com

*Prout, W. Cadman –
[(RE) T 1940; F 1942] 1940 school; 1941 Highland Park: Trinity (assoc); 1942 Royal Oak: St. John's; 1949 Livonia; 1953 Four Towns; 1955 Attorney, Friend of the Court, Oakland County; 1963 Sabbatical; 1964 Voluntary Location; **1981 Retired.**<> Home: (Jun-Nov) 4216 Chipmunk, Lincoln 48742; (Nov-Jun) 618 Deerwood Ave., Englewood FL 34223

*Puckett, Timothy R. (Esther) –
[(RL) PL-2011; RL 2020] Frontier (PTLP ¼) 2011; Frontier/Osseo (PTLP ½) 01/01/2012; North Adams/ Jerome (PTLP ¼) 2014; w/o appointment Jan 1, 2020; **Retired Jun 1, 2020.**<> Home: 10445 Folks Rd, Hanover 49241 (859) 421-8931. timpuckett761@yahoo.com

Query, Todd J. –

[(FD) PD-2003; FD-2008] Transferred from Detroit Conf 2004; Holland: First (Assoc) 2003; Appointed in Other Annual Conferences (¶331.8, ¶346.1) Virginia Conference, Williamsburg First 2006; Transitional Leave 12/31/2012; Personal Leave 01/01/2014; Deacons Appointed Beyond the Local Church(¶331.1a) Freelance Curriculum Writer/ Contributer, Sparkhouse, Augsburg Fortess Publishers (LTFT ½) and Wellspring UMC, Virginia Conference (LTFT ¼) 2015; **Transitional Leave Jan 1, 2020**.<> Home: 2620 Sir Thomas Way, Williamsburg VA 23185 (757) 208-0207. deacontodd08@gmail.com

*Rader, Blaine B. (Sharon) –

[(RE) D-1958; FE-1964; R-2004] Transferred from Northern IL Conf 1978; Other Valid Ministries (¶344.1d) Executive Director, Samaritan Counseling Center, Battle Creek 1978; Other Valid Ministries (¶344.1d) Comprehensive Psychological Services, Grand Rapids 1983; Other Valid Ministries (¶344.1d) Clinical Director, Samaritan Counseling Center of Central Michigan 01/01/1987; Other Valid Ministries (¶344.1d) Clinical Director, Samaritan Counseling Center of Central Michigan (LTFT ½) and Pastoral Counseling and Consultation (LTFT ½) 1990; Leave of Absence 09/01/1992; Other Valid Ministries (¶344.1d) Private Practice of Pastoral Counseling 01/27/1993; Other Valid Ministries (¶344.1d) Executive Director, Samaritan Counseling Center of Southern Wisconsin 01/01/1995; Appointed in Other Annual Conferences (¶337.1) Wisconsin Conf, Good Shepherd UMC 1997; Appointed in Other Annual Conferences (¶337.1) Wisconsin Conf, Madison: Bethany 2001; Retired 2004.<> Home: 450 Davis St #362, Evanston IL 60201 (312) 255-8544. Raderbb@aol.com

Radtke, Clifford L. (Beverly) –

[(PL) PL 2018] Lawrence 2006; Lawrence (PTLP ¾) 2015; Galien/Olive Branch (LTFT ¾) 2016; **Port Austin, Pinnebog (LTFT ¾) 2018**.<> (PA) 8625 Arch, Box 129, Port Austin 48467 (989) 738-5322. (P) 4619 N. Pinnebog Rd., Kinde 48445. Home: 114 Washington, Port Austin 48467 (989) 738-6322. parsoncliff@aol.com

Rafferty, Cathy Lynne –

[(FE) PE 1999; FE 2002; transfer to Detroit Conference 2010] 1999 Grandville (assoc); 2001 Chaplain Clark Retirement Community (¶344.1b,c); Feb 24, 2010 Chaplain, Chelsea Retirement Community (¶344.1b,c); Dec 4, 2017 Chaplain, Adrian Dominican Sisters (¶344.1b,c); **2019 Gladstone: Memorial**.<> 1920 Lake Shore Dr., Gladstone 49837 (906) 428-9311. Home: 1006 Lake Shore Dr., Gladstone 49837 (906) 420-8449. mail4cr@yahoo.com

Raineri, Jacqueline L. –

[(FL) FL 2012] Wisner 2012; Webberville, Williamston: Crossroads 2016; Millville, New Church Start 2017; Millville Jan 1, 2018; DownRiver 2018; **Clare 2020**.<> 105 E Seventh Street, Clare 48617-1301 (989) 386-2591. Home: 714 S Rainbow Dr, Clare 48617 (989) 386-7683. pastorjackieumc@gmail.com

Ralston, Douglas E. (Sharon) –

[(FE) PL 2000; PE 2004; FL Aug 1, 2009; PE 2011; FE 2013] Nov 1, 2000 LaSalle: Zion; 2004 LaSalle: Zion (LTFT ¾), Lambertville (assoc); Apr 1, 2007 discontinued; Aug 1, 2009 reinstated; Aug 1, 2009 East Side Covenant Cooperative Parish: St. Clair Shores: Good Shepherd; 2014 Dearborn: Good Shepherd; 2016 Trenton: Faith; **2019 Retired**.<> Home: 147 Borgess Ave, Monroe 48162 (734) 676-7079. dougralston@gmail.com

Ramsey, Michael J. (Kathy) –
[(FL) PL-2010; FL-2017] Carlisle (PTLP ½) 2010; Carlisle (PTLP ¾) 01/01/2011; Kent City Chapel Hill 2017; **Grand Rapids: South 2020**.<> 4500 Division Ave S, Grand Rapids 49548 (616) 534-8931. Home: 4777 10th St, Wayland 49348 (616) 293-9831. pastorramsey@att.net

*Randels, Jeanne M. (Paul Hartman) –
[(RE) D-1982; FR-1984; R-2014] Marshall (Assoc) 1981; Plainfield 02/23/1988; Albion: First 08/16/1991; Okemos Community Church 10/16/1998; Retired 01/01/2014; Lansing: Faith & S Lansing Ministries (LTFT ½) 2015-12/31/2015; Potterville (LTFT ½) 2016-08/31/2016.<> Home: 3786 Yosemite Dr, Okemos 48864 (517) 349-3595. jeannerandels@gmail.com

Ravi, Latha –
[(FE) P 1997; FE 1999] 1997 Ypsilanti: First (assoc); Jan 1, 2001 Flint: Central; 2002 Detroit: Central (assoc); 2005 Canton: Cherry Hill; 2008 Rochester St. Paul's (assoc); 2017 sabbatical leave; 2018 appoint. to attend school, U of M, School of Social Work (¶338.4); Jan 1, 2019 Transitional Leave; **2019 Detroit: Cass Community (assoc) (LTFT ¼)**.<> 3901 Cass Ave, Detroit 48201 (313) 833-7730. Home: 533 Hill St, Rochester 48307 (248) 464-4600. revlatharavi@gmail.com

*Ray, David Evans (Janie Marie) –
[(RE) P 1985; F 1988] 1986 Erie; 1991 Livonia: Newburg (assoc); 1992 Hazel Park: First; 1994 Corunna; 1996 Leave of Absence; Aug 1, 2000 South Central Cooperative Ministry: Halsey/South Mundy; 2006 leave of absence; **2012 Retired**.<> Home: 840 Georgia St., Williamston 48895

*Ray, Kenneth Bradley (Diane) –
[(RE) P 1992, on recognition of orders, Church of God; F 1994] 1989 North Street; 1992 Cass City: Salem; 1994 Roseville: Trinity; 2000 Alpena; 2003 Waterford: Trinity; 2004 Oxford; 2006 Redford: New Beginnings; 2007 Stony Creek; **2010 Retired**.<> Home: 186 Murphys Trail, Kalamazoo 49009 (269) 348-1089

*Reece, Wayne G. (Jo) –
[(RE) D-1958; FE-1960; R-2000] Transferred from North Indiana Conf 1963; Appointed to Extension Ministries (¶344.1b,c) Field Worker Conf; Board of Education 1963; Bangor 1966; Appointed to Extension Ministries (¶344.1b,c) General Board of Education 1970; Appointed in Other Annual Conferences (¶331.8, ¶346.1) Board of Discipleship, Section of Curriculum Resources 1973; Appointed in Other Annual Conferences (¶331.8, ¶346.1) Board of Discipleship, Curriculum Resources Committee 1977; Kalamazoo: First (Assoc) 02/15/1979; Big Rapids: First 1985; Mason: First 1992; Retired 2000.<> Home: 12 McKendree Circle, Hermitage TN 37076 (615) 818-0272. wayne.reece@comcast.net

Reed, David Allen –
[(PE) PE 2017 on recognition of orders from Missionary] **2017 North Street**.<> 4580 North Rd., Clyde 48049 (810) 385-4027. Home: 4584 North Rd., Clyde 48049 (810) 385-8366. david.reed68@gmail.com

Reed, Nathan T. –
[(FL) FL 2011] 2011 Crystal Falls: Christ, Amasa: Grace; 2015 Coleman: Faith; **2019 L'Anse, Sidnaw, Zeba**.<> (L) 304 N. Main, L'Anse 49946 (906) 524-7939. (S) S 121 W. Milltown Rd., Sidnaw 49961. (Z) 16024 Zeba Rd., L'Anse 49946 (906) 524-6967. Home: 227 N. Front, L'Anse 49946 (906) 524-7936. natereed1977@gmail.com

*Rees, Dianna Lynn (Forrest) –
[(RE) PE 2003; FE 2006; RE 2020] Armada, West Berlin 2003; Imlay City 2011; Wyandotte: First 2013; **Retired 2020**.<> Home: 2210 20th St., Wyandotte 48192 (586) 201-3681. diannarees@hotmail.com

*Reeves, Kenneth C. (Susanne) –
[(RE) D-1978; FE-1982; R-2006] Transferred from Detroit Conf 1995; Riverdale: Lincoln Road 1995; Burnips/ Monterey Center 1997; Marion/Cadillac: South Community 2004; Retired 2006; Marion/Cadillac: South Community 2006-2007.<> Home: 201 James Drive, Roscommon 48653 (989) 821-8504. kcreeves1@frontier.com

*Regan, Jeffery D. (Linda) –
[(RE) P 1974; F 1977] 1976 Lakeville, Leonard; 1979 Midland: First (assoc); Sept 1982 Grayling; 1989 Utica; 1994 Saginaw Bay District Superintendent; 1998 Conference Council Director; Feb 1, 2001 Rochester: St. Paul's; **2013 Retired**.<> 51781 Colonial Dr, Shelby Township 48316 (586) 803-0124. jeffery.regan@me.com

Reichle, Walter P. –
[(FL) FL 2012] **Oct 2012 Iron Mountain: First, Quinnesec**.<> (IM)106 Fourth St., Iron Mountain 49801 (906) 774-3586. (Q) 677 Division, PO Box 28, Quinnesec 49876 (906) 774-7971. Home: 901 Fairbanks St., Iron Mountain 49801 (906) 828-1228. pastorwalterr@gmail.com

Reinhardt, Keith –
[(PL) PL Dec 1, 2014] Dec 1, 2014 Wilber; **Sept 1, 2016 Wilber, Glennie (LTFT ¼)**.<> (W) 3278 N. Sherman Rd., East Tawas 48730 (989) 362-7860. (G) 3170 State St., PO Box 189, Glennie 48737. Home: 7620 Spruce, Hale 48739 (989) 710-1976. pkrwilber@gmail.com

Reinker, Heidi C. –
[(FE) P 1986; F 1988] Sept 5, 1986 Seymour Lake; 1989 honorable location; 1996 reinstated 1996 Old Mystic United Methodist Church, Old Mystic CT (LTFT); 2003 leave of absence; Nov 1, 2003 Richford, Troy Conference; 2010 Waterville Union Church, Waterville VT; **2016 Trenton: First**.<> 2610 W. Jefferson, Trenton 48183 (734-676-2066. Home: 2604 Lenox Rd., Trenton 48183 (734) 676-0041. hcreinker@gmail.com

*Reisinger, Jaye Annette (Alan) –
[(RD) CRT, 1981; CON (CE), 1982; FD 2002; RD 2018] 1981 Clio: Bethany; 1985 Leave of Absence; 1986 Saginaw Bay District Project Director; 1992 Medical Leave; 1994 Leave of Absence; 1999 Freeland (LTFT ¼); 2003 Freeland (deacon) (LTFT ½); **2018 Retired**.<> Home: 7485 N. River Rd., Freeland 48623 (989) 239-1820. jayealan@tm.net

Reissmann, Paul C. (Ashleigh) –
[(PE) PE 2020] **Wayland 2020**.<> 200 Church St, Wayland 49348-1203 (269) 792-2208. Home: *220 Church St, Wayland 49348 (269) 621-5333. paul.c.reissmann@gmail.com

*Rencontre, James A. (Jean) –
[(RA) PL 1989; FL 1990; AM 1995] 1989 Upper Peninsula Native American Ministry; 1990 Iron River: Wesley; 1993 Decker, Argyle, Shabbona (LTFT ¾); **1997 Retired**.<> Home: 709 Garvey St., Ironwood 49938 (906) 932-0470. revumc@charter.net

*Rencontre, Jean B. (James) –
[(RL) PL 1993; FL 1997] 1993 Decker, Argyle, Shabbona (part-time); 1997 Decker, Argyle, Shabbona; 2000 Ironwood: Wesley, Wakefield; **2008 Retired**.<> Home: 709 Garvey St., Ironwood 49938 (906) 932-0470. jbrencontre42@gmail.com

Reynolds, Jonathan E. (Lindsey Hall) –
[(FE) FL Jan 9, 2014; PE 2015; FE 2019] Rochester: St. Paul (assoc) Jan 9, 2014; Detroit: Cass Community (assoc) 2018; **Brighton: First (co-pastor, Whitmore Lake Campus) 2020**.<> 400 E. Grand River, Brighton 48116 (810) 229-8561. Home: 7608 Brookview Ct., Brighton 48116. (248) 891-2788. jreynolds@brightonfumc.org

*Rhinesmith, James Lyon –
[(RE) T Newark, 1946; F NY East, 1951] 1946 Paterson NJ: Hamilton Avenue; 1947 school; 1949 Trans. to NY East Conf, Oceanside; 1951 Long Island: Central Islip; 1953 Norwalk: South Norwalk; 1956 Trans. to Detroit Conf, Detroit: Messiah; 1959 Sandusky; 1963 Marine City; 1965 Oak Park: Faith; 1969 Sabbatical; **1969 Retired**; Jan 15, 1986-Dec 1987 Trenton: Faith (assoc) (LTFT).<> Home: 404 Cheswick Place, #252, Rosemont PA 19010

*Rhoades, Stephen E. (Debra) –
[(RE) P 1994 on recognition of orders, Wesleyan Church; F 1997; RE 2019] 1983 Madison, Good Shepherd Wesleyan Church; Feb 16, 1994 transf to Detroit Conf, Crystal Falls, Amasa: Grace; 2000 Marquette: First; 2004 Crystal Falls: Christ, Amasa: Grace; 2011 L'Anse, Sidnaw, Zeba; **2019 Retired**.<> Home: 126 S Shore Rd, Crystal Falls 49920 (906) 367-4587. srhoades@up.net

*Rice, Clifford –
[(RE) SP 1993; PE 1998; FE 2002] 1993 Detroit: West Outer Drive (LTFT); **2002 Retired**.<> Home: 20539 Woodward, Clinton Twp. 48035 (586) 791-4396. Clifford496@cs.com

*Rice, Philip A. (Charlene) –
[(RE) P 1969; F 1972] 1971 Hillman, Spratt; May 1975 Homer; 1979 Freeland; 1987 Essexville: St. Luke's; 1997 Cass City; **2002 Retired**.<> Home: 6074 Old Hickory Dr., Bay City 48706 (989) 684-2629. Ricepc@chartermi.net

Richards, Robert Grant –
[(FL) FL 1993] Dec 16, 1993 Tawas (assoc); 1997 Monroe: East Raisinville Frenchtown; 2001 Saginaw: Swan Valley; 2013 Saginaw: Swan Valley, LaPorte; **2019 Saginaw: Swan Valley, LaPorte, Hemlock, Nelson**.<> (SV) 9265 Geddes Rd, Saginaw 48609, (L) 3990 Smith's Crossing, Freeland 48623 (989) 695-9692, (H) 406 W. Saginaw St., PO Box 138, Hemlock 48626, (N) 5950 S Hemlock Rd., PO Box 138, Hemlock 48626. Home: 16344 Northern Pintail Trail, Hemlock 48626 (989) 642-4560. robertgrichards@chartermi.net

*Rickard, O'Ryan –
[(RL) PL-2004; PE-2005; RL-2013] Morris Chapel 2003; Townline/Breedsville 2004; Salem/Greenbush/Lowe 2005; Salem/Lowe/Maple Rapids 2006; Coloma/Watervliet 2007; Niles: Portage Prairie/Arden 2009; PE Discontinued 2013; **Retired 2013**; Niles: Portage Prairie/Arden (LTFT ¼) 2013; Arden (LTFT ¼) 2014-Feb 9, 2020.<> Home: 9241 W Broward Blvd Apt 3308, Plantation FL 33324. orr6148@aol.com

Riegler, Anne W. (Michael) –
[(FL) PL-2010; FL-2017; AM-2019] LP w/o Appointment 2007; Amble (PTLP) 08/15/2009; Mears/Shelby 2017.<> (M) PO Box 100, 1990 N Joy St, Mears 49436 (231) 873-0875. (S) 68 E 3rd St, Shelby 49455 (231) 861-2020. Home: 5181 Hancock St, Montague 49437 (231) 631-0573. pastoranne09@gmail.com

Riegler, Michael A. (Anne) –
[(FE) FL-2006; AM-2012; PE-2015; FE-2017] Big Rapids: Third Avenue/Paris/Rodney 09/11/2005; Edmore: Faith 2011; Montague 2017.<> 8555 Cook St, Montague 49437 (231) 894-5789. Home: 5181 Hancock St, Montague 49437 (231) 631-4712. pastormikeriegler@gmail.com

*Riley, Richard M. (Janis) –
[(RE) D-1975; FE-1979; R-2014] Sturgis (Assoc) 1977; Middleton/Maple Rapids 1980; Kalkaska 1984; Rockford 1993; Retired 2014.<> Home: 4307 Rezen Ct, Rockford 49341 (616) 648-4340. dick.riley52@gmail.com

*Ritter, John F. (Delcina) –
[(RL) FL-1978; PL-1980; FL-1984; RL-2001] Ashley / Bannister 10/16/1978; Rosebush (LTFT PT) 1980; Edwardsburg: Hope 03/01/1984; Smith Corners / Crystal Valley / Walkerville 1988; Carlisle 09/01/1990; Girard / Ellis Corners 1994; Turk Lake 07/08/1996; Retired 11/01/2001.<> Home: 2490 E Levering Rd, Levering 49755 (231) 537-2777

*Ritter, William Anthony (Kristine) –
[(RE) T 1963; F 1967] 1965 Dearborn: First (assoc); 1969 Livonia: Newburg; 1980 Farmington: Nardin Park; 1993 Birmingham: First; **2005 Retired**.<> Home: 940 Scott Court, Northville 48176 (248) 308-3216. billritter65@yahoo.com

Robbins, Patrick Doyle (Karen) –
[(FL) FL 1998] 1998 Cole, Omard; 2000 Omard; 2001 Sutton-Sunshine, Bethel, Akron; 2011 Grayling: Michelson Memorial; 2014 Yale; **2019 Brown City, Omard**.<> (BC) 7043 Lincoln, PO Box 39, Brown City 48416 (810) 346-2010. (O) 2055 Peck Rd., Brown City 48416 (810) 346-3448. Home: 6931 George St., Brown City 48416 (810) 346-2555. suttonsunshine@hotmail.com

*Roberts, Archie Ted –
[(RE) T 1961; F 1963] 1961 school; 1962 Franklin (assoc); 1963 Dixboro; 1965 Chaplain, Army, Vietnam; 1966 Chaplain, Air Defense, Cleveland OH; 1968 Chaplain, Alaska; 1971 Chaplain School; 1972 CPE Student, Englewood Federal Prison; 1973 Military Police School Faculty; 1977 Chaplain, Korea; 1978 Division Chaplain, 24th Div., Ft. Stewart GA; 1982 Chaplain School, Director of Training, Ft. Monmouth NJ; 1990 Staff Chaplain, Chapel of Four Chaplains, Valley Forge PA; **1997 Retired**.<> Home: G-08 Road, W 6555, Wallace 49893

Roberts, Richard D. (Lucinda) –
[(PL) PL-2015] Fountain 2012; Free Soil-Fountain (DSA) (LTFT ¼) 2013; Free Soil-Fountain (LTFT ¼) 12/01/2015.<> PO Box 173, 2549 E Michigan St, Free Soil 49411(231) 690-4591. Home: 2415 E Michigan St, Free Soil 49411 (231) 233-8954. onchristthesolidrockistandd@gmail.com

Robertson, James C. (Jean) –
[(PL) PL-2014] Townline (LTFT ¼) 2014.<> 41470 24th Ave, Bloomingdale 49026 (269) 521-4559. Home: 55130 County Rd 384, Grand Junction 49056 (269) 838-3500. jc.robertson@ymail.com

*Robertson, Stanley Joe (Mary Ellen) –
[(RE) T 1967; F 1970] 1969 Detroit: Redford (assoc); 1970 Homer; 1973 school; 1975 Chaplain, CPE Supervisor, Chillicothe Correctional Institution; 1981 Port Huron: Gratiot Park, Washington Avenue; 1985 Cass City: Trinity; Jan 1, 1990 Tawas; 2001 sabbatical leave; **2002 Retired.**<> Home: 907 Monument, Tawas City 48763 (989) 362-5881. sjmrobertson@charter.net

*Robinson, Beatrice K. –
[(RE) D-1990; FE-1992; R-2007] Pokagon (Part Time) 1988; Riverdale: Lincoln Road 1990; Holland: First (Assoc) 1995; Jackson: Trinity 1998; Bath/Gunnisonville 2006; Retired 2007.<> Home: 706 Huntington Blvd, Albion 49224 (517) 629-5881. bearobin@sbcglobal.net

*Robinson, William T. (Joyce) –
[(RE) T S. Caro, Central Jurisd., 1964; F S. Caro, Central Jurisd., 1966] 1966 Forest City; 1968 Trans. to Detroit Conf, Detroit: East Grand Boulevard; 1970 Detroit: East Grand Boulevard, Urban Missioner; 1971 Urban Missioner; 1974 Ann Arbor: Glacier Way; Oct 1978 General Board of Global Ministries; 1998 Saginaw Bay District Superintendent; **2004 Retired.**<> Home: 3310 Corvair Lane, Saginaw 48602 (989) 792-7552. TJMROB@aol.com

*Robinson-Fisher, Carolyn A. (Don) –
[(RL) PL-1988; FL-1991; RL-2011] Williamston: Wheatfield (LTFT ¼) 1988; Middleton / Maple Rapids 1991; Millville 1997; Three Rivers: Ninth Street / Jones 07/14/1998; Battle Creek: Christ 2007; **Retired 2011;** Battle Creek: Christ Jul 1-22, 2020.<> Home: 20908 Collier Rd, Battle Creek 49017 (269) 589-6487

Roe, Jacquelyn –
[(FE) P 1994; F 1997] Gwinn 1995; Gladstone: Memorial 2006; Cass City 2010; Milan: Marble Memorial 2018; **God's Country Cooperative Parish: Newberry, Engadine 2020.**<> (N) 110 W Harrie St, Newberry 49868 (906) 293-5711. (E) 13970 Park Ave, PO Box 157, Engadine 49827 (906) 477-9989. Home: PO Box 157, N6828 Elm St, Engadine 49827 (906) 293-5497. revjackieroe@gmail.com

Roosa, Kayla J. –
[(PE) PL 2015; FL 2017; PE 2019] Poseyville Nov 1, 2015; **Freeland 2017.**<> 205 E. Washington, PO Box 207, Freeland 48623 (989) 695-2101. Home: 7801 N. River Rd, Freeland 48623 (989) 573-8357. kroosa42@gmail.com

*Roose, Randall E. (LaVonna) –
[(RA) AM-1986; RA-1993] [Church of the Brethren] Weidman 01/01/1986; Retired 1993; Leaton (DSA) 08/01/1999-2016.<> Home: 3380 S Genuine Rd, Mt Pleasant 48858 (989) 772-1001. rlroose60@gmail.com

*Ross, Edward C. (Monika) –
[(RE) D-1976; FE-1980; R-2012] Mt Pleasant: First (Assoc) 1978; Gull Lake 1981; Jackson: First 1994; Retired 2012; Lansing: Christ (Interim) 12/31/2012; Waterloo Village (LTFT ¼) 2013; Three Rivers Ninth St (LTFT ¼) 2017.<> 16621 Morris Ave, Three Rivers 49093 (269) 273-2065. Home: 4231 Persian Dr, Kalamazoo 49006 (269) 382-0870. edward.c.ross45@gmail.com

*Roth, Robert H., Jr. –
[(RE) West Michigan; trans to Detroit Conf Jan 1, 2015] 2009 Ann Arbor: First (assoc), Director of Wesley Foundation (2010 came out of retirement);2014 Chaplain-Director, Wesley Foundation, University of Michigan; **2018 Retired**.<> Home: 270 E 14th St, Holland 49423 (734) 369-8068. bobjazzrr@gmail.com

Rourke, LuAnn L. (Patrick) –
[(FE) FL 2006; PE 2007; FE 2011] Swartz Creek (assoc) 2006; Seymour Lake 2009; Clio: Bethany 2015; Port Huron: First 2017; **Heritage District Superintendent 2020**.<> PO Box 128, St. Clair Shores 48080 (734) 663-3939. Home: 6493 S Sheridan Ave, Durand 48429 (734) 660-4887. lrourke@michiganumc.org

Rouse, Ronald W. (Donna) –
[(PL) PL Nov 9, 2013] **Nov 9, 2013 Attica**.<> 26789 Dayton Rd., Richmond 48062 (810) 724-0690. Home: (248) 379-2509

*Rowe, Edwin A. (Nida Donar). –
[(RE) P 1968; F 1972] 1971 Pontiac: Central (assoc); 1974 Pontiac Ecumenical Ministry; 1979 Director, Wesley Foundation, Wayne State University; 1981 Detroit: Cass Avenue; July 1, 1994 Detroit: Central; **Dec 31, 2014 Retired**.<> 2023 Hyde Park, Detroit 48207 (313) 268-0068. whereisthepastor@yahoo.com

*Rowe, Gregory E. (Karen Kay) –
[(RE) SP 1984; P 1986; F 1988] 1984 Spartanburg (N. IN Conf); 1986 L'Anse, Sidnaw, Zeba; 1990 Macon; 1993 Caring Covenant Group Ministry: Otisville, West Forest; Feb 1, 1995 Redford: Rice Memorial; 2000 Redford: Rice Memorial, Lola Valley; Jan 26, 2005 Redford: New Beginnings; 2006 Bad Axe: First; 2008 Wayne-Westland: First; 2011 Atherton, Phoenix; **2016 Retired**.<> Home: 9704 Baywood Dr., Plymouth 48170 (734) 656-8226. revgrowe@gmail.com

*Rubingh, Larry W. (Linda) –
[(RE) D-1981; FE-1987; R-2012] Camden/Montgomery/Stokes Chapel 1983; Stevensville (Assoc) 1987; Holton 1988; Battle Creek: Convis Union 01/01/1992; Jackson Calvary 1997; Grass Lake 1999; Stockbridge/Munith 2007; Munith (LTFT ¼) 10/15/2010; Medical Leave 09/06/2011; **Retired 2012**; Allen 2017; **Allen, Quincy 2020**.<> (A) PO Box 103; 167 W Chicago Rd, Allen 49227 (517) 200-8416. (Q) 32 W. Chicago St., Quincy 49082 (517) 639-5035. Home: 2480 N Portage Rd, Jackson 49201 (517) 812-6636. lsrlwr@aol.com

*Rule, James Lloyd (JoAn) –
[(RE) P 19__; F 1984] 1982 Decker, Shabbona, Argyle; 1986 God's Country Cooperative Parish: Newberry; June 1, 1996 Freeland; **2012 Retired**.<> Home: 10955 Carter Rd., Freeland 48623 989-695-2672. jlrule43@gmail.com

*Rupe, Meredith –
[(RE) P 1964 W.MI; F 1966 W.MI] school 1964; Elkhart-Hillcrest (N. IN) 1966; Keeler, Sliver Creek (N. IN) 1968; transf. from N. IN to W. MI 1969; Three Oaks Nov 1, 1970; Chaplain, Marquette Prison/House of Corrections Nov 15, 1975; Wesley Foundation, Ferris State University 1979; Iron Mountain: Trinity 1998 (2003 transf. to Detroit Conf); **Retired 2006**; Grant Center (LTFT ¼) 2018-2020.<> Home: 620 Birch Circle Dr E, Boyne Falls 49713 (231) 549-3142. meredithrupe@ballstate.bsu.edu

*Rupert, James Russell –

[(RE) P 1972; F 1975] 1974 Ferndale: First (assoc); Dec 1975 Clinton; 1977 Leave of Absence; 1981 Hillman, Spratt; 1984 Pontiac: Aldersgate, Elmwood; Jan 1985 Pontiac: Aldersgate, Rochester Hills: First; 1987 Rochester Hills: First; 1990 Dryden, Attica; Oct 1, 1995 Birmingham: Embury; 1997 Burton: Emmanuel; 2000 Burton: Emmanuel, Flint: Asbury; July 16, 2006 Hancock: First; **2009 Retired**.<> Home: 3445 Saginaw, National City 48748 (989) 820-9383

Rush, Albert –

[(PL) PL Oct 8, 2007] Oct 8, 2007 Detroit: West Outer Drive; **2012 Eastside Covenant Cooperative Parish – Eastpointe: Immanuel**.<> 23715 Gratiot, Eastpointe 48021 (586) 776-7750. Home: 22839 Linwood, Eastpointe 48021 (586) 871-2025. arushy2k@yahoo.com

*Russell, Donald A. –

[(RE) D-1958; FE-1962; HL-1977; FE-1980; R-1996] Transferred from Kentucky Conf 1960; Byron Center 1960; Byron Center/Market Street 1964; Lawton/Porter 1966; Watervliet 1971; Sabbatical Leave 1975; Appointed in Other Annual Conferences (¶331.8, ¶346.1) Wellspring Mission Group, Church of the Savior, Washington DC 1976; Honorable Location 1977; Readmitted, Appointed in Other Annual Conferences (¶331.8, ¶346.1) The Church of the Savior, Washington DC 1980; Retired 1996.<> Home: 4651 County Rd 612 NE, Kalkaska 49646 (231) 258-6728

*Sailor-Petit, Deanna M. –

[(RL) PL Jan 1, 1999] Jan 1, 1999 Detroit: West Outer Drive (assoc); 2000 Inkster: Christ (LTFT ½); 2005 Inkster: Christ (LTFT ¼); **Oct 11, 2006 Retired**.<> Home: 2927 Lyndhurst Place, Chester VA 23831. thesailorgroup@comcast.net

Sampson, Frederick G., III –

[(OF), National Baptist Convention] Bloomfield Hills: St. Paul 2013; Bloomfield Hills: St. Paul, Hazel Park 2016; **Medical Leave Jan 1, 2020**.<> Home: 208 Barrington Rd, Bloomfield Hills 48302 (248) 542-5598. pastorfgsampson@gmail.com

*Sanders, William P. (Manila) –

[(RE) D-1980; FE-1985; R-2003] Transferred from Detroit Conference Bellevue/Kalamo 1988; Buchanan: First 02/02/1996; **Retired 2003**; Appointed in Other Annual Conferences (¶331.8, ¶346.1) Detroit Conference, Wisner 2010; Appointed in Other Annual Conferences (¶331.8, ¶346.1) Detroit Conference, Standish/Saganing Indian 2012-01/01/2013; Appointed in Other Annual Conferences (¶331.8, ¶346.1) Detroit Conference, Fairgrove/Watrousville 2013; **Watrousville Sept 1, 2014**.<> PO Box 56 (4446 W Caro Rd, Caro 48723), Fairgrove 48733 (989) 673-3434. Home: 6116 Slocum St, Unionville 48767 (989) 674-2421. Chaplainbill4msp@aol.com

Sandlin, Margaret K. [Mallory] (Josh) –

[(FL) SP-2017; FL-2018] Mendon (¶318.3 LTFT) 2017; Battle Creek: Baseline/Bellevue 2018; Bellevue, BC: Convis Union 2020.<> (B) 122 W Capital Ave, Bellevue 49021 (269) 793-9421. (CU) 18990 12 Mile Rd, Battle Creek 49014 (269) 965-3787. Home: 523 Sherwood Rd, Bellevue 49021 (989) 387-1494. revmkm2017@gmail.com

Sawicki, Michael T. (Patricia) –

[(FE) PE 2001; FE 2004] Asbury Theological Seminary; June 1, 2001 Pigeon: Salem; 2009 FaithWay; **2013 Midland: Aldersgate**.<> 2206 Airfield Lane, Midland 48642 (989) 631-1151. Home: 415 Coolidge Dr., Midland 48642 (989) 492-4465. MichaelTSawicki@gmail.com

*Sayer, Cecilia Lee –
[(RL) PL Nov 2013; NL 2017; RL 2019] Nov 19, 2013 New Lothrop; 2017 no appointment; **2019 Retired**.<> Home: 7404 Cross Creek Dr., Swartz Creek 48473 (810) 635-8117. jolee5053@gmail.com

*Scavella, Donald Alexander, Sr. (Freddie) –
[(RE) T GA, 1963; F OH W., 1967] 1965 Inner City Project Director, Cincinnati OH; 1967 Shepherd; 1969 Trans. to Detroit Conf, Detroit: Scott Memorial; 1977 Detroit East District Superintendent; Oct 1982 Associate Council Director: Church Extension, New Church Development, United Methodist Union of Greater Detroit; 1993 Executive Director, United Methodist Union of Greater Detroit; **Dec 31, 2005 Retired**.<> Home: 24040 Roanoke, Oak Park 48237 (313) 861-0895

*Schippert, Ellen O. –
[(RL) PL 2007; NL 2015; PL 2019; RL 2020] Forester 2007; no appointment May 18, 2015; Applegate, Buel, Croswell: First (LTFT ¾) Jan 1, 2019; **Retired 2020**.<> . Home: 7350 N Lakeshore Rd, Palms 48465 (989) 864-3791. schippertellen@gmail.com

Schleicher, Andrew John (Lilamani) –
[(FD) PD 2004; FD 2010] 2004 Communications Specialist, UMPH; Aug 1, 2007 leave of absence; June 15, 2009 Director of CEF Services, Consulting Ministry of Religious Journalism and Communications; **Jan 1, 2015 Project Coordinator, United Methodist Communications**.<> 810 12th Ave., S, Nashville TN 37202 (615) 742-5145. Home: 594 Huntington Pkwy., Nashville TN 37211 (615) 837-3330. aschleicher93@gmail.com

*Schleicher, John Gordon (Margery) –
[(RE) PL 1983; SP 1985; P 1987; F 1989] 1983 Willow; 1985 South Lyon (part-time (assoc); 1987 Carsonville, Applegate, Watertown: Zion; 1991 Fowlerville: First; August 15, 1992, Chaplain, Chelsea Retirement Home; 2000 Sterling, Alger; 2002 Sterling, Garfield, Alger; 2003 Middlebury (LTFT ½); 2005 Middlebury, Bennington; **2006 Retired**.<> Home: 1586 Hagadorn Road, Mason 48854 (517) 833-4988. gschleicher1@wowway

*Schleicher, Margery Ann Taber (Gordon) –
[(RE) P 1981; F 1983] 1980 (PL) Livonia: Newburg (assoc); 1981 Romulus: Community, Willow; Sept 1983 Romulus: Community; 1987 Sandusky; 1991 Livingston Circuit: Plainfield, Trinity; May 16, 1995 Denton: Faith; 2000 AuGres; 2003 St. Johns: First; **2007 Retired**.<> Home: 1586 Hagadorn Road, Mason 48854 (517) 833-4988. mschleicher@wowway.com

Schlimm, Matthew R. (Melanie) –
[(FE) PE-2002; FE-2005] Clergy Appointed To Attend School, Duke University 2003; Other Valid Ministries (¶344.1d) Asst Professor, Univ Dubuque Theological Seminary 09/01/2008; Appointed to Extension Ministries (¶344.1b,c) Associate Professor, Old Testament, University of Dubuque Theological Seminary 2015.<> 2000 University Ave, Dubuque IA 52001 (563) 589-3101. Home: 2130 Fairway Drive, Dubuque IA 52001 (563) 589-3101. matthew.schlimm@duke.edu

Schmidt, Marcus V. (Jody) –
[(PL) CC-2015; PL-2016] Grand Rapids: Cornerstone (Assoc) South Wyoming Campus (LTFT ½) 05/01/2016.<> 2730 56th St SW, Wyoming 49418 (616) 698-3170. Home: 5482 Fieldstone Dr SW, Wyoming 49418 (616) 443-9257. marcuss@cornerstonemi.org

Schneider, John Henry, Jr. (Debra) –
[(FE) P 1993; F 1995] 1993 Morrice, Bennington, Pittsburg; 1997 Wisner; Sept 1, 1999 Monroe: First; 2005 Lincoln Park: Dix, Taylor: West Mound; **2013 Hardy**.<> 6510 E. Highland Rd., Howell 48843 (517) 546-1122. Home: 6520 E. Highland Rd., Howell 48843 (517) 579-2626. johnhenryschneider@yahoo.com

*Schneider, Terrill M. (Linda) –
[(RA) PL-2000; FL-2001; AM-2004; R-2018] Scottdale 06/01/1995; Scottdale/Bridgman Faith 05/01/2000; Retired 10/01/2018.<> Home: 73239 Cinder Ct, South Haven 49090 (269 767-7218. schneider4276@comcast.net

*Schoenhals, Robert David (Jill Warren) –
[(RE) P 1973; F 1976; RE 2020] Bethel UCC 1970; Chaplain, Green's Chapel 1972; Armada, Omo: Zion 1975; Seven Churches United Group Ministry: Byron 1983; Parish Director, Seven Churches United Group Ministry: Byron 1990; Wesley Foundation, University of Michigan 1995; Indianapolis: Central Avenue 2002; Grayling: Michelson Memorial 2004; leave of absence Feb 1, 2006; Bloomfield Hills: St. Paul 2007; West Bloomfield 2010; Lincoln Park: First 2012; Ferndale: First 2013; **Retired Jan 1, 2020; Ferndale: First 2020**.<> 22331 Woodward Ave., Ferndale 48220 (248) 545-4467. Home: 657 W. Oakridge, Ferndale 48220 (248) 542-5598. rschoenhals@sbcglobal.net

*Schoenherr, Leonard R. (Janette) –
[(RE) D-1973; FE-1975; R-2013] Transferred from North Indiana Conf 1987; Watervliet 06/09/1987; Coloma/Watervliet 02/16/1996; Marshall 1999; Retired 06/30/2013; Galesburg (LTFT ½) 2013; Galesburg (LTFT ¼) 01/01/2014; Galesburg (LTFT 45%) 01/26/2015; Gull Lake (LTFT 45%) (Co-pastor) 2016; **Almena 2020 (LTFT ½)**.<> 27503 County Rd 375, Paw Paw 49079 (269) 668-2811. Home: 4500 Mountain Ash Ln, Kalamazoo 49004 (269) 903-2182. schoenherrlen@gmail.com

*Schomaker, W. Thomas (Patricia) –
[(RE) T 1967; F 1969] 1967 Columbus (OH): Gates, Fourth UMC; 1969 Linden; Jan 1976 Wesley Foundation, University of Michigan; 1981 Detroit: Jefferson Avenue; 1990 Troy: Fellowship; 1998 St. Clair: First; **Aug 1, 2004 Retired**.<> Home: 5656 Firethorne Drive, Bay City 48706 (989) 450-5291. asktherev@mac.com

*Schoonover, William Dale (Norma) –
[(RE) T 1966; F 1968] 1959 Brent Creek, West Vienna; 1962 Elba; 1965 school; 1965 Culloden, Yatesville, Rogers (N. GA Conf); Mar 1, 1968 Norway, Faithorn; 1974 Negaunee, Palmer; 1982 Flint: Asbury; Feb 16, 1990 Ontonagon, Greenland, Rockland: St. Paul's; **1992 Retired;** 1994-95 Menominee: First (LTFT).<> Home: (May-Sept) N 15957 Henderson Lane, Vulcan 49892 (906) 250-2138. (Oct-Apr) 5591 Goldenrod St, Kalamazoo 49009. Schoonover49892@aol.com

*Schrock, Jeffrey J. (Kathi) –
[(RL) FL-2000; RL-2016] Marion / Cadillac: South Community 06/04/2000; Sunfield / Sebewa Center 2004; Moorestown-Stittsville / Merritt-Butterfield 2012; Retired 2016.<> Home: 7500 E Boon Rd, Cadillac 49601. pastorjs@centurytel.net

Schroeder, Clifford James, III (Rachel) –
[(FE) FL 1999; PE 2004; FE 2009] Feb 1, 1999 Dryden, Attica; Jan 1, 2001 Attica; 2007 Birch Run; 2010 Birch Run, Burt; **2012 Holly: Calvary**.<> 15010 N. Holly Rd., Holy 48442 (248) 634-9711. Home: 3464 Quick Rd., Holly 48442 (248) 245-9125. cliff.schroeder@gmail.com

Schumann, William –
[(PL) PL 2000] 2000 Melvindale: New Hope; 2007 Allen Park: Trinity, Melvindale: New Hope; **2011 Retired**.<> Home: 1386 Dulong, Madison Heights 48971 (313) 551-4003. revbillnancy@comcast.net

Schwandt, James P. (Yvonne) –
[(FE) P 1975; F 1978] 1977 Deckerville, Minden City; 1980 Genesee, Thetford Center; 1987 Rochester: St. Paul's (assoc); 1988 Pigeon: First; Sept 1, 1994 Tecumseh; 1999 Harper Woods: Redeemer; **Feb 15, 2008 incapacity leave**.<> Home: 2566 Sunny Creek SE, Kentwood 49508 (616) 554-9181. jpschwandt@yahoo.com

*Schweizer, Allen F. –
[(RL) FL 1989] 1989 Ogden; 1992 Whittemore, Prescott; June 1, 1996 Pontiac Cooperative Parish: Four Towns; 1998 Ironwood: Wesley, Wakefield; Oct 1, 1999 Deerfield, Wellsville; **Nov 1, 2000 Retired**.<> Home: 9440 Forestview Circle, Grand Blanc 48439 (810) 655-2454. mom3@mycidco.com

Scott, John A. (Rebecca) –
[(FE) FL-2000; PE-2001; FE-2004] Girard/Ellis Corners 2000; Girard/Ellis Corners/Quincy (Co-Pastor) 09/01/2003; Traverse Windward Community New Church Start 2007; Lakeview: New Life 2011; Manistee 2015.<> 387 1st St, Manistee 49660 (231) 723-6219. Home: 819 Elm St, Manistee 49660 (231) 723-3304. jtentmaker@mac.com

*Scott, Sharon G. –
[(RE) P 1989; F 1991] Jan 1, 1989 Detroit: Zion; 1992 Warren: First (assoc); 1995 Detroit: St. Timothy (assoc); 1998 Waterford: Four Towns; **Sep1 1, 2001 Retired**.<> Home: 33133 Orchard St., Farmington 48336 (248) 476-1411. sharongscott1939@gmail.com

*Scroggins, Nicholas William (Lorna) –
[(RA) SP 1987; FL 1990; AM 1996] 1988 Painesdale: Albert Paine; 1990 Republic, Woodland; 1993 Henderson, Chapin; 1998 Britton: Grace; 2002 Hemlock, Nelson; 2009 Marquette: Grace, Skanda; **2010 Retired**.<> Home: 12306 Conde Dr., Brooksville FL 35213. pscroggins@charter.net

*Seaver, Howard D. (Judy) –
[(RA) FL-2000; AM-2001; RA-2012] Fife Lake/Boardmans Parish (DSA) 1994; Fife Lake/Boardmans Parish 11/16/1994; Retired 2012.<> Home: 3932 Deater Dr NW, Rapid City 49676 (231) 331-6867. seaver@torchlake.com

*Secrist, Robert B. (Mary Evelyn) –
[(RE) T 1952; F 1955] 1955 Dearborn: First (assoc); 1956 Southfield; 1962 Standish; 1966 Dearborn: Warren Valley; 1967 Pontiac: St. James; 1971 Pontiac: St. James, Covert; 1973 Hudson; 1980 Burton: Emmanuel; 1985 Blissfield: Emmanuel; 1987 Fowlerville: First; **1991 Retired**.<> Home: 12612 St Paul Rd, Chambersburg PA 17202 (931) 787-7513

Seitz, William R. (Kristen Coates) –
[(FE) FL 1991; P 1992; F 1996] Owosso: Burton, Carland 1991; Iron Mountain: First June 1, 1996; Davisburg Feb 1, 2004; Sault Ste. Marie, Algonquin 2011; **Oscoda, Oscoda Indian Mission 2014**.<> (O) 120 W. Dwight, Oscoda 48750 (989) 739-8591. (OIM) 7994 Alvin Rd., Mikado 48750. Home: 108 W Dwight St, Oscoda 48750 (989) 739-5213. pbsinseitz@gmail.com

*Selleck, David A. (Anne) –
[(RE) D-1972; FE-1975; R-2015] St Joseph First (Assoc) 1974; Constantine 04/01/1976; Stockbridge 09/16/1979; Hillsdale: First 1987; Leave of Absence 12/01/1988; Honorable Location 1993; Readmitted 2002; Muskegon Lakeside 2002; Martin/Shelbyville 2009; Manistee 2012; **Retired 2015; Ravenna 2020**.<> PO Box 191, 12348 Stafford St, Ravenna 49451 (231) 853-6688. Home: 13687 Pinewood Dr, Grand Haven 49417 (231) 299-5374. dselleck2000@gmail.com

*Selleck, Gerald L. (Claudia) –
[(RE) D-1977; FE-1981; R-2018] Somerset Center/Moscow Plains 1979; Kalamazoo: First (Assoc) 1982; Courtland - Oakfield 12/01/1984; Hartford 1990; Manistee 1998; Leave of Absence 2002; Holton 2006; Retired 2018.<> Home: 1121 Kelsey St NE, Grand Rapids 49505 (231) 225-2856. jerryselleck@comcast.net

*Selleck, Richard A. (Eloise) –
[(RE) D-1961; FE-2063; R-1996] Ogdensburg (Old Mission Peninsula) 1955; Oakdale 1963; Rockford 1966; Muskegon Heights 1970; Appointed to Extension Ministries (¶344.1b,c) District Superintendent, Kalamazoo District 1977; Appointed to Extension Ministries (¶344.1b,c) West MI Conference Council Director 1983; Lansing: Christ 03/01/1987; Sand Lake/South Ensley 1992; Retired 1996.<> Home: 1551 Franklin St SE, 1024 Terrace, Grand Rapids 49506 (616) 248-7982. Rselleck0426@yahoo.com

*Seward, Edward Charles –
[(RL) FL 1985] 1983 Glennie, Curran and Wilber; 1985 Snover: Trinity, Moore, Elmer; July 1, 1987 Berrien Springs (W. MI); Apr 1, 1990 Litchfield (W. MI). 1990 Harrisville, Lincoln; **Dec 31, 2004 Retired**.<> Home: 6503 N. Towerline Rd., Hale 48739 (989) 728-2866. tippicanoe90@hotmail.com

*Seymour, Merton Wallace –
[(RE) T 1959; F 1961] 1960 Norway; 1963 St. Ignace; 1968 St. Clair; 1975 Alpena; 1983 Davison; 1987 Detroit West District Superintendent; 1993 Plymouth: First; 1995 Royal Oak: First; **1999 Retired**.<> Home: (summer) 11077 Hillman Rd., Lakeview 48850 (989) 352-6805; (winter) Country Park 508, 2331 Belleair Rd., Clearwater FL 33764. mseym@hotmail.com

*Seymour, Philip Merritt (Julie) –
[(RE) T 1968; F 1972] 1970 Novi; 1975 Ypsilanti: First (assoc); 1977 Saginaw: Sheridan Avenue, Warren Avenue; Jan 1980 Saginaw: Sheridan Avenue, Burt; 1980 Dearborn: Good Shepherd; 1988 Birmingham: Embury; Sept 1, 1995 Escanaba: Central; 1997 Taylor: West Mound, Melvindale: New Hope; 2000 leave of absence; **2011 Retired**.<> Home: 14272 Greentrees, Riverview 48192 (734) 479-2739. thatcounselor@yahoo.com

Shabazz, Rahim O. (Cheryl) –
[(FE) PL 2005; PE 2012; FE 2016] 2005 Detroit: Henderson Memorial; 2006 River Rouge: John Wesley; **2012** Poseyville, Saginaw: West Michigan Avenue; 2015 Romulus: Community; 2017 Detroit: St. Timothy, Westland: St. James; **2018 Detroit: Peoples, Westland: St. James**.<> (DP) 19370 Greenfield Rd, Detroit 48235 (313) 342-7868. (W) 30055 Annapolis, Westland 48186 (734) 729-1737. Home: 3722 Heritage Parkway, Dearborn 48124 (313) 570-6292. rcshabazz623@comcast.net

Shafer, Todd W. (Noreen) –
[(FL) DSA-2010; FL-2010] Mancelona/Alba (DSA) 07/15/2010; Mancelona/Alba 11/01/2010; Indian River 2017.<> PO Box 457, 956 Eagles Nest Rd, Indian River 49749 (231) 238-7764. Home: 5954 Berry Ln, Indian River 49749 (231) 587-8461. tshafer7@gmail.com

Shaler, Joseph D. (Terri) –
[(FE) PE-2001; FE-2003] Otsego 2001.<> PO Box 443, 223 E Allegan St, Otsego 49078 (269) 694-2939. Home: 411 Walden Dr, Otsego 49078 (269) 806-9087. revshalerjosephd@gmail.com

*Shapley, Jane B. (Allen) –
[(RE) D-1984; FE-1987; R-1996] Kalamazoo: First (Assoc) 1985; Oakdale 1987; Retired 1996.<> Home: PO Box 345, Malahat BC VOR 2LO, Canada (250) 743-1199. ajshap@telus.net

*Sharai, Maurice DeMont, Jr. (Susan) –
[(RE) P 1969; F 1972] 1971 Redford (assoc); 1977 Manchester; 1980 Flushing; 1989 Adrian: First; **2005 Retired**.<> Home: 3 Maumee Ct., Adrian 49221. Msharai@tc3net.com

*Shatz, Connie E. (Eugene) –
[(RL) PL-1999; RL-2012] Belding (LTFT < ¼) 06/21/1999; Retired 2012.<> Home: 11448 Heintzelman NE, Rockford 49341 (616) 754-8023. shatzconnie@yahoo.com

Shaw, Esrom –
[(PL) PL Nov 2013] Detroit: Mt. Hope Nov 9, 2013; **Birmingham: Embury (PTLP ¼) 2020**.<> 1803 E. 14 Mile Rd., Birmingham 48009 (248) 644-5708. 29600 Franklin #40, Southfield 48034 (313) 868-1352. sirrome3039@yahoo.com

*Sheen, Brian K. (Bonnie) –
[(RA) AM-2000; RA-2004] St John Pilgrim 1970; Leave of Absence 11/17/1983; Lansing: Central Free Methodist (assoc) 1985; Withdrew to Unite with the Free Methodist Church 1987; Davidson Free Methodist 1990; Owosso Free Methodist 1993-1995; Received from Free Methodist 1998; Sunfield 1998; Retired 2004.<> Home: 3170 Crudup Rd, Attalla AL 35954 (989) 224-6181. bonniesheen@gmail.com

*Sheffield, Alice Jean –
[(RL) PL 1995; FL 1997] 1995 Melvindale: New Hope; Dec 1, 1996 Owendale, Gagetown; 2001 North Lake; **2012 Retired**.<> Home:37505 Barkridge Circle, Westland 48185 (734) 649-3749. ajsheffield@gmail.com

Sherrill, Scott Leonard (Deborah) –
[(FE) PE 2016; FE 2019] **Vassar: First 2016**.<> 139 N. Main, Box 71, Vassar 48768 (989) 823-8811. scott@mtu.edu

*Shin, Isaac Yong-Choel (Ellen) –
[(RE) P, MN, 1986; F, MN, 1989] 1987 Jordan: Immanuel; Apr 1, 1992 Trans. to Detroit Conf, Ann Arbor: Korean; **2010 Retired**.<> Home: 33333 South River Bend Rd., Black Canyon City AZ 85324 (734) 649-7788. isaacyshin@yahoo.com

Shin, Tae Gyu –
[(PE) FL 2016; PE 2019] Troy: Korean (assoc) 2016; **Big Rapids: First 2020**.<> 304 Elm Street, Big Rapids 49307 (231) 796-7771. Home: 14080 Wildwood Dr, Big Rapids 49307 (909) 472-7802. bigrapidsfumcpastor@gmail.com

*Shiplett, Gary Ronald (Carol) –
[(RE) P, FL 1964; F, FL, 1966] 1964 Fieldsboro (NJ); 1865 Coronado (FL); 1966 Roscoe (N. IL); 1969 Naperville: Wesley (assoc); 1970 school; 1973 Leland, Suydam (N. IL); 1874 Frankfort; 1980 Woodale Community; 1991 sabbatical; 1992 Munising (LTFT) (Det. Conf); 1994 Gladstone: Memorial; **2000 Retired**.<> 4156 12th Rd., Escanaba 49829

*Shrout, Larry R. (Sheila) –
[(RE) D-1970; FE-1977; R-1998] Transferred from Nebraska Conf 1980; Colon 1980; St Johns: Pilgrim 1983; Retired 1998.<> Home: 237 W Slope Way, Canton GA 30115 (770) 704-0711. lrshrout@gmail.com

Shumaker, Anthony C. (Linda) –
[(FL) PL-2003; FL-2004; PL-2009; FL-2012] Almena (DSA) 2002; Almena 12/01/2002; LP w/o Appointment 2003; Burnips/ Monterey Center 2004; Otsego: Trowbridge (PTLP ¾) 2008; Middleville/Snow 2012; Middleville 2017.<> PO Box 400, 111 Church St, Middleville 49333 (269) 795-9266. Home: 1497 120th Ave, Hopkins 49328 (269) 650-5112. tshu59@gmail.com

*Sielaff, Robert J. (Darlene) –
[(RE) PL Apr 1998; PM on recognition from Missouri Lutheran, 1999; FE 2001; RE 2018] Dearborn Heights: Warren Valley Apr 1, 1998; Dearborn Heights: Stephens, Warren Valley 1999; Walled Lake 2012; New Hudson 2016; **Retired 2018;** Dearborn: Good Shepherd (LTFT ½) 2018-2020.<> Home: 42054 Baintree Circle, Northville 48168. sielaffrobert@gmail.com

Simmons, Gary L. (BethAnn Perkins-Simmons) –
[(FE) FL-2011; PE-2014; FE-2018] Mulliken (PTLP ¼) / Barry County: Woodland (LTFT ¼) 2011; Barry-Eaton Cooperative Ministry: Nashville (PTLP ½) and Vermontville (PTLP ¼) Barry County: Woodland (PTLP ¼) 2013; Barry-Eaton Cooperative Ministry: Nashville (LTFT ½) and Vermontville (LTFT ¼) Barry County: Woodland (LTFT ¼) 2014; Ithaca/Beebe 2015.<> 327 E Center St, Ithaca 48847 (989) 875-4313. Home: 601 N Union St, Ithaca 48847 (517) 388-2286. pastorgarysimmons@gmail.com

Simon, Corey M. (Ellyn) –
[(PE) FL 2016; PE 2018] 2016 Ida, Samaria: Grace; **2019 Martin, Shelbyville**.<> (M) 969 E Allegan, PO Box 154, Martin 49070 (269) 672-7097, (S) 938 124th Ave, Shelbyville 49344 (269) 672-7097. Home: 948 Lee St, Martin 49070 (231) 622-2070. pastorcoreysimon@gmail.com

*Simon, Michael J. (Beth) –
[(RL) PL-2006; FL-2013; RL-2017] Chase: Barton / Grant Center 2006; Harrison: The Gathering 2010; Lake Ann 2013; Retired 2017.<> (231) 349-1914

*Six, Jay Kendall (Linda) –
[(RE) P W. VA, 1976; F W. VA, 1979] Oct 1979 Trans. to Detroit Conf, Lake Linden, Painesdale; 1981 Controller, OMS International, Inc; **2016 Retired**.<> Home: 890 Ironwood Trail, Greenwood IN 46143 (317) 882-5385. jayksix@gmail.com

*Skutar, Cynthia A. (Jerry Welborn) –
[(RE) D-1987; FE-1990; RE 2020] Hersey 1988; Kalamazoo: First (Assoc) 1992; Three Rivers: First 1997; Muskegon: Lake Harbor 2000; Coldwater 2004; Mt Pleasant: First 2010; Grand Ledge: First 2013; **Retired 2020**.<> Home: 6680 Ambassador Ave Apt 112, Grand Ledge 48837 (517) 627-7347. cindyskutar@gmail.com

*Slate, Edward H. (Patsy) –
[(RE) D-1974; FE-1978; R-2012] Whitehall/Claybanks 1976; Leave of Absence 04/17/1983; Comstock 1984; South Haven: First 1989; Stanwood: Northland 1995; Evart 2006; Niles: Wesley 2008; Retired 2012; Buchanan: Faith (LTFT ½) 2012.<> 728 N Detroit St, Buchanan 49107 (269) 695-3261. Home: 1358 Honeysuckle Ln, Niles 49120 (269) 262-0011. faithoffice@sbcglobal.net

*Slater, Harold Jon (Karen) –
[(RE) T MI, 1963; F 1969] 1963 Gilead Circuit; 1966 Ebeneezer Presb., OH; 1967 Oran UCC, OH; 1969 Port Huron: Gratiot Park; 1970 Denton: Faith; Jan 1972 Lola Valley; Oct 1973 Ecumenical Institute; Feb 1975 Calumet, Laurium, Mohawk-Ahmeek; 1978 Jeddo, Lakeport; 1980 Four Towns, Keego Harbor; Aug 1, 1986 Four Towns (LTFT ¾), Oakland County Jail Ministry (LTFT ¼); 1989 Freeland; 1992 Hope, Edenville; 2002 St. Charles, Brant; Jan 1, 2008 Reese; **Mar 1, 2010 Retired**.<> Home: 3927 Lincoln Woods Dr., Midland 48642 989-486-3559. HSlatotrailwulf@aol.com

*Slattery, Dennis E. (Karen) –
[(RE) D-1982; FE-1985; R-2012] Ravenna 1983; Climax/Scotts 04/01/1987; Appointed to Extension Ministries (¶344.1b,c) Chaplain, Army Fort Hood TX 10/01/1988; Keeler/Silver Creek 1990; Marcellus/Wakelee 1992; Marcellus: Wakelee 1995; Ludington: St Paul 1998; LeValley/Berlin Center 2007; Retired 2012; Grass Lake (LTFT ¼) 2012-2018.<> Home: 6209 Montgomery Dr., Shelby Twp 48316 (616) 755-3554. den98@juno.com

*Slaughter-Titus, Linda J. –
[(RE) PL 1987; SP 1988; P 1991; FE 1999] 1987 Detroit: Thoburn; 1990 Detroit: Christ, Jefferson Avenue (assoc); 1991 Oak Park: Faith; 1995 Detroit: Cass Community (assoc); 1997 Detroit: Henderson Memorial, Ferndale: St. Paul's; 2000 Detroit: Henderson Memorial; 2001 Detroit: Conant Avenue; Jan 1, 2003 incapacity leave; 2005 Highland Park: Berea-St. Paul's; Mar 1, 2007 voluntary leave of absence; **2010 Retired**.<> Home: 1108 Suwannee Dr., Waycross GA 31501. 19titus10@gmail.com

*Small, Stephen C. (Karen) –
[(RE) PE-2001; FE-2004; R-2004] Glenn 11/16/1998; Center Park 2001; Brookfield Eaton 2004; Retired 10/01/2004; Riverside 2009-2014.<> Home: 9658 Allen Court, South Haven 49090 (269) 637-1692. karesmall@msn.com

Smalls, Benjamin Kevin –
[(OE) Baltimore/Washington Conf] June 1, 2016 Southfield: Hope; **2018 Southfield: Hope, Detroit: St. Timothy**.<> (SH) 26275 Northwestern Hwy., Southfield 48076 (248) 356-1020, (ST) 15888 Archdale, Detroit 48227 (313) 837-4070. Home: 5704 N. Pinnacle, West Bloomfield 48322 (301) 512-4075. kevinsmalls@aol.com

*Smith, Betty A. (Bill Biergans) –
[(RE) D-1990; FE-1992; R-2004] Ludington United (Assoc) 1990; Wacousta Community 1992; Coldwater 1998; Retired 2004; Potter Park (DSA) 10/16/2004-2005; Grand Ledge: First (Interim) 01/01/2013-03/31/2013; Sunfield and Mulliken (LTFT 45%) 2015-2016.<> Home. 1551 Franklin St SE Apt 2803, Grand Rapids 49506. revbet@comcast.net

*Smith, Charles W. (Arlene) –

[(RE) D-1971; FE-1976; R-2011] Transferred from North Indiana 1974; Centreville/ Nottawa 1974; Centreville 1976; East Lansing Chapel Hill/Gunnisonville 1984; Shepardsville/Price 1988; Courtland-Oakfield 1996; Ravenna 2008; Retired 2011.<> Home: 341 Guy St, Cedar Springs 49319 (616) 970-6269. Smith_chuckw@yahoo.com

Smith, Devin R. (Brittany) –

[(FE) PE 2014; FE 2019] Blissfield: Emmanuel, Lambertville (assoc) 2015; **Romeo, Leonard 2020.**<> (R) 280 North Main St., Romeo 48065 (586) 752-9132. (L) 245 E. Elmwood, Box 762, Leonard 48367(248) 628-7983. Home: 289 North Bailey St., Romeo 48065 (734) 707-1792. smith.devinr@gmail.com

*Smith, James Allen –

[(RE) T 1959; F 1962] 1960 Rockville (assoc) (Baltimore Conf); Feb 1962 Frankenmuth; 1966 Pinconning; 1969 Detroit: Jefferson Avenue; Oct 1970 Commerce; 1976 Oscoda, Oscoda Indian Mission; Jan 1983 Birmingham: Embury; 1988 Sanford; **1993 Retired.**<> Home: 5995 Weiss Rd., #4, Saginaw 48603 (989) 799-3323

Smith, Jean M. (Gary) –

[(AM) FL-2002; PL-2003; FL-2006; PL-2009; AM-2010] Saugatuck (DSA) 2001; Saugatuck 12/01/2001; Saugatuck/Ganges 01/16/2005; Ganges/Glenn 2005; Lake City 09/01/2010; Evart/Sears 2019.<> (E) 619 N Cherry St, PO Box 425, Evart 49631 (231) 734-2130. (S) 4897 Pratt St, Sears 49679 (231) 734-2733. Home: 8543 7 Mile Rd, Evart 49631 (231) 734-2003. smithjean56@gmail.com

*Smith, Jerome K. (Mary) –

[(RE) P 1969; F 1972] 1971 Livonia: St. Matthew's (assoc); 1975 Livingston Circuit: Plainfield, Trinity; Jan 1981 Goodrich; Jan 15, 1986 Detroit: Metropolitan (assoc); 1991 West Bloomfield; Sept 1, 1997 Garden City: First; 2006 Caro; **2011 Retired.**<> 586 Porta Rosa Circle, St. Augustine FL 32092 904-671-5034. jksmio46@yahoo.com

*Smith, Kathleen (Dennis) –

[(RL) FL-2002; R-2012] Vermontville/Gresham 2002; Retired 12/31/2012; Lake Odessa: Lakewood (Assoc) (LTFT ¼) 07/15/2014-2015; Lake Odessa: Lakewood (Assoc) (LTFT ¼) and Barry County: Woodland (LTFT ¼) 2015.<> (L) 10265 Brown Rd, Lake Odessa 48849 (269) 367-4800. (W) 203 N Main St, Woodland 48897 (269) 367-4061. Home: 7500 Bayne Rd, Woodland 48897 (269) 367-4123. kdsmith868@gmail.com

*Smith, Russell Lawrence (Ruth) –

[(RE) T 1959; F 1963] 1959 school; 1963 Dearborn: Mt. Olivet (assoc); 1967 Highland, Clyde; 1974 Dearborn: Good Shepherd; 1980 Houghton Lake; 1986 Ann Arbor: First (assoc); **1994 Retired.**<> Home: 801 W. Middle St., #362, Chelsea 48118 (734) 433-1435. smith.russell962@gmail.com

Smith, Scott B. –

[(FL) FL-2013] Weidman 2013; Niles: Portage Prairie 2019.<> 2450 Orange Rd, Niles 49120 (269) 695-6708. Home: 3310 W Chicago R, Niles 49120. nilesmando23@live.com

*Smith, William Michael (Janet) –

[(RE) T 1966; F 1969] 1968 Detroit: Aldersgate (assoc); Jan 1974 Harbor Beach, Port Hope; Nov 1978 Dundee; 1992 Clinton; **2005 Retired.**<> Home: 6231 Clinton-Macon Rd., Clinton 49236 (517) 423-6480. janetandwilliam@gmail.com

Smith, Willie Frank (Dianne Jefferson-Smith) –
[(FE) PL 2008; PE 2011; FE 2014] 2008 Westland: St. James; **2015 Detroit: Conant Avenue**.<> 18600 Conant Ave., Detroit 48234 (313) 891-7237. Home: 16876 Braile, Detroit 48219 (313) 566-7226. smittyo48@aol.com

Smith-Jang, Barbara L. (Soo Chan) –
[(FE) D-1993; FE-1996] Grand Ledge: First (Assoc) 1994; Family Leave 1997; UM Connectional Structures (¶344.1a,c) GBGM Missionary to Korea 2000; Other Valid Ministries (¶344.1d) Pastoral Counselor, Taejon Christian International School 2003.<> Home: Yeolmea Apt 802-901, Yusong-gu No-eun-dong 520-1, Taejon City South Korea, 305-325, Republic of Korea. smithjang@hotmail.com

*Snedeker, Kathryn Sue (Haldon Ferris) –
[(RE) P 1984; F 1987; RE 2020] Flushing (assoc) 1985; Dearborn: Good Shepherd 1988; Saginaw: First (co-pastor) June 16, 1996; Saginaw: First 2002; Traverse Bay 2016; **Retired 2020**.<> Home: 7364 Williams Court, Elk Rapids 49629 (989) 239-9267. queenrev1@aol.com

Snodgrass, Robert L. (Kathe) –
[(PL) PL-2014; FL-2017] Morris Chapel (DSA ¼ Time) 2014; Morris Chapel (PTLP ¼ Time) 11/10/14; Niles: Grace (LTFT 45%) 2016; Niles Wesley/Morris Chapel/Niles Grace 2017 (Niles: Grace merged w/ Wesley, renamed Niles: New Journey 1/1/20).<> (NNJ) 302 Cedar St, Niles 49120 (269) 683-7250. (MC) 11721 Pucker St, Niles 49120 (269) 684-5194. Home: 16270 Lewis Rd, Vandalia 49095 (574) 261-5139. rsnod-grass72@gmail.com

*Snogren, Dorraine S. (Ruth) –
[(RE) T 1955; F 1958] 1953 Seaford, Long Island (assoc); 1956 Onaway; 1962 West Branch; 1968 Flint: Calvary; **1990 Retired**.<> Home: 24 Chapin St., Bethel ME 04217 (207) 595-8087. drsnogren@coopresources.net

Snook, Edwin D. (Ellen) –
[(FL) FL-2003] Big Rapids: Third Ave/Paris/Rodney (DSA) 2002; Big Rapids: Third Ave/Paris/ Rodney 12/01/2002; Elsie 07/16/2005; White Cloud 2012.<> PO Box 188, 1125 E Newell St, White Cloud 49349 (231) 689-5911. Home: 718 E Pine Hill Ave, White Cloud 49349 (231) 689-6774. snookedwin@yahoo.com

*Snyder, David Paul –
[(RE) P 1986; F 1991] 1987 Ishpeming: Salisbury, Palmer, Director, Wesley Foundation, Northern Michigan University (LTFT ¼); 1988 Ishpeming, Salisbury, Palmer; 1990 Calumet, Mohawk-Ahmeek; 1993 L'Anse, Sidnaw, Zeba; Oct 1, 2003 leave of absence; Mar 1, 2004 Iron Mountain: First; Aug 1, 2006 Iron Mountain: First, Quinnesec; 2009 Gladwin; 2012 Sebewaing; **2014 Retired**.<>. pastordave48@yahoo.com

*Snyder, Jean R. –
[(RE) P 1997; FE 1999] Lexington, Bethel 1997; Armada 2000; **Retired Sept 1, 2002;** Birmingham: Embury (LTFT ¼) 2018-2020.<> Home: 1582 Millecoquins Ct., Rochester 48307 (248) 650-5888. jeansnyder@ameritech.net

Snyder, Thomas L. (Lizbeth) –
[(FD) PD 2014; FD 2017] **2014 Dexter (deacon)**.<> 7643 Huron River Dr., Dexter 48130 (734) 426-8480. Home: 8650 Huron River Dr., Dexter 48130 (734) 476-8954. tomsnyder@dexterumc.org

Song, Jinny Lee (Solomon) –
[(PD) PD 2016] **2016 Troy: Korean**.<> 42693 Dequindre, Troy 48085 (248) 879-2240. jinnys@sbcglobal.net

*Sonquist, G. Charles (Jane Parchem) –
[(RE) T 19__; F 1968] 1967 Royal Oak: First (assoc); 1970 Southfield: United; 1980 Troy: Fellowship; 1990 Livonia: St. Matthew's **Sept 1, 2002 Retired**.<> Home: 1152 Timberview Trail, Bloomfield 48304 (248) 844-7178. sonquist@att.net

Sorden, Karen J. –
[(FE) FL-2005; PE-2007; FE-2012] Baldwin: Covenant Community/Luther 2005; Lake Odessa: Central 2012; Cedar Springs 2017; St. Charles Dec 1, 2017.<> PO Box 87, 301 W. Belle Ave., St. Charles 48655 (989) 865-9091. Home: 510 Christy Drive, St. Charles 48655 (989) 865-8144. ksorden@sbcglobal.net

*Sorensen, Harlan E. (Luann) –
[(RE) FL 1999; PE 2001; FE 2004] 1996 Gratis, Somerville OH (W. OH). 1999 Seven Churches United Group Ministry: Gaines, Duffield; Nov 15, 2004 Blissfield: Emmanuel; Nov 15, 2005 school; June 1, 2006 leave of absence; **2006 Retired**.<> Home: 2109 Magnolia Parkway, Grovetown GA 30813 (706) 447-2441. luannsorensen@rocketmail.com

*Spachman, Donald E. (Shelly) –
[(RE) D-1982; FE-1984; RE 2020] Grawn 1982; Shepherd/Pleasant Valley 1992; Shepherd 1997; Keswick 2004; Hastings: First 2010; Greenville: First, Turk Lake/Belding Cooperative Parish 2014; **Retired 2020**.<> Home: 170 Witbeck Dr, Clare 48617 (231) 499-9578. dspachman@yahoo.com

*Spackman, Joseph L. (Nona) –
[(RE) D-1985; FE-1989; R-2013] Mulliken (Ad Interim) 1982; Mulliken/Sebewa Center 1987; St Johns Parish: Salem/Greenbush/Lowe 1991; Allegan 1999; Paw Paw 2007; Retired 2013; Delta Mills (LTFT ¼) 2013.<> 6809 Delta River Dr, Lansing 48906 (517) 321-8100. Home: 3806 Cornice Falls Dr Apt 6, Holt 48842 (517) 694-8346. nspackman12@gmail.com

*Spahr, Sandra L. (Michael) –
[(RE) PE-2000; FE-2003; R-2006] Newaygo 2000; Retired 2006; Jackson Trinity/Parma (DSA) 2006; Webberville (DSA) 2007-12/31/2007; Appointed in Other Annual Conferences (¶385.6) Rocky Mountain Conference, Monte Vista/Bowen (LTFT ½) 2010; Appointed in Other Annual Conferences (¶331.8, ¶346.1) Rocky Mountain Conference, Avondale (LTFT ½) 2013.<> Home: 3229 Northridge Dr, Pueblo CO 81008 (719) 568-5858

*Spalenka, Gordon E. (Nancy) –
[(RE) D-1957; FE-1960; R-1993] Griffith (Assoc), Griffith IN 1957; Holton/Twin Lake 1959; Muskegon: Lake Harbor 1961; Boyne Falls/Boyne City 1964; Ovid United Church 1965; Leslie/ Felt Plains 1969; Bronson/Snow Prairie 10/15/1969; Arden 1972; Bear Lake/Arcadia/Pleasanton 1975; Mt Pleasant: Trinity/Chippewa 1980; Centerville 1984; Bellaire: Community 1987; Mulliken/Sebewa Center 1991; Retired 1993.<> Home: 2119 Waldron St SW, Wyoming 49519 (616) 249-0513. gnspalenka@sbcglobal.net

Speiran, Laura Crawford (Ross) –
[(FD) PD 2007; FD 2010] Saline: First (deacon) 2007; Clarkston (deacon) (LTFT ¾) 2014; **Medical Leave May 1, 2020**.<> Home: 7801 Hoffman, Waterford 48327 (248) 242-6159. Lauraspeiran@gmail.com

Spencer, George Raymond (Donna) –
[(FE) FL (recognition of orders, Church of the Nazarene), 1997; AM 1999; PE 2005; FE 2007] 1987-1995 Warrenton Church of the Nazarene, Warrenton OR; 1995-1996 Springwater Church of the Nazarene, Springwater NY; 1996 trans to Detroit Conf, Hope, Mount Vernon; 1999 North Central Macomb Regional Ministry: Mount Vernon, New Hope, Washington; Jan 1, 2002 New Hope, Mt. Vernon; June 1, 2002 New Hope; Jan 1, 2002 New Hope; 2010 Trenton: Faith; **2016 Houghton Lake**.<> 7059 W. Houghton Lake Dr., Houghton Lake 48629 (989) 422-5622. Home: 316 Superior, Houghton Lake 48629 (989-422-4365. Umcgeorge@aol.com

*Spencer, Mary E. –
[(RL) FL 1995] Flint: Eastwood 1995; **Retired Jan 1, 2009**.<> Home: 6140 Myrtle Grove Rd, Wilmington NC 28409 910-352-5575

Sperling, Donald R. (Rosalie) –
[(FE) P Wyo., 19__; F 19__; HL 1996; PL Apr 1, 2008; AM 2009; FE 2009] Transf. to Detroit Conf, Port Huron: Gratiot Park, Washington Avenue 1988; Honorable Location 1996; Oro: Zion (ad interim LTFT ¼) Apr 1, 2008 (restored to full membership May 14, 2009); **Livonia: Clarenceville 2010**.<> 20300 Middlebelt, Livonia 48152 (248) 474-3444. Home: 34184 Haldane, Livonia 48152 (248) 615-1435. lambsway@hotmail.com

Sperry, Donna J. (George) –
[(FL) DSA-2014; PL-2014; FL-2016] Ionia: Easton (DSA) 2014; Ionia: Easton (PTLP ½) 11/1/2014; Ionia: Easton (PTLP ½) and Turk Lake/Belding 2016.<> (IE) 4970 Potters Rd, Ionia 48846 (616) 527-6529. (TL) 8900 Colby Rd, Greenville 48838 (616) 745-3718. (B) 301 Pleasant St, Belding 48809 (616) 794-1244. Home: 319 Pearl St, Ionia 48846 (586) 255-6228. pastordonnasperry@gmail.com

Spina, Stephen –
[(OF) DSA 2017; OF 2018 Presbyterian USA] Corunna, New Lothrop: First (DSA) 2017; **Corunna, New Lothrop: First May 3, 2018**.<> (C) 200 W McArthur St, Corunna 48817 (989) 743-5050. (NL) 7495 Orchard St, PO Box 247, New Lothrop 48460 (810) 638-5702. Home: 225 W Corunna Ave, Corunna 48817 (989) 472-3850. 320phenix@gmail.com

*Spragg, Carolin S. –
[(RE) D-1991; FE-1994; R-2013] Parma/North Parma 1992; Paw Paw 1999; Fremont 2007; Retired 2013.<> Home: 1063 Gale Rd, Eaton Rapids 48827 (517) 604-0755. carolinspragg1946@gmail.com

*Srock, Robert A. (Barb) –
[(RL) PL 1994; FL 2002] Nov 16, 1994 Ubly; 2000 Minden City, Forester; 2002 Jeddo, Buel; Dec 1, 2003 incapacity leave; **2012 Retired** <> Home: 4706 Stone, Deckerville 48427 (810) 376-8022. rasbas2g@gmail.com

*Stallworth, Lynnette –
[(RE) P 1980; F 1984 W.MI] 1982 Trans. to W. MI Conf, Muskegon Heights: Temple; 1984 Trans. to Detroit Conf, Detroit: Faith Bethany; 1988 Detroit: Trinity, Faith Bethany; 1989 Director, Wesley Foundation, Wayne State University **Jan 16, 2002 Retired**.<> Home: 125 Shell Falls Drive, Apollo Beach FL 33572 (813) 641-0565

Stanley-Hook, Luanne M. –
[(PD) PD-2019] Holland First: UMC Director of Community Involvement (Deacon) 2019.<> 57 W 10th St, Holland 49423 (616) 396-5205. Home: 6618 Butternut Dr, West Olive 49460 (616) 994-0085. luanne@fumcholland.org

*Stark, Robert W. (Mary) –
[(RE) D-1998; FE-2002; R-2008] North Evart/Sylvan (DSA) 11/01/1990; Pine River Parish (DSA) 1991; Pine River Parish: Leroy/Ashton/Luther 08/01/1991; Pine River Parish: Leroy/Ashton/ Luther 05/01/1993; Girard/Ellis Corners 1996; Kalkaska 2000; Retired 2008; Grant (LTFT ¼) 07/01-11/01/2011.<> Home: 11649 E 14 1/2 Rd, Manton 49663 (231) 824-3294. Winter: 8108 Lake Dr, Palmetto FL 34221 (231) 564-0677. serenityridge61@yahoo.com

Starkey, Nathaniel R. (Amy) –
[(FL) FL 2017] Stony Creek 2017; **Edwardsburg: Hope 2020**.<> PO Box 624, 69941 Elkhart Rd, Edwardsburg 49112 (269) 663-5321. Home: 69862 Roy Dr, Edwardsburg 49112 (586) 229-5767. pastornatestarkey@gmail.com

*Stears, Ethel Z. (Robert Richards) –
[(RE) D-1978; FE-1981; R-1999] Springport/Lee Center 1979; Grand Rapids: Trinity (Assoc) 09/16/1983; Plainfield 1986; Appointed to Extension Ministries (¶344.1b,c) Director of Development, Clark Home 01/01/1988; Appointed to Extension Ministries (¶344.1b,c) Chaplain, M.J. Clark Memorial Home 1989; Sabbatical Leave 01/15/1994; Grand Rapids: Saint Paul 1994; Retired 1999.<> Home: 414 Bush Blvd, Three Rivers 49093 (616) 328-4043. e.z.stears@gmail.com

Steele, Brian E. –
[(PE) West Michigan Conf] Battle Creek Christ (LTFT ¾) 2015; Battle Creek Christ/Washington Heights 2017; **New Baltimore: Grace 2018**.<> 49655 Jefferson, New Baltimore 48047 (586) 725-1054. Home: 33840 Hooker Rd., New Baltimore 48047 (586) 648-6242. besteele@gmail.com

Steen, Kathryn M. –
[(FE) D-1994; FE-1997] Big Rapids Third Ave/Paris/Rodney 1994; Mancelona/Alba 2000; Clergy Appointed to Attend School CPE, Bronson Methodist Hospital, Kalamazoo 2007; Leave of Absence 09/01/2008; Other Valid Ministries (¶344.1d) Chaplain, Munson Medical Center 11/10/2008.<> 1105 Sixth St, Traverse City 49684 (231) 935-7163. Home: 951 Hammond Place S, Traverse City 49686 (231) 499-3652. steenkathy@yahoo.com

*Steinberg, Bruce R. (Patti) –
[(RL) FL 2011; RL 2018] Ontonagon, Greenland, Rockland: St. Paul 2011; **Retired 2018**.<> Home: 142 Indian Lake Dr, Crystal Falls 49920 906-367-2128. byooper@gmail.com

Step, Gary G. (Lori) –
[(FE) PE-2000; FE-2003] Indian River 2000; UM Connectional Structures (¶344.1a,c) Director of New Church Development and Congregational Transformation, West Michigan Conference 2012; UM Connectional Structures (¶344.1a,c) Michigan Area Director of Congregational Excellence and New Church Development 01/01/2016; UM Connectional Structures (¶344.1a,c) Associate Director for Congregatonal Vibrancy 2018.<> 207 Fulton St E, Ste 6, Grand Rapids 49503 (517) 347-4030 ext. 4093. Home: 6666 Crown Point Drive, Hudsonville 49426 (231) 420-2676. gstep@michiganumc.org

Stephan, Brittney D. –
[(PE) Indiana Conference] **Associate Director for Multi-Cultural Vibrancy 2108.**<> 1161 E Clark Rd, Ste 212, DeWitt 48820 (517-357-4030 ext. 4073). Home: 40703 Long Horn Dr, Sterling Heights 48313. bstephan@michiganumc.org

Stephan, Linda J. –
[(PE) PE-2018] Williamston 2018.<> 211 S Putnam St, Williamston 48895 (517) 655-2430. Home: 733 Orchard Dr, Williamston 48895 (616) 617-9419. ljstephan@gmail.com

*Sternaman, John R. (Linda) –
[(RL) FL-1997; RL-2002] Riverside 12/01/1997; Retired 2002.<> Home: 5792 Clymer Rd, Coloma 49038 (269) 468-6454

*Stevens, Gary Ian –
[(ROF) Congregational] 2000 Republic, Woodland; 2004 Ishpeming: Salisbury; Jan 1, 2005 Munising (LTFT ½); **Jan 1, 2009 Retired.**<> Home: 801 Pine St., Marquette 49855 (906) 225-1730. revgstevens@sbcglobal.net

*Stewardson, Jerry Leo (Ardith) –
[(RE) P Cent. IL, 19__; F Cent. IL, 19__] 19__ Trans. to Detroit Conf, Professor of Religion and Philosophy, Adrian College; **Retired 2003.**<> Home: 1328 University Ave., Adrian 49221 (517) 263-7554

*Stewart, Carlyle Fielding, III (Jeane) –
[(RE) P (on recognition of orders) 1985; F 1987] Trans. from Baptist Church, Southfield: Hope 1985; **Retired 2014.**<> cspirit@cs.com

*Stewart, David Kirk, Sr. (Ellen) –
[(RE) P 1985; F 1989; RE 2020] Peck, Buel, Melvin 1986; Plymouth: First (assoc) June 1, 1990; Beaverton: First, Dale 1991; Wayne-Westland: First Aug 1, 2000; Hale: First 2008; Pigeon: Salem 2013; **Retired 2020; Pigeon: Salem 2020** (until 9/1/2020).<> Home: 533 W Brownlee Rd, Sanford 48657 (734) 904-7218. dkspreaches@gmail.com

*Stilwell, James W. (Pamela) –
[(RL) PL-2005; FL-2006; RL-2017] Olivet 3/1/2005; Arden / Benton Harbor Peace Temple 2006; Pleasant Valley 2009-2015; Three Rivers: Ninth Street 2009-2017; Three Rivers: First 2015-2017; Retired 2017.<> Home: 4329 William Ave., Celina OH 45822 (269) 365-7923

*Stoddard, Linda D. –
[(RE) D-1970; FE-1973; R-2017] Oshtemo/Northwest 1972; Bainbridge New Hope/Scottdale 10/15/1976; Battle Creek: Convis Union 05/16/1983; Leave of Absence 01/01/1992; Other Valid Ministries (¶335.1d) Staff Chaplain, Battle Creek Health System (LTFT ¼) 2000; Battle Creek: Maple (LTFT ¼) 2008; Retired 01/01/2017; Battle Creek: Maple (LTFT ¼) 01/01/2017.<> 342 Capital Ave NE, Battle Creek 49017 (269) 964-1252. Home: 126 Heather Ridge, Battle Creek 49017 (269) 965-1671. mapleumc@yahoo.com

Stoll, Matthew T. (Amy) –
[(FE) FL-2002; PE-2003; FE-2006] Epsilon/Emmett County: New Hope 2003; Lowell: Vergennes 2010; Holton 2018.<> 9530 Holton Duck Lake Rd, Holton 49425 (231) 821-2323. Home: 8670 Ward St, Holton 49425 (231) 821-0374. pastormattstoll@gmail.com

*Stone, Arthur R. (Judith) –
[(RE) PL Nov 1, 1996; PE 1999; FE 2002] Nov 1, 1996 New Haven-Meade: Faith; 1999 school (Methesco). Nov 1, 1998 Brown City; 2004 Sebewaing: Trinity (Intentional Interm ¶329.3); **2006 Retired**.<> 2847 Quincy Dr., Troy 48085 (248) 835-1301. artintroy@wowway.com

*Stone, Diane E.
[(RL) FL-1996; PL-2004; RL-2010] Camden / Montgomery / Stokes Chapel 11/16/1996; Springport (LTFT PT) / Lee Center (LTFT PT) 2004; Retired 2010.<> Home: 234 S Clemens Ave, Lansing 48912 (517) 775-0286

Stone, Eric Alan (Sherry Lee) –
[(FE) P 1993; F 1996] Farmington: Orchard (assoc) 1994; Wesley Foundation: University of Illinois Feb 1, 1998; Waterford: Central (assoc) 1999; Chaplain/Director: Wesley Foundation, Central Michigan University Dec 1, 2001; Chaplain/Director U of M Wesley Foundation 2006; Essexville: St. Luke's 2009; **Adrian: First 2020**.<> 1245 W. Maple Ave., Adrian 49221 (517) 265-5689. Home: 4580 S. Clubview Dr., Adrian 49221 (734) 355-7486. reveastone@sbcglobal.net

Stover, Colin P. (Annette) –
[(FE) PE 2002 (on recognition of orders from United Church of Canada), FE 2005] 1999 Imlay City, West Goodland-Lum; Jan 1, 2002 Imlay City; 2002 Lapeer: Trinity (assoc); June 1, 2005 Sandusky: First; **2011 incapacity leave**.<> 922 Elizabeth Ct., Lapeer 48446 (810) 660-8359. revstover@yahoo.com

*Stover, Robert P. (Kathleen) –
[(RE) D-1975; FE-1977; R-2012] Camden/Montgomery/Stokes Chapel 1976; Niles: Portage Prairie 1980; Portage Prairie 1982; Cedar Springs/East Nelson 1987; Ludington: St Paul 1989; Grand Rapids: South 1998; Napoleon 2004; Allegan 2007; Retired 2012; Calhoun County: Homer/Lyon Lake (LTFT ¾) 2012.<> (CCH) 101 E Adams St, Homer 49245 (517) 568-4001. (LL) 8493 17 Mile Rd, Marshall 49068 (269) 789-0017. Home: 105 E Adams St, Homer 49245 (517) 568-1126. rpstover48@gmail.com

*Strall, Dana Ray (Sandy) –
[(RE) P 1977; F 1979] 1977 Port Huron: First (assoc); Oct 1980 Lakeville, Leonard; 1985 Midland: First (assoc); 1988 South Rockwood (LTFT ¾), Flat Rock: First (assoc) (LTFT ¼); 1990 South Rockwood; Aug 1, 1997 Coleman: Faith; 1999 Erie; 2011 Flat Rock: First; **2017 Retired**.<> Home: 12638 Dixie Hwy, PO Box 1, South Rockwood 48179 (734) 379-9680. Dstrall@hotmail.com

*Streevy, Michael P. –
[(RE) D-1987; FE-1995; R-2010] Elk Rapids/Kewadin 04/01/1987; Jonesville/Allen 1988; Battle Creek: Sonoma/ Newton 1995; Galesburg 11/16/1999; Parma/North Parma 2003; North Parma (LTFT ¾) 11/01/2005; North Parma 2008; Litchfield/Quincy 2009; Retired 2010.<> Home: PO Box 89, Sodus NY 14551 (585) 943-4328. Dad0kkaj@gmail.com

*Strobe, David Randall (Mary) –
[(RE) P 1980; F 1984] 1982 North Lake; May 1, 1984 Farmington: Nardin Park (assoc); Apr 15, 1989 Houghton: Grace; 1995 Milford; Dec 1, 1997 disability leave; 1998 Linden, Argentine; Feb 1, 2001 Hartland; Feb 1, 2006 incapacity leave; 2007 Corunna; **2013 Retired**; Oct 31, 2014 Burton: Christ (LTFT ¼).<> 4428 Columbine Ave, Burton 48529 (810) 743-1770. Home: 5930 Augusta Ln, Grand Blanc 48439 (248) 933-3602. dstrobe@comcast.net

*Strobe, Donald Bovee –
[(RE) T 1956 W.MI; F 1959 W.MI] 1972 Trans. to Detroit Conf, Ann Arbor: First; **1990 Retired**.<> Home: 19191 Harvard Ave. #401A, Irvine CA 92612 (949) 679-9900. Dstrobe925@aol.com

*Strong, David Tull (Marcia) –
[(RE) T 1959; F 1961] 1960 Dearborn: First (assoc); 1964 Richmond; 1969 Troy: Fellowship; 1980 Livonia: St. Matthews 1990 Detroit: Central; 1994 Belleville; **1998 Retired**.<> Home: 21870 River Ridge Trail, Farmington Hills 48335 (248) 888-9848. strongdt11@aol.com

Stull-Lipps, Linda K. (David Lipps) –
[(FE) FL-2006; PE-2007; FE-2015] Parma 01/15/2006; Center Park 2006; Potterville 2011; Riverdale: Lincoln Road (LTFT ¾) 2016.<> 9479 W Lincoln Rd, Riverdale 48877 (989) 463-5704. Home: 9437 W Lincoln Rd, Riverdale 48877. pastorlynelr@gmail.com

*Stybert, Stanley Patrick (Janet) –
[(RL) PL 1992] Jan 1, 1993 Seven Churches United Group Ministry: Lennon; June 1, 1996 Flint: Bristol, Dimond; 2000 Fowlerville: First; 2007 Flint: Asbury, Burton: Emmanuel; **2010 Retired**; 2012 Owosso: Carland; July 1-Oct 31, 2018 Oregon, Elba (LTFT ½).<> Home: 647 Basswood, Flint 48506 (810) 715-9331. thegoodword1@att.net

Sudduth, Steven T. –
[(OF)] Crystal Falls: Christ, Amasa: Grace 2016; **no appointment Feb 6, 2018**.<> Home: 504 Blossom St, Iron River 49935 (859) 329-9371

*Summers, Verne C. (Dawn) –
[(RE) D-1955; FE-1964; R-1992] Beaverton/Dale 1956; Elk Rapids 1963; Elk Rapids Parish 1965; Jackson: Brookside 1966; Charlotte 09/01/1974; Okemos Community Church 1987; Mason: First 1989; Retired 1992.<> Home: 13119 Farm Ln, DeWitt 48820 (517) 669-2815. dvsumm@juno.com

Sutton, Tara Renee –
[(FE) P (on recognition of orders, AME) 1998; FE 2001] 1991 Dolton IL: Holy Trinity AME; 1998 Flint: Oak Park; Dec 1, 2002 Waterford: Central (interm assoc); 2001 Waterford: Central (assoc); 2005 Flint: Bethel; 2012 Crossroads District Superintendent; **2016 Halsey, South Mundy.**<> (H) 10006 Halsey Rd., Grand Blanc 48439 (810) 694-9243. (SM) 10018 S. Linden Rd., Grand Blanc 48439. Home: PO Box 1181, Grand Blanc 48480. angelicspirit8272@gmail.com

Swainston, Jeffrey A. –
[(PL) CC-2017; DSA-2017; PL-2018] Manton (DSA) (½ time) 2017; Manton (PL) (PTLP ½) 12/01/2017; Manton (PTLP ¾) 2018.<> 02 N. Michigan Ave, PO Box B, Manton 49663 (231) 824-3593. Home: PO Box 77, 102 N. Michigan, Manton 49663 (616) 813-8746. jeffswainston@gmail.com

Swanson, Reed P. (Juliana) –
[(FE) P 1995; F 1998] 1995 Detroit: Metropolitan (assoc); Aug 1, 1998 Richmond: First; 2004 Tawas; 2008 Clarkston (assoc); 2010 Stony Creek; 2017 Frankenmuth; Feb 7, 2018 Crystal Falls: Christ, Amasa: Grace (LTFT ½); **2018 Pinckney: Arise.**<> 11211 Dexter-Pinckney Rd., Pinckney 48169 (734) 878-1928. Home: 11267 Dexter-Pinckney Rd., Pinckney 48169 (586) 202-1894. lxxmt@yahoo.com

Swanson, Sherri L. (Brad Bartelmay) –
[(FE) D-1987; FE-1994] Transferred from Iowa Conf 1991; Galien/Olive Branch 1991; Galien/Olive Branch (LTFT ¾) 1993; Berrien County: Lakeside (LTFT ¼) 1995; Three Oaks 09/01/1999; Grand Rapids: Faith 2017; Georgetown 2018.<> 2766 Baldwin St, Jenison 49428 (616) 669-0730. Home: 6105 Balcom Ln, Allendale 49401 (269) 405-0002. sherriswanson61@gmail.com

Sweet, Mary A. (Jeffrey) –
[(PE) PE-2015] Harbor Springs/Alanson 2011; Whitehall/Muskegon: Crestwood 2014; Litchfield/ Jonesville 2017; Jonesville/Napoleon 2019.<> (J) 203 Concord Rd, Jonesville 49250 (517) 849-9565. (N) 210 Nottawasepee, PO Box 337, Napoleon 49261 (517) 536-8609. Home: 10014 Sunset Dr, Jackson 49201 (231) 881-7367. pastormarysweet@aol.com

Sykes, Lori J. (Gary) –
[(FE) PE-2007; FE-2010] St Johns: First 2007; Lansing: First 07/15/2012; **Alma 2020.**<> 501 Gratiot Ave, Alma 48801 (989) 463-4305. Home: 627 Woodworth Ave, Alma 48801 (517) 775-6556. pastorlori@almaumc.com

*Synwolt, Royal J. (Constance) –
[(RE) D-1952; FE-1954; R-1997] Coloma/Riverside 10/01/1951; Portage 1955; Lansing: Mount Hope 1962; Muskegon: Central 1966; Appointed In Other Annual Conferences (¶331.8, ¶346.1) (Director) Staff ProgTransferred to Detroit Conf 1971; Transferred from Detroit Conf 1983; Kalamazoo: First 1983; Retired 1991.<> Home: 11214 Morning Side Dr, Boyne Falls 49713 (231) 549-2547. Winter: 870 NW Sarria Ct, Port St Lucie FL 34986 (772) 873-0949. consyn@live.com

*Tabor, Kenneth E. (Eldonna) –
[(RL) PL-1999; FL-2006; RL-2010] Free Soil / Fountain 11/1/1999; Walkerville / Crystal Valley 2000; Ludington 2004; Retired 2010; Crystal Valley / Walkerville 12/1/2015-12/1/2016.<> Home: 1243 Blue Heron Dr., Ludington 49431 (231) 845-6101. taborek@charter.net

*Tarpley, Thomas E., Sr. (Gloria) –
[(RE) PL 1997; PE 2001; FE 2004] 1997 Detroit: Cass Community (assoc); 2003 Flint: Trinity; Jan 1, 2007 Flint: Trinity (LTFT ¾), Flint: Faith (LTFT ¼); 2007 Fowlerville; **2015 Retired**.<> Home: 209 Addison Cr., Fowlerville 48836 (313) 407-4151. tthiwayman@att.net

Taveirne, Edmond G. (Beth) –
[(FE) P 1970, N IL; F 1984 N.IL.] 1982 Lansing (IL): First (assoc); 1984 Park Hill: Grace; Elmhurst: First; 1996 Wheaton: Gary Memorial; 2007 transfer to Detroit Conference Fenton; Apr 30, 2011 voluntary leave of absence; 2013 Bethany Methodist Communities; 2014 voluntary leave of absence; 2017 personal leave; **Nov 15, 2018 Retired**.<> Home: 102 Indian Trail Dr., Westmont IL 60559 (312) 888-6380. taveirne@att.net

Taylor, Thomas L. (Carmen) –
[(FE) P 1996; F 1998] 1995 Oak Park: Faith; 1998 Saginaw: Calvary; 2000 Pontiac: First (LTFT ½), Pontiac: Baldwin Avenue (assoc) (LTFT ½). 2001 Pontiac: First; 2008 Madison Heights; Feb 15, 2011 incapacity leave; 2011 Harper Woods: Redeemer, Detroit: Henderson Memorial; **Jan 31, 2013 medical leave**.<>. Janese28@aol.com

Terhune, AmyLee Brun (T. Bradley) –
[(FE) PE 1999; FE 2002] 1999 Port Huron: First (assoc); 2002 Caring Covenant Group Ministry: Columbiaville; Dec 1, 2006 Caring Covenant Group Ministry: Columbiaville, Parish Director; 2009 Hancock: First; **2016 Saginaw: First**.<> 4790 Gratiot, Saginaw 48638 (989) 799-0131. Home: 4674 Village Drive, Saginaw 48638 (989) 793-5880. pastoramy@clergy.net

Terhune, T. Bradley (AmyLee) –
[(FE) PM 1998; FE 2003] Algonac: Trinity 1999; Caring Covenant Group Ministry: Richfield, Otter Lake 2002; Caring Covenant Group Ministry: Richfield Sept 1, 2004; voluntary leave of absence 2007; Painesdale: A. Paine Memorial 2014; Arbela 2016; Saginaw: Kochville, Mapleton Oct 1, 2017; Medical Leave Sept 1, 2018; **Personal Leave 2020**.<> Home: 4674 Village Drive, Saginaw 48638 (906) 231-1495. tbradley.terhune726@gmail.com

*Testolin, Roy G. (Sandy) –
[(RE) D-1974; FE-1976; R-2013] Battle Creek: First, Staff Pastoral Counselor (¶337.1) 1990; Transferred from Wisconsin Conf 1999; Appointed to Extension Ministries (¶344.1b,c) Pastoral Counselor, Heritage Interfaith Counseling Center, Battle Creek 1999; Retired 11/01/2013; Appointed to Extension Ministries (¶344.1b,c) Pastoral Counselor, Heritage Interfaith Counseling Center, Battle Creek 11/01/2013.<> Home: 12884 E Dr S, Marshall 49068 (269) 781-9257. rt232@yahoo.com

Thomas, Crystal C. –
[(FL) PL Nov 2013; FL 2014] Flint: Dimond 2013; Linden, Flint: Dimond 2014; Linden 2015; Battle Creek: Christ, Battle Creek: Washington Heights 2018; **Somerset Center, Hillside 2020**.<> (H) 6100 Folks Rd, Horton 49246 (517) 563-2835. (SC) PO Box 277, 12095 E Chicago Rd, Somerset Center 49282 (517) 688-4330. Home: 6094 Folks Rd, Horton 49246 (517) 563-8920. athisservice2008@gmail.com

Thomas, Deborah S. –
[(FE) PE 2000; FE 2003] Plymouth: First (assoc) June 1, 2000; Royal Oak: St. John's 2004; Iron Mountain: Trinity 2006; Bay City: First 2011; Alma 2013; **DeWitt: Redeemer (co-pastor) 2020**.<> 13980 Schavey Rd, DeWitt 48820 (517) 669-3430. Home: 3505 W Clark Rd R103, DeWitt 48820 (989) 285-4212. pastordebthomas@gmail.com

*Thomas, Wayne N. (Janet) –
[(RE) P 1973; F 1976] 1975 Jasper, Weston; 1976 Monroe: St. Paul's (assoc); 1978 Sutton-Sunshine, Bethel; 1982 Rochester: St. Luke's; 1984 leave of absence; 1988 Durham NC: Trinity (assoc) (NC Conf, para. 426.1); 1989 transf to Holson Conf, Seymour TN: Seymour (assoc); 1992 Axley's Chapel, Williamson Chapel; 1995 Axley's Chapel, Binfield; 1996 leave of absence; 1997 trans from N. IN Conf Royal Oak: First (assoc); 2002 Seven Churches United Group Ministry: Durand: First; **2010 Retired**.<> Home: 1408 Bonita Drive, Knoxville TN 37918 (248) 842-5366. orggardner@aol.com

*Thompson, James M. (Judith) –
[(RE) P 1970; F 1975] 1972 Richmondale Charge (W. OH Conf); 1974 Oregon, Elba; 1976 Davison Area Group Ministry (parish director): Oregon, Elba; 1980 Hardy; Jan 3, 1984 Pinconning; Jan 16, 1990 Midland: Homer; 1996 Eastern Thumb Cooperative Parish: Port Sanilac, Deckerville (parish director); 1999 Marysville; **2006 Retired**.<> Home: 5975 Mill Point Court, Kentwood 49512 (616) 656-3492. thompsonfive@hotmail.com

*Thompson, Jeffrey Todd (Jodi) –
[(RE) D-1989; FE-1992; R-2010] Alto/Bowne Center 1990; Muskegon Wolf Lake/Unity 1995; Muskegon Wolf Lake 1998; Charlevoix 2000; Retired 2010.<> Home: 4354 M 66 N, Charlevoix 49720 (231) 675-2135

*Thompson, John Ross (Ellen Brubaker) –
[(RE) D-1966; FE-1968; R-2010] Transferred from Western Pennsylvania Conf 1995; Grandville 1995; UM Connectional Structures (¶344.1a,c) West MI Conference Director 1998; East Lansing: University 2006; Retired 12/31/2010; Grand Rapids: Trinity (Assoc) (LTFT 1/8) 2015-09/01/2016; Grand Rapids Genesis (Part Time) 01/01/2017-2018.<> Home: 4114 Sawkaw NE, Grand Rapids 49525 (517) 812-9679. johnellen5@comcast.net

Thompson, Mark E. –
[(FE) D-1988; FE-1990] Riverside/Scottdale 01/01/1987; Niles: Grace 11/16/1992; Bellevue/Kalamo 1996; Keeler/Silver Creek 2004; Grand Rapids: Faith 2009; Lansing Central 2017; **St. Ignace 2020**.<> 615 W US Highway 2, PO Box 155, Saint Ignace 49781 (906) 643-8088. Home: 90 Spruce St, St Ignace 49781 (269) 591-0731. mark757984@gmail.com

*Thompson, R. John (Sheryl) –
[(RE) D-1998; FE-2003; R-2010] Hudsonville 1997; Hudsonville/Holland: First (Assoc) 1998; Litchfield 04/01/2001; Kent City: Chapel Hill 2005; Retired 2010; Muskegon: Unity (LTFT ¼) 11/01/2011-2014.<> Home: 2418 Valleywood Ct, Muskegon 49441 (231) 563-6417. rjohnthompson@gmail.com

*Thompson, Ronald J. (Hope) –
[(RE) D-1961; FE-1963; R-1995] Transferred from Detroit Conf 1975; DeWitt: Redeemer 10/15/1975; Marshall 04/05/1983; Mt Pleasant: First 1989; Retired 1995.<> Home: 707-A McLaughlin St, Eaton Rapids 48827 (989) 506-3225

Thon, Dorothy Jean (Duane) –
[(FE) PE 2002; FE 2005] 2002 Pinconning; 2007 Mayville; 2011Bethel (BASS), Akron, Sutton-Sunshine; **2017 Retired**.<> Home: 1514 Kent Dr, Davison 48423 (989) 245-8837. djthon@hotmail.com

*Thon, Duane G. (Dorothy) –
[(RE) LP 1997; PM 1998; FE 2000] 1997 Saginaw: West Michigan Avenue, Sheridan Avenue; Sept 15, 2005 Saginaw: West Michigan Avenue; **2007 Retired**.<> Home: 1514 Kent Dr, Davison 48423 (989) 245-8837. dgthon@mailstation.com

Thurston-Cox, Hillary (Vaughn) –
[(PE) OE-2014; PE-2019] [Free Methodist, Elder] Epsilon/New Hope/Harbor Springs/Alanson (Assoc) 2014; Epsilon/Harbor Springs/Alanson (Assoc) (LTFT ¾) 01/01/2015; Wacousta Community 2016.<> 9180 W Herbison Rd, Eagle 48822 (517) 626-6623. Home: 9590 Looking Glass Brook Dr, Grand Ledge 48837 (231) 250-8142. hillary.thurstoncox@gmail.com

Thurston-Cox, Vaughn W. (Hillary) –
[(PE) OE-2008; PE-2020] [Free Methodist, Elder] UM Connectional Structures (¶344.1a,c) Director, Ferris State University Wesley Foundation 2008; Epsilon/New Hope of Emmett County 2010; Epsilon/New Hope/Harbor Springs/Alanson 2014; Epsilon/Harbor Springs/ Alanson (LTFT ¾) 2015; Mulliken/Sunfield 2016; Mulliken 2017; Grand Rapids: South Jan 19, 2020; transferred from Free Methodist Church 2020; **Lake Odessa: Central 2020**.<> PO Box 485, 912 4th Ave, Lake Odessa 48849 (616) 374-8861. Home: 9590 Looking Glass Brook Dr, Grand Ledge 48837 (231) 250-3924. dr.thurstoncox@gmail.com

*Timm Potrykus, Paula M. (Jon) –
[(RE) P 1990; F 1993; RE 2020] Hillman, Spratt 1990; Flint: Court Street (assoc) 1992; Redford: Lola Valley Apr 16, 1994; leave of absence Jan 1, 1997; Grand Blanc: Phoenix 1997; Royal Oak: St. John's 2001; Harbor Beach, Port Hope 2004; **Oak Grove 2011; Retired 2020**.<> Home: 5460 Sergent Rd., Gladwin 48624 (989) 324-7930. revtimm2011@att.net

Timmons, Faith Elizabeth Green (Gregory) –
[(FE) PL 2000; PE 2000; FE 2005] 2000 Southfield: Hope; Sept 1, 2002 school (Yale); Aug 1, 2004 Detroit: Metropolitan (assoc); 2008 Holly: Calvary; 2012 Flint: Bethel; **Apr 1, 2018 medical leave (¶356)**.<> Home: 2327 Limestone Ln, Flushing 48433. fegisme@aol.com

Timmons, Gregory E. (Faith Elizabeth Green Timmons) –
[(PL) PL Jan 1, 2019] Flint: Calvary (DSA) (LTFT ½) 2018; **Flint: Calvary (LTFT ½) Jan 1, 2019**.<> 2111 Flushing Rd, Flint 48504 (810) 238-7685. Home: 2327 Limestone Ln, Flushing 48433 (810) 922-2257. timmons2c@gmail.com

Tipken, Douglas A. (Dana) –
[(FL) DSA-2018; CLM-2018; FL-2019] Fennville/ Fennville: Pearl (DSA) 06/01/2018; Fennville/Fennville: Pearl 01/01/2019.<> (F) 5849 124th Ave, Fennville 49408 (269) 561-5048. (FP) 1689 56th St, PO Box 407, Fennville 49408 (269) 561-5048. Home: 687 W Fennville St, Fennville 49408 (269) 873-0014. dougtipken@live.com

PASTORAL RECORDS

Titus, Beth D. (Dale) –
[(FE) PL 2002; PE 2004; FE 2008] Sept 1, 2002 Denton: Faith (LTFT ½); 2008 Ann Arbor: Calvary; 2013 Voluntary leave; **Feb 1, 2015 Farmington Hills: Nardin Park (assoc)**.<> 29887 W. 11 Mile, Farmington Hills 48336 (248) 474-6573. Home: 6771 Kestrel Ridge, Brighton 48116 (810) 231-6436. bdtitus@sbcglobal.net

Titus, Christopher G.L. (Tina) –
[(FL) PL 2010; FL 2019] Nov 2010 Cole; 2011 Cole, Melvin; **2019 Armada, West Berlin**.<> (A) 23200 E Main St, PO Box 533, Armada 48005–0533 (586) 784-5201, (W) 905 Holmes Rd, PO Box 91, Allenton 48002 (810) 395-2409. Home: 23234 E Main, Armada 48005 (586) 784-9484

To, Karen Hien Thi Vo (Ut VanTo) –
[(FE) P 1995; F 1998] 1995 Dearborn Heights: Warren Valley 1996 school; 1997 Detroit: Cass Community (assoc); 2001 General Board of Global Ministries, Program Director, Vietnam; **2018 Retired**.<> Home: 15273 Paris St, Allen Park 48101. Karenvoto@hotmail.com

Tomasino, Anthony J. (Cordelia) –
[(FE) P N. IL 19; FE 2001] 1998 trans to Detroit Conf from N. IL Conf; 1998 Flint: Lincoln Park; 2002 Negaunee: Mitchell; 2003 Associate Professor, Bethel College, Mishawaka IN (para 335.1); **2016 Caro**.<> 670 Gilford, Caro 48723 (989) 673-2246. Home: 208 W. Burnside, Caro 48723 (989) 673-4355. tomasinos4@juno.com

*Tommy, Dominic A. (Comfort) –
[(RE) PL-1997; FL-1999; PE-2000; FE-2003; RE 2020] Grand Rapids: First (DSA) (Assoc) 1997; Grand Rapids: First (PTLP) (Assoc)11/16/1997-04/13/1999; Olivet (Assoc) 04/16/1999; Alto/Bowne Center 2000; Berrien Springs/Arden 2002; Stanwood: Northland 2006; Hopkins/South Monterey 2014; Lake Odessa Central 2017; **Retired 2020**.<> Home: 2840 Riley Ridge Rd, Holland 49424 (269) 941-3787. pastordominic61@gmail.com

*Torrey, William J. (Eileen) –
[(RE) D-1952; FE-1955; R-1993] Oshtemo 1951; Wayland 1956; Wacousta Community 1960; Battle Creek: Chapel Hill 1964; South Haven: First 1968; Ludington 1974; Jackson: Brookside 09/15/1978; Portage: Chapel Hill 1985; Rockford 1989; Retired 1993; Portage: First (Assoc LTFT) 1993-05/01/1996.<> Home: 28 Owl Brook Rd, Ashland NH 03217 (603) 968-6348. eileen@weisshouse.net

*Toshalis, Gerald L. (Barbara) –
[(RE) D-1968; FE-1973; R-2006] Voluntary Location 1971; Readmitted 1972; Other Valid Ministries (¶344.1d) Personal Growth Ministry, Grand Rapids Community Counseling 1972; Other Valid Ministries (¶344.1d) Director, Samaritan Health and Living Center 1979; Appointed in Other Annual Conferences (¶426.1) First UMC, San Diego CA 1990; Grand Rapids: Trinity (Assoc) 1992; Grandville 2001; Grand Rapids: Aldersgate (Interim) 2005; Retired 2006.<> Home: Stillpoint, 4305 Persianwood Dr, Kalamazoo 49006 (269) 365-0313. jtoshalis@gmail.com

Totty, Darryl E. (Anita) –
[(FE) PL 1998; FL 1999; PE 2002; FE 2008] 1998 Eastside Covenant Cooperative Parish: Detroit: Christ (assoc), Jefferson Avenue; Sept 1, 2003 Eastside Covenant Cooperative Parish: Detroit: Conant Avenue; **2015 Detroit: Second Grace**.<> 18700 Joy Rd., Detroit 48228 (313) 838-6475. Home: 29193 Northwestern Hwy., Unit #388, Southfield 48034 (313) 215-3841. entj2@aol.com

*Tousley, Kenneth Lee (Doris) –
[(RE) T N.IN., 1958; F N.IN., 1960] 1955 Prairie: Bethel; 1957 Keystone: Blanche Chapel; 1959 Keystone Parish; 1960 Robinson: Wesley; 1965 Trans. to Detroit Conf, Saginaw: Ames (assoc); 1968 Tawas; 1982 Adrian; 1989 Port Huron District Superintendent; **1995 Retired**.<> Home: 1235 Wintergreen St., East Tawas 48730 (989) 362-6554

*Tousley, Philip L. (Laurie) –
[(RE) P 1993; F 1995; RE 2020] transf to Detroit Conf from Rocky Mountain Conf 1998; Menominee: First 1998; Bad Axe: First 2011; Bad Axe: First, Minden City, Ubly 2019; Bad Axe: First, Minden City Sept 30, 2019 (Ubly closed 9-30-2019); **Retired 2020; Columbiaville (LTFT ½) 2020**.<> 4696 Pine, PO Box 98, Columbiaville 48421 (810) 793-6363. Home: 216 East Woodworth, Bad Axe 48413 (989) 553-3790. pastorphil@live.com

Townley, Alice Fleming (Michael) –
[(FE) D-1997; FE-2000] Center Park 1997; Family Leave 2001; Williamston 07/15/2008; Family Leave 2009; Other Valid Ministries (¶344.1d) Assoc for Parish Life, Okemos Presbyterian Church 02/01/2010.<> 2258 Bennett Rd, Okemos 48823 (517) 507-5117. Home: 1035 Prescott Drive, East Lansing 48823 (517) 324-5432. aftownley@yahoo.com

*Townsend, Raymond J. (Joyce) –
[(RE) D-1987; FE-1990; R-2009] Appointed in Other Annual Conferences (¶331.8, ¶346.1) Detroit Conference, Samaria and Lulu 1984; Plainwell: First (Assoc) 1988; Leighton 1991; Sparta 2006; Retired 2009.<> Home: 7178 Cornerstone Dr SE, Caledonia 49316 (616) 204-3495. shamu25revenge@yahoo.com

*Townsend, Ted Paul –
[(RE) T 1955; F 1957] 1956 Raub IN; 1957 Seward AK; 1963 Ann Arbor: West Side (assoc); 1968 Ferndale: First (assoc); 1969 Board of Missions, World Division, Professor of Old Testament, Leonard Theological Seminary, India; Oct 1989 Theological Hall, Sierra Leone; 1995 Missionary in Residence, Methodist Theological School in Ohio; 1996 General Board of Global Ministries, Russia; **1998 Retired**.<> Home: PO Box 1018, Penney Farms FL 32079 (904) 284-8441. tedrotown@juno.com

*Trebilcock, Douglas Robert (Catherine Ann) –
[(RE) T 1966; F 1969] 1967 Hardy; 1969 Rochester: St. Paul's (assoc); Dec 1972 Bloomfield Hills: St. Paul; 1975 St. Clair; 1985 Clarkston; 2004 Midland: Aldergate; **2006 Retired**.<> Home: 2212 Cranbrook Drive, Midland 48642 (989) 837-7087. DRTMidland@aol.com

Treman, Colleen T. (Keith) –
[(FD) DM-1984; FD-1997] Transferred from West Ohio Conf 1985; Muskegon: Central, Director of Christian Education 09/01/1985; Muskegon Lakeside, Director of Christian Education 01/01/1990; Kalamazoo: First, Coordinator of Children's Ministries 1990; Leave of Absence 01/15/1998; Sturgis (Deacon) (LTFT ½) 1998; Lansing: Mount Hope (Deacon) Children's Coordinator (LTFT ½) 2008; Transitional Leave 2015.<> Home: 5393 Woodrush Ave, Kalamazoo 49009 (269) 625-0511. ctreman@yahoo.com

*Treman, Keith R. (Colleen) –
[(RE) D-1983; FE-1987; R-2015] Whitehall/Claybanks 1985; Kalamazoo: First (Assoc) 1990; Sturgis 01/15/1998; Portland 2008; Retired 2015.<> Home: 5393 Woodrush Ave, Kalamazoo 49009 (269) 358-3966. ktreman@fastmail.fm

Triebwasser, Amy –
[(PE) PL Jan 2016; FL 2017; PE 2019] Salem Grove Jan 1, 2016; **Flat Rock 2017**.<>
28400 Evergreen, Flat Rock 48134 (734) 782-2565. 29451 Evergreen, Flat Rock
48134

*Trinidad, Saul Camargo –
[(RE) P Costa Rica Conf, 19_; F Costa Rica, 19_] Trans. from Methodist Church of
Costa Rica 1990; Detroit: El Buen Pastor 1990; Consultant on Hispanic Ministries Sept
1, 1998; **Retired 2013**.<> Home: 1216 Creek Knoll, San Antonio TX 78253 (210) 679-
9736. strinidad@juno.com

Trommater, Timothy W. (Erin) –
[(FE) PE-2015; FE-2018] Jackson: First (Assoc) 2015; DeWitt Redeemer (Assoc)
2017; **Personal Leave Apr 3, 2020**.<> Home: 1302 W. Webb Rd, DeWitt 48820 (517)
614-9321. tim.trommater@gmail.com

Trowbridge, Susan J. (Roger) –
[(FE) D-1987; FE-1990] Peace/Quimby (DSA) 04/01/1993; Transferred from Detroit
Conf 1994; Peace/Quimby (LTFT ¾) 1994; Peace 1998; Leave of Absence 03/15/2005;
Munith and Stockbridge (LTFT ½) 2014; Battle Creek: First (LTFT ½) 2019.<> 111 E
Michigan Ave, Battle Creek 49014 (269) 963-5567. Home: 329 S Main St, PO Box
151, Vermontville 49096 (517) 667-8414. suetrowbridgeart744@gmail.com

*Trudgeon, Theodore A. –
[(RA) PL 2004; AM 2019; RA 2019] Bergland, Ewen, Wakefield 2004; **Retired 2019**.<>
Home: 20126 Trudgeon Rd, Ewen 49925 (906) 988-2533. aa8yf@yahoo.com

*Turner, Arthur R. (Johncie Palmer Turner) –
[(RE) D-1968; FE-1972; R-2006] Scottdale/Bridgman 04/01/1970; Manton/Fife
Lake/East Boardman/South Boardman 1971; Potter Park 1976; Battle Creek: Baseline
1981; Ashley/Bannister 1984; Other Valid Ministries (¶344.1d) Handicapper Information
Advocate, Handicapper Information Council & Patient Equipment Locker 1990; Honorable Location 1991; Appointed in Other Annual Conferences (¶331.8, ¶346.1) Detroit
Conference, Morrice/Bennington/Pittsburg (Ad-Interim) 1998; Appointed in Other Annual Conferences (¶337.1) Detroit Conference, Morrice/Bennington/ Pittsburg
06/02/1999; Munith/Pleasant Lake 2004; Medical Leave 11/15/2005; **Retired 2006;**
North Adams/Jerome (LTFT ¼) 02/01/2012-2014.<> Home: 1039 Crestwood Ln, Jackson 49203 (517) 769-2329. arthurturn@gmail.com

*Turner, Johncie Kay [Palmer] (Arthur R. Turner) –
[(RD) Con CE (E. Ohio) 1991; CRT CE (E. Ohio) 1992; FD 1997] Church of the Savior,
Canton, Ohio 1990; Goshen IN: First 1993; Ypsilanti: First Presbyterian 1996; transf
to Memphis Conference; Dyersburg (TN): First Jan 15, 1998; transf to Detroit Conf
Chelsea: First, Minister of Christian Education and S.E.N.I.O.R.S. Ministries Sept 1,
1999; **Retired Aug 31, 2008**.<> Home: 1039 Crestwood Ln, Jackson 49203 (734) 972-
7186. johnciekay@gmail.com

PASTORAL RECORDS

*Turner, Molly C. –

[(RE) D-1969; FE-1972; R-2012] Manton/Fife Lake/East Boardman/South Boardman (Assoc) 1971; Lansing: Mount Hope (Assoc) 1976; Vermontville/Gresham 1979; Breckenridge 1983; Appointed to Extension Ministries (¶344.1b,c) District Superintendent, Central District 1990; UM Connectional Structures (¶344.1a,c) Clergy Assistant to the Bishop 1993; Grand Ledge: First 2003; Retired 2012; Grand Ledge First (Interim) 07/01/2012-12/31/2012.<> Home: 1873 Hamilton Rd, Okemos 48864 (517) 214-6308. mollycturner@gmail.com

*Turner, Richard A. (Mary Lee) –

[(RE) T N.IN 1957; F N.IN. 1960] 1954 Windsor, Rehobeth; 1957 Losantville, Blountsville; 1960 Trans. to Detroit Conf, Bay Port; 1965 Millington, Arbela; 1971 Pinconning; Dec 1, 1983 Saginaw: West Michigan Avenue; Mar 1, 1987 Saginaw: West Michigan Avenue, Sheridan Avenue; 1991 Onaway, Millersburg; **1995 Retired**.<> Home: H.C.R. 01, Box 285, Bois Blanc Island 49775

*Tuttle, James Edward (Linda) –

[(RE) P 1972; F 1976] 1972 Calumet; Feb 1975 Detroit: Metropolitan (assoc); 1977 Ypsilanti: St. Matthew's; Jan 15, 1985 Livonia: Clarenceville; 1990 Flint: Calvary; 1999 Saline; **2016 Retired**.<> Home: 1450 Maplewood Dr., Saline 48176 (734) 944-8081. jet.tuttle@juno.com

*Vale, Diane "Dia" E. (Marc) –

[(RE) D-1973; FE-1977; R-1990] Fife Lake/Boardmans Parish 1976; Lawton 10/15/1977; Other Valid Ministries (¶344.1d) Institute for Advanced Pastoral Studies, Bloomfield Hills 05/01/1980; Sabbatical Leave 1983; Weidman 1984; Leave of Absence 07/15/1985; **Retired 1990**.<> Home: 17600 Garvey Rd, Chelsea 48118 (734) 475-9526. diavale@juno.com.

Van, Lanette S. –

[(OE) OE 2020 Iowa Conf, para. 346.1] **Constantine, White Pigeon 2020**.<> (C) 285 White Pigeon St., Constantine 49042 (269) 435-8151. (WP) PO Box 518, 204 N Kalamazoo St, White Pigeon 49099 (269) 483-9054. Home: 265 White Pigeon St, Constantine 49042. pastorlanette@gmail.com

VanBeek, Craig H. (Laura) –

[(FL) DSA-2017; CLM-2017; FL-2019] Burnips/Monterey Center (DSA) 2017; Burnips/Monterey Center 01/01/2019.<> (B) 4237 30th St, PO Box 30, Burnips 49314 (616) 896-8410. (MC) 3022 130th Ave, Hopkins 49328 (616) 896-8410. Home: 4290 Summer Creek Dr., Dorr 49323 (616) 299-6668

*VanConant, Earleen A. –

[(RL) FL 1988] Omard 1989; Cole, Omard (LTFT) Jan 1, 1992; White Pine, Bergland, Ewen, Trout Creek Presb (LTFT ½) 1993; Port Austin, Grindstone/Pinnebog 1997; **Retired Jan 1, 2000**.<> Home: 55209 Fallbrooke Dr., Macomb 48042 (586) 243-6176. c.vanconant@yahoo.com

*VandenBrink, Sandra Kay (Trevor) –

[(RL) PL-2001; RL-2013] Hudsonville 5/31/2001; Bradley Indian Mission / Salem Indian Mission 1/16/2005; Bradley Indian Mission / Salem Indian Mission 2013-10/1/2014; Retired 2013; Kewadin Indian Mission 2015-12/31/2016.<> Home: 3933 Kerri Ct., Holland 49424 (616) 886-3579. sandravandenbrink20@gmail.com

*VanderBilt, Herbert J. (Emmy) –
[(RL) PL-2004; NL-2016; RL-2017] East Nelson 2004; Not Appointed 2016; Retired 12/01/2017.<> Home: 2204 Gee Dr, Lowell 49331 (616 460-0997. hvanderbilt@comcast.net

Vanderlip, Joyce L. –
[(PE) PE 2020] **Centreville 2020**.<> 305 E Main Street, Centreville 49032 (269) 467-8645. Home: 304 East Market St, Centreville 49032 (810) 813-9200. pastorjoyce.umc@gmail.com

VanderSande, Ruth A. (Dennis Eric Irish) –
[(PE) PL Sept 7, 2017; PE 2019] Macon (PTLP ½) Sept 7, 2017; Britton Grace, Macon 2019; **Midland: First (assoc) 2020**.<>. 315 W. Larkin St., Box 466, Midland 48640 (989) 835-6797. Home: (810) 335-3962. pastorruthiv@gmail.com

VanDessel, Joan E. –
[(PE) PE-2019] Grand Rapids: First (assoc and Director of Mission and Outreach).<> 227 Fulton St E, Grand Rapids 49503 (616) 451-2879. Home: 2005 Collingwood Ave SW, Wyoming 49519 (616) 818-9295. joanv@grfumc.org

VanDop, Jonathan D. (Darcie) –
[(FE) FL-2008; PE-2009; FE-2014] Rosebush 2008; Ionia: First 2014; Lyons-Muir 01/01/2016; Leave of Absence (¶353.2a) 2017; Appointed to Extension Ministries (¶344.1b) Chaplain, West Texas VA Health Care System 08/19/2018; Appointed to Extension Ministries by GBHEM (¶344.1b,c) **Chaplain, Veterans Administration, William S.-Middleton Veterans Hospital, Madison, WI Jun 21, 2020**.<> 2500 Overlook Terrace, Madison WI 53705 Home: 2500 Overlook Terrace, Madison 53705 (989) 954-7099. uscgemt@yahoo.com

*VanLente, Charles R. (Linda) –
[(RA) SP-1963; FL-1970; AM-1976; RA-2010] Ashton Charge 09/01/1963; Morris Chapel/Niles 12/01/1964-09/01/1965; St Johns: Salem 01/15/1970; Maple Hill 1972; Honorable Location 08/15/1976; Holton/Sitka/Twin Lake (Ad Interim) 1978; Readmitted 1982; Holton/Sitka/Twin Lake 1982; Cassopolis 1983; Kalkaska 1993; Grand Rapids: Northlawn 1996; Retired 2010.<> Home: 2103 Shetland Dr NE, Grand Rapids 49505 (616) 719-1833. chucksmemo@gmail.com

*VanMarter, Dianne Helene (Merl) –
[(RL) PL 2002] Omard 2001; Omard, Peck (LTFT ¾) 2002; Omard, Peck (LTFT ½) Jan 1, 2004; Peck 2005; New Haven: Faith (LTFT ½), Omo: Zion (LTFT ¼) 2011; New Haven: Faith Jan 1, 2014; **Retired 2015; Macomb: Faith 2015** [New Haven: Faith renamed Macomb: Faith Dec 6, 2015].<> 56370 Fairchild Rd., Macomb 48042 (586) 749-3147. Home: 20100 Cushing, Detroit 48205 (810) 488-0608. deerev@aol.com

VanOudheusden, Melodye Surgeon (John) –
[(FE) D-1994; FE-2005] Family Leave 1996; Marcellus 2002; Jackson Trinity/Parma 2007; Evart 2012; Evart/Sears 2017; Monroe: St. Paul's 2019.<> 201 S Monroe St, Monroe 48161 (734) 242-3000. Home: 212 Hollywood Dr, Monroe 48162 (517) 250-1879. pastormelodye@yahoo.com

Vasey, Bradley R. –
[(PL) PL 2019] **Deerfield, Wellsville (LTFT ½) 2019**.<> (D) 110 Williams St, Deerfield 49238 (517) 447-3420. (W) 2509 S Wellsville Hwy, Blissfield 49228 (517) 486-4777. Home: 4322 Corey Hwy, Blissfield 49228 (419) 704-1884. brickvase@yahoo.com

*Ventura, Oscar A. (Naomi) –
[(RE) D-1975; FE-1978; R-2009] Transferred from Wisconsin Conf 1996; Grand Rapids: La Nueva Esperanza 12/05/1996; Involuntary Leave of Absence 09/25/2002; Grand Rapids: La Nueva Esperanza 03/17/2003; Retired 2009.<> Home: Calle Carlos Lassy #13, Apartado Postal 97, Barahona 82000, Dominican Republic

Verhelst, Weatherly Burkhead (Craig) –
[(FE) P 1993; F 1996] 1994 Flint: Court Street (assoc); 1998 Middlebury; 2003 Saginaw: State Street; Aug 1, 2009 Utica (assoc); **2015 Troy: First**.<> 6363 Livernois, Troy 48098 (248) 879-6363. Home: 6339 Vernmoor, Troy 48098 (989) 598-6506. revwow@charter.net

*Verhelst, William A. (Suzanne) –
[(RE) T 1966; F 1968] 1963 Republic Charge; 1966 Wellington (Cent. IL Conf); 1968 Gladstone; Apr 1974 Beverly Hills; 1979 Flint: Central; Oct 15, 1987 Associate Council Director, Parish Development and Global Ministries; 1997 Detroit West District Superintendent; 2004 Detroit: Metropolitan (Intentional Interim, ¶329.3); **2006 Retired**.<> Home: 14763 W. Brady, Chesaning 48616 (989) 845-5007. wsverhelst@centurytel.net

*Vernon, Douglas W. (Jane) –
[(RE) D-1967; FE-1970; R-2010] Niles Trinity 1969; Kalamazoo: First (Assoc) 1971; Stockbridge 11/01/1974; Transferred to Detroit Conf 1979; Transferred from Detroit Conf 2000; Retired 2010; Kalamazoo: First 2000; Retired 2010; Lawton: St Paul's (LTFT ¼) 2011-2014; Battle Creek: First (Assoc) (LTFT ¼) 2015-2016.<> Home: 793 Red Maple Lane, Wixom 48393 (248) 859-2986. dvernon@fumcnorthville.org

*Veska, Rony S. (Ivor) –
[(RE) P 1997; FE 2000] 1997: Ann Arbor: First (assoc); 1998 Poseyville; Mar 1, 2001 Rochester: St. Paul's (assoc); 2008 Ferndale: First; **2013 Retired**.<> 31 W. Los Reales Rd., #167, Tucson AZ 85756. rveska@yahoo.com

*Vincent, Alonzo Elliott (Elmira) –
[(RE) P W. OH, 1966; F W. OH, 1968] 1961 McCabe Chapel (N. Little Rock AR; 1962 Sweet Home, Lone Oak Circuit AR; 1966 Chicago: St. Matthew's (assoc); 1967 Evanston IL: Sherman Avenue; 1968 Cincinnati: Marbly Memorial; 1973 Cincinnati: Marbly, Bond Hill, St. Mark Parish; 1979 Trans. to Wisconsin Conf, Director of Urban Strategy, Milwaukee; 1983 Southcentral District Superintendent; July 1984 Trans. to Detroit Conf, Detroit: Cass Avenue (assoc); 1986 Highland Park: Berea-St. Paul's; 1991 Flint: Bethel; 2005 Birch Run; 2007 Attica; 2008 Mt. Morris: First; **2013 Retired**.<> Home: 9197 Liverpool Ct., Grand Blanc 48439 (810) 953-9917. esmithvinc@aol.com

*Vittoz, Irene L. (Gary) –
[(RL) PL-2005; RL-2018] Brookfield Eaton (DSA) 10/01/2004; Brookfield Eaton (PTLP) 11/15/2005; Brookfield Eaton (PTLP) and Pope (PTLP) 2008; Brookfield Eaton (PTLP ¼) and Lee Center (PTLP ¼) 2010; Brookfield Eaton (PTLP ¼) 2014; Retired 2018.<> Home: 5503 Long Hwy, Eaton Rapids 48827 (517) 543-4225. ilv@vcconsulting.com

Vollmer, Michael W. (Sarah) –
[(PE) FL 2014; PE 2016] Hemlock, Nelson 2014; Centreville 2019; **Clinton, Stony Creek 2020**.<> (C) 10990 Tecumseh-Clinton Rd, Clinton 49236 (517) 456-4972. (SC) 8635 Stony Creek Rd, Ypsilanti 48197 (734) 482-0240. Home: 5493 Willis Rd, Ypsilanti 48197 (989) 600-6148. revmwv@gmail.com

Vorenkamp, Mark A. –
[(PL) PL 2020] **Oak Grove (PTLP ¾) 2020**.<> 6686 Oak Grove Rd., Oak Grove 48855 (517) 546-3942. Home: 6893 Sanford Rd., Howell 48855 (810) 772-1987. anabsurd-lylongscarf@gmail.com

*Wachterhauser, Paul Thomas (Beth) –
[(RE) P 1969; F 1973 W.MI] 1971 Burr Oak; 1974 Trans. to Detroit Conf, Midland: First (assoc); 1979 Cass City; Sept 1, 1983 Ann Arbor: First (assoc); 1997 Caring Covenant Group Ministry: Davison; **2009 Retired**.<> Home: 716 Surfwood, Davison 48423 (810) 653-4459. twachterhauser@yahoo.com

Waggoner, Katherine C. (Scott) –
[(FL) PL 2011; FL 2016] Monroe: E. Raisinville Frenchtown (became Heritage UMC, 2012) 2011; Heritage (¼), Monroe: First (¾) 2013; **Alden, Central Lake 2020**.<> (A) PO Box 130, 9015 Helena, Alden 49612 (231) 331-4132. (CL) PO Box 213, 8147 W State Rd, Central Lake 49622. Home: 9022 Franklin, Alden 49612 (517) 215-4846. PastorKatieW@gmail.com

Waggy, Jenaba –
[(PE) PE 2020] **Essexville: St. Luke's 2020**.<> 206 Scheurmann St, Essexville 48732 (989) 893-8031. Home: 212 Hart St., Essexville 48732 (989) 894-2453. waggyj09@alumni.hanover.edu

Wagner, Charlene S. –
[(PL) DSA-2018; PL 2019] Carland (DSA) (LTFT ¼) 2018; Carland (LTFT ¼) 01/01/2019.<> 4002 N Carland Rd, Elsie 48831 (989) 494-7763. Home: 587 N Baldwin Rd, Owosso 48867 (989) 494-7763. thewagners2@gmail.com

*Wagner, Glenn M. (Nancy) –
[(RE) D-1976; FE-1982; R-2017] Transferred from Northern Illinois Conf 1992; N Muskegon: Community 1992; Holt 2006; Church of The Dunes 2014; Retired 01/01/2017.<> Home: 1284 Oakhampton Rd, Holland 49424 (616) 842-3586. gnmbwagner@aol.com

*Wagner, Lynn W. –
[(RE) D-1965; FE-1970; R-2002] Hillsdale: First (Assoc) 1966; Niles: Wesley (Assoc) 1969; Howard City Circuit 09/15/1970; Evart Circuit 03/01/1971; Keeler/Silver Creek 10/15/1973; Mulliken/ Grand Ledge: First (Assoc) 1975; Dowling: Country Chapel/Banfield 1977; Nashville 1984; Middleville/Parmelee 1988; Battle Creek: Maple 1996; Lyons-Muir/Ionia: Easton 2001; Retired 09/01/2002.<> Home: 26685 Elk Run E, New Hudson 48165 (269) 986-2876

*Wales, Gary S. (Cynthia Kaye) –
[(RE) D-1988; FE-1990; RE 2020] Fife Lake/Boardman 1987; Otsego: Trowbridge 1994; Kingsley 2008; Charlotte: Lawrence Ave 2013; **Retired 2020**.<> Home: 350 E Kalamo Hwy, Charlotte 48813 (269) 650-5656. gcts86@gmail.com

*Walker, James J. (Susan) –
[(RE) P 1985 W.MI; F 1987 W.MI; RE 2020] Lansing: Christ (assoc) 1985; Trans. to Detroit Conf, Brown City: First, Immanuel 1989; Utica (assoc) 1996; Wyandotte: First 1998; Belleville: First 2007**; Retired 2020**.<> Home: 854 S. Center Park Dr. SW #25, Byron Center 49315 (734) 934-0007. jim2016walker@gmail.com

Walkup, Kenny Ray, Jr. (Michelle) –
[(PL) PL 2015] South Lyon (associate) Nov 23, 2015; **Walled Lake 2020 (PTLP ¾).**<> 313 Northport St., Walled Lake 48390 (248) 624-2405. Home: 1115 Paddock Dr, South Lyon 48178 (248) 361-6658. kennywalkup@gmail.com

*Wallace, Joyce E. –
[(RE) P; F MO W. Conf Wesley Foundation, Lincoln University; transfer from Missouri West Conference, Detroit: Central (assoc) 1995; Detroit: Conant Avenue 1997; Detroit: Scott Memorial 2001; Hardy 2005; **Retired 2013;** Middlebury, Pittsburg 2015-2018; **Lennon 2020.**<> 1014 Oak St, PO Box 19, Lennon 48449 (810) 621-3676. Home: 9921 Belcrest Blvd, Fenton 48430 (810) 208-0648. rapturewks@sbcglobal.net

Waller, Tom J. –
[(FL) FL Jan 2015] Dearborn Heights: Stephens, Warren Valley Jan 1, 2015; **Richmond: First 2018.**<> 69495 Main St., Box 293, Richmond 48062 (586-727-2622. Home: 35675 Pound Rd., Richmond 48062 (586-727-655. waller0307@yahoo.com

Wallis, David Michael (Lisa) –
[(FE) SP 1990; P 1994; F 1997] Norway: Grace, Faithhorn 1995; **Mackinaw City: Church of the Straits 2006.**<> PO Box 430, 307 N. Huron, Mackinaw City 49701 (231) 436-8682. Home: 309 East Jamet, PO Box 901, Mackinaw City 49701 (231) 436-5484. norev@juno.com

*Walls, Suzanne B. (John) –
[(RE) SP 1994; PE 1999; FE 2003] Feb 16, 1995 Inkster: Christ; 2000 Ortonville; 2005 Wyandotte: Glenwood; 2013 Berkley: First, Beverly Hills; **2016 Retired.**<> Home: 225 Munger Rd., Holly 48442 (248) 459-6851. pastorsuew@yahoo.com

*Walsworth, Lowell F. (Jessica) –
[(RE) D-1959; FE-1962; R-2002] Hastings Parish 1957; Lyon Lake/Marengo 1959; Kalamazoo: First (Assoc) 1962; Bellevue/Kalamo 1966; Grand Rapids: First (Assoc) 1971; Edwardsburg/Niles Trinity 1973; Battle Creek: Trinity 1978; Vicksburg 1981; Sturgis 1993; Other Valid Ministries (¶344.1d) Assoc Professor, Olivet College 1995; Retired 2002.<> Home: 1412 E Hatch St, Sturgis 49091 (269) 659-4688. Ljwalsworth@charter.net

Walther, Joel L. (Megan) –
[(FE) FL 2011; PE 2012; FE 2015] Petersburg, LaSalle: Zion 2011; **Goodrich 2017.**<> 8071 S. State Road, Goodrich 48438 8071 S. State Road, Goodrich 48438 (810) 636-2444. Home: 7228 Chapel View Dr., Clarkston 48346 (734) 636-2444. pastorjoel@charter.net

Walther, Megan Jo Crumm (Joel) –
[(FE) PE 2011; FE 2014] Erie 2014; **Clarkston (assoc) 2017.**<> 6600 Waldon Rd., Clarkston 48346 (248) 625-1611. Home: 7228 Chapel View Dr., Clarkston 48346 (734) 751-6836. rev.megan.walther@gmail.com

*Walworth, Maurice E. (Sally) –
[(RE) D-1985; FE-1989; R-2006] Transferred from Southwest Texas Conf 1993; Battle Creek: Baseline 11/01/1993; Lansing: Christ 1996; Jackson Calvary 2003; Retired 2006; Munith/ Pleasant Lake 2006; Pleasant Lake 2007-09/30/2007; Somerset Center 2008-2009; Munith 09/06/2011-2012.<> Home: PO Box 612, 257 Lake Heights, Grass Lake 49240 (517) 522-3936. mewjr1@juno.com

*Ward, George F. (Alice) –

[(RE) P 1969; F 1971] 1970 Dearborn: Mt. Olivet (assoc); 1972 Southfield: Magnolia; Mar 1976 Clayton, Rollin Center; Nov 1, 1981 Croswell; 1988 Franklin: Community (assoc); 1993 Chesaning: Trinity; 2002 Cass City; **2006 Retired**.<> 995 N. Baywood, Holland 49424 616-786-4761. Gfward@hotmail.com

*Ward, Kenneth Edwin (Sue) –

[(RE) P E.OH 1968; F E.OH 1970] 1970 Waynesburg: Centenary; 1973 Ashland: Christ; Mar 1978 Trans. to Detroit Conf, Director-Manager, Judson Collins Camp; Jan 1, 1982 Detroit Conference Staff: Outdoor Education; 1992 Marquette District Superintendent; 1998 Dearborn: First; **2005 Retired**.<> Home: (May-Oct): 18585 Red Pine Dr., Hillman 49746 (989) 742-2133, (Nov-Apr): 905 Conway, #18, Las Cruces NM 88005 575-541-0982. ksward88005@gmail.com

*Washburn, Grant A. (Patricia) –

[(RE) P 1968; F 1971] 1970 Port Huron: Gratiot Park; 1972 Flushing (assoc); 1975 Mio; 1980 Saginaw: Swan Valley; 1983 Bay City: Madison Avenue; Sept 1, 1987 Burton: Atherton; 1993 Sterling Heights; **Aug 1, 1995 Retired**.<> 8378 West Bluefield Avenue, Peoria AZ 85382 (623) 215-7849. gwashburn2@cox.net

*Webster, Brent L. (Mary) –

[(RE) P 1974; F 1977] 1976 Davison Group Ministry: Richfield; Nov 1978 Harbor Beach, Port Hope; 1983 Washington, Davis; Sept 1, 1997 West Bloomfield; 2010 Carleton; **2012 Retired**; May 1-June 30, 2019 West Bloomfield.<> Home: 7863 Academy Court E., Waterford 48329 (248) 742-1092. brent1949@live.com

*Webster, Roy LaVere (Zola) –

[(RE) T 1957; F 1963] 1955 Indian River; 1957 school; 1962 New Hudson; 1966 Birmingham: First (assoc); 1968 West Branch; 1973 Holly; 1976 Berkley; 1979 Royal Oak: St. John's; 1988 East Detroit: Immanuel; 1991 Belleville: First; June 30, 1994 disability leave; **1995 Retired**.<> Home: 1160 W. South Boulevard, Rochester Hills 48309 (248) 227-7619. Laverew@aol.com

*Weemhoff, Harold E., Jr. (Chris) –

[(RE) P W. OH, 1970; F W. OH, 1973] May 1977 Trans. to Detroit Conf, Birmingham: First (assoc); 1980 Leave of Absence; 1982 Whittemore, Prescott; 1984 Gladwin; 1986 Laingsburg, Middlebury; 1990 Ann Arbor: Glacier Way; Mar 1, 1992 Taylor: West Mound; Dec 1, 1997 Taylor: West Mound, Melvindale: New Hope; 1997 Eastpointe: Immanuel; Jan 1, 2000 Rochester: St. Paul's (assoc); 2008 Troy: First; **2015 Retired**.<> Home: 5800 Thorny Ash, Rochester 48306 (313) 418-2748. drhalw@sbcglobal.net

*Wegner, Glenn R. (Evelyn) –

[(RE) D-1975; FE-1978; R-2004] Transferred from Deroit Conf 1984; Woodland/Welcome Corners 1984; Epsilon/ Levering 1987; Appointed in Other Annual Conferences (¶426.1) West Ohio Conf, Seaman 09/01/1992; Battle Creek: Baseline 1996; Retired 2004.<> Home: 3788 Bass Rd, Williamsburg OH 45176 (269) 967-3850

Weiler, Cara B.A. (John Matthew) –
[(FD) PD-2007; FD-2011] Portage: Chapel Hill (Deacon) (LTFT ¼) 10/01/2007; Transferred from Northern Illinois Conf 2008; Kalamazoo: Sunnyside (Deacon) (LTFT ¼) 10/01/2009; Deacons Appointed w/in UM Connectional Structure (¶331.1b) Kalamazoo: Sunnyside (LTFT ¼) and SW MI Children's Trauma Assessment Center (LTFT ½) 11/18/2009. **Associate Director of Site Services, Communities In Schools of Kalamazoo (para 331.4a) Jan 17, 2017.**<> 125 W Exchange Pl, Kalamazoo 49007 (269) 337-1601. Home: 3090 Vliet Ln, Kalamazoo 49004. cara.weiler@gmail.com

Weiler, John Matthew (Cara) –
[(FE) FL-2007; PE-2009; FE-2013] Portage: Chapel Hill (Assoc) 2007; Portage: Chapel Hill (Assoc) (LTFT ½) and Kalamazoo: Sunnyside (LTFT ½) 2009; Kalamazoo: Sunnyside 2011; **Kalamazoo: First (assoc) 2020.**<> 212 South Park Street, Kalamazoo 49007 (269) 381-6340. Home: 3090 Vliet Ln, Kalamazoo 49004 (269) 599-2274. mweiler@umc-kzo.org

*Weinberger, Stephan –
[(RE) D-1985; FE-1987; R-2016] Indian River/Pellston 1984; St Johns: First 1990; Lansing: First 2000; Other Valid Ministries (¶344.1d) Oaks Correctional Facility 2004; Lansing Calvary/Potter Park 2005; Lansing Calvary 2006; Lansing Calvary/Wheatfield 08/01/2006; Mancelona/Alba 2007; Muskegon: Lakeside/Crestwood 2010; Pierson Heritage 2014; Retired 03/01/2016; Dimondale 02/01/2019; Stockbridge (LTFT ¼), Munith (LTFT ¼) 2019.<> (M) 224 N Main St, PO Box 189, Munith 49259 (517) 596-2441. (S) 219 E Elizabeth St, Stockbridge 49285 (517) 851-7676. Home: 3880 Lone Pine Dr, Apt 03, Holt 48842 (517) 242-5020. revsteve75@hotmail.com

*Weiss, Edward C., Jr. –
[(RE) LP 1976; FM 1998] 1968 Wellsville; 1972 Springville; 1974 Crystal Falls, Amasa; 1985 St. Charles, Brant; **Sept 1, 1994 Retired.**<> Home: 952 W. Maple Ave., Adrian 49221 (517) 265-7259

*Weiss, James Dewey (Sara) –
[(RE) T 1954; F 1957] 1955 Rea, Cone; 1956 Samaria; 1958 Stephens; 1963 Dearborn Heights: Stephens; 1966 Berkley; 1969 Lincoln Park: First; Aug 1975 Detroit: Trinity; Oct 1982 Lincoln Park: Dix; 1989 St. Clair Shores: Good Shepherd; 1992 Auburn; **1993 Retired.**<> Home: 56645 Cardinal Dr., Macomb 48042. JDEWeiss@comcast.net

*Welbaum, Barbara Ellen –
[(RE) P 1988; F 1991; RE 2019] 1989 Port Austin, Grindstone City, Pinnebog; Mar 1, 1992 Ann Arbor: Glacier Way; 1994 Pontiac Cooperative Parish: Aldersgate, St. James; 1997 Detroit: Redford; 2000 Livonia: Newburg (assoc); 2006 Marysville; **Retired 2019.**<> Home: 4258 Berkshire Dr, Sterling Hts 48314 (586) 219-5263. bewelbaum@att.net

*Welch, Karen Alayne [Mars] –
[(RE) SP 1993; P 1994; F 1997] Jan 1, 1994 Dearborn Heights: Warren Valley; 1995 Morenci; Nov 1, 2000 Chelsea Retirement Community: Chaplain; July 15, 2002 leave of absence; 2003 God's Country Cooperative Parish: Grand Marals, Germfask, McMillan; 2006 Hillman, Spratt; **2008 Retired.**<> Home: 9099 Pembrook Dr, Davison 48423 (231) 590-2551. kwelch1941@gmail.com

PASTORAL RECORDS

*Welsch, P. Kay –
[(AF) D-1986; FE-1992; RE-2004; AF-2004] [Wisconsin Conf, Retired Elder] Turk Lake (DSA LTFT) 7/16/2005-2012.<> Home: PO Box 318, 9440 Cutler Road, Lakeview 48850 (989) 352-1209. kwelsch80@gmail.com

*Welsh, Gerald L. (Martha Gene) –
[(RE) D-1957; FE-1960; R-1994] Sand Lake Circuit 1953; Alma (Assoc) 01/01/1960; Carson City 1961; Harbor Springs 09/01/1965; Stevensville 1968; Bellaire: Community 10/15/1969; Martin/ Shelbyville 1976; Evart/Avondale 1984; Bronson: First 1990; Retired 1994.<> Home: 35 Roberts Ct, Coopersville 49404 (616) 837-7157. gwelsh449@gmail.com

Wenburg, Ryan L. (Kathleen "Beth") –
[(FE) PE-2015; FE-2018] Hartford/Keeler 2015; Hartford 01/01/2017; Frankenmuth 2019.<> 346 E Vates St, Frankenmuth 48734 (989) 652-6858. Home: 326 E Vates St, Frankenmuth 48734. PastorRyanWenburg@gmail.com

*Wendell, Donald R. (Violet) –
[(RL) PL-1993; FL-2009; RL-2010] Moscow Plains (DSA) (LTFT PT) 01/01/1993; Moscow Plains (LTFT PT) 1993; Nottawa (LTFT PT) 01/01/1996; Jackson: Zion (LTFT PT) 07/15/2003; Not Appointed 03/15/2006; Bloomingdale (LTFT ¼) 2006; Mt Pleasant: Trinity / Countryside / Leaton 11/30/2008; Retired 11/01/2009.<> Home: 137 W Michigan Ave, Galesburg 49053 (269) 200-5205

*Wessman, Robert L. –
[(FL)– FL-2018] Mason: First (Assoc) 1979; Caledonia 1984; Allegan 1990; Retired 1999.<> Home: 6476 Castle Ave, Holland 49423 (616) 335-8983

West, Brian Gregory (Stephanie) –
[(FE) PE 2012; FE 2015] Laingsburg 2012; Laingsburg, Pittsburg (¶206.3) 2018; **Grand Blanc 2020**.<> 515 Bush Ave, Grand Blanc 48439 (810) 694-9040. Home: 12110 Francesca Dr, Grand Blanc 48439 (586) 419-1178. pastorbrianwest@gmail.com

*West, Charles Henry (Margaret) –
[(RE) P 1978; F 1981] 1979 Richfield, Otter Lake; 1985 Parish Director, Caring Covenant Group Ministry: Richfield, Otter Lake; Mar 1, 1988 White Pine Circuit: White Pine, Bergland, Ewen (LTFT ½); 1993 Marquette: Grace, Skandia; **2009 Retired**.<> Home: 440 E. Prospect, Marquette 49855. mqtchaz@gmail.com

*West, Margaret Helen Rodgers (Charles) –
[(RE) P 1982; F 1985] 1982 Flint: Hope (assoc); 1983 Dryden, Attica; Mar 1, 1988 White Pine Circuit: White Pine, Bergland, Ewen (LTFT ½); 1993 family leave; Sept 1, 1993 Director: Wesley Foundation, N. MI University ¼ Time; 1994 family leave 1999 Chaplain/Director, Wesley Foundation, Northern Michigan University; **2009 Retired**.<> Home: 440 E. Prospect, Marquette 49855. margiewest@earthlink.net

West, Matthew J. (Melissa) –
[(FL) FL 2018] Girard 2018; **Milan: Marble Memorial 2020**.<> 8 Park Ln, Milan 48160 (734) 439-2421. Home: 835 Faith Court, Milan 48160. (269) 967-4444. PastorMattWest@gmail.com

*Wheat, Karen S. (Vincent) –
[(RE) D-1972; FE-1975; R-2015] Niles: Wesley (Assoc) 1974; Gobles/Kendall 09/15/1976; Jackson: Trinity 1986; Battle Creek: First 1998; Charlotte: Lawrence Ave 2002; Schoolcraft 2010; Retired 2015.<> Home: 2933 Hunters Pl, Kalamazoo 49048 (517) 588-9184. WheatKS@aol.com.

*Wheelock, Calvin H. –
[(RL) PL 1999; RL 2019] Dec 16, 1999 Caring Covenant Group Ministry: Arbela; Apr 1, 2005 Parish Director, Caring Covenant Group Ministry: Arbela; Nov 1, 2006 Henderson, Chapin; 2011 Henderson, Chapin, Owosso; **2019 Retired**.<> Home: 14405 Vassar Rd, Millington 48746 (810) 624-0795. pastorherbw@aol.com

*Whitcomb, Randy James (Michelle Gentile) –
[(RE) P MN, 1984; F 1987; RE 2019] 1985 Trans. to Detroit Conf, Detroit: Aldersgate (assoc); 1988 Canton: Cherry Hill; 1993 Flint: Bristol, Dimond; June 1, 1996 Lake Orion (assoc); Feb 15, 2001 incapacity leave (para 355.1); 2004 leave of absence; Oct 1, 2007 Chaplain, Great Lakes Caring – Hospice; **Jan 1, 2019 Retired; Jan 1, 2019 Chaplain, Great Lakes Caring – Hospice**.<> Home: 2772 Roundtree Drive, Troy 48083 (248) 979-6677. arejayrev@aol.com

White, Christina Miller (Jason Michael White) –
[(FD) PD 2015; FD 2018] Midland: First (deacon) 2015; Flint: Court Street (deacon), Crossroads District (deacon) 2017; Flint: Court Street (deacon), East Winds District (deacon) Jan 1, 2019; Coordinator of Discipleship Formation of East Winds District Jan 1, 2020; Flint: Court Street (assoc) Mar 1, 2020; **Flint: Court Street (deacon), missional (LTFT ¼), Youth Ministry Initiatives Coordinator (LTFT ½) 2020**.<> (FCS) 225 W. Court St., Flint 48502 (810) 235-4651. Home: 7191 Birchwood Dr, Mount Morris 48458 (989) 488-3347. cmillerwhite@michiganumc.org

White, Irene R. –
[(PL) PL 1997] 1997 Escanaba: First (assoc); Sept 1, 1997 Escanaba: First (assoc), Trenary; Jan 1, 2000 Trenary; Jan 1, 2009 Munising, Trenary; **2011 Norway: Grace, Faithorn**.<> (N) 130 O'Dill Dr., Norway 49870 (906) 563-8917. (F) W8601 Blum Rd, Vulcan 49892. Home: 725 Norway St., Norway 49870 (906) 563-9877. irene@up.net

White, Reggie Allen –
[(OF) Progressive National Baptist Convention, OF 2019] **Southfield: Hope (assoc), Detroit: St. Timothy (assoc) (LTFT ¼) 2019**.<> (SH) 26275 Northwestern Hwy., Southfield 48076 (248) 356-1020. (DST) 15888 Archdale St., Detroit 48227 (313) 837-4070. reggieallenwhite4609@gmail.com

*White, Robert Alan –
[(RE) FE Great Rivers] 2000 trans. from Illinois Great Rivers, Keweenaw Charge: Calumet, Mohawk-Ahmeek, Lake Linden, Laurium; **2016 Retired**.<> Home: 311 Eckart St., Antigo WI 54409 (309) 370-7227. bwhite@up.net

*Whitely, Betty (Theodore) –
[(RL) PL 2000; RL 2007] 1998 Southfield: Hope (assoc); 2000 Saginaw: Burt. Appointment ended May 1, 2007; **2017 Retired**.<> Home: 17156 Shervilla Place, Southfield 48075 (248) 557-4688. BettyTedWhitely@aol.com

*Whitely, Theodore DeLeon, Sr. (Betty) –
[(RE) Elder, AME Zion, 1979; P 1986; F 1988] 1978-83 St. Paul AME Zion, Carnegie PA; 1984 Trans. to Detroit Conf, Westland: St. James; Mar 1, 1987 Detroit: Calvary; 1992 Detroit: St. Paul's; 1996 Detroit: Jefferson Ave; 1998 Southfield: Hope (assoc); 2000 Saginaw: Calvary; 2003 Saginaw: Calvary; 2004 Burton: Christ; 2006 Detroit: Calvary, Henderson Memorial; 2011 Detroit: Calvary; 2013 Birmingham: Embury, Troy: Fellowship, Waterford: Trinity; 2014 Pontiac: Grace and Peace Community, Waterford: Four Towns; **2015 Retired**.<> Home: 17156 Shervilla Place, Southfield 48075 (248) 557-4688. BettyTedWhitely@aol.com

*Whitlock, Bobby Dale –
[(RE) D-1977; FE-1980; R-2009] Transferred from Oklahoma Conf 1985; Remus/Halls Corners/Mecosta 09/16/1985; Dansville/Vantown 05/16/1987; Caledonia 1990; Scottville 01/06/1996; Big Rapids: First 2004; Robbins 2008; Retired 2009; Wolf Lake (LTFT ½) 2011; Wolf Lake (LTFT 45%) 01/01/2014-9/1/2014.<> Home: 4512 S Quarterline Rd, Muskegon 49444 (231) 457-4705. the.whitlocks81@yahoo.com

Whittemore, Inge E. –
[(PL) PL-2016] East Nelson (PTLP ½) 2016.<> 9024 18 Mile Rd NE, Cedar Springs 49319 (616) 696-0661. Home: 590 Wildview, Lowell 49331 (616) 897-6525. ingeandray@aol.com

Wichert, David Allen (Janet) –
[(FE) PE 2002; FE 2008] 2002 Fairgrove, Gilford; 2006 Plymouth: First (assoc); 2010 Seven Churches United Group Ministry: Gaines, Duffield; 2013 AuGres, Twining: Trinity; [AuGres and Twining: Trinity merged in 2015 forming Arenac County: Christ] **2019 Saginaw: Ames**.<> 801 State St., Saginaw 48602 (989) 754-6373. Home: 1477 Vancouver, Saginaw 48638 (989) 876-0148. WichertDG@yahoo.com

Wicks, Jeremy J. (Toinette) –
[(FL) PL-2011; FL-2013] Dansville (DSA ¼ Time) 2011; Dansville (PTLP ¼) 11/13/2011; Dansville and Wheatfield (PTLP ½) 2012; M-52 Cooperative Ministry: Millville (½ Time) and Dansville (¼ Time) and Wheatfield 2013; M-52 Cooperative Ministry: Millville (½ Time) and Dansville (¼ Time) and New Church Start (¼ Time) 2014; Millville and New Church Start (FTLP) 01/01/2015-2017; Traverse City Mosaic (New Church Start) 2017.<> 1249 Three Mile Rd S, Traverse City 49696 (231) 943-3048. Home: PO Box 395, 449 N. Brownson St, Kingsley 49649 (517) 851-1494. jeremy_wicks@yahoo.com

Wieland, Ryan B. (Stacey MB) –
[(FE) PE-2007; FE-2010] Dowling: Country Chapel (LTFT ¾) 2011; Transferred from Iowa Conf 2013; Grandville 2016.<> 3140 Wilson Ave SW, Grandville 49418 (616) 538-3070. Home: 2000 Frontier Ct. SW, Wyoming 49519 (616) 258-2001. grandvillepastor@gmail.com

Wierman, Colleen A. (Brian) –
[(FL) FL-2014] Brethren: Epworth (PTLP ¼) 2011; Brethren: Epworth/Grant (PTLP ½) 11/27/2011; Grawn (PTLP ½) and Grant (PTLP ¼) Kingsley (Assoc) (PTLP ¼) 2014; Kingsley 2017.<> PO Box 395, 113 W Blair St, Kingsley 49649 (231) 263-5278. Home: 8658 Hency Rd, Kingsley 49649 (231) 263-4145. cawierman1964@gmail.com

*Wik, Carolyn S. –
[(RD) DM 2000; FD 2003] Farmington: First (deacon) 2000; **Retired 2014**.<> Home: 32850 Ten Mile Rd., Farmington Hills 48336 (248) 474-2032. carolynwik@ymail.com

Wik, Lawrence Allen (Jenny) –
[(FE) P 1993; F 1996] Detroit: Ford Memorial July 1, 1994; Canton: Cherry Hill 1998; Manchester 2005; **Lake Orion 2012**.<> 140 East Flint, Lake Orion 48362 (248) 693-6201. Home: 3691 Hi Crest, Lake Orion 48360 (248) 732-7739. larry.wik@lakeorion-umc.org

*Wiliford, Lawrence J. (Terry) –
[(OR) Retired Elder Upper New York Conf, OR 2019] **Grass Lake (LTFT ¼) 2019**.<> 449 E Michigan Ave., Grass Lake 49240 (517) 522-8040. Home: 4273 Indian Trl., Jackson 49201 (585) 409-3546. holytroubador@comcast.net

*Wiliford, Terry S. (Lawrence) –
[(OR) Retired Elder Upper New York Conf, OR 2019] **Jackson: Calvary (LTFT ½) 2019-Oct 14, 2019**.<> Home: 4273 Indian Trl., Jackson 49201 (585) 645-4554. pastorterryw@gmail.com

William, Monica L. –
[(FE) PE 2005; FE 2008] Ashton IL (Northern Illinois conference) 2004; Birmingham: First (assoc) (LTFT ½) 2009; Northville: First (assoc) (LTFT ½) 2012; **West Bloomfield 2019**.<> 4100 Walnut Lake Rd., West Bloomfield 48323 (248) 851-2330. Home: 5553 Fox Hunt Lane, West Bloomfield 48322 (248) 851-0149. pastor@westbloomfieldumc.org

Williams, Alicea Lynn (Chris) –
[(FD) PD 2006; FD 2010] Flint: Court Street (deacon) 2007; Port Huron: First (deacon) Oct 1, 2007; family leave Oct 25, 2007; transitional leave 2016; **Mount Clemens: First (deacon) Dec 12, 2016**.<> 57 S.B. Gratiot Ave., Mt. Clemens 48043 (586) 468-6464. Home 21515 Bay Hills Rd., Macomb 48044 (586) 746-4650. alwharpist30@yahoo.com

Williams, Beverley J. (Harry) –
[(FL) FL-2012] Mesick/Harrietta (DSA) 2012; Mesick/Harrietta 11/10/2012; Mesick/Harrietta/ Brethren: Epworth 12/01/2015; Climax/Scotts 2016.<> (C) PO Box 125, 133 East Maple, Climax 49034 (269) 746-4023. (S) PO Box 112, 8458 Wallene, Scotts 49088 (269) 626-9757. Home: 331 Prairie Drive, Climax 49034 (269) 438-1514. bvwllm526@gmail.com

Williams, Caleb B. (Colleen) –
[(FD) PD-2015; FD-2018] Portage: Chapel Hill (Deacon) 2015; Royal Oak: First (Deacon, Minister of Music and Arts) Sep. 1, 2016; **Transitional Leave Jan 5, 2020**.<> Home: 817 Dobbin Dr, Kalamazoo 49006 (231) 313-9005. caleb.b.williams@gmail.com

Williams, Charles A. –
[(FE) FD-1995; FE-2000] Mesick/Harrietta 1992; Belding 02/15/1997; Quincy 01/01/1999; Alden/Central Lake 2003; Keswick 2010; Leave of Absence 2011; Appointed in Other Annual Conferences (¶331.8, ¶346.1) Detroit Conference, Houghton: Grace 2013; Houghton: Grace / Painesdale: Albert Paine Memorial 2019; **Hartland 2020**.<> 10300 Maple St., Hartland 48353 (810) 632-7476. Home: 1403 Odetta, Hartland 48353 (810) 991-1032. chuckawilla@gmail.com

Williams, Jeffrey C. (Beverly) –

[(FE) D-1987; FE-1991] Center Park 08/01/1989; UM Connectional Structures (¶344.1a,c) Director, WMC Wesley Foundation 02/16/1993; New Church Start/Rockford (Assoc) 2002; White Pines New Church Start 2004; White Pines and Courtland-Oakfield 2009; Hartford 2011; Wayland 2014; **Greenville 2020**.<> 204 W Cass St, Greenville 48838 (616) 754-8532. Home: 405 W Grant St, Greenville 48838 (269) 944-9231. jeffwrev@gmail.com

Williams, Jeremy P.H. (Tamara) –

[(FE) D-1996; FE-2001] Arden 1995; Berrien Springs/Arden 1998; Traverse City: Asbury 2002; Traverse Bay 01/01/2005 (Asbury and Emmanuel merged 01/2005); Albion: First 2009; North Muskegon Community 2017.<> 1614 Ruddiman Dr, N Muskegon 49445 (231) 744-4491. Home: 2317 Marquard Ave, North Muskegon 49445 (517) 554-1836. pastorjeremywilliams@gmail.com

Williams, Karen B. (H. Lawrence) –

[(FL) PL 2003; FI 2005] Mt. Bethel 2003; Flint: Lincoln Park 2005; Waterford: Central (assoc) 2009; **Caring Covenant Group Ministry: Genesee, Thetford Center 2010**.<> (G) 7190 N. Genesee Rd., Box 190, Genesee 48437 (810) 640-2280. (TC) G-11394 N. Center Rd., Genesee 48437 (810) 687-0190. Home: 7472 Roger Thomas Dr., Mt. Morris 48458 (810) 640-3140. pastorkaren5@comcast.net

*Williams, Myron K. (Maudy) –

[(RE) D-1953; FE-1956; R-1994] Ludington (EUB) 1956; Sodus/Chapel Hill (EUB) 1960; Vicksburg 1969; Holt 1972; Hastings: First 1982; Wyoming: Wesley Park 1985; Retired 1994.<> Home: 5430 E Arbor Ave, Mesa AZ 85206 (517) 896-4788. Summer: 1743 S Stebbins Rd, White Cloud 49349 (231) 689-1689. myronmaudy@hotmail.com

*Williams, Nolan R. (Sandra) –

[(RA) D-1970; RA-2000] Coral/Amble 1966; Stanwood/Higbe 1967; Stanwood: Northland 1971; Ionia: Zion/Easton 1974; Ithaca/Beebe 10/01/1980; Niles: Wesley 1991; Retired 01/01/2000.<> Home: 4231 Embassy Dr SE, Grand Rapids 49546 (616) 957-3222. nolanraywilliams37@yahoo.com

Williams, Richard K. (Susan) –

[(RE) D-1969; FE-1972; HL-1976; FE-1977; R-2001] Benton Harbor Peace Temple (Assoc) 1971; Constantine 04/01/1973; Honorable Location 1976; Galien/Olive Branch (Ad Interim) 02/01/1977; Wolf Lake 10/01/1979; Lansing: Trinity (Assoc) 11/01/1983; Hesperia/Ferry 1985; Leave of Absence 10/01/1997; Retired 2001.<> Home: 332 Birch St, Fremont 49412 (231) 854-3005. williric@verizon.net

Williams, Tamara S.M. (Jeremy) –

[(FE) D-1987; FE-1990] Transferred from Baltimore-Washington Conf 1993; Stevensville (Assoc) 1993; Traverse City: Central (Assoc) 2002; UM Connectional Structures (¶344.1a,c) District Superintendent, Albion District 2009; Medical Leave 2017.<> Home: 2317 Marquard Ave, Muskegon 49445 (269) 967-7104. Pastortamara@hotmail.com

Williamson, Ronald Todd –

[(FL)–DSA-2016; FL-2017] Salem: Indian Mission (DSA) (LTFT ½) 01/01/2016; Bradley: Indian Mission (DSA) (LTFT ½) 01/01/2016; Salem: Indian Mission / Bradley: Indian Mission (FL) 12/01/2017.<> (SIM) 3644 28th St, Hopkins 49328 (616) 738-9030. (BIM) 695 128th Ave, Shelbyville 49344 (616) 738-9030. Home: 1146 Nicolson St., Wayland 49348 (616) 460-1918. revrtwilliamson@gmail.com

Willingham, Brian Kendall (Rhonda) –
[(PL) PL Dec 1, 2014] Dec 1, 2014 Flint: Charity, Dort Oak Park Neighborhood House; 2015 Flint Charity, Faith; 2018 Flint: Bristol (LTFT ¾); **May 1, 2019 Flint: Bristol (LTFT ½), Burton: Christ (LTFT ¼).**<> (FB) G-5285 Van Slyke Rd., Flint 48507 (810) 238-9244, (BC) 4428 Columbine Ave, Burton 48529 (810) 743-1770. Home: 1884 Springfield Street, Flint 48503 (810) 513-1407. pastorbkwillingham@gmail.com

*Willobee, Sondra Blanche (Edwin) –
[(RE) P 1979; F 1984] 1982 Detroit: Whitefield-Grace; 1985 Detroit: Whitefield-Grace ((LTFT ½); Nov 15, 1985 North Lake (LTFT ½); 1990 North Lake (LTFT ¾); 1991 Editorial Consultant, Ecumenical Theological Seminary; 1994 leave of absence; 1999 Farmington: First (assoc) (LTFT ½); 2007 South Lyon: First; **2017 Retired.**<> Home: 11553 McGregor Road, Pinckney 48169 (248) 915-8364. sondrawillobee@gmail.com

*Willson, Roberta –
[(RL) PL 2008] 2008 Iron River: Wesley; **2014 Retired.**<> Home: 203 W. Iron St., Bessemer 49911. randrwillson@charter.net

Wilsey, Melene E. –
[(FL) DSA 2015; FL 2017] 2015 Saginaw: West Michigan Avenue (DSA); **2017 Saginaw: New Heart.**<> 1802 W. Michigan Ave., Saginaw 48602 (989) 792-4689. Home: 1304 W. Stewart, Midland 48640 (989) 839-4798. pastormelene@aol.com

Wilsdon, Coleen –
[(FL) FL-2017] Morrice, Bancroft (DSA) 2017; **Morrice, Bancroft (PTLP ½) Dec 1, 2017.**<> (M) PO Box 301, 204 Main St, Morrice 48857 (517) 625-7715. (B) 101 S Beach St, Bancroft 48414 (989) 634-5291. Home: 8452 E Cole Rd, Durand 48429 (989) 413-9850. Luv2cookmom@hotmail.com

Wilson, Janet S. (Mark) –
[(FL) FL-2018] Battle Creek: Chapel Hill (assoc) 01/01/2018; **Battle Creek: Chapel Hill (assoc), Battle Creek: Christ (¾+¼) Sept. 8, 2020.**<> (CH) 157 Chapel Hill Dr, Battle Creek 49015 (269) 963-0231. (C) 65 Bedford Road N, Battle Creek 49037 (269) 965-3251. Home: 20515 Bedford Rd N, Battle Creek 49017 (269) 317-5591. pastor-janet@thehillbc.com

*Wilson, Margaret E. Halls –
[(RE) D-1984; FE-1989; R-2009] Alto/Bowne Center 1985; Niles: Portage Prairie 1989; Marshall (Assoc) 1994; Otsego 1998; Evart 2000; Grawn 2006; Retired 11/01/2009.<> Home: 615 Bay Hill Drive Apt 5, Traverse City 49684 (231) 743-0119. megarev44@gmail.com

*Wilson, Richard D. –
[(RE) D-1963; FE-1967; R-2008] Muskegon: Unity/Twin Lake 1965; Cadillac Selma Street/South Community 10/01/1966; Big Rapids Parish 11/01/1968; Howard City/Coral/Maple Hill 03/01/1971; Howard City First/Coral 1972; Lane Boulevard 1975; Muskegon Lakeside 1981; Buchanan: Faith/Morris Chapel 1987; Sodus: Chapel Hill 1996; Battle Creek Sonoma/Newton 2003; **Retired 2008**; Quincy (½ Time) 2017-2020.<> Home: 548 East Dr, Marshall 49068 (269) 781-4082. PastorMan127@yahoo.com

*Wingeier, Douglas E. –
[(RE) D-1951; FE-1954; R-2000] Transferred from Wisconsin Conf 2000; Retired 2000.<> Home: 266 Merrimon Ave, Asheville NC 28801 (828) 456-3857. dcwing@dnet.net

*Winslow, David Allen (Doribell) –
[(RE) T 1965; F 1973] 1969 All Saints Episcopal Church, Millington NJ; 1970 Marble Collegiate NY; 1971 Trinity UMC, Jersey City NJ; 1973 West Side UMC, Patterson NJ; 1975 Chaplain School, 1st Marine Air Wing FMF Pac, Japan; 1976 Chaplain NTC, San Diego CA; 1978 Chaplain, USS Worden, CG-18; 1980 Chaplain USS Reeves, CG-24; 1981 Chaplain, 1st Marine Division, FMF Pac; 1981 Chaplain, 3rd Marine Division, FMF Pac; 1982 Chaplain 1st Marine Division, FMF Pac; 1984 Chaplain Navy Station, Long Beach CA; 1987 Chaplain, 3rd Marine Air Wing, FMF Pac; 1987 Chaplain, 11th Marine Expeditionary Unit FMF Pac; 1988 Chaplain, 3rd Marine Air Wing, El Toro CA; 1991 Chaplain, USS Wichita AOR-1; 1993 Chaplain, USNS Mercy, TAH-19 and Navy Hospital, Oakland CA; 1995 USN Retired; 1997 Chaplain and Board Member, Interfaith Ministries, San Jose CA, San Jose International Airport and Disaster Service Consultant, Church World Service 1997-2000; **2008 Retired**.<> Home: 3845 Pleasant Springs Dr., Naples FL 34119 (408) 784-2850

Wisenbaugh, Jeanne Harmon –
[(OF) OF 4-1-2020, Christian Church] Oregon, Elba (DSA) (½ time) Nov. 1, 2018. **Oregon, Elba (½ time) Apr 1, 2020**.<> (O) 2985 German Rd, Columbiaville 48421 (810) 793-6828. (E) 154 S Elba Rd, Lapeer 48446 (810) 664-5780. Home: 1457 Westerrace Dr, Flint 48532 (810) 732-8123. revjeannemarie@gmail.com

Wojewski, Donald L. –
[(FL) FL Jan 1, 2005] Dec 1, 2004 Memphis: First, Lamb; Jan 1, 2005 Omo: Zion; 2005 Rose City: Trinity, Churchill; Jan 1, 2008 Rose City: Trinity (LTFT ½); 2008 Rose City: Trinity, Glennie; 2011 Standish: Community, Saganing Indian Church; 2012 Jeddo, Buel; 2013 Avoca, Jeddo, Ruby; Dec 21, 2017 Jeddo, Avoca; Caseville 2018; **Caseville (60%), Hayes (40%) 2020**.<> (C) 6490 Main St., Box 1027, Caseville 48725 (989) 856-4009. (H) 7001 Filion Rd., Pigeon 48755 (989) 553-2161. Home: PO Box 1027, 6474 Main St, Caseville 48725 (989) 856-2626. donaldlouis51@yahoo.com

Wolfgang, Donald W. (Jacqueline) –
[(FE) OE-2016; FE 2018] Portage: Pathfinder 2016 (Transferred from S. Georgia Conf 2018).<> 8740 S Westnedge Ave, Portage 49003 (269) 327-6761. Home: 8731 Newhouse St, Portage 49024 (912) 674-8155. BroDon@PathfinderChurch.com

*Won, Chong Youb –
[(RE) P 1991; F 1995] 1992 South Central Cooperative Ministry: Halsey, South Mundy; 1995 Warren: First (assoc); Sept 1, 1998 Lapeer: Trinity (assoc); 2002 Lincoln Park: First; 2005 Oak Grove; 2011 Algonac: Trinity, Marine City; 2012 Dearborn Heights: Stephens, Warren Valley; **Jan 1, 2015 Retired**.<> Home: 704 S. Brady St., #A, Dearborn 48124. pastorjoywon@yahoo.com

Woo, Yong Choel –
[(FE) Korean Methodist, OF Feb 1, 2009; PE 2012; FE 2014] 2008 Troy: Korean (assoc) (2012 Transferred to DAC); Jan 15, 2015 Madisonville: Korean (W OH); **2019 Kalkaska**.<> 2525 Beebe Rd., Kalkaska 49646 (231) 258-2820. Home: 2301 Shawn Rd. NW, Kalkaska 49646 (231) 258-5995. mrwoo19@gmail.com

*Wood, Gregory B. (Beverly) –
[(RE) D-1980; FE-1984; R-2015] New Buffalo/Berrien County: Lakeside 02/01/1982; Lansing: Trinity (Assoc) 1985; Manistee 1990; Portage: First 1998; Retired 2015.<> Home: 1578 Rupal St, Kalamazoo 49009 (269) 365-5101. gwood1950@gmail.com

*Woodford, Steven L. (Ann) –
[(RE) P 1996; F 1998; RE 2020] Reese 1996; school 2000; Chaplain, Spiritual Care Coordinator, Heartland Hospice (335.1) 2001; Vassar: First May 1, 2002; [called to active duty chaplaincy May 1, 2007]; Readjustment Counselor, Veterans Administration 2008; **Retired 2020**.<> Home: 4658 N. Steel Rd., Hemlock 48626 (989) 928-3845. skypilot927@gmail.com

Woolley, Marsha Marie (Charles) –
[(FE) P 1984 W.MI; F 1987] 1985 Trans. to Detroit Conf, Ypsilanti: First (assoc); Nov 1, 1991 Manchester; 1994 Ann Arbor: First (assoc); 2006 Livonia: Newburg; **2013 Northville: First**.<> 777 W. 8 Mile Rd., Northville 48167 (248) 349-1144. Home: 20490 Lexington, Northville 48167 (734) 349-1143. mwoolley@fumcnorthville.org

*Woolum, Donald –
[(RL) FL-1997; RL-2003] Mulliken / Sebewa Center 08/28/1997; Retired 2003.<> Home: 1104 Clark Rd, Lansing 48917 (517) 649-8689

Worley, Ronald L. (Shelly) –
[(PL) PL-2004] Crystal Valley/Walkerville (PTLP ½) 2004; LP w/o Appointment 12/01/2013; Muskegon: Unity (PTLP ¼) 2014-Jan. 18, 2020; **Amble 2020**.<> 15207 Howard City Edmore Rd., Howard City 49329 (231) 580-6304. Home: PO Box 254, 76 W Muskegon St NW, Kent City 49330 (616) 485-4441. revronworley@gmail.com

Woycik, Timothy S. (Chris Schwind) –
[(FE) P NY 19__; F 1986] Sept 1, 1983 Whitmore Lake: Wesley; 1993 Ortonville; 1998 Saginaw: State Street; 2003 AuGres, Twining: Trinity; **2012 Chesaning: Trinity**.<> 1629 W. Brady, Chesaning 48616 (989) 845-3157. Home: 1701 W. Brady, Chesaning 48616 (989) 845-2227. pastortim1953@yahoo.com

Wright, Christina L. –
[(FD) PD-2009; FD-2012] Deacons Appointed w/in UM Connectional Structure (¶331.1b) Advance Directives Coordinator, Cleveland Clinic 06/07/2009; Clergy Appointed to Attend School (¶326.1) University of West Georgia 08/01/2009; Deacons Appointed w/in UM Connectional Structure (¶331.1b) University of West Georgia 2015; Deacons Appointed Beyond the Local Church (¶331.1a) Chaplain, University of Michigan Health Care Systems and Missional: Royal Oak 08/10/2015; Deacons Appointed Beyond the Local Church (¶331.1a), Associate Director, Department of Spiritual Care, Michigan Medicine, University of Michigan and Missional: Royal Oak 02/01/2019.<> 1138 Lariat Loop #104, Ann Arbor 48108 (734) 936-4041. Home: 45677 Spinning Wheel Dt, Canton 48187 (617) 875-6955. cwright1223@gmail.com

*Wright, Robert Denecke (Jenneth) –
[(RE) P 1982; F 1985] 1983 Port Huron: First (assoc); 1985 Marine City; Feb 1, 1988 Bay City: Christ; 1992 Cheboygan: St. Paul's; 1994 Rochester: St. Paul's (assoc); 1999 Grosse Pointe; 2008 Flint: Court Street; **2015 Retired**; 2016 Alto, Bowne Center (LTFT ½); **Jan 1, 2019 Bowne Center (LTFT ¼)**.<> 12051 84th St SE, Box 122, Alto 49302 (616) 868-7306. Home: 10187 Mulberry Dr, Middleville 49333 (269) 205-2609. rdwcsumc@gmail.com

Wright, Timothy B. (Paula) –
[(FE) PE-2005; FE-2008] Horton Bay/Charlevoix: Greensky Hill 2005; Grand Rapids: Northlawn 2013; Gladstone: Memorial 2018, Lakeview: New Life 2019.<> 6584 W Howard City Edmore Rd, Six Lakes 48886 (989) 352-7788. Home: 8544 Howard City Edmore Rd, Lakeview 48850 (989) 352-6728. wright.tim.b@gmail.com

*Wright, William Robert (Dayna) –
[(RE) P 1980; F 1983] 1981 Lake Linden, Painesdale; Jan 15, 1985 Birmingham: First (assoc); 1990 Bad Axe: First; 2006 Sebewaing: Trinity; 2012 Port Huron: First; **2017 Retired**.<> Home: 6094 Jeddo Road, Jeddo 48032 (810) 858-7033. justwright54@gmail.com

*Wyatt, Christine Elizabeth (Robert) –
[(RD) CON 1999; FD 2002] 1993 Grand Blanc; Dec 1, 1999 Director: Skills on Wheels (LTFT ½);1999 Clarkston (deacon) (LTFT ½). 2004 Clarkston (deacon); **2015 Retired**.<> Home: 8181 Deerwood, Clarkston 48348 (248) 625-5326. deaconchris1@gmail.com

*Wylie-Kellermann, William A. –
[(RE) P 1972; F 1980; RE 2017] 1975 Greenway Non-Violent Community; 1979 Detroit: Waterman, Preston; 1981 Leave of Absence; Sept 1, 1981 Detroit: Cass Community (LTFT ½); 1988 Whitaker School of Theology, Detroit; Sept 1, 1997 Director of M.Div Program, Seminary Consortium of Urban Pastoral Education (LTFT ¾); 2006 St. Peter's Episcopal, Detroit; **2017 Retired**.<> Home: 4691 Larkins, Detroit 48210 (313) 841-7554. bwkellermann@gmail.com

Wyllys, Deane Brian (Nancy) –
[(FE) P 1981; F 1985] 1983 White Pine, Bergland, Ewen; Feb 15, 1988 Marine City; 1992 Gladwin: First; Sept 2, 2002 family leave; 2004 Commerce; **2018 Owosso: First**.<> 1500 N. Water St., Owosso 48867 (989) 725-2201. Home: 1415 N. Water St., Owosso 48867. dwyllys@sbcglobal.net

Yoo, Joonshik (Hyangmi Yoo) –
[(PE) OE 2003 Korean Methodist Church; PE 2013] May 1, 2003 Amen Korean; 2015 Korean Church of Dayton (¶346.1 W OH Conf); **Aug 1, 2019 Ann Arbor: Korean**.<> 1526 Franklin St, Ann Arbor 48103 (734) 662-0660. Home: 1811 Avondale, Ann Arbor 48103 (248) 974-5459. joonys@gmail.com

*Youells, Richard A. (Carol) –
[(RE) D-1960; FE-1963; R-1995] Silver Creek 1958; Bridgman 1963; UM Connectional Structures (¶344.1a,c) Director, CMU Wesley Foundation 1965; UM Connectional Structures (¶344.1a,c) Director, Flint Wesley Foundation 1969; Potterville/West Benton/ Dimondale 1970; South Haven: First 1974; Olivet 08/16/1979; Muskegon Heights: Temple 1989; Church of the Dunes (Assoc) 1991; Retired 1995.<> Home: 740 Clark Crossing SE, Grand Rapids 49506 (616) 243-3759. gryouells@gmail.com

Youmans, Susan M. (Dennis) –
[(FE) PE 2005; FE 2008] 2005 Caring Covenant Group Ministry: Davison (assoc); 2008 Farmington: Nardin Park (assoc); 2012 Warren: First; **2018 Lexington**.<> 5597 Main St, Lexington 48450 (810) 359-8215. Home: 7051 Greenbush Ln, Lexington 48050. smyoumans@gmail.com

Young, Melanie S. –
[(FE) D-1993; FE-1995] Weidman 1993; Muskegon: Central (Assoc) 1994; Leave of Absence 1996; Grovenburg 1997; Quincy 1998; UM Connectional Structures (¶344.1a,c) Director, Wesley Foundation Ferris State University 10/01/1998; Burr Oak (LTFT ½) 2003; Clergy Appointed to Attend School 2006; Constantine 2007; Leave of Absence 2009; Pentwater: Centenary 2014; Ovid, Middlebury (LTFT ¾) 2018; **Ovid, Middlebury (full-time) Jan 1, 2020.**<> (O) 131 Front St, PO Box 7, Ovid 48866 (989) 834-5958. (M) 8100 W Hibbard Rd, PO Box 7, Ovid 48866 (989) 834-2573. Home: 141 W Front St, Ovid 48866 (231) 301-2055. msyoung14760@gmail.com

Young, Steven R. (Kathy) –
[(FE) D-1982; FE-1985] Turk Lake 1982; Muskegon Lakeside 1987; Sparta 1993; Ithaca/Beebe 2006; Coldwater 2010; Hart 2015.<> 308 S State St, Hart 49420 (231) 873-3516. Home: 3818 Melody Lane, Hart 49420 (231) 873-4766. SYoung4152@aol.com

*Youngs, David L. (Doris) –
[(RL) PL-1976; RL-2006] Townline (LTFT PT) 03/14/1976; Bloomingdale (LTFT PT) 03/14/1976; Retired 2006; Breedsville (LTFT PT) 2007; Townline (LTFT PT) 01/03/2008-6/1/2008.<> Home: 1108 Barton St, Otsego 49078 (269) 694-9125

Yum, Jung Eun (Somi Nam) –
[(FE) FL Jan 2006; PE 2007; FE 2010] Jan 1, 2006 Troy: Korean (assoc); Jan 2, 2011 MN Conf, Woodbury: Christ Korean; **2014 Midland: First (assoc)**.<> 315 W. Larkin St., Box 466, Midland 48640 (989) 835-6797. Home: 1010 Pepperidge Ct., Midland 48640 (989) 486-9307. jeyum@hotmail.com

*Zaagman, Gayle S. (John) –
[(RL) PL-2001; FL-2002; RL-2014] Muskegon: Unity (DSA) (LTFT PT) 09/16/1999; Muskegon: Unity (LTFT PT) 02/01/2001; Reading 09/01/2001; Claybanks / Whitehall 2006; Retired 2014.<> Home: 3662 Courtland Dr, Muskegon 49441 (231) 780-3119. booger99@chartermi.net

*Zachman, Lee F. (Barbara) –
[(RE) D-1974; FE-1981; R-2010] Eaton Rapids: First (Assoc) 01/15/1977; North Adams/Jerome 1980; Martin/ Shelbyville 1984; Wyoming Park 04/16/1994; Middleville/Parmelee 1996; Parmelee (LTFT ½) 2004; Retired 12/01/2010.<> Home: 3645 Lakeshore Dr, Shelbyville 49344 (269) 397-1243. revleezachman@gmail.com

*Zawodni, Kelly-Marie [Vergowven] –
[(FL) DSA-2017; PL-2017; FL-2020] Willow (DSA) July 1-Nov 11, 2017; Willow (PTLP ½) Nov 12, 2017; **Blissfield: Emmanuel, Macon 2020**.<> (B) 215 E. Jefferson St., Blissfield 49228 (517) 486-3020. (M) 11964 Macon Hwy., Clinton 49236 (517) 423-8270.Home: 302 E. Jefferson St., Blissfield 49228 (734) 497-3560. kmzawodni@gmail.com

*Zeigler, Karl L. (Carmen) –
[(RE) T 1968; F 1970] 1964 Wheatfield, Williamston Center; 1967 Columbus OH: North Broadway (assoc); 1968 Camden, Montgomery (W.MI Conf); 1969 Price, Shepardsville (W.MI Conf); 1970 Detroit: Christ (assoc); 1972 Allen Park; 1975 Novi; 1979 Executive Director, United Methodist Foundation; Nov 1, 1988 President, Bethany Methodist Foundation; Sept 1, 1990 Leave of Absence; 1991 Richmond: First; Aug 1, 1998 Franklin Community; Nov 1, 2000 Goodrich; **2010 Retired**.<> Home: 4273 Port Austin Rd, Caseville MI 48725 (248) 904-8816. zeigler.karl@yahoo.com

*Zender, Mark E. –
[(RL) PL Jan 1, 2005; FL Jan 1, 2008; RL 2019] Jan 1, 2005 Willow (LTFT ¾); Jan 1, 2008 Willow; 2011 Canton: Cherry Hill, Denton: Faith; 2014 Britton: Grace; **2019 Retired**.<> Home: 7962 Selph Rd, Hillsboro OH 45133 (313) 690-7248. revmark zender@sbcglobal.net

Ziegler, Timothy R. (Lisa) –
[(FE) FL 2003; PE 2006; FE 2010] 2003 Ann Arbor: First (assoc); 2009 Lexington; **2013 Ann Arbor: West Side**.<> 900 S. Seventh, Ann Arbor 48103 (734-663-4164. Home: 3023 Appleridge, Ann Arbor 48103. revtimziegler@westside-umc.org

*Zienert, Ellen K. –
[(RE) PL-2005; PE-2010; FE-2013; R-2018] Chapel Hill East Lansing (DSA) 2005; Chapel Hill East Lansing (Part-Time) 11/15/2005; East Lansing Chapel Hill (LTFT ¼) and Williamston: Crossroads (LTFT ¼) 2010; St Johns: First 07/15/2012; St Johns: First (LTFT ¾) 01/01/2018; Retired 2018.<> Home: 13015 Cedar St, Charlevoix 49720 (517) 515-9500. ekzienert@gmail.com

Zimmerman, Teresa "Tina" J. (Greg) –
[(FD) PD 2010; FD 2014] Jan 1, 2012 Manchester: First (deacon); Dec 4, 2017 Manchester: First (deacon), Interim Director of Spiritual Life Chelsea Retirement Community; **2019 Associate Director of Spiritual Life Chelsea Retirement Community, Manchester Missional Charge Conference (para 331.1a)**.<> 805 W. Middle St., Chelsea 48118 (734) 433-1000. Home: 5450 Sharon Hollow, Manchester 48158 (734) 417-3117. tinajzimm@gmail.com

Zimmerman, Thomas Harold (Julie) –
[(FE) P 1986; F 1989] 1987 Ironwood: Wesley, Wakefield; 1991 Royal Oak: First (assoc); 1997 Lambertville; **2016 Saline**.<> 1200 N. Ann Arbor St., Saline 48176 (734) 429-4730. Home: 3020 Aspen Lane, Ann Arbor 48108 (419) 262-5575. tzimmerman@fumc-saline.org

Zundel, Jill Hardt (Gary) –
[(FE) P 1991; F 1995] 1992 Detroit: Zion; 1994 Hazel Park: First; 1999 Clarkston (assoc); 2006 New Baltimore: Grace; **2014 Detroit: Central**.<> 23 E. Adams, Detroit 48226 (313) 965-5422. Home: 2013 Hyde Park, #33, Detroit 48207 (313) 393-8899 RevDrJill@hotmail.com

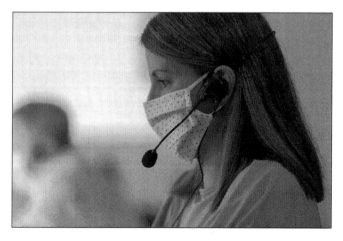

— MAC Photos

CLERGY ON HONORABLE and
ADMINISTRATIVE LOCATION

This Pastoral Record indicates appointments, but is not necessarily a pension record. The date given following each appointment represents the initial year of that appointment, with changes occurring immediately following Annual Conference unless otherwise noted. The record is maintained by the Michigan Conference Ezra Database Specialist. Correspondence can be sent to pstewart@michiganumc.org

HL=Honorable Location
RHL=Retired Honorable Location
AL=Administrative Location

*Boyd, Gordon B. –
[(RHL) trans. from Independent Assemblies of God, 1978; F 1984; HL 2015; RHL 2016] Aug., 1979 Lapeer: Trinity (assoc.); 1981 Carsonville, Applegate, Watertown; July 15, 1984 Owosso: Trinity; Oct., 15, 1987 Capac: First, Zion; 1991 Springville; Dec 1, 1992 LaPorte, Mapleton; Sep 1, 1994 North American Study Center; 1997 Counselor-Professor, Baker College, North American Study Center; Integrative Mental Health Center; 2015 Honorable Location; **2016 Honorable Location, Retired**.<> Home: 26110 Nagel, Roseville 48066 (586) 774-8293. Taccess4@yahoo.com

*Brady, William Hugh –
[(RHL) T 1961 NE OH; F 1963 NE OH; HL 1976] 1959 Clarksfield; 1961 Vickery; Sep 1963 trans to Detroit Conf, Pontiac: Central (assoc.); 1966 Four Towns; 1967 Genesee; 1970 National Council of Alcoholism, Flint; 1974 Insight, Inc.; 1976 Honorable Location; **2012 Honorable Location, Retired**

*Carruth, Hayden Kenna, Jr. (Sylvia) –
[(RHL) P 1980; F 1983; HL 1992] 1981 Decker, Elmer, Shabbona; Apr. 1982 Shabbona, Argyle, Decker; 1982 Owosso: First (Assoc.); 1984 Manchester; 1989 Hardy; Feb 15, 1992 Honorable Location; **2016 Honorable Location, Retired**.<> Home: 459 Dupont Ave, Ypsilanti 48197 (734) 434-4072. carruth1973@att.net

*Clapp, Jon Marvin (Karen) –
[(RHL) T 1961; F 1964; HL 1981; RHL 2002] 1962 Farmington Hills: Nardin Park (assoc.); 1965 Detroit: Lola Valley; 1972 Counselor, Macomb County Drug Council; 1973 Case Worker, Oakland County Juvenile Court; 1981 Honorable Location; **2002 Honorable Location, Retired**.<> Home: 2344 Eaton Gate Rd, Lake Orion 48360 (248) 391-0391. jkclapp@hotmail.com

*Crossman, Thomas A. –
[(RHL) FL-1980; FD-1983; FE-1986; HL-1991; RHL-2016] Leaton 08/16/1980; Mt Pleasant: First (Assoc) 08/01/1981; Leave of Absence 06/30/1986; Honorable Location 1991; **Honorable Location, Retired 2016**.<> Home: 687 W 204th Street #6J, New York NY 10034 (212) 567-0437. t_crossman@verizon.net

^Dempsey, Bruce W. (Anne) –
[(RHL) D-1979; FE-1983; HL-1993; RHL-2018] Edwardsburg: Hope 1981; Wolf Lake 11/01/1983; Leave of Absence 11/01/1988; Honorable Location 1993; Wolf Lake (Ad Interim) 09/01/2017-07/01/2018; **Honorable Location, Retired 2018**.<> Home: 3950 Westbrook Dr, Muskegon 49444 (616) 847-5145. bwdempsey90@gmail.com

*Draggoo, David L. –
[(RHL) D-1962; FE-1966; HL-1986; RHL-2009] Morris Chapel 1962; Sturgis (Assoc) 11/01/1964; Burr Oak 1967; Shaftsburg 1971; Perry 1971; Personal Leave 1981; Honorable Location 1986; **Honorable Location, Retired 2009**.<> Home: 9637 Jason Rd, Laingsburg 48848 (517) 651-6846. dldraggoo@wowway.com

Easlick, Robert James (LuAnn) –
[(HL) P 1986; F 1989; HL Sep 1, 2004] 1987 Calumet, Mohawk-Ahmeek; 1990 Laingsburg, Middlebury; 1993 Whitmore Lake: Wesley; 2001 incapacity leave; 2002 Blissfield: Emmanuel; **Sep 1, 2004 Honorable Location; Linden (Ad Interim) 2020**.<> 201 S. Bridge St., PO Box 488, Linden 48430 (810) 735-5858. Home: 701 Tickner, Linden 48451 (810) 397-1376. bob.easlick@hotmail.com

*Elliott, James Kyle –
[(RHL) T 1959; F 1962; HL 1964] 1954 Highland Park: Trinity (assoc.); 1957 Rochester (assoc.); 1961 Ortonville; 1963 supernumerary; 1964 Honorable Location; **2012 Honorable Location, Retired**.<> Home: Rocky Ridge Retirement Center, 3517 Lorna Rd #3, Hoover AL 35216 (205) 989-9230

*Ellis, Ronald Fred –
[(RHL)] 1971 Honorable Location; **2012 Honorable Location, Retired**.<> Home: 2516 Middlebridge Lane, Charlotte NC 28270 (980) 819-5824. ellis4445@gmail.com

*Ford, Harold G. –
[(RHL) T 1965 N IN; F 1967 N IN; HL 1974] 1965 Warsaw: First (assoc.); 1967 trans to Detroit Conf, Franklin (assoc.); 1969 Detroit: Greenfield; 1974 Honorable Location; **2013 Honorable Location, Retired**.<> Home: 6855 Dublin Fair, Troy 48098 (248) 813-0347

Frost, Mary Elizabeth Isaacs –
[(HL) P 1976; F 1980; HL 1989] 1978 Grosse Pointe (assoc.); 1980 Gaines; Oct, 1982 Midland: First (assoc.); 1986 leave of absence; **1989 Honorable Location**.<> Home: 827 Guthrie Ct, Winter Park FL 32792 (407) 227-7601. jib73@aol.com

*Hainer, C. David (Rhonda) –
[(RHL) D-1981; FE-1985; HL-1996] Bainbridge Newhope 1983; Scottdale 1983; Belding 11/01/1983; Kent City: Chapel Hill 10/01/1988; Leave of Absence 03/01/1991; Honorable Location 1996; **Honorable Location, Retired 2019**.<> Home: 163 Southmoor Shrs, Saint Marys OH 45885 (616) 706-4496. david.hainer@yahoo.com

Hall, Melvin Foster –
[(HL) P N IN; F 1981; HL 1986] 1979 trans to Detroit Conf, Detroit: Cass Avenue; 1984 leave of absence; **1986 Honorable Location**.<> Home: 1302 Honan Dr, South Bend IN 46014 (574) 532-4935. mhall520@comcast.net

*Herndon, Leon William –
[(RHL) P 19__ IA; F 19__] 1998 Oak Park: Faith (1999 trans to Detroit); Apr 1, 2004 incapacity leave; 2010 Honorable Location; **2012 Honorable Location, Retired**.<> Home: 18501 Cherrylawn, Detroit 48221 (313) 861-2733

Hill, Valerie Marie –
[(AL) D-1979; FE-1983; AL-1999] Hinchman 1981; Oronoko 1981; Bear Lake 03/01/1983; Arcadia 03/01/1983; Osseo 1985; Frontier 1985; Comstock 1989; Leave of Absence 1991; Lee Center 1996; Springport 1996; Ashton 1998; Leroy 1998; **Administrative Location 1999**.<> Home: 1527 West State St #108, Belding 48809 (616) 808-6100

*Howard, Mary Evelynn –
[(RHL) P 1971; F 1974; HL 1978; RHL 2010] 1973 Mt. Clemens: First (assoc.); 1974 New Haven: Meade; 1976 Detroit: Waterman, Simpson; 1977 Detroit: Woodmere, Simpson; 1978 Honorable Location; **2010 Honorable Location, Retired**.<> Home: PO 452541, Garland TX 75044 (972) 530–0197. bdiggs@earthlink.net

*Long, Michael E. (Jean) –
[(RHL) PE-1983; FE-1986; HL-1998; RHL-2018] Rosebush (Rosebush 3/4 Time And Clare 1/4 Time 7/1/84) (LTFT ¾) 1984; Clare (Assoc) (LTFT ¼) 1984; Rosebush 1990; Appointed In Other Annual Conferences (¶331.8, ¶346.1) Detroit Conference, Geneva Hope 1990; Grawn 1992; Somerset Center 1996; Honorable Location 1998; **Honorable Location, Retired 2018; Twin Lake (Ad Interim) (LTFT ½) Jan 5, 2020**.<> 5940 S Main St, PO Box 352, Twin Lake 49457 (231) 828-4083. Home: 1303 6th St, Muskegon 49441 (231) 645-9584. PastorMikeLong@gmail.com

*MacArthur, Terry L. –
[(RHL) PE-1974; FE-1977; HL-6/15/1985; RHL-2018] Appointed In Other Annual Conferences (¶331.8, ¶346.1) In School, Sparta/Bloomfield, OH 1974; St Johns: Salem 1976; Lowe 1976; Greenbush 1976; Three Oaks 10/16/1979; Leave of Absence 1984; Honorable Location 06/15/1985; **Honorable Location, Retired 2018**.<> Home: 17 Chemin Taverney, CH-1218 Grand Saconnex, Switzerland. tmacarthur@bluewin.ch

McKinven-Copus, Clinton E. (Laurie) –
[(HL) D-1984; FE-1987; HL-2007] South Boardman 1985; East Boardman 1985; Fife Lake 1985; West Mendon 1987; Leslie 1990; Felt Plains 1990; Leave of Absence 09/16/1991; Perry 02/01/1992; Shaftsburg 02/01/1992; Olivet 01/01/1995; Other Valid Ministries (¶344.1D) Executive Director Secom Ministries (¶335.1D) 01/01/2001; Leave of Absence 02/15/2005; **Honorable Location 2007**.<> Home: 5480 S Lakeshore Dr, Ludington 49431 (231) 723-6201. clintone@outlook.com

*McKinven-Copus, Laurie J. (Clinton) –
[(RHL) D-1984; FE-1987; HL-2005; RHL-2013] Manton 1985; Nottawa (LTFT) 1987; Leonidas 1987; Pleasant Lake 1990; Munith 1990; Personal Leave 09/16/1991; Other Valid Ministries (¶344.1D) United Methodist Community House, Church & Community Liaison 1996; Honorable Location 04/02/2005; **Honorable Location, Retired 2013**.<> Home: 5480 S Lakeshore Dr, Ludington 49431 (231) 845-9414. office@ludingtonumc.org

*McNary, Charles D. (Sandra Hoffman McNary)
[(RHL) D-1965; FE-1968; HL-1977; RHL-1995] Winn 1961; Coomer 1961; Millbrook 1961; Casnovia 1964; Kent City: Chapel Hill 1964; Kent City: Chapel Hill 1967; Bangor: Simpson 1970; Honorable Location 1977; **Honorable Location, Retired 1995;** Morris Chapel (DSA) 2002-2003.<> Home: 6117 Santa Fe Trail NE, Rio Rancho NM 87144 (269) 427-0766. charlesdmcnary@live.com

*Meredith, Thurlan E. –
[(RHL) D-1966; FE-1969; HL-1993; RHL-2008] Gladwin Parish 01/01/1960; Courtland-Oakfield 11/01/1903, Martin 1970; Shelbyville 1970; Grand Rapids: Northlawn 1976; Lake Odessa: Central 1984; Medical Leave 1986; Personal Leave 1988; Honorable Location 1993; Lowell: Snow (Ad Interim) 1995; **Honorable Location, Retired 2008**.<> Home: 541 Alles Dr SW, Byron Center 49315 (616) 785-8494. temric@peoplepc.com

*Myers, Allen C. (Janice) –
[(RHL) FE-1970; HL-1980; RHL-2016] Honorable Location 1980; **Honorable Location, Retired 2016**.<> Home: 2011 Orville St SE, Grand Rapids 49506 (616) 452-5339. amyers@eerdmans.com

*Otter II, Louis Ernest –
[(RHL) T 1961 NE OH; F 1963; HL 1971; RHL 1994] 1961 North Canton; 1962 Pavonia; 1963 trans to Detroit Conf., Kochville; 1968 Plymouth: St. Luke's; 1971 Honorable Location; **1994 Honorable Location, Retired**.<> Home: 14735 Richfield, Livonia 48154 (734) 464-3319

*Otto, Edward F. (Nancy) –
[(RHL) PE-1968; FE-1970; HL-1978; RHL-2012] Gunnisonville (Transferred from Wisconsin Conference 1969) 1969; Chapel Hill East Lansing 1969; Wacousta Community 12/15/1971; Honorable Location 10/01/1978; **Honorable Location, Retired 2012**.<> Home: 1335 S Prairie Ave #405, Chicago IL 60605 (312) 945-3966. ted@tedottogroup.com

*Porter, Robert Lewis –
[(RHL) P 1969; F 1972; HL 1980; RHL 2003] 1971 AuGres, Prescott, Turner, Twining; 1973 Britton: Grace, Wellsville; 1976 Dearborn: First (assoc.); 1978 Munising, Trenary; 1980 Honorable Location; **2003 Honorable Location, Retired**.<> Home: 2345 Oxford Apt 229, Berkley 48072 (248) 548-4016

Rafferty, Brian F. (Andrea) –
[(HL) D-1993; FE-1995; HL-2016] Burr Oak 1991; Grant 1993; Kingsley 1993; Church of The Dunes (Assoc) West Olive Area New Church Start 1999; New Foundation 2002; Cedar Springs / East Nelson 2003; Cedar Springs 2004; Williamston: Crossroads 2008; Family Leave 2010; **Honorable Location 2016**.<> Home: 244 Church Hill Downs Blvd, Williamston 48895 (517) 648-8747. brian.f.rafferty@gmail.com

*Rahn, David Philip –
[(RHL) P 1978; F 1980; HL 1988] 1978 Monroe: St. Paul (assoc); 1980 Halsey, Mt. Bethel; 1987 Caring Covenant Group Ministry: Genesee, Theford Center; 1988 honorable location; 2001 Caring Covenant Group Ministry: Fostoria, West Deerfield; **Oct 10, 2007 Honorable Location, Retired**.<> Home: 425 Old Bridge, Grand Blanc 48439 (810) 694-2725. revdavefwd@yahoo.com

Rawson, Rodney E. –
[(HL) P 1971; F 1974; HL 1979] 1973 Riley Center, Berville, West Berlin; 1976 River Rouge: Epworth; **1979 Honorable Location**.<> Home: 3615 Gillia Circle E, Bartlett TN 38135 (901) 373-3785. rerawson@aol.com

*Schark, Donald Christian (Rhonda) –
[(RHL) LP 1979; P 1983; F 1986 HL 1995] Whittemore, Prescott, Maple Ridge Presbyterian 1978-82; Azalia, London 1984; Menominee 1986; Leave of Absence Nov 15, 1991; Honorable Location 1995; **Honorable Location, Retired 2020**.<> Home: 800 11th Ave, Menominee 49858 (906) 864-3502. dschark@new.rr.com

*Scheibner, Paul K. (Elaine) –
[(RHL) D-1959; FE-1963; HL-1983; RHL-1993] Girard 1959; In School 1960; Concord 1962; Martin 1965; Shelbyville 1965; Dansville 1970; Vantown 1970; Gunnisonville 1974; Chapel Hill East Lansing 1974; Personal Leave 1978; Honorable Location 1983; **Honorable Location, Retired 1993**.<> Home: 631 Nixon Blvd, Roscommon 48653 (989) 821-9723. paul_scheibner@yahoo.com

*Silvernail, Carl G. –
[(RHL) HL 1969; RHL 1994] 1969 Honorable Location; **1994 Honorable Location, Retired.**<> Home: 6910 E Sanilac Rd, Kingston 49741. cgsil@centurytel.net

*Silvis, Donald Roy –
[(RHL) P 1964 MI; F 1966 MI; HL 1972; RHL 1996] 1964 Marcellues Circuit; 1967 Boyne City; 1969 Snover: Moore, Trinity; 1972 Honorable Location; **1996 Honorable Location, Retired.**<> Home: 230 N Jefferson, Lowell 49331

*Small, David E. (Elaine Lewis-Small) –
[(RHL) D-1982; FE-1985; HL-1999; RHL-2012] Brandywine Trinity (Niles Trinity Re-Named Brandywine Trinity 1982) 1981; Appointed In Other Annual Conferences (¶331.8, ¶346.1) Northern New Jersey Conf., Morristown Umc (¶425.1); In School, Drew University 1988; Appointed In Other Annual Conferences (¶331.8, ¶346.1) Northern New Jersey Conf: Anderson And Asbury Umcs (¶337.1) 1998; Honorable Location 1999; Appointed In Other Annual Conferences (¶331.8, ¶346.1) Pacific Northwest Conf: Nooksack Valley, Everson, Wa (Ad Interim) 2008; **Honorable Location, Retired 2012**; Paw Paw (Ad Interim) 2016; **Paw Paw (Ad Interim) (LTFT ½) Jan 1, 2020.**<> Home: 52333 Ackley Terrace, Paw Paw 49079 (269) 657-7727. desmall62@gmail.com

*Steele, Philip P. –
[(RHL) D-1964; FE-1968; HL-1971; RHL-2006] Schoolcraft 1961; Sitka 1964; Wolf Lake 1964; Other Valid Ministries (¶344.1D) Cooper UCC 1965; Portage: Pathfinder (Assoc) 05/03/1966; Coopersville 03/01/1968; Battle Creek: Birchwood 1970; Honorable Location 1971; **Honorable Location, Retired 2006**; Lane Boulevard (DSA) 10/08/2006-1/1/2007.<> Home: 5768 Comstock Ave, Kalamazoo 49048 (269) 668-3973. bro.philip.osl2@verizon.net

*Strawn, Charles Edward –
[(RHL) T 1964; F 19__; HL 1979] 1964 Kingston, Deford; 1966 Flint: Bristol; 1969 Detroit: Bethany; 1979 Honorable Location; **2012 Honorable Location, Retired.**<> Home: Amsterdam, The Netherlands. cstrawn@etrusca.net

*Tallman, Ronald William –
[(RHL) T 1966; F 1969; HL 1981; RHL 2005] 1968 Pontiac: Central (assoc.); 1971 Saginaw: Epworth; 1974 Detroit: St. Andrew's; 1981 Honorable Location; **2005 Honorable Location, Retired.**<> Home: 2914 S Scranton, S Aurora CO 80014 (303) 369-8877. ron@denvercounselor.com

Tuthill, Timothy J. (Susan) –
[(HL) D-1998; FE-2001; HL-2017] Mason: First 1993; MSU Wesley Foundation 2006; Clark Retirement Community, Chaplain, Director of Pastoral Care 2010; Clark Retirement Community, Director of Life Enrichment 2013; Clark Retirement Community, Director of Resident Services 2015; Christian Living Services, Manager of Care Resources 2016; **Honorable Location, Director of Congregational Care at GR First 2017.**<> 227 Fulton St E, Grand Rapids 49503 (616) 452-1568. Home: 2139 Glen Echo Dr SE, Grand Rapids 49545 (517) 449-4965. tim.tuthill@gmail.com

*Vermeulen, Bertram W. –
[(RHL) – D-1958; FE-1962; HL-1984; RHL-1998] Bloomingdale 1954; Three Rivers: Ninth Street 1957; Litchfield 1961; Lansing: Mount Hope (Assoc) 1965; Dewitt: Redeemer 1967; Fremont 10/15/1969; Leave of Absence 01/01/1979; Honorable Location 1984; Honorable Location, Retired 1998.<> Home: 4715 Trillium Spring Blvd Apt 112, Fremont 49412 (231) 335-2171. bvermeulen0910@sbcglobal.net

HON-ADMIN LOCATION

*Versteeg, George William –
[(RHL) T 1960; F 1963; HL 1976] 1960 school; 1962 Lambertville; 1966 Plymouth: St. Luke's; 1968 Flint: Burton; 1971 University of Detroit; 1976 Honorable Location; **2012 Honorable Location, Retired**.<> Home: 11460 Wells Rd, Petersburg 49270 (734) 854-1928. georgeversteeg@aol.com

*Vostry, Robert Melvin –
[(RHL) P 1974; F 1979; HL 1991] 1975 school; Aug, 1975 General Board of Ministries: Alaska Pipeline Chaplaincy; Oct, 1976 school; 1977 Board of Global Ministries, Alaska National Division; 1981 leave of absence; Feb 1982 Board of Global Ministries, Alaska Missionary Conference, Ketchikan; 1986 leave of absence; 1991 Honorable Location; **2018 Honorable Location, Retired**.<> Home: PO Box 523, Palmer AK 99645 (907) 715-4631. Mel_Vostry@yahoo.com

*Warren, Harvard James –
[(RHL) T 1966; F 1964; HL 1972; RHL 1994] 1966 Imlay City, Attica; 1972 Honorable Location; **1994 Honorable Location, Retired**.<> Home: 1801 SE 24th Rd Apt 119, Ocala FL 34471 (941) 747-8948

*Whited, Harold Vaughn –
[(RHL) T IN 1949; F 1951; HL 1964; RHL 1985] 1947 Cratherville; 1948 Fairview; 1950 trans to Detroit Conference, Clinton; 1956 school; Feb 1, 1957 Ann Arbor: West Side; Sep 1, 1963 sabbatical; 1964 Honorable Location; **1985 Honorable Location, Retired**.<> Home: 524 SE 14th Ct, Gresham OR 97080

*Whiting, Lawrence C. –
[(RHL) P 1971; F 1973; HL 1981; RHL 1994] 1972 Sutton; 1976 Otisville, West Forest, Otter Lake; 1977 school, Marquette University; 1981 Honorable Location; **1994 Honorable Location, Retired**.<> Home: 723 Creekwood Circle, Vassar 48768 (989) 823-8677

*Wightman, Galen Edward –
[(RHL) T 1961; F 1964; RHL 1970] 1961 Charlestown, Educational Assistant (W VA); 1962 Wolfstown, (PA Conf.); 1964 Munith; 1967 West Bloomfield; **1970 Honorable Location, Retired**.<> Home: 6005 Brookland Rd, Alexandria VA 22310 (703) 921-9447. 1orin@verizon.net

Wisdom-Long, Michelle M. (Richard Long) –
[(HL) D-1996; FE-1998; HL-2011] Kalamazoo: First (Assoc) 11/20/1998; Family Leave 2000; Pleasant Valley (LTFT ¼) 2001; Pleasant Valley (LTFT ½) 01/01/2007; Leave of Absence 2008; Kalamazoo: First (Assoc) (LTFT ½) 2010; **Honorable Location 2011**.<> Home: 6071 Thunder Bluff Rd, Kalamazoo 49009 (269) 808-0279. Revshelly@hotmail.com

*Woodside, Kenneth B. –
[(RHL) T 1966 NE; F 1968 NE; HL 1991] 1968 trans to Detroit Conf., Detroit: Christ (assoc.); 1970 Highland Park: Trinity; Nov 1976 Detroit Industrial Mission; 1978 leave of absence; 1991 Honorable Location; **2012 Honorable Location, Retired**.<> Home: 6632 Telegraph #344, Bloomfield Hills 48301 (248) 645-9898. drkwoodsideforum@aol.com

HON-ADMIN LOCATION

*Yordy, David –
[(RHL) T 1964 Rock River; F 1968; HL 1970; RHL 1994] Trans to Detroit Conf, Wesley Foundation, Flint; 1969 Director, Wesley Foundation, Northern Michigan University; 1970 Honorable Location; **1994 Honorable Location, Retired.**<> Home: 1257 Grace Dr, Sycamore IL 60178 (815) 991-9313. david@yordy.net

DSA SERVICE RECORD

This DSA Service Record indicates assignments by District Superintendents to serve on a weekly basis. The date given following each assignment represents the initial year of that assignment, with changes occurring immediately following Annual Conference unless otherwise noted. The record is maintained by the Michigan Conference Database Manager. Correspondence can be sent to khippensteel@michiganumc.org.

DSA = District Superintendent Assignment

Adkins, Theodore A. –
[DSA-2020] North Branch: First, Silverwood (DSA) (½ time) 2020.<> (NB) 4195 Huron St., PO Box 156, North Branch 48461 (810) 688-2610. (S) PO Box 556, Mayville 48744 (989) 761-7599. Home: 1506 S Townline Rd, Sandusky 48471 (810) 837-1646. gogreengowhite79@gmail.com

Angarita-Oviedo, Ricardo –
[DSA-2020] Iglesia Metodista Unida La Nueva Esperanza (DSA) 2020.<> 1005 Evergreen St SE, Grand Rapids 49507 (616) 560-4207. Home: 324 Griswold SE, Grand Rapids 49507 (734) 680-5185. vida7plena@gmail.com

Brooks, Mary D –
[DSA-2013] Paradise/Hulbert: Tahquamenon (DSA) (½ time) 2013.<> (P) 7087 N M123, PO Box 193, Paradise 49768 (906) 492-3585. (HT) 10505 Maple St, PO Box 91, Hulbert 49748. Home: 207 W Ave B, Newberry 49868 906) 293-1966. marybrooks729@gmail.com

Clark, Beverly –
[DSA-2020] North Adams, Jerome (CLM/DSA) (½ time) Jan 1, 2020. [North Adams disaffiliated 7/1/2020] <> (J) 8768 Jerome Rd, Jerome 49249. Home: PO Box 355, 216 Spink St, Hanover 49241 (517) 474-2679 beverlyjclark@frontier.com

Cori Raylene Clevenger –
[DSA-2020] Colon and Battle Creek: Newton (DSA) (¾ time) Jul 15, 2020.<> (C) PO Box 646, 224 N. Blackstone, Colon 49040 (269) 432-2783. (N) 8804 F Drive South, Ceresco 49033 (269) 979-2779. Home: 403 Maple St, Colon 49040 (936) 391-2204. pastorcori.umc@gmail.com

Cousino, Mickey Ann –
[DSA-2015; CLM-2015] Hastings: Welcome Corners (CLM/DSA) (¼ time) 2015; Nashville: Peace (CLM/DSA) (¼ time) 09/01/2015-12/31/2017; Freeport (CLM/DSA) (¼ time) 09/01/2015.<> 3185 N M43 Hwy, Hastings 49058 (517) 852-1993. Home: 1713 W Sisson Rd, Hastings 49058 (616) 765-5322. macousino1@gmail.com

Davis, Morgan William "Bill" –
[DSA-2019] Big Rapids: Third Avenue/Paris/Rodney (DSA) (¾ time) 2019.<> (TA) 226 N Third Ave, Big Rapids 49307 (231) 796-4157. (P) 109 Lincoln, Paris 49338 (231) 796-4157. (R) PO Box 14, 12135 Charles St, Rodney 49342 (231) 796-4157. Home: 1764 Kettle Lake Rd, Kalkaska 49646 (231)384-0040. wg1billd@gmail.com

Dover, Jason –
[DSA-2020] Duffield (DSA) 2020.<> 7001 Duffield Rd, PO Box 19, Durand 48449 (810) 621-3676. Home: 5222 Don Shenk Dr, Swartz Creek 48473 (810) 635-9067. dov5222@hotmail.com

Fetterly, Joseph –
[DSA-2020] Applegate, Avoca (DSA) 2020.<> (Ap) 133 W State St, Croswell 48422 (810) 633-9700. (Av) PO Box 7, Jeddo 48032 (810) 327-6144. Home: 2844 17th Ave, Port Huron 48060 (810) 982-0798. josephfet@msn.com

Gagne, Jeff –
[DSA 2020] Hermansville (DSA) 2020.<> W 5494 Second St., Hermansville 49847. Home: N14020 Co Rd. 577, Vulcan 49852 (906) 438-2252. gagnej@alphacomm.net

Gillings, Gary –
[DSA-2019] Whittemore (DSA) (¼ time) 07/01/2019.<> Box 155, 110 North St, Whittemore 48770 (989) 756-2831. Home: 205 W State St, Whittemore 48770 (989) 756-3981. gary338@centurytel.net

Harriman, Karen A. (Mark A. Harriman) –
[DSA-2020] Jeddo, Buel (DSA) (½ time) 2020.<> (J) PO Box 7, Jeddo 48032 (810) 327-6644. (B) 133 W State St, Croswell 48422. Home: 2990 Applegate Rd, Applegate 48401 (810) 633-9374. shepherdsacre@hotmail.com

Heiple, Bradley K. –
[DSA 2020] Bridgman: Faith (DSA) (¼ time) 2020.<> PO Box 414, 9156 Red Arrow Hwy, Bridgman 49106 (269) 465-3696. Home: 2909 Yankee, Niles 49120 (517) 270-1664. bkheiple@juno.com

Heldt, Christopher J. –
[DSA 2020] New Baltimore: Grace, Algonac: Trinity (DSA) (½ time) 2020.<> (NBG) 49655 Jefferson, New Baltimore 48047 (586) 725-1054. (AT) 424 Smith St., Algonac 48001 (810) 794-4379. Home: 43748 Donley Dr, Sterling Heights 48314 (586) 206-2684. cjheldt2000@yahoo.com

Henderson, Merry –
[DSA-2019] Bentley (DSA) (¼ time) 01/01/2019; Bentley, Garfield (DSA) (¼ time) 2020.<> (B) 7209 Main St, Bentley 48613, PO Box 1, Rhodes 48652 (989) 233-5529. (G) 701 N. Garfield Rd, Linwood 48634 (989) 879-6992. Home: 10601 Carr Rd, St Charles 48655 (989) 447-1874. merryyankee@aol.com

Lawrence, Devin T. –
[DSA-2019] God's Country Cooperative Parish: Grand Marais, Germfask, McMillian (DSA) 2019.<> (GM) N 14226 M-77, PO Box 268, Grand Marais 49839 (906) 494-2751. (G) 1212 Morrison St, PO Box 135, Germfask 49836 (906) 586-3162. (M) 7406 Co Rd 415, PO Box 54, McMillan 49853 (906) 293-8933. Home: 719 Garden Ave, Manistique 49854 (906) 202-3231. heydevin@hotmail.com

LePalm, Kristen –
[DSA-2020] Thomas (DSA) (¼ time) 2020.<> 504 First St., PO Box 399, Oxford 48371 (248) 628-7636. Home: 10266 E Stanley Rd, PO Box 307, Davison 48423 (810) 429-3269. lepalmkristen@gmail.com

Melton, Terry –
[DSA-2020] Pittsburg (DSA) (part-time) Feb 1, 2020.<> c/o Janet Demerly, Treasurer, 3888 W Brewer Rd, Owosso 48867 (810) 208-0648. Home: 5069 Bell Oak Rd, Webberville 48892 (517) 468-0113. tcmelton@aol.com

McClintic, Ray –
[DSA 2020] Harrison: The Gathering (DSA) (½ time) Sept 1, 2020.<>. PO Box 86, 426 N. First, Suite 106, Harrison 48625. Home: 3781 Peninsular Drive, Gladwin 48624 (989) 249-6158. raymcclintic@hotmail.com

Miller, Alexander (Sandy) –
[DSA-2003] Nottawa (DSA) (¼ time) 2003.<> 25838 M-86, PO Box 27, Nottawa 49075 (269) 467-7134. Home: 61616 Filmore Rd, Sturgis 49091 (269) 467-7134. umcnottawa1893@gmail.com

Molloy, Larry –
[DSA-2019] Mohawk Ahmeek (DSA) (¼ time) 2019.<> 120 Stanton Ave, PO Box 76, Mohawk 49950 (906) 337-2710. Home: 226 Fourth St, Eagle Harbor 49950 (906)284-4221. pastormolloy@gmail.com

Paik, Jung Du
[DSA-2020] Elsie, Shepardsville (DSA) (½+¼ time) Jul 15, 2020.<> (E) PO Box 189, 160 W Main St, Elsie 48831 (989) 862-5239. (S) 6990 Winfield Rd, Ovid 48866 (989) 834-5104. Home: 2653 N Elm St, Onaway 49765 (989) 733-8434. jdpaik@gmail.com

Pamp, George –
[DSA-1/1/2017] Kewadin: Indian Mission (DSA) (¼ time) 01/01/2017.<> 7250 Carin Hwy, Kewadin 49648 (616) 886-3579. Home: 851 W. Conway Rd, Harbor Springs 49740 (231) 838-9375. gpamp@live.com

Pease, Christine L. –
[CLM-2014] Pleasant Lake (CLM/DSA) (¼ time) 2014.<> 4815 E Territorial Rd, PO Box 82, Pleasant Lake 49272 (517) 543-5618. Home: 340 Pleasant St, Charlotte 48813 (517) 543-5618. peasechris@yahoo.com

Pinto, Michael A. (Susan) –
[DSA-2006; PL-2007; DSA-2019] Lacota (DSA) 2006; Lacota (PTLP ¼ time) 2007; Discontinued Apr 9, 2019; Lacota (DSA) (¼ time) Apr 9, 2019.<> 01160 CR 681, PO Box 7, Lacota 49063 (269) 385-4154. Home: 2321 Tamarack, Kalamazoo 49006 (269) 207-2095. m2pinto@hotmail.com

Poirier, Russell W. –
[DSA-2020] Mesick, Brethren Epworth (DSA) (½ time) 2020.<> (M) 121 S Alvin St, PO Box 337, Mesick 49668 (231) 885-1699 (BE) PO Box 177, 3939 High Bridgo Rd, Brethren 49619 (231) 477-5486. Home: PO Box 325, Onekama 49675. russ_poirier@yahoo.com

Shaffer, Janet –
[DSA-2019] Alger (DSA) (¼ time) 2019; Alger, Pinconning (DSA) (½ time) 2020.<> (A) 7786 Newberry St, Alger 48610; PO Box 167, Sterling 48659 (989) 836-2291. (P) 314 Whyte St., Pinconning 48650 (989) 879-3271. Home: 7786 Newberry St, Alger 48610 (989) 362-6536. jshaffertumc4842@gmail.com

Shimek, Stephen J. –
[DSA 2020] Three Oaks (DSA) (½ time) 2020.<> 2 Sycamore Street E, Three Oaks 49128 (269) 756-2053. Home: 112 E Sycamore, Three Oaks 49128 (269) 756-3724. sjshimek@comcast.net

Slocum, Vincent –
[DSA-2020] Lake Fenton (DSA) (¼ time) 2020.<> 2581 N Long Lake Rd, Fenton 48430 (810) 629-5161. Home: 11494 Torrey Rd, Fenton 48430 810-210-8589. vs-locum83@gmail.com

Tucker, Marcia A –
[DSA-2014] Ganges (DSA) (¼ time) 2014.<> 2218 68th St, PO Box 511, Fennville 49408 (269) 543-3581. Home: 6948 Colver, Fennville 49408 (269) 857-4797. friar.tuck2009@live.com

Veilleux, Cynthia L –
[PL-2011; FL-2015; DSA-2018] Frontier/Osseo (DSA) 11/01/2010; Bronson (PTLP ¾ time) 2011; Union City/Athens 2015; Discontinued 2018; Galien/Olive Branch (DSA) (½ time) 2018.<> (G) 200 Ellen St, PO Box 95, Union City 49094 (517) 741-7028. (OB) 123 N Clark St, PO Box 267, Athens 49011 (269) 729-9370. Home: 201 N Cleveland Ave, Galien 49113 (517) 741-9041. clveilleux@yahoo.com

Vorel, Richard –
[DSA-Jan 1, 2020] Saugatuck (DSA) (¼ time) Jan 1, 2020.<> 250 Mason St, PO Box 647, Saugatuck 49453 (269) 857-2295. Home: 2315 Forest Trail Circle, Fennville 49408 (616) 990-4717. rvorel@tpbr.com

Wagner, Melissa S. –
[DSA-2020] Fenwick, Palo, Vickeryville (DSA) (¼ time) 2020.<> (F) 235 W Fenwick Rd, Sheridan 48884 (989) 291-5547. (P) 8445 Division St, Palo 48870 (989) 291-5547. (V) PO Box 241, 6850 S Vickeryville Rd, Sheridan 48884 (989) 291-5547. Home: 10963 Sundog Trail, Perrinton 48871 (989) 682-4779. 141 Lafayette St, Ionia 48846 (616) 302-3406. melissasuewagner@gmail.com

Walters, William –
[DSA-2018] Pokagon/Berrien Springs (DSA) 2018.<> (P) 31393 Kansas St, Dowagiac 49047 (269) 683-8515. (BS) 310 W Mars, Berrien Springs 49103 (269) 471-7220. Home: 609 Rynearson St, Buchanan 49107 (269) 479-5561. wwalters1965@yahoo.com

Zinger, Gary Melvin –
[CLM-2017; DSA-2017] Carlisle (CLM/DSA) (¾ time).<> 1084 76th St SW, Byron Center 49315 (616) 878-1836. Home: 6559 Burlingame Ave SW, Byron Center 49315 (616) 890-2744. garyzinger@gmail.com

DIACONAL MINISTER SERVICE RECORD

(ACE)—Associate in Christian Education; (CCW)—Church and Community Worker; (CE)—Christian Education; (DE)—Deaconess; (SM)—Sacred Music; (WDM)—World Division Missionary; (YM)—Youth Ministry.

Status abbreviations: COM—Commissioned; CON—Consecrated; CRT—Certified.

*Brooks, Barbara Ann
[(DR) CON N GA (DE)]. Oct 14, 1994 trans. to Detroit Conf.; Oct 14, 1994 Co-operative Ministries/Church and Community Worker; 1998 Church and Community Worker/Teacher, Colegio Americano; 2007 Retired
(H) 1610 Gregory, Ypsilanti 48197 (734-547-9120)

*Caldwell, Janice
[(DR) DE COM W.MI, 1962; CRT W.MI, 1971; CON 1977; reinst (CE), 1987]. 1957 Spartansburg, SC; 1962 Chattanooga, TN; 1969 Hastings, MI; 1975 Trans. to Detroit Conf., Pontiac: Central; 1983 Voluntary Termination; 1986 Director of Christian Education, Waterford: Central; 1999 Retired
caldwellpresumc@yahoo.com
(H) 900 N Cass Lake Rd Apt 124, Waterford 48328-2385 (248-499-8272)

*Case, Jane
[(DR) CON June 1995] Organist, Napoleon UMC 1995; Retired 2011
PO Box 146, 113 West, Napoleon, MI 49261 (517) 536-8781

*Childress, Thelma (John)
[(DR) CRT, 1971; CON (CE), 1977]. 1966 Rochester: St. Paul's. 1994 Retired
(H) 1661 Bedford Square Dr., #101, Rochester Hills 48306 (248-935-7775)
(H) 610 Burgundy Dr, Madison, TN 37115-3502

*Flegal, Daphna (Gary)
[(DR) CON June 1978] Transferred from North Georgia Conf.; Director of Christian Education, Lansing First and East Lansing University, Dec. 1, 1987; Diaconal Minister of Program, Lansing First 1991; Editor of Children's Publications, General Board of Discipleship 1992; Retired 02/18/2018
(H) 610 Burgundy Dr, Madison, TN 37115-3502 (615) 885-6621

*Foster, Margaret L.
[(DR) CON June 1986] Staff Support, Dyslexia Resource Center; Retired 1999
(H) 660 Lake Dr, Altamonte Springs, FL 32701-5412

Gossett, Timothy (Katherine)
[(DM) CRT 1999]

Griffin, Diane Mary-Allen (Kevin)
[(DM) CRT 1996; CON (CE) 1997]. 1996 Director of Program and Interpretation, Board of Outdoor and Retreat Ministries; Jan 1, 1998 leave of absence; Aug 1, 1999 Iglesia Metodista de Costa Rica; Jan 14, 2003 Methodist Church of Peru, trainer of lay persons; Jan 1, 2006 Howell: First, Director of Educational Ministries
diane@howellfumc.com
(O) 1230 Bower St., Howell 48843 (517-546-2730)
(H) 247 S. Mill St., Pinckney 48169 (734-878-9414)

*Gish, George (Yoko)
[(DR) COM GBGM, 1968; CON (WDM)1983]. 1968 Fransiscan School of Japanese Studies, Tokyo; 1970 Naganuma School, Tokyo; 1973 Kyodan Information Center, Tokyo; 1998 Aoyama Gakuin University; 2003 Retired

gygishjr@iris.ocn,ne.jp

(H) 6-10-8 Minami Aoyama, Minoto-Ku, Tokyo 107-0062, Japan (03-3486-8353)

Packer, Matthew J. (Kristina)
[(DM) CON W. MI, 1999; PE 2011; DM 2016]. 1986 Farwell; 1987 St. Bartholomew's Episcopal; 1988 Flint: Central; 1990 Clare; Nov 16, 1999 transf to Detroit Conf., Fenton: Director of Music; May 1, 2006 Flushing: Director of Music; Jun 8, 2016 Surrendered Credentials; Nov 15, 2017 Fenton: Chancel Choir Director, Music Coordinator (LTFT ¼)

mpack65@yahoo.com

(O) 119 S. Leroy St., Fenton 48430 (810-629-2132)

(H) 6020 Creekside Dr., Swartz Creek 48473 (810-610-3692)

*Quick, Mary Levack
[(DR) CON (SM), 1990]. 1984 Detroit: Metropolitan 1997 Leave of Absence; 2002 Retired

marylevack@aol.com

(H) 1941 Wellesley Dr., Detroit 48203 (313-891-2861)

*Rice, Beverly (Charles)
[(DR) CRT, 1984; CON (CE), 1989]. Jan 1, 1978 Port Huron District Project Director. Jan 1, 1982 Director Skills on Wheels; Dec 31, 1997 Retired

(H) 47840 Jefferson, New Baltimore 48047 (586-949-9348)

*Denotes retired person.

— MAC Photos

DEACONESS SERVICE RECORD

*Brooks, Barbara Ann
[(DR) CON N GA (DE)]. Oct 14, 1994 trans. to Detroit Conf.; Oct 14, 1994 Co-operative Ministries/Church and Community Worker; 1998 Church and Community Worker/Teacher, Colegio Americano; 2007 Retired
(H) 1610 Gregory, Ypsilanti 48197 (734-547-9120)

*Caldwell, Janice
[(DR) DE COM W.MI, 1962; CRT W.MI, 1971; CON 1977; reinst (CE), 1987]. 1957 Spartansburg, SC; 1962 Chattanooga, TN; 1969 Hastings, MI; 1975 Trans. to Detroit Conf., Pontiac: Central; 1983 Voluntary Termination; 1986 Director of Christian Education, Waterford: Central; 1999 Retired
(H) 900 N Cass Lake Rd Apt 124, Waterford 48328-2385 (248-499-8272)

Hillman, Anne M.
Worship and Discipleship Assistant, Grand Rapids: Trinity; Detroit: Central
annem.hillman@gmail.com
(O) 23 E. Adams, Detroit 48226 (313) 965-5422

Mossman-Celestin, Valerie
U.S. Executive Director, HAPI (Haitian Artisans for Peace International.
CC: Grand Rapids: Trinity
valeriemcelestin@gmail.com
(H) 2828 Keystone Dr, Hudsonville MI 49426-7720

*Reynolds, Phoebe
Study leave. Retired
(H) 3095 Ewald Circle, Detroit 48238 (313-934-5047)

*Denotes retired person.

— MAC Photos

MISSIONARIES

MISSION PERSONNEL WITHIN
THE MICHIGAN ANNUAL CONFERENCE

Sonya Luna
General Advance #3019618

Sonya Luna's missionary status ends effective September 1, 2020. She served as Michigan Conference Hispanic/Latino(a) Missionary. She continues to serve on the Michigan Conference staff.

The Michigan Conference is no longer receiving funds for this missionary. Please select another missionary to support.

Randy Hildebrant
General Advance #982961

Serving God's County Cooperative Parish in Newberry, MI.

Randy Hildebrant is a Church and Community Worker and assigned to God's Country Cooperative Parish in the Michigan Conference Randy has served as a Church and Community worker for 13 years, serving the Rural Revitalization Project of the Elkhorn Valley District in the Nebraska Conference and the Jubilee Project, an Appalachian ministry based in Sneedville, Tennessee in the Holston Annual Conference. He has a strong commitment to rural ministry and a commitment to bring self-esteem, hope and faith to all God's children throughout the vast parish.

GLOBAL MISSION FELLOWS/US-2S

Michael Bennett
General Advance #3022617

Global Mission Fellow (2020-2022)

Serving at Wesley Foundation of Kalamazoo; began service August 17, 2020.

Michael W. Bennett III is a Global Mission Fellow with the United Methodist General Board of Global Ministries, engaged in a two-year term of service. He was commissioned in August 2020.

The Global Mission Fellows program takes young adults ages 20-30 out of their home environments and places them in new contexts for mission experience and service. The program has a strong emphasis on faith and justice. Global Mission Fellows become active parts of their new local communities. They connect the church in mission across cultural and geographical boundaries. They grow in personal and social holiness and become strong young leaders working to build just communities in a peaceful world.

Michael is from Lakeland, Florida. He is a member of the Wesley Fellowship of Florida Southern College, Lakeland, in the Florida Annual Conference. He holds a Bachelor of Science Degree in Political Economy and Business and Free Enterprise with minors in Religion and Economics and Finance from Florida Southern College. While in school, he was a member of Wesley Fellowship and served in various leadership roles in campus ministries.

Michael's earliest memories come from the church. "I grew up in the church, I learned in the church, I cried in the church, and I encountered God in the church," he said. "Because I had spent so much of my childhood in the church, I knew a lot of Scripture, but I was never taught how to apply the Scripture."

When Michael started being sexually abused at age 12, he thought that God was allowing it to happen and that because his prayers didn't seem to make a difference, he must not be very faithful. However, as a young adult, he started seeing the gospel in a fresh way and learned how much God really loves him.

"Through meeting with the campus minister," he said, "my faith has been strengthened. I stepped out in faith and began to share my story of my childhood sexual abuse with youth from around the United States. God really started to work in this area of my life. My prayer through college was that God would teach me to forgive like Jesus did, so that I could move past the emotional and spiritual baggage that came with the six years of sexual abuse.

"I identify as a Christian, a follower of Christ, but have also embraced my identity as a sexual abuse survivor. My experience with and triumph over childhood sexual abuse has shaped my faith and has made me a better servant to the gospel of Jesus Christ. The Lord has used the story of my faith journey to inspire others to open up about their individual experiences with sexual abuse and have led them to resuming their faith journeys."

The call to mission, Michael said, "has been a long journey of wrestling with God." For years, he planned to become a lawyer. "I had the grades and the experience to pursue this dream," he explained, "but one day, the Lord completely removed this desire from my heart." Driving through his childhood neighborhood, he realized that God did not call him to live an ordinary life.

"A crucial part to responding to this call to mission," he said, "was that this was act of faith and service rather than a last resort that I was forced to accept. I was not going to go into ministry because I wanted to but because my faith called me to. No matter where God sends me, God's will, still being perfect, will be done."

Emily Burns
General Advance #3022426

Global Mission Fellow/US-2 (2018-2020)

Serving at Sunnyside UMC in Kalamazoo; service ending around August 1, 2020.

Emily Burns (was) a Global Mission Fellow with the United Methodist General Board of Global Ministries, engaged in a two-year term of service with the Michigan Annual Conference. She was commissioned in August 2018.

Emily is from Ohio and a member of the Community Methodist Church in Circleville, a congregation of the West Ohio Annual Conference. She holds a Bachelor of Arts degree in economics from Ohio Wesleyan University in Delaware, Ohio. She has worked as a peer mentor at Ohio Wesleyan and a servant leader intern at Freedom Schools of the Church for All People in Columbus.

"My call to mission has not been dramatic; it has become a 'gut feeling' or a sense of the natural next step. It feels more like a thread that has been woven through my classes, jobs, and relationships that has led me toward and into a life of mission."

Lauren Norton
Advance # 3022515

Global Mission Fellow/US-2 (2019-2021)

Serving at Motor City Wesley & Motown Mission in Detroit

Lauren Elizabeth Norton is a Global Mission Fellow with the United Methodist General Board of Global Ministries, engaged in a two-year term of service. She was commissioned on Aug. 23, 2019.

Born in Conyers, Georgia, Lauren is a member of Carrollton First United Methodist Church, North Georgia Annual Conference. She holds a Bachelor of Science degree in early childhood education from the University of West Georgia, Carrollton. She has worked in the children's ministry program and as an office assistant at her church, as well as in the food-service industry.

Active in church since eighth grade, Lauren said, "My faith truly kicked off during my sophomore year of college. Becoming involved in a local church taught me that life was never meant to be about me. It is about serving others. Through Carrollton First UMC, I have been given opportunities to connect with so many people and built life-changing relationships. My faith has become the most important part of my life, and I would not be where I am without the grace and love of God. Through the Global Mission Fellows program, I will continue to serve with people to help make disciples as I grow as a disciple. I truly believe that my calling in life is to act justly, love mercy and walk humbly with God."

Emily Palm
Advance # 3022618

Global Mission Fellow/US-2 (2020-2022)

Serving at NOAH Project, Detroit; began service on August 17, 2020.

Emily K. Palm is a Global Mission Fellow with the United Methodist General Board of Global Ministries, engaged in a two-year term of service. She was commissioned in August 2020.

Emily is from Rockford, Illinois. She is a lifelong member of Christ United Methodist Church, Rockford, in the Northern Illinois Annual Conference. She holds a Bachelor of Science degree, with a psychology major and a biology minor, from Wisconsin Lutheran College in Milwaukee.

"I am passionate about missions and helping people in need," Emily said. "I have experience working with youth and at-risk populations, as well as extensive mission work. When faced with stress or adversity, I have learned to use mindfulness, meditation and prayer, which have helped me to take care of myself better and, ultimately, become a better leader."

Kathryn Sappington
Advance # 3022516

Global Mission Fellow/US-2 (2019-2021)

Serving at First United Methodist Church in Kalamazoo, MI

Kathryn Anne Sappington is a Global Mission Fellow with the United Methodist General Board of Global Ministries, engaged in a two-year term of service. She was commissioned on Aug. 23, 2019.

Born in Tupelo, Mississippi, Kathryn is a member of Rolling Fork United Methodist Church, Mississippi Annual Conference. She studied child development at Delta State University, Cleveland, Mississippi, and elementary education at Itawamba Community College, Fulton, Mississippi. She has worked as an intern, Delta State Wesley Foundation; a youth minister, St. Luke United Methodist Church, Cleveland; and a summer intern, Delta Grace, Sunflower, Mississippi.

Volunteering for community-outreach programs as a child and youth, Kathryn didn't realize God was leading her into the future. "I thought I was just having fun," she admitted. "Recently, I was praying about my future and pleading with God to show me what to do."

Jinnia Siironen
General Advance #3022429

Global Mission Fellow/US-2 (2018-2020)

Serving at The NOAH Project in Detroit, MI; service ending around August 1, 2020.

Jinnia Siironen (was) a Global Mission Fellow with the United Methodist General Board of Global Ministries, engaged in a two-year term of service with the Michigan Annual Conference. She was commissioned in August 2018.

Jinnia is from Franklinville, North Carolina, where she is a member of Grays Chapel United Methodist Church in the Western North Carolina Annual Conference. She holds a degree in culinary arts from Guilford Technical Community College in Jamestown, North Carolina and has worked as a cook and in summer camping programs.

A call to mission service came to Jinnia in a "small and quiet voice," and she is excited to see how God will use her in the future.

MISSIONARIES

Asti White

General Advance #3022366

Global Mission Fellow/US-2 (2018-2020)

Serving at Wesley Foundation of Kalamazoo; service ending around August 1, 2020.

Asti Nicholas White (was) a Global Mission Fellow with the United Methodist General Board of Global Ministries, engaged in a two-year term of service with the Michigan Annual Conference. He was commissioned in August 2018.

Asti is from Grayson, Georgia, and is a member of the Trinity on the Hill United Methodist Church in LaGrange, Georgia, in the North George Annual Conference. He holds a Bachelor of Arts degree in nonprofit leadership from LaGrange College where he also traveled to the Philippines and El Salvador for service and sustainability efforts. He has served in several annual conference youth and young adult leadership programs.

His call to mission emerged along with an expanding awareness of world issues and needs that affect daily lives, such as injustice, homelessness, inadequate health care, racial tensions and poverty. "Justice, mercy and love, he says, "are all important, and, as I see the rise of injustice, I have a responsibility to uproot it."

Yeo Jin Yun

Advance # 3022513

Global Mission Fellow/US-2 (2019-2021)

Serving at Methodist Federation for Social Action (MFSA) in Detroit, MI

Yeo Jin Yun is a Global Mission Fellow with the United Methodist General Board of Global Ministries, engaged in a two-year term of service. She was commissioned on Aug. 23, 2019.

Born in South Korea, Yeo Jin is a member of Grace-Bethel United Methodist Church, Leonia, New Jersey, Greater New Jersey Annual Conference. She holds Bachelor of Arts degrees in peace and conflict studies and in ethnic and area studies, with a concentration in Asian studies, from Messiah College, Grantham, Pennsylvania. She has worked as a research/development and marketing team member, MANE Concept, and as an English-language instructor, Campus Education.

"Raised in a Christian household," Yeo Jin said, "I grew up with Jesus as a friend. Between the years singing 'Jesus Loves Me' in Sunday school and the years spent in meetings and in front of computer screens, my faith journey had its share of highs and lows." Feeling unhappy and unfulfilled in her job after college, Yeo Jin had an opportunity to attend the 2018 United Methodist Women's Assembly. "During those days in Columbus, Ohio," she said, "I was instilled with a desire to live boldly for God. My heart undeniably heard the call. A month later, I resigned and began my application for Global Mission Fellows. Now, I'm filled with an uncharacteristically high amount of confidence and a genuine excitement for what God has in store for me."

BEYOND THE MICHIGAN ANNUAL CONFERENCE

MISSION PERSONNEL IN AFRICA

Delbert and Sandy Groves

General Advance #12150Z – Delbert

General Advance #12151Z – Sandra

Serving at New Life Center in Kitwe, Zambia.

Delbert and Sandy Groves are United Methodist missionaries with the General Board of Global Ministries based in Kitwe, Zambia since August 2000. They serve at the New Life Center which offers numerous outreach and training ministries within the Provisional Annual Conference of Zambia.

David Paye Guinkpa

General Advance #15089Z

Serving as the treasurer for the Liberia Annual Conference.

David Guinkpa is a missionary with the General Board of Global Ministries of The United Methodist Church serving as the treasurer for the Liberia Annual Conference. He recently served as the mission finance/auditor for Central Africa, based in Nairobi, Kenya. Mission finance auditors work with church leaders, mission partners and institutions, and Global Ministries personnel in ensuring that funds are distributed and utilized in appropriate ways. Commissioned as a missionary in 2007, Mr. Guinkpa formerly worked in mission finance in Uganda. "As a Christian, my responsibility is to serve God, the church, and humanity," he says. "I am from a loving family that was very supportive of my work. I believe that 'God's time is the best.' We are all called to be servants and custodian of the Word of God."

Princess Jusu

General Advance #13037Z

Serving at the Women's Leadership Training Center in Monrovia, Liberia.

Princess M. Jusu is a missionary with the Board of Global Ministries of The United Methodist Church serving in Monrovia, Liberia, as an instructor at the United Methodist Women's Leadership Training Center. "I am hopeful and prayerful that my service will be one that contributes to a more positive environment and will be productive for the women and children that I can assist while on assignment."

Emmanuel and Florence Ogugua Mefor

General Advance #13990Z – Emmanuel
General Advance #13991Z – Florence

Serving as a medical doctor in Mutambara, Zimbabwe – Emmanuel

Serving as a nurse and midwife in Mutambara, Zimbabwe – Florence

Dr. Emmanuel Ufonna Mefor, a medical doctor, and Florence Ogugua Mefor, a nurse and mid-wife, are missionaries with the Board of Global Ministries of The United Methodist Church currently assigned to Mutambara, Zimbabwe.

Helen Roberts-Evans

General Advance #3021129

Serving as the director of the Department of General Education & Ministry of The United Methodist Church in Liberia.

Helen Roberts-Evans is a missionary of the General Board of Global Ministries of The United Methodist Church, serving as director of the Department of General Education and Ministry of the United Methodist Church in Liberia. Helen's work includes meeting needs in such areas as teacher training, scholarships, resources, new school construction, and school building renovation and repair. "I want to share the love of Christ with each child because I know that His love brings peace and gives strength to overcome life's challenges."

Temba Nkomozepi

General Advance #3022400

Serving at Mujila Falls Agricultural Centre in Kanyama, Zambia.

Temba Nkomozepi is a missionary with the United Methodist General Board of Global Ministries serving as an agriculturalist at Mujila Falls Agriculture Center in Kanyama, Zambia. He was commissioned in October 2017.

Temba takes part in a range of agricultural, education, and health projects, as well as church growth and development. Mujila Falls raises essential crops, such as corn, and engages in small animal husbandry, cattle and goat milking, fruit culture, tree nurseries, fish culture, and research.

MISSION PERSONNEL IN ASIA

Chin Cho
General Advance #3022047

Serving as coordinator of the United Methodist Mission in Mongolia, based in Ulaanbaatar.

Chin Cho is a missionary with the General Board of Global Ministries serving as the coordinator of the United Methodist Mission in Mongolia, based in Ulaanbaatar. He was commissioned in June 2015. As the country coordinator, Chin oversees the several aspects of ministry, working with local Mongolian United Methodist leaders and other missionaries. He engages in the training of indigenous clergy, who study at the Mongolia Trinity Bible College, where he teaches Wesleyan studies.

Debbie and Lester Dornon
General Advance #10920Z – Debbie
General Advance #10919Z – Lester

Serving as coordinator of expatriate service at Tensen Hospital in western Nepal – Debbie

Serving as senior physician at Tensen Hospital in western Nepal – Lester

Deborah Dornon and Lester Dornon, M.D., are missionaries with the General Board of Global Ministries, Tansen Hospital in western Nepal in Asia. Deborah is assigned as coordinator of expatriate services at the hospital. Lester is assigned as senior physician at the hospital. Lester and Deborah returned to Nepal and Tansen as missionaries in mid-2012, having served there from 1990 to 2002. The hospital in Tansen is related to the United Mission to Nepal, established in 1954 as a partnership between the people of Nepal and a coalition of 20 Christian organizations on four continents.

Hyo-Won Park
General Advance #3021822

Serving as a new church planter in St. Petersburg, Russia.

The Rev. Hyo-Won Park is a missionary with the General Board of Global Ministries serving as a new church planter in St. Petersburg, Russia. He was commissioned in June 2013.

Familiar with the area from time previously spent there, Rev. Park is working with the leadership of the St. Petersburg District in identifying opportunities for new congregations. Methodism returned to St. Petersburg, where it had existed prior to the Communist Revolution, with the dissolution of the Soviet Union almost 25 years ago. Likely constituents for new churches are the young people who come to the city looking for jobs and educational opportunities.

Adam Shaw

General Advance #3021347

Serving as International Linkages Coordinator for Korea at the Asia Pacific Regional Office, based in Seoul, South Korea.

Adam Shaw is a missionary with the General Board of Global Ministries of The United Methodist Church serving as the International Linkages Coordinator for Korea at the Asia Pacific Regional Office, based in Seoul, South Korea. In light of the continuing Korean Conflict, he works with various churches and community organizations to further efforts for justice and peace, to seek ways toward community and healing, and build national networks to better understand each other.

MISSION PERSONNEL IN CENTRAL AMERICA

José Roberto Peña
General Advance #14026Z

Serving as pastor at Danli Central UMC in Honduras.

The Rev. José Roberto Peña-Nazario is a missionary with the General Board of Global Ministries of The United Methodist Church assigned as Pastorate, United Methodist Mission in Honduras. He serves as pastor at Danli Central UMC and works at developing new churches and new leaders for Christ's ministry.

Mbwizu Ndjungu and Nkemba Ndjungu
General Advance #12909Z – Mbwizu
General Advance #12910Z – Nkemba

Serving the Methodist Church of Belize.

For the past 10 years Nkemba and Mbwizu Ndjungu have provided leadership in the Cameroon Initiative of The United Methodist Church. Now they leave Africa for service in Central America.

Nkemba reports in a recent email: "We have received a new assignment to serve as missionaries in Belize. We arrived September 10. The Methodist Church of Belize is part of The Methodist Church in the Caribbean and the Americas, composed of Belize, Honduras and Haiti. My task is supervising the work in the Stan Creek Circuit, to groom pastors spiritually. Mbwizu will serve as Director of Christian Education. Our prayer and hope is that you will continue to support us in this new adventure."

Kristen Brown

Kristen Brown is no longer a missionary with the General Board of Global Ministries of the United Methodist Church.

The Michigan Conference is no longer receiving funds for this missionary.

Please select another missionary to support.

MISSION PERSONNEL IN NORTH AMERICA

Paul Webster
General Advance #11865Z

Serving in agricultural mission work here in the USA and also consulting beyond our borders.

Rev. Paul L. Webster, commissioned in 1992, is a missionary with the Board of Global Ministries of The United Methodist Church who served at the Mujila Falls Agriculture Centre in Kanyama, Zambia until 2018. The projects he developed and oversaw served the needs of the poor, rural people. "As a rural development specialist, I am attacking the root causes of poverty, disease, and hopelessness through education and training in small animal husbandry, cattle and goat milking, animal traction, tree nurseries, fruit culture, gardening and fish culture at our research and demonstration station. The goal is for families who can provide balanced nutrition for themselves and an income from small-scale, family-based production." Now, Paul is applying these basic principles here in the USA. He is based in his home conference in Wisconsin.

— MAC Photos

CHURCH PASTORAL HISTORIES

In Church Pastoral Histories the dates given following each name indicate a pastoral change at the time of Annual Conference unless otherwise noted. These records begin with the pastor serving each church at the time of the 1968 EUB-Methodist merger. Questions and correspondence about Church Pastoral Histories can be sent to Kathy Hippensteel at khippensteel@michiganumc.org. Physical Address (P), Mailing Address (M), Same Address for Physical and Mailing (P/M). The state is MI in the addresses unless otherwise entered. The district the church is in appears as *[District]*.

Adrian: First UMC *[Heritage]*   adrianfumc@adrianfumc.org
(P/M) 1245 W. Maple Ave., Adrian 49221   (517) 265-5689
　　Robert P. Ward 1965-1969; Warren S. Webb (assoc) 1966-1970; Robert C. Brubaker 1969-1974; Bruce W. Garner (assoc) 1970-1973; Robert W. Boley 1974-1982; Howard C. Emrick (assoc) 1974-1975; John N. Hamilton (assoc) 1980-1981; Kenneth L. Tousley 1982-1989; Maurice D. Sharai Jr. 1989-2005; Jack R. Lancaster (assoc) 1989-Mar 31, 1992; Robert W. Boley (assoc) Sep 1, 1992-1998; Gary C. Dawes 2005-2014; Wilson A. (Drew) Hart 2014-2020; Eric A. Stone 2020-

Alba UMC *[Northern Waters]*   mance1@mancelonaumc.org
(P) 5991 Barker St, Alba 49611; (M) PO Box 301, Mancelona 49659-0301   (231) 587-8461
　　M. Helen Jackson 1968-1972; George Gierman 1972-1975; Curtis Jensen 1975-1983; Timothy Graham 1983-1990; Gary Coates 1990-Aug. 1991; Pulpit Supply Sept.-Oct. 1991; Wayne Gorsline Nov. 1991-June 15, 1992; John W. Boley June 16, 1992-1997; Carolyn C. Floyd 1997-2000; Kathryn M. Steen 2000-2007; Stephan Weinberger 2007-2010; Zawdie K. Abiade July 1-July 4, 2010; Todd Shafer (DSA) July 15, 2010; Todd Shafer Nov. 1, 2010-2017; Bryan K. Kilpatrick 2017-

Albion: First UMC *[Heritage]*   office@albionfumc.org
(P/M) 600 E Michigan Ave, Albion 49224-1849   (517) 629-9425
　　Don Baker Jan. 1966-1969; Lynn A. DeMoss 1969-1979; David S. Evans 1979-1985; Randall R. Hansen (Assoc.) 1983-1985; John W. Ellinger 1985-1990; Dean L. Francis 1990-1991; Jeanne M. Randels Aug. 1991-Oct. 15, 1998; Gregory J. Martin Dec. 1, 1998-2002; Dwayne E. Bagley 2002-2009; Jeremy PH Williams 2009-2017; Leslee J. Fritz 2017-

Alden UMC *[Norther Waters]*   aldenumc@outlook.com
(P) 9015 Helena Street, Alden 49612; (M) PO Box 130, Alden 49612-0130   (231) 331-4132
　　Leonard Yarlott 1968-1970; Paul Hartman 1970-1974; Daniel Miles 1974-1976; Chris Schroeder 1976-1982; David Cheyne 1982-1991; Wayne Gorsline (interim) July-Nov. 1991; Peter H. Shumar Nov. 1991-May 1992; Richard A. Morrison 1992-1995; Richard L. Matson 1995-2003; Charles A. Williams 2003-2010; Daniel W. Biteman, Jr. 2010-2020; Katherine C. Waggoner 2020-

Alger UMC *[Central Bay]*   pastorjimpayne@gmail.com
(P) 7786 Newberry St, Alger 48610; (M) PO Box 167, Sterling 48659-0167   (989) 836-2291
　　Byron Coleman 1969-1974; Lynn Chappell 1974-1981; Janet M. Larner 1981-1982; John J. Britt 1982-1990; Zina B. Bennett Jr. 1990-1993; Jan L. Beaderstadt 1993-Feb 15, 2000; J. Gordon Schleicher 2000-2003; Jon W. Gougeon 2003-Feb 28, 2010; James A. Payne Mar 1, 2010-June 30, 2019; Janet Shaffer (DSA) 2019- [Pinconning, Alger became 2-point charge 2020]

Algonac: Trinity UMC *[Greater Detroit]*   tumc@mich1.net
(P/M) 424 Smith St, Algonac 48001   (810) 794-4379
　　Bruce W. Garner 1967-1970; Douglas K. Mercer 1970-1974; Gary Beeker 1974-1984; David S. Stiles 1984-90; Susan B. Stiles 1986-1990; James E. Britt 1990-1992; Wayne C. Ferrigan 1992-1999; T. Bradly Terhune 1999-2002; Dennis E. Irish 2002-2011; Chong Youb Won 2011-2012; Matthew Osborne 2012-2013; Carol Floyd 2013-2014; Mary Beth BeeBe 2014-Sep 1, 2014; Donna Cartwright Sep 1, 2014-2015; John Pajak 2015-2020; Christopher J. Heldt (DSA) 2020-

Algonquin UMC *[Northern Skies]* centralumc632@sbcglobal.net
(P) 1604 W 4th Ave, Sault Ste Marie 49783; (M) 111 E Spruce St, Sault Ste Marie 49783
(906) 632-8672
Robert L. Brown 1967-1972; Theodore E. Doane 1972-1980; John C. Huhtala, Sr. 1980-1992; David M. Liscomb 1992-1993; George A. Luciani 1993-1998; James H. McLaurin 1998-Feb 1, 2001; John N. Hamilton Jun 16, 2001-2004; Steven A. Miller 2004-Nov 15, 2010; John Huhtala, Sr. (Interim) Jan 9, 2011-2011; William R. Seitz 2011-2014; Larry Osweiler 2014-2018; Victoria L Hadaway 2018-

Allegan UMC *[Greater Southwest]* secretary@allumc.org
(P/M) 409 Trowbridge St, Allegan 49010-1230 (269) 673-4236
Lester Clough 1968-1973; Paul Patterson 1973-1979; Clarence Hutchens 1979-1983; Robert L. Pumfery 1983-1990; Robert L. Wessman 1990-1999; Joseph L. Spackman 1999-2007; Robert P. Stover 2007-2012; Robert K. Lynch 2012-

Allen UMC *[Heritage]* allen.umc@aol.com
(P) 167 W Chicago Rd, Allen 49227; (M) PO Box 103, Allen 49227-0103 (517) 200-8416
Wayne Fleenor 1967-1970; Peter Kunnen 1970-1972; Morris Reinhart 1972-1974; William Johnson 1974-1977; Derryl Cook 1977-1978; M. John Palmer 1978-1982; Lloyd Walker 1982-1985; Jack Kraklan 1985-1988; Michael Baker-Streevy 1988-1995; Reva Hawke 1995-1997; Nelson Ray 1997-2000; Craig A. Pahl 2000-2014; [Jonesville/Allen became single charges 2014] Eric Iden (DSA) 2014-2015; Robert M. Hughes (DSA) 2015-2016; Clare W. Huyck (RLA) 2016-2017; Larry W. Rubingh (Ret.) 2017- [Allen, Quincy became 2-point charge 2020]

Allendale: Valley UMC *[Midwest]* mbistayi@valleychurchallendale.org
(P/M) 5980 Lake Michigan Dr, Allendale 49401
[new church start 2009] Matthew Bistayi 2009- [chartered 9-22-2013]

Alma UMC *[Mid-Michigan]* office@almaumc.com
(P/M) 501 Gratiot Ave, Alma 48801-1708 (989) 463-4305
George Elliott 1967-Nov. 1975; Donald Scranton Dec. 1975-1981; Charles D. Grauer 1981-1989; David S. Yoh 1989-1995; Phillip J. Friedrick 1995-2012; Melanie J. Baker July 15, 2012-2013; Deborah S. Thomas 2013- ; Zachary D. McNees (Assoc.) 2019-2020; Lori J. Sykes 2020-

Almena UMC *[Greater Southwest]* office@almenaumc.com
(P/M) 27503 County Road 375, Paw Paw 49079-9425 (269) 668-2811
Raymond Carpenter 1966-1977; Philip Steele 1977-1980; C. Nesseth 1980-1981; Dean Francis 1981-1985; Beverly Gaska 1985-1987; Billie R. Dalton 1987-1995; Claudette K. Haney 1995-1996; Carol Newman (Assoc.) 1995-1996; Carol A. Newman 1996-2002; Anthony C. Shumaker 2002-2003; Cindy E. Holmquist 2003-Dec. 31, 2005; Donna J. Keyte Jan. 1, 2006-2019; [Gobles / Almena became a circuit 2019] Lawrence James French 2019-2020; [Almena became single station 2020] Leonard R. Schoenherr 2020-

Alpena: First UMC [Northern Water] pastor@alpenafumc.org
(P/M) 167 S Ripley Blvd, Alpena 49707 (989) 354-2490
Verle J. Carson 1965-1972; Louis Ellinger 1972-1975; Merton W. Seymour 1975-1983; Clive H. Dickins 1983-1995; Kenneth L. Christler 1995-2000; Kenneth E. Ray Aug 1, 2000-2003; David A. Diamond 2003-2006; Eugene K. Bacon 2006-2016; Susan E. Platt 2016-2018; Seok Nam Lim 2018

Amasa: Grace UMC *[Northern Skies]* cumc@up.net
(P) 209 Pine St, Amasa 49903; (M) PO Box 27, Crystal Falls 49920-0027 (906) 875-3123
W. Frederick Worth 1961-1971; Frank Bishop 1971-1974; Edward C. Weiss 1974-1985; Nancy G. Sparks 1985-1993; Paul J. Mallory 1993-Jan 1994; Stephen Rhoades Feb 1, 1994-2000; Elbert P. Dulworth 2000-2004; Stephen E. Rhoades 2004-2011; Nathan T. Reed 2011-2015; Steven T. Sudduth 2016-Feb 6, 2018; Reed P. Swanson Feb 7-Jun 30, 2018; Vicky Prewitt (DSA) 2018-

Amble UMC *[Midwest]*   andyhollander122@yahoo.com
(P) 15207 Howard City Edmore Rd, Howard City 49329; (M) PO Box 392, Howard City 49329
(231) 580-6304
   Albert Rill 1968-Nov. 1971; Larry Dekema Jan. 1972-1975; Joseph Shaw 1975-1979; John Gurney
   1979-Nov. 8, 1981; David England Oct. 1, 1982-1984; Ben Lester 1988-1995; Mark Mitchell (DSA)
   1995-July 31, 1999; Charles W. Fullmer (DSA) Aug. 1, 1999-Oct. 31, 2001; Bryan Schneider-
   Thomas Nov. 1, 2001-2009; Anne W. Riegler Aug. 15, 2009-2017; Andrew Benjamin Hollander
   (DSA) 2017-Nov. 30, 2017; Andrew Benjamin Hollander (LTFT) Dec. 1, 2017-2020; Ronald L.
   Worley 2020-

Ann Arbor: First UMC *[Heritage]*   tina@fumc-a2.org
(P/M) 120 S State St, Ann Arbor 48104   (734) 662-4536
   Hoover Rupert 1959-1972; L. Burlin Main (assoc) 1958-1970; Kendall W. Cowing (assoc) 1959-
   1973; Joseph A. Pia (assoc) 1960-1962; Melbourne Johnson (assoc) 1963-1969; Fred B. Maitland
   (assoc) 1970-1983; Donald B. Strobe 1972-1990; Kenneth R. Colton (assoc) 1973-1975; E. Jack
   Lemon (assoc) 1976-1978; Gerald R. Parker (assoc) 1978-1986; P. Thomas Wachterhauser (assoc)
   1983-1997; Russell L. Smith (assoc) 1986-1994; Alfred T. Bamsey 1990-2000; Marsha M. Woolley
   (assoc) 1994-2006; Sherry Parker (assoc) 1995-1997; David A. Eardley (assoc) 1997-2000; Rony
   S. Hallstrom (assoc) 1997-1998; Stanley McKinnon (assoc) 1998-Nov 30, 1998; John E. Harnish
   2000-2005; Michael Mayo-Moyle (assoc) 2001-Jan 31, 2003; Timothy R. Ziegler (assoc) Jul 16,
   2003-2009; J. Douglas Paterson 2005-2018; Joanne R. Bartelt (assoc.) 2006-2009; Robert H. Roth,
   Jr. (assoc.) 2009-2014; Nancy S. Lynn (assoc.) 2010-2018; Nancy S. Lynn 2018- ; Nicolas R
   Berlanga (assoc.) 2018-

Ann Arbor: First UMC - Green Wood Campus *[Heritage]*
(P) 1001 Green Rd, Ann Arbor 48105; (M) 120 S State St, Ann Arbor 48104
   J. Douglas Paterson 2005-2018; Joanne R. Bartelt (assoc.) 2006-2009; Robert H. Roth, Jr. (assoc.)
   2009-2014; Nancy S. Lynn (assoc.) 2010-2018; Nancy S. Lynn 2018- ; Nicolas R Berlanga (assoc.)
   2018-

Ann Arbor: Korean UMC *[Heritage]*   pastor.hjcho@gmail.com
(P/M) 1526 Franklin St, Ann Arbor 48103   (734) 662-0660
   Yohan Choi 1980-1981; Woo-Hyun Jung 1981-1988; Jae (John) H. Lee 1988-Mar 15, 1992; Isaac
   Y. Shin Apr 1, 1992-2010; Steven H. Khang (assoc) 2007-2014; Hyun Jun Cho 2010-July 31, 2019;
   Joonshik Yoo Aug 1, 2019-

Ann Arbor: West Side UMC *[Heritage]*   westside@westside-umc.org
(P/M) 900 S 7th St, Ann Arbor 48103-4769   (734) 663-4164
   Milton H. Bank 1968-1975; Wallace Robinson (assoc) 1968-1970; King W. Hanna (assoc) 1970-
   1972; Duane E. Snyder (assoc) 1972-1974; Frank A. Cozadd 1975-1982; W. Cardwell Prout (assoc)
   1976-1986; Elwood J. Berkompas 1982-1995; Nancy A. Woycik (assoc) 1987-Jul. 31, 1990;
   Jacqueline E. Holdsworth (assoc) 1991-1995; Gary L. Sanderson 1995-1999; Eric Hammer (assoc)
   1995-1999; Tracy N. Huffman 1999-2013; Frederick P. Cooley (assoc) 2001-2006; W. Vincent
   McGlothlin-Ellers (assoc) 2006-2008; Wilson (Drew) Hart (assoc) 2008-2014; Timothy R. Ziegler
   2013-

Applegate UMC *[East Winds]*   ngenoff@rocketmail.com
(P) 4792 Church St, Applegate 48401; (M)133 W State St, Croswell 48422   (810) 633-9700
   Wallace Zinnecker 1969-1971; Max D. Weeks 1971-1973; John E. Naile 1973-1985; Mary F. Neil
   1985-1987; J. Gordon Schleicher 1987-1991; Darrel Tallman 1991-1994; Victor L. Studaker 1994-
   2000; Emerson W. Arntz 2000-2002; Maureen V. Baker 2002-2007; James E. Barnett 2007-2013;
   Nicholas K. Genoff 2013-Dec 31, 2018; Ellen O. Schippert Jan 1, 2019-2020; [Applegate, Avoca
   became 2-point charge 2020] Joseph Fetterly (DSA) 2020-

Arbela UMC *[Central Bay]* bruce.malicoat@gmail.com
(P) 8496 Barnes Rd, Millington 48746; (M) PO Box 252, Millington 48746   (989) 793-5880
Richard A. Turner 1965-1971; Arthur V. Norris 1971-1976; Paul L. Amstutz 1976-1982; Keith B.
Colby 1982-1985; Ronald Figgins Iris 1985-Aug. 31, 1991; Max D. Weeks Sept. 1, 1991-1994;
Thomas F. Keef 1994-Dec 31, 1995; Kenneth R. Andrews Jan 1, 1996-Dec 1, 1998; David P. Rahn
Jan 1, 1999-Dec 1, 1999; Calvin H. Wheelock Dec 16, 1999-2006; Bruce Malicoat Nov 1, 2006-
2016; T. Bradley Terhune 2016-Sept 30, 2017; Dainel J. Wallington Nov 1, 2017-2018; Gloria
Haynes (Ret.) 2018-

Arcadia UMC *[Northern Waters]* blumc316@gmail.com
(P) 3378 Division, Arcadia 49613; (M) PO Box 72, Arcadia 49613-0072   (231) 864-3680
Stephen Hubbell 1967-1969; Richard Matson 1969-1971; Ken Curtis 1971-March 1975; Raymond
Roe April-June 1975; Gordon Spalenka 1975-1980; Donald Vuurens 1980-1983; Valerie Hill 1983-
1985; John Backoff 1985-1989; William Carr 1989-1993; Pulpit Supply July-Nov. 1993; Arthur C.
Murphy Dec. 1, 1993-1999; Mark D. Anderson Feb. 1, 2000-2006; William F. Dye 2006-2011;
Roberta W. Cabot 2011-2014; Jane D. Logston 2014-Aug. 31, 2018 [Bear Lake / Arcadia became
signle point charges 11-1-2018]; Kenneth D. VanderLaan (DSA) May 1-Dec 1, 2019

Arden UMC *[Greater Southwest]* orr6148@aol.com
(P) 6891 US Highway 31, Berrien Springs 49103; (M) 6891 M 139, Berrien Springs 49103
(269) 429-4931
Frederick Fischer 1965-1970; Harrison Harnden 1970-1972; Gordon Spalenka 1972-1975; Wayne
Gorsline 1975-1980; John Moore 1980-1988; Jesse Schoebell 1988-1995; Jeremy P.H. Williams
1995-2002; Dominic A. Tommy 2002-2006; James W. Stilwell 2006-2009; [Portage Prairie/Arden
two-point charge 2009] O'Ryan Rickard (RLA) 2009-Feb 9, 2020 [Arden single-point charge 2014]

Arenac Cnty: Christ UMC *[Central Bay]* arenacchristumc@gmail.com
(P) 3322 E Huron Rd, AuGres 48703; (M) PO Box 145, AuGres 48703   (989) 876-7449
Stephen N. Meeks (w/Twining: Trinity) 1967-1971; Robert Porter (w/Twining: Trinity) 1971-1973;
Dale E. Brown (w/Twining: Trinity) 1973-1979; Gilbert James MacDonald (w/Twining: Trinity) 1979-
1985; Lillian G. Richards (w/Twining: Trinity) 1985-1993; Lillian G. Richards 1993-1995; Priscilla J.
Seward 1995-1996; Douglas Coone 1996-2000; Margery A. Schleicher 2000-2003; Timothy S.
Woycik 2003-2012; Marcel A. Lamb 2012-2013; Donald Wichert 2013-2019; (AuGres merged with
Christ and new name.) James A. Payne 2019-

Armada UMC *[East Winds]* armadaumc@yahoo.com
(P) 23200 E Main St, Armada 48005; (M) PO Box 533, Armada 48005   (586) 784-5201
Edger M. Smith 1965-1970; Donald W. Brown 1970-1972; Elmer J. Snyder 1972-1974; Ira L. Wood
1974-1975; Robert D. Schoenhals 1975-1983; Robert Thornton 1983- 2000; Jean R. Snyder 2000-
Sep 1, 2002; Dianna L. Rees 2003-2011; Curtis Clarke Nov 12, 2011-2019; Christopher G.L. Titus
2019-

Ashley UMC *[Mid-Michigan]* abgumc@gmail.com
(P) 112 N New St, Ashley 48806; (M) PO Box 7, Ashley 48806-0007   (989) 862-4392
Wayne Sparks 1966-1970; William Cox 1970-1972; Marjorie Matthews June-Sept. 1972; Joseph
Dudley Sept. 1972-1973; Miriam DeMint 1973-1975; Emmett Kadwell 1975-Oct. 1978; John Ritter
Oct. 1978-1980; Mark Johnston 1980-1982; Donald McLellan 1982-1984; Arthur R. Turner 1984-
1990; Glenn C. Litchfield 1990-1996; Robert J. Besemer Sept. 1, 1996-1999; Jana L. Jirak
1999-2003; Diane L. Gordon 2003-2006; Jon L. Pohl 2006-2011; Mona J. Dye 2011-Sept. 30, 2017;
[Ashley/Bannister realigned with Pompeii to become Ashley/Bannister/Pompeii charge 2016] Zella
Marie Daniel (DSA) Oct. 3, 2017-Dec. 31, 2018; Zella Marie Daniel Jan. 1, 2019-

Athens UMC *[Greater Southwest]*   athensumc@att.net
(P) 123 Clark St, Athens 49011; (M) PO Box 267, Athens 49011-0267   (269) 729-9370
  Garold L. Simison Sept. 1965-1969; James Gerhardt 1969-1970; Dwight Benner 1970-1972; John
  Bauer 1972-Jan. 1974; Gary Kintigh Feb. 1974-1977; Walter Rothfuss 1977-1978; Wendy S. Pratt
  1978-Dec. 1979; Terry Howard Dec. 1979-1980; Richard Young Aug. 1980-1986; Robert G.
  Woodring 1986-1987; David Minger Sept. 1987-1991; Sandra J. Gastian 1991-Dec. 31, 2010; Allen
  Pebley (DSA) date?-2011; Robert D. Nystrom (1/4 time) 2011-2012; [Union City / Athens became
  two-point charge 2012] Seung Ho Baek (1/4 time) 2012-2015; Cynthia L. Veilleux 2015-2018; James
  Palaszeski 2018- [Union City and Athens realigned to become UnionCity/Athens charge 2018]

Atherton UMC *[East Winds]*   athertonumc@gmail.com
(P/M) 4010 Lippincott Blvd, Burton 48519   (810) 742-5644
  Emil E. Haering 1967-1975; Donald W. Joiner 1975-Dec. 1977; Charles R. Marble Jan. 1978-1985;
  James R. McCallum 1985-Sept. 1, 1987; Grant A. Washburn Sept. 1, 1987-1993; Bruce L. Billing
  1993-2011; Gregory E. Rowe 2011-2016; Sang Yoon (Abraham) Chun 2016-

Attica UMC *[East Winds]*   atticamethodist@gmail.com
(P/M) 27 Elk Lake Rd, Attica 48412   (810) 724-0690
  Harvard J. Warren 1969-1972; H. Reginald Cattell 1972-1974; Dale L. Vorman 1974-1977; Bufford
  C. Coe 1977-1983; Margaret H. Rodgers-West 1983-1988; Zina Braden Bennett, Jr. 1988-1990;
  James R. Rupert 1990-Sep 30, 1995; Dennis Madill Nov 16, 1995-Sep 8, 1998; Clifford J.
  Schroeder, III Feb 1, 1999-2007; Alonzo Vincent 2007-2008; Margaret E. Bryce Aug 1, 2008-2013;
  Ronald W. Rouse 2013-2018; Robert D Nystrom 2018-

Auburn UMC *[Central Bay]*   auburnumc@sbcglobal.net
(P/M) 207 S Auburn, Auburn 48611   (989) 662-6314
  Harold D. Dakin 1967-1972; Arthur R. Parkin 1972-1977; John E. Marvin (interim); Phillip D. Miles
  1977-1980; Joseph H. Ablett 1980-1985; Donald P. Haskell 1985-1992; James D. Weiss 1992-
  1993; Lawson D. Crane 1993-2009; Duane M. Harris 2009-2018; Robert D Nystrom 2018-

Augusta: Fellowship UMC *[Greater Southwest]*   augustafellowshipumc@gmail.com
(P) 103 N. Webster, Augusta 49012; (M)PO Box 337, Augusta 49012-0337   (269) 731-4222
  Marvin Rosa 1967-Feb. 1972; Richard Cobb March 1972-1976; Matthew Walkotten Aug. 1976-Sept.
  1977; Herbert Lowes Feb. 1978-Dec. 1983; Robert Tomlinson Feb. 1984-87; Lloyd Hansen 1987-
  1988; Nelson Ray 1988-May 1993; Sue Gay 1993-2007; Nelson Hall 2007-2013; Jennifer J. Wheeler
  2013-Jan. 16, 2017; Scott M. Bouldrey Jan. 18, 2017-

Avoca UMC *[East Winds]*   juliekrauss@hotmail.com
(P) 8905 Avoca Rd, Avoca 48006; (M) PO Box 7, Jeddo 48032-0007   (810) 327-6144
  John Thomas 1969-1972; Stephen Chapko 1972-1977; Merle M. Nichols 1977-1978; Darrel Tallman
  1978-1988; Victor L. Studaker 1989-1994; Robert D. Chapman 1994-Oct 15, 2000; Robert I. Kreger
  2001-2003; Donna J. Osterhout 2003-2007; Nicholas J. Genoff 2007-2013; Donald L. Wojewski
  2013-2018; Julie Krauss 2018-2020; [Applegate, Avoca became 2-point charge 2020] Joseph
  Fetterly (DSA) 2020-

Avondale UMC *[Northern Waters]*
(P) 6976 14 Mile Rd, Evart 49631; (M) PO Box 388, Evart 49631-0388
  Edward R. Jones 1967-1969; Walter Easton 1969-1971; Daniel L. Reedy 1971-1972; H. Howard
  Fuller 1973-1975; Laurence Waterhouse June-Oct. 1975; Stanley Hayes Oct. 1975-March 1984;
  Gerald Welsh 1984-1990; Donald L. Buege 1990-Jan. 2006; Jon Pohl Jan. 15 - June 30, 2006;
  Jean A. Crabtree (DSA) Nov. 5, 2006-July 2007; Russell Morgan (DSA) July 8, 2007-2012; Kara
  Lynne Burns (CLM) July 22, 2012-2014; TBS

Azalia UMC *[Heritage]* christopherbutson@live.com
(P) 9855 Azalia Rd, Azalia 48110; (M) PO Box 216, Milan 48160-0216 (734) 529-3731
John McNaughton 1968-1969; Gary R. Imms 1969-1976; John J. Landon 1976-Mar. 1978; James B. Lumsden - Mar. 1978-Dec. 1978; D. Byron Coleman Dec. 1978-1982; Mildred M. Hiner 1982-1984; Donald C. Schark 1984-1986; David W. Purdue 1986-1991; William Michael Clemmer (interim Jun-Aug, 1991); Diana K. Goudie Sep. 1, 1991-Aug 31, 1994; William Michael Clemmer Sep 1, 1994-Feb 16, 2003; Richard E. Burstall Mar 1, 2003-2007; Edward L. Tam 2007-Oct 31, 2007; Ruth A. McCully Nov 1, 2007-Nov 15, 2009; Courtney D. Williams Nov 16, 2009-Dec 31, 2013; Christopher Butson Jan 1, 2014-2019; Beatrice S. Alghali 2019-

Bad Axe: First UMC *[East Winds]* office@badaxefumc.org
(P/M) 216 E Woodworth St, Bad Axe 48413 (989) 269-7671
Jack E. Giguere 1969-1971; Byron G. Hatch 1971-1972; Ross N. Nicholson 1972-1977; Kenneth R. Colton 1977-1978; David A. Stout 1978-1990; William R. Wright 1990-2006; Gregory E. Rowe 2006-2008; Mary Jean Love 2008-Dec 1, 2010; Donna J. Cartwright (interm) Jan 1., 2011-2011; Philip Tousley 2011-2020 [Ubly Regional Church 2018; Bad Axe: First / Minden City / Ubly formed Bad Axe Cooperative Parish 07/01/2019] Timothy G. Callow 2020-

Baldwin: Covenant Community UMC *[Northern Waters]* ljball6@hotmail.com
(P) 5330 S M-37, Baldwin 49304; (M) PO Box 250, Baldwin 49304-0250 (231) 745-3232
Rebecca Neal Niese 1984-1988; Dale Peter Ostema 1988-Jan. 1993; Reva Hawke May 1993-1995; Mary S. Brown 1995-Oct 15, 1998; David A. Cheyne Jan. 16, 1999-June 30, 1999; Nelson Hall 1999-2005; Karen J. Sorden 2005-2012; James A. Richie 2012-Jan. 31, 2015; [Baldwin: Covenant Community / Chase-Barton became cross-district circuit 2015] Lyle J. Ball (LTFT) 2015-

Bancroft UMC *[Mid-Michigan]* bancroftmorricepastor@gmail.com
(P) 101 S Beach St, Bancroft 48414; (M) PO Box 301, Morrice 48857-0301 (989) 634-5291
Lawrence C. Brooks 1969-1970; Meldon E. Crawford 1970-1975; Thomas E. Hart 1975-Aug. 1980; Willard A. King Sept., 1980-March 15, 1985; Raymond D. Field 1985-1988; Katherine J. Rairick 1988-1990; Philip D. Voss 1990-Jul 31, 1997; James M. Mathews Aug 1, 1997-Sep 30, 2001; Frederic G. Heath Oct 1, 2001-2003; Richard B. Brown 2003-2005; Jeremy T. Peters 2005-2008; Jeremy P. Benton 2008-2011; Patricia Elliott 2011-2015; Robert Forsyth Dec 1, 2015-Mar 31, 2017; Terry A Euper Apr 1-Jun 30, 2017; Coleen Wilsdon 2017-

Bangor: Simpson UMC *[Greater Southwest]* simpsonumcbangor@gmail.com
(P/M) 507 Joy St ,Bangor 49013-1123 (269) 427-7725
Wayne C. Reece Oct. 1966-1970; Charles D. McNary 1970-1977; Lawrence D. Higgins 1977-1981; Robert C. Carson 1981-1984; Morris J. Reinhart 1984-1987; Robert E. Tomlinson 1987-1989; James E. Hodge 1989-1994; Sandra B. Hoffman 1994-2007; Thomas A. Davenport 2007-2016; Mona K. Joslyn 2016-

Bannister UMC *[Mid-Michigan]* abgumc@gmail.com
(P/M) 103 E Hanvey St, Bannister 48807 (989) 862-4392
Wayne Sparks 1966-1970; William Cox 1970-1972; Marjorie Matthews June-Sept. 1972; Joseph Dudley Sept. 1972-1973; Miriam DeMint 1973-1975; Emmett Kadwell 1975-Oct. 1978; John Ritter Oct. 1978-1980; Mark Johnston 1980-1982; Donald McLellan 1982-1984; Arthur R. Turner 1984-1990; Glenn C. Litchfield 1990-1996; Robert J. Besemer Sept. 1, 1996-1999; Jana L. Jirak 1999-2003; Diane L. Gordon 2003-2006; Jon L. Pohl 2006-2011; Mona J. Dye 2011-Sept. 30, 2017; [Ashley/Bannister realigned with Pompeii to become Ashley/Bannister/Pompeii charge 2016] Zella Marie Daniel (DSA) Oct. 3, 2017-Dec. 31, 2018; Zella Marie Daniel Jan. 1, 2019-

Bark River UMC *[Northern Skies]*   1chris1cross1@att.net
(P/M) 3716 D Rd, Bark River 49807   (989) 634-5291
   David M. Liscomb 1969-1973; Walter David 1973-1978; Jack Lancaster 1978-1980; Michael L.
   Peterlin 1980-1991; Christine J. Bergquist 1991-2020; [Escanaba: First, Bark River became 2-point
   charge 2020] Ryan C. Edwardson 2020-

Barnard UMC *[Northern Waters]*   cappahl@netzero.net
(P) 15645 Klooster Rd, Charlevoix 49720; (M) PO Box 878, East Jordan 49727   (231) 547-5269
   Stanley Hayes 1967-1970; Lester Priest 1970-Jan. 1974; Daniel Minor April 1974-1981; Betty Burton
   1981-1982; Glenn Britton 1982-1983; Supply pastor 1983-Aug. 1985; Robert Bellairs Aug. 1985-
   1996; Bernard W. Griner (DSA) 1996-1997; Eugene L. Baughan 1997-2002; D. Michael Maurer
   2002-Nov. 10, 2008; Ralph Posnik (DSA) Nov. 23, 2008; Ralph Posnik Nov. 15, 2009-2014; Craig
   A. Pahl 2014-

Barry County: Woodland UMC *[Mid-Michigan]*   kdsmith868@gmail.com
(P/M) 203 N Main St, Woodland 48897-9638   (269) 367-4061
   Claude Ridley 1968-1972; Richard Erickson 1972-1976; Clinton Bradley-Galloway 1976-1981;
   Constance Hefflefinger 1981-1984; Glenn Wegner 1984-1987; Robert Kersten 1987-1991; Carl
   Litchfield 1991-2000; Geraldine M. Litchfield (Assoc.) Jan. 1993-1994; Soo Han Yoon Aug. 1, 2000-
   Jan. 31, 2001; Robert E. Smith Feb. 1, 2001-Dec. 31, 2003; Mary Schippers-DeMunter (DSA)
   2004-2008; James E. Fox (DSA) July 22, 2008-2011; Gary L. Simmons (1/4 time) 2011-2015;
   [Barry-Eaton Cooperative Ministry 2013] Kathleen Smith (RLA) 2015-

Barryton: Faith UMC *[Midwest]*   brookscornersparish@gmail.com
(P/M) 95 E Marion Ave, Barryton 49305   (989) 382-5431
   Thomas Tarrant 1967-March 1969; Isaac Sayers March 1969-1975; Altha Barnes 1975-1979; Lyle
   Heaton 1979-1984; Jean Crabtree 1984-1990; Pulpit Supply 1990-1991; Arthur C. Murphy 1991-
   Dec. 1, 1993; William W. Dornbush Jan. 1-June 30, 1994; Timothy J. Miller 1994-1995; Kevin
   Parkins 1995-1998; Robert E. Smith July 16, 1998-Feb. 1, 2001; James E. Cook (DSA) 2001-Feb.
   28, 2002; Merged with Chippewa Lake Jan. 1, 2002 (See Barryton-Chippewa Lake for current
   listings); Brian R. Bunch Mar. 1, 2002-2005; name changed to Barryton Faith 2005; Ronald DeGraw
   Aug. 1, 2005-Nov. 6, 2005; James L. Breithaupt Mar. 15, 2006-Oct. 19, 2009; Joseph Beavan Jan.
   15, 2010-2014; Bryan K. Kilpatrick 2014-2017; Raymond Johnson (DSA) (LTFT 1/4) Dec. 1, 2017-
   June 30, 2018; TBS [Barryton: Faith became single station 2017]

Bath UMC *[Mid-Michigan]*   pastor@unitedch.com
(P) 13777 Main St, Bath 48808; (M) PO Box 308, Bath 48808-0308   (517) 641-6551
   Alma Glotfelty 1968-1970; Tom Daggy 1970-1971; Clarence Keith 1971-1976; Dan Miles June-
   Dec. 1976; Tom Peters Feb. 1977-1993; Raymond D. Field 1993-1998; Nancy L. Besemer
   1998-2003; Thomas L. Truby Oct. 15, 2003-2006; Beatrice K. Robinson 2006-2007; Mark G.
   Johnson 2007-2015; Matthew D. Kreh 2015-

Battle Creek: Baseline UMC *[Greater Southwest]*   baselineum@gmail.com
(P/M) 9617 Baseline Rd, Battle Creek 49017-9766   (269) 763-3201
   Richard Budden 1966-1969; Paul Mazur 1969-Sept. 1972; Charles Grauer Sept.-Dec. 1972; Marvin
   Iseminger Jan. 1973-1977; Harold Diepert 1977-1978; Sharon Rader 1978-1981; Arthur Turner
   1981-1984; Gregory J. Martin Sept. 1984-1987; Robert Woodring Sept. 1987-1990; Joy Jittaun
   Moore 1990-Aug. 15, 1993; Maurice E. Walworth, Jr. Nov. 1, 1993-1996; Glenn R. Wegner 1996-
   2004; Virginia L. Heller 2004-2011; Peggy J. Baker 2011-2018; Margaret Mallory Sandlin 2018-2020;
   [BC: Baseline became single station 2020]

Battle Creek: Chapel Hill UMC *[Greater Southwest]*   office@thehillbc.com
(P/M) 157 Chapel Hill Dr, Battle Creek 49015-4631   (269) 963-0231
  Royce Robinson 1968-1973; William J. Richards 1973-May 1976; Heath T. Goodwin May 1976-1981; Donald Scranton 1981-1985; Joseph J. Bistayi 1985-1993; James M. Gysel 1993-2011; Robert J. Mayo 2011-2013; Chad M. Parmalee 2013- ; Janet Sue Wilson (Assoc.) Jan. 1, 2018- [Battle Creek: Birchwood / Battle Creek: Trinity UMC merged with Battle Creek: Chapel Hill 07-01-2018]

Battle Creek: Christ UMC *[Greater Southwest]*   BCChristUMC@comcast.net
(P/M) 65 Bedford Rd N, Battle Creek 49037-1837   (269) 965-3251
  Gaylord Howell 1966-1973; Chester Erickson 1973-1978; Morris Bauman 1973-Jan. 1983; Kenneth Vaught Jan. 1983-1986; B. James Varner 1986-July 1992; John Charter Nov. 1992-Jan. 1, 1999; Bruce R. Kintigh Jan. 1, 1999-2007; Carolyn A. Robinson-Fisher 2007-2011; Scott M. Bouldrey 2011-2015; Brian E. Steele 2015-2018; [BC: Christ / BC: Washington Heights became a two-point charge 2017] Crystal C. Thomas 2018-2020; Carolyn Robinson-Fisher Jul 1-22, 2020; [BC: Christ became single station 2020] Janet Sue Wilson Sept. 8, 2020-

Battle Creek: Convis Union UMC *[Greater Southwest]*   convisunionumc@gmail.com
(P/M) 18990 12 Mile Rd, Battle Creek 49014   (269) 965-3787
  Howard McDonald 1968-1973; Willard Gilroy 1973-1979; Dennis Paulson 1979-Apr. 1983; Linda D. Stoddard May 1983-Dec. 1991; Larry W. Rubingh Jan. 1992-1997; Lewis A. Buchner 1997-2001; David L. Litchfield 2001-2006; Sueann Hagan 2006-2017; Eric Iden (DSA) Aug. 1, 2017-Dec. 31, 2017; Andrea L Johnson Jan. 1, 2018-2020; [Bellevue, BC: Convis Union became 2-point charge 2020] Margaret M. Sandlin 2020-

Battle Creek: First UMC *[Greater Southwest]*   jharveyclark@firstumcbc.org
(P/M) 111 E Michigan Ave, Battle Creek 49014   (269) 963-5567
  John Tennant 1966-Jan. 1973; David Lee Miles (Assoc.) 1967-1971; Charles Fry Jan. 1973-1978; Howard Lyman 1978-1982; Neil Bintz July-Nov. 1982; Merle Broyles (interim) Nov. 1982-Jan. 1983; Dale Brown Jan. 1983-1993; Ron L. Keller 1993-1998; Karen S. Wheat 1998-2002; William P. Myers, Jr. 2002-Apr. 15, 2007; Donald R. Ferris 2007- ; Billie R. Dalton Mar. 1, 2009-Mar. 5, 2014; David L. Morton (Ret.) Mar. 5-June 30, 2014; Marshall C. Murphy 2014- ; Scott M. Bouldrey 2014-2015; Douglas W. Vernon (Assoc.) (Ret.) 2015-2016; Michael T. Conklin (Ret.) 2016-2018; Linda J. Farmer-Lewis (Ret.) 2018-2019; Susan Jo Arnold Trowbridge 2019-

Battle Creek: Maple UMC *[Greater Southwest]*   mapleumc@yahoo.com
(P/M) 342 Capital Ave NE, Battle Creek 49017   (269) 964-1252
  Donald Sailor 1966-1972; Jack Baumgart 1972-1980; Curtis Strader 1980-1986; David L. Morton 1986-1996; Lynn W. Wagner 1996-2001; Charles D. Farnum 2001-2006; Theresa Little Eagle Sayles 2006-2008; Linda D. Stoddard (Ret.) 2008-

Battle Creek: Newton UMC *[Greater Southwest]*   NewtonChurch@aol.com
(P/M) 8804 F Drive South, Ceresco 49033   (269) 979-2779
  Howard Moore May 1968-1970; Ray Grienke 1970-Jan. 1974; Ray McBratnie Jan. 1974-1976; Kenneth Curtis 1976-1981; Harry Johnson 1981-1985; Gary Kintigh 1985-1993; Charles M. Shields 1993-1995; Michael Baker-Streevy 1995-Nov. 16, 1999; Charles Edward Rothy 2000-2003; Richard Duane Wilson 2003-2008; Nancy G. Powers 2008-2012; Sally Harrington (Ret.) 2012-2016; Robert J. Freysinger 2016-2019; Connor James Bailey (DSA) 2019-2020; Cori R. Clevenger (DSA) Jul 15, 2020-

Battle Creek: Washington Heights UMC *[Greater Southwest]*
washingtonheightsumc@gmail.com
(P/M) 153 Wood St N, Battle Creek 49037-2271   (269) 968-8773
Donald Grant 1967-1972; John L. Thompkins Sept. 1972-1975; Pulpit Supply 1975-1976; Clifton Bullock 1976-Feb. 1991; Herbert Griffin (Assoc.) 1990-1993; Russell McReynolds 1991-1996; Howard (Rick) McKire 1996-Feb. 27, 1997; Curnell Graham 1997-2002; James A. Richie 2002-2009; Sandra V. Douglas (1/4 time) 2009-2011; Marshall C. Murphy 2011-2017; Brian E. Steele 2017-2018; [BC: Christ / BC: Washington Heights became a two-point charge 2017] Crystal C. Thomas 2018-2020; [BC: Washington Hts became single station 2020] Cleora French 2020-

Bay City: Grace UMC *[Central Bay]*   office@baycitygracechurch.org
(P/M) 4267 2 Mile Rd, Bay City 48706   (989) 684-1101
[New Church Start Jul 1, 2013] Leonard Clevenger 2013-2015; Eric Kieb 2015-

Bay City: Grace – East Campus *[Central Bay]*   office@baycitygracechurch.org
(P) 510 Fremont St, Bay City 48708; (M) 4267 2 Mile Rd, Bay City 48706   (989) 684-1101
[Bay City: Grace merged with Bay City: Fremont Jun 30, 2016] Eric Kieb 2016-

Bay Port UMC *[Central Bay]*   bayporthayesumc@att.net
(P/M) 836 N 2nd St, Bay Port 48720   (989) 656-2151
Donald W. Brown 1965-1970; Louis E. Reyner 1970-1975; Richard Andrus 1975-1979; Frederick P. Cooley 1979-1984; Randy A. Chemberlin 1984-1986; Alger T. Lewis 1986-1992; S. Douglas Leffler 1992-1994; Norman R. Beckwith 1994-1998; Barbra Franks 1998-2000; Alan W. DeGraw 2000-2003; Douglas E. Mater 2003-2010; Bruce L. Nowacek 2010-2012; Karl L. Zeigler 2012 (interm)-Dec 31, 2012; Brian K. Johnson Jan 1, 2013-2016; Matthew D. Chapman 2016-2020; [Sebewaing: Trinity, Bay Port became 2-point charge 2020] Heather M. Nowak 2020-

Bear Lake UMC *[Northern Waters]*   blumc316@gmail.com
(P) 7861 Main St, Bear Lake 49614; (M) PO Box 157, Bear Lake 49614   (231) 864-3680
Stephen Hubbell 1967-1969; Richard Matson 1969-1971; Ken Curtis 1971-March 1975; Raymond Roe April-June 1975; Gordon Spalenka 1975-1980; Donald Vuurens 1980-1983; Valerie Hill 1983-1985; John Backoff 1985-1989; William Carr 1989-1993; Pulpit Supply July-Nov. 1993; Arthur C. Murphy Dec. 1, 1993-1999; Mark D. Anderson Feb. 1, 2000-2006; William F. Dye 2006-2011; Roberta W. Cabot 2011-2014; Jane D. Logston 2014-Aug. 31, 2018; [Bear Lake / Arcadia became single charges 11-1-2018] Cynthia Corey (DSA) Nov 18, 2018; Cynthia Montague-Corey Jan 1, 2020-

Beaverton: First UMC *[Central Bay]*   beavertonumc@gmail.com
(P/M) 150 W Brown St, Beaverton 48612   (989) 435-4322
A. H. Keesler 1967-1970; Zina B. Bennett Jr. 1970-1975; Vernon Wyllys 1975-1979; Bruce C. Hatch 1979-1986; Janet M. Larner 1986-1991; David K. Stewart Sr. 1991-Jul 31, 2000; Frederick LaMere Aug 1, 2000-2002; Linda Jo Powers 2002-2009; Lynn F. Chappell 2009-

Beebe UMC *[Mid-Michigan]*   pastorgarysimmons@gmail.com
(P) 2975 N. Baldwin, Ithaca 48847; (M) 327 E Center St, Ithaca 48847
Wayne Sparks 1968-1970; Larry Uhrig 1970-1971; Ralph Kline 1971-Sept. 1974; Supply pastor Sept. 1974-1976; David Nelson 1976-Sept. 1980; Nolan Williams Oct. 1980-1991; David McBride 1991-2006; Steven R. Young 2006-2010; Cynthia Greene 2010-2015; Gary L. Simmons 2015-[Ithaca / Beebe became a two-point charge 2018]

Belding UMC *[Midwest]* beldingu@att.net
(P/M) 301 Pleasant St, Belding 48809 (616) 794-1244
   Ross E. Tracy 1966-1972; Eugene A. Lewis 1972-1977; Richard A. Strait 1977-1981; Ellen A. Brubaker 1981-1983; William D. Carr July-Oct. 1983; C. David Hainer Nov. 1983-Oct. 1988; Theodore F. Cole Oct. 1988-1991; Nathaniel W. Johnson 1991- Aug. 31, 1996; Charles A. Williams Feb. 15, 1997-Jan. 1, 1999; Connie Shatz 1999-2012; [Turk Lake / Belding became two-point charge 2012] Kimberly A. DeLong Aug. 15, 2012-2013; [Greenville First, Turk Lake/Belding Cooperative Parish 2013] Kimberly A. DeLong (Deacon) 2013-2015; Stephen MG Charnley 2013-2014; Stephen F. Lindeman 2013-2014; Donald E. Spachman 2014- ; Eric Mulanda Nduwa (Assoc.) Feb. 15-Aug. 1, 2015 [cooperative parish re-named Flat River Cooperative Parish 2015]; Joseph K. Caldwell (CLM/DSA) Aug. 1, 2015-2016; Donna Jean Sperry 2016-

Bellaire: Community UMC *[Northern Waters]*
(P) 401 N. Bridge St, Bellaire 49615; (M) PO Box 235, Bellaire 49615 (231) 533-8133
   James Lavengood Sept. 1965-Sept. 1969; Gerald Welsh Oct. 1969-1976; Alan Volkema 1976-1977; Garth Smith 1977-1981; David Litchfield 1981-1987; Gordon Spalenka 1987-1991; Richard A. Powell 1991-1998; D.S. Assignment 1998; Mary S. Brown Oct. 16, 1998-2009; Carl Q. Litchfield 2009-2013; Peggy A. Boltz 2013-July 16, 2014; Eric M. Falker Sept. 24, 2014-2019; Daniel J.W. Phillips 2019-

Belleville: First UMC *[Heritage]* bellevilleumc48111@yahoo.com
(P/M) 417 Charles St, Belleville 48111 (734) 697-9288
   Allen B. Rice II 1965-1969; Charles Dibley 1969-1973; Joy E. Arthur 1973-1982; George E. Spencer 1982-1989; Mary E. Hoff (assoc) 1983-1987; Edwin C. Hoff (assoc) 1983-Jan 4, 1999; Richard O. Griffith 1989-1991; R. LaVere Webster 1991-Jun 30, 1994; David Strong Jul 1, 1994-1998; John N. Grenfell, III 1998-2007; James J. Walker 2007-2020; Mary K. Loring 2020-

Bellevue UMC *[Greater Southwest]* office@bellevueumc.org
(P/M) 122 W Capital Ave, Bellevue 49021 (269) 763-9421
   Lowell F. Walsworth 1966-1971; Laurence R. Grubaugh 1971-1973; Milton J. Tenhave 1973-1977; David L. Johnston 1977-May 1983; James William Schoette May 1983-1988; William P. Sanders 1988-Feb. 1996; Mark E. Thompson 1996-2004; Virginia L. Heller 2004-2011; Peggy J. Baker 2011-2018; Margaret M. Sandlin 2018- [Bellevue, BC: Convis Union became 2-point charge 2020]

Bentley UMC *[Central Bay]* bentleyumc@live.com
(P) 7209 Main St, Bentley 48613; (M) PO Box 1, Rhodes 48652-0001 (989) 233-5529
   (With Sterling and Alger) Byron Coleman 1969-1974; Lynn Chappell 1974-1981; Janet M. Larner 1981-1982; John J. Britt 1982-1990; Zina B. Bennett Jr. 1990-1993; Jan L. Beaderstadt 1993-1995; (Single point charge) Charles Cerling 1995-2000; David LaBeau 2001-2009; John Tousiuck Nov 8, 2009-2011; Cheryl L. Mancier 2011-Oct 31, 2016; David LaBeau (DSA) Dec 1, 2016-Dec 31, 2018; Merry Henderson (DSA) Jan 1, 2019- ; [Bentley, Garfield became 2-point charge 2020]

Bergland UMC *[Northern Skies]* aa8yf@yahoo.com
(P) 108 Birch, Bergland 49910; (M) PO Box 142, Bergland 49910-0142 (906) 988-2533
   Zina Bennett 1966-1970; Lloyd Christler 1970-1972; James Hilliard 1970-1971; Lawrence Brooks 1971-1975; Roger Gedcke 1972-1979; Lillian Richards 1971-1976; Wayne E. Sparks 1975-1980; Myra Sparks 1976-1980; Ed Hingelburg 1979-1981; Robert Thorton 1981-1983; Deane Wyllys 1983-1987; Charles H. West 1987-1993; Margaret H. West 1987-1993; Earleen VanConant 1993-1997; Clarence VanConant 1993-1997; Timothy C. Dibble 1997-2000; Cherrie A. Sporleder 2000-Jun 15, 2002; Theodore A. Trudgeon 2003-2019; [White Pine Community / Ewen / Bergland three-point charge 7-1-2019] Rosemary R. DeHut 2019-

Berrien Cnty: Lakeside UMC *[Greater Southwest]*　　　　　geolawton@csinet.net
(P) 14970 Lakeside Rd, Lakeside 49116; (M) PO Box 402, Union Pier 49129　　　(269) 469-8468
　Robert Carson 1958-1964; Laurence R. Grubaugh 1964-1968; John Bullock 1968-1974; Robert
　Pumfery 1974-1979; Pulpit Supply 1979-1981; Charles Tooman 1981-1982; Gregory Wood 1982-
　1985; B. Gordon Barry 1985-1988; Steven Pearson 1988-1990; Ruth Haynes-Merrifield 1990-1995;
　Sherri L. Swanson 1995-Sept. 1, 1999; George W. Lawton (DSA) Sept. 1, 1999-2001; George W.
　Lawton (PL) 2001-2007; George W. Lawton (RLA) 2007-Sept. 2, 2019; George W. Lawton (RLA)
　Dec. 1, 2019-2020; Brenda L. Ludwig 2020-

Berrien Springs UMC *[Greater Southwest]*
(P/M) 310 W Mars St, Berrien Springs 49103　　　　　　　　　　　　(269) 471-7220
　David Lutz, March 1967-1969; William A. Wurzel 1969-Feb. 1975; Dennis Buwalda March 1975-
　Sept. 1978; Gaylord Howell Sept. 1978-1983; Curtis Jensen 1983-1987; Edward & Priscilla Seward
　1987-March 1990; Ross Bunce Jr. (Interim) 1990-1991; Wayne H. Babcock 1991-1998; Jeremy
　P.H. Williams 1998-2002; Dominic A. Tommy 2002-2006; Cynthia M. Parsons 2006-2012; [Berrien
　Springs / Hinchman / Oronoko became three-point charge 2012] Jane D. Logston (part-time) 2012-
　2014; [Berrien Springs/Pokagon became a 2-point charge 2014] Brenda E. Gordon 2014-2018;
　William Walters (DSA) 2018-

Beverly Hills UMC *[Greater Detroit]*　　　　　　　　　　　　admin@bhumc.org
(P/M) 20000 W 13 Mile Rd, Beverly Hills 48025　　　　　　　　　　　(248) 646-9777
　Robert Boley 1961-1970; Howard Childs 1970-1974; William Verhelst 1974-1979; John W. Bray
　1979-1989; Scott Wilkinson 1989-1995; Samuel V. White, III 1995-Nov 24, 1996; Juanita J.
　Ferguson 1997-1998; Stephen K. Perrine 1998-2003; John K. Benissan 2003-Jul 31, 2008; David
　E. Huseltine Aug 1, 2008-2013; Suzanne Walls 2013-2015; Anthony J. Ballah 2016-

Big Rapids: First UMC *[Midwest]*　　　　　　　　　bigrapidsfirstumc@gmail.com
(P/M) 304 Elm St, Big Rapids 49307　　　　　　　　　　　　　　　(231) 796-7771
　James E. Leach 1965-1972; J. Leon Andrews 1972-1980; Richard Johns 1980-1985; Wayne G.
　Reece 1985-1992; Marvin R. Rosa 1992-March 31, 1993; Keith W. Heifner 1993-1996; Robert E.
　Jones 1996-2004; Bobby Dale Whitlock 2004-2008; Dean N. Prentiss 2008-2011; Rebecca K.
　Morrison 2011-2019; Devon R. Herrell 2019-2020; Tae Gyu Shin 2020-

Big Rapids: Third Avenue UMC *[Midwest]*
(P) 226 N Third Ave, Big Rapids 49307; (M) 628 S Warren Ave, Big Rapids 49307　(231) 796-4157
　Richard D. Wilson 1968-1971; Lynn Chapel 1971-1979; John Buker 1979-Jan. 1981; Elaine Buker
　Jan. 1981-1986; Kendall Lewis 1986-1990; J. Robert Collins 1990-Oct. 1991; Albert Frevert (interim)
　Jan.-June 1992; David Hills 1992-1994; Kathryn M. Steen 1994-2000; Dawn A. Beamish Jan. 1,
　2001-2002; Edwin D. Snook 2002-2005; Michael A. Riegler Sept. 11, 2005-2011; Ed Milam (DSA)
　July 1-Nov. 12, 2011; Ed Milam Nov. 12, 2011-2014; David J. Cadarette Sr. 2014-April 12, 2015;
　Kimberly A. DeLong 2015-2017; Devon R. Herrell (LTFT 1/2) 2017-2019; Morgan William (Bill)
　Davis (DSA) 2019-

Birch Run UMC *[Central Bay]*　　　　　　　　　　　godopensdoors@gmail.com
(P) 12265 Church St, Birch Run 48415; (M) PO Box 277, Birch Run 48415　　　(989) 624-9340
　Peyton E. Loy 1962-1970; Gordon D. Everett Jan. 1970-1973; Thomas J. Wood 1973-1980; James
　D. Jacobs 1980-1989; Dale E. Brown 1989-1999; Sang Yoon (Abraham) Chun 1999-2005; Alonzo
　E. Vincent 2005-2007; Clifford J. Schroeder, III 2007-2013; Paul G. Donalson 2013-2015; Rey C.
　B. Mondragon 2015-2020; Laura E. Feliciano 2020-

Birmingham: Embury UMC *[Greater Detroit]*   emburyumc@yahoo.com
(P/M) 1803 E 14 Mile Rd, Birmingham 48009   (248) 644-5708
  Albert E. Hartoog 1966-1969; Timothy R. Hickey 1969-1973; James D. Parker 1973-1979; Haxton H. Patterson 1979-Dec 1981; William E. Frayer Jan 1982-Oct 1982; James A. Smith Jan. 1983-1988; Philip Seymour 1988-Sep 1, 1995; James R. Rupert Oct 1, 1995-1997; Linda J. Donelson 1997-Sep 30, 2000; Mary Lynch Mallory Feb 1, 2001-2006; Elizabeth A. Hill 2006-2010; Carter Cortelyou 2010-2013; Theodore Whitely 2013-2014; Jean Snyder 2014-2015; Karen Y. Noel 2015-2018; Jean Snyder 2018-2020; Esrom Shaw 2020-

Birmingham: First UMC *[Greater Detroit]*   office@fumcbirmingham.org
(P/M) 1589 W Maple Rd, Birmingham 48009   (248) 646-1200
  G. Ernest Thomas 1962-1972; William Lovejoy (assoc) 1960-1969; James W. Wright 1972-1982; William H. Fraser (assoc) 1967-1969; John Bunce 1968-1978 (assoc); G. Bryn Evans (assoc) 1970-1981; J. Bruce Brown (assoc) 1971-1973; Thomas H. Beaven (assoc) 1973-1979; Hal Weemhoff (assoc) 1977-1980; Douglas Vernon (assoc) 1979-1984; Robert Paul Ward 1982-1993; Evans C. Bentley (assoc) 1980-1983; Charles H. Beynon (assoc) 1983-Dec, 1995; Ronald K. Fulton (assoc) 1983-Feb. 1988; William R. Wright (assoc) 1985-1990; Juanita Ferguson (assoc) 1990-1993; Bruce Denton (assoc) 1988-1995; Bruce Petrick (assoc) 1993-1995; William Ritter 1993-2005; Matthew J. Hook (assoc.) 1995-2002; Melody P. Hurley (assoc.) 1995-1998; Mariane Meir (assoc.) 1995-1997; Linda J. Farmer-Lewis (assoc) Jun 1, 1998-Jan 1, 1999; Lisa M. McIlvenna (assoc) Sep 1, 1999-2004; Scott A. Harmon (assoc) 2002-2003; Taek H. Kim (assoc) 2002-2004; Lynn M. Hasley (assoc) 2004-Oct 1, 2008; Jeffrey S. Nelson (assoc) 2004-2009; Carl T. Gladstone (deacon) 2004-2008; John E. Harnish 2005-2013; Brian William (assoc) 2009-2012; Monica L. William (assoc) 2009-2012; Gary Haller (co-pastor) 2013-2017; Laurie Haller (co-pastor) 2013-Jul 14, 2016; Lindsey M. Hall (assoc) 2013-2020; Zack Dunlap (assoc.; Path One Internship) 2015- ; Daniel J.C. Hart (assoc) 2016-2019; Elbert Dulworth Jun 11, 2017- ; Shawn Lewis-Lakin (sr assoc) 2017- ; Susanne E. Hierholzer (assoc) 2019- ; Sarah Nadeau Alexander (deacon) 2019- ; Rachael M. Dunlap (assoc) 2020-

Blanchard-Pine River UMC *[Central Bay]*
(P/M) 7655 W Blanchard Rd, Blanchard 49310   (989) 561-2864
  Harold E. Arman 1968-1969; Leslie D. Smith 1969-1977; James C. Sabo-Shuler 1977-1980; James W. Burgess 1980-1986; M. Christopher Lane 1986-1990; Paula Jane Duffey 1990-1998; Dale A. Golden 1998-2005; Paulette G. Cheyne 2005-2006; Melody Lane Olin (DSA) 2006; Melody Olin Nov. 15, 2006-2010; Lawrence Wonsey 2010-2014; Russell D. Morgan 2014-2016; [Blanchard-Pine River became a single-point charge 2016; Shepherd / Blanchard-Pine River became 2-point charge 2017] Janet M. Larner 2017-2020 [Blanchard-Pine River / Shepherd became a single-point charges 01/01/2019] William W. Chu 2020-

Blissfield: Emmanuel UMC *[Heritage]*   pastor@emmanuel-godwithus.org
(P/M) 215 E Jefferson St, Blissfield 49228   (517) 486-3020
  Rupert H. Lindley 1961-1974; Robert N. Hicok 1974-1976; Kenneth L. Harris 1976-1981; David J. Hill 1981-1985; Mark D. Miller (assoc) 1984-May 1, 1989; Robert B. Secrist 1985-1987; Lawrence E. Van Slambrook 1987-1990; Thomas A. Davenport (assoc) 1989-Sep. 15, 1990; John N. Hamilton 1990-1995; Kevin Miles 1995-2002; Robert J. Easlick 2002-Aug 31, 2004; James G. Simmons (interm) Sep1, 2004-Nov 14, 2004; Harlan E. Sorensen Nov 15, 2004-Nov 15, 2005; Aaron Kesson 2006-2012; Lawson D. Crane 2012-Dec 31, 2013; Zachary L. Dunlap Jan 1, 2013-2015; Devin Smith 2015-2020; [Blissfield: Emmanuel, Macon two-point charge 7-1-2020] Kelley-Marie Zawodni 2020-

Blissfield: First UMC *[Heritage]*   blissfumc@gmail.com
(P/M) 201 W Adrian St, Blissfield 49228   (517) 486-4040
Floyd A. Ellison 1967-1973; Charles E. Sutton 1973-1980; Arthur V. Norris 1980-1983; Ralph H. Pieper II 1983-1989; Robert P. Garrett 1989-1994; Walter H. Miller 1994-Dec 1, 2002; Michael Mayo-Moyle Feb 1, 2003-2010; Paul G. Donelson 2010-2013; Kristen I. (Parks) Coristine 2013-2019; Gun Soo Jung 2019-

Bloomfield Hills: St. Paul UMC *[Greater Detroit]*   st.paul.bh@sbcglobal.net
(P/M) 165 E Square Lake Rd, Bloomfield Hills 48302-0669   (248) 338-8233
Sam Seizert 1965-1970; Harold Diehl 1970-1972; Douglas Trebilcock Dec.1972-1975; Roger Ireson 1975-1979; David Truran 1979-1983; Guenther Branstner 1983-1989; Pauline S. Hart 1989-1995; James E. Greer, II 1995-Nov 15, 2000; Steven Gjerstad Nov 16, 2000-2002; Alan J. Hanson 2002-2007; Robert D. Schoenhals 2007-2010; Leonard Clevenger 2010-2013; Frederick Sampson, III 2013-Dec 31, 2019; Joseph J. Bistayi (interim) Mar 15-Jun 30, 2020; Maurice R. Horne 2020-

Bowne Center UMC *[Midwest]*   rdwcsumc@gmail.com
(P) 12051 84th St SE, Alto 49302; (M) PO Box 122, Alto 49302   (616) 868-7306
Beulah Poe 1962-1971; Carter Miller 1971-1973; John Eversole 1973-1977; Keith Avery June-Oct. 1977; Albert Sprauge Oct. 1977-Jan. 1978; Herb Kinsey Jan. 1978-May 1979; Martin Fox May 1979-Oct. 1982; Herb Kinsey Oct. 1982-1983; Harold Diepert 1983-March 1985; Margaret Peterson 1985-1989; Jill Rose July-Dec. 1989; Lloyd Hansen Dec. 1989-1990; Todd Thompson 1990-1995; Bryan Schneider-Thomas 1995-2000; Dominic A. Tommy 2000-2002; Dean Irwin Bailey (Ret.) 2002-2014; Andrew Jackson (Ret.) 2014- ; Robert D. Wright (Ret.) 2016-

Boyne City UMC *[Northern Waters]*   bcbfumc@me.com
(P/M) 324 S Park St, Boyne City 49712   (231) 582-9776
R.J. McBratnie 1965-1970; Bruce Pierce 1970-Dec. 1973; Ray Grienke Jan. 15, 1974-1981; Forest Crum 1981-1983; Michael T. Conklin 1983-1989; John Backoff 1989-April 1991; Max Gladding (retired) April-June 1991; Gary D. Bondarenko 1991-2000; Carl Q. Litchfield 2000-2005; Wayne E. McKenney 2005-2014; Michael Neihardt 2014-2015; Eun Sik Poy Sept. 1, 2015- [Boyne City / Boyne Falls realigned w/ Boyne City / Boyne Falls / Epsilon 2016]

Boyne Falls UMC *[Northern Waters]*   bcbfumc@me.com
(P) 3057 Mill St, Boyne Falls 49713; (M) 324 S Park St, Boyne City 49712   (231) 582-9776
R.J. McBratnie 1965-1970; Bruce Pierce 1970-Dec. 1973; Ray Grienke Jan. 15, 1974-1981; Forest Crum 1981-1983; Michael T. Conklin 1983-1989; John Backoff 1989-April 1991; Max Gladding (retired) April-June 1991; Gary D. Bondarenko 1991-2000; Carl Q. Litchfield 2000-2005; Wayne E. McKenney 2005-2014; Michael Neihardt 2014-2015; Eun Sik Poy Sept. 1, 2015- [Boyne City / Boyne Falls realigned w/ Boyne City / Boyne Falls / Epsilon 2016]

Bradley: Indian Mission of the UMC *[Midwest]*   revrtwilliamson@gmail.com
(P) 695 128th Ave, Shelbyville 49344; (M) 1146 Nicolson St, Wayland 49348   (616) 738-9030
Lewis White Eagle Church 1972-1990; Pulpit Supply 1990-1992; David G. Knapp 1992-1995; Timothy J. Miller 1995-1999; John Pesblakal (DSA)1999-Aug. 31, 2001; Calvin Hill Sept. 1, 2001-2003; Wesley S. Rehberg (DSA) 2003-2005; Sandra VandenBrink, Jan. 16, 2005-2013; Sandra VandenBrink, (Ret.) Director, Senior Meals Program 2013- ; Nancy L. Boelens (Ret.) 2013-Dec. 15, 2015; Ronald Todd Williamson (DSA) Jan. 1, 2016-Nov. 30, 2017; Ronald Todd Williamson Dec. 1, 2017

Breckenridge UMC *[Mid-Michigan]* breckenridgeumc@yahoo.com
(P) 125 3rd St, Breckenridge 48615; (M) PO Box 248, Breckenridge 48615 (989) 842-3632
Allen Wittrup 1966-1969; Gilbert Heaton 1969-1972; Birt Beers 1972-1977; Philip Brown 1977-1983; Molly Turner 1983-1990; Stanley Hayes 1990-1994; David L. Miles 1994-1999; Emilie Forward 1999-2005; Dale A. Golden 2005-2013; Paul W. Thomas 2013-Aug. 3, 2015; William F. Dye Sept. 1, 2015-2017; Mark G. Johnson (Ret.) 2017-2019; Cleoria M. French 2019-2020; [St. Louis: First, Breckenridge became 2-point charge 2020] Billie Lou Gillespie 2020-

Brethren: Epworth UMC *[Northern Waters]* anikakasper@gmail.com
(P) 3939 High Bridge Rd, Brethren 49619; (M) PO Box 177, Brethren 49619 (231) 477-5486
Ward Pierce 1967-1971; Floyd Soper 1986-1993; Russell M. Garrigus (Ret) (DSA) 1993-2002; Lemuel O. Granada 2003-2005; Carl Greene (DSA) 2005; Carl Greene, Nov. 12, 2005-2011; Colleen A. Wierman (1/4 time) 2011-2014; [Brethren Epworth / Grant became single-point charges 2014] Judy Coffey (DSA) 2014-Dec. 1, 2015; Beverley J. Williams, Dec. 1, 2015-2016; Laurie M. Koivula 2016-2018; [Mesick /Harrietta/Brethren became a three-point charge 2016] Laurie M. Koivula (LTFT) 2018-2019; [Mesick/Brethren became a two-point charge 2018] Anika Kasper (DSA) July 14, 2019-2020; Russell W. Poirier (DSA) 2020-

Bridgman: Faith UMC *[Greater Southwest]* schneider4276@comcast.net
9156 Red Arrow Hwy, Bridgman 49106; (M) PO Box 414, Bridgman 49106 (269) 465-3696
Walter Easton 1968-1969; David Lutz 1969-Jan. 1970; Arthur & Molly Turner April 1970-1971; Merritt Edner 1971-1972; Wayne Babcock 1972-Dec. 1974; Stanley Buck Jan. 1975-Dec. 1981; Daniel Graber Jan. 1982-1983; Joan Hamlin 1983-1985; Laura Truby 1985-Jan. 1987; Richard Bates March-Nov. 1987; Ross Bunce Nov. 1987-1988; B. Gordon Barry 1988-1993; Bradley S. Bartelmay 1993-May 1, 2000; Terrill M. Schneider May 1, 2000-October 1, 2018; Ashlei K. Horn (DSA) October 28, 2018 [Bridgman became a single point charge 10-1-2018] Ashlei K. Horn Jan 1-Jun 30, 2020; Bradley K. Heiple (DSA) 2020-

Brighton: First UMC *[Heritage]* wendy@brightonfumc.org
(P/M) 400 E Grand River Ave, Brighton 48116 (810) 229-8561
Robert C. Brubaker 1964-1969; W. Herbert Glenn 1969-1973; Kearney Kirkby 1973-1977; Richard C. Cheatham 1977-1988; Benjamin Bohnsack 1988-1997; Karen D. Poole (assoc) 1988-1993; Patricia A. Green (assoc.) 1993-1995; Kristine J. Sigal (assoc.) 1995-2000; Gilson M. Miller 1997-2008; Adam W. Bissell (assoc) 2000-2003; Jennifer Browne (assoc.) 2003-2006; Scott Crostek (assoc.) 2006-2009; Loretta M. Job (deacon) 2007-2018; Sherry L. Parker-Lewis 2008-2020; John W. Ball (assoc) 2009-2013; Paul S. Hahm (assoc.) 2013-2015; Robert F. Fuchs (assoc.) 2017-2020; Lindsay M. Hall (co-pastor) 2020- ; Jonathan E. Reynolds (co-pastor) 2020-

Brighton: First - Whitmore Lake: Wesley Campus *[Heritage]* wumcwhitmorelake@gmail.com
(P) 9318 Main St, Whitmore Lake 48189; (M) PO Box 431, Whitmore Lake 48189-0431
Walter R. Damberg 1968-1970; Robert C. Strobridge 1970-1972; Dwight W. Murphy 1972-1976; Larry J. Peacock 1976-1979; Ronald K. Fulton 1979-1983; Timothy S. Woycik 1983-1993; Robert J. Easlick 1993-2001; Sandra L. Tannery 2001-Aug 15, 2009; Fred Cooley (interim) Aug 16, 2009-Sep 20, 2009; Frederick M. Hatfield Sep 21, 2009-2018; Robert F. Fuchs (campus pastor) 2017-2020; Lindsay M. Hall (co-pastor) 2020- ; Jonathan E. Reynolds (co-pastor) 2020-

Britton: Grace UMC *[Heritage]*　　　　　　　　　　brittongraceumc@yahoo.com
(P/M) 9250 E Monroe Rd, Britton 49229　　　　　　　　　　(517) 451-8280
John D. Lover, 1966-1969; Lauren J. Strait 1969-1972; Gerald R. Parker 1972-1973; Robert L. Porter 1973-1976; John D. Roach 1976-1979; Kenneth C. Reeves 1979-1982; Thomas E. Sumwalt 1982-1985; Martha C. Gregg Ball 1985-Mar. 31, 1991; Stuart L. Proctor May 1, 1991-1993; David A. Eardley 1993-1997; Marianne M. Meier 1997-1998; Nicholas W. Scroggins 1998-2002; Amy Mayo-Moyle 2002-2010; Richard E. Burstall 2010-2014; Mark Zender 2014-2019; [Britton: Grace / Macon two-point charge 7-1-2019] Ruth A. VanderSande 2019-2020; [Britton: Grace became single station 2020] William R. Lass 2020-

Bronson: First UMC *[Greater Southwest]*　　　　　　　　umcb@frontier.com
(P/M) 312 E Chicago St, Bronson 49028　　　　　　　　　　(517) 369-6555
Lloyd A. Phillips 1961-Oct. 1969; Gordon E. Spalenka Oct. 1969-1972; Charles W. Richards 1972-1977; Eldon C. Schram 1977-Oct. 1980; Paul Walter Oct.-Dec. 1980; A. Edward Perkins Dec. 1980-April 1987; Marilyn Barney April-May 1987; Milton John Palmer May 1987-1990; Gerald L. Welsh 1990-1994; Robert D. Nystrom 1994-1998; Mona Joslyn 1998-2006; Matthew Bistayi 2006-2009; Shane Chellis (DSA) 2009-2010; Shane Chellis (part-time) May 25, 2010-2011; Cindy Veilleux 2011-2015; Samuel C. Gordy 2015- [Bronson: First became single station 2020]

Brookfield Eaton UMC *[Mid-Michigan]*　　　　　　　　ilv@vcconsulting.com
(P) 7681 Brookfield Rd, Charlotte 48813; (M) PO Box 430, Charlotte 48813　　　(517) 420-3903
John H. King, Jr. 1967-1971; Miriam DeMint 1971-1973; John Morse 1973-March 1976; James Allred March 1976-Sept. 1979; Pulpit Supply Sept. 1979-1980; Robert Hundley 1980-1982; Pulpit Supply July-Oct. 1982; Robert Freysinger Oct. 1982-1985; Ronald Brooks 1985-1988; Robert Roth 1988-1990; Isabel Deppe 1990-1991; Charlene Minger 1991-1995; Geraldine M. Litchfield 1995-2000; Kevin E. Hale 2000-2004; Stephen C. Small 2004-Oct. 1, 2004; Irene Vittoz (DSA) Oct. 1, 2004; Irene Vittoz Nov. 15, 2005-2018; Cari A. Godbehere (DSA) 2018-Dec 31, 2018; Cari A. Godbehere Jan 1, 2019-Dec 31, 2019; [Robbins, Brookfield Eaton became 2-point charge 2020] Peggy A. Katzmark 2020-

Brooks Corners UMC *[Northern Waters]*　　　　　　brookscornersparish@gmail.com
(P/M) 5951 30th Ave, Sears 49679　　　　　　　　　　(231) 734-2733
Carter Miller 1968-March 1971; Lynn Wagner March 1971-Oct. 1973; Pulpit Supply Nov. 1973-1974; Darryl Cook 1974-May 1977; Kenneth Kline 1977-1986; Carl Q. Litchfield 1986-1991; Eugene L. Baughan 1991-1997; Brian R. Bunch 1997-2005; Ronald DeGraw Aug. 1, 2005-Nov. 6, 2005; James L. Breithaupt Mar. 15, 2006-Oct. 19, 2009; Joseph L. Beavan Jan. 15, 2010-2014; Bryan K. Kilpatrick 2014-2017; Irene Elizabeth Starr Jul. 1-Oct. 22, 2017 [Grant Center / Brooks Corners became a two-point charge 2017] Timothy Locker (DSA) Jan. 1 – June 30, 2019; Douglas Mochama Obwoge (DSA) July 7, 2019-Dec 31, 2019; Douglas Mochama Obwoge Jan 1, 2020-

Brown City UMC *[East Winds]*　　　　　　　　　　browncityumc@gmail.com
(P) 7043 Lincoln St, Brown City 48416; (M) PO Box 39, Brown City 48416　　　(810) 346-2010
Gloria Haynes 1996-Sep 30, 1998; Arthur R. Stone Nov 1, 1998-2004; Lance E. Ness Aug 1, 2004-2007; Maureen V. Baker 2007-2013; Dennis Irish 2013-2019; Patrick D. Robbins 2019- [Brown City Cooperative Parish: Brown City and Omard formed 07/01/2019]

Buchanan: Faith UMC *[Greater Southwest]*　　　　　　faithoffice@sbcglobal.net
(P/M) 728 N Detroit St, Buchanan 49107　　　　　　　　　　(269) 695-3261
D. Keith Laidler 1968-1972; Kenneth L. Snow 1972-1982; Richard C. Kuhn 1982-1987; Richard D. Wilson 1987-1996; Zawdie K. Abiade 1996-2002; Ralph K. Hawkins 2002-2004; Christopher A. Kruchkow 2004-Feb. 15, 2012; [Buchanan Faith UMC became single point charge 2012] Edward H. Slate (Ret.) (1/2 time) 2012-

Buchanan: First UMC *[Greater Southwest]*   fumcbuchanan@att.net
(P/M) 132 S Oak St, Buchanan 49107   (269) 695-3282
     C. Robert Carson 1966-1972; Ronald Entenman 1972-1979; Ward D. Pierce 1979-1985; Paul D. Mazur 1985-1987; Curtis E. Jensen 1987-Jan. 1996; William P. Sanders Feb. 2, 1996-2003; David W. Meister 2003-2006; Rob A. McPherson 2006-2018; Ellen Dannelley Beirlein 2018-

Buel UMC *[East Winds]*
(P) 2165 Peck Rd, Croswell 48422; (M) 133 W State St, Croswell 48422
     William J. Burgess 1968-1973; Martin Caudill 1973-1976; Willard A. King 1976-1980; J.D. Landis 1980-1986; David K. Stewart 1986-1990; Louise R. Ott 1990-1992; Michael F. Bossingham 1992-1994; Thomas K. Spencer 1994-1998; David C. Freeland (co-pastor) 1998-2002; Susan K. Freeland (co-pastor) 1998-2000; Robert A. Srock 2002-Dec 1, 2003; Catherine W. J. Hiner 2004-2009; Micheal P. Kelley 2009-2012; Donald L. Wojewski 2012-2013; Nicholas K. Genoff 2013- Dec 31, 2018; Ellen O. Schippert Jan 1, 2019-2020; [Jeddo, Buel became 2-point charge 2020] Karen A. Harriman (DSA) 2020-

Burnips UMC *[Greater Southwest]*   secretary.bumc@gmail.com
(P) 4237 30th St, Burnips 49314; (M) PO Box 30, Burnips 49314-0030   (616) 896-8410
     Ron Smith Oct. 1991-1997; Kenneth C. Reeves 1997-2004; Anthony Carrol Shumaker 2004-2008; Richard A. Fritz 2008-2014; Nancy J. Patera 2014-2017; Craig H. VanBeek (DSA) 2017- Dec. 31, 2018; Craig H. VanBeek Jan. 1, 2019-

Burr Oak UMC *[Greater Southwest]*
(P) 105 S. Fourth St, Burr Oak 49030; (M) PO Box 91, Burr Oak 49030   (269) 489-2985
     David Draggoo 1967-1971; P.T. Wachterhauser 1971-1974; Larry D. Higgins 1974-1977; Harold Tabor 1977-1978; Wade S. Panse 1978-March 1982; Dan Bennett 1982-1983; Timothy Boal 1983-1986; John Buker 1986-1988; William Bills 1988-1991; Brian Rafferty 1991-1993; Ruth A. Bonser 1993-1994; Emilie Forward 1994-1999; Martin Cobb 1999-2001; William Chu 2001-2003; Melanie S. Young (1/2 time) 2003-2006; Donald J. Graham 2007-2012; John Sterner 2012-2018; Carl Q Litchfield (Ret.) Feb. 15-Jun. 30, 2018; Carl Q Litchfield (Ret.) Oct. 1, 2018-

Burt UMC *[Central Bay]*
(P) 12799 Nichols Rd, Burt 48417; (M) PO Box 96, Burt 48417-0096   (989) 770-9948
     Martin G. Seitz 1968-1972; Ronald Brunger 1972-1976; Kyle Ballard 1976-1979; Philip Seymour 1979; Alan Weeks 1979-1982; Martin G. Seitz 1983-1990; Lois E. Glenn 1990-Dec 31, 1994; Sandra Uptegraff Jan 1, 1994-2000; Betty Whitely 2000-2006; Michael P. Kelley 2006-2009; James O. Bowen 2009-Oct, 2009; Clifford J. Schroeder III, 2010-2013; Paul G. Donalson 2013-2015; Rey C. B. Mondragon 2015-2020; Laura E. Feliciano 2020-

Burton: Christ UMC *[East Winds]*   ChristUMCBurton@att.net
(P/M) 4428 Columbine Ave, Burton 48529   (810) 743-1770
     Peyton E. Loy Jan. 1970-1975; Ralph H. Pieper 1975-1982; William B. Cozadd 1982-1988; Thomas F. Keef 1988-1994; Trevor A. Herm 1994-2004; Theodore D. Whitely 2004-2006; Janet M. Engler 2006-Mar 1, 2009; Kenneth C. Bracken 2009-Dec1, 2010; Naylo T. Hopkins 2011-2014; David Leinke 2014-Oct 30, 2014; David R. Strobe (interim) Nov 1, 2014-Apr 30, 2019; Brian Kendall Willingham May 1, 2019- [Flint: Bristol / Buron: Christ became a two-point charge on May 1, 2019]

Byron Center UMC *[Midwest]*   secretary@byroncenterchurch.org
(P/M) 2490 Prescott St 3W, Byron Center 49315   (616) 878-1618
     Max Gladding 1966-1975; James C. Grant 1975-1985; Fred Hamlin 1985-1987; William H. Doubblestein 1987-2004; Cynthia S.L. Greene 2004-2010; Lawrence A. Nichols 2010-2016; Jeffrey O. Cummings 2016-

Byron: First UMC *[East Winds]* byronumc@byronumc.com
(P) 101 S Ann St, Byron 48418; (M) PO Box 127, Byron 48418-0127 (810) 266-4976
Lorenz Stahl 1969-1973; Dalton Bishop 1973-1975; Harry R. Weeks 1975-1979; Martin G. Seitz 1979-1983; Robert D. Schoenhals 1983-1995; Marilyn C. DeGraw 1995-Jan 28, 2000; G. Fred Finzer 2000-2006; Jack E. Johnston 2006-2010 Michael Mayo-Moyle 2010-2012; Nathan J. Jeffords 2012-2016; Barbara S. Benjamin 2016-

Cadillac: South Community UMC *[Northern Waters]* jim.mort@sbcglobal.net
(P/M) 11800 47 Mile Rd, Cadillac 49601 (231) 775-3067
Richard Wilson Nov. 1966-Nov. 1968; Richard Matson Dec. 1968-Oct. 1969; Edward Eidins Oct. 1969-1971; Robert R. Boyer 1971-1977; Kendall A. Lewis 1977-1981; Donald Fry 1981-1994; James C. Grant 1994-1999; Howard H. Harvey 1999-2000; Jeffrey Schrock 2000-2004; Kenneth C. Reeves 2004-2006; Kenneth C. Reeves (DSA) 2006-7; James J. Mort 2007-

Cadillac UMC *[Northern Waters]* umccadillac@gmail.com
(P) 1020 E Division St, Cadillac 49601; (M) PO Box 37, Cadillac 49601 (231) 775-5362
George Grettenberger Nov. 1967-1980; Richard Wilson 1980-1990; Allen D. McCreedy 1990-2000; Dale P. Ostema 2000-2007; Thomas E. Ball 2007- ; Travis Heystek (Assoc.) 09/01/2018-

Caledonia UMC *[Midwest]* office@caledoniaumc.org
(P/M) 250 Vine St SE, Caledonia 49316 (616) 891-8669
Edward D. Passenger 1966-1969; Robert Boyer 1969-1971; Lloyd Van Lente 1971-1976; Adam Chyrowski 1976-1980; Robert Tomlinson 1980-1984; Robert Wessman 1984-1990; Bobby Dale Whitlock 1990-Jan. 1996; Norman C. Kohns 1996-2005; James E. Hodge 2005-2012; Jodie R. Flessner 2012-2019; Elizabeth Ann Hurd 2019-

Calhoun County: Homer UMC *[Heritage]* homlyl@rocketmail.com
(P/M) 101 E Adams St, Homer 49245 (517) 568-4001
Ronald Wise 1968-1969; Orvel Lundberg 1969-1970; E. Lenton Sutcliffe 1970-1971; Daniel D. Corl 1971-1973; John T. Charter 1973-1978; Harold Deipert 1978-1983; Walter Rothfuss 1983-1987; Linda Farmer-Lewis Sept. 1987-Dec. 1992; Claudette Haney Apr. 16, 1993-1995; Nelson Ray 1995-1997; Linda J. Burson 1997-Jan. 1, 2000; Mark Mitchell 2000-2008; Thomas P. Fox 2008-2012; Robert P. Stover (Ret.) 2012-

Calumet UMC *[Northern Skies]* calumc@pasty.net
(P/M) 57235 Calumet Ave, Calumet 49913 (906) 337-2720
Alan DeGraw 1967-1972; James Tuttle 1972-1975; Harold Slater 1975-1978; Wayne Hutson 1978-1983; Dennis N. Paulson 1983-1987; Robert J. Easlick 1987-1990; David P. Snyder 1990-1993; Nancy G. Sparks 1993-2000; Robert A. White 2000-2016; Richard B. Brown (assoc) 2000-2003; James Palaszeski 2016-2018; Gunsoo Jung 2018-2019; [Keweenaw Parish: Calumet / Lake Linden 7-1-2019] James M. Mathews (Ret.) 2019-

Camden UMC *[Heritage]* pastortrevor1@gmail.com
(P) 205 S Main St, Camden 49232; (M) PO Box 155, Camden 49232-0155 (517) 368-5406
Karl L. Zeigler 1968-1969; John H. Gurney 1969-Aug. 1970; Joseph Huston Aug. 1970-1972; Richard Huskey 1972-1974; J. Brian Selleck 1974-Feb. 1976; Robert P. Stover March 1976-1980; Stephen Beech 1980-1983; Larry W. Rubingh 1983-1987; Frederick G. Hamlin 1987-1994; Russell K. Logston 1994-1996; Diane Stone Nov. 16, 1996-2004; Edward Mohr 2004-2010; Trevor McDermont 2010-2013; Frederick G. Cain (Ret.) (part-time) 2013-

Canton: Cherry Hill UMC *[Heritage]*   secretarycherryhillumc@yahoo.com
(P/M) 321 S Ridge Rd, Canton 48188-1011   (734) 495-0035
   Reinhardt E. Niemann 1961-1969; Dwight W. Murphy 1969-1972; Leonard C. Ritzler 1972-1977;
   Bert Hosking 1977-1986; John R. Henry 1986-1988; Randy J. Whitcomb 1988-1993; Marjorie H.
   Munger 1993-1998; Lawrence A. Wik 1998-2005; Latha Ravi 2005-2008; Frederick M. Hatfield
   2008-Aug 15, 2008; Merlin H. Pratt Aug 15, 2008-2011; Mark Zender 2011-2014; Naylo T. Hoplkins
   2014-2016; Michael Desotell 2016-

Canton: Friendship UMC *[Heritage]*   church@firendshipchurchinfo.com
(P/M) 1240 N Beck Rd, Canton 48187   (734) 710-9370
   Michael K. Norton 1997-

Canton: Friendship – Shelby Twp Campus UMC *[Heritage]*
(P) 53245 VanDyke, Shelby Twp 48316; (M) 1240 N Beck Rd, Canton 48187   (734) 710-9370
   [Satellite of Canton: Friendship stared 01/01/2017] Michael K. Norton Jan. 1, 2017-

Capac UMC *[East Winds]*   capacumparish@yahoo.com
(P/M) 14952 Imlay City Rd, Capac 48014   (810) 395-2112
   Roy G. Forsyth 1967-1972; Raymond S. Burkett 1972-1981; Otto F. Flachsmann 1981-1984; Donald
   L. Bates 1984-Oct. 1987; Gordon B. Boyd 1987-1991; Patricia A. Van Wormer 1991-1996; Harold
   V. Phillips 1996-2006; Lisa J. Clark (assoc) Oct 1, 2000-2008; Steven A. Gjerstad 2006-Dec 7,
   2006; James E. Paige, Jr. Jan 1, 2007-2007; Dale E. Brown 2007-2011; Lisa J. Clark 2011-

Carland UMC *[Mid-Michigan]*   thegoodword1@att.net
(P) 4002 N Carland Rd, Elsie 48831; (M) 587 N Baldwin, Owosso 48867   (989) 494-7763
   Horace N. Freeman 1969-1974; Homer VanBuren 1974-1983; Billy J. McKown 1983-1989; M.
   Shirley Jones 1989-1991; Howard M. Jones (assoc) 1989-1991; William R. Seitz 1991-Jan 1, 1996;
   Jean M. Scroggins Jun 16, 1996-Dec 31, 2000; Lance E. Ness Jan 1, 2000-Jul 31, 2004; Michael
   S. McCoy Aug 1, 2004-2006; Carole A. Brown Aug 1, 2006-2011; Calvin H. Wheelock 2011-2013;
   Stanley P. Stybert 2013-2018; Charlene S. Wagner (DSA) 2018-Dec 31, 2018; Charlene S. Wagner
   Jan 1, 2019-

Carleton UMC *[Heritage]*   carletonumc@carletonumc.com
(P) 11435 Grafton Rd, Carleton 48117; (M) PO Box 327, Carleton 48117   (734) 654-2833
   David A. Russell 1966-1971; Albert E. Hartoog 1971-1974; Howard M. Montgomery 1974-1979;
   Thomas P. Macaulay 1979-1984; James G. Simmons 1984-1986; Martha H. Cargo 1986-1987;
   Frederick O. Timm 1987-1993; George H. Lewis 1993-1998; Carman J. Minarik 1998-Aug 31, 2002;
   Donna J. Minarik (assoc) 1998-Aug 31, 2002; Robert D. Brenner Sep 1, 2002-2010; Kathy
   Charlefour (assoc) Sep 1, 2003-Oct 31, 2005; Brent L. Webster 2010-2012; Taek H. Kim 2012-

Carlisle UMC *[Midwest]*   secretary@carlisleumc.com
(P/M) 1084 76th St SW, Byron Center 49315   (616) 878-1836
   John Rothfuss 1968-1971; Curtis Cruff 1971-1975; Leonard Yarlott 1975-1979; Timothy Graham
   1979-1983; John Buker 1983-1986; Larry Mannino 1986-1990; John Ritter 1990-1994; Andrew
   Jackson 1994-2006; Craig L Adams 2006-Dec. 1, 2009; Andrew Jackson (DSA) Dec. 1, 2009-2010;
   Mike Ramsey 2010-2017; Gary M. Zinger (LM/DSA) 2017-

Caro UMC *[Saginaw Bay]*   secretarycumc@centurytel.net
(P/M) 670 W Gilford Rd, Caro 48723   (989) 673-2246
   Benjamin C. Whaley (Caro: First) 1968-1971; G. Charles Ball (Caro & Fairgrove EUB) 1966-1971;
   Benjamin C. Whaley & G. Charles Ball (merged) 1971-1972; Ronald Thompson 1972-1975; John
   Marvin (interim) Clive Dickins 1975-1983; Brian Kundinger (assoc) 1978-1981; Bonnie Welch
   (assoc) 1981-1983; John Bunce 1983-1988; Calvin Blue 1988-1999; Duane E. Miller 1999-2006;
   Jerome K. Smith 2006-2011; Gregory M. Mayberry 2011-2016; Anthony J. Tomasino 2016-

CHURCH HISTORIES

Carson City UMC *[Mid-Michigan]*   carsoncityumc@gmail.com
(P) 119 E Elm St, Carson City 48811; (M) PO Box 298, Carson City 48811   (989) 584-3797
   Raymond D. Flessner 1970-1978; Paul D. Mazur 1978-1985; A. Ray Grienke 1985-Aug. 16, 1999;
   Richard A. Powell Aug. 16, 1999-Dec. 16, 1999; Robert E. Horton (DSA) Dec. 16, 1999-July 1,
   2000; Kenneth J. Nash 2000-2006; Ronald K. Brooks 2006-2008; Andrew L. Croel 2008-2014;
   Charles Edward Milam 2014-Feb. 17, 2016; Larry W. Nalett (RLA) Feb. 22-June 30, 2016; Charles
   R. Kaliszewski (Ret.) 2016-Dec. 31, 2017; Patricia L Brook (Ret) (LTFT 1/4) 2018- ; Todd W Butler
   (DSA) (LTFT 1/4) (Pastoral Assistant) 2018-2019; Ian S. McDonald 2019-

Carsonville UMC *[East Winds]*   mcrgegorumc@airadvantage.net
(P) 3953 W Sheldon Rd, Carsonville 48419; (M) 5791 Paldi Rd, Peck 48466
   John Edmund Naile Jan 1, 1997-Jan 1, 1077' Gordon B. Boyd Jun 16, 1981-Jul 14, 1984; Jerry D.
   Griggs 1998-

Casco UMC *[Greater Southwest]*   cascoumcoffice@gmail.com
(P/M) 880 66th St, South Haven 49090   (269) 227-3328
   Lawrence Lee 1968-1970; O.I. Lundberg 1970-1971; Adam Chyrowski 1971-1977; Athel Lynch
   1977-1979; Dan Graber 1979-1980; John Fisher 1980-1986; Theodore Cole 1986-Sept. 1988;
   Willard Gilroy Oct. 1988-April 15, 1993; Michael J. Tupper April 16, 1993-2001; Cynthia M. Parsons
   2001-2006; David W. Meister 2006-2016; Donald J. Graham 2016-2019; Jodi M. Cartwright 2019-

Caseville UMC *[Central Bay]*   cumc@airadv.net
(P) 6490 Main St, Caseville 48725; (M) PO Box 1027, Caseville 48725-1027   (989) 856-4009
   G. William Dunstan 1968-1977; Warren D. Pettis 1977-1980; Wayne E. Sparks 1980-1981; Brent
   L. McCumons 1981-1986; John N. Hamilton 1986-1990; Gregory M. Mayberry 1990-Apr 30, 1998;
   Michael L. Quayle May 1, 1998-2004; Philip D. Voss 2004-2010; Linda L. Fuller 2010-2018; Donald
   L. Wojewski 2018- [Caseville, Hayes became 2-point charge 2020]

Cass City UMC *[Central Bay]*   ccumc@airadv.net
(P/M) 5100 Cemetery Rd, Cass City 48726   (989) 872-3422
   Ira L. Wood 1966-1974; Donald Turbin 1968-1970; Elizabeth D.K. Isaacs 1970-1976; Eldred L.
   Kelly 1974-1983; Byron Hatch 1976-1979; Paul T. Wachterhauser 1979-1983; Clare Patton 1983-
   1989; James Mc Callum 1983-1985; S. Joe Robertson 1985-Jan. 1990; Donald J. Daws 1989-1992;
   Kenneth B. Ray 1992-1994; Robert P. Garrett (assoc) 1994-1997; Richard W. Sheppard 1990-
   1997; Philip A. Rice 1997-2002; George F. Ward 2002-2006; Paul G. Donelson 2006-2010;
   Jacquelyn Roe 2010-2018; Robert Paul Demyanovich (DSA) 2018-

Cassopolis UMC *[Greater Southwest]*   casscumc@frontier.com
(P) 209 S Rowland St, Cassopolis 49031; (M) PO Box 175, Cassopolis 49031   (269) 445-3107
   Fred W. McNeil 1960-63; Joseph Wood 1966-1976; James G. Crosby 1976-1983; Charles Van
   Lente 1983-1993; Donald R. Ferris 1993-2000; Claudette Haney 2000-2005; Glenn Litchfield 2005-
   2009; James A. Richie 2009-2012; Dawn Laupp 2012-Dec, 31, 2012; Benjamin D. Hutchison Jan.
   1, 2013-July 15, 2015; Wade S. Panse (Ret.) Aug. 23, 2015-

Cedar Springs UMC *[Midwest]*   office@cedarspringsumc.org
(P) 140 S Main St, Cedar Springs 49319; (M) PO Box K, Cedar Springs 49319   (616) 696-1140
   Leo Bennett 1965-1970; Stanley Hayes 1970-Oct. 1975; Ralph Kallweit Jan. 1976-1980; Lloyd
   Hansen 1980-1983; Arthur Jackson 1983-1987; Robert Stover 1987-1989; William Haggard 1989-
   1995; Ben B. Lester 1995-2003; Brian F. Rafferty 2003-2008; Mary Letta-Bement Ivanov 2008-2014;
   Stephen F. Lindeman 2014-Mar. 14, 2017; Karen J. Sorden 2017-Nov. 30, 2017; William C. Johnson
   (Ret) (LTFT 1/4) Jan. 1, 2018-2020; [Cedar Springs, KC: Chapel Hill became 2-point charge 2020]
   Lawrence J. French 2020-

Central Lake UMC *[Northern Waters]*　　　　　　　　　　dbiteman@outlook.com
(P) 8147 W State Rd, Central Lake 49622; (M) PO Box 213, Central Lake 49622-0213
　Leonard Yarlott 1967-1969; Paul Hartman 1970-1974; Daniel Miles 1974-1976; Chris Schroeder
　1976-1982; David Cheyne 1982-1991; Celia Hastings, June-Nov. 1991; Peter H. Shumar Nov.
　1991-May 1992; Richard A. Morrison June 1992-1995; Richard L. Matson 1995-2003; Charles A.
　Williams 2003-2010; Daniel W. Biteman, Jr. 2010-2020; Katherine C. Waggoner 2020-

Central Lakeport UMC *[East Winds]*
(P) 3597 Milwaukee Rd, Lakeport 48059; (M) c/o Marysville UMC, 721 W Huron Blvd,
Marysville 48040
　Darrel W. Tallman 1967-1973; Mark K. Smith 1973-1976; Daniel R. Fenton 1976-1978; Harold J.
　Slater 1978-1980; James E. & Peggy Paige 1980-1985; Georg F.W. Gerritsen 1985-1988; Donald
　H. Francis 1988-1992; Emerson W. Arntz 1992-2000; Jimmy S. Barnet (co-pastor) 2000-2001;
　Pamela Barnett (co-pastor) 2000-2001; Susan K. Freeland Montenegro 2001-2003; Ralph T. Barteld
　2003-2016; [Marysville / Central Lakeport formed Marysville Cooperative Parish 07/01/2019] Curtis
　B. Clarke 2019-

Centreville UMC *[Greater Southwest]*　　　　　　　　cumchurch@comcast.net
(P/M) 305 E Main St, Centreville 49032　　　　　　　　　　　(269) 467-8645
　Rudy A. Wittenbach 1967-1974; Charles W. Smith 1974-1984; Gordon E. Spalenka 1984-1987;
　Paul G. Donelson 1987-1989; Michael T. Conklin 1989-Aug. 1, 1997; David W. Meister Aug. 16,
　1997-2003; Karin Orr 2003-2014; Emily K. (Beachy) Slavicek Hansson 2014-Dec. 31, 2018; Debra
　L. Eisenbise (DSA) Feb. 9-Jun. 30, 2019; Michael W. Vollmer 2019-2020; Joyce L. Vanderlip 2020-

Chapin UMC *[Mid-Michigan]*　　　　　　　　　　　　pastorherbw@aol.com
(P) 19848 S Chapin Rd, Elsie 48831; (M) 218 E Main, Henderson 48841-9765　　　(989) 661-2497
　Monroe J. Frederick 1968-1972; T. K. Foo Sep 18, 1972-1976; Wayne A. Rhodes 1976-1978; James
　B. Lumsden 1978-1982; David S. Stiles 1982-1984; James P. James 1984-1989; J. Robert
　Anderson 1989-1993; Nicholas W. Scroggins 1993-1998; Paul B. Lim 1998-2000; Billie Lou Gillespie
　2000-Oct 14, 2006; Calvin H. Wheelock Nov 1, 2006-2019; [Henderson / Chapin / Owosso: Trinity
　formed three-point charge 7-1-2019] Steffani Glygoroff (DSA) 2019-

Charlevoix UMC *[Northern Waters]*　　　　　　　　　　chxumc@gmail.com
(P/M) 104 State St, Charlevoix 49720　　　　　　　　　　　(231) 547-2654
　Leona Winegarden 1965-1969; Elmer J. Faust 1969-1975; Austin Regier 1975-1981; David Yingling
　1981-1988; Benton R. Heisler 1988-Nov. 15, 1992; Dale Peter Ostema Feb. 1, 1993-2000; J. Todd
　Thompson 2000-2010; Gregory P. Culver 2010-2017; [Charlevoix / Horton Bay became a two-point
　charge 2016; Charlevoix became a single station 2017] Randall J. Hitts (LTFT 1/2) 2017-

Charlevoix: Greensky Hill UMC *[Northern Waters]*　　　　jonmays7@gmail.com
(P/M) 8484 Green Sky Hill Rd, Charlevoix 49720　　　　　　　(231) 547-2028
　Leona Winegarden 1965-1969; Elmer J. Faust 1969-1975; Austin Regier 1975-1981; David Yingling
　1981-1988; Benton R. Heisler 1988-Nov. 15, 1992; Dale Peter Ostema Feb. 1, 1993-Feb. 1, 1998;
　Kathryn S. Slaughter Feb. 1, 1998-2000; Geraldine M. Litchfield 2000-2005; Timothy B. Wright
　2005-2013; [became single-point charge 2013] Jonathan D. Mays (DSA) 2013-2015; Jonathan D.
　Mays (LTFT) 2015-

Charlotte: Lawrence Avenue UMC *[Mid-Michigan]*　　　　laumc@ameritech.net
(P) 210 E Lawrence Ave, Charlotte 48813; (M) PO Box 36, Charlotte 48013　　　(517) 543-4070
　Forrest E. Mohr 1966-1970; Lester Bailey 1970-1974; Verne Summers Sept. 1974-1987; James
　Mitchum (Assoc.) Apr. 1983-May 1987; George W. Fleming 1987-2002; Don Entenman (Assoc.)
　1987-1988; Gary Bondarenko (Assoc.) 1988-1991; Edna Fleming (Assoc.) 1995-2002; Karen S.
　Wheat 2002-2010; Terry Fisher 2010-2013; Gary S. Wales 2013-2020; John J. Conklin 2020-

Chase: Barton UMC *[Northern Waters]* ljball6@hotmail.com
(P) 6957 S Depot St, Chase 49623; (M) PO Box 104, Chase 49623-0104 (231) 832-5069
Michael Nicholson 1988-Dec. 1991; Paul Patterson (ret.) Jan.-June 1992; Deborah R. Miller June
1, 1992-1995; Wayne McKinney (DSA) 1995-July 31, 2002; Timothy W. Doubblestein Sept. 1, 2002-
Sept. 15, 2003; Sueann K. Hagan Oct. 16, 2003-2006; Michael J. Simon 2006-2010; Lyle J. Ball
(LTFT) 2010- [Baldwin: Covenant Community / Chase-Barton became cross-district circuit 2015]

Cheboygan: St. Paul's UMC *[Northern Skies]* chebstpauls531@att.net
(P/M) 531 E Lincoln Ave, Cheboygan 49721 (231) 627-5262
Carol O. Oswald 1963-1972; R. Edward McCracken 1972-1978; Ralph T. Barteld 1979-1985; Clare
M. Tosch 1985-1988; John F. Greer 1988-1992; Robert D. Wright 1992-1994; Jeffry W. Dinner
1994-1998; George H. Lewis 1998-2010; Trevor A. Herm 2010-2017; John D. Bailey 2017-

Chelsea: First UMC *[Heritage]* jbarrett@chelseaumc.org
(P/M) 128 Park St, Chelsea 48118 (734) 475-8119
Robert M. Worgess 1967-1970; Clive H. Dickens 1970-1975; Marvin H. McCallum 1975-1983;
David W. Truran 1983-1986; Gerald R. Parker 1986-Jul. 15, 1992; Richard L. Dake Sep. 1 1992-
2004 ; Rebecca Foote (assoc.) 1992-1998; Margaret Garrigues-Cortelyou (assoc) 1998-2000;
Johncie (Zellers) Palmer (deacon) Sep 1, 1999-2008; Jennifer W. Williams (assoc) 2000-2003; Joy
A. Barrett 2004- ; Barbara Lewis-Lakin (assoc) 2004-2010; Annalissa Gray-Lions (deacon) Jan 1,
2007-2010;

Chesaning: Trinity UMC *[East Winds]* cumc@centurytel.net
(P/M) 1629 Brady St, Chesaning 48616 (989) 845-3157
Charles E. Jacobs 1962-1970; Walter T. Ratcliffe 1970-1974; Lewis P. Compton 1974-1986; Brent
L. McCumons 1986-1993; George F. Ward 1993-2002; Sherry L. Parker Sep 1, 2002-2008; Mark
G. Johnston 2008-2012; Timothy S. Woycik 2012-

Churchill UMC *[Central Bay]* reidr@ziggnet.com
(P) 501 E State Rd, West Branch 48661; (M) Box 620, West Branch 48661 (989) 312-0105
Fred Timm 1965-1975; James R. Balfour II 1975-1982; David Baize 1982-1983; John R. Crotser
1983-1987; Jeffrey Hildebrand 1987-1989; Barbra Franks 1989-1994; Carter Garrigues-Cortelyou
Sep 1, 1994-1998; Thomas K. Spencer 1998-2005; Donald J. Wojewski 2005-Dec 31, 2007; Cindy
L. Gibbs Jan 1, 2008-2010; Ronald Cook Sep 20, 2010-2011; Janet M. Larner 2011-2013; Brenda
K. Klacking 2013-2020; Michelle N. Forsyth 2020-

Clare UMC *[Central Bay]* jbailey@clareumc.org
(P/M) 105 E 7th St, Clare 48617 (989) 386-2591
Donald Winegar 1966-Sept. 1973; C. William Martin Oct. 1973-1979; Marvin R. Rosa 1979-1986;
Eugene A. Lewis 1986-1994; Gregory R. Wolfe 1994-2003; Mark R. Payne (Assoc. 1/4 time) 1995-
1996; Dennis B. Bromley 2003-2013; John G. Kasper 2013-2020; Jaqueline L. Raineri 2020-

Clarkston UMC *[East Winds]* cumcoffice@clarkstonumc.org
(P/M) 6600 Waldon Rd, Clarkston 48346 (248) 625-1611
Frank A. Cozadd 1967-1975; Paul M. Cargo 1975-Dec. 1975; James R. Balfour Jan. 1976-1985;
Douglas R. Trebilcock 1985-2004; Carole A. Massey (assoc) 1986-1987; Tracy Lynne Huffman
(assoc.) 1995-1999; Jill H. Zundel (assoc) 1999-2006; Christine E. Wyatt (deacon) 1999-2014;
Richard L. Dake 2004- ; Matthew L. Pierce (assoc.) 2006-Oct 8, 2007; Reed P. Swanson (assoc)
2008-2010; Amy E. Mayo-Moyle (assoc.) 2010-2015; Laura Speiran (deacon) 2014-2020; Kyle
Bucholtz (assoc) 2015-Dec 31, 2015; Megan Walther (assoc) 2017-

Clawson UMC *[Greater Detroit]*   clawsonumchurch@wowway.com
(P/M) 205 N Main St, Clawson 48017   (248) 435-9090
Clyde E. Smith 1968-1973; David A. Stout (assoc) 1968-1971; W. Herbert Glenn 1973-1982; Frank A. Cozadd 1982-1985; Archie H. Donigan 1985-Mar.12-1988; Gordon E. Ackerman 1988-2001; Thomas F. Keef 2001-2010; Margaret Garrigues 2010-Sept 1, 2016; Murphy S. Ehlers (deacon) Jan 1, 2016-Dec 30, 2017; Yoo Jin Kim Sept 1, 2016-2018; Harris M. Dunn Jul 1-Nov 30, 2018; Michael R. Perez (DSA) Jan 1, 2019; Michael R. Perez 2019-

Claybanks UMC *[Midwest]*   claybanksumc@gmail.com
(P) 9197 S 56th Ave, Montague 49437; (M) PO Box 104, Montague 49437   (231) 923-0573
Charles Dunbar 1965-1971; Richard Matson 1971-1975; Bernard Randolph 1975-1976; Edward Slate 1976-1983; Steve Smith 1983-1985; Keith Treman 1985-1990; Kay B. Bosworth 1990-1998; Anita Hahn 1998-2006; Gayle Berntsen 2006-2014; [Claybanks realigned from Whitehall/Claybanks to Shelby/Claybanks 2014] Terri L. Cummins 2014-2016; Gary L. Peterson (RLA) 2016- [Claybanks became a single-point charge 2016]

Clayton UMC *[Heritage]*   clayton.rollincenter@gmail.com
(P) 3387 State St, Clayton 49235; (M) PO Box 98, Clayton 49235-0098   (517) 445-2641
Lawson D. Crane 1967-1975; Heath T. Goodwin 1975-1976; George F. Ward 1976- 1981; Walter H. Miller Nov 1, 1981-1994; Craig A. Pillow 1994-2009; Linda Jo Powers 2009-2012; Robert W. Dister 2012-

Climax UMC *[Greater Southwest]*   cxssumc@gmail.com
(P) 133 E Maple St, Climax 49034; (M) PO Box 125, Climax 49034-0125   (269) 746-4023
Garth Smith 1965-1971; Pulpit Supply July-Nov. 1971; Wilbur Williams Nov. 1971-Aug. 1973; Paul Mazur Sept. 1973-1978; Pulpit Supply July-Dec. 1978; Donald Robinson Dec. 1978-Aug. 1979; James Allred Sept. 1979-Dec. 1986; Pulpit Supply Jan.-Apr. 1987; Dennis Slattery Apr. 1987-Oct. 1988; Pulpit Supply Oct.-Dec. 1988; Thomas E. Ball Dec. 1988-1994; David F. Hills 1994-Aug. 1, 1999; Sally J. LaFrance Oct. 1, 1999-2001; Thomas L. Truby 2001-March 1, 2003; David G. Knapp 2003-2009; Glenn C. Litchfield 2009-2016; Beverley J. Williams 2016-

Clinton UMC *[Heritage]*   clinltonumc@frontier.net
(P/M) 10990 Tecumseh Clinton Rd, Clinton 49236   (517) 456-4972
David M. Liscomb 1967-1969; Dean W. Parker 1969-1971; David A. Stout 1971-1974; Ronald K. Corl 1974-1975; James R. Rupert 1975-1977; Thomas A. Kruchkow 1977-Dec. 1979; Jack R. Lancaster Jan. 1980-1989; Roy A. Syme 1989-1992; William M. Smith 1992-2005; A. Faye McKinstry 2005-2014; Pamela A. Beedle-Gee 2014-2018; Robert P. Blanchard 2018-2020; [Clinton, Stony Creek became 2-point charge 2020] Michael W. Vollmer 2020-

Clio: Bethany UMC *[East Winds]*   bethanyumcclio@gmail.com
(P) 353 E Vienna St, Clio 48420; (M) PO Box 327, Clio 48420-0327   (810) 686-5151
S. D. Kinde 1968-1976; John D. Rozeboom 1976-1981; Calvin H. Blue 1981-1988; Thomas G. Badley 1988-1997; Roger F. Gedke 1997-2010; John D. Bailey 2010-2015; LuAnn L. Burke 2015-2017; Catherine (Cathi) M Huvaere 2017-

Coldwater UMC *[Greater Southwest]*   coldwaterum@cbpu.com
(P/M) 26 Marshall St, Coldwater 49036   (517) 279-8402
Mark D. Graham 1968-Sept. 1974; Lester C. Bailey Sept. 1974-1982; James M. Morgan 1982-1988; Royce R. Robinson 1988-1989; Charles W. Richards 1989-1988; Betty A. Smith 1998-2004, Mark Babb (Deacon) 2002-2006; Cynthia Ann Skutar 2004-2010; Denise J. Downs (Assoc.) 2007-2008; Steven R. Young 2010-2015; Edrye A. Maurer 2015-Jan. 1, 2017; David L. Morton (Ret.) Jan. 1, 2017-June 30, 2017; Julie Yoder Elmore 2017-

Cole UMC *[East Winds]*

(P/M) 7015 Carson Rd, Yale 48097   (810) 387-4400

Roy C. Forsyth 1969-1972; Harvard Warren 1972-1988; William D. Wood Jan 1989-Jan, 1992; Earleen A. (Hamblen) VanConant 1992-1993; Harold V. Phillips 1993-1996; Patrick D. Robbins 1998-2000; Debra K. Brown 2000-2010; Christopher G.L. Titus 2010-2019; [Yale / Cole / Melvin became a three-point charge 07/01/2019] Dennis Eric Irish 2019-Mar 30, 2020; Julia A. Cramer (assoc) (DSA) 2019-Dec 31, 2019; Julia A. Cramer (PL) Jan 1, 2020- [Cole, Melvin became 2-point charge 04/01/2020]

Coleman: Faith UMC *[Central Bay]*   colemanfaithumc@sbcglobal.net

(P) 310 N 5th St, Coleman 48618; (M) PO Box 476, Coleman 48618-0476   (989) 465-6181

R. A. Edwards (w/Geneva Hope) 1969-1971; T. H. Bennink (w/Geneva Hope) 1971-1974; James S. Ritchie (w/Geneva Hope) 1976-1980; Roger L. Colby (w/Geneva Hope) 1980-1986; Stephen Cartwright (w/Geneva Hope) 1986-1988; Joy E. Arthur (w/Geneva Hope) 1988-1990; Joy E. Arthur 1991-1992; Donald J. Daws 1992-Jul 31, 1997; Dana R. Strall Aug 1, 1997-1999; David K. Koski 1999-2008; Caroline F. Hart 2008-2015; Nathan T. Reed 2015-2019; Scott W. Marsh 2019-

Coloma UMC *[Greater Southwest]*   office.colomaumc@gmail.com

(P) 144 S Church St, Coloma 49038; (M) PO Box 670, Coloma 49038   (269) 468-6062

George W. Chaffee 1968-1971; Carl Hausermann 1971-1977; Elizabeth Perry Nord (Assoc.) 1976-1981; Dwight Benner 1977-Sept. 1981; Timothy Closson Jan. 1982-Oct. 1986; Laura C. Truby Jan. 1987-1991; Richard Rossiter 1992-Feb. 4, 1996; Leonard R. Schoenherr Feb. 16, 1996-1999; David F. Hills Aug. 1, 1999-2007; O'Ryan Rickard 2007-2009; William W. Chu 2009-2011; Ronald D VanLente 2011-2018 [Watervliet UMC merged w/ Coloma UMC 6-26-11]; David L. Haase (assoc.) 2014-2016; Christine Marie Beaudoin 2018-

Colon UMC *[Greater Southwest]*   colonumcsecretary19@gmail.com

(P) 224 N Blackstone Ave, Colon 49040; (M) PO Box 646, Colon 49040   (269) 432-2783

Leon Shaffer 1967-Nov. 1, 1973; Larry R. Sachau March 15, 1974-1979; Theodore Bennink 1979-1980; Larry R. Shrout 1980-1983; Jack Kraklan 1983-1985; Lawrence Hubley Nov. 1, 1985-1991; Raymond D. Flesner 1991-1999; Arthur C. Murphy 1999-Jan. 15, 2007; Donald J. Graham 2007-2012; John Sterner 2012-2015; Carl Q. Litchfield (Ret.) Feb. 15-Jun. 30, 2018; Samuel C. Gordy 2018-2020; [Colon became single station 2020] Cori R. Clevenger (DSA) Jul 15, 2020-

Columbiaville UMC *[East Winds]*   columc@frontier.net

(P) 4696 Pine St, Columbiaville 48421; (M) PO Box 98, Columbiaville 48421   (810) 793-6363

Theodore H. Bennink 1969-1971; John F. Greer 1971-1982; Lawrence C. Brooks 1982-1985; Stephen E. Wenzel 1985-1993; Frederick O. Timm 1993-1998; Margaret A. Paige 1998-2002; AmyLee Brun Terhune 2002-2009; Kim D. Spencer 2009-2010; Kristen I. Parks 2010-2013; Esther A. Irish 2013-2020; Philip L Tousley 2020-

Commerce UMC *[Heritage]*   commerceumc@sbcglobal.net

(P/M) 1155 N Commerce Rd, Commerce Twp 48382   (248) 363-3935

George MacDonald Jones 1963-1969; John W. Smith 1969-1970; James A. Smith 1970-1976; Gary R. Imms 1976-1981; John G. Park 1981-1992; Dwight W. Murphy 1992-Jan 31, 2004; Janet Gaston Petty (interim) Feb 1, 2004-2004; Deane B. Wyllys 2004-2018; Donald S Weatherup 2018-Jan. 31, 2019; Andrew H. Lee 2019-

Concord UMC *[Heritage]*   concordumc1@hotmail.com

(P) 119 S Main St, Concord 4923; (M) PO Box 366, Concord 49237-0366   (517) 524-6156

Everett Love 1967-1969; Daniel Miles 1969-Dec. 1971; Pulpit Supply Jan.-June 1972; Joseph Huston 1972-1975; Ronald Grant 1975-1982; John McNaughton 1982-1984; Pulpit Supply 1984-1986; David Hansen 1986-1989; Ed Dahringer (interim) July-Dec. 1989; Barbara M. Flory Jan. 1990-1998; Harris J. Hoekwater 1998-2006; Melany A. Chalker 2006-2013; David Elmore 2013-2016; Robert M. Hughes (DSA) 2016-2019; Robert M. Hughes 2019-

Constantine UMC *[Greater Southwest]* umcconstantine@yahoo.com
(P) 285 White Pigeon St, Constantine 49042; (M) 265 E Third St, Constantine 49042 (269) 435-8151
Adam Chyrowski 1966-1971; Roger Wittrup 1971-April 1973; Richard Williams April 1973-April 1976; David Selleck April 1976-Sept. 1979; R. Paul Doherty Dec. 1979-1987; Walter Rothfuss 1987-1989; Gerald Hagans 1989-Aug. 1991. James W. Barney Sept. 1991-1998; Russell K. Logston 1998-2001; Mark R. Erbes 2001-2007; Melanie Young 2007-2009; Scott E. Manning 2009-2016 [Constantine / White Pigeon became a two-point charge 2009]; Khristian A. McCutchan 2016-2017; Tiffany M. Newsom 2017-2020; Lanette S. Van 2020-

Coopersville UMC *[Midwest]* office@coopersvilleumc.org
(P/M) 105 68th Ave N, Coopersville 49404 (616) 997-9225
Philip P. Steele 1968-1969; Vernon L. Michael 1970-1980; David L. Flagel 1980-1989; Paul D. Mazur 1989-1990; Martin M. DeBow 1990-1997; Michael T. Conklin Aug. 1, 1997-1999; John D. Morse 1999-2012; Cori Lynn Cypret Conran 2012-

Corunna UMC *[East Winds]* corunna.mi.umc@gmail.com
(P/M) 200 W McArthur St, Corunna 48817 (989) 743-5050
J. Paul Pumphrey 1968-1973; John W. Simpson 1973-1982; Leonard W. Gamber 1982-1990; Paul G. Donelson 1990-1992; Donald P. Haskell 1992-1994; David E. Ray 1994-1996; William R. Maynard 1996-2001; Michael L. Peterlin 2001-Oct 1, 2006; Douglas K. Mercer (interm) Jan 1, 2007-2007; David R. Strobe 2007-2013; Janet M. Larner 2013-2017; Stephen Spina (DSA) 2017-May 2, 2018; Stephen Spina May 3, 2018;

Corunna: Northwest Venice UMC *[East Winds]* nbeckwithsr@msn.com
(P/M) 6001 Wilkinson Rd, Corunna 48817 (989) 661-2377
Fred W. Knecht 1969-1972; Charles F. Kitchenmaster Feb., 1972-1981; Keith Rasey 1981-1984; To be supplied-DS Assignment; Harry M. Brakeman 1987-1991; Richard O. Griffith 1991-1992; Donald O. Crumm 1992-2002; Douglas D. Sheperd 2003-2006; Betty Kay Leitelt 2006-2010; Cheryll Warren Aug 1, 2010-2014; Norman R. Beckwith, Sr. Nov 2, 2014-2020; David Owen Jul 15, 2020-

Croswell: First UMC *[East Winds]* ngenoff@rocketmail.com
(P/M) 13 N Howard Ave, Croswell 48422 (810) 679-3595
John Allan 1966-1979; C. William Bollinger 1979-1981; John Tagenhorst Jun-Aug 1981; George F. Ward 1981- 1988; Grant R. Lobb 1988-1996; Leonard W. Gamber 1996-1999; Elmer A. Armijo 1999-2001; Jerry P. Densmore 2001-2009; Nickolas K. Genoff 2009- Dec 31, 2018; Ellen O. Schippert Jan 1, 2019-2020; [Croswell became single station 2020] Linda L. Fuller 2020-

Courtland-Oakfield UMC *[Midwest]* courtland.oakfieldumc@gmail.com
(P/M) 10295 Myers Lake Ave NE, Rockford 49341 (616) 866-4298
T.E. Meredith 1968-1970; Richard E. Cobb 1970-March 1972; William J. Bildner 1972-1977; Wendell Stine 1977-1983; Forest H. Crum 1983-Sept. 1984; Gerald Selleck Dec. 1984-1990; Charles K. Stanley Nov. 1, 1990-1996; Charles W. Smith 1996-2008; Michael T. Conklin 2008-2009; Jeffrey C. Williams 2009-2011; Robert Eckert 2011-Oct. 21, 2016; William C. Johnson (Ret.) Nov. 8, 2016-June 30, 2017; Kimberly A. DeLong 2017- [Wyoming Park / Courtland-Oakfield became a two-point charge 2017]

Crystal Falls: Christ UMC *[Northern Skies]* cumc@up.net
(P) 500 Marquette Ave, Crystal Falls 49; (M) PO Box 27, Crystal Falls 49920 (906) 875-3123
W. Frederick Worth 1961-1971; Frank Bishop 1971-1974; Edward C. Weiss 1974-1985; Nancy G. Sparks 1985-1993; Paul J. Mallory 1993-Jan, 1994; Stephen M. Rhoades Feb 1, 1994-2000; Elbert P. Dulworth 2000-2004; Stephen E. Rhoades 2004-2011; Nathan T. Reed 2011-2015; Steven T. Sudduth 2016- Feb 6, 2018; Reed P. Swanson Feb 7-Jun 30, 2018; Vicky Prewitt (DSA) 2018-

Crystal Valley UMC *[Midwest]* gooey@tir.com
(P) 1547 E Hammett Rd, Hart 49420; (M) PO Box 125, Walkerville 49459 (231) 873-5422
Hubert Bengsten 1965-1974; Pulpit supply 1974-1975; Charles Bowman 1975-Jan. 1977; Harry Parker Feb. 1977-1980; Rebecca Neal Niese 1980-1984; Michael Nicholson 1984-1988; John Ritter 1988-Sept. 1990; Max Gladding Sept.-Oct. 1990; A. Ruth Bonser Oct. 1990-1993; Nancy Bugajski 1993-Oct. 1995; Donald J. Vuurens (DSA) 1996-1998; Steven J. Hale 1998-Nov. 8, 1999; Ronald A. Houk (DSA) Nov. 8, 1999-2000; Kenneth E. Tabor 2000-2004; Ronald L. Worley 2004-Nov. 30, 2013; Ronald Iris (Ret.) Dec. 1, 2013-2015; Theresa Fairbanks (DSA) Jun. 1, 2015-Nov. 14, 2016; Kenneth E. Tabor (RLA) Dec. 1, 2015-Dec. 1, 2016; Theresa Fairbanks (LTFT) Nov. 15, 2016-2018; David O Pratt (Ret) (LTFT) 2018

Dale UMC *[Central Bay]* phope000@centuryte.net
(P) 4688 Freeman Rd, Beaverton 48612; (M) PO Box 436, Beaverton 48612 (989) 435-4829
A. H. Keesler 1967-1970; Zina B. Bennett Jr. 1970-1975; Vernon Wyllys 1975-1979; Bruce C. Hatch 1979-1986; Janet M. Larner 1986-1991; David K. Stewart Sr. 1991-Jul 31, 2000; Frederick LaMere Aug 31, 2000-2002; Linda Jo Powers 2002-2005; Patrick R. Poag 2005-

Davisburg UMC *[East Winds]* davisburgumc803@aol.com
(P/M) 803 Broadway, Davisburg 48350 (248) 634-3373
Henry W. Powell 1969-1972; Charles R. Jacobs 1972-1976; Otto F. Flachsmann 1976-1981; Melvin Leach 1981-Dec 31, 1994; Steven A. Miller Feb 1, 1995-1999; David D. Amstutz 1999-2001; William R. Maynard 2001-Jan 1, 2004; William R. Seitz Feb 1, 2004-2011; David L. Fleming 2011-Feb 15, 2014; Eric J. Miller Feb 16, 2014-2018; Thomas C. Hartley, Sr. (DSA) 2018-2019; Thomas C. Hartley, Sr. 2019-

Davison UMC *[East Winds]* umchurchoffice.davison@;gmail.com
(P/M) 207 E 3rd St, Davison 48423 (810) 653-5272
John W. Bray 1963-1975; Sam E. Yearby, Jr. 1975-1983; Brent Webster (assoc) 1976-Oct. 1978; Merton W. Seymour 1983-1987; Dwayne L. Kelsey 1987-1991; Daniel J. Wallace 1991-1997; P. Thomas Wachterhauser 1997-2009; Susan M. Youmans (assoc.) 2005-2008; Deborah A. Line 2009-2014; Kevin L. Miles 2014-2017; Bo Rin Cho 2017-

Dearborn: First UMC *[Greater Detroit]* fumcod@aol.com
(P/M) 22124 Garrison St, Dearborn 48124 (313) 563-5200
Frederick C. Vosburg 1961-1976; Daniel J. Wallace (assoc) 1970-1976; Richard MacCanon (assoc) 1969-1974; John W. Mulder 1976- 1980; Robert L. Porter 1976-1978; Patricia Meyers (assoc) 1978-1980; Richard L. Myers 1978-1980; William D. Mercer 1980-1986; Michael L. Raymo (assoc) 1980-1985; Ralph W. Janka 1986-1994; Michelle A. Gentile (assoc) 1985-1988; Timothy P. Wohlford (assoc) 1988-1990; Shawn P. Lewis-Lakin (assoc) 1990-1994; Robert L. Selberg 1994-1998; Mary J. Scifres (assoc) 1994-Oct 31, 1995; Judith A. May Feb 5, 1996-1998; Kenneth E. Ward 1998-2005; Pamela S. Kail (assoc) 1998-2001; Julius Del Pino 2005-2008; Marshal G. Dunlap (co-pastor) 2008-2011 ; Susan DeFoe Dunlap (co-pastor) 2008-2011; Susan DeFoe Dunlap 2011-2013; Tracy N. Huffman 2013-2018; David Nellist 2018- ; Carl T. S. Gladstone (deacon) 2019-

Dearborn: Good Shepherd UMC *[Greater Detroit]* gshepherdumc@att.net
(P/M) 1570 Mason St, Dearborn 48124 (313) 278-4350
Arthur L. Spafford 1966-1974; Russell L. Smith 1974-1980; Philip M. Seymour 1980-1988; Kathryn S. Snedeker 1988-Jun 15, 1996; Dwayne L. Kelsey 1996-Dec 31, 1999; Nancy K. Frank 2000-Oct 1, 2005; Kathy R. Charlefour Nov 1, 2005-2014; Douglas Ralston 2014-2016; Seok Nam Lim 2016-2018; Robert J Sielaff 2018-2020; Stephen K. Perrine 2020-

Deckerville UMC *[East Winds]*
(P/M) 3346 Main St, Deckerville 48427-9798 (810) 376-2029
Alan W. Weeks 1964-1974; Harry M. Brakeman 1974-1977; James P. Schwandt 1977-1980; Basel W. Curtiss 1980-1983; Zinna Braden Bennett 1983-1985; Richard J. Richmond 1985-1991; Max L. Gibbs 1991-1996; James M. Thompson 1996-1999; Catherine W. J. Hiner Jan 1, 1999-2004; John H. Rapson 2004-2010; Monique R. Carpenter 2010-2015; Dale Barber Nov 1, 2015-2016;

Deerfield UMC *[Heritage]* wmclemmer@hotmail.com
(P) 110 Williams St, Deerfield 49238; (M) 2509 S Wellsville Hwy, Blissfield 49228 (517) 447-3420
Philip D. Miles 1967-1970; Donald L. Bates 1971-1976; Basil W. Curtiss 1976-1980; Howard L. Deardorff 1980-1981; William Michael Clemmer 1981-1984; Thomas C. Anderson 1984-Dec. 31, 1989; Max L. Gibbs Feb. 1, 1990-1991; June M. Westgate 1991-1996; Gerald M. Sever, Jr. 1996-1999; Wilson C. Bailey 1999-Aug 31, 1999; Allen F. Schweitzer Oct 1, 1999-Oct 31, 2000; Edward C. Weiss Nov 1, 2000-2005; William Michael Clemmer 2005-Dec 31, 2013; Samuel Pooley 2014-Dec 31, 2016; David R. McKinstry (Ret.) Jan 8-Jun 30, 2017; William T. Kreichbaum 2017-2019; Bradley R. Vasey 2019-

Delta Mills UMC *[Mid-Michigan]* nspackman12@gmail.com
(P/M) 6809 Delta River Dr, Lansing 48906 (517) 321-8100
Donald H. Thomson 1963-1969; Bruce Pierce Aug. 1969-1970; Raymond J. McBratnie 1970-1973; Dave Morton 1973-1982; William Dornbush 1982-1986; Clarence W. Hutchens Nov. 1986-Jan. 1987; Janelle E.R. Gerkin Jan. 1987-1990; Lyle D. Heaton 1990-Jan. 1, 1999; D. Keith Laidler Jan. 1, 1999-June 30, 1999; Robert J. Besemer 1999-2002; Kathleen S. Kursch 2003-Aug. 31, 2004; Keith Laidler 2005-2007; Paulette G. Cheyne 2007-2013; Joseph L. Spackman (Ret.) (1/4 time) 2013-

Delton: Faith UMC *[Greater Southwest]* faithumc@mei.net
(P) 503 S Grove St, Delton 49046; (M) PO Box 467, Delton 49046-0467 (269) 623-5400
Earl Champlin 1968-1971; Gordon Showers 1971-1975; Elmer Faust 1975-1990; William A. Hertel 1990-2001; Daniel B. Hofmann 2001-2007; David F. Hills 2007-2010; Gary L. Bekofske 2010-2012; Brian R. Bunch 2012-

Denton: Faith UMC *[Ann Arbor]* faithchur1@sbcglobal.net
(P/M) 6020 Denton Rd, Belleville 48111 (734) 483-2276
Clive H. Dickens 1963-1970; Harold J. Slater 1970-1972; Norman R. Beckwith 1972-1976; Susan K. DeFoe Dunlap 1976-1983; Hoon Hee Wong 1983-1988; Michelle A. Gentile 1988-1990; Gerald S. Hunter 1990-May 15, 1995; Margery A. Schleicher May 16, 1995-2000; Robert D. Brenner 2000-Aug 31, 2002; Beth D. Titus Sep 1, 2002-2008; Michael Rudd 2008-Aug 1, 2008; D. Kay Pratt Aug 15, 2008-2010; Merlin H. Pratt 2010-2011; Mark Zender 2011-2014; Naylo T. Hopkins 2014-2016; Mannah Harris Dunn 206-2018; Arthur D. Korlapati (DSA) 2018-Dec 31, 2019; Arthur D. Korlapati Jan 1, 2020-

Detroit: Calvary UMC *[Greater Detroit]* detroitcalvaryumc@yahoo.com
(P/M) 15050 Hubbell St, Detroit 48227 (313) 835-1317
Lloyd Houser 1966-1977; Bishop S. Thompson (assoc) 1974-1977; Edmund Millet Aug. 1977-1984; Robert C. Williams 1984-1986; Theodore Whitely 1987-1992; Wilfred E. Johnson Sr. 1992-1997; Hilda L. Harris 1997-Aug 31, 2004; Jennifer Whatley Williams Sep 1, 2004-2006; Theodore B. Whitely, Sr. 2006-2013; Bruce D. Johnson (DSA) 2013-2014; Carter Grimmett Nov 1, 2013-2014; Will G. Council 2014-

Detroit: Cass Community UMC *[Greater Detroit]*   ccumcac@aol.com
(P) 3901 Cass Ave, Detroit 48201; (M) 11850 Woodrow Wilson St, Detroit 48206   (313) 883-2277
Lewis L. Redmond 1953-1981; Edwin A. Rowe 1981-Jun 30, 1994; Juanita Ferguson (assoc) 1972-1973; Melvin Hall (assoc) 1979-1984; Alonzo E. Vincent (assoc) 1984-1986; William A. Kellermann (assoc) 1981; Lyle Kett (assoc) 1900-1900; Harry Watson 1989-1990; Gloria Gerald (assoc) 1990-1991; Norman Allen, III (assoc) 1991-1993; Bea Soots Fraser (assoc) 1991-1994; Lamarr Gibson (assoc) 1993-1995; Faith E. Fowler Jul 1, 1994- ;Linda Slaughter (assoc.) 1995-1997; Karen Vo To (assoc) 1997-2001; Thomas E. Tarpley, Sr. (assoc) 1997-Aug 31, 2003; Sue Pethoud (deacon) 2014-Jan 1, 2016; Jonathan E. Reynolds (assoc) 2018- ; Latha Ravi 2019-

Detroit: Cass Community – World Bldg Campus UMC *[Greater Detroit]*
(P) 11745 Rosa Parks Blvd, Detroit 48206; (M) 3901 Cass Ave, Detroit 48201-1721
[Satellite of Dtroit: Cass Community founded 07/01/2017] Faith E. Fowler 2017- ; Jonathan E. Reynolds (assoc.) 2018-

Detroit: Central UMC *[Greater Detroit]*   centralumcdetroit@yahoo.com
(P/M) 23 E Adams Ave, Detroit 48226   (313) 965-5422
Dwight Large 1967-1970; William Mate (assoc) 1968-1971; James Cochran 1968-1969; Richard Devor 1971-1979; Daniel Krichbaum (assoc) 1972-1976; Robert Walton (assoc) 1977-1980; David Kidd 1980-1985; Lester Mangum (assoc) 1984-1985; Barbara Byers Lewis (assoc) 1986-1990; David Strong 1990-Jun 30, 1994; Linda Lee (assoc) 1990-1992; Emmanuel J. Giddings (assoc) 1992-1995; Edwin A. Rowe Jul 1, 1994-2014 ;Joyce E. Wallace (assoc.) 1995-1997; Victoria McKenze (assoc) 1997-1998; DaVita McCallister (assoc) Jun 16, 2001-2002; Latha Ravi (assoc) 2002-2005; Jill Hardt Zundel 2014-

Detroit: Centro Familiar Cristiano UMC (formerly El Buen Pastor) *[Greater Detroit]*
(P/M) 1270 Waterman St, Detroit 48209   (734) 482-8374
Eduardo Cartes 1982-1984; Geraldo Silva 1984-1985; Saul C. Trinidad 1985-1998; Marcos A. Gutierrez Sep 1, 1998-Apr 15, 2005; Dora Gutierrez (assoc) Sep 1, 1998-Dec 31, 2004; Luis M. Collazo 2007-2012; Patricia Gandarilla 2012-

Detroit: Conant Avenue UMC *[Greater Detroit]*   conantave@sbcglobal.net
(P/M) 18600 Conant St, Detroit 48234   (313) 891-7237
W. E. Teague 1967-1977; Bishop S. Thompson 1977-1984; Phylemon D. Titus 1984-1988; Hydrian Elliott (assoc) 1985-Feb. 1986; James D. Cochran 1988-1992; Linda Lee 1992-1995; Emmanuel J. Giddings, Sr. 1995-1997; Joyce E. Wallace 1997-2001; Linda Slaughter-Titus 2001-Jan 1, 2003; Carter Grimmett Jan 1, 2003-Jun 30, 2003; Darrel E. Totty Sep 2, 2003-2015; Willie F. Smith 2015-
[Mt. Hope merged w/ Conant Ave 7-1-2020]

Detroit: French UMC *[Greater Detroit]*   frenchumcd@yahoo.com
(P/M) 1803 E 14 Mile Rd, Birmingham 48009
[New Church Start 07/01/2018] Gertrude Mwadi Mukalay 2018- ; John Kabala Ilunga 2018-

Detroit: Ford Memorial UMC *[Greater Detroit]*   office@fordmemorial.org
(P/M) 16400 W Warren Ave, Detroit 48228   (313) 584-0035
Edward Fulcher 1965-1974; D. Clyde Carpenter 1974-1978; Juanita J. Ferguson 1978-1986; Faith E. Fowler 1986-Jun 30, 1994; Lawrence A. Wik Jul 1, 1994-1998; Olaf Ludums 1998-Nov 15, 1999; Kenneth Bryant, Jr. May 1, 2000-Mar 1, 2016; Donald Beasley (DSA) 2016; Donald Beasley Jan 1, 2020-

Detroit: Metropolitan UMC *[Greater Detroit]* 　　　serving@metroumc.org
(P/M) 8000 Woodward Ave, Detroit 48202 　　　(313) 875-7407
　Robert H. Bodine 1962-1973; William K. Quick 1974-1998; Allen B. Rice (assoc) 1966-1967; William L. Stone (assoc) 1968-1969; Arthur E. Smith (assoc) 1970-1971; Carter W. Preston (assoc) Feb. 1972-Dec. 1974; James E. Tuttle (assoc) Feb 1975-1977; Joseph D. Huston (assoc) 1975-Oct. 1977; Gary L. Damon (assoc) 1977-Jan. 1986; Scott Wilkinson (assoc) 1981-1985; Jerome K. Smith (assoc) 1986-1991; William Michael Clemmer (assoc) 1987-Dec, 1987; William Mercer (assoc) 1990-1993; Charles S.G. Boayue (assoc) 1990-1992; Robert L. Selberg (assoc) 1991-1994; John D. Landis (assoc) 1994-2000; Reed Swanson 1995-Aug 31, 1999; Julius E. Del Pino 1998-Dec 31, 2003; Demphna Krikorian (assoc) 1998-2000; Terry W. Allen (assoc) 2000-2002 ; Amy Mayo-Moyle (assoc) 1999-2002; Janet Gaston Petty (assoc) 2002-Dec 31, 2003 ; Bonnie J. Light (deacon) Aug 16, 2002-Dec 31, 2003; William A. Verhelst (Intentional interim) Jan 1, 2004-2006 ; Faith E. (Green) Timmons (assoc) Aug 1, 2004-2008; Tonya M. Arnesen 2006-2011; Catherine J. Miles (deacon) May 17, 2009-2013; Ray T. McGee 2011-2016; Janet Gaston Petty (interim) 2016-

Detroit: People's UMC *[Greater Detroit]* 　　　peoplesumcdetroit@outlook.com
(P/M) 19370 Greenfield Rd Detroit 48235 　　　(313) 342-7868
　Andrew A. Allie 1976-1980; Frederick B. Moore 1980-1992; Lester Mangum 1992-Jan 1, 2003; Julius Nelson Jan 1, 2003-Jun 30, 2003; Jennifer W. Williams 2003-2004; Gary A. Williams 2004-2008; Carter M. Grimmett 2008-2014; Marva Pope 2014-2018; Rahim O. Shabazz 2018-

Detroit: Resurrection UMC *[Greater Detroit]* 　　　resurrectionumc@gmail.com
(P) 8150 Schaefer Hwy, Detroit 48228; (M) 15391 Griggs, Detroit 48238 　　　(313) 582-7011
　Charles Jones 1986-1992; Hydrian Elliott 1992-Jan 1, 1998; Henry Williams Feb 1, 1998-2010; Margaret Martinez-Ventura 2010-2019; Carolyn A. Jones 2019-

Detroit: St. Paul UMC *[Greater Detroit]* 　　　StPaulUMCdet@aol.com
(P/M) 8701 W 8 Mile Rd, Detroit 48221 　　　(313) 342-4656
　Thomas Tinsley 1965-1983; Janet Gaston Petty 1983-1989; Wilford Johnson 1989-1992; Theodore Whitely Sr. 1992-1996; Julius A. McKanders 1996-Nov 5, 2000; Victoria McKenze Nov 16, 2000-2001; Karen Y. Noel 2001-2010; Henry D. Williams, Jr., 2010-Aug 1, 2013; William Reese, Jr. 2014-Feb 3, 2015; Anthony J. Ballah Apr 15, 2016-2018; Kenneth Johnson 2018-

Detroit: St. Timothy UMC *[Greater Detroit]* 　　　sttimothysecretary@yahoo.com
(P/M) 15888 Archdale St, Detroit 48227 　　　(313) 837-4070
　Frank R. Leineke 1977-1979; John Hinkle (assoc) 1978-1980; Roger W. Ireson 1979-Jan. 1 1988; William P. Sanders (assoc) 1981-1982; Anthony Cutting (assoc) 1982-1986; Wilfred E. Johnson, Sr. (assoc) 1986-1989; Douglas W. Vernon Jan. 1, 1988-1991; W. Steven Boom (assoc) 1989-1991; Thomas E. Hart 1991-1995; Philip Burks (assoc) 1991-1993; Hilda L. Harris (assoc) 1993-1995; Phylemon D. Titus 1995-Dec 31, 2002; Sharon G. Niefert (assoc.) 1995-1998; Lester Mangum Jan 1, 2003-2013; Christopher M. Grimes 2013-

Detroit: Scott Memorial UMC *[Greater Detroit]* 　　　scottumc@yahoo.com
(P/M) 15361 Plymouth Rd, Detroit 48227 　　　(313) 836-6301
　Donald A. Scavella 1969-1977; George E. Rice 1977-1980; Quincy D. Copper July 1980-1987; Anthony J. Shipley 1987-Mar. 1, 1992; Samuel V. White, III (assoc) 1987-1990; Charles Knight (assoc) 1990-1991; Marquis D. Lyles (assoc) 1991-1994; Andrew A. Allie May 1, 1992-2001; Joyce E. Wallace 2001-2005; Anthony R. Hood 2005-2016; Cornelius Davis, Jr. 2016-

Detroit: Second Grace UMC *[Greater Detroit]*   secondgraceumc@gmail.com
(P/M) 18700 Joy Rd, Detroit 48228   (313) 838-6475
  Alvin Burton 1958-1971; Henry E. Johnson 1971-1974; Chester Trice, Sr. 1974-1980; George E.
  Rice 1980-1984; Carroll Felton 1984-1986; Anthony Cutting 1986-1993; Emmanuel F. Bailey 1993-
  1999; Charles S. G. Boayue, Jr. 1999-2015; Murphy Ehlers (deacon) Oct 1, 2011-Nov 20, 2015;
  Darryl E. Totty Nov 30, 2015-

Detroit: Trinity-Faith UMC *[Greater Detroit]*   trinityfaith@ameritech.com
(P/M) 19750 W McNichols Rd, Detroit 48219   (313) 533-0101
  Sam S. Tatem 1989-1990; Samuel V. White III 1990-1995; Robert G.Williams 1995-Jan 1, 1998;
  Hydrian Elliott Jan 16, 1998-Apr 30, 2000; Lamarr V. Gibson Jun 1, 2000-2001; Emmanuel F. Bailey
  2001-Aug 31, 2006; Janet J. Brown 2007-2018; Markey C Gray 2018-

DeWitt: Redeemer UMC *[Mid-Michigan]*   office@dewittredeemer.org
(P/M) 13980 Schavey Rd, Dewitt 48820   (517) 669-3430
  Rodney J. Kalajainen 1988-; Patricia L. Brook (Assoc.) 1999-Jan. 31, 2002; Timothy W. Trommater
  (Assoc.) 2017-Apr 2, 2020; Deborah S. Thomas (Co-Pastor) 2020-

DeWitt: Redeemer UMC - St Johns: First Campus *[Mid-Michigan]*   sjfumc@4wbi.net
(P/M) 200 E State St, Saint Johns 48879   (989) 224-6859
  [St Johns: First was adopted and became a satellite campus of DeWitt: Redeember July 1, 2018]
  Rodney J. Kalajainen 2018-; Timothy W. Trommater (Assoc.) 2018-Apr 2, 2020; Deborah S. Thomas
  (Co-Pastor) 2020-

Dexter UMC *[Heritage]*   secretary@dexterumc.org
(P/M) 7643 Huron River Dr, Dexter 48130   (734) 426-8480
  William J. Rosemurgy 1965-1971; James L. Hynes 1971-1979; John E. Harnish 1979-1990; Leland
  E. Penzien 1990-Jan. 17, 1993; Eric S. Hammar (interim Jan.-Jun); Jacqueline E. Holdsworth
  (assoc) 1991-Aug 31, 1992; William R. Donahue Jr. Jun. 1, 1993-2003; Anna Marie Austin (assoc)
  1993-1996; G. Fred Finzer (assoc) 1996-2000; Matthew J. Hook 2003- ; Thomas Snyder (deacon)
  2014- ; [Ann Arbor: Calvary merged with Dexter 7/1/2020]

Dimondale UMC *[Mid-Michigan]*   dimondaleumc@gmail.com
(P) 6801 Creyts Rd, Dimondale 48821; (M) PO Box 387, Dimondale 48821   (517) 646-0641
  Tom Peters 1967-1970; Richard Youells 1970-1974; Thomas Weber 1974-Apr. 1978; John Ristow
  Apr. 1978-1979; Daryl Boyd 1979-May 1981; Heidi Joos 1981-1983; Glenn Herriman 1983-1985;
  Richard Powell 1985-1988; Bonnie Yost-McBain 1988-Nov. 1990; Donald D. Entenman 1991-Jan.
  31, 1994; Joyce DeToni-Hill Feb. 16, 1994-Oct. 15, 1999; Lillian T. French Nov. 16, 1999-2002;
  Robert David Nystrom 2002-2004; Thomas Peters (DSA) 2004-2005; Andrew L. Croel 2005-2008;
  Kimberly A. Tallent 2008-2009; Joseph D. Huston (Ret.) (LTFT) 2009-Feb. 1, 2019; [Dimondale
  became a single point station 2017] Stephan Weinberger (Ret.) (LTFT) Feb. 2, 2019-2019; Linda
  J. Farmer-Lewis (Ret.) 2019-

Dixboro UMC *[Heritage]*   dumc@dixborochurch.org
(P/M) 5221 Church Rd, Ann Arbor 48105   (734) 665-5632
  Robert C. Strobridge 1968-1970; Dwayne Summers 1970-1974; Haldon D. Ferris 1974-1985;
  Charles R. Marble 1985-1992; James D. Cochran 1992-1998; John C. Ferris 1998-2006; John G.
  Park 2006-2011; Catherine M. Freeman (deacon) 2008-2014; Tonya M. Arneson 2011-2019; Mary
  Hagley (deacon) 2013- ; E. Jeanne Garza 2019-

Dorr: CrossWind Community UMC *[Midwest]*   office@crosswindcc.org
(P/M) 1683 142nd Ave, Dorr 49323   (616) 681-0302
  [new church start 2004; chartered 2009] Scott K. Otis, Oct. 1, 2004-2017; Kevin K. Guetschow
  2017-

Dowagiac First UMC *[Greater Southwest]*   fumcdowagiac@gmail.com
(P) 326 N Lowe St, Dowagiac 49047; (M) PO Box 393, Dowagiac 49047   (269) 782-5167
   John H. Ristow 1966-1978; Dale Benton 1979-1980; Clyde Miller 1980-1983; Claude Ridley 1983-1987; R. Paul Doherty 1987-2004; William H. Doubblestein 2004-2006; John K. Kasper 2006-2013; David A. Price 2013-Jan. 1, 2015; Kellas D. Penny III, Feb. 1, 2015-2017; Jodi M. Cartwright 2017-2019; Christopher P. Momany 2019-

Dowling: Country Chapel UMC *[Greater Southwest]*   office@mei.net
(P) 9275 S M 37 Hwy, Dowling 49050; (M) PO Box 26, Dowling 49050   (269) 721-8077
   Marvin Iseminger 1968-1973; Kendall Lewis 1973-1977; Lynn Wagner 1977-1984; Carl Olson 1984-1985; James Cook 1985-1986; Mary Horn (Schippers) 1986-1991; Merlin Pratt 1991-1996; Kay Pratt (co-pastor) 1992-1996; DeAnn J. Dobbs 1996-Oct. 1, 2000; Dianne D. Morrison Feb. 1, 2001-2004; Patricia Anne Harpole 2004-2009; Kimberly A. Tallent 2009-2011; Ryan Wieland 2011-2016; Richard J. Foster 2016-

DownRiver UMC *[Greater Detroit]*   office@drumc.org
(P/M) 14400 Beech Daly, Taylor 48180   (734) 442-6100
   Margaret E. Bryce 2013-2018; Keith Lenard (assoc) 2016- ; Jaqueline L Raineri 2018-2020; Robert L. Fuchs 2020-

Dryden UMC *[East Winds]*   pastorpatty@hughes.net
(P) 5400 Dryden Rd, Dryden 48428; (M) PO Box 98, Dryden 48428-0098   (810) 796-3341
   Paul Doherty 1966-1970; Lois Glenn 1970-1974; Dale L. Vroman 1974-1977; Bufford C. Coe 1977-1983; Margaret H. Rodgers-West 1983-1988; Zina Braden Bennett, Jr. 1988-1990; James R. Rupert 1990-Sep 30, 1995; Dennis Madill Nov 16, 1995-Sep 8, 1998; Clifford Schroeder III Feb 1, 1999-Dec 31, 2000; Frederick O. Timm Jan 1, 2001-2003; Carol S. Walborn 2003-Sep 15, 2008; Patricia A. Hoppenworth Oct 1, 2008-

Duffield UMC *[East Winds]*
(P/M) 7001 Duffield Rd, PO Box 19, Durand 48449   (810) 621-3676
   Donald D. McLellan 1967-1970; Gary L. Sanderson 1970-1979; Paul I. Greer 1979-1981; Meredith T. Moshauer 1981-1988; James R. Allen 1988-1992; Myra Lee Sparks 1992-1995; David L. Fleming 1995-1999; Harlan E. Sorensen 1999-Nov 14, 2004; John D. Bailey 2005-2010; David A. Wichert 2010-2013; Eric L. Johnson 2013-2018; Duane A Lindsey (DSA) 2018-Dec 31, 2019; Duane A Lindsey Jan 1, 2019-2020; [Lake Fenton / Lennon / Duffield three-point charge 7-1-2019] [Duffield became single station 2020] Jason Dover (DSA) 2020-

Dundee UMC *[Heritage]*   office.dundeeumc@comcast.net
(P/M) 645 Franklin St, Dundee 48131   (734) 529-3535
   Richard L. Beemer 1968-1975; Joseph J. Bistayi 1975-1978; William M. Smith 1978-1992; Linda J. Donelson 1992-1997; Sherry L. Parker 1997-Jul 31, 2002; Kathleen A. Groff Sep 1, 2002-2008; Douglas K. Olsen 2008-2015; Seung H. (Andy) Baek 2015-2018; Bradley S. Luck 2018-

Durand UMC *[East Winds]*   durandfumc@frontier.com
(P/M) 10016 E Newburg Rd, Durand 48429   (989) 288-3880
   Donald D. McLellan 1967-1970; Gary L. Sanderson 1970-1979; Ronald W. Tallman 1979-1981; R. Edward McCracken 1981-Dec. 1989; Thomas C. Anderson Jan. 1, 1990-1995; William P. McBride 1995-2002; Wayne N. Thomas 2002-2010; Beverly L. Marr 2010-2017; Aaron B. Kesson 2017-

East Jordan UMC *[Northern Waters]*   eastjordanumc@gmail.com
(P) 201 4th St, East Jordan 49727; (M) PO Box 878, East Jordan 49727   (231) 536-2161
   Stanley L. Hayes Nov. 1966-1970; Lester E. Priest 1970-Jan. 1974; Daniel J. Minor April 1974-1981; Phillip W. Simmons Sept. 1981-1984; Brian Secor 1984-1986; Merlin K. Delo 1986-1997, Eugene L. Baughan 1997-2002; D. Michael Maurer 2002-Nov. 10, 2008; Ralph Posnik (DSA) Nov. 23, 2008; Ralph Posnik Nov. 15, 2009-2014; Craig A. Pahl 2014-

East Lansing: Peoples Church *[Mid-Michigan]* office@thepeopleschurch.com
(P/M) 200 W Grand River Ave, East Lansing 48823 (517) 332-5073
   Andrew Pomerville 2000-Jun. 18, 2018; [Served by other demoniation.]

East Lansing: University UMC *[Mid-Michigan]* office@eluumc.org
(P/M) 1120 S Harrison Rd, East Lansing 48823 (517) 351-7030
   Alden Burns 1966-1971; Arno Wallschlaeger (Assoc.) 1968-1977; Donn Doten 1971-1979; Jon
   Powers (Assoc.) 1974-1978; Tom Pier-Fitzgerald (Assoc.) 1978-1982; Keith Pohl 1980-1986; Robert
   Hundley (Assoc.) 1982-1990; Sharon Z. Rader 1986-1989; Gessel Berry, Jr. 1989-1991; William
   Dobbs 1991-1996; Marguerite M. Rivera (Assoc.) April 16, 1995-1996; Frank W. Lyman, Jr. & Carole
   S. Lyman (co-pastors) 1996-2006; John Ross Thompson 2006-Dec. 31, 2010; Kennetha Bigham-
   Tsai (Assoc.) 2006-2011; Jennifer Browne 2011-2016; William W. Chu (Assoc.) 2011- ; William C.
   Bills 2016-

East Nelson UMC *[Midwest]* eastnelsonumc@yahoo.com
(P/M) 9024 18 Mile Rd NE, Cedar Springs 49319 (616) 696-0661
   Leo Bennett 1965-1970; Stanley Hayes 1970-Oct. 1975; Ralph Kallweit Jan. 1976-1980; Lloyd
   Hansen 1980-1983; Arthur Jackson 1983-1987; Robert Stover 1987-1989;William Haggard 1989-
   1995; Ben B. Lester 1995-2003; Brian F. Rafferty 2003-2004; Herbert VanderBilt 2004-2016; Inge
   E. Whittemore (LTFT) 2016-

Eastpointe: Immanuel UMC *[Greater Detroit]* secretary@ImmanuelEastpointe.org
(P/M) 23715 Gratiot Ave, Eastpointe 48021 (586) 776-7750
   Arthur E. Smith 1960-1970; John N. Howell 1970-1972; Archie H. Donigan 1972-1980; William D.
   Rickard 1980-1988; R. LaVere Webster 1988-1991; David Gladstone 1991-1997; Harold E.
   Weemhoff 1997-Dec 31, 1999; Demphna Krikorian 2000-2003; Christopher D. Cowdin (assoc)
   2001-2003; Adam W. Bissell 2003-2007; Sang C. Park 2007-Sep 1, 2008; Lynn Marie Hasley Oct
   1, 2008-Jan 9, 2012; Albert Rush 2012-

Eaton Rapids: First UMC *[Mid-Michigan]* dsfumer@gmail.com
(P/M) 600 S Main St, Eaton Rapids 48827 (517) 663-3524
   Ronald A. Houk Oct. 1971-Jan. 1982; Eric S. Beck (Assoc.) Dec. 1980-1983; Robert E. Betts Feb.
   1982-1988; Larry W. Mannino (Assoc.) 1983-1986; Larry E. Irvine 1988-Oct. 15, 1993; Howard
   (Rick) McKire (Assoc.) Jan. 1993-; Thomas J. Evans Feb. 1, 1994-2007; Daniel B. Hofmann 2007-
   2014; Martin M. DeBow 2014-

Edenville UMC *[Central Bay]* phopeooo@centurytel.net
(P) 455 W Curtis Rd, Edenville 48620; (M) PO Box 125, Edenville 48620 (989) 689-6250
   William Cozadd 1965-1980; Cleon Abbott 1980-1985; Donald Crumm 1985-1992; Harold J. Slater
   1992-2002; Patrick R. Poag 2002-

Edmore Faith UMC *[Midwest]* churchmouse833@gmail.com
(P/M) 833 S 1st St, Edmore 48829 (989) 427-5575
   C. William Martin 1965-1969; Eldon Eldred 1969-1973; Howard McDonald 1973-1976; David
   Yingling 1976-1981; Stanley Finkbeiner 1981-Feb. 1987; Stephen Charnley (interim) Feb.-April
   1987; Joseph Graybill April 1987-1997; Connie R. Bongard 1997-Jan. 1, 2007; Esther R. Barton
   (DSA) Jan. 1-June 30, 2007; Susan E. Poynter 2007-2011; Michael A. Riegler 2011-2017; Daniel
   L. Barkholz 2017-

Edwardsburg: Hope UMC *[Greater Southwest]* hopeumc2@hope-umc.us
(P) 69941 Elkhart Rd, Edwardsburg 49112; (M) PO Box 624, Edwardsburg 49112 (269) 663-5321
   (Formerly Adamsville and Edwardsburg); Jeffrey L. Reese Dec. 1, 1997-Dec. 31, 2016; Evan Lash
   Feb. 1-June 30, 2017; Scott K. Otis 2017- 2020; Nathaniel R. Starkey 2020-

Elba UMC *[East Winds]* jbja4047@hotmail.com
(P/M) 154 S Elba Rd, Lapeer 48446 (810) 664-5780
Emmett E. Coons 1969-1974; James M. Thompson 1974-1980; David R. McKinstry 1980-1988; Georg F. W. Gerritsen 1988-1996; Wayne E. Samson 1996-1998; James E. Paige, Jr. 1998-Oct 1, 2003; James B. Montney 2004-2014; Barbara Benjamin 2014-2016; Marybelle Haynes 2016-2018; Stanley Patrick Stybert Jul 1-Oct 31, 2018; Jeanne Harmon Wisenbaugh (DSA) Nov 1., 2018; Jeanne Harmon Wisenbaugh Apr 1, 2020-

Elberta UMC *[Northern Waters]* feumc@att.net
(P) 555 Lincoln Ave, Elberta 49628; (M) PO Box 405, Elberta 49628-0405 (231) 352-4311
Richard M. Wilson 1967-1971; John Melvin Bricker 1971-1980; Richard C. Kuhn 1980-1982; John D. Morse 1982-1987; Paul D. Mazur 1987-April 1989; Donald R. Ferris April 1989-1993; John W. McNaughton 1993-1996; Marvin R. Rosa 1996-1999; Kathryn M. Coombs 1999-2002; Gregory P. Culver 2002-2010; Barbara J. Fay 2010-Dec 31, 2019; Nancy Conrad (DSA) Jan 1-Jun 30, 2020; Penny L. Parkin May 1, 2020-

Elkton UMC *[Central Bay]* elktonumc@yahoo.com
(P) 150 S Main St, Elkton 48731; (M) PO Box 9, Elkton 48731-0009 (989) 375-4113
Thomas J. Wood 1965-1970; O. William Cooper 1970-1974; Albert E. Hartoog 1974-1978; Joel W. Hurley 1978-1983; Ronald L. Iris 1983-1985; James P. Kummer 1985-1989; James P. James 1989-1992; Sang Yoon (Abraham) Chun 1992-1996; W. Peter Crawford 1996-2006; David C. Collins 2006-Apr 15, 2009; John W. Ball Apr 15, 2009-2009; Craig A. Pillow 2009-Oct 31, 2016; Won Dong Kim Jan 1, 2017

Elsie UMC *[Mid-Michigan]* elsieumc@mutualdata.com
(P) 160 W Main St, Elsie 48831; (M) PO Box 189, Elsie 48831-0189 (989) 862-5239
Gordon Showers 1965-1970; David Litchfield 1970-1976; David Miles 1976-1983; Joe Glover 1983-1985; Fred Fischer 1985-1996; Merlin Pratt 1996-2003; David C. Blair 2003-2004; Jayme L. Kendall 2004-2005; Edwin D. Snook July 16, 2005-2012; Mona Kindel (3/4 time) 2012-2013; Donald R. Ferris-McCann (3/4 time) 2013-2016 [Elsie/Salem became a charge 5-1-14]; Robert D. Nystrom 2016-2018; [Elsie / Ovid became a two-point charge 2016] Ara R Williams (DSA) (LTFT 1/2) 2018-2020; Jung Du Paik Jul 15, 2020-

Emmett Cnty: New Hope UMC *[Northern Skies]* newhopeofemmet@gmail.com
(P) 4516 US Highway 31, Levering 49755; (M) PO Box 72, Levering 49755 (231) 537-2000
Matthew Todd Stoll 2003-2010; Vaughn Thurston-Cox 2010-2015; [Epsilon/New Hope/Harbor Springs/Alanson became a 4-point charge 2014] Hillary Thurston-Cox (Assoc.) 2014-Jan. 1, 2015; [New Hope UMC of Emmett County became a single-point charge 2015] Everett L. Harpole 2015-Dec. 1, 2015; Michelle K. Merchant (DSA) Dec. 1, 2015-Nov. 14, 2016; Michelle K. Merchant (LTFT) Nov. 15, 2016-

Empire UMC *[Northern Waters]* empireumc@centurytel.net
(P) 10050 W Michigan St, Empire 49630; (M) PO Box 261, Empire 49630 (231) 326-5510
Elmer J. Faust 1966-1969; Edward R. Jones 1969-1971; Alvin Doten 1971-1976; Harry R. Johnson 1976-Sept. 1978; Emmett Kadwell Jr. Oct. 1978-1982; Andrew Weeks 1982-1985; Melanie Baker-Streevy 1985-1988; Kenneth Curtis 1988-1991; Kathryn M. Coombs 1991-1998; William (Will) McDonald 1998-Jan. 31, 2003; William F. Dye Feb. 1, 2003-2006; Brenda E. Gordon 2006-2014; Russell K. Logston 2014-2019; Melody L. Olin 2019-

Engadine UMC *[Northern Skies]*   engadineumc@yahoo.com
(P) 13970 Park Ave, Engadine 49827; (M) 110 W Harrie St, Newberry 49868   (906) 477-9989
  Vernon D. Wyllys 1969-1975; James Lumsden 1975-1976; Audrey M. Dunlap 1976-1985; Ramona
  Cowling 1985-1987; Phillip D. Voss 1987-1991; Bo L. Lange 1991-1997; Ronald O. Piette 1997-
  2000; Max D. Weeks 2000-2003; Saundra J. Clark 2003-2013; Timothy G. Callows 2013-2020;
  Jacquelyn A. Roe 2020-

Epsilon UMC *[Northern Waters]*   cloud.sik@asburyseminary.edu
(P/M) 8251 E Mitchell Rd, Petoskey 49770   (231) 347-6608
  Norman Crotser 1968-1969; Seward Walton 1969-1976; John Gurney 1976-1979; Marvin Iseminger
  1979-1981; Jerry Jaquish 1981-1987; Glenn Wegner 1987-Aug. 1992; John F. Greer Sept.-Nov.
  1992; Dennis Bromley Jan. 1993-2003; Matthew Todd Stoll 2003-2010; Vaughn Thurston-Cox 2010-
  2016; [Epsilon/New Hope/Harbor Springs/Alanson became a 4-point charge 2014] Hillary
  Thurston-Cox (Assoc.) 2014-2016; Eun Sik Poy 2016- [Epsilon realigned w/ Boyne City / Boyne
  Falls / Epsilon 2016]

Erie UMC *[Heritage]*
(P/M) 1100 E Samaria Rd, Erie 48133   (734) 856-1453
  James L. Hynes 1968-1971; James A. Wagoner 1971-1972; John D. Roach 1972- 1976; Norman
  R. Beckwith, Sr. 1976-1981; Larry J. Werbil 1981-1985; David L. Baize 1985-1986; David E. Ray
  1986-1991; Kenneth C. Reeves 1991-1995; Patricia A. Green 1995-1999; Dana R. Strall 1999-
  2011; Megan J. Walther 2011-2017; Mary Hyer 2017-2018; Janet J Brown 2018-

Escanaba: Central UMC *[Northern Skies]*   churchoffice@escanabacentral.org
(P/M) 322 S Lincoln Rd, Escanaba 49829-1342   (906) 786-0643
  Joseph Ablett 1969-1971; Clem Parr 1971-1980; James Hilliard 1980-1985; Ralph Barteld 1985-
  1991; Daniel M. Young 1991-1995; Philip M. Seymour Sep 1, 1996-1997; Bo L. Lange 1997-2003;
  Scott A. Harmon 2003-2013; Donna J. Minarik 2013-2016; Elise Rodgers Low Edwardson 2016-

Escanaba: First UMC *[Northern Skies]*   firstmet@escanabafirstumc.com
(P/M) 302 S 6th St, Escanaba 49829-3917   (906) 786-3713
  David M. Liscomb 1969-1973; Walter David 1973-1978; Jack Lancaster 1978-1980; Michael L.
  Peterlin 1980-2001; Eileen Kuehnl (assoc) 1995-1997; Philip B. Lynch (assoc) 1997-May 15,2000
  ; Irene R. Peterlin (assoc) 1997-Dec 31,1999; Mary G. Laub 2001-2010; Margaret H. Host 2010-
  2013; Carman Minarik 2013-2016; Ryan C. Edwardson 2016- [Single point charge 7-1-2019]
  [Escanaba: First, Bark River two-point charge 2020]

Essexville: St. Luke's UMC *[Central Bay]*   stlukes-umc@sbcglobal.net
(P/M) 206 Scheurmann St, Essexville 48732-1626   (989) 893-8031
  Glenn Atchinson 1966-1972; Alan DeGraw 1972-1975; Robert Hastings 1975-1980; Warren Pettis
  1980-1987; Philip A. Rice 1987-1997; Duane M. Harris 1997-2005; Juanita J. Ferguson 2005-2009;
  Eric A. Stone 2009-2020; Jenaba Waggy 2020-

Evart UMC *[Northern Waters]*   evartunitedchurch@yahoo.com
(P) 619 N Cherry St, Evart 49631; (M) PO Box 425, Evart 49631-0425   (231) 734-2130
  Milton TenHave 1967-1970; Marjorie Matthews Feb.-Oct. 1970; Laurence Waterhouse Oct. 1970-
  Oct. 1975; Stanley Hayes Oct. 1975-March 1984; Gerald Welsh 1984-1990; Donald Buege
  1990-2000; Margaret Halls Wilson 2000-2006; Edward H. Slate, 2006-2008; Mark Mitchell 2008-
  2012; Melodye Surgeon (Rider) VanOudheusden 2012-2019; [Evart / Sears became a two-point
  charge 2017] Jean M. Smith 2019-

Ewen UMC *[Northern Skies]*   aa8yf@yahoo.com
(P) 621 M 28, Ewen 49925; (M) PO Box 142, Bergland 49910-0142   (906) 988-2533
   Zina B. Bennett 1965-1970; James R. Hilliard 1970-1971; Lawrence Brooks 1971-1975; Roger
   Gedcke 1972-1979; Lillian Richards 1971-1976; Wayne E. Sparks 1975-1980; Myra Sparks 1976-
   1980; Ed Hingelburg 1979-1981; Robert Thorton 1981-1983; Deane Wyllys 1983-1987; Charles
   H. West 1987-1993; Margaret H. West 1987-1993; Earleen VanConant 1993-1997; Clarence
   VanConant 1993-1997; Timothy C. Dibble 1997-2000; Cherrie A. Sporleder 2000-Jun 15, 2002;
   Theodore A. Trudgeon 2003-2019; [White Pine Community / Ewen / Bergland three-point charge
   7-1-2019] Rosemary R. Dehut 2019-

Fairgrove UMC *[Central Bay]*   fgumc@att.net
(P) 5116 Center St, Fairgrove 48733; (M) PO Box 10, Fairgrove 48733   (989) 693-6564
   David L. Saucier 1965-1972; Donald P. Haskell 1972-1978; John G. Park 1978-1981; C. William
   Bollinger 1981-1984; Otto Flachsmann 1984-1992; David G. Mulder 1992-1996; Kevin Harbin Jan
   1, 1997-1999; Kevin C. Zaborney 1999-Aug 26, 1999; Fredric Heath May 1, 2000-Sep 30, 2001;
   David A. Wichert 2002-2006; Daniel Gonder 2006-2013; William Sanders 2013-Aug 31, 2014;
   Penny L. Parkin Sep 1, 2014-May 31, 2020; James Butler Jun 1, 2020-

Faithorn UMC *[Northern Skies]*   gumc@norwaymi.com
(P) W8601 Blum Rd, Vulcan 49892; (M) 130 O'Dill Dr, Norway 49870
   William D. Schoonover 1967-1974; Emmett Coons 1974-1977; Mark Karls 1977-1983; Ray D. Field
   1983-1985; Carl R. Doersch 1985-1991; Nancy K. Frank 1991-Oct 31, 1994; Deborah R. Jones
   Feb 16, 1995-1996; David M. Wallis 1996-2006; James E. Britt Aug 16, 2006-2011; Irene R. White
   2011-

Farmington: First UMC *[Greater Detroit]*   ann5@farmingtonfumc.org
(P) 33112 Grand River Ave, Farmington 48336; (M) PO Box 38, Farmington 48332 (248) 474-6573
   Hugh C. White 1969-1972; B. Bryce Swiler (assoc) 1967-1971; John N. Howell 1972-1978; R.
   Howard F. Snell (assoc) 1971-1977; Charles H. Beynon 1978-1983; Arthur L. Spafford 1983-1991;
   Edward L. Duncan 1991-1995; Wayne T. Large 1995-Jun 1, 2001; Sondra B. Willobee (assoc)
   1999-2007; Jeffrey R. Maxwell 2001-2010; Carolyn S. Wik (deacon) 2000-2014; Robert D. Brenner
   2010-2013; Marshal G. Dunlap 2013-Feb 1, 2016; Cornelius Davis, Jr., Feb 1, 2016-2016; Anthony
   R. Hood 2016-

Farmington: Nardin Park UMC *[Greater Detroit]*   LMcDoniel@NardinPark.org
(P/M) 29887 W 11 Mile Rd, Farmington Hills 48336   (248) 476-8860
   William D. Mercer 1963-1980; Meredith T. Moshauer (assoc) 1969- 1977; Robert C. Laphew (assoc)
   1970-1972; James F. Thomas (assoc) 1972-1982; William E. Frayer (assoc) 1977-1982; William
   A. Ritter 1980-1993; Jeffry W. Dinner (assoc) 1982-Nov. 1983; David Strobe (assoc) 1984-1989;
   George Kilbourn (R. assoc) 1984-1992; David Penniman (assoc) 1989-1993; Karen D. Poole
   (assoc) 1993-1997; Richard A. Peacock 1993-1997; Benjamin Bohnsack 1997-2006; Kathleen
   Groff (assoc) 1997-Aug 31, 2002; Jane A. Berquist (deacon) 1997-2006; Mary Ann Shipley (assoc)
   Nov 1, 2002-2008; Dale M. Miller 2006-2016; Susan M. Youmans (assoc) 2008-2012; Beth Titus
   (assoc.) Feb 1, 2015-; Melanie Lee Carey 2016-

Farmington: Orchard UMC *[Greater Detroit]*   info@orchardumc.org
(P/M) 30450 Farmington Rd, Farmington Hills 48334   (248) 626-3620
   Eric S. Hammar 1967-1977; William M. Hughes (assoc) 1967-1972; James F. Thomas (assoc)
   1972-1982; Robert L.S. Brown 1977-1985; Nancy A. Woycik (assoc) 1982-1987; Paul F. Blomquist
   1985-1996; James E. Greer II (assoc) 1987-1990; David Huseltine (assoc) 1990-1994; Eric A.
   Stone (assoc) 1994-Feb 1, 1998; Carol J. Johns 1996-2015; Margo B. Dexter (deacon) 1998-Apr,
   2012; Suzanne K. Goodwin (deacon) 2008-2019; Amy Mayo-Moyle 2015- ; Nicholas E. Bonsky
   (assoc) 2019-

Farwell UMC *[Central Bay]* office@farwellumc.org
(P) 281 E Ohio St, Farwell 48622; (M) PO Box 709, Farwell 48622-0709 (989) 588-2931
Leroy Howe 1967-Dec. 1967; Eldon K. Eldred Dec. 1967-1969; George B. Rule 1969-Feb. 1970;
Altha M. Barnes Feb. 15-June 1970; Miriam F. DeMint 1970-1971; Chester J. Erickson 1971-1974;
John W. Bullock 1974-1978; Dwight J. Burton 1978-1983; David L. Miles 1983-1994; Thomas E.
Ball 1994-2000; Jane Ellen Johnson 2000-Jan. 1, 2007; Connie R. Bongard Jan. 1, 2007-2015;
Michael Neihardt 2015-Sept. 25, 2016; Martin T. Cobb 2017-

Felt Plains UMC *[Mid-Michigan]* feltplainsumc@wowway.biz
(P) 3523 Meridian Rd, Leslie 49251; (M) 401 S Main St, Leslie 49251 (517) 589-9211
William Wurzel 1966-1969; Gordon E. Spalenka June-Oct. 1969; Arthur A. Jackson Oct. 1969-
1972; Wayne E. Sparks 1972-1975; James M. Morgan 1975-1982; Max J. Gladding 1982-1990;
Clinton McKinven-Copus 1990-Oct. 1991; Reva Hawke Oct. 1991-April 1993; Derek DeToni-Hill
1993-Oct. 15, 1999; Janet Sweet-Richardson Nov. 1, 1999-2003; Carroll Arthur Fowler 2003-Jan.
1, 2006; Donald L. Buege Jan. 15, 2006-2014; Kelly M. Wasnich July 1-Aug. 10, 2014; Frederick
H. Fischer (Ret.) Sept. 14, 2014-2015; Daniel J.W. Phillips 2015-2017; [Grovenburg / Jackson:
Zion / Felt Plains / Williamston: Wheatfield became multi-point charge 2017] John Kabala Ilunga
2017-2018 ; Gertrude Mwadi Mukalay 2017-2018; Paul A Damkoehler (LTFT) 2018-2020 [Leslie /
Felt Plains became a two-point charge 2018] [Millville, Leslie, Felt Plains became 3-point charge
2020] Rhonda J. Osterman 2020-

Fenton UMC *[East Winds]* kim.chase@fentonumc.com
(P/M) 119 S Leroy St, Fenton 48430 (810) 629-2132
Eskil H. Fredrickson 1966-1972; G. Russell Nachtrieb 1972-1974; Theodore I. Hastings 1974-Nov.
1979; James L. Hynes Nov. 1979-1985; Keith Rasey (assoc) 1980-1981; Ellis Fenton (assoc) Nov.
1988-1990; David W. Truran 1986-Dec 6, 2006; Zack A. Clayton (assoc) 1990-1992; Margaret R.
Garrigues-Cortelyou (assoc) 1992-Aug 31, 1994; Nancy A. Frank (assoc.) Nov 1, 1994-1996; Carol
M. (Blair) Bouse (assoc) Oct 1, 1996-2001; David G. Mulder (assoc) 2001-2008; Matthew J. Packer
(diaconal) 2000-2006; Edmond G. Taverine 2007-Apr 30, 2011; Jeremy T. Peters (assoc) 2008-
2015; William R. Donahue, Jr. 2011-Mar 11, 2014; Terry Euper (interim) Mar 15, 2014-2014; Jeffry
J. Jaggers 2014-; Michelle N. Forsyth (assoc.) 2015- [Fenton became single station 2020]

Fennville UMC *[Greater Southwest]* fenumc@frontier.com
(P) 5849 124th Ave, Fennville 49408; (M) PO Box 407, Fennville 49408 (269) 561-5048
Lloyd R. VanLente 1968-1971; Matthew Walkotten 1971-1976; Miriam DeMint 1976-1978; Ronald
Hansen 1978-1984; Stanley Hayes 1984-1990; James Fox 1990-1992; Randall R. Hansen 1992-
2000; Jane A. Crabtree 2000-2002; Jean Crabtree (DSA) (Assoc.) 2000-2002; Robert L. Hinklin
(DSA) 2002-2003; Raymond R. Sundell 2003-2008; Gary L. Peterson 2008-2016; Daniel L.
Barkholz 2016-2017; Eric Perry (DSA) 2017-May 30, 2018; Douglas Allan Tipken (DSA) Jun. 1-
Dec. 31, 2018; Douglas Allan Tipken Jan. 1, 2019-

Fennville: Pearl UMC *[Greater Southwest]* fenumc@frontier.com
(P) 1689 56th St, Fennville 49408 (M) PO Box 407, Fennville 49408 (269-)561-5048
Ronald Wise 1968-1969; Harold Arman 1969-1971; Arthur Beadle 1971-1973; Matthew Walkotten
1973-1976; Miriam DeMint 1976-1978; Ronald Hansen 1978-1984; Stanley Hayes 1984-1990;
James Fox 1990-1992; Randall R. Hansen 1992-2000; Jane A. Crabtree 2000-2002; Jean Crabtree
(DSA) (Assoc.) 2000-2002; Robert L. Hinklin (DSA) 2002-; Raymond R. Sundell 2003-2008; Gary
L. Peterson 2008-2016; Daniel L. Barkholz 2016-2017; Eric Perry (DSA) 2017-May 30, 2018;
Douglas Allan Tipken (DSA) Jun. 1-Dec. 31, 2018; Douglas Allan Tipken Jan. 1, 2019-

Fenwick UMC *[Midwest]*   fenwickumc@cmsinter.net
(P) 235 W Fenwick Rd, Fenwick 48834; (M) PO Box 241, Sheridan 48884   (989) 291-5547
  John H. Gurney 1970-1976; Norman Crotser 1976-Dec. 1978; Daniel R. Bennett 1979-March 1982;
  Mark G. Johnson March 1982-1986; James E. Cook 1986-1991; Howard H. Harvey 1991-1996;
  Patrick Glass 1996-1998; Larry W. Nalett 1998-Aug. 9, 2004; Charles E. Cerling Aug. 10, 2004-
  2009; Jolennda Cole (DSA) 2009-2010; Jolennda Cole 2010-2011; William F. Dye 2011-2012;
  Russell D. Morgan (CLM) July 15, 2012-2014; Gerald A Erskine 2014-2020; Melissa S. Wagner
  (DSA) 2020-

Ferndale: First UMC *[Greater Detroit]*   ferndalefirstumc@ameritech.net
(P/M) 22331 Woodward Ave, Ferndale 48220   (248) 545-4467
  William N. Mertz 1965-1969; Joseph T. Edwards 1969-1974; James M. Morgan (assoc) 1969-1970;
  Arthur L. Spafford 1974-1983; David Stiles (assoc) 1970-1974; James Rupert (assoc) 1974-Dec
  1975; Douglas K. Olsen (assoc) 1976-1981; Terry W. Allen 1983-1989; George Spencer 1989-Feb
  21, 1997; Patricia A. Meyers 1997-1999; Dennis N. Paulson 1999-2008; Rony Veska 2008-2013;
  Robert Schoenals 2013-

Fife Lake UMC *[Northern Waters]*   jack49668@gmail.com
(P) 206 Boyd St, Fife Lake 49633; (M) PO Box 69, Fife Lake 49633-0069   (231) 920-2908
  Gerald L. Hedlund 1966-1971; Arthur and Molly Turner (co-pastors) 1971-1976; Diane Vale 1976-
  Oct. 1977; Marion Nye Dec. 1977-1978; Pulpit Supply 1978-1979; Athel Lynch 1979-1981; Pulpit
  Supply 1981-1983; Daniel Biteman, Jr. 1983-1985; Clinton McKinven-Copus 1985-1987; Gary
  Wales 1987-1994; Howard Seaver 1994-2012; Mark E. Mitchell 2012-2014; Donald L. Buege 2014-
  2017; [Williamsburg and (Fife Lake Boardman Parish) Fife Lake / East Boardman / South Boardman
  became multi-point charge 2017] John J. Conklin 2017-2020 [2018 Williamsburg, Fife Lake, East
  Boardman, South Boardman formed the Unified Parish] John D. Messner 2020-

Flat Rock: First UMC *[Greater Detroit]*   flatrockumc@sbcglobal.net
(P/M) 28400 Evergreen St, Flat Rock 48134   (734) 782-2565
  Floyd P. Braun 1967-1970; Ronald D. Carter 1970-1979; Clyde E. Smith 1979-1981; John W. Hinkle
  1981-1989; Gary R. Imms 1989-1991; Alan W. DeGraw 1991-1995; Evans C. Bentley 1995-2004;
  David E. Huseltine 2004-Jul 31, 2008; John K. Benissan Aug 1, 2008-2011; Dana R. Strall 2011-
  2017; Amy Triebwasser 2017-

Flint: Asbury UMC *[East Winds]*   flintasburyumc@gmail.com
(P/M) 1653 Davison Rd, Flint 48506   (810) 235-0016
  Paul I. Greer 1969-1971; Albert C. Fennell 1971-1976; Eskil H. Fredrickson 1976-1982; William D.
  Schoonover 1982-Feb. 16, 1990; Grant Wessel (associate) 1985-1987; Leonard W. Gamber 1990-
  1996; Gary A. Allward 1996-2000; James R. Rupert 2000-Jul 31, 2006; Michael L. Quayle Aug 1,
  2006-2007; S. Patrick Stybert 2007-2010; Tommy L. McDoniel 2010-

Flint: Bethel UMC *[East Winds]*   bchr@att.net
(P/M) 1309 N Ballenger Hwy, Flint 48504   (810) 238-3843
  Donald E. Morris 1969-1973; Russell F. McReynolds 1973-1991; Alonzo E. Vincent 1991-2005;
  Tara R. Sutton 2005-2012; Faith E. Green Timmons 2012-Mar 30, 2018; Andrew Amadu Allie (Ret.)
  Apr 1-Jun 30, 2018; Joy Jittaun Moore 2018-2019; Andrew Amadu Allie (Ret.) (interm) 2019-2020;
  James I. Cogman 2020-

Flint: Bristol UMC *[East Winds]*   bristolchurch2015@gmail.com
(P/M) 5285 Van Slyke Rd, Flint 48507   (810) 238-9244
  Nelson D. Cushman 1969-1971; Fred W. Knecht 1971-1973; Robert T. Koch 1973-1981; Gary
  Imms May, 1981-1982; Eugene K. Bacon 1982-1988; Hoon Hee Wong 1988-1991; Marjorie H.
  Munger 1991-1993; Randy J. Whitcomb 1993-Apr 30, 1996; S. Patrick Stybert Jun 16, 1996-2000;
  Elizabeth M. Gamboa 2000-2003; Olaf R. Lidums 2003-2007; Melvin L. Herman Oct 1, 2007-2018;
  Brian K. Willingham 2018- [Flint: Bristol / Buron: Christ became a two-point charge on May 1, 2019]

CHURCH HISTORIES

Flint: Calvary UMC *[East Winds]*   flintclavary@gmail.com
(P/M) 2111 Flushing Rd, Flint 48504-4722   (810) 238-7685
  Dorraine S. Snogren 1968-1990; James P. Kummer (assoc) Apr. 15, 1989-Jan. 31, 1992; James
  E. Tuttle 1990-1999; Steven A. Miller 1999-2004; Ray T. McGee 2004-2011; James E. Britt 2011-
  2018; Gregory E. Timmons (DSA) 2018-Dec 31, 2018; Gregory E. Timmons Jan 1, 2019- [Fliint:
  Charity merged w/ Flint: Calvary 7-1-2020]

Flint: Court Street UMC *[East Winds]*   courtstreetumc@comcast.net
(P/M) 225 W Court St, Flint 48502-1130   (810) 235-4651
  Robert P. Ward 1969-1972, Jack E. Price (assoc) 1966-1974; Andrew A. Michelson (assoc) 1968-
  1972; Kenneth R. Callis 1972-1977; H. Emery Hinkston (assoc) 1972-1974; Douglas K. Mercer (assoc)
  1974-1977; Kenneth A. Kohlmann (assoc) 1974-1977; Ralph W. Janka 1977-1986; Donald E. Hall
  (assoc) 1977-1986; Theodore E. Doane 1986-1990; James D. Cochran (assoc) 1986-1988; Horace
  L. James (assoc) 1985-; David G. Mulder (assoc) 1988-1992; John E. Harnish 1990-1993; Paula M.
  Timm (assoc) 1992-Apr 15, 1994; Steven J. Buck 1993-2008; Weatherly A. Burkhead Verhelst (assoc)
  1994-1998; Shirley A. Cormicle (assoc) 1999-Jan 1, 2003; Murphy S. Ehlers (deacon) Oct 1, 2000-
  Dec 1, 2002; Margie R. Crawford (assoc.) 2005-2008; Alicea Williams (deacon) 2007-Sep 30, 2008;
  Robert D. Wright 2008-2015; Jeremy T. Peters 2015-

Flint: Hope UMC *[East Winds]*   flinthopeumc@yahoo.com
(P/M) G-4467 Beecher Rd, Flint 48532-8532   (810) 732-4820
  Gerald H. Fisher 1969-Mar. 1974; Howard B. Childs Mar. 1974-1980; M. Clement Parr 1980-1985;
  Margaret Rodgers West (assoc) 1982-1983; Frank A. Cozadd 1985-1989; Ralph H. Pieper II 1989-
  1996; John G. Park 1996-2006' John C. Ferris 2006-2012; John H. Amick 2012-2013; Carol Blair
  Bouse 2013-

Flushing UMC *[East Winds]*   flumc@sbcglobal.net
(P/M) 413 E Main St, Flushing 48433-2029   (810) 659-5172
  Thomas F. Jackson 1968-1971; Jack E. Giguere 1971-1980; Grant A. Washburn (assoc) 1972-
  1975; Stephen K. Perrine (assoc) 1975-Oct. 1977; Eugene K. Bacon (assoc) 1978-1982; Maurice
  D. Sharai 1980-1989; Cherie R. Boeneman (assoc) 1982-1983; David L. Baize (assoc) 1983-1985;
  Kathryn S. Snedeker (assoc) 1985-1988; Susan Jo Arnold Word (assoc) 1988-1991; Gary L.
  Sanderson 1989-1995; Nanette D. Myers (assoc) 1991-Jan 1, 1997; Adam W. Bissell (assoc) 1997-
  1998; Bruce M. Denton 1995-2004; Donald S. Weatherup (assoc) 2002-2006; Jeffrey L. Jaggers
  2004-2014; Matthew Packer (diaconal) 2008- ; Deborah A. Line Yencer 2014-

Forester UMC *[East Winds]*   eos@globali.us
(P) 2481 N Lakeshore Rd, Carsonville 48419; (M) 7209 Main St, Port Sanilac 48469   (810) 366-0369
  James B. Lumsden 1969-1973; J. Paul Pumphrey 1973-1977; Glenn R. Wegner 1977-1980; James
  P. Kummer Dec. 1980-1985; Kenneth C. Reeves 1985-1991; Gloria Haynes 1991-1996; Ellen Burns
  1996-2000; Robert A. Srock 2000-2002; John H. Rapson 2002-2004; Clarence W. VanConant 2004-
  2007; Ellen O. Schippert 2007-2014; Mark Harriman 2016-2018; Anika Bailey 2018-

Fostoria UMC *[East Winds]*   pastor.kay@live.com
(P) 9115 Fostoria Rd, Fostoria 48435; (M) PO Box 125, Otisville 48463   (810) 631-8395
  Donald L. Lichtenfelt 1969-1970; Ralph T. Barteld 1970-1979; Dale E. Brown 1979-1984; Allen J.
  Lewis Inter.; Wayne C. Ferrigan 1984-1986; William J. Maynard 1986-1992; Bonny J. Lancaster 1992-
  1997; Donald Fairchild Jan 1, 1998-2001; David P. Rahn 2001-2009; Peggy Garrigues-Cortelyou May
  10, 2009-2010; Betty Kay Leitelt 2010-

Fowlerville: First UMC *[Ann Arbor]* fumc201@sbcglobal.net
(P) 201 S 2nd St, Fowlerville 48836; (M) PO Box 344, Fowlerville 48836 (517) 223-8824
  Ronald A. Brunger 1965-1971; Ralph A. Edwards 1971-1975; Emil E. Haering 1975-1982; Paul L. Amstutz 1982-1987; Robert B. Secrist 1987-1991; J. Gordon Schleicher 1991-Aug. 14, 1992; Donald H. Francis Sep. 15, 1992-2000; S. Patrick Stybert 2000-2007; Thomas E. Tarpley 2007-2015; Robert Freysinger 2015-2016; Scott A. Herald 2016-

Fowlerville: Trinity Livingston Circuit UMC *[Heritage]* livcirumc@gmail.com
(P/M) 8201 Iosco Rd, Fowlerville 48836-9265 (517) 223-3803
  Harry Gintzer 1966-1969; Roger A. Parker 1969-1970; Thomas E. Hart 1970-1975; Jerome K. Smith 1975-1981; Meredith T. Moshauer 1981-Dec. 31, 1981; William R. Donahue Jr. Jan. 14, 1982-Dec. 31, 1987; Richard W. Sheppard Jan. 15, 1988-Dec. 31, 1989; Paul F. Bailey Jan. 1, 1990-1991; Margery A. Schleicher 1991-1995; Myra L. Sparks 1995-Aug 31, 1997; Darrel L. Rice Jan 1, 1998-2003; Malcolm L. Greene 2003-Aug 31, 2004; Steven A Gjerstad Sep 1, 2004-2006; Judith M. Darling 2006-2009; Alan DeGraw (interim) 2009-Dec 31, 2009; Robert A. Miller Jan 1, 2010-2013; David C. Freeland 2013-2017; Mark Huff Nov 12, 2017-

Frankenmuth UMC *[Central Bay]* fmuthumc@airadv.net
(P/M) 346 E Vates St, Frankenmuth 48734 (989) 652-6858
  Gordon E. Ackerman 1969-1983; G. Charles Ball 1983-1996; Douglas K. Mercer 1996-2000; Kenneth L. Christler 2000-2006; David A. Eardley 2006-2013; Scott Harmon 2013-2017; Reed P. Swanson 2017-Feb 6, 2018; Mark A Karls (Ret.) Feb 7, 2018-2019; Ryan L. Wenburg 2019-

Frankfort UMC *[Northern Waters]* feumc@att.net
(P) 537 Crystal Ave, Frankfort 49635; (M) PO Box 1010, Frankfort 49635 (231) 352-7427
  Richard M. Wilson 1967-1971; John Melvin Bricker 1971-1980; Richard C. Kuhn 1980-1982; John D. Morse 1982-1987; Paul D. Mazur 1987-April 1989; Donald R. Ferris April 1989-1993; John W. McNaughton 1993-1996; Marvin R. Rosa 1996-1999; Kathryn M. Coombs 1999-2002; Gregory P. Culver 2002-2010; Barbara J. Fay 2010-Dec 31, 2019; Nancy Conrad (DSA) Jan 1-Jun 30, 2020; Penny L. Parkin May 1, 2020-

Franklin: Community UMC *[Greater Detroit]* ffranklincc@aol.com
(P/M) 26425 Wellington Rd, Franklin 48025 (248) 626-6606
  Frank B. Cowick 1967-1980; Roger M. Ireson (assoc) 1970-1975; Jack Stubbs (assoc) 1976-1980; Samuel F. Stout 1980-1988; J. Douglas Parker (R. assoc) 1985-; William P. Sanders (assoc) 1987-1988; Richard C. Cheatham 1988-Aug 31, 1998; George F. Ward (assoc) 1988-1993; Bruce E. Petrick 1997-1998; Karl L. Zeigler Sep 1, 1998-Oct 31, 2000; Murphy Ehlers (diaconal) Nov 1, 1998-Sep 30, 2000; James E. Greer Nov 16, 2000-2013; Lynn M. Hasley 2013-2016; David Huseltine 2016-

Fraser: Christ UMC *[Greater Detroit]* cumcfraser@msn.com
(P/M) 34385 Garfield Rd, Fraser 48026 (586) 293-5340
  Eric G. Wehrli 1967-1993; Stephen E. Wenzel 1993-Jul 1, 1994; Melvin Leach Jan 1, 1995-2015; Catherine Miles (deacon) Aug 1, 2013-2015; Kevin J. Harbin 2015-Mar 26, 2020; Dennis E. Irish Apr 1, 2020-

Freeland UMC *[Central Bay]* freelandumc@gmail.com
(P) 205 E Washington Rd, Freeland 48623; (M) PO Box 207, Freeland 48623 (989) 695-2101
  Howard Montgomery 1967 1974; David Truran 1974-1979; Philip A. Rice 1979-1987; Dennis N. Paulson 1987-1989; Harold J. Slater 1989-1992; Paul B. Lim 1992-Mar 31, 1996; James L. Rule Jun 1, 1996-2012; Jaye Reisinger (deacon) 1999-; Lynda F. Frazier 2012-Feb 14, 2014; Elizabeth Librande Feb 15, 2014-2017; Kayla J. Roosa 2017-

Free Soil - Fountain UMC *[Northern Waters]*   onchristthesolidrockistandd@gmail.com
(P) 2549 E Michigan St, Free Soil 49411; (M) PO Box 173, Free Soil 49411   (231) 690-4591
  Viola Norman 1967-1971; Robert Doner June-Dec. 1971; Lewis Buchner Jan. 1972-Aug. 1972;
  Russell Garrigus Sept. 1972-1993; Warren Wood (DSA) 1993-Nov. 1, 1999; Kenneth E. Tabor Nov.
  1, 1999-2000; Janet Lynne O'Brien (DSA) 2001-Nov. 30, 2001; Janet Lynne O'Brien (part-time)
  Dec. 1, 2001-2009; Mona Dye 2009-2011; Joyce A. Theisen (DSA) 2011-2013; Richard D. Roberts
  (DSA) 2013-11/30/2015; Richard D. Roberts (PL) 12/01/2015

Free Soil - Fountain UMC – Fountain Campus *[Northern Waters]*
(P) 5043 N Foster St, Fountain 49410; (M) PO Box 173, Free Soil 49411   (231) 690-4591
  Viola Norman 1967-1971; Robert Doner June-Dec. 1971; Lewis Buchner Jan. 1972-Aug. 1972;
  Russell Garrigus Sept. 1972-1993; Warren Wood (DSA) 1993-Nov. 1, 1999; Kenneth E. Tabor Nov.
  1, 1999-2000; Janet Lynne O'Brien (DSA) 2001-Nov. 30, 2001; Jan O'Brien (part-time) Dec. 1,
  2001-2002; Lemuel O. Granada 2002-2003; Lemuel Granada 2005-Nov. 30, 2007; Mona J. Dye
  (part-time) Dec. 1, 2007-2011; Joyce A. Theisen (DSA) 2011-2013; Richard D. Roberts (DSA) 2013-
  11/30/2015; Richard D. Roberts (PL) 12/01/2015

Freeport UMC *[Mid-Michigan]*   macousino1@gmail.com
(P) 193 Cherry St, Freeport 49325; (M) PO Box 142, Freeport 49325-0142   (616) 765-5316
  Harold M. Taber 1966-1969; Charles W. Martin 1969-Oct. 1973; Harold R. Simon Nov. 1973-Oct.
  1976; Arthur D. Jackson Apr. 1977-1981; Bradley P. Kalajainen Jan. 1981-1985; Gilbert R. Boersma
  1985-Jan. 1989; Janet K. Sweet 1989-1991; Carroll A. Fowler 1991-April 15, 1995; Paulette Cheyne
  June 1, 1995-1999; Richard A. Powell 1999-Aug. 15, 1999; Deborah R. Miller Aug. 16, 1999-Jan.
  31, 2002; Paul Peterson (DSA) 2002-2004; Scott E. Manning 2004-2006; Susan D. Olsen 2006-
  2015; Mickey Ann Cousino (CLM/DSA) Sept. 1, 2015-

Fremont UMC *[Midwest]*   umcfremont@att.net
(P/M) 351 Butterfield St, Fremont 49412   (231) 924-0030
  Lynn DeMoss 1966-1969; Bertram Vermeulen 1969-1978; Constance Heffelfinger (Assoc.) 1978-
  1981; Eldon K. Eldred 1979-1987; A. Edward Perkins 1987-1990; Harold F. Filbrandt 1990-1994;
  Daniel M. Duncan 1994-2003; Lawrence R. Wood 2003-2007; Carolin S. Spragg 2007-2013; Martin
  T. Cobb 2013-2017; Julie E. Fairchild 2017-2020; Donna J. Minarik 2020-

Frontier UMC *[Heritage]*
(P) 9925 Short St, Frontier 49239; (M) PO Box 120, Frontier 49239-0120   (269) 223-0631
  Kenneth Karlzen 1966-1968; Charles D. Grauer 1968-1970; Daniel W. Harris 1970-1971; Robert
  E. Jones 1971-Nov. 15, 1973; Marion V. Nye Nov. 15, 1973-1976; Daniel R. Bennett Feb. 1, 1977-
  1979; Leonard J. Yarlott 1979-1982; Gilbert R. Boersma 1982-1985; Valerie M. Hill 1985-1989;
  Jerry L. Hippensteel 1989-1994; Susan Deason 1994-1998; Kathy L. Nitz 1998-Aug. 15, 1999;
  Donald Lee (DSA) 2002-2010; Cynthia Veilleux (DSA) Nov. 1, 2010-2011; Timothy R. Puckett (part-
  time) 2011-2014; Martin Johnston Sept. 1, 2014-2017; Donald Lee 2017-

Gaines UMC *[East Winds]*   dadj@hotmail.com
(P) 117 W. Clinton St, Gaines 48436; (M) PO Box 125, Gaines 48436   (989) 271-9131
  John M. Miller 1969-1970; John D. Roach 1970-1972; Verne W. Blankenburg 1972-1977; David S.
  Stiles 1977-1980; Mary Isaacs Frost 1980-Oct. 1982; Harry R. Weeks Oct. 1982-Feb. 15, 1986;
  Larry J. Werbil 1986-Aug. 15, 1989; Dorothy Rossman (Interim part-time); Myra Lee Sparks Oct.
  16, 1989-1995; David L. Fleming 1995-1999; Harlan E. Sorensen 1999-Nov 14, 2004; John D.
  Bailey 2005-2010; David A. Wichert 2010-2013; Eric L. Johnson 2013-2018; Barbara Benjamin
  2018-

Galesburg UMC *[Greater Southwest]*   galesburgumc@att.net
(P) 111 W Battle Creek St, Galesburg 49053; (M) PO Box 518, Galesburg 49053   (269) 665-7952
Laurence R. Lowell 1968-1969; Pulpit Supply 1969-1970; Milton J. TenHave 1970-1973; Jack Scott
1973-1977; Allan Valkema 1977-1980; Larry Grubaugh 1980-1988; Rochelle Ray 1988-1992; John
L. Moore 1992-1995; Charles M. Shields 1995-1997; Janet Sweet-Richardson 1997-Nov. 1, 1999;
Michael Baker-Streevy Nov. 16, 1999-2003; Keith W. Heifner 2003-2006; Mona K. Joslyn 2006-
2010; [Comstock UMC merged w/ Galesburg UMC 04-29-07]; Sally K. Harrington (DSA) Nov. 1,
2010-2012; John L. Moore (DSA) (1/2 time) 2012-2013; Leonard R. Schoenherr (Ret.) 2013-2016;
Leonard E. Davis 2016-

Galien UMC *[Greater Southwest]*   galienandolivebranch@gmail.com
(P) 208 N Cleveland Ave, Galien 49113; (M) PO Box 266, Galien 49113   (269) 665-7952
Lawrence Smith 1967-1969; Willard Gilroy 1969-1973; Arthur Beadle 1973-1976; Gordon Everett
(interim) July-Nov. 1976; Richard Williams Dec. 1976-Oct. 1979; Paul Smith Nov. 1979-March 1980;
Joseph Wood (interim) March-June 1980; William Doubblestein 1980-1983; William Carr 1983-
April 1986; Joseph Wood (interim) April-June 1986; Phillip Friedrick 1986-1991; Sherri Swanson
1991-1995; Charlene A. Minger 1995-1999; Valerie Fons 1999-2001; John G. Kasper 2001-2006;
Russell K. Logston 2006-2011; Jeffrey O. Cummings Jan. 1, 2012-2016; Clifford L. Radtke 2016-
2018; Cynthia L. Veilleux (DSA) 2018-

Galien: Olive Branch UMC *[Greater Southwest]*   galienandolivebranch@gmail.com
(P) 2289 Olive Branch Rd, Galien 49113; (M) PO Box 266, Galien 49113   (269) 545-2275
Leslie Smith 1965-1969; Willard Gilroy 1969-1973; Arthur Beadle 1973-1976; Gordon Everett
(interim) July-Nov. 1976; Richard Williams Dec. 1976-Oct. 1979; Paul Smith Nov. 1979-March 1980;
Joseph Wood (interim) March-June 1980; William Doubblestein 1980-1983; William Carr 1983-
April 1986; Joseph Wood (interim) April-June 1986; Phillip Friedrick 1986-1991; Sherri Swanson
1991-1995; Charlene A. Minger 1995-1999; Valerie Fons 1999-2001; John G. Kasper 2001-2006;
Russell K. Logston 2006-2011; Jeffrey O. Cummings Jan. 1, 2012-2016; Clifford L. Radtke 2016-
2018; Cynthia L. Veilleux (DSA) 2018-

Ganges UMC *[Greater Southwest]*   gangumc@frontier.com
(P) 2218 68th St, Fennville 49408; (M) PO Box 511, Fennville 49408-0511   (269) 543-3581
Lloyd R. Van Lente Jan. 1966-1971; Matthew Walkoton 1971-1973; Douglas L. Pederson 1973-
1975; Richard W. McLain 1975-1979; Craig L. Adams 1979-1984; Constance L. Heffelfinger
1984-Jan. 1990; Aurther D. Jackson Jan. 1990-Jan. 1991; Leonard Coon Jan.-June 1991; John
Burgess 1991-1994; Marcia L. Elders 1994-1997; Barbara Jo Fay 1997-Dec.31, 2004; Jean M.
Smith Jan. 16, 2005-Sept. 1, 2010; Jack E. Balgenorth Sept. 1, 2010-2014; [Ganges/Glenn became
single charges 2014] Marcia A. Tucker (DSA) 2014-

Garden City: First UMC *[Greater Detroit]*   fumcgc@hotmail.com
(P/M) 6443 Merriman Rd, Garden City 48135   (734) 421-8628
Glen E. L. Kjellberg 1970-1977; Robert C. Grigereit 1977-1987; David A. Russell 1987-1990; Gary
L. Damon 1990-Jul 31, 1997; Jerome K. Smith Sep 1, 1997-2006; Kenneth C. Bracken 2006-2009;
Pamela Beedle-Gee 2009-2014; Bea Barbara Fraser-Soots 2014-2015; Jonathan Combs Dec 1,
2016-

Garfield UMC *[Central Bay]*
(P) 1701 N Garfield Rd, Linwood 48634; (M) 314 Whyte St, Pinconning 48650   (989) 879-6992
Byron G. Hatch (w/Pinconning) 1969-1972; Richard A. Turner (w/Pinconning) 1971-1981; Jeffrey
R. Maxwell 1982-1984; Eldon C. Schram 1984-1996; Michael Luce 1996-2001; J. Gordon
Schleicher 2001-2003; Jon W. Gougeon 2003-2010; James A. Payne 2010-2013; John Tousciuk
2013-Aug 3, 2016; Heather M. Nowak (DSA) Oct 1, 2016-Sept 30, 2017; Heather M. Nowak Dec
1, 2017-2020; [Bentley, Garfield became 2-point charge 2020] Merry Henderson (DSA) 2020-

Gaylord: First UMC *[Northern Waters]* fumcoffice@winntel.net
(P) 215 S Center Ave, Gaylord 49735; (M) PO Box 617, Gaylord 49734 (989) 732-5380
Raymond Roe 1968-1971; Dwayne Summers 1971-1978; John H. Bunce 1978-1983; Donna J. Lindberg 1983-1989; Warren D. Pettis 1989-1998; John E. Naile 1998-2014; Daniel J. Bowman 2014-2020; Paul J. Gruenberg 2020-

Genesee UMC *[East Winds]* geneseethetford@sbcglobal.net
(P) 7190 N Genesee Rd, Genesee 48437; (M) PO Box 190, Genesee 48437 (810) 640-2280
William H. Brady 1967-1970; John P. Hitchens 1970-1972; Ralph H. Pieper II 1972-1975; Roger L. Colby 1975-1980; James P. Schwandt 1980-1987; David P. Rahn 1987-Nov. 1, 1987; Willard A. King Nov. 1, 1987-Aug 31, 1994; Lorrie E. Plate Sep 1, 1994-1998; Malcolm L. Greene 1998-2003; Bruce L. Nowacek 2003-2010; Karen B. Williams 2010-

Georgetown UMC *[Midwest]* info@gumonline.org
(P/M) 2766 Baldwin St, Jenison 49428 (616) 669-0730
Robert Hinklin Feb. 1, 1976-1984; John R. Smith 1984-Feb. 18, 1999; Joseph J. Bistayi Aug. 16,1999-2005; Joseph D. Huston 2005-2007; William C. Bills 2007-2016; Jennifer Browne 2016-2018; Sherri L Swanson 2018-

Germfask UMC *[Northern Skies]* pastorimcdonald@outlook.com
(P) 1212 Morrison St, Germfask 49836; (M) PO Box 268, Grand Marais 49839 (906) 586-3162
Vernon D. Wyllys 1969-1975; James Lumsden 1975-1976; Audrey Dunlap 1976-1985; Ramona Cowling 1985-1987; John N. Grenfell III 1987-1992; Mary G. Laub 1992-1998; Tracy L. Brooks Aug 16, 1998-2003; Karen A. Mars 2003-2006; Paul J. Mallory 2006-2011; Meredith Rupe Oct 15, 2011-2012; Ian S. McDonald 2012-2019; Devin T. Lawrence (DSA) 2019-

Girard UMC *[Greater Southwest]* girardumcsecretary@gmail.com
(P/M) 990 Marshall Rd, Coldwater 49036 (517) 279-9418
C. Jack Scott 1968-1970; William E. Miles 1970-1971; Harold M. Deipert 1971-1973; Norman A. Charter 1973-1976; Densel G. Fuller 1976-1981; Jerry L. Hippensteel 1981-1984; Thomas E. Ball 1984-Nov. 1988; Stanley Fenner Dec. 1988-1989; Stacy R. Minger 1989-1994; John F. Ritter 1994-1996; Robert Stark 1996-2000; John Scott 2000-Sept. 1, 2003; John A. Scott & Rebecca Scott (CoPastors) Sept 2003-2007; Bruce R. Kintigh 2007-2010; Emily (Slavicek) Beachy Sept. 1, 2010-2014; Cydney Idsinga 2014-2018; Matthew J West 2018-2020; Sean LaGuire 2020-

Gladstone: Memorial UMC *[Northern Skies]* mumc@uplogon.com
(P/M) 1920 Lake Shore Dr, Gladstone 49837 (906) 428-9311
William Verhelst 1968-1974; Wayne T. Large 1974-1981; Dale M. Miller 1981-1988; Douglas K. Mercer 1988-1990; Jeffry W. Dinner 1990-1994; Gary R. Shiplett 1994-2000; Joanne R. Bartelt 2000-2006; Jacquelyn Roe 2006-2010; Elizabeth A. Hill 2010-2015; Caroline F. Hart 2015-2018; Timothy B. Wright 2018-2019; Cathy L. Rafferty 2019-

Gladwin: First UMC *[Central Bay]* fumcgladwin@cynergycomm.net
(P/M) 309 S M 18, Gladwin 48624 (989) 426-9619
John Cermak Sr. 1966-1972; Byron G. Hatch 1972-1976; Donald Bates 1976-1984; Harold Weemhoff 1984-1986; Joel W. Hurley 1986-1992; Deane B. Wyllys 1992-Sep 1, 2002; Jill Bair (diaconal) 1999-2001; Charles Marble Sep 15, 2002-Apr 30, 2003 (interm); Lynn F. Chappell May 1, 2003-2009; David P. Snyder 2009-2012; David D. Amstutz 2012-2018; Carmen Cook 2018-

Glenn UMC *[Greater Southwest]* harold77020@comcast.net
(P) 1391 Blue Star Hwy, Glenn 49416; (M) PO Box 46, Glenn 49416-0046 (269) 227-3930
Lloyd Van Lente 1968-1969; Harold Arman 1969-1971; Arthur Beadle 1971-1973; Pulpit Supply 1973-1974; O. Bernard Strother 1974-1998; Stephen Small Nov. 16, 1998-2001; John R. Cantwell (DSA) 2002-2005; Jean A. Smith 2005-Sept. 1, 2010; Jack E. Balgenorth Sept. 1, 2010-2014; [Ganges/Glenn became single charges 2014] Harold F. Filbrandt (Ret.) 2014-Dec. 31, 2018; Philip S. Harrington 2019-

Glennie UMC *[Central Bay]*
(P) 3170 State St, Glennie 48737; (M) PO Box 189, Glennie 48737-0189
Donald Daws 1965-1971; James Gerzetich 1971-1974; Byron Coleman 1974-1979; Norman Horton 1979-1983; Priscilla Seward 1983-1985; Margaret A. Paige 1985-1986; Margaret A. Paige (1/2 time) 1986-1991; James E. Paige Jr. (1/2 time) 1986-1991; George H. Morse 1991-2000; Brenda K. Klacking 2000-2008; Donald Wojewski 2008-2012; Linda Jo Powers 2012-2014; Mary Soderhold (DSA) Nov 1, 2014-Sept 30, 2015; Charles Soderholm (DSA) Oct 1, 2015-Sept 30, 2016;

Gobles UMC *[Greater Southwest]* info@goblesumc.org
(P) 210 E Exchange St, Gobles 49055; (M) PO Box 57, Gobles 49055-0057   (269) 628-2263
James Boehm 1967-1970; Allen Valkema 1970-1971; William Miles 1971-1974; Rudolph Wittenback 1974-1976; Karen S. Slager-Wheat 1976-1986; John McNaughton 1986-1987; Judy K. Downing 1987-1998; Susan Olsen 1998-2004; Mary Beth Rhine 2004-2010; Edward Mohr L. 2010-Sept. 11, 2012; Daniel J. Minor (Ret.) Sept. 16, 2012-June 30, 2013; Nelson L. Hall 2013-2015; John M. Brooks 2015-2019; [Gobles / Almena became a circuit 2019] Lawrence James French 2019-2020; [Gobles became single station 2020] Ashlei K. Horn 2020-

Goodrich UMC *[East Winds]* office@goodrichumc.org
(P/M) 8071 S State Rd, Goodrich 48438 (810) 636-2444
Gary L. Sanderson 1966-1970; Donald O. Crumm 1970-Jan. 1981; Jerome K. Smith Jan. 1981-Jan. 15, 1986; John W. Elliott Mar. 1, 1986-Jun 30, 1994; Steven A. Gjerstad Jul 1, 1994-Nov 15, 2000; Karl L. Zeigler Nov 16, 2000-2010; Jeremy P. Africa 2010-2015; Won Dong Kim 2015-Dec 31, 2016; Steven J. Buck Jan 1-Jun 30, 2017; Joel L. Walther 2017-

Gordonville UMC *[Central Bay]* gordonvilleumc@parishonline.tv
(P/M) 76 E Gordonville Rd, Midland 48640 (989) 486-1064
H. Emery Hinkston 1969-1972; Robert Moore 1972-1980; Robert Kersten 1980-1982; Paul Riegle 1982-1983; Joy A. Barrett 1983-1988; Charles Keyworth 1988-Aug 31, 1994; Janet M. Larner Sep 1, 1994-2002; Phillip D. Voss 2002-Apr 15, 2003; Tracy L. Brooks 2003-2005; Lynda F. Frazier 2005-Jun 20, 2011; Thomas W. Schomaker (interm) Jun 21, 2010-2015; Josheua Blanchard 2015-Aug 31, 2017; Ernesto Mariona Oct 1, 2017-2020; Michael P. Kelley 2020-

Grand Blanc UMC *[East Winds]* gbumc515@gmail.com
(P/M) 515 Bush Ave, Grand Blanc 48439 (810) 694-9040
James A. Craig 1967-1971; Frank R. Leineke 1971-1977; John S. Jury 1977-1982; James F. Thomas 1982-Jan. 1, 1990; R. Edward McCracken Jan. 1, 1990-1998; Roger L. Colby 1998-2008; Christine E. Wyatt (diaconal) 1999-2002; G. Patrick England 2008-2016; Julius Del Pino 2016-2020; Brian G. West 2020-

Grand Blanc: Phoenix UMC *[East Winds]* phoenixumc@att.net
(P/M) 4423 S Genesee Rd, Grand Blanc 48439-7958 (810) 743-3370
George W. Versteeg 1968-1971; Horace L. James 1971-1975; Louis E. Reyner 1975-1978; Steven Gjerstad 1979-1983; Bonnie D. Byadiah 1983-1992; Colon R. Brown 1992-1997; Paula M. Timm 1997-2001; Bruce L. Billing 2001-2011; Gregory E. Rowe 2011-2016; Sang (Abraham) Chun 2016-

Grand Haven Church of the Dunes *[Midwest]* jblanchard@umcdunes.org
(P/M) 717 Sheldon Rd, Grand Haven 49417 (616) 842-7980
Albert W. Frevert 1965-1972; David Miles (Assoc.) 1971-1976; Charles F. Garrod 1972-1978; Lawrence Wiliford (Assoc.) 1976-1978; Gerald A. Pohly 1978-1980; Victor Charnley (Assoc.) 1978-1984; Robert Gillette (Assoc.) 1984-1991; Ellen A. Brubaker 1989-1992; Richard Youells (Assoc.) 1991-1995; Eldon K. Eldred 1992-2003; Brian F. Rafferty (Assoc.) 1999-2003; Daniel M. Duncan 2003-2014; Glenn M. Wagner 2014-Dec. 31, 2016; John E. Harnish (Ret.) Jan. 1-June 30, 2017; Louis W. Grettenberger 2017-

Grand Ledge: First UMC *[Mid-Michigan]*   glfumc.secretary@comcast.net
(P/M) 411 Harrison St, Grand Ledge 48837   (517) 627-3256
   H. James Birdsall 1967-1973; Royce R. Robinson 1973-1983; Philip L. Brown 1983-1989; Lynn E. Grimes 1989-1993; Robert H. Roth, Jr. (Assoc.) 1991-1994; William J. Amundsen 1993-2003; Barbara Smith Jang (Assoc.) 1994-1997; Jana L. Almeida (Assoc.) 1997-Oct. 15, 1999; Kathleen S. Kursch (Assoc.) Feb. 1, 2000-Aug. 31, 2004; Molly C. Turner 2003-2012; Molly Turner (DSA) July-Dec. 31, 2012; Gregory W. Lawton (Deacon) 2007-2011; Betty A. Smith (Interim) Jan. 1-Mar. 31, 2013; Terry A. Euper Apr. 1-June 30, 2013; Cynthia Skutar 2013-2020; Ronald K. Brooks 2020-

Grand Marais UMC *[Northern Skies]*   thevicar@jamadots.com
(P) N14226 M 77, Grand Marais 49839; (M) PO Box 34, Grand Marais 49839   (906) 494-2653
   Carl Shamblen 1966-1969; Vernon D. Wyllys 1969-1975; James Lumsden 1975-1976; Audrey Dunlap 1976-1981; John N. Grenfell III 1987-1992; Mary G. Laub 1992-1998; Tracy L. Brooks Aug 16, 1998-2003; Karen A. Mars 2003-2006; Paul J. Mallory 2006-2011; Meredith Rupe Oct 15, 2011-2012; Ian S. McDonald 2012-

Grand Rapids: Aldersgate UMC *[Midwest]*   aumcoffice@gmail.com
(P/M) 4301 Ambrose Ave NE, Grand Rapids 49525   (616) 363-3446
   Clinton Galloway 1967-Dec. 1973; Norman Kohns Jan. 1974-1981; William Johnson 1981-1992; Thomas B. Jones (Assoc.) 1990-Dec. 31, 1995; Ellen A. Brubaker 1992-Jan. 1, 2002; Cathi M. Gowin Feb. 1, 2002-2005; Gerald L. Toshalis 2005-2006; Gregory J. Martin 2006-2012; [Grand Rapids Aldersgate / Plainfield became two-point charge 2012] Laurie A. Haller 2012-2013; [became single-point charge 2013] James E. Hodge 2013-

Grand Rapids: Cornerstone UMC *[Midwest]*   infogroup@cornerstonemi.org
(P/M) 1675 84th St SE, Caledonia 49316   (616) 698-3170
   [new church start 1990] Bradley P. Kalajainen 1990- ; Scott Keith Otis (Assoc.) 2003-Oct. 1, 2004; Kenneth J. Nash (Assoc.) 2006-2016; Alejandro D. Fernandez (Heritage Hill Campus Pastor) Jan. 1, 2015- ; Marcia L. Elders (South Wyoming Campus Pastor) Jan. 1-June 30, 2015 [South Wyoming UMC merged w/ Cornerstone UMC Jan. 1, 2015]; Marcus V. Schmidt (South Wyoming Campus Pastor) May 1, 2016-

Grand Rapids: Cornerstone UMC - Heritage Hill Campus *[Midwest]*
(P) 48 Lafayette Ave SE, Grand Rapids 49503; (M) 1675 84th St SE, Caledonia 49316
                                             (616) 698-3170
   [Cornerstone UMC - Heritage Hill Campus launched October 2013] Alejandro D. Fernandez Jan. 1, 2015-

Grand Rapids: Cornerstone UMC - South Wyoming Campus *[Midwest]*
(P) 2730 56th St SW, Wyoming 49418; (M) 1675 84th St SE, Caledonia 49316   (616) 698-3170
   Marcus V. Schmidt May 1, 2016-

Grand Rapids: Faith UMC *[Midwest]*   secretary@grfaithumc.org
(P/M) 2600 7th St NW, Grand Rapids 49504   (616) 453-0693
   Second UMC and Valley UMC merged in 1977 to become Faith UMC. Eugene Lewis 1977-1984; Paul Patterson 1984-1987; Douglas Pedersen 1987-Feb. 15, 1994; Kim L. Gladding 1994-1998; Geoffrey L. Hayes 1998-2009; Mark E. Thompson 2009-2017; Sherri L. Swanson 2017-2018; Daniel M Bilkert (Ret.) 2018-

Grand Rapids: First UMC *[Midwest]*   firstchurch@grandrapidsfumc.org
(P/M) 227 Fulton St E, Grand Rapids 49503   (616) 451-2879
Donald B. Strobe 1964-1972; Carl L. Hausermann (Assoc.) 1967-1971; Lowell F. Walsworth (Assoc.) 1971-1973; John S. Jury 1972-Nov. 1974; Geoffrey L. Hayes (Assoc.) 1973-1978; William W. DesAutels Dec. 1974-1981; Robert E. Jones (Assoc.) 1978-1983; Robert C. Brubaker 1981-Nov. 1987; Darwin R. Salisbury (Assoc.) 1983-1985; Bradley P. Kalajainen (Assoc.) 1985-1990; Lynn A. DeMoss April 1988-1993; Joyce DeToni-Hill (Assoc.) 1990-1991; Derek DeToni-Hill (Assoc.) 1990-1993; Gary T. Haller (Co-pastor) 1993-2013; Laurie A. Haller (Co-pastor) 1993-2006; Dominic A. Tommy (Assoc.) 1997-1999; Jennifer Browne (Assoc.) 2006-2011; Kim DeLong (Deacon - Director of Education)(1/2 time) 2009-2012; Martha Beals (Deacon) (part-time) July 1-Nov. 20, 2009; Janet Carter (Deacon) (part-time) 2009- ; Letisha Bowman (Assoc.) 2011-2015; Robert L. Hundley 2013- ; Amee A. Paparella (Assoc.) 2017-Feb. 27, 2018; Joan Van Dessel (Assoc.) 2019-

Grand Rapids: Genesis UMC *[Midwest]*   info@genesisumc.org
(P/M) 3189 Snow Ave, Lowell 49331   (616) 974-0400
[new church start 1995] M. Christopher Lane & Jane R. Lippert (co-pastors) 1995-2007; Susan M. Petro 2007-2014; DeAnn J. Dobbs 2014-Dec. 31, 2016; Georgia N. Hale (Deacon) 2015- ; John Ross Thompson (Ret.) Jan. 1, 2017-

Grand Rapids: Iglesia Metodista Unida La Nueva Esperanza *[Midwest]*
(P/M) 1005 Evergreen St SE, Grand Rapids 49507   (616) 560-4207
Miguel A. Rivera 1983-1986; Francisco Diaz 1986-1991; Juan B. Falcon 1992-Sep. 1995; Oscar Ventura Sept. 1995-Sept. 2002; Isidro Carrera Sept. 2002-March 16, 2003; Oscar Ventura Mar. 16, 2003-2009; Jorge Rodriguez 2009-2013; Nohemi Ramirez 2013-2018; Laura E. Feliciano 2018-2020; Ricardo Angarita-Oviedo (DSA) 2020-

Grand Rapids: Northlawn UMC *[Midwest]*   office@northlawnumc.org
(P/M) 1157 Northlawn St NE, Grand Rapids 49505   (616) 361-8503
Ivan Niswender 1966-1969; Leonard Putnam 1969-1973; Carlton Benson 1973-1976; Thurlan Meredith 1976-1984; Vance Dimmick, Jr. 1984-1992; Stanley Finkbeiner 1992-1996; Charles R. VanLente 1996-2010; James C. Noggle 2010-2013; Timothy B. Wright 2013-2018; Janice T. Lancaster (Deacon) Feb. 1, 2014-Mar. 31, 2017; Craig L. Adams (Ret.) 2018-2019; Zachary D. McNees 2019-

Grand Rapids: Resotration *[Midwest]*   rccchurch20181@yahoo.com
(P/M) 2730 56th St SW, S Wyoming 49418   (616) 589-4793
[new church start 01/01/2018] Banza Mukalay Jan. 1, 2018-

Grand Rapids: South UMC *[Midwest]*   grsouthumc@comcast.net
(P/M) 4500 Division Ave S, Grand Rapids 49548   (616) 534-8931
Donald Cozadd 1967-1969; Kenneth McCaw 1969-1975; Clarence Hutchens 1975-1979; Ray Burgess 1979-1988; Thomas M. Pier-Fitzgerald 1988-1998; Robert P. Stover 1998-2004; Kathleen S. Kursch Sept. 1, 2004-2007; Mack C. Strange 2007-Jan 18, 2020; Vaughn Thurston-Cox Jan 19-Jun 30, 2020; Michael J. Ramsey 2020-

Grand Rapids: St Paul's UMC *[Midwest]*   grstpaulsumc@gmail.com
(P/M) 3334 Breton Rd SE, Grand Rapids 49512   (616) 949-0880
John S. Myette 1964-1969; William A. Hertell 1969-1974; Robert E. Betts 1974-1982; Edward Trimmer (Assoc.) 1981-1982; Joseph D. Huston 1982-1989; Andrew Jackson (Assoc. part-time) Sept. 1-1986-1994; Theron E. Bailey 1989-1994; Ethel Z. Stears 1994-1999; Robert J. Mayo 1999-2005; Cathi M. Huvaere (formerly Catherine M. Gowin) 2005-2012; Erin L. Fitzgerald 2012-2018; Virginia L. Heller 2018-

Grand Rapids: Trinity UMC *[Midwest]*　　　office@grtumc.org
(P/M) 1100 Lake Dr SE, Grand Rapids 49506　　　(616) 456-7168
　Donn P. Doten 1962-1971; Philip A. Carpenter (Assoc.) 1966-1972; Lawrence R. Taylor 1971-1978; Marvin R. Rosa (Assoc.) Feb. 1972-1979; Charles F. Garrod 1978-1984; William John Amundsen (Assoc.) 1979-1982; Edward A. Trimmer (Assoc.) 1982-1983; Ethel Stears (Assoc.) Sept. 1983-1986; Charles Fry 1984-1989; Timothy P. Boal (Assoc.) 1986-1992; Gerald A. Pohly 1989-1996; Gerald Toshalis (Assoc.) 1992-2001; A. Edward Perkins 1996-2006; Robert Cook (Assoc.) 2001-2006; Carole and Frank Lyman (Co-pastors) 2006-2010; David Nellist 2010-2018; Julie Dix (Assoc.) Nov. 8, 2010-2015; Ellen A. Brubaker and John Ross Thompson (Assoc.) 2015-Sept 1, 2016; Mariel Kay DeMoss 2016- ; Steven W. Manskar 2018-

Grand Rapids: Vietnamese UMC *[Midwest]*　　　dhfishing@yahoo.com
(P/M) 212 Bellevue St SE, Wyoming 49548　　　(616) 534-6262
　Vinh Q. Tran Sept.1, 1987-2004; Cuong Nguyen 2004-2008; Sanh Van Tran 2008-2012; Dung Q. Nguyen 2012-

Grandville UMC *[Midwest]*　　　office@grandvilleumc.com
(P/M) 3140 Wilson Ave SW, Grandville 49418　　　(616) 538-3070
　Dale Brown 1964-Feb. 1973; L. George Babcock (Assoc.) 1967-1972; E. William Wiltse March 1973-1977; William H. Doubblestein (Assoc.) 1974-Aug. 1977; Charles Fullmer 1977-1986; Leon Andrews 1986-1989; Barry Petrucci (Assoc.) 1986-1989; Kim L. Gladding (Assoc.) 1989-1994; J. Melvin Bricker 1989-1995; Rob McPherson (Assoc.) 1994-1999; John Ross Thompson 1995-1998; Robert L. Hinklin 1998-2001; Cathy Rafferty (Assoc.) 1999-2001; Gerald L. Toshalis 2001-; James Edward Hodge (Assoc.) 2001-2005; Thomas M. Pier-Fitzgerald 2005-2016; Ryan B. Wieland 2016-

Grant UMC *[Northern Waters]*　　　grantumcbuckley@gmail.com
(P) 10999 Karlin Rd, Buckley 49620; (M) PO Box 454, Interlochen 49643　　　(231) 269-3981
　Marion Nye 1966-1970; Silas H. Foltz 1970-1971; Lewis (Bud) Buckner 1972-1978; Wayne Babcock 1978-1983; Beverly Prestwood-Taylor 1983-1986; Beverly Prestwood Taylor (3/4 time) 1986-May 1988; Bruce Prestwood-Taylor (3/4 time) 1986-May 1988; Bruce Kintigh 1988-1993; Brian F. Rafferty 1993-1999; Craig South 1999-2002; James L. Breithaupt (1/4 time) 2002-2004; James L. Breithaupt (1/2 time) 2004-Mar. 15, 2006; Carl Greene, Mar. 15, 2006-2011; Robert W. Stark (DSA) 2011; Colleen A. Wierman (1/4 time) Nov. 27, 2011-2017 [Brethren Epworth / Grant became single-point charges 2014]; Sean T. Barton 2017-2018; Daniel L. Gonder 2018-2019; TBS

Grant Center UMC *[Midwest]*
(P/M) 15260 21 Mile Rd, Big Rapids 49307　　　(231) 796-8006
　David A. Cheyne 1977-1982; Wesley E. Smith 1982-Feb.1984; Martin D. Fox May 1984-Sept. 1986; Nelson Ray Dec. 1986-1988; Michael Nicholson 1988-Dec. 1991; Paul Patterson (ret.) Jan.-June 1992; Deborah R. Miller June 1, 1992-1995; Wayne McKinney (DSA) 1995-July 31, 2002; Timothy W. Doubblestein Sept. 1, 2002-Sept. 15, 2003; Sueann K. Hagan Oct. 16, 2003-2006; Michael J. Simon 2006-2010; Lyle J. Ball 2010-2015 [Grant Center became single-point charge 2015] Paula Jane Duffey (Ret.) Aug. 1, 2015-2016; Irene Elizabeth Starr 2016- Oct 27, 2017; [Grant Center / Brooks Corners became a two-point charge 2017] Meredith Rupe (Ret.) (LTFT ¼) Dec. 1, 2017-2020; TBS

Grass Lake UMC *[Heritage]*　　　glumc@modempool.com
(P/M) 449 E Michigan Ave, Grass Lake 49240　　　(517) 522-8040
　Kenneth Harris Dec. 1966-1969; Dale Culver 1969-Dec. 1972; Charles Grauer Jan. 1973-1976; Howard McDonald 1976-1979; Kenneth Lindland 1979-Sept. 1983; Gregory Wolfe Nov. 1983-1994; Stanley L. Hayes 1994-1999; Larry W. Rubingh 1999-2007; D. Gunnar Carlson 2007-2010; Esther Barton (DSA) 2010-2012; Dennis E. Slattery (DSA) (1/4 time) 2012-Sept 30, 2018; Gerald S. Hunter (Ret.) (LTFT ¼) Oct. 1-29, 2018; David Carlson Dec 1, 2018-2019; Lawrence J, Wiliford (Ret.) 2019-

Grawn UMC *[Northern Waters]*   grawnumc@gmail.com
(P) 1260 S West Silver Lake Rd, Traverse City 49685; (M) PO Box 62, Grawn 49637
           (231) 943-8353
   Carter Miller 1968-1969; Richard LaCicero 1969-Nov. 1970; Russell J. Lautner Nov. 1970-1982;
Don Spachman 1982-1992; Michael E. Long 1992-1996; Daniel W. Biteman, Jr. 1996-2006;
Margaret Halls Wilson 2006-Nov. 1, 2009; Mary S. Brown, Nov. 1, 2009-2014; Colleen A. Wierman
(1/2 time) 2014-2017; Sean T. Barton 2017-2018; Sean Thomas Barton 2018-

Grayling: Michelson Memorial UMC *[Northern Waters]*   mmumc@12k.net
(P/M) 400 E Michigan Ave, Grayling 49738   (989) 348-2974
   Paul C. Frederick 1969-1976; George E. Spencer 1976-1982; Jeffery D. Regan 1982-1989; Dennis
N. Paulson 1989-1993; J. Douglas Paterson 1993-1998; Jeffery L. Jaggers 1998-2004; Robert D.
Schoenhals 2004-Feb 1, 2006; Ralph W. Janka (interm) Feb 18, 2006-2006; William A. Cargo 2006-
2011; Patrick D. Robbins 2011-2014; Richard M. Burstall 2014-

Greenland UMC *[Northern Skies]*   ontmeth@jamadots.com
(P) 1002 Ridge Rd, Greenland 49929; (M) PO Box 216, Ontonagon 49953   (906) 883-3141
   Lloyd Christler 1968-1972; James Hillard 1970-1971; James Gerzetich 1971; Lawrence Brooks
1971-1975; Roger Gedcke 1972-1979; Lillian Richards 1971-1976; Wayne E. Sparks 1975-1980;
Myra Sparks 1976-1980; Ed Hingelburg 1976-1980; Brian Marshall 1980-1984; Donald J. Emmert
1984-Feb 15, 1990; William D. Schoonover Feb 16, 1990-1991; Mel D. Rose 1992-1994; Lance E.
Ness Jul 1, 1994-Dec 31, 2000; Christine Bohnsack May 1, 2000-2004; Cherrie A. Sporleder 2004-
2010; Bruce R. Steinberg 2010-2018; Nelson L. Hall 2018-

Greenville: First UMC *[Midwest]*   office@greenvillefumc.org
(P/M) 204 W Cass St, Greenville 48838   (616) 754-8532
   Darwin R. Salisbury 1964-March 1970; Howard A. Smith March 1970-1972; Harold A. Jayne 1972-
Sept. 1977; Kenneth W. Karlzen Sept. 1977-March 1982; Harold L. Mann March 1982-1988; Laren
J. Strait (Assoc.) 1980-; Harry R. Johnson 1988-2007; Joy Jittaun Moore 2007-2008; Stephen MG
Charnley 2008-14; Stephen F. Lindeman 2013-14; Kimberly A. DeLong (Deacon) 2013-2015;
[Greenville First, Turk Lake/Belding Cooperative Parish 2013] Donald E. Spachman 2014-2020;
Eric Mulanda Nduwa (Assoc.) Feb. 15-Aug. 1, 2015 [cooperative parish re-named Flat River
Cooperative Parish 2015] ; Joseph K. Caldwell (CLM/DSA) Aug. 1, 2015-2016; Jeffrey C. Williams
2020-

Gresham UMC *[Mid-Michigan]*   hauble23@gmail.com
(P) 5055 Mulliken Rd, Charlotte 48813; (M) 235 Dunham St, Sunfield 48890
   David C. Haney 1967-1969; William R. Tate 1969-1972; Gary V. Lyons 1972-April 1976; Gerald A.
Salisbury April 1976-1979; Molly C. Turner 1979-1983; Glenn C. Litchfield 1983-1990; Richard W.
Young 1990-1991; Robert L. Kersten 1991-1995; Jeffrey J. Bowman 1995-2002; Kathleen Smith
2002-Dec. 31, 2012; [Vermontville/Gresham no longer two-point charge 2013] [Barry-Eaton
Cooperative Ministry 2013] Bryce E. Feighner 2013-2017; [Gresham/Sunfield became two-point
charge 2017] Heather L. Nolen (DSA) 2017-

Griffith UMC *[Heritage]*   bralembury@myfrontiermail.com
(P/M) 9537 S Clinton Trl, Eaton Rapids 48827   (517) 663-6262
   Lambert G. McClintic 1952-1995; Jack Fugate 1995-July 15, 2008; Charlene A. Minger (1/4 time)
2009-2013; David H. Minger (Ret.) (1/4 time) 2013-Oct. 16, 2014; Larry Embury Jan. 1, 2015-

Gull Lake UMC *[Greater Southwest]*   gulllakeumc@gmail.com
(P/M) 8640 Gull Rd, Richland 49083   (269) 629-5137
   Keith Heifner Sept. 1980-1981; Edward C. Ross 1981-1994; Stephen M.G. Charnley 1994-2008; Susan M. Petro (Assoc.) 1994-Dec. 31, 1997; Dianne Doten Morrison (Assoc.) 1998-Feb. 1, 2001; David Nellist 2008-2010; Mona K. Joslyn 2010-2015; Rebecca L. Wieringa 2015-2016; Leonard R. Schoenherr (Ret.) 2016-2020; Michael James Tupper (Assoc.) Jan. 1, 2019-Apr 30, 2020; Ian J. Boley 2020-

Gunnisonville UMC *[Mid-Michigan]*   pastor@unitedch.com
(P/M) 2031 Clark Rd, Bath 48808   (517) 482-7987
   Stephen Beach 1968-1969; Edward F. Otto 1969-Dec. 1972; Daniel Miles Dec. 1972-1974; Paul K. Scheibner 1974-1978; J. Lynn Pier-Fitzgerald 1978-May 1984; Thomas M. Pier-Fitzgerald (co-pastor) 1982-May 1984; Charles W. Smith May 1984-1988; Carl W. Staser 1988-Jan. 1991; Thomas Peters Jan. 1, 1991-1993; Raymond D. Field 1993-1998; Nancy L. Besemer 1998-2003; Thomas L. Truby Oct. 15, 2003-2006; Beatrice K. Robinson 2006-2007; Mark G. Johnson 2007-2015; Matthew D. Kreh 2015-

Grosse Pointe UMC *[Greater Detroit]*   office@gpumc.org
(P/M) 211 Moross Rd, Grosse Pointe Farms 48236-2950   (313) 886-2363
   Perry A. Thomas 1966-1978; Robert P. Ward 1978-1982; Mary Frost (assoc) 1978-1980; David Penniman (assoc) 1980-1984; Robert W. Boley 1982-1989; Jack Mannschreck (assoc) 1984-1992; Jack Giguere 1989-1999; David J. Leenhouts (assoc) 1992-1996; Mary Ann Shipley (assoc) 1996-Oct 31, 2002; Robert D. Wright 1999-2008; Pamela A. Beedle-Gee (assoc) 2003-2009; Judith A. May 2008-2016; Daniel Hart (assoc) 2012-2016; Ray McGee 2016- ; Sari L. Brown (assoc) 2016-2017; Keith A. Lenard, Jr. (assoc) 2017-

Gwinn UMC *[Northern Skies]*   gwinnumc@aol.com
(P) 251 W Jasper, Gwinn 49841; (M) PO Box 354, Gwinn 49841-0354   (906) 346-6314
   Konstantine Wipp 1969-1975; Bruce Pierce 1975-1977; Duane E. Miller 1977-1986; Paul Lim 1986-1987; Max Weeks 1987-1991; Ronald F. Iris 1991-1995; Jacquelyn Roe 1995-2006; Geraldine G. Hamlen 2006-2014; Robert A. Fike 2014-

Hale: First UMC *[Central Bay]*   haleumc@gmail.com
(P) 201 W Main, Hale 48739; (M) PO Box 46, Hale 48739-0046   (989) 728-9522
   Arthur R. Parkin 1963-1972; Henry W. Powell 1972-1973; Willis E. Braun 1973-1979; Theodore I. Hastings 1979-1985; Willard A. King 1985-1987; William Donahue Jr. 1988-1993; G. Patrick England 1993-2008; David Stewart 2008-2013; David J. Goudie 2013-Aug 31, 2017; Melvin Leroy Leach Sept 1, 2017

Halsey UMC *[East Winds]*   halkathphillips@sbcglobal.net
(P/M) 10006 Halsey Rd, Grand Blanc 48439   (810) 694-9243
   Dudley C. Mosure 1969-1977; Susan Bennett Stiles 1977-1980; David P. Rahn 1980-1987; Martha H. Cargo 1987-1992; Chong Youb Won 1992-1995; Robin G. Gilshire 1995-Jul 31, 2000; David E. Ray Aug 1, 2000-2006; Harold V. Phillips 2006-2016; Tara R. Sutton 2016-

Hancock: First UMC *[Northern Skies]*   hfumc@hotmail.com
(P) 401 Quincy St, Hancock 49930; (M) PO Box 458, Hancock 49930   (906) 482-1401
   Nelson Cushman 1967-1968; George A. Luciani 1968-1980; Charles R. Jacobs 1980-1984; Thomas G. Badley 1984-1988; Fredrick P. Cooley 1988-1995; Eugene K. Bacon Jul 1, 1995-2006; James R. Rupert Jul 16, 2006-2009; AmyLee Terhune 2009-2016; Scott Lindenberg 2016-

Harbor Beach UMC *[East Winds]*   revsaribrown@gmail.com
(P) 253 S. First St, Harbor Beach 48441; (M) PO Box 25, Harbor Beach 48441   (989) 479-6053
Carl Shamblen 1968-1970; Thomas C. Badley 1970-1973; William M. Smith 1974-1978; Brent L.
Webster 1978-1983; Wayne A. Hawley 1983-1991; Kris S. Kappler 1991-1997; Victoria M. Webster
1997-1999; Clarence W. VanConant 1999-2004; Paula M. Timm 2004-2011; Donna J. Cartwright
Oct 1, 2011-2012; Mark E. Ryan 2012-Sept 18, 2016; Sari L. Brown 2017-

Harbor Springs UMC *[Northern Waters]*   harborspringsumc@gmail.com
(P/M) 343 E Main St, Harbor Springs 49740   (231) 526-2414
Phillip Howell 1968-1971; Philip Brown 1971-1977; Milton TenHave 1977-1979; Richard Matson
1979-1987; Catherine Kelsey 1987-1990; Claudette Haney 1990-April 1993; Birt A. Beers May
1993-1995; Lawrence R. Wood 1995-2003; Kathryn S. Cadarette 2003-2011; Mary A. Sweet 2011-
2014; Vaughn Thurston-Cox 2014-2016; [Epsilon/New Hope/Harbor Springs/Alanson became a
4-point charge 2014] Hillary Thurston-Cox (Assoc.) 2014-2016; Randall J. Hitts 2016-2017; Susan
E. Hitts 2016- [Harbor Springs / Alanson realigned 2016]

Hardy UMC *[Heritage]*   hardyumcsecy@sbcglobal.net
(P/M) 6510 E Highland Rd, Howell 48843   (517) 546-1122
Douglas R. Trebilcock 1967-1969; W. Harold Pailthorpe 1969-1970; William J. Rosemurgy 1970-
1973; Benjamin Bohnsack 1973-1980; James M. Thompson 1980-1983; Dale E. Brown 1984-1989;
Hayden K. Carruth Jr. 1989-Feb. 14, 1992; James E. McCallum Mar. 1, 1992-1994; Sherry Parker
(assoc—Hardy/Hartland) 1994-1995; Ronda L. (Beebe) Hawkins 1995-Jun 1, 2000; Barbra Franks
2000-2005; Joyce E. Wallace 2005-2013; John H. Schneider, Jr. 2013-

Harper Woods: Redeemer UMC *[Greater Detroit]*   hwredeemer@att.net
(P/M) 20571 Vernier Rd, Harper Woods 48225   (313) 884-2035
Ralph Edwards 1967-1969; Jack Lancaster 1969-1976; Charles Jacobs 1976-1980; Donald L.
Lichtenfelt 1980-1988; Ronald Corl 1988-1999; James P. Schwandt 1999-Feb 15, 2008; Marshall
G. Dunlap 2008-2011; Thomas Taylor 2011-2013; Thomas Priest, Jr. 2013-Feb 1, 2017; Judith A.
May (Ret.) Feb 1-Jun 30, 2017; Marshall C. Murphy 2017-

Harrietta UMC *[Northern Waters]*   harriettaumc@yahoo.com
(P) 116 N Davis St, Harrietta 49638; (M) PO Box 13, Harrietta 49638-0013   (231) 389-0267
Ward Pierce 1967-1972; Bill Amundsen 1972-1979; Jean Crabtree 1979-Aug. 1980; Donald Buege
Sept. 1980-Jan. 1984; Bruce Prestwood-Taylor Jan. 1984-1986; Thomas P. Fox 1986-1992; Charles
A. Williams 1992-Feb 14, 1997; J. David Thompson Nov. 16, 1997-2001; John J. Conklin (DSA)
2001-Nov. 30, 2001; John J. Conklin Dec. 1, 2001-2009; Mona L. Kindel 2009-2012; Beverley
Williams 2012-2016; Laurie M. Koivula 2016-2018; [Mesick/Harrietta/ Brethren became a three-
point charge 2016] [Harrietta became a sigle point charge 2018] Travis Heystek 09/01/2018-

Harrison: The Gathering *{Central Bay]*   gatheringumc@gmail.com
(P) 426 First St S Ste 106, Harrison 48625; (M) PO Box 86, Harrison 48625   (989) 539-1445
[new church start 2004; mission congregation 2009; became 3-point charge: The Gathering
(WMAC) & Wagarville/Wooden Shoe UMCs (DAC-Saginaw District) 2009] James C. Noggle 2004-
2010; Michael J. Simon 2010-2013; Kellas D. Penny (1/2 time) July 1-Dec.31, 2013; Vincent J.
Nader May 1, 2014-2016; Cheryl Lynn Mancier Nov. 1, 2016-Aug. 31, 2020; Ray McClintic (DSA)
Sept. 1, 2020-

Harrisville UMC *[Central Bay]*　　　　　　　　　　UMCinHarrisvilleMI@charter.net
(P/M) 217 N State St, Harrisville 48740　　　　　　　　　　　　(989) 724-5450
　　Carl J. Litchfield 1969-1971; G. MacDonald Jones 1971-1972; Luren J. Strait 1972-1978; Bruce
　　M. Denton 1978-1983; William L. Stone 1983-1990; Edward C. Seward 1990-Dec 31, 2004; William
　　P Sanders (interm) Aug 31, 2004-Dec 31, 2004; William Omansiek Jan 1, 2005-2005; Travis DeWitt
　　Sep 1, 2005-2007; Tracy Brooks 2007-2012; Lynda Jo Powers 2012-Oct 31, 2014; Mary Soderholm
　　Nov 1, 2014-Jun 10, 2017; Charles Sheldon (DSA) Sept 1, 2017-2018; Eric Lee Johnson 2018-
　　2020; Angela M. Lovegrove 2020-

Hart UMC *[Midwest]*　　　　　　　　　　　　　　　　hartumc@gmail.com
(P/M) 308 S State St, Hart 49420　　　　　　　　　　　　　　(231) 873-3516
　　Theron Bailey 1966-Dec. 1969; Edward Passenger Dec. 1969-1971; Jack Kraklan 1971-1979;
　　Lloyd Walker 1979-1982; Kenneth Snow 1982-1989; Laurie Haller 1989-1993; Bruce R. Kintigh
　　1993-Jan. 1, 1999; Harvey Prochnau Feb. 1, 1999-2003; Ben Bill Lester 2003-2011; Rebecca
　　Farrester Wieringa 2011-2015; Steven R. Young 2015-

Hartford UMC *[Greater Southwest]*　　　　　　　　　hartfordmethodist@gmail.com
425 E Main St, Hartford 49057　　　　　　　　　　　　　　(269) 621-4103
　　Morris Reinhart 1967-1972; Jean Crabtree 1972-1979; John Hice 1979-1987; David L. Crawford
　　1987-1990; Gerald L. Selleck 1990-1998; Richard A. Powell 1998-1999; Ronald W. Hansen 1999-
　　2011; Jeffrey C. Williams 2011-2014; Rey Mondragon 2014-2015; [Hartford/Keeler became a
　　two-point charge 2015] Ryan L. Wenburg 2015-2019; [Keeler UMC merged with Hartford UMC
　　12-31-16] Stephanie Elaine Norton 2019-

Hartland UMC *[Heritage]*　　　　　　　　　　　　hartlandumc@sbcglobal.net
(P/M) 10300 Maple Rd, Hartland 48353　　　　　　　　　　　(810) 632-7476
　　Charles Kitchenmaster 1966-Jan. 1972; Ted P. Townsend (interim) Feb. 1972-Jun. 1972; Ronald
　　L. Figgins Iris 1972-1975; Horace L. James 1975-1979; John R. Crotser 1979-1983; Mark E. Spaw
　　1983- (as Hardy/Hartland 1994-95) 1999; Gerald S. Hunter 1999-Sep 17, 2000; Gerald R. Parker
　　(interim) Oct 1, 2000-Jan 31, 2001; David R. Strobe Feb 1, 2001-Feb 1, 2006; Thomas Hart (interm)
　　Mar 1, 2006-Jun 30, 2006; G. Fred Finzer 2006-2012; Paul J. Gruenberg 2012-2020; Charles A.
　　Williams 2020-

Hastings: First UMC *[Mid-Michigan]*　　　　　　　　hastingsfumc@gmail.com
(P/M) 209 W Green St, Hastings 49058　　　　　　　　　　(269) 945-9574(P)
　　Emeral Price 1967-March 1969; Stanley Buck April 1969-Dec. 1972; Sidney Short Jan. 1973-1982;
　　Myron Williams 1982-May 1985; David Nelson 1985-1989; Philip L. Brown 1989-1994; Bufford W.
　　Coe 1994-Oct. 15, 2000; Kathy E. Brown Feb. 1, 2001-2010; Donald E. Spachman 2010-2014;
　　Mark R. Payne 2014-Dec. 31, 2016; Thomas J. Evans Jan. 1, 2017-June 30, 2017; Bryce E.
　　Feighner 2017-

Hastings: Hope UMC *[Mid-Michigan]*　　　　　　　　hastingshopeumc@gmail.com
(P) 2920 S M 37 Hwy, Hastings 49058; (M) PO Box 410, Hastings 49058-0410
　　Kenneth Vaught 1968-January 1983; Jack Bartholomew February 1983-February1986; Robert
　　Mayo April 1986-1992; James E. Fox 1992-1995; Laurence E. Hubley 1995-2000; Richard D. Moore
　　2000-2015; Marcia L. Elders 2015-2017; Kimberly S. Metzer 2017-

Hastings: Welcome Corners UMC *[Mid-Michigan]*   macousino1@gmail.com
(P/M) 3185 N M 43 Hwy, Hastings 49058   (269) 945-2654
John Jodersma 1967-Nov. 1968; Stanley Finkbeiner Nov. 1968-1969; Esther Cox 1969-1975; Richard Erickson 1975-1976; Clinton Bradley-Galloway 1976-1981; Constance Heffelfinger 1981-1984; Glenn Wegner 1984-1987; Robert Kersten 1987-1991; Carl Q. Litchfield 1991-2000; Geraldine M. Litchfield (Assoc.) Jan. 1993-1994; Soo Han Yoon Aug. 1, 2000-Jan. 31, 2001; Robert E. Smith Feb. 1, 2001-Dec. 31, 2003; Robert E. Smith (part-time) Dec. 31, 2003-2006; Susan D. Olsen 2006-2015; Mickey Ann Cousino (DSA) 2015-

Hayes UMC *[Central Bay]*   bayporthayes@att.net
(P) 7001 Filion Rd, Pigeon 48755; (M) 836 N 2nd St, Bay Port 48720-9630   (989) 553-2161
Donald W. Brown 1965-1970; Louis E. Reyner 1970-1975; Richard Andrus 1975-1979; Frederick P. Cooley 1979-1984; Randy A. Chemberlin 1984-1986; Alger T. Lewis 1986-1992; S. Douglas Leffler 1992-1994; Norman R. Beckwith 1994-1998; Barbra Franks 1998-2000; Alan W. DeGraw 2000-2003; Douglas E. Mater 2003-2010; Bruce L. Nowacek 2010-2013; Brian K. Johnson 2013-2016; Matthew D. Chapman 2016-2020; [Caseville, Hayes became 2-point charge 2020] Donald L. Wojewski 2020-

Hazel Park: First UMC *[Greater Detroit]*   hazelparkfirst@wowway.com
(P/M) 315 E 9 Mile Rd, Hazel Park 48030   (248) 546-5955
Bryn Evans 1961-1970; Sam Yearby 1970-1975; Reginald Cattell 1975-Feb. 1979; Donna Lindberg 1979-Apr.1983; Robert C. Hastings 1983-1987; Paul Lim 1987-1992; David Ray 1992-1994; Jill H. Zundel 1994-1999; James R. McCallum 1999-Apr 30, 2002; Mary Ellen Chapman May 1, 2002-2010; Cherrie A. Sporleder 2010-2013; Rochelle J. Hunter 2013-2015; Frederick G. Sampson, III 2016- Dec 31, 2019; Joseph J. Bistayi (interim) Mar 15-Jun 30, 2020; Maurice R. Horne 2020-

Hemlock UMC *[Central Bay]*   hemlockumc@frontier.com
(P) 406 W Saginaw St, Hemlock 48626; (M) PO Box 138, Hemlock 48626   (989) 642-5932
A. Theodore Halsted 1965-1970; John C. Huhtala 1970-1975; Terry W. Allen 1976-1978; Tom Brown 1978-1984; Steven A. Gjerstad 1984-Jun 30, 1994; Arthur V. Norris Jul 1, 1994-2001; Karen L. Knight 2001-Jan 1, 2002; Nicholas W. Scroggins 2002-2009; Jerry F. Densmore 2009-2014; Michael W. Vollmer 2014-2019; Robert G. Richards 2019- (Swan Valley (lead church) / LaPorte charge and Hemlock / Nelson charge formed new four point charge July 1, 2019)

Henderson UMC *[East Winds]*   pastorherbw@aol.com
(P) 302 E Main St, Henderson 48841; (M) 218 E Main, Henderson 48841   (989) 723-5729
Monroe J. Frederick 1968-1972; T. K. Foo Sep 18, 1972-1976; Wayne A. Rhodes 1976-1978; James B. Lumsden 1978-1982; David S. Stiles 1982-1984; James P. James 1984-1989; J. Robert Anderson 1989-1993; Nicholas W. Scroggins 1993-1998; Paul B. Lim 1998-2000; Billie Lou Gillespie 2000-Oct 14, 2006; Calvin H. Wheelock Nov 1, 2006-2019; [Henderson / Chapin / Owosso: Triity frmed three-point charge 07/01/2019] Steffani Glygoroff (DSA) 2019-

Hermansville UMC *[Northern Skies]*   1chris1cross1@att.net
(P) W5494 Second S, Hermansville 49847; (M) 3716 D Rd, Bark River 49807
Calvin Rice 1967-1974; James Paige 1974-1975; John Henry 1975-1981; John Hamilton 1981-1986; David Leenhouts 1986-1992; W. Peter Bartlett 1992-1996; Kenneth C. Dunstone 1996-Dec 15, 1999; Jean M. Larson Jan 1, 2000-Nov 15, 2001; James A. Fegan Dec 1, 2001-May 31, 2002; Cherrie A. Sporleder Jun 16, 2002-2004; James M. Mathews 2004-2011; Christine J. Berquist 2011-2020; [Hermansville became single station 2020] Jeff Gagne (DSA) 2020-

Hersey UMC *[Northern Waters]*   herseyumc1@outlook.com
(P) 200 W 2nd St, Hersey 49639; (M) PO Box 85, Hersey 49639-0085   (231) 832-5168
Otto Flachsmann 1964-1969; M.K. Matter 1969-1977; David A. Cheyne 1977-1982; Wesley E. Smith 1982-1984; Martin D. Fox 1984-Sept. 1986; Nelson Ray Dec. 1986-1988; Cynthia A. Skutar 1988-1992; Timothy J. Miller 1992-1994; Pulpit Supply July 1994; John G. Kasper Aug. 1, 1994-2001; Raymond D. Field 2001-2003; Lawrence A. Nichols 2003-2010; Mary Beth Rhine 2010-2012; Lemuel O. Granada (1/4 time) July 29, 2012-

Hesperia UMC *[Midwest]*   humchesp@frontier.com
(P/M) 187 E South Ave, Hesperia 49421   (231) 854-5345
Merlin Delo 1966-1978; William Bowers 1978-1980; David Dryer 1980-1984; Richard Williams 1984-Oct. 1, 1997; Pulpit Supply Oct. 1, 1997 - Dec. 31, 1997; Susan Olsen Jan. 1, 1998-July 1, 1998; Raymond D. Field 1998-1999; James Bradley Brillhart 1999-2007; Dianne D. Morrison 2007-2011; Richard D. Morrison (DSA) 2007-2011; Paul E. Hane 2011-2018; Paul E. Hane (Ret.) (LTFT) 2018-Apr 26, 2020; [Ferry merged w/ Hesperia 4-26-2020] Donna J. Minarik 2020-

Highland UMC *[Heritage]*   phaskell@humc.us
(P/M) 680 W Livingston Rd, Highland 48357   (248) 887-1311
Russell L. Smith 1967-1974; H. Emery Hinkston 1974-1983; Gilson M. Miller 1983-1992; David E. Church 1992-1995; James P. Kummer 1995-2016; Thomas Anderson 2016-

Hillman UMC *[Northern Waters]*   hillmanumc@outlook.com
(P) 111 Maple St, Hillman 49746; (M) PO Box 638, Hillman 49746-0638   (989) 742-3014
Howard E. Shaffer 1964-1971; Philip A. Rice 1971-1975; Robert Kersten 1975-1978; Harold F. Blakely 1978-1981; James R. Rupert 1981-1984; R. Wayne Hutson 1984-1990; Paula Timm 1990-1992; Jack E. Johnston 1992-Nov 1, 2005; George Morse (interm) Nov 1, 2005-Jun 30, 2006; Karen A. Mars 2006-2008; Donald R. Derby 2008-2013; Lisa L. Kelley 2013-2020; Duane A. Lindsey 2020-

Hillsdale First UMC *[Heritage]*   office.hillsdalefirstumc@gmail.com
(P/M) 45 N Manning St, Hillsdale 49242   (517) 437-3681
John Francis 1968-1971; David S. Evans 1971-1979; William V. Payne 1979-1987; David A. Selleck 1987-Dec. 1988; Hugh C. White (Interim) Dec. 1988-1989; Gary L. Bekofske 1989-1996; Mark G. Johnson 1996-2003; Curtis Eugene Jensen 2003-2010; Patricia L. Brook 2010-2018; Rob A. McPherson 2018-

Hillside UMC *[Heritage]*   hillsideunited1@frontiernet.net
(P/M) 6100 Folks Rd, Horton 49246   (517) 563-2835
Eugene Lewis 1966-1972; Paul Mazur 1972-1974; Tom Jones 74-78; Jon Powers 78-81; Larry Wiliford 81-83; Lawrence Hodge 1983-1991; Laurence E. Hubley 1991-1995; David A. Cheyne 1995-1998; Marilyn B. Barney 1998-2008; Denise J. Downs 2008-2009; [Hillside/Somerset Center two-point charge 2009] E. Jeanne Koughns 2009-2014; Patricia A. Pebley 2014-2020; Crystal C. Thomas 2020-

Hinchman UMC *[Greater Southwest]*   hinchmanumc@hotmail.com
(P/M) 8154 Church St, Berrien Springs 49103   (269) 471-5492
Robert Strauss 1968-1981; Valerie Hill 1981-March 1983; Leonard Haynes 1983-1986; Leo Bennett 1986-1989; Walter J. Rothfuss 1989-2000; Brenda Gordon 2000-2006; Jane D. Logston (part-time) 2006-14; [Berrien Springs / Hinchman / Oronoko became 3-point charge 2012] [Hinchman / Oronoko became 2-point charge 2014] Linda R. Gordon 2014-2017; Brenda E. Gordon 2017-2018; Dawn Oldenbury (DSA) (LTFT ½) 2018- [Hinchman / Scottdale beacme two-point charge 10-1-2018]

Holland: First UMC *[Midwest]* office@fumcholland.org
(P/M) 57 W 10th St, Holland 49423 (616) 396-5205
Hilding W. Kilgren 1963-1970; Paul E. Robinson (Assoc.) 1965-1972; Darwin R. Salisbury 1970-1977; Brent Phillips (Assoc.) 1972-1973; John L. Francis 1977-1987; William C. Johnson (Assoc.) 1977-1981; Heath T. Goodwin (part-time) 1981-1983; Robert S. Treat (part-time) 1983-1988; Harold F. Filbrandt 1987-1990; Susan J. Hagans (Assoc.) 1988-1995; John W. Ellinger 1990-1996; Beatrice K. Rose (Assoc.) 1995-1998; William E. Dobbs 1996-2005; R. John Thompson (Assoc.) 1998-Apr. 1, 2001; Karen A. Tompkins (Assoc.) 1998-2003; Todd J. Query (Deacon) 2003-2006; J. Lynn Pier-Fitzgerald 2005-2017; Janice T. Lancaster (Assoc. Pastor of Congregational Care) 2010-Jan. 30, 2014; Bradley S. Bartelmay 2017- ; Tania J. Dozeman (Assoc.) 2018- ; LuAnne M. Stanley-Hook (Deacon) 2019-

Holly: Calvary UMC *[East Winds]* hollycalvarychurch@gmail.com
(P/M) 15010 N Holly Rd, Holly 48442 (248) 634-9711
Robert F. Davis 1968-1973; R. LaVere Webster 1973-1976; Michael Grajcar, Jr. 1976-1982; Harley L. Siders 1982-1990; Jeffrey R. Maxwell 1990-2001; Mary Jean Love 2001-2008; Faith E. Timmons 2008-2012; Clifford J. Schroeder III 2012-

Holly: Mt. Bethel UMC *[East Winds]* scottclark714@msn.com
(P/M) 3205 Jossman Rd, Holly 48442 (248) 627-6700
Donald E. Hall 1969-1970; Dudley C. Mosure 1970-1977; Susan Bennett Stiles 1977-1980; David Rahn 1980-1981; David Davenport 1981-Sept., 1986; Scott Harper 1986-1988; Gerald E. Mumford 1988-1993; Donald Woolum 1993-Sep 30, 1996; Robert Watt Oct 1, 1996-2001; Karen B. Williams 2001-2005; Patricia A. Harton Feb 1, 2006-2010; Pam Kail 2010-2012; Scott Clark 2012-2018; Leah Caron 2018-

Holt UMC *[Mid-Michigan]* holtumc@acd.net
(P) 2321 Aurelius Rd, Holt 48842; (M) PO Box 168, Holt 48842-0168 (517) 694-8168
Philip R. Glotfelty, Jr. 1964-1970; Douglas A. Smih 1970-1972; Myron K. Williams 1972-1982; Dennis Buwalda 1982-1989; Joseph D. Huston 1989-1999; Barbara J. Flory (Assoc.) 1998-2000; Lynn E. Grimes 1999-2006; Glenn M. Wagner 2006-2014; Mark R. Erbes 2014-

Holton UMC *[Midwest]* humcoffice@frontier.com
(P/M) 9530 Holton Duck Lake Rd, Holton 49425 (231) 821-2323
Ira J. Noordhof 1967-1975; Donald Vuurens 1975-Jan. 1978; Pulpit Supply Jan.-June 1978; Charles Van Lente 1978-1983; David McBride 1983-1988; Larry Rubingh 1988-Dec. 1991; Pulpit Supply Jan.-June 1992; Kenneth Bremer 1992-2006; Gerald Selleck 2006-2018; Matthew Todd Stoll 2018-

Hopkins UMC *[Greater Southwest]* hsmumc@hotmail.com
(P) 322 N Maple St, Hopkins 49328; (M) PO Box 356, Hopkins 49328-0356 (269) 793-7323
Glenn Britton 1968-Jan. 1970; Stanley Finkbeiner Feb. 1970-1974; Densel Fuller 1974-1976; Brent Phillips 1976-1978; David Knapp 1978-Oct. 15, 1982; Robert J. Stillson Nov. 1982-1989; Robert D. Nystrom 1989-1992; Marjory A. Berkompas 1992-June 13, 1996; David S. Yoh (DSA) 1996-1999; Raymond D. Field 1999-2001; Reva H. Daniel 2001-2005; Linda J. Burton 2005-2014; Dominic A. Tommy 2014-2017; Joel T. Fitzgerald 2017-2018; Andrew Ryan Phillips 2018-2020; Kelsey Burns French 2020-

Horton Bay UMC *[Northern Waters]* barneyfife@torchlake.com
(P/M) 4961 Boyne City Rd, Boyne City 49712 (231) 582-9262
Seward Walton 1968-1976; John Gurney 1976-1978; Steve Tower 1978-1979; Carl Staser 1979-1980; Allen Valkema 1980-1982; Martin Fox 1982-1984; Craig Adams 1984-1994; Kathryn S. Slaughter 1994-2000; Geraldine M. Litchfield 2000-2005; Timothy B. Wright 2005-2013; [Horton Bay became single-point charge 2013] Michael R. Neihardt 2013-2015; Eun Sik Poy Sept. 1, 2015-2016; Gregory P. Culver 2016-2017; [Charlevoix / Horton Bay became a two-point charge 2016; Horton Bay became a single station 2017] Michael R. Neihardt 2017-2020; Kathryn S. Cadarette (Ret.) 2020-

Houghton: Grace UMC *[Northern Skies]* churchoffice@houghtongraceumc.org
(P/M) 201 Isle Royale St, Houghton 49931 (906) 482-2780
Carter W. Preston 1968-1972; James H. McLaurin 1972-1978; Alan R. George 1978-1987; Ronald K. Fulton 1987-1988; David R. Strobe 1988-1995; Thomas C. Anderson 1995-2009; David J. Goudie Aug 1, 2009-20-13; Charles A. Williams 2013-2020; [Houghton: Grace / Painesdale: Albert Paine Mem. two-point charge 7-1-2019] Eric M. Falker 2020-

Houghton Lake UMC *[Northern Waters]* hlumc@gmail.com
(P/M) 7059 W Houghton Lake Dr, Houghton Lake 48629 (989) 422-5622
Troy Lemmons 1966-1971; James R. Hilliard 1971-1980; Russell L. Smith 1980-1986; Roger L. Colby 1986-1992; Charles R. Marble 1992-2000; Calvin D. Long 2000-2009; Thomas C. Anderson Aug 1, 2009-2016; George R. Spencer 2016-

Howarth UMC *[Greater Detroit]* howarthumc@att.net
(P/M) 550 E Silverbell Rd, Lake Orion 48360 (248) 373-2360
Elmer J. Snyder 1967-1972; Georg Gerritsen 1972-1978; Dwayne Lee Kelsey 1978-1981; Bruce L. Billing 1982-1993; David K. Koski 1993-1998; Sylvia A. Bouvier 1998-2006; Stephen Fraser-Soots 2006-2009; Thomas M. Sayers 2009-2016; Carolyn Jones 2016-2018; Marvin L. Herman 2018-

Howell: First UMC *[Heritage]* fumcwl@ameritech.net
(P/M) 1230 Bower St, Howell 48843 (517) 546-2730
Allan G. Gray 1962-1973; Lewis C. Sutton 1973-1985; Gary L. Damon 1986-1990; Margaret R. Garrigues-Cortelyou (assoc) 1990-1992; David A. Russell 1990-1997; Charles R. Jacobs 1997-2010; Diane Griffin (deacon) Jan 1, 2006- ; George H. Lewis 2010-2020; Scott K. Otis 2020-

Hudson: First UMC *[Heritage]* pastorcjabbott@frontier.com
(P/M) 420 W Main St, Hudson 49247 (517) 448-5891
Roland F. Liesman 1965-1973; Robert B. Secrist 1973-1980; James G. Simmons 1980-1984; Ralph C. Pratt 1984-1985; Myra L. Sparks 1985-Oct. 14, 1989; Francis F. Anderson Nov. 1, 1989-1991; Melanie L. Carey 1991-1993; Martha C. Ball Jul. 16, 1993-Jan 15, 1996; Benjamin B. Ball (assoc) Jul. 16, 1993-Jan 15, 1996; Mark G. Johnston Feb 1, 1996-2008; Raymond D. Wightman 2008-2010; Fredrick D. Neumann 2010-2013; Bradley S. Luck 2013-2018; Carol J. Freeland (Abbott) 2018-

Hulbert: Taquamenon UMC *[Northern Skies]* marybrooks729@gmail.com
(P) 10505 Maple St, Hulbert 49748; (M) PO Box 91, Hulbert 49748
Wayne T. Large 1967-1970; Vernon D. Wyllys 1970-1975; James Lumsden 1975-1976; Audrey N. Dunlap 1976-1979; David J. Hill 1979-1980; David K. Campbell 1980-1981; J. Douglas Paterson 1981-1982; James W. Robinson 1982-1983; Julaine A. Hays 1983-1984; Ramona E. Cowling 1984-1985; Melinda R. Cree 1985-1986; Ray S. Peterson 1986-1989; Jan L. Beaderstadt 1989-1991; Audrey M. Dunlap 1991-1993; Donald Bates 1993-Sep 30, 1996; Barbra Franks Oct 1, 1996-1998; Donald L. Bates 1998-2001; Virginia B. Bell 2001-Oct 30, 2005; Sandra J. Kolder Dec 4, 2005-2011; Lowell Peterson 2011-2013; Mary D. Brooks (DSA) 2013-

Ida UMC *[Heritage]*   sachun1128@cs.com
(P) 8124 Ida St, Ida 48140; (M) PO Box 28, Ida 48140   (734) 269-6127
   Paul R. Crabtree 1951-1969; Ferris S. Woodruff 1969-1973; Henry W. Powell 1973-1977; Robert E.
   Burkey 1977-1982; Jack Edward Fulcher 1982-1984; J. Robert Anderson 1984-1989; John M. Mehl
   Jr. 1989-2001; Wayne A. Hawley 2001-2007; Sang Yoon (Abraham) Chun 2007-2016; Corey M. Simon
   2016-2019; Robert J. Freysinger 2019-

Imlay City UMC *[East Winds]*   icumc@yahoo.com
(P/M) 210 N Almont Ave, Imlay City 48444   (810) 724-0687
   Harvard J. Warren 1969-1972; H. Reginald Cattell 1972-1975; Lawrence C. Brooks 1975-1980;
   Donald J. Daws 1980-1989; James A. Govatos 1989-1998; Colin P. Stover 1998-2002; Rodney L.
   Sanderson-Smith (assoc.) 2000-Mar 31, 2002; Jimmy S. Barnett (assoc) 2001-2002; Pamela K.
   Barnett (assoc) 2001-2002; Kevin J. Harbin 2002-2011; Dianna L. Rees 2011-2013; Marcel A. Lamb
   2013-

Indian River UMC *[Northern Waters]*   indianriverumc@gmail.com
(P) 956 Eagles Nest Rd, Indian River 49749; (M) PO Box 457, Indian River 49749   (231) 238-7764
   Gerald Janousek 1968-1970; Argle Leesler 1970-1972; Robert Elder 1972-1976; Morris Reinhart
   1976-1984; Steve Weinberger 1984-1990; Larry Mannino 1990-1994; John D. Lover 1994-2000;
   Gary G. Step 2000-2012; O. Jay Kendall (Assoc.) 2007-Aug. 31, 2012; DeAnn J. Dobbs 2012-
   2014; Patricia A. Harpole 2014-2017; Everett L. Harpole (Assoc.) 2016-2017; Todd W. Shafer 2017-
   ; Noreen S. Shafer (Assoc.) 2017-

Ionia: Easton UMC *[Midwest]*   eastonoffice@gmail.com
(P/M) 4970 Potters Rd, Ionia 48846   (616) 527-6529
   George W. Chaffee 1971-1974; Nolan Williams 1974-Oct. 1980; Eldon Schram Oct. 1980-Sept.
   1984; Kathryn M. Williams Sept. 1984-Nov. 1986; Kathryn M. Coombs Nov. 1986-1990; Scott K.
   Otis 1990-1993; David J. Blincoe 1993-Aug. 15, 1994; Supplied by Presbyterian Church Sept.
   1994; Don Wells (Presbyterian) 1995-Jan. 6, 1999; Judy K. Downing 1999-2001; Lynn W. Wagner
   2001-Sept. 1, 2002; Paul F. Bailey (DSA) April 13, 2003; Thomas R. Reaume Sept 1, 2004-Jan. 1,
   2007; Nancy J. Patera, Jan. 1, 2007-2014; Donna Jean Sperry 2014-

Ionia: First UMC *[Midwest]*   ioniafirst@gmail.com
(P/M) 105 E Main St, Ionia 48846   (616) 527-1860
   Lester C. Bailey 1964-1970; Charles W. Fullmer 1970-1977; Carl L. Hausermann 1977-1983; John
   F. Sorensen 1983-1985; Keith A. Bovee 1985-1991; Lawrence E. Hodge 1991-2000; Martin H.
   Culver 2000-2006; Lawrence P. Brown 2006-2014; Jonathan D. Van Dop 2014-2017; [Ionia First
   / Lyons-Muir became a two-point charge 2016] Jonathan E. Bratt Carle 2017-

Ionia Parish: Berlin Center UMC *[Midwest]*   levalleybc@gmail.com
(P) 3042 Peck Lake Rd, Saranac 48881; (M) 4018 Kelsey Hwy, Ionia 48846   (616) 527-1480
   Luther Brokaw 1967-1971; Donald Fry 1971-1973; Lloyd Walker 1973-Aug. 1979; Willis Braun Aug.
   16, 1979-Feb. 1989; David L. Flagel March 1989-2003; Mark G. Johnson 2003-2007; Dennis E.
   Slattery 2007-2012; Raymond R. Sundell 2012-Nov. 30, 2016; Mark G. Johnson (Ret.) Dec. 1,
   2016-June 30, 2017; Nancy J. Patera 2017-

Ionia Parish: LeValley UMC *[Midwest]*   levalleybc@gmail.com
(P/M) 4018 Kelsey Hwy, Ionia 48846   (616) 527-1480
   Luther Brokaw 1967-1971; Donald Fry 1971-1973; Lloyd Walker 1973-Aug. 1979; Willis Braun Aug.
   16, 1979-Feb. 1989; David L. Flagel March 1989-2003; Mark G. Johnson 2003-2007; Dennis E.
   Slattery 2007-2012; Raymond R. Sundell 2012-Nov. 30, 2016; Mark G. Johnson (Ret.) Dec. 1,
   2016- June 30, 2017; Nancy J. Patera 2017-

Ionia: Zion UMC *[Midwest]*   zionumcsecretary@gmail.com
(P/M) 423 W Washington St, Ionia 48846   (616) 527-1910
   Chester Erickson 1967-1971; George Chaffee 1971-1974; Nolan Williams 1974-Oct. 1980; Eldon Schram Oct. 1980-1984; Kathryn Williams (Coombs) 1984-Sept. 1986; William Dornbush Nov. 1986-Dec. 31, 1993; Pulpit Supply Jan. 1- June 30, 1994; Craig L. Adams 1994-Sept. 15, 1999; Arlo Vandlen (DSA) Jan. 24, 2000-2001; Donald Graham 2001-2007; Cliff Allen (DSA) 2007; Cliff Allen, Nov. 10, 2007-2018; Larry W. Nalett (Ret.) (LTFT ½) 2018-

Iron Mountain: First UMC *[Northern Skies]*   imfirstumc@att.net
(P/M) 106 4th St, Iron Mountain 49801   (906) 774-3586
   Richard Reese 1967-1971; Monroe Fredrick 1971-1976; John Moore 1976-1980; James Hall 1980-1983; Paul Doering 1983-1984; James Mathews 1984-1989; Douglas J. McMunn 1989-Dec 31, 1995; William R. Seitz Jan 1, 1996-Feb 1, 2004; David P. Snyder Feb 15, 2004-2009; Margaret A.W. Paige 2009-2012; Walter P. Reichle 2012-

Iron Mountain: Trinity UMC *[Northern Skies]*   imtrinityumc@gmail.com
(P/M) 808 Carpenter Ave, Iron Mountain 49801   (906) 774-2545
   Tom Brown II 1968-1973; David M. Liscomb 1973-1982; John F. Greer 1982-1986; John C. Stubbs 1986-1991; Arthur V. Norris 1991-Jun 30, 1994; James A. McLaurin Jul 1, 1994-1998; Scott A. Harmon (assoc) 1996-1998; Meredith Rupe 1998-2006; Philip B. Lynch (assoc) Oct 1, 2000-2003; Deborah S. Thomas 2006-2011; Paul J. Mallory 2011-2014; Geraldine G. Hamlin 2014-

Ironwood: Wesley UMC *[Northern Skies]*   iwumc@charter.net
(P) 500 E McLeod Ave, Ironwood 49938; (M) PO Box 158, White Pine 49971   (906) 932-3900
   Thomas H. Beaven 1966-1970; Lillian G. Richards 1970; David A. Russell 1971-1977; Troy Lemmons 1977-1980; Gary A. Allward 1980-1987; Thomas H. Zimmerman 1987-1991; Carl R. Doersch 1991-1995; Pamela S. Kail 1995-1998; Allen F. Schweitzer 1998-Sep 30, 1999; Cherrie A. Sporleder Feb 1, Jun 30, 2000; Jean B. Rencontre 2000-2008; Rosemary R. DeHut 2008-Aug. 31, 2018; Keith Paul Mullikin (DSA) Oct. 1, 2018-Jan 21, 2020; Keith Paul Mullikin Jan 22, 2020- [Ironwood Wesley / Wakefield two-pooint charge 7-1-2019]

Ishpeming: Wesley UMC *[Northern Skies]*   church@ishpemingwesley.org
(P) 801 Hemlock St, Ishpeming 49849; (M) PO Box 342, Ishpeming 49849   (906) 486-4681
   Stanley A. Bailey 1967-1976; Paul C. Frederick 1976-1980; Robert Kersten (assoc) 1978-1980; George A. Luciani 1980-1993; Donna J. Lindberg 1993-1997; Lawrence C. Brooks 1997-1999; Bruce C. Hatch 1999-2001; Paul G. Donelson Oct 1, 2001-2006; Scott P. Lindenberg 2006-2014; Jeremiah J. Mannschreck 2014-2018; Matthew Osborne 2018-

Ithaca UMC *[Mid-Michigan]*   office@Ithacaumc.org
(P/M) 327 E Center St, Ithaca 48847   (989) 875-4313
   John F. Sorensen 1967-1972; David B. Nelson, Jr. 1972-1980; Nolan R. Williams 1980-1991; David L. McBride 1991-2006; Steven R. Young 2006-2010; Cynthia Greene 2010-2015; Gary L. Simmons 2015- [Ithica / Beebe became a two-point charge 2018]

Jackson: Brookside UMC *[Heritage]*   brooksideumc@gmail.com
(P/M) 4000 Francis St, Jackson 49203   (517) 782-5167
   Verne Summers 1966-Aug. 1974; Verner Kilgren Sept. 1974-Sept. 15, 1978; William Torrey Sept. 15, 1978-1985; Richard Johns 1985-1992; David L. Johnston 1992-2005; Charles Campbell July 15, 2005-Sept 1, 2005; Chad M. Parmalee Sept 1, 2005-2013; Ronald K. Brooks 2013-2020 [Jackson Brookside/Trinity became a two-point charge 2015] Jennifer J. Jue 2020-

Jackson: Calvary UMC *[Heritage]*   jaxcalumc@gmail.com
(P/M) 925 Backus St, Jackson 49202   (517) 782-0543
  J. Leon Andrews 1968-1972; Haven UMC merged with Calvary in 1972; Donald P. Sailor 1972-
1977; Claude Ridley 1977-1983; Carl L. Hausermann 1983-1989; George R. Grettenberger
1989-1992; Timothy P. Boal 1992-1997; Linda J. Carlson (Assoc.) 1993-Feb. 16, 1999; Michael T.
Conklin 1999-2003; Maurice E. Walworth, Jr. 2003-2006; Linda H. Hollies 2006-Aug. 18, 2007;
Lillian T. French Jan. 1, 2008-Sept. 1, 2010; Edrye Maurer Sept. 1, 2010-2015; [Jackson Calvary
& Zion became two-point charge 2013] Eric Iden (DSA) 2015-2017; [Jackson: Calvary became
single station 2017] Mary K. Loring 2017-2019; Terry S. Wiliford (Ret.) 2019-Oct 14, 2019; Ronald
K. Brooks Nov 1, 2019-2020; Jennifer J. Jue 2020-

Jackson: First UMC *[Heritage]*   church@firstumcjackson.org
(P/M) 275 W Michigan Ave, Jackson 49201   (517) 787-6460
  Robert C. Smith 1966-1971; E. Lenten Sutcliffe (Assoc.) 1968-1971; Richard A. Morrison (Assoc.)
1969-1971; Merle D. Broyles 1971-1981; Wilbur A. Williams (Assoc.) 1971-1973; David C. Brown
(Assoc.) 1971-1973; Ivon Gonsor (Assoc.) 1973-1974; George Chaffee (Assoc.) 1974-1984; John
Ellinger (Assoc.) Jan. 1972-1976; Richard Erickson (Assoc.) 1976-1982; Larry Taylor 1981-1987;
David Morton (Assoc.) 1982-1986; Ted Cole (Assoc.) 1984-1986; Linda Farmer-Lewis (Assoc.)
1986-1987; David Knapp (Assoc.) 1986-1989; Joy Moore 1988-1990; John Cermak 1987-1994;
Leo E. Bennett (Assoc.) 1989-1993; Donette Bourke (Deacon) 1990- 2003; John D. Morse (Assoc.)
1993-1999; Edward C. Ross 1994-2012; Sanda Sanganza (Assoc.) 1999-2001; Charles Campbell
(Assoc.) 2003-2007; Susan Babb (Assoc.) 2004-2015; Mark Babb (Deacon-Spiritual Formation
Consultant) June 1, 2010-2015; Eric S. Beck 2012-2019; Timothy W. Trommater (Assoc.) 2015-
2017; Mary K. Loring (Assoc.) 2017-2019; Tonay M. Arnesen 2019- ; Gregory W. Lawton (Deacon,
Minister of Spiritual Formation) Aug. 15, 2020-

Jackson: Trinity UMC *[Heritage]*   jacksontrinity@sbcglobal.net
(P/M) 1508 Greenwood Ave, Jackson 49203   (517) 782-7937
  (Jackson Trinity is a merged congregation of Greenwood Ave. UMC, Greenwood Park EUB and
Francis Street EUB); James Crosby 1968-1969; Harold Kirkenbauer 1968-1969; Harold Taber 1969-
1972; Dale Crawford 1972-1977; B. James Varner 1977-1986; Karen Slager Wheat 1986-1998;
Beatrice K. Robinson 1998-2006; [Jackson Trinity / Parma became a charge 2006] Sandra L. Spahr
(DSA) 2006-2007; Melodye Surgeon Rider 2007-2012; Patricia A. Pebley (1/2 time) 2012-2014;
[Jackson Trinity became single-point charge 2014] Robert Q. Bailey (Ret.) 2014-2015; [Jackson
Brookside/Trinity became a two-point charge 2015] Ronald K. Brooks 2015-2020; Jennifer J. Jue
2020-

Jackson: Zion UMC *[Heritage]*   jacksonZionUMC@gmail.com
(P/M) 7498 Cooper St, Jackson 49201   (517) 769-2570
  Amos R. Bogart Jan. 1968-1969; Frederick W. Werth 1969-1971; Charles R. Campbell 1971-1981;
D. David Ward 1981-Jan. 7, 1994; Lawrence A. Nichols Feb. 1, 1994-2003; Donald R. Wendell
July 15, 2003-Mar. 15, 2006; William Lang (DSA), Oct. 1, 2006-2007; [Pleasant Lake & Jackson
Zion became two-point charge 2008] David H. Minger (DSA) 2008-2013; [Jackson Calvary & Zion
became two-point charge 2013] Edrye A. Eastman Maurer 2013-2015; Eric Iden (DSA) 2015-2017;
[Grovenburg / Jackson: Zion / Felt Plains / Williamston: Wheatfield became multi-point charge 2017]
John Kabala 2017-2018; Gertrude Mwadi Mukalay 2017-2018; TBS

Jeddo UMC *[East Winds]*   juliekrauss@hotmail.com
(P) 8533 Wildcat Rd, Jeddo 48032; (M) PO Box 7, Jeddo 48032   (810) 327-6644
    William J. Burgess 1968-1973; Mark K. Smith 1973-1976; Daniel R. Fenton 1976-1978; Harold J.
    Slater 1978-1980; James E.& Peggy Paige 1980-1985; Georg F.W. Gerritsen 1985-1988; Donald
    H. Francis 1988-1992; Emerson W. Arntz 1992-2002; Robert A. Srock 2002-Dec 1, 2003; Catherine
    W. J. Hiner 2004-2009; Micheal P. Kelly 2009-2012; Donald L. Wojewski 2012-2018; Julie Krauss
    2018-2020; [Jeddo, Buel became 2-point charge 2020] Karen A. Harriman (DSA) 2020-

Jerome UMC *[Heritage]*   najumcs@yahoo.com
(P/M) 8768 Jerome Rd, Jerome 49249
    Kenneth W. Karlzen 1968-1971; Thomas R. Jones 1971-Aug. 1974; David Flagel Sept. 1975-1980;
    Lee F. Zachman 1980-1984; Donald McLellan 1984-Sept. 1988; Melanie Baker-Streevy Oct. 1988-
    1995; Rochelle Ray 1995-2000; Tim Doubblestein 2000-Aug. 31, 2002; Charles Richards Sept.
    1-Dec. 31, 2002; Paul Hane Jan. 1, 2003-2011; Kimberly A. Metzger July 1-Dec. 19, 2011; Arthur
    R. Turner (DSA) Feb. 1, 2012-2014; Timothy R. Puckett 2014-Dec 31, 2019; Beverly Clark
    (CLM/DSA) Jan 1, 2020-

Jonesville UMC *[Heritage]*   jonesvilleunitedmethodist@gmail.com
203 Concord Rd, Jonesville 49250   (517) 849-9565
    Densel Fuller 1968-1974; William Johnson 1974-1977; Derryl Cook 1977-1978; M. John Palmer
    1978-1982; Lloyd Walker 1982-1985; Jack Kraklan 1985-1988; Michael Baker-Streevy 1988-1995;
    Reva Hawke 1995-1997; Nelson Ray 1997-2000; Craig Pahl 2000-2014; [Jonesville/Allen became
    single charges 2014] Jennifer Ward (DSA) 2014-2017; [Litchfield / Jonesville became two-point
    charge 2017] Mary A. Sweet 2017- [Jonesville / Napoleon became two-point charege 2019]

Juddville UMC *[Mid-Michigan]*   juddvilleunitedmethodistchurch@hotmail.com
(P/M) 3907 N Durand Rd, Corunna 48817   (810) 638-7498
    Paul L. Amstutz 1964-1971; Clifford J. Furness 1971-1976; Donald W. Brown 1976-1978; Linda
    Susan Garment 1978-1980; Verne W. Blankenburg 1980-1983; Robert J. Henning 1983-Jul. 1990;
    Mary Thoburn Tame Oct. 16, 1990-Aug 31, 1997; James M. Downing Sep 1, 1997-Aug 16, 1999;
    Olaf Lidums Nov 16, 2000-2003; David L. Fleming 2003-2011; Janet M. Engler 2011-2013; Danny
    Bledsoe 2013-2015; Dan Wallington 2015-2018; Wallace Peter Crawford (Ret.) 2018-

Kalamazoo: First UMC *[Greater Southwest]*   KalamazooFUMC@umc-kzo.org
(P/M) 212 S Park St, Kalamazoo 49007   (269) 381-6340
    James W. Wright 1964-1972; J. Melvin Bricker (Assoc.) 1966-1971; O. Lavern Merritt (Assoc.)
    1968-1970; Ray R. Fassett (Assoc.) 1970-1974; Hoover Rupert 1972-1983; Douglas W. Vernon
    (Assoc.) 1971-1974; Marvin Zimmerman (Assoc.) 1974-1976; Donald Ludman (Assoc.) 1974-1978;
    William Richards (Assoc.) 1976-1979; Richard Beckett (Assoc.) 1977-1987; Mac Kelly (Assoc.)
    1978-1982; Wayne Reece (Assoc.) 1979-1985; Gerald Selleck (Assoc.) 1982-1984; Royal Synwolt
    1983-1991; Jane Shapley (Assoc.) 1985-1987; Dean Francis (Assoc.) 1985-1990; Richard Rossiter
    (Assoc.) 1987-1992; George Hartmann (Assoc.) 1987-1994; Keith Treman (Assoc.) 1990-1998;
    Kenneth McCaw 1991-Jan. 1, 2000; Cynthia A. Skutar (Assoc.) 1992-1997; Cynthia M. Schaefer
    (Assoc.) 1997-2001; Michelle Wisdom-Long (Assoc.) 1998-2000; Ron Keller (interim senior pastor)
    Jan. 1, 2000-July 1, 2000; Douglas W. Vernon 2000-2010; Dale A. Hotelling (Assoc.) July 16, 2000-
    2004; Matthew J. Bistayi (Assoc.) 2002-2006; Julie Dix (Assoc.) 2006-2010; John W. Boley
    2010-2014; Michelle M. Wisdom-Long (Assoc.) 2010-2011; Stephen MG Charnley 2014-2020;
    Manohar A. Joshi (assoc) 2019-Nov 30, 2019; Julie A. Kline (assoc) 2019-2020; Julie A. Kline 2020-
    ; J. Matthew Weiler (assoc) 2020-

Kalamazoo: Milwood UMC *[Greater Southwest]*   office@milwoodunitedmethodistchurch.org
(P/M) 3919 Portage St, Kalamazoo 49001   (269) 381-6720
   Richard C. Miles 1966-1970; Heath T. Goodwin 1970-1971; Alden B. Burns 1971-Dec. 1981; John H. Hice (Assoc.) 1977-1979; Ron L. Keller Jan. 1982-1988; James M. Morgan 1988-1999; Robert K. Lynch 1999-2006; Martin H. Culver 2006-2011; Kennetha J. Bigham-Tsai 2011-2013; Heather A. (McDougall) Molner 2013-Feb. 8, 2016; David A. Newhouse (Ret.) Mar. 1, 2016-2017; Bille R. Dalton (Ret.) 2017-

Kalamazoo: Northwest UMC *[Greater Southwest]*   markroberts1903@yahoo.com
(P/M) 3140 N 3rd St, Kalamazoo 49009   (269) 290-1312
   Ray Carpenter 1967-1972; Linda Stoddard 1972-1976; Dorcas Lohr 1976-1982; Pulpit supply 1982-1983; Alden B. Burns 1983-1996; Carol A. Newman 1996-2000; John W. McNaughton 2000-2003; Calvin Y. Hill 2003-2007; Sheila F. Baker 2007-2012; Ronald W. Hansen (DSA) (1/4 time) 2012-2013; Samuel C. Gordy (1/4 time) 2013-2015; Nelson L. Hall 2015-2018; Mark Robers (LTFT ¼) 2018-

Kalamazoo: Sunnyside UMC *[Greater Southwest]*   office@sunnysideumc.com
(P/M) 2800 Gull Rd, Kalamazoo 49048   (269) 349-3047
   Allen D. McCreedy 1967-1973; Robert H. Conn 1973-1976; John W. Ellinger 1976-1981; Norman C. Kohns 1981-1985; Paul L. Hartman 1985-1992; John W. Fisher 1992-2004; Billie R. Dalton 2004-Feb. 28, 2009; Linda J. Burson, Mar. 1-July 1, 2009; John Matthew Weiler (1/2 time) 2009-2020; Cara Weiler (deacon 1/4 time) Oct. 1, 2009-Jan 16, 2020; Amee A. Paparella 2020-

Kalamazoo: Westwood UMC *[Greater Southwest]*   info@westwood-umc.org
(P/M) 538 Nichols Rd, Kalamazoo 49006   (269) 344-7165
   A.R. Davis 1968-1973; Allen D. McCreedy 1973-1977; E. William Wiltse 1977-1980; Merged with Kalamazoo Simpson 1980; Jack H. Baumgart 1980-1984; Larry E. Irvine 1984-1988; Kenneth W. Karlzen 1988-July 31, 1995; Eric S. Beck Aug. 1, 1995-2007; Wayne A. Price 2007-2019; Sandra Douglas (Deacon) (1/4 time) 2011- ; Sean K. Kidd 2019-

Kalamo UMC *[Mid-Michigan]*   office@kalamochurch.org
(P/M) 1475 S Ionia Rd, Vermontville 49096   (517) 588-8415
   Lowell F. Walsworth 1966-1971; Laurence R. Grubaugh 1971-1973; Milton J. Tenhave 1973-1977; David L. Johnston 1977-May 1983; James William Schoettle May 1983-1988; William P. Sanders 1988-Feb. 1996; Mark E. Thompson 1996-2004; Bryce Feighner 2004-2013; [Barry-Eaton Cooperative Ministry 2013] Dan Phillips 2013-2015; Jerry J. Bukoski (LTFT) 2015-

Kalkaska UMC *[Northern Waters]*   KalkaskaUMC@yahoo.com
(P/M) 2525 Beebe Rd NW, Kalkaska 49646   (231) 258-2820
   Richard M. Riley 1984-1993; Charles R. VanLente 1993-1996; Charles K. Stanley 1996-Oct. 1, 1999; Stanley Lee Hayes (DSA) Oct. 1, 1999-July 1, 2000; Robert W. Stark 2000-2008; Gregory R. Wolfe 2008-2013; Robert J. Freysinger 2013-2015; John Paul Murray 2015-2019; Yong Choel Woo 2019-

Kendall UMC *[Greater Southwest]*   info@goblesumc.org
(P) 26718 County Road 388, Gobles 49055; (M) PO Box 6, Kendall 49062   (269) 628-2263
   James Boehm 1967-1970; Allen Valkema 1970-1971; William Miles 1971-1974; Rudolph Wittenback 1974-1976; Karen S. Slager-Wheat 1976-1986; John McNaughton 1986-1987; Judy K. Downing 1987-1998; Susan Olsen 1998-2004; Mary Beth Rhine 2004-2010; Edward Mohr L. 2010-Sept. 11, 2012; Daniel J. Minor (Ret.) Sept. 16, 2012-June 30, 2013; Nelson L. Hall 2013-2015; John M. Brooks 2015-2019; Glenn C Litchfield 2019-

Kent City: Chapel Hill UMC *[Midwest]*   mary.chapelhillkc@gmail.com
(P/M) 14591 Fruit Ridge Ave, Kent City 49330   (616) 675-7184
     Charles McNary 1964-1970; David Morton 1970-Jan. 1974; Stanley Finkbeiner 1974-1981; Ray
     Grienke 1981-1985; Willard Gilroy 1985-Oct. 1988; David Hainer Oct. 1988-March 1991; Mark
     Johnson May 1991-1996; Glenn C. Litchfield 1996-2005; R. John Thompson 2005-2010; Kevin
     Guetschow 2010-2017; Michael J. Ramsey 2017-2020; [Cedar Springs, KC: Chapel Hill became
     2-point charge 2020] Lawrence J. French 2020-

Keswick UMC *[Northern Waters]*   office@keswickchurch.com
(P/M) 3376 S Center Hwy, Suttons Bay 49682   (231) 271-3755
     Dale Crawford 1968-Oct. 1971; Richard Kuhn Oct. 1971-1980; John Myette 1980-1984; Tom Evans
     1984-1988; Wayne Gorsline 1988-1991; Martin H. Culver 1991-1999; Wayne A. Price 2000-2004;
     Donald E. Spachman 2004-2010; Charles A. Williams 2010-2011; Patricia A. Haas 2011-

Kewadin: Indian Mission UMC *[Northern Waters]*   gpamp@live.com
(P) 7250 Cairn Hwy, Kewadin 49648; (M) 851 W Conway Rd, Harbor Springs 49740   (231) 347-9861
     Harry John Sr. Jan. 1975-1993; Owen White-Pigeon (DSA) 1993-1994; Cletus Marshall 1994-Feb.
     5, 1995; Pulpit Supply Feb. 6-June 1995; Delfred White-Crow (DSA) 1995-Nov. 15, 1997; Delfred
     White-Crow (part-time) Nov. 16, 1997-Apr. 16, 1998; Thomas H. John Jr 1998-2015; [Kewadin
     Indian Mission became single-point charge 2015] Sandra K. VandenBrink (RLA) 2015-Dec. 31,
     2016; George Pamp (DSA) Jan. 1, 2017-

Kewadin UMC *[Northern Waters]*   kewadinumc@gmail.com
(P) 7234 Cairn Hwy, Kewadin 49648; (M) PO Box 277, Kewadin 49648   (231) 264-9640
     Glenn Loy 1968-Sept. 1970; Russell Lautner (Assoc.) 1968-Oct. 1970; Gordon Showers Oct. 1970-
     Nov. 1971; Robert Doner Dec. 1971-1976; Bernard Randolph 1976-1978; Jack Bartholomew
     1978-Feb. 1983; Stephen Beach Feb. 1983-Nov. 1986; Michael Baker-Streevy Dec. 1986-1988;
     Charles M. Shields 1988-1993; Raymond R. Sundell 1993-1998; Kathryn M. Coombs 1998-1999;
     Janilyn McConnell (Deacon) 1998-2003; Thomas M. Pier-Fitzgerald 1999-2005; William W. Chu &
     Julie A. Greyerbiehl (Chu) 2005-2009; Mary S. Brown July 1-Nov. 1, 2009; Eugene L. Baughan
     (Ret.) Nov. 1, 2009-2015; Howard Harvey 2015-

Kilmanagh UMC *[Central Bay]*   pastorbilloumc@outlook.com
(P/M) 2009 S Bay Port Rd, Bay Port 48720   (989) 975-1500
     Harold F. Blakely 1957-1978; William R. Maynard 1978-1980; Donald McLellan 1980-1982; Robert
     L. Kersten 1982-1986; Jeffrey R. Maxwell 1986-1990; George H. Lewis 1990-1993; Nancy Goings
     1993-Dec 31, 1995; Ronald O. Pietta Jan 1, 1996-1997 Clarence VanConant 1997-1999; Alger T.
     Lewis 1999-Mar 1, 2011; Duane G. Thon 2011-2017; William Cleland 2017-

Kingsley UMC *[Northern Waters]*   kumcadmin@kingsleyumcmi.org
(P) 113 Blair St, Kingsley 49649; (M) PO Box 39,5 Kingsley 49649-0395   (231) 263-5278
     Marion Nye 1966-1970; Silas H. Foltz 1970-1971; Lewis (Bud) Buckner 1972-1978; Wayne Babcock
     1978-1983; Beverly Prestwood-Taylor 1983-1986; Beverly Prestwood Taylor (3/4 time) 1986-May
     1988; Bruce Prestwood-Taylor (3/4 time) 1986-May 1988; Bruce Kintigh 1988-1993; Brian F. Rafferty
     1993-1999; Charlene A. Minger 1999-2008; Gary S. Wales 2008-2013; Carl Q. Litchfield 2013-
     2017; Colleen A. Wierman (Assoc.)(1/4 time) 2014-2017; Colleen A. Wierman 2017-

Kingston UMC *[Central Bay]*   kingstonumchurch@gmail.com
(P) 3453 Washington St, Kingston 48741; (M) PO Box 196, Kingston 48741   (989) 683-2832
     Verne W. Blankenburg 1968-1972; Robert Bryce 1972-1973; Joel W. Hurley 1973-1978; Gilson M.
     Miller 1978-1983; Lawrance D. Higgins 1983-1984; C. Wm Bollinger 1984-1989; Lynn F. Chappell
     1989-1996; Kwang Min Lee 1996-1997; Margaret Pettit Passenger 1997-2001; Terry D. Butters
     2001-2005; Richard B. Brown 2005-2010; Debra K. Brown 2010-Mar 15 1, 2015; Margaret
     Passenger (interim) Apr 15, 2015-2015; Carol Joan Abbott 2015-2018; Mark Harriman 2018-

L'Anse UMC *[Northern Skies]*   lumc@up.net
(P/M) 304 N Main St, Lanse 49946   (906) 524-7939
William Kelsey 1968-1970; Lillian Richards 1971; Howard E Shaffer 1971-1981; John R. Henry 1981-1986; Gregory Rowe 1986-1990; James M. Mathews 1990-1993; David P. Snyder 1993-Oct 1, 2003; John R. Henry 2004-2011; Stephen E. Rhoades 2011-2019; Nathan T. Reed 2019-

Lacota UMC *[Greater Southwest]*   m2pinto@hotmail.com
(P) 01160 CR 681, Lacota 49063; (M) PO Box 7, Lacota 49063-0007   (269) 207-2095
Robert Victor 1966-1969; John Hagans 1969-1974; Pulpit Supply 1974-1977; Joseph Pratt 1977-1980; Carl C. Nisbet 1980-Aug. 31, 2003; Donna Jean Keyte Sept. 1, 2003-Jan. 1, 2006; Michael A. Pinto (DSA) 2006-2007; Michael A. Pinto 2007-Apr. 8, 2019; Michael A. Pinto (DSA) April 9, 2019-

Laingsburg UMC *[Mid-Michigan]*   lumc@cablespeed.com
(P/M) 210 Crum St, Laingsburg 48848   (517) 651-5531
Dale Ferris 1969-1972; Brian D. Kundinger 1972-1977; David K. Koski 1977-1982; L. Michael Pearson 1982-1986; Harold E. Weemhoff 1986-1990; Robert J. Easlick 1990-1993; J. Robert Anderson 1993-1999; Gerald M. Sever Jr., 1999-2006; Elbert P. Dulworth 2006-2012; Brian West 2012-2020; [Laingsburg became single station 2020] Tiffany M. Newsom 2020-

Lake Ann UMC *[Northern Waters]*   church@lakeannumc.com
(P/M) 6583 1st St, Lake Ann 49650   (231) 275-7236
Carter Miller 1966-1969; Richard LoCicero 1969-1970; Russell J. Lautner Oct. 1970-1982; William E. Haggard 1982-1989; Charles J. Towersey 1989-Apr. 15, 2008; James L. Breithaupt (Assoc. 1/2 time) 2004-Mar. 15, 2006; Devon R. Herrell June 15, 2008-2013; Michael J. Simon 2013-2017; Joshua Manning 2017-

Lake City UMC *[Northern Waters]*   lcumc301@gmail.com
(P) 301 E John St, Lake City 49651; (M) PO Box - Drawer P, Lake City 49651   (231) 839-2123
J. William Schoettle 1965-Feb. 1970; Leonard J. Yarlott Feb. 1970-1972; Ward D. Pierce 1972-Aug. 1976; Ross Bunce Aug. 1976-1979; Willard Gilroy 1979-1985; David L. Dryer 1985-1996; Jane A. Crabtree 1996-2000; Edrye (Eastman-Sealey) Maurer 2000-Sept. 1, 2010; Jean M. Smith Sept. 1, 2010-2019; Russell K. Logston 2019-

Lake Fenton UMC *[East Winds]*   pastorcshay@gmail.com
(P/M) 2581 N Long Lake Rd, Fenton 48430   (810) 629-5161
Dwight E. Reibling 1968-1970; Donald C. Turbin 1970-1973; David G. Knapp Dec. 1973-1976; Clifford J. Furness 1976-Sep 30, 1998; Gloria Haynes Oct 1, 1998-2002; Emerson W. Arntz 2002-2009; Pamela S. Kail 2009-2012; Jeremy Peters 2012-2015; Charmaine Shay 2015-2019; Duane A. Lindsey 2019-2020 [Lake Fenton / Lennon / Duffield three-point charge 7-1-2019] [Lake Fenton became single station 2020] Vincent Slocum (DSA) 2020-

Lake Linden UMC *[Northern Skies]*   calumc@up.net
(P/M) 57235 Calumet Ave, Calumet 49913   (906) 337-2720
J. Howard Wallis 1967-1968; Robert Barry 1969-1970; Lillian Richards; 1970; John Moore 1970-1976; Martin Caudill 1976-1979; Jay Six 1979-1981; William Wright 1981-1985; W. Peter Bartlett 1985-1987; Pamela J. Scott; Jack E. Johnston 1989-1992; Mary L. Rose 1992-1994; Christine F. Bohnsack 1994-Feb 29, 2000; Robert A. White Mar 16, 2000- ; Richard B. Brown (assoc) Mar 16, 2000 2003; Robert A. White 2000 2016; James Palaazcaki 2016-2018; Gun Soo Jung 2018-2019; [Keweenaw Parish: Calumet / Lake Linden 7-1-2019] James M. Mathews (Ret.) 2019-

Lake Odessa: Central UMC *[Mid-Michigan]*   info@centralchurch-lakeo.org
(P) 912 4th Ave, Lake Odessa 48849; (M) PO Box 485, Lake Odessa 48849   (616) 374-8861
Marvin F. Zimmerman 1967-1974; William A. Hertel 1974-Sept. 1980; Steve Keller 1980-1984; Thurlan E. Meredith 1984-1986; Charles W. Richards 1986-1989; D. Keith Laidler 1989-1992; Emmett H. Kadwell, Jr. 1992-Jan. 1, 2000; Charles M. Shields Feb. 1, 2000-July 1, 2000; Donald R. Ferris 2000-2007; Eric S. Beck 2007-2012; Karen J. Sorden 2012-2017; Dominic A. Tommy 2017-2020; Vaughn W. Thurston-Cox 2020-

Lake Odessa: Lakewood UMC *[Mid-Michigan]*   juliew@lakewoodmiumc.org
(P/M) 10265 Brown Rd, Lake Odessa 48849   (269) 367-4800
Wilbur A. Williams 1967-1971; Charles A. Dunbar 1971-1978; James R. Hulett 1978-1985; Ward D. Pierce 1985-2001; Curtis E. Jensen 2001-2003; David Lee Flagel 2003-2013; James C. Noggle 2013-2015; Kathleen Smith (RLA) (Assoc.) July 15, 2014- ; Cynthia Greene 2015-2017; Steven C. Place 2017-

Lake Orion UMC *[East Winds]*   loumc1@sbcglobal.net
(P/M) 140 E Flint St, Lake Orion 48362   (248) 693-6201
Robert Hudgins 1962-1971; Edward L. Duncan 1971-1982; W. Harold Pailthorp (assoc) 1973-1984; Mary Margaret Eckhardt (assoc) 1978-1983, 1985-1990; Richard A Peacock 1982-1993; Bruce E. Petrick (assoc) 1990-1993; Robert Davis 1993-1997; Wilson Andrew Hart (assoc) 1993-Apr 30, 1996; Randy J. Whitcomb (assoc) May 1, 1996-Feb 15, 2001; Thomas P. Macaulay 1997-2004; Carol M. Blair Bouse (assoc) 2001-2002; Marjorie H. Munger (assoc) 2002-2013; Bruce M. Denton 2004-2012; Lawrence A. Wik 2012- ; John Ball (assoc.) 2013-

Lakeview: New Life UMC *[Midwest]*   newlifeumc6584@gmail.com
(P/M) 6584 W Howard City Edmore Rd, Six Lakes 48886   (989) 352-7788
Lawrence P. Brown Jan. 1, 1998-2006; Richard J. Duffy (co-pastor) Jan. 1, 1998-June 30, 1998; Anita Hahn 2006-2011; John A. Scott 2011-2015; Susan J. Babb 2015-2019; Mark R. Babb (Deacon) 2016-2019; Timothy B. Wright 2019-

Lamb UMC *[East Winds]*   huff1@aol.com
(P) 1209 Cove Rd, Wales 48027; (M) PO Box 29, Memphis 48041-0029   (810) 392-2294
Max Weeks 1965-1971; Duane E. Miller 1972-1977; Paul W. Reigle 1977-1982; Wayne C. Ferrigan 1982-1984; Martin Caudill 1984- 1987; Oct. Donald L. Bates 1987-1991; Douglas M. Choate 1992-1993; Catherine W. Hiner 1993-1999; David L. Fleming 1999-2001; Janet M. Engler 2001-2004; Donald L. Wojewski Nov 1, 2004-Dec 31, 2004; James E. Huff, Jr. Jan 1, 2005-2020; Luis M. Collazo 2020-

Lambertville UMC *[Heritage]*   office@labertvilleumc.org
(P) 8165 Douglas Rd, Lambertville 48144; (M) PO Box 232, Lambertville 48144

(734) 847-3944
Leonard C. Ritzler 1966-1972; Harry Gintzer (assoc) 1971-1972; A. Edward Perkins 1972-1974; Dean A. Klump 1974-1981; James R. McCallum 1981-1983; Jeffry W. Dinner 1983-1990; David D. Amstutz 1990-1997; Thomas H. Zimmerman 1997-2016; Douglas E. Ralston (assoc) 2004-Mar 28, 2007; King W. Hanna (interim-assoc) May 1, 2007-Jul 31, 2007; James O. Bowen (assoc) Aug 1, 2007-2008; Aaron B. Kesson (assoc) 2008-2012; Zachary Dunlap (assoc.) Jan 1, 2013-2015; Devin Smith (assoc.) 2015-2020; Gene Patrick England 2016-2018; James E. Britt 2018-

Lansing: Asbury UMC *[Mid-Michigan]*   asburyumclansing@gmail.com
(P/M) 2200 Lake Lansing Rd, Lansing 48912   (517) 484-5794
Douglas A. Smith 1960-1970; John S. Myette 1970-1978; Geoffrey L. Hayes 1978-1987; William A. Hertel 1987-1990; Charles F. Garrod 1990-Oct. 1992; Benton R. Heisler Nov. 1992-1997; Deborah M. Johnson 1997-2008; Martin M. DeBow 2008-2014; Bo Rin Cho 2014-2017; Jon L. Pohl 2017-

Lansing: Central UMC *[Mid-Michigan]* adminassistant@lansingcentralumc.net
(P/M) 215 N Capitol Ave, Lansing 48933 (517) 485-9477
Howard A. Lyman Feb. 1967-1978; Francis F. Anderson (Assoc.) 1966-1970; Peter H. Kunnen (Assoc.) 1968-1970; Robert E. Betts (Assoc.) 1970-1974; Charles Grauer (Assoc.) 1970-1972; Paul L. Hartman (Assoc.) 1974-Jan. 1980; Samuel H. Evans (Assoc.) 1975-1977; Lloyd VanLente (Assoc.) 1977-1982; Neil F. Bintz 1978-1982; Robert H. Roth, Jr. (Assoc.) May 1980-1983; Sidney A. Short 1982-1993; James M. Gysel (Assoc.) 1983-1993; Lynn A. DeMoss 1993-1997; Pegg Ainslie (Assoc.) 1993-1997; John W. Boley 1997-2002; Russell F. McReynolds 2002-2007; Joseph D. Huston 2007-2009; Ronald K. Brooks 2009-2013; Linda J. Farmer-Lewis 2013-2017; Mark E. Thompson 2017-2020; Naylo T. Hopkins 2020-

Lansing: First UMC *[Mid-Michigan]* office@lansingfirst.org
(P/M) 3827 Delta River Dr, Lansing 48906 (517) 321-5187
Francis C. Johannides 1968-1972; John F. Sorensen 1972-Sept. 1978; Theron E. Bailey Sept. 1978-March 1982; Kenneth W. Karlzen March 1982-1988; Mark D. Graham 1988-1996; Robert L. Hundley 1996-2000; Stephan Weinberger 2000-2004; Melanie J. Baker 2004-2012; Lori J. Sykes July 15, 2012-2020; Robert P. Blanchard 2020-

Lansing: Grace UMC *[Mid-Michigan]* lgraceumc@gmail.com
(P/M) 1900 Boston Blvd, Lansing 48910 (517) 482-5750
Clarence W. Hutchens 1967-1975; Paul F. Albery 1975-1981; John W. Ellinger 1981-1985; David L. Johnston 1985-1992; Richard E. Johns 1992-1996; Gary L. Bekofske 1996-2005; Timothy P. Boal 2005-2006; Jane Ellen Johnson Jan. 1, 2007-2016; Paul SungJoon Hahm 2016- ; Nancy V. Fancher (Deacon) 2017-

Lansing: Mt Hope UMC *[Mid-Michigan]* office@mounthopeumc.org
(P/M) 501 E Mount Hope Ave, Lansing 48910 (517) 482-1549
Donald Merrill 1967-Oct. 1975; George Elliott Nov. 1975-1979; Lloyd Phillips 1979-1984; Robert Hinklin 1984-Feb. 1987; Wade Panse May 1987-Oct. 1992; Paul C. Frederick Dec. 1992-1999; Pamela J. Mathieu (Deacon) 1995- Ronald K. Brooks (Assoc.) 1998-1999; Ronald K. Brooks 1999-2000; Linda H. Hollies 2000-2001; William Earl Haggard 2002-2012; Lansing Calvary UMC merged w/ Mt. Hope UMC 07-01-07]; Colleen Treman (Deacon, Children's Coordinator) 2008-2015; Robert B. Cook 2012- ; Eric Nduwa Mulanda Aug. 1, 2015- ; Nancy V. Fancher (Deacon) (LTFT ½) 2018-

Lansing: Sycamore Creek UMC *[Mid-Michigan]* office@sycamorecreekchurch.org
(P/M) 1919 S Pennsylvania Ave, Lansing 48910 (517) 394-6100
[new church start 2000] Barbara J. Flory 2000-2009; Thomas F. Arthur 2009- [Potterville UMC merged w/ Sycamore Creek UMC and became Sycamore Creek Potterville Campus 12-31-16] Mark Aupperlee (Assoc.) Jan 1, 2018-

Lansing: Sycamore Creek UMC - Potterville Campus *[Mid-Michigan]*
(P) 105 N Church St, Potterville 48876; (M) 1919 S Pennsylvania Ave, Lansing 48910
(517) 645-7701
Thomas F. Arthur Dec. 31, 2016- ; [Potterville UMC merged w/ Sycamore Creek UMC and became Sycamore Creek Potterville Campus 12-31-16] Mark Aupperlee (Assoc.) Jan 1, 2018-

Lapeer: Trinity UMC *[East Winds]*   trinumc@trinitylapeer.org
(P/M) 1310 N Main St, Lapeer 48446   (810) 664-9941
   Arthur B. Howard 1968-1973; Norman R. Beckwith (assoc) 1970-1972; Floyd W. Porter (assoc)
   1972-1976; Garfield H. Kellermann 1973-1976; James R. Timmons 1976-1994; David J. Hill (assoc)
   1976-1979; Gordon B. Boyd (assoc) 1979-1981; Allen J. Lewis (assoc) 1979-1981; Donald E.
   Washburn (assoc) 1981-1984; David C. Dupree (assoc) 1984-1987; Michael O. Pringle (assoc)
   1987-1991; W. Steven Boom (assoc) 1991-Nov 1, 1994; Terry A. Euper 1994-2003; Daniel J.
   Bowman (assoc) Jan 1, 1995-Aug 31, 1998; Chong Youb Won (assoc) Sep 1, 1998-2002; Colin P.
   Stover (assoc) 2002-May 31, 2005; Ralph H. Pieper, II 2003-2012; Gloria Haynes (assoc) 2005-
   2009; Grant R. Lobb 2012-

LaPorte UMC *[Central Bay]*   laportepastor@aol.com
(P/M) 3990 Smith's Crossing, Freeland 48623   (989) 695-9692
   Karl Patow 1969-1971; Richard Mansfield 1971; John Eversole 1971-1973; Max Weeks 1973-1977;
   Leon Smith 1977-1979; Leonard Gamber 1979-1982; Kenneth Reeves 1982-1985; Edwin M.
   Collver 1985-1992; Gordon B. Boyd 1993-Aug 31, 1994; Barbra Franks Sep 1, 1994-Sep 30, 1996;
   Timothy Hastings Dec 1, 1996-Dec 15, 2003; Elin A. Peckham Dec 16, 2003-Jun 30, 2007; Bonita
   Davis Sep 16, 2007-2008; L. Cecille Adams Aug 1, 2008-2013; Robert G. Richards 2013- [Swan
   Valley (lead church) / LaPorte charge and Hemlock / Nelson charge formed new four point charge
   July 1, 2019]

LaSalle: Zion UMC *[Heritage]*   lasallezionumc@yahoo.com
(P) 1603 Yargerville Rd, La Salle 48145; (M) 1607 Yargerville Rd, La Salle 48145
   Tony Johnson 1968-1969; Paul W. Hoffmaster 1969-1972; John G. Park 1972-1975; Donald J.
   Daws 1975-1980; Stephen E. Wenzel 1980-1982; Robert Worgess 1982-1984; Grant R. Lobb 1984-
   1988; Craig A. Smith Aug. 1, 1988-Aug. 16, 1990; Daniel J. Bowman Sep. 16, 1990-Dec 31, 1994;
   Ray T. McGee Jan 1, 1995-Aug 15, 2000; Judy Link Fuller Sep 1, 2000-Oct 31, 2000; Douglas E.
   Ralston Nov 1, 2000-Mar 28, 2007; King W. Hanna (interim) May 1, 2007-Jul 31, 2007; James O.
   Bowen Aug 1, 2007-2009; Janet L. Luchs 2009-2011; Joel Walther 2011-2017; Daniel Hyer 2017-
   2018; Carter Louis Cortelyou 2018-2020;

Lawrence UMC *[Greater Southwest]*   lawrenceunitedmethodist@gmail.com
(P) 122 S Exchange St, Lawrence 49064; (M) PO Box 276, Lawrence 49064   (269) 674-8381
   Kenneth Snow 1967-1972; Norman Crotser 1972-1976; George Gierman 1976-1979; Leo Bennett
   1979-1986; Mark Johnson 1986-Apr. 1991; Ronald K. Brooks May 1991-1998; Wayne H. Babcock
   1998-Dec. 31, 2002; David S. Yoh (DSA) Jan. 1, 2003-July 1, 2003; Jane D. Logston 2003-2006;
   Clifford L. Radtke 2006-2016; Wayne E. McKenney 2016- [Lawrence / Lawton St. Paul's became
   a two-point charge 2016]

Lawton St Paul's UMC *[Greater Southwest]*   st.paulsoffice2018@gmail.com
(P) 63855 N M 40, Lawton 49065; (M) PO Box 456, Lawton 49065-0456   (269) 624-1050
   Donald Russell 1968-1971; Roger Nielson 1971-1974; Al Sprague 1974-1977; Diane Vale 1977-
   1980; Jeff Edwards 1980-1981; Dean Francis 1981-1985; Beverly Gaska 1985-1987; Billie R. Dalton
   1987-1995; Claudette I. Haney 1995-2000; Ronald K. Brooks 2000-2006; Daniel W. Biteman 2006-
   2010; Peggy A. Boltz 2010-2011; Douglas W. Vernon (DSA) (1/4 time) 2011-2014;
   [LifeSpring/Lawton St. Paul's became 2-point charge 2014] Wayne E. McKenney 2014- [Lawrence
   / Lawton St. Paul's became a two-point charge 2016]

Leaton UMC *[Central Bay]*   fatpastor@cmsinter.net
(P/M) 6890 E Beal City Rd, Mt Pleasant 48858   (989) 773-3838
Paul Peet 1968-1969; Fred Fischer 1969-1978; David Meister 1978-1979; Pulpit Supply 1979-1980; Thomas Crossman 1980-1981; Pulpit Supply 1981-Jan. 1984; Dale Barry Jan.-Aug. 1984; Tim Girkin Oct.-Nov. 1984; Byron Coleman Nov. 1984-Jan. 1992; Connie Bongard Jan. 1992-1994; Thomas R. Jones (retired) 1994-July 31, 1999; Randall E. Roose (DSA) Aug. 1, 1999-2004; Susan D. Olsen July 16, 2004-2006; Sharyn K. Osmond Aug. 1, 2006-Nov. 30, 2008; Donald R. Wendell Nov. 30, 2008-Nov. 1, 2009; Craig L. Adams Dec. 1, 2009-2010; David Michael Palmer 2010-2016; Russell D. Morgan 2016-2018; Deborah A. Line Yencer (Ret.) (LTFT ¼) 2018-

Lee Center UMC *[Heritage]*   lackcv@yahoo.com
(P/M) 23058 21 Mile Rd, Olivet 49076   (517) 857-3447
Lynn Chapel 1965-March 1971; Beulah Poe March 1971-1976; Robert Doner 1976-1978; Joel Campbell 1978-1979; Ethel Stears 1979-Sept. 16, 1983; William Doubblestein Oct. 16, 1983-1987; Eugene Baughan 1987-1991; David H. Minger 1991-1995; Wayne Willer 1995-1996; Valerie Hill 1996-1998; David L. Litchfield 1998-2001; David Blair 2001-2003; Diane E. Stone 2004-2010; Irene L. Vittoz 2010-2014 [Lee Center UMC became single-point charge 7-1-10]; James Gysel (Ret.) 2014-

Leighton UMC *[Midwest]*   office@leightonchurch.org
(P/M) 4180 2nd St, Caledonia 49316   (616) 891-8028
James Sherwood 1965-1972; Keith Laidler 1972-1977; Curtis Cruff July-Dec. 1977; Donald Vuurens Jan. 1978-1980; Richard W. McClain 1980-1986; Kenneth Vaught 1986-May 31, 1991; Raymond Townsend 1991-2006; David L. McBride 2006-

Leland UMC *[Northern Waters]*   office@lelandcommunityumc.org
(P) 106 N 4th St, Leland 49654; (M) PO Box 602, Leland 49654-0602   (231) 256-9161
Elmer J. Faust 1966-1969; Edward Jones 1969-1971; Richard Kuhn Nov. 1971-1980; John Myette 1980-1984; Tom Evans 1984-Jan. 31, 1994; Doug L. Pedersen Feb. 16, 1994-1997; Joseph M. Graybill 1997-2011; Linda J. Farmer-Lewis 2011-2013; Virginia L. Heller 2013-2014; Daniel B. Hofmann 2014-

Lennon UMC *[East Winds]*   dualind@yahoo.com
(P) 1014 Oak St, Lennon 48449; (M) PO Box 19, Lennon 48449-0019   (810) 621-3676
Herbert W. Thompson 1969-1978; Ralph C. Pratt 1978-1979; Paul I. Greer 1979-1981; Meredith T. Moshauer 1981-1988; James R. Allen 1988-1992; S. Patrick Stybert 1992-1996; Paul L. Amstutz 1998-2007; Ron Keller 2007-Nov, 2007; Kathy M. Phillips Dec 1, 2007-2016; Barbara S. Benjamin 2016-2018; Duane A. Lindsey (DSA) 2018-Dec 31, 2018; Duane A. Lindsey Jan 1, 2019-2020 [Lake Fenton / Lennon / Duffield three-point charge 7-1-2019] [Lennon became single station 2020] Joyce E. Wallace (Ret.) 2020-

Leonard UMC *[East Winds]*   pastorpatty@att.net
(P) 245 E Elmwood, Leonard 48367; (M) 3645 Grant Ave, Fort Gratiot 48059   (248) 628-7983
Elmer J. Snyder 1974-1976; Jeffery D. Regan 1976-1979; James W. Burgess 1979-1980; Dana R. Strall 1980-1985; Sylvia A. Bouvier 1985-1987; Emerson W. Arntz 1987-1992; Rothwell W. Mc Vety 1992-1996; Harry Brakeman 1996-1997; Ralph Barteld 1997-2002; Ruthmary King (assoc) 1998-2001; Harold C. Nelson (assoc) 2001-Jan 1, 2003; Harold C. Nelson 2003-Apr 1, 2006; Carol S. Walborn Apr 1, 2006-2008; Patricia A. Hoppenworth 2008-2020; Devin R. Smith 2020- [Romeo and Leonard formed cooperative parish 2020]

Leslie UMC *[Mid-Michigan]*   leslieumc@wowway.biz
(P/M) 401 S Main St, Leslie 49251   (517) 589-9211
   William Wurzel 1966-1969; Gordon E. Spalenka June-Oct. 1969; Arthur A. Jackson Oct. 1969-
   1972; Wayne E. Sparks 1972-1975; James M. Morgan 1975-1982; Max J. Gladding 1982-1990;
   Clinton McKinven-Copus 1990-Oct. 1991; Reva Hawke Oct. 1991-April 1993; Derek DeToni-Hill
   1993-Oct. 15, 1999; Janet Sweet-Richardson Nov. 1, 1999-2003; Carroll Arthur Fowler 2003-Jan.
   1, 2006; Donald L. Buege Jan. 15, 2006-2014; Kelly M. Wasnich July 1-Aug. 10, 2014; Frederick
   H. Fischer (Ret.) Sept. 14, 2014-2015; Paul A. Damkoehler (LTFT) 2015-2020 [Leslie / Felt Plains
   became a two-point charge 2018] [Millville, Leslie, Felt Plains became 3-point charge 2020] Rhonda
   J. Osterman 2020-

Lexington UMC *[East Winds]*   lexingtonumc@gmail.com
(P/M) 5597 Main St, Lexington 48450   (810) 359-8215
   Kenneth L. Harris 1969-1977; John D. Lover 1977-1982; Max D. Weeks Jan. 1983-1987; Donna
   J. Osterhout 1987-1991; Richard F. Kriesch 1991-1997; Jean R. Snyder 1997-2000; Linda Jo
   Powers 2000-2002; Betty Montei Blair 2002-Jan 30, 2009; Timothy R. Ziegler 2009-2013; Maureen
   Baker 2013-2017; David G. Gladstone (Ret.) 2017-2018; Susan M. Youmans 2018-

Lincoln UMC *[Central Bay]*   UMCinLincolnMI@charter.net
(P) 101 E Main St, Lincoln 48742; (M) PO Box 204, Lincoln 48742   (989) 736-6910
   Carl J. Litchfield 1969-1971; G. MacDonald Jones 1971-1972; Luren J. Strait 1972-1978; Bruce
   M. Denton 1978-1983; William L. Stone 1983-1990; Edward C. Seward 1990-Dec 31, 2004; William
   P. Sanders (interm); Travis DeWitt Sep 1, 2005-2007; Tracy Brooks 2007-2012; Linda Jo Powers
   2012-Oct 31, 2014; Mary Soderholm Nov 1, 2014-Jun 10, 2017; Charles Sheldon Sept 1, 2017-
   2018; Eric Lee Johnson 2018-2020; Angela M. Lovegrove 2020-

Linden UMC *[East Winds]*   lumc01@aol.com
(P) 201 S Bridge St, Linden 48451; (M) PO Box 488, Linden 48451-0488   (810) 735-5858
   W. Thomas Schomaker 1969-Dec. 1975; James G. Simmons 1976-1980; Dale B. Ward 1980-
   1981; John M. Mehl, Jr. 1981-1989; Linda J. Donelson 1989-1990; Carter Garrigues-Cortelyou
   1990-Aug 31, 1994; Shirley A. Cormicle Sep 1, 1994-1998; David R. Strobe 1998-Jan 31, 2001;
   Janet M. Stybert 2001-2004; Margaret A. Kivisto 2004-2014; Crystal C. Thomas 2014-2018;
   Michelle N. Forsyth 2018-2020; [Linden became single station 2020] Robert J. Easlick 2020-

Livingston Circuit: Plainfield, Trinity UMC *[Heritage]*   livcirumc@gmail.com
(P) 17845 MI State Rd 36, Gregory 48137; (M) 8201 Iosco Rd, Fowlerville 48836
                                                                        (517) 223-3803
   Harry Gintzer 1966-1969; Roger A. Parker 1969-1970; Thomas E. Hart 1970-1975; Jerome K.
   Smith 1975-1981; Meredith T. Moshauer 1981-Dec. 31, 1981; William R. Donahue Jr. Jan. 14,
   1982-Dec. 31, 1987; Richard W. Sheppard Jan. 15, 1988-Dec. 31, 1989; Paul F. Bailey Jan. 1,
   1990-1991; Margery A. Schleicher 1991-1995; Myra L. Sparks 1995-Aug 31, 1997; Darrel L. Rice
   Jan 1, 1998-2003; Malcolm L. Greene 2003-Aug 31, 2004; Steven A Gjerstad Sep 1, 2004-2006;
   Judith M. Darling 2006-2009; Alan DeGraw (interim) 2009-Dec 31, 2009; Robert A. Miller Jan 1,
   2010-2013; David C. Freeland 2013-2017; Mark Huff Nov 12, 2017-

Livonia: Clarenceville UMC *[Greater Detroit]*   clarencevillechurch@gmail.com
(P/M) 20300 Middlebelt Rd, Livonia 48152   (248) 474-3444
   Elsie A. Johns 1941-1973; Gerald H. Fisher 1973-1985; James E. Tuttle Jan. 15 1985-1990;
   Lawrence E. VanSlambrook 1990-Feb. 2, 1992; M. Lester McCabe (assoc) 1990-1992; James P.
   Kummer Feb. 2, 1992-1995; M. Jean Love 1995-2001; James E. Britt 2001-Aug 14, 2006; Elizabeth
   A. Librande Aug 15, 2007-2010; Donald L. Sperling 2010-

Livonia: Newburg UMC *[Greater Detroit]* judy@newburgumc.org
(P/M) 36500 Ann Arbor Trl, Livonia 48150 (734) 422-0149
  William A. Ritter 1969-1980; Benjamin Bohnsack (assoc) 1970-1973; Donna J. Lindberg (assoc) 1973-March 1974; Duane E. Snyder 1974-1976; John Ferris (assoc) 1976-Apr. 1979; Jack E. Giguere 1980-1984; Roy G. Forsyth (assoc) 1981-1991; Edward C. Coley 1984-1988; David Church 1988-1992; David E. Ray (assoc) 1991-1993; Gilson M. Miller 1992-1997; Melanie L. Carey (assoc) 1993-2000; Thomas G Badley 1997-2002; Barbara E. Welbaum (assoc) 2000-2006; Terry W. Allen 2002-Sep 1, 2005; Marsha M. Woolley 2006-2013; Paul Perez (deacon) 2008-2013; Steven E. McCoy 2013- ; Rebecca Wilson (deacon) 2014-Jan 1, 2105;

Livonia: St. Matthews UMC *[Greater Detroit]* ekemoli@stmatthewslivonia.com
(P/M) 30900 6 Mile Rd, Livonia 48152 (734) 422-6038
  Paul T. Hart 1968-1971; Jerome K. Smith (assoc) 1971-1975; William D. Rickard 1971-1980; David T. Strong 1980-1990; Kearney Kirby (R. assoc) 1989-1992; G. Charles Sonquist 1990-Aug 31, 2002; Mary Margaret Eckhardt Sep 1, 2002-2010; George E. Covintree, Jr. 2010-2015; Jeremy P. Africa 2015-

London UMC *[Heritage]* christopherbutson@live.com
(P/M) 11318 Plank Rd, Milan 48160 (734) 439-2680
  Gary R. Imms 1969-1976; John J. Landon 1976-Mar. 1978; James B. Lumsden Mar. 1978-Dec. 1978; D. Byron Coleman Dec. 1978-1982; Mildred M. Hiner 1982-1984; Donald C. Schark 1984-1986; David W. Purdue 1986-1991; William Michael Clemmer (interim Jun-Aug. 1991); Diana K. Goudie Sep. 1, 1991- Aug 31, 1994; William Michael Clemmer Sep 1, 1994-Feb 16, 2003; Richard E. Burstall 2003-2007; Edward L. Tam 2007-Oct 31, 2007; Ruth A. McCully Nov 1, 2007-Nov 15, 2009; Courtney D. Williams Nov 16, 2009-Dec 31, 2013; Christopher Butson Jan 1, 2014-2019; Beatroce S. Alghali 2019-

Lowell: First UMC *[Midwest]* office@lowellumc.com
(P/M) 621 E Main St, Lowell 49331 (616) 897-5936
  G. Robert Webber 1965-1969; Hartwell Gosney (Assoc.) 1968-Oct. 1972; Dean E. Bailey 1969-1979; Gerald R. Bates 1979-Apr. 1982; Donald L. Buege (Assoc.) 1979-Aug. 1980; Beulah P. Poe (Assoc.) Sept. 1980-1982; William J. Amundsen 1982-1993; B. Gordon Barry 1993-2003; Michael T. Conklin 2003-2008; Richard W. Blunt 2008-2014; Cheryl A. Mulligan (Deacon) Jan. 1, 2014- ; James Bradley Brillhart 2014-

Lowell: Vergennes UMC *[Midwest]* vergennes.secretary@gmail.com
(P/M) 10411 Bailey Dr NE, Lowell 49331 (616) 897-6141
  William Vowell 1968-1969; Phillip Carpenter 1969-1977; Luren Strait 1978-1979; Donald Buege 1979-Sept. 1, 1980; Stanley Forkner Sept. 1, 1980-1986; Daniel Duncan 1986-1989; Tracy Taylor 1989-1990; Lloyd Hansen 1990-1991; Mary Schippers 1991-March 31, 1995; Pulpit Supply April-June 1995; David F. Stout 1995-1996; Nathaniel W. Johnson Sept. 1, 1996-2010; Matthew Stoll 2010-2018; Thomas C. Fifer 2018-

Ludington: St Paul UMC *[Northern Waters]* stpaulumc333@gmail.com
(P/M) 3212 W Kinney Rd, Ludington 49431 (231) 843-3275
  Jack Kraklan 1967-1971; Bernard Randolph 1971-1974; Forest Crum 1974-1981; Ray D. Flessner 1981-1989; Robert P. Stover 1989-1998; Dennis E. Slattery 1998-2007; Robert J. Henning 2007-2011; Jon L. Pohl 2011-2017; Bradley E. Bunn (DSA) 2017-

Ludington United UMC *[Northern Waters]*   office@ludingtonumc.org
(P/M) 5810 Bryant Rd, Ludington 49431   (231) 843-8340
   Harold F. Filbrandt 1967-1974; William J. Torrey 1974-1978; John F. Sorensen Sept. 15, 1978-
   1983; William D. Dobbs 1983-1991; Laurie A. Haller (Assoc.) 1985-1989; Paul E. Lowley 1991-2000;
   Betty A. Smith (Assoc.) 1990-1992; Joe D. Elenbaas 2000-Nov 30, 2006; Kenneth E. Tabor (Assoc.)
   2004-2010; Thomas J. Evans 2007-2013; Dennis B. Bromley 2013-

Lulu UMC *[Heritage]*   vmoree@msn.com
(P) 12810 Lulu Rd, Ida 48140; (M) PO Box 299, Ida 48140-0299   (734) 269-9076
   Ferris S. Woodruff 1967-1973; Harry Gintzer 1973-1974; Keith Rasey 1974-1976; William Michael
   Clemmer 1976-1980; J. Robert Anderson 1980-1984; Raymond J. Townsend 1984-1988; Patricia
   A. VanWormer 1988-1991; Doris Crocker 1991-1998; Ruth McCully 1998-2003; Judith M. Darling
   Sep 16, 2003-2006; Bonnie M. Frey 2006-Jan 7, 2018; William R. Lass (DSA) Jan 15-Dec 31,
   2018; William R. Lass Jan 1, 2019-2020; Robert J. Freysinger 2020-

Lyon Lake UMC *[Heritage]*   homlyl@rocketmail.com
(P) 8493 17 Mile Rd, Marshall 49068; (M) 101 E Adams St, Homer 49245   (269) 789-0017
   A. Ray Noland Sept. 1968-1973; John T. Charter 1973-1978; Harold Deipert 1978-1983; Walter
   Rothfuss1983-1987; Linda Farmer-Lewis Sept. 1987-Dec. 1992; Claudette Haney April 16, 1993-
   1995, Nelson Ray 1995-1997; Linda J. Burson 1997-Jan. 1, 2000; Mark Mitchell 2000-2008;
   Thomas P. Fox 2008-2012; Robert P. Stover (Ret.) 2012-

Lyons-Muir Church *[Midwest]*   info@lyonsmuirchurch.com
(P/M) 1074 Olmstead Rd, Muir 48860   (989) 855-2247
   Richard Strait 1972-1977; George Matter 1977-1979; Howard McDonald 1979-1982; Byron
   Coleman 1982-1984; Bette Dobie 1984-1988; Scott Otis 1988-1993; David J. Blincoe 1993-Aug.
   15, 1994; Supplied by Presbyterian Church Sept. 1994; Don Wells (Presbyterian) 1995-Jan. 6,
   1999; Judy K. Downing 1999-2001; Lynn W. Wagner 2001-Sept. 1, 2002; Kathy Jean Clark Aug.
   1, 2003-?Jan. 1,2005; Forrest B. Nelson Jan. 1, 2005- Jan. 1, 2016; Jonathan D. VanDop, Jan. 1,
   2016-2017; [Ionia First / Lyons-Muir became a two-point charge 2016] Jonathan E. Bratt Carle
   2017-

Mackinaw City: Church of the Straits UMC *[Northern Skies]*   office@churchofthestaits.com
(P) 307 N Huron, Mackinaw City 49701; (M) PO Box 430, Mackinaw City 49701   (231) 436-8682
   Raymond C. Provost (Presb.) 1965-1984; Douglas W. Vernon 1984-1988; William J. McGuinness
   (Presb) 1988-Apr 30, 1996; Wilson "Drew" Andrew Hart May 1, 1996-2001; C. Jack Richardson
   (Presb) 2001-2002; Maria Rutland Price (Presb) 2002-2006; David M. Wallis 2006-

Macomb: Faith UMC *[Greater Detroit]*   faith_umc@yahoo.com
(formerly New Haven: Faith; also New Haven Meade)
(P/M) 56370 Fairchild Rd, Macomb 48042   (586) 749-3147
   Joan D. Roach 1965-1970; Forrest Pierce 1970-1972; Donald L. Linchtenfelt 1972-1973; Ronald
   Leisman 1973; Donald L. Lichtenfelt 1973-1974; Mary Howard (Rawson) 1974-1976; Donald L.
   Lichtenfelt 1976-1980; Thomas F. Keef 1980-1982; Mary F. Neil 1982-1984; John J. Rodgers 1984-
   1991; Marion A. Pohly Jan.1, 1992-1996; Arthur Stone Nov 16, 1996-Oct 31, 1998; Marion A. Pohly
   Nov 1, 1998-Apr 28, 2011; Dianna H. Van Marter 2011- [New Haven: Faith re-named Macomb:
   Faith 12-6-2015]

Macon UMC *[Heritage]* maconumc@frontier.com
(P/M) 11964 Macon Hwy, Clinton 49236 (517) 4238270
Thomas G. Badley 1968-1970; Robert E. Burkey 1970-1973; John W. Vance 1973-1975; Albert F. Raloff 1975-1979; Martha H. Cargo 1979-1982; Robert C. Strobridge 1982-1983; Robin G. Gilshire 1983-1990; Gregory E. Rowe 1990-1993; Ramona E. Cowling 1993-Aug 31, 1997; C. Michael Madison Sep 1, 1997-1999; Bonnie J. Lancaster 1999-2001; Alan J. Hanson 2001-2002; Dale E. Brown 2002-2007; Lance E. Ness 2007-2017; Ruth A. VanderSande Sept 7, 2017-2020 [Britton: Grace / Macon two-point charge 7-1-2019] [Blissfield: Emmanuel, Macon two-point charge 7-1-2020] Kelley-Marie Zawodni 2020-

Madison Heights: First UMC *[Greater Detroit]* rhonda8776@gmail.com
(P/M) 246 E 11 Mile Rd, Madison Heights 48071 (248) 544-3544
Ross N. Nicholson 1967-1972; Robert H. Bough 1972-1975; Kenneth A. Kohlmann 1981-Sept. 1985; Ronald K. Corl 1975-1988; Eugene K. Bacon 1988-1995; Faye McKinstry Jul 1, 1995-1999; Patricia A. Green 1999-2008; Thomas L. Taylor 2008-Feb 15, 2011; Juanita J. Ferguson 2011-Sep 30, 2011; G. Charles Sonquist Oct 17, 2011-2012; Rhonda J. Osterman 2012-2020; Rodney K. Diggs 2020-

Madison Heights: Korean First Central UMC *[Greater Detroit]* gsj0925@yahoo.com
(P/M) 500 W Gardenia Ave, Madison Heights 48071 (248) 545-5554
Mu-Young Kim Nov. 1 1984-1992; Jae H. Lee 1992-Jan 31, 2004; Chul-Goo Lee Mar 1, 2004-2013; Sang Hyu Han (interim) August 1, 2013-Oct 1, 2013; Gunsoo Jung Oct 1, 2013-2018; Yoo Jin Kim (assoc) 2016-2018; Daeki Kim 2018-

Madison Heights: Vietnamese Ministry UMC *[Greater Detroit]* ducnhan234@yahoo.com
(P) 500 W Gardenia Ave, Madison Heights 48071; (M) 38108 Charwood Dr, Sterling Heights 48312
Nhan Duc Nguyen Apr 1, 2016-

Mancelona UMC *[Northern Waters]* mance1@mancelonaumc.org
(P) 117 E Hinman St, Mancelona 49659; (M) PO Box 301, Mancelona 49659 (231) 587-8461
M. Helen Jackson 1968-1972; George Gierman 1972-1975; Curtis Jensen 1975-1983; Timothy Graham 1983-1990; Gary Coates 1990-Aug. 1991; Pulpit Supply Sept.-Oct. 1991; Wayne Gorsline Nov. 1991-June 15, 1992; John W. Boley June 16, 1992-1997; Carolyn C. Floyd 1997-2000; Kathryn M. Steen 2000-2007; Stephan Weinberger 2007-2010; Zawdie K. Abiade July 1-July 4, 2010; Todd Shafer (DSA) July 15, 2010; Todd Shafer Nov. 1, 2010-2017; Bryan K. Kilpatrick 2017-

Manchester UMC *[Heritage]* office@manchesterumchurch.org
(P/M) 501 Ann Arbor St, Manchester 48158 (734) 428-8495
O. William Cooper Jr. 1965-1970; Walter R. Damberg 1970-1977; Maurice D. Sharai Jr. 1977-1980; David A. Spieler 1980-1981; Thomas E. Hart 1981-1984; Hayden K. Carruth Jr. 1984-1989; Peggy Ainslie 1989-Oct. 31, 1991; Marsha M. Woolley Nov. 1, 1991-1994; Thomas Davenport 1994-Dec 1, 1998; Frank Leineke (interim) Jan 1, 1999-Jun 30, 1999; A. Faye McKinstry 1999-2005; Lawrence A. Wik 2005-2012; Tersea Zimmerman (deacon) Jan 1, 2012- ; Aaron B. Kesson 2012-2017; Dillion S. burns 2017-

Manchester: Sharon UMC *[Heritage]* RevPHarris@aol.com
(P) 19980 Pleasant Lake Rd, Manchester 48158; (M) PO Box 543, Manchester 48158
(734) 428-7714
Charles R. Fox 1967-1969; O. William Cooper Jr. 1969-1970; John C. Huhtala (assoc) 1969-1970; Michael L. Peterlin 1970-1976; Wayne C. Ferrigan 1976-1980; Ronald L. Figgins Iris 1980-1983; Evans C. Bentley 1983-1987; Vernon D. Jones (DSA) Jan-Jun 1988; Erik J. Alsgaard 1988-Sep. 30, 1991; Margaret A. Paige Nov 15, 1991-1998; Carter L. Garrigues-Cortelyou 1998-2007; Peter S. Harris 2007-

Manistee UMC *[Northern Waters]*   mumc@t-one.net
(P/M) 387 1st St, Manistee 49660   (231) 723-6219
   Carleton A. Benson Sept. 1968-1971; Richard M. Wilson 1971-1980; Gilbert B. Heaton 1980-1982;
   Richard R. Erickson 1982-1990; Gregory B. Wood 1990-1998; Gerald L. Selleck 1998-2002; Jerry
   Lee Jaquish 2002-2012; David A. Selleck 2012-2015; John A. Scott 2015-

Manistique: First UMC *[Northern Skies]*   1stumcmanistique@gmail.com
(P/M) 190 N Cedar St, Manistique 49854   (906) 341-6662
   Theodore E. Doane 1968-1972; Marvin McCallum 1972-1975; Audrey Dunlap 1975-1976; Michael
   Peterlin 1976-1980; Max D. Weeks 1980-1983; Timothy Hastings 1983-1986; Stuart L. Proctor
   1986-1991; Raymond D. Wightman 1991-1997; Donna J. Lindberg 1997-2004; Donald E. Bedwell
   2004-2020; B.J. Ash 2020-

Manton UMC *[Northern Waters]*   umcmanton@charter.net
(P) 102 N Michigan Ave, Manton 49663; (M) PO Box B, Manton 49663   (231) 824-3593
   Eduard Eidens 1967-1969; J. William Schoette 1969-1970; Leonard J. Yarlott 1970-1971; Arthur
   R. Turner 1971-1976; Molly C. Turner (Assoc.) 1971-1976; Norman Charter 1976-1977; J.T. Wood
   1977-1981; Deborah Johnson 1981-1985; Laurie McKinven-Copus 1985-1987; Louis W.
   Grettenberger 1987-1993; Richard W. Blunt 1993-Feb. 1, 1999; Linda J. Carlson Feb. 16, 1999-
   2009; Beth A. Reum 2009-2013; Noreen S. Shafer 2013-2017; Jeff A. Swainston (DSA) 2017-Nov
   30, 2017; Jeff A. Swainston (LP) Dec 1, 2017-

Maple River Parish: Lowe UMC *[Mid-Michigan]*   mapleriverumccharge@gmail.com
(P/M) 5485 W Lowe Rd, Saint Johns 48879   (989) 224 -4460
   William Tate 1967-1969; Robert Boyer 1969-1970; Charles VanLente 1970-1972; Everett Love
   June-Dec. 1972; Harold McGuire 1973-1974; Terry MacArthur 1976-Oct. 15, 1979; Robert Gillette
   Jan. 1980-1984; Merritt Bongard 1984-1991; Joseph Spackman 1991-1999; James Dibbet 1999-
   2005; O'Ryan Rickard 2005-2007; Kathryn L. Leydorf (DSA) 2007; Kathryn L. Leydorf Nov. 10,
   2007- [Salem/Maple Rapids/Lowe charge re-aligned 5-1-14 to Maple Rapids/Lowe charge; Maple
   Rapids / Lowe became Maple River Parish 2015]

Maple River Parish: Maple Rapids UMC *[Mid-Michigan]*   mapleriverumccharge@gmail.com
(P) 330 S Maple Ave, Maple Rapids 48853; (M) 5485 W Lowe Rd, St. Johns 48879   (989) 224 -4460
   William Tate 1967-1969; Robert Boyer 1969-Feb. 1970; Charles VanLente Feb. 1970-May 1972;
   Abe Caster May 1972-Jan. 1973; Eldon Schram Feb.-June 1973; J. Thomas Churn 1973-1979;
   Richard Whale 1979-1980; Richard Riley 1980-1984; Lyle Heaton 1984-1990; Tim Wohlford 1990-
   1991; Carolyn Robinson 1991-1997; Charles D. Farnum 1997-2001; Martin Cobb 2001-2006;
   O'Ryan Rickard 2006-2007; Kathryn L. Leydorf (DSA) 2007; Kathryn L. Leydorf Nov. 10, 2007-
   [Salem/Maple Rapids/Lowe charge re-aligned 5-1-14 to Maple Rapids/Lowe charge; Maple Rapids
   / Lowe became Maple River Parish 2015]

Marcellus UMC *[Greater Southwest]*   jdmessner@gmail.com
(P) 197 W Main St, Marcellus 49067; (M) PO Box 396, Marcellus 49067   (269) 646-5801
   Ira Fett 1968-1969; Donald Ludman 1969-1974; Wayne Babcock 1975-1978; Derryl Cook 1978-
   1981; Robert Mayo 1981-1986; Kenneth I. Kline 1986-1992; Dennis E. Slattery 1992-1995; Peggy
   A. Boltz 1995-2002; Melodye Surgeon Rider 2002-2007; John D. Messner (DSA) 2007; John D.
   Messner Jan. 1, 2008-2020;

Marcellus: Wakelee UMC *[Greater Southwest]*   jdmessner@gmail.com
(P/M) 15921 Dutch Settlement Rd, Marcellus 49067   (269) 646-2049
   Ira Fett 1968-1969; Donald Ludman 1969-1974; Wayne Babcock 1975-1978; Derryl Cook 1978-
   1981; Robert Mayo 1981-1986; Kenneth I. Kline 1986-1992; Dennis E. Slattery 1992-1998; Gregory
   L. Buchner (DSA) 1998-Nov. 16, 1999; Gregory L. Buchner Nov. 16, 1999-2005; Nelson L. Hall
   2005-2007; John D. Messner (DSA) 2007; John D. Messner Jan. 1, 2008-

CHURCH HISTORIES

Marion UMC *[Northern Waters]* marionmiumc@yahoo.com
(P) 216 W Main St, Marion 49665; (M) PO Box C, Marion 49665-0703 (231) 743-2834
  Edward R. Jones 1967-1969; Walter S. Easton 1969-1971; Robert R. Boyer 1971-1977; Kendall A. Lewis 1977-1981; Donald R. Fry 1981-1994; James C. Grant 1994-1999; Howard H. Harvey 1999-2000; Jeffrey Schrock 2000-2004; Kenneth C. Reeves 2004-2006; Kenneth C. Reeves (DSA) 2006-2007; James J. Mort 2007-

Marlette: First UMC *[East Winds]* fumcmarlette@centurytel.net
(P/M) 3155 Main St., Marlette 48453 (989) 635-2075
  Rex M. Dixon 1966-1970; A. Theodore Halsted 1970-1975; Theodore H. Bennink 1975-1979; John R. Allan 1979-Aug 31, 1998; Daniel J. Bowman Sep 1, 1998-2014; David G. Mulder 2014-2018; Larry Osweiler Jul 1-Sept 5, 2018; George H. Ayoub Oct 1, 2018-

Marne UMC *[Midwest]* secretary@marneumc.com
(P) 14861 Washington St, Marne 49435; (M) PO Box 85, Marne 49435 (616) 677-3957
  Kenneth E. Curtis 1967-1969; Don W. Eddy 1969-1971; Kenneth W. Karlzen 1971-1973; Donald Fry 1973-1977; Douglas Knight 1977-1980; Vernon Michael 1980-1982; Keith Bovee 1982-1985; Deborah M. Johnson 1985-1990; Timothy W. Graham 1990-1993; Cathi M. Gowin 1993-Jan. 31, 2002; Patricia L. Brook Feb. 1, 2002-2010; James Thomas Boutell 2010-2018; Cydney M. Idsinga 2018-

Marquette: Hope UMC *[Northern Skies]* office@mqthope.com
(P/M) 111 E Ridge, Marquette 49855 (906) 225-1344
  Ralph Janka 1967-1971; Robert D. Dobson (assoc) 1968-1972; Alan J. Hanson (assoc.) 1972-1973) Samuel F. Stout 1971-1975; Gilson M. Miller (assoc) 1973-1975; Webley Simpkins 1975-1980; John C. Huhtala (assoc) 1976-1980; Lawrence C. Brooks (assoc) 1980-1982; Benjamin Bohnsack 1980-1988; Steven J. Buck 1988-1993; Stanley A. Bailey, Jr. (assoc) 1989-; Gordon S. Nusz 1993-2000; Stephen E. Rhoades 2000-2004; Elbert P Dulworth 2004-2006; Steven E. McCoy 2006-2013; Alan J. Hansen (interim) 2013-2014; Kristine K. Hintz 2014- ; Christopher Hintz 2016-

Marquette: Hope - Connection Center Campus UMC *[Northern Skies]* office@mqthope.com
(P) 927 W Fair Ave, Marquette 49855; (M) 111 E Ridge, Marquette 49855
  [Formerly Marquette: Hope – Grace Campus. Satellite of Marquette: Hope founded 07/01/2016] Kristine K. Hintz 2014- ; Christopher Hintz 2016-

Marquette: Hope - Skandia Campus UMC *[Northern Skies]* office@mqthope.com
(P) 189 Kreiger Dr, Skandia 49885; (M) 111 E Ridge, Marquette 49855
  UMC [Satellite of Marquette: Hope founded 07/01/2016] Kristine K. Hintz 2014- ;Christopher Hintz 2016-

Marshall UMC *[Heritage]* rah@umcmarshall.org
(P/M) 721 Old US 27N, Marshall 49068 (269) 781-5107
  Charles Manker 1968-1970; Ralph Witmer 1970-1974; Harold Filbrandt 1974-1983; Jeanne Randels (Assoc.) 1981-1988; Ronald Thompson 1983-1989; David McBride (Assoc.) 1988-1991; Leon Andrews 1989-1992; William Bills (Assoc.) 1991-1994; William Johnson 1992-1996; Margaret H. Peterson (Assoc.) 1994-1998 ; Keith W. Heifner 1996-1999; Judy K. Downing (Assoc.) 1998-1999; Leonard R. Schoenherr 1999-2013; Melany A. Chalker 2013-

Martin UMC *[Greater Southwest]* martinumc@sbcglobal.net
(P) 969 E Allegan St, Martin 49070; (M) PO Box 154, Martin 49070-0154 (269) 672-7097
  Paul Scheibner 1965-1970; Thurlan Meridith 1970-1976; Gerald L. Welsh 1976-1984; Lee F. Zachman 1984-April 15, 1994; William C. Bills 1994-2007; Christopher L. Lane 2007-2009; David A. Selleck 2009-2012; Donald J. Graham 2012-2014; Sean K. Kidd 2014-2019; Corey M. Simon 2019-

Marysville UMC *[East Winds]*   office@umcmarysville.com
(P/M) 721 Huron Blvd, Marysville 48040   (810) 364-7391
Howard F. Snell 1965-1971; Joseph H. Ablett 1971-1980; Webley J. Simpkins 1980-1985; Cleon F. Abbott Jr. 1985-1991; Ralph T. Barteld 1991-1997; David D. Amstutz 1997-1999; James M. Thompson 1999-2006; Barbara E. Welbaum 2006-2019; [Marysville / Central Lakeport formed Marysville Cooperative Parish 07/01/2019] Curtis B. Clarke 2019-

Mason: First UMC *[Mid-Michigan]*   info@masonfirst.org
(P/M) 201 E Ash St, Mason 48854   (517) 676-9449
Keith L. Hayes 1966-1980; Robert L. Wessman (Assoc.) 1979-1984; George R. Grettenberger 1980-1989; Donald R. Ferris (Assoc.) 1984-1989; Verne C. Summers 1989-1992; Charles B. Hodges (Assoc.) 1989-March 1991; Wayne G. Reece 1992-2000; Robert K. Lynch (Assoc.) 1992-1995; Jane D. Logston (Assoc.) 1996-1998; Timothy Tuthill (Assoc.) 1998-2006; Robert L. Hundley 2000-2009; Dwayne E. Bagley 2009-2016; Donna Jo Minarik 2016-2019; Suzanne K. Goodwin 2019-

Mayville UMC *[Central Bay]*   mayvilleumc@att.net
(P) 601 E Ohmer Rd, Mayville 48744 (M) PO Box 189, Mayville 48744   (989) 843-6151
Donald L. Lichtenfelt 1968-1970; Ralph T. Barteld 1970-1979; Dale E. Brown 1979-1984; Allen J. Lewis Inter.; Wayne C. Ferrigan 1984-1986; William J. Maynard 1986-1992; Bonny J. Lancaster 1992-1999; John W. Ball 1999-2007; Dorothy J. Thon 2007-2011; Carole A. Brown 2011-2019; Nathan J. Jeffords 2019-

McGregor UMC *[East Winds]*   mcrgegorumc@airadvantage.net
(P) 2230 Forester Rd, Deckerville 48427; (M) 5791 Paldi Rd, Peck 48466   (810) 378-5686
James B. Lumsden 1969-1973; J. Paul Pumphrey 1973-1977; Glenn R. Wegner 1977-1980; James P. Kummer Dec. 1980-1985; Kenneth C. Reeves 1985-1991; Gloria Haynes 1991-1996; Malcolm L. Green 1996-1998; Jerry D. Griggs 1998-

McMillan UMC *[Northern Skies]*   pastorimcdonald@outlook.com
(P) 7406 Co Rd 415, McMillan 49853; (M) PO Box 268, Grand Marais 49839   (906) 293-8933
Vernon D. Wyllys 1969-1975; James Lumsden 1975-1976; Audrey M. Dunlap 1976-1985; Ramona Cowling 1985-1987; Phillip D. Voss 1987-1991; Bo L. Lange 1991-1997; Ronald O. Piette 1997-1998; Tracy L. Brooks 1998-2003; Karen A. Mars 2003-2006; Paul J. Mallory 2006-2012; Ian S. McDonald 2012-2019; Devin T. Lawrence (DSA) 2019-

Mears UMC *[Midwest]*   office@mearsumc.org
(P) 1990 N. Joy St, Mears 49436; (M) PO Box 100, Mears 49436-0100   (231) 873-0875
Kenneth L. Snow 1990-1993; Kenneth Vanderlaan (DSA) 1993-2017; [Mears and Shelby became a multi-station circuit 2016]; Anne W. Riegler 2017-

Mecosta: New Hope UMC *[Midwest]*   newhope.mecosta@gmail.com
(P/M) 7296 9 Mile Rd, Mecosta 49332   (231) 972-2838
Gordon L. Terpening 1968-1971; Norman Charter 1971-1973; Pulpit Supply 1973-1974; Michael Nickerson 1974-1977; Ilona Sabo-Schuler 1977-1982; B. Gordon Barry 1982-1985; Pulpit Supply July-Oct. 1985; Bobby Dale Whitlock Oct. 1985-Apr. 1987; Pulpit Supply April-June 1987; Remus, Mecosta and Halls Corners merged to form New Hope in 1987; Christopher Momany 1987-1993; Scott K. Otis 1993-1997; James C. Noggle 1997-2004; Victor D. Charnley 2004-2013; Gregory L. Buchner 2013-2019; Carman J. Minarik 2019-

Melvin UMC *[East Winds]*   marlettelawfirm@yahoo.com
(P/M) 1171 E Main St, Melvin 48454   (810) 376-4518
Earl S. Geer 1969-1973; Martin Caudill 1973-1976; Willard A. King 1976-1980; J.D. Landis 1980-1986; David K. Stewart 1986-1990; Louise R. Ott 1990-1992; Michael F. Bossingham 1992-1994; Thomas K. Spencer 1994-1998; David C. Freeland (co-pastor) 1998-2002; Susan K. Freeland (co-pastor) 1998-Dec 31, 1999; Debra K. Brown 2002-2010; Christopher G.L. Titus 2010—2019; [Yale / Cole / Melvin became a three-point charge 07/01/2019] Dennis Eric Irish 2019-Mar 30, 2020; Julia A. Cramer (assoc) (DSA) 2019-Dec 31, 2019; [Cole, Melvin became 2-point charge 04/01/2020] Julia A. Cramer (PL) Apr 1, 2020-

Memphis: First UMC *[East Winds]*   huff11@aol.com
(P) 81265 Church St, Memphis 48041; (M) PO Box 29, Memphis 48041   (810) 392-2294
Max Weeks 1965-1971; Donald L. Lichtenfelt Inter.; Duane E. Miller March 1972-Nov. 1977; Paul W. Reigle 1977-1982; Wayne C. Ferrigan 1982-1984; Martin Caudill 1984- 1987; Donald L. Bates Oct. 1987-1991; Douglas M. Choate 1991-1993; Catherine W. Hiner 1993-1999; David L. Fleming 1999-2001; Janet M. Engler 2001-2004; Thomas G. Badley (interm Aug 1, 2004-Oct 31, 2004; Donald L. Wojewski Nov 1, 2004-Dec 31, 2004; James E. Huff, Jr. Jan 1, 2005-2020; Luis M. Collazo 2020-

Mendon UMC *[Greater Southwest]*   mendonmethodist@gmail.com
(P) 320 W Main St, Mendon 49072; (M) PO Box 308, Mendon 49072-0308   (269) 496-4295
Marcius Taber 1968-1969; David Litchfield 1969-1970; Harold Simon 1970-Nov. 1973; Robert Jones Nov. 1973-1978; John Charter 1978-1981; Ira Noordhoff 1981-Jan. 1985; Kendall Lewis Jan. 1985-1986; Elaine Buker 1986-1992; Rochelle Ray 1992-1995; Thomas L. Truby 1995-2001; Ward D. Pierce (DSA) 2001-Dec. 2, 2012 (died); David G. Knapp (interim) Jan. 1-June 30, 2013; [Three Rivers First / Mendon became two-point charge 2013] Robert D. Nystrom 2013-2015; [Mendon / West Mendon became two-charge 2015] Thoreau May 2015-2017; Margaret K. Mallory 2017-2018; Carl Q. Litchfield (LTFT ¼) 2018-

Menominee: First UMC *[Northern Skies]*   menomineeumc@gmail.com
(P) HCR 1 US 41 E, Michigamme 49861; (M) PO Box 323, Menominee 49858   (906) 864-2555
Everett D. Erickson 1964-1976; Robert D. Dobson 1976-1986; Donald C. Schark 1986-1991; John N. Grenfell III 1991-1994; William D. Schoonover 1994-1995; John N. Grenfell, III 1995-1998; Philip L. Tousley 1998-2011; Dale E. Brown 2011-2014; Bruce L. Nowacek 2014-2016; Ryan C. Edwardson 2016-2019; [Menominee: First / Stephenson two-point charge 7-1-2019] John R. Murray 2019-

Mesick UMC *[Northern Waters]*   mesickumc@gmail.com
(P) 121 S Alvin St, Mesick 49668; (M) PO Box 337, Mesick 49668-0337   (231) 885-1699
Ward Pierce 1967-1972; Bill Amundsen 1972-1979; Jean Crabtree 1979-Aug. 1980; Donald Buege Sept. 1980-Jan. 1984; Bruce Prestwood-Taylor Jan. 1984-1986; Thomas P. Fox 1986-1992; Charles A. Williams 1992-Feb. 14, 1997; J. David Thompson Nov. 16, 1997-2001; John J. Conklin (DSA) 2001-Nov. 30, 2001; John J. Conklin Dec. 1, 2001-2009; Mona L. Kindel 2009-2012; Beverley Williams 2012-2016; ; [Mesick/Harrietta/ Brethren became a three-point charge 2016] Laurie M. Koivula 2016-2018 [Mesick/Brethren became a two-point charge 2018] Anika Kasper (DSA) July 14, 2019-2020; Russell W. Poirier (DSA) 2020-

Michigamme: Woodland UMC *[Northern Skies]*   woodumc@gmail.com
(P/M) 3533 US 41E , Michigamme, MI 49861   (906) 323-6151
James Mathews 1978-1984; Charles Keyworth 1984-1988; Robert Duggan 1988-1990; Nicholas W. Scroggins 1990-1993; Fred A. LaMere 1993-1996; Terry J. Kordish 1996-2000l; Gary I. Stevens 2000-2004; James A. Fegan 2004-2009; Mark E. Ryan 2009-2012; Terri L. Branstrom 2012-2016; Peter A. LeMoine 2016-

Middlebury UMC *[Mid-Michigan]*   middleburyunitedmethodist@gmail.com
(P) 8100 W Hibbard Rd, Ovid 48866; (M) PO Box 7, Ovid 48866-0007   (989) 834-2573
Dale Ferris 1969-1972; Brian D. Kundinger 1972-1977; David K. Koski 1977-1982; L. Michael Pearson 1982-1986; Harold E. Weemhoff 1986-1990; Robert J. Easlick 1990-1993; J. Robert Anderson 1993-1996; Nancy L. Bessemer Sep 1, 1996-1998; Weatherly A. Burkehead Verhelst 1998-2003; J. Gordon Schleicher 2003-2006; Carl R. Cooke Jan 1, 2007-Dec 31, 2008; Norman R. Beckwith, Jr., Jan 1, 2009-Apr 10, 2010; Don Wentz May 1, 2010-2015; Joyce Wallace Oct 1, 2015-2016-2018; Melanie S. Young 2018-

Middleville UMC *[Midwest]*   middlevilleumc@gmail.com
(P) 111 Church St, Middleville 49333; (M) PO Box 400, Middleville 49333   (269) 795-9266
Harold M. Taber 1964-1969; C. William Martin 1969-1973; Harold Simon Nov. 1973-Oct. 1976; Arthur Jackson April 1977-Aug. 1983; Bradley Kalajainen (Assoc.) Jan. 1981-1985; Carl Staser Oct. 1983-1988; Lynn W. Wagner 1988-1996; Lee F. Zachman 1996-2004; Scott E. Manning 2004-2009; [Middleville/Snow two-point charge 2009] Michael T. Conklin 2009-2012; Anthony C. Shumaker 2012- [Middleville became single station 2017]

Midland: Aldersgate UMC *[Central Bay]*   admin@aumcmidland.org
(P/M) 2206 Airfield Ln, Midland 48642   (989) 631-1151
Harold W. Diehl 1965-1970; Zack A. Clayton 1970-1990; David A. Stout 1990-Oct 1, 2003; Douglas R. Trebilcock 2004-2006; Mark D. Miller 2006-2013; Michael T. Sawicki 2013- [Poseyville UMC merged with Midland: Aldersgate UMC 08/01/2018]

Midland: Aldersgate - Saginaw: Kochville Campus UMC *[Central Bay]*   office@kumcsag.com
(P) 6030 Bay Rd, Saginaw 48604; (M) 2206 Airfield Ln, Midland 48642   (989) 792-2321
[Satellite of Midland: Aldersgate started 09/01/2018] Michael T. Sawicki Aug. 1, 2018-

Midland Cnty: Hope UMC *[Central Bay]*   phope000@centurytel.net
(P/M) 5278 N Hope Rd, Hope 48628   (989) 689-3811
William Cozadd 1965-1980; Cleon Abbott 1980-1985; Donald Crumm 1985-1992; Harold J. Slater 1992-2002; Patrick R. Poag 2002-

Midland: First UMC *[Central Bay]*   tsimons@fumcmid.org
(P/M) 315 W Larkin St, Midland 48640   (989) 835-6797
Wayne E. North 1965-1973; Webley Simpkins (assoc) 1966-1970; Herbert C. Brubaker (assoc) 1968-1971; S. H. Evans (assoc) 1968-1971; Wayne Large (assoc) 1970-1974; Ira A. Bush (assoc) 1971-1995; John W. Parrish (assoc) 1973-1985; Carl E. Price 1973-1998; P. Thomas Wachterhauser (assoc) 1974-1979; Jeffery D. Regan (assoc) 1979-1982; Arthur B. Howard (assoc) 1979-1985; Mary Isaacs Frost (assoc) 1982-1986; Dana Strall (assoc) 1985-1988; Robert Grigereit (assoc) 1987-1999; Duane M. Harris (assoc) 1988-1997; Kevin C. Zaborney (assoc) 1997-1999; Brent L. McCumons 1998-2011;Charles W. Keyworth (assoc) 1999- ; Susan M. Kingsley (assoc) Sep 1, 1999-2008; Steven E. McCoy (assoc) 1999-2006; Jeremy P. Africa (assoc.) 2006-2010; Pamela Buckholtz (deacon) 2006-2013; Lisa McIlvenna (assoc) 2008-2013;Catherine Christman (assoc.) 2010-2013; John D. Landis 2011-2019; Jung Eun Yum (assoc.) 2014-; Christina Miller-Black (assoc.) 2015-2017; Anita K. Hahn 2019- ; Ruth A. VanderSande (assoc) 2020-

Midland: Homer UMC *[Central Bay]*   homeroffice@gmail.com
(P/M) 507 S Homer Rd, Midland 48640-8369   (989) 835-5050
Dale Lantz 1967-1970; S. Joe Robertson 1970-1973; Robert Adams 1973-1975; Walter Radcliffe (interim); Philip A. Rice 1975-1979; Henry Powell 1979-1982; Donald Goold & Arthur Howard (interim); Kenneth Christler 1983-1988; Paul Bailey 1988-1990; James M. Thompson 1990-1996; Kenneth A. Kohlmann 1996-2001; Raymond A. Jacques 2001-2008; David G. Mulder 2008-2014; Josheua Blanchard 2014-Aug 31, 2017; Ernesto Mariona Oct 1, 2017-2020; Michael P. Kelley 2020-

Milan: Marble Memorial UMC *[Heritage]*   marblemumc@sbcglobal.net
(P/M) 8 Park Ln, Milan 48160   (734) 439-2421
  George Q. Woomer 1966-1969; Charles W. Cookingham 1969-1973; Clare M. Tosch 1973-1983; Diana K. Goudie (assoc) 1983-Aug. 31, 1991; Robert F. Goudie 1983-Aug 31, 1994; King W. Hanna Sep 1, 1994-2003; Kristine J. Sigal 2003-Oct 1, 2007; Thomas E. Hart (interim) Oct 1, 2007-2008; Patricia A. Green 2008-2013; Robert A. Miller, Jr. 2013-2018; Jacquelyn A. Roe 2018-2020; Matthew J. West 2020-

Milford UMC *[Heritage]*   churchoffice@milfordumc.net
(P/M) 1200 Atlantic St, Milford 48381   (248) 684-2798
  Archie H. Donigan 1966-1972; Wayne W. Brookshear 1972-1983; James C. Braid 1983-1995; David R. Strobe 1995-Dec 1, 1997; Paul Blomquist (interim) Dec 1, 1997-Apr 30, 1998; Gregory M. Mayberry May 1, 1998-2011; Douglas J. McMunn 2011- ; Sherry Foster (deacon) 2008-

Millersburg UMC *[Northern Waters]*   onawayumc@voyager.net
(P) 5484 Main St, Millersburg 49759; (M) PO Box 258, Millersburg 49759   (989) 745-4479
  Charles R Fox (Onaway) 1969-1972; N. Ralph Guilliat (Millersburg) 1967-1972; G. Charles Ball 1972-1983; Roy A. Syme 1983-1989; Michael Grajcar Jr. 1989-1991; Richard A. Turner 1991-1995; John N. Hamilton 1995-Jun 15, 2001; W. Peter Bartlett 2001-2011; Josheua Blanchard 2011-2014; Carman Cook 2014-2018; Yoo Jin Kim 2018-

Millington UMC *[Central Bay]*   millingtonumc@millingtonumc.com
(P) 9020 State Rd, Millington 48746; (M) PO Box 321, Millington 48746   (989) 871-3489
  Richard A. Turner 1965-1971; Arthur V. Norris 1971-1976; Paul L. Amstutz 1976-1982; Keith B. Colby 1982-1985; Ronald Figgins Iris 1985-Aug. 31, 1991; Max D. Weeks Sept. 1, 1991-1994; Thomas F. Keef 1994-2001; Wilson Andrew Hart 2001-2006; W. Peter Crawford 2006-2015; John J. Britt 2015-2020; Nickolas K. Genoff 2020-

Millville UMC *[Mid-Michigan]*   millvillechurch@yahoo.com
(P/M) 1932 N M 52, Stockbridge 49285   (517) 851-7853
  Daniel Harris 1965-1970; Dorr Garrett 1970-1973; Lester Priest Jan. 15, 1974-1980; Robert Stillson 1980-Nov. 15, 1982; Donald Vuurens Feb. 1983-1986; Richard Young 1986-1990; Jeffrey Wright 1990-Jan. 1993; James C. Noggle March 1993-1997; Carolyn A. Robinson 1997-1998; Richard A. Tester 1998-2004; Robert J. Freysinger 2004-2013; [M-52 Cooperative Ministry 2013; re-named Connections Cooperative Ministry 2015] Jeremy J. Wicks (1/2 time) 2013-2017; [Dansville UMC merged with Millville UMC 12-31-14] Jaqueline L. Raineri 2017-2018; Theresa Fairbanks 2018-2020 [Millville / Williamston: Wheatfield became multi-point charge 2018] [Millville, Leslie, Felt Plains became 3-point charge 2020] Rhonda J. Osterman 2020-

Minden City UMC *[East Winds]*   dcbarber229@att.net
(P) 3346 Main St, Minden City 48456; (M) PO Box 126, Minden City 48456   (810) 648-4155
  Alan W. Weeks 1964-1974; Harry M. Brakeman 1974-1977; James P. Schwandt 1977-1980; Basel W. Curtiss 1980-1983; Zina Braden Bennett 1983-1985; Richard J. Richmond 1985-1991; Max L. Gibbs 1991-1996; Ellen Burns Nov, 1996-2000; Robert A. Srock 2000-2002; John H. Rapson 2002-2010; Monique R. Carpenter 2010-2015; Dale Barber Dec 15, 2015-Mar 30, 2019; Philip L. Tousley 2019-2020 [Seperated as a two-point charge from Minden City 07/01/2019; Bad Axe: First / Minden City / Ubly formed Bad Axe Cooperative Parish 07/01/2019] Timothy G. Callow 2020-

Mio UMC *[Central Day]*   office@mioumc.org
(P/M) 1101 W 8th St, Mio 48647   (989) 826-5598
  Robert Kersten 1969-1975; Grant Washburn 1975-1980; David Diamond 1980-1986; Lois Glenn 1986-1990; John J. Britt 1990-2005; Kenneth Tousley (interim) 2005-Sep 15, 2005; Marcel Lamb, Sep 16, 2005-2012; Tracy Brooks 2012-2014; Brenda K. Klacking 2014-2020; Michelle N. Forsyth 2020-

Mohawk-Ahmeek UMC *[Northern Skies]*   calumc@up.net
(P) 120 Stanton, Mohawk 49950; (M) 57235 Calumet Ave, Calumet 49913   (906) 337-2720
Alan DeGraw 1967-1972; James Tuttle 1972-1975; Harold Slater 1975-1978; Wayne Hutson 1978-1983; Dennis N. Paulson 1983-1987; Robert J. Easlick 1987-1990; David P. Snyder 1990-1993; Nancy G. Sparks 1993-2000; Robert A. White 2000-2016; Richard B. Brown (assoc) 2000-2003; James Palaszeski 2016-2018; Gun Soo Jung 2018-2019; Larry Molloy (DSA) 2019-

Monroe: Calvary UMC *[Heritage]*   monroecalvaryumc@yahoo.com
(P/M) 790 Patterson Dr, Monroe 48161   (734) 242-0145
Otto F. Hood 1968-1974; J. Edward Fulcher 1974-1977; Gary A. Allward 1977-1980; Georg F. W. Gerritsen 1980-1985; William P. McBride 1985-1995; Paul G. Donalson 1995-1997; James E. Armbrust (co-pastor) 1997-1999; Judith A. Armbrust (co-pastor) 1997-1999; David J. Goudie 1999-2004; Janet M. Engler 2004-2006; William T. Kreichbaum 2006-2016; Steven Perrine 2016-2020; Andrea L. Johnson 2020-

Monroe: Faith UMC (formerly Monroe: First) *[Heritage]*   monroefumc@gmail.com
(P/M) 790 Patterson Dr, Monroe 48161   (734) 242-0145
Elwood J. Berkompas 1965-1972; George E. Spencer 1972-1975; Robert F. Goudie 1975-1983; Robert C. Watt 1983-1987; Warren D. Pettis 1987-1989; James D. Jacobs 1989-Aug 31, 1999; John H. Schneider, Jr. Sep 1, 1999-2005; Sang Yoon (Abraham) Chun 2005-2007; Clarence W. VanConant 2007-2010; Phillip D. Voss 2010-2011; Bradford Lewis 2011-2013; Katherine C. Waggoner 2013-2020; [Monroe: Heritage merged w/ Monroe: First, re-named Faith 7-1-2020] Andrea L. Johnson 2020-

Monroe: St. Paul's UMC *[Heritage]*   stpaulsmonroe@sbcglobal.net
(P/M) 201 S Monroe St, Monroe 48161   (734) 242-3000
Raymond R. Lamb 1966-1969; M. Clement Parr (assoc) 1968-1971; William N. Mertz 1969-1978; Roy A. Syme (assoc) 1971-1973; E. Jack Lemon (assoc) 1973-1976; Wayne N. Thomas (assoc) 1976-1978; Hugh C. White 1978-1983; David Rahn (assoc) 1978-1980; Marvin H. McCallum 1983-1991; Karen D. Poole (assoc) 1986-1988; Claire A. Clingerman (assoc) 1988-1990; Dean A. Klump 1991-1995; Jacqueline E. Holdsworth (co-pastor) 1995-2003; John W. Kershaw (co-pastor) 1995-2003; Jacqueline E. Holdsworth 2003-2004; Evans C. Bentley 2004-2018; Tracy N. Huffman 2018-2019; Melodye Surgeon VanOudheusden 2019-

Montague UMC *[Midwest]*   montagueumc@gmail.com
(P/M) 8555 Cook St, Montague 49437   (231) 894-5789
Wirth G. Tennant 1965-1972; Gilbert B. Heaton 1972-1977; Birt A. Beers 1977-1983; Robert E. Jones, Jr. 1983-1992; D. Keith Laidler 1992-1997; Timothy P. Boal 1997-2005; Gary Bekofske 2005-2009; Randall R. Hansen 2009-2014; Mary S. Brown 2014-Nov. 30, 2016; David "Gunnar" Carlson Dec. 1, 2016-June 30, 2017 [Whitehall UMC merged with Montague UMC, 6-02-17] Michael A. Riegler 2017-

Monterey Center UMC *[Greater Southwest]*   secretary.bumc@gmail.com
(P) 3022 130th Ave, Hopkins 49328; (M) PO Box 30, Burnips 49314-0030   (616) 896-8410
Ron Smith Oct. 1991-1997; Kenneth C. Reeves 1997-2004; Anthony Carrol Shumaker 2004-2008; Richard A. Fritz 2008-2014; Nancy J. Patera 2014-2017; Craig H. VanBeek (DSA) 2017-Dec. 31, 2018; Craig H. VanBeek Jan. 1, 2019-

Montgomery UMC *[Heritage]*　　　　　　　　　　　pastortrevor1@gmail.com
(P) 218 S Michigan St, Montgomery 49255; (M) PO Box 155, Camden 49232　　　(517) 269-4232
　Karl L. Zeigler 1968-1969; John H. Gurney 1969-Aug. 1970; Joseph Huston Aug. 1970-1972;
　Richard Huskey 1972-1974; J. Brian Selleck 1974-Feb. 1976; Robert P. Stover March 1976-1980;
　Stephen Beech 1980-1983; Larry W. Rubingh 1983-1987; Frederick G. Hamlin 1987-1994; Russell
　K. Logston 1994-1996; Diane Stone Nov. 16, 1996-2004; Edward Mohr 2004-2010; Trevor
　McDermont 2010-2013; Frederick G. Cain (Ret.) (part-time) 2013-

Montrose UMC *[East Winds]*　　　　　　　　　　　montroseumc1@gmail.com
(P) 158 E State St, Montrose 48457; (M) PO Box 3237, Montrose 48457　　　(810) 639-6925
　Dalton Bishop 1967-1973; Robert C. Watt 1973-Nov., 1980; Richard L. Beemer Jan., 1981-1993;
　Dennis N. Paulson 1993-Jan 16, 1997; David C. Collins 1997-2006; Wayne C. Ferrigan 2006-2012;
　Norman R. Beckwith, Sr. 2012-2013; Susan Bennett Stiles 2013-2016; Harold V. Phillips 2016-

Morenci UMC *[Heritage]*　　　　　　　　　　　donagalloway@msn.com
(P) Corner of S Summit & Main, Morenci 49256; (M) 111 E Main St, Morenci 49256　(517) 458-6923
　Emmett E. Coons 1966-1969; Cleon F. Abbott Jr. 1969-1973; Alan J. Hanson 1973-1981; Richard
　W. Sheppard 1981-Jan 14, 1988; Evans C. Bentley Jan. 15, 1988-1995; Karen A. (Welch) Mars
　1995-Oct 31, 2000; Earl Eden (interim) Nov 1, 2000-Jun 15, 2001; Elmer A. Armijo Jun 16, 2001-
　2003; Dorothy J. Okray 2003-2007; Richard E. Burstall 2007-2010; Donna Galloway 2010-

Morrice UMC *[Mid-Michigan]*　　　　　　　　　bancroftmorricepastor@gmail.com
(P) 204 Main St, Morrice 48857; (M) PO Box 301, Morrice 48857　　　　　(517) 625-7715
　Richard Andrus 1969-1972; Terry A. Euper 1972-1976; James E. Paige, Jr. (co-pastor) 1976-1980;
　Margaret A. Paige (Co-Pastor) 1977-1980; Charles J. Bamberger 1980-1990; Donald Woolum
　1990-1993; John H. Schneider, Jr. 1993-1997; Penney Meints 1997-1998; Arthur R. Turner 1998-
　2004; Jeremy T. Peters 2004-2008; Jeremy P. Benton 2008-2011; Patricia Elliott 2011-2015; Robert
　Forsyth 2015-Mar 31, 2017; Terry A. Euper (Ret.) Apr 1, 2017-2017; Coleen Wilsdon (DSA) 2017-
　Nov 30, 2017; Coleen Wilsdon Dec 1, 2017-

Morris Chapel UMC *[Greater Southwest]*　　　　　　rsnodgrass72@gmail.com
(P) 11721 Pucker St, Niles 49120; (M) 1730 Holiday Dr, Niles 49120　　　(269) 684-5194
　Albert O'Rourke 1968-1970; Douglas Vernon 1970-1971; Pulpit Supply 1971-1972; Kenneth L.
　Snow 1972-1982; Richard C. Kuhn 1982-1987; Richard D. Wilson 1987-1996; Zawdie K. Abiade
　1996-2002; Charles D. McNary (DSA) 2002-2003; O'Ryan Rickard 2003-2004; Christopher A.
　Kruchkow 2004-Feb. 15, 2012; [Morris Chapel UMC became single point charge 2012] Samuel
　Gordy (1/4 time) Mar. 11, 2012-2013; Rob Snodgrass 2014- [Morris Chapel / Niles Grace became
　a two-point charge 2016; Niles Wesley / Morris Chapel / Niles Grace became a 3-point charge
　2017]

Mount Clemens: First UMC *[Greater Detroit]*　　　　office@mountclemensumc.org
(P/M) 57 Southbound Gratiot Ave, Mt Clemens 48043　　　　　　　(586) 468-6464
　Ronald Cornwell (assoc) 1963-1971; James R. Balfour 1969-1976; Robert Adams (assoc) 1971-
　1973; Mary E. Howard (assoc) 1973-1974; John W. Elliott (assoc) 1974-1977; Stanley A. Bailey
　1976-1986; Kenneth A. Kohlmann (assoc) 1977-1981; Thomas R. Kinney (assoc) 1981-1984;
　Frederick P. Cooley (assoc) 1984-1988; David M. Liscomb 1986-1992; Richard C. Andrus 1992-
　1999; William D. Rickard (assoc) 1991-1993; Patricia A. Meyers 1999-2006; G. Charles Sonquist
　(interim) 2006-2007; Carman J. Minarik (co-pastor) 2007-2013; Donna J. Minarik (co-pastor) 2007-
　2013; Mary G. (Gibson) McInnes 2013-2017; Maureen V. Baker 2017-2019; Daniel J.C. Hart 2019-

Mt. Morris: First UMC *[East Winds]*   rmpieper@aol.com
(P/M) 808 E Mt Morris Rd, Mt Morris 48458   (810) 686-3870
   Ellis A. Hart 1968-1973; Charles C. Cookingham 1973-1976; Jack Lancaster 1976-Aug., 1978;
   Walter David Aug., 1978-1986; Donald E. Hall 1986-Aug., 1992; William R. Maynard Aug. 1992-
   1996; Robert E. Burkey 1996-2003; Elizabeth M. Gamboa 2003-2008; Alonzo Vincent 2008-2013;
   Janet M. Engler 2013-Oct 1, 2015; Bruce Lee Billing (Ret.) Oct 1, 2015-2018; Ralph H Pieper II
   (Ret.) 2018-

Mt Pleasant: Chippewa Indian UMC *[Central Bay]*   CWhite-Pigeon@sagchip.org
(P) 7529 E Tomah Rd, Mount Pleasant 48858; (M) 3490 S Leaton Rd, Mt Pleasant 48858
   Joseph Sprague 1974-1986; Maynard Hinman DSA 1986-1987; Joseph Sprague 1984-1986; Chris
   Cavender DSA 1990-Dec. 31, 1991; James Burgess Jan.1992-June1992; Joseph Sprague June
   15, 1992-1994; Carla Sineway (1/3 time) 1994-Nov. 1, 2003; Matthew Sprague (1/3 time) 1994-
   Nov. 15, 1995; Owen White-Pigeon (1/3 time) 1994; Owen White-Pigeon (DSA) 2011-Aug 26, 2019

Mt Pleaseant: Countryside UMC *[Central Bay]*
(P) 4264 S Leaton Rd, Mt Pleasant 48858; (M) 202 S Elizabeth St, Mt Pleasant 48858
                                                                   (989) 773-0359
   George Rule 1968-1970; Joseph Dudley 1970-Sept. 1972; Daren C. Durey Oct. 1972-Jan. 1977;
   Robert E. Tomlinson Feb. 1977-1980; Gordon Spalenka 1980-1984; Janelle Gerken 1984-Jan.
   1987; Michael J. Kent May 1987-Jan. 1991; James Cook 1991-1995; Dean Prentiss 1995-Sept.
   14, 1999; Susan D. Olsen July 16, 2004-2006; Sharyn K. Osmond Aug. 1, 2006-Nov. 30, 2008;
   Donald R. Wendell Nov. 30, 2008-Nov. 1, 2009; Craig L. Adams Dec. 1, 2009-2010; David Michael
   Palmer 2010-2016; Russell D. Morgan 2016-2018; Martin T. Cobb Oct 1, 2019-

Mt Pleasant: First UMC *[Central Bay]*   office@mtpfumc.org
(P/M) 400 S Main St, Mt Pleasant 48858   (989) 773-6934
   Paul Albery 1966-1970; Neil Bintz 1970-1978; Albert W. Frevert 1978-1989; Edward C. Ross
   (Assoc.) 1978-1981; Rodney J. Kalajainen (Assoc.) 1981-1984; Thomas Crossman (Assoc.) 1984-
   1986; Steven M. Smith (Assoc.) 1986-1991; Ronald J. Thompson 1989-1995; Janet K. Sweet
   (Assoc.) 1991-1994; Connie R. Bongard (Assoc.) Aug. 1, 1994-1997; Wade S. Panse 1995-1997;
   Benton R. Heisler 1997-2002; Mark R. Erbes (Assoc.) 1997-2001; Michelle LaMew (Assoc.) 2001-
   ; John W. Boley 2002-2010; Charles D. Farnum (Assoc.) July 16, 2006-2007; Cynthia A. Skutar
   2010-2013; Diane Gordon 2013-2018; Julie A. Greyerbiehl 2018-

Mt Pleasant: Trinity UMC *[Central Bay]*
(P/M) 202 S Elizabeth St, Mt Pleasant 48858   (989) 772-5690
   G.B. Rule 1967-1969; J.A. Dudley 1969-1972; Daren C. Durey 1972-1977; Robert E. Tomlinson
   1977-1980; Gordon E. Spalenka 1980-1984; Janelle E. Gerken 1984-1987; Michael J. Kent 1987-
   1991; James Cook 1991-1995; Dean Prentiss 1995-Sept. 14, 1999; Jana Lynn Almeida Oct. 16,
   1999-2004; Susan D. Olsen July 16, 2004-2006; Sharyn K. Osmond Aug. 1, 2006-Nov. 30, 2008;
   Donald R. Wendell Nov. 30, 2008-Nov. 1, 2009; Craig L. Adams Dec. 1, 2009-2010; David Michael
   Palmer 2010-2016; Russell D. Morgan 2016-2018; Martin T. Cobb Oct 1, 2019-

Mt. Vernon UMC (formerly New Beginnings) *[Greater Detroit]*   bwmtvernon@gmail.com
(P/M) 3000 28 Mile Rd, Washington 48094   (248) 650-2213
   [merger of Davis and Mount Vernon, Oct 22, 2009] Douglas J. Shephard 2009-Nov 30, 2011; Jacque
   Hodges Dec 1, 2011-2017; Cherlyn McKanders 2017-

Munising UMC *[Northern Skies]*   umcmunising@jamadots.com
(P/M) 312 Lynn St, Munising 49862   (906) 387-3394
  Norman C. Kohns 1969-1973; Konstantin Wipp 1974-1978; Robert L. Porter 19778-1980; William F.
  Bowers 1980-1983; Joel W. Hurley 1983-1986; Mary B. Willoughby 1986-1989; Ray S. Peterson 1989-
  1991; Gary R. Shiplett 1992-1994; James M. Downing 1994-Aug 31, 1997; Rosemarie O. Fahrion
  1997-Dec 31, 2004; Gary I. Stevens Jan 1, 2005-Jan 1, 2009; Irene R. White Jan 1, 2009-2011; Sandra
  J. Kolder 2011-

Munith UMC *[Mid-Michigan]*   MunithUMC@gmail.com
(P) 224 N Main St, Munith 49259; (M) PO Box 189, Munith 49259-0189   (517) 596-2441
  Frederick Werth 1967-1971; Bert L. Cole March 1972-1973; Larry Irvine 1973-1975; Thomas Adams
  1976-1978; James Barney 1979-1983; Linda Farmer-Lewis 1983-1986; Milton TenHave 1986-1990;
  Laurie McKinven-Copus 1990-Sept. 1991; Robert Marston Oct. 1991-1998; Judith A. Nielson 1998-
  2000; Charles Cerling 2000-Aug. 9, 2004; Arthur R. Turner 2004-Nov. 15, 2005; Kenneth Karlzen
  (DSA) Dec. 2005-2006; Maurice Walworth (DSA) 2006-2007; Larry W. Rubingh 2007-Sept. 6, 2011;
  Maurice E. Walworth, Jr. (pulpit supply) Sept. 6, 2011-2012; Jeanne M. Laimon (1/4 time) 2012-
  2014 [M-52 Cooperative Ministry 2013-2014]; Susan J. Trowbridge 2014-2019; Stephan Weinberger
  (Ret.) 2019-

Muskegon: Central UMC *[Midwest]*   cumc@muskegoncentralumc.org
(P/M) 1011 2nd St, Muskegon 49440   (231) 722-6545
  Royal J. Synwolt 1966-1971; Robert H. Jongeward 1971-1979; Lynn A. DeMoss 1979-1988; Ron
  L. Keller 1988-1993; Daniel M. Duncan (Assoc.) 1989-1994; Ray W. Burgess 1993-2000; Melanie
  S. Young (Assoc.) 1994-1996; Virginia L. Heller (Assoc.) 1996-1998; Gregory P. Culver (Assoc.)
  1998-2002; Randall R. Hansen 2000-2009; M. Kay DeMoss (Deacon) 2003-2015; Gary L. Bekofske
  2009-2010; Diane Gordon 2010-2013; Mark D. Miller 2013-2020; Robert B. Cook 2020-

Muskegon: Crestwood UMC *[Midwest]*   judyccstk@yahoo.com
(P/M) 1220 Creston St, Muskegon 49442   (231) 773-9696
  Carl B. Strange 1962-1969; John S. Myette 1969-1970; Phillip R. Glotfelty, Jr. 1970-1973; Kenneth
  W. Karlzen 1973-1977; David G. Showers 1977-1980; Lawrence E. Hodge 1980-1983; Birt A. Beers
  1983-1990; M. Chris Lane 1990-1995; Victor D. Charnley 1995-2004; Dianne D. Morrison 2004-
  2007; Diane M Bowden 2007-2008; Dale Hotelling 2008-2010; Stephan Weinberger 2010-2014;
  [Muskegon Crestwood realigned from Lakeside/Crestwood to Whitehall/Crestwood 2014] Mary A.
  Sweet 2014-2017; Jennifer J. Wheeler 2017-2020 [Whitehall and Crestwood became multi-station
  circuit 2014; Crestwood became a single station 2017] William F. Dye (Ret.) 2020-

Muskegon Hts: Temple UMC *[Midwest]*   templeumcmkht@gmail.com
(P/M) 2500 Jefferson St, Muskegon Heights 49444   (231) 733-1065
  Verner Kilgren 1962-1970; Richard Selleck 1970-1977; Dale Crawford 1977-1979; Robert Pumfrey
  1979-1983; Don Eddy 1983-1989; Richard Youells 1989-1991; Gerald F. Hagans 1991-Sept. 1,
  2006; Robert B. Cook Sept. 1, 2006-2012; Jeffrey J. Bowman, Sr. 2012-

Muskegon: Lake Harbor UMC *[Midwest]*   Office@LakeHarborUMC.org
(P/M) 4861 Henry St, Norton Shores 49441
  Wayne Speese 1964-1975; Harold Kirchenbauer Oct. 1975-1981; Frank Lyman 1981-1991; Carole
  Lyman (Assoc.) 1984-1991; Jack Stubbs 1991-1995; Susan J. Hagans 1995-2000; Cynthia Ann
  Skutar 2000-2004; Richard A. Morrison 2004-2007; Mark R. Erbes 2007-2014; Mary Letta-Bement
  Ivanov 2014- [Muskegon Lakeside merged w/ Muskegon Lake Harbor 07-01-16]

Napoleon UMC *[Heritage]*   napoleonunited@att.net
(P) 210 Nottawasepee, Napoleon 49261; (M) PO Box 337, Napoleon 49261   (517) 536-8609
   Robert Kersten 1967-1969; Robert Hinklin 1969-1972; Douglas Smith 1972-1973; Marjorie
   Matthews 1973-Dec. 1975; J. Brian Selleck March 1976-Sept. 1978; Francis Anderson Sept. 1978-
   Sept. 1980; Wayne Gorsline Sept. 1980-1988; Robert J. Freysinger 1988-2004; Robert P. Stover
   2004-2007; Jennifer Jue 2007-2013; Gregory R. Wolfe (Ret.) 2013-2019; Mary A. Sweet 2019-
   [Jonesville / Napoleon became two-point charege 2019]

Nashville UMC *[Mid-Michigan]*   numcoffice@att.net
(P) 210 Washington St, Nashville 49073; (M) PO Box 370, Nashville 49073   (517) 852-2043
   James Crosby 1969-1975; Leonard F. Putnam 1975-1984; Lynn Wagner 1984-1988; Ronald K.
   Brooks 1988-May 15, 1991; Kenneth Vaught June 1, 1991-1994; James L. Hynes 1994-2000; Gail
   C. Patterson 2000-Dec. 31, 2001; Dianne M. Bowden January 16, 2002-2007; Cathy M. Christman
   2007-2010; Nancy J. Bitterling 2010-2013; Gary L. Simmons 2013-2015; [Barry-Eaton Cooperative
   Ministry 2013] Nancy V. Fancher (Deacon) 2014-2015; Karen L. Jensen-Kinney 2015-

Nashville: Peace UMC *[Mid-Michigan]*   macousino1@gmail.com
(P/M) 6043 E M 79 Hwy, Nashville 49073   (517) 852-1993
   Robert E. Boyer 1968-1969; Marion R. Putnam 1969-Jan. 1970; E.F. Rhoades Feb.-July 1970;
   Michael Williams Aug. 1970-1971; William P. Reynders 1971-Feb. 1972; Thomas Churn March
   1972-April 1973; Thomas Peters May 1973-Aug. 1976; Dale D. Spoor Sept. 1976-Dec. 1979;
   Steven Reid Jan. 1980-Jan. 1984; Mary Curtis March 1984-1989; James Noggle 1989-Feb. 1993;
   Susan A. Trowbridge March 1993-March 15, 2005; Nancy V. Fancher (DSA) March 16, 2005-March
   31, 2006; Susan D. Olsen 2006-2015; Mickey Ann Cousino (CLM/DSA) Sept. 1, 2015-

Negaunee: Mitchell UMC *[Northern Skies]*   mitchellumc@sbcglobal.net
(P) 207 N Teal Lake Ave, Negaunee 49866; (M) PO Box 190, Negaunee 49866
                                                                              (906) 475-4861
   Albert F. Roloff 1965-1974; William D. Schoonover 1974-1982; King Wm. Hanna 1982-Aug 31,
   1994; John Bunce Sep 1, 1994-1998; Scott A. Harmon 1998-2002; Anthony J. Tomasino 2002-
   2003; Eric D. Kieb 2003-2010; Douglas E. Mater 2010-2016; J. Albert Barchue 2016-Aug 31, 2020
   [merged w/ Marquette: Hope 9/1/2020]

Nelson UMC *[Northern Water]*   hemlockumc@frontier.net
(P) 5950 S Hemlock Rd, Hemlock 48626; (M) PO Box 138, Hemlock 48626   (989) 642-8285
   A. Theodore Halsted 1965-1970; John C. Huhtala 1970-1975; Terry W. Allen 1976-1978; Tom Brown
   1978-1984; Steven A. Gjerstad 1984-Jun 30, 1994; Arthur V. Norris Jul 1, 1994-2001; Karen L.
   Knight 2001-Jan 31, 2002; Nicholas W. Scroggins 2002-2009; Jerry F. Densmore 2009-2014;
   Michale W. Vollmer 2014-2019; Robert G. Richards 2019- (Swan Valley (lead church) / LaPorte
   charge and Hemlock / Nelson charge formed new four point charge July 1, 2019)

NE Missaukee Parish: Merritt-Butterfield UMC *[Northern Waters]* m-mchurches@centurytel.net
(P/M) 428 S Merritt Rd, Merritt 49667   (231) 328-4598
   Athel Lynch 1968-1970; Marion Nye 1970-1973; Eugene Baughan 1974-1987; Bernard Griner
   1988-1989; Cynthia Schaefer 1989-1993; (Merritt and Butterfield merged on July 1, 1991.) Pulpit
   Supply July 1-Aug. 31, 1993; O. Jay Kendall Sept. 1, 1993-2005; Brian R Bunch, Aug. 1, 2005-
   2012; Jeffrey J. Schrock 2012-2016; Joshua Henderson Sept. 1, 2016-July 31, 2019; Hyun-Jun
   Cho Aug. 1, 2019-

NE Missaukee Parish: Moorestown-Stittsville UMC *[Northern Waters]*
m-mchurches@centurytel.net
(P/M) 4509 E Moorestown Rd, Lake City 49651   (231) 328-4598
Athel Lynch 1968-1970; Marion Nye 1970-1973; Eugene Baughan 1974-1987; Bernard Griner 1988-1989; Cynthia Schaefer 1989-1993; Stittsville merged with Moorestown in 1993; O. Jay Kendall Sept. 1, 1993-2005; Brian R Bunch, Aug. 1, 2005-2012; Jeffrey J. Schrock 2012-2016; Joshua Henderson Sept. 1, 2016-July 31, 2019; Hyun-Jun Cho Aug. 1, 2019-

New Baltimore: Grace UMC *[Greater Detroit]*   gumcnb@comcast.net
(P/M) 49655 Jefferson Ave, Chesterfield 48047   (586) 725-1054
Robert C. Andrus 1979-1987; David D. Amstutz 1987-1990; James E. Greer II 1990-1995; Donald J. Emmert 1995-May 31, 2000; Tonya M. Arneson Jun 1, 2000-2006; Jill Hardt Zundel 2006-2014; Jean-Pierre Duncan 2014-2018; Brian E. Steele 2018- ; Christopher J. Heldt (DSA) 2020-

New Buffalo: Water's Edge UMC *[Greater Southwest]*   betty@h2oedge.org
(P/M) 18732 Harbor Country Dr, New Buffalo 49117   (269) 469-1250
John Bullock 1968-1974; Robert Pumfery 1974-1979; Joseph Beattie 1979-1980; Ken Vanderlaan 1980-1981; Charles Tooman 1981-Jan. 1982; Gregory B. Wood Feb. 1, 1982-1985; B. Gordon Barry 1985-1993; Bradley S. Bartelmay 1993-2017; [01/01/12 New Buffalo First UMC renamed New Buffalo: Water's Edge UMC] Kellas D. Penny III 2017-

New Hudson UMC *[Heritage]*   newhudsonumc@sbcglobal.net
(P) 56730 Grand River Ave, New Hudson 48165; (M) PO Box 803, New Hudson 48165
(248) 437-6212
Robert A. Mitchinson 1966-2002; Gerald S. Hunter 2002-Oct 15, 2015; Thomas Tarpley Oct 15, 2015-2016; Robert J. Sielaff 2016-2018; Seung (Andy) Ho Baek 2018-2020; John J. Pajak 2020-

New Lothrop: First UMC *[Mid-Michigan]*   umc7495@centurytel.net
(P) 7494 Orchard Street, New Lothrop 48460; (M) PO Box 247, New Lothrop 48460 (810) 638-5702
Paul L. Amstutz 1964-1971; Clifford J. Furness 1971-1976; Donald W. Brown 1976-1978; Linda Susan Garment 1978-1980; Verne Blankenburg 1980-1983; Robert J. Henning 1983-Jul., 1990; Mary Thoburn Tame 1990-Aug 3, 1997; James M. Downing Sep 1, 1997-Aug 16, 1999; Olaf Lidums Nov 16, 2000-2003; David L. Fleming 2003-2011; Janet M. Engler 2011-2013; Cecillia Lee Sayer 2013-2017; Stephen Spina (DSA) 2017-May 2, 2018; Stephen Spina May 3, 2018-Correct in Ezra

Newaygo UMC *[Midwest]*   umcnew@newaygoumc.com
(P) 101 State Rd, Newaygo 49337; (M) PO Box 366, Newaygo 49337-0366   (231) 652-6581
Jean Crabtree 1967-1972; Paul E. Robinson 1972-1975; James W. Boehm 1975-1984; John S. Myette 1984-1988; Stephen M.G. Charlney 1988-1994; Donald R. Fry 1994-1999; Sandra L. Spahr 2000-2006; Patricia L. Bromberek 2006-2011; Kathy Groff (Ret.) 2011-2017; Eric L. Magner (DSA) 2017-Nov 30, 2017; Eric L. Manger (PL) (THFT ¾) Dec 1, 2017-

Newberry UMC *[Northern Skies]*   nbyumc@up.net
(P/M0) 110 W Harrie St, Newberry 49868   (906) 293-5711
Wayne T. Large 1967-1970; Robert N. Hicok 1970-1974; William E. Miles 1974-1975; Ralph A. Edwards 1975-1979; David J. Hill 1979-1981; June M. Westgate 1981-1986; James L. Rule 1986-1996; Wm. Peter Bartlett 1996-2001; Jane D. Logston 2001-2003; Saundra J. Clark 2003-2013; Timothy G. Callow 2013-2020; Jacquelyn A. Roe 2020-

Niles: Portage Prairie UMC *[Greater Southwest]*   ppumcs@aol.com
(P/M) 2450 Orange Rd, Niles 49120   (269) 695-6708
     Darrell Osborn 1968-1970; Robert Welfare 1970-1974; Robert Stillson 1974-1980; Robert Stover 1980-1987; Morris Reinhart 1987-1989; Margaret Peterson 1989-1994; Larry W. Mannino 1994-1995; David H. Minger 1995-1999; Thomas P. Fox 1999-2008; Theresa Little Eagle Sayles 2008-Apr. 15,2009; [Portage Prairie/Arden two-point charge 2009] O'Ryan Rickard 2009-2014; Ralph A. Posnik Jr 2014-2019; [Portage Prairie single-point charge 2014] Scott B. Smith 2019-

Niles: New Journey UMC (formerly Niles: Wesley) *[Greater Southwest]*
            johnwesley2561@sbcglobal.net
(P/M) 302 Cedar St, Niles 49120   (269) 683-7250
     Robert Trenery 1968-1974; Mark Graham 1974-1984; Lloyd Phillips 1984-1991; Nolan R. Williams 1991-Jan. 1, 2000; Emmett H. Kadwell, Jr. Jan. 1, 2000-2008; Edward H. Slate 2008-2012; Cathi M. Huvaere 2012-2017; [Niles Wesley / Morris Chapel / Niles Grace became a 3-point charge 2017] Robert L. Snodgrass II 2017- [Niles: Grace merged with Niles: Wesley, re-named Niles: New Journey 1-1-2020]

North Branch UMC *[East Winds]*   nblumc@gmail.com
(P) 4195 Huron St, North Branch 48461; (M) PO Box 156, North Branch 48461   (810) 688-2610
     John D. Lover 1969-1977; Henry W. Powell 1977-1979; Roger F. Gedcke 1979-1997; C. Michael Madison 1997-Aug 31, 1997; Mary T. Tame Sep 1, 1997-1999; Wayne C. Ferrigan 1999-2006; Michael S. McCoy 2006-Mar 31, 2009; Ronald G. Hutchinson Apr 16, 2009-2020; Theodore A. Adkins (DSA) 2020-

North Lake UMC *[Heritage]*   secretary.nlumc@gmail.com
(P/M) 14111 N Territorial Rd, Chelsea 48118   (734) 475-7569
     George T. Nevin 1964-1969; George Q. Woomer 1969 (interim); Frederick Atkinson Oct. 1, 1969-Feb. 4, 1971; Harry R. Weeks Mar. 1971-1973; John W. Todd 1973-1974; David S. Stiles 1974-1977; John W. Elliott 1977-1982; David R. Strobe 1982-1984; David C. Collins 1984-1985; Sondra B. Willobee 1985-1991; Wayne A. Hawley 1991-2001; Alice J. Sheffield 2001-2012; Anna Moon 2012-2016; Todd Wesley Jones 2016-

North Muskegon Community UMC *[Midwest]*   wendy@communitychurchumc.org
(P/M) 1614 Ruddiman Dr, North Muskegon 49445   (231) 744-4491
     David S. Yoh 1968-Sept. 1978; Dennis Buwalda Sept. 1978-1982; Laurence L. Waterhouse 1982-1986; John W. Fisher 1986-1992; Glenn M. Wagner 1992-2006; Robert K. Lynch 2006-2012; Phillip J. Friedrick July 15, 2012-2017; Jeremy P.H. Williams 2017-

North Parma UMC *[Heritage]*
(P) 11970 Devereaux, Parma 49269; (M) PO Box 25, Parma 49269-0025   (517) 531-4619
     Edward Dahringer 1968-Sept. 1980; Jean Crabtree Nov. 1980-Jan. 1984; Jerry Hippensteel 1984-1989; Charlotte Lewis 1989-1992; Carolin S. Spragg 1992-1999; Keith W. Heifner 1999-2003; Michael P. Baker-Streevy 2003-2009; Melissa Claxton 2009-2018; [North Parma / Springport became two-point charge 7-1-10] Mark E. Mitchell 2018-

Northport: Indian Mission UMC *[Northern Waters]*   pastor@NorthportIndianumc.org
(P) 8626 N Manitou Trl, Northport 49670; (M) PO Box 401, Northport 49670   (231) 715-1280
     Marshall Collins (DSA) 1991-2001; Kathryn Coombs (DSA) 2003-2005; Thomas H. John Jr. 2005-2015; [Northport Indian Mission became single-point charge 2015] Terry M. Wildman (DSA) 2015-Nov 30, 2017; Terry M Wildman (PL) (LTFT 1/2) Dec 1, 2017-2019; Mary Wava Hofmann (DSA) Apr. 1, 2019-Jan 31, 2020; Mary Wava Hofmann (PL) Feb 1, 2020-

North Street UMC *[East Winds]* northstreetumc@gmail.com
(P/M) 4580 North Rd, North Street 48049 (810) 385-4027
Herbert Griffith 1963-1981; David D. Amstutz 1981-1987; David C. Dupree 1987-1989; Kenneth B. Ray 1989-1992; Alger T. Lewis 1992-1999; Fredrick D. Neumann 1999-2002; William P. McBride 2002-Oct 31, 2014; David A. Reed Dec 12, 2014-

Northville: First UMC *[Heritage]* fumc777@fumcnorthville.org
(P/M) 777 W 8 Mile Rd, Northville 48167 (248) 349-1144
Guenther C. Branstner 1968-1983; Eric S. Hammar 1983-1991; Douglas W. Vernon 1991-2000; Arthur L. Spafford (assoc) Mar. 1, 1992-Aug 31, 1999; Thomas M. Beagan (assoc) 1992-2000; Cynthia A. Loomis-Abell 1999-2000; John E. Hice 2000-2008; Gordon W. Nusz (assoc) 2000-May 1, 2002; Jennifer L Bixby (assoc) 2000-2004; Lisa L. Cook (assoc) 2004-2009; Steven J. Buck 2008-2013; Stephan A. D'Angelo (assoc) 2009-2012; Monica L. William (assoc) 2012-2019; Marsha M. Woolley 2013- ; Alice K. Ford (assoc) 2020-

Norway: Grace UMC *[Northern Skies]* gumc@norwaymi.com
(P/M) 130 O'Dill Dr, Norway 49870 (906) 563-8917
William D. Schoonover 1967-1974; Emmett Coons 1974-1977; Mark Karls 1977-1983; Ray D. Field 1983-1985; Carl R. Doersch 1985-1991; Nancy K. Frank 1991-Oc 31, 1994; Deborah R. Jones Feb 16, 1995-1996; David M. Wallis 1996-2006; James E. Britt Aug 16, 2006-2011; Irene R. White 2011-

Norwood UMC *[Northern Waters]*
(P/M) 00667 4th St. Norwood Village, Charlevoix 49720
Stanley Hayes 1967-1970; Lester Priest 1970-Jan. 1974; Daniel Minor April 1974-1981; Betty Burton 1981-1982; Glenn Britton 1982-1983; Supply pastor 1983-Aug. 1985; Robert Bellairs Aug. 1985-1996; Bernard W. Griner (DSA) 1996-1997; Eugene L. Baughan 1997-2002; D. Michael Maurer 2002-Nov. 10, 2008; Ralph Posnik (DSA) Nov. 23, 2008; Ralph Posnik Nov. 15, 2009-2014; Craig A. Pahl 2014-2017; Haldon Dale Ferris 2017-Aug 31, 2017; TBS

Nottawa UMC *[Greater Southwest]* umcnottawa1893@gmail.com
(P) 25838 M 86, Nottawa 49075; (M) PO Box 27, Nottawa 49075-0027 (269) 467-7134
Rudy A. Wittebach 1967-1974; Charles W. Smith 1974-1976; Elanor Carpenter 1976-Nov. 1980; Carl Leth Nov. 1980-Oct. 1983; David H. Minger Oct. 1983-1987; Laurie J. McKinven-Copus 1987-1990; Emilie Forward 1990-1994; Pulpit Supply July-Sept. 1994; Mona Joslyn (DSA) Oct. 1994-1996; Donald R. Wendell Jan. 1996-July 15, 2003; Alexander Miller (DSA) (LTFT ¼) 2003-

Novi UMC *[Heritage]* admin@umcnovi.com
(P/M) 41671 W 10 Mile Rd, Novi 48375 (248) 349-2652
Albert E. Hartoog 1969-1970; Philip M. Seymour 1970-1975; Karl L. Zeigler 1975-1979; Richard O. Griffith 1979-1984; Kearney Kirkby (assoc) 1982-1989; Charles R. Jacobs 1984-1997; Louise R. Ott 1997-2004; Jacqueline E. Holdsworth 2004-Mar 1, 2007; Alan W. DeGraw (interim) Mar 1, 2007-2007; June M. Marshall Smith 2007-2020; Carter L. Cortelyou 2020-

Oak Grove UMC *[Heritage]* oakgrove3395@att.net
(P/M) 6686 Oak Grove Rd, Howell 48855 (517) 546-3942
Robert M. Stoppert 1967-1969; James S. Ritchie 1969-1975; Lawson D. Crane 1975-1986; David A. Diamond 1986-1988; M. Jean Love 1988-1995; Alan W. DeGraw 1995-Jul 31, 2000; Robin G. Gilshire Aug 1, 2000-2001; June M. Westgate 2001-2005; Chong Y. Won 2005-2011; Paula M. Timm 2011-2020; Mark A. Vorenkamp 2020-

Okemos: Community Church *[Mid-Michigan]*   office@OkemosOCC.org
(P) 4734 Okemos Rd, Okemos 48864; (M) PO Box 680 ,Okemos 48805   (517) 349-4220
John E. Cermak 1966-1987; Lynn E. Grimes (Assoc.) 1983-1986; Verne C. Summers 1987-1989;
Richard C. Sneed (Assoc.) 1989-1991; Charles D. Grauer 1989-1996; Pegg Ainslie (Assoc.) 1991-
1993; Joyce DeToni-Hill (Assoc.) 1993-Feb. 15, 1994; James W. Boehm 1996-Sept. 1, 1998;
Jeanne M. Randels Oct. 16, 1998-Jan. 1, 2014; Richard W. Blunt 2014-

Old Mission Peninsula UMC *[Northern Waters]*   melodyolin@yahoo.com
(P/M) 16426 Center Rd, Traverse City 49686   (231) 223-4393
Richard W. Blunt 1986-1993; Orin L. Daniels 1993-1995; Dale Hotelling 1995-July 16, 2000; Sally
J. LaFrance 2001-2002; Stanley Lee Hayes (DSA) 2002-Jan. 31, 2003; David H. Minger Feb. 1,
2003-2006 (Church changed name from Ogdensburg to Old Mission Peninsula 2004); Martin Cobb
2006-2010; Melody Lane Olin 2010-2019; Zelphia J. Mobley 2019-

Omard UMC *[East Winds]*   omardumc@yahoo.com
(P/M) 2055 Peck Rd, Brown City 48416   (810) 346-3448
Basil W. Curtiss 1968-1971; Allen J. Lewis 1971-1979; Donald L. Casterline 1979-1986; Milton E.
Stahl 1987-1988; Earleen A. (Hamblen) Van Conant 1988-1993; Harold V. Phillips 1993-1996;
Rothwell McVety 1996-1997; Patrick D. Robbins May 1, 1998-2001; Dianne H. VanMarter 2001-
2005; Marvin H. McCallum (interm) 2005-2007; Peggy A. Katzmark 2007-2014; Daniel William
Surbrook (DSA) 2014-2015; Thomas G. Badley (Ret.) Aug 9-Nov 2, 2015; Patrick D. Robbins 2019-
[Brown City Cooperative Parish: Brown City and Omard formed 07/01/2019]

Omo: Zion UMC *[Greater Detroit]*   omozionumc@hotmail.com
(P) 63020 Omo Rd, Lenox 48050; (M) PO Box 344, Richmond 48062   (586) 428-7988
Edgar M. Smith 1969-1970; Donald W. Brown 1970-1972; Elmer J. Snyder 1972-1974; Ira L. Wood
1974-1975; Robert D. Schoenhals 1975-1983; Robert Thornton 1983-2000; Victor Studaker 2000-
Dec 31, 2004; Donald L. Wojewski Jan 1, 2005-2005; Susan K. Montenegro 2005-Oct 7, 2007;
Donald R. Sperling Nov 1, 2007-2010; Marianne M. McMunn 2010-2011; Dianna H. Van Marter
2011-Dec 31, 2013; Donna J. Zuhlke Jan 1, 2014-Sept 1, 2018; Mary Ellen Chapman (Ret.) Sep
3, 2018- [Omo: Zion / Washington became signle point charges 7-1-2019]

Onaway UMC *[Northern Waters]*   onawayumc@src-milp.com
(P) 3647 N Lynn St, Onaway 49765; (M) PO Box 762, Onaway 49765   (989) 745-4479
Charles R Fox (Onaway) 1969-1972; N. Ralph Guilliat (Millersburg) 1967-1972; G. Charles Ball
1972-1983; Roy A. Syme 1983-1989; Michael Grajcar Jr. 1989-1991; Richard A. Turner 1991-1995;
John N. Hamilton 1995-Jun 15, 2001; W. Peter Bartlett 2001-2011; Josheua Blanchard 2011-2014;
Carman Cook 2014-2018; Yoo Jin Kim 2018-

Ontonagon UMC *[Northern Skies]*   ontmeth@jamadots.com
(P) 109 Greenland Rd, Ontonagon 49953; (M) PO Box 216, Ontonagon 49953   (906) 884-4556
Lloyd Christler 1968-1972; James Hillard 1970-1971; Lawrence Brooks 1971-1975; Roger Gedcke
1972-1979; Lillian Richards 1971-1976; Wayne E. Sparks 1975-1980; Myra Sparks 1976-1980; Ed
Hingelburg 1976-1980; Brian Marshall 1980-1984; Donald J. Emmert 1984-Feb 1, 1990; William
D. Schoonover Feb 16, 1990-1991; Mel D. Rose 1992-1994; Lance E. Ness Sep 1, 1994-Dec 31,
1999; Christine F. Bohnsack Mar 1, 2000-2004; Cherrie A. Sporleder 2004-2010; Bruce R. Steinberg
2010-2018; Nelson L. Hall 2018-

Oregon UMC *[East Winds]*
(P) 2985 German Rd, Columbiaville 48421; (M) 2971 German Rd, Columbiaville 48421
(810) 793-6828
Emmett E. Coons 1969-1974; James M. Thompson 1974-1980; David R. McKinstry 1980-1988; Georg F. W. Gerritsen 1988-1996; Wayne E. Samson 1996-1998; James E. Paige, Jr. 1998-Oct 1, 2003; Carole A. Brown Sep 1, 2004-Jul 31, 2006; Marybelle Haynes Aug 1, 2006-2018; Stanley Patrick Stybert (Ret.) Ju 1-Oct 31, 2018; Jeanne Harmon Wisenbaugh (DSA) Nov 1., 2018; Jeanne Harmon Wisenbaugh Apr 1, 2020-

Ortonville UMC *[East Winds]*   ortonvilleumc@gmail.com
(P) 93 N Church St, Ortonville 48462; (M) PO Box 286, Ortonville 48462   (248) 627-3125
Horace Murry 1969-1973; Alan R. George 1973-1978; Richard A. Peacock 1978-Jul., 1982; R. Stanley Sutton Aug., 1982-1984; Daniel M. Young 1984-1991; Gary R. Imms 1991-1993; Timothy S. Woycik 1993-1998; Frederick O. Timm 1998-2000; Suzanne B. Walls 2000-2005; Timothy C. Dibble 2005-2011; Jeremy Benton 2011-2013; David O. Pratt 2013-Mar 1, 2016; W. Peter Crawford mar 1, 2016-2016; Brian K. Johnson 2016-

Oscoda UMC *[Central Bay]*   umcoscoda@gmail.com
(P/M) 120 W Dwight St, Oscoda 48750   (989) 739-8591
William Stone 1969-1976; James A. Smith 1976-1983; F. Richard MacCanon 1983-1988; William A. Cargo 1988-2006; Briony E. Peters-Desotell 2006-2014; William R.Seitz 2014-

Oscoda Indian Church UMC *[Central Bay]*   umcoscoda@gmail.com
(P) 7994 Alvin Rd, Mikado 48745; (M) 120 W Dwight St, Oscoda 48750   (989) 739-8591
William Stone 1969-1976; James A. Smith 1976-1983; F. Richard MacCanon 1983-1988; William A. Cargo 1988-2006; Briony E. Peters-Desotell 2006-2014; William R. Seitz 2014-

Oshtemo: LifeSpring UMC *[Greater Southwest]*   lifespring.churchoffice@gmail.com
(P/M) 1560 S 8th St, Kalamazoo 49009   (269) 353-1303
[new church start 2001] Mark R. Payne 2001-2009; Patricia A. Harpole 2009-2014; [LifeSpring/Lawton St. Paul's became 2-point charge 2014] Wayne E. McKenney 2014-2016; Jason E. Harpole 2016- [LifeSpring became a single-point charge 2016]

Oshtemo UMC *[Greater Southwest]*   oshumc@att.net
(P) 6574 Stadium Dr, Kalamazoo 49009; (M) PO Box 12, Oshtemo 49077   (269) 375-5656
Jay Gunnett Apr. 1968-1971; Laurence Dekema 1971-Jan. 1972; Linda Stoddard 1972-Oct. 1976; Pulpit Supply Oct. 1976-1977; Dorcas Lohr 1977-1982; Kenneth H. Kline 1982-1987; David L. Litchfield 1987-1992; Lewis A. Buchner 1992-1997; Charles M. Shields 1997-Feb. 1, 2000; Suzanne Kornowski 2000-2011 (Kalamazoo: Oakwood merged with Oshtemo on October 27, 2002) Peggy Boltz 2011-2013; John W. Fisher (Ret.) 2013-

Ossineke UMC *[Northern Waters]*   ossinekemiumc@gmail.com
(P) 13095 US Hwy 23 S, Ossineke 49766; (M) 7770 Scott Rd, Hubbard Lake 49747   (989) 471-2334
Kyle Ballard 1968-1970; John Miller 1970-1982; James Lumsden 1982-1988; Stephen Cartwright 1988-1990; Priscilla Seward 1990-1994; Fredrick D. Neumann Aug 1, 1994-1999; John D. Bailey 1999-2005; Stephen T. Euper 2005-2010; Jack E. Johnston 2010-2012; Micheal P. Kelley 2012-2020; Angela M. Lovegrove 2020-

Otisville UMC *[East Winds]*   otisvilleunitedmethodistchurch@yahoo.com
(P) 200 W Main St, Otisville 48463; (M) PO Box 125, Otisville 48463   (810) 631-2911
Beatrice Townsend 1969-1971; Basel W. Curtiss 1971-1976; Lawrence C. Whiting 1976-1977; Bruce L. Billing 1977-1982; Janice I. Martineau 1982-1985; G. Patrick England Sept. 1, 1985-1993; Gregory E. Rowe 1993-Feb 28, 1995; Billy J. McKown Mar 1, 1995-2005; James P. James 2005-2007; Carter Garrigues-Cortelyou 2007-2010; Betty Kay Leitelt 2010-

Otsego UMC *[Greater Southwest]*   office@otsegoumc.org
(P) 223 E. Allegan St, Otsego 49078; (M) PO Box 443, Otsego 49078-0443   (269) 694-2939
Birt Beers 1967-1972; Leonard Yarlott 1972-1975; J. William Schoettle 1975-1983; Robert H. Roth, Jr. 1983-1985; James C. Grant 1985-March 1992; Emerson Minor (interim) March-August 1992; James C. Grant 1992-1994; Philip L. Brown 1994-1998; Margaret H. Peterson 1998-2000; Joseph D. Shaler 2001-

Ovid: United Church *[Mid-Michigan]*   sue@unitedchurchofovid.com
(P) 131 W Front St, Ovid 48866; (M) PO Box 106, Ovid 48866-0106   (989) 834-5958
Claude B. Ridley, Jr. 1972-1977; Gilbert B. Heaton 1977-1980; Carl W. Staser 1980-Oct. 1983; Ronald W. Hansen Feb. 1, 1984-1993; Richard L. Matson 1993-1995; Steven D. Pearson 1995-1997; Robert L. Pumfery 1997-1999; Rob A. McPherson 1999-2006; Donald R. Fry 2006-2008; Gregory L. Buchner 2008-2013; Paul A. Damkoehler 2013-2015; Robert D. Nystrom 2015-2018 [Elsie / Ovid became a two-point charge 2016] Melanie S. Young 2018- [Middlebury / Ovid became a two-point charge 2018]

Owendale UMC *[Central Bay]*   bcleland@comcast.net
(P) 7370 Main St, Owendale 48754; (M) PO Box 98, Owendale 48754   (989) 678-4172
Clifford M. DeVore 1968-1971; Paul L. Amstutz 1971-1976; Carl J. Litchifeld 1976-1978; William P. Mc Bride 1978-1980; Myra L. Sparks 1980-1985; Zina B. Bennett 1985-1988; Mary F. Neil 1988-1991; Lisa M. McIlvenna 1991-1995; Carol M. Blair 1995-Sep 30, 1996; Allice J. Sheffield Dec 1, 1996-2001; John Heim 2001-2012; Cynthia M. Parsons 2012-2014; William C. Cleland 2014-

Owosso: First UMC *[Mid-Michigan]*   firstumc@michonline.net
(P/M) 1500 N Water St, Owosso 48867   (989) 725-2201
Ivan O. Gonser 1968-1972; Arthur V. Norris (assoc) 1969-1971; David G. Knapp (assoc) 1971-Dec. 1973; Paul T. Hart Jan., 1972-1977; Thomas G. Butcher (assoc) Dec. 1975-1977; Norbert W. Smith 1977-1985; J. Michael Pearson (assoc) 1977-1980; Susan Bennett Stiles (assoc) 1980-1982; Hayden K. Carruth (assoc) 1982-1984; Peter S. Harris (assoc) 1984-1986; Carol J. Johns 1985-1996; John W. Simpson (assoc) 1986-1989; Grant R. Lobb 1996-2005; Eric D. Kieb (assoc) 2001-2003; Duane M. Harris 2005-2009; Calvin D. Long 2009-2018; Deane B. Wyllys 2018-

Owosso: Trinity UMC *[Mid-Michigan]*   trinityumc@michonline.net
(P/M) 720 S Shiawassee St, Owosso 48867   (989) 723-2664
Clyde R. Moore 1968-1974; Alan W. Weeks 1974-1980; Ralph C. Pratt 1980-July 15, 1984; Gordon B. Boyd July 15, 1984-1987; Martin R. Caudill Oct. 15, 1987-1988; Mark D. Miller May 1, 1989-1998; Norman R. Beckwith, Sr. 1998-2008; Susan M. Kingsley 2008-2016; Carman J. Minarik 2016-2019; [Henderson / Chapin / Owosso: Triity frmed three-point charge 7-1-2019] Steffani Glygoroff (DSA) 2019-

Oxford UMC *[East Winds]*   oumc.office@sbcglobal.net
(P/M) 21 E Burdick St, Oxford 48371   (248) 628-1289
Marvin H. Mc Callum 1966-1972; J. Edward Cherryholmes 1972-1973; Donald H. Hall 1973-1977; David A. Russell 1977-1985; Dwight W. Murphy 1985-1992; Jack L. Mannschreck 1992-2002; Joseph R. Baunoch 2002-2004; Kenneth B. Ray 2004-2006; Douglas J. McMunn 2006-2011; Jean Snyder 2011-2012; Kevin L. Miles 2012-2014; Jennifer Jue 2014-2020 [Oxford / Thomas 2-point charge 2019] [Oxford became single station 2020] Julius E. Del Pino Sept 1, 2020-

Painesdale: Albert Paine Mem. UMC *[Northern Skies]*   revlaub@charter.net
(P) 54385 Iroquois, Painesdale 49955; (M) 204 W Douglass, Houghton 49931   (906) 482-1470
   A. P. Young 1962-1970; John Moore 1970-1976; Martin Caudill 1976-1979; Jay Six 1979-1981; William Wright 1981-1985; W. Peter Bartlett 1985-1987; Nicholas W. Scroggins 1987-1990; Mary G. Laub 1990-1992; Christine F. Bohnsack 1992-1995; Lillian G. Richards 1995-Oct 15, 2012; Mary G. Laub Nov 1, 2012-2014; T. Bradley Terhune 2014-2016; Mary Laub 2016-2019; [Houghton: Grace / Painesdale: Albert Paine Mem. Two-point charge 7-1-2019] Charles A. Williams 2019-2020; Eric M. Falker 2020-

Paint Creek UMC *[Greater Detroit]*   howarthumc@att.net
(P/M) 4420 Collins Rd, Rochester 48306   (248) 373-2360
   Elmer J. Snyder 1967-1972; Harold S. Morse 1972-1977; Paula Barker 1977-1979; Jeffery W. Dinner 1979-1982; Bruce L. Billing 1982-1993; David K. Koski 1993-1998; Sylvia A. Bouvier 1998-2006; Stephen Fraser-Soots 2006-2009; Thomas M. Sayers 2009-2016; Carolyn Jones 2016-2018; Marvin L. Herman 2018-

Palo UMC *[Midwest]*   fenwickumc@cmsinter.net
(P) 8445 Division St, Palo 48870; (M) PO Box 241, Sheridan 48884-0241   (989) 291-5547
   John H. Gurney 1970-1976; Norman Crotser 1976-Dec. 1978; Daniel R. Bennett 1979-March 1982; Mark G. Johnson March 1982-1986; James E. Cook 1986-1991; Howard H. Harvey 1991-1996; Patrick Glass 1996-1998; Larry W. Nalett 1998-Aug. 9, 2004; Charles E. Cerling Aug. 10, 2004-2009; Jolennda Cole (DSA) 2009-2010; Jolenda Cole 2010-2011; William F. Dye 2011-2012; Russell D. Morgan (CLM) July 15, 2012-2014; Gerald A Erskine (DSA) 2014-Nov. 9, 2014; Gerald A Erskine Nov. 10, 2014-2020; Melissa S. Wagner (DSA) 2020-

Paradise UMC *[Northern Skies]*   marybrooks729@gmail.com
(P) 7087 N M123, Paradise 49768; (M) PO Box 193, Paradise 49768   (906) 492-3585
   Wayne T. Large 1968-1970; Robert N. Hicok 1970-1974; William E. Miles 1974-1975; Ralph A. Edwards 1975-1979; David J. Hill 1979-1980; David K. Campbell 1980-1981; Douglas Paterson 1981-1982; James W. Robinson 1982-1983; Julaine A. Hays 1983-1984; Ramona E. Cowling 1984-1985; Melinda R. Cree 1985-1986; Ray S. Peterson 1986-1989; Jan L. Beaderstadt 1989-1991; Audrey M. Dunlap 1991-1993; Donald Bates 1993-Sep 30, 1996; Barbra Franks Oct 1, 1996-1998; Donald L. Bates 1998-2001; Virginia B. Bell 2001-Oct 30, 2005; Sandra J. Kolder Dec 4, 2005-2011; Lowell Peterson 2011-2013; Mary D. Brooks (DSA) 2013-

Parchment UMC *[Greater Southwest]*   parchmentumc@tds.net
(P/M) 225 Glendale Blvd, Parchment 49004   (269) 234-40125
   Wayne Groat Feb. 1968-Feb. 1969; James W. Dempsey March 1969-1973; Gaylord D. Howell 1973-1978; David S. Yoh Sept. 1978-1989; Daniel J. Minor 1989-2011; Michael J. Tupper 2011-2016; Thomas A. Davenport 2016-

Paris UMC *[Midwest]*
(P) 109 Lincoln, Paris 49338; (M) 226 N Third Ave, Big Rapids 49307   (231) 796-4157
   Richard Wilson 1968-1971; Lynn Chapel 1971-1979; John Buker 1979-1981; Elaine Buker 1981-1986; Kendall Lewis 1986-1990; J. Robert Collins 1990-Oct. 1991; David F. Hills 1992-1994; Kathryn M. Steen 1994-2000; Dawn A. Beamish Jan. 1, 2001-2002; Edwin D. Snook 2002-2005; Michael A. Riegler Sept. 11, 2005-2011; Ed Milam (DSA) July 1-Nov. 12, 2011; Ed Milam Nov. 12, 2011-2014; David J. Cadarette Sr. 2014-April 12, 2015; Kimberly A. DeLong 2015-2017; Devon R. Herrell 2017-2019; Morgan William (Bill) Davis (DSA) 2019-

Parmelee UMC *[Midwest]*   wvcleggjr@gmail.com
(P) 9266 W Parmalee Rd, Middleville 49333; (M) PO Box 237, Middleville 49333   (269) 795-8816
Edward D. Passenger 1966-1969; Robert Boyer 1969-1971; Lloyd Van Lente 1971-1976; Adam Chyrowski 1976-1980; Robert Tomlinson 1980-1981; Arthur Jackson 1981-Aug. 1983; Carl Staser Oct. 1983-1988; Lynn W. Wagner 1988-1996; Lee F. Zachman 1996-2004; Lee F. Zachman (1/2 time) 2004-Nov. 30, 2010; Vance Dimmick (DSA) (1/4 time) Nov. 28, 2010-Nov. 5, 2012; William V. Clegg, Jr (Ret.) (1/4 time) Nov. 11, 2012-

Paw Paw UMC *[Greater Southwest]*   pawpawunitedmethodistchurch@gmail.com
(P/M) 420 W Michigan Ave, Paw Paw 49079   (269) 657-7727
William Payne 1965-1979; Paul Patterson 1979-1984; Keith Laidler 1984-1989; Ward N. Scovel 1989-1995; Robert K. Lynch 1995-1999; Carolin S. Spragg 1999-2007; Joseph L. Spackman 2007-2013; Trevor J. McDermont 2013-2016; David E. Small 2016-

Pentwater Centenary UMC *[Midwest]*   pentwaterumc@gmail.com
(P) 82 S Hancock, Pentwater 49449; (M) PO Box 111, Pentwater 49449   (231) 869-5900
W. Jackson 1967-1970; Glenn B. Britton 1970-1973; Clyde Miller 1973-1979; Charles M. Johnson 1979-1982; Milton John Palmer 1982-1985; Gary T. Haller 1985-1993; Christopher P. Momany 1993-Dec. 31, 1996; Curtis E. Jensen Jan. 16, 1996-2001; Michael J. Tupper 2001-2006; Harris J. Hoekwater 2006-2012; Gary L. Bekofske 2012-2014; Melanie S. Young 2014-2018; William E. Haggard 2018-

Perry UMC *[Mid-Michigan]*   pastornancy@live.com
(P) 131 Madison St, Perry 48872; (M) PO Box 15, Perry 48872-0015   (517) 625-3444
Karl W. Patow 1962-1969; Ivan Niswender 1969-1971; David Draggoo 1971-1981; Jeff Siker-Giesler 1981-1983; Harris Hoekwater 1983-Jan. 1992; Clinton McKinven-Copus Feb. 1992-Dec. 31, 1994; Pulpit Supply Jan. 1-April 15, 1995; Carroll A. Fowler April 16, 1995-2003; Carolyn C. Floyd 2003-2008; Raymond R. Sundell 2008-2012; Nancy G. Powers 2012-2020; Rey C. Mondragon 2020-

Petersburg UMC *[Heritage]*   pastor@petersburgumc.org
(P) 152 Saline St, Petersburg 49270; (M) PO Box 85, Petersburg 49270   (734) 279-1118
Philip D. Miles 1967-1970; Donald L. Bates 1971-1976; Basil W. Curtiss 1976-1980; Howard L. Deardorff 1980-1981; William Michael Clemmer 1981-1984; Thomas C. Anderson 1984-Dec. 31, 1989; Max L. Gibbs Feb. 1, 1990-1991; June M. Westgate 1991-1996; John M. Mehl, Jr. 1996-Oct 1, 2008; King W. Hanna (interim) Oct 15, 2008-Jan 15, 2009; Robert Dister (interim) Jan 28, 2009-Mar 1, 2009; King W. Hanna Mar 1, 2009-Dec 31, 2009; Janet L. Luchs Jan 1, 2010-2011; Joel Walther 2011-2017; Daniel Hyer 2017-2018; Carter Louis Cortelyou 2018

Petoskey UMC *[Northern Waters]*   info@petoskeyumc.org
(P/M) 1804 E Mitchell Rd, Petoskey 49770   (231) 347-2733
Ralph P. Witmer 1964-Sept. 1970; Charles L. Manker Sept. 1970-Oct. 15, 1975; Donald H. Merrill Oct. 15, 1975-1986; Charles W. Fullmer 1986-April 30, 1994; Don W. Eddy March 1, 1994-Dec. 1996; James P. Mitchum 1997-

Pickford UMC *[Northern Skies]*   pickfordumc@gmail.com
(P) 115 E Church St, Pickford 49774; (M) PO Box 128, Pickford 49774   (906) 647-6195
Ralph H. Pieper 1969-1975; Richard Beemer 1975-1981; Howard Shaffer 1981-1986; Lawson D. Crane 1986-1993; James M. Mathews 1993-1996; Lynn F. Chappell 1996-May 1, 2003; Paul J. Gruenberg 2003-2012; Larry D. Osweiler 2012-2014; Timothy T. Bashore 2014-

Pierson: Heritage UMC *[Midwest]*   church.heritageumc@gmail.com
(P/M) 19931 W Kendaville Rd, Pierson 49339   (231) 937-4310
Richard D. Moore Aug. 1 1999-2000; Mark Mitchell (Assoc.) Aug. 1, 1999-2000; Thomas E. Ball 2000-2007; James Bradley Brillhart, 2007-2014; Stephan Weinberger 2014-Mar. 1, 2016; Charles R. Kaliszewski (DSA) Mar. 1-June 30, 2016; Terri L. Cummins 2016-

Pigeon: First UMC *[Central Bay]* pigeonfirstumc@gmail.com
(P) 7102 Michigan Ave, Pigeon 48755; (M) PO Box 377, Pigeon 48755 (989) 453-2475
Meldon E. Crawford 1966-1970; Webley J. Simpkins 1970-1975; Martin G. Seitz 1975-1979; Ralph C. Pratt 1979-1980; Gordon Wayne Nusz 1980-1988; James P. Schwandt 1988-Aug 31, 1994; Willard A. King Sep 31, 1994-1998; Karen L. Knight 1998-2001; Margaret A. Passenger 2001-2005; John J. Britt 2005-2015; Cindy L. Gibbs 2015-

Pigeon: Salem UMC *[Central Bay]* salemumc@avci.net
(P) 23 Mabel St, Pigeon 48755; (M) PO Box 438, Pigeon 48755-0438 (989) 453-2552
Raymond F. Roe 1968-1971; Sam H. Evans 1971-1975; Ralph H. Pieper II 1975-1983; Mark A. Karls 1983-1986; Timothy S. Hastings 1986-1990; Steven A. Miller 1990-Jan 31, 1995; Calvin Long Jun 1, 1995-2000; Gary A. Allward 2000-Nov 30, 2000; Michael T. Sawicki 2001-2009; Gloria Haynes 2009-2012; John K. Benissan 2012-2013; David K. Stewart, Sr. 2013; David K. Stewart, Sr. (Ret.) Jul 1-Aug 31, 2020; J. Albert Barchue Sept 1, 2020-

Pinckney: Arise UMC *[Heritage]* arise@arisechurch.org
(P/M) 11211 Dexter Pinckney Rd, Pinckney 48169 (734) 878-1928
Douglas J. McMunn Jan 1, 1996-2006; Donald S. Weatherup 2006-2018; Reed P. Swanson 2018-

Pinconning UMC *[Central Bay]* pumchurch@centurytel.net
(P/M) 314 Whyte St, Pinconning 48650-8606 (989) 879-3271
Byron G. Hatch (w/Garfield) 1969-1971; Richard Turner (w/Garfield) 1971-1981; Richard Turner 1981-1983; James M. Thompson 1983-1990; Donald Emmert Feb 16, 1990-1995; Gerald S. Hunter 1995-1999; Lawrence C., Brooks 1999-2002; Dorothy J. Thon 2002-2007; Charles Marble (interim) 2007-2008; Donald Mosher 2008-2010; John Tousciuk 2011- Agu 31, 2016; Heather M. Nowak (DSA) Oct 1, 2016 - Nov 30, 2017; Heather M. Nowak Dec 1, 2017-2020; [Pinconning, Alger became 2-point charge 2020] Janet Shaffer (DSA) 2020-

Pine River Parish: Ashton UMC *[Northern Waters]* srloomis1@gmail.com
(P) 20862 11 Mile Rd, Leroy 49655; (M) PO Box 38, Leroy 49655-0038 (231) 832-8347
David Dryer April 1968-1974; Ilona Sabo-Schuler 1974-1977; Robert Boyer 1977-1979; Harold R. Simon 1979-1983; Mark Gaylord-Miles 1983-Jan. 1985; Pulpit Supply Jan.-June 1985; Douglas Kokx 1985-1991; Robert W. Stark 1991-1996; Valerie M. Sisson Sept. 16, 1996-1998; Valerie M. Hill 1998-1999; David A. Cheyne 1999-2003; Jodie R. Flessner 2003-2012; Scott R. Loomis 2012-

Pine River Parish: LeRoy UMC *[Northern Waters]* srloomis1@gmail.com
(P) 310 West Gilbert St, LeRoy 49655; (M) PO Box 38, Leroy 49655-0038 (231) 768-4512
David Dryer 1968-1974; Ilona Sabo-Schuler 1974-1977; Robert Boyer 1977-1979; Harold R. Simon 1979-1983 Mark Gaylord-Miles 1983-Jan. 1985; Pulpit Supply Jan.-June 1985; Douglas Kokx 1985-1991; Robert Stark 1991-1996; Valerie M. Sisson Sept. 16, 1996-1998; Valerie M. Hill 1998-1999; David A. Cheyne 1999-2003; Jodie R. Flessner 2003-2012; Scott R. Loomis 2012-

Pine River Parish: Luther UMC *[Northern Waters]* srloomis1@gmail.com
(P) 315 State St, Luther 49656; (M) PO Box 175, Luther 49656-0175 (231) 797-0073
David Dryer 1968-1974; Ilona Sabo-Schuler 1974-1977; Robert Boyer 1977-1979; Harold Simon 1979-1983; Mark Gaylord-Miles 1983-Dec. 1984; Pulpit Supply Jan.-June 1985; Douglas Kokx 1985-1991; Robert Stark 1991-April 1993; Reva Hawke May 1993-1995; Mary S. Brown 1995-Oct. 15, 1998; David A. Cheyne Jan. 16, 1999-June 30, 1999; Nelson Hall 1999-2005; Karen J. Sorden 2005-2012; James A. Richio 2012 Jan. 31, 2015; [Luther was added to Pine River Parish: Ashton/Leroy/Luther 2015] Scott R. Loomis 2015-

Pinnebog UMC *[Central Bay]* pacharge@hotmail.com
(P/M) 4619 Pinnebog Rd, Kinde 48445 (989) 738-5322
Elizabeth D.K. Isaacs 1969-1970; Robert P. Garrett 1970-1989; Barbara E. Welbaum 1989-1992; Raymond A Jacques 1992-1997; Earleen VanConant 1997-Dec 31, 1999; Robert P. Garrett 2000-2002; David C. Freeland 2002-2013; Nancy J. Bitterling 2013-2018; Clifford L. Radtke 2018-

Pittsburg UMC *[East Winds]*   heiligj@michonline.net
(P) 2960 W Grand River Rd, Owosso 48867; (M) c/o Janet Demerly, Treasurer, 3888 W Brewer Rd,
Owosso 48867   (810) 208-0648
   Lawrence C. Brooks 1969-1972; Terry A. Euper 1972-1976; James E. Paige, Jr. 1976-1980;
   Margaret A. Paige (Co-Pastor) 1977-1980; Charles J. Bamberger 1980-1990; Donald Woolum
   1990-1993; John H. Schneider, Jr. 1993-1997; Penney Meints 1997-1998; Arthur R. Turner 1998-
   2004; Jeremy T. Peters 2004-2008; Jeremy P. Benton 2008-2011; Don Wentz 2011-2015; Joyce
   Wallace Oct 1, 2015-2018; Brian G. West 2018-2020; [Pittsburg became single station 2-1-2020]
   Terry Melton (DSA) Feb 1, 2020- ;

Plainwell First UMC *[Greater Southwest]*   plainwellumc@gmail.com
(P) 200 Park St, Plainwell 49080; (M) PO Box 85, Plainwell 49080-0085   (269) 685-5113
   Emerson B. Minor 1964-1984; James W. Boehm 1984-1989; Raymond Townsend (Assoc.) 1988-
   1991; David B. Nelson, Jr. 1989-1991; Frank W. Lyman, Jr. and Carole Strobe Lyman (co-pastors)
   1991-1996; Charles D. Grauer 1996-2003; Cindy E. Holmquist (Assoc.) 2001-June 30, 2003;
   Harvey K. Prochnau 2003-2010; Barbara Jo Fay (Assoc.) 2007-2010; Kathy E. Brown 2010-

Pleasant Lake UMC *[Heritage]*   peasechris@yahoo.com
(P) 4815 E Territorial Rd, Pleasant Lake 49272; (M) PO Box 83, Pleasant Lake 49272
                                                                         (517) 543-5618
   Frederick Werth 1967-1971; Bert L. Cole March 1972-1973; Larry Irvine 1973-1975; Thomas Adams
   1976-1978; James Barney 1979-1983; Linda Farmer-Lewis 1983-1986; Milton TenHave 1986-1990;
   Laurie McKinven-Copus 1990-Sept. 1991; Robert Marston Oct. 1991-1998; Judith A. Nielson 1998-
   2000; Charles E. Cerling 2000-Aug. 9, 2004; Arthur R. Turner 2004-Nov. 15, 2005; Kenneth Karlzen
   (DSA) Dec. 2005-2006; Maurice Walworth (DSA) 2006-Sept. 30, 2007; Thomas Peters (DSA) Oct.
   1, 2007-Apr. 23, 2008; [Pleasant Lake & Jackson Zion became two-point charge 2008] David H.
   Minger (DSA) 2008-2013; [Pleasant Lake became single-point charge 2013] [M-52 Cooperative
   Ministry 2013-2014] Jeanne M. Laimon (1/4 time) 2013-2014; Christine L. Pease (DSA) 2014-

Pleasant Valley UMC *[Heritage]*   jrhumenik@gmail.com
(P) 9300 West XY Ave, Schoolcraft 49087; (M) PO Box 517, Schoolcraft 49087   (269) 679-5352
   Robert J. Stillson 1963-1969; Vern Michael 1969-1970; Roger Nielson 1970-1971; Lay Speakers
   1971-1972; Dale Benton 1972-1978; John W. Fisher 1978-1980; Dale Crawford 1980-1983; Dwight
   J. Burton 1983-1992; Laura Truby 1992-1996; Ronald S. Scholte 1996-2000; Larry Reeves 2000;
   Michelle Wisdom-Long 2001-2008; [Schoolcraft Pleasant Valley / White Pigeon became a two-
   point charge 2008] Janet Luchs 2008-2009; [Three Rivers Ninth / Schoolcraft Pleasant Valley
   became a two-point charge 2009] James W. Stilwell 2009-2015; [Schoolcraft/Pleasant Valley
   became a charge 2015] Julia R. Humenik 2015-

Plymouth: First UMC *[Heritage]*   liz@pfumc.org
(P/M) 45201 N Territorial Rd, Plymouth 48170   (734) 453-5280
   Ronald K. Corl (assoc) 1967-1971; Paul M. Cargo 1968-1975; Dean A. Klump (assoc) 1971-1974;
   Samuel F. Stout 1975-1980; Dale M. Miller (assoc) 1974-1976; Dwayne L. Kelsey (assoc) 1976-
   1978; Frederick C. Vosburg (assoc) 1976-1993; Frank W. Lyman Jr. (assoc) 1978-1981; John N.
   Grenfell Jr. 1980-1993; Thomas E. Sumwalt (assoc) 1980-1982; Stephen E. Wenzel (assoc) 1982-
   1985; Larry J. Werbil (assoc) 1985-1986; Douglas J. McMunn (assoc) 1986-Feb. 1990; David K.
   Stewart Sr. (assoc) 1990-1991; Kevin L. Miles (assoc) 1991-1995; Merton W. Seymour 1993-1995;
   Dean A. Klump 1995-2007; Tonya M. Arnesen (assoc.) 1995-May 31, 2000; Deborah S. Thomas
   (assoc) Jun 1, 2000-2004; Jeremy P. Africa (assoc.) Jun 1, 2005-2006; David Allen Wichert (assoc.)
   2006-2010; John N. Grenfell, III 2007-2018; Elizabeth A. Librande (assoc.) 2010-Feb 15, 2014;
   Nicholas R. Berlanga Feb 15, 2014-2018; Robert A. Miller Jr. 2018- ; Suzanne L. Hutchison (assoc.)
   2018-

Pokagon UMC *[Greater Southwest]* PokagonUMC@aol.com
(P/M) 31393 Kansas St, Dowagiac 49047 (269) 683-8515
Albert A. O'Rourke 1962-1974; Harold Deipert 1974-1977; Gary D. Kintigh 1977-1981; Michael Conklin 1981-1983; Theodore H. Bennink (retired, part-time) 1983-1984; Reva Hawke 1984-1988; Beatrice Rose 1988-1990; Claude Ridley (retired) May 1-Nov. 1, 1990; Theodore Bennink (retired) Nov. 1, 1990-April 30, 1991; Claude Ridley (retired May 1-Nov. 1, 1991; Richard Muessig (DSA) Nov. 1, 1991-April 30, 1992; Claude Ridley (retired) May 1-Aug. 30, 1992; Richard Muessig Sept. 1992-2001; Valerie Fons 2001-2003; Patrica Ann Haas 2003-2011; Sean K. Kidd (DSA) (1/2 time) 2011-2014; [Berrien Springs/Pokagon became a 2-point charge 2014] Brenda E. Gordon 2014-2018; William Walters (DSA) 2018-

Pompeii UMC *[Mid-Michigan]* billmona3@gmail.com
(P) 135 Burton St, Pompeii 48874; (M) PO Box 125, Pompeii 48874-0125 (989) 838-4159
Robert E. Tomlinson 1974-Jan. 1977; Donald L. Warmouth Feb. 1977-1978; Glenn Britton 1978-1979; Lois H. Gremban 1979-1981; Dale F. Jaquette Aug. 1981-April 1990; T. Ried Martin 1990-1993; Karen E. Nesius 1993-1994; Jodie Flessner 1994-2003; William F. Foldesi Nov. 16, 2003-Apr. 7, 2007; Clare Huyck (DSA) 2007; Clare Huyck Nov. 10, 2007-2012; William F. Dye July 15, 2012-Sept. 1, 2015 ; Mona J. Dye 2011-Sept. 30, 2017; [Ashley/Bannister realigned with Pompeii to become Ashley/Bannister/Pompeii charge 2016] Zella Marie Daniel (DSA) Oct. 3, 2017-Dec. 31, 2018; Zella Marie Daniel Jan. 1, 2019-

Pontiac: Grace & Peace Cmnty UMC *[Greater Detroit]* lward@graceandpeace.comcastbiz.net
(P/M) 451 W Kennett Rd, Pontiac 48340 (248) 334-3280
Dudley Mosure 1967-1969; Donald Bates 1969-1970; John Kershaw 1970-1975; Thomas Badley 1975-1978; Donald McClennan 1978-1979; Martin Caudill 1979-1984; James R. Rupert 1984-1987; Sylvia Bouvier 1987-1992; James Allen 1992-1994; Barbara E. Welbaum 1994-1997; Kenneth L. Bracken 1997-2006; Bea Barbara Fraser-Soots 2006-2014; Theodore D. Whitely, Sr. 2014-2015; Zelphia J. Mobley 2015-2019; Laurie M. Koivula 2019-

Pontiac: St. John UMC *[Greater Detroit]* st.johnpontiac@sbcglobal.net
(P/M) 620 University Dr, Pontiac 48342 (248) 338-8933
C.R. Trice 1968-1974; Henry Johnson 1975-1980; Andrew Allie 1981- May 1991; Frederick Moore, Sr. 1992-2008; Johnnie L. Dyer (assoc) 2000-2004; Gary A. Williams 2008-2009; Andrew Allie 2009-2010; Karel Y. Noel 2010-Sep 15, 2013; Lester Mangum Oct 1, 2013-

Pope UMC *[Heritage]*
(P) 10025 N Parma Rd, Springport 49284; (M) PO Box 419, Eaton Rapids, MI 48827
(517) 857-3655
Lambert G. McClintic 1952-1995; Jack Fugate 1995-July 15, 2008; Irene Vittoz (part-time) 2009-2010; Robert S. Moore-Jumonville 2010-2018; Lawrence J. Embury 2018-

Portage: Chapel Hill UMC *[Greater Southwest]* office@pchum.org
(P/M) 7028 Oakland Dr, Portage 49024 (269) 327-6643
David Nelson 1968-1972; Dow Chamberlain 1972-1978; Jon Powers July-August 1978; Joseph Bistayi Sept. 1978-1985; William Torrey 1985-1989; Carl Hausermann 1989-2001; Julie A. Liske (Assoc.) 1994-Nov. 30, 1997; Susan M. Petro (Assoc.) Jan. 1, 1998-2007; Barry Thayer Petrucci 2001- ; John M. Weiler (Assoc.) 2007-2011; Cara Weiler (deacon 1/4 time) Oct. 1, 2007-Oct. 1, 2009; Virginia L. Heller (Assoc.) 2011-2013; Caleb B. Williams (Deacon) 2015-Sept. 1, 2016; Patricia L. Catellier (Deacon) Jan. 1, 2016-2020; Jessica M. Davenport (assoc) 2020-

CHURCH HISTORIES

Portage: Pathfinder UMC *[Greater Southwest]*   office@pathfinderchurch.com
(P/M) 8740 S Westnedge Ave, Portage 49002   (269) 327-6761
    Donald Scranton 1967-1970; Paul Albery 1970-1975; Kenneth McCaw 1975-1983; Logan Weaver (Assoc.) Oct. 1, 1980; Royce Robinson 1983-Dec. 1986; Robert Hinklin March 1987-1998; Logan Weaver (Pastor Emeritus, Assoc.) Jan. 1, 1988; William J. Torrey (Ret. Assoc.) 1993-1995; Gregory B. Wood 1998-2015; John L. Moore (Ret. Assoc.) (DSA), Oct. 1, 2006-2013; Ronald W. Hansen (Ret.) 2015-2016; Donald W. Wolfgang 2016-

Portland UMC *[Mid-Michigan]*   portlandmiumc@gmail.com
(P/M) 310 E Bridge St, Portland 48875   (517) 647-4649
    Raymond Norton 1967-1969; Donald Cozadd 1969-1971; Carlton Benson 1971-1973; Harold Homer 1973-1978; C. Dow Chamberlain 1978-Nov. 1985; David Evans (interim) Nov. 1985-Feb. 1986; Dale Crawford Feb.-Oct. 1986; David Evans (interim) Oct. 1986-Feb. 1987; Stanley Finkbiener 1987-1992; Elaine M. Buker 1992-1997; Scott K. Otis 1997-2003; Gregory Ryan Wolfe 2003-2008; Keith R. Treman 2008-2015; Letisha M. Bowman 2015-

Port Austin U.P.C. UMC *[Central Bay]*   pacharge@hotmail.com
(P) 8625 Arch; Port Austin 48467; (M) PO Box 129, Port Austin 48467   (989) 738-5322
    William Small 1967-1968; Robert P. Garrett 1968-1989; Barbara E. Welbaum 1989-1992; Raymond A Jacques 1992-1997; Earleen VanConant 1997-Dec 31, 1999; Robert P. Garrett 2000-2002; David C. Freeland 2002-2013; Nancy J. Bitterling 2013-2018; Clifford L. Radtke 2018-

Port Hope UMC *[East Winds]*
(P) 4521 Main St, Port Hope 48468; (M) PO Box 25, Harbor Beach 48441   (989) 479-6053
    Robert P. Garrett 1968-1970; Thomas G. Badley 1970-1973; William M. Smith 1974-1978; Brent L. Webster 1978-1983; Wayne A. Hawley 1983-1991; Kris S. Kappler 1991- 1997; Victoria M. Webster 1997-1999; Clarence W. VanConant 1999-2004; Paula M. Timm 2004-2011; Mark E. Ryan 2012-Sept 18, 2016; Sari L. Brown 2017-

Port Huron: First UMC *[East Winds]*   phfumc@advnet.net
(P/M) 828 Lapeer Ave, Port Huron 48060   (810) 985-8107
    John N. Grenfell Jr. 1968-1974; William Schlitts (assoc) 1968-1972; Donna J. Lindberg (assoc) 1972-1973; Harry R. Weeks (assoc) 1973-1975; O. William Cooper Jr. 1974-1979; James D. Jacobs (assoc) 1975-1977; Dana R. Strall (assoc) 1977-1980; Paul F. Blomquist 1979-1985; William G. Wager (assoc) 1980-1984; Jacqueline E. Holdsworth (assoc) 1981-1983; Robert D. Wright (assoc) 1983-1985; Richard D. Lobb 1985-1992; Trevor A. Herm (assoc) Jan. 1 1986-1989; Jeffery L. Jaggers (assoc) Jan 1 1990-1994; John C. Huhtala 1992-1996; Kevin C. Zaborney (assoc) 1994-1997; Ralph H. Pieper, II 1996-2003;Connie S. Porter (assoc) 1997-Nov 1, 1998; AmyLee Brun Terhune (assoc) 1999-2002; David G. Gladstone 2003-2012; Alicea L. Williams (deacon) Oct 1, 2007-Oct 25, 2011; William R. Wright 2012-2017; LuAnn Lee Rourke 2017-2020; Wilson A. (Drew) Hart 2020-

Port Huron: Gratiot Park UMC *[East Winds]*
(P/M) 811 Church St, Port Huron 48060   (810) 985-6206
    Harold J. Slater 1969-1970; Grant A. Washburn 1970-1973; Lloyd E. Christler 1973-1978; John N. Howell 1978-1981; S. Joe Robertson 1981-1985; Robert E. Burkey 1985-1988; Donald R. Sperling 1988-1996; Georg F. W. Gerritsen 1996-Dec 31, 1999; Susan K. Freeland Jan 1, 2000-2001; Robert D. Chapman 2001-2014; Penelope P. Nunn 2014-2018; [Port Huron: Wasihton Ave. UMC merged with Port Huron: Gratiot Park 07/01/2018] Eric J. Miller-2018

Port Sanilac UMC *[East Winds]*
(P) 7225 Main St, Port Sanilac 48469; (M) 7209 Main St, Port Sanilac 48469   (810) 622-0001
James B. Lumsden 1969-1973; J. Paul Pumphrey 1973-1977; Glenn R. Wegner 1977-1980; James P. Kummer Dec. 1980-1985; Kenneth C. Reeves 1985-1991; Gloria Haynes 1991-1996; James M. Thompson 1996-1999; Catherine W. J. Hiner 1999-2004; Clarence W. VanConant 2004-2007; Eric L. Johnson 2007-2012; Ellen Burns 2013-2016; Mark Harriman 2016-2018; Anika Bailey 2018-

Quincy UMC *[Heritage]*   umcquincy@gmail.com
(P/M) 32 W Chicago St, Quincy 49082   (517) 639-5035
W. Ernest Combellack 1967-1969; Jack Bartholomew 1969-1974; Bruce Keegstra 1974-1977; Kay Williams 1977-1979; Jim Gysel 1979-1983; James Barney 1983-1987; Joan Hamlin 1987-1994; Jane D. Logston 1994-1996; John Knowlton 1996-1998; Melanie S. Young 1998-Oct. 1, 1998; Charles A. Williams Jan. 1, 1999-2003; John A. Scott & Rebecca Scott (CoPastors) Sept. 2003-2007; Geraldine M. Litchfield 2007-2009; [Litchfield/Quincy two-point charge 2009] Michael P. Baker-Streevy 2009-2010; Martin T. Cobb 2010-2013; Julie Elmore 2013-2017; [Quincy UMC became single station 2017] Richard D. Wilson (Ret.) 2017-2020; [Allen, Quincy became 2-point charge 2020] Larry W. Rubingh (Ret.) 2020-

Quinnesec: First UMC *[Northern Skies]*   QuinnesecUMC@yahoo.com
(P) 677 Division, Quinnesec 49876; (M) PO Box 28, Quinnesec 49876   (906) 774-7971
Richard Reese 1967-1971; Monroe Fredrick 1971-1976; John Moore 1976-1980; James Hall 1980-1983; Paul Doering 1983-1984; James Mathews 1984-1989; Douglas J. McMunn 1989-Dec 31, 1995; Scott A. Harmon 1996-1998; Pauline E. Rupe Aug 16,1998-2006; David P. Snyder Aug 1, 2006-2009; Margaret A.W. Paige 2009-2012; Walter P. Reichle 2012-

Ravenna UMC *[Midwest]*   ravennaumc@gmail.com
(P) 12348 Stafford St, Ravenna 49451; (M) PO Box 191, Ravenna 49451   (231) 853-6688
Harry R. Johnson 1967-Dec. 1968; William Foster Dec. 1968-1973; William Bowers 1973-1978; Lewis Buchner 1978-1983; Dennis Slattery 1983-1987; Kenneth Curtis 1987-1988; Rick Powell 1988-1991; Pamela Kail 1991-1994; Daniel B. Hofmann 1994-2001; Mary Bement Ivanov 2001-2008; Charles W. Smith 2008-2011; Carleton R. Black (DSA) 2011; Carleton R. Black Nov. 12, 2011-2020; David A. Selleck 2020-

Reading UMC *[Heritage]*   office@readingumc.com
(P) 312 E Michigan St, Reading 49274; (M) PO Box 457, Reading 49274-0457
Harold Cox 1968-Sept. 1969; William Bowers Sept. 1969-1972; Eric Johnson 1972-1975; Dennis Paulson 1975-1979; Altha M. Barnes 1979-1983; Harold R. Simon 1983-March 1990; Dale F. Jaquette April 1990-1992; Thomas P. Fox 1992-1999; Kathy L. Nitz Aug. 16, 1999-July 31, 2001; Gayle Berntsen Sept. 1, 2001-2006; Nancy G. Powers 2006-2008; DeAnn J. Dobbs 2008-2012; Robert M. Hughes 2012-2014; Deborah S. Cole Sept. 1, 2014-

Redford: Aldersgate UMC *[Greater Detroit]*   redfordaldersgatge@sbcglobal.net
(P/M) 10000 Beech Daly Rd, Redford 48239   (313) 937-3170
William G. Wager 1966-1980; William W. Smith (assoc) 1968-1974; David K. Koski (assoc) 1974-1977; Thomas F. Keef (assoc.) 1977-1980; Archie H. Donigan 1980-1985; Barbara J. Byers Lewis (assoc) 1981-1985; Randy J. Whitcomb (assoc) 1985-1988; M. Clement Parr 1985-Aug 31, 1994; Troy Douthit (assoc) 1988-1990; Bufford Coe (assoc) 1990-1994; Diana Goudie (co-pastor) Sep 1, 1994-2003; Robert Goudie co-pastor Sep 1, 1994-2003; Diana Goudie 2003-2009; [merged with Redford: Redford, 2005]; Jeffrey S. Nelson 2009-2016; Jonathan Combs (assoc) 2015- ; Benjamin Bower 2016-

Redford: Aldersgate - Brightmoore Campus UMC *[Greater Detroit]*
(P) 12065 W Outer Dr, Detroit 48223; (M) 10000 Beech Daly Rd, Redford 48239   (313) 937-3170
[Satellite of Redford: Aldersgate] Jonathan Combs (assoc) 2015-

Redford: New Beginnings UMC *[Greater Detroit]*   newbeginningsumc@sbcglobal.net
(P/M) 16175 Deleware Ave, Redford 48240   (313) 255-6330
   Gregory E. Rowe Jan 1, 2005-2006; Kenneth B. Ray 2006-2007; John H. Amick 2007-2008; Ronald
   L.F. Iris 2008-Apr 1, 2009; John J. Pajak Apr 1, 2009-2015; Diane Covington 2015-

Reed City UMC *[Heritage]*   office@readingumc.com
(P/M) 503 S Chestnut St, Reed City 49677   (231) 832-9441
   Charles W. Fullmer 1966-1970; Forrest E. Mohr 1970-1977; Allen D. McCreedy 1977-1990; Richard
   L. Matson 1990-1993; Gregory J. Martin 1993-Dec. 1, 1998; Jennifer Browne (Assoc.) Jan. 15,
   1997-Dec. 1, 1998; Richard W. Blunt Feb. 1, 1999-2008; Emmett H. Kadwell, Jr. 2008-2011; Kathryn
   S. Cadarette 2011-2019; Kristen I. Coristine 2019-

Reese UMC *[Central Bay]*   pastorgougeon@gmail.com
(P) 1968 Rhodes St, Reese 48757; (M) PO Box 7, Reese 48757-0007   (989) 868-9957
   Donald Pinner 1968-1970; Edgar M. Smith 1970-1976; Monroe J. Frederick 1976-1988; Sang Yoon
   (Abraham) Chun 1988-1992; James P. James 1992-1996; Steven J. Woodford 1996-2000;
   Raymond D. Wightman 2000-2003; Jean M. Larson 2003-Dec 31, 2007; Harold J. Slater 2008-
   Feb 28, 2010; Jon W. Gougeon Mar 1, 2010-

Republic UMC *[Northern Skies]*   hdrider2@chartermi.net
(P) 216 Front, Republic 49879; (M) PO Box 395, Republic 49879   (906) 376-2389
   Michael Peterlin 1969-1970; Ronald Lindner 1970-1972; Alden Thomas 1972-1974; Alan Larsen
   1974-1978; James Mathews 1978-1984; Charles Keyworth 1984-1988; Robert Duggan 1988-1990;
   Nicholas W. Scroggins 1990-1993; Fred A. LaMere 1993-1996; Terry J. Kordish 1996-2000; Gary
   I. Stevens 2000-2004; James A. Fegan 2004-2009; Mark E. Ryan 2009-2012; Terri L. Branstrom
   2012-2016; Peter A. LeMoine 2016-

Richfield UMC *[East Winds]*   pastorshellyRUMC@comcast.net
(P) 10090 E Coldwater Rd, Davison 48423; (M) PO Box 307, Davison 48423   (248) 417-1196
   Beatrice Townsend 1969-1971; Basel W. Curtiss 1971-1976; Brent Webster 1976-1979; Charles
   H. West 1979-Mar. 1988; Dennis Norris 1988-1989; Paul G. Donelson 1989-1990; Robert D. Harvey
   1990-1994; Dorothy J. Rossman Nov 16, 1994-2002; T. Bradly Terhune 2002-2007; James E.
   Paige, Jr. 2007-2008; Jannie L. Plum 2008-2012; Barbara Benjamin Aug 1, 2012-2012; Barbara
   Benjamin 2012-2016; Shelly Ann Long 2016-

Richmond: First UMC *[East Winds]*   fumc@methodist.comcastbiz.net
(P) 69495 N Main St, Richmond 48062; (M) PO Box 293, Richmond 48062   (586) 727-2622
   Richard L. Myers 1969-1973; Roy Syme 1973-1983; Steven Gjerstad 1983-1984; Gary Beeker
   1984-1991; Karl L. Zeigler 1991-Aug 31, 1998; Reed P. Swanson Sep 1, 1998-2004; Trevor A.
   Herm 2004-2010; Thomas F. Keef 2010-2014; Suzanne L. Hutchison 2014-2018; Thomas Waller
   2018-

Riverdale: Lincoln Road UMC *[Mid-Michigan]*   lincolnroadumc@casair.net
(P/M) 9479 W Lincoln Rd, Riverdale 48877   (989) 463-5704
   John Buckner 1966-1972; Eldon Schram 1973-1977; Marvin Iseminger 1977-1979; Milton TenHave
   1979-1986; Jane Lippert 1986-1990; Beatrice Rose 1990-1995; Kenneth C. Reeves 1995-1997;
   Lois M. Munn 1997-2000; Charles M. Shields 2000-2002; Nancy J. Bitterling 2002-2010; Jana Lynn
   Almeida 2010-2016; Linda (Lyne) K. Stull-Lipps 2016-

Riverside UMC *[Greater Southwest]* riverside_umc@att.net
(P) 4401 Fikes Rd, Benton Harbor 49022; (M) PO Box 152, Riverside 49084 (269) 849-1131
George Chaffee 1968-1971; Carl L. Hausermann 1971-1977; Elizabeth Perry Nord 1976-Oct. 1986;
Mark Thompson Jan. 1987-Nov. 15, 1992; Norman C. Kohns Nov. 16, 1992-1993; Jackie Bralick
1993-Feb. 1, 1995; Pulpit Supply Feb.-April 1995; Alan D. Stover May 1, 1995-Sept. 25, 1997; John
Sternaman Dec. 1, 1997-2002; Michael R. Bohms 2002-Dec. 31, 2003; Thomas Meyer (DSA) Feb.
1, 2004-June 30, 2004; Sheila F. Baker 2004-2005; Russell K. Logston 2005-2006; Walter G.
Gerstung (DSA) July 1, 2006; David S. Yoh (DSA), Oct. 4, 2006-2009; Stephen C. Small (DSA)
2009-2014; David L. Haase 2014-

Riverview UMC *[Greater Detroit]* TheRiverviewUMC@att.net
(P/M) 13199 Colvin St, Riverview 48193 (734) 284-2721
Robert C. Watt 1968-1973; J. Bruce Brown 1973-1981; William A. Cargo 1981-1988; Michael
Grajcar 1988-1989; Gary A. Allward 1989-1996; June M. Westgate 1996-2001; David D. Amstutz
2001-2012; Gloria Haynes 2012-Aug 1, 2015; Alan Hansen Aug 1, 2015-2016; Keith Lenard 2016-
2017; Daniel J.W. Phillips 2017-2019; Carol Ann Middel 2019-

Robbins UMC *[Mid-Michigan]* robbins@robbinsumc.org
(P/M) 6419 Bunker Rd, Eaton Rapids 48827 (517) 663-5226
Maurice Glasgow 1966-1977; Joseph Huston 1977-1982; Wade Panse 1982-1987; James P.
Mitchum 1987-1997; Martin M. DeBow 1997-2008; Bobby Dale Whitlock 2008-2009; Mark R. Payne
2009-2014; Peggy A. Katzmark 2014- [Robbins, Brookfield Eaton became 2-point charge 2020]

Rochester Hills: St. Luke's UMC *[Greater Detroit]* stlukesrh@gmail.com
(P/M) 3980 Walton Blvd, Rochester Hills 48309 (248) 373-6960
David E. Church 1968-1970; Daniel Krichbaum 1970-1972; Harold Morse 1972-1977; R. Stantley
Sutton 1977- Aug. 1982; Wayne N. Thomas Oct. 1982-Jan. 1984; David B. Penniman May 1, 1984-
1989; Jeffrey B. Hildebrand 1989-1990; Johnny S. Liles Mar. 1990-2004; Sharyn K. Osmond (assoc)
Jan 16, 1999-2002; Lynda B. Hamilton (deacon) 1999- ; Murphy S. Ehlers (deacon) 2002-Dec 1,
2002; Lisa M. McIlvenna 2004-2008; Julius Del Pino 2008-2016; Scott E. Manning 2016-

Rochester: St. Paul's UMC *[Greater Detorit]* rachel@stpaulsrochester.org
(P) 620 Romeo Rd, Rochester 48307; (M) PO Box 80307, Rochester 48308 (248) 651-9361
William Richards 1967-1973; Timothy Hickey 1973-Sep 30, 2000; Athanasius P. Rickard (assoc)
1963-1975; Howard Short (assoc) 1967-1968; Loren Strait (assoc) 1968-1969; Douglas Trebilcock
(assoc) 1969-1973; Dale Lindsey (assoc) 1973; Thomas Badley (assoc) 1973-1975; Gilson Miller
(assoc) 1975-1978; Ronald Brunger (assoc) 1975-1979; Duane J. Hicks (assoc) 1978-1981; Ralph
A. Edwards (assoc) 1979-1985; Devin S. Chisholm (assoc) 1981-1983; James E. Greer, II (assoc)
1983-1987; James R. Hilliard (assoc)1985-1988; James P. Schwandt (assoc) 1987-1988; David
A. Diamond (assoc) 1988-1994; Samuel Stout (assoc) 1988-1990; Robert D. Wright (assoc) 1994-
1999; Joanne Bartelt (assoc) 1996-2000; Harold E. Weemhoff, Jr. (assoc) Jan 1, 2000-2008; Jeffrey
D. Regan Feb 1, 2001-2013; Rony S. (Hallstrom) Veska (assoc) Mar 1, 2001-2008; John Amick
(assoc) 2008-2012; Latha Ravi (assoc) 2008-2017; David A. Eardley 2013- ; Jon Reynolds (assoc.)
Jan 9, 2014-2018; Carter M. Grimmett (assoc.) 2017-2020; Erin L. Fitzgerald (assoc.) 2018-

Rockford UMC *[Midwest]* office@rockfordumc.org
(P/M) 159 Maple St, Rockford 49341 (616) 866-9515
Richard A. Selleck 1966-1970; Ron L. Keller 1970-1973; George A. Belknap 1973-1978; John S.
Myette 1978-1980; J. Melvin Bricker 1980-1989; Leonard F. Putnam (Assoc. part-time) 1984-1994;
William J. Torrey 1989-1993; Richard M. Riley 1993-2014; Jeffrey Charles Williams (Assoc.) 2002-
2004; Kenneth J. Bremer 2014-2017; Cynthia S.L. Greene 2017-2019; Gregory L. Buchner 2019-

Rockland: St. Paul UMC *[Northern Skies]*   ontmeth@jamadots.com
(P) 50 National Ave, Rockland 49960; (M) PO Box 216, Ontonagon 49953   (906) 886-2851
  Lloyd Christler 1968-1972; James Hillard 1970-1971; James Gerzetich 1971; Lawrence Brooks
  1971-1975; Roger Gedcke 1972-1979; Lillian Richards 1971-1976; Wayne E. Sparks 1975-1980;
  Myra Sparks 1976-1980; Ed Hingelburg 1976-1980; Brian Marshall 1980-1984; Donald J. Emmert
  1984-Feb 15, 1990; William D. Schoonover Feb 16, 1990-1991; Mel D. Rose 1992-1994; Lance E.
  Ness Sep 1, 1994-Dec 31, 1999; Christine F. Bohnsack Mar 1, 2000-2004; Cherrie A. Sporleder
  2004-2010; Bruce R. Steinberg 2010-2018; Nelson L. Hall 2018-

Rodney UMC *[Midwest]*
(P) 12135 Charles St, Rodney 49342; (M) PO Box 14, Rodney 49342-0014   (231) 796-4157
  Richard Wilson 1968-1971; Lynn Chapel 1971-1979; John Buker 1979-1981; Elaine Buker 1981-
  1986; Kendall Lewis 1986-1990; J. Robert Collins 1990-Oct. 1991; David F. Hills 1992-1994; Kathryn
  M. Steen 1994-2000; Dawn A. Beamish Jan. 1, 2001-2002; Edwin D. Snook 2002-2005; Michael
  A. Riegler Sept. 11, 2005-2011; Ed Milam (DSA) July 1-Nov. 12, 2011; Ed Milam Nov. 12, 2011-
  2014; David J. Cadarette Sr. 2014-April 12, 2015; Kimberly A. DeLong 2015-2017; Devon R. Herrell
  2017-2019; Morgan William (Bill) Davis (DSA) 2019-

Rollin Center UMC *[Heritage]*   clayton.rollincenter@gmail.com
(P) 3988 Townley Hwy, Manitou Beach 49253; (M) PO Box 98, Clayton 49235   (517) 445-2641
  Lawson D. Crane 1967-1975; Heath T. Goodwin 1975-1976; George F. Ward 1976- 1981; Walter
  H. Miller Nov 1, 1981-1994; Craig A. Pillow 1994-2009; Linda Jo Powers 2009-2012; Robert W.
  Dister 2012-

Romeo UMC *[East Winds]*   romeounited@sbcglobal.net
(P/M) 280 N Main St, Romeo 48065   (586) 752-9132
  J. Douglas Parker 1969-1973; Calvin Blue 1973-1981; Dean A. Klump 1981-1991; Dwayne L.
  Kelsey 1991-1996; Gary R. Glanville 1996-2015; John D. Bailey 2015-2017; Trevor A. Herm 2017-
  2020; Devin R. Smith 2020- [Romeo and Leonard formed cooperative parish 2020]

Romulus: Community UMC *[Greater Detroit]*   office@communityunited.comcastbiz.net
(P/M) 11160 Olive St, Romulus 48174   (734) 941-0736
  Frank R. Lieneke 1966-1971; Haldon D. Ferris 1971-1974; Paul I. Greer 1974-1977; Floyd A. Ellison
  1977-1981; Margery A. Schleicher 1981-1987; John D. Landis 1987-1994; Bradford K. Lewis 1994-
  1998; William Kren 1998-2006; Mark A. Miller 2006-2010; Cindy L. Gibbs 2010-2015; Rahim O.
  Shabazz 2015-2017; Rochelle J. Hunter 2017-Feb 28, 2018; James Reinker Mar 1, 2018-

Roscommon: Good Shepherd UMC *[Nothern Waters]*   office@gsumc-roscommon.com
(P/M) 149 W Robinson Lake Rd, Roscommon 48653   (989) 275-5577
  Kenneth L. Christler 1988-1995; Joel W. Hurley 1995-1998; Bradford K. Lewis 1998-2010; Eric D.
  Kieb 2010-2015; James C. Noggle 2015-Mar 31, 2019; Thomas Leo Hoffmyer Apr 1, 2019-

Rosebush UMC *[Central Bay]*   rosebushumc@gmail.com
(P) 3805 School Rd, Rosebush 48878; (M) PO Box 187, Rosebush 48878   (989) 433-2957
  Paul Peet 1968-1969; Fred Fischer 1969-1978; David Meister 1978-1980; John Ritter 1980-1984;
  Michael Long 1984-1992; Mark R. Payne 1992-2001; Brian Charles LaMew 2001-May 1, 2005;
  Gregory L. Buchner 2005-2008; Jonathan D. Van Dop 2008-2014; Joseph L. Beavan 2014-

Rose City: Trinity UMC *[Central Bay]*   N_Jeffords@yahoo.com
(P) 125 West Main St, Rose City 48654; (M) PO Box 130, Rose City 48654   (989) 685-2350
  Fred Timm 1965-1975; James R. Balfour II 1975-1982; David Baize 1982-1983; John R. Crotser
  1983-1987; Jeffrey Hildebrand 1987-1989; Barbra Franks 1989-Aug 31, 1994; Carter Garrigues-
  Cortelyou Sep 1, 1994-1998; Thomas K. Spencer 1998-2005; Donald J. Wojewski 2005-2011;
  Joseph Coon 2011-2016; Nathan J. Jeffords 2016-2019; Helen Alford (DSA) 2019-

Roseville: Trinity UMC *[Greater Detroit]*   rosevilletrinity@gmail.com
(P/M) 18303 Common Rd, Roseville 48066   (586) 776-8828
  James W. Deeg 1967-1973; Tom Brown II 1973-1978; Thomas G. Badley 1978-1984; Sam Yearby Jr. 1984-1994; Kenneth B. Ray 1994-2000; Paul G. Donelson 2000-Sep 30, 2001; James A. Mathews Oct 1, 2001-2002; Kevin L. Miles 2002-2012; Stephen T. Euper 2012-

Royal Oak: First UMC *[Greater Detroit]*   office@rofum.org
(P/M) 320 W 7th St, Royal Oak 48067   (248) 541-4100
  Everett Seymour 1963-1974; Charles Songquist (assoc) 1967-1969; David W. Truran (assoc) 1970-1972; Samuel Seizert (assoc) 1970- 1981; James R. Balfour, II (assoc) 1972-1975; John G. Park (assoc) 1975-1978; Brent L. McCumons (assoc) 1978-1981; Gerald Fuller (assoc) 1981-1984; Steven J. Buck (assoc) 1982-1988; Thomas Rousseau (assoc.) 1984-1987; Raymond R. Lamb 1974-1987; Edward L. Duncan July 1987-1991; Nanette Myers (assoc) 1987-1992; Thomas H. Zimmerman (assoc) 1991-1997; Marvin H. McCallum 1991-1995; Merton W. Seymour 1995-1999; Wayne N. Thomas (assoc) 1997-2002; Marshall Dunlap (co-pastor) 1999-2008; Susan K. Defoe Dunlap (co-pastor) 1999-2008; Wayne T. Large (assoc) 2002-2003; John H. Hice 2008-2016; Jeffrey S. Nelson 2016- ; Caleb Williams (deacon) Sep 1, 2016-Jan 4, 2020; Myra Moreland Jan 1, 2018- ; George Marck (assoc) Jan. 1, 2020-

Saginaw: Ames UMC *[Central Bay]*   office@ameschurch.org
(P/M) 801 State St, Saginaw 48602   (989) 754-6373
  Richard D. Lobb 1967-1985; Warren Pettis (assoc) 1968-1971; Eldred Kelley (assoc) 1971-1974; Steve Patton (assoc) 1974-1977; Richard Sheppard (assoc) 1977-1981; Gary Glanville (assoc) 1981-1983; Calvin Long (assoc) 1981-1987; O. William Cooper Jr. 1985-1989; Steven Miller (assoc) 1987-1990; John Hinkle 1989-1994; Timothy Hastings (assoc) 1990-1994; Lawrence C. Brooks 1994-1997; Mark A. Karls 1997-2014; Scott P. Lindenberg 2014-2016; Douglas E. Mater 2016-2019; David A. Wichert 2019-

Saginaw: First UMC *[Central Bay]*   firstumsag@aol.com
(P/M) 4790 Gratiot Rd, Saginaw 48638   (989) 799-0131
  Norbert W. Smith 1967-1972; Lois Glenn (assoc) 1966-1970; A. Edward Perkins (assoc) 1970-1972; Robert L. S. Brown 1972-1977; Carol J. Johns (assoc) 1972-1978; Paul T. Hart 1977-1980; Gary W. Bell (assoc) 1978-1980; Frank B. Cowick 1980-1990; Tim Hastings (assoc) 1980-1983; Gary Dawes (assoc) 1983-1987; Steven E. Poole (assoc) 1988-1990; Karen Knight Ott (assoc) 1990-1993; James F. Thomas 1990-Aug 31, 1994; M. Clement Parr Sep 1, 1994-Dec 26, 1995; Walter David (interim) Jan 1, 1996-Jun 14, 1996; Haldon D. Ferris (co-pastor) Jun 16, 1996-2002; Kathryn S. Snedeker (co-pastor) Jun 16, 1996-2002; Kathryn S. Snedeker 2002-2016; Amylee B. Terhune 2016-

Saginaw: New Heart UMC (formerly Saginaw: West Michigan Ave) *[Central Bay]*
     wmaumc@yahoo.com
(P/M) 1802 W Michigan Ave, Saginaw 48602   (989) 792-4689
  Clare M. Tosch 1968-1973; A. Claire Wolfe 1973-1975; Donald W. Pinner 1975-1978; Georg Gerritsen 1978-1980; Troy Lemmons 1980-1983; Richard Turner 1983-1987; Richard Turner 1987-1991; David C. Collins 1991-1997; Duane G. Thon 1997-2007; Micheal P. Kelley 2007-2009; George A. Dorado 2009-2010; Rahim O. Shabazz 2012-2015; Melene E. Wilsey (DSA) 2015-2017; Melene E. Wilsey 2017-

Saginaw: Swan Valley UMC *[Central Bay]*   svumc_48609@yahoo.com
(P/M) 9265 Geddes Rd, Saginaw 48609   (989) 781-0860
  Charles Kolb (org. 1969) 1969-1974; Gordon Nusz 1974-1980, Grant Washburn 1980-1983; Gary Glanville 1983-1987; Calvin Long 1987-1991; W. Peter Crawford 1991-1996; Nancy K. Frank 1996-2000; Robert Harvey (interim) 2000-2001; Robert G. Richards 2001- (Swan Valley (lead church) / LaPorte charge and Hemlock / Nelson charge formed new four point charge July 1, 2019)

Salem Grove UMC *[Heritage]*　　　　　cmbeau81@aol.com
(P/M) 3320 Notten Rd, Grass Lake 49240　　　　　(734) 475-2370
George T. Nevin 1964-1969; George Q. Woomer 1969 (interim); Frederick Atkinson Oct. 1, 1969-Feb. 4, 1971; Harry R. Weeks Mar. 1971-1973; John W. Todd 1973-1974; Richard C. Stoddard 1974-1975; Gerald R. Parker 1975-1978; Ferris S. Woodruff 1978-1979; Ronald A. Brunger 1979-1981; Dale B. Ward 1981-1984; David C. Collins 1984-1985; Donald Woolum 1985-1990; Michael F. Bossingham 1990-Dec. 31, 1991; James E. Paige Jr. Jan. 1, 1992-1998; Carolyn G. Harris (co-pastor) 1998-2003; Daniel W. Harris (co-pastor) 1998-2003; Carolyn G. Harris 2003-2013; Christine Beaudoin 2013-2015; Amy Triebwasser 2015-2017; Mary J. Barrett 2017-

Salem: Indian Mission of the UMC *[Midwest]*　　　　　revrtwilliamson@gmail.com
(P) 3644 28th St, Hopkins 49328; (M) 103 Mason St SW, Byron Center 49315　　　(616) 738-9030
Lewis White Eagle Church 1948-1990; Pulpit Supply 1990-1992; David G. Knapp 1992-1995; Timothy J. Miller 1995-1999; John Pesblakal (DSA)1999-Aug. 31, 2001; Calvin Hill Sept. 1, 2001-2003; Wesley S. Rehberg (DSA) 2003-2005; Sandra VandenBrink, Jan. 16, 2005-2013; Sandra VandenBrink, (Ret.) Director, Senior Meals Program 2013- ; Nancy L. Boelens (Ret.) 2013-Dec. 15, 2015; Ronald Todd Williamson (DSA) Jan. 1, 2016-Nov. 30, 2017; Ronald Todd Williamson Dec. 1, 2017-

Saline: First UMC *[Heritage]*　　　　　office@fumc-salinle.org
(P/M) 1200 N Ann Arbor St, Saline 48176　　　　　(734) 429-4730
George Saucier 1967-1969; Ira L. Fett 1969-1976; Daniel J. Wallace 1976-1984; Lloyd E. Christler 1984-Jul. 15, 1992; Eric S. Hammar (interim); Paul G. Donelson (assoc) 1992-1995; Gerald R. Parker Jul. 16, 1992-1994; John Hinkel 1994-1999; James E. Tuttle 1999-2016; Tyson G. Ferguson (assoc) 2002-2004; Laura C. Speiran (deacon) 2007-2014; Thomas H. Zimmerman 2016-

Samaria: Grace UMC *[Heritage]*　　　　　sachun1128@cs.com
(P) 1463 Samaria, Samaria 48177; (M) PO Box 28, Ida 48140-0028　　　　　(734) 856-6430
John C. Huhtala 1968-1969; James L. Hynes 1969-1971; Ronald K. Corl 1971-1974; Thomas G. Butcher 1974-1976; Willilam Michael Clemmer 1976-1980; J. Robert Anderson 1980-1984; Raymond J. Townsend 1984-1988; Patricia A. VanWormer 1988-1991; Doris Crocker 1991-1998; Ruth A. McCully 1998-2001; Wayne A. Hawley 2001-2007; Sang Yoon (Abraham) Chun 2007-2016; Corey M. Simon 2016-2019; Robert J. Freysinger 2019-

Sand Lake UMC *[Midwest]*　　　　　seumc@charter.net
(P) 65 W Maple St, Sand Lake 49343; (M) PO Box 97, Sand Lake 49343　　　(616) 636-5673
Jerry L. Hippensteel 1977-1981; Richard Strait 1981-1984; Richard Fairbrother 1984-1989; Mary Curtis 1989-91; Richard Sneed 1991-1992; Richard A. Selleck 1992-1996; Howard H. Harvey 1996-1999; Nathan D. Junius 1999-Feb. 1, 2002; Lloyd R. Hansen Feb. 1, 2002-June 30, 2002; Donald Turkelson (DSA)(part-time) 2002 - Nov. 30, 2007; Darryl Miller (DSA) (1/2 time) Jan. 1, 2007; Darryl Miller (part-time) Dec. 1, 2007-

Sandusky: First UMC *[East Winds]*　　　　　sfumc@avci.net
(P/M) 68 Lexington St, Sandusky 48471　　　　　(810) 648-2606
Horace James 1966-1971; Clifford M. De Vore 1971-1975; Frederick O. Timm 1975-1987; Margery A. Schleicher 1987-1991; Michael O. Pringle 1991-1997; Donald D. Gotham 1997-Aug 31, 2004; Georg F. W. Gerritsen (interim) Sep 1-15, 2004; John N. Grenfell, Jr. (interim) Sep 16, 2004-Jan 1, 2005; Marvin H. McCallum (interim) Jan 1, 2005-Feb 28, 2005; John N. Grenfell, Jr. (interim) Mar 1, 2005-May 31, 2005; Colin P. Stover Jun 1, 2005-Jan 1, 2011; Ellen Burns Jan 1, 2011-2012-Eric L. Johnson 2012-2013; Matthew Osborne 2013-2018; Susan E. Platt 2018-

Sanford UMC *[Central Bay]* sanumc@tds.net
(P/M) 2560 N West River Rd, Sanford 48657 (989) 687-5353
James C. Braid 1969-1983; Clare M. Tosch 1983-1985; Haldon D. Ferris 1985-1988; James A. Smith 1988-1993; Bruce C. Hatch 1993-1999; J. Robert Anderson 1999-Oct 15, 2002; Ronald G. Cook Oct 16, 2002-Jun 30, 2003 (interm); Janet M. Larner 2003-2011; Anthony Cutting 2011-2014; Lisa Cook 2014-2020; Lisa L. Kelley 2020-

Saugatuck UMC *[Greater Southwest]* saugatuckumc@i2k.com
(P) 250 Mason St, Saugatuck 49453; (M) PO Box 647, Saugatuck 49453 (269) 857-2295
C. Dow Chamberlain 1967-1969; Harold Arman 1969-1971; Arthur Beadle 1971-1973; Douglas L. Pedersen Oct. 1973-Aug. 1975; Richard W. McClain Aug. 1975-1979; Craig L. Adams 1979-1984; Constance L. Heffelfinger 1984-1996; Fred & Joan Hamlin (DSA) 1996-1998; Karen A. Tompkins 1998-2001; Jean Smith (DSA) 2001; Jean Smith Dec. 1, 2001-2005; Letisha Bowman (DSA) 2005-2007; Letisha Bowman (part-time) 2007-2011; John Huenink July 1-Aug. 31, 2011; Emmett H. Kadwell, Jr. (Ret.) (1/4 time) Sept. 1, 2011-Dec 31, 2019; Richard Vorel (DSA) Jan 1, 2020-

Sault Ste. Marie: Central UMC *[Nothern Skies]* centralumc632@sbcvglobal.net
(P/M) 111 E Spruce St, Sault Sainte Marie 49783 (906) 632-8672
Robert L. Brown 1967-1972; Theodore E. Doane 1972-1980; John Huhtala, Sr. 1980-1992; David M. Liscomb 1992-1993; George A. Luciani 1993-1998; James H. McLaurin 1998-Feb 1, 2001; John N. Hamilton Jun 16, 2001-2004; Steven A. Miller 2004-Nov 15, 2011; John Huhtala, Sr., (interim) Jan 9, 2011-2011; William R. Seitz 2011-2014; Larry D. Osweiler 2014-2018; Victoria L. Hadaway 2018-

Schoolcraft UMC *[Greater Southwest]* office@schoolcraftumc.com
(P) 342 N Grand Ave, Schoolcraft 49087; (M) PO Box 336, Schoolcraft 49087 (269) 679-4845
Robert J. Stillson 1963-1969; Vern Michael 1969-1970; Roger Nielson 1970-1971; Lay Speakers 1971-1972; Dale Benton 1972-1978; John W. Fisher 1978-1980; Dale Crawford 1980-1983; Dwight J. Burton 1983-1992; Laura C. Truby 1992-1998; Marilyn M. Sanders 1998-Jan. 16, 2000; Pete Love (DSA) 2000-; David Nellist 2000-2008; Seung Ho "Andy" Baek 2008-2010; Karen S. Wheat 2010-2015; [Schoolcraft/Pleasant Valley became a charge 2015] Julia R. Humenik 2015-

Scottdale UMC *[Greater Southwest]* schneider4276@comcast.net
(P) 4271 Scottdale Rd, St Joseph 49085; (M) 4276 Scottdale Rd, St Joseph 49085 (269) 429-7270
David Litchfield 1966-1969; David Lutz 1969-1970; Arthur Turner 1970-1971; Merritt Edner 1971-1972; Wayne Babcock 1972-1975; Ross Bunce 1975-1977; Linda Stoddard 1977-1983; C. David Hainer 1983-1984; Elizabeth Perry Nord 1984-Oct. 1986; Mark Thompson Jan. 1987-Nov. 15, 1992; Norman C. Kohns Nov. 16, 1992-1993; Jackie Bralick 1993-Feb. 1, 1995; Pulpit Supply Feb.-May 1995; Terrill M. Schneider June 1, 1995-Oct. 1, 2018; Dawn Marie Oldenburg (DSA) Oct. 1, 2019- [Hinchman / Scottdale beacme two-point charge 10-1-2018]

Scotts UMC *[Greater Southwest]* cxssumc@ctsmail.net
(P) 8458 Wallene, Scotts 49088; (M) PO Box 112, Scotts, 49088-0112 (269) 626-9757
Garth Smith 1965-1971; Pulpit Supply July-Nov. 1971; Wilbur Williams Nov. 1971-Aug. 1973; Paul Mazur Sept. 1973-1978; Pulpit Supply July-Dec. 1978; Donald Robinson Dec. 1978-Aug. 1979; James Allred Sept. 1979-Dec. 1986; Pulpit Supply Jan.-Apr. 1987; Dennis Slattery Apr. 1987-Oct. 1988; Pulpit Supply Oct.-Dec. 1988; Thomas E. Ball Dec. 1988-1994; David F. Hills 1994-Aug. 1, 1999; Sally J. LaFrance Oct. 1, 1999-2001; Thomas L. Truby 2001-March 1, 2003; David G. Knapp 2003-2009; Glenn C. Litchfield 2009-2016; Beverley J. Williams 2016-

Scottville UMC *[Northern Waters]* secretary@thesumc.com
(P/M) 114 W State St, Scottville 49454 (231) 757-3567
  Bernard Fetty 1964-Jan. 1970; J. William Schoettle Feb. 1970-1975; Harold Taber 1975-Jan. 1976; Lloyd R. Hansen Feb. 1976-Oct. 1980; William Mathae Nov. 1980-Dec. 1983; D. Hubert Lowes Jan. 1984-1993; Merritt F. Bongard 1993-Aug. 16, 1995; Pulpit Supply Aug. 1995-Jan. 1996; Bobbie Dale Whitlock Jan. 1996-2004; Robert Ellery Jones 2004-2009; John J. Conklin 2009-2017; Richard J. Hodgeson 2017-

Sears UMC *[Northern Waters]* brookscornersparish@gmail.com
(P) 4897 Pratt St, Sears 49679; (M) PO Box 425, Evart 49631-0425 (231) 734-2733
  Dan Reedy 1968-1969; Carter Miller 1969-March 1971; Lynn Wagner March 1971-Oct. 1973; Eugene Baughn Oct. 1973-March 1974; Daryl Cook 1974-1977; Kenneth Kline 1977-1986; Carl Litchfield 1986-1991; Eugene L. Baughan 1991-1997; Brian R. Bunch 1997-2005; Ronald DeGraw Aug. 1, 2005-Nov. 6, 2005; James L. Breithaupt Mar. 15, 2006-Oct. 19, 2009; Joseph L. Beavan Jan. 15, 2010-2014; Bryan K. Kilpatrick 2014-2017; Melodye Surgeon (Rider) VanOudheusden 2017-2019; [Evart / Sears became a two-point charge 2017] Jean M. Smith 2019-

Sebewaing: Trinity UMC *[Central Bay]* tumc.sebewaing@gmail.com
(P/M) 513 Washington St, Sebewaing 48759 (989) 883-3350
  Conrad Lee Higdon 1968- Dec. 1969; Robert Worgess 1970-1976; Elizabeth D.K. Isaacs 1976-1980; Donald O. Crumm Jan. 1981-1985; Lawrence C. Brooks 1985-1994; Michael K. Norton 1994-1997; Richard F. Kriesch 1997-2000; Ray T. McGee Aug 15, 2000-2004; Arthur R. Stone 2004-2006; William R. Wright 2006-2012; Daniel P. Snyder 2012-2014; Cynthia M. Parson 2014-2018; Pamela A. Beedle-Gee 2018-2020; [Sebewaing: Trinity, Bay Port became 2-point charge 2020] Heather M. Nowak 2020-

Seymour Lake UMC *[East Winds]* office@seymourlakeumc.org
(P) 3050 S Sashabaw Rd, Oxford 48371; (M) 3100 S Sashabaw Rd, Oxford 48371 (248) 572-4200
  W. Howard Nichols 1969-1975; Lorenz Stahl 1975-1979; Kenneth L. Christler 1979-Jan. 1983; J. Douglas Paterson 1983-Sept. 15, 1986; Heidi C. Reinker Sept. 15, 1986-1988; Karen L. Knight Apr. 15, 1989-1990; R. Wayne Hutson 1990-1991; Erik J. Alsgaard Oct. 1, 1991-Dec 31, 1994; John Martin Mar 1, 1995-Aug 4, 1998; Duane E. Miller Jan 1, 1999-Jun 30, 1999; Deborah A. Line 1999-2009; LuAnn Lee Rourke 2009-2014; Danny Bledsoe (assoc.) Jan 9, 2014-2015; Janine Plum 2015-

Shaftsburg UMC *[Mid-Michigan]* pastornancy@live.com
(P) 12821 Warner Rd, Shaftsburg 48882; (M) PO Box 161, Shaftsburg 48882-0161 (517) 675-1567
  Karl Patow 1962-1969; Ivan Niswender 1969-1971; David Draggoo 1971-1981; Jeff Siker-Geisler 1981-1983; Harris Hoekwater 1983-Jan. 1992; Clinton McKinven-Copus Feb. 1992-Dec. 31, 1994; Pulpit Supply Jan. 1-April 15, 1995; Carroll A. Fowler April 16, 1995-2003; Carolyn C. Floyd 2003-2008; Raymond R. Sundell 2008-2012; Nancy G. Powers 2012-2020; Rey C. Mondragon 2020-

Shelby UMC *[Midwest]* shelbyumc@gmail.com
(P/M) 68 E 3rd St, Shelby 49455 (231) 861-2020
  Ronald Houk Jan. 1966-Oct. 1971; James Fox Nov. 1971-Aug. 1977; Robert Carson Sept. 1977-1981; Daniel Minor 1981-1989; Ray Flessner 1989-1991; Keith Bovee 1991-1994; James E. Hodge 1994-2001; Lewis A. Buchner 2001-Feb. 1, 2002; Peggy A. Boltz 2002-2010; Terri Cummins 2010-2016 [Shelby became a two-point charge Shelby/Claybanks 2014]; Kenneth D. Vanderlaan (DSA) 2016-2017 [Mears and Shelby became a multi-station circuit 2016]; Anne W. Riegler 2017-

Shelbyville UMC *[Greater Southwest]* martinumc@sbcglobal.net
(P) 938 124th Ave, Shelbyville 49344; (M) PO Box 154, Martin 49070-0154 (269) 672-7097
Paul Scheibner 1965-1970; Thurlan Meridith 1970-1976; Gerald L. Welsh 1976-1984; Lee F. Zachman 1984-April 15, 1994; William C. Bills 1994-2007; Christopher L. Lane 2007-2009; David A. Selleck 2009-2012; Donald J. Graham 2012-2014; Sean K. Kidd 2014-2019; Corey M. Simon 2019-

Shepardsville UMC *[Mid-Michigan]* pastorjudy777@gmail.com
(P/M) 6990 Winfield Rd, Ovid 48866 (989) 834-5104
Leroy Howe 1968-1969; Karl Ziegler 1969-1970; Roger Wittrup 1970-1971; Darold Boyd 1971-1978; Rodney Kalajainen 1979-1981; Bruce Kintigh 1981-1988; Charles Smith 1988-1996; D. Kay Pratt 1996-2004; Rob McPherson (Administrative Pastor) 2005; Gordon Schleicher (Administrative Pastor) 2006; Cheryll Warren (DSA) 2007; Cheryll Warren Nov. 10, 2007-June 30, 2009; Judy A. Hazle (DSA) Aug. 1, 2009-2020; Jung Du Paik Jul 15, 2020-

Shepherd UMC *[Central Bay]* office@shepherdumcmi.org
(P) 107 W Wright Ave, Shepherd 48883; (M) PO Box 309, Shepherd 48883 (989) 828-5866
G. Albert Rill 1971-1976; Joseph Dudley 1976-Aug. 1979; Michael L. Selleck Aug. 1979-1986; Leonard B. Haynes 1986-1992; Donald E. Spachman 1992-2004; Wayne Allen Price 2004-2007; Kathleen S. Kursch 2007- 2017 [Shepherd / Blanchard-Pine River became 2-point charge 2017] Janet M. Larner 2017-2020 [Blanchard-Pine River / Shepherd became a single-point charges 01/01/2019] William W. Chu 2020-

Sidnaw UMC *[Nothern Skies]* lumc@up.net
(P) 6071 W Milltown Rd, Sidnaw 49961; (M) 304 N Main St, Lanse 49946
Zina B. Bennett, Jr. 1966-1971; William Kelsey 1970; Howard E Shaffer 1971-1981; John R. Henry 1981-1986; Gregory Rowe 1986-1990; James M. Mathews 1990-1993; David P. Snyder 1993-Oct 1, 2003; John R. Henry 2004-2011; Stephen E. Rhoades 2011-2019; Nathan T. Reed 2019-

Silver Creek UMC *[Greater Southwest]* silvercreekumc@gmail.com
(P/M) 31994 Middle Crossing Rd, Dowagiac 49047 (269) 782-7061
Meredith Rupe 1968-Nov. 1970; Gary Gamble Nov. 1970-May 1973; Supply pastor June-Oct. 1973; Lynn Wagner Oct. 1973-1975; Daniel Barker 1975-Sept. 1978; Gregory Wolfe Oct. 1978-Nov. 1983; Donald Buege Jan. 1984-1990; Dennis Slattery 1990-1992; David L. Litchfield 1992-1988; Virginia L. Heller 1998-2004; Mark E. Thompson 2004-2009; Julie A. Greyerbiehl 2009-2011; Heather McDougall 2011-2013; Beth A. Reum 2013-Jan. 15, 2016 [Silver Creek became single-point charge 2015]; Sara Louise Carlson Feb. 2, 2016-

Silverwood UMC *[East Winds]* ronhutchinson50@aol.com
(P) 2750 Clifford Rd, Silverwood 48760; (M) PO Box 556, Mayville 48744 (989) 761-7599
Donald L. Lichtenfelt 1968-1970; Ralph T. Barteld 1970-1979; Dale E. Brown 1979-1984; Allen J. Lewis Inter.; Wayne C. Ferrigan 1984-1986; William J. Maynard 1986-1992; Bonny J. Lancaster 1992-1998; Ronald G. Hutchinson 1998-Apr 15, 2009-2020; Theodore A. Adkins (DSA) 2020-

Sitka UMC *[Midwest]* francis1491@aol.com
(P/M) 9606 Dickinson Rd, Holton 49425 (231) 744-1767
Kenneth D. McCaw 1967-1968; Austin W. Regier 1969; Ira J. Noordhof 1971-1975; Donald J. Vuurens, Oct. 15, 1975-Dec. 31, 1977; Wayne Speese (Pulpit Supply) Jan. 1, 1978-June 1978; Charles R. VanLente 1978-1983; Steven D. Pearson 1983-1988; Kathryn B. Robotham 1988-1990; Michael A. Van Horn 1990-1991; Leonard Coon 1991-Nov. 1, 1999; Milton Stahl (interim) Nov. 1, 1999-July 1, 2000; Patrick Cameron 2000-Nov. 30, 2001; James Meines December 1, 2001-2005; Brian M. McLellan (DSA) 2005-Feb. 15, 2006; James Meines (DSA) Apr. 15, 2006-Oct. 31, 2006; Nancy L. (Besemer) Boelens Nov. 1, 2006-2008; Paul Lynn (part-time) 2008-Nov. 15, 2009; Gerald F. Hagans (DSA) (1/4 time) Nov. 15, 2009-2019; TBS

Snover: Heritage UMC *[East Winds]*   heritageumchurch@gmail.com
(P) 3329 W Snover Rd, Snover 48472; (M) PO Box 38, Snover 48472   (810) 672-9101
Michael K. Norton 1990-1994; Jeffery L. Jaggers 1994-1998; Mary G. Laub 1998-2001; David L. Fleming 2001-2003; David O. Pratt 2003-2013; Donald R. Derby 2013-2018; Penelope R. Nunn 2018-

Sodus: Chapel Hill UMC *[Greater Southwest]*   chumcsodus@comcast.net
(P/M) 4071 Naomi Rd, Sodus 49126   (269) 927-3454
Myron Kent Williams 1960-1969; B. James Varner 1969-1973; Leonard Putnam 1973-1975; George Fleming 1975-1987; William V. Payne 1987-1996; Richard D. Wilson 1996-2003; David A. Cheyne 2003-2005; James A. Dibbet 2005-2011; Russell K. Logston 2011-2014; Mark E. Mitchell 2014-2018; Brenda E. Gordon 2018-

Somerset Center UMC *[Heritage]*   somersetcentermethodist@frontiernet.net
(P) 12095 E. Chicago Rd, Somerset Center 49282; (M) PO Box 277, Somerset Center 49282
(517) 688-4330
Richard Stoddard 1968-1974; David Showers 1974-1976; Martin Fox 1976-1979; Gerald Selleck 1979-1982; Mark Kelly 1982-1983; Dr. Campbell 1983-1984; Jim Hodge 1984-1989; Lawrence P. Brown 1989-1996; Michael E. Long 1996-1998; James W. Barney 1998-2005; Geraldine M. Litchfield 2005-2007; Denise J. Downs 2007-2008; Maurice Walworth Jr. (DSA) 2008-2009; [Hillside/Somerset Center two-point charge 2009] E. Jeanne Koughns 2009-2014; Patricia A. Pebley 2014-2020; Crystal C. Thomas 2020-

South Boardman UMC *[Northern Waters]*   jack49668@gmail.com
(P) 5488 Dagle St SW, S Boardman 49680; (M) PO Box 112, S Boardman 49680   (231) 879-6055
Gerald L. Hedlund 1966-1971; Arthur and Molly Turner (co-pastors) 1971-1976; Diane Vale 1976-Oct. 1977; Marion Nye Dec. 1977-1978; Pulpit Supply 1978-1979; Athel Lynch 1979-1981; Pulpit Supply 1981-1983; Daniel Biteman, Jr. 1983-1985; Clinton McKinven-Copus 1985-1987; Gary Wales 1987-1994; Howard Seaver 1994-2012; Mark E. Mitchell 2012-2014; Donald L. Buege 2014-2017; [Williamsburg and (Fife Lake Boardman Parish) Fife Lake / East Boardman / South Boardman became multi-point charge 2017] John J. Conklin 2017-2020 [2018 Williamsburg, Fife Lake, East Boardman, South Boardman formed the Unified Parish] John D. Messner 2020-

South Ensley UMC *[Midwest]*   seumc@charter.net
(P) 13600 Cypress Ave, Sand Lake 49343; (M) PO Box 97, Sand Lake 49343   (616) 636-5659
Jerry L. Hippensteel 1977-1981; Richard Strait 1981-1984; Richard Fairbrother 1984-1989; Mary Curtis 1989-91; Richard Sneed 1991-1992; Richard A. Selleck 1992-1996; Howard H. Harvey 1996-1999; Nathan D. Junius 1999-Feb. 1, 2002; Lloyd R. Hansen Feb. 1, 2002-June 30, 2002; Donald Turkelson (DSA)(part-time) 2002-Nov. 30, 2007; Darryl Miller (DSA) (1/2 time) Jan. 1, 2007; Darryl L. Miller (part-time) Dec. 1, 2007-

South Haven: First UMC *[Greater Southwest]*   southhavenmethodist@gmail.com
(P/M) 429 Michigan Ave, South Haven 49090   (269) 637-2502
William Torrey 1968-1974; Richard Youells 1974-Aug. 15, 1979; Larry Irvine Sept. 16, 1979-1984; C. William Martin 1984-1989; Edward Slate 1989-1995; Billie R. Dalton 1995-2004; John W. Fisher 2004-2013; Devon R. Herrell 2013-2014; Virginia L. Heller 2014-2018; Ronald D. VanLente 2018-2020; TBS

South Lyon: First UMC *[Heritage]* slfumc@sbcglobal.net
(P/M) 640 S Lafayette St, South Lyon 48178 (248) 437-0760
  Roger W. Merrell 1966-1970; Donald D. McLellan 1970-1975; Milton H. Bank 1975-1977; Douglas K. Mercer 1977-1988; J. Gordon Schleicher (assoc) 1985-1987; Ralph A. Edwards (assoc) 1987-1991; Alan R. George 1988-1995; Nina C. Weaver (assoc) Sep. 1, 1992-1995; Pauline S. Hart (co-pastor) 1995-2002; Thomas E. Hart (co-pastor) 1995-Aug 31, 2002; Carman J. Minarik (co-pastor) Sep 1, 2002-2007; Donna J. Minarik (co-pastor) Sep 1, 2002-Sep 15, 2006; Sondra B. Willobee 2007-2017; Kenny Walkup (assoc) Nov 23, 2016- ; Mary G. McInnes 2017-

South Monterey UMC *[Greater Southwest]* crowemitzi@yahoo.com
(P) Corner of 26th St & 127th Ave, Hopkins 49328; (M) PO Box 356, Hopkins 49328
  (269) 793-7323
  Glenn Britton 1968-Jan. 1970; Stanley Finkbeiner Feb. 1970-1974; Densel Fuller 1974-1976; Brent Phillips 1976-1978; David Knapp 1978-Oct. 15, 1982; Robert J. Stillson Nov. 1982-1989; Robert D. Nystrom 1989-1992; Marjory A. Berkompas 1992-June 13, 1996; David S. Yoh (DSA) 1996-1999; Raymond D. Field 1999-2001; Reva H. Daniel 2001-2005; Linda J. Burton 2005-2014; Dominic A. Tommy 2014-2017; Joel T. Fitzgerald 2017-2018; Andrew R. Phillips 2018-2020; Kelsey Burns French 2020-

South Mundy UMC *[East Winds]* smhumc01@gmail.com
(P) 10018 Linden Rd, Grand Blanc 48439; (M) 10006 Halsey Rd, Grand Blanc 48439
  (810) 655-4184
  T. Thornley Eddy 1962-1978; Ralph C. Pratt 1978-1979; Stephen K. Perrine 1979-1980; David P. Rahn 1980-1987; Martha H. Cargo 1987-1992; Chong Youb Won 1992-1995; Robin G. Gilshire 1995-Jul 31, 2000; David E. Ray Aug 1, 2000-2006; Harold V. Phillips 2006-2016; Tara R. Sutton 2016-

South Rockwood UMC *[Heritage]* sperrine@sbcglobal.net
(P) 6311 S Huron Rvr Dr, S Rockwood 48179; (M) 23435 Oak Glen Dr, Southfield 48033
  (734) 379-3131
  Zina B. Bennett, Jr. 1975-1983; Robert C. Strobridge 1983-1988; Dana R. Strall 1988-Jul 31, 1997; Philip D. Voss Aug 31, 1997-2002; Elizabeth A. Librande 2002-Aug 14, 2006; Stephen K. Perrine Aug 15, 2006-2020; Ann Birchmeier 2020-

Southfield: Hope UMC *[Greater Detroit]* kevinsmalls@aol.com
(P/M) 26275 Northwestern Hwy, Southfield 48076 (248) 356-1020
  G. Charles Sonquist 1970-1980; Terry W. Allen 1980-1983; Carlyle F. Stewart, III 1983-2014; Hilda L. Harris (assoc.) 1995-1997; Lamarr V. Gibson (assoc) 1997-May 30, 2000; Vivian C. Bryant (assoc) 1997-2003; Theodore D. Whitely (assoc) 1998-2000; Betty Whitely (assoc) 1998-2000; Troy M. Benton (assoc) 2000-2003; Faith Green (assoc) 2000-Sep 1, 2002; Anthony R. Hood (assoc) Oct 1, 1999-2002; Gary A. Williams (assoc) 2000-2004; Kenny J. Waldon (assoc) 2003-2005; Janet Gaston Petty (assoc) 2004-2012; Cornelius Davis, Jr. 2014-Sep 22, 2015; Benjamin K. Smalls 2016- ; Christopher Michael Grimes (assoc) 2017- ; Rosaline D. Green (Ret. 2019) Dec 1, 2017- ; Dale R. Milford (assoc) 2019- ; Reggie Allen White (assoc) 2019-

Sparta UMC *[Midwest]* spartaumc@spartaumc.com
(P/M) 54 E Division St, Sparta 49345 (616) 887-8255
  Paul Patterson 1968-1973; Eldon K. Eldred 1973-April 1979; Ronald Entenman 1979-1985; James R. Hulett 1985-1993; Steven R. Young 1993-2006; Raymond J. Townsend 2006-2009; Louis W. Grettenberger 2009-2017; Phillip J. Friedrick 2017-

Spratt UMC [Nothern Waters]   pastorlisakelley@outlook.com
(P) 7440 M 65 S, Lachine 49753; (M) PO Box 323, Lachine 49753   (989) 742-4372
   Howard E. Shaffer 1964-1971; Philip A. Rice 1971-1975; Robert Kersten 1975-1978; Harold F. Blakely 1978-1981; James R. Rupert 1981-1984; R. Wayne Hutson 1984-1990; Paula Timm 1990-1992; Jack E. Johnston 1992-Oct 30, 2005; George Morse (interim) Nov 1, 2005-Jun 30, 2006; Karen A. Mars 2006-2008; Donald R. Derby 2008-2013; Lisa L. Kelley 2013-2020; Duane A. Lindsey 2020-

Springport UMC [Heritage]
(P) 127 W Main St, Springport 49284   (517) 857-2777
   Lynn Chapel 1965-March 1971; Beulah Poe March 1971-1976; Robert Doner 1976-1978; Joel Campbell 1978-1979; Ethel Stears 1979-Sept. 16, 1983; William Doubblestein Oct. 16, 1983-1987; Eugene Baughan 1987-1991; David H. Minger 1991-1995; Wayne Willer 1995-1996; Valerie Hill 1996-1998; David L. Litchfield 1998-2001; David Blair 2001-2003; Diane E. Stone 2004-2010; Melissa Claxton 2010-2018; [North Parma / Springport became two-point charge 7-1-10] Mark E. Mitchell 2018-

Springville UMC [Heritage]   sumchurch@springvilleumc.us
(P/M) 10341 Springville Hwy, Onsted 49265   (517) 467-4471
   Ford Baker 1968-1969; Harold R. Krieg 1969-1971; Edward C. Weiss Jr. 1972-1973; Juanita J. Ferguson 1973-1978; Donald W. Brown 1978-1980; Richard L. Dake 1980-1985; William P. McKnight 1985-1991; Gordon B. Boyd 1991-Nov. 30, 1992; James G. Simmons (interim); C. Earl Eden Jr. Mar. 1, 1993-1999; Victoria M. Webster 1999-May 19, 2000; Melany A. Chalker 2000-2006; Margery H. Host 2006-2010; Ronald A. Fike 2010-2014; Julius Nagy 2014-2018; Evans C. Bentley (Ret.) 2018-

St. Charles UMC [Central Bay]   stcharlesumc@att.net
(P) 301 W Belle Ave, Saint Charles 48655; (M) PO BOX 87, Saint Charles 48655   (989) 865-9091
   George Jones 1966-1971; John Crotser 1971-1979; William Omansiek 1979-1985; Edward C. Weiss Jr. 1985-Aug 31 1, 1994; Charles W. Keyworth Sep 1, 1994-1999; Kevin J. Harbin 1999-2002; Harold J. Slater 2002-2008; Ernesto Mariona 2008-Sept 30, 2017; Karen J. Sorden Dec 1, 2017-

St. Clair: First UMC [East Winds]   scfumc@sbcglobal.net
(P/M) 415 N 3rd St, Saint Clair 48079   (810) 329-7186
   Merton W. Seymour 1968-1975; Douglas R. Trebilcock 1975-1985; John E. Naile 1985-1998; W. Thomas Schomaker 1998-Jul 31, 2004; Marvin H. McCallum (interim) Aug 1-31, 2004; Donald D. Gotham Sep 1, 2004-2011; Margie R. Crawford 2011-2018; John Nicholas Grenfell III 2018-

St. Ignace UMC [Nothern Skies]   umethstig@att.net
(P) 615 W US Highway 2, St Ignace 49781; (M) PO Box 155, St Ignace 49781   (906) 643-8088
   Howard R. Higgins 1968-1973; Dale Lantz 1973-1977; John E. Naile 1977-1985; David A. Russell 1985-1987; Robert C. Watt 1987-Jun 30, 1994; John Elliott Jul 1, 1994-Apr 15, 2002; James R. Balfour II 2002-2010; Erik J. Alsgaard 2010-2013; Susanne E. Hierholzer 2013-2019; Eric M. Falker 2019-2020; Mark E. Thompson 2020-

St Johns: Pilgrim UMC [Mid-Michigan]   office@pilgrimumchurch.com
(P/M) 2965 W Parks Rd, Saint Johns 48879   (989) 224-6865
   Eugene Friesen 1966-1970; Brian K. Sheen 1970-1983; Larry R. Shrout 1983-1998; Raymond R. Sundell 1998-2003; Merlin H. Pratt 2003-2006; D. Kay Pratt (Assoc.) 2004-2006; Price UMC merged with St Johns Pilgrim 2005; Kenneth J. Bremer 2006-2014; Andrew L. Croel 2014-

St Joseph: First UMC *[Greater Southwest]*   office@sjfirstumc.org
(P/M) 2950 Lakeview Ave, St Joseph 49085   (269) 983-3929
   Sidney A. Short Feb. 1968-Jan. 1973; Richard E. Johns (Assoc.) Apr. 1968-Apr. 1969; Gary Gamble (Assoc.) 1969-1971; Douglas L. Pedersen (Assoc.) 1971-Oct.1973; Dale D. Brown Feb. 1973-Dec. 1982; David A. Selleck (Assoc.) 1974-Mar. 1976; Harold F. Filbrandt Feb. 1983-Mar. 1987; Benton R. Heisler (Assoc.) 1986-Aug. 1988; Ronald A. Houk 1987-1997; Charles K. Stanley (Assoc.) Oct. 1988-Oct. 1990; Shelley L. Caulder (Assoc.) Dec. 1991-1996; Thomas C. Nikkel (Assoc.) 1996-2000; Wade S. Panse 1997-Jan. 1, 2012; James W. Kraus, Jr. (Deacon) 2001- ; Terry Euper (DSA) Jan. 1, 2012; Harris J. Hoekwater 2012-2018; Daniel R. Colthorp (Deacon) 2016-2018; Daniel R. Colthopr 2018-

St Louis: First UMC *[Mid-Michigan]*   stlouisfumc@yahoo.com
(P/M) 116 S Franklin St, Saint Louis 48880   (989) 681-3320
   Harold L. Mann 1972-March 1982; Gerald R. Bates April 1982-1987; Richard C. Kuhn 1987-1998; Robert D. Nystrom 1998-2002; Lillian T. French 2002-Dec. 31, 2007; [Pleasant Valley UMC merged w/ St. Louis UMC 01-01-08] Terri L. Bentley Feb. 1, 2008-2020; [St. Louis: First, Breckenridge became 2-point charge 2020] Billie Lou Gillespie 2020-

Standish: Beacon of Light UMC (formerly Standish: Community) *[Central Bay]*   cumcch@att.net
(P) 201 S Forest St, Standish 48658; (M) PO Box 186, Standish 48658   (989) 846-6277
   Albert Johns, 1967-1972; C. William Bollinger 1972-1977; Paul Greer 1977-1979; Byron G. Hatch 1979-1983; Devin S. Chisholm 1983-2011; Donald J. Wojewski 2011-2012; William P. Sanders 2012-2013; James A. Payne 2013- [Sterling UMC merged into Standish: Community UMC 04/01/2019 to become Standish: Beacon of Light]

Stanwood: Northland UMC *[Midwest]*   secretary@northlandumc.org
(P) 6842 Northland Dr, Stanwood 49346; (M) PO Box 26, Stanwood 49346   (231) 823 -2300
   Nolan Williams 1967-1974; Bernard Randolph 1974-March 1975; Max Gladding March 1975-1982; Emmett Kadwell 1982-1992; Jack Bartholomew 1992-1995; Edward H. Slate 1995-2006; Dominic A. Tommy 2006-2014; Gary D. Bondarenko 2014-

Stephenson UMC *[Northern Skies]*   sumc111@att.net
(P) S 111 Railroad St, Stephenson 49887; (M) PO Box 205, Stephenson 49887   (906) 753-6363
   Calvin Rice 1967-1974; James Paige 1974-1975; John Henry 1975-1981; John Hamilton 1981-1986; David Leenhouts 1986-1992; W. Peter Bartlett 1992-1996; Kenneth C. Dunstone 1996-Dec 15, 1999; Jean M. Larson Jan 1, 2000-Nov 15, 2001; James A. Fegan Dec 1, 2001-May 31, 2002; Cherrie A. Sporleder Jun 16, 2002-2004; James M. Mathews 2004-2019; John P. Murray 2019-

Sterling Heights UMC *[Greater Detroit]*   shumc@wowway.com
(P/M) 11333 16 1/2 Mile Rd, Sterling Heights 48312   (586) 268-3130
   Walter David 1967-1973; Richard L. Myers 1973-1978; Donald P. Haskell 1978-1985; Michael L. Raymo 1985-1988; Joy A. Barrett 1988-1993; Grant A. Washburn 1993-Aug 1, 1995; Kwang M. Lee Aug 1, 1995-1996; David J. Leenhouts 1996-Sep 19, 1998; Elizabeth A. Macaulay Jun 16, 1999-2008; Robert I. Kreger 2008-2013; Norma Taylor 2013-Mar 1, 2016; Karen Y. Noel 2016-2018; Joel Thomas Fitzgerald 2018-

Stevensville UMC *[Greater Southwest]*   office@stevensvilleumc.org
(P/M) 5506 Ridge Rd, Stevensville 49127   (269) 429-5911
   Gerald Welsh 1968-Oct. 1969; Lloyd Phillips Oct. 1969-1979; Dean Bailey 1979-1987; Steve Emery (Assoc.) 1981-1987; Geoffrey Hayes 1987-March 23, 1994; Larry Rubingh (Assoc.) 1987-1988; Jeffrey Wright (Assoc.) 1988-1990; Bradley Bartelmay (Assoc.) 1990-1993; Tamara S.M. Williams (Assoc.) 1993-2002; Eugene A. Lewis 1994-2003; Terri L. Bentley (Assoc.) 2002-Feb. 1, 2008; Beryl Gordon Barry 2003-2015; David F. Hills Aug. 1, 2015-

Stockbridge UMC *[Mid-Michigan]*   sumcaa@aol.com
(P/M) 219 E Elizabeth St, Stockbridge 49285   (517) 851-7676
   William Frayer 1965-1969; Raymond Norton 1969-1971; Dale Spoor 1971-Sept. 1974; Douglas
   Vernon Oct. 1974-Sept. 1979; David Selleck Oct. 1979-1987; Richard Matson 1987-1990; Birt
   Beers 1990-1993; Stuart L. Proctor 1993-Sept. 1995; Robert J. Henning 1996-2007; Larry W.
   Rubingh 2007-Oct. 15, 2010; Galen L. Goodwin (Retired Elder, Greater New Jersey Conf), Interim
   Pastor, Oct. 24, 2010-July 1, 2011; Robert J. Freysinger 2011-2013; [M-52 Cooperative Ministry
   2013-2014] Jeanne M. Laimon (1/4 time) 2013-2014; Susan J. Trowbridge 2014-2019; Stephan
   Weinberger (Ret.) 2019-

Stokes Chapel UMC *[Heritage]*   revfgcain@yahoo.com
(P) 201 Main St, Montgomery 49255; (M) PO Box 155, Camden 49232   (517) 368-5406
   Karl L. Zeigler 1968-1969; John H. Gurney 1969-Aug. 1970; Joseph Huston Aug. 1970-1972;
   Richard Huskey 1972-1974; J. Brian Selleck 1974-Feb. 1976; Robert P. Stover March 1976-1980;
   Stephen Beech 1980-1983; Larry W. Rubingh 1983-1987; Frederick G. Hamlin 1987-1994; Russell
   K. Logston 1994-1996; Diane Stone Nov. 16, 1996-2004; Edward Mohr 2004-2010; Trevor
   McDermont 2010-2013; Frederick G. Cain (Ret.) (part-time) 2013-

Stony Creek UMC *[Heritage]*   SCumc8635@gmail.com
(P/M) 8635 Stony Creek Rd, Ypsilanti 48197   (734) 482-0240
   Robert N. Hicok 1967-Sep 30, 1970; Roger A. Parker Oct 1, 1970-1976; Dale M. Miller 1976-1981;
   Douglas K. Olsen 1981-1996; Peter S. Harris 1996-2007; Kenneth B. Ray 2007-2010; Reed P.
   Swanson 2010-2017; Nathaniel R. Starkey 2017-2020; [Clinton, Stony Creek became 2-point
   charge 2020] Michael W. Vollmer 2020-

Sturgis UMC *[Greater Southwest]*   fumcsturgis@gmail.com
(P/M) 200 Pleasant St, Sturgis 49091   (269) 651-5990
   Charles B. Hahn 1966-1970; Hilding Kilgren 1970-1977; Miriam DeMint (Assoc.) 1969-1970; David
   Dunn (Assoc.) 1970-1973; Dennis Paulsen (Assoc.) 1973-1975; Edward Boase (Assoc.) 1975-
   1977; George Hartmann 1977-1987; Richard Riley (Assoc.) 1977-1980; Mark Graham 1987-1988;
   Susan Adsmond Fox July-Sept. 1987; Ray W. Burgess 1988-1993; Lowell F. Walsworth 1993-1995;
   Richard A. Morrison 1995-Jan. 1, 1998; Dianne Morrison (Assoc.) Jan. 1996-Jan. 1, 1998; Keith
   R. Treman Jan. 15, 1998-2008; Colleen T. Treman (Deacon) 1998-2008; J. Robert Keim (Assoc.)
   Dec. 16, 1999-Dec. 31, 2011; Deborah M. Johnson 2008-2014; E. Jeanne Koughn 2014-2019;
   Susan J. Babb 2019- ; Mark R. Babb (deacon) 2019-

Sunfield UMC *[Mid-Michigan]*   sumcoffice@centurytel.net
(P) 227 Logan St, Sunfield 48890; (M) PO Box 25, Sunfield 48890-0025   (517) 566-8448
   Marjorie S. Matthews June-Sept. 1968; Robert Keith Sept. 1968-1971; Ralph G. Kallweit 1971-
   Jan. 1976; John Morse Feb. 1976-1982; J. Chris Schroeder 1982-Jan. 1992; Harris J. Hoekwater
   Jan. 1992-1998; Brian K. Sheen 1998-2004; Jeffrey J. Schrock 2004-2012; Clare W. Huyck 2012-
   2015 [Sunfield/Sebewa Center no longer two-point charge 2013] [Barry-Eaton Cooperative Ministry
   2013] Betty A. Smith (Ret.) 2015-Dec. 31, 2015; Lyle D. Heaton Jan. 1-June 30, 2016; Vaughn W.
   Thurston-Cox 2016-2017; [Gresham and Sunfield became two-point charge 2017] Heather L. Nolen
   (DSA) 2017; Heather L. Nolen (FL) Dec 1, 2017-

Sutton Sunshine UMC *[Central Bay]*   pastorpennyparkin@gmail.com
(P) 2996 Colwood Rd, Caro 48723; (M) 2988 Colwood Rd, Caro 48723   (989) 673-6695
   Wallis E. Braum 1964-1970; Carl Shamblen 1970-1972; Lawrence C. Whiting 1972-1975; Peyton
   E. Loy 1975-1978; Wayne N. Thomas 1978-1982; Janet M. Larner 1982-1986; Duane M. Harris
   1986-Nov. 1988; Billy J. McKown 1989-Feb 28, 1995; Donald D. Gotham Oct 1, 1996-1997;
   Raymond A. Jacques 1997-2001; Patrick D. Robbins 2001-2011; Dorothy J. Thon 2011-2017; Penny
   L. Parkin 2017-May 31, 2020; James Butler Jun 1, 2020-

Swartz Creek UMC *[East Winds]* office@umc-sc.org
(P/M) 7400 Miller Rd, Swartz Creek 48473 (810) 635-4555
Harold A. Nessel 1970-1974; John W. Murbach 1974-Oct., 1983; H. Reginald Cattell Nov. 1, 1983-Aug 31, 1994; Emil E. Haering (assoc) 1990-1991; James F. Thomas Sep 1, 1994-2000; John D. Landis 2000-2011; LuAnn L. Rourke (assoc.) 2006-2009; Matthew Packer (deacon) May 1,2006-2008; Kevin J. Harbin 2011-2015; Gary R. Glanville 2015-Aug 31, 2020; Aaron B. Kesson (assoc) 2017-2020; Daniel J. Bowman 2020-

Tawas UMC *[Central Bay]* tawasumc@sbcglobal.net
(P/M) 20 E M 55, Tawas City 48763 (989) 362-4288
Kenneth L. Tousley 1968-1982; Ralph D. Churchill 1982-1984; Ronald D. Carter 1984-1990; S. Joe Robertson 1990-2001; Robert Richards (assoc) Jan 1, 1994-1997; Lisa L. (Okrie) Cook (assoc) 1997-Apr 30, 2000; David E. Huseltine 2001-2004; Reed P. Swanson 2004-2008; Mary Ann Gibson 2008-2013; Daniel Gonder 2013-2018; Kris Stewart Kappler 2018-

Tecumseh UMC *[Heritage]* tumc@tc3net.com
(P/M) 605 Bishop Reed Dr, Tecumseh 49286 (517) 423-2523
Donald C. Porteous 1962-1973; Allan G. Gray 1973-1983; Gordon E. Ackerman 1983-1988; Stuart L. Proctor (assoc) 1984-1986; John H. Bunce 1988-Aug 31, 1994; James Schwandt Sep 1, 1994-1999; David R. McKinstry 1999-2010; Mark A. Miller 2010-

Thetford Center UMC *[East Winds]* geneseethetford@sbcglobal.net
(P) G-11394 North Center Rd, Clio 48420; (M) PO Box 190, Genesee 48437 (810) 640-2280
Fred E. Wager 1969-1970; John P. Hitchens 1970-1972; Ralph H. Pieper II 1972-1975; Roger L. Colby 1975-1980; James P. Schwandt 1980-1987; David P. Rahn 1887; Willard A. King Nov 1, 1987-Aug 31, 1994; Lorrie E. Plate Sept 1, 1995-1998; Malcom L. Greene 1998- 2003; Bruce L. Nowacek 2004-2010; Karen B. Williams 2010-

Thomas UMC *[East Winds]* thomasumc504@gmail.com
(P) 504 First St, Oxford 48371; (M) PO Box 399, Oxford 48371-0399 (248) 628-7636
Fred Clark 1954-1972; George F. W. Gerritsen 1972-1978; Dwayne L. Kelsey 1978-Oct. 1981; Donald H. Francis 1981-1988; Mary Margaret Eckhardt 1988-2002; Gloria Haynes 2002-2005; Thomas K. Spencer 2005-Dec 1, 2006; Donald H. Francis (interim) Dec 1, 2006-Dec 31, 2006; Carla Ann Jepson Jan 1, 2007-2016; Mark Huff (DSA) 2016-2017; Carol Ann Middel (DSA) 2017-2019; [Oxford / Thomas 2-point charge 2019] Jennifer J. Jue 2019-2020; [Thomas became single station 2020] Kristen LePalm 2020-

Three Oaks UMC *[Greater Southwest]* toumc@att.net
(P/M) 2 Sycamore St E, Three Oaks 49128 (269) 756-2053
Larry Waterhouse Apr. 1966-Oct. 1970; Meredith Rupe Nov. 1970-Nov. 1975; Larry Irvine Nov. 1975-Sept. 1979; Terry MacArthur Sept. 1979-1983; Ross Bunce 1983-1985; Lloyd Walker 1985-1988; Steven Pearson 1988-1995; Orin L. Daniels 1995-1998; David A. Cheyne 1998-Jan. 16, 1999; Sherri L. Swanson Sept. 1, 1999-2017; Susan D. Martin 2017-2018; Brenda Lee Ludwig (LTFT ¾) 2018-2020; Stephen J. Shimek (DSA) 2020-

Three Rivers: Center Park UMC *[Greater Southwest]* officemcp@gmail.com
(P/M) 18662 Moorepark Rd, Three Rivers 49093 (269) 279-9109
Richard Darhing 1969-1970; Douglas Pederson 1970-1971; Luther Brokaw 1971-1975; Logan Weaver 1975-1978; Albert O'Rourke Sept. 1978-April 1982; Jesse Schwoebell 1982-1988; Dwight Stoner 1988-1989; Jeffrey Williams August 1989-Feb. 1993; Nelson Ray June 1993-1995; John L. Moore 1995-1997; Alice Fleming Townley 1997-2001; Stephen C. Small 2001-2004; Patricia L. Bromberek 2004-2006; Linda K. Stull-Lipps 2006-2011; Martin Culver (RLA) 2011-2019; [Center Park and Three Rivers First became multi station circuit 2017] Derl G. Keefer 2019-

Three Rivers: First UMC *[Greater Southwest]*   trfumc@live.com
(P/M) 215 N Main St, Three Rivers 49093   (269) 278-4722
   Richard H. Beckett 1968-1976; Charles D. Grauer 1976-1981; Raymond McBratnie (Assoc.) 1976-1980; James Patrick McCoy (Assoc.) Oct. 1980-1983; Frank B. Closson 1981-April 1985; John A. Backoff (Assoc.) 1983-1985; James E. Fox May 1985-1990; Robert L. Pumphery 1990-1997; Cynthia A. Skutar 1997-2000; Donald R. Fry 2000-2006; Maria L. Rutland Nov. 1, 2006-2012; Robert D. Nystrom (1/2 time) 2012-2015; [Three Rivers First / Mendon became two-point charge 2013; Three Rivers First / Ninth Street became two-point charge 2015] James W. Stilwell 2015-2017; [Center Park and Three Rivers First became multi station circuit 2017] Martin H. Culver (RLA) 2017-2018; Derl Keefer 2018-2019; Heather Ann McGougall 2019-

Three Rivers: Ninth Street UMC *[Greater Southwest]*
(P) 700 9th St, Three Rivers 49093; (M) 16621 Morris Ave, Three Rivers 49093   (269) 273-2065
   Eugene Moore 1968-1972; Helen Jackson 1972-Jan. 1974; Albert A. O'Rourke Nov. 1974-1976; Charles Grauer 1976-1981; Raymond McBratnie (Assoc.) 1976-Aug. 1980; James Patrick McCoy (Assoc.) Oct. 1980-1983; Frank Closson 1981-April 1985; John A. Backoff (Assoc.) 1983-1985; Phillip Simmons 1985-1988; Reva Hawke 1988-Oct. 1991; Marilyn B. Barney Oct. 1991-1998; Carolyn A. Robinson 1998-2007; Thomas R. Reaume (part-time) 2007-2009; [Three Rivers Ninth / Schoolcraft Pleasant Valley became a two-point charge 2009] James W. Stilwell 2009-2017 [Three Rivers First / Ninth Street became two-point charge 2015; Three Rivers Ninth Street became single station 2017]; Edward C. Ross (Ret.) 2017-

Townline UMC *[Greater Southwest]*   townlineumc@gmail.com
(P/M) 41470 24th Ave, Bloomingdale 49026   (269) 521-4559
   John Gurney 1965-1969; Wayne Babcock 1969-1971; Gerald Hudlund 1971-1972; Wayne Barrett 1972-1974; Pulpit Supply 1974-1976; David Youngs 1976-1978; Lloyd Bronson 1978-1985; Dwight Stoner 1985-1988; Donald Williams 1988-1990; William Brady 1990-1991; Kenneth J. Littke 1991-1998; D.S. Assignment 1998; Jana Jirak Sept. 16, 1998-1999; Robert L. Pumfery 1999-October 31, 2002; Patricia Anne Harpole November 1, 2002-2004; O'Ryan Rickard 2004-2005; Sheila F. Baker 2005-Jan. 3, 2008; David L. Youngs Jan. 3, 2008 - June 2008; David L. Haase (DSA) (1/4 time) Jan. 3, 2008; David L. Haase (1/4 time) July 1, 2008-2014; James C. Robertson (1/4 time) 2014- [Bloomingdale merged w/Townline 01-01-2020]

Traverse Bay UMC *[Northern Waters]*   tbumc@traversebaychurch.org
(P/M) 1200 Ramsdell St, Traverse City 49684   (231) 946-5323
   Traverse City Asbury & Emmanuel merged to become Traverse Bay UMC January 2005; [ASBURY: Dale E. Crawford 1967-Oct. 1971; Wilson Tennant Nov. 1971-May 1976; Richard E. Cobb 1976-Aug. 1980; Wirth G. Tennant (Assoc.) 1978-Sept. 1983; William A. Hertel Sept. 1980-1987; John H. Hice 1987-1995; William E. Haggard 1995-2002; Jeremy P.H. Williams 2002- ;] [Emmanuel: George Belknap 1966-1973; B. James Varner 1973-1977; Kenneth A.O. Lindland 1977-1979; Jack Kraklan 1979-1983; Steven Averill 1983-April 1989; Lewis Buchner 1989-1992; Robert J. Mayo 1992-1999; David H. Minger 1999-Jan. 31, 2003; Douglas L. Pedersen Feb. 1, 2003- ;] Jeremy P.H. Williams 2002-2009; Douglas L. Pedersen Feb. 1, 2003-2005; Devon R. Herrell (Assoc.) 2005-2008; Jeanne E. Koughn (Assoc.) 2008-2009; Jane R. Lippert 2009-Sept. 1, 2015; John E. Harnish Sept. 1, 2015-2016; Kathryn Sue Snedeker 2016-2020; Matthew D. Chapman 2020-

Traverse City: Central UMC *[Northern Waters]*   office@tccentralumc.org
(P/M) 222 Cass St, Traverse City 49684   (231) 946-5191
   William N. DesAutels 1968-Nov. 1974; Robert C. Brubaker Dec. 1974-1981; Ellen A. Brubaker (Assoc.) 1975-1981; Joanne Parshall (Assoc.) 1981-Sept. 1982; David L. Crawford 1981-1987; Gary T. Haller (Assoc.) 1981-1985; Kathy E. Brown (Assoc.) 1985-1990; Dean I. Bailey 1987- 2002; Steven R. Emery-Wright (Assoc.) Aug. 1990-May 1992; Robert D. Nystrom (Assoc.) 1992-1994; John W. Ellinger 2002-2007; Tamara S.M. Williams (Assoc.) 2002-2009; Dale Ostema 2007- ; Christopher M. Lane (Assoc.) 2009-

Traverse City: Mosaic *[Northern Waters]*   jeremy_wicks@yahoo.com
(P/M) 1249 Three Mile Rd S, Traverse City 49696   (231) 946-3048
    [New Church Start Jul 1, 2017] Jeremy J. Wicks 2017-

Trenary UMC *[Nothern Skies]*   skolder@att.net
(P) N1133 ET Rd, Trenary 49891; (M) PO Box 201, Trenary 49891   (906) 446-3599
    Norman Kohns 1969-1973; William Verhelst 1973-1974; Wayne Large 1974-1977; Robert Porter
    1977-1979; William Bowers 1979-1983; George Thompson 1983-1985; James Ritchie 1985-1992;
    Gail P. Baughman 1993-1994; James M. Downing 1994-1997; Irene R. White Sep 1, 1997-2011;
    Sandra J. Kolder 2011-

Trenton: Faith UMC *[Greater Detroit]*   trentonfaithumc@sbcglobal.net
(P/M) 2530 Charlton Rd, Trenton 48183   (734) 671-5211
    Robert L. Selberg 1969-1978; Edward C. Coley 1978-1984; Richard O. Griffith 1984-1989; James
    L. Rhinesmith (assoc) 1984-1988; Marshall G. Dunlap (co-pastor) 1989-1999; Susan K. DeFoe
    Dunlap (co-pastor) 1989-1999; Mark E. Spaw 1999-2010; George R. Spencer 2010-2016; Douglas
    E. Ralston 2016-2019; Wayne A. Price 2019-

Trenton: First UMC *[Greater Detroit]*   trentonfumc@gmail.com
(P/M) 2610 W Jefferson Ave, Trenton 48183   (734) 676-2066
    Walter C. B. Saxman 1962-1971; Robert J. Hudgins 1971-1976; Ira L. Fett 1976-1985; Webley J.
    Simpkins 1985-1994; Shawn P. Lewis-Lakin 1994-1997; Karen D. Poole 1997-2003; Raymond D.
    Wightman 2003-2008; Elizabeth A. Macaulay 2008-Apr 1, 2013; Mary Beth Beebe Apr 15, 2013-
    2013; Benjamin Bower 2013-2016; Heidi C. Reinker 2016-

Troy: Big Beaver UMC *[Greater Detroit]*   bbumc@bbumchurch.org
(P/M) 3753 John R Rd, Troy 48083   (248) 689-1932
    Michael Grajcar Jr. 1969-1976; Terry Euper 1976-1989; Daniel J. Wallace 1989-1991; Edwin
    Hingelberg 1991-Feb 26, 1997; H. Emory Hinkston 1997-2002; Jack L. Mannschreck 2002-2013-
    David E. Huseltine 2013-2016; Gregory M. Mayberry 2016-

Troy: First UMC *[Greater Detroit]*   troyfirst@sbcglobal.net
(P/M) 6363 Livernois Rd, Troy 48098   (248) 879-6363
    Robert M. Clune 1967-1969; Alfred T. Bamsey 1969-1976; Elwood J. Berkompas 1976-1982; David
    M. Liscomb 1982-1986; William D. Mercer 1986-1990; Terry Allen 1990-1997; Richard A. Peacock
    1997-2008; Harold E. Weemhoff, Jr. 2008-2015; Weatherly Burkhead Verhelst 2015-

Troy: Korean UMC *[Greater Detroit]*   bibisisi@gmail.com
(P/M) 42693 Dequindre Rd, Troy 48085   (248) 879-2240
    Young B. Yoon 1978-Dec 31, 1994; Kwang Min Lee (assoc) Dec. 1989-1991; Paul Lee (assoc)
    1992-1994; Dongil Chang (assoc) 1994-1997; Hoon K. Lee Jan 1, 1995-2013; Sang K. Choi (assoc)
    1996-Mar 31, 2001; Jin Young Oh (assoc) Jan 1, 1998-Aug 1, 2002; Min Hyuk Woo (assoc) Jun 1,
    2001-2011; S. David Ryn (assoc.) Jul 12, 2004-2006; Jung Eun Yum (assoc.) Jan 1, 2006-2011;
    Youngchoel Woo (assoc) 2008-Jan 15, 2015; David Inho Kim (assoc) 2008-2016; Chan Joung
    Jang 2013-Jan 31, 2018; In Boem Oh (assoc.) 2013-2016; Se Jin Bae (assoc.) Mar 1, 2015- ; Tae
    Gyu Shin (assoc) 2016-2020; Anna Mi-Hyun Moon (assoc) 2016- ; Jinny L. Song (deacon) 2016-
    ; Kyunglim Shin Lee Feb 9, 2018- Dec 31, 2018; Eung Yong Kim Jan 1, 2019-

Troy: Korean – Hope Campus UMC *[Greater Detroit]*   troyhopeministry@gmail.com
(P/M) 42693 Dequindre Rd, Troy 48085   (248) 879-2240
    [New Church Start] Anna Mi-Hyun Moon (assoc) 2016-

Turk Lake UMC *[Midwest]*   pastordonnasperry@gmail.com
(P/M) 8900 Colby Rd, Greenville 48838   (616) 754-3718
   George Fleming 1965-1975; Douglas Pedersen 1975-1979; Jim Hartman 1979-1982; Steven Young
   1982-1987; Joyce DeToni-Hill 1987-1990; Jane Crabtree 1990-1996; John F. Ritter 1996-Nov. 1,
   2001; Ronald W. DeGraw Nov. 1, 2001-2005; Kay Welsch (DSA) July 16, 2005-2012; [Turk Lake /
   Belding became two-point charge 2012] Kimberly A. DeLong Aug. 15, 2012-2013; [Greenville First,
   Turk Lake/Belding Cooperative Parish 2013] Kimberly A. DeLong (Deacon) 2013-2015; Stephen
   MG Charnley 2013-14; Stephen F. Lindeman 2013-14; Donald E. Spachman 2014- ; Eric Mulanda
   Nduwa (Assoc.) Feb. 15-Aug. 1, 2015 [cooperative parish re-named Flat River Cooperative Parish
   2015] ; Joseph K. Caldwell (CLM/DSA) Aug. 1, 2015-2016; Donna Jean Sperry 2016-

Twin Lake UMC *[Midwest]*   jdm14879@gmail.com
(P) 5940 S Main St, Twin Lake 49457; (M) PO Box 352, Twin Lake 49457   (231) 828-4083
   Kenneth D. McCaw 1967-1968; Austin W. Regier 1969; Alma H. Glotfelty 1970; Ira J. Noordhof
   1971-1975; Donald J. Vuurens, Oct. 15, 1975-Dec. 31, 1977; Wayne Speese (Pulpit Supply) Jan.
   1, 1978-June 1978; Charles R. VanLente 1978-1983; Steven D. Pearson 1983-1988; Kathryn B.
   Robotham 1988-1990; Michael A. Van Horn 1990-1991; Leonard Coon 1991-Oct. 31, 1999; Milton
   Stahl (interim) Nov. 1, 1999-July 1, 2000; Patrick Cameron 2000-2002; Sally J. LaFrance 2002-
   Oct. 1, 2004; Paul R. Doherty (DSA) Nov. 1, 2004-2010; Mary Loring 2010-2013; John D. Morse
   (Ret.) 2013-2018; William F. Dye 2018-2020; Michael E. Long Jan 5, 2020-

Union City UMC *[Greater Southwest]*   unioncityumc@frontier.com
(P) 200 Ellen St, Union City 49094; (M) PO Box 95, Union City 49094-0095   (517) 741-7028
   Philip L. Brown 1966-1971; Walter J. Rothfuss 1971-1973; Larry Grubaugh 1973-1980; Adam
   Chyrowski 1980-1986; Eric S. Beck 1986-July 31, 1995; David W. Meister Aug. 1, 1995-Aug. 15,
   1997; D.S. Assignment Aug. 16, 1997; John L. Moore (DSA) Aug. 17, 1997-2004; Robert M. Hughes
   2004-2012; [Union City / Athens became two-point charge 2012] Seung Ho Baek (3/4 time) 2012-
   2015; Cynthia L. Veilleux 2015-2018; James Palaszeski 2018-

Utica UMC *[Greater Detroit]*   charlotte@uticaumc.org
(P/M) 8650 Canal Rd, Sterling Heights 48314   (586) 731-7667
   Samuel F. Stout 1966-1971; Paul S. Durham (assoc) 1969-1971; Robert E. Horton 1971-1977;
   Kenneth R. Callis 1977-1989; Richard A. Peacock (assoc) 1973-1978; William R. Donahue (assoc)
   1979-1982; John R. Walters (assoc) 1982-1983; Thomas M. Beagan (assoc) 1983-1987; Gary R.
   Glanville (assoc) 1987-1989; Christopher D. Cowdin (assoc) 1989-1996; Jeffery D. Regan 1989-
   1994; David Diamond 1994-2003; James J. Walker (assoc) 1996-1998; Vincent P. Facione (assoc)
   1998- Nov 30, 1999; William R. Donahue, Jr. 2003-2011; David J. Goudie (assoc) 2004-2009;
   Weatherly Burkhead Verhelst (assoc) 2009-2015; Donald D. Gotham 2011-

Vassar: First UMC *[Central Bay]*   vassarfumc@sbcglobal.net
(P) 139 N Main St, Vassar 48768; (M) PO Box 71, Vassar 48768-0071   (989) 823-8811
   Robert Bough 1968-1972; Clare Patton 1972-1983; Alan DeGraw 1983-1991; Charles Knight 1991-
   Dec 31, 1996; Richard W. Sheppard 1997-Oct 26, 2001; Steven L. Woodford May 1, 2002-2010;
   William Sanders (interim) May 1, 2007-2008; Tyson G. Ferguson 2010-2013; Catherine Christman
   2013-2016; Scott Sherrill 2016-

Vernon UMC *[East Winds]*   nbeckwithsr@msn.com
(P) 202 E Main St, Vernon 48476; (M) PO Box 155, Vernon 48476   (989) 288-4187
   Ralph D. Harper 1968-1970; Meldon E. Crawford 1970-1975; Thomas E. Hart 1975-1980; Willard
   A. King Sept., 1980-Mar. 15, 1985; Raymond D. Field 1985-1988; Katherine J. Rairick 1988-1991;
   Philip D. Voss 1991-Jul 31, 1997; James M. Mathews Aug 1, 1997-Sep 30, 2001; Frederic G. Heath
   Oct 1, 2001-2003; Richard B. Brown 2003-2006; Billy J. McKown 2006-Jun 6, 2007; Gerald M.
   Sever, Jr., 2007-2015; Norman R. Beckwith, Sr. 2016-2020; David Owen Jul 15, 2020-

Vickeryville UMC *[Midwest]*   fenwickumc@cmsinter.net
(P) 6850 S Vickeryville Rd, Sheridan 48884; (M) PO Box 241, Sheridan 48884   (989) 291-5547
John H. Gurney 1970-1976; Norman Crotser 1976-Dec. 1978; Daniel R. Bennett 1979-March 1982;
Mark G. Johnson March 1982-1986; James E. Cook 1986-1991; Howard H. Harvey 1991-1996;
Patrick Glass 1996-1998; Larry W. Nalett 1998-Aug. 9, 2004; Charles E. Cerling Aug. 10, 2004-
2009; Jolennda Cole (DSA) 2009-2010; Jolennda Cole 2010-2011; William F. Dye 2011-2012;
Russell D. Morgan (CLM) July 15, 2012-2014; ;Gerald A Erskine (DSA) 2014-Nov. 9, 2014; Gerald
A Erskine Nov. 10, 2014-2020; Melissa S. Wagner (DSA) 2020-

Vicksburg UMC *[Greater Southwest]*   reception@vicksburgumc.org
(P/M) 217 S Main St, Vicksburg 49097   (269) 649-2343
Dean Bailey (Methodist) 1966-1969; David Morton (EUB) 1965-1969; Myron K. Williams 1969-
1972; C. Robert Carson 1972-Oct. 1977; Francis C. Johannides Oct. 1977-1981; Lowell F.
Walsworth; 1981-1993; Lawrence R. Wood (Assoc.) 1991-1995; James R. Hulett 1993-1997; Jana
Lynn Almeida (Assoc.) 1995-1997; Isabell M. Deppe 1998-Sept. 2000; Bufford W. Coe, Oct. 15,
2000-2017; Gregory P. Culver 2017-

Wacousta: Community UMC *[Mid-Michigan]*   office@wacoustaumc.org
(P/M) 9180 W Herbison Rd, Eagle 48822   (517) 626-6623
Dale Spoor 1967-1971; Edward Otto 1971-1977; John R. Smith 1977-1984; Eugene Lewis 1984-
1986; James Hynes 1986-1992; Betty A. Smith 1992-1998; D.S. Assignment 1998; Lyle D. Heaton
Jan. 1, 1999-2013; Amee A. Paparella 2013-2016; Hillary Thurston-Cox 2016-

Gladwin: Wagarville Community UMC *[Central Bay]*
(P/M) 2478 Wagarville Rd, Gladwin 48624   (989) 426-2971
George Saucier & Bob Bryce 1969-1973; Wayne D. Jensen 1973-1985; Wayne D. Jensen
(w/Wooden Shoe) 1985-1991; Sherry Parker (w/Wooden Shoe) 1991-1994; Janet M. Larner 1994-
Aug 31, 1994; Margaret Garrigues-Cortelyou Sep 1, 1994-1995; Donald P. Haskell 1995-Dec 31,
2004; Kim Spencer Jan 1, 2005-2005; Linda Jo Powers 2005-2009; Jim Noggle 2009-2012; Michael
J. Simon 2011-2013; Dennis Paulson 2013-2014; Vincent Nader 2014-Sept 1, 2016; Doug E. Hasse
(DSA) Sept 1, 2017- Dec 31, 2018; Doug E. Hasse Jan 1, 2019-

Wakefield UMC *[Nothern Skies]*   aa8yf@yahoo.com
(P/M) 706 Putnam St, Wakefield 49968   (906) 988-2533
J. Harold Wallis 1971-1976; Lillian G. Richards 1976-1984; Gary A. Allward 1984-1987; Thomas
H. Zimmerman 1987-1991; Carl R. Doersch 1991-1995; Pamela S. Kail 1995-1998; Allen F.
Schweitzer 1998-Sep 30, 1999; Cherrie A. Sporleder Feb 1, 2000-Jun 30, 2000; Jean B. Rencontre
2000-2008; Theodore A. Trudgeon 2008-2019; [Ironwood Wesley / Wakefield two-pooint charge
7-1-2019] Keith Paul Mullikin (DSA) 2019- Jan 21, 2020; Keith Paul Mullikin Jan 22, 2020-

Walkerville UMC *[Midwest]*   gooey@tir.com
(P) 189 E Main St, Walkerville 49459; (M) PO Box 125, Walkerville 49459   (231) 873-4236
A. Ruth Bonser Oct. 1990-1993; Nancy Bugajski 1993-1996; Donald J. Vuurens (DSA) 1996-1998;
Steven J. Hale 1998-Nov. 8, 1999; Ronald A. Houk (DSA) Nov. 8, 1999-2000; Kenneth E. Tabor
2000-2004; Ronald L. Worley 2004-Nov. 30, 2013; Ronald Iris (Ret.) Dec. 1, 2013-2015; Theresa
Fairbanks (DSA) Jun. 1, 2015-Nov. 14, 2016; Kenneth E. Tabor (RLA) Dec. 1, 2015-Dec. 1, 2016;
Theresa Fairbanks Nov. 15, 2016-2018; David O Pratt (Ret) (LTFT) 2018-

Walled Lake UMC *[Heritage]*   walledlakeumc@sbcglobal.net
(P/M) 313 Northport St, Walled Lake 48390   (248) 624-2405
  Horace G. Thurston 1968-1970; David E. Church 1970-1978; Lloyd E. Christler 1978-1984; Leland
  E. Penzien 1984-1990; John R. Crotser (assoc) 1987-1990; Tat-Khean Foo 1990-1997; Samuel
  D. Fry, Jr. 1997-1998; Judith A. May 1998-2003; Demphna R. Krikorian 2003-Aug 1, 2003; Gordon
  Ackerman (interm) Aug 1, 2003-2004; Taek H. Kim 2004-2012; Robert J. Sielaff 2012-2016; Ian J.
  Boley 2016-2020; Kenny R. Walkup Jr. 2020-

Warren: First UMC *[Greater Detroit]*   contact@warrenfirstumc.org
(P/M) 5005 Chicago Rd, Warren 48092   (586) 264-4701
  Douglas Parker 1968-1969; Harold Johnson (assoc) 1967-1968; Paul F. Blomquist 1969-1973;
  Robert Davis 1973-1979; Randall Vinson (assoc) 1980 Mar 1982; John Britt (assoc) 1982-Nov
  1982; M. Jean Love (assoc) 1984; O. William Cooper 1979-1985; Norbert W. Smith 1985-1990;
  Johnny S. Liles (assoc) 1988-Mar 1990; Richard Andrus (assoc) Jan. 1990-1992; Thomas P.
  Macaulay July 1990-1997; Sharon G. Scott-Niefert (assoc) 1992-1995; Chong Yaub Won (assoc.)
  1995-Aug 31, 1998; David G. Gladstone 1997-2003; Carolyn F. Hart (assoc) 1999- ; Murphy Ehlers
  (deacon) Dec 1, 2002-2003; Judith A. May 2003-2008; Dennis N. Paulson 2008-2012; Susan M.
  Youmans 2012-2018; Melissa J. Claxton 2018-

Washington UMC *[Greater Detroit]*
(P) 58430 Van Dyke Rd, Washington 48094; (M) PO Box 158, Washington 48094   (586) 781-9662
  Harry M. Brakeman 1968-1974; John E. Harnish 1974-1979; John C. Stubbs 1979-1983; Brent L.
  Webster 1983-Aug 31, 1997; Bea B. Soots Sep 1, 1997-Dec 31, 1998; George R. Spencer Jan 1,
  1999-2002; James E. Barnett (assoc) 2000-Jun 1, 2002; James E. Barnett Jun 1, 2002-Feb 1,
  2007; Arthur R. Stone (interim) Jan 14, 2007-Feb 28, 2007; Jean R. Snyder (interim) Mar 1, 2007-
  2007; Cheryl Mancier 2007-2011; William C. Schumann 2011-2014; Donna J. Zuhlke 2014-Sept
  1, 2018; Mary Ellen Chapman (Ret.) Sep 3, 2018-2019; [Omo: Zion / Washington became signle
  point charges 7-1-2019] Cherlyn E. McKanders 2019-

Waterford: Central UMC *[Greater Detroit]*   info@waterfordcumc.org
(P/M) 3882 Highland Rd, Waterford 48328   (248) 681-0040
  (Previously: Pontiac: Central)—Carl E. Price 1968-1973; Richard L. Clemans (assoc) 1963-1969;
  James H. McLaurin (assoc) 1966-1968; Ronald Tallman (assoc) 1968- 1971; Edwin A. Rowe (assoc)
  1971-1974; Alan DeGraw (assoc) 1975-1978; Max L. Gibbs (assoc) 1978-1980; Richard L. Myers
  (assoc) 1980-1989; Ralph D. Churchill 1973-1982; W. Herbert Glenn 1982-1992 (changed church
  to Waterford: Central 1992); W. Herbert Glenn 1982-1992; George Covintree (assoc.) 1989-1993;
  Dale Miller 1992-Sep 30, 2000; Susan Bennett Stiles (assoc) Apr 15, 1994-May 1, 1999; Eric A.
  Stone (assoc) 1999-Nov 30, 2001; James G. Kellermann Nov 1, 2000-2013; Tara R. Sutton (assoc)
  Dec 31, 2001-2005; Wendy Lyons Chrostek (assoc.) 2006-2009; Kathryn L. Pittenger (deacon)
  2008-2018; Karen B. Williams (assoc) 2009-2010; Jack L. Mannschreck 2013- ;

Waterford: Four Towns UMC *[Greater Detroit]*   fourtownsumc@gmail.com
(P/M) 6451 Cooley Lake Rd, Waterford 48327   (248) 682-0211
  Daniel L. Rial 1968-1969; Frank Dennis 1969-1971; Troy Lemmons 1971-1977; Dale Ferris 1977-
  1979; Leroy E. Philbrook 1979-1980; Harold Slater 1980-1989; Judith A. May 1989-Jan 1, 1996;
  Allen F. Schweizer Jun 1, 1996-1998; Sharon S. Niefert 1998-Aug 31, 2001; Cynthia Loomis-Able
  Sep 1, 2001-2004; Karen D. Poole 2004-2006; Bea Barbara Fraser-Soots 2006-2014; Theodore
  D. Whitely, Sr. 2014-2015; Dale R. Milford (DSA) 2015-2019; Sean LaGuire (DSA) 2019-Dec 31,
  2019; Sean LaGuire Jan 1-June 30, 2020; George Marck 2020-

Waterford: Trinity UMC *[Greater Detroit]*   wtrinityumc@juno.com
(P/M) 6440 Maceday Dr, Waterford 48329   (248) 623-6860
   Timothy Hickey 1967-1969; Don Crumm 1969-1970; Bob Goudie 1970- 1976; Tat-Khean Foo 1976-1990; John C. Ferris 1990-1998; Juanita J. Ferguson 1998-2003; Kenneth B. Ray 2003-2004; Karen D. Poole 2004-2006; Kim D. Spencer 2006-2009; Carter Cortelyou 2010-2013; Theodore Whitely, Sr. 2013-2015; Zelphia J. Mobley 2015-2019; Michael R. Perez, Jr. 2019-

Waterloo Village UMC *[Heritage]*   waterloovillageumc@gmail.com
(P/M) 8110 Washington St, Grass Lake 49240   (734) 475-1171
   Wilbur Silvernail 1960-1969; Donald R. Fry 1969-1970; Altha M. Barnes 1970-1975; Richard M. Young 1975-1976; Glenn Kjellburg 1976-1978; Pulpit Supply 1978-1979; L. A. Nichols 1979-1988; Merlin Pratt 1988-1991; Wayne Willer 1991-1995; Pulpit Supply 1995; Kathleen A. Groff Dec. 1995-July 31, 1997; Mona Joslyn Aug. 1, 1997-1998; Kathleen S. Kursch 1998-Feb. 1, 2000; Georgiana M. Dack (1/4 time) Feb. 1, 2000-2013; [Waterloo Village/First no longer two-point charge 2013] Edward C. Ross (Ret.) (1/4 time) 2013-2016; Mary J. Barrett 2016-

Watrousville UMC *[Central Bay]*   chaplainbill4msp@aol.com
(P) 4446 W Caro Rd, Caro 48723; (M) 2076 1st St, Vassar 48768   (989) 673-3434
   Donald Pinner 1968-1970; Edgar M. Smith 1970-1976; Monroe J. Frederick 1976-1988; Sang Yoon (Abraham) Chun 1988-1992; James P. James 1992-1996; Martin G. Seitz 1996-1998; Wayne C. Samson 1998-2005; James A. Payne 2005-Feb 28, 2010; Daniel Gonder Mar 1, 2010-2013; William Sanders 2013-

Wayland UMC *[Midwest]*   office@waylandumc.org
(P/M) 200 Church St, Wayland 49348   (269) 792-2208
   H. Forest Crum, 1960-66; Bernard R. Randolph 1966-1970; Leo E. Bennett 1970-1979; Richard W. Barker 1979-1982; Douglas L. Pedersen 1982-1987; James W. Barney 1987-Sept. 1991; Wendell R. Stine Sept. 1991-1995; Stacy R. Minger 1995-Jul. 31, 2001; Julie A. Dix Aug. 1, 2001-2003; Nancy L. Besemer 2003-Nov. 1, 2006; Gary D. Bondarenko Nov. 15, 2006-2014; Jeffrey C. Williams 2014-2020; Paul C. Reissman 2020-

Wayne-Westland: First UMC *[Greater Detroit]*   fumcww@yahoo.com
(P/M) 3 Towne Square St, Wayne 48184   (734) 721-4801
   Russell W. Sursaw 1966-1970; Charles E. Jacobs 1970-1984; Daniel J. Wallace 1984-1989; Martha C. Gregg (Ball) (assoc) 1984-1985; John W. Kershaw 1989-1995; Fredrick P. Cooley 1995-Jul 31, 2000; David K. Stewart Sr. Aug 1, 2000-2008; Gregory E. Rowe 2008-2011; Paul S. Hahm 2011-2013; Jennifer Jue 2013-2014; Carter L. Cortelyou 2014-2018; Marva Pope 2018-

Webberville UMC *[Mid-Michigan]*   webbervillechurch@gmail.com
(P/M) 4215 E Holt Rd, Webberville 48892   (517) 521-3631
   Gary Lyons 1968-1969; Milford Bowen 1969-1973; John McNaughton 1973-1979; Ross Bunce 1979-1983; Wayne Babcock 1983-1991; David Cheyne 1991-1995; Dwayne E. Bagley 1995-2002; Wayne E. McKenney Aug. 1, 2002-2005; Robert D. Nystrom 2005-2007; Sandra L. Spahr (DSA) 2007-Dec. 31, 2007; Paul A. Damkoehler, Jan. 1, 2008-2013; [M-52 Cooperative Ministry 2013; renamed Connections Cooperative Ministry 2015] Richard J. Foster (3/4 time) 2013-2016; Jacqueline L. Raineri 2016-2017; Martin A. Johnston 2017-

CHURCH HISTORIES

Weidman UMC *[Central Bay]*   weidmanumc@yahoo.com
(P) 3200 N Woodruff Rd, Weidman 48893; (M) PO Box 98, Weidman 48893   (989) 644-3148
James Linton 1967-1969; Lawrence R. Smith 1969-1970; Athel J. Lynch 1970-1977; Vance M. Dimmick, Jr. 1977-1984; Diane E. Vale 1984-1985; Pulpit supply July 1985-Jan. 1986; Randall E. Roose Jan. 1986-1993; Melanie S. Young 1993-1994; Jerry L. Hippensteel 1994-March 26, 1995; Pulpit Supply April-June 1995; James H.K. Lawrence 1995-May 10, 1999; Craig L. Adams Sept. 16, 1999-2006; David Price (DSA) 2006-Nov. 15, 2006; David Price Nov. 15, 2006-2013; Scott B. Smith 2013-2019; Cynthia S.L. Greene 2019-

Wellsville UMC *[Heritage]*   wmclemmer@hotmail.com
(P/M) 2509 S Wellsville Hwy, Blissfield 49228-9554   (517) 486-4777
Edward C. Weiss 1968-1972; Gerald R. Parker 1972-1973; Robert L. Porter 1973-1976; John D. Roach 1976-1979; Kenneth C. Reeves 1979-1982; Thomas C. Sumwalt 1982-1984; Mark D. Miller 1984-1989; Thomas A. Davenport 1989-Sep. 15, 1990; Benjamin B. Ball Sep. 16, 1990-1991; Kimberly A. Barker 1991-May 31, 1992; Bradford K. Lewis Jun. 1, 1992-1994; Gerald M. Sever, Jr. 1994-1999; Wilson C. Bailey 1999-Aug 31, 1999; Allen W. Schweitzer Oct 1, 1999-Oct 31, 2000; Edward C. Weiss Nov 1, 2000-2005; William Michael Clemmer 2005-Dec 31, 2013; Samuel Pooley 2014-Dec 31, 2014; David R McKinstry Jan 8-Jun 30, 2017; William T. Kreichbaum 2017-2019; Bradley R. Vasey 2019-

West Berlin UMC *[East Winds]*   cbclarke95@gmail.com
(P) 905 Holmes Rd, Allenton 48002; (M) PO Box 533, Armada 48005   (810) 395-2409
Paul Jarvis 1967-1970; Victor L. Studaker 1970-1973; Rodney E. Rawson 1973-1976; James B. Limsden 1976-1978; David D. Amstutz 1978-1981; Emerson W. Arntz 1982-1991; Rothwell W. McVety 1991-1997; Ralph Barteld 1997-2003; Ruthmary King (assoc) 1998-2001; Harold Nelson (assoc) 2001-2003; Dianna L. Rees 2003-2011; Curtis Clarke (DSA) Jul 1,-Nov 11, 2011-Curtis Clarke Nov 12, 2011-2019; Christopher G.L. Titus 2019-

West Bloomfield UMC *[Greater Detroit]*   wbumc@sbcglobal.net
(P/M) 4100 Walnut Lake Rd, West Bloomfield 48323   (248) 851-2330
Leland E. Penzien 1969-1984; Thomas E. Hart 1984-1991; Jerome K. Smith 1991-Jul 31, 1997; Brent L. Webster Sep 1, 1997-2010; Robert D. Schoenals 2010-2012; Brian K. William 2012-Apr 16, 2019; Brent L. Webster (Ret.) May 1-Jun30, 2019; Monica L. William 2019-

West Branch: First UMC *[Central Bay]*   office@westbranchfumc.org
(P/M) 2490 W State Rd, West Branch 48661   (989) 345-0210
R. LaVere Webster 1968-1973; Howard R. Higgins 1973-1977; Walter R. Damberg 1977-1983; Bruce M. Denton 1983-1988; Gordon W. Nusz 1988-1993; David Penniman 1993-Dec 17, 1997; Kenneth Tousley (interim) Dec 18, 1997-1998; Mark D. Miller 1998-2006; Mary Lynch Mallory 2006-2009; Lisa L. Cook 2009-2014; Timothy C. Dibble 2014-

West Deerfield UMC *[East Winds]*   pastor.kay@live.com
(P) 383 Otter Lake Rd, Fostoria 48435; (M) PO Box 185, Fostoria 48435
John F. Greer 1971-1976; Gerald E. Mumford 1976-1989; Ginethea D. McDowell 1989-1992; Nobel R. Joseph 1992-Dec 31, 1996; David M. Fairchild Jan 1, 1997-2001; David P. Rahn 2001-May 1, 2009; Peggy Garrigues-Cortelyou 2009-2010; Betty Kay Leitelt 2010-

West Forest UMC *[East Winds]*   smithsk1962@gmail.com
(P) 7297 Farrand Rd, Millington 48746; (M) 129 E Vates, Frankenmuth 48734   (989) 871-3456
Gerald E. Mumford 1964-1976; Lawrence C. Whiting 1976-1977; Bruce L. Billing 1977-1982; Janice I. Martineau 1982-1985; G. Patrick England Sept. 1, 1985-1993; Gregory E. Rowe 1993-Feb 28, 1995; Billy J. McKown Mar 1, 1995-2005; James P. James 2005-2007; Carter L. Garrigues-Cortelyou 2007-2010; Bruce E. Malicoat 2010-2020; [West Vienna, West Forest became 2-point charge 2020] Christopher M. Grimes 2020-

West Vienna UMC *[East Winds]*   westviennaumc@gmail.com
(P/M) 5485 W Wilson Rd, Clio 48420   (810) 686-7480
John N. Grenfell, Sr. 1968-1973; Melvin Leach 1973-1981; William B. Cozadd 1981-1982; David K. Koski 1982-1986; Wayne C. Ferrigan 1986-1992; James E. Britt 1992-2001; Bonny J. Lancaster 2001-2006; Billie Lou Gillespie Oct 15, 2006-2020; [West Vienna, West Forest became 2-point charge 2020] Christopher M. Grimes 2020-

Westland: St. James UMC *[Greater Detroit]*   stsjamesumcwestland@att.net
(P/M) 30055 Annapolis Rd, Westland 48186-5372   (734) 729-1737
Bradley F. Watkins 1968-1971; Clarence Acklin 1971-1974; Charles A. Talbert (part-time R) 1974-1979; Janet Gaston Petty 1980-1984; Theodore Whitely 1984-1986; Robert G. Williams 1986-1995; Elias Mumbiro 1995-Oct 31, 1999; Cheryl Myhand Nov 16, 1999-Apr 30, 2000; Hydrian Elliott May 1, 2000-2003; Carter M. Grimmett Sep 1, 2003-2008; Willie Frank Smith 2008-2015; Christopher M. Grimes 2015-2017; Rahim O. Shabazz 2017-

Weston UMC *[Heritage]*   donagalloway@msn.com
(P) 4193 Weston Rd, Weston 49289; (M) PO Box 96, Weston 49289   (517) 436-3492
Robert Hinklin 1968-1969; John F. Price 1969-1971; Ronald Hart 1971-1972; Richard C. Andrus 1972-1975; Wayne N. Thomas 1975-1976; Donald A. Wittbrodt 1977-1978; Mark K. Smith 1978-2012; David McKinstry 2012-2014; Lawson Crane 2014-2015; Tyler Kleeberger 2015-2016; Dona Galloway 2016-

White Cloud UMC *[Midwest]*   whitecloudumc@att.net
(P/M) 1125 E Newell St, White Cloud 49349   (231) 689-5911
William A. Hertel 1966-1969; Kenneth E. Curtis 1969-1971; Allan R. Valkema 1971-1976; Peter H. Kunnen 1976-Jan. 1984; Thomas and Lynn Pier-Fitzgerald (co-pastors) May 1984-1988; Jerry L. Jaquish 1988-2002, Jeffrey J. Bowman 2002-2012; Edwin D. Snook 2012-

White Pigeon UMC *[Greater Southwest]*
(P) 204 N Kalamazoo St, White Pigeon 49099; (M) PO Box 518, White Pigeon 49099
    (269) 483-9054
Lyle Chapman 1965-1969; Robert Stillson 1969-1975; Daniel Wolcott 1975-Sept. 1977; Donald Fry Nov. 1977-1981; Kendall Lewis 1981-Jan. 1985; Wesley Smith Jan. 1985-Sept. 1990; Charles Vizthum Nov. 1990-July 31, 1995; Mary Pieh 1996-1998; Patrick Glass 1998-Sept. 15, 2001; Linda J. Burton (DSA) 2001-2002; Linda J. Burton 2002-2005; Ronna L. Swartz 2005-2007; Janet L. Luchs (part-time) 2007-2009 [Schoolcraft Pleasant Valley / White Pigeon became a two-point charge 2008]; Scott E. Manning 2009-2016 [Constantine / White Pigeon became a two-point charge 2009]; Khristian A. McCutchan 2016-2017; Tiffany M. Newsom 2017-2020; Lanette S. Van 2020-

White Pine UMC Community *[Northern Skies]*   wpcumc@yahoo.com
(P) 9 Tamarack, White Pine 49971; (M) PO Box 158, White Pine 49971   (906) 885-5419
Lloyd E. Christler 1968-1972; James Hilliard 1970-1971; Lawrence Brooks 1971-1975; Roger Gedcke 1972-1979; Lillian Richards 1971-1976; Wayne E. Sparks 1975-1980; Myra Sparks 1976-1980; Ed Hingelberg 1979-1981; Robert Thornton 1981-1983; Deane Wyllys 1983-1987; Charles H. West 1987-1993; Margaret H. West 1987-1993; Earleen VanConant 1993-1997; Clarence VanConant 1993-1997; Timothy C. Dibble 1997-2000; Cherrie A. Sporleder 2000-Jun 15, 2002; Rosemary R. DeHut Aug 1, 2002- [White Pine Community / Ironwood: Wesley became single point charges 9-1-2018] [White Pine Community / Ironwood: Wesley became single point charges 9-1-2018] [White Pine Community / Ewen / Bergland three-point charge 7-1-2019]

Whittemore UMC *[Central Bay]*   whittemoreumc@yahoo.com
(P) 110 North St, Whittemore 48770; (M) PO Box 155, Whittemore 48770   (989) 756-2831
Arthur Parkin (Whittemore) 1963-1972; Henry Powell (Whittemore) 1972-1973; Stephen Meeks (Prescott) 1967-1971; Robert L. Porter (Prescott) 1971-1973; Merle Nichols 1973-1978; Donald Shark 1978-1982; Harold Weemhoff 1982-1984; Lynn Chappell 1984-1989; Donald Milano 1989-1992; Allen Schweizer 1992-May 31, 1996; Linda Jo Powers Jun 16, 1996-2000; Kim Spencer 2000-Aug 31, 2002; Donald R. Derby Nov 1, 2002-2005; Bruce A. Mitchell 2005-2008; Brenda K. Klacking 2008-2014; Joseph Coon 2014-2016; Nathan J. Jeffords 2016-2019; Gary Gillings (DSA) 2019-

Wilber UMC *[Central Bay]*   pkrwilber@gmail.com
(P) 3278 Sherman Rd, East Tawas 48730; (M) 7620 Spruce St, Hale 48739   (989) 362-7860
Charles Hanley 1969-1974; L. Susan Garment 1974-1975; Clifford DeVore 1975-1980; William Stone 1980-1983; Priscilla Seward (w/Glennie, Curran) 1983-1985; Margaret A. Paige (w/Glennie, Curran) 1985-1986; Margaret A. Paige (w/Glennie, Curran) (1/2 time) 1986-1991; James E Paige Jr. (w/Glennie, Curran) (1/2 time) 1986-1991; Charles Bamberger 1991-1992; Deborah Lewis 1992-1993; Thomas Spencer 1993-1994; Charles J. Bamberger Oct 1, 1994-2008; Brenda K. Klacking 2008-2014; Keith Reinhardt 2014-

Williamsburg UMC *[Northern Waters]*   wumctoday@gmail.com
(P) 5750 Williamsburg Rd, Williamsburg 49690; (M) PO Box 40, Williamsburg 49690
                    (231) 267-5792
Merritt F. Bongard 1991-1993; Cynthia W. Schaefer 1993-1997; Douglas L. Pedersen 1997-2005; William W. Chu & Julie A. Greyerbiehl (Chu) 2005-2009; Geraldine M. Litchfield 2009-2014 [Elk Rapids UMC merged w/ Williamsburg UMC 4-1-11] Nathaniel R. Starkey 2014-2017; [Williamsburg and (Fife Lake Boardman Parish) Fife Lake / East Boardman / South Boardman became multi-point charge 2017] John J. Conklin 2017-2020 [2018 Williamsburg, Fife Lake, East Boardman, South Boardman formed the Unified Parish] John D. Messner 2020-

Williamston Crossroads UMC *[Mid-Michigan]*   office.umccrossroads@gmail.com
(P/M) 5491 Zimmer Rd, Williamston 48895   (517) 655-1466
Williamston: Center and Bell Oak merged to become Williamston: Crossroads UMC June 14, 2000; Patricia A. Skinner June 14, 2000-2002; DeAnn J. Dobbs 2002-2008; Brian F. Rafferty 2008-2010; Ellen K. Zienert 2010-2012; Richard J. Foster (1/4 time) Aug. 1, 2012- [M-52 Cooperative Ministry 2013-2016; re-named Connections Cooperative Ministry 2015] Jacqueline L. Raineri 2016-2017; Martin A. Johnston 2017-

Williamston UMC *[Mid-Michigan]*   julie@williamstonumc.org
(P/M) 211 S Putnam St, Williamston 48895   (517) 655-2430
Ferris S. Woodruff 1966-1979; Harold A. Kirchenbauer 1969-Oct. 1975; Laurence L. Waterhouse Oct. 1975-1982; Ilona R. Sabo-Shuler 1982-1994; Robert H. Roth, Jr. 1994-1999; Dean Prentiss Sept. 15, 1999-2008; Alice Fleming Townley (3-6 months interim, para. 338.3b) July 15, 2008-2009; Amee Anne Miller 2009-2011; Julie A. Greyerbiehl 2011-2018; Linda J. Stephan 2018-

Williamston: Wheatfield UMC *[Mid-Michigan]*
(P/M) 520 Holt Rd, Williamston 48895 (517) 851-7853
Eugene Tate Oct.-Dec. 1968; Dennis Ferris Dec. 1968-April 1969; Wayne Gorsline April 1969-1975; Millard Wilson 1975-1977; Marcel Elliott 1977-Jan. 1978; Thomas Butcher Jan. 1978-Oct. 1979; Dennis Demond Oct. 1979-1980; Fred Fischer 1980-1985; Susan Adsmand 1985-1987; David Wendland 1987-1988; Carolyn Hare Robinson 1988-1991; Paulette Cheyne 1991-1995; Valerie Fons 1995-1999; Stephen F. Ezop 1999-June 30, 2002; Sharyn K. Osmond 2002-2006; Stephan Weinberger Aug. 1, 2006-2007; Jeanne Laimon (DSA) 2007; Jeanne Laimon (1/4 time) Dec. 1, 2007-2012; Jeremy J. Wicks (1/4 time) 2012-2014 [M-52 Cooperative Ministry 2013-2014]; Richard J. Ahti (DSA) 2014-2015; Daniel J.W. Phillips 2015-2017; [Grovenburg / Jackson: Zion / Felt Plains / Williamston: Wheatfield became multi-point charge 2017] John Kabala 2017-2018 ; Gertrude Mwadi Mukalay 2017-2018; Theresa Fairbanks 2018-2020; [Millville / Williamston: Wheatfield became multi-point charge 2018] [Wmstn: Wheatfield became single station 2020] TBS

Willow UMC *[Heritage]* willowumc@gmail.com
(P) 36925 Willow Rd, New Boston 48164; (M) PO Box 281, New Boston 48164 (734) 654-9020
David A. Russell 1965-1969; Harry Gintzer 1969-1971; Keith C. Chappell 1971-1973; Richard F. Venus-Madden 1973-1976; John W. Walter 1976-1977; Norman A. Charter 1977-1979; Dale M. Miller 1979-1981; Margery A. Schleicher 1981- Aug. 31, 1983; J. Gordon Schleicher Sep. 1, 1983-Dec. 31, 1984; Fred B. Maitland (interim) Jan - Jun 1985; Jack Edward Fulcher 1985-1989; Charles W. Booth 1989-Feb. 1991; Edward Coley (interim) Mar-Jun 1991; Hoon Hee Wong 1991-Nov 1, 1994; Otto Hood Nov 1, 1994-2000; Elizabeth A. Librande 2000-2004; Mark E. Zender 2004-2011; Marianne M. McMunn 2011-Feb 1, 2016; Bradford K. Lewis (Ret.) Feb 1, 2016-2017; Kelly Vergowven (DSA) Jul 1-Nov 11, 2017; Kelly-Marie Zawodni [Vergowven] Nov 12, 2017-2020; Ann Birchmeier 2020-

Winn UMC *[Central Bay]* wumc8187@yahoo.com
(P/M) 8187 S. Winn Rd, Mt Pleasant 48858 (989) 866-2440
Harold Arman 1968-1969; Lawrence Smith 1969-1970; Athel J. Lynch 1970-1973; Joseph A. Dudley 1973-1974; Kathy Nickerson 1974-1977; James C. Sabo-Schuler 1977-1980; James W. Burgess 1980-1986; M. Christopher Lane 1986-1990; Paula Jane Duffey 1990-1994; Philip Bacon 1994-1997; Ron Smith 1997-1999; Paulette Cheyne 1999-2006; Melody Lane Olin (DSA) 2006; Melody Olin Nov. 15, 2006-2010; Lawrence Wonsey 2010-2014; Russell D. Morgan 2014-2016; [Coomer/Winn realigned to a two-point charge 2016; previously w/ Blanchard-Pine River] Raymond W. Francis (DSA) 2016-Dec 31, 2019; Raymond W. Francis Jan 1, 2020- [Coomer merged w/ Winn 3-8-2020]

Wisner UMC *[Central Bay]* wisnerumc@wisnerumc.com
(P/M) 5375 Vassar Rd, Akron 48701 (989) 691-5277
Clare Patton 1967-1972; E. Neil Sheridan 1972-1981; Lynn Chappell 1981-1984; Shirley & Howard Jones 1984-1986; Mark Karls 1986-1997; John H. Schneider, Jr. 1997-Aug 31, 1999; Wilson C. Bailey Sep 1, 1999-2005; William W. Omansiek 2005-2006; Frederick D. Neumann 2006-2010; William Sanders 2010-2012; Jacqueline L. Raineri 2012-2016; In Boem Oh 2016-

Wolf Lake UMC *[Midwest]* secretarywolflakeumc@frontier.com
(P/M) 378 Vista Terrace, Muskegon 49442 (231) 788-3663
Kenneth McCaw Nov. 1966-1969; Austin Reiger 1969-1975; Craig Adams 1975-Aug. 1979; Richard Williams Sept. 1979-Nov. 1983, Bruce Dempsey Nov. 1983-Nov. 1988, Gilbert Boersma Jan. 1989-Jan. 31, 1995; Pulpit Supply Feb.-June 1995; J. Todd Thompson 1995-2000; Laurence E. Hubley 2000-Nov. 15, 2001; Roberta W. Cabot Nov. 16, 2001-2011; Bobby Dale Whitlock (Ret.) 2011-Sept. 1, 2014; Susan J. Hagans (Ret.) Sept. 1, 2014-2018; Mona Joann Dye (Ret.) (LTFT ½) 2018-

Worth: Twp Bethel UMC (Worth Twp.) *[East Winds]*
(P) 8020 Babcock Rd, Croswell 48422; (M) PO Box 143, Croswell 48422   (810) 327-1440
Kenneth L. Harris 1969-1977; John D. Lover 1977-1982; Max D. Weeks Jan. 1983-1987; Donna J. Osterhout 1987-1991; Richard F. Kriesch 1991-1997; Jean R. Snyder 1997-1999; Linda L. Fuller, 1999-2010; Kevin Fick Apr 26, 2011-Jan, 2013; Timothy T. Bashore Nov 9, 2013-2014; Mark Harriman 2014-2018; Donald Derby 2018-

Wyandotte: First UMC *[Greater Detroit]*   fumcoffice@sbcglobal.net
(P/M) 72 Oak St, Wyandotte 48192   (734) 282-9222
James R. Timmons 1970-1976; H. H. Patterson 1976-1979; Gary Sanderson 1979-1988; Otto F. Hood (assoc) 1988-1994; Richard L. Myers 1988-1998; James J. Walker 1998-2007; Alan J. Hanson 2007-2013; Dianna L. Rees 2013-2020; Mark D. Miller 2020-

Wyoming Park UMC *[Midwest]*   wyomingparkumc@gmail.com
(P/M) 2244 Porter St SW, Wyoming 4951   (616) 532-7624
James W. Dempsey 1965-1969; Gerald A. Pohly 1969-Feb. 1973; John P. Hitchens (Assoc.) 1972-1985; Stanley H. Forkner March 1, 1973-1979; C. William Martin 1979-1984; Ward N. Scovel 1984-1989; Don Eddy 1989-Feb. 28, 1994; Lee F. Zachman April 16, 1994-1996; William C. Johnson 1996-2012; Robert Eckert (Assoc.) Apr. 1, 2006-2008; Joel T. Fitzgerald 2012-2017; Kimberly A. DeLong 2017- [Wyoming Park / Courtland-Oakfield became a two-point charge 2017]

Wyoming: Wesley Park UMC *[Midwest]*   info@wesleypark.org
(P/M) 1150 32nd St SW, Wyoming 49509   (616) 988-6738
Kenneth Lindland 1968-Dec. 1969; Theron Bailey Dec. 1969-Sept. 1977; James E. Fox Sept. 1977-April 1985; (Griggs St. UMC merged with Wesley Park in Jan. 1979. Ward Pierce was pastor of Griggs St.)Ward Pierce Jan.-March 1979; Douglas Pedersen (Assoc.) 1979-1982; Myron K. Williams 1985-1994; William V. Clegg 1994-2011; Dean N. Prentiss 2011-

Yale UMC *[East Winds]*   office@yaleumc.org
(P/M) 2 S Main St, Yale 48097   (810) 387-3962
D. Olney White 1969-1972; Charles R. Fox 1972-1977; Steven J. Buck 1977-1982; Charles R. Vinson 1982-1986; Donald Milano 1986-1989; Trevor A. Herm 1989-1994; Ginethea D. McDowell 1994-Dec 1, 1998; John R. Allan Jan 1, 1999-2008; Marvin H. McCallum (interm) Jan 1, 2009-2009; Bernadine Wormley-Daniels 2009-2012; Bruce L. Nowacek 2012-Feb 1, 2014; John C. Huhtala, Sr. Feb 15, 2014-2014; Patrick D. Robbins 2014—2019; [Yale / Cole / Melvin became a three-point charge 07/01/2019]; Dennis Eric Irish 2019-Mar 30, 2020; Julia A. Cramer (assoc) (DSA) 2019-Dec 31, 2019; Julia A. Cramer (PL) Jan 1, 2020-Mar 30, 2020 [Yale became single station 04/01/2020] Joseph R. Baunoch Apr 1, 2020-

Ypsilanti: First UMC *[Heritage]*   fumcypsi@fumcypsi.org
(P/M) 209 Washtenaw Rd, Ypsilanti 48197   (734) 482-8374
Kenneth R. Callis 1965-1972; Timothy R. Hickey (assoc) 1965-1967; Charles R. Kishpaugh (assoc) 1967-1969; Charles R. Jacobs (assoc) 1969-1972; L. LaVerne Finch (assoc) 1969-1971; Hugh C. White 1972-1978; Joseph J. Bistayi (assoc) 1972-1975; Philip M. Seymour (assoc) 1975-1977; Tom G. Burdette (assoc) 1977-1983; Perry A. Thomas 1978-1990; William P. McKnight (assoc) 1983-1985; Marsha M. Woolley (assoc) 1985-Oct. 31, 1991; David E. Kidd 1990-1997; Louise R. Ott (assoc) Jan 1, 1992-1997; Terry W. Allen 1997-2000; Latha Ravi (assoc) 1997-Dec 31, 2000 ; Melanie L. Carey 2000-2011; Judith Y. Mayo (deacon) 2001-Dec 5, 2007; Ventra Asana (deacon), 2001-Jan 25, 2003; Rey Carlos Mondragon (assoc) 2008-2013; Timothy C. Dibble 2011-2014; Briony Desotell 2014- ; Patricia Ganderilla (assoc.) 2015-2017

Ypsilanti: Lincoln Community UMC *[Heritage]* pastormaryellen@wowway.com
(P/M) 9074 Whittaker Rd, Ypsilanti 48197 (734) 482-4446
   Bernard Hearl 1964-1977; C. William Bollinger 1977-1979; Howard M. Montgomery 1979-1983;
   Tom G. Burdette 1983-1985; David C. Collins 1985-1991; Donna J. Osterhout 1991-1996; Walter
   B. Fenton 1996-2003; Beverly L. Marr 2003-2010; Mary Ellen Chapman 2010-2016; Merlin H. Pratt
   2016-2019; Christopher A. Butson 2019-

Ypsilanti: St. Matthew's UMC *[Heritage]* saintmattsumc@gmail.com
(P/M) 1344 Borgstrom Ave, Ypsilanti 48198 (734) 483-5876
   William A. Kendall 1967-1969; Thomas H. Beaven 1969-1973; P. Glen Trembath 1973-1977; James
   E. Tuttle 1977-1984; Richard L. Dake 1984-Aug. 31, 1992; Ronald K. Fulton (interim) Sept 1, 1992-
   Nov 30, 1992; Gary C. Dawes Dec 1, 1992-1996; David G. Mulder 1996-2001; Pamela S. Kail
   2001-2009; Steven H. Khang 2009-2014; Michael Desotell 2014-

Zeba UMC *[Northern Skies]* lumc@up.net
(P) Zeba Rd, L'anse 49946; (M) 304 N Main St, Lanse 49946 (906) 524-6967
   William Kelsey 1968-1970; Lillian Richards 1971; Howard E Shaffer 1971-1981; John R. Henry
   1981-1986; Gregory Rowe 1986-1990; James M. Mathews 1990-1993; David P. Snyder 1993-Oct
   1, 2003; John R. Henry 2004-2011; Stephen E. Rhoades 2011-2019; Nathan T. Reed 2019-

MERGED CHURCHES

Alanson UMC *[Northern Waters]* harborspringsumc@gmail.com
(P) 7330 Chicago St, Alanson 49706; (M) 343 E Main St, Harbor Springs 49740 (231) 548-5709
   Phillip Howell 1968-1971; Philip Brown 1971-1977; Milton TenHave 1977-1979; Richard Matson
   1979-1987; Catherine Kelsey 1987-1990; Claudette Haney 1990-April 1993; Birt A. Beers May
   1993-1995; Lawrence R. Wood 1995-2003; Kathryn S. Cadarette 2003-2011; Mary A. Sweet 2011-
   2014; Vaughn Thurston-Cox 2014-2016; [Epsilon/New Hope/Harbor Springs/Alanson became a
   4-point charge 2014] Hillary Thurston-Cox (Assoc.) 2014-2016; Randall J. Hitts 2016-2017; Susan
   E. Hitts 2016- [Harbor Springs / Alanson realigned 2016] [Alanson merged w/ Harbor Springs
   1/1/2020]

Ann Arbor: Calvary UMC *[Heritage]*
(P/M) 1415 Miller Ave, Ann Arbor 48103
   Robert C. Grigereit 1968-1976; Dwight W. Murphy 1976-1985; Ira L. Fett 1985-1989; Gary R.
   Glanville 1989-1996; Douglas K. Olsen 1996-2008; Beth D. Titus 2008-2013; Andrew Lee 2013-
   2019; Mary K. Loring 2019-2020 [Ann Arbor: Calvary merged with Dexter 7/1/2020]

Battle Creek: Birchwood UMC *[Greater Southwest]*
(P/M) 3003 Gethering Rd, Battle Creek 49015
   Ron L. Keller 1966-1970; Philip P. Steele 1970-1971; Lawrence E. Hodge 1971-1980; Ward N.
   Scovel 1980-1984; Rodney J. Kalajainen 1984-1988; David W. Yingling 1988-1991; Phillip J.
   Friedrick 1991-1995; Melanie J. Baker-Streevy 1995-2003; Karen A. Tompkins 2003-Jan. 1, 2007;
   David Dryer Jan. 1-June 30, 2007; Robert D. Nystrom 2007-2011; Robert D. Nystrom (3/4 time)
   2011-2012; [Battle Creek Birchwood / Trinity became two-point charge 2012] Bruce R. Kintigh (1/2
   time) 2012-2018; [Battle Creek: Birchwood / Battle Creek: Trinity UMC merged with Battle Creek:
   Chapel Hill 07-01-2018]

Battle Creek: Trinity UMC *[Greater Southwest]*
   Harold L. Mann 1968-1973; Wirth G. Tennant 1973-1978; Lowell Walsworth 1978-1981; Lloyd M.
   Schloop 1981-1984; Victor Charnley 1984-1995; Joy Jittaun Moore 1995-1996; David L. Dryer
   1996-2006; Diane Gordon 2006-2010; Bruce R. Kintigh 2010-2012; [Battle Creek Birchwood / Trinity
   became two-point charge 2012] Bruce R. Kintigh (1/2 time) 2012-2018; [Battle Creek: Birchwood /
   Battle Creek: Trinity UMC merged with Battle Creek: Chapel Hill 07-01-2018]

Bloomingdale UMC *[Greater Southwest]*
(P) 201 E Pine St, Bloomingdale 49026
Wayne Babcock 1969-1971; Gerald Hudlund 1971-1972; Wayne Barrett 1972-1973; Pulpit supply 1973-1976; David L. Youngs 1976-2006; Donald R. Wendell 2006-Nov. 30, 2008; John W. McNaughton Dec. 8-31, 2008; Eugene B. Moore, Jan. 1, 2009, 2012; Carol A. Newman (DSA 1/4), Sept. 23, 2012-Sept 30, 2019 [Bloomingdale merged w/Townline 01-01-2020]

Comstock UMC *[Kalamazoo]*
Wilbur Courter 1967-Jan. 1973; David Dunn Jan. 1973-Dec. 1973; David Charter Feb. 1974-Feb. 1976; Thomas Evans 1976-1984; Edward Slate 1984-1989; Valerie Hill 1989-1991; Mary Curtis 1991-1998; Peggy J. Baker 1998-2006; Paulette G. Cheyne 2006-Nov. 15, 2006; [Comstock UMC merged w/ Galesburg UMC 04-29-07]

Coomer UMC *[Central Bay]*
(P) 5410 S Vandecar Rd, Mt Pleasant 48858;
Harold Armon 1968-1969; Lawrence Smith 1969-1970; Athel Lynch 1970-1973; Joseph Dudley 1973-1974; Kathy Nickerson 1974-1977; James Sabo-Schuler 1977-1980; James Burgess 1980-1986; M. Christopher Lane 1986-1990; Paula Jane Duffey 1990-1998; Dale A. Golden 1998-2005; Paulette G. Cheyne 2005-2006; Melody Lane Olin (DSA) 2006; Melody Olin Nov. 15, 2006-2010; Lawrence Wonsey 2010-2014; Russell D. Morgan 2014-2016; [Coomer/Winn realigned to a two-point charge 2016; previously w/ Blanchard-Pine River] Raymond W. Francis (DSA) (LTFT 1/4) 2016-Dec 31, 2019; Raymond W. Francis Jan 1, 2020- [Coomer merged w/ Winn 3-8-2020]

Dansville UMC *[Lansing]*
Silas Foltz 1968-1970; Paul Schreibner 1970-1974; David Dryer 1974-1980; Joseph Graybill 1980-May 1987; Bobby Dale Whitlock 1987-May 1990; Clyde Miller (interim) May-Sept. 1990; Genevieve DeHoog Oct. 1990-1994; Pulpit Supply July-Aug. 1994; DeAnn J. Dobbs Sept. 1, 1994-1996; Russell K. Logston 1996-1998; DSA 1998-1999; Stephen F. Ezop 1999-June 30, 2002; Sharyn K. Osmond 2002-2006; Kimberly A. Tallent Aug. 1, 2006-2008; Donald R. Fry (DSA) (1/4 time) 2008-2011; Jeremy J. Wicks (1/4 time) 2011-Dec, 31, 2014 [M-52 Cooperative Ministry 2013] [Dansville UMC merged with Millville UMC 12-31-14]

Detroit: Mt. Hope UMC *[Greater Detroit]*   mh_methodist@sbcglobal.net
(P/M) 15400 E Seven Mile Rd, Detroit 48205   (313) 371-8540
Rudolph H. Boyce 1969; Lloyd O. Houser 1981; John N. Howell 1981; Susan DeFoe Dunlap 1983; John Martin 1989-Feb 28, 1995; Bea B. Soots Mar 1, 1995-Aug 31, 1997; Sanda Sangaza Sep 15, 1997-1999; Maurice R. Horne 1999-2004; Margaret Martinez-Ventour 2005-2010; Henry D. Williams, Jr. 2010-2012; Jean Snyder Sep 2, 2012-2013; Esron Shaw Nov 9, 2014-2020 [Mt. Hope merged w/ Conant Ave 7-1-2020]

Elk Rapids UMC *[Grand Traverse]*
Lawrence Hodge 1966-Nov. 1968; Glen Loy Oct. 1968-Oct. 1970; A.J. Lynch (Assoc.) June-Oct. 1968; R.J. Lautner (Assoc.) 1968-Oct. 1970; Gordon Showers Oct. 1970-Oct. 1971; Robert Doner Dec. 1971-1976; Bernard Randolph 1976-1978; Jack Barthlomew 1978-Feb. 1983; Stephen Beach April 1983-Nov. 1986; Michael Baker-Streevy Dec. 1986-1988; Charles Shields 1988-1993; Raymond R. Sundell 1993-1998; Kathryn M. Coombs 1998-1999; Thomas M. Pier-Fitzgerald 1999-2005; William W. Chu & Julie A. Greyerbiehl (Chu) 2005-2009; Geraldine M. Litchfield 2009- [Elk Rapids UMC merged w/ Williamsburg UMC 04-01-11]

Ferry UMC *[Midwest]*
(P) 2215 Main St, Shelby 49455
Merlin Delo 1966-1978; William Bowers 1978-1980; David Dryer 1980-1984; Richard Williams 1984-Oct 1, 1997; Pulpit Supply Oct. 1, 1997 - Dec. 31, 1997; Susan Olsen Jan. 1, 1998-July 1, 1998; Raymond D. Field 1998-1999; James Bradley Brillhart 1999-2007; Dianne D. Morrison 2007-2011; Richard D. Morrison (DSA) 2007-2011; Paul E. Hane 2011-2018; Paul E. Hane (Ret.) (LTFT) 2018-Apr 26, 2020 [Ferry UMC merged w/ Hesperia 04- 26-2020]

Flint: Charity UMC *[East Winds]* dopnh@gfn.org
(P/M) 4601 Clio Rd, Flint 48504-6012 (810) 789-2961
Emmanuel F. Bailey 1988-1993; Julius A. McKanders 1993-1996; Philip Burks 1996-Dec 6, 1999; Russel Von Sutton Dec 16, 2000-2003; Hydrian Elliott 2003-2011; David Lieneke 2011-2014; Brian Willingham 2014-2018; Frederick Bowden (DSA) 2018- [Fliint: Charity merged w/ Flint: Calvary 7-1-2020]

Keeler UMC *[Kalamazoo]*
Meredith Rupe 1968-Nov. 1970; Gary E. Gamble Nov. 1970-1973; Supply pastor June-Oct. 1973; Lynn W. Wagner Oct. 1973-1975; Daniel R. Barker 1975-Sept. 1978; Gregory R. Wolfe Oct. 1978-Nov. 1983; Donald L. Buege Jan. 1984-1990; Dennis E. Slattery 1990-1992; David L. Litchfield 1992-1998; Virginia L. Heller 1998-2004; Mark E. Thompson 2004-2009; Julie A. Greyerbiehl 2009-2011; Heather McDougall 2011-2013; Beth A. Reum 2013-2015; [Hartford/Keeler became a two-point charge 2015] Ryan L. Wenburg 2015- [Keeler UMC merged with Hartford UMC 12-31-16]

Lansing Calvary UMC *[Lansing]*
Morris Bauman 1965-1973; H. James Birdsall 1973-1978; William Dobbs 1978-1983; Dale Crawford 1983-Feb. 1986; Jack M. Bartholomew Feb. 1986-1992; Leonard B. Haynes 1992-1998; Paula Jane Duffey 1998-2005; Stephan Weinberger 2005-2007; [Lansing Calvary UMC merged w/ Mt. Hope UMC 07-01-07]

Monroe: Heritage UMC (formerly E. Raisinville Frenchtown) *[Heritage]*
(P/M) 4010 N Custer Rd, Monroe 48162
Paul R. Crabtree 1951-1969; Otto F. Hood 1969-1974; J. Edward Fulcher 1974-1977; Paul W. Crabtree 1977-1985; Daniel W. Harris 1985-1995; M. Lester McCabe 1988-1990; Mary T. Tame 1990-Oct. 15, 1990; Robert L. S. Brown (interim); Calvin D. Long Apr. 1, 1991-1995; Carolyn Harris (co-pastor) 1995-1997; Daniel W. Harris (co-pastor) 1995-1997; Robert G. Richards 1997-2001; Kathy R. Charlefour 2001-Oc 31, 2005; Margaret A. Passenger Nov 1, 2005-2011; Katherine C. Waggoner 2011-2020 [Monroe: Heritage merged w/ Monroe: First, re-named Faith 7-1-2020]

Muskegon Lakeside UMC *[Midwest]*
Robert Treat 1967-1981; Richard D. Wilson 1981-1987; Steven R. Young 1987-1993; William P. Myers, Jr. 1993-2002; David A. Selleck 2002-2009; Zawdie K. Abiade 2009-2010; Stephan Weinberger 2010-2014; [Lakeside became a single-point charge 2014] Donald J. Graham 2014-2016 [Muskegon Lakeside merged w/ Muskegon Lake Harbor 07-01-16]

Niles: Grace UMC *[Greater Southwest]* nilesgraceumc@att.net
(P/M) 501 Grant St, Niles 49120 (269) 683-8770
Leonard Putnam 1964-1969; Orin M. Bailey 1969-1971; Don Cozadd 1971-1976; David Litchfield 1976-1981, John Charter 1901-Nov. 1992; Mark E. Thompson Nov. 1992-1996; Glenn McNeil 1996-2000; Nancy J. Bitterling 2000-2002; Patricia L. Bromberek (SP-DSA) 2002-2004; Anthony Tomasino (DSA) Oct. 17, 2004-2016; [Morris Chapel / Niles Grace became a two-point charge 2016; Niles Wesley / Morris Chapel / Niles Grace became a 3-point charge 2017] Robert L. Snodgrass II 2016- [Niles: Grace merged with Niles: Wesley, re-named Niles: New Journey 1-1-2020]

Osseo UMC *[Albion]*
William F. Bowers 1966-Sept. 15, 1969; Charles D. Grauer Sept. 15, 1969-1970; Daniel W. Harris 1970-1971; Robert E. Jones 1971-Nov. 15, 1973; Marion V. Nye Nov. 15, 1973-1976; Daniel R. Bennett Feb. 1, 1977-1979; Leonard J. Yarlott 1979-1982; Gilbert R. Boersma 1982-1985; Valerie M. Hill 1985-1989; Jerry L. Hippensteel 1989-1994; Susan Deason 1994-1998; Kathy L. Nitz 1998-Aug. 15, 1999; Clarence Able (DSA) 2001-2002; Donald E. Lee 2003-2010; Cynthia Veilleux (DSA) Nov. 1, 2010-2011; Kimberly A. Metzger July 1-Dec. 19, 2011; Timothy Puckett (part-time) Jan. 1, 2012- [Osseo UMC merged w/ North Adams UMC 04-06-14]

Pleasant Valley UMC *[Heartland]*
G. Albert Rill 1971-1976; Joseph Dudley 1976-Aug. 1979; Michael L. Selleck Aug. 1979-1986; Leonard B. Haynes 1986-1992; Donald E. Spachman 1992-1997; Doris Lyon 1997-Jan. 1, 2008 [Pleasant Valley UMC merged w/ St. Louis UMC 01-01-08]

Port Huron: Washington Avenue UMC *[East Winds]*
Douglas K. Mercer 1968-1970; Richard C. North 1970-1972; Lloyd E. Christler 1972-1978; John N. Howell 1978-1981; S. Joe Robertson 1981-1985; Robert E. Burkey 1985-1988; Donald R. Sperling 1988-1996; Georg F. W. Gerritsen 1996-Dec 31, 1999; Susan K. Freeland Montenegro Jan 1, 2000-Dec 1, 2003; Nickolas K. Genoff Jan 1, 2004-2009; Robert D. Chapman 2009-2014; Penelope P. Nunn 2014-2018; [Port Huron: Washington Ave. UMC merged with Port Huron: Gratiot Park 07/01/2018]

Poseyville UMC *[Central Bay]*
H. Emery Hinkston 1969-1972; Robert Moore 1971-1980; Robert Kersten 1980-1982; Paul Riegle 1981-1983; John W. Elliott 1981-1986; Bruce C. Hatch 1986-1993; Karen L. Knight 1993-1998; Rony S. Hallstrom 1998-Feb 29, 2001; Michael W. Luce 2001-2012; Rahim O. Shabazz 2012-2015; Karen Knight Price 2015-Nov 1, 2015; Kayla J. Roosa Nov 1,2015-2017; Lynda F. Frazier 2017-July 31, 2018 [Poseyville UMC merged with Midland: Aldersgate UMC 08/01/2018]

Potterville UMC *[Lansing]*
Thomas Peters 1967-1970; Richard Youells 1970-1974; Gregory Wolfe 1974-Oct. 1978; J. Thomas Churn Oct. 1978-1982; Austin Regier 1982-1987; Beverly Gaska 1987-Jan. 1991; Charles B. Hodges March 1991-March 1992; Milton J. TenHave (interim) March-July 1992; John Buker 1992-1995; Paul F. Bailey 1995-May 1, 2001; Rebecca K. Morrison Jan. 16, 2002-2011; Lyne Stull-Lipps 2011-2016; Jeanne M. Randels (Ret.) July 1-Sept. 1, 2016; [Potterville UMC merged w/ Sycamore Creek UMC 6/21/2017 and became Sycamore Creek Potterville Campus 12-31-16]

South Wyoming UMC *[Midwest]*
Walter Rothfus 1968-1971; Curtis Cruff 1971-1975; Leonard Yarlott 1975-1979; Edward Trimmer 1979-1981; Ben Chapman 1981-1982; Howard Harvey 1982-1988; John Myette 1988-March 15, 1991; Arthur D. Jackson March 15, 1991-Dec. 31, 1993; John Myette Jan. 1, 1994-1995; Lois M. Munn 1995-1997; Donald D. Entenman 1997-Sept. 30, 1997; Rhonda J. Prater Nov. 16, 1997-2003; Marcia L. Elders (part-time) 2003-2015 [merged with Cornerstone UMC 1-1-15; re-named Cornerstone UMC-South Wyoming Campus, building temporarily closed May 31, 2015 to re-open in fall 2015]

Sterling UMC *[Central Bay]*
Byron Coleman 1969-1974; Lynn Chappell 1974-1981; Janet M. Larner 1981-1982; John J. Britt 1982-1990; Zina B. Bennett Jr. 1990-1993; Jan L. Beaderstadt 1993-Feb 15, 2000; J. Gordon Schleicher 2000-2003; Jon W. Gougeon 2003-2010; James A. Payne 2010-Apr. 1, 2019; [Sterling UMC merged into Standish: Community UMC 04/01/2019 to become Standish: Beacon of Light]

St Johns: First UMC *[Heartland]*
Harold Homer 1968-1972; Francis Johannides 1972-1977; Keith Laidler 1977-1984; Mark Graham 1984-1987; Paul Patterson 1987-1990; Stephan Weinberger 1990-2000; Carolyn C. Floyd 2000-2003; Margery A. Schleicher 2003-2007; Lori J. Sykes 2007-2012; Ellen K. Zienert July 15, 2012-2018 [merged with DeWitt: Redeemer and became DeWitt: Redeemer – St. Johns: First Campus 07-01-18]

Watervliet UMC *[Kalamazoo]*
Lawrence Grubaugh 1968-1971; Donald Russell 1971-1975; Joseph Wood 1975-1978; Lawrence Wiliford 1978-Sept. 1981; Katherine Williams (Coombs) Dec. 1981-Sept. 1984; Fred Hamlin Nov. 1984-1985; Kenneth Curtis 1985-May 1987; Len Schoenherr 1987-1999; David F. Hills Aug. 1, 1999-2007; O'Ryan Rickard 2007-2009; William W. Chu 2009-2011; Ron Van Lente 2011- [Watervliet UMC merged w/ Coloma UMC 06-26-11]

Whitehall UMC *[Midwest]*
Charles Dunbar 1965-1971; Richard Matson 1971-1975; Bernard Randolph 1975-1976; Edward Slate 1976-1983; Steve Smith 1983-1985; Keith Treman 1985-1990; Kay B. Bosworth 1990-1998; Anita Hahn 1998-2006; Gayle Berntsen 2006-2014; [Whitehall realigned from Whitehall/Claybanks to Whitehall/Crestwood 2014] Mary A. Sweet 2014-2017 [Whitehall and Crestwood became multi-station circuit 2014] [Whitehall UMC merged with Montague UMC, 07-01-17]

CLOSED CHURCHES

Congregations closed in accordance with ¶2549 of *The Book of Discipline, 2016.*

Alto UMC *[Midwest]*
Beulah Poe 1962-1971; Carter Miller 1971-1973; John Eversole 1973-1977; Keith Avery June-Oct. 1977; Albert Sprauge Oct. 1977-Jan. 1978; Herb Kinsey Jan. 1978-May 1979; Martin Fox May 1979-Oct. 1982; Herb Kinsey Oct. 1982-1983; Harold Diepert 1983-March 1985; Margaret Peterson 1985-1989; Jill Rose July-Dec. 1989; Lloyd Hansen Dec. 1989-1990; Todd Thompson 1990-1995; Bryan Schneider-Thomas 1995-2000; Dominic A. Tommy 2000-2002; Dean Irwin Bailey (Ret.) 2002-2014; Andrew Jackson (Ret.) 2014-2016; Robert D. Wright (Ret.) 2016-Dec 31, 2018. [Alto UMC closed 12-31-2018]

Battle Creek: Sonoma UMC *[Albion]*
Howard Moore May 1968-1970; Ray Grienke 1970-Jan. 1974; Ray McBratnie Jan. 1974-1976; Kenneth Curtis 1976-1981; Harry Johnson 1981-1985; Gary Kintigh 1985-1993; Charles M. Shields 1993-1995; Michael Baker-Streevy 1995-Nov. 16, 1999; Charles Edward Rothy 2000-2003; Richard Duane Wilson 2003-2008; Nancy G. Powers 2008-2012; Sally Harrington (Ret.) 2012- [Sonoma UMC discontinued 06-30-14]

Benton Harbor Peace Temple UMC *[Kalamazoo]*
George Hartman 1966-1971; Carlos Page 1971-1989; Dow Chamberlain 1989-Nov. 30, 1993; Donald Entenman Feb. 1, 1994-1995; David G. Knapp 1995-2003; Deborah R. Miller 2003-Nov. 14, 2003; David S. Yoh (DSA) Nov. 15, 2003-2006; James W. Stilwell 2006-2009; Sandra V. Douglas (Deacon) (1/4 time) 2008-2009 [Benton Harbor: Peace Temple UMC discontinued 06-30-09]

Brandywine: Trinity UMC *[Kalamazoo]*
Vernon L. Michaels 1967-1969; Douglas Vernon 1969-1971; Robert Wellfare 1971-1973; Lowell T. Walsworth 1973-1978; Raymond D. Flessnor 1978-1981; David E. Small 1981-1987; Arthur C. Murphy Aug. 1987-1991; Edward A. Friesen 1991-1993; Patricia A. Myles 1993-Apr. 17, 1994; Richard L. Eslinger 1994-Nov. 1, 1998; Matthew Bistayi Jan. 1, 1999-2002; Allen J. Duyck 2002-Sept. 22, 2003; Carl Harrison Feb. 1, 2004-2008; Christopher A Kruchkow (DSA) 2008-2009 [Brandywine: Trinity UMC discontinued 08-30-08]

CHURCH HISTORIES

Breedsville UMC *[Kalamazoo]*
Lloyd Bronson 1967-1978; Lloyd Bronson 1978-1981; Charles McNary 1981-1991; James Hodge 1991-1992; Kenneth J. Littke 1992-1998; D.S. Assignment 1998; Jana Jirak Sept. 16, 1998-1999; Robert L. Pumfery 1999-October 31, 2002; Patricia Anne Harpole November 1, 2002-2004; O'Ryan Rickard 2004-2005; Sheila F. Baker 2005-2007; David L. Youngs 2007-2008; David L. Haase (DSA) (1/4 time) Jan. 3, 2008; David L. Haase (1/4 time) July 1, 2008-2014; Jason E. Harpole (1/4 time) 2014-2016 [Breedsville UMC discontinued 11-12-16]

Dearborn Heights: Stephens UMC *[Detroit Renaissance; Greater Detroit]*
Charles F. Davenport 1968-1977; Roy G. Forsyth 1977-1981; Edwin C. Hingelberg 1981-1988; Robert C. Hastings 1988-1994; James R. McCallum 1994-1999; Robert J. Sielaff 1999-2012; Chong Yuob Won 2012-Dec 31, 2014; Tom Waller Jan 1, 2015-2018; Carolyn A. Jones Jul 1-Dec 31, 2018. [Dearborn Heights: Stephens UMC closed 12-31-2018]

Eagle UMC *[Lansing]*
William Cox 1968-1970; Raymond J. McBratnie 1970-1974; David Morton 1974-1982; William Dornbush 1982-Nov. 1986; Janell E.R. Gerken Jan. 1987-1988; Raymond D. Field 1988-1993; Larry W. Nalott 1993-1998; Stephen F. Ezop 1998-1999; D. Michael Maurer Aug. 16, 1999-2002; Judith Lee Scholten 2003-2011 [Eagle UMC discontinued 10-15-11]

East Boardman UMC *[Northern Waters]*
(P) 2082 Boardman Rd SW, S Boardman 49680
Gerald L. Hedlund 1966-1971; Arthur and Molly Turner (co-pastors) 1971-1976; Diane Vale 1976-Oct. 1977; Marion Nye Oct. 1977-1985; Clinton McKinven-Copus 1985-1987; Gary Wales 1987-1994; Howard Seaver 1994-2012; Mark E. Mitchell 2012-2014; Donald L. Buege 2014-2017; [Williamsburg and (Fife Lake Boardman Parish) Fife Lake / East Boardman / South Boardman became multi-point charge 2017] John J. Conklin 2017-2020 [2018 Williamsburg, Fife Lake, East Boardman, South Boardman formed the Unified Parish] [East Boardman disaffiliated/closed 7-1-2020]

East Lansing Aldersgate UMC *[Lansing]*
William Clegg 1984-1994; David W. Meister 1994-July 31, 1995; Kenneth W. Karlzen Aug. 1, 1995-2000; Gary D. Bondarenko 2000-Nov. 15, 2006; Paulette G. Cheyne Nov. 15, 2006-Apr. 1, 2008 [East Lansing Aldersgate UMC discontinued 04-01-08]

East Lansing Chapel Hill UMC *[Lansing]*
Stephen Beach 1968-1969; Edward F. Otto 1969-Dec. 1972; Daniel Miles Dec. 1972-1974; Paul K. Scheibner 1974-1978; J. Lynn Pier-Fitzgerald 1978-May 1984; Thomas M. Pier-Fitzgerald (co-pastor) 1982-May 1984; Charles W. Smith May 1984-1988; Carl W. Staser 1988-Jan. 1991; Beverly E. Gaska Jan. 1991-July 31, 1995; D. Michael Maurer Aug. 1, 1995-2002; Robert David Nystrom 2002-Jan. 15, 2004; Robert David Nystrom (1/2 time) Jan. 16, 2004-2005; Ellen K. Zienert 2005-2012; [East Lansing Chapel Hill discontinued 06-24-12]

Ellis Corners UMC *[Albion]*
Logan Weaver 1968-1976; Densel G. Fuller 1976-1981; Jerry L. Hippensteel 1981-1984; Thomas E. Ball 1984-Nov. 1988; Stanley Fenner Dec. 1988-1989; Stacy R. Minger 1989-1994; John F. Ritter 1994-1996; Robert Stark 1996-2000; John Scott 2000-Sept. 1, 2003; John A. Scott & Rebecca Scott (CoPastors) Sept. 2003-2007; Bruce R. Kintigh 2007- ; [Ellis Corners UMC discontinued 12-31-07]

Grand Rapids Mosaic UMC *[Grand Rapids]*
[new church start 1997; "Michigan Suhbu Korean UMC" re-named "Church of All Nations", 2006; renamed "Mosaic UMC" 2012] Seung Ho Baek July 16, 1997-2008; Robert Eckert (part-time) 2008-2009; Trevor McDermont 2009-2010; Steven C. Place Jan. 1, 2011-2017 [Mosaic UMC closed 07-01-17]

Grand Rapids Oakdale UMC *[Grand Rapids]*
Arthur Jackson 1966-Oct. 1969; Kenneth Lindland Dec. 1969-1973; Brent Phillips 1973-1976; Douglas Knight 1976-1978; Charles Dunbar 1978-1979; Ed Trimmer 1979-1982; Cathy Kelsey 1982-1987; Jane Shapley 1987-1996; Marguerite R. Bermann 1996-1999; Calvin Hill Aug. 16, 1999-2003; Theresa Little Eagle Oyler-Sayles 2003-2006; Andy Baek 2006-2008 [Oakdale UMC discontinued 06-30-08]

Grand Rapids Olivet UMC *[Grand Rapids]*
Grand Orin Bailey 1964-1969; Allen Wittrup 1969-1977; C. Jack Scott 1977-1979; Richard Youells Aug. 1979-1989; Barry T. Petrucci 1989-Dec. 31, 1994; Clinton McKinven-Copus Jan. 1, 1995-Jan. 1, 2001; Dominic A. Tommy (Assoc.) Apr. 16, 1999-2000.; Robert Eckert (DSA) 2001-2005; James Stilwell March 1, 2005-2006; Gary Peterson (DSA) 2006-2008; James Thomas Boutell (part-time) 2008-2010; Jean & Jane Crabtree (DSA) 2010- [discontinued 12-12-10]

Grand Rapids Plainfield UMC *[Grand Rapids]*
K.C. Downing 1967-1969; C. Dow Chamberlain 1969-1972; Don W. Eddy (Assoc.) 1971-1979; Robert L. Hinklin 1972-1976; Marvin F. Zimmerman 1976-1978; Wayne C. Barrett 1978-1982; Neal M. Kelly 1982-1984; John McNaughton 1984-1986; Ethel Z. Stears 1986-1988; Jeanne Randels 1988-1991; Lynn Pier-Fitzgerald 1991-1999; Neil Davis 1999-2002; Robert R. Cornelison 2002-2005; Joyce F. Gackler June 1, 2005-2012; [Grand Rapids Aldersgate / Plainfield became two-point charge 2012] Laurie A. Haller 2012-2013 [Plainfield UMC discontinued 06-30-13]

Greenbush UMC *[Heartland]*
William Tate 1967-1969; Robert Boyer 1969-1970; Charles VanLente 1970-1972; Everett Love June-Dec. 1972; Norman Wood 1973-1976; Terry MacArthur 1976-Oct. 15, 1979; Robert Gillette Jan. 1980-1984; Merritt Bongard 1984-1991; Joseph Spackman 1991-1999; James Dibbet 1999-2005; O'Ryan Rickard 2005-2006; Jon L. Pohl 2006-2011; Mona J. Dye 2011-2015 [Greenbush UMC discontinued 09-28-15]

Grovenburg UMC *[Lansing]*
Maurice Glasgow 1966-1978; Paul Mergener (Assoc.) 1976-Oct. 1978; Joseph Huston Oct. 1978-Oct. 1981; Paul Wehner Oct. 1981-1986; Marty DeBow 1986-1990; Kyewoon Choi 1990-1997; Melanie S. Young 1997-1998; Richard J. Duffey 1998-2005; Andrew L. Croel 2005-2008; Kimberly A. Tallent 2008-2009; Joseph D. Huston (Ret.) 2009-2017; [Grovenburg / Jackson: Zion / Felt Plains / Williamston: Wheatfield became multi-point charge 2017] John Kabala 2017- ; Gertrude Mwadi Mukalay 2017-2018; [Grovenburg UMC discontinued 06-30-2018]

Hudsonville UMC *[Grand Rapids]*
Deborah Johnson Sept. 1990-1997; R. John Thompson 1997-Apr. 1, 2001; Sandra K. VandenBrink 2001-Jan. 1, 2005; [Hudsonville UMC discontinued 01-01-05]

Jones UMC *[Albion]*
Reva Hawke 1988-Oct. 1991; Marilyn B. Barney Oct. 1991-1998; Carolyn A. Robinson 1998-2007; Thomas R. Reaume (part-time) 2007-2009; Jack Balgenorth 2009-Sept. 1, 2010 [discontinued 09-01-10]

Kalamazoo Lane Blvd UMC *[Kalamazoo]*
Marion Burkett 1966-1969; James Lavengood 1969-1972; Harold Taber 1972-1975; Richard D. Wilson 1975-1981; Gary Kintigh 1981-1985; Robert Freysinger 1985-1988; Daniel Biteman 1988-1996; John W. McNaughton 1996-Jan. 16, 2000; James Dyke (DSA) 2000-2006; David S. Yoh (DSA), July 1, 2006-Oct. 4, 2006; Philip P. Steele (DSA), Oct. 8, 2006; Kevin E. Hale (DSA), Jan. 1, 2007; Martin H. Culver (DSA), Mar. 18, 2007-Mar. 25, 2008 [Lane Boulevard UMC discontinued 03-25-08]

Kalamazoo Stockbridge Avenue UMC *[Kalamazoo]*
Lloyd Schloop 1968-1973; Kenneth O. Lindland 1973-1977; Charles W. Richards 1977-1986; Curtis Strader 1986-1988; John Moore 1988-1992; Dwight J. Burton 1992-1998; John W. McNaughton 1998-2003; Calvin Y. Hill 2003-2007; John L. Moore (DSA) 2007-2010; Ronald D. Slager 2010-2015; Sara L. Carlson 2015-Jan. 31, 2016 [Stockbridge Avenue UMC discontinued 07-01-16]

Lansing Christ UMC *[Lansing]*
Wilson Tennant 1966-1969; Meinte Schuurmans (Assoc) 1966-1980; David L. Crawford 1969-1977; Thomas L. Weber (Assoc) 1974-1978; Donald P. Sailor 1977-February 1983; Clyde E. Miller April 1983-March 1987; Eric Burrows (Assoc) 1983-1984; Philip Simmons (Assoc) 1984-1985; James J. Walker (Assoc) 1985-1989; Richard A. Selleck March 1987-1992; Rebecca N. Niese (Assoc) 1991-October 31, 1994; Robert E. Jones 1992-1996; Maurice E. Walworth, Jr. 1996-2003; Charles David Grauer 2003-Dec. 31, 2012; Edward C. Ross (Interim), Jan. 1-June 30, 2013; Lyle D. Heaton 2013-Dec. 31, 2015 [Lansing Christ UMC discontinued 12-31-15]

Lansing Faith UMC *[Lansing]*
J. Edward Cherryholmes Apr. 1964-Apr. 1969; Richard E. Johns Apr. 1969-1980; David B. Nelson Jr. 1980-1985; John Palmer 1985-May 1987; Kenneth W. Bensen May 1987-2003; James A. Richie (Assoc.) 2000-2002; Cornelius Davis (Assoc. 1/4 time) 2003-2008; (Lansing Faith merged with South Lansing Ministries 2005); Russell F. McReynolds (Ret.) 2008-2015; Jeanne M. Randels (Ret.) July 1-Dec. 31, 2015 [Lansing Faith UMC discontinued 12-31-15]

Lansing: Korean UMC *[Lansing]*
Young Ho Ahn 1984-Sept. 1985; Chung Soon Chang Sept. 1985-1988; Hyo Nam Hwang Oct. 1988-1998; Jung Kee Lee 1998-Dec. 31, 2003; Bo Rin Cho Mar. 1, 2004-2014; Seok Nam Lin 2014-2016 [Lansing: Korean UMC discontinued 07-01-16]

Lansing Potter Park UMC *[Lansing]*
Ronald Entenman 1967-1972; Peter Kunnen 1972-1976; Arthur Turner 1976-1981; Clinton Bradley-Galloway 1981-1983; Lewis Buchner 1983-1986; Zawdie Abiade 1986-1988; Donald Entenman 1988-1991; Isabell Deppe 1991-Dec. 31, 1997; D. Michael Maurer (Pastor Interim, part time) Jan. 1, 1998-June 30, 1998; Grace Kathleen O'Connor 1998-2001; Lamarr V. Gibson 2001-2004; Betty A. Smith (DSA) October 16, 2004-2005; Stephan Weinberger 2005-2006; [Potter Park UMC discontinued 06-30-06]

Lansing: Trinity UMC *[Lansing]*
James E. Fox 1968-1971; Gerald R. Bates 1971-1979; Larry Sachua 1979-1989; Richard Williams (Assoc.) 1983-1985; Gregory Wood (Assoc.) 1985-1990; Dennis Buwalda 1989-1992; Paul C. Frederick (Assoc.) 1990-Dec. 1992; Leicester Longden 1992-2001; Linda J. Farmer-Lewis (Assoc.) Jan. 1993-1994; Joy J. Moore (Assoc.) 1995-1997; Cynthia S.L. Green (Assoc.) May 1, 1998-2004; Rae L. Franke (Deacon) 1998-2003; William Beachy 2001-2014; Steve J. Buck 2014-2015 [Lansing Trinity UMC discontinued 07-01-15]

Lansing: Vietnamese UMC *[Mid-Michigan]*
Vinh Q. Tran, Jan. 1, 1986 - 2004; Cuong M. Nguyen 2004-2008; Tho Van Phan (DSA) 2009-Oct. 15, 2009 [Lansing: Vietnamese UMC discontinued 10-15-2009]

Litchfield UMC *[Heritage]*
Dorr Garrett 1968-1970; Peter Kunnen 1970-1972; Morris Reinhart 1972-1976; Stephen Keller 1976-Dec. 1979; Paul Hartman Jan. 1980-1985; David Meister 1985-March 1990; Kathy Brown 1990-Feb. 1, 2001; R. John Thompson Apr. 1, 2001-2005; Carl Q. Litchfield 2005-2009; [Litchfield/Quincy two-point charge 2009] Michael P. Baker-Streevy 2009-2010; Martin T. Cobb 2010-2013; Julie Elmore 2013-2017; [Litchfield / Jonesville became two-point charge 2017] Mary A. Sweet 2017-2019 [Litchfield closed 06-30-2019]

Mapleton UMC *[Central Bay]*
   Karl Patow 1969-1971; Richard Mansfield 1971; John Eversole 1971-1973; Max Weeks 1973-1977; Leon Smith 1977-1979; Leonard Gamber 1979-1982; Kenneth Reeves 1982-1985; Edwin M. Collver 1985-1992; Gordon B. Boyd 1993-Aug 31, 1994; Barbra Franks Sep 1, 1994-Sep 30, 1996; Timothy Hastings Dec 1, 1996-2004; Michael P. Kelley 2004-2007; Leonard Clevenger 2007-2010; L. Cecile Adams 2010-2013; Richard J. Hodgeson 2013-2017; T. Bradley Terhune Oct 1, 2017-Aug 31, 2018; Leonard Clevenger Oct 1, 2018-2019 [Mapleton UMC closed 06-30-2019]

Marengo UMC *[Albion]*
   Stanley Fenner 1989-Aug. 8, 2000; Gerry Retzloff (DSA) Jan. 1, 2010- [Marengo UMC discontinued 07-01-16]

Middleton UMC *[Heartland]*
   De Layne Hersey 1967-1969; Herald Cox Sept. 1969-Sept. 1971; Lloyd Hansen Sept. 1971-May 1972; Abe Caster May 1972-Jan. 1973; Eldon Schram Feb.-June 1973; J. Thomas Churn 1973-1979; Richard Whale 1979-1980; Richard Riley 1980-1984; Lyle Heaton 1984-1990; Tim Wohlford 1990-1991; Carolyn A. Robinson 1991-1997; Charles D. Farnum 1997-2001; Martin Cobb 2001-2006; William F. Foldesi 2006-Apr. 7, 2007; Clare Huyck (DSA) 2007; Clare Huyck Nov. 10, 2007-2012; William F. Dye July 15, 2012-Aug. 31, 2015; Larry W. Nalett (RLA) Sept. 15-Nov. 29, 2015 [Middleton UMC discontinued 12-01-15]

Moscow Plains UMC *[Albion]*
   Densel Fuller Feb. 1969-1974; David Showers 1974-1976; Martin Fox 1976-1979; Gerald Selleck 1979-1982; Mark Kelly 1982-1983; Dr. Campbell 1983-1984; Jim Hodge 1984-1989; Lawrence P. Brown 1989-Dec. 1992; Donald R. Wendell Jan 1, 1993-Dec. 31, 1995; Bernice Taylor-Alley (DSA) 1996-2001; Craig Pahl 2001-2007; [Moscow Plains UMC discontinued 06-30-07]

Mulliken UMC *[Mid-Michigan]*
(P/M) 400 Charlotte St, Mulliken 48861
   Everatt Love 1968-1972; David A. Cheyne 1972-1975; Lynn Wagner 1975-1977; John Eversole 1977-1982; Joseph Spackman 1982-1983; Ken Lindland 1983-1987; Joseph Spackman 1987-1991; Gordon Spalenka 1991-1993; Robert Besemer 1993-Aug. 31, 1996; Donald Woolum Sept. 16, 1996-2003; Judith Lee Scholten 2003-2011; Gary L. Simmons 2011-2013; [Barry-Eaton Cooperative Ministry 2013] Claire W. Huyck 2013-2015; Betty A. Smith (Ret.) 2015-Dec. 31, 2015; Lyle D. Heaton Jan. 1-June 30, 2016; Vaughn W. Thurston-Cox 2016-Jan 18, 2020 [Mulliken became single station 2017] [Mulliken closed 3/1/2020]

Muskegon: Unity UMC *[Midwest]*
(P/M) 1600 N Getty St, Muskegon 49445
   Kenneth McCaw Dec. 1966-1969; Austin Regier 1969-1975; Joseph Glover 1975-1983; Eric Beck 1983-1986; Susan Krill (Hagans) 1986-Nov. 1988; Ronald Carl Robotham Jan. 1989-1990; Jane Lippert 1990-1995; J. Todd Thompson 1995-1998; Kimberly A. DeLong 1998-Sept. 16, 1999; Gayle Berntsen Sept, 16, 1999-Sept. 1, 2001; James Meines Dec. 1, 2001-2005; Brian M. McLellan (DSA) 2005-Feb. 15, 2006; James Meines (DSA) Apr. 15, 2006-Oct. 31, 2006; Nancy L. (Besemer) Boelens Nov. 1, 2006-Dec. 31, 2008; Gilbert R. Boersma (1/4 time) 2009-Oct. 31, 2011; R. John Thompson (DSA) (1/4 time) Nov. 1, 2011-2014; Ronald L. Worley 2014 [Unity closed 12/31/2019]

North Adams UMC *[Heritage]*
228 E Main St, North Adams 49262;
Kenneth W. Karlzen 1968-1971; Thomas R. Jones 1971-Aug. 1974; David Flagel Sept. 1975-1980; Lee F. Zachman 1980-1984; Donald McLellan 1984-Sept. 1988; Melanie Baker-Streevy Oct. 1988-1995; Rochelle Ray 1995-2000; Tim Doubblestein 2000-Aug. 31, 2002; Charles Richards Sept. 1-Dec. 31, 2002; Paul Hane Jan. 1, 2003-2011; Kimberly A. Metzger July 1-Dec. 19, 2011; Arthur R. Turner (DSA) Feb. 1, 2012-2014 [Osseo UMC merged w/ North Adams UMC 4-6-14] Timothy R. Puckett 2014-Dec 31, 2019; Beverly Clark (CLM/DSA) Jan 1-Jun 30, 2020 [North Adams disaffiliated / closed 7-1-2020]

North Evart UMC *[Heartland]*
Carter Miller 1968-March 1971; Lynn Wagner March. 1971-Oct. 1973; Pulpit Supply Nov. 1973-1974; Darryl Cook 1974-May 1977; Kenneth Kline 1977-1981; Pulpit Supply June-Aug. 1981; Dwight Benner Sept. 1981-1983; Purlin Wesseling Aug. 1983-1986; Frank Closson 1986-Jan. 1988; Jane Crabtree Jan. 1988-1990; Pulpit Supply July-Nov. 1991; Robert Stark Nov. 1990-Aug. 1991; Carol Lynn Bourns Sept. 1991-Dec. 31, 1994; Pulpit Supply Jan. 1995-1996; Jean Crabtree (DSA) 1996-2000; Donald L. Buege 2000-Jan. 2006; Jon Pohl Jan. 15 - June 30, 2006; Jean A. Crabtree (DSA) Nov. 5, 2006-July 2007; Russell Morgan (DSA) July 8, 2007-2012; Kara Lynne Burns (CLM) July 22, 2012- [North Evart UMC discontinued 07-01-14]

North Star UMC *[Heartland]*
Robert E. Tomlinson 1974-Jan. 1977; Donald L. Warmouth Feb. 1977-1978; Glenn Britton 1978-1979; Lois H. Gremban 1979-1981; Dale F. Jaquette Aug. 1981-April 1990; T. Ried Martin 1990-1993; Karen E. Nesius 1993-1994; Jodie Flessner 1994-2003; William F. Foldesi Nov. 16, 2003-Apr. 7, 2007; Clare Huyck (DSA) 2007; Clare Huyck Nov. 10, 2007-2012; William F. Dye July 15, 2012- [North Star UMC discontinued 07-01-15]

Oronoko UMC *[Kalamazoo]*
Robert Strauss 1968-1981; Valerie Hill 1981-March 1983; Leonard Haynes 1983-1986; Leo Bennett 1986-1989; Walter J. Rothfuss 1989-2000; Brenda Gordon 2000-2006; Jane D. Logston (part-time) 2006-14; [Berrien Springs/Hinchman/Oronoko became 3-point charge 2012] [Hinchman/Oronoko became 2-point charge 2014] Linda R. Gordon 2014-2017; Brenda E. Gordon Jul 1-Dec 27, 2017. [Oronoko UMC discontinued 12-27-17]

Otsego: Trowbridge UMC *[Greater Southwest]*
Henry Houseman 1962-1974; Leon Shaffer 1974-1981; R. Ivan Niswender 1981-1994; Gary S. Wales 1994-2008; Anthony C. Shumaker (part-time) 2008-2012; Sheila F. Baker (1/2 time) 2012-Feb. 2, 2014; John L. Moore (Ret.) 2014-2017 [Otsego: Trowbridge UMC closed 12-31-2018]

Outland *[Albion]*
[new church start 2006] Peggy J. Baker 2006-2011; Stacy Caballero 2011-Mar. 1, 2012 [Outland discontinued 02-29-12]

Owosso: Burton UMC *[Mid-Michigan]*
(P) 510 N Baldwin Rd, Owosso 48867
Horace N. Freeman 1969-1974; Homer VanBuren 1974-1983; Billy J. McKown 1983-1989; M. Shirley Jones 1989-1991; Howard M. Jones (assoc) 1989-1991; William R. Seitz 1991-Jan 1, 1996; Jean M. Scroggins Jun 16, 1996-Dec 31, 1999; Lance E. Ness Jan 1, 2000-Jul 31, 2004; Michael S. McCoy Aug 1, 2004-2006; Carole A. Brown Aug 1, 2006-2011; Calvin H. Wheelock 2011-2019; [Single point charge 07/01/2019] [Owosso: Burton closed 6/30/2019]

Parma UMC *[Albion]*
Edward Dahringer 1968-Sept. 1980; Jean Crabtree Nov. 1980-Jan. 1984; Jerry Hippensteel 1984-1989; Charlotte Lewis 1989-1992; Carolin S. Spragg 1992-1999; Keith W. Heifner 1999-2003; Michael P. Baker-Streevy 2003-Nov. 1, 2005; Lynn Stull-Lipps Jan. 15-June 30, 2006; [Jackson Trinity / Parma became a charge 2006] Sandra L. Spahr (DSA) 2006-2007; Melodye Surgeon Rider 2007-2012; Patricia A. Pebley (1/2 time) 2012-2014 [Parma UMC discontinued 07-01-14]

Pawating Magedwin UMC *[Grand Rapids]*
David G. Knapp 1992-1995; Timothy J. Miller 1995-Jan. 31, 2002; Deborah R. Miller Feb. 1, 2002-2003; Theresa Little Eagle Oyler-Sayles 2003-2006; [Pawating Magedwin UMC discontinued 07-01-06]

Perrinton UMC *[Heartland]*
Robert E. Tomlinson 1974-Jan. 1977; Donald L. Warmouth Feb. 1977-1978; Glenn Britton 1978-1979; Lois H. Gremban 1979-1981; Dale F. Jaquette Aug. 1981-April 1990; T. Ried Martin 1990-1993; Karen E. Nesius 1993-1994; Jodie Flessner 1994; William F. Foldesi Nov. 16, 2003-Apr. 7, 2007; Clare Huyck (DSA) 2007; Clare Huyck Nov. 10, 2007-2012; William F. Dye July 15, 2012-Aug. 31, 2015 [Perrinton UMC discontinued 09-02-15]

Quimby UMC *[Lansing]*
John Joldersma 1965-1970; Esther Cox 1970-1971; William P. Reynders 1971-Feb. 1972; Thomas Churn March 1972-April 1973; Thomas Peters May 1973-Aug. 1976; Dale D. Spoor Sept. 1976-Dec. 1979; Steven Reid Jan. 1980-Jan. 1984; Mary Curtis March 1984-1989; James Noggle 1989-Feb. 1993; Susan A. Trowbridge, March 1993-1998; Kenneth R. Vaught (DSA) 1998-2011; Bryce E. Feighner 2011-2013; [Barry-Eaton Cooperative Ministry 2013] Jerry Bukoski 2013-2018 [Quimby UMc discontinued 06-30-18]

Saginaw: State Street UMC *[Central Bay]*
Kearney Kirkby 1967-1973; Donald C. Porteous 1973-1983; H. Emery Hinkston 1983-1988; Phillip Miles 1988-1993; Joy A. Barrett 1993-1998; Timothy Woycik 1998-2003; Weatherly Burkhead Verhelst 2003-2009; Elias N. Mumbrio Aug 1,2009-2015; Monique Tuner 2015-2019 [Closed 06-30-2019]

Salem UMC *[Heartland]*
William Tate 1967-1969; Robert Boyer 1969-1970; Charles VanLente 1970-1972; Everett Love June-Dec. 1972; Paul Jones 1973-1975; Douglas Jones 1975-1976; Terry MacArthur 1976-Oct. 15, 1979; Robert Gillette Jan. 1980-1984; Merritt Bongard 1984-1991; Joseph Spackman 1991-1999; James Dibbet 1999-2005; O'Ryan Rickard 2005-2007; Kathryn L. Leydorf (DSA) 2007; Kathryn L. Leydorf Nov. 10, 2007-2014; [Elsie/Salem became a charge 5-1-14] Donald R. Ferris-McCann May 1, 2014-Aug. 2, 2015 [Salem UMC discontinued 12-31-15]

Sebewa Center UMC *[Lansing]*
Marjorie Matthews June-Sept. 1968; Robert D. Keith Sept. 1968-1971; Ralph Kallweit 1971-Jan. 1976; John Morse Feb. 1976-1982; Chris Schroeder 1982-Nov. 1984; Kenneth A.O. Lindland Nov. 1984-1987; Joseph L. Spackman 1987-1991; Gordon Spalenka 1991-1993; Robert Besemer 1993-Aug. 31, 1996; Donald Woolum Sept. 16, 1996-2003; Judith Lee Scholten 2003-2004; Jeffrey J. Schrock 2004-2012; Clare W. Huyck 2012-2013 [Sunfield/Sebewa Center no longer two-point charge 2013] [Barry-Eaton Cooperative Ministry 2013] [Sebewa Center UMC discontinued 12-31-14]

Shabbona UMC *[East Winds]*
(P/M) 4455 Decker Rd, Decker 48426
Stephen Chapko 1968-1972; Carl Shamblen 1972-1973; Carl Silvernail (interim); William J. Burgess (interim); Wayne A. Rhodes 1974-1976; John E. Tatgenhorst 1976-1981; Hayden K. Carruth 1981-1982; James L. Rule 1982-1986; Wallace Peter Crawford 1986-1991; Jan L. Beaderstadt 1991-1993; James A. Rencontre 1993-1997; Jean B. Rencontre 1993-2000; Ellen Burns 2000-2010; John Heim (assoc) 2000-2001; Frederick J. McDowell (assoc) 2001-2003; Pamela K. Barnett 2010-2014; James Palaszecki 2014-2016; Dale Barber 2016-Mar 30, 2019; [Seperated as a two-point charge from Minden City 2019] Nancy J. Bitterling 2019-2020 [Shabbona disaffiliated 7/1/2020]

Snow UMC *[Grand Rapids]*
Ralph Tweedy 1967-1969; Wayne Barrett 1969-1972; Steven Beach 1972-1974; Ed Passenger 1974-1977; Allen Wittrup 1977-1985; Richard Strait 1985-1986; Dan Duncan 1986-1989; Tracey Taylor 1989-1990; Lloyd Hansen 1990-1991; Mary (Horn) Schippers 1991-March 31, 1995; Pulpit Supply April-June 1995; Thurland Meredith (ad interim) 1995-2008; Vance Dimmick (DSA) 2008-2009; [Middleville/Snow two-point charge 2009] Michael T. Conklin 2009-2012; Anthony C. Shumaker 2012-2017 [Snow UMC closed 07-01-17]

Sylvan UMC *[Heartland]*
Kenneth I. Kline 1977-1981; Pulpit Supply June-Aug. 1981; Dwight Benner Sept. 1981-1983; Purlin Wesseling Aug. 1983-1986; Frank Closson 1986-Jan. 1988; Jane Crabtree Jan. 1988-1990; Pulpit Supply July-Nov. 1991; Robert Stark Nov. 1990-Aug. 1991; Carol L. Bourns Sept. 1991-Dec. 31, 1994; Pulpit Supply Jan. 1995-1996; Jean Crabtree (DSA) 1996-2000; Donald L. Buege 2000-Jan. 2006; Jon Pohl Jan. 15 - June 30, 2006; Jean A. Crabtree (DSA) Nov. 5, 2006-July 2007; Russell Morgan (DSA) July 8, 2007-Nov. 9, 2009; Pat Robinson (DSA) Nov. 9, 2009 [Sylvan UMC became single-point charge Nov. 9, 2009] [discontinued 12-31-11]

Traverse City: Christ UMC *[Grand Traverse]*
John D. Morse 1987-1993; Louis W. Grettenberger 1993-2009; Mary S. Brown July 1-Nov. 1, 2009; Hal Ferris (DSA) Nov. 1-30, 2009; John W. Ellinger (DSA) Dec. 1, 2009-June 1, 2010; Kathryn M. Coombs (DSA) 2010-2011; Dianne Doten Morrison 2011- Jan. 1, 2016; Paul Cole (DSA) Oct. 1, 2015-Mar. 11, 2016 [Traverse City: Christ UMC discontinued 06-30-17]

Traverse City Windward *[Grand Traverse]*
[new church start 2007] John A. Scott 2007-2011; Rebecca Scott (Assoc.) Nov. 1, 2008-2010 [Windward new church start discontinued 05-15-11]

Ubly UMC *[East Winds]*
(P) 4496 Pike St, Ubly 49475
Maynard Q. Kent 1964-1977; Emerson W. Arntz 1977-1982; Carl A. Renter 1982-1987; Earleen A. VanConant 1987-1989; Rothwell McVety 1989-1991; Catherine W. Hiner 1991-1993; Robert A. Srock 1993-2000; Ellen Burns 2000-2010; John Heim (assoc) 2000-2001; Fredrick J. McDowell (assoc) 2001-2001; Pamela K. Barnett 2010-2014; James Palaszeski 2014-2016; Philip L. Tousley 2019-2020 [Bad Axe: First / Minden City / Ubly formed Bad Axe Cooperative Parish 07/01/2019] [Ubly UMC closed 9-30-2019]

Vermontville UMC *[Lansing]*
David C. Haney 1967-1969; William R. Tate 1969-1972; Gary V. Lyons 1972-April 1976; Gerald A. Salisbury April 1976-1979; Molly C. Turner 1979-1983; Glenn C. Litchfield 1983-1990; Richard W. Young 1990-1991; Robert L. Kersten 1991-1995; Jeffrey J. Bowman 1995-2002; Kathleen Smith 2002-Dec. 31, 2012; [Vermontville/Gresham no longer two-point charge 2013] [Barry-Eaton Cooperative Ministry 2013] Gary L. Simmons (1/4 time) 2013-2015; Nancy V. Fancher (Deacon) 2014-2015; Karen L. Jensen-Kinney 2015-Dec 31, 2017 [Vermontville UMC discontinued 12-31-17]

Village Church (New Church Start) *[Lansing]*
[M-52 Cooperative Ministry 2014; re-named Connections Cooperative Ministry 2015] Jeremy J. Wicks 2014-2017; Jaqueline L. Raineri 2017-2018 [Millville: Village Church Campus discontinued 10-31-17]

Waterloo First UMC *[Lansing]*
Wilbur Silvernail 1960-1969; Donald R. Fry 1969-1970; Altha M. Barnes 1970-1975; Richard M. Young 1975-1976; Glenn Kjellburg 1976-1978; Pulpit Supply 1978-1979; L. A. Nichols 1979-1988; Merlin Pratt 1988-1991; Wayne Willer 1991-1995; Pulpit Supply 1995; Kathleen A. Groff Dec. 1995-July 31, 1997; Mona Joslyn Aug. 1, 1997-1998; Kathleen S. Kursch 1998-Feb. 1, 2000; Georgiana M. Dack (1/4 time) Feb. 1, 2000-2013; [Waterloo Village/First no longer two-point charge 2013] [M-52 Cooperative Ministry 2013] Jeanne M. Laimon (1/4 time) 2013-2014 [Waterloo First UMC was discontinued 07-01-14]

West Mendon UMC *[Albion]*
William Foster 1965-Dec. 1968; David Litchfield Dec. 15, 1968-1971; Harold Simon 1971-1973; William Dobbs 1973-1978; Frank Closson 1978-1981; Larry Higgins 1981-1983; Lloyd Hansen 1983-1987; Clinton McKinven-Copus 1987-1990; Carolyn Floyd 1990-1997; Reva Hawke 1997-2001; Ward D. Pierce (DSA) 2001-Dec. 2, 2012 (died); David G. Knapp (interim) Jan. 1, 2013-June 30, 2013; [West Mendon became single-point charge 2013] Thoreau May 2013-2017; [Mendon / West Mendon became a multi-charge 2015] [West Mendon UMC discontinued 07-01-2017]

White Pines UMC *[Grand Rapids]*
[new church start 2004] Jeffrey C. Williams 2004-2011; Dale A. Hotelling 2011-Aug. 31, 2012 [White Pines new church start discontinued 08-31-12]

— MAC Photos

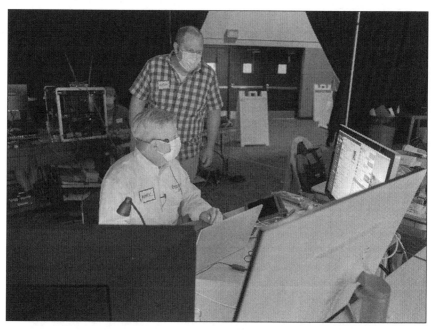

— MAC Photos

STATISTICAL INFORMATION

sowing**seeds**

ROOTING | TENDING | REAPING

2020 Virtual Annual Conference Statistician Report

Local Church Data for 2019

Michigan Conference
The United Methodist Church

STATISTICAL INFORMATION

CB

CONFERENCE Number	CHURCH NAME	Total professing members reported at the close of last year (1)	TOTAL PROFESSING MEMBERS reported at the close of this year (4)	Average attendance at all weekly worship services (7)	Total Baptized Members who have not become Professing Members (9)	Number of other constituents of the church (10)	TOTAL Christian Formation Group Participants (Total of lines 11a-d) (11)	Average weekly attendance (all ages) in Sunday Church School or other weekly education classes (13)	Membership in United Methodist Men (18a)	Membership in United Methodist Women (19a)	Number of persons sent out on UMVIM teams from this local church (20b)	Total Number of community ministries for outreach, justice, and mercy offered by this local church (21)	Value of church assets and buildings (24 & 25)	Church Debt (26 & 27)	Amount APPORTIONED to the local church by the CONFERENCE (28a)	Amount PAID by the local church to the CONFERENCE for all apportioned causes (29a)
CLOSED	MAPLETON	18	18	12	0	17	18	9	0	0	0	0	570000	0	3342	2005
CLOSED	SAGINAW: STATE STREET	156	156	70	0	60	72	14	0	0	0	2	2829138	247384	19597	1379
CLOSED	STERLING	96	96	30	5	9	19	5	0	0	0	0	434125	0	6190	0
CLOSED	UBLY	28	28	14	0	0	0	3	0	0	0	0	233337	60	1885	1697
CLOSED	LITCHFIELD	107	107	37	0	100	42	6	0	6	0	7	1753405	3664	11226	0
CLOSED	OWOSSO: BURTON	25	25	9	5	0	7	5	0	0	0	0	1002000	0	3100	1860
CLOSED	MUSKEGON: UNITY	24	20	13	8	4	7	0	0	0	0	0	502000	0	4083	4083
	CENTRAL BAY DISTRICT															
33001	ALGER	20	20	120	0	3	10	12	0	1	0	3	205591	0	3889	3889
33002	ARBELA	61	61	20	0	0	13	14	0	0	0	0	111000	295	4036	4036
33003	ARENAC CNTY: CHRIST	74	72	50	21	80	30	10	0	10	0	2	1807471	0	12749	200
33004	AUBURN	172	166	88	21	32	59	35	7	49	5	5	3657416	20392	27417	3120
33005	BAY CITY: GRACE	444	401	224	44	248	259	36	20	91	0	9	5386980	0	43581	39261
33006	BAY PORT	78	78	27	0	20	26	8	0	0	0	0	994000	0	6240	1000
33007	BEAVERTON: FIRST	61	57	45	7	31	8	5	0	10	0	3	1142000	0	6632	6632
33008	BENTLEY	39	35	21	0	0	4	5	0	0	0	3	966000	0	3563	3563
33009	BIRCH RUN	97	95	30	0	0	5	5	2	15	0	2	785000	0	9510	5706
33010	BLANCHARD-PINE RIVER	24	24	10	0	0	1	0	0	0	0	5	0	0	3187	0
33011	BURT	49	49	20	0	1	10	2	0	14	0	0	200000	0	3631	1300

CONFERENCE Number	30-38 Church Benevolence Giving	39a Total ASKED for clergy pension	39b Total PAID for clergy pension	41a Base compensation paid to/for the Senior Pastor or other person assigned or appointed in the lead pastoral role to the church	41b Base compensation paid to/for all Associate Pastor(s) and other pastoral staff assigned or appointed to the church. Include deacons and other clergy in this role	41c & 42c Deacons salary/benefits	40,42a-44 Pastoral Benefits	45 Total amount paid in salary and benefits for all other church staff and diaconal ministers	46 Total amount spent for local church program expenses	47 Total amount spent for other local church operating expenses	48 & 49 Local Church capital expenses	50 TOTAL CHURCH EXPENSES (Sum of Lines 29a through 49)	51 Number of giving units	52 Total income for annual budget/spending plan	53 Total income for designated causes including capital campaign and other special projects	54 Total income from connectional and other institutional sources outside the local church
CLOSED	2108	500	500	9300	0	0	730	725	3481	11500	0	30349	10	35500	0	800
CLOSED	1750	2773	0	36967	0	0	14218	28152	7264	55595	33726	179051	64	161504	2714	800
CLOSED	0	1433	1433	22542	0	0	0	0	523	14560	0	39058	46	47812	127	0
CLOSED	0	675	675	6000	0	0	0	14212	3517	4402	7037	16291	7	21940	0	0
CLOSED	100	1634	1114	14135	0	0	22446	0	3312	23067	0	85423	41	100670	32602	1900
CLOSED	306	601	601	10021	0	0	0	5450	2000	10000	0	24788	10	53100	4000	0
CLOSED	583	765	765	13051	0	0	13820		768	8322	0	34156	9	28823	0	0
33001	257	768	768	6851	0	0	2285	0	1256	18369	5000	38675	20	20915	100	0
33002		600	600	12000	0	0	0	0	897	5940	0	23473	10	28172	400	0
33003	717	4941	2500	23500	0	0	13456	0	477	13133	8933	53983	35	64922	13739	0
33004	3762	7097	7097	38992	0	0	26629	37617	6975	53230	12318	186355	99	179886	35927	0
33005	5366	8510	7801	57834	0	0	33220	156943	38622	104524	0	455889	311	386722	2478	0
33006	701	2676	2676	16270	0	0	13247	2027	1245	8425	3400	45591	35	50088	3297	0
33007	1720	870	870	17400	0	0	4801	1546	3912	19976	0	60257	40	62496	0	0
33008	1877	240	240	5200	0	0	5200	0	800	8700	0	25580	12	24494	6856	0
33009	1930	5103	5103	47313	0	0	1923	15054		22665		99694	40	104801	1975	0
33010	0	630	473	4149	0	0	1000	330	1450	5186	2485	15073	9	10354	140	0
33011	24	851	851	11828	0	0	5344	1606	500	8537	7200	37190	25	28842		0

STATISTICAL INFORMATION

CB

CONFERENCE Number	CHURCH NAME	1 Total professing members reported at the close of last year	4 TOTAL PROFESSING MEMBERS reported at the close of this year	7 Average attendance at all weekly worship services	9 Total Baptized Members who have not become Professing Members	10 Number of other constituents of the church	11 TOTAL Christian Formation Group Participants (Total of lines 11a-d)	13 Average weekly attendance (all ages) in Sunday Church School or other weekly education classes	18a Membership in United Methodist Men	19a Membership in United Methodist Women	20b Number of persons sent out on UMVIM teams from this local church	21 Total Number of community ministries for outreach, justice, and mercy offered by this local church	24 & 25 Value of church assets and buildings	26 & 27 Church Debt	28a Amount APPORTIONED to the local church by the CONFERENCE	29a Amount PAID by the local church to the CONFERENCE for all apportioned causes
33012	CARO	325	320	121	2	25	63	19	0	52	0	5	2754625	0	24855	19914
33013	CASEVILLE	147	150	53	0	33	12	0	0	0	0	2	2019539	0	14433	14433
33014	CASS CITY	180	175	95	25	50	98	35	0	25	0	0	2159306	110940	16676	2791
33015	CHURCHILL	92	90	29	7	29	6	5	0	14	0	1	404100	0	7253	7253
33016	CLARE	270	259	115	0	40	180	60	0	24	0	8	3500617	198380	29632	11853
33017	COLEMAN: FAITH	137	127	97	2	67	82	24	15	12	12	13	3908420	0	17897	17897
33018	COOMER	21	20	12	0	0	0	0	0	0	0	0	80059	0	2272	1818
33019	DALE	23	21	20	14	17	25	2	0	10	0	0	1008000	0	4042	4042
33020	EDENVILLE	27	27	15	0	4	5	5	0	12	0	2	336500	0	3740	3740
33021	ELKTON	174	183	85	7	14	41	18	0	12	0	5	230000	0	16239	10761
33022	ESSEXVILLE: ST LUKE'S	256	249	79	52	68	89	25	0	40	0	5	3603309	154149	25344	7430
33023	FAIRGROVE	54	53	21	22	24	5	3	12	6	0	4	1608139	6100	7016	3506
33024	FARWELL	120	113	63	0	77	56	10	0	15	0	4	178000	90000	13382	6283
33025	FRANKENMUTH	483	486	159	0	82	129	9	0	35	8	0	4525152	15313	40430	40430
33026	FREELAND	184	188	84	0	90	57	12	0	0	0	3	2345930	0	25802	7741
33027	GARFIELD	46	47	25	2	6	14	6	0	0	0	0	231710	0	2934	2934
33028	GLADWIN: FIRST	141	147	105	3	67	94	37	19	6	319	10	2664779	1125	20622	20622
33081	GLADWIN: WAGARVILLE COMMUNITY	59	46	45	0	28	0	0	0	0	2	2	744190	0	6858	6858
33029	GLENNIE	22	20	15	0	11	0	0	0	12	0	1	474064	45000	1684	1684

CONFERENCE Number	Church Benevolence Giving (30-38)	Total ASKED for clergy pension (39a)	Total PAID for clergy pension (39b)	Base compensation paid to/for the Senior Pastor or other person assigned or appointed in the lead pastoral role to the church (41a)	Base compensation paid to/for all Associate Pastor(s) and other pastoral staff assigned or appointed to the church. Include deacons and other clergy in this role (41b)	Deacons salary/benefits (41c & 42c)	Pastoral Benefits (40, 42a-44)	Total amount paid in salary and benefits for all other church staff and diaconal ministers (45)	Total amount spent for local church program expenses (46)	Total amount spent for other local church operating expenses (47)	Local Church capital expenses (48 & 49)	TOTAL CHURCH EXPENSES (Sum of Lines 29a through 49) (50)	Number of giving units (51)	Total income for annual budget/spending plan (52)	Total income for designated causes including capital campaign and other special projects (53)	Total income from connectional and other institutional sources outside the local church (54)
33012	9170	9860	9860	51600	0	0	15589	75432	12073	35442	146027	375107	133	222004	85206	130
33013	7265	5770	5770	39681	0	0	12656	1140	7371	30347	11500	130163	46	102326	3087	0
33014	2831	4365	4365	36375	0	0	22500	12480	2000	45168	24515	153025	100	142925	0	1720
33015	1195	1748	1748	19035	0	0	7219	5437	3772	14961	45657	60620	46	46442	0	0
33016	11901	7491	7491	49938	0	0	29973	65989	2979	65989	342	291770	177	235337	6773	0
33017	7836	5585	5585	37832	0	0	22963	25845	3884	54306		176490	85	166866	74450	2000
33018	0	600	500	3500	0	0	0	2000	80	7300	0	15198	8	16782	0	0
33019	5162	1468	1468	10611	0	0	4042		783	11923	0	38031	19	41857	110	0
33020	785	1557	1557	10175	0	0	7135	1680	157	5923	70	31222	17	28478	123	2000
33021	1954	8900	4119	43500	0	0	31487	13912	1413	13912	4665	125723	65	151444	659	0
33022	6323	7820	7820	52135	0	0	33278	21517	4769	49289	18414	200975	91	147606	38778	0
33023	1039	2504	2504	18734	0	0	5057	6047	2446	9729	3752	52814	22	53818	4472	0
33024	1005	6025	6025	37750	0	0	8350	2631	5240	64078	45573	176935	51	125954	2850	0
33025	34166	5825	5825	51321	0	0	20065	78327	88429	86674	155896	561133	163	411383	86493	4000
33026	1412	6450	6450	41810	0	0	22649	34234	9194	45406	0	168896	115	151709	5671	0
33027	804	1865	1710	12485	0	0	2689	0	143	3143	0	23908	25	26293	440	0
33028	21077	5700	5700	39640	0	0	30121	22606	6373	39631	10099	195869	132	1813217	4654	0
33081	2144	341	341	9960	170	0	5290	8300	3610	9154	2329	47986	35	65300	3255	0
33029	750	1100	1100	6501	0	0	2050	0	250	8253	10891	31649	25	23452	425	0

STATISTICAL INFORMATION

CB

CONFERENCE Number	CHURCH NAME	Total professing members reported at the close of last year	TOTAL PROFESSING MEMBERS reported at the close of this year	Average attendance at all weekly worship services	Total Baptized Members who have not become Professing Members	Number of other constituents of the church	TOTAL Christian Formation Group Participants (Total of lines 11a-d)	Average weekly attendance (all ages) in Sunday Church School or other weekly education classes	Membership in United Methodist Men	Membership in United Methodist Women	Number of persons sent out on UMW teams from this local church	Total Number of community ministries for outreach, justice, and mercy offered by this local church	Value of church assets and buildings	Church Debt	Amount APPORTIONED to the local church by the CONFERENCE	Amount PAID by the local church to the CONFERENCE for all apportioned causes
		1	4	7	9	10	11	13	18a	19a	20b	21	24 & 25	26 & 27	28a	29a
33030	GORDONVILLE	113	106	52	0	5	29	15	0	20	0	3	723140	0	11786	11786
33031	HALE: FIRST	184	186	105	178	194	110	31	0	0	0	4	2379662	50000	22778	22778
33032	HARRISON: THE GATHERING	47	49	22	0	8	13	5	12	0	0	1	7000	0		
33033	HARRISVILLE	56	55	26	0	0	6	4	0	0	0	3	1445300	0	5650	4600
33034	HAYES	76	76	20	0	41	50	6	0	31	0	0	545823	0	7417	7417
33035	HEMLOCK	136	143	35	0	10	8	2	0	15	0	0	2800000	9037	14215	14215
33036	KILMANAGH	31	33	17	0	4	0	0	0	0	0	0	258874	0	2965	2965
33037	KINGSTON	121	114	60	0	13	43	18	0	0	0	4	1530000	0	9772	5863
33038	LAPORTE	36	42	32	8	11	17	12	0	7	0	4	916231	0	3459	3459
33039	LEATON	40	40	22	0	7	7	12	6	8	0	1	1116500	0	5476	5476
33040	LINCOLN	65	64	45	0	24	20	16	0	0	0	7	1036500	0	4629	4629
33042	MAYVILLE	187	187	97	79	99	46	38	16	36	0	26	2886425	172514	16761	16761
33043	MIDLAND CNTY: HOPE	68	68	42	10	10	16	5	0	5	0	0	522910	0	9417	9417
33044	MIDLAND: ALDERSGATE	427	408	254	20	144	154	49	0	0	20	34	3640293	0	37757	37757
33046	MIDLAND: FIRST	1869	1838	426	14	216	504	202	0	45	88	6	26688931	0	194735	194735
33045	MIDLAND: HOMER	125	126	51	12	20	73	35	0	0	0	6	1775130	1228	18367	0
33047	MILLINGTON	234	233	82	0	119	151	42	8	28	0	11	3356500	0	20512	20512
33048	MIO	101	80	30	0	25	10	10	31	16	0	3	1230000	0	8352	4176
33050	MT PLEASANT: COUNTRYSIDE	53	59	25	0	0	19	12	0	8	0	6	489200	8988	6372	6372

CONFERENCE Number	Church Benevolence Giving (30-38)	Total ASKED for clergy pension (39a)	Total PAID for clergy pension (39b)	Base compensation paid to/for the Senior Pastor or other person assigned or appointed in the lead pastoral role to the church (41a)	Base compensation paid to/for all Associate Pastor(s) and other pastoral staff assigned or appointed to the church. Include deacons and other clergy in this role (41b)	Deacons salary/benefits (41c & 42c)	Pastoral Benefits (40, 42a-44)	Total amount paid in salary and benefits for all other church staff and diaconal ministers (45)	Total amount spent for local church program expenses (46)	Total amount spent for other local church operating expenses (47)	Local Church capital expenses (48 & 49)	TOTAL CHURCH EXPENSES (Sum of Lines 29a through 49) (50)	Number of giving units (51)	Total income for annual budget/spending plan (52)	Total income for designated causes including capital campaign and other special projects (53)	Total income from connectional and other institutional sources outside the local church (54)
33030	5709	3670	3670	19570	0	0	15579	7552	3681	26706	1500	95753	53	103805	6054	2000
33031	9904	1270	1270	13400	0	0	19577	41429	13070	19090	93629	234147	96	194616	8710	0
33032	0	2000	0	0	0	0	4020	0	340	13794	9000	27154	24	24385	0	20000
33033	758	1713	1570	12500	0	0	13116	12500	500	13600	2500	48528	36	49525	893	0
33034	2399	3271	3271	21699	0	0	28374	2028	1104	18344	0	69378	32	65205	8636	0
33035	256	3801	3801	25639	0	0	6030	20534	3200	26000	73200	195219	47	121300	0	0
33036	0	1121	1121	9549	0	0	14469	0	548	68	1800	22081	11	29415	553	0
33037	2218	5675	5675	37832	0	0	3525	3568	2000	15000	4087	90712	50	87642	3845	0
33038	3922	1116	1116	8400	0	0	1011	0	1160	15363	0	36945	25	36856	26531	2000
33039	6375	650	650	13000	0	0	1130	1690	1050	19586	0	48838	15	37175	2489	0
33040	3700	1713	1713	12500	25000	0		10500	550	14300	55000	104022	62	59464	9440	0
33042	9610	5810	5810	38468	0	0	16112	30884	9531	26493	46290	199959	69	171797	4385	0
33043	5283	4718	4718	31630	0	0	15266	3000	973	11500	0	81787	49	82914	27581	2000
33044	26155	12744	12744	85000	0	0	33686	170906	74750	77594	169798	713390	313	593731	156587	50074
33046	241357	22390	22390	97916	93355	0	75937	608567	142108	264581	71788	1812734	437	1681461	267546	3064
33045	3119	4720	4720	29540	0	0	23587	23254	916	23805	5977	114918	54	104590	25187	2000
33047	12522	7803	7153	52000	0	0	28412	18736	2258	25177	14676	181446	57	166810	30636	0
33048	2935	3569	3569	26597	0	0	9402	929	3020	14943	0	65571	34	80440	561	0
33050	4073	1283	83	10000	0	0	1204	1300	2099	31006	4415	60552	20	40490	414	0

STATISTICAL INFORMATION

CB

CONFERENCE Number	CHURCH NAME	Total professing members reported at the close last year (1)	TOTAL PROFESSING MEMBERS reported at the close of this year (4)	Average attendance at all weekly worship services (7)	Total Baptized Members who have not become Professing Members (9)	Number of other constituents of the church (10)	TOTAL Christian Formation Group Participants (Total of lines 11a-d) (11)	Average weekly attendance (all ages) in Sunday Church School or other weekly education classes (13)	Membership in United Methodist Men (18a)	Membership in United Methodist Women (19a)	Number of persons sent out on UMW/M teams from this local church (20b)	Total Number of community ministries for outreach, justice, and mercy offered by this local church (21)	Value of church assets and buildings (24 & 25)	Church Debt (26 & 27)	Amount APPORTIONED to the local church by the CONFERENCE (28a)	Amount PAID by the local church to the CONFERENCE for all apportioned causes (29a)
33051	MT PLEASANT: FIRST	342	322	150	34	102	204	35	0	75	0	13	4243630	157441	49512	49512
33052	MT PLEASANT: TRINITY	39	39	18	0	0	19	11	0	0	0	0	575000	13324	5028	0
33053	NELSON	91	88	40	10	10	10	7	25	15	0	1	593707	0	6288	6288
33054	OSCODA	211	210	102	0	78	69	25	0	17	0	0	1537952	0	18741	6087
33055	OSCODA: INDIAN MISSION	87	87	10	0	10	11	8	0	0	0	0	40553		1591	1591
33056	OWENDALE	69	80	44	0	37	18	8	0	34	0	1	399141	144592	5652	5652
33057	PIGEON: FIRST	172	161	57	21	30	54	16	18	18	0	7	1660865	0	15627	15627
33058	PIGEON: SALEM	153	160	90	20	14	143	93	0	0	0	2	695000	0	26034	26034
33059	PINCONNING	92	87	22	0	7	11	6	0	15	0	3	1245000	0	8399	106
33060	PINNEBOG	15	17	22	0	15	5	2	0	0	0	0	351000	0	3355	3355
33061	PORT AUSTIN UPC	39	40	32	0	23	12	0	0	11	0	5	550682	0	5550	5550
33063	REESE	135	133	65	39	67	37	18	0	17	0	11	1021000	0	12625	12625
33064	ROSE CITY: TRINITY	98	92	57	0	38	35	20	0	22	0	0	1012132	12195	9638	921
33065	ROSEBUSH	110	104	90	1	151	26	4	10	13	0	1	1927000	0	20102	20102
33066	SAGINAW: AMES	254	248	191	21	88	95	81	0	38	0	8	3602066	0	43879	8736
33067	SAGINAW: FIRST	353	341	125	38	68	70	9	15	58	6	5	9852200	0	40547	40547
33069	SAGINAW: NEW HEART	58	56	45	0	76	78	0	0	0	0	9	345211	0	11247	0
33071	SAGINAW: SWAN VALLEY	124	120	49	36	33	45	4	0	28	0	0	1504554	0	17210	13000
33072	SANFORD	172	167	67	15	49	23	7	9	17	0	2	1725443	0	19496	19496

CONFERENCE Number	30-38 Church Benevolence Giving	39a Total ASKED for clergy pension	39b Total PAID for clergy pension	41a Base compensation paid to/for the Senior Pastor or other person assigned or appointed in the lead pastoral role to the church	41b Base compensation paid to/for all Associate Pastor(s) and other pastoral staff assigned or appointed to the church. Include deacons and other clergy in this role	41c & 42c Deacons salary/benefits	40,42a-44 Pastoral Benefits	45 Total amount paid in salary and benefits for all other church staff and diaconal ministers	46 Total amount spent for local church program expenses	47 Total amount spent for other local church operating expenses	48 & 49 Local Church capital expenses	50 TOTAL CHURCH EXPENSES (Sum of Lines 29a through 49)	51 Number of giving units	52 Total income for annual budget/spending plan	53 Total income for designated causes including capital campaign and other special projects	54 Total income from connectional and other institutional sources outside the local church
33051	45215	8250	8250	50769	0	0	14449	119721	36595	91853	67037	483401	312	328277	121564	0
33052	1494	1283	83	10000	0	0	7190	0	580	14065	4550	37962	9	37702	2560	0
33053	2455	1720	1720	13601	0	0	5210	6000	300	5000	164	40738	32	57506	1500	0
33054	4494	6746	6184	48750	0	0	33367	17098	14761	26571	38762	196074	124	190461	2839	0
33055	625	539	539	3000	0	0	0	0	2220	7022	0	14997		11005	0	0
33056	2092	4163	4163	22875	0	0	16491	0	2009	12838	226760	292880	29	71104	63064	0
33057	4301	6543	6543	43620	0	0	30474	24435	4231	23554	10196	162981	83	173469	24058	0
33058	36053	7783	7783	53748	0	0	37796	48373	23912	29819	18414	281932	90	253393	0	0
33059	387	3730	933	24872	0	0	4349	6253	1055	12348	0	50303	25	46127	453	5000
33060	243	1498	1498	9900	0	0	9116	0	50	3962	0	28124	10	29950	0	0
33061	2958	3002	3002	20010	0	0	19524	0	107	8007	0	59158	34	62704	2481	0
33063	2771	7012	7012	45000	0	0	21996	0	8129	17384	8108	123025	69	122326	240	0
33064	1836	3343	3343	26176	0	0	16275	0	4358	35545	18715	107169	44	113217	2394	0
33065	11294	6750	6750	45000	0	0	28237	17154	4774	20208	26262	179781	79	185579	3375	0
33066	4542	7834	7834	52225	0	0	30218	80450	20084	56103	2619	262811	94	257949	16015	0
33067	37689	9644	9644	64767	0	0	33452	118203	16489	108750	185764	615305	104	362981	121460	0
33069	525	4221	4221	35483	0	0	0	13728	14472	33950	0	102379	73	81333	25000	0
33071	2303	6900	6900	42823	0	0	14106	27116	8045	18470	2706	135469	75	144502	1442	1050
33072	6243	7409	7409	49890	0	0	30128	39663	949	24728	58691	237197	91	156406	4236	2000

STATISTICAL INFORMATION

CB

EW

CONFERENCE Number	CHURCH NAME	1 Total professing members reported at the close last year	4 TOTAL PROFESSING MEMBERS reported at the close of this year	7 Average attendance at all weekly worship services	9 Total Baptized Members who have not become Professing Members	10 Number of other constituents of the church	11 TOTAL Christian Formation Group Participants (Total of lines 11a-d)	13 Average weekly attendance (all ages) in Sunday Church School or other weekly education classes	18a Membership in United Methodist Men	19a Membership in United Methodist Women	20b Number of persons sent out on UMVIM teams from this local church	21 Total Number of community ministries for outreach, justice, and mercy offered by this local church	24 & 25 Value of church assets and buildings	26 & 27 Church Debt	28a Amount APPORTIONED to the local church by the CONFERENCE	29a Amount PAID by the local church to the CONFERENCE for all apportioned causes
33073	SEBEWAING: TRINITY	197	191	52	41	43	102	27	11	11	0	18	8388381	0	17506	1000
33074	SHEPHERD	84	79	42	0	22	16	10	0	0	0	3	507262	0	15275	15275
33075	ST CHARLES	139	144	65	16	25	41	12	0	14	0	13	3499878	6786	15780	15780
33076	Standish: Beacon of Light	51	69	39	3	5	24	12	0	15	0	7	1543200	0	4893	4893
33077	STERLING	96	96	30	5	9	19	5	0	0	0	0	434125	0	6190	0
33078	SUTTON-SUNSHINE	78	74	31	3	20	11	3	0	12	0	5	1084886	0	5513	5513
33079	TAWAS	226	224	125	0	111	34	45	0	27	2	10	3376107	636043	22802	22802
33080	VASSAR: FIRST	182	175	86	4	170	124	25	0	0	0	2	2840916	1787	21863	4553
33082	WATROUSVILLE	119	121	45	18	0	12	10	0	33	0	1	512751	0	4774	4774
33083	WEIDMAN	108	110	67	0	0	75	20	0	3533	0	2	1050000	0	12379	9919
33084	WEST BRANCH: FIRST	213	192	95	0	102	355	21	15	18	0	16	1929656	0	24850	24850
33085	WHITTEMORE	64	65	40	38	8	25	15	0	17	0	3	971030	0	5377	5377
33086	WILBER	24	24	18	0	15	17	15	0	8	0	0	450000	0	2747	2747
33087	WINN	40	39	23	0	0	0	0	0	0	0	0	320950	0	4767	4767
33088	WISNER	163	166	80	60	73	68	21	0	0	3	1	2364245	0	16428	16428
	EAST WINDS DISTRICT															
36001	APPLEGATE	93	91	27	0	0	8	3	12	10	0	4	328522	0	3806	3806
36002	ARMADA	119	116	53	62	26	60	24	0	10	0	2	1011000	0	12790	12790
36003	ATHERTON	180	157	45	0	18	33	25	7	7	0	2	4282416	0	13948	3932

CONFERENCE Number	30-38 Church Benevolence Giving	39a Total ASKED for clergy pension	39b Total PAID for clergy pension	41a Base compensation paid to/for the Senior Pastor or other person assigned or appointed in the lead pastoral role to the church	41b Base compensation paid to/for all Associate Pastor(s) and other pastoral staff assigned or appointed to the church. Include deacons and other clergy in this role	41c & 42b Deacons salary/benefits	40,42a-44 Pastoral Benefits	45 Total amount paid in salary and benefits for all other church staff and diaconal ministers	46 Total amount spent for local church program expenses	47 Total amount spent for other local church operating expenses	48 & 49 Local Church capital expenses	50 TOTAL CHURCH EXPENSES (Sum of Lines 29a through 49)	51 Number of giving units	52 Total income for annual budget/spending plan	53 Total income for designated causes including capital campaign and other special projects	54 Total income from connectional and other institutional sources outside the local church
33073	2908	7344	7344	48960	0	0	8181	16442	5469	26313	34100	150717	84	139401	2988	5000
33074	8934	6750	6750	45000	0	0	24491	11137	1856	28159	0	141602	50	142117	0	0
33075	4843	6900	6900	49169	0	0	18933	33233	3981	30314	47575	210728	90	160376	109034	2826
33076	221	2361	2361	31870	0	0	25260	0	500	10700	35300	111105	36	51030	18420	750
33077	0	1433	1433	22542	0	0	0	0	523	14560	6000	39058	46	47812	127	0
33078	8504	1873	1873	18734	0	0	5785	700	1107	16884	65532	65100	50	80899	6477	0
33079	2173	6832	6832	45547	0	0	27804	38141	4989	89424	4147	303244	0	212903	0	0
33080	5131	6405	6405	42700	0	0	27826	20531	14884	40511	20791	166688	71	150644	14263	1500
33082	6541	1176	1176	23520	0	0	1053	3120	7356	8692		77023	40	44826	20886	0
33083	11053	5767	5767	46385	0	0	1500	18900	1400	88600	28855	183524	50	61725	1593	8835
33084	8140	7488	6864	48741	200	0	33319	54228	5427	46095	0	227864	139	199335	11047	0
33085	124	1429	1429	12188	0	0	9095	0	950	15222	10422	73240	40	73902	339	0
33086	40	551	600	8500	0	0	0	0	500	7000		18787	10	33000	400	0
33087	277	600	600	6000	0	0	2330	2880	1350	12200	0	40826	16	41932	275	0
33088	19615	6472	6472	44629	0	0	34975	20449	14007	23310	0	179885	65	159974	27846	0
36001	30	1624	1624	10070	0	0	4574	0	250	8791	0	29145	26	38019	16	0
36002	4605	4867	4867	36529	0	0	24499	5781	1661	23851	0	114583	89	106615	10312	1335
36003	1458	4588	4588	30585	0	0	19200	16877	2520	30331	5300	114791	58	96929	114485	0

STATISTICAL INFORMATION

EW

CONFERENCE Number	CHURCH NAME	1 — Total professing members reported at the close of last year	4 — TOTAL PROFESSING MEMBERS reported at the close of this year	7 — Average attendance at all weekly worship services	9 — Total Baptized Members who have not become Professing Members	10 — Number of other constituents of the church	11 — TOTAL Christian Formation Group Participants (Total of lines 11a-d)	13 — Average weekly attendance (all ages) in Sunday Church School or other weekly education classes	18a — Membership in United Methodist Men	19a — Membership in United Methodist Women	20b — Number of persons sent out on UMVIM teams from this local church	21 — Total Number of community ministries for outreach, justice, and mercy offered by this local church	24 & 25 — Value of church assets and buildings	26 & 27 — Church Debt	28a — Amount APPORTIONED to the local church by the CONFERENCE	29a — Amount PAID by the local church to the CONFERENCE for all apportioned causes
36004	ATTICA	78	67	53	1	13	20	12	11	19	0	5	899250	30304	11096	11096
36005	AVOCA	44	42	42	35	11	0	10	0	12	0	2	678760	0	4451	4451
36006	BAD AXE: FIRST	236	251	93	29	9	75	27	16	29	0	9	3909244	0	19739	19739
36007	BROWN CITY	120	124	66	0	35	30	20	8	31	0	2	550000	0	11973	11973
36008	BUEL	63	61	30	17		18	18	12	12	0	5	275000	0	3532	3532
36009	BURTON: CHRIST	71	70	31	0	44	32	14	0	10	0	0	1431184	21405	8636	4000
36010	BYRON: FIRST	100	96	75	18	35	54	28	0	18	0	12	3057611	3127	15237	15237
36011	CAPAC	109	109	42	2	16	35	13	0	0	0	3	750000	0	12495	0
36012	CARSONVILLE	12	11	10	15	3	0	0	0	0	0	1	28838	0	2636	2636
36013	CENTRAL LAKEPORT	40	39	25	0		0	0	0	10	0	1	1106508	0	4205	4205
36014	CLARKSTON	1609	1619	442	278	819	1415	220	75	50	0	0	13717542	4028706	133636	133636
36015	CLIO: BETHANY	269	275	135	75	6	94	12	6	0	0	1	5348843	0	35447	35447
36016	COLE	89	90	55	5	201	33	12	0	20	0	0	170000	0	7480	3480
36017	COLUMBIAVILLE	175	176	49	13	110	15	7	13	18	0	10	1897500	0	11316	500
36018	CROSWELL: FIRST	63	62	41	31	28	19	10	7	18	0	10	1772000	34821	6773	6773
36019	DAVISBURG	53	46	23	0	15	8	8	0	0	0	6	2032000	0	10949	5630
36020	DAVISON	241	243	128	0	52	58	35	10	93	0	6	3213844	23808	40536	40537
36021	DECKERVILLE	24	24	18	0	8	6	4	0	0	0	15	283706	0	3116	3116
36022	DRYDEN	70	61	26	0	20	13	10	0	0	0	0	2496000	0	10946	10946

CONFERENCE Number	Church Benevolence Giving (30.38)	Total ASKED for clergy pension (39a)	Total PAID for clergy pension (39b)	Base compensation paid to/for the Senior Pastor... (41a)	Base compensation paid to/for all Associate Pastor(s)... (41b)	Deacons salary/benefits (41c & 42e)	Pastoral Benefits (40.42a-44)	Total amount paid in salary and benefits for all other church staff and diaconal ministers (45)	Total amount spent for local church program expenses (46)	Total amount spent for other local church operating expenses (47)	Local Church capital expenses (48 & 49)	TOTAL CHURCH EXPENSES (Sum of Lines 29a through 49) (50)	Number of giving units (51)	Total income for annual budget/spending plan (52)	Total income for designated causes including capital campaign and other special projects (53)	Total income from connectional and other institutional sources outside the local church (54)
36004	4372	3150	3150	27500	0	0	12241	0	1150	21509	25846	106864	26	78010	7510	5000
36005	927	1662	1662	11383	0	0	2391	0	183	18284	5309	44590	40	39622	3135	0
36006	6043	8891	8891	57954	0	0	23009	36984	14448	39135	0	206203	121	193824	8490	0
36007	429	7613	7613	42708	0	0	17439	6125	3871	15941	28622	134721	105	142373	4430	0
36008	12669	1624	1624	10070	0	0	4574	0	545	11225		44239	30	32888		0
36009	100	1044	740	10324	0	0	2928		225	28719	5919	52955	32	40014	1220	0
36010	4383	3272	3000	21816	0	0	4048	53318	19785	31500	13710	166797	70	122413	1945	0
36011	1953	6150	6150	41000	0	0	12100	7150	1935	17026	11380	98694	44	82910	608	0
36012	120	1210	1210	12095	0	0	2600	0	320	3585	0	22566	11	22222	0	0
36013	6	900	900	6000	0	0		9562	1192	9911	0	31776	19	35084	1313	0
36014	62577	18410	18410	113893	52039	37601	40834	555028	59621	294716	623938	1992293	504	1370080	891775	0
36015	9343	8343	8343	55620	0	0	13696	70590	8210	60806	369500	631555	130	293636	8962	0
36016	866	3891	3891	25578	1820	0	6907	0	3235	17390	0	63167	58	67435	855	0
36017	1300	5908	3692	40623	0	0	80	15496	500	24644		86835	58	87698	1175	0
36018	338	1624	1624	10070	0	0	7099	6717	491	21117	15200	69429	35	67064	16429	0
36019	418	467	467		0	0	10600	20000	1200	31390	7460	77165	22	61181	350	0
36020	16738	8768	8768	58451	0	0	30535	90873	8198	59136	20829	334065	162	308798	33152	0
36021	11177	900	900	6000	0	0	900	4770	167	7563		34593	18	25182	8123	0
36022	3399	4287	4287	20816	0	0	6288	4962	323	21330	0	72351	20	69647	0	0

STATISTICAL INFORMATION

EW

CONFERENCE Number	CHURCH NAME	1	4	7	9	10	11	13	18a	19a	20b	21	24 & 25	26 & 27	28a	29a
36023	DUFFIELD	47	48	28	0	15	0	0	0	8	0	0	1204800	16000	4171	4171
36024	DURAND: FIRST	128	128	77	40	141	67	8	23	15	0	3	3470300	355787	15479	7287
36025	ELBA	30	29	22	0	0	17	1	0	6	0	4	65097	0	3463	3463
36026	FENTON	867	692	249	150	505	225	75	15	62	0	16	16459091	648746	68271	68271
36027	FLINT: ASBURY	136	125	30	36	0	25	7	6	7	0	8	487384	0	16915	0
36028	FLINT: BETHEL	260	260	120	0	0	59	75	15	25	0	1	6717170	0	31297	31297
36029	FLINT: BRISTOL	60	70	45	0	0	4	0	5	20	0	0	950000	0	9766	1283
36030	FLINT: CALVARY	101	102	68	0	28	51	35	0	0	0	5	714506	0	42411	10000
36031	FLINT: CHARITY	78	78	34	0	4	18	6	7	11	0	2	6828967	53003	4517	4517
36032	FLINT: COURT STREET	501	487	166	114	60	146	56	27	70	139	8	15332074	0	63725	63725
36034	FLINT: HOPE	160	159	81	0	22	54	5	14	0	0	3	3983963	0	24654	2465
36035	FLUSHING	313	311	166	0	180	85	50	0	90	0	10	4880000	0	38691	38691
36036	FORESTER	51	29	11	0	13	7	7	0	6	0	0	310000	0	3163	3163
36037	FOSTORIA	39	39	19	0	32	12	10	0	8	0	1	700380	49883	3667	3667
36038	GAINES	63	63	37	0	0	27	25	30	15	0	3	1468451	0	10093	10093
36039	GENESEE	71	65	28	5	39	50	13	9	12	0	6	1530026	0	6266	6266
36040	GOODRICH	355	265	112	81	46	84	32	6	46	0	4	7038627	527220	31120	12935
36041	GRAND BLANC	329	336	136	0	0	142	52	60	53	0	0	3816104	190947	33556	33556
36042	GRAND BLANC: PHOENIX	34	34	16	8	14	21	5	0	0	0	2	2034772	0	6422	6422

Column key:
- 1: Total professing members reported at the close of last year
- 4: TOTAL PROFESSING MEMBERS reported at the close of this year
- 7: Average attendance at all weekly worship services
- 9: Total Baptized Members who have not become Professing Members
- 10: Number of other constituents of the church
- 11: TOTAL Christian Formation Group Participants (Total of lines 11a-d)
- 13: Average weekly attendance (all ages) in Sunday Church School or other weekly education classes
- 18a: Membership in United Methodist Men
- 19a: Membership in United Methodist Women
- 20b: Number of persons sent out on UMW teams from this local church
- 21: Total Number of community ministries for outreach, justice, and mercy offered by this local church
- 24 & 25: Value of church assets and buildings
- 26 & 27: Church Debt
- 28a: Amount APPORTIONED to the local church by the CONFERENCE
- 29a: Amount PAID by the local church to the CONFERENCE for all apportioned causes

EW

CONFERENCE Number	30-38 Church Benevolence Giving	39a Total ASKED for clergy pension	39b Total PAID for clergy pension	41a Base compensation paid to/for the Senior Pastor or other person assigned or appointed in the lead pastoral role to the church	41b Base compensation paid to/for all Associate Pastor(s) and other pastoral staff assigned or appointed to the church. Include deacons and other clergy in this role	41c & 42c Deacons salary/benefits	40,42a-44 Pastoral Benefits	45 Total amount paid in salary and benefits for all other church staff and diaconal ministries	46 Total amount spent for local church program expenses	47 Total amount spent for other local church operating expenses	48 & 49 Local Church capital expenses	50 TOTAL CHURCH EXPENSES (Sum of Lines 29a through 49)	51 Number of giving units	52 Total income for annual budget/spending plan	53 Total income for designated causes including capital campaign and other special projects	54 Total income from connectional and other institutional sources outside the local church
36023	0	1219	1219	10063	0	0	625	2625	75	2153	7711	28642	15	32864	1982	0
36024	1134	3153	3153	49440	0	0	23458	12012	1500	29548	39470	167002	50	135331	2000	0
36025	2297	971	971	9713	0	0	375	2440	906	7903	0	28068	18	36724	0	0
36026	32705	18460	18460	92635	30748	0	26672	203773	21895	615775	256749	1367683	288	718126	15104	0
36027	236	5713	1428	39653	12000	0	24917	7700	8000	136108	0	218042	26	138838	255	0
36028	892	5551	5551	28000	0	0	27519	93000	10000	57000	34000	299259	145	191955	460	2500
36029	3462	3561	3310	24846	0	0	4200	15000	900	19400	1600	74001	41	82800	4000	0
36030	89343	2500	2500	20000	0	0	14048	69319	9029	56279	12570	283088	74	187087	56564	1500
36031	574	763	763	9488	0	0	2609	1680	600	30000	7328	57559	15	57700	1832	33450
36032	36028	16925	16925	73136	21657	6750	55759	209408	29780	136681	128006	777855	126	580117	105043	0
36034	5003	7275	7275	48500	0	0	35175	26155	3644	72201	27485	227903	52	184250	25005	38457
36035	28875	7200	7200	48000	0	0	26698	81474	8271	85680	0	324889	193	294718	32600	0
36036	903	1275	1275	10404	0	0	3780	50	2000	4958	0	22753	14	23982	113	3000
36037	679	1487	1487	9910	0	0	5044	0	383	15139	10440	45485	25	42305	3048	0
36038	9089	3272	3272	21816	0	0	10043	16262	4124	25727	10520	105947	37	94596	5073	0
36039	1130	3093	3093	20620	0	0	24518	5084	1752	8767	1518	58273	32	61511	1387	500
36040	16515	6900	6900	46000	0	0	28101	51722	41510	59324	145942	405366	179	265582	190920	0
36041	21469	7673	7673	65894	0	0	12643	82515	6106	70256	96467	412037	187	321673	84707	0
36042	2412	3059	3059	20390	0	0		-10321	1500	18059	67038	141844	13	112413	5274	0

CONFERENCE Number	CHURCH NAME	1	4	7	9	10	11	13	18a	19a	20b	21	24 & 25	26 & 27	28a	29a
36043	HALSEY	91	86	60	20	49	32	16	0	35	0	3	1433353	0	8923	8923
36044	HARBOR BEACH	42	47	34	0	0	12	7	6	7	0	2	936238	0	5885	5885
36045	HOLLY: CALVARY	148	136	109	0	88	162	45	6	17	0	4	3231662	288419	25396	12707
36046	HOLLY: MT BETHEL	57	56	27	9	10	15	9	0	0	0	2	167375	0	4399	3959
36047	IMLAY CITY	95	86	68	2	69	72	37	0	20	0	10	2226217	0	15187	606
36048	JEDDO	107	55	35	0	0	0	17	0	10	0	32	1048600	0	7379	7379
36049	LAKE FENTON	182	179	33	0	12	0	0	0	16	0	0	1855134	64950	9217	9217
36050	LAKE ORION	595	542	162	330	524	242	23	20	36	0	14	5433548	993117	68166	30675
36051	LAMB	41	36	25	0	15	0	1	0	5	0	1	639000	0	3941	3941
36052	LAPEER: TRINITY	469	448	296	56	190	237	32	21	25	34	4	6393298	0	50971	50971
36053	LENNON	66	66	22	0	22	18	15	0	8	0	0	640000	0	5599	5599
36054	LEONARD	34	34	12	0	0	0	4	0	0	0	0	450702	0	2261	0
36055	LEXINGTON	142	146	118	17	70	56	25	15	34	3	28	2584109	0	17504	17504
36056	LINDEN	113	105	40	12	19	28	2	0	20	0	0	1470336	0	10695	10695
36057	MARLETTE: FIRST	161	170	110	1	203	122	25	7	11	0	4	2400425	0	24444	4000
36058	MARYSVILLE	273	271	84	64	65	98	8	0	6	0	19	3314482	0	25191	25191
36059	MCGREGOR	80	80	90	14	96	52	18	0	15	0	0	242848	0	5397	5397
36060	MELVIN	27	27	44	0	82	0	4	0	0	1	0	37042	7200	4291	2117
36061	MEMPHIS: FIRST	45	46	25	17	26	18	5	0	0	0	4	1482644	0	4473	4473

EW

CONFERENCE Number	30-38 Church Benevolence Giving	39a Total ASKED for clergy pension	39b Total PAID for clergy pension	41a Base compensation paid to/for the Senior Pastor or other person assigned or appointed in the lead pastoral role to the church	41b Base compensation paid to/for all Associate Pastor(s) and other pastoral staff assigned or appointed to the church, include deacons and other clergy in this role	41c & 42c Deacons salary/benefits	40,42a-44 Pastoral Benefits	45 Total amount paid in salary and benefits for all other church staff and diaconal ministers	46 Total amount spent for local church program expenses	47 Total amount spent for other local church operating expenses	48 & 49 Local Church capital expenses	50 TOTAL CHURCH EXPENSES (Sum of Lines 29a through 49)	51 Number of giving units	52 Total income for annual budget/spending plan	53 Total income for designated causes including capital campaign and other special projects	54 Total income from connectional and other institutional sources outside the local church
36043	2422	3860	3860	22658	0	0	13550	11386	6650	24245	488	94182	55	88348	200	350
36044	1792	2767	2767	18631	0	0	10607	3500	1165	6270	18771	69388	23	68103	9748	3150
36045	1613	9843	8233	62477	0	0	9294	42053	3592	25657	70404	236030	97	205928	15301	0
36046	1655	540	540	11440	0	0	540	1925	325	8434	123195	28818	18	25180	7868	0
36047	3383	7654	140	51026	0	0	27264	11712	1345	19051	0	237722	72	113364	851797	0
36048	2207	2493	2493	16623	0	0	2490	712	244	21340	6990	52776	30	59232	3777	0
36049	2862	2333	2333	18135	0	0	0	10754	1826	32895	0	85012	76	63001	1935	0
36050	43403	17366	17366	69800	45967	0	63075	140135	22119	101579	176956	711075	330	674640	33194	0
36051	1008	1586	1586	9918	0	0	2772	1200	874	19397	0	40696	22	27200	4217	0
36052	11858	11139	11139	74263	0	0	25732	205533	24490	67428	0	471414	241	468634	21234	0
36053	269	1219	1103	10063	0	0	625	8011	1208	7722	0	34600	13	45623	830	0
36054		1661	280	7553	0	350	0	0	100	4043	0	12326	14	22242	0	200
36055	12627	7650	7650	51000	8761	22573	28257	24440	13198	31485	1916	188077	87	168292	9486	0
36056	1337	761	761	12471	0	0	7211	22525	0	38802	20691	145827	0	90930	4547	0
36057	4170	8175	8175	56000	0	0	33327	35359	3024	49579	5506	199140	158	211816	3971	0
36058	9486	9833	9833	40437	0	0	26171	47137	9614	29825	16673	214367	100	216544	22405	0
36059	10437	4345	4345	24190	1820	0	16575	0	3282	8837	0	73063	66	82076	0	0
36060	100	882	882	7902	0	0	810	0	200	21569	1031	36431	0	31483	0	0
36061	304	1566	1566	12530	0	0	5435	3300	658	10048	1098	39412	25	36170	3193	7200

CONFERENCE Number	CHURCH NAME	1. Total professing members reported at the close last year	4. TOTAL PROFESSING MEMBERS reported at the close of this year	7. Average attendance at all weekly worship services	9. Total Baptized Members who have not become Professing Members	10. Number of other constituents of the church	11. TOTAL Christian Formation Group Participants (Total of lines 11a-d)	13. Average weekly attendance (all ages) in Sunday Church School or other weekly education classes	18a. Membership in United Methodist Men	19a. Membership in United Methodist Women	20b. Number of persons sent out on UMW/UMM teams from this local church	21. Total Number of community ministries for outreach, justice, and mercy offered by this local church	24 & 25. Value of church assets and buildings	26 & 27. Church Debt	28a. Amount APPORTIONED to the local church by the CONFERENCE	29a. Amount PAID by the local church to the CONFERENCE for all apportioned causes
36062	MINDEN CITY	24	22	17	0	9	0	0	0	0	0	6	110000	0	1606	1606
36063	MONTROSE	138	142	106	3	57	31	30	0	0	0	4	2783000	0	14997	3000
36064	MT MORRIS: FIRST	126	124	34	7	65	13	9	0	12	0	0	849000	51667	11543	11543
36065	NORTH BRANCH: FIRST	121	110	46	25	45	16	0	0	10	0	0	1610610	0	8758	8758
36066	NORTH STREET	136	139	60	73	72	67	28	0	31	0	12	1923070	151613	14325	0
36067	OMARD	70	68	42	0	16	46	20	10	14	0	5	55214	0	2715	2715
36068	OREGON	96	103	40	0	0	44	8	0	9	0	0	544861	0	4220	4220
36069	ORTONVILLE	129	139	73	23	66	64	17	10	30	0	4	788027	0	15971	0
36070	OTISVILLE	67	60	38	0	59	5	6	0	21	0	8	1795000	0	6353	6353
36071	OXFORD	135	125	44	92	47	22	4	8	12	0	6	3630248	0	17830	1783
36072	PORT HOPE	53	50	45	9	50	25	13	0	8	0	8	556665	0	5900	5900
36073	PORT HURON: FIRST	637	574	180	5	75	98	38	36	117	20	8	7395525	0	52830	52830
36074	PORT HURON: GRATIOT PK	58	53	30	0	8	19	4	0	11	0	4	764770	0	4708	0
36076	PORT SANILAC	56	56	29	2	17	10	12	0	10	0	0	850000	0	3926	3926
36077	RICHFIELD	65	66	46	2	11	49	26	4	13	0	4	752742	0	5671	5671
36078	RICHMOND: FIRST	211	204	72	31	75	18	5	11	30	11	5	1963000	0	16334	8167
36079	ROMEO	254	233	131	76	112	140	20	0	40	0	44	4492844	557263	35941	35941
36081	SANDUSKY: FIRST	196	212	86	38	2	93	75	4	8	1	3	811786	0	18862	18862
36082	SEYMOUR LAKE	125	105	84	50	0	63	33	0	0	0	1	957918	306000	20902	20902

STATISTICAL INFORMATION

EW

CONFERENCE Number	30-38 Church Benevolence Giving	39a Total ASKED for clergy pension	39b Total PAID for clergy pension	41a Base compensation paid to/for the Senior Pastor or other person assigned or appointed in the lead pastoral role to the church	41b Base compensation paid to/for all Associate Pastor(s) and other pastoral staff assigned or appointed to the church. Include deacons and other clergy in this role	41c & 42c Deacons salary/benefits	40,42a-44 Pastoral Benefits	45 Total amount paid in salary and benefits for all other church staff and diaconal ministers	46 Total amount spent for local church program expenses	47 Total amount spent for other local church operating expenses	48 & 49 Local Church capital expenses	50 TOTAL CHURCH EXPENSES (Sum of Lines 29a through 49)	51 Number of giving units	52 Total income for annual budget/spending plan	53 Total income for designated causes including capital campaign and other special projects	54 Total income from connectional and other institutional sources outside the local church
36062	3982	894	894	6342	0	0	700	3700	200	2700	0	20124	9	17200	0	0
36063	7682	2781	2781	22509	0	0	38787	30214	14464	27614	9427	156478	86	137490	6223	500
36064	1031	850	850	17000	0	0	0	1516	1499	42397	0	75836	24	55020	23909	0
36065	1275	2333	2333	23328	0	0	1400	21717	2653	19639	5036	86139	46	83462	25122	0
36066	1702	6286	6286	41909	0	0	16900	8350	4012	36696	18911	134766	75	121846	23127	500
36067	1502	900	900	6000	0	0	297	1200	3500	9399	11088	36601	20	39578	2733	0
36068	736	1923	1923	9683	0	0	9551	1328	4708	14201	0	46350	35	34401	2429	0
36069	6181	6064	6064	40425	0	0	27668	14418	8248	26929	92670	222603	81	148380	117831	0
36070	2469	2676	2676	17838	0	0	6965	10451	809	10412	0	57973	57	46910	6008	0
36071	2156	6374	6374	42303	0	0	29331	24121	2173	24219	3808	136268	72	112143	11556	14000
36072	6244	3382	3382	22772	0	0	13591	4490	2060	7893	295	66627	39	77519	8852	2200
36073	14978	9889	9889	65928	0	0	9792	150182	35493	79736	34742	453570	229	444787	153378	0
36074	1842	1800	1800	4630	0	0	13000	3000	989	15600	275	41136	19	44708	6568	0
36076	1233	1250	1250	10404	0	0	850	0	850	5307	0	23820	27	26500	6648	0
36077	2034	1830	1830	19258	0	0	3450	5111	400	15265	5963	58982	25	42133	21605	6750
36078	31270	5040	5040	38064	0	0	31441	19104	1642	24025	1800	160553	105	132761	9489	7500
36079	9116	9000	9000	60000	0	0	19066	72469	6217	72826	71561	356196	166	346714	13760	0
36081	12036	6930	6930	46200	0	0	31467	17666	14973	30372	16989	195495	106	161781	97120	0
36082	8970	7020	7020	43300	0	0	12610	31949	22600	49598	69344	266293	81	203745	7448	5076

CONFERENCE Number	CHURCH NAME	Total professing members reported at the close last year (1)	TOTAL PROFESSING MEMBERS reported at the close of this year (4)	Average attendance at all weekly worship services (7)	Total Baptized Members who have not become Professing Members (9)	Number of other constituents of the church (10)	TOTAL Christian Formation Group Participants (Total of lines 11a-d) (11)	Average weekly attendance (all ages) in Sunday Church School or other weekly education classes (13)	Membership in United Methodist Men (18a)	Membership in United Methodist Women (19a)	Number of persons sent out on UMW/UMM teams from this local church (20b)	Total Number of community ministries for outreach, justice, and mercy offered by this local church (21)	Value of church assets and buildings (24 & 25)	Church Debt (26 & 27)	Amount APPORTIONED to the local church by the CONFERENCE (28a)	Amount PAID by the local church to the CONFERENCE for all apportioned causes (29a)
36083	SHABBONA	86	90	40	9	20	34	28	5	20	0	0	245990	0	5936	5936
36084	SILVERWOOD	38	36	15	0	5	0	0	0	16	0	0	546587	0	2813	2813
36085	SNOVER: HERITAGE	112	112	75	76	56	59	40	10	23	0	4	2725188	0	19947	12000
36086	SOUTH MUNDY	110	107	59	32	43	71	27	0	0	0	8	1572522	0	9112	9112
36080	ST CLAIR: FIRST	311	309	77	32	65	63	45	0	25	0	1	4103605	3090	23753	23753
36087	SWARTZ CREEK	561	464	276	47	71	195	80	40	30	0	0	6917460	0	62143	62143
36088	THETFORD CENTER	63	63	24	5	53	41	13	0	10	0	6	936592	0	5714	5714
36089	THOMAS	31	30	20	0	8	17	6	0	0	0	0	451876	0	4843	1200
36090	UBLY	28	28	14	0	11	9	3	0	12	0	0	233337	60	1885	1697
36091	WEST BERLIN	45	43	28	0	9	9	6	0	11	0	3	745547	0	4621	4621
36092	WEST DEERFIELD	52	49	43	4	80	37	10	15	11	0	10	514500	0	2502	2502
36093	WEST FOREST	77	76	45	42	98	53	4	0	0	0	9	856019	0	5688	5688
36094	WEST VIENNA	84	75	60	13	38	56	20	0	33	0	18	2813234	0	15781	2760
36095	WORTH TWP: BETHEL	66	66	24	0	26	6	6	10	14	0	0	425000	0	4842	2643
36096	YALE	94	75	43	0	9	22	7	5	12	0	2	300000	0	17151	0
	GREATER DETROIT DISTRICT															
39001	ALGONAC: TRINITY	83	77	42	0	17	9	1	8	8	0	6	2709000	15970	7805	1760
39002	BEVERLY HILLS	72	72	38	0	24	17	2	0	10	1	1	2553000	12669	12669	12669
39003	BIRMINGHAM: EMBURY	43	32	21	11	10	11	1	0	0	0	3	2762568	13877	13967	13967

CONFERENCE Number	Church Benevolence Giving	Total ASKED for clergy pension	Total PAID for clergy pension	Base compensation paid to/for the Senior Pastor or other person assigned or appointed in the lead pastoral role to the church	Base compensation paid to/for all Associate Pastor(s) and other pastoral staff assigned or appointed to the church. Include deacons and other clergy in this role	Deacons salary/benefits	Pastoral Benefits	Total amount paid in salary and benefits for all other church staff and diaconal ministers	Total amount spent for local church program expenses	Total amount spent for other local church operating expenses	Local Church capital expenses	TOTAL CHURCH EXPENSES (Sum of Lines 29a through 49)	Number of giving units	Total income for annual budget/spending plan	Total income for designated causes including capital campaign and other special projects	Total income from connectional and other institutional sources outside the local church
	30-38	39a	39b	41a	41b	41c & 42c	40,42a-44	45	46	47	48 & 49	50	51	52	53	54
36083	123	1471	1471	12184	0	0	2730	0	1778	11772	26846	62840	29	60576	795	0
36084	25	788	788	10138	0	0	900	0	238	7207	6764	28873	17	6044	21	0
36085	3178	6000	6000	36624	0	0	15793	13959	4268	28108	0	119930	77	146679	12942	0
36086	4246	4182	4182	25734	0	0	5861	12415	2476	25380	0	89406	60	86027	580	700
36080	8027	7920	7920	47961	0	0	37655	53514	4817	36770	19637	240054	101	255361	3165	0
36087	16399	16711	16711	76160	45664	0	21992	190819	13485	101729	101111	646213	256	498917	83339	0
36088	466	3351	3351	20620	0	0	9893	5877	485	7045	45	53496	25	50564	2763	0
36089	0	1711	1711	16054	0	0	3747	4075	1025	12656	0	40468	11	39393	480	0
36090	0	675	675	6000	0	0	0	0	3517	4402	0	16291	7	21940	0	0
36091	1809	2148	2148	11321	0	0	10112	0	1468	9976	6443	47898	34	38304	4465	0
36092	1307	1820	1820	11892	0	0	4397	1800	920	5468	22862	52968	30	34507	1111	0
36093	705	4758	4758	39653	0	0	0	0	4450	8801	0	64055	47	67392	1866	0
36094	13210	7178	6580	46795	0	0	22600	20000	4000	27575	300	143820	55	125611	20889	0
36095	312	650	650	13000	0	0	3078	0	1530	9001	13987	44201	15	29519	597	0
36096	2608	5474	5474	36658	1820	0	16028	9927	500	21350	0	94365	28	72676	0	3496
39001	2839	2456	2456	19644	0	0	3535	8390	745	28284	9429	77082	47	64887	1533	0
39002	2505	5400	5400	36000	0	0	25843	41743	295	40412	0	164867	72	152906	2980	0
39003	1535	750	750	15000	0	0	510	41247	1585	40803	3780	119177	22	132740	1065	0

STATISTICAL INFORMATION

GD

CONFERENCE Number	CHURCH NAME	Total professing members reported at the close of last year [1]	TOTAL PROFESSING MEMBERS reported at the close of this year [4]	Average attendance at all weekly worship services [7]	Total Baptized Members who have not become Professing Members [9]	Number of other constituents of the church [10]	TOTAL Christian Formation Group Participants (Total of lines 11a-d) [11]	Average weekly attendance (all ages) in Sunday Church School or other weekly education classes [13]	Membership in United Methodist Men [18a]	Membership in United Methodist Women [19a]	Number of persons sent out on UMVIM teams from this local church [20b]	Total Number of community ministries for outreach, justice, and mercy offered by this local church [21]	Value of church assets and buildings [24 & 25]	Church Debt [26 & 27]	Amount APPORTIONED to the local church by the CONFERENCE [28a]	Amount PAID by the local church to the CONFERENCE for all apportioned causes [29a]
		2816	2742	716	591	974	1348	167	81	186	11	62	55725047	0	377126	377126
39004	BIRMINGHAM: FIRST	68	62	34	10	26	13	7	10	10	0	5	4615101	0	16433	2080
39005	BLOOMFIELD HLS: ST PAUL	79	48	33	0	27	34	8	0	17	0	3	2290891		21879	2600
39006	CLAWSON	369	382	121	67	40	90	19	0	25	0	8	6645412	60000	44146	31521
39008	DEARBORN: FIRST	136	130	66	39	90	31	2	11	0	0	2	4268500	0	21438	21438
39009	DEARBORN: GOOD SHEPHERD	140	117	51	0	4	30	6	0	0	0	6	4627300	55852	11782	1068
39010	DETROIT: CALVARY	97	99	85	10	10	43	12	8	5	10	2	7805434	166000	17146	17146
39011	DETROIT: CASS CMNTY	273	261	100	9	48	77	32	13	24	0	0	14091166	135046	60983	6098
39012	DETROIT: CENTRAL	129	130	60	0	0	56	58	0	45	0	1	955000	52000	25573	1520
39014	DETROIT: CONANT AVE	21	21	22	8	15	16	10	6	0	0	0	814100	111874	13240	0
39015	DETROIT: FORD MEMORIAL	356	323	192	38	51	81	25	0	43	2	17	43774400	397800	71401	7800
39016	DETROIT: METROPOLITAN	56	51	34	0	2	8	10	0	0	0	5		32695	11673	0
39017	DETROIT: MT HOPE	71	68	27	0	4	19	7	0	20	0	3	456000	80000	22571	226
39018	DETROIT: PEOPLE'S	114	69	30	1	0	11	10	0	0	0	0	400000	32000	8981	200
39019	DETROIT: RESURRECTION			150	2	121	72	28	0	0	0	6		4810	200	8286
39020	DETROIT: SCOTT MEMORIAL	327	289	112	0	7	360	49	42	52	0	3	1009000	130500	37759	10000
39021	DETROIT: SECOND GRACE	367	363	41	0	5	12	10	40	51	0	0	5660034	738219	28234	0
39022	DETROIT: ST PAUL	98	99	31	2	0	21	5	10	17	0	0	575000	6420	8086	783
39023	DETROIT: ST TIMOTHY	76	73	58	3	27	21	7	5	15	0	0	305000	48786	20320	783
39024	DETROIT: TRINITY-FAITH	155	157						13	20	0	4	2437800	139417	20708	5000

CONFERENCE Number	Church Benevolence Giving [30-38]	Total ASKED for clergy pension [39a]	Total PAID for clergy pension [39b]	Base compensation paid to/for the Senior Pastor or other person assigned or appointed in the lead pastoral role to the church [41a]	Base compensation paid to/for all Associate Pastor(s) and other pastoral staff assigned or appointed to the church. Include deacons and other clergy in this role [41b]	Deacons salary/benefits [41c & 42b]	Pastoral Benefits [40,42a-44]	Total amount paid in salary and benefits for all other church staff and diaconal ministers [45]	Total amount spent for local church program expenses [46]	Total amount spent for other local church operating expenses [47]	Local church capital expenses [48 & 49]	TOTAL CHURCH EXPENSES (Sum of Lines 29a through 49) [50]	Number of giving units [51]	Total income for annual budget/spending plan [52]	Total income for designated causes including capital campaign and other special projects [53]	Total income from connectional and other institutional sources outside the local church [54]
39004	438561	55538	55538	130047	258031	0	142905	1615073	458713	559571	244082	4309647	1022	2704340	646191	0
39005	2488	2458	2458	19666	0	0	19861	36219	3561	37421	0	123754	30	116206	3264	5000
39006	1714	750	750	12000	0	0	588	60786	17000	44931	8000	131369	45	134844	0	2000
39008	11482	10893	10893	62620	31000	0	32554	104354	13645	79479	65000	445903	190	361099	65000	0
39009	10090	2224	2224	35000	0	0	125	30695	2058	62577		175794	72	176526	22996	0
39010	507	3460	3460	19000	0	2550		17481	250	52541	3856	96511	153	90018	4062	0
39011	3695	15318	15318	55667	45500	0	62295	53760	2266	57908	73854	387943	43	162809	23881	57500
39012	294	10900	10900	69669	0	0	45489	125846	8188	148438	10800	419800	54	418123	144365	0
39014	1362	8040	8040	55144	4800	0	12000	45434	200	5625	9507	151620	49	157980	20459	5000
39015	0	450	450	9000	0	2000	2000	8943		48414	5500	76507	12	30214	15153	4500
39016	43238	4580	4199	73302	0	0	13492	184610	24586	344322	499344	1194893	127	739459	738	0
39017	0	567	567	9000	0	0	510244	22000	300	40000	3000	585111	30	70911	0	0
39018	0	3070	2814	22135	0	0	5477	9200	7689	61511	3685	112737	32	117206	0	0
39019	75	2055	350	17000	0	0	7000	16080	440	14200	0	55345	66	55848	0	2500
39020	32	9000	8250	62400	0	0	33186	91915	4567	82987	62051	353674	144	306715	43800	16500
39021	1346	12453	10378	83833	0	0	18830	37490	38221	58760	46626	305484	140	289546	1671	0
39022	0	840	840	11000	0	0	3000	16068	850	27600	0	59358	60	62055	263	0
39023	52	1170	0	6000	9000	0		15837	311	40655		72638	102	60598	0	7000
39024	4093	5280	5280	37000	0	0	24947	40938	12226	38183	21061	188728	99	179229	3827	0

STATISTICAL INFORMATION

GD

Conference Number	CHURCH NAME	Total professing members reported at the close of last year (1)	TOTAL PROFESSING MEMBERS reported at the close of this year (4)	Average attendance at all weekly worship services (7)	Total Baptized Members who have not become Professing Members (9)	Number of other constituents of the church (10)	TOTAL Christian Formation Group Participants (Total of lines 11.a-d) (11)	Average weekly attendance (all ages) in Sunday Church School or other weekly education classes (13)	Membership in United Methodist Men (18a)	Membership in United Methodist Women (19a)	Number of persons sent out on UMVIM teams from this local church (20b)	Total Number of community ministries for outreach, justice, and mercy offered by this local church (21)	Value of church assets and buildings (24 & 25)	Church Debt (26 & 27)	Amount APPORTIONED to the local church by the CONFERENCE (28a)	Amount PAID by the local church to the CONFERENCE for all apportioned causes (29a)
39025	DOWNRIVER	234	228	88	1	60	49	18	0	20	0	3	3123754	500000	28700	5740
39026	EASTPOINTE: IMMANUEL	135	136	87	1	25	22	10	0	0	0	0	2750000	60000	16530	9918
39027	FARMINGTON: FIRST	366	344	160	45	15	91	57	39	44	11	3	4367712	202987	53061	1400
39028	FARMINGTON: NARDIN PARK	792	795	197	39	170	356	20	0	0	0	34	8649548	0	80417	30000
39029	FARMINGTON: ORCHARD	645	640	254	182	237	367	100	0	0	0	14	7664776	326668	75058	75058
39030	FERNDALE: FIRST	158	163	58	129	71	42	14	0	38	0	24	11802581	0	28455	15191
39031	FLAT ROCK: FIRST	168	173	97	15	56	76	44	12	28	0	11	3939346	0	20646	20646
39032	FRANKLIN: COMMUNITY	207	194	750	10	19	45	12	0	31	0	1	5121811	0	40269	5667
39033	FRASER: CHRIST	194	180	157	65	50	107	70	0	25	0	10	4038900	0	37009	0
39034	GARDEN CITY: FIRST	132	132	70	0	27	14	6	12	0	0	8	2923223	0	16474	2300
39035	GROSSE POINTE	570	580	160	63	81	216	45	8	121	32	24	7046620	0	71847	71847
39036	HARPER WOODS: REDEEMER	60	60	40	0	23	11	7	0	0	0	2	2912867	0	19136	19136
39037	HAZEL PARK: FIRST	54	56	41	0	23	11	6	0	0	0	0	1510000	0	8701	8701
39038	HOWARTH	41	39	31	14	38	8	3	0	6	0	2	109220	0	6495	6495
39039	LIVONIA: CLARENCEVILLE	111	108	68	7	35	73	52	0	0	0	0	7520266	2112	34565	0
39040	LIVONIA: NEWBURG	560	553	205	111	131	484	113	0	4	64	22	8874350	32767	46835	23418
39041	LIVONIA: ST MATTHEWS	419	406	95	59	141	127	50	0	63	10	4	4872420	0	30122	30122
39042	MACOMB: FAITH	50	55	31	5	14	62	3	0	14	0	1	1467000	0	4791	4791
39043	MADISON HTS	58	55	45	16	0	23	22	0	0	0	2	1662000	17000	9158	2478

CONFERENCE Number	30-38 Church Benevolence Giving	39a Total ASKED for clergy pension	39b Total PAID for clergy pension	41a Base compensation paid to/for the Senior Pastor or other person assigned or appointed in the lead pastoral role to the church	41b Base compensation paid to/for all Associate Pastor(s) and other pastoral staff assigned or appointed to the church. Include deacons and other clergy in this role	41c & 42c Deacons salary/benefits	40,42a-44 Pastoral Benefits	45 Total amount paid in salary and benefits for all other church staff and diaconal ministers	46 Total amount spent for local church program expenses	47 Total amount spent for other local church operating expenses	48 & 49 Local Church capital expenses	50 TOTAL CHURCH EXPENSES (Sum of Lines 29a through 49)	51 Number of giving units	52 Total income for annual budget/spending plan	53 Total income for designated causes including capital campaign and other special projects	54 Total income from connectional and other institutional sources outside the local church
39025	1200	6885	6885	45900	0	0	27036	56414	14563	45835	32750	236323	101	128488	65673	20000
39026	511	6064	6064	40424	0	0	21912	23113	2011	34132	0	138085	120	133012	14000	0
39027	7539	9750	9750	65000	31013	0	37983	174190	12067	98571	40450	446950	200	399648	9866	15000
39028	36616	15461	15461	82400	43101	0	23650	243799	29909	200746	843055	1566649	316	576430	313186	0
39029	12218	17041	17041	70830	0	0	61052	289218	24172	170915	224816	988421	326	713505	216993	0
39030	6196	9134	9134	60892	0	0	25189	49611	5138	94024	16192	281567	52	203793	19940	0
39031	10060	5700	5700	38000	0	0	8312	31379	10041	52900	39871	216909	129	213541	31561	0
39032	6461	7725	7725	51500	0	0	24082	123889	6701	76656	9697	312378	87	276261	4193	0
39033	13908	9483	9483	63678	0	0	23440	97375	11514	63499	1340	284237	195	346120	1500	15000
39034	9511	5054	5054	26089	0	0	5778	35040	1400	54674	7200	147046	90	121207	2895	0
39035	15012	18495	18495	65392	42353	0	55840	135066	17762	238611	65200	725581	0	586300	139358	0
39036	4884	6105	6105	40700	0	0	6837	46855	1573	58234	1243	185567	39	168021	21771	0
39037	374	2458	2458	17126	0	0	8967	15612	3565	18990	22510	98303	50	95175	230	0
39038	3853	2153	2153	17940	0	0	855	10380	4565	20931	8919	76091	23	48584	169	0
39039	6199	7284	7284	48523	20702	0	29521	39760	41586	92879	4634	270386	65	195116	36600	0
39040	50992	11264	10436	66217	0	0	46076	188582	9205	96496	62075	574199	301	437480	62758	0
39041	6021	8041	8041	23001	0	0	28056	51197	12302	84753	33220	307317	125	290318	11201	0
39042	268	1150	1150	23001	0	0	925	0	126	15991	6500	52752	21	26741	19196	1350
39043	1246	2959	2959	23669	0	0	3000	12762	5000	46000	4500	101614	47	74671	13642	0

STATISTICAL INFORMATION

GD

CONFERENCE Number	CHURCH NAME	1	4	7	9	10	11	13	18a	19a	20b	21	24 & 25	26 & 27	28a	29a
		Total professing members reported at the close of last year	TOTAL PROFESSING MEMBERS reported at the close of this year	Average attendance at all weekly worship services	Total Baptized Members who have not become Professing Members	Number of other constituents of the church	TOTAL Christian Formation Group Participants (Total of lines 11a-d)	Average weekly attendance (all ages) in Sunday Church School or other weekly education classes	Membership in United Methodist Men	Membership in United Methodist Women	Number of persons sent out on UMVIM teams from this local church	Total Number of community ministries for outreach, justice, and mercy offered by this local church	Value of church assets and buildings	Church Debt	Amount APPORTIONED to the local church by the CONFERENCE	Amount PAID by the local church to the CONFERENCE for all apportioned causes
39044	MADISON HTS: KOREAN FIRST CENTRAL	176	166	131	18	4	184	35	0	0	0	10	3385000	1019395	32379	12000
39046	MT CLEMENS: FIRST	277	260	124	5	163	96	6	0	0	16	5	1150000	318521	35015	21010
39047	MT VERNON	59	50	16	0	12	16	3	15	14	0	8	1155628	174000	10660	10660
39048	NEW BALTIMORE: GRACE	193	185	102	55	45	127	36	0	0	0	0	2959204	237000	26663	15500
39049	OMO: ZION	74	70	24	0	3	13	10	0	10	0	0	191216	0	2100	2100
39050	PAINT CREEK	54	48	35	3	8	13	9	0	0	0	3	863483	0	5594	5594
39051	PONTIAC: GRACE AND PEACE CMNTY	111	105	40	1	45	13	0	0	8	0	5	1844800	0	10387	130
39052	PONTIAC: ST JOHN	107	102	50	18	32	31	10	25	30	0	10	1742225	2000	23212	7600
39053	REDFORD: ALDERSGATE	341	335	154	13	1000	114	40	23	49	0	20	9830987	0	52530	4000
39054	REDFORD: NEW BEGINNINGS	23	24	22	7	28	18	16	0	0	0	9	2007000	2400	9302	0
39055	RIVERVIEW	84	81	23	0	8	3	0	0	0	0	0	1084000	0	9058	8480
39056	ROCHESTER HLS: ST LUKE'S	143	129	55	12	49	18	4	15	5	0	5	3940088	29248	30113	0
39057	ROCHESTER: ST PAUL'S	2182	2171	495	445	463	833	61	80	214	24	3	13044630	0	167287	99600
39058	ROMULUS: COMMUNITY	72	70	35	0	4	8	7	0	0	0	0	2880500	15032	15170	3117
39059	ROSEVILLE: TRINITY	173	158	103	48	21	51	62	8	40	0	4	3324054	0	28311	26675
39060	ROYAL OAK: FIRST	771	806	380	14	473	567	107	0	64	38	5	7152046	30171	78708	48065
39061	SOUTHFIELD: HOPE	1018	1093	380	0	55	55	50	15	50	0	0	14582291	4196133	184857	0
39062	STERLING HEIGHTS: FIRST	66	65	21	0	24	10	5	6	13	0	3	1388756	23273	11214	2200
39063	TRENTON: FAITH	442	433	144	3	192	107	18	0	228	0	3	2281763	236719	35268	35268

GD

CONFERENCE Number	Church Benevolence Giving (30-38)	Total ASKED for clergy pension (39a)	Total PAID for clergy pension (39b)	Base compensation paid to/for the Senior Pastor or other person assigned or appointed in the lead pastoral role to the church (41a)	Base compensation paid to/for all Associate Pastor(s) and other pastoral staff assigned or appointed to the church. Include deacons and other clergy in this role (41b)	Deacons salary/benefits (41c & 42c)	Pastoral Benefits (40,42a-44)	Total amount paid in salary and benefits for all other church staff and diaconal ministers (45)	Total amount spent for local church program expenses (46)	Total amount spent for other local church operating expenses (47)	Local Church capital expenses (48 & 49)	TOTAL CHURCH EXPENSES (Sum of Lines 29a through 49) (50)	Number of giving units (51)	Total income for annual budget/spending plan (52)	Total income for designated causes including capital campaign and other special projects (53)	Total income from connectional and other institutional sources outside the local church (54)
39044	25525	6975	6975	46500		0	42190	31836	37930	94788	54899	379643	0	395151	0	0
39046	7481	10350	10350	55000	27000	0	21979	53246	18288	84934	165914	459202	207	417609	36354	0
39047	2300	2916	2916	18060	21000	0	9715	2892	689	15275	800	63307	38	60639	22653	0
39048	10638	6600	6600	44000	0	0	25531	60766	5744	32560	48921	250260	103	229583	8739	0
39049	13	450	450	9000	0	0	13588	11835	436	2067	0	909654	17	17291	0	0
39050	3821	2153	2153	17939	0	0	1198	0	2787	21141	0	66468	38	56019	23403	22200
39051	355	2601	2601	15542	0	0	19536	51522	468	43196	0	62292	17	77997	17061	0
39052	4845	7024	7024	49165	0	0	20100	92565	8961	35723	987	184376	140	136467	21510	0
39053	600	7695	7054	45300	15000	0	500	5200	5174	89846	8000	280626	199	282499	3280	0
39054	300	1337	1003	21378	0	0	2000	8000	750	25600	0	62731	25	59645	0	0
39055	316	2400	2400	20000	0	0	42174	37608	800	50309	2820	53996	37	68100	900	0
39056	2550	8572	8572	57000	94086	0			2733			203766	96	246538	461	
39057	45099	29256	29256	77639	0	0	132510	455461	200410	242597	69229	1445887	700	1357033	398779	0
39058	4507	2800	2800	20000	0	0	14139	20332	8847	47412	17598	138752	0	141186	927	0
39059	1763	10037	10037	48241	0	0	29235	49383	4374	38511	71993	280212	0	227336	4138	0
39060	21012	18069	18069	75100	22640	53467	40560	314857	86197	481300	2279952	3441219	442	1090885	131241	0
39061	5760	14660	3375	96772	61517	0	616003	510244	261117	400000	449059	2403847	800	1363499	22865	20000
39062	144	6078	6078	45025	0	0	11322	10860		23817		100485	23	101124	2697	16600
39063	9134	8356	8356	59000	0	0	23615	152131	11501	91516	67728	458249	194	322207	64466	6000

STATISTICAL INFORMATION

GD

GS

Conf. No.	CHURCH NAME	1	4	7	9	10	11	13	18a	19a	20b	21	24 & 25	26 & 27	28a	29a
39064	TRENTON: FIRST	105	99	45	21	67	37	8	0	0	0	4	2785521	0	15922	15922
39065	TROY: BIG BEAVER	350	327	162	56	82	131	43	10	47	0	10	3390105	0	39305	39305
39066	TROY: FIRST	402	363	165	3	64	222	34	32	72	0	26	11255669	1483813	46472	35000
39067	TROY: KOREAN	1111	1157	1350	0	0	1043	325	480	590	0	5	9582305	2239678	129423	129423
39068	UTICA	281	255	190	137	93	234	85	25	44	0	9	7879991	0	57068	57068
39069	WARREN: FIRST	265	258	94	26	19	71	11	10	78	0	9	4652584	0	33979	6796
39070	WASHINGTON	37	36	21	0	29	0	0	0	0	0	2	136306	0	4169	4169
39071	WATERFORD: CENTRAL	454	439	162	66	567	200	7	0	0	0	17	17466065	0	77944	34171
39072	WATERFORD: FOUR TOWNS	20	20	20	0	37	0	0	0	8	0	0	861590	15207	4489	450
39073	WATERFORD: TRINITY	41	40	24	3	5	6	2	0	0	0	0	809219	0	7558	7558
39074	WAYNE-WESTLAND: FIRST	78	75	33	22	68	17	19	0	40	0	0	1600000	0	19940	9000
39075	WEST BLOOMFIELD	154	149	63	9	10	36	19	0	0	0	16	3044612	30481	18363	18363
39076	WESTLAND: ST JAMES	80	84	35	9	53	27	1	19	17	0	3	1069000	0	8521	883
39077	WYANDOTTE: FIRST	297	296	140	0	53	104	20	0	54	0	50	5997017	0	36635	36635
	GREATER SOUTHWEST DISTRICT															
37001	ALLEGAN	302	295	95	1	750	77	23	12	70	0	4	2751000	0	29721	233
37002	ALMENA	92	90	53	3	29	18	24	10	0	0	0	1613080	0	9552	9552
37003	ARDEN	16	16	13	0	8	8	7	0	0	0	0	557900	0	5107	1000
37004	ATHENS	32	29	21	24	21	9	9	0	5	0	0	782222	0	4592	4592

STATISTICAL INFORMATION

CONFERENCE Number	Church Benevolence Giving (30-38)	Total ASKED for clergy pension (39a)	Total PAID for clergy pension (39b)	Base compensation paid to/for the Senior Pastor or other person assigned or appointed in the lead pastoral role to the church (41a)	Base compensation paid to/for all Associate Pastor(s) and other pastoral staff assigned or appointed to the church. Include deacons and other clergy in this role (41b)	Deacons salary/benefits (41c & 42c)	Pastoral Benefits (40, 42a-44)	Total amount paid in salary and benefits for all other church staff and diaconal ministers (45)	Total amount spent for local church program expenses (46)	Total amount spent for other local church operating expenses (47)	Local Church capital expenses (48 & 49)	TOTAL CHURCH EXPENSES (Sum of Lines 29a through 49) (50)	Number of giving units (51)	Total income for annual budget/spending plan (52)	Total income for designated causes including capital campaign and other special projects (53)	Total income from connectional and other institutional sources outside the local church (54)
39064	2340	5218	5218	34789	0	0	23897	33773	4929	27485	0	148353	65	172155	3626	0
39065	17278	9375	9375	62500	0	0	18355	111428	16019	70622	36532	381414	156	317813	54847	0
39066	14099	9074	9074	60490	0	0	40687	119878	22926	109804	160255	572213	152	490698	201432	11250
39067	70160	34786	34786	78704	274568	0	212387	64843	317096	349116	200360	1731443	605	1547907	0	0
39068	30817	10800	10800	72000	0	0	19363	109872	33345	120195	78543	532003	196	439226	281564	13249
39069	7093	7500	7500	50016	0	0	28673	93081	7120	89213	33026	322518	120	231392	21341	5000
39070	964	550	550	9700	0	0	620	3583	768	22297		42651	17	56659	0	0
39071	38619	18044	18044	78087	0	48539	55621	246517	19614	163945	0	733157	285	539816	116066	11584
39072	2008	629	629	10000	0	0	4133	12935	300	23190	0	53645	20	23326	0	0
39073	2283	2010	2010	15304	0	0	7302	10700	862	17253	0	63272	29	72682	25	0
39074	3260	3100	3100	22000	0	0	31866	23683	4985	57699	25048	180641	80	340561	0	0
39075	10288	6931	6931	51715	0	0	13051	27443	11451	11572	11448	162262	55	164284	10977	0
39076	118	3070		25750	0	0	2500	0	0	20341	0	49592	30	0	0	0
39077	17381	8565	8565	57103	0	0	30337	126036	10934	73254	110226	470471	168	301488	77923	0
37001	6078	8657	8657	57710	0	0	31250	69000	18000	43000	33800	267728	106	194270	38500	5800
37002	8746	3065	3065	18401	0	0	14092	9830	5267	19999	1731	90683	50	77169	72737	0
37003	515	807	807	16250	0	0	0	6664	577	6954	1617	34384	9	32999	8235	0
37004	1363	1492	1492	9945	0	0	6525	0	612	12966	5371	42866	29	40189	1165	0

GD

GS

CONFERENCE Number	CHURCH NAME	1 Total professing members reported at the close of last year	4 TOTAL PROFESSING MEMBERS reported at the close of this year	7 Average attendance at all weekly worship services	9 Total Baptized Members who have not become Professing Members	10 Number of other constituents of the church	11 TOTAL Christian Formation Group Participants (Total of lines 11a-d)	13 Average weekly attendance (all ages) in Sunday Church School or other weekly education classes	18a Membership in United Methodist Men	19a Membership in United Methodist Women	20b Number of persons sent out on UMW/MW teams from this local church	21 Total Number of community ministries for outreach, justice, and mercy offered by this local church	24 & 25 Value of church assets and buildings	26 & 27 Church Debt	28a Amount APPORTIONED to the local church by the CONFERENCE	29a Amount PAID by the local church to the CONFERENCE for all apportioned causes
37005	AUGUSTA: FELLOWSHIP	46	47	33	0	30	21	0	0	0	0	6	860000	0	4343	4343
37006	BANGOR: SIMPSON	147	139	50	0	21	55	14	12	20	0	8	2156000	357488	13029	1229
37007	BATTLE CREEK: BASELINE	81	78	50	49	100	32	35	0	0	0	1	1700000	0	12101	12101
37009	BATTLE CREEK: CHAPEL HILL	435	412	119	6	199	388	56	0	0	16	5	7703797	20458	44770	44770
37010	BATTLE CREEK: CHRIST	87	87	46	0	10	38	3	0	0	0	5	289122	0	15695	0
37011	BATTLE CREEK: CONVIS UNION	54	45	29	0	13	0	0	0	0	0	3	1639365	0	8641	8641
37012	BATTLE CREEK: FIRST	166	170	75	0	20	65	5	0	0	0	8	4680000	0	21238	7303
37013	BATTLE CREEK: MAPLE	67	65	41	2	55	15	8	0	0	0	2	3223500	0	9346	9346
37014	BATTLE CREEK: NEWTON	78	77	45	26	18	11	6	0	5	0	0	1046307	0	8097	8097
37016	BATTLE CREEK: WASHINGTON HTS	24	24	7	0	0	8	0	0	5	0	0	2013625	0	7401	7161
37017	BELLEVUE	124	121	47	0	29	15	9	12	15	0	1	3058727	0	9573	9573
37018	BERRIEN CNTY: LAKESIDE	35	32	16	2	19	0	0	0	0	0	0	737213	0	4962	4962
37019	BERRIEN SPRINGS	29	25	22	5	3	13	13	0	0	0	0	4086540	0	9811	2865
37020	BLOOMINGDALE	21	21	6	0	16	0	2	0	0	0	1	392000	0		
37021	BRIDGMAN: FAITH	39	39	14	0	0	0	0	0	0	0	6	352500	0	5390	5390
37022	BRONSON: FIRST	60	57	30	0	27	32	16	0	0	0	4	2266669	0	11441	11441
37023	BUCHANAN: FAITH	122	121	72	32	29	0	26	0	10	0	0	2853000	0	9806	4976
37024	BUCHANAN: FIRST	149	151	58	39	43	29	25	0	0	0	3	3077935	0	18028	18028
37025	BURNIPS	61	63	78	2	27	20	6	0	0	0	4	1070000	0	9944	7200

STATISTICAL INFORMATION

GS

CONFERENCE Number	30-38 Church Benevolence Giving	39a Total ASKED for clergy pension	39b Total PAID for clergy pension	41a Base compensation paid to/for the Senior Pastor or other person assigned or appointed in the lead pastoral role to the church	41b Base compensation paid to/for all Associate Pastor(s) and other pastoral staff assigned or appointed to the church. Include deacons and other clergy in this role	41c & 42c Deacons salary/benefits	40,42a-44 Pastoral Benefits	45 Total amount paid in salary and benefits for all other church staff and diaconal ministers	46 Total amount spent for local church program expenses	47 Total amount spent for other local church operating expenses	48 & 49 Local Church capital expenses	50 TOTAL CHURCH EXPENSES (Sum of Lines 29a through 49)	51 Number of giving units	52 Total income for annual budget/spending plan	53 Total income for designated causes including capital campaign and other special projects	54 Total income from connectional and other institutional sources outside the local church
37005	478	450	450	12500	0	0	4950	4605	828	11866	20150	60170	18	44100	3075	0
37006	4997	7375	7375	48192	0	0	32256	3975	1209	14063	33515	146811	37	143878	1196	0
37007	853	2756	2756	18370	0	0	15252	29611	8456	15380	27745	130524	45	103122	4761	0
37009	96510	14029	14029	48060	36910	0	46992	148977	51643	133580	26168	647639	239	480771	565150	5000
37010	1679	4297	4297	25372	0	0	23191	20138	1527	31078	9650	116932	44	87068	31663	0
37011	1961	2296	2296	19079	0	0	6864	10816	1947	13970	22550	88124	31	67485	2423	0
37012	0	2868	0	18600	0	0	20525	74579	868	83097	0	204104	80	184535	0	0
37013	885	1061	1061	4451	0	0	18901	16291	3479	30372	1800	83975	46	69385	2590	0
37014	3870	864	864	9900	7500	0	0	3929	300	16577	0	54216	39	43535	2174	0
37016	3959	1432	1432	8457	0	0	1625	15500	2513	27500	15000	80934	18	31300	27000	24800
37017	275	2756	2756	18370	0	0	12028	11696	1498	83147	0	137845	52	93789	2008	0
37018	8465	410	410	1480	0	0	13585	6080	100	14166	8922	51661	15	50676	6383	0
37019	885	1297	973	20180	7697	0	13361	3834	499	7566	0	104812	15	75636	25146	0
37020	0	0	0	5485	0	0	0	0	2053	20596	0	13151	15	10688	0	0
37021	8361	540	540	10300	0	0	4350	11800	1453	20747	0	45686	15	51996	7329	0
37022	3986	2910	2910	19402	0	0	10000	20747	6239	40535	24095	100784	25	74826	4372	0
37023	6699	1394	1394	19875	0	0	7636	40535	2488	31337	4138	89070	51	104409	6529	0
37024	11389	5400	5400	35544	0	0	6172	28512	6239	31337	6518	150603	90	168069	1395	0
37025	1899	3769	3769	21450	0	0	6172	7942	2488	7508	9430	67858	49	102455	5455	0

STATISTICAL INFORMATION

GS

CONFERENCE Number	CHURCH NAME	Total professing members reported at the close last year (1)	TOTAL PROFESSING MEMBERS reported at the close of this year (4)	Average attendance at all weekly worship services (7)	Total Baptized Members who have not become Professing Members (9)	Number of other constituents of the church (10)	TOTAL Christian Formation Group Participants (Total of lines 11a-d) (11)	Average weekly attendance (all ages) in Sunday Church School or other weekly education classes (13)	Membership in United Methodist Men (18a)	Membership in United Methodist Women (19a)	Number of persons sent out on UMVIM teams from this local church (20b)	Total Number of community ministries for outreach, justice, and mercy offered by this local church (21)	Value of church assets and buildings (24 & 25)	Church Debt (26 & 27)	Amount APPORTIONED to the local church by the CONFERENCE (28a)	Amount PAID by the local church to the CONFERENCE for all apportioned causes (29a)
37026	BURR OAK	32	32	10	0	0	5	0	0	0	0	0	302000	0	4028	0
37027	CASCO	152	144	66	61	150	50	30	6	25	0	4	3410060	0	17899	17899
37028	CASSOPOLIS	60	64	60	0	42	51	5	0	0	0	14	326230	0	11697	1000
37029	CENTREVILLE	191	184	67	21	29	19	19	0	0	0	15	985000	0	19578	19578
37030	CLIMAX	92	79	59	1	64	23	8	0	20	0	6	708852	1739	12173	12173
37031	COLDWATER	243	235	121	55	97	85	11	26	64	0	6	7374234	0	27779	27779
37032	COLOMA	156	153	61	12	14	34	11	0	0	0	8	956564	0	22047	16607
37033	COLON	67	63	33	0	28	10	2	0	0	0	2	842453	0	8823	8823
37034	CONSTANTINE	133	128	31	33	33	20	10	0	0	0	1	2892938	0	10079	10079
37035	DELTON: FAITH	174	172	101	0	60	119	48	0	0	13	3	1187352	0	26160	22213
37036	DOWAGIAC: FIRST	165	154	73	0	52	55	13	0	0	0	3	1201196	0	18891	18891
37037	DOWLING: COUNTRY CHAPEL	172	172	99	0	64	78	32	0	0	0	4	1604737	0	13622	0
37038	EDWARDSBURG: HOPE	456	447	140	148	435	89	20	0	0	0	34	1441418	125313	29912	29912
37039	FENNVILLE	73	73	40	7	26	26	5	0	20	0	3	1977400	12664	12204	2150
37040	FENNVILLE: PEARL	30	29	28	0	13	4	2	0	0	0	2	348900	0	3067	0
37041	GALESBURG	76	77	45	0	12	0	0	0	11	0	12	617955	0	9708	9708
37042	GALIEN	49	49	40	0	0	9	3	0	0	0	0	600500	0	5030	0
37043	GALIEN: OLIVE BRANCH	75	70	24	0	0	6	4	0	0	0	3	600001	0	4818	3373
37044	GANGES	83	88	37	36	40	8	8	0	33	0	0	561000	0	4702	3130

CONFERENCE Number	Church Benevolence Giving (30-38)	Total ASKED for clergy pension (39a)	Total PAID for clergy pension (39b)	Base compensation paid to/for the Senior Pastor or other person assigned or appointed in the lead pastoral role to the church (41a)	Base compensation paid to/for all Associate Pastor(s) and other pastoral staff assigned or appointed to the church. Include deacons and other clergy in this role (41b)	Deacons salary/benefits (41c.&42c)	Pastoral Benefits (40,42a-44)	Total amount paid in salary and benefits for all other church staff and diaconal ministers (45)	Total amount spent for local church program expenses (46)	Total amount spent for other local church operating expenses (47)	Local Church capital expenses (48 & 49)	TOTAL CHURCH EXPENSES (Sum of Lines 29a through 49) (50)	Number of giving units (51)	Total income for annual budget/spending plan (52)	Total income for designated causes including capital campaign and other special projects (53)	Total income from connectional and other institutional sources outside the local church (54)
37026	0	575	400	9500	0	0	1500	2500	600	14500	0	29000	22	29500	0	0
37027	20064	5491	5491	32604	0	0	19988	30235	2696	39412	0	168389	80	110354	38020	0
37028	8158	1392	1392	25747	0	0	2342	23447	2911	23350	0	88347	51	90374	10540	0
37029	26136	3451	3451	41214	0	0	21849	29708	2796	21289	3891	169912	70	150139	65596	6372
37030	3183	3663	3663	24419	0	0	18356	8598	436	24968	1739	97535	29	94451	24395	0
37031	29488	7488	7488	49920	0	0	28879	38467	12466	79714	0	274201	138	242614	54136	0
37032	11482	6750	6750	45000	0	0	8657	41559	6146	29631	1279	167111	83	186075	6317	0
37033	8638	2910	2910	19402	0	0	3723	11952	1789	22708	3871	83816	36	72023	9674	0
37034	2862	4140	4140	27602	0	0	18981	1817	1895	14605	0	81981	35	72753	0	0
37035	39835	7050	7050	42200	0	0	27064	12763	13224	39338	1788	205475	90	71451	39478	0
37036	30	5276	5276	36969	0	0	20698	22061	1628	53687	4761	164001	63	155056	19980	0
37037	4445	6000	6000	40000	0	0	31171	4233	6167	41937	8090	142043	84	119119	0	0
37038	12497	9984	9984	65195	0	0	40733	50458	12850	37862	96794	356285	152	232831	86856	0
37039	3351	6244	6244	27750	0	0	7427	10222	2180	20139	13853	93316	42	85510	22770	0
37040	184	1740	1740	9250	0	0	3576	2917	63	5072	8230	31032	25	30180	0	0
37041	1001	990	990	12400	0	0	16415	21600	2260	53951	0	118325	43	53177		0
37042	801	750	750	12000	0	0	119	3380	113	7254	0	24417	16	32474	887	0
37043	5873	750	750	12000	0	0	0	6760	185	7332	0	36273	43	32572	0	0
37044	2634	250	250	5000	0	0	0	13055	1321	25298	36158	86846	12	40391	11790	0

STATISTICAL INFORMATION

GS

CONFERENCE Number	CHURCH NAME	1 Total professing members reported at the close last year	4 TOTAL PROFESSING MEMBERS reported at the close of this year	7 Average attendance at all weekly worship services	9 Total Baptized Members who have not become Professing Members	10 Number of other constituents of the church	11 TOTAL Christian Formation Group Participants (Total of lines 11a-d)	13 Average weekly attendance (all ages) in Sunday Church School or other weekly education classes	18a Membership in United Methodist Men	19a Membership in United Methodist Women	20a Number of persons sent out on UMW/UMM teams from this local church	20b Number of persons sent out on UMW/UMW teams from this local church	21 Total Number of community ministries for outreach, justice, and mercy offered by this local church	24 & 25 Value of church assets and buildings	26 & 27 Church Debt	28a Amount APPORTIONED to the local church by the CONFERENCE	29a Amount PAID by the local church to the CONFERENCE for all apportioned causes
37045	GIRARD	84	59	56	0	25	46	6	6	20	0	0	6	1225000	0	10996	10996
37046	GLENN	17	17	29	0		8	4	0	10	0	0	9	974394	0	3215	2750
37047	GOBLES	57	62	42	0	1	14	9	0	19	0	3	9	480428	283931	7752	7752
37048	GULL LAKE	265	264	112	20	30	119	25	0	15	0	25	3	2170342	0	24908	24908
37049	HARTFORD	253	242	127	0	104	42	8	0	0	0	0	5	2650594	0	21242	21242
37050	HINCHMAN	59	53	15	0	9	40	16	0	15	0	0	0	873730	0	3179	3179
37051	HOPKINS	65	74	41	7	18	40	16	0	14	0	12	8	3731685	0	7204	7204
37052	KALAMAZOO: FIRST	861	878	294	173	223	636	70	0	106	0	0	13	27500000	318930	116649	116649
37053	KALAMAZOO: MILWOOD	142	134	84	0	54	61	4	0	0	0	0	6	3827535	0	20997	6352
37054	KALAMAZOO: NORTHWEST	23	23	25	25	75	8	16	0	0	0	0	5	711453	0	3948	3948
37055	KALAMAZOO: SUNNYSIDE	106	112	119	2	85	146	57	0	0	4	4	0	1631353	0	23014	23014
37056	KALAMAZOO: WESTWOOD	201	199	177	4	4	59	57	0	0	0	0	8	5136477	296272	38933	29200
37057	KENDALL	22	20	14	0	0	1	12	0	0	0	0	0	275000	0	3862	3862
37058	LACOTA	30	27	22	0	25	5	15	0	0	0	0	0	366600	0	2883	2883
37059	LAWRENCE	110	107	40	1	70	40	11	0	5	0	0	3	650929	0	9982	0
37060	LAWTON: ST PAUL'S	85	82	56	17	28	48	10	0	0	0	0	4	1034307	0	11436	11436
37061	MARCELLUS	68	68	30	0	15	30	8	0	4	0	0	0	900000	0	9148	0
37062	MARCELLUS: WAKELEE	77	55	38	0	32	14	14	0	0	0	0	2	350000	0	6727	6727
37063	MARTIN	117	105	55	0		10	5	0	0	0	0	2	1210821	0	14537	1260

CONFERENCE Number	Church Benevolence Giving (30-38)	Total ASKED for clergy pension (39a)	Total PAID for clergy pension (39b)	Base compensation paid to/for the Senior Pastor or other person assigned or appointed in the lead pastoral role to the church (41a)	Base compensation paid to/for all Associate Pastor(s) and other pastoral staff assigned or appointed to the church. Include deacons and other clergy in this role (41b)	Deacons salary/benefits (41c & 42b)	Pastoral Benefits (40,42a-44)	Total amount paid in salary and benefits for all other church staff and diaconal ministers (45)	Total amount spent for local church program expenses (46)	Total amount spent for other local church operating expenses (47)	Local Church capital expenses (48 & 49)	TOTAL CHURCH EXPENSES (Sum of Lines 29a through 49) (50)	Number of giving units (51)	Total income for annual budget/spending plan (52)	Total income for designated causes including capital campaign and other special projects (53)	Total income from connectional and other institutional sources outside the local church (54)
37045	1366	5768	5768	26375	0	0	4076	4295	500	27650	1384	82410	32	124696	3850	0
37046	628	773	773	10800	0	0	0	0	0	9317	3759	28027	31	31923	0	0
37047	3299	3764	3764	25095	0	0	8874	1608	8004	15563	4153	78112	40	76217	2707	0
37048	15432	2500	2500	15000	15000	0	21525	58586	12210	65697	58347	289205	95	273427	18741	0
37049	8368	6450	6450	43000	0	0	30447	24671	16947	33119	6759	191003	169	158960	18313	3000
37050	3900	600	600	25836	0	0	0	3696	1914	13050	0	52175	14	51436	991	0
37051	428	3746	3746	28213	0	0	4920	5332	15575	13697	2915	82030	45	86652	693	1307
37052	208538	17215	17215	77250	45000	0	37155	466094	145047	179297	270203	1562448	360	912696	476218	0
37053	0	1486	1486	7000	0	0	27203	58535	2325	56197	91973	251071	103	173007	275	0
37054	9916	1500	1500	500	0	0	26750	0	252	14180	2155	59201	22	32029	0	0
37055	145	8028	0	48240	2965	0	43511	16219	802	36181	4539	172651	80	176708	5905	14750
37056	39280	9400	9400	50757	0	0	37170	89999	24887	104113	161852	549623	135	285271	102475	0
37057	1609	998	998	3990	0	0	8005	1530	416	8030	144	28584	10	32000	1399	0
37058	2024	470	470	9000	0	0	0	0	375	14275	0	29027	16	17363	1424	0
37059	0	4500	4125	25953	0	0	17550	0	6618	29869	29171	113286	28	74678	91213	0
37060	609	4644	4644	28500	0	0	20285	17065	6433	26556	5933	121461	62	106374	7867	0
37061	356	2763	2533	37400	0	0	9500	3500	800	34000	0	87733	38	60000	0	0
37062		2763	2763	17350	0	0	300	5000	1000	23000	0	56496	15	70000	0	0
37063	10454	4490	4490	29934	0	0	19694	14935	2060	18869	5571	107267	40	94554	3400	3883

STATISTICAL INFORMATION

GS

CONFERENCE Number	CHURCH NAME	Total professing members reported at the close of last year (1)	TOTAL PROFESSING MEMBERS reported at the close of this year (4)	Average attendance at all weekly worship services (7)	Total Baptized Members who have not become Professing Members (9)	Number of other constituents of the church (10)	TOTAL Christian Formation Group Participants (Total of lines 11a-d) (11)	Average weekly attendance (all ages) in Sunday Church School or other weekly education classes (13)	Membership in United Methodist Men (18a)	Membership in United Methodist Women (19a)	Number of persons sent out on UMW/UMM teams from this local church (20b)	Total Number of community ministries for outreach, justice, and mercy offered by this local church (21)	Value of church assets and buildings (24 & 25)	Church Debt (26 & 27)	Amount APPORTIONED to the local church by the CONFERENCE (28a)	Amount PAID by the local church to the CONFERENCE for all apportioned causes (29a)
37064	MENDON	73	66	35	0	0	23	12	6	0	0	5	1054999		8074	8074
37065	MONTEREY CENTER	47	46	47	1	3	21	21	0	0	0	1	585000	0	5336	534
37066	MORRIS CHAPEL	23	23	20	2	14	0	0	0	0	0	5	355001	0	4096	4096
37067	NEW BUFFALO: WATER'S EDGE	182	188	97	2	8	125	26	0	0	0	1	2523997	0	28355	28355
37068	NILES: GRACE	58	31	19	0	0	29	3	0	0	0	0	2211000	0	5568	3341
37069	NILES: PORTAGE PRAIRIE	157	155	68	0	37	50	38	0	0	0	6	2455001	0	11784	0
37070	NILES: WESLEY	150	119	58	0	15	25	25	0	19	0	4	4730833	0	18814	18814
37071	NOTTAWA	11	8	9	0	45	9	9	0	0	0	3	40000	0	1963	1963
37072	OSHTEMO	104	97	55	0	0	9	14	0	20	0	5	2512697	2420	13749	3700
37073	OSHTEMO: LIFESPRING	55	33	38	0	0	18	5	0	0	0	3	504000	484718	8953	1120
37074	OTSEGO	360	380	311	2	292	235	113	15	27	0	0	3362042	30179	28156	28156
37076	PARCHMENT	241	233	78	0	63	30	14	12	43	0	4	4928000	42291	22372	13683
37077	PAW PAW	111	103	50	0	51	31	0	0	0	42	3	3725480	0	16820	16820
37078	PLAINWELL: FIRST	172	168	92	74	112	49	16	0	0	0	4	4833238	419082	27065	13539
37079	PLEASANT VALLEY	55	53	25	8	30	6	6	0	0	0	3	651492	0	5271	5271
37080	POKAGON	96	82	47	0	30	54	24	0	15	0	15	42000	0	10008	5553
37081	PORTAGE: CHAPEL HILL	507	513	232	179	295	248	137	0	29	0	9	5594353	421993	77684	77684
37082	PORTAGE: PATHFINDER	385	372	227	75	304	348	55	0	0	0	9	5002432	719437	60110	60110
37083	RIVERSIDE	69	63	40	0	42	13	5	0	0	0	4	2122400	0	5847	5847

STATISTICAL INFORMATION

GS

CONFERENCE Number	Church Benevolence Giving (30-38)	Total ASKED for clergy pension (39a)	Total PAID for clergy pension (39b)	Base compensation paid to/for the Senior Pastor or other person assigned or appointed in the lead pastoral role to the church (41a)	Base compensation paid to/for all Associate Pastor(s) and other pastoral staff assigned or appointed to the church. Include deacons and other clergy in this role (41b)	Deacons salary/benefits (41c & 42c)	Pastoral Benefits (40,42a-44)	Total amount paid in salary and benefits for all other church staff and diaconal ministers (45)	Total amount spent for local church program expenses (46)	Total amount spent for other local church operating expenses (47)	Local Church capital expenses (48 & 49)	TOTAL CHURCH EXPENSES (Sum of Lines 29a through 49) (50)	Number of giving units (51)	Total income for annual budget/spending plan (52)	Total income for designated causes including capital campaign and other special projects (53)	Total income from connectional and other institutional sources outside the local church (54)
37064	12493	1200	1200	24000	0	0	2095	15117	1130	15862	0	79971	29	90212	94839	0
37065	995	3200	3200	17550	0	0	5541	7771	266	5471	868	42196	46	92225	3355	0
37066	0	1584	1584	10200	0	0	4674	0	1325	9090	23601	54570	17	36400	4000	0
37067	35879	5972	5972	37248	0	0	34018	70250	20359	81958	0	314039	53	264107	26239	8406
37068	3570	1584	1584	13200	0	0	1310	11328	200	8946	0	43479	16	26100	300	0
37069	7548	6076	6076	35000	0	0	0	13558	2227	32298	0	96707	157	112957	0	0
37070	6186	3888	3888	20400	0	0	17242	24124	1993	41576	39454	173677	62	133572	33525	0
37071	952	325	325	6500	0	0	1470	0	25	13855	7742	32832	8	8868	2083	0
37072	4625	2469	2469	5002	0	0	30851	15409	12950	21924	2527	99457	63	97372	37112	0
37073	3	900	900	15000	0	0	825	0	1435	22516	41448	83247	12	74868	0	0
37074	6708	9135	9135	54900	0	0	32072	86237	13540	64535	91276	386559	224	108814	19367	0
37076	5195	9000	9000	59000	0	0	19700	34850	3427	31860	0	176715	44	174880	344	0
37077	0	2813	0	45000	0	0	0	45499	1335	48649	0	140483	50	127696	0	0
37078	5132	9538	9538	60203	0	0	25487	53771	4589	45278	80342	297879	98	227378	82613	4086
37079	3114	1883	1883	12631	0	0	8227	2320	483	10341	2347	46617	20	44372	420	0
37080	1666	1297	0	18270	0	0	12089	3697	14749	19691	3697	79412	58	74251	2100	0
37081	15409	11231	11231	79487	16975	0	54066	185040	21627	210719	76041	748279	273	732915	9540	0
37082	20240	9893	9893	64200	0	0	12404	179720	15018	113817	868532	1343934	200	425669	294405	0
37083	2608	992	992	9470	0	0	7000	9450	1700	17213	39200	93480	39	56203	662	0

CONFERENCE Number	CHURCH NAME	1 — Total professing members reported at the close of last year	4 — TOTAL PROFESSING MEMBERS reported at the close of this year	7 — Average attendance at all weekly worship services	9 — Total Baptized Members who have not become Professing Members	10 — Number of other constituents of the church	11 — TOTAL Christian Formation Group Participants (Total of lines 11a-d)	13 — Average weekly attendance (all ages) in Sunday Church School or other weekly education classes	18a — Membership in United Methodist Men	19a — Membership in United Methodist Women	20b — Number of persons sent out on UMW teams from this local church	21 — Total Number of community ministries for outreach, justice, and mercy offered by this local church	24 & 25 — Value of church assets and buildings	26 & 27 — Church Debt	28a — Amount APPORTIONED to the local church by the CONFERENCE	29a — Amount PAID by the local church to the CONFERENCE for all apportioned causes
37084	SAUGATUCK	51	47	22	0	5	14	12	0	0	0	0	722741	0	6135	6135
37085	SCHOOLCRAFT	95	91	49	1	23	62	26	20	18	0	5	3054999	34421	14297	14297
37086	SCOTTDALE	52	52	25	11	14	23	4	0	12	0	6	848000	3000	7085	0
37087	SCOTTS	31	27	26	1	27	8	2	0	10	0	2	305000	0	5724	2712
37088	SHELBYVILLE	60	56	43	0	37	17	4	0	18	0	2	1036000	0	5722	5722
37089	SILVER CREEK	86	84	45	2	52	21	12	0	0	0	0	774469	0	8838	8838
37090	SODUS: CHAPEL HILL	176	169	61	50	70	55	34	0	0	0	0	460248	0	20213	3818
37091	SOUTH HAVEN: FIRST	125	125	69	6	70	55	34	9	5	0	13	906000	0	25423	12712
37092	SOUTH MONTEREY	34	36	21	4	5	6	0	0	0	0	1	217000	0	3894	3894
37093	ST JOSEPH: FIRST	343	309	149	8	70	154	131	0	0	0	12	4850757	2904	60889	45667
37094	STEVENSVILLE	434	396	157	8	325	137	16	0	100	0	0	6483700	0	39182	39182
37095	STURGIS: FIRST	316	309	100	11	25	57	34	0	0	0	16	8152614	0	44790	44790
37096	THREE OAKS	124	117	64	0	12	32	5	0	0	0	0	423211	0	12911	12911
37097	THREE RIVERS: CENTER PARK	127	128	92	42	126	48	25	0	0	0	7	2581500	0	11509	11509
37098	THREE RIVERS: FIRST	135	130	40	9	10	46	7	0	32	0	9	4301619	16042	14881	8606
37099	THREE RIVERS: NINTH STREET	52	53	20	22	27	28	3	0	8	0	0	822353	1299	4558	4558
37100	TOWNLINE	67	65	53	41	50	30	8	0	0	0	5	874080	0	4309	4309
37101	UNION CITY	92	88	71	0	58	24	13	4	29	0	3	2001114	0	13987	4196
37102	VICKSBURG	280	261	120	0	80	131	30	0	94	0	6	2105616	578974	42524	3358

STATISTICAL INFORMATION

GS

CONFERENCE Number	Church Benevolence Giving (30-38)	Total ASKED for clergy pension (39a)	Total PAID for clergy pension (39b)	Base compensation paid to/for the Senior Pastor or other person assigned or appointed in the lead pastoral role to the church (41a)	Base compensation paid to/for all Associate Pastor(s) and other pastoral staff assigned or appointed to the church, Include deacons and other clergy in this role (41b)	Deacons salary/benefits (41c & 42c)	Pastoral Benefits (40,42a-44)	Total amount paid in salary and benefits for all other church staff and diaconal ministers (45)	Total amount spent for local church program expenses (46)	Total amount spent for other local church operating expenses (47)	Local Church capital expenses (48 & 49)	TOTAL CHURCH EXPENSES (Sum of Lines 29a through 49) (50)	Number of giving units (51)	Total income for annual budget/spending plan (52)	Total income for designated causes including capital campaign and other special projects (53)	Total income from connectional and other institutional sources outside the local church (54)
37084	6346	1080	1080	0	0	0	23000	5181	5909	14364	0	62015	23	59533	1981	0
37085	6404	3767	3767	25111	0	0	16103	16861	2377	20530	20974	126424	50	97534	21081	0
37086	383	683	383	0	0	0		26475	1014	12139	0	40394	66	31455	64624	0
37087	2284	2151	2151	14341	0	0	9516	4615	483	9363	16175	61640	32	40492	3140	10839
37088	2733	1924	1924	12828	0	0	8687	10936	3297	5749	13581	65457	34	69374	7584	4905
37089	7090	781	781	11700	0	0	15420	13442	4106	16846	9315	87538	41	83182	13000	0
37090	43542	7579	7579	48852	0	0	35858	21228	8145	35931	17492	222445	116	178121	23335	0
37091	6222	7350	6738	49000	0	0	26984	33552	3413	47965	6758	193344	72	186328	6727	0
37092	80	2129	2129	18172	0	51476	3798	3886	1474	8177	0	41610	10	35784	0	0
37093	23616	11706	11706	40000	0	0	57664	107313	55863	67540	220887	681732	156	443651	182642	0
37094	21230	10478	10478	69855	0	0	35750	93009	7924	61072	17155	355872	169	341418	14904	0
37095	24904	8902	8902	54265	0	0	31750	84745	6897	48287	12686	317226	93	301093	24911	350
37096	1939	2501	2501	41002	0	0	15464	7009	1776	16789	0	99391	70	101644	11337	0
37097	8628	1526	1526	7782	0	0	18073	30110	2301	59004	3676	142609	52	129148	14409	0
37098	3023	1430	1430	26042	1000	0	2894	24528	4065	30242	63242	165072	66	120940	0	0
37099	730	703	703	3852	400	0	10731	2814	659	9969	22897	57313	28	33200	16630	0
37100	4500	587	587	0	0	0	9775		6804	11518	2825	40318	47	45526	11456	0
37101	145	4475	4475	39780	0	0	3673	18959	1778	30805	67260	171071	48	80218	657	0
37102	10022	8681	8681	52500	0	0	41021	143264	5997	74812	163495	503150	129	266293	39876	75000

STATISTICAL INFORMATION

CONFERENCE Number	CHURCH NAME	Total professing members reported at the close of last year (1)	TOTAL PROFESSING MEMBERS reported at the close of this year (4)	Average attendance at all weekly worship services (7)	Total Baptized Members who have not become Professing Members (9)	Number of other constituents of the church (10)	TOTAL Christian Formation Group Participants (Total of lines 11a-d) (11)	Average weekly attendance (all ages) in Sunday Church School or other weekly education classes (13)	Membership in United Methodist Men (18a)	Membership in United Methodist Women (19a)	Number of persons sent out on UMVIM teams from this local church (20b)	Total Number of community ministries for outreach, justice, and mercy offered by this local church (21)	Value of church assets and buildings (24 & 25)	Church Debt (26 & 27)	Amount APPORTIONED to the local church by the CONFERENCE (28a)	Amount PAID by the local church to the CONFERENCE for all apportioned causes (29a)
37103	WHITE PIGEON	45	43	16	0	29	0	0	0	8	0	0	1954540	0	5691	5691
	HERITAGE DISTRICT															
38001	ADRIAN: FIRST	462	445	115	39	106	158	38	35	101	0	12	10090224	0	57761	57761
38002	ALBION: FIRST	231	220	70	6	46	54	37	0	40	0	5	8993779	12738	22647	22647
38003	ALLEN	46	52	38	0	300	15	0	0	0	0	0	600000	0	3864	1915
38004	ANN ARBOR: CALVARY	64	62	17	0	6	10	0	0	0	0	1	2142600	0	14061	4000
38005	ANN ARBOR: FIRST	1009	967	443	99	265	576	117	0	222	110	9	20412700	673160	156376	93826
38006	ANN ARBOR: KOREAN	210	210	180	0	0	236	60	80	76	0	0	1530097	824651	30678	0
38007	ANN ARBOR: WEST SIDE	260	236	105	67	66	152	50	0	50	10	0	5011775	323438	49809	49809
38008	AZALIA	26	26	18	6	8	2	0	0	0	0	2	973943	0	3695	3695
38009	BELLEVILLE: FIRST	298	294	131	26	78	148	40	75	87	10	4	8098278	44800	35221	35221
38010	BLISSFIELD: EMMANUEL	50	49	41	0	39	78	23	0	0	0	4	757000	0	15063	3346
38011	BLISSFIELD: FIRST	143	138	52	0	0	8	9	0	0	0	2	1971180	0	13175	660
38012	BRIGHTON: FIRST	764	765	312	163	258	605	15	0	143	4	6	10005283	306347	71237	50661
38013	BRITTON: GRACE	150	148	35	36	20	13	20	0	14	0	3	912569	0	12922	0
38014	CALHOUN COUNTY: HOMER	45	43	34	15	21	31	16	6	3	0	0	2287450	0	7103	0
38015	CAMDEN	11	11	8	0	0	0	5	6	0	0	0	590001	0	3878	3878
38016	CANTON: CHERRY HILL	66	64	31	0	0	7	4	0	0	0	0	1127758	0	14022	1900
38017	CANTON: FRIENDSHIP	270	289	228	78	155	321	35	0	0	22	12	2815000	524000	46967	23484

CONFERENCE Number	Church Benevolence Giving (30-38)	Total ASKED for clergy pension (39a)	Total PAID for clergy pension (39b)	Base compensation paid to/for the Senior Pastor or other person assigned or appointed in the lead pastoral role to the church (41a)	Base compensation paid to/for all Associate Pastor(s) and other pastoral staff assigned or appointed to the church. Include deacons and other clergy in this role (41b)	Deacons salary/benefits (41c & 42c)	Pastoral Benefits (40, 42a-44)	Total amount paid in salary and benefits for all other church staff and diaconal ministers (45)	Total amount spent for local church program expenses (46)	Total amount spent for other local church operating expenses (47)	Local Church capital expenses (48 & 49)	TOTAL CHURCH EXPENSES (Sum of Lines 29a through 49) (50)	Number of giving units (51)	Total income for annual budget/spending plan (52)	Total income for designated causes including capital campaign and other special projects (53)	Total income from connectional and other institutional sources outside the local church (54)
37103	922	2039	2039	13562	0	0	9135	0	4200	14785	4876	55210	30	44220	15885	0
38001	25041	9329	9329	62190		0	32510	144278	29415	112241	0	472765	145	449597	29465	0
38002	20357	5280	5280	35202		0	28010	46953	3901	42556	6594	211500	92	229464	402921	0
38003	3409	960	880	19800	0	0		3900	1000	7244	7244	45392	27	44257	9062	0
38004	0	6496	6496	42620	0	0	28300	10400	3000	37000	0	131816	22	112235	12512	0
38005	94725	22442	22442	96500	53114	0	71168	618886	80622	143391	243063	1517737	563	1415732	344908	0
38006	16175	14832	14832	47275	38920	0	43015	0	54099	33833	72328	320477	85	328897	18529	0
38007	32525	8523	8523	50727	0	36972	40654	113037	13162	134691	83234	563334	110	390960	280053	4405
38008	3130	1084	1084	9960	0	0	1200	0	300	5700	0	25069	19	21566	0	0
38009	7024	10990	10990	73264	0	0	26349	86114	8848	38304	16293	302407	140	269505	5616	0
38010	23	2744	2516	21960	0	0	17826	19316	5950	31222	0	102159	44	80451	2000	0
38011	3978	6925	6925	41644	44125	0	22949	13524	758	27640	0	118078	58	108817	3146	0
38012	82229	18833	18833	79603	0	0	25479	232219	68835	112942	159953	874879	411	740105	78041	40000
38013	2002	4848	4848	43470	0	0	17167	2520	265	26373	0	96645	55	76935	2940	0
38014	1562	776	679	14610	0	0	15652	10842	2185	13452	0	58982	24	57927	2541	0
38015	16	570	570	9000	0	0	900	0	603	11590	350	26907	8		0	0
38016	2144	3306	3306	22038	0	0	1087	14409	1181	4824	10800	61689	25	78221		0
38017	9928	10286	10286	56114	0	0	50592	125955	86270	76657	255038	694324	167	454425	126870	0

STATISTICAL INFORMATION

Conference Number	CHURCH NAME	1 — Total professing members reported at the close of last year	4 — TOTAL PROFESSING MEMBERS reported at the close of this year	7 — Average attendance at all weekly worship services	9 — Total Baptized Members who have not become Professing Members	10 — Number of other constituents of the church	11 — TOTAL Christian Formation Group Participants (Total of lines 11a-d)	13 — Average weekly attendance (all ages) in Sunday Church School or other weekly education classes	18a — Membership in United Methodist Men	19a — Membership in United Methodist Women	20b — Number of persons sent out on UMVIM teams from this local church	21 — Total Number of community ministries for outreach, justice, and mercy offered by this local church	24 & 25 — Value of church assets and buildings	26 & 27 — Church Debt	28a — Amount APPORTIONED to the local church by the CONFERENCE	29a — Amount PAID by the local church to the CONFERENCE for all apportioned causes
38018	CARLETON	267	269	109	88	190	70	50	10	8	0	0	3637766	0	22420	22420
38019	CHELSEA: FIRST	649	645	225	0	181	463	28	11	0	0	22	1784076	227243	68486	68486
38020	CLAYTON	36	43	29	0	32	8	8	0	12	0	6	1156632	0	7007	7007
38021	CLINTON	118	108	57	21	6	39	9	9	0	0	7	3111909	309123	15066	892
38022	COMMERCE	639	366	211	137	112	72	20	15	70	0	0	3013239	1141943	53079	53079
38023	CONCORD	100	87	68	1	70	134	33	18	15	0	9	2158827	186877	17225	17225
38024	DEERFIELD	14	14	10	0	0	8	5	0	0	0	0	112000	0	2672	
38025	DENTON: FAITH	19	20	15	0	7	7	0	0	0	0	2	0	0	6631	5950
38026	DEXTER	1218	1184	535	151	5	1245	86	140	0	0	9	10042912	3695265	127292	127292
38027	DIXBORO	214	204	83	27	70	75	35	0	26	0	26	571593	0	23780	23780
38028	DUNDEE	262	263	88	66	112	68	33	12	0	0	1	4255298	12502	18089	18089
38029	ERIE	144	139	51	20	0	56	37	0	12	0	7	1801263	0	10623	5862
38030	FRONTIER	38	38	27	2	0	9	15	0	20	0	7	385447	0	4425	4425
38031	GRASS LAKE	126	126	64	22	40	20	11	7	0	0	2	2195289	0	11325	11325
38032	GRIFFITH	39	34	25	0	14	19	18	0	0	0	5	688000	243749	5301	0
38033	HARDY	115	118	49	0	88	35	15	15	20	0	7	2818808	0	15743	15743
38034	HARTLAND	119	118	56	0	54	22	52	16	14	0	0	3007601	133737	21108	3400
38035	HIGHLAND	444	394	225	0	185	206		1	0	8	17	3678958	361838	60427	0
38036	HILLSDALE: FIRST	151	148	80	0	75	27	0	0	0	0	10	7805489	357955	21053	21053

Column headers:
- 54 — Total income from connectional and other institutional sources outside the local church
- 53 — Total income for designated causes including capital campaign and other special projects
- 52 — Total income for annual budget/spending plan
- 51 — Number of giving units
- 50 — TOTAL CHURCH EXPENSES (Sum of Lines 29a through 49)
- 48 & 49 — Local Church capital expenses
- 47 — Total amount spent for other local church operating expenses
- 46 — Total amount spent for local church program expenses
- 45 — Total amount paid in salary and benefits for all other church staff and diaconal ministers
- 40, 42a-44 — Pastoral Benefits
- 41c & 42c — Deacons salary/benefits
- 41b — Base compensation paid to/for all Associate Pastor(s) and other pastoral staff assigned or appointed to the church, Include deacons and other clergy in this role
- 41a — Base compensation paid to/for the Senior Pastor or other person assigned or appointed in the lead pastoral role to the church
- 39b — Total PAID for clergy pension
- 39a — Total ASKED for clergy pension
- 30-38 — Church Benevolence Giving

CONFERENCE Number	30-38	39a	39b	41a	41b	41c & 42c	40, 42a-44	45	46	47	48 & 49	50	51	52	53	54
38018	973	8032	8032	53544	0	0	29458	32951	12128	27049	24370	210925	162	196327	20810	0
38019	19826	13456	13456	80039	0	20731	21764	283725	31850	102814	130735	773426	279	642102	73961	0
38020	9175	2919	2919	19462	0	0	17670	4995	5636	14131	0	80995	21	79448	5473	0
38021	44	5880	5880	40593	0	0	36002	0	1849	28456	40460	154176	89	123934	15024	10000
38022	11907	7802	7802	50109	0	0	18213	102825	121487	62143	177531	605096	231	544292	25396	0
38023	6767	4946	4946	37424	0	0	2045	37354	925	37737	77460	221883	45	115009	2588	0
38024	675	545	431	3000	0	0	4561	0	769	5199	0	13435	6	8529	0	0
38025	0	431	431	9094	0	0	681	9578		20745	0	47248	0	49439	0	0
38026	222552	21006	21006	92190	34356	0	68594	653308	90835	199683	825959	2335775	473	1637848	432253	0
38027	9514	10517	10517	62458	21671	0	34997	28262	3882	34184	20581	249846	134	216362	13952	0
38028	1436	7500	7500	43954	0	0	29397	27880	4782	34008	30552	197598	104	223138	13095	0
38029	5357	2438	2438	39000	0	0	4830	3300	2989	31694	52219	147689	43	88726	9444	0
38030	1388	1932	1932	6284	0	0	14837	0	100	9316	0	38282	25	32260	1842	0
38031	9947	865	865	17976	0	0	3888	10535	5928	45275	38648	144387	68	138827	19092	6743
38032	724	1000	1000	0	0	0	10000		1625	24500	29464	67313	36	61876	558	0
38033	519	7971	7971	52098	0	0	10896	22630	4210	38400	76293	228760	40	71831	675	0
38034	2533	7650	7650	51000	0	0	32058	23234	199	50531	24300	194905	67	181848		0
38035	11207	9707	9707	39407	0	0	43744	175412	48820	70460	174310	603067	150	386831	116498	0
38036	40435	7800	7800	52000	0	0	26246	230680	38521	134669	127782	679186	65	128557	502810	0

STATISTICAL INFORMATION

HG

CONFERENCE Number	CHURCH NAME	1 Total professing members reported at the close of last year	4 TOTAL PROFESSING MEMBERS reported at the close of this year	7 Average attendance at all weekly worship services	9 Total Baptized Members who have not become Professing Members	10 Number of other constituents of the church	11 TOTAL Christian Formation Group Participants (Total of lines 11a-d)	13 Average weekly attendance (all ages) in Sunday Church School or other weekly education classes	18a Membership in United Methodist Men	19a Membership in United Methodist Women	20b Number of persons sent out on UMVIM teams from this local church	21 Total Number of community ministries for outreach, justice, and mercy offered by this local church	24 & 25 Value of church assets and buildings	26 & 27 Church Debt	28a Amount APPORTIONED to the local church by the CONFERENCE	29a Amount PAID by the local church to the CONFERENCE for all apportioned causes
38037	HILLSIDE	115	113	44	36	36	23	4	7	3	0	10	641665	0	12354	12354
38038	HOWELL: FIRST	526	534	250	63	108	328	50	20	112	51	8	8302000	1067882	55559	55559
38039	HUDSON: FIRST	123	119	45	5	34	44	19	0	49	1	5	4243000	0	13370	2271
38040	IDA	86	82	22	7	20	25	0	0	24	0	8	470556	0	10757	10757
38041	JACKSON: BROOKSIDE	145	140	73	2	30	91	30	0	0	0	3	2580000	0	22440	18473
38042	JACKSON: CALVARY	107	99	45	43	31	91	6	0	10	0	21	4939810	11800	21893	21893
38043	JACKSON: FIRST	650	639	196	290	130	267	55	0	150	23	0	6968599	0	74250	74250
38044	JACKSON: TRINITY	48	49	32	3	10	24	14	10	0	0	0	4032967	0	8063	7257
38045	JACKSON: ZION	13	13	14	0	30	9	5	0	7	0	0	263038	0	2371	2371
38046	JEROME	23	22	14	0	18	5	0	2	9	0	7	117544	0	3436	3436
38047	JONESVILLE	112	109	45	0	20	25	12	12	10	0	4	809249	0	9704	2169
38048	LA SALLE: ZION	76	73	31	18	0	0	9	0	17	0	1	1810000	0	5195	2598
38049	LAMBERTVILLE	408	386	121	26	400	74	5	0	0	0	3	4008352	0	31400	31400
38050	LEE CENTER	58	58	34	10	50	27	5	0	0	0	4	153146	0	3743	3743
38052	LONDON	78	75	30	5	28	22	12	0	22	0	2	415000	1294	4152	4152
38053	LULU	32	32	7	0	0	9	6	0	0	0	1	672905	0	2481	2481
38054	LYON LAKE	38	38	36	0	0	3	2	5	0	0	0	1108000	14000	5527	5527
38055	MACON	59	61	35	21	11	5	8	0	0	0	6	1085238	0	8870	8870
38056	MANCHESTER: FIRST	172	168	74	61	28	52	8	15	30	0	19	1047851	111200	20563	20563

HG

CONFERENCE Number	Church Benevolence Giving (≤0-38)	Total ASKED for clergy pension (39a)	Total PAID for clergy pension (39b)	Base compensation paid to/for the Senior Pastor or other person in the lead pastoral role (41a)	Base compensation paid to/for all Associate Pastor(s) and other pastoral staff (41b)	Deacons salary/benefits (41c & 42c)	Pastoral Benefits (40,42a-44)	Total amount paid in salary and benefits for all other church staff and diaconal ministers (45)	Total amount spent for local church program expenses (46)	Total amount spent for other local church operating expenses (47)	Local Church capital expenses (48 & 49)	TOTAL CHURCH EXPENSES (Sum of Lines 29a through 49) (50)	Number of giving units (51)	Total income for annual budget/spending plan (52)	Total income for designated causes including capital campaign and other special projects (53)	Total income from connectional and other institutional sources outside the local church (54)
38037	6161	4320	4320	28798	0	0	27228	16285	7113	21581	13045	136885	41	125511	15434	0
38038	21356	11388	11388	64635	0	0	18898	251699	30835	96282	236679	787331	126	559789	243689	0
38039	1628	5730	5252	38197	0	0	16545	4010	523	23805	9827	102058	57	130081	470	0
38040	2393	3405	3405	19512	0	0	17231	7867	5000	18768	3965	88898	35	99210	14011	0
38041	4566	6110	6110	39060	0	0	14408	43178	3137	32746	0	161678	37	157551	2896	0
38042	2487	1421	1421	15710	0	0	4716	55179	389	55614	27695	186104	66	127713	9174	0
38043	26069	13441	13441	61717	1000	0	56702	256864	10575	128762	76519	726107	356	577503	9491	6540
38044	300	3055	3055	26211	0	0	1566	11675	2681	29182	0	81927	35	73676	0	0
38045	908	240	240	5000	0	0	240	0	193	10838	0	19790	14	16225	3448	0
38046	493	944	944	7731	0	0	12802		2058	5327	0	32791	23	29305	1085	0
38047	788	3143	3143	20801	0	0	12990	15316	2203	19803	0	77213	61	63788	32009	0
38049	794	3501	3501	23343	21208	0	6622	2965	734	13021	0	53578	25	47097	4097	0
38048	30096	11229	11229	56000	21040	0	46315	51712	26439	92563	12400	379194	210	300592	54177	0
38050	5400	920	920	18400	0	0	1790		9210	4290	3375	47128	22	48484	3040	0
38052	1718	1084	1084	9641	0	0	3027	2450	794	11687	0	34553	36	35637	4220	0
38053	229	564		9400	0	0	600		75	5000	0	17785	12	18488	1015	0
38054	1287	1067	1067	14610	0	0	14356	8700	2290	15577	9500	66043	16	68812	10715	0
38055	2729	2686	2686	21657	0	0	11179		2600		0	65298	46	76016	1169	0
38056	6602	5184	6184	41229	0	0	28319	47385	12007	28478	41194	231961	75	208468	17806	0

STATISTICAL INFORMATION

CONFERENCE Number	CHURCH NAME	Total professing members reported at the close of last year (1)	TOTAL PROFESSING MEMBERS reported at the close of this year (4)	Average attendance at all weekly worship services (7)	Total Baptized Members who have not become Professing Members (9)	Number of other constituents of the church (10)	TOTAL Christian Formation Group Participants (Total of lines 11a-d) (11)	Average weekly attendance (all ages) in Sunday Church School or other weekly education classes (13)	Membership in United Methodist Men (18a)	Membership in United Methodist Women (19a)	Number of persons sent out on UMWM teams from this local church (20b)	Total Number of community ministries for outreach, justice, and mercy offered by this local church (21)	Value of church assets and buildings (24 & 25)	Church Debt (26 & 27)	Amount APPORTIONED to the local church by the CONFERENCE (28a)	Amount PAID by the local church to the CONFERENCE for all apportioned causes (29a)
38057	MANCHESTER: SHARON	129	133	50	17	40	42	20	0	19	1	13	420438	0	16177	3235
38058	MARSHALL	451	437	259	0	223	157	45	0	0	13	30	10739779	531517	52568	36798
38059	MILAN: MARBLE MEMORIAL	288	278	71	47	48	29	18	0	55	0	6	3091908	0	19150	5000
38060	MILFORD	242	225	103	106	100	47	5	0	35	0	4	1291181	162551	30371	30371
38061	MONROE: CALVARY	57	53	28	3	12	16	8	0	0	0	2	707443	0	10001	10001
38062	MONROE: FIRST	75	64	31	24	30	31	6	0	0	0	0	1737000	16000	9082	8131
38063	MONROE: HERITAGE	44	56	35	0	18	31	10	0	0	0	0	594300	0	3569	3569
38064	MONROE: ST PAUL'S	541	534	129	1	100	101	50	0	22	0	0	12545589	2767	39925	39925
38065	MONTGOMERY	21	22	12	0	0	0	0	0	4	0	0	1297114	0	2808	2808
38066	MORENCI	90	88	28	0	10	6	4	0	0	0	5	3025620	27463	8790	0
38067	NAPOLEON	92	78	48	1	15	2	22	0	11	0	6	1713196	0	12872	6316
38068	NEW HUDSON	86	76	41	0	43	18	10	0	12	3	1	1286220	0	15960	1800
38069	NORTH ADAMS	47	32	26	0	33	5	5	10	10	0	9	183030	10152	4781	4781
38070	NORTH LAKE	114	111	46	24	39	42	8	30	40	13	0	1534020	0	12196	12196
38071	NORTH PARMA	75	65	18	0	10	27	15	0	1	0	2	540000	0	6682	4009
38072	NORTHVILLE: FIRST	1028	1038	421	93	321	781	211	46	0	75	16	13336456	629555	109629	109629
38073	NOVI	129	125	45	0	25	51	38	15	0	0	4	1267170	489970	26083	6995
38074	OAK GROVE	93	91	43	11	11	61	12	7	37	0	10	1669311	0	11915	0
38075	PETERSBURG	84	83	33	0	46	16	0	0	0	0	0	2370690	0	6553	6553

STATISTICAL INFORMATION

CONFERENCE Number	Church Benevolence Giving (30-38)	Total ASKED for clergy pension (39a)	Total PAID for clergy pension (39b)	Base compensation paid to/for the Senior Pastor or other person assigned or appointed in the lead pastoral role to the church (41a)	Base compensation paid to/for all Associate Pastor(s) and other pastoral staff assigned or appointed to the church. Include deacons and other clergy in this role (41b)	Deacons salary/benefits (41c & 42c)	Pastoral Benefits (40, 42a-44)	Total amount paid in salary and benefits for all other church staff and diaconal ministers (45)	Total amount spent for local church program expenses (46)	Total amount spent for other local church operating expenses (47)	Local Church capital expenses (48 & 49)	TOTAL CHURCH EXPENSES (Sum of Lines 29a through 49) (50)	Number of giving units (51)	Total income for annual budget/spending plan (52)	Total income for designated causes including capital campaign and other special projects (53)	Total income from connectional and other institutional sources outside the local church (54)
38057	19025	7103	6511	53189	0	0	15027	17562	4974	26739	302708	448970	84	176530	106535	0
38058	52314	8640	8640	57000	0	0	39178	196552	41028	102958	97322	631790	246	524779	73678	0
38059	10757	7354	7354	49028	0	0	17917	33665	3637	22247	35800	185405	117	176251	3631	0
38060	12340	8991	8991	50685	0	0	46877	56294	5858	80393	24717	316526	150	271581	26241	0
38061	2107	4152	4152	27600	0	0	8150	12890	1519	24714	8016	99149	30	79030	8660	0
38062	2335	3739	3739	29617	0	0	5451	21482	550	18632	42818	132755	30	78503	34537	0
38063	33	1000	1000	4932	0	0	1500	4000	310	9834	0	25178	16	36503	0	0
38064	14338	8187	8187	47377	0	0	35647	106282	8658	72188	8008	340610	175	309653	52941	800
38065	53068	570	570	9394	0	0	4846	0	943	8663	18520	98812	12	11756	11644	0
38066	269	2974	744	17451	0	0	17140	11411	499	15553	5972	69039	20	57723	694	8084
38067	3872	2257	1993	18297	0	0	1758	12695	13678	30759	20956	110324	44	69046	124013	0
38068	3049	8181	8181	54537	0	0	7237	13318	1453	34965	21630	146170	69	127169	17337	0
38069	3592	944	944	7731	0	0	11920	739	727	13398	5158	48990	20	48864	3873	0
38070	10012	6127	6127	40845	0	0	10386	14640	3207	15774	0	113187	70	128447	10696	0
38071	21	2813	2813	20500	0	0	0	2400	2865	6766	4230	43604	23	61862	25	0
38072	78015	18818	18818	99807	17630	0	21276	505083	68719	197444	306954	1423375	406	1002401	175581	0
38073	8264	7375	7375	50612	0	0	20881	43049	9344	58967	71256	276743	63	258308	5247	0
38074	4221	7254	7254	39545	0	0	14803	7944	1624	19606	2100	97097	28	94034	4310	3876
38075	4505	3501	3501	23343	0	0	6622	1900	715	22745	3900	73784	36	94563	6754	0

HG

STATISTICAL INFORMATION

HG

CONFERENCE Number	CHURCH NAME	Total professing members reported at the close of last year (1)	TOTAL PROFESSING MEMBERS reported at the close of this year (4)	Average attendance at all weekly worship services (7)	Total Baptized Members who have not become Professing Members (9)	Number of other constituents of the church (10)	TOTAL Christian Formation Group Participants (Total of lines 11a-d) (11)	Average weekly attendance (all ages) in Sunday Church School or other weekly education classes (13)	Membership in United Methodist Men (18a)	Membership in United Methodist Women (19a)	Number of persons sent out on UMVIM teams from this local church (20b)	Total Number of community ministries for outreach, justice, and mercy offered by this local church (21)	Value of church assets and buildings (24 & 25)	Church Debt (26 & 27)	Amount APPORTIONED to the local church by the CONFERENCE (28a)	Amount PAID by the local church to the CONFERENCE for all apportioned causes (29a)
38076	PINCKNEY: ARISE	92	90	88	0	0	17	9	0	0	0	0	1185247	40620	16436	0
38077	PLEASANT LAKE	30	29	8	8	8	0	0	0	0	0	0	532902	0	2270	681
38078	PLYMOUTH: FIRST	596	517	258	37	127	195	27	0	0	0	7	12282740	0	108338	108338
38079	POPE	24	23	33	11	50	10	4	0	0	0	1	571094	0	2781	2781
38080	QUINCY	53	50	46	0	37	28	11	0	0	0	0	678688	0	12505	12505
38081	READING	111	106	65	26	99	41	36	0	35	1	11	2912873	0	13210	13210
38082	ROLLIN CENTER	44	42	23	0	26	10	10	0	4	0	5	425506	0	6159	333
38083	SALEM GROVE	35	35	17	0	14	15	10	0	7	0	1	340000	0	4753	4753
38084	SALINE: FIRST	706	701	309	102	564	414	160	0	61	20	27	10495359	0	87730	87730
38085	SAMARIA: GRACE	36	36	17	0	16	12	1	0	7	0	0	490998	8031	4571	60
38086	SOMERSET CENTER	38	35	16	0	0	0	0	0	3	0	28	1119046	0	4553	4553
38087	SOUTH LYON: FIRST	614	576	229	101	190	429	110	75	0	23	5	7862438	308926	54835	24676
38088	SOUTH ROCKWOOD	119	111	54	12	15	31	16	0	20	0	3	787855	0	8328	8328
38089	SPRINGPORT	63	64	32	0	15	18	5	0	0	0	5	500000	0	6023	6023
38090	SPRINGVILLE	142	142	32	38	53	11	5	7	14	0	5	929602	900	5450	5450
38091	STOKES CHAPEL	18	20	25	19	0	9	9	0	13	0	0	445598	0	3145	3145
38092	STONY CREEK	139	128	45	0	25	33	10	0	0	0	2	2025000	3000	16452	2045
38093	TECUMSEH	269	264	62	0	0	13	20	0	0	0	0	6679672	148608	21690	5757
38094	WALLED LAKE	145	133	46	17	29	18	16	0	0	0	0	1578000	0	25743	25743

STATISTICAL INFORMATION

CONFERENCE Number	Church Benevolence Giving (30-38)	Total ASKED for clergy pension (39a)	Total PAID for clergy pension (39b)	Base compensation paid to/for the Senior Pastor or other person assigned or appointed in the lead pastoral role to the church (41a)	Base compensation paid to/for all Associate Pastor(s) and other pastoral staff assigned or appointed to the church. Include deacons and other clergy in this role (41b)	Deacons salary/benefits (41c & 42c)	Pastoral Benefits (40.42a-44)	Total amount paid in salary and benefits for all other church staff and diaconal ministers (45)	Total amount spent for local church program expenses (46)	Total amount spent for other local church operating expenses (47)	Local Church capital expenses (48 & 49)	TOTAL CHURCH EXPENSES (Sum of Lines 29a through 49) (50)	Number of giving units (51)	Total income for annual budget/spending plan (52)	Total income for designated causes including capital campaign and other special projects (53)	Total income from connectional and other institutional sources outside the local church (54)
38076	1930	7482	0	52287	0	0	23400	17265	6200	21255	27000	149337	103	134760	1793	0
38077	157	689	172	13321	0	0	0	0	917	5897	0	21145	7	11347	126	0
38078	35843	7875	7875	80000	46000	0	27615	287497	75483	159468	51859	879978	278	879967	32745	15703
38079	1182	1000	1000	0	0	0	10260	375	1016	11861	4865	33340	24	26012	1688	0
38080	4949	1000	1000	2000	0	0	20417	18630	4457	17835	3376	85169	60	73674	12588	0
38081	7266	9710	9710	37832	0	0	27647	11350	1912	18294	18905	146126	78	106092	39480	0
38082	523	2919	2919	19462	0	0	19750	2380	1916	4085	0	51368	28	44483	2334	5417
38083	720	2760	2760	23000	0	0	5020	575	700	7340	1000	45868	20	52130	0	0
38084	53861	11247	11247	64727	0	0	29669	314565	53772	161716	69422	846709	407	742038	94350	0
38085	262	3179	801	21195	0	0	1153	780	310	5979	3507	34047	15	32979	943	0
38086	559	1440	1440	9600	28949	0	9204	6889		16745	3418	52408	19	23556	1083	0
38087	28960	13032	13032	63720	0	0	52658	191014	29755	97577	68422	598763	273	532114	68542	3000
38088	987	4152	4152	27600	0	7000	1150	3900	8630	9443	11210	82400	35	73979	35616	0
38089	8298	3938	3938	22208	0	0	25404	2400	664	14774	0	83709	30	71370	4078	0
38090	806	950	950	18985	0	0	0	0	356	11953	12309	50809	51	45318	0	0
38091	1587	570	570	8366	0	0	3659	0	300	8588	32	26247	12	43027	215	0
38092	6051	5909	5909	39390	0	0	29565	8520	4285	53128	4292	153185	52	118393	25486	0
38093	1415	7236	7236	48241	0	0	19084	46777	3532	41838	43625	217505	95	173171	113999	0
38094	11535	5566	5566	37597	0	0	27601	54586	4178	36585	7000	184648	73	153771	5791	0

HG

STATISTICAL INFORMATION

CONFERENCE Number	CHURCH NAME	1 Total professing members reported at the close of last year	4 TOTAL PROFESSING MEMBERS reported at the close of this year	7 Average attendance at all weekly worship services	9 Total Baptized Members who have not become Professing Members	10 Number of other constituents of the church	11 TOTAL Christian Formation Group Participants (Total of lines 11a-d)	13 Average weekly attendance (all ages) in Sunday Church School or other weekly education classes	18a Membership in United Methodist Men	19a Membership in United Methodist Women	20a Number of persons sent out on UMW teams from this local church	20b Total Number of community ministries for outreach, justice, and mercy offered by this local church	21	24 & 25 Value of church assets and buildings	26 & 27 Church Debt	28a Amount APPORTIONED to the local church by the CONFERENCE	29a Amount PAID by the local church to the CONFERENCE for all apportioned causes
38095	WATERLOO VILLAGE	56	55	15	1	30	7	5	0	0	0	0	6	511227	0	3962	2377
38096	WELLSVILLE	38	38	25	0	15	0	12	0	0	0	0	0	275000	0	3938	0
38097	WESTON	104	100	45	0	12	29	18	0	0	0	0	2	742648	0	6936	6936
38098	WILLOW	93	93	54	4	12	42	9	0	43	0	0	5	1365600	0	7071	7071
38099	YPSILANTI: FIRST	351	351	107	0	27	120	42	0	78	0	0	4	10749141	0	44033	44033
38100	YPSILANTI: LINCOLN CMNTY	58	52	41	4	23	35	20	0	0	0	0	4	3421490	0	11286	11286
38101	YPSILANTI: ST MATTHEWS	109	109	30	0	14	14	14	0	0	0	0	0	962350	0	7394	7394
	MID-MICHIGAN DISTRICT																
35001	ALMA	217	217	116	1	62	84	20	23	42	0	0	2	4039717	4552	25088	25088
35002	ASHLEY	28	31	20	0	23	10	10	0	10	0	0	0	130000	0	4527	4527
35003	BANCROFT	61	59	26	0	8	15	10	8	10	0	0	5	508627	0	4101	4101
35004	BANNISTER	43	42	28	0	15	15	10	0	15	0	0	15	389160	0	4265	4265
35005	BARRY COUNTY: WOODLAND	58	55	28	0	41	12	18	0	10	0	0	0	140000	0	4292	4292
35006	BATH	90	91	73	7	74	132	15	0	0	0	0	5	1249077	46685	7292	7292
35007	BEEBE	10	18	17	0	0	0	0	0	0	0	0	0	468266	0	1735	1735
35008	BRECKENRIDGE	128	123	60	13	18	17	10	0	16	0	0	2	2453422	0	13755	8000
35009	BROOKFIELD EATON	31	31	22	1	0	5	2	0	6	0	0	0	149610	0	4619	4619
35010	CARLAND	18	18	25	3	11	14	3	0	0	0	0	0	324228	0	2425	2425
35011	CARSON CITY	286	287	158	2	126	66	46	0	25	0	0	0	1263335	156874	18315	18315

CONFERENCE Number	Church Benevolence Giving	Total ASKED for clergy pension	Total PAID for clergy pension	Base compensation paid to/for the Senior Pastor or other person assigned or appointed in the lead pastoral role to the church	Base compensation paid to/for all Associate Pastor(s) and other pastoral staff assigned or appointed to the church. Include deacons and other clergy in this role	Deacons salary/benefits	Pastoral Benefits	Total amount paid in salary and benefits for all other church staff and diaconal ministers	Total amount spent for local church program expenses	Total amount spent for other local church operating expenses	Local Church capital expenses	TOTAL CHURCH EXPENSES (Sum of Lines 29a through 49)	Number of giving units	Total income for annual budget/spending plan	Total income for designated causes including capital campaign and other special projects	Total income from connectional and other institutional sources outside the local church
	30-38	39a	39b	41a	41b	41c & 42c	40,42a-44	45	46	47	48 & 49	50	51	52	53	54
38095	10	1435	1435	0	0	0	11957	0	50	10388	1070	27287	20	24900	9932	0
38096	0	848	242	11649	0	0	729	0	950	11910	0	25480	22	43485	0	0
38097	6265	2974	2974	19827	0	0	11447	5280	9342	11170	0	73241	45	61492	8963	0
38098	136	2541	2541	27720	0	0	3300	3000	1000	8000	3000	55768	30	67000	500	0
38099	37455	8022	8022	51150	0	0	10282	95733	33139	95519	10111	385444	155	363128	97559	0
38100	8333	6547	6547	38730	0	0	25000	10084	1348	27839	0	129167	36	121907	7428	0
38101	2231	3168	3168	23038	0	0	7806	19039	1324	25611	0	89611	45	71643	5708	0
35001	7134	8568	8568	57120	0	0	28735	54598	28446	51456	49510	310655	125	245930	76194	0
35002	596	695	695	12600	0	0	0	1900	1000	10000	0	31318	0	0	0	0
35003	9618	929	929	9285	0	0	2638	8800	502	11572	0	47445	0	68859	3172	0
35004	5192	695	695	6182	0	0	1667	2812	1047	12125	0	33985	28	34227	1647	0
35005	1331	515	515	0	0	0	10566	5455	816	15467	0	38442	24	39115	87831	0
35006	5072	2572	2572	16934	0	0	18489	11096	1135	13075	12065	87730	88	86912	697	9000
35007	546	356	356	4000	0	0	0	3183	0	4214	0	14034	18	12672	2000	0
35008	777	3100	3100	28124	0	0	26627	15821	1134	29837	0	113420	55	112722	28068	0
35009	4993	546	546	7110	0	0	10551	2985	1870	4757	1085	38516	25	31040	1474	0
35010	1421	551	551	9192	0	0	0	275	528	2709	0	17101	16	17137	310	0
35011	5152	3582	3582	26289	1769	0	2589	16215	3163	37187	86956	201217	65	194202	4146	13000

STATISTICAL INFORMATION

MM

CONFERENCE Number	CHURCH NAME	1 Total professing members reported at the close of last year	4 TOTAL PROFESSING MEMBERS reported at the close of this year	7 Average attendance at all weekly worship services	9 Total Baptized Members who have not become Professing Members	10 Number of other constituents of the church	11 TOTAL Christian Formation Group Participants (Total of lines 11a-d)	13 Average weekly attendance (all ages) in Sunday Church School or other weekly education classes	18a Membership in United Methodist Men	19a Membership in United Methodist Women	20b Number of persons sent out on UMVIM teams from this local church	21 Total Number of community ministries for outreach, justice, and mercy offered by this local church	24 & 25 Value of church assets and buildings	26 & 27 Church Debt	28a Amount APPORTIONED to the local church by the CONFERENCE	29a Amount PAID by the local church to the CONFERENCE for all apportioned causes
35012	CHAPIN	73	69	36	0	49	22	4	0	17	0	8	219623	0	4864	4864
35013	CHARLOTTE: LAWRENCE AVE	227	224	100	0	0	0	0	10	36	0	3	1655613	0	31824	20000
35014	CHESANING: TRINITY	313	296	114	0	79	56	35	9	30	0	0	3357000	0	24559	12680
35015	CORUNNA	73	73	40	0	0	0	44	0	0	0	1	2832638	0	14074	900
35016	CORUNNA: NORTHWEST VENICE	15	15	14	5	10	12	0	0	8	0	0	310000	0	1927	1927
35017	DELTA MILLS	57	42	39	7	6	15	9	0	17	0	7	880216	0	6210	6210
35018	DEWITT: REDEEMER	848	826	549	261	561	990	15	0	40	0	16	9097700	0	116420	116420
35019	DIMONDALE	61	61	50	1	48	14	201	7	0	2	4	2200158	9216	10074	10074
35021	EAST LANSING: UNIVERSITY	459	464	245	2	75	320	0	36	34	0	5	4298505	748366	63888	63888
35022	EATON RAPIDS: FIRST	312	322	230	5	270	160	47	14	61	10	2	6844742	229439	68947	38855
35023	ELSIE	109	101	55	0	109	22	20	0	0	0	4	1081500	0	12125	2000
35024	FELT PLAINS	14	10	16	0	11	5	22	0	0	0	30	580000	0	3697	3697
35025	FOWLERVILLE: FIRST	120	115	54	41	42	70	20	8	18	0	6	3658494	0	18802	11633
35026	FOWLERVILLE: TRINITY	68	61	25	0	50	24	5	8	8	0	0	1142000	0	8519	8519
35027	FREEPORT	5	5	5	7	2	0	0	0	0	0	1	941984	0	3484	3484
35028	GRAND LEDGE: FIRST	275	251	130	25	76	101	14	20	12	0	3	5380040	0	37937	37937
35029	GRESHAM	62	62	58	44	28	27	10	0	13	0	0	194500	0	6344	6344
35031	GUNNISONVILLE	58	62	56	0	26	54	4	0	0	0	4	936592	0	10879	10879
35032	HASTINGS: FIRST	201	203	218	47	50	58	60	0	10	0	4	8036445	0	31565	31565

CONFERENCE Number	Church Benevolence Giving (30-38)	Total ASKED for clergy pension (39a)	Total PAID for clergy pension (39b)	Base compensation paid to/for the Senior Pastor or other person assigned or appointed in the lead pastoral role to the church (41a)	Base compensation paid to/for all Associate Pastor(s) and other pastoral staff assigned or appointed to the church. Include deacons and other clergy in this role (41b)	Deacons salary/benefits (41c & 42c)	Pastoral Benefits (40,42a-44)	Total amount paid in salary and benefits for all other church staff and diaconal ministers (45)	Total amount spent for local church program expenses (46)	Total amount spent for other local church operating expenses (47)	Local Church capital expenses (48 & 49)	TOTAL CHURCH EXPENSES (Sum of Lines 29a through 49) (50)	Number of giving units (51)	Total income for annual budget/spending plan (52)	Total income for designated causes including capital campaign and other special projects (53)	Total income from connectional and other institutional sources outside the local church (54)
35012	3874	1118	1118	6067	0	0	1500	0	4000	12000	4000	37423	49	47408	4135	0
35013	8078	8505	8505	56700	0	0	38200	42560	4500	70000	35000	283543	94	228360	53923	0
35014	14854	8033	8033	42314	0	0	142374	49102	8140	32744	32115	342356	99	238054	127281	0
35015	1048	2919	2919	19462	0	0	9761	16942	1019	28102	5041	85194	45	83179	1352	0
35016	322	596	596	8808	0	0	1200	600	700	3000	0	17153	8	16000	0	0
35017	13671	950	950	21360	47249	0	1200	7860	1815	14836	36862	104764	33	60450	5112	0
35018	261261	21552	21552	92901	0	0	92513	569591	67760	222431	67593	1559271	848	1496535	267509	0
35019	5688	1575	1575	30300	0	0	4760	20349	2000	28918	43805	147469	44	108938	13326	34500
35021	20297	10959	10959	63330	0	0	44241	215477	27644	110088	195883	751807	230	587693	277539	0
35022	43105	8868	8868	52910	0	0	28866	180024	51001	106430	38284	548343	244	469116	134042	0
35023	30	1125	0	20558	0	0	13287	18902	4162	24535	14407	97881	32	86355	10638	0
35024	868	1296	1296	13600	0	0	3000	2485	2498	8530	12350	45826	11	42008	0	0
35025	3632	5369	5369	39341	0	0	8060	27825	911	29180	8745	136283	60	128053	2440	0
35026	423	1136	1136	22200	0	0	0	16316	4961	17410	0	66915	12	76563	1037	0
35027	43780	326	326	6523	0	0	396	0	6460	5601	7794	72865	8	18749	9871	531
35028	7233	9825	9825	65500	0	0	30881	72259	2500	70088	2362	302545	85	275395	661196	0
35029	702	2949	2949	13602	0	0	21248	4940	8643	11500	62265	126050	45	73657	22920	0
35031	6225	3353	3353	21618	0	0	19558	9708	15623	18268	0	98252	58	109996	4272	0
35032	23000	9600	9600	64000	0	0	22924	62045		66893	54492	350142	158	298749	56212	0

STATISTICAL INFORMATION

MM

Conference Number	Church Name	Total professing members reported at the close of last year (1)	TOTAL PROFESSING MEMBERS reported at the close of this year (4)	Average attendance at all weekly worship services (7)	Total Baptized Members who have not become Professing Members (9)	Number of other constituents of the church (10)	TOTAL Christian Formation Group Participants (Total of lines 11a-d) (11)	Average weekly attendance (all ages) in Sunday Church School or other weekly education classes (13)	Membership in United Methodist Men (18a)	Membership in United Methodist Women (19a)	Number of persons sent out on UMVIM teams from this local church (20b)	Total Number of community ministries for outreach, justice, and mercy offered by this local church (21)	Value of church assets and buildings (24 & 25)	Church Debt (26 & 27)	Amount APPORTIONED to the local church by the CONFERENCE (28a)	Amount PAID by the local church to the CONFERENCE for all apportioned causes (29a)
35033	HASTINGS: HOPE	70	75	52	0	31	27	30	0	0	0	1	1634275	174607	17166	15550
35034	HASTINGS: WELCOME CORNERS	25	29	15	0	12	0	0	0	7	0	0	75493	0	4578	4578
35035	HENDERSON	53	50	20	4	36	11	10	0	0	0	0	614512	0	4738	4738
35036	HOLT	388	359	200	0	340	214	50	0	70	0	5	5039737	0	52040	52040
35037	ITHACA	129	125	73	2	39	57	17	0	0	0	3	395000	0	15067	12054
35038	JUDDVILLE	40	39	26	0	14	5	0	0	16	0	1	3380309	0	4838	4838
35039	KALAMO	53	49	25	4	49	10	0	0	7	0	4	110487	0	3910	3910
35040	LAINGSBURG	116	123	83	34	86	56	15	0	14	0	7	2195483	122038	15884	15885
35041	LAKE ODESSA: CENTRAL	130	127	64	26	40	36	23	0	34	0	2	4743954	0	21957	17566
35042	LAKE ODESSA: LAKEWOOD	235	227	170	2	193	678	130	0	0	0	32	5473800	445697	44890	44890
35043	LANSING: ASBURY	143	134	60	0	9	10	10	0	0	0	4	4658647	0	23289	18631
35044	LANSING: CENTRAL	307	307	97	3	200	209	54	0	12	3	3	21215000	0	52756	8993
35045	LANSING: FIRST	128	116	66	7	46	34	0	0	12	1	2	4290000	0	27301	15235
35046	LANSING: GRACE	215	213	106	32	101	134	44	0	25	0	1	1473640	182000	27992	27992
35047	LANSING: MOUNT HOPE	284	288	243	123	90	336	119	0	25	0	5	5108047	0	48390	48390
35048	LANSING: SYCAMORE CRK	290	290	259	0	85	59	51	0	8	3	9	4086695	169261	41449	41449
35049	LESLIE	55	55	26	0	18	9	0	0	13	0	0	1476435	0	6038	6038
35050	LIVINGSTON CIRCUIT: PLAINFIELD	41	41	28	0	58	0	0	0	0	0	0	1043040	0	6809	0
35051	LOWE	70	74	60	1	0	0	12	0	0	0	0	810000	0	6835	6835

CONFERENCE Number	30-38 Church Benevolence Giving	39a Total ASKED for clergy pension	39b Total PAID for clergy pension	41a Base compensation paid to/for the Senior Pastor or other person in the lead pastoral role	41b Base compensation paid to/for all Associate Pastor(s) and other pastoral staff	41c & 42c Deacons salary/benefits	40, 42a-44 Pastoral Benefits	45 Total salary and benefits for all other church staff and diaconal ministers	46 Total amount spent for local church program expenses	47 Total amount spent for other local church operating expenses	48 & 49 Local Church capital expenses	50 TOTAL CHURCH EXPENSES (Sum of Lines 29a through 49)	51 Number of giving units	52 Total income for annual budget/spending plan	53 Total income for designated causes including capital campaign and other special projects	54 Total income from connectional and other institutional sources outside the local church
35033	1218	5511	5511	36739	0	0	6198	18455	1897	32329	42480	160377	46	159690	10628	0
35034	883	652	652	14596	0	0	0	0	0	21858	26000	68567	16	25446	8829	0
35035	760	1118	1118	9466	0	0	1984	4820	288	13638	10320	47132	29	45143	857	0
35036	39746	10091	10091	67275	0	0	30198	161892	13246	93144	9075	476707	285	425253	83882	0
35037	7333	6972	6972	46546	0	0	24251	15270	511	19013	19743	131950	75	158703	11154	0
35038	18817	655	655	13100	0	0	0	12450	10727	17127	9976	97457	30	98032	11727	4763
35039	9266	1932	1932	11688	0	0	9041	4919	2985	4511	36192	58228	22	30660	10188	0
35040	3266	5941	5941	47000	0	0	30833	22165	3098	28260	22784	192640	92	148935	4486	0
35041	11423	6958	6958	41715	0	0	33469	39945	3210	36546	110194	213616	126	324523	24957	0
35042	20477	7419	7419	43705	0	0	37097	54974	10944	79764	40866	409464	136	414348	24507	0
35043	6182	6186	6186	35136	0	0	30518	61624	1040	1040	14000	200183	80	134689	15000	0
35044	7022	6186	6186	52000	0	0	22000	137000	16000	162000	10940	425201	85	329600	10000	0
35045	2911	7425	7425	49500	0	0	22253	37440	19278	34226	97287	199208	96	173193	9223	0
35046	11058	7650	7650	51000	43313	39597	28777	75042	16764	52568	17032	368138	110	209714	38830	0
35047	34419	19251	19251	61200	37572	0	70200	167698	22286	70122	125583	593508	196	481650	16071	47000
35048	21955	12530	12530	47636	0	0	32899	119079	16003	53264	9487	507970	298	256644	233375	0
35049	2225	1296	1188	12822	0	0	5938	10188	2139	15537	0	65562	30	44841	2791	0
35050	136	1136	1136	22200	0	0	0	16316	153	9457		49398	15	42370	220	0
35051	4437	2533	2533	19250	0	0	8625	3944	2926	15801		64351	45	56711	1410	0

STATISTICAL INFORMATION

MM

Conference Number	CHURCH NAME	1	4	7	9	10	11	13	18a	19a	20b	21	24 & 25	26 & 27	28a	29a
35052	MAPLE RAPIDS	34	30	35	0	25	10	0	0	0	0	0	445000	0	5159	5159
35053	MASON: FIRST	433	403	137	42	329	162	45	0	84	0	12	5561920	256497	46018	38398
35054	MIDDLEBURY	38	37	14	0	18	0	0	0	14	0	0	625041	0	3121	3121
35055	MILLVILLE	113	111	62	0	33	29	22	4	20	0	0	2600000	0	18150	18150
35056	MORRICE	70	69	15	0	0	0	0	0	4	0	0	921289	0	4266	4266
35057	MULLIKEN	29	28	19	0	25	5	0	0	0	0	3	220000	14028	4725	473
35058	MUNITH	39	37	29	0	0	10	6	4	0	0	0	1041000	0	6161	6161
35060	NASHVILLE: PEACE	24	23	20	1	28	3	3	0	9	0	0	442000	0	3176	3176
35061	NEW LOTHROP: FIRST	75	75	33	0	0	26	7	8	21	0	7	988923	0	8458	8458
35062	OKEMOS: COMMUNITY CHURCH	448	441	150	0	152	76	30	0	30	0	17	6817271	0	61842	41511
35063	OVID UNITED CHURCH	83	80	65	0	0	36	0	0	0	0	1	2148276	6965	8746	8746
35065	OWOSSO: FIRST	268	268	132	60	136	140	66	26	69	0	9	7865088	0	34663	20313
35066	OWOSSO: TRINITY	122	122	49	43	27	18	7	8	20	0	2	2057000	0	14038	8500
35067	PERRY	47	47	37	5	44	37	14	0	7	0	4	600610	0	6619	6619
35068	PITTSBURG	27	38	15	0	28	4	0	0	7	0	2	257000	0	1902	1902
35069	POMPEII	36	35	27	6	33	32	6	0	20	2	22	1273000	0	4409	4409
35070	PORTLAND	228	219	90	6	29	44	20	0	25	0	6	2631348	0	30629	18377
35072	RIVERDALE: LINCOLN ROAD	117	117	45	0	34	25	15	0	8	0	5	1012246	0	14759	14759
35073	ROBBINS	121	118	50	13	21	52	23	0	0	0	4	1839500	0	19087	7234

Column key:
- 1: Total professing members reported at the close of last year
- 4: TOTAL PROFESSING MEMBERS reported at the close of this year
- 7: Average attendance at all weekly worship services
- 9: Total Baptized Members who have not become Professing Members
- 10: Number of other constituents of the church
- 11: TOTAL Christian Formation Group Participants (Total of lines 11a-d)
- 13: Average weekly attendance (all ages) in Sunday Church School or other weekly education classes
- 18a: Membership in United Methodist Men
- 19a: Membership in United Methodist Women
- 20b: Number of persons sent out on UMVIM teams from this local church
- 21: Total Number of community ministries for outreach, justice, and mercy offered by this local church
- 24 & 25: Value of church assets and buildings
- 26 & 27: Church Debt
- 28a: Amount APPORTIONED to the local church by the CONFERENCE
- 29a: Amount PAID by the local church to the CONFERENCE for all apportioned causes

CONFERENCE Number	30-38 Church Benevolence Giving	39a Total ASKED for clergy pension	39b Total PAID for clergy pension	41a Base compensation paid to/for the Senior Pastor or other person assigned or appointed in the lead pastoral role to the church	41b Base compensation paid to/for all Associate Pastor(s) and other pastoral staff assigned or appointed to the church. Include deacons and other clergy in this role	41c. & 42c. Deacons salary/benefits	40.42a-44 Pastoral Benefits	45 Total amount paid in salary and benefits for all other church staff and diaconal ministers	46 Total amount spent for local church program expenses	47 Total amount spent for other local church operating expenses	48 & 49 Local Church capital expenses	50 TOTAL CHURCH EXPENSES (Sum of Lines 29a through 49)	51 Number of giving units	52 Total income for annual budget/spending plan	53 Total income for designated causes including capital campaign and other special projects	54 Total income from connectional and other institutional sources outside the local church
35052	2905	2533	2533	19250	0	0	8000	3900	500	12102	0	54349	25	49260	520	0
35053	9783	8250	8250	50000	0	0	21123	138687	14015	74329	96038	450623	167	367701	121946	2997
35054	346	1218	1218	9020	0	0	9661	2236	0	10780	0	36382	17	32748	1482	0
35055	25115	4156	2770	27691	0	0	5184	19387	46	660	0	99003	50	114217	6601	0
35056	2696	929	929	14547	0	0	2275	0	1279	13497	4699	44188	25	30341	3389	225
35057	1	3100	517	29576	0	0	8354	0	1175	14460	0	54556	34	34501	1325	7047
35058	3249	1365	1365	12466	0	0	8829	3595	1220	14976	0	51861	25	30941	5754	0
35060	2894	505	505	11590	0	0	170	0	300	7062	0	25697	20	21857	1676	0
35061	2335	2919	2919	19462	0	0	8570	6606	9314	24404	5124	87192	29	79451	8548	0
35062	70210	10800	10800	62840	0	0	58381	184911	35268	77941	2264	544126	158	442410	513397	0
35063	4651	3206	3206	23750	0	0	16966	24921	5039	36646	29000	152925	65	117163	74954	0
35065	30537	9150	9150	61000	0	0	28226	90417	7988	75025	103816	426472	130	322429	25154	0
35066	4390	3935	3935	23682	0	0	6512	13371	8720	13923	0	83033	58	91858	1845	0
35067	3043	4011	4011	23748	0	0	15522	4789	4327	7785	3996	73840	27	69954	3294	0
35068	1094	1485	1485	6650	1000	0	0	2660	341	16144	0	30276	19	26753	550	0
35069	2664	695	695	0	0	0	7915	2333	2131	12139	736	34022	38	46260	1988	0
35070	5742	9600	9600	59675	0	0	5526	40605	6036	49514	0	195075	60	226047	6591	0
35072	7977	5909	5909	39395	0	0	7018	14458	3177	46268	7099	146060	42	126267	13320	5800
35073	12697	5812	5812	38746	0	0	24051	21050	1707	24739	1000	137036	42	119949	19504	0

MM

STATISTICAL INFORMATION

CONFERENCE Number	CHURCH NAME	1	4	7	9	10	11	13	18a	19a	20b	21	24 & 25	26 & 27	28a	29a
35074	SHAFTSBURG	50	50	40	31	55	41	23	0	0	0	5	841659	0	7778	7778
35075	SHEPARDSVILLE	34	28	25	10	30	28	0	0	0	0	21	314500	0	3822	2622
35076	ST JOHNS: PILGRIM	236	257	236	16	200	208	86	15	0	0	1	2451187	0	31960	31960
35077	ST LOUIS: FIRST	207	202	69	3	82	60	4	0	37	0	4	3047113	0	16218	16218
35078	STOCKBRIDGE	39	39	29	0	0	16	7	0	12	0	4	679845	0	7107	7107
35079	SUNFIELD	46	45	44	0	50	30	6	0	0	0	0	1185000	0	12360	1955
35080	VERNON	25	25	15	0	16	6	3	0	5	0	0	1120000	5765	2412	2412
35081	WACOUSTA COMMUNITY	258	257	104	0	315	84	20	0	20	1	8	2975472	35717	16833	16833
35082	WEBBERVILLE	114	122	80	0	44	54	32	8	35	0	8	2620645	134150	16151	8200
35083	WILLIAMSTON	153	147	72	0	54	45	3	0	0	0	15	4342117	0	18883	18883
35084	WILLIAMSTON: CROSSROADS	38	33	37	8	8	35	9	0	20	0	7	2150000	0	7323	7323
35085	WILLIAMSTON: WHEATFIELD	46	46	16	0	14	0	4	0	0	0	7	259853	0	3687	3687
	MIDWEST DISTRICT															
34001	ALLENDALE: VALLEY CHURCH	129	155	160	0	0	249	35	0	0	0	4	600000	60000	24379	22100
34003	AMBLE	63	64	40	2	21	19	6	0	0	0	3	389000	0	7002	7002
34004	BARRYTON: FAITH	23	21	15	0	10	15	12	0	7	0	0	280833	0	4130	50
34005	BELDING	35	34	13	8	20	16	6	0	0	0	4	1200000	0	2736	1567
34006	BERLIN CENTER	48	43	22	0	0	0	0	0	12	0	0	145094	0	5650	0
34007	BIG RAPIDS: FIRST	276	276	125	47	150	104	48	0	0	0	3	992176	0	32380	32380

CONFERENCE Number	Church Benevolence Giving (30-38)	Total ASKED for clergy pension (39a)	Total PAID for clergy pension (39b)	Base compensation paid to/for the Senior Pastor or other person assigned or appointed in the lead pastoral role to the church (41a)	Base compensation paid to/for all Associate Pastor(s) and other pastoral staff assigned or appointed to the church. Include deacons and other clergy in this role (41b)	Deacons salary/benefits (41c & 42c)	Pastoral Benefits (40,42a-44)	Total amount paid in salary and benefits for all other church staff and diaconal ministers (45)	Total amount spent for local church program expenses (46)	Total amount spent for other local church operating expenses (47)	Local Church capital expenses (48 & 49)	TOTAL CHURCH EXPENSES (Sum of Lines 29a through 49) (50)	Number of giving units (51)	Total income for annual budget/spending plan (52)	Total income for designated causes including capital campaign and other special projects (53)	Total income from connectional and other institutional sources outside the local church (54)
35074	5727	3703	3703	23748	0	0	19579	4430	6123	12128	0	83216	37	82039	17636	0
35075	5000	605	0	10080	0	0	0	1330	2561	15800	3859	41252	22	29418	3635	0
35076	34994	8436	8436	45851	0	0	32308	100006	40477	54636	27890	376558	212	371228	13349	0
35077	4829	5955	5955	29096	0	0	17407	19439	3522	41508	2715	140689	104	163023	21982	0
35078	68	1365	1365	11486	0	0	9168	11239	1792	13972	1846	58043	35	55452	1684	0
35079	15826	3048	3048	14589	0	0	16901	21454	3632	7905	0	85310	43	90335	16297	0
35080	1400	497	497	12000	0	0	1400	1500	300	1500	0	21009	20	35000	50	0
35081	6117	6724	6724	44629	0	0	28226	38963	5116	32906	21979	201493	108	191260	35478	0
35082	5321	4450	4450	7536	0	0	41136	18734	4598	53886	17924	161785	62	144101	28292	18720
35083	4036	5801	5801	37042	0	0	25711	33894	6700	43629	37320	213016	830	181810	80389	0
35084	5838	2036	2036	3768	0	0	20583	6003	7748	15670		68969	30	78377	4665	0
35085	698	1154	1039	8148	0	0	6007	3710	870	9762	268	34189	20	33061	920	375
34001	2500	7824	7824	46600	11125	0	6400	76596	31500	28000	11648	244293	100	238314	60797	5000
34003	5665	4358	4358	25190	0	0	30938	0	4751	13658	9275	100837	37	67281	11093	0
34004	0	240	40	4550	0	0	0	1575	179	7989	0	14383	10	20272	897	0
34005	1263	1546	1546	9549	0	0	1443	9614	337	19628	0	35333	22	28343	18	0
34006	2253	1167	1167	1513	0	0	13504	9614	591	12066	6572	47280	19	54009	2634	0
34007	12535	7950	7950	53000	0	0	24794	66310	35535	74456	4709	311669	138	291262	63009	0

MM

MW

MW

STATISTICAL INFORMATION

MW

Conference Number	Church Name	1	4	7	9	10	11	13	18a	19a	20b	21	24 & 25	26 & 27	28a	29a
34008	BIG RAPIDS: THIRD AVENUE	51	46	46	4	27	8	0	0	0	0	8	215630	0	4015	4015
34009	BOWNE CENTER	94	94	49	0	0	24	10	0	4	0	0	958000	0	6077	6077
34010	BRADLEY: INDIAN MISSION	28	28	22	0	5	6	3	0	0	0	0	373500	0	2073	0
34012	BYRON CENTER	159	154	68	0	161	38	6	0	0	0	0	995986	98000	19393	10338
34013	CALEDONIA	169	164	84	0	66	66	25	0	6	0	16	1155838	0	21798	5480
34014	CARLISLE	91	65	63	0	51	10	10	0	0	0	0	840000	28825	14504	14504
34015	CEDAR SPRINGS	154	152	98	0	182	22	30	9	0	0	26	3394508	0	21153	21153
34016	CLAYBANKS	49	48	43	0	51	14	12	0	0	0	0	1393892	0	4348	4348
34017	COOPERSVILLE	96	96	94	1	145	131	13	0	0	0	6	465000	223600	15316	1315
34018	COURTLAND-OAKFIELD	102	98	60	0	60	41	11	0	0	0	1	828449	0	12589	12589
34019	CRYSTAL VALLEY	21	21	14	0	20	7	0	0	5	0	6	454414	0	2208	2208
34020	DORR: CROSSWIND CMNTY	67	81	125	66	380	63	35	0	0	0	3	425399	261748	20463	1500
34021	EAST NELSON	105	109	69	0	38	14	8	0	0	0	5	1276776	0	12862	12862
34022	EDMORE: FAITH	157	152	80	0	40	31	17	0	20	0	2	1538636	0	13745	13745
34023	FENWICK	11	11	15	0	13	4	4	0	8	0	0	692796	0	1787	1787
34024	FERRY	39	36	21	0	8	20	0	0	0	0	3	154000	0	5164	5164
34025	FREMONT	350	337	98	135	183	225	35	0	52	5	14	4033187	0	29709	29709
34026	GEORGETOWN	426	392	250	122	203	247	62	0	54	12	17	4735241	0	54784	54784
34027	GRAND HAVEN: CHURCH OF THE DUNES	555	535	259	32	115	269	84	45	75	0	4	7690177	93940	64985	64985

STATISTICAL INFORMATION

CONFERENCE Number	30-38 Church Benevolence Giving	39a Total ASKED for clergy pension	39b Total PAID for clergy pension	41a Base compensation paid to/for the Senior Pastor or other person assigned or appointed in the lead pastoral role to the church	41b Base compensation paid to/for all Associate Pastor(s) and other pastoral staff assigned or appointed to the church. Include deacons and other clergy in this role	41c & 42c Deacons salary/benefits	40,42a-44 Pastoral Benefits	45 Total amount paid in salary and benefits for all other church staff and diaconal ministers	46 Total amount spent for local church program expenses	47 Total amount spent for other local church operating expenses	48 & 49 Local Church capital expenses	50 TOTAL CHURCH EXPENSES (Sum of Lines 29a through 49)	51 Number of giving units	52 Total income for annual budget/spending plan	53 Total income for designated causes including capital campaign and other special projects	54 Total income from connectional and other institutional sources outside the local church
34008	5438	780	780	8377	0	0	5422	568	1487	7053	0	33140	43	36931	4799	0
34009	7981	925	848	12500	0	0	3348	4845	806	14853	20651	71909	45	40527	1831	0
34010	1200	3269	0	31500	0	0	0	2640	50	6478	500	42368	6	25000	0	0
34012	1876	6368	6368	42452	0	0	30376	13080	8997	27472	20542	161501	68	115056	19749	0
34013	8620	6915	6915	46097	0	0	27270	46059	1957	29562	36561	171960	100	170190	16621	0
34014	7753	0	0	0	0	0	210	21056	3248	27019	0	110351	67	124197	32968	0
34015	21803	1250	1250	25000	0	0	2552	35551	14003	67196	5780	188508	182	182669	45215	0
34016	5812	700	700	12600	0	0	4446	5572	1086	8464	32205	48808	42	62323	5819	1525
34017	2143	6694	6694	41232	0	0	27717	18543	2409	13101	8563	145359	64	107621	34259	0
34018	2943	2957	2957	23192	0	0	12142	29373	8021	29786	854	129566	51	109783	9269	0
34019	255	438	438	2035	0	0	9550	33586	392	5642	34778	21374	15	21067	421	0
34020	500	7920	7260	46000	0	0	38878	21585	9321	18134	23094	189957	82	184912	3442	0
34021	8211	2320	2320	18200	0	0	27319	26652	7969	43671	1498	165231	69	170759	750	0
34022	8723	5813	5813	35074	0	0	6908			18364		118005	60	158397		2400
34023	440	240	240	4000	0	0	626	0	1228	6811	0	14008	9	12677	289	0
34024	9502	587	587	6237	0	0	2914	5636	104	7927	0	37967	22	42461	999	0
34025	9132	6000	6000	40000	0	0	17174	66456	11724	37139	114014	331348	115	249906	87974	0
34026	25994	9959	9959	70992	0	0	26431	172371	24931	87368	28569	501399	252	488403	63148	0
34027	65719	10627	10627	67700	0	0	30559	204541	29376	110027	72940	656474	295	568905	159975	0

MW

STATISTICAL INFORMATION

MW

CONFERENCE Number	CHURCH NAME	1 Total professing members reported at the close of last year	4 TOTAL PROFESSING MEMBERS reported at the close of this year	7 Average attendance at all weekly worship services	9 Total Baptized Members who have not become Professing Members	10 Number of other constituents of the church	11 TOTAL Christian Formation Group Participants (Total of lines 11a-d)	13 Average weekly attendance (all ages) in Sunday Church School or other weekly education classes	18a Membership in United Methodist Men	19a Membership in United Methodist Women	20b Number of persons sent out on UMVIM teams from this local church	21 Total Number of community ministries for outreach, justice, and mercy offered by this local church	24 & 25 Value of church assets and buildings	26 & 27 Church Debt	28a Amount APPORTIONED to the local church by the CONFERENCE	29a Amount PAID by the local church to the CONFERENCE for all apportioned causes
34028	GRAND RAPIDS: ALDERSGATE	170	167	89	0	80	187	30	0	0	0	3	2112225	0	23293	23293
34029	GRAND RAPIDS: CORNERSTONE	1651	1690	1953	9	2500	3780	976	0	0	51	18	18721903	761005	305417	305417
34030	GRAND RAPIDS: FAITH	147	102	63	4	20	20	0	0	0	0	0	3237038	0	24198	13000
34031	GRAND RAPIDS: FIRST	914	908	475	143	90	642	210	0	0	32	12	42625154	224061	163419	116442
34032	GRAND RAPIDS: GENESIS	170	132	72	4	0	39	13	0	0	0	2	735689	36026	31926	832
34033	GRAND RAPIDS: LA NUEVA ESPERANZA	70	73	30	1	0	21	8	0	0	0	2	500001	0	3278	0
34034	GRAND RAPIDS: NORTHLAWN	182	164	86	6	47	55	55	14	0	0	0	2610823	74576	20551	400
34036	GRAND RAPIDS: SAINT PAUL'S	176	163	88	8	0	8	36	16	0	0	15	1868000	57600	22555	22555
34037	GRAND RAPIDS: SOUTH	120	126	60	6	28	92	36	0	15	0	2	1225574	0	20995	20995
34038	GRAND RAPIDS: TRINITY	502	472	150	115	88	140	30	0	60	6	6	11381203	0	57947	2300
34039	GRAND RAPIDS: VIETNAMESE	120	115	97	0	8	60	40	0	30	7	1	300000	0	10080	10080
34040	GRANDVILLE	248	176	139	0	52	92	19	0	49	0	15	4874412	0	30517	30517
34041	GRANT CENTER	21	22	18	0	20	15	9	5	15	0	10	656940	0	3177	3177
34042	GREENVILLE: FIRST	580	550	90	71	105	56	54	0	59	0	12	3825780	1098252	29949	1080
34043	HART	123	110	56	34	92	95	10	22	21	0	0	2584380	0	19980	19980
34044	HESPERIA	69	64	51	65	51	16	9	0	14	0	12	557200	0	9611	9611
34045	HOLLAND: FIRST	592	594	330	2	581	436	225	0	129	0	0	12428904	18709	66685	66685
34046	HOLTON	209	209	152	4	178	109	28	0	0	0	0	2344870	0	25369	25369
34047	IONIA: EASTON	78	75	34	0	39	28	0	0	12	0	5	1240559	0	6170	6170

CONFERENCE Number	Church Benevolence Giving (30-38)	Total ASKED for clergy pension (39a)	Total PAID for clergy pension (39b)	Base compensation paid to/for the Senior Pastor or other person assigned or appointed in the lead pastoral role to the church (41a)	Base compensation paid to/for all Associate Pastor(s) and other pastoral staff assigned or appointed to the church. Include deacons and other clergy in this role (41b)	Deacons salary/benefits (41c & 42c)	Pastoral Benefits (40,42a-44)	Total amount paid in salary and benefits for all other church staff and diaconal ministers (45)	Total amount spent for local church program expenses (46)	Total amount spent for other local church operating expenses (47)	Local Church capital expenses (48 & 49)	TOTAL CHURCH EXPENSES (Sum of Lines 29a through 49) (50)	Number of giving units (51)	Total income for annual budget/spending plan (52)	Total income for designated causes including capital campaign and other special projects (53)	Total income from connectional and other institutional sources outside the local church (54)
34028	10363	8837	8837	58640	0	0	10104	51465	5666	47988	6977	223333	75	223880	20661	0
34029	257637	31706	31706	116488	60535	0	77891	1349109	292765	331850	453410	3286808	1471	2869798	1230016	0
34030	2466	2356	2356	19891	0	0	27234	45500	1632	65279	0	177358	60	185361	25393	0
34031	56964	17122	17122	83700	20600	0	68130	555181	62591	218930		1209660	239	1162856	0	0
34032	4215	7366	7366	46385	0	0	18802	45183	8378	27886	26113	185160	59	180149	27558	0
34033	0	4500	4125	17575	0	0	5000	0	5000	25000	0	56700	12	6203	1000	31000
34034	3804	2841	2841	28228	0	0	5553	13610	12259	60552	124800	252047	73	151985	123570	0
34036	16843	6900	6900	41000	0	0	26912	37176	3847	59049	52517	266799	74	212998	41086	0
34037	13403	3381	3381	54101	0	0	12675	27501	26848	39631	12222	210757	61	143929	18402	0
34038	36252	10496	10496	67831	0	0	33373	242354	46679	94006	118098	651389	213	469266	407649	27970
34039	4668	6131	5620	38703	0	0	33910		44000	33000	5500	175481	34	76700	5500	45000
34040	38816	8127	8127	50117	0	0	29526	73765	15300	78268	41530	365966	161	346183	31424	0
34041	2933	500	500	10000	0	0	661	4435	2208	7434	0	31348	21	36423	3338	0
34042	14597	9375	9375	59000	0	0	21120	49389	506	49396	130872	335335	133	169146	61192	0
34043	3927	7050	7050	47000	0	0	28210	40988	10423	24433	43382	225393	41	143436	147972	0
34044	2518	1140	1140	18240	0	0	6463	13834	770	19629	0	72205	57	76311	2735	0
34045	31603	18620	18620	71070	60890	0	65725	190140	28410	192962	52341	778446	359	798200	43134	0
34046	10965	7950	7950	55581	0	0	30440	34431	17174	57830		239740	138	228907		0
34047	1948	3148	3148	19099	0	0	8186	5643	1108	11672	0	56974	40	58590	1341	0

MW

STATISTICAL INFORMATION

MW

CONFERENCE Number	CHURCH NAME	1 Total professing members reported at the close of last year	4 TOTAL PROFESSING MEMBERS reported at the close of this year	7 Average attendance at all weekly worship services	9 Total Baptized Members who have not become Professing Members	10 Number of other constituents of the church	11 TOTAL Christian Formation Group Participants (Total of lines 11a-d)	13 Average weekly attendance (all ages) in Sunday Church School or other weekly education classes	18a Membership in United Methodist Men	19a Membership in United Methodist Women	20b Number of persons sent out on UMW/UMW teams from this local church	21 Total Number of community ministries for outreach, justice, and mercy offered by this local church	24 & 25 Value of church assets and buildings	26 & 27 Church Debt	28a Amount APPORTIONED to the local church by the CONFERENCE	29a Amount PAID by the local church to the CONFERENCE for all apportioned causes
34048	IONIA: FIRST	101	97	66	21	33	21	14	0	11	0	5	3679531	84630	18237	12250
34049	IONIA: ZION	78	64	41	2	12	8	7	0	0	0	5	2375753	0	12061	2895
34050	KENT CITY: CHAPEL HILL	144	139	45	0	12	36	24	15	0	11	1	1951830	0	14485	2824
34051	LAKEVIEW: NEW LIFE	215	213	83	40	71	41	25	0	15	0	4	2645548	0	24095	24095
34052	LEIGHTON	135	142	125	0	40	299	72	0	0	0	17	4316682	0	26770	20083
34053	LEVALLEY	148	145	76	1	0	46	16	0	12	0	3	510826	0	17445	17445
34054	LOWELL: FIRST	350	349	142	0	168	155	11	0	65	0	3	4765652	0	32059	32059
34055	LOWELL: VERGENNES	106	104	90	11	131	95	38	0	0	0	12	526472	0	22923	22923
34056	LYONS-MUIR	64	59	41	0	12	21	13	0	9	0	0	1399802	0	8795	1798
34057	MARNE	94	91	76	0	32	17	10	0	10	0	2	872098	0	13646	8188
34058	MEARS	91	92	69	3	18	2	2	5	15	0	4	858000	0	13001	13001
34059	MECOSTA: NEW HOPE	226	216	99	2	67	200	37	20	28	0	3	847703	255265	30307	5500
34060	MIDDLEVILLE	222	220	157	0	100	58	25	27	0	0	15	1300000	316841	21308	17415
34061	MONTAGUE	367	367	135	10	30	69	32	2	0	0	10	6531000	7075	28154	28154
34062	MUSKEGON HEIGHTS: TEMPLE	126	124	55	10	56	47	12	8	6	0	8	380258	0	24402	24402
34063	MUSKEGON: CENTRAL	218	203	82	0	37	5	0	0	0	0	1	3753567	35000	59646	2460
34064	MUSKEGON: CRESTWOOD	67	105	42	10	28	24	10	0	15	0	0	2312000	19500	7941	271
34065	MUSKEGON: LAKE HARBOR	393	386	182	48	71	107	37	0	0	0	4	3256501	0	41755	41755
34066	MUSKEGON: UNITY	24	20	13	8	4	7	0	0	0	0	0	502000	0	4083	4083

CONFERENCE Number	30-38 Church Benevolence Giving	39a Total ASKED for clergy pension	39b Total PAID for clergy pension	41a Base compensation paid to/for the Senior Pastor or other person assigned or appointed in the lead pastoral role to the church	41b Base compensation paid to/for all Associate Pastor(s) and other pastoral staff assigned or appointed to the church. Include deacons and other clergy in this role	41c & 42c Deacons salary/benefits	40,42a-44 Pastoral Benefits	45 Total amount paid in salary and benefits for all other church staff and diaconal ministers	46 Total amount spent for local church program expenses	47 Total amount spent for other local church operating expenses	48 & 49 Local Church capital expenses	50 TOTAL CHURCH EXPENSES (Sum of Lines 29a through 49)	51 Number of giving units	52 Total income for annual budget/spending plan	53 Total income for designated causes including capital campaign and other special projects	54 Total income from connectional and other institutional sources outside the local church
34048	7645	3600	3000	40000	0	0	15100	50289	20838	38300	84533	271955	56	171428	27860	0
34049	520	1100	1100	22510	0	0		13526	308	21663	0	62522	20	81252	0	0
34050	625	5893	1473	36013	0	0	14362	9255	1566	14360	3070	83548	66	85031	4700	0
34051	5748	7332	7332	41116	6185	0	29823	49212	7511	46374	2507	219903	90	207232	16924	0
34052	21945	10598	10598	64422	0	0	27846	40887	17794	61838	20230	285643	88	265742	14637	0
34053	55207	3500	3500	8885	0	0	46560	23316	3339	39789	24660	232701	50	156764	30127	0
34054	31908	8851	8851	60365	0	0	34318	69200	74581	67026	47155	425463	147	335747	55051	0
34055	9320	7080	7080	39000	0	0	43570	39009	9192	24402	63713	258209	57	207560	17434	0
34056	1649	2400	750	16000	0	0	6040	8722	7261	14487	16000	72707	28	56760	0	0
34057	1120	6300	6300	42000	0	0	27421	19816	5351	38828	32963	181987	60	144415	12482	0
34058	14984	4586	4586	25601	0	0	13405	8059	11140	17320	4586	112682	39	140743	0	4710
34059	2736	8266	8266	63629	0	0	23573	39173	15312	67293	37380	262862	123	225323	16553	0
34060	8073	7162	7162	45868	0	0	45410	29378	5408	31939	70666	261319	141	257547	33866	0
34061	5796	8280	8280	55200	0	0	16437	77401	13320	62852	132440	399880	120	251304	15300	1200
34062	7672	7393	7393	49288	0	0	29682	50269	5626	34210	2200	210742	85	205650	1649	0
34063	14714	9486	9486	58650	0	0	44317	120762	23898	144573	38722	457582	106	355319	35753	0
34064	380	1171	1171	15312	0	0		7220	500	21195	75460	121509	35	57050	2500	0
34065	24969	10363	10363	69089	0	0	8975	122537	24524	55239	73563	431014	184	371192	13927	0
34066	948	765	765	13051	0	0	769	5450	768	8322	0	34156	9	28323	0	0

MW

STATISTICAL INFORMATION

MW

Conf. No.	Church Name	1	4	7	9	10	11	13	18a	19a	20b	21	24 & 25	26 & 27	28a	29a
34067	NEWAYGO	83	78	70	13	131	41	38	0	27	0	2	1161808	0	15149	15149
34068	NORTH MUSKEGON: COMMUNITY	355	348	106	0	65	135	50	10	20	32	3	1045000	0	27046	27046
34069	PALO	12	11	6	0	4	9	9	0	0	0	0	464485	0	1282	100
34070	PARIS	36	35	26	0	30	9	0	0	0	0	1	810171	0	4521	4521
34071	PARMELEE	50	43	23	0	0	0	0	0	0	0	0	229603	0	4007	4007
34072	PENTWATER: CENTENARY	141	134	74	11	0	25	8	0	17	0	5	2546829	0	21218	21218
34073	PIERSON: HERITAGE	211	208	89	0	84	72	10	0	0	0	6	921914	114728	18720	18720
34074	RAVENNA	62	62	41	0	9	36	11	0	0	0	3	509500	0	13454	1487
34075	ROCKFORD	415	401	227	0	8	253	39	0	0	0	5	6969814	525939	64608	64607
34076	RODNEY	16	15	10	0	15	13	0	3	0	0	0	139760	0	1540	1540
34077	SALEM: INDIAN MISSION	24	24	12	0	0	13	6	0	0	0	30	358795	9150	1994	0
34078	SAND LAKE	14	14	23	0	14	59	5	0	0	0	0	41886	0	2299	2299
34079	SHELBY	66	61	47	3	4	16	6	0	5	0	5	1775000	56497	11071	2500
34080	SITKA	26	26	15	0	0	26	13	0	0	0	0	700000	0	2173	2173
34081	SOUTH ENSLEY	47	49	32	0	115	15	13	0	7	0	0	106879	0	5347	5347
34082	SPARTA	190	176	121	0	90	33	50	20	44	0	3	1410219	0	35450	18109
34083	STANWOOD: NORTHLAND	126	128	95	37	0	108	58	0	20	0	3	2222225	0	18197	16842
34084	TURK LAKE	35	35	20	0	0	17	13	0	0	0	4	1394001	0	4091	4091
34085	TWIN LAKE	87	89	45	3	12	21	19	0	0	0	2	1657230	0	6056	6056

Column key:
1 — Total professing members reported at the close of last year
4 — TOTAL PROFESSING MEMBERS reported at the close of this year
7 — Average attendance at all weekly worship services
9 — Total Baptized Members who have not become Professing Members
10 — Number of other constituents of the church
11 — TOTAL Christian Formation Group Participants (Total of line 11a-d)
13 — Average weekly attendance (all ages) in Sunday Church School or other weekly education classes
18a — Membership in United Methodist Men
19a — Membership in United Methodist Women
20b — Number of persons sent out on UMVIM teams from this local church
21 — Total Number of community ministries for outreach, justice, and mercy offered by this local church
24 & 25 — Value of church assets and buildings
26 & 27 — Church Debt
28a — Amount APPORTIONED to the local church by the CONFERENCE
29a — Amount PAID by the local church to the CONFERENCE for all apportioned causes

STATISTICAL INFORMATION

CONFERENCE Number	30-38 Church Benevolence Giving	39a Total ASKED for clergy pension	39b Total PAID for clergy pension	41a Base compensation paid to/for the Senior Pastor or other person assigned or appointed in the lead pastoral role to the church	41b Base compensation paid to/for all Associate Pastor(s) and other pastoral staff assigned or appointed to the church. Include deacons and other clergy in this role	41c & 42c Deacons salary/benefits	40, 42a-44 Pastoral Benefits	45 Total amount paid in salary and benefits for all other church staff and diaconal ministers	46 Total amount spent for local church program expenses	47 Total amount spent for other local church operating expenses	48 & 49 Local Church capital expenses	50 TOTAL CHURCH EXPENSES (Sum of Lines 29a through 49)	51 Number of giving units	52 Total income for annual budget/spending plan	53 Total income for designated causes including capital campaign and other special projects	54 Total income from connectional and other institutional sources outside the local church
34067	2530	4433	0	29580	0	0	9178	27576	2150	44069	350	130582	76	112076	4529	0
34068	25948	9000	9000	60000	0	0	5949	48731	5976	46431	2500	231581	130	224253	10429	0
34069	0	240	240	4000	0	0	626	0	104	4895	175	10140	7	6424		0
34070	5955	780	780	12506	0	0	6264	795	0	5135	0	35956	35	47708	2292	0
34071	450	957	957	19136	0	0	187	0	425	9857	11089	35019	24	37655	0	0
34072	6836	1938	1938	55000	0	0	6369	19018	17309	30841	13992	169618	105	165270	39225	0
34073	191	5893	5893	39289	0	0	25730	15335	1323	28332	4131	148805	52	149794	35528	0
34074	8107	5941	4951	36490	0	0	13023	10528	5670	15843		100230	62	94071	5440	0
34075	30783	8928	8928	51356	0	0	33405	189591	28267	165523	125636	698096	300	634107	21922	0
34076	632	780	780	2690	0	0	1756	292	160	303	61	8214	15	9839	798	0
34077	2000	3269		10700	0	0	2500	2000	200	5000	1000	23400	5	11950	2949	500
34078	2235	573	573	1814	0	0	1003	575	2009	11842	4330	26680	19	28362	330	0
34079	5750	1784	1784	11261	0	0	4535	7390	3230	16554	0	53004	48	59910	900	0
34080	1516	148	148	3125	0	0	712	0	1163	4675	290	13802	15	10461	1167	0
34081	4990	1205	1205	3771	0	0	7530	4180	5333	11188	8319	43544	42	49874	3469	0
34082	3458	10097	10097	68661	0	0	32218	58336	8205	53374	2164	260777	120	270122	23539	0
34083	3432	9818	9818	52031	0	0	20429	32850	3012	18844	0	159422	95	168699	2566	0
34084	2247	1146	1146	9552	0	0	1439	3975	778	9170	4082	32398	14	35537	4052	0
34085	3062	1300	1300	10000	0	0	17570	8800	4592	16937		72399	44	62745		0

MW

Conference Number	CHURCH NAME	Total professing members reported at the close of last year (1)	TOTAL PROFESSING MEMBERS reported at the close of this year (4)	Average attendance at all weekly worship services (7)	Total Baptized Members who have not become Professing Members (9)	Number of other constituents of the church (10)	TOTAL Christian Formation Group Participants (Total of lines 11a-d) (11)	Average weekly attendance (all ages) in Sunday Church School or other weekly education classes (13)	Membership in United Methodist Men (18a)	Membership in United Methodist Women (19a)	Number of persons sent out on UMVIM teams from this local church (20b)	Total Number of community ministries for outreach, justice, and mercy offered by this local church (21)	Value of church assets and buildings (24 & 25)	Church Debt (26 & 27)	Amount APPORTIONED to the local church by the CONFERENCE (28a)	Amount PAID by the local church to the CONFERENCE for all apportioned causes (29a)
34086	VICKERYVILLE	12	8	6	0	5	0	0	0	0	0	0	495143	0	1475	1475
34087	WALKERVILLE	11	10	22	10	32	8	8	0	0	0	9	446746	0	3312	3312
34088	WAYLAND	113	113	53	101	70	76	25	0	0	0	0	3115518	0	13825	9863
34089	WHITE CLOUD	126	123	101	52	78	77	49	10	0	0	1	2827000	0	18670	18670
34090	WOLF LAKE	102	102	45	4	26	68	19	0	0	0	7	2568800	0	13169	5926
34091	WYOMING PARK	116	76	64	0	24	74	60	0	0	0	5	3053000	239368	16381	9450
34092	WYOMING: WESLEY PARK	283	282	180	124	120	41	30	0	15	0	8	4993436	448969	41626	24976
	NORTHERN SKIES DISTRICT															
31001	ALGONQUIN	54	58	23	0	1	10	0	0	10	0	2	260000	0	5227	5227
31002	AMASA: GRACE	25	24	13	2	0	4	4	0	0	0	5	35222	0	2021	2021
31003	BARK RIVER	77	76	17	0	15	23	18	0	0	0	5	182045	0	2716	2716
31004	BERGLAND	14	15	15	0	16	1	0	0	0	0	0	229275	1377	2723	2723
31005	CALUMET	99	98	45	0	0	0	0	0	24	0	1	689500	0	6403	6403
31006	CHEBOYGAN: ST PAUL'S	249	249	107	0	91	72	25	12	40	0	0	3051689	0	20753	14170
31007	CRYSTAL FALLS: CHRIST	125	125	42	1	0	70	0	15	16	0	0	1806586	0	9474	9474
31008	EMMETT CNTY: NEW HOPE	45	64	46	0	54	35	4	0	0	0	8	1010348	0	7537	7537
31009	ENGADINE	41	41	28	0	54	55	6	0	15	1	0	633160	0	5155	5155
31010	ESCANABA: CENTRAL	176	173	59	21	38	53	38	0	0	0	5	1406039	0	17575	17575
31011	ESCANABA: FIRST	107	108	45	20	39	19	8	0	0	0	4	1949889	744	11392	0

CONFERENCE Number	30-38 Church Benevolence Giving	39a Total ASKED for clergy pension	39b Total PAID for clergy pension	41a Base compensation paid to/for the Senior Pastor or other person assigned or appointed in the lead pastoral role to the church	41b Base compensation paid to/for all Associate Pastor(s) and other pastoral staff assigned or appointed to the church. Include deacons and other clergy in this role	41c & 42c Deacons salary/benefits	40,42a-44 Pastoral Benefits	45 Total amount paid in salary and benefits for all other church staff and diaconal ministers	46 Total amount spent for local church program expenses	47 Total amount spent for other local church operating expenses	48 & 49 Local Church capital expenses	50 TOTAL CHURCH EXPENSES (Sum of Lines 29a through 49)	51 Number of giving units	52 Total income for annual budget/spending plan	53 Total income for designated causes including capital campaign and other special projects	54 Total income from connectional and other institutional sources outside the local church
34086	153	240	240	4000	0	0	626	0	104	6454	240	13292	6	10868	469	0
34087	53	438	438	3465	0	0	10083	0	0	12854	0	30205	12	29369	1282	0
34088	1859	8973	8973	57548	0	0	11648	21371	1793	21890	0	134945	44	130781	9365	0
34089	3773	7501	7501	45000	0	0	80513	25999	7062	40863	6000	235381	61	173806	2190	0
34090	1459	1316	1316	5789	0	0	17366	24398	12825	32789	0	101868	30	106619	12580	0
34091	7722	2813	2813	23192	0	0	12913	25589	1580	44186	48273	175718	33	149269	18443	0
34092	5174	9508	9508	60694	0	0	39842	108645	18466	63307	108994	439606	129	430959	4019	0
31001	1735	1080	1080	7200	0	0	2730	1490	3792	4424	0	27678	18	27341	2360	0
31002	200	600	250	3401	0	0	350	0	0	7000	0	13222	20	15834	0	0
31003	1416	1645	1645	13535	0	0	5799	0	1024	3334	0	29469	28	22051	27750	0
31004	200	852	852	5097	0	0	1250	0	400	3203	910	14635	14	13005	699	0
31005	16	2157	2157	12994	0	0	3009	4865	0	27843	0	57287	55	49337	1000	0
31006	2903	7575	7575	50500	0	0	26251	32009	5468	27161	6249	172286	150	167500	20893	0
31007	1958	5456	5356	0	0	0	3183	6744	1872	14789	0	41504	70	58400	600	0
31008	3630	2340	2340	21503	0	0	34198	0	3581	17482	6929	95491	37	79195	12129	0
31009	8468	3012	3012	18604	0	0	6481			8258	9514	63073	35	58033		3600
31010	1696	6210	6210	41403	0	0	16705	25219	5867	36212	2986	153873	90	156425	9678	0
31011	16757	2502	2502	20022	0	0	12207	10207	3226	23373	6114	94408	33	67476	25303	2333

STATISTICAL INFORMATION

NS

Conference Number	CHURCH NAME	1 Total professing members reported at the close of last year	4 TOTAL PROFESSING MEMBERS reported at the close of this year	7 Average attendance at all weekly worship services	9 Total Baptized Members who have not become Professing Members	10 Number of other constituents of the church	11 TOTAL Christian Formation Group Participants (Total of lines 11a-d)	13 Average weekly attendance (all ages) in Sunday Church School or other weekly education classes	18a Membership in United Methodist Men	19a Membership in United Methodist Women	20b Number of persons sent out on UMVIM teams from this local church	21 Total Number of community ministries for outreach, justice, and mercy offered by this local church	24 & 25 Value of church assets and buildings	26 & 27 Church Debt	28a Amount APPORTIONED to the local church by the CONFERENCE	29a Amount PAID by the local church to the CONFERENCE for all apportioned causes
31012	EWEN	23	23	15	4	16	7	1	0	0	0	0	186000	0	2159	2159
31013	FAITHORN	30	27	24	6	19	7	0	0	0	0	0	93500	0	1508	1508
31014	GERMFASK	24	25	19	0	0	0	0	0	8	0	3	513852	0	2543	0
31015	GLADSTONE: MEMORIAL	277	266	91	42	47	60	24	0	0	0	19	3491703	0	22057	14715
31016	GRAND MARAIS	11	11	10	0	31	2	0	0	0	0	6	557005	0	2799	540
31017	GREENLAND	41	41	21	0	15	0	0	0	11	0	5	382000	0	2043	2043
31018	GWINN	225	224	80	37	172	136	26	0	32	0	5	2795000	5000	17047	17047
31019	HANCOCK: FIRST	298	298	81	44	49	90	42	0	27	0	21	4264000	2291	20969	20969
31020	HERMANSVILLE: FIRST	65	67	23	3	0	0	5	0	0	0	0	173295	0	4105	3211
31021	HOUGHTON: GRACE	254	118	98	10	36	58	15	0	0	0	0	1691481	0	17931	0
31022	HULBERT: TAHQUAMENON	7	7	8	0	36	6	6	0	0	0	0	376332	0	1040	1040
31023	IRON MOUNTAIN: FIRST	66	64	34	25	30	29	16	10	18	0	17	1872385	59681	8701	8701
31024	IRON MOUNTAIN: TRINITY	304	299	99	28	137	62	17	0	39	16	4	4386131	131389	25877	25877
31025	IRONWOOD: WESLEY	126	128	47	0	0	7	7	0	21	0	2	103385	0	8653	8653
31026	ISHPEMING: WESLEY	550	535	125	0	0	102	29	0	0	0	5	5390923	0	28040	28040
31027	LAKE LINDEN	122	108	34	52	51	7	5	0	15	0	1	630000	0	4190	4190
31028	L'ANSE	196	197	51	20	20	43	21	0	30	0	0	1418324	0	12623	12623
31029	MANISTIQUE: FIRST	112	108	117	0	20	79	43	20	0	0	3	1449833	0	10845	10845
31030	MACKINAW CITY: CHURCH OF THE STRA	154	152	45	1	0	22	16	0	24	0	3	30614	0	9569	9569

STATISTICAL INFORMATION

CONFERENCE Number	30-38 Church Benevolence Giving	39a Total ASKED for clergy pension	39b Total PAID for clergy pension	41a Base compensation paid to/for the Senior Pastor or other person assigned or appointed in the lead pastoral role to the church	41b Base compensation paid to/for all Associate Pastor(s) and other pastoral staff assigned or appointed to the church. Include deacons and other clergy in this role	41c & 42c Deacons salary/benefits	40.42a-44 Pastoral Benefits	45 Total amount paid in salary and benefits for all other church staff and diaconal ministers	46 Total amount spent for local church program expenses	47 Total amount spent for other local church operating expenses	48 & 49 Local Church capital expenses	50 TOTAL CHURCH EXPENSES (Sum of Lines 29a through 49)	51 Number of giving units	52 Total income for annual budget/spending plan	53 Total income for designated causes including capital campaign and other special projects	54 Total income from connectional and other institutional sources outside the local church
31012	1833	852	852	8147	0	0	0	585	150	2373	0	16099	20	12638	10075	0
31013	1900	780	780	5200	0	0	2643	0	270	4612	0	16913	10	32278	0	0
31014	700	1074	1074	12548	0	0	5429	0	0	5100	0	24851	20	33303	0	0
31015	10859	7229	7229	48193	0	0	42148	43144	11684	35950	19574	233496	110	229471	59746	0
31016	678	1556	1556	12548	0	0	5387	0	100	4512	3892	29213	8	25891	1150	0
31017	2223	1271	1271	8075	0	0	3044	0	704	4823	805	22988	14	24919	1694	0
31018	1660	6788	6788	45255	0	0	8914	22295	6108	39615	9970	157652	117	135054	3712	500
31019	12801	7362	6749	48311	0	0	31338	23143	5363	43332	0	192006	83	187079	9577	0
31020	3939	1645	1645	13535	0	0	6130	0	41	7786	9804	46091	22	25918	1285	0
31021	5560	7365	6769	51361	0	0	26451	8324	3113	49098	0	150676	80	134592	4447	0
31022	1621	178	178	3522	3085	0	482	0	675	0	130	11170	23	12059	0	0
31023	4597	3551	3551	23676	0	0	8689	6642	2232	14709	21135	93932	35	79695	8007	9913
31024	18538	7371	7371	61421	0	0	29545	62937	4762	37442	9279	257172	160	214767	25567	3000
31025	3706	500	500	10000	0	0	2451	6592	250	22159	25771	80082	52	76287	1854	0
31026	8202	6732	6732	44017	0	0	40721	55928	33906	49676	56545	323767	93	304080	12913	0
31027	281	1068	1068	11341	0	0	7403	2350	1509	5379	1787	36884	44	40338	0	0
31028	7181	5329	5329	35524	0	0	18452	9350	9276	10664	6706	107338	36	104604	10975	0
31029	32130	9262	9262	61750	0	0	31589	46872	938	30751	0	232475	120	234932	2215	0
31030	4383	2283	2283	26620	0	0	12825	12107	0	29036	1163	98924	51	107277	19639	0

NS

CONFERENCE Number	CHURCH NAME	Total professing members reported at the close of last year (1)	TOTAL PROFESSING MEMBERS reported at the close of this year (4)	Average attendance at all weekly worship services (7)	Total Baptized Members who have not become Professing Members (9)	Number of other constituents of the church (10)	TOTAL Christian Formation Group Participants (Total of lines 11a-d) (11)	Average weekly attendance (all ages) in Sunday Church School or other weekly education classes (13)	Membership in United Methodist Men (18a)	Membership in United Methodist Women (19a)	Number of persons sent out on UMW/UMVIM teams from this local church (20b)	Total Number of community ministries for outreach, justice, and mercy offered by this local church (21)	Value of church assets and buildings (24 & 25)	Church Debt (26 & 27)	Amount APPORTIONED to the local church by the CONFERENCE (28a)	Amount PAID by the local church to the CONFERENCE for all apportioned causes (29a)
31031	MARQUETTE: HOPE	314	334	145	32	115	144	20	16	34	0	5	9642000	0	23183	8755
31032	MCMILLAN	14	14	7	0	10	0	8	0	10	0	2	357500	0	3061	3061
31033	MENOMINEE: FIRST	86	76	51	0	0	36	10	10	33	0	0	1495040	297761	13395	13395
31034	MICHIGAMME: WOODLAND	22	22	15	0	12	1	1	0	0	0	0	553013	0	3131	3131
31035	MOHAWK AHMEEK	27	30	15	5	31	47	8	0	0	0	0	112000	0	3331	0
31036	MUNISING	71	69	34	46	17	33	27	0	0	0	11	1100017	0	7026	7026
31037	NEGAUNEE: MITCHELL	213	212	56	0	0	24	7	12	18	0	3	4615495	0	20943	2000
31038	NEWBERRY	90	90	32	34	26	8	3	0	12	0	5	1119500	0	8969	8969
31039	NORWAY: GRACE	148	145	60	0	3	8	0	0	0	0	0	836000	0	10208	5083
31040	ONTONAGON	131	130	25	9	26	8	0	0	15	0	0	1575346	0	5851	5851
31041	PAINESDALE: ALBERT PAINE MEM.	42	42	17	0	26	8	0	0	0	0	4	109184	0	1948	1948
31042	PARADISE	31	31	22	42	75	31	0	0	0	0	6	753000	0	3391	3391
31043	PICKFORD	209	208	157	0	17	12	25	0	0	0	0	2233113	0	16986	13589
31044	QUINNESEC	56	50	25	0	19	7	4	3	0	0	6	663000	0	5430	5430
31045	REPUBLIC	43	41	17	2	18	0	0	0	16	0	7	250000	0	4500	4500
31046	ROCKLAND: ST PAUL'S	66	64	22	67	60	90	20	0	0	0	0	1092395	0	3476	3476
31047	SAULT STE MARIE: CENTRAL	162	167	85	0	0	7	0	0	31	12	5	6980972	0	21589	21589
31048	SIDNAW	16	15	13	0	7	0	0	0	0	0	0	137521	0	1870	1870
31049	ST IGNACE	171	170	75	13	77	40	15	0	30	0	4	1602252	0	17580	17580

STATISTICAL INFORMATION

CONFERENCE Number	Church Benevolence Giving (30-38)	Total ASKED for clergy pension (39a)	Total PAID for clergy pension (39b)	Base compensation paid to/for the Senior Pastor or other person assigned or appointed in the lead pastoral role to the church (41a)	Base compensation paid to/for all Associate Pastor(s) and other pastoral staff assigned or appointed to the church. Include deacons and other clergy in this role (41b)	Deacons salary/benefits (41c & 42c)	Pastoral Benefits (40, 42a-44)	Total amount paid in salary and benefits for all other church staff and diaconal ministers (45)	Total amount spent for local church program expenses (46)	Total amount spent for other local church operating expenses (47)	Local Church capital expenses (48 & 49)	TOTAL CHURCH EXPENSES (Sum of Lines 29a through 49) (50)	Number of giving units (51)	Total income for annual budget/spending plan (52)	Total income for designated causes including capital campaign and other special projects (53)	Total income from connectional and other institutional sources outside the local church (54)
31031	4931	16972	16972	55105	55105	0	28610	77263	18978	98282	18252	382253	121	231309	16742	30000
31032	1518	1074	1074	12548	0	0	5387	0	350	4512	0	28450	10	25612	3588	0
31033	3555	2486	2486	19124	0	0	9146	21250	3330	23475	30465	126226	59	110186	16203	0
31034	2352	1110	1110	9300	2871	0	2552	1029	794	5612	0	24851	16	29286	0	0
31035	410	1348	1348	4763	0	0	4561	7827	250	3786	0	19018	12	15670	0	0
31036	5889	1253	1253	23574	0	0	7331	37201	3149	13756	4684	69805	48	62163	6508	2300
31037	5426	7249	7249	48379	0	0	33760	5235	2226	19722	19251	160647	78	146193	628	0
31038	5247	3682	3682	24546	0	0	8855	5500	2123	17060	0	94968	50	84814	7573	0
31039	3179	5220	5220	34800	0	0	16849	1686	1110	16636	82640	88377	57	93529	0	0
31040	1528	2917	2917	18512	0	0	808	723	500	15008	1762	128642	35	45590	2076	5000
31041	1645	659	659	10000	0	0	33	29	804	7371	0	25720	24	32061	1796	0
31042	506	398	398	9400	0	0	26228		0	8932	13080	22689	30	33845	41624	1000
31043	22004	8006	8006	53372	0	0	4519	32458	23171	54097	3380	246005	110	208720	428	0
31044	4279	2368	2368	15792	0	0	3303	4360	1138	14624	0	55890	23	48254	0	0
31045	150	1110	1110	9300	0	0		3725	311	5527	0	27926	28	28620	3694	0
31046	1950	1856	1856	0	0	0		24564	620	6166	21466	38632	20	28590	3063	0
31047	21093	5670	5670	36913	0	0	15991	37621	17891	34243	6120	212467	71	239103	915	0
31048	1725	355	355	4737	0	0	780	1390	1480	7242	0	25699	11	20383	5710	0
31049	7169	6413	6413	37946	0	0	31621	19591	10670	22455	22949	176394	102	147419		

SI

STATISTICAL INFORMATION

CONFERENCE Number	CHURCH NAME	1 Total professing members reported at the close of last year	4 TOTAL PROFESSING MEMBERS reported at the close of this year	7 Average attendance at all weekly worship services	9 Total Baptized Members who have not become Professing Members	10 Number of other constituents of the church	11 TOTAL Christian Formation Group Participants (Total of lines 11a-d)	13 Average weekly attendance (all ages) in Sunday Church School or other weekly education classes	18a Membership in United Methodist Men	19a Membership in United Methodist Women	20b Number of persons sent out on UMVIM teams from this local church	21 Total Number of community ministries for outreach, justice, and mercy offered by this local church	24 & 25 Value of church assets and buildings	26 & 27 Church Debt	28a Amount APPORTIONED to the local church by the CONFERENCE	29a Amount PAID by the local church to the CONFERENCE for all apportioned causes
31050	STEPHENSON	62	60	33	13	10	9	5	5	15	0	1	821771	0	7869	7869
31051	TRENARY	21	20	15	0	9	5	0	0	0	0	4	643423	0	2432	2432
31052	WAKEFIELD	28	32	23	0	8	4	4	0	0	0	1	272000	0	2595	2595
31053	WHITE PINE COMMUNITY	72	70	35	11	14	13	12	0	20	0	3	913652	0	4586	4586
31054	ZEBA	29	33	20	0	10	0	0	0	0	0	0	398666	0	3248	3248
	NORTHERN WATERS DISTRICT															
32001	ALANSON	34	36	20	0	0	0	0	0	0	0	0	509264	23334	6281	0
32002	ALBA	25	23	10	0	51	14	4	0	0	0	0	111000	0	3394	0
32003	ALDEN	59	65	33	9	30	16	6	0	24	7	2	1478000	0	11919	11919
32004	ALPENA: FIRST	241	228	82	0	22	30	13	8	0	0	2	4317384	0	25352	0
32005	ARCADIA	17	17	16	0	20	4	4	0	8	0	0	160000	0	2777	2222
32006	ASHTON	34	32	19	0	0	3	2	0	0	0	0	682755	0	4110	4110
32007	AVONDALE	8	8	14	0	0	0	0	0	0	0	5	131237	0	899	899
32008	BALDWIN: COVENANT CMNTY	37	36	38	0	33	21	2	0	0	0	3	755000	0	8911	8911
32009	BARNARD	65	64	43	0	35	15	12	0	17	0	0	506218	0	2952	2952
32010	BEAR LAKE	74	74	40	0	20	25	0	0	10	0	1	1458774	0	14003	4624
32011	BELLAIRE: COMMUNITY	150	134	101	0	146	76	10	0	0	0	1	472829	0	16844	16844
32012	BOYNE CITY	60	56	42	0	0	31	1	0	0	0	0	964824	24314	9354	6901
32013	BOYNE FALLS	25	24	19	0	0	9	0	0	10	0	1	274730	0	3647	3085

CONFERENCE Number	30-38 Church Benevolence Giving	39a Total ASKED for clergy pension	39b Total PAID for clergy pension	41a Base compensation paid to/for the Senior Pastor or other person assigned or appointed in the lead pastoral role to the church	41b Base compensation paid to/for all Associate Pastor(s) and other pastoral staff assigned or appointed to the church. Include deacons and other clergy in this role	41c & 42b Deacons salary/benefits	40, 42a-44 Pastoral Benefits	45 Total amount paid in salary and benefits for all other church staff and diaconal ministers	46 Total amount spent for local church program expenses	47 Total amount spent for other local church operating expenses	48 & 49 Local Church capital expenses	50 TOTAL CHURCH EXPENSES (Sum of Lines 29a through 49)	51 Number of giving units	52 Total income for annual budget/spending plan	53 Total income for designated causes including capital campaign and other special projects	54 Total income from connectional and other institutional sources outside the local church
31050	6197	2223	2223	22205	0	0	5506	5431	865	15094	0	65390	29	62985	7298	0
31051	643	537	493	10008	0	0	2395			4710	0	20681	24	18632	3873	0
31052	7948	952	952	10000	0	0	11596	3170	1200	7926	0	45387	19	38712	1315	0
31053	3154	1396	1396	16463	3300	0	6584	2086	369	10485	5644	54067	50	47615	13003	3300
31054	760	1421	1421	9473	0	0	6160	840	1474	4618	0	27994	27	27900	260	0
32001	2148	1551	1551	12482	0	0	4403	10940	1919	9493	1050	43986	1	29896	3162	0
32002	0	1739	1304	11283	0	0	3447	1000	208	5000	0	22234	10	30500	0	0
32003	14609	5141	5141	35100	0	0	23558	10510	208	19344	0	120389	44	95421	25074	0
32004	5255	6347	6347	42310	0	0	29453	40434	3042	39881	0	166722	122	136292	14940	2000
32005	594	240	240	9275	0	0	7407	1175	998	3570	0	18074	22	4877	586	0
32006	1335	1459	1459	10506	0	0	0	1366	289	9752	55	36224	23	31621	2782	0
32007	820	240	240	0	0	0		2425	267	3432	0	8138	12	9632	495	0
32008	1606	2333	2333	19645	0	0	19461	0	1230	11004	30900	95090	33	85147	4390	10000
32009	4515	1940	1940	12936	0	0	8988	1588	1374	5998	15765	56056	49	40080	9160	0
32010	5040	650	650	12000	0	0	1472	17992	200	31692	4334	73670	75	77489		0
32011	5905	5675	5675	37000	0	0	29281	21154	6777	27864	0	154834	129	153436	3702	0
32012	6127	2567	2567	17113	0	0	11804	20693	3170	16534	0	84909	42	68962	4746	0
32013	822	1284	1284	8557	0	0	5145	5381	793	4277	0	29344	14	29552	529	0

STATISTICAL INFORMATION

NW

Conference Number	Church Name	Total professing members reported at the close of last year (1)	TOTAL PROFESSING MEMBERS reported at the close of this year (4)	Average attendance at all weekly worship services (7)	Total Baptized Members who have not become Professing Members (9)	Number of other constituents of the church (10)	TOTAL Christian Formation Group Participants (Total of lines 11a-d) (11)	Average weekly attendance (all ages) in Sunday Church School or other weekly education classes (13)	Membership in United Methodist Men (18a)	Membership in United Methodist Women (19a)	Number of persons sent out on UMVIM teams from this local church (20b)	Total Number of community ministries for outreach, justice, and mercy offered by this local church (21)	Value of church assets and buildings (24 & 25)	Church Debt (26 & 27)	Amount APPORTIONED to the local church by the CONFERENCE (28a)	Amount PAID by the local church to the CONFERENCE for all apportioned causes (29a)
32014	BRETHREN: EPWORTH	36	34	15	2	23	21	11	0	0	0	0	1042822	0	3444	2985
32077	BROOKS CORNERS	25	23	27	0	49	0	20	0	0	0	0	560000	0	6368	6368
32015	CADILLAC	383	365	114	142	58	53	10	10	71	0	1	3206565	0	34013	24311
32016	CADILLAC: SOUTH COMMUNITY	34	34	32	0	0	0	10	0	0	0	11	770643	0	4665	4665
32017	CENTRAL LAKE	25	24	13	0	1	6	0	0	0	0	0	827000	0	3501	3501
32018	CHARLEVOIX	86	82	31	0	0	8	0	0	21	0	0	3479180	0	11289	11101
32019	CHARLEVOIX: GREENSKY HILL	103	114	36	10	40	25	12	12	7	0	3	668478	0	6664	5666
32020	CHASE: BARTON	12	12	13	0	20	10	0	0	0	0	0	770000	0	5730	5730
32021	EAST BOARDMAN	26	26	35	0	0	23	14	0	0	0	2	541000	0	5295	0
32022	EAST JORDAN	112	111	50	61	40	27	8	0	10	0	2	1460162	0	11501	11501
32023	ELBERTA	27	30	31	25	0	0	0	0	0	0	2	571780	0	4020	4020
32024	EMPIRE	79	77	46	5	31	48	18	0	23	0	3	1588991	0	14224	14224
32025	EPSILON	42	42	38	0	16	22	9	0	20	0	0	424944	0	7139	7139
32026	EVART	80	81	47	0	60	14	5	0	0	0	3	467602	0	17134	750
32027	FIFE LAKE	36	35	50	0	33	8	13	0	10	0	2	874476	0	7379	7379
32028	FRANKFORT	106	111	77	50	0	7	10	0	75	0	0	2064970	0	19540	19540
32029	FREE SOIL - FOUNTAIN	30	30	15	5	35	7	10	0	0	0	12	909000	6000	2300	0
32030	GAYLORD: FIRST	579	551	265	205	142	147	43	15	0	0	3	4233070	0	39311	39311
32031	GRANT	61	52	52	0	13	30	9	0	0	0	3	624268	0	5376	5376

STATISTICAL INFORMATION

CONFERENCE Number	Church Benevolence Giving (30-38)	Total ASKED for clergy pension (39a)	Total PAID for clergy pension (39b)	Base compensation paid to/for the Senior Pastor or other person assigned or appointed in the lead pastoral role to the church (41a)	Base compensation paid to/for all Associate Pastor(s) and other pastoral staff assigned or appointed to the church. Include deacons and other clergy in this role (41b)	Deacons salary/benefits (41c & 42b)	Pastoral Benefits (40, 42a-44)	Total amount paid in salary and benefits for all other church staff and diaconal ministers (45)	Total amount spent for local church program expenses (46)	Total amount spent for other local church operating expenses (47)	Local Church capital expenses (48 & 49)	TOTAL CHURCH EXPENSES (Sum of Lines 29a through 49) (50)	Number of giving units (51)	Total income for annual budget/spending plan (52)	Total income for designated causes including capital campaign and other special projects (53)	Total income from connectional and other institutional sources outside the local church (54)
32014	382	771	771	9250	200	0	4308	3000	1387	7139	0	29422	34	45680	0	0
32077	17393	970	970	15600	0	0	2555	0	697	16055	1772	61410	17	56208	18636	0
32015	13726	11417	10466	59990	18188	0	37197	49291	10663	72228	37053	333113	260	253690	49944	0
32016	2912	3206	3206	21373	0	0	2179	1500	2512	8071	2534	48952	22	43277	3278	0
32017	1008	1714	1714	11425	0	0	10532	0	200	6086	0	34466	10	29980	500	0
32018	2108	2645	2645	21682	0	0	21977	16687	1095	12853	19373	109521	23	74621	30186	1500
32019	2153	3177	1324	12943	0	0	23549	3944	5238	17106	973	72896	98	42947	0	18500
32020	1110	1719	1473	9822	0	0	9730	0	1640	28468	0	57973	12	46557	1435	0
32021	1200	1377	1377	15598	0	0	8096	1158	1244	7814	1000	37487	35	49150	1500	0
32022	9480	4990	4990	33264	0	0	24624	19493	1411	12704	4557	122024	54	121364	13390	0
32023	2864	1611	1611	10742	0	0	2756	8937	3237	13674	4935	52776	45	45287	5514	4000
32024	3522	6954	6954	44696	0	0	26986	18751	4777	24787	3500	148197	47	141785	2485	0
32025	7095	2567	2567	17113	0	0	2504	4800	355	11994	12073	58501	20	44544	16449	20749
32026	4055	4945	4945	48177	0	0	17199	19961	1955	31093	13450	141585	43	132720	0	12445
32027	12912	1722	1722	11477	2987	0	7565	1523	1192	2071	635	49463	40	61355	230	5000
32028	9891	6445	6445	42966	0	0	8833	49967	8897	54911	50514	251964	104	179742	41493	0
32029	0	780	0	2715	0	0	0	0	1500	8400	2000	14615	18	14619	0	0
32030	13233	12097	12097	76482	0	0	41043	114693	22780	90071	11776	421486	304	471544	10174	0
32031	48	315	315	4500	10500	0	850	2400	5416	5131	0	34536	23	35875	745	0

NW

STATISTICAL INFORMATION

CONFERENCE Number	CHURCH NAME	1	4	7	9	10	11	13	18a	19a	20b	21	24 & 25	26 & 27	28a	29a
		Total professing members reported at the close of last year	TOTAL PROFESSING MEMBERS reported at the close of this year	Average attendance at all weekly worship services	Total Baptized Members who have not become Professing Members	Number of other constituents of the church	TOTAL Christian Formation Group Participants (Total of lines 11a-d)	Average weekly attendance (all ages) in Sunday Church School or other weekly education classes	Membership in United Methodist Men	Membership in United Methodist Women	Number of persons sent out on UMVIM teams from this local church	Total Number of community ministries for outreach, justice, and mercy offered by this local church	Value of church assets and buildings	Church Debt	Amount APPORTIONED to the local church by the CONFERENCE	Amount PAID by the local church to the CONFERENCE for all apportioned causes
32032	GRAWN	98	99	70	0	42	50	24	0	0	0	4	1031912	0	8724	8724
32033	GRAYLING: MICHELSON MEM.	226	218	103	0	83	24	0	0	42	0	5	2152450	17000	18887	6600
32034	HARBOR SPRINGS	72	54	40	0	0	0	0	0	18	0	1	2386269	38702	11226	0
32035	HARRIETTA	52	52	32	0	0	8	3	0	0	0	0	668000	0	6088	4867
32036	HERSEY	76	76	35	13	23	20	7	0	0	0	10	500800	0	6466	6466
32037	HILLMAN	101	103	61	27	35	71	12	0	4	0	4	564795	0	8249	8249
32038	HORTON BAY	32	32	30	0	0	10	8	0	0	0	0	423678	0	5122	5122
32039	HOUGHTON LAKE	426	367	157	8	127	91	19	0	26	4	6	2212000	2800	32007	18948
32040	INDIAN RIVER	267	252	212	7	306	179	45	0	0	54	12	1565112	157680	29164	29164
32041	KALKASKA	125	82	71	3	38	48	7	12	22	0	14	478162	247819	15433	11597
32042	KESWICK	60	54	57	0	82	55	35	1	0	0	9	972025	85576	14244	14244
32043	KEWADIN	43	37	31	4	30	0	3	0	18	0	0	1029369	0	7490	5999
32044	KEWADIN: INDIAN MISSION	20	20	10	0	0	0	0	0	0	0	0	500500	0	3235	3235
32045	KINGSLEY	142	145	126	1	35	90	35	0	0	0	7	1465451	0	10266	10266
32046	LAKE ANN	165	168	110	0	128	101	40	20	12	0	11	1803053	135000	18091	4636
32047	LAKE CITY	162	161	75	4	38	43	16	0	40	0	2	758847	49046	15796	15796
32048	LELAND	315	313	116	0	152	152	26	0	0	0	1	2658446	162699	33244	23271
32049	LEROY	83	80	40	0	151	9	3	0	0	0	2	879215	0	8017	8017
32050	LUDINGTON: ST PAUL	142	143	71	2	48	33	27	0	0	0	6	1980000	0	18502	13000

Column key:
- 30-38: Church Benevolence Giving
- 39a: Total ASKED for clergy pension
- 39b: Total PAID for clergy pension
- 41a: Base compensation paid to/for the Senior Pastor or other person assigned or appointed in the lead pastoral role to the church
- 41b: Base compensation paid to/for all Associate Pastor(s) and other pastoral staff assigned or appointed to the church. Include deacons and other clergy in this role
- 41c & 42c: Deacons salary/benefits
- 40, 42a-44: Pastoral Benefits
- 45: Total amount paid in salary and benefits for all other church staff and diaconal ministers
- 46: Total amount spent for local church program expenses
- 47: Total amount spent for other local church operating expenses
- 48 & 49: Local Church capital expenses
- 50: TOTAL CHURCH EXPENSES (Sum of Lines 29a through 49)
- 51: Number of giving units
- 52: Total income for annual budget/spending plan
- 53: Total income for designated causes including capital campaign and other special projects
- 54: Total income from connectional and other institutional sources outside the local church

CONFERENCE Number	30-38	39a	39b	41a	41b	41c & 42c	40, 42a-44	45	46	47	48 & 49	50	51	52	53	54
32032	9652	5511	5511	36739	0	0	22125	0	545	26769	25791	135856	56	88484	5806	0
32033	1988	6826	6826	45505	0	0	19807	28645	6645	36542	60400	212958	120	139043	19587	0
32034	0	2881	2641	23180	0	0	9005	14428	5197	28961	8777	92189	87	88410	1968	0
32035	0	2419	2419	9994	0	0	4347		2111	11047	0	34785	29	49577	4238	0
32036	1410	1302	1302	18692	0	0	6127	5495	2803	11646	3591	57532	41	56941	9433	0
32037	7181	2313	2313	18500	0	0	9449	13015	939	17832	6135	83613	51	75989	2365	0
32038	25	1170	1170	15600	5000	0	3596	350	1140	13852	0	40855	24	43884	10000	0
32039	5749	9000	9000	60000	0	0	38120	71403	14102	46231	20938	284491	137	246731	71015	5000
32040	16126	6810	6273	43000	0	0	33765	66698	22419	56613	94437	373495	135	127576	10866	4000
32041	2825	6125	5572	40831	0	0	27857	11252	3100	26749	47039	176822	25	147827	4810	0
32042	1963	6694	6694	40627	0	0	30702	5558	1234	17497	27494	146013	44	142289	4053	0
32043	2662	1200	1200	20000	0	0	2203	11360	1268	15764	0	60456	47	47006		23500
32044	0	900	0	10000	0	0	1200	0	50	4000	0	18485	0	0	0	24438
32045	880	5963	3479	39694	0	0	16535	26101	40535	26611	5719	169820	57	137394	17891	0
32046	10582	6183	6183	40000	0	0	24535	25909	6856	40248	26610	185559	100	180247	0	36529
32047	7220	6696	6696	55801	0	0	29593	12552	6666	25099	47591	207014	53	99071	3353	0
32048	6907	10120	10120	67465	0	0	20952	83587	12125	73734	53113	351274	136	298302	13756	0
32049	1944	3502	3502	23436	0	0	16813	3809	1856	11722	0	71099	29	72891	1660	0
32050	3200	5803	5803	40000	0	0	21800	27082	2500	15989	0	129374	64	142505	20897	0

STATISTICAL INFORMATION

Conference Number	CHURCH NAME	Total professing members reported at the close of last year (1)	TOTAL PROFESSING MEMBERS reported at the close of this year (4)	Average attendance at all weekly worship services (7)	Total Baptized Members who have not become Professing Members (9)	Number of other constituents of the church (10)	TOTAL Christian Formation Group Participants (Total of lines 11a-d) (11)	Average weekly attendance (all ages) in Sunday Church School or other weekly education classes (13)	Membership in United Methodist Men (18a)	Membership in United Methodist Women (19a)	Number of persons sent out on UMVIM teams from this local church (20b)	Total Number of community ministries for outreach, justice, and mercy offered by this local church (21)	Value of church assets and buildings (24 & 25)	Church Debt (26 & 27)	Amount APPORTIONED to the local church by the CONFERENCE (28a)	Amount PAID by the local church to the CONFERENCE for all apportioned causes (29a)
32051	LUDINGTON: UNITED	316	315	182	31	249	117	22	0	129	8	15	4529662	73418	39066	39066
32052	LUTHER	25	23	18	0	31	21	0	0	0	0	1	252699	0	3318	3318
32053	MANCELONA	97	89	45	0	131	13	6	0	21	0	22	612670	0	10805	10805
32054	MANISTEE	323	320	153	8	237	99	14	0	70	0	6	1360314	2054	32608	32120
32055	MANTON	123	117	78	0	27	16	8	0	0	0	0	1327000	5	9632	9632
32056	MARION	94	93	38	0	0	0	8	0	12	0	0	915055	0	6781	6781
32057	MERRITT-BUTTERFIELD	55	52	59	0	80	0	12	0	0	0	0	1229080	0	8481	8481
32058	MESICK	57	53	20	0	16	5	4	0	0	0	6	315813	0	6190	600
32059	MILLERSBURG	61	61	22	0	0	5	0	0	2	0	2	125000	0	4171	0
32060	MOORESTOWN-STITTSVILLE	43	43	45	0	0	16	5	0	0	0	2	458606	0	4709	4709
32061	NORTHPORT: INDIAN MISSION	50	43	20	0	0	0	0	0	0	0	0	415000	0	1996	1996
32062	NORWOOD	8	8	5	0	0	4	4	0	0	0	0	300400	0	1631	0
32063	OLD MISSION PENINSULA	95	86	40	0	25	36	17	0	0	0	7	1077187	0	12901	12901
32064	ONAWAY	200	199	73	0	62	105	15	0	40	0	3	509560	0	14389	2865
32065	OSSINEKE	101	101	48	15	30	40	14	0	10	0	0	1119179	4800	12399	7439
32066	PETOSKEY	469	478	138	84	182	78	4	0	60	15	4	1868973	175335	44337	44337
32067	REED CITY	285	234	86	19	145	48	8	0	0	0	4	3060000	0	21761	15750
32068	ROSCOMMON: GOOD SHEPHERD	220	205	151	0	67	41	8	0	0	0	4	3346565	387281	27692	2769
32069	SCOTTVILLE	123	124	789	9	50	46	23	0	76	0	8	3288494	49292	15971	65

NW

CONFERENCE Number	Church Benevolence Giving (30-38)	Total ASKED for clergy pension (39a)	Total PAID for clergy pension (39b)	Base compensation paid to/for the Senior Pastor or other person assigned or appointed in the lead pastoral role to the church (41a)	Base compensation paid to/for all Associate Pastor(s) and other pastoral staff assigned or appointed to the church. Include deacons and other clergy in this role (41b)	Deacons salary/benefits (41c & 42c)	Pastoral Benefits (40, 42a-44)	Total amount paid in salary and benefits for all other church staff and diaconal ministers (45)	Total amount spent for local church program expenses (46)	Total amount spent for other local church operating expenses (47)	Local Church capital expenses (48 & 49)	TOTAL CHURCH EXPENSES (Sum of Lines 29a through 49) (50)	Number of giving units (51)	Total income for annual budget/spending plan (52)	Total income for designated causes including capital campaign and other special projects (53)	Total income from connectional and other institutional sources outside the local church (54)
32051	28562	10225	10225	68015	0	0	28919	80899	9526	142821	101038	509071	192	330871	94693	0
32052	771	875	875	5837	0	0	4203	425	538	9100	14908	39975	13	26154	8091	0
32053	8279	4056	4056	27043	0	0	19214	6711	1793	24185	2542	104628	64	95324	15759	0
32054	23884	8968	8968	56158	0	0	11667	116413	37499	40116	4929	331754	137	316483	46789	0
32055	125	4174	3826	27828	0	0	12612	12383	2000	22851	1200	92457	56	115757	0	0
32056	2844	3918	3918	25022	0	0	0	3755	1510	13426	0	57256	22	44560	2925	0
32057	5757	5540	5540	26942	0	0	15304	7566	4967	15613	10271	100441	49	80557	14878	5500
32058	225	771	771	7500	0	0	4704	0	3575	9898	0	27273	25	35730	1438	0
32059	928	1845	1845	11150	0	0	7441	3384	1467	11430	0	37645	26	32985	1405	0
32060	18618	3118	2396	21168	0	0	12023	1819	6763	10023	4500	82019	35	54783	18598	4400
32061	50	3437	2266	20458	0	0	4248	0	6850	14869	0	50737	40	16115	4242	34000
32062	200	240	0	3000	0	0	1000	0	200	4000	0	8400	5	10300	100	0
32063	5609	5990	5990	39932	0	0	21650	5027	267	23820	0	115196	33	117335	10000	1500
32064	7207	4305	4305	28698	0	0	21370	10938	2962	22980	21789	123114	67	95020	18458	3250
32065	908	6543	6543	40934	0	0	20145	12460	792	16041	313	105575	51	103144	100	0
32066	36027	11193	11193	74620	0	0	28607	130751	12793	80328	86595	505251	241	369826	108700	0
32067	3752	7558	7558	48766	0	0	25128	29634	1800	50453	0	182841	124	173428	12948	0
32068	6807	7300	6700	52824	0	0	24028	74277	5849	41546	58898	273698	0	0	69290	0
32069	2766	5382	5382	35880	0	0	31210	22255	5214	25308	17760	145840	80	136608	12728	0

STATISTICAL INFORMATION

NW

CONFERENCE Number	CHURCH NAME	Total professing members reported at the close of last year (1)	TOTAL PROFESSING MEMBERS reported at the close of this year (4)	Average attendance at all weekly worship services (7)	Total Baptized Members who have not become Professing Members (9)	Number of other constituents of the church (10)	TOTAL Christian Formation Group Participants (Total of lines 11a-d) (11)	Average weekly attendance (all ages) in Sunday Church School or other weekly education classes (13)	Membership in United Methodist Men (18a)	Membership in United Methodist Women (19a)	Number of persons sent out on UMVIM teams from this local church (20b)	Total Number of community ministries for outreach, justice, and mercy offered by this local church (21)	Value of church assets and buildings (24 & 25)	Church Debt (26 & 27)	Amount APPORTIONED to the local church by the CONFERENCE (28a)	Amount PAID by the local church to the CONFERENCE for all apportioned causes (29a)
32070	SEARS	11	11	14	0	18	9	4	0	0	0	1	50000	0	1736	0
32071	SOUTH BOARDMAN	10	10	12	0	30	5	5	0	0	0	2	509490	0	1117	1117
32072	SPRATT	70	69	38	2	21	13	0	0	12	0	0	731224	0	6870	6870
32073	TRAVERSE BAY	191	167	131	157	58	50	42	0	0	5	10	827000	0	28847	28847
32074	TRAVERSE CITY: CENTRAL	1070	1011	483	0	305	505	207	0	92	0	8	5150066	0	120077	120077
32076	WILLIAMSBURG	63	61	57	0	57	14	8	0	0	0	2	678863	0	13350	13350
	DISTRICT TOTALS															
	CLOSED	454	450	185	13	190	165	42	0	6	0	9	7324005	251108	49423	11024
	CENTRAL BAY	12247	12007	5450	973	3593	4545	1489	251	4742	465	372	163533839	1855629	1307631	1007522
	EAST WINDS	14704	13974	6394	2253	5477	5770	1910	643	1668	209	476	219240230	8407136	1551832	1192732
	GREATER DETROIT	20941	20511	9536	2538	6386	8924	2181	1081	2625	219	547	400223802	13335871	2769805	1550938
	GREATER SOUTHWEST	12969	12517	6322	1363	5784	5068	1675	150	983	115	414	222659466	4173555	1588004	1192225
	HERITAGE	19455	18636	8202	2359	6098	9044	2230	711	1907	388	532	304034203	12965602	2275063	1710537
	MID-MICHIGAN	10690	10504	6071	940	5147	5521	1678	216	1138	22	373	193921649	2741857	1432942	1170857
	MIDWEST	15368	14911	9138	1409	7720	10013	3166	241	992	150	445	233809172	5149304	2066161	15786650
	NORTHERN SKIES	6021	5854	2461	590	1478	1572	545	98	566	29	188	79336376	498243	490273	396105
	NORTHERN WATERS	9478	9060	5656	0	3905	2959	995	78	1014	93	263	94994950	1642155	1040422	800991
	MICHIGAN CONFERENCE TOTALS	122327	118424	59415	13346	45778	53581	15911	3469	15641	1690	3619	1919077692	51020460	14571556	10611581

STATISTICAL INFORMATION

CONFERENCE Number	Church Benevolence Giving 30-38	Total ASKED for clergy pension 39a	Total PAID for clergy pension 39b	Base compensation paid to/for the Senior Pastor or other person assigned or appointed in the lead pastoral role to the church 41a	Base compensation paid to/for all Associate Pastor(s) and other pastoral staff assigned or appointed to the church. Include deacons and other clergy in this role 41b	Deacons salary/benefits 41c & 42c	Pastoral Benefits 40,42a-44	Total amount paid in salary and benefits for all other church staff and diaconal ministers 45	Total amount spent for local church program expenses 46	Total amount spent for other local church operating expenses 47	Local Church capital expenses 48 & 49	TOTAL CHURCH EXPENSES (Sum of Lines 29a through 49) 50	Number of giving units 51	Total income for annual budget/spending plan 52	Total income for designated causes including capital campaign and other special projects 53	Total income from connectional and other institutional sources outside the local church 54
32070	12000	1773	0	0	0	0	0	0	1000	1800	0	14800	10	14300	100	0
32071	2358	492	492	3280	854	0	2161		99	3894		14255	17	16007	0	0
32072	225	2010	2010	20100	0	0	9815	6818	450	9569	3198	59055	29	54825	0	0
32073	5663	8270	8270	46918	0	0	21679	106395	6677	35390	0	259839	125	233787	162861	0
32074	120217	23370	23370	86845	64945	840	87932	424641	64319	222735	160451	1376372	574	1116855	60651	2500
32076	2233	4489	4489	23940	5388	0	15740	18042	381	27976	34613	146152	42	109515	4550	0
	5847	8381	5088	112016	0	0	51214	48539	20865	127446	40763	409116	187	449349	39443	3500
	719492	368048	349978	2516154	118725	0	1273585	2288032	701377	2534424	1994196	13503485	5639	12952373	1568782	117949
	675784	436975	418428	2823397	222296	67274	1268113	3097115	548366	3609132	2963480	16886117	6729	13453610	3320174	137364
	1171848	577839	551884	3209832	1001311	106556	2956879	7100861	1919470	6468240	6387105	33306924	9952	22967485	3513255	257233
	967933	390129	373107	2631643	133447	51476	1522582	2996644	676307	3426794	3021881	16994039	6368	12669398	3030279	168498
	1308700	557222	541161	3460396	328013	64703	1818666	6026852	12716629	4129827	4464248	25124741	8978	20248963	4237365	104568
	985640	356957	351035	2301565	130903	39597	1440821	3237974	582455	2668854	1740146	14649847	6973	12653430	3412694	143958
	1108540	467538	447084	3022888	159335	0	1651858	5061368	1165539	3697825	2571989	20464993	8261	17926496	3324193	119305
	270730	182300	180597	1221563	64361	0	628379	673782	199114	994947	428956	5062833	2702	4556970	409565	60946
	528630	327848	314015	2149944	108062	840	1166233	1932600	408045	2005575	1168889	10585391	5077	8568286	1136527	218811
	7743081	3673237	3532377	23449398	2266453	330446	13778330	32463767	7493167	29663064	24781653	156987486	60866	126446360	23992277	1332132

NW

— MAC Photos

MICHIGAN CONFERENCE PLAN OF ORGANIZATION

The Michigan Conference equips and connects through:
Christ-Centered Mission and Ministry;
Bold and Effective Leaders;
Vibrant Congregations.

§ 1 AGENCIES RELATING TO CHRIST-CENTERED MISSION AND MINISTRY

1.1 COMMISSION ON THE ANNUAL CONFERENCE SESSION
  1.1.1   Purpose – Arrange and plan the annual conference session.
  1.1.2   Duties.
    1.1.2.1   Manage the order and flow of the entire annual conference session, including business/plenary sessions, for all matters.
    1.1.2.2   Facilitate the business sessions of the annual conference.
    1.1.2.3   Coordinate the daily schedule of the annual conference business sessions.
    1.1.2.4   Plan, coordinate, and implement the worship and program content of the annual conference session.
    1.1.2.5   Appoint the following for the annual conference session:
      1.1.2.5.1   Worship planning task force in consultation with the Worship Coordinator.
      1.1.2.5.2   Any other people or task forces as the commission may deem necessary.
    1.1.2.6   Ensure the Committee on the Journal (§ 1.3, below), which is amenable to it, is fulfilling its responsibilities pursuant to *The Book of Discipline* and the Plan of Organization and direction of the annual conference.
    1.1.2.7   Executive Committee duties: implement the actions of the full commission between sessions of the full commission; interface with all vendors; establish and monitor annual budget; assist chairperson as requested in setting agenda for full commission.
  1.1.3   Membership.
    1.1.3.1   Eight voting members shall be nominated by the Committee on Nominations, in consultation with the Executive Team, who shall be either clergy members of the annual conference or lay people who are members of a local church within the annual conference.
    1.1.3.2   Annual Conference Coordinator/Coordinator for Event Planning.
      1.1.3.2.1   Gives project management assistance to the Commission.
      1.1.3.2.2   Creates systems for event planning an assists conference-sponsored event planning teams in setting up their event registration processes.

1.1.3.2.3   Negotiates venue terms and options.

1.1.3.2.4   Reports directly to the Director of Connectional Ministries (see *The Book of Discipline*, ¶ 608).

1.1.3.3 *Ex officio* with vote.

1.1.3.3.1   Resident bishop (or representative).

1.1.3.3.2   Conference lay leader (or representative).

1.1.3.3.3   Conference secretary.

1.1.3.3.4   Chair of the Committee on Rules.

1.1.3.3.5   A district superintendent designated by the cabinet.

1.1.3.3.6   Legislative Coordinator.

1.1.3.3.7   Conference facilitator.

1.1.3.3.8   A representative of the Board of Ordained Ministry.

1.1.3.4 *Ex officio* with voice, but no vote.

1.1.3.4.1   Director of Connectional Ministries (see *The Book of Discipline*, ¶ 608).

1.1.3.4.2   Director of Communications (see *The Book of Discipline*, ¶ 609).

1.1.4 Organization.

1.1.4.1 The Commission shall elect from among its membership the following:

1.1.4.1.1   Chairperson.

1.1.4.1.2   Vice chairperson.

1.1.4.1.3   Head Usher.

1.1.4.1.4   Worship Coordinator.

1.1.4.2 The Legislative Coordinator shall have the following duties:

1.1.3.2.1   Receive new business in accordance with the rules of order (§ 5, below).

1.1.3.2.2   Assign business to legislative committees as appropriate in consultation with the Executive Team.

1.1.3.2.3   Maintain and revise (as necessary) the schedule of legislative process for the annual conference session in consultation with the rest of the Executive Committee (see § 1.1.4.5, below).

1.1.3.2.4   Manage the flow of the legislative work of the annual conference session in consultation with the Executive Team.

1.1.4.3 The conference secretary shall serve as the secretary of the commission.

1.1.4.4 Members shall serve four-year terms, renewable twice, in annually staggered classes.

1.1.4.5 The Executive Committee shall be composed of the persons serving in the following capacities:

1.1.4.5.1   Bishop.

1.1.4.5.2   Clergy Assistant to the Bishop.

	1.1.4.5.3	Chairperson.
	1.1.4.5.4	Worship Coordinator.
	1.1.4.5.5	Director of Connectional Ministries (see *The Book of Discipline*, ¶ 608).
	1.1.4.5.6	Legislative Coordinator.
	1.1.4.5.7	Director of Communications (see *The Book of Discipline*, ¶ 609).
	1.1.4.5.8	Conference Secretary.
	1.1.4.5.9	Annual Conference Coordinator.

1.2 COMMISSION ON COMMUNICATIONS

1.2.1 Purpose – Assist the conference Director of Communications (see *The Book of Discipline*, ¶ 609) in communicating (via various forms of media) news and information about the annual conference and its ministries to the local churches of the conference and to the wider world.

1.2.2 Duties.

    1.2.2.1 As determined by the conference director of communications.

    1.2.2.2 Fulfill all other responsibilities enumerated in ¶ 650 of *The Book of Discipline*.

1.2.3 Membership.

    1.2.3.1 Four persons who shall be clergy members or local pastors of the annual conference (if clergy) or professing members of a local church within the annual conference (if laity).

    1.2.3.2 Members shall serve four-year terms, renewable once, in annually staggered classes.

    1.2.3.3 *Ex officio* with vote.

        1.2.3.3.1 Bishop or clergy assistant to the Bishop (at the Bishop's discretion).

        1.2.3.3.2 Conference lay leader.

        1.2.3.3.3 Any board member of United Methodist Communications residing within the bounds of the annual conference.

    1.2.3.4 *Ex officio* with voice, but no vote.

        1.2.3.4.1 Senior editor of conference communications.

        1.2.3.4.2 I.T. data manager (or representative).

        1.2.3.4.3 Conference Director of Communications (see *The Book of Discipline*, ¶ 609).

        1.2.3.4.4 Director of Connectional Ministries (see *The Book of Discipline*, ¶ 608).

    1.2.3.5 Members shall be nominated by the Committee on Nominations, in consultation with the director of communications.

1.2.4 Organization – The Conference Director of Communications (see *The Book of Discipline*, ¶ 609) shall chair the commission.

1.2.5 Amenability – The commission shall be amenable to the Conference Leadership Council (§ 2.1, below).

PLAN OF ORGANIZATION

1.2.6   Relationship – The board shall relate to United Methodist Communications.

1.3 COMMITTEE ON THE JOURNAL
    1.3.1   Purpose – Compile and cause to be published the journal of the annual conference.
    1.3.2   Duties.
        1.3.2.1   Review the format and content of the conference journal, ensuring compliance with *The Book of Discipline*.
        1.3.2.2   Prepare a report for inclusion in the conference journal reviewing that legislation that requires follow-up or implementation by the conference or any agency thereof.
        1.3.2.3   Cause the conference journal to be printed and distributed to all members (clergy and lay) of the annual conference and all local churches of the annual conference.
    1.3.3   Membership.
        1.3.3.1   Four people who shall be members of the annual conference (if clergy) or professing members of a local church within the annual conference (if laity).
        1.3.3.2   Members shall serve four-year terms, renewable once, in annually staggered classes.
        1.3.3.3   Members shall be nominated by the Committee on Nominations.
        1.3.3.4   *Ex officio* with vote – Conference secretary.
        1.3.3.5   *Ex officio with voice, but no vote* – Conference Director of Communications (see *The Book of Discipline*, ¶ 609).
    1.3.4   Organization.
        1.3.4.1   The conference secretary shall serve as chairperson and secretary.
        1.3.4.2   The committee shall elect from among its members a vice chairperson.
    1.3.5   Amenability – The committee shall be amenable to the Commission on the Annual Conference Session (§ 1.1, above).

1.4 BOARD OF JUSTICE
    1.4.1   Purpose.
        1.4.1.1   Relate the gospel to the world by showing that the reconciliation of humans to God effected through Jesus Christ involves personal, social, and civic righteousness.
        1.4.1.2   Challenge and equip the agencies of the annual conference to a full and equal participation of racial and ethnic constituencies in the total life and mission of the church.
        1.4.1.3   Challenge the annual conference and its local churches and agencies to a continuing commitment to the full and equal responsibility and participation of women in the total life and mission of the church.

1.4.1.4 Advocate for the role of persons with disabilities in ministry and the leadership of the annual conference.

1.4.2 Duties.

1.4.2.1 Division of Church and Society.

1.4.2.1.1 Implement the Social Principles and the annual conference's policy statements on social issues within the annual conference.

1.4.2.1.2 Provide forthright witness and action on issues of human well-being, justice, peace, and the integrity of creation.

1.4.2.1.3 Develop, promote, and distribute resources to inform, motivate, train, and organize people toward issues of social justice.

1.4.2.1.4 Fulfill all other responsibilities enumerated in ¶ 629 of *The Book of Discipline*.

1.4.2.2 Division on Religion and Race.

1.4.2.2.1 Review and make appropriate recommendations for racial and ethnic inclusiveness and equity within the annual conference staff and on all annual conference agencies.

1.4.2.2.1.1 Review and make appropriate recommendations for total inclusiveness an equity among conference staff and on all conferences agencies, reporting annually to the annual conference.

1.4.2.2.1.2 Provide resources through collaboration and training to enable the work of the local church ministry area of religion and race, with particular emphasis placed on pastors and congregations involved in cross-racial/cross-cultural ministry.

1.4.2.2.2 Consult with the Board of Ordained Ministry and the cabinet to ensure racial/ethnic inclusion and equity in the recruitment, credentialing, and itineracy processes of the annual conference. The executive committee of the Board of Ordained Ministry and cabinet shall meet at least once per year in joint sessions with the Commission on Religion and Race to create and assess long-term plans for identifying and developing clergy leaders who will serve the growing racial and ethnic populations of the church.

1.4.2.2.3 Consult with local churches of the annual conference whose neighborhoods are experiencing changing racial/ethnic demographics in their neighborhoods and that desire to be in ministry with those changing neighborhoods, but coordinating conference leadership in support of racial and social justice movements impacting local communities, in consultation and partnership with other entities within and outside the boundaries of the annual conference.

1.4.2.2.4 Support and provide programs of education in areas of cultural competency and racial justice and reconciliation.

1.4.2.2.4.1 Support and provide programs of education in areas of intercultural competency, institutional equity, and vital conversation at every level of the conference.

1.4.2.2.4.2 Partner with the Board of Justice and other agencies as they seek to develop vital conversations, programs, and policies of racial/institutional equity and intercultural competency.

1.4.2.2.5 Partner with appropriate agencies and entities, and denominational bodies to assist in the resolution of complaints of racial/ethnic discrimination made by clergy or laity.

1.4.2.2.6 Fulfill all other responsibilities enumerated in ¶ 643 of *The Book of Discipline*.

1.4.2.3 Division on the Status and Role of Women.

1.4.2.3.1 Be informed about the status and role of all women in the total life of the annual conference.

1.4.2.3.2 Assist the resident bishop and cabinet in focusing on issues related to women such as sexual harassment.

1.4.2.3.3 Fulfill all other responsibilities enumerated in ¶ 644 of *The Book of Discipline*.

1.4.2.4 Division on Disability Concerns.

    1.4.2.4.1 Develop programs that meet the needs of persons with disabilities.

    1.4.2.4.2 Assist the resident bishop and cabinet in focusing on issues important to persons with disabilities.

    1.4.2.4.3 Provide resources to local churches seeking to develop ministries that are attitudinally and architecturally accessible.

    1.4.2.4.4 Fulfill all other responsibilities enumerated in ¶ 653 of *The Book of Discipline*.

1.4.3 Membership.

    1.4.3.1 Division of Church and Society.

        1.4.3.1.1 Four people who shall be members of the annual conference (if clergy) or professing members of a local church within the annual conference (if laity).

        1.4.3.1.2 Members shall serve four-year terms, renewable once, in annually staggered classes.

        1.4.3.1.3 Members shall be nominated by the Committee on Nominations.

        1.4.3.1.4 *Ex officio* with vote:

            1.4.3.1.4.1 The mission coordinator for social action of the conference United Methodist Women.

            1.4.3.1.4.2 Any member of the General Board of Church and Society residing within the bounds of the annual conference.

            1.4.3.1.4.3 The conference peace with justice coordinator, who shall be named by the Division of Church and Society and shall serve at the division's pleasure for up to eight years.

    1.4.3.2 Division on Religion and Race.

        1.4.3.2.1 Two clergy members of the annual conference.

        1.4.3.2.2 Two laymen who shall be professing members of a local church within the annual conference.

        1.4.3.2.3 Two laywomen who shall be professing members of a local church within the annual conference.

        1.4.3.2.4 Members shall serve four-year terms, renewable once, in annually staggered classes.

1.4.3.2.5   Members shall be nominated by the Committee on Nominations.

1.4.3.2.6   *Ex officio* with vote – Any member of the General Commission on Religion and Race residing within the bounds of the annual conference.

1.4.3.3   Division on the Status and Role of Women.

1.4.3.3.1   Two clergy women who shall be members of the annual conference.

1.4.3.3.2   A clergyman who shall be a member of the annual conference.

1.4.3.3.3   Three laymen who shall be professing members of a local church within the annual conference.

1.4.3.3.4   Three laywomen who shall be professing members of a local church within the annual conference.

1.4.3.3.5   Members shall serve four-year terms, renewable once, in annually staggered classes.

1.4.3.3.6   Members shall be nominated by the Committee on Nominations.

1.4.3.3.7   *Ex officio* with vote – Any member of the General Commission on the Status and Role of Women residing within the bounds of the annual conference.

1.4.3.4   Division on Disability Concerns.

1.4.3.4.1   Four people who shall be members of the annual conference (if clergy) or professing members of a local church within the annual conference (if laity).

1.4.3.4.2   Members shall serve four-year terms, renewable once, in annually staggered classes.

1.4.3.4.3   Members shall be nominated by the Committee on Nominations.

1.4.3.4.4   At least one member of the division shall have a physical disability.

1.4.3.4.5   At least one member of the division shall have a mental disability.

1.4.4   Organization.

1.4.4.1   The board shall be organized in four divisions as enumerated above.

1.4.4.2   Each division shall elect from among its members a convener.

1.4.4.2.1   The convener of the Division on the Status and Role of Women shall be a woman.

1.4.4.2.2   One of the conveners shall serve as vice chairperson of the board. The conveners shall decide amongst themselves who this shall be.

1.4.4.3 In addition to the members enumerated above, an additional person, nominated by the Committee on Nominations, shall serve as the chairperson of the board. This chairperson shall be a member of the annual conference (if clergy) or a professing member of a local church within the annual conference (if laity).

1.4.5 Amenability – The board shall be amenable to the Conference Leadership Council (§ 2.1, below).

1.4.6 Relationship – The board shall relate to the following general agencies:

1.4.6.1 General Board of Church and Society.

1.4.6.2 General Commission on Religion and Race.

1.4.6.3 General Commission on the Status and Role of Women.

1.5 BOARD OF GLOBAL MINISTRIES

1.5.1 Purpose – Engage the annual conference and its local churches in ministry with persons and in places around the world.

1.5.2 Duties.

1.5.2.1 Act as a conduit for interpretation, support, and programming between the annual conference and the General Board of Global Ministries.

1.5.2.2 Plan, promote, and develop a spirit of global ministry within the annual conference and its local churches.

1.5.2.3 Encourage and support specialized urban and town and country ministries.

1.5.2.4 Envision and develop new forms of mission appropriate to the changing needs of the world.

1.5.2.5 Appoint and train conference disaster relief coordinators.

1.5.2.6 Recruit and support missionaries.

1.5.2.7 Promote Christian, financial, and professional standards in health and welfare ministries within the annual conference.

1.5.2.8 Fulfill all other responsibilities enumerated in ¶ 633 of *The Book of Discipline*.

1.5.3 Membership.

1.5.3.1 Twelve people who shall be members of the annual conference (if clergy) or professing members of a local church within the annual conference (if laity).

1.5.3.2 Members shall serve four-year terms, renewable once, in annually staggered classes.

1.5.3.3 Members shall be nominated by the Committee on Nominations.

1.5.3.4 *Ex officio* with vote:

1.5.3.4.1 Mission coordinator for education and interpretation of the conference United Methodist Women.

1.5.3.4.2   The conference secretary of global ministries, who shall be appointed by the board and shall serve at its pleasure for up to eight years.

1.5.3.4.3   Conference disaster response coordinator (selected by the Board of Global Ministries).

1.5.3.4.4   Any member of the General Board of Global Ministries residing within the bounds of the annual conference.

1.5.3.4.5   Conference VIM coordinator.

1.5.3.4.6   Chair of the Town and Country group, or their designee.

1.5.4   Organization – The board shall elect the following officers from among its members:

1.5.4.1   Chairperson.

1.5.4.2   Vice chairperson.

1.5.5   Amenability – The board shall be amenable to the Conference Leadership Council (§ 2.1, below).

1.5.6   Relationship – The board shall relate to the General Board of Global Ministries.

1.6 COMMISSION ON ARCHIVES AND HISTORY

1.6.1   Purpose – Collect and preserve the records and historical data of the annual conference.

1.6.2   Duties.

1.6.2.1   Maintain a fire-safe historical and archival depository for the records and items of historical nature of the annual conference.

1.6.2.2   Liaise with shrines, landmarks, and historical sites related to the annual conference and its churches and ministries.

1.6.2.3   Work with the Commission on the Annual Conference Session in the planning of historical observances at the annual conference session.

1.6.2.4   Encourage and assist local churches in the preservation and compilation of records and history.

1.6.2.5   Fulfill all other responsibilities enumerated in ¶ 641 of *The Book of Discipline*.

1.6.3   Membership.

1.6.3.1   Four clergy members of the annual conference.

1.6.3.2   Four lay persons who shall be professing members of a church within the annual conference.

1.6.3.3   Members shall be nominated by the Committee on Nominations.

1.6.3.4   Members shall serve four-year terms, renewable once, in annually staggered classes.

1.6.3.5   The archivists of the conference archives shall serve as ex-officio members with voice and vote.

1.6.3.6   The president of the Michigan Area United Methodist Church Historical Society shall serve as an ex-officio member with voice and vote.

1.6.3.7　Any member of the General Commission on Archives and History shall serve as an ex officio member with voice and vote.

1.6.4　Organization – The commission shall elect from among its members the following officers:

1.6.4.1　Chairperson.

1.6.4.2　Vice chairperson.

1.6.4.3　Secretary.

1.6.4.4　Treasurer.

1.6.5　Amenability – The commission shall be amenable to the Conference Leadership Council (§ 2.1, below).

1.6.6　Relationship – The commission shall relate to the General Commission on　Archives and History and the Michigan United Methodist Church Historical Society.

§ 2　AGENCIES RELATING TO BOLD AND EFFECTIVE LEADERS

2.1　CONFERENCE LEADERSHIP COUNCIL.

2.1.1　Purpose – The basic governing council of the annual conference.

2.1.2　Duties.

2.1.2.1　Implementation of the vision and direction of the annual conference.

2.1.2.2　Ensuring that the following agencies, which are amenable to it, are fulfilling their responsibilities pursuant to *The Book of Discipline* and the Plan of Organization and direction of the annual conference:

2.1.2.2.1　Board of Congregational Life (§ 3.5, below).

2.1.2.2.2　Board of Global Ministries (§ 1.5, above).

2.1.2.2.3　Board of Justice (§ 1.4, above).

2.1.2.2.4　Board of Laity (§ 3.3, below).

2.1.2.2.5　Board of Young People's Ministries (§ 3.4, below).

2.1.2.2.6　Commission on Archives and History (§ 1.6, above).

2.1.2.2.7　Commission on Communications (§ 1.2, above).

2.1.2.2.8　Committee on African-American Ministry (§ 3.9, below).

2.1.2.2.9　Committee on Asian-American Ministry (§ 3.7, below).

2.1.2.2.10　Committee on the Episcopacy (§ 2.4, below).

2.1.2.2.11　Committee on Hispanic/Latino Ministry (§ 3.6, below).

2.1.2.2.12　Committee on Human Resources (§ 2.5, below).

2.1.2.2.13   Committee on Native American Ministry (§ 3.8, below).

2.1.2.2.14   Protection Policy Implementation Team (§ 2.6, below).

2.1.2.3   Ensuring that all agencies amenable to it (see § 2.1.2.2, above) are functioning with values and goals that are aligned with the vision for ministry set by the annual conference.

2.1.2.4   Evaluation of the fruitfulness and effectiveness of the work of all agencies amenable to it (see § 2.1.2.2, above).

2.1.2.5   Ensuring that all agencies amenable to it (see § 2.1.2.2, above) compile a list (that shall be published in the conference journal) of all non-conference entities to which they have provided funding (and which are thereby responsible for ensuring the appropriate use of such funding).

2.1.2.6   At its discretion, the council may create and define the positions of additional conference directors (beyond those defined in *The Book of Discipline*).

2.1.2.7   The council may create task forces, work groups, and *ad hoc* committees as needed in order to ensure that its work is being done.

2.1.3   Membership.

2.1.3.1   With voice and vote.

2.1.3.1.1   Four clergy members of the annual conference, at least one of whom shall be a member of the Board of Ordained Ministry.

2.1.3.1.2   Five lay people who are professing members of a congregation within the annual conference.

2.1.3.2   *Ex officio* with voice and vote.

2.1.3.2.1   Conference lay leader.

2.1.3.2.2   President of the Council on Finance and Administration.

2.1.3.2.3   A representative of the Division on Religion and Race of the Board of Justice.

2.1.3.2.4   Any member of the Connectional Table residing within the bounds of the Annual Conference.

2.1.3.2.5   Chair of the Conference Board of Trustees or their designee.

2.1.3.2.6   Chair of the Conference Human Resources Committee or their designee.

2.1.3.2.7   Chair of the Conference Board of Pension and Benefits or their designee.

2.1.3.3   *Ex officio* with voice only.

2.1.3.3.1   Director of Administrative Services and Conference Treasurer (see *The Book of Discipline*, ¶ 619).

2.1.3.3.2   Director of Connectional Ministries (see *The Book of Discipline*, ¶ 608).

2.1.3.3.3   Director of Communications (see *The Book of Discipline*, ¶ 609).

2.1.3.3.4   Bishop or clergy assistant to the Bishop (at the Bishop's discretion).

2.1.3.3.5   Dean of the appointive cabinet.

2.1.3.3.6   Director of Benefits and Human Resources.

2.1.3.3.7   Any other directors whose position may be created by the Conference Leadership Council (see § 2.1.2.6, above).

2.1.3.4   Members shall be nominated by the Committee on Nominations.

2.1.3.5   Members shall serve three-year terms, renewable thrice, in annually staggered classes.

2.1.3.6   Except for *ex officio* members listed hereinabove, chairpersons of conference agencies and employees of conference agencies shall be ineligible for membership on the council.

2.1.4   Organization.

2.1.4.1   The council, in consultation with the Bishop, shall elect from among its voting members a president, vice president, and secretary.

2.1.4.2   The Director of Administrative Services and Conference Treasurer (see *The Book of Discipline*, ¶ 619) shall be the council treasurer.

2.2 BOARD OF ORDAINED MINISTRY.

2.2.1   Purpose – To counsel and guide the equipping and qualification of candidates for ordained ministry and conference membership.

2.2.2   Duties.

2.2.2.1   Assume the primary responsibility for the enlistment and recruitment of ordained clergy by working in consultation with the cabinet and the General Board of Higher Education and Ministry to study and interpret the clergy needs and resources of the annual conference.

2.2.2.2   Renew a culture of call in the church by giving strategic leadership to the annual conference, local churches, and other ministry settings.

2.2.2.3   Seek from schools of theology information about the personal and professional qualities of candidates for ministry.

2.2.2.4   Appoint and train clergy mentors.

2.2.2.5   Examine all applicants as to their qualification and fitness for the following:

2.2.2.5.1   Annual election as local pastor.

2.2.2.5.2   Election to associate membership.

2.2.2.5.3   Election to provisional membership.

2.2.2.5.4   Election to full membership.

2.2.2.6   Interview and make recommendations for applicants/those formally recommended for a change in conference relationship.

2.2.2.7   Provide support services for the career development, continuing education, morale, and preparation for retirement of clergy.

2.2.2.8   Provide means of evaluating the effectiveness of clergy in the annual conference.

2.2.2.9   Provide continuing support and management of diaconal ministers.

2.2.2.10 Administer the conference ministerial education fund.

2.2.2.11 Collaborate with the director of clergy excellence in the development of bold and effective leaders.

2.2.2.12 Fulfill all other responsibilities enumerated in ¶ 635 of *The Book of Discipline*.

2.2.3   Membership.

2.2.3.1   With voice and vote.

2.2.3.1.1   At least twenty-five full (*i.e.*, ordained) clergy members of the annual conference.

2.2.3.1.1.1   At least one of whom shall be engaged in extension ministry.

2.2.3.1.1.2   At least one of whom shall be age thirty-five or younger.

2.2.3.1.1.3   At least two-thirds of whom shall be graduates of theological schools listed by the University Senate.

2.2.3.1.1.4   At least one of whom shall be retired.

2.2.3.1.2   At least three clergy persons who are either associate members or local pastors who have completed course of study.

2.2.3.1.3   At least twelve lay people who are professing members of a local church within the annual conference.

2.2.3.2   *Ex officio* with voice and vote.

2.2.3.2.1   Chairpersons of the following:

2.2.3.2.1.1   Order of Elders.

2.2.3.2.1.2   Order of Deacons.

2.2.3.2.1.3   Fellowship of Local Pastors and Associate Members.

2.2.3.2.2   A district superintendent named by the Bishop.

2.2.3.2.3   Director of Clergy Excellence.

2.2.3.3   Members shall be nominated by the Bishop.

2.2.3.4 Members shall serve four-year terms (starting at the close of the annual conference session following General Conference), renewable twice, with quadrennially staggered classes.

2.2.4 Organization.

2.2.4.1 The board shall elect from among its members the following officers:

2.2.4.1.1 Chairperson.

2.2.4.1.2 Vice chairperson.

2.2.4.1.3 Secretary.

2.2.4.1.4 At least one registrar.

2.2.4.2 The conference relations committee of the board shall be chaired by the vice chairperson of the board and shall be composed of as many members as the board shall decide. District superintendents may not serve on the conference relations committee.

2.2.4.3 The board may establish further committees of itself as it may deem necessary.

2.3 COMMITTEE ON NOMINATIONS

2.3.1 Purpose – Preparation and presentation to the annual conference a slate of nominees for the conference agencies, giving careful consideration to racial/ethnic, geographic, demographic, age, and gender balance.

2.3.2 Duties.

2.3.2.1 Preparation of a slate of nominees for presentation to the annual conference. The committee shall have the duty, whenever necessary, to assign nominees to specific classes within an agency.

2.3.2.2 Assist other agencies with the following:

2.3.2.2.1 Identifying the skill sets and perspectives needed to perform the agency's work.

2.3.2.2.2 Auditing the skill sets of current and prospective members.

2.3.2.3 Except as otherwise provided by *The Book of Discipline*, filling agency vacancies that occur between sessions of the annual conference.

2.3.2.4 By a three-fourths vote, the committee may remove from office any member of an agency for whose nominations it is responsible should that member fail to perform the duties required.

2.3.3 Membership.

2.3.3.1 Two persons nominated by the annual conference session.

2.3.3.2 Ten persons nominated by the Conference Leadership Council.

2.3.3.3 *Ex officio* with vote.

2.3.3.2.1 A district superintendent designated by the cabinet.

2.3.3.2.2   Conference lay leader (or designated representative).

2.3.3.2.3   Chairperson (or representative) of the Committee on Rules.

2.3.3.2.4   Secretary of the annual conference.

2.3.3.4   *Ex officio* with voice, but no vote – Director of Connectional Ministries (see *The Book of Discipline*, ¶ 608).

2.3.3.5   Members shall serve four-year terms, renewable once, staggered annually.

2.3.4   Organization – The committee shall elect the following officers from among its members:

2.3.4.1   Chairperson.

2.3.4.2   Vice chairperson.

2.3.4.3   Secretary.

2.4 COMMITTEE ON THE EPISCOPACY

2.4.1   Purpose – Provide personal support and counsel to the resident bishop.

2.4.2   Duties.

2.4.2.1   Support the resident bishop in the oversight of the spiritual and temporal affairs of the church, with special reference to areas in which the bishop has presidential responsibility.

2.4.2.2   Be available to provide counsel to the resident bishop.

2.4.2.3   Make determinations and appropriate recommendations concerning the episcopal needs of the conference.

2.4.2.4   Advise the bishop as to conditions within the annual conference.

2.4.2.5   Interpret the nature and function of the episcopal office to the annual conference.

2.4.2.6   Engage in annual consultation and appraisal concerning the balance of the resident bishop's relationship to and responsibilities within the annual conference and its agencies.

2.4.2.7   Report the annual conference's needs concerning episcopal leadership to the jurisdictional committee on the episcopacy via the committee's representatives thereto. The committee's representatives to the jurisdictional committee on the episcopacy shall ensure that this report includes profiles of the annual conference's assets, limits, and strengths, and that it shall be used when the jurisdictional committee assigns bishops to episcopal areas.

2.4.2.8   Ensuring that the Committee on the Episcopal Residence (§ 4.7, below), which is amenable to it, is fulfilling its responsibilities pursuant to *The Book of Discipline* and the Plan of Organization and direction and of the annual conference.

2.4.2.9 Fulfill all other responsibilities enumerated in ¶ 637 of *The Book of Discipline.*

2.4.3 Membership.

    2.4.3.1 Members nominated by the Committee on Nominations.

        2.4.3.1.1 Six clergy members of the conference.

        2.4.3.1.2 Five lay persons who shall be professing members of a local church within the conference.

    2.4.3.2 The Conference Lay Leader

    2.4.3.3 Three members appointed by the resident bishop who, if laity, shall be professing members of a local church within the conference and, if clergy, shall be members of the annual conference.

    2.4.3.4 Members of the jurisdictional committee on the episcopacy who reside within the bounds of the conference shall be *ex officio* members with vote.

    2.4.3.5 No staff person of the annual conference or any agency thereof, nor an immediate family member of such staff person shall serve as a member of the committee, except that this prohibition shall not apply to the conference lay leader nor to members of the jurisdictional committee on the episcopacy residing within the bounds of the conference.

    2.4.3.6 Members shall serve four-year terms, renewable once, in annually staggered classes.

2.4.3 Organization – The committee shall elect from among its members the following officers:

    2.4.3.1 Chairperson.

    2.4.3.2 Vice chairperson.

    2.4.3.3 Secretary.

2.4.4 Amenability – The committee shall be amenable to the Conference Leadership Council (§ 2.1, above).

2.5 PROTECTION POLICY IMPLEMENTATION TEAM

2.5.1 Purpose – Train and certify those who will work with children, youth, or vulnerable adults at conference events.

2.5.2 Duties.

    2.5.2.1 Propose changes to the conference protection policy (§ 8, below) as needed.

    2.5.2.2 In accordance with the policies and procedures of the conference protection policy (§ 8, below), train and certify volunteers to work with children, youth, and vulnerable adults at conference events.

    2.5.2.3 In accordance with the policies and procedures of the conference protection policy (§ 8, below), train volunteer certification trainers.

    2.5.2.4 In accordance with the policies and procedures of the conference protection policy (§ 8, below), process and certify (or decline, as appropriate) applications for protection policy certification.

2.5.3   Membership.
    2.5.3.1   Eight adults (at least 18 years of age) who shall be members of the annual conference (if clergy) or professing members of a local church within the annual conference (if laity).
    2.5.3.2   Members shall serve four-year terms, renewable once, in annually staggered classes.
    2.5.3.3   Members shall be nominated by the Committee on Nominations.
2.5.4   Organization – The committee shall elect the following officers from among its members:
    2.5.4.1   Chairperson.
    2.5.4.2   Vice chairperson.
2.5.5   Amenability – The committee shall be amenable to the Conference Leadership Council (§ 2.1, above).

§ 3   AGENCIES RELATING TO VIBRANT CONGREGATIONS

3.1   UNITED METHODIST WOMEN

3.1.1   Purpose – To know God and to experience freedom as whole persons through Jesus Christ; to develop a creative, supportive fellowship; and to expand concepts of mission through participation in the global ministries of the church.
3.1.2   Duties.
    3.1.2.1   Work with the district and local units of United Methodist Women in developing programs to meet the needs and interests of women and the concerns and responsibilities of the global church.
    3.1.2.2   Promote the plans and responsibilities of the national office of United Methodist Women.
    3.1.2.3   Fulfill all other responsibilities enumerated in ¶ 647 of *The Book of Discipline*.
3.1.3   Membership.
    3.1.3.1   The membership shall be composed of all of the members of the local United Methodist Women units existing within the bounds of the conference.
    3.1.3.2   *Ex officio* with vote
        3.1.3.2.1   Resident bishop.
        3.1.3.2.2   Members of the board of directors of the national office of United Methodist Women residing within the bounds of the conference.
        3.1.3.2.3   Members of the United Methodist Women Program Advisory Group residing within the bounds of the conference.
        3.1.3.2.4   Members of the North Central Jurisdiction United Methodist Women leadership team residing within the bounds of the conference.
3.1.4   Organization – The United Methodist Women shall elect from among its members the following positions:

3.1.4.1 President.

3.1.4.2 Treasurer.

3.1.4.3 Secretary.

3.1.4.4 A committee on nominations whose membership shall be determined by the membership of the United Methodist Women.

3.1.4.5 Any other committees that the membership may create.

3.1.5 Relationship – The conference United Methodist Women shall relate to the national organization of United Methodist Women.

3.2. UNITED METHODIST MEN

3.2.1 Purpose – A creative, supportive fellowship of men who seek to know God and Jesus Christ that meets the inspirational needs of men in evangelism, mission, and spiritual discipline.

3.2.2 Duties.

3.2.2.1 Promote the objectives and responsibilities of the General Commission on United Methodist Men.

3.2.2.2 Establish, support, and maintain local church units of United Methodist Men.

3.2.2.3 Empower personal witness and evangelism in men.

3.2.2.4 Encourage the involvement of men in mission.

3.2.2.5 Promote the scouting movement and other youth organizations recognized by the General Commission on United Methodist Men.

3.2.2.6 Fulfill all other responsibilities enumerated in ¶ 648 of *The Book of Discipline*.

3.2.3 Membership.

3.2.3.1 The membership of the United Methodist Men shall be made up of all men who are professing members of local churches within the bounds of the annual conference.

3.2.3.2 *Ex officio* members.

3.2.3.2.1 Any member of the North Central Jurisdiction United Methodist Men residing within the bounds of the conference.

3.2.3.2.2 Any member of the General Commission on United Methodist Men residing within the bounds of the annual conference.

3.2.3.2.3 Conference lay leader (or designated representative).

3.2.3.2.4 Resident bishop.

3.2.4 Organization.

3.2.4.1 The organization shall elect the following officers from among its members:

3.2.4.1.1 President.

3.2.4.1.2 Vice-president.

3.2.4.1.3 Secretary.

3.2.4.1.4 Treasurer.

3.2.4.2 The resident bishop shall serve as the honorary president.
3.2.4.3 The organization may elect additional officers and committees as its members may direct.
3.2.5 Relationship – The conference United Methodist Men shall relate to the General Commission on United Methodist Men.

3.3 BOARD OF LAITY
3.3.1 Purpose.
3.3.1.1 Foster an awareness of the role of laity in the church.
3.3.1.2 Develop and promote stewardship within the annual conference.
3.3.1.3 Provide for the training of lay members of the annual conference.
3.3.1.4 Provide support and direction for the ministry of the laity at all levels of the church.
3.3.1.5 Provide organization and support for the development of local church leaders.
3.3.2 Duties.
3.3.2.1 Develop and promote programs to cultivate the further understanding of the theological and biblical basis for the ministry of the laity.
3.3.2.2 Give direction and guidance to lay programs within the conference.
3.3.2.3 Give support and direction to the conference for local church leadership development.
3.3.2.4 Advocate for the needs of lay people within all levels of the church.
3.3.2.5 Organize a conference committee on lay servant ministries in accordance with ¶¶ 266-268 of *The Book of Discipline*.
3.3.2.6 Fulfill all other responsibilities enumerated in ¶ 631 of *The Book of Discipline*.
3.3.3 Membership.
3.3.3.1 Conference lay leader.
3.3.3.2 Conference associate lay leader.
3.3.3.3 The district lay leaders.
3.3.3.4 The associate district lay leaders.
3.3.3.5 Conference director of lay servant ministries.
3.3.3.6 President of the United Methodist Men (or representative).
3.3.3.7 President of the United Methodist Women (or representative).
3.3.3.8 Convener of the Division of Young Adult Ministry of the Board of Young People's Ministries.
3.3.3.9 Convener of the Division of Youth Ministry of the Board of Young People's Ministries.
3.3.3.10 Conference scouting coordinator.
3.3.3.11 Director of Connectional Ministries (see *The Book of Discipline*, ¶ 608).
3.3.3.12 A district superintendent designated by the cabinet.

3.3.4   Organization.
         3.3.4.1   The conference lay leader shall be the chairperson of the board.
         3.3.4.2   The conference associate lay leader shall be the vice chairperson of the board.
3.3.5   Amenability – The board shall be amenable to the Conference Leadership Council (§ 2.1, above).

3.4 BOARD OF YOUNG PEOPLE'S MINISTRIES

3.4.1   Purpose.
         3.4.1.1   Strengthen youth ministry in the local churches of the annual conference.
         3.4.1.2   Strengthen young adult ministry in the local churches of the annual conference.
         3.4.1.3   Interpret and promote United Methodist ministries in higher education.
3.4.2   Duties.
         3.4.2.1   Division of Youth Ministry.
                  3.4.2.1.1   Initiate and support plans, activities, and projects that are of particular interest to youth.
                  3.4.2.1.2   Support and facilitate the formation of youth caucuses.
                  3.4.2.1.3   Recommend to the Committee on Nominations qualified youth for conference agency membership.
                  3.4.2.1.4   Elect representatives to jurisdictional youth events.
                  3.4.2.1.5   Assist graduating youth entering college with transition to campus ministries.
                  3.4.2.1.6   Set policy and give direction for the conference Youth Service Fund.
                  3.4.2.1.7   Recommend to the General and Jurisdictional Conference delegation qualified youth for general and jurisdictional agency membership.
                  3.4.2.1.8   Facilitate an Adult Workers network for designing training for workers with youth ministries in local churches.
                  3.4.2.1.9   Fulfill all other responsibilities enumerated in ¶ 649 of *The Book of Discipline*.
         3.4.2.2   Division of Young Adult Ministry.
                  3.4.2.2.1   Initiate and support plans, activities, and projects that are of particular interest to young adults (age 18-30).
                  3.4.2.2.2   Support and facilitate the formation of young adult caucuses.
                  3.4.2.2.3   Recommend to the Committee on Nominations qualified young adults for conference agency membership.

3.4.2.2.4   Assist graduating college students with transition to adult congregational life.

3.4.2.2.5   Recommend to the General and Jurisdictional Conference delegation qualified young adults for general and jurisdictional agency membership.

3.4.2.2.6   Fulfill all other responsibilities enumerated in ¶ 650 of *The Book of Discipline*.

3.4.2.3   Division of Higher Education and Campus Ministry.

3.4.2.3.1   Make recommendations concerning annual conference policies in the area of higher education.

3.4.2.3.2   Train and provide resources for the local churches of the annual conference in them areas of higher education and campus ministry.

3.4.2.3.3   Evaluate schools, colleges, universities, and campus ministries related to the annual conference, with concern for the quality of their performance, the integrity of their mission, and their response to the missional goals of the annual conference.

3.4.2.3.4   Advocate for the financial needs of conference-related schools, colleges, universities, and campus ministries.

3.4.2.3.5   Monitor the annual conference's fiduciary and legal relationships with United Methodist-related schools, colleges, universities, and campus ministries.

3.4.2.3.6   Assist colleges and universities affiliated with the annual conference in raising funds and attracting students.

3.4.2.3.7   Encourage participation in campus ministries.

3.4.2.3.8   Provide resources and training for campus ministries.

3.4.2.3.9   Fulfill all other responsibilities enumerated in ¶ 634 of *The Book of Discipline*.

3.4.3   Membership.

3.4.3.1   Division of Youth Ministry.

3.4.3.1.1   Two clergy persons appointed in the annual conference, who shall serve four year terms, renewable once, in biennially staggered classes.

3.4.3.1.2   Two adult (*i.e.*, age 18 or older) laypersons who shall be professing members of a local church within the annual conference, who shall serve four-year terms, renewable once, in biennially staggered classes.

3.4.3.1.3   Ten youth (age 13-17), who shall be professing members of a local church within the annual conference, who shall serve one-year terms, renewable as long as they are under age 18 at the start of a new term.

3.4.3.1.4   Members shall be nominated by the Committee on Nominations.

3.4.3.2   Division of young adult ministry.

3.4.3.2.1   Two young adult (age 18-30) clergy persons of the annual conference who shall be nominated by the committee on nominations.

3.4.3.2.2   Four young adult lay persons (age 18-30) who shall be nominated by the committee on nominations and who shall be professing members of a local church within the annual conference.

3.4.3.2.3   Members shall serve one-year terms, renewable as long as they are age 30 or under at the start of the new term.

3.4.3.3   Division of Higher Education and Campus Ministry.

3.4.3.3.1   Six people who shall be members of the annual conference (if clergy) or professing members of a local church within the annual conference (if laity).

3.4.3.3.2   Members shall serve four-year terms, renewable once, in annually staggered classes.

3.4.3.3.3   Members shall be nominated by the Committee on Nominations.

3.4.3.3.4   *Ex officio* with vote – any member of the General Board of Higher Education and Ministry residing within the bounds of the annual conference.

3.4.4   Organization.

3.4.4.1   The board shall be organized in three divisions as enumerated above.

3.4.4.2   Each division shall elect from among its members a convener.

3.4.4.3   One of the conveners shall serve as vice chairperson of the board. The conveners shall decide amongst themselves who this shall be.

3.4.4.4   In addition to the members enumerated above, an additional person, nominated by the Committee on Nominations, shall serve as the chairperson of the board. This chairperson shall be a member of the annual conference (if clergy) or a profession member of a local church within the annual conference (if laity).

3.4.4.5   *Ex officio* with voice, but no vote – A representative of the Michigan Area United Methodist Camping Board.

3.4.5   Amenability – The board shall be amenable to the Conference Leadership Council (§ 2.1, above).
3.4.6   Relationship – The board shall relate to the following general agencies.
3.4.6.1   General Board of Higher Education and Ministry.
3.4.6.2   Discipleship Ministries.

3.5 BOARD OF CONGREGATIONAL LIFE

3.5.1   Purpose.
3.5.1.1   Lead and assist the local churches of the annual conference in their efforts to communicate and celebrate the redeeming love of God as revealed in Jesus Christ and to invite persons into discipleship through this love.
3.5.1.2   Inform the conference and its agencies of the needs an opportunities of small membership churches.
3.5.1.3   Interpret and advocate for the unity of the Christian church, while encouraging dialog and cooperate with persons of other religions, starting at the local church level.
3.5.1.4   Promote and interpret ethnic local church concerns to the annual conference.
3.5.1.5   Collaborate with the director of congregational vibrancy in overseeing any staff and processes related to the development of vital congregations and new church development.
3.5.2   Duties.
3.5.2.1   Division of Congregational Vibrancy.
3.5.2.1.1   Develop a unified and comprehensive program for leadership training to serve all age groups in the home, church, and community.
3.5.2.1.2   Develop and promote a comprehensive program of Christian education for all ages.
3.5.2.1.3   Provide training for local church confirmation leaders.
3.5.2.1.4   Plan and promote an effective, comprehensive ministry of evangelism for persons of all ages.
3.5.2.1.5   Promote the use of *The United Methodist Hymnal* and *The United Methodist Book of Worship* in all local churches of the conference.
3.5.2.1.6   Promote seminars and training events in the area of worship, including music and other arts.
3.5.2.1.7   Plan and promote a comprehensive program of stewardship for all age groups.

3.5.2.1.8 Develop programming for the local church regarding ecology and the environment.

3.5.2.1.9 Promote and provide training regarding spiritual formation and devotional life for persons of all ages.

3.5.2.1.10 Fulfill all other responsibilities enumerated in ¶ 630 of *The Book of Discipline*.

3.5.2.2 Division on the Small-Membership Church.

3.5.2.2.1 Assist the Committee on Nominations in ensuring that laity and clergy from small-membership churches are included in the decision-making agencies of the annual conference.

3.5.2.2.2 Assist the resident bishop and cabinet in focusing on issues related to small membership churches.

3.5.2.2.3 Fulfill all other responsibilities enumerated in ¶ 645 of *The Book of Discipline*.

3.5.2.3 Division on Christian Unity and Interreligious Relationships.

3.5.2.3.1 Recommend to the annual conference goals, objectives, and strategies for the development of ecumenical relationships.

3.5.2.3.2 Encourage participation by the local churches of the annual conference in ecumenical ministries and missions.

3.5.2.3.3 Fulfill all other responsibilities enumerated in ¶ 642 of *The Book of Discipline*.

3.5.3 Membership.

3.5.3.1 Division of Congregational Vibrancy.

3.5.3.1.1 Four people who shall be members of the annual conference (if clergy) or professing members of a local church within the annual conference (if laity).

3.5.3.1.2 Members shall serve four-year terms, renewable once, in annually staggered classes.

3.5.3.1.3 Members shall be nominated by the Committee on Nominations.

3.5.3.1.4 *Ex officio* with vote – any member of Discipleship Ministries residing within the bounds of the annual conference.

3.5.3.2 Division on the Small-Membership Church.

3.5.3.2.1 Four people who shall be members of the annual conference (if clergy) or professing members of a local church within the annual conference (if laity).

3.5.3.2.2   Members shall serve four-year terms, renewable once, in annually staggered classes.

3.5.3.2.3   Members shall be nominated by the Committee on Nominations.

3.5.3.3   Division on Christian Unity and Interreligious Relationships.

3.5.3.3.1   Six persons who shall be members of the annual conference (if clergy) or professing members of a local church within the annual conference (if laity), one of whom shall serve as the district coordinator for Christian unity and interreligious relationships.

3.5.3.3.2   Members shall serve four-year terms, renewable once, in annually staggered classes.

3.5.3.3.3   Members shall be nominated by the Committee on Nominations.

3.5.3.3.4   *Ex officio* with vote – any United Methodists residing within the bounds of the annual conference who are members of the following:

3.5.3.3.4.1   The Office of Christian Unity and Interreligious Relationships of the Council of Bishops.

3.5.3.3.4.2   The governing board of the National Council of the Churches of Christ in the U.S.A.

3.5.3.3.4.3   The World Methodist Council.

3.5.3.3.4.4   The United Methodist delegation to the most recent World Council of Churches Assembly.

3.5.3.3.4.5   The United Methodist delegation to the most recent plenary meeting of Churches Uniting in Christ.

3.5.4   Organization.

3.5.4.1   The board shall be organized in four divisions as enumerated above.

3.5.4.2   Each division shall elect from among its members a convener. One of the conveners shall serve as vice chairperson of the board; the conveners shall decide amongst themselves who this shall be.

3.5.4.3   In addition to the members enumerated above, an additional person, nominated by the Committee on Nominations, shall serve as the chairperson of the board.

This chairperson shall be a member of the annual conference (if clergy) or a professing member of a local church within the annual conference (if laity).

        3.5.4.4   The director of congregational vibrancy shall be an *ex officio* member of the board with vote.

3.5.5   Amenability – The board shall be amenable to the Conference Leadership Council (§ 2.1, above).

3.5.6   Relationship – The board shall relate to Discipleship Ministries.

3.6 COMMITTEE ON HISPANIC/LATINO MINISTRY

3.6.1   Purpose.

        3.6.1.1   Implement the National Plan for Hispanic Ministry within the bounds of the conference.

        3.6.1.2   Provide direction and leadership for Hispanic/Latino ministries within the conference.

3.6.2   Duties – The committee shall, in keeping with its purpose (as set forth in § 3.6.1, above), define its duties in any way it sees fit, subject to the approval of the Conference Leadership Council.

3.6.3   Membership – The committee shall define its membership in any way it sees fit, subject to the approval of the Conference Leadership Council.

3.6.4   Organization – The committee shall organize itself in any way it sees fit, subject to the approval of the Conference Leadership Council.

3.6.5   Amenability – The committee shall be amenable to the Conference Leadership Council (§ 2.1, above).

3.7 COMMITTEE ON ASIAN-AMERICAN MINISTRY

3.7.1   Purpose.

        3.7.1.1   Develop and support leadership for Asian-American churches and communities within the annual conference.

        3.7.1.2   Train, support, and empower Asian-American clergy and lay leadership for effective ministry in their churches, their communities, and the world.

3.7.2   Duties – The committee shall, in keeping with its purpose (as set forth in § 3.7.1, above), define its duties in any way it sees fit, subject to the approval of the Conference Leadership Council.

3.7.3   Membership – The committee shall define its membership in any way it sees fit, subject to the approval of the Conference Leadership Council.

3.7.4   Organization – The committee shall organize itself in any way it sees fit, subject to the approval of the Conference Leadership Council.

3.7.5   Amenability – The committee shall be amenable to the Conference Leadership Council (§ 2.1, above).

3.8 COMMITTEE ON NATIVE AMERICAN MINISTRY
    3.8.1   Purpose – Monitor and promote Native American ministries within the annual conference.
    3.8.2   Duties.
        3.8.2.1   Manage the distribution of the Native American Ministries Sunday offering.
        3.8.2.2   Fulfill all other responsibilities enumerated in ¶ 654 of *The Book of Discipline.*
        3.8.2.3   The committee shall, in keeping with its purpose (as set forth in § 3.8.1, above), define any other duties in any way it sees fit, subject to the approval of the Conference Leadership Council.
    3.8.3   Membership.
        3.8.3.1   Insofar as possible, the majority of the committee's members should be Native Americans.
        3.8.3.2   Taking into account the mandate of § 3.8.3.1, above, the committee shall define its membership in any way it sees fit, subject to the approval of the Conference Leadership Council.
    3.8.4   Organization – The committee shall organize itself in any way it sees fit, subject to the approval of the Conference Leadership Council.
    3.8.5   Amenability – The committee shall be amenable to the Conference Leadership Council (§ 2.1, above).

3.9 COMMITTEE ON AFRICAN-AMERICAN MINISTRY
    3.9.1   Purpose.
        3.9.1.1   Develop and support leadership for African-American churches and communities within the annual conference.
        3.9.1.2   Train, support, and empower African-American clergy and lay leadership for effective ministry in their churches, their communities, and the world.
    3.9.2   Duties – The committee shall, in keeping with its purpose (as set forth in § 3.9.1, above), define its duties in any way it sees fit, subject to the approval of the Conference Leadership Council.
    3.9.3   Membership – The committee shall define its membership in any way it sees fit, subject to the approval of the Conference Leadership Council.
    3.9.4   Organization – The committee shall organize itself in any way it sees fit, subject to the approval of the Conference Leadership Council.
    3.9.5   Amenability – The committee shall be amenable to the Conference Leadership Council (§ 2.1, above).

§ 4 ADMINISTRATIVE AGENCIES

4.1 COUNCIL ON FINANCE AND ADMINISTRATION.
    4.1.1   Purpose – To develop, maintain, and administer a comprehensive and coordinated plan of fiscal and administrative policies,

procedures, and management services for the annual conference.

4.1.2   Duties.

4.1.2.1   Cooperation with the Conference Leadership Council in the development of the conference benevolences budget pursuant to ¶ 612.7 of *The Book of Discipline*.

4.1.2.2.   Presentation to the annual conference of a budget, developed in conjunction with the recommendations of the Conference Leadership Council.

4.1.2.3   Development of a ministry share formula for approval by the annual conference.

4.1.2.4   Ensure that appropriate compensation is provided for Clergy Assistant to the Bishop, the district superintendents, and the director of connectional ministries.

4.1.2.5   Develop policies for clergy moves undertaken in connection with a change in appointment.

4.1.2.6   Make a recommendation to the annual conference regarding any request for a conference-wide financial appeal.

4.1.2.7   Ensuring that the Commission on Equitable Compensation (§ 2.14, below), is fulfilling its responsibilities pursuant to *The Book of Discipline* and the direction of the annual conference.

4.1.2.7.1   Create and define, in consultation with the Committee on Human Resources, the position of Director of Conference Benefits and Human Resources.

4.1.2.8   Fulfill all other responsibilities enumerated in ¶¶ 613-618 of *The Book of Discipline*.

4.1.3   Membership.

4.1.3.1   With voice and vote.

4.1.3.1.1   Six clergy members of the annual conference.

4.1.3.1.2   Seven lay people who are professing members of a local church within the annual conference.

4.1.3.1.3   At least one of the thirteen members enumerated above shall be appointed to (in the case of a clergy person) or a member of (in the case of a lay person) a church with fewer than two hundred members.

4.1.3.2   *Ex officio* with voice and vote – Any member of the General Council on Finance and Administration who resides within the bounds of the annual conference.

4.1.3.3   *Ex officio* with voice only.

4.1.3.3.1   Director of Administrative Services and Conference Treasurer (see *The Book of Discipline, ¶ 619*).

4.1.3.3.2   Resident Bishop or clergy assistant to the Bishop (at the Bishop's discretion).

4.1.3.3.3 A district superintendent chosen by the Cabinet.

4.1.3.3.4 Director of Connectional Ministries (see *The Book of Discipline,* ¶ 608).

4.1.3.3.5 Director of Benefits and Human Resources.

4.1.3.3.6 Any other conference directors as the Conference Leadership Council shall designate.

4.1.3.3.7 Any director level benefits officer as determined by the Board of Pension and Health Benefits.

4.1.3.3.8 Chair of the Board of Trustees or their designee.

4.1.3.4 Members shall be nominated by the Committee on Nominations.

4.1.3.5 Members shall serve four-year terms (starting at the close of the annual conference session following General Conference), renewable once, with quadrennially staggered classes.

4.1.4 Organization.

4.1.4.1 The council shall elect from among its voting members a president, a vice president, and a secretary.

4.1.4.2 The Director of Administrative Services and Conference Treasurer (see *The Book of Discipline,* ¶ 619) shall be the council treasurer.

4.1.5 Relationship – The council shall relate to the General Council on Finance and Administration.

4.2 BOARD OF PENSION AND HEALTH BENEFITS

4.2.1 Purpose – Have charge of the interests and work of providing pension benefits and health insurance coverage to the clergy and eligible lay employees of the annual conference.

4.2.2 Duties.

4.2.2.1 Provide retirement, disability, and death benefits for all clergy members of the annual conference, their surviving spouses, and their dependent children.

4.2.2.2 Work with the Clergy Retirement Security Program of the General Board of Pension and Health Benefits.

4.2.2.3 Provide health insurance coverage for all clergy members, full-time local pastors, and full-time lay employees of the annual conference.

4.2.2.4 Continuously evaluate the quality and cost of the conference health insurance plan.

4.2.2.5 Provide information regarding conference health insurance benefits to all persons upon request.

4.2.2.6 Fulfill all other responsibilities enumerated in ¶ 639 of *The Book of Discipline*.

4.2.3 Membership.

4.2.3.1 Six clergy members of the annual conference.

4.2.3.2 Six lay persons who shall be professing members of a local church within the annual conference.

4.2.3.3 Members shall be nominated by the Committee on Nominations.

4.2.3.4 Members shall serve one non-renewable eight-year term, in annually staggered classes.

4.2.3.5 *Ex officio* with vote.

4.2.3.5.1 Any board member of Wespath Benefits and Investments residing within the bounds of the annual conference.

4.2.3.5.2 A district superintendent designated by the cabinet.

4.2.3.6 *Ex officio* with voice, but no vote.

4.2.3.6.1 Director of Administrative Services and Conference Treasurer (see *The Book of Discipline,* ¶ 619).

4.2.3.6.2 Director of Benefits and Human Resources.

4.2.3.6.3 Any other conference directors as the Conference Leadership Council shall designate.

4.2.3.6.4 Any director level benefits officer as determined by the Board.

4.2.4 Organization.

4.2.4.1 The committee shall elect from among its members the following officers:

4.2.4.1.1 Chairperson.

4.2.4.1.2 Vice chairperson.

4.2.4.1.3 Secretary.

4.2.4.2 The Director of Administrative Services and Conference Treasurer (see *The Book of Discipline,* ¶ 619) shall serve as the treasurer of the board.

4.2.4.3 The executive committee of the board shall be composed of the four officers enumerated above.

4.2.5 Relationship – The board shall relate to Wespath Benefits and Investments.

4.3 ADMINISTRATIVE REVIEW COMMITTEE

4.3.1 Purpose – To ensure that the disciplinary procedures for involuntary changes in conference relationship are followed.

4.3.2 Duties.

4.3.2.1 Review the entire administrative process leading to the action for a change in conference relationship.

4.3.2.2 Report to the clergy session on the finding of its review.

4.3.2.3 Fulfill all other responsibilities enumerated in ¶ 636 of *The Book of Discipline.*

4.3.3 Membership.

4.3.3.1 Three full clergy members of the annual conference.

4.3.3.2 Two additional full clergy members of the annual conference who shall serve as alternate committee members.

4.3.3.3   None of the foregoing shall be a district superintendent (or a relative thereof) or a member of the Board of Ordained Ministry (or a relative thereof).

4.3.3.4   Members shall be nominated by the Bishop.

2.5.3.5   Members shall serve four-year terms, renewable once.

4.4 BOARD OF TRUSTEES

4.4.1   Purpose – Management of property owned by the annual conference.

4.4.2   Duties.

4.4.2.1   Receive and hold in trust for the benefit of the annual conference all donations and bequests of real property and tangible personal property made to the annual conference.

4.4.2.2   Maintain all conference property.

4.4.2.3   Sell any conference property as may be directed by the annual conference or allowed by *The Book of Discipline*.

4.4.2.4   In conjunction with the conference chancellor, manage any legal affairs related to any conference property.

4.4.2.5   The Board of Trustees shall serve as the Board of Directors of the Michigan Conference of The United Methodist Church, a Michigan ecclesiastical corporation.

4.4.2.5   Fulfill all other responsibilities enumerated in ¶ 2512 of *The Book of Discipline*.

4.4.3   Membership.

4.4.3.1   Six clergy members of the annual conference.

4.4.3.2   Six lay persons who are professing members of a local church within the annual conference.

4.4.3.3   *Ex officio* with voice, but not vote.

     4.4.3.3.1   Director of Administrative Services and Conference Treasurer (see *The Book of Discipline*, ¶ 619).

     4.4.3.3.2   Director of Connectional Ministries (see *The Book of Discipline*, ¶ 608).

     4.4.3.3.3   President of the Council on Finance and Administration, or their designee.

4.4.3.4   All board members must be at least eighteen years of age.

4.4.3.5   All board members must fulfill any other criteria for serving on the board of directors of a corporation that the laws of the State of Michigan may require.

4.4.3.6   Members shall be nominated by the Committee on Nominations.

4.4.3.7   Except as otherwise required by law, members shall be elected to four-year terms, renewable once, with annually staggered classes.

4.4.4   Organization.

4.4.4.1   Except as otherwise required by law, the board shall elect the following from among its members:

1.5.4.1.1   Chairperson.

1.5.4.1.2   Vice chairperson.

1.5.4.1.3   Secretary.

4.4.4.2   Except as otherwise required by law, the Director of Administrative Services and Conference Treasurer (see *The Book of Discipline,* ¶ 619) shall serve as the board treasurer.

4.5 COMMITTEE ON INVESTIGATION

4.5.1   Purpose – Consideration of judicial complaints against clergy members of the annual conference, clergy on location within the bounds of the annual conference, local pastors, and diaconal ministers.

4.5.2   Duties.

    4.5.2.1   Conduct an investigation into the allegations made in a judicial complaint made against any of the persons enumerated above.

    4.5.2.2   Issue a bill of charges and specifications against the respondent to a judicial complaint upon a finding of reasonable grounds.

    4.5.2.3   Fulfill all other responsibilities enumerated in ¶¶ 2703-2706 of *The Book of Discipline.*

4.5.3   Membership.

    4.5.3.1   Four ordained clergy members of the annual conference.

    4.5.3.2   Three lay people who are professing members of a local church within the annual conference.

    4.5.3.3   Three ordained clergy members of the annual conference shall serve as alternate members.

    4.5.3.4   Six lay people – three of whom, if possible, shall be diaconal ministers – who are professing members of a local church within the annual conference shall serve as alternate members.

    4.5.3.5   Members shall be nominated by the resident bishop.

    4.5.3.6   Members shall serve a one-quadrennium term.

    4.5.3.7   Members of the following entities and their immediate family members shall be ineligible for membership of the committee:

        4.5.3.7.1   Cabinet.

        4.5.3.7.2   Board of Ordained Ministry.

4.5.4   Organization.

    4.5.4.1   The committee shall elect a chairperson from among its membership.

    4.5.4.2   Seven members (or alternate members seated as members) shall constitute a quorum.

    4.5.4.3   For the investigation of complaints against a diaconal minister, two alternate lay members shall be seated (bringing the total of lay members to five).

4.6 COMMITTEE ON RULES

4.6.1   Purpose.

    4.6.1.1   In consultation with the Conference Leadership Council, maintain the efficient functionality and disciplinary compliance of the annual conference plan of organization.

4.6.1.2 Consult with the Commission on the Annual Conference Session to ensure the efficient and orderly flow of the legislative process in preparation for and at the annual conference session.

4.6.2   Duties.

4.6.2.1 Initiate and propose revisions of the annual conference plan of organization as appropriate.

4.6.2.2 Initiate and propose revisions of the rules of order (§ 5, below) as appropriate.

4.6.2.3 Assign and train legislative committee chairs and recorders.

4.6.3   Membership.

4.6.3.1 Eight voting members who shall be either clergy members of the annual conference or lay people who are members of a local church within the annual conference.

4.6.3.2 *Ex officio* with vote.

    4.6.3.2.1 Legislative Coordinator (Selected by the Commission on the Annual Conference Session)

    4.6.3.2.2 Annual Conference Facilitator.

    4.6.3.2.3 A district superintendent designated by the cabinet.

    4.6.3.2.4 Annual Conference Secretary.

    4.6.3.2.5 Conference parliamentarian (if one is appointed by the bishop).

4.6.3.3 *Ex officio* with voice, but no vote – Director of Connectional Ministries (see *The Book of Discipline*, ¶ 608).

4.6.3.4 Members shall be nominated by the Committee on Nominations.

4.6.3.5 Members shall serve four-year terms, renewable twice, in annually staggered classes.

4.6.4   Organization.

4.6.4.1 The committee shall elect from among its members the following officers:

    4.6.4.1.1 Chairperson.

    4.6.4.1.2 Vice-chairperson.

    4.6.4.1.3 Secretary.

4.7 EPISCOPAL RESIDENCE COMMITTEE

4.7.1   Purpose – Give oversight in matters of upkeep, maintenance, improvements, and insurance for the episcopal residence.

4.7.2   Duties.

4.7.2.1 Make recommendations regarding the purchase or sale of an episcopal residence.

4.7.2.2 Prepare a proposed annual budget for the cost of providing the episcopal residence.

4.7.2.3 Supervise the expenditure of funds related to the maintenance and upkeep of the episcopal residence.

       4.7.2.4 Fulfill all other responsibilities enumerated in ¶ 638 of *The Book of Discipline.*

4.7.3   Membership.

       4.7.3.1 Chairperson of the Committee on the Episcopacy (or representative).

       4.7.3.2 President of the Council on Finance and Administration (or representative).

       4.7.3.3 Chairperson of the Board of Trustees (or representative).

       4.7.3.4 Others may be co-opted, with voice but without vote, as needed.

4.7.4   Amenability – The committee shall be amenable to the Committee on the Episcopacy (§ 2.10, above).

4.8 COMMISSION ON EQUITABLE COMPENSATION

4.8.1   Purpose – Recommend conference standards for pastoral support and administer funds used to supplement pastoral support in instances where a charge is unable to meet its support requirements.

4.8.2   Duties.

       4.8.2.1 Submit to the annual conference session a recommended schedule of the required minimum salary for appointed pastors.

       4.8.2.2 Recommend to the annual conference standards and guidelines to be used in determining whether a charge qualifies for equitable compensation support.

       4.8.2.3 Administer the equitable compensation fund in accordance with the standards and guidelines adopted by the annual conference.

       4.8.2.4 Fulfill all other responsibilities enumerated in ¶ 625 of *The Book of Discipline.*

4.8.3   Membership.

       4.8.3.1 Four clergy members of the annual conference, at least one of whom shall be appointed to a church with fewer than 200 members.

       4.8.3.2 Four lay persons who shall be professing members of a church within the annual conference, at least one of whom shall be a member of a church with fewer than 200 members.

       4.8.3.3 Members shall serve four-year terms, renewable once, in annually staggered classes.

       4.8.3.4 Members shall be nominated by the Committee on Nominations.

       4.8.3.5 *Ex officio* with vote.

          4.8.3.5.1 A district superintendent appointed by the cabinet.

          4.8.3.5.2 A member of the Council on Finance and Administration.

       4.8.3.6 *Ex officio* with voice, but no vote – Director of Administrative Services and Conference Treasurer (see *The Book of Discipline,* ¶ 619).

4.8.4   Organization.
  4.8.4.1   The commission shall elect from among its members
    the following officers:
    4.8.4.1.1   Chairperson.
    4.8.4.1.2   Vice chairperson.
    4.8.4.1.3   Secretary.
  4.8.4.2   The Director of Administrative Services and Confer-
    ence Treasurer (see *The Book of Discipline,* ¶ 619)
    shall serve as the treasurer of the commission.
4.8.5   Amenability – The board shall be amenable to the Council on
  Finance and Administration (§ 4.1, above).

4.9   COMMITTEE ON HUMAN RESOURCES

4.9.1   Purpose – Provide adequate program and support staff to carry
  out the purposes, goals, and responsibilities of the annual conference.

4.9.2   Duties.
  4.9.2.1   The committee shall be amenable to the Council on
    Finance and Administration with respect to adminis-
    trative human resources policies and procedures.
    While the committee is primarily an administrative
    committee, it has a critical role in the programming
    functions of the conference. It is the responsibility of
    the committee to constantly evaluate the conference's
    staffing needs vis-à-vis the vision and mission of the
    conference.
  4.9.2.2   The committee shall also be amenable to the Confer-
    ence Leadership Council, having input and taking di-
    rection on conference staffing as it relates to the
    mission and vision of the conference.
  4.9.2.3   Consult and collaborate with director level staff and
    the appointive cabinet (as needed) on the hiring, eval-
    uation, support, training, and termination of non-ex-
    empt and exempt staff.
  4.9.2.4   Guide the annual evaluation of director level staff.
  4.9.2.5   Oversee the implementation of conference human
    resources policies and procedures handbook.
  4.9.2.6   Oversee the editing and maintenance of the confer-
    ence employee handbook.
  4.9.2.7   Defines the role and functions of the Director of Bene-
    fits and Human Resources in consultation with the
    Council on Finance and Administration.

4.9.3   Membership.
  4.9.3.1   Eight people who shall be members of the annual
    conference (if clergy) or professing members of a
    local church within the annual conference (if laity).
  4.9.3.2   Members shall serve four-year terms, renewable
    once, in annually staggered classes.
  4.9.3.3   Members shall be nominated by the Committee on
    Nominations.
  4.9.3.4   *Ex officio* with vote.

4.9.3.4.1   Bishop or clergy assistant to the Bishop (at the Bishop's discretion).

4.9.3.4.2   A district superintendent chosen by the cabinet.

4.9.3.5   *Ex officio* with voice, but no vote.

4.9.3.5.1   Director of Connectional Ministries (see *The Book of Discipline*, ¶ 608).

4.9.3.5.2   Director of Administrative Services and Conference Treasurer (see *The Book of Discipline*, ¶ 609).

4.9.3.5.3   Director of Benefits and Human Resources.

4.9.3.5.4   Chair of the personnel committee of the Council on Finance and Administration.

4.9.4   Organization.

4.9.4.1   A chairperson chosen by the Committee on Nominations from among the members.

4.9.4.2   A vice-chairperson chosen by the Committee on Human Resources from among its membership.

4.9.4.3   A secretary chosen by the Committee on Human Resources from among its membership.

4.9.5   Amenability – The committee shall be amenable to the Council on Finance and Administration (§ 4.1., above) and the Conference Leadership Council (§ 2.1, above) as expounded in §§ 4.9.2.1 and 4.9.2.2, above.

§ 5   RULES OF ORDER

5.1   PRE-CONFERENCE

5.1.1   Reports.

5.1.1.1   All agencies that are directly amenable to the annual conference (enumerated hereinabove) and director-level staff of the annual conference are required to submit an annual report to the conference secretary no later than February 15. These reports shall be available on the conference website no later than April 1 and shall be included in the conference journal. Each agency's report shall include the report of any agencies amenable to it. (See § 5.1.1.4, below.)

5.1.1.2   Notwithstanding § 5.1.1.1, the Board of Pension and Health Benefits and the Director of Administrative Services and Conference Treasurer shall submit an annual report no later than March 31.

5.1.1.3   Notwithstanding § 5.1.1.1, the Committee on Nominations shall submit an annual report no later than the start of the annual conference session.

5.1.1.4   All agencies not directly amenable to the annual conference (enumerated hereinabove) shall submit a report to the agency to which they are amenable no later than January 20. These reports shall be included in the reports of those supervising agencies as specified in § 5.1.1.1, above.

5.1.1.5 The report of the conference statistician shall be available on the conference website no later than March 31 and shall be printed in the Journal.

5.1.1.6 The proposed plan of organization of the annual conference shall be made available on the conference website no later than April 15 and shall be printed in the Journal.

5.1.2 Resolutions.

5.1.2.1 A resolution – a motion to initiate new business in the annual conference session – may be submitted by any of the following:

5.1.2.1.1 A clergy member of the annual conference.

5.1.2.1.2 A professing member of a local church within the annual conference.

5.1.2.1.3 A specific person on behalf of an agency or other subdivision of the annual conference.

5.1.2.1.4 A specific person on behalf of a local church or ministry setting of the annual conference or a committee thereof.

5.1.2.2 All resolutions, upon being introduced in the annual conference session, must be presented by a member (clergy or lay) of the annual conference. The presenter of the resolution need not be the author of the resolution.

5.1.2.3 All resolutions must be submitted in writing to the Legislative Coordinator no later than February 15.

5.1.2.4 A copy of any resolution that would require an expenditure of more than $1000 must be sent to the Council on Finance and Administration, along with a five-year cost projection, no later than February 1.

5.1.2.5 If a resolution is submitted by multiple persons or entities, only the name of the person(s) actually signing it shall be published as the submitter. If more than two people actually sign a resolution, only the first two names will be published, along with the total number of additional signers.

5.1.2.6 Resolutions may be accompanied by a rationale, which shall not exceed 300 words.

5.1.2.7 The Committee on Rules reserves the right to edit any resolution for grammar, spelling, and clarity. The committee's edits shall not substantively alter the resolution.

5.1.2.8 Anyone submitting a resolution that affects other people or other entities is strongly encouraged to consult with the affected parties before submitting the resolution.

5.1.2.9 Anyone wishing to introduce a resolution (that was not timely submitted) directly in the plenary at the Annual Conference session must (in addition to requesting a suspension of the rules [§ 5.1.2.3]) have brought the following:

5.1.2.9.1   At least 1700 paper copies of the resolution.

5.1.2.9.2   A copy of the resolution on a thumb drive.

5.1.3   All resolutions and other items that must be voted or acted upon by the annual conference shall be posted to the conference website no later than April 15.

5.1.4   All requests for presentation time at the annual conference session must be made to the Commission on the Annual Conference Session no later than February 15. The granting of such requests shall be at the discretion of the Commission on the Annual Conference Session.

5.2 MEMBERSHIP

5.2.1   The annual conference membership shall be composed of the following:

5.2.1.1   Clergy members as defined in ¶¶ 32 and 602 of *The Book of Discipline.*

5.2.1.2   At least one lay person elected by each charge.

5.2.1.2.1   A charge that has more than one church with 101 or more professing members shall elect one lay member for each church with 101 or more professing members.

5.2.1.2.2   Each charge with more than one clergy person under episcopal appointment shall be entitled to as many lay members as it has clergy under episcopal appointment.

5.2.1.2.3   Churches with more than 167 professing members shall be entitled to at least one lay member for every 167 professing members or major fraction thereof.

5.2.1.2.4   Lay members shall have been professing members of The United Methodist Church for at least two years and shall have been active participants in The United Methodist Church for at least four years.

5.2.1.2.5   The rule that lay members shall have been professing members of The United Methodist Church for at least two years (§ 5.2.1.2.4, above) shall not apply in the case of youth (under age 18).

5.2.1.3   Deaconesses and home missioners under episcopal appointment within the bounds of the annual conference.

5.2.1.4   Diaconal ministers who are members of a local church within the annual conference.

5.2.1.5   Presidents of the conference United Methodist Women and United Methodist Men.

5.2.1.6   Conference lay leader.

5.2.1.7   District lay leaders.

5.2.1.8   Convener of the Division of Youth Ministry of the Board of Young People's Ministries.

5.2.1.9   Convener of the Division of Young Adult Ministry of the Board of Young People's Ministries.

5.2.1.10 One person between the ages of 12 and **18,** inclusive, **from each district.**

5.2.1.11 One person between the ages of 18 and 30, inclusive, **from each district.**

5.2.1.12 Conference director of lay servant ministries.

5.2.1.13 Conference secretary of global ministries.

5.2.2   In order to equalize lay and clergy membership as required by ¶¶ 32 and 602.4 of *The Book of Discipline*, the following persons, when laity, shall be members of the annual conference in the order listed below.

5.2.2.1   Conference secretary.

5.2.2.2   Conference chancellor.

5.2.2.3   Annual Conference Coordinator.

5.2.2.4   Director of Administrative Services/Conference Treasurer (see *The Book of Discipline,* ¶ 619).

5.2.2.5   Conference parliamentarian.

5.2.2.6   Associate conference lay leader.

5.2.2.7   Director of Connectional Ministries (see *The Book of Discipline,* ¶ 608).

5.2.2.8   Any other conference director.

5.2.2.9   Any conference associate director.

5.2.2.10 Chairperson of the Committee on the Episcopacy.

5.2.2.11 Persons serving on general or jurisdictional agencies or the Connectional Table.

5.2.2.12 Delegates to General and Jurisdictional Conferences for the four Annual Conference sessions following their election.

5.2.2.13 Conference statistician.

5.2.2.14 Members of the Committee on Rules.

5.2.2.15 Members of the Conference Leadership Council.

5.2.2.16 Members of the Council on Finance and Administration.

5.2.2.17 Trustees of the annual conference.

5.2.2.18 Legislative coordinator.

5.2.2.19 Conference facilitator.

5.2.2.20 Members of the Commission on the Annual Conference Session.

5.2.2.21 Members of the Committee on the Journal.

5.2.2.22 Members of the Board of Ordained Ministry.

5.2.2.23 Chairpersons of other conference agencies (enumerated in §§ 1-4, above).

5.2.3   Any remaining lay members necessary for equalization shall be selected by the Board of Laity.

5.2.4   The following, if laity, shall be granted voice but not vote:

     5.2.4.1   A representative from each of the affiliate entities enumerated in § 10, below.

     5.2.4.2   Affiliate clergypersons.

5.3 RESPONSIBILITY FOR THE COST OF ATTENDANCE

5.3.1   Active clergy – The local church or ministry to which clergy are appointed shall pay for registration, room, and board.

5.3.2   Retired clergy (except as stated in § 5.3.7, below).

     5.3.2.1   The annual conference shall pay for registration.

     5.3.2.2   Retired clergy shall pay for their own room and board.

5.3.3   Laity representing charges – The charge shall pay for registration, room, and board.

5.3.4   Laity attending by virtue of office (enumerated in §§ 5.2.1.3 through 5.2.1.13 and 5.2.2, above) – The annual conference shall pay for registration, room, and board.

5.3.5   Laity selected by the Board of Laity (as per § 5.2.3, above) – The annual conference shall pay for registration, room, and board.

5.3.6   Those who are being received into provisional membership and who are not currently serving as local pastors – the Board of Ordained Ministry shall pay for registration, room, and board.

5.3.7   Notwithstanding § 5.3.2, above, the Board of Ordained Ministry shall pay for registration, room, and board for retired clergy serving on the Board of Ordained Ministry.

5.4 THE ANNUAL CONFERENCE SESSION

5.4.1   In accordance with ¶ 603.2 of *The Book of Discipline*, the Bishop shall determine the time of the annual conference session.

5.4.2   The Commission on the Annual Conference Session shall determine the place and the program for the annual conference session.

5.4.3   In addition to the business (plenary) sessions of the annual conference, the following sessions shall also be held:

     5.4.3.1   An orientation session for lay members of the annual conference shall be held early in the conference session. It is recommended that this be done as early as possible.

     5.4.3.2   Clergy session.

         5.4.3.2.1   A clergy session shall be held at which questions relating to matters of ordination, character, and conference relations of clergy shall be attended to.

         5.4.3.2.2   Ordained clergy and lay members of the Board of Ordained Ministry shall have voice and vote in the clergy session.

         5.4.3.2.3   Non-ordained clergy shall have voice, but no vote in the clergy session.

         5.4.3.2.4   Lay persons, other than those serving on the Board of Ordained Ministry, shall not be admitted to the clergy session unless the clergy session shall expressly authorize otherwise.

5.4.3.3   Corporate session.

     5.4.3.3.1   A corporate session shall be held to handle any corporate matters that may be required by the laws of the State of Michigan and any other business specified by the Board of Trustees.

     5.4.3.3.2   The chair of the Board of Trustees shall preside at the corporate session.

5.4.4   All materials distributed by the ushers at the annual conference session must be approved by either the Commission on the Annual Conference Session or the Committee on Rules.

5.4.5   Voting area.

     5.4.5.1   At the first business session of the annual conference session, a voting bar shall be fixed. All members of the annual conference, lay and clergy, must display a membership badge in order to be admitted to the bar of the conference.

     5.4.5.2   Except for volunteers assisting with the functioning of the annual conference session (*e.g.*, ushers and pages), paid personnel acting within the course of their duties (*e.g.*, audio-visual technicians and facilities staff), area office staff, and anyone entitled to voice but not vote in the annual conference session (as enumerated in § 5.2.4, above), no one who is not a voting member of the annual conference shall be allowed in the bar of the conference when the conference is in session.

     5.4.5.3   Except by leave of the annual conference, no member who is not within the bar of the conference at the time a question is called for shall be allowed to vote.

5.4.6   Accessibility – Handicap accessible seating areas shall be clearly marked at all Annual Conference business sessions.

5.4.7   Voting procedure.

     5.4.7.1   All voting shall be by show of colored placards unless otherwise directed by the presiding officer. A division of the house shall occur upon motion for same, supported by at least one-fifth of the members present and voting.

     5.4.7.2   Except as otherwise directed by *The Book of Discipline* or by these rules, all questions shall be decided by a simple majority of those present and voting.

5.4.8   No later than 11:00 a.m., the minutes of the previous day's proceedings shall be made publicly available for viewing, by posting in a conspicuous place at the site of the conference session, posting to the conference website, or e-mailing to conference members.

5.4.9   Reports timely submitted for approval need not be read aloud or read into the record before being voted upon.

5.4.10 Introductions of speakers shall be limited to two minutes.

5.4.11 Opportunity shall be given for announcements to be read by the conference secretary at the close of each business session.

5.4.12 Procedures governing speeches from the floor of the business session.

    5.4.12.1 Microphones shall be placed around the conference floor so that members may speak from near their seats.

    5.4.12.2 Any member desiring to speak in debate, present any matter, or make any motion shall raise the provided colored placard while seated and wait to be recognized by the chair.

    5.4.12.3 Upon being recognized by the chair, members shall proceed to the microphone to which they were directed and before saying anything else shall give their name and the church or extension ministry to which they are appointed (in the case of active clergy), church (in the case of laity representing their local church pursuant to § 5.2.1.2, above), agency or position (in the case of laity who are members by virtue of office pursuant to § 5.2.2, above), equalization status (in the case of laity selected by the Board of Laity pursuant to § 5.2.3, above), or retired status (in the case of retired clergy).

    5.4.12.4 After identifying themselves, members speaking to a motion shall state whether they are speaking for or against said motion.

    5.4.12.5 Any member desiring to speak on a question of privilege shall, upon being recognized by the chair, briefly state the question but shall proceed only when the chair has decided it to be a privileged question.

    5.4.12.6 No member shall speak more than twice as to the same motion.

    5.4.12.7 Speeches shall be no longer than three minutes in duration. This time period shall begin after a speaker has been properly recognized by the Chair and has properly introduced himself/herself.

    5.4.12.8 Except for non-debatable motions, no resolution, report, or motion shall be adopted or a question relating thereto decided without opportunity having been given for at least three speeches in favor thereof and three speeches against.

    5.4.12.9 Before debate on any resolution begins, the presenter or his/her representative shall have the opportunity to speak for up to three minutes.

    5.4.12.10 At the conclusion of debate on any main motion, the presenter of said motion or his/her representative shall be entitled to speak up to one minute even after the previous question has been called.

5.4.13   Legislative committees.

    5.4.13.1 The Committee on Rules shall, in consultation with the Commission on the Annual Conference Session, decide the number of legislative committees into which the annual conference will be divided.

    5.4.13.2 The conference registrar shall randomly assign all members to a legislative committee, with care being given to make certain that members with disabilities be assigned to a committee meeting in a room with barrier-free access.

    5.4.13.3 All resolutions to come before the annual conference shall be assigned by the Committee on Rules to any of the legislative committees. The Committee on Rules may, at its discretion assign resolutions directly to the plenary, by-passing legislative committees. Such an action should only be taken in cases where a resolution is non-controversial and/or highly technical in nature.

    5.4.13.4 All resolutions, upon initially being brought to the floor (whether in a legislative committee or in the plenary) shall be introduced by a presenter who must be a member of the annual conference. The presenter shall have up to three minutes to speak to the resolution before debate begins. At the conclusion of debate, the presenter of said motion shall be entitled to speak up to one minute even after the previous question has been called. No resolution shall be considered by its assigned committee unless a presenter is present at the committee session. In the event no presenter for a resolution is present, no one may designate himself/herself as a presenter.

    5.4.13.5 All rules governing debate in the plenary session shall govern debate in legislative committees.

    5.4.13.6 Notwithstanding § 5.4.13.2, the chairperson and recorder of a given legislative committee shall be members (with all privileges appertaining thereto) of that committee only.

    5.4.13.7 Notwithstanding § 5.4.13.2, the presenter of a resolution being considered by a given legislative committee shall be a member of that committee only.

    5.4.13.8 If a resolution has more than one presenter, only one of those presenters shall be entitled to voice and vote in the committee (except for presenters who were originally selected by the registrar as members of that committee).

    5.4.13.9 When a legislative committee votes in favor of a resolution, the resolution shall come before the plenary as perfected for ordinary debate and discussion in accordance with all applicable rules.

    5.4.13.10 When a legislative committee votes against a resolution, the question of whether to consider that resolution notwithstanding the vote of the legislative committee shall be brought to the plenary. Only in the event that at least 20% of the plenary votes in favor of consideration shall the resolution then be considered by the plenary.

5.4.13.11 When the question of consideration of a resolution notwithstanding the vote of the legislative committee is brought before the plenary in accordance with § 5.4.13.11, the presenter of the resolution shall not have the opportunity to speak before the vote on whether to consider the resolution is taken. Should the plenary vote to consider a resolution notwithstanding the vote of the legislative committee, the presenter shall then have the opportunity to speak for up to three minutes before debate begins and shall have the right to give a concluding speech (§ 5.4.12.10).

5.4.13.12 A legislative committee may only consider business assigned to it by the Committee on Rules, except that any substitute resolution duly moved by a member of the legislative committee shall be considered by the committee.

5.4.13.13 At the discretion of the Commission on the Annual Conference Session, a non-legislative discussion item may be assigned to the several legislative committees provided that such discussion advances a clearly defined purpose.

5.4.13.14 After the legislative committees have concluded their business, the Legislative Coordinator shall compile a written report of their work, to be presented to the plenary as soon as possible. The report shall contain the following:

5.4.13.15.1 Editorial corrections to any resolutions.

5.4.13.15.2 Proposed amendments (to any resolutions or substitute resolutions), including the results of the votes thereon.

5.4.13.15.3 Proposed secondary amendments (to any resolutions or substitute resolutions), including the results of the votes thereon.

5.4.13.15.4 Proposed substitute resolutions, including the results of the votes thereon.

5.4.13.15.5 The results of the final votes taken on all resolutions (or substitutes thereto).

5.4.13.15.6 The names of the committee chairs and recorders.

5.4.13.15.7 A listing of which resolutions have been placed on the consent calendar (see § 5.4.14, below).

5.4.13.15 Once adopted, all resolutions shall be valid until the close of the Annual Conference session eight years thence (unless otherwise prohibited by The Book of Discipline).

PLAN OF ORGANIZATION

5.4.14 Consent calendar.
    5.4.14.1 Any resolution (or substitute resolution) that sustains a vote of concurrence by at least nine-tenths of its legislative committee shall be placed on the conference consent calendar.
    5.4.14.2 All resolutions placed on the conference consent calendar shall be considered *en masse* by the plenary, whose consideration of the consent calendar shall not be subject to debate, amendment, or substitution.
    5.4.14.3 Notwithstanding § 5.4.14.2, any resolution may be removed from the consent calendar by a vote of at least two-fifths of the plenary. Any resolution, upon being removed from the consent calendar, shall be considered as an ordinary item of business.
    5.4.14.4 The consent calendar shall not be brought to a vote until at least two hours after it has been distributed to the members of the conference.

5.4.15 Adopted resolutions.
    5.4.15.1 All adopted resolutions shall be published on the conference website as soon as is practical.
    5.4.15.2 The conference secretary shall determine which resolutions require action by an agency, officer, or employee of the annual conference and shall, as soon as is practical after the close of the annual conference session, submit the relevant resolution(s) to the parties of whom action is required.
    5.4.15.3 Any resolution or any portion of a resolution subsequently ruled by a bishop's decision of law to be null, void, and/or of no effect shall immediately be removed from the conference website, and all conference action thereon shall immediately cease. In the event that the Judicial Council fails to sustain the ruling of the Bishop in whole or in part, any reinstated portion of the resolution shall immediately be returned to the conference website, and all conference action thereon shall immediately resume.
    5.4.15.4 Except as otherwise specified either therein or by *The Book of Discipline*, all resolutions adopted by the annual conference shall be valid from the close of the annual conference session until the close of the following annual conference session.

5.5 NOMINATIONS
5.5.1 Each agency shall annually review its membership to identify members who have not functioned. After consultation with the person(s) so identified, a written request for replacement shall be sent to the Committee on Nominations no later than January 10, with a copy of such request sent to the person(s) so identified.
5.5.2 Any agency wishing to suggest nominees may do so by submitting the request in writing to the Committee on Nominations no later than January 10.

5.5.3   Except as otherwise required by *The Book of Discipline,* all terms of office shall begin at the close of the annual conference session.

5.5.4   Aside from *ex officio* membership, no one may serve on more than two agencies at once.

5.5.5   The Committee on Nominations, when nominating persons for agency membership, shall give primary consideration to aptness, experience, diversity, inclusiveness, and efficiency.

5.5.6   Aside from *ex officio* membership, no employee of the annual conference shall be eligible to serve on an agency that has supervisory responsibility over the area of that employee's work.

5.5.7   Except as otherwise provided herein, no district superintendent shall serve on a conference agency.

5.5.8   At the annual conference session immediately following General Conference, the annual conference shall elect people – nominated by the Committee on Nominations in consultation with the Conference Leadership Council – to the following positions:

     5.5.8.1   Secretary.

     5.5.8.2   Director of Administrative Services and Conference Treasurer (see *The Book of Discipline,* ¶ 619).

     5.5.8.3   Statistician.

5.5.9   For purposes of organization each council, board, commission, division or committee required to elect its own officers as provided in the Plan of Organization shall be convened on call by a person named by the Director of Connectional Ministries. The convener shall be someone other than a member of such group and shall conduct the election of the officers to be elected.

5.6 DEPENDENT CARE

5.6.1   While carrying out the responsibilities of the annual conference or any agency thereof, members may be reimbursed for dependent care provided in their homes. Such reimbursement shall not exceed ten hours per day and shall not exceed minimum wage.

5.6.2   Each agency shall be responsible for budgeting for appropriate dependent care expenses when considering its membership and time requirements.

5.6.3   Dependent care expenses shall be vouchered and reimbursed.

5.6.4   Local churches are encouraged to support members in need of dependent care for conference responsibilities by volunteering to provide dependent care whenever possible.

5.6.5   Agency members are encouraged to enlist family members and friends for dependent care whenever possible.

5.6.6   Conference agencies may choose to provide on-site childcare. In such cases, parents shall be responsible for bringing necessary items (*e.g.*, toys, lunches) for their children. The conference protection policy (§ 8, below) shall be strictly followed.

PLAN OF ORGANIZATION

5.7 GENERAL AND JURISDICTIONAL CONFERENCES

5.7.1   Nomination of candidates for General and Jurisdictional Conference delegation.

5.7.1.1   Nomination forms designed by the Committee on Rules and the Order of Business shall be made available on the conference website no later than October 15 of the calendar year preceding delegate elections.

5.7.1.2   Candidates may be nominated by themselves or by another clergy member of the annual conference (in the case of clergy) or by another professing member of a local church within the annual conference (in the case of laity).

5.7.1.3   The names of the candidates and the information on their nomination forms shall be posted to the conference website no later than April 1.

5.7.2   Election of delegates.

5.7.2.1   Elections shall occur at the annual conference session in the calendar year immediately preceding General Conference.

5.7.2.2   The Commission on the Annual Conference Session shall appoint a group of tellers, who shall be composed of people ineligible (as per ¶¶ 35-36 of *The Book of Discipline*) and/or unwilling to serve as delegates.

5.7.2.3   The election of General Conference delegates and Jurisdictional Conference delegates shall constitute a single process, with General Conference delegates being elected first.

5.7.2.4   Eligible voters may vote for as many different people as are being elected on a particular ballot.

5.7.2.5   In order to be elected, a candidate must receive a vote on a simple majority of valid (*i.e.*, non-defective) ballots cast.

5.7.2.6   Clergy and laity ballots shall be taken separately, alternating between the two.

5.7.2.7   After the designated number of delegates for General Conference has been elected, the election of Jurisdictional Conference delegates shall begin on the following ballot.

5.7.2.8   The Jurisdictional Conference delegates shall serve as reserve delegates to General Conference in the order elected.

5.7.2.9   After the designated number of delegates for Jurisdictional Conference has been elected, an additional ballot shall be taken, on which the two highest vote-getters (regardless of whether their vote totals constitute a majority) shall be elected as reserve delegates to Jurisdictional Conference.

5.7.2.10 Ties shall be broken by the casting of lots.

5.7.2.11 All conference members must be seated in the bar of the conference at the time a vote is taken in order to vote.

5.7.2.12 A ballot that includes more votes than people being elected on that ballot shall be invalid and shall not be counted in the vote total.

5.7.2.13 After each vote, the secretary of the conference (or a person designated by him/her) shall announce the number of votes received by all candidates who received at least 10 votes.

5.7.2.14 Additional candidates may be nominated from the floor prior to the first ballot only, provided the name being offered meets the requirements set forth in ¶¶ 35-36 of *The Book of Discipline*.

5.7.2.15 Candidates' names need not be spelled correctly on a ballot. Any ballot on which the intent of the voter can be reasonably discerned will be counted.

5.7.3   Petitions to General and Jurisdictional Conferences.

5.7.3.1   Anyone eligible to submit a resolution to the annual conference may submit a proposed petition to General or Jurisdictional Conferences for endorsement by the annual conference.

5.7.3.2   Petitions to General or Jurisdictional Conferences shall be treated like resolutions except that they shall not be subject to amendment (although they shall be subject to substitution, and substitute motions shall be subject to amendment).

5.7.4   Endorsement of episcopal nominees.

5.7.4.1   At the session of the annual conference immediately prior to Jurisdictional Conference, the annual conference may endorse any number of episcopal nominees, up to the number of bishops being elected.

5.7.4.2   The Jurisdictional Conference delegation, at its discretion, may nominate candidates for endorsement.

5.7.4.3   Immediately following the presentation of the candidates for endorsement recommended by the Jurisdictional Conference delegation, any conference member may make a nomination from the floor.

5.7.4.4   Any full elder eligible for the office of bishop may be endorsed for election. A full elder need not be a member of the annual conference or a declared candidate for the episcopacy in order to be endorsed.

5.7.4.5   A ballot shall be taken no less than four hours after nominations are made.

5.7.4.6   Members may vote for up to the number of episcopal vacancies in the jurisdiction or the number of nominations, whichever is fewer. Provision shall be made on each ballot for a vote of no endorsement.

5.7.4.7   A nominee must receive a vote on at least 60% of the valid (*i.e.*, non-defective) ballots in order to receive the endorsement of the annual conference.

5.7.4.8   The number of ballots taken shall be equal to the number of episcopal vacancies, except that no further ballots shall be taken if either of the following occurs:

5.7.4.8.1   The number of candidates who have received the endorsement of the annual conference has reached the number of episcopal vacancies.

5.7.4.8.2   At least 60% of the valid (*i.e.*, non-defective) ballots cast are for a vote of no endorsement.

5.8 PARLIAMENTARY AUTHORITY

5.8.1   The proceedings of the annual conference shall be governed by the following in order of priority and precedence:

5.8.1.1   *The Book of Discipline.*

5.8.1.2   The acts of the preceding North Central Jurisdictional Conference.

5.8.1.3   The Plan of Organization of the Michigan Annual Conference.

5.8.1.4   *Robert's Rules of Order Newly Revised* (11th edition).

5.8.2   The Plan of Organization of the Michigan Annual Conference shall remain in force and effect until repealed, amended, or superseded by a vote of at least two-thirds of the annual conference.

5.8.3   Notwithstanding § 5.8.2, if any portion of the Plan of Organization of the Michigan Annual Conference be invalidated, either directly or indirectly, by General Conference, the Judicial Council, or an episcopal ruling of law, the remaining portions of the Plan of Organization shall remain in effect.

§ 6 OFFICERS OF THE ANNUAL CONFERENCE

6.1 SECRETARY

6.1.1   Election.

6.1.1.1   At the first session of the annual conference following General Conference, the annual conference shall elect a secretary, nominated by the Committee on Nominations in consultation with the Bishop, who shall take office immediately following the adjournment of that session of the annual conference.

6.1.1.2   Notwithstanding the foregoing, the outgoing secretary shall still be responsible for the completion of that year's conference journal.

6.1.1.3   The secretary shall serve a four-year term, renewable once.

6.1.1.4   If the secretary wishes to retire after one term, he/she must notify the Committee on Nominations and the Bishop by January 1 of the year preceding General Conference.

6.1.2   The secretary, after certifying the number of lay members necessary for equalization with clergy members, shall determine the distribution of lay members (in accordance with the rules hereinabove) and shall notify the proper persons no later than January 10.

6.1.3   Duties.

       6.1.3.1   Serve as the chair of the Committee on the Journal.

       6.1.3.2   Receive all required agency annual reports and shall ensure that they contain no action items or budget proposals.

       6.1.3.3   Keep a fair and accurate record of the proceedings of the annual conference session.

       6.1.3.4   Preserve the journals and papers of the annual conference.

       6.1.3.5   Receive and review any written notices of corrections and additions to the conference journal as published, incorporating them into the permanent records of the annual conference as appropriate.

       6.1.3.6   Serve *ex officio* on the Commission on the Annual Conference Session and the Committee on Rules and the Order of Business.

6.2 STATISTICIAN

6.2.1   The statistician shall be elected, upon nomination of the Committee on Nominations in consultation with the Bishop and Conference Treasurer, at the session of the annual conference immediately following General Conference.

6.2.2   The statistician shall report directly to the conference treasurer.

6.2.3   The statistician shall serve a four-year term, renewable once.

6.3 FACILITATOR

6.3.1   The conference shall elect, upon nomination of the Committee on Nominations, a layperson to serve as facilitator.

6.3.2   The facilitator shall serve a four-year term, renewable once.

6.3.3   The facilitator shall be seated at an announced location on the floor of the annual conference session and shall have the duties of assisting anyone who needs assistance in understanding and using procedures and resources of the conference session.

6.3.4   The facilitator shall serve as an *ex officio* member of the Commission on the Annual Conference Session and the Committee on Rules.

6.3.5   Nominated by the Committee on Nominations and elected by the annual conference for a four-year term, renewable once.

6.4 PARLIAMENTARIAN

6.4.1   The Bishop may, at his or her discretion, appoint a conference parliamentarian.

6.4.2   The parliamentarian shall assist the Bishop in ensuring that the annual conference session is run in accordance with the rules of order set forth hereinabove.

6.4.3   The parliamentarian, should one be chosen, shall serve at the Bishop's pleasure.

6.5 CHANCELLOR

6.5.1   The conference shall designate a chancellor, who shall be nominated by the Bishop and elected quadrennially by the annual conference.

6.5.2   The chancellor shall be a member of a local church within the annual conference and shall also be a member in good standing of the State Bar of Michigan.

6.5.3   Except as prohibited by the Michigan Rules of Professional Conduct, the chancellor shall serve as legal advisor to the Bishop and to the annual conference.

6.6 DIRECTOR OF ADMINISTRATIVE SERVICES AND CONFERENCE TREASURER

6.6.1   Coordinates and collaborates with the Council on Finance and Administration regarding the conference budget process and the oversight of the treasury staff.

6.6.2   Coordinates with the Board of Trustees regarding facility contracts and concerns.

6.6.3   Oversees information technology (I.T.) contracts in consultation with the director of communications.

6.6.4   Elected by the annual conference at the first session following each General Conference.

6.6.5   Directly amenable to the Council on Finance and Administration (§ 1.2, above).

6.6.6   Fulfills all other responsibilities enumerated in ¶ 619 of *The Book of Discipline*.

6.7 LAY LEADER

6.7.1   Fosters awareness of the role of the laity within the congregation and through their ministries in the home, workplace, community, and world.

6.7.2   Advocates for the role of the laity in the life of the church, encouraging laypersons in the general ministry of the church.

6.7.3   Meets with the cabinet when matters relating to the coordination, implementation, or administration of the conference program, or other matters as the cabinet may determine.

6.7.4   Fulfills all other responsibilities enumerated in ¶ 607 of *The Book of Discipline*.

6.7.5   Nominated by the Bishop in consultation with the Board of Laity, and elected for one four-year term.

§ 7 FINANCIAL POLICIES

[*Determined by the Council on Finance and Administration.*]
See pages 182-201.

§ 8 PROTECTION POLICY

[*Provided by the Protection Policy Implementation Team.*]
https://michiganumc.org/resources/conference-administration/protection-policy/

§ 9 HUMAN RESOURCES POLICIES

[*Provided by the Committee on Human Resources.*]
https://michiganumc.org/resources/conference-administration/human-resources/

§ 10 AFFILIATE ENTITIES OF THE ANNUAL CONFERENCE

10.1 AFFILIATED VIA THE BOARD OF GLOBAL MINISTRIES
   10.1.1 Bronson Health Group.
   10.1.2 Clark Retirement Community.
   10.1.3 Methodist Children's Home Society.
   10.1.4 United Methodist Community House.
   10.1.5 United Methodist Retirement Communities, Inc.

10.2 AFFILIATED VIA THE BOARD OF YOUNG PEOPLE'S MINISTRIES
   10.2.1 Adrian College.
   10.2.2 Albion College.
   10.2.3 Bay Shore Evangelical Association.
   10.2.4 Michigan Area United Methodist Camping (MAUMC).
   10.2.5 Lake Louise Christian Community.

10.3 AFFILIATED VIA THE COMMISSION ON ARCHIVES AND HISTORY – Michigan Area United Methodist Church Historical Society, Inc.

10.4 AFFILIATED VIA THE COUNCIL ON FINANCE AND ADMINISTRATION
   10.4.1 Michigan Area Loan Funds.
   10.4.2 United Methodist Foundation of Michigan.

§ 11 DISTRICTS

11.1. Nine Districts. There shall be nine (9) Districts in the Michigan Conference. The boundaries shall be determined from time to time by the Bishop. (2016 Discipline ¶ 415.4)

11.2 *Book of Discipline.* At all times, operation of the Districts in the Michigan Conference shall be subject to the *Book of Discipline*, as amended from time to time, and this Plan of Organization.

11.3. Incorporation. All Districts shall be separately incorporated and shall comply with the Michigan Non-Profit Corporation Act. (*Book of Discipline* ¶ 2518.2). The bylaws shall describe the duties of the Officers and Directors. The District Leadership Team shall be the Board of Directors of the corporation. The officers of the District Leadership Team shall be the officers of the corporation.

11.4. Basic District Structure. The following shall be the basic structure of each District.

11.4.1   District Conference. Each District shall hold a District Conference at least annually at a time and place selected by the District superintendent in consultation with the District Leadership Team and in a manner consistent with the Discipline. (2016 Discipline ¶ 658-659). Membership of the District Conference shall be all clergy members of the Michigan Conference appointed or residing in the District, and the professing members of all congregations located in the District. No congregation shall be represented by more than ten (10) professing members.

11.4.2   District Leadership Team. Each District shall have a District Leadership Team.

     11.4.2.1 Membership. The team shall consist of between six (6) and fifteen (15) members as nominated by the District Nominating Committee and as elected by the District Conference. The members shall serve for three (3) year terms, and no member may serve for more than three consecutive terms. The District Conference may stagger the terms in its discretion. The District Superintendent and the Lay Leader shall be members with voice and vote. The District Leadership Team shall elect its own officers; a Chair, Secretary and Treasurer, who shall also be the officers of the Corporation. It may elect such additional officers as it deems appropriate.

     11.4.2.2. Vision Team. Prior to and at the commencement of each new District, and for a reasonable time thereafter, in the discretion of the District Superintendent, a Vision Team may be organized to do visioning for the District. The members shall be appointed by the District Superintendent. This Vision Team will disband after it has done its initial visioning work and a District Leadership Team is properly elected by the District Conference. The Vision Team shall perform the functions of the District Leadership Team until the District Leadership Team is properly elected by the District Conference.

     11.4.2.3. Roles and Responsibilities. The District Leadership Team shall be the primary programmatic, fiduciary and administrative agency of District. It may create such subcommittees as it deems appropriate.

          11.4.2.3.1.   The District Leadership Team officers shall serve as the Board of Trustees for the District and perform all functions inherent in a Board of Trustees, including the owning of any District real estate and being the party to any legal contracts.

(*Book of Discipline* ¶2518). Unless the District Leadership Team is directed by the Annual Conference Board of Trustees, the Annual Conference Board of Trustees shall be responsible for the sale of all closed church buildings and parsonages in the District or owned by the District.

11.4.2.3.2. The District Leadership Team shall serve as the District Board of Missions. It shall receive and manage all invested and budgeted funds held by the District. Invested funds shall consist of funds currently held by District Boards of Mission and Church Extension, or their equivalent, prior to January 1, 2019. Additional invested funds may be received through gift, fundraising, or the receipt of the proceeds of the sale of closed church property, as determined by the Annual Conference. With the advice of the District Superintendent and the Conference Leadership Council, the District Leadership Team shall make all decisions regarding the use of invested and budgeted funds in the mission and ministry of the District.

11.4.2.3.3. Exception. The United Methodist Union of Greater Detroit shall serve as the Board of Missions for the District(s) which includes the City of Detroit.

11.4.3 Committees Required by Discipline. All Districts shall have a District Committee on the Superintendency, District Committee on Ministry, and District Committee on Church Location and Building. The makeup, meetings, and authority of these committees shall be as required by the Discipline. They shall report regularly to the District Conference and District Leadership Team.

11.4.4 Nominating Committee. There shall be a District Nominating Committee to make recommendations to the District Conference. It shall consist of between four (4) and ten (10) members. The District Superintendent shall be the chair of the Committee and the Lay Leader shall be a member. Members shall be elected to three (3) year terms, with no member serving more than three consecutive terms. Members shall be elected by the District Conference and may be in staggered classes as directed by the District Conference. In making nominations for all District agencies, care shall be taken to have an inclusive membership and that is otherwise representative of the District

11.4.5   Reporting and Accountability. The District Leadership Team shall make oral and written annual reports to the District Conference and such reports as requested to the Michigan Conference of all of its activities, including the receipt, investment, management and disbursement of assets. The District Leadership Team shall also be amenable to the Conference Leadership Council, and shall be amenable to the Conference Board of Trustees for property related matters and to the Conference Council on Finance and Administration for all financial matters.

11.5   Other Agencies. The District may have such other agencies as the District Conference may determine from time to time not inconsistent with the Discipline or this Plan of Organization.

INDEX – PLAN OF ORGANIZATION

PLAN OF ORGANIZATION

— MAC Photos

INDEX – GENERAL

Made in the USA
Monee, IL
22 July 2021